The Handbook of Family Psychology and Therapy

Volume II

The Handbook of Family Psychology and Therapy

Volume II

Edited by
Luciano L'Abate
Georgia State University

Dorsey
Professional
Books

THE DORSEY PRESS
Chicago, Illinois   60604

© THE DORSEY PRESS, 1985

ISBN 0–256–03488–5

Library of Congress Catalog Card No. 84–73505

Printed in the United States of America

2 3 4 5 6 7 8 9 0 K 2 1 0 9 8 7 6

Foreword

Historically, psychologists have been largely concerned with the individual and only in the recent past have begun to consider the significance of family members as agents of influence on the individual. In developmental psychology, for instance, the subject of study first of all was the child himself, and then the mother/child dyad. Later, theorists and practitioners began to consider the role of the father as an important determinant in the development of the child. Still later, other family members, most notably siblings and grandparents, were added to this influential triad. So the system known as the family has become increasingly more differentiated and, as a totality, has become a primary focus of investigation.

As we deal with the complexity of the family, we must utilize a systems approach in the development of models on which to build our theories. We must also keep in mind that as complex as the family system is, it does not exist in isolation but at the intersect of all of our other societal institutions—the schools, the media, the health system, the world of work, and government at all levels—and is therefore influenced by them. The social ecology of the family has been increasingly noted as a major determinant of family concerns and problems. One of the most dramatic of these problems is that of child abuse, which (as all figures indicate) is increasing at an alarming rate, indicative of both a dramatic breakdown of the nurturant function of the family in this country and rapidly growing social stresses (poverty and rising unemployment, for instance). Underlying such problems are breakdowns in, or difficulties with, the links between family members and between families and society.

These connections and their dynamics constitute the central theme in family psychology. The underlying assumption is that people must be viewed and, where necessary, treated with regard to their roles as family members. The family must be seen as a dynamic and multifaceted whole. Family psychology also recognizes a lifespan approach to psychology; the examination of family relationships as they change over time is essential to this field. Finally, a systems approach demands that the family continually be conceptualized as a part of a larger system, namely, the society in which the family is embedded.

This *Handbook* appears at a time when demand for such a text is becoming increasingly apparent. The striking change in the demographics of our society underline the need for attention to a family psychology. Almost 20 percent of all American families (and 50 percent of black American families) are headed by single parents. Future thinking concerning the family must increasingly deal with family forms other than the conventional nuclear family. Similarly, the rising rate of divorce and subsequent increase in the number of issues related to remarriage, custody, and the roles of family members affected by divorce ("custody" issues for grandparents, for example) are not fully recognized by traditional psychology or sociology texts. The growing number of mothers in the work force and of two-income families and the impact of the workplace on family life are all phenomena with which the social sciences must be concerned. An expanding need for, and reliance on, day care in America, a new mobility that may separate family members by great distances, changing housing patterns, and the splitting of families along generational lines all affect the interactions of family members with one another and with their communities.

The importance of family-related issues to many professionals and the need to address these issues have outstripped the availability of thoughtfully produced resources. Academicians, service providers, clinicians, and social policy analysts, among others, should find *The Handbook of Family Psychology and Therapy* a useful contribution to our understanding of the family. Such a comprehensive publication as this will have widespread appeal, being appropriate for established professionals as well as new adherents to family psychology. Many of the chapters combine the practical with the theoretical, and these volumes will be immediately useful to social psychologists, developmental psychologists, and family counselors.

The relationship of the individual to the family has been too long neglected as a subject of study for psychologists. Generally considered the domain of sociology, family studies in psychology have for the most part been confined to the field of child development. To undertake the task of making this the subject of a psychological text is admirable, and Luciano L'Abate has done a laudable job of choosing topics and subtopics pertinent to this theme. The book represents a novel conjoining of issues that are inherently related, distilling information from the great amount of research already completed. The contributors to this book succeed in covering a wide range of topics concerning both normal and pathological family functions.

A final aim of the editor and authors of this publication is the integration of knowledge from many disciplines. If we are to maximize our accomplishments in the field of family psychology, it must be through the cooperation and efforts of a broad array of workers in the fields of psychology, sociology, education, medicine, and law. We must be willing to work towards an ever greater convergence of these disciplines around family-related issues and to take an interdisciplinary approach to the study of families.

The principal functions served by this *Handbook* seem to be fourfold. First, it serves to circumscribe an emerging field of study. Secondly, these volumes highlight the role of the family as a source of developmental influence, an agent of change, and an appropriate and necessary unit of preventive and remedial intervention. Thirdly, students of the field and those for whom the concept of family psychology is a new one will find in this work a splendid introduction to the field. Finally, this text, with its wide scope of focus, has considerable value as a source of new inquiry and theorizing.

As in the evolution of all thought, fields of study within psychology are born, mature, and sometimes vanish. This *Handbook* may well constitute the formal birth of the field of family psychology. It is a movement of the present that can only increase in importance over the coming decades. Future thinking will be characterized by an ecological approach in which the individual is characterized as behaving within a family which in turn is embedded in a broad social environment. This *Handbook* points us towards the future of psychological thought, and as such is a seminal work.

Edward Zigler
Sterling Professor of Psychology
Yale University

Preface

The purpose of this reference work is to put together under one cover information about the relationship of the individual to the family. The branch of psychology that deals with this relationship is called *family psychology*, linking concern for the individual, which has been the task of psychology, with concern for the family, which as a whole has been a task of sociology.

A recent survey by Burr and Leigh (1982) pointed out that, according to titles, at least 25 different names were being used to designate family-oriented departments. By contrast, the title and the definition of family psychology are clear enough. To paraphrase a cliché, it's the name—without the game.

The lack of an academic and professional field of family psychology is an anachronism when we consider that at least two thirds of our waking and sleeping time is usually spent with someone we care about or who cares for us. Psychology and psychoanalysis have paid lip service to the family's early influence on the individual. Yet, family references in psychology textbooks (except for child development textbooks, where such references may reach up to 15 percent of the total) may be totally absent in textbooks representing the fields of personality, theories of personality, and especially social psychology—as if personality and social psychology originated and are being maintained in a vacuum (Dunne & L'Abate, 1978).

It is the recognition of the importance of the family context *through-out the life span* (L'Abate, 1976) that makes such bypassing unbelievable to commonsense readers, even those who know nothing about psychology. The family, as an aggregate of individual members, has been relatively neglected by psychology as a science and as a profession (L'Abate, 1983). Fortunately, there are many signs that this neglect is decreasing considerably. *The Handbook of Family Psychology and Therapy* demonstrates that interest does indeed exist. Yet, in collaborating on this manuscript, we have been aware that family psychology as an academic discipline is practically nonexistent. As a clinical profession, family psychology remains ill-defined, except perhaps for the Academy of Psychologists Interested in Sex, Marital, and Family Therapy (now called the Academy of Family Psychology). The *Handbook*, then, has at least two functions: first, to collect under one cover what we know about the relationship of the individual with the family; second, to serve as a springboard for a more effective and clearly defined discipline of family psychology by summarizing past findings, theories, and applications.

The *Handbook* thus describes a field that is academically nonexistent and professionally ill-defined. Its purpose is to define this field in ways that show the continuity if not the congruence of individual psychology and family psychology. Contributors to the *Handbook* were asked to rely as much as possible on studies in which the relationships of family members (e.g., parents, sibs) have been investigated.

The field of family psychology is so undeservedly unrecognized and ignored by psychology that it has nowhere to go but up! The family does need recognition as a legitimate unit of psychological study and practice (Thaxton & L'Abate, 1982), and the *Handbook* represents such recognition.

Conger's (1981) article was an articulate and much needed summary of the state of the American family. Although this important and relevant statement included the family as a unit of psychological study and practice, Conger did not go far enough in the implications of what the family field means to psychology as a science and as a profession.

In the first place, psychologists are not prepared, conceptually or practically, to deal with families. As already noted, a recent survey (Dunne & L'Abate, 1978) showed that most textbooks in general, social, personality, and abnormal psychology have had very few or no references to family concepts (e.g., parents, marriage, parent-child interaction). The only exception was developmental psychology.

In the second place, with the exception of the AAMFT-approved Georgia State University clinical program (L'Abate, Berger, Wright, & O'Shea, 1979), no institutions grant a Ph.D. in family psychology. In fact, the term *family psychology* is relatively new (L'Abate, 1983). Contrast this state of affairs to the number of programs in social psychology, which as a whole has been extremely uninterested in dealing with marriage and the family. If there is a field of family psychology, it is still a clinically applied one. As far as I know, there is no academic program in family psychology.

In the third place, most clinical programs remain stuck at the individual level of training, along with whatever the level may imply (i.e., linear, noncontextual approaches that use outmoded clinical tests and procedures). In other words, most clinical training is still very traditional, clinging to World War II models and ignoring most of the advances that have been made in the past quarter of a century in mental health services (L'Abate & Thaxton, 1981).

In the fourth place, the current status of the family, which Conger (1981) aptly described as changed and still changing, requires the application of new educational tools for educators as well as trainers. We need preventive rather than solely therapeutic models which will allow us to deal with families in toto, not in parts as we have done thus far.

The jump that is required in order to move from the individual to the family might be described as a quantum leap. Although that description may seem an exaggeration, the process does require thinking in circular, contextual, and dialectical fashions that most of us are neither trained for nor accustomed to (Weeks & L'Abate, 1982). The jump is not an easy one. It will be resisted mostly by those whose linearity and rigidity in thinking do not permit alternatives. The family is an alternative that has caught psychology with its pants down, so to speak. We'd better hurry and pull them up, along with our bootstraps. We are singularly unprepared, academically and clinically, to deal with families. More than Conger's thoughtful address will be needed to move psychologists toward different models of thinking and training.

Fortunately, psychologists are becoming increasingly more involved in the field of family therapy (Thaxton & L'Abate, 1982). Despite the shortcomings already mentioned, we, as latecomers to this relatively new field, can learn from errors made by other disciplines and add a dimension that is still in short supply, that is, rigor both in theory and in research.

Even the respected critics of psychological trends and theories (Sarason, 1981) who have recently decried psychology's focus on the individual without historical and cultural contexts, have failed to mention the family as the vital nexus between the individual and society. Although this connection was recognized early by Murphy (1947), the recognition within the field of personality development remained unheeded in theory and practice.

The *Handbook* is an attempt to fill a large gap that the science and profession of psychology has allowed: the relationship of the individual with the family. By no means as comprehensive as it might be, the *Handbook* is nevertheless an attempt to represent, as much as possible, the field of family psychology. Psychologists of all persuasions and specialties will, we hope, concede that the attempt was needed.

Luciano L'Abate

REFERENCES

Burr, W. R., & Leigh, G. K. *Newsletter: National Council for Family Relations,* 1982, *27,* 1–5.

Conger, J. J. Freedom and commitment: Families, youth, and social change. *American Psychologist,* 1981, *36,* 1475–1484.

Dunne, E. E., & L'Abate, L. The family taboo in psychology textbooks. *Teaching of Psychology,* 1978, *5,* 115–117.

L'Abate, L. *Understanding and helping the individual in the family.* New York: Grune & Stratton, 1976.

L'Abate, L. *Family psychology: Theory, therapy, and training.* Washington, D.C.: University Press of America, 1983.

L'Abate, L., Berger, M., Wright, L., & O'Shea, M. Training in family studies: The program at Georgia State University. *Professional Psychology,* 1979, *10,* 58–64.

L'Abate, L., & Thaxton, M. L. Differentiation of resources in mental health delivery: Implications for training. *Professional Psychology,* 1981, *12,* 761–768.

Murphy, G. *Personality.* New York: Harper & Row, 1947.

Sarason, S. B. *Psychology misdirected.* New York: Free Press, 1981.

Thaxton, M. L., & L'Abate, L. The second wave and the second generation: Characteristics of new leaders in family therapy. *Family Process,* 1982, *21,* 359–362.

Weeks, G. R., & L'Abate, L. *Paradoxical psychotherapy: Theory and practice with individuals, couples, and families.* New York: Brunner/Mazel, 1982.

Acknowledgments

Lucy Rau Ferguson is responsible for helping to change the title of the training program at Georgia State University from *Family Studies* to *Family Psychology*. At the first Mailman Center Conference on Applied Child Psychology in January 1980 in Miami, her questioning led me to assert that, indeed, *family psychology* was not an empty term (the term had not, to my knowledge, been used until then). Despite that historical acknowledgment, I cannot believe that we waited until 1980 to coin the term. Surely, someone must have used it earlier— I would like to know who that someone is so that his or her contribution can be acknowledged.

A former Dorsey Press editor deserves the credit for conceiving the idea of this *Handbook*. A matter of being in the right place at the right time: He suggested it to me, and by return mail, I sent him an outline of possible topics. From that initial, rather skimpy outline, a larger one grew, and potential contributors were contacted. Originally, we thought about a board of consultants; however, many persons, approached with a fait accompli, begged off. Among the many who helped with their support and ideas were George Levinger at the University of Massachusetts, Norma Radin at the University of Michigan, Bernard Murstein at Connecticut College, Robert Woody at the University of Nebraska at Omaha, Norman Garmezy at the University of Minnesota, Gerald Zuk of New Orleans, as well as many other colleagues and students whose response to the idea of *The Handbook of Family Psychology and Therapy* was "Why not? Other, less-relevant fields are receiving much more recognition than this one." I cannot cite all of them—the list would be too long. The strong support of contributors, colleagues, and consultants kept me going throughout the writing and editing of the manuscript. Their support has meant, to mean, a great deal to me. I hope that any whom I have failed to name will not feel slighted.

I am grateful to Amy Alexander, Billy Sue Groutas, Leila L'Abate, and Lisa Reddy for their help with the Author and Subject Indexes.

Marie Morgan deserves credit for *really* editing many of the chapters that my associates and I wrote and for suggesting improvements in all of them. The *Handbook* would have not materialized without her careful typing, proofing, and improving.

L. L.

LIST OF CONTRIBUTORS

Stephen I. Abramowitz
Division of Clinical Psychology
Department of Psychiatry
Davis Medical Center
University of California
Sacramento, California

James F. Alexander
Department of Psychology
University of Utah
Salt Lake City, Utah

Dennis A. Bagarozzi
School of Social Work
East Carolina University
Greenville, North Carolina

Cole Barton
Department of Psychology
Davidson College
Davidson, North Carolina

Steven R. H. Beach
Department of Psychology
State University of New York at
Stony Brook
Stony Brook, New York

Kathryn Beckham
Department of Child and
   Family Development
College of Home Economics
University of Georgia
Athens, Georgia

Jay Belsky
College of Human Development
The Pennsylvania State University
University Park, Pennsylvania

Audrey Berger
Rochester Regional Forensic Unit
Rochester, New York

Michael Berger
Department of Psychology
Georgia State University
Atlanta, Georgia

Stephen D. Berger
School of Human Services
New Hampshire College
Manchester, New Hampshire

Andrew Christensen
Department of Psychology
University of California at Los
   Angeles
Los Angeles, California

Victor G. Cicirelli
Department of Psychological
   Sciences
Purdue University
West Lafayette, Indiana

Teresa Cooney
College of Human Development
The Pennsylvania State University
University Park, Pennsylvania

Mary Crawford
Department of Psychology
Michigan State University
East Lansing, Michigan

Jeri A. Doane
Yale Psychiatric Institute
Yale University of Medicine
New Haven, Connecticut

Bernice T. Eiduson
Family Styles Project
Neuropsychiatric Institute
Center for the Health Sciences
Los Angeles, California

Doris R. Entwisle
Department of Psychology
The Johns Hopkins University
Baltimore, Maryland

Beverley Fehr
Psychology Department
The University of British Columbia
Vancouver, British Columbia,
* Canada*

Lucy Rau Ferguson
Private Practice
Berkeley, California

Hiram E. Fitzgerald
Department of Psychology
Michigan State University
East Lansing, Michigan

Martha Foster
Department of Psychology
Georgia State University
Atlanta, Georgia

Joseph Frey III
Department of Psychiatry
Medical College of Georgia
Augusta, Georgia

Gary F. Ganahl
Department of Psychiatry
West Virginia University Medical
* Center*
Morgantown, West Virginia

Richard Gilbert
Department of Psychology
University of California at Los
* Angeles*
Los Angeles, California

Jeffrey A. Giordano
Gerontology Department
University of South Florida
Tampa, Florida

Frances K. Grossman
Department of Psychology
Boston University
Boston, Massachusetts

Bernard G. Guerney, Jr.
College of Human Development
The Pennsylvania State University
University Park, Pennsylvania

Louise Guerney
College of Human Development
The Pennsylvania State University
University Park, Pennsylvania

Russell W. Irvine
Department of Educational
  Foundations
Georgia State University
Atlanta, Georgia

Edgar H. Jessee
St. Mary's Hospital
Knoxville, Tennessee

Gregory J. Jurkovic
Department of Psychology
Georgia State University
Atlanta, Georgia

Kenneth Kaye
Department of Psychiatry
Northwestern University
Chicago, Illinois

Luciano L'Abate
Department of Psychology
Georgia State University
Atlanta, Georgia

Robert A. Lewis
Department of Child Development
  and Family Studies
Purdue University
West Lafayette, Indiana

Robert M. Milardo
Human Development
University of Maine at Orono
Orono, Maine

Daniel R. Miller
Department of Psychology
Wesleyan University
Middletown, Connecticut

Nancy E. Moss
Division of Clinical Psychology
Department of Psychiatry
Davis Medical Center
University of California
Sacramento, California

Clifford I. Notarius
Department of Psychology
The Catholic University of America
Washington, D.C.

K. Daniel O'Leary
Department of Psychology
State University of New York at
*   Stony Brook*
Stony Brook, New York

Gerald R. Patterson
Oregon Social Learning Institute
Eugene, Oregon

Daniel Perlman
Department of Family Studies
The University of British Columbia
Vancouver, British Columbia,
*   Canada*

William S. Pollack
McLean Hospital
Harvard Medical School
Boston, Massachusetts

Gary R. Racusin
Yale Child Study Center
New Haven, Connecticut

Mark W. Roosa
Center for Family Studies
Arizona State University
Tempe, Arizona

R. Barry Ruback
Department of Psychology
Georgia State University
Atlanta, Georgia

Jennifer E. Sade
Department of Psychology
The Catholic University of America
Washington, D.C.

Jill D. Sanders
Department of Psychology
University of Utah
Salt Lake City, Utah

Victor D. Sanua
Department of Psychology
St. John's University
Jamaica, New York

Sadell Sloan
Private Practice
Atlanta, Georgia

Michael T. Smith
Department of Psychology
Georgia State University
Atlanta, Georgia

Monta P. Smith
Associate School Psychologist
Walton County Public Schools
Monroe, Georgia

George Sobelman
Rechovot, Israel

Joseph Stevens
Early Childhood Education
Georgia State University
Atlanta, Georgia

Barbara Strudler-Wallston
Department of Psychology and
    Human Development
George Peabody College for Teachers
Vanderbilt University
Nashville, Tennessee

Clifford H. Swenson, Jr.
Department of Psychological Sciences
Purdue University
West Lafayette, Indiana

Lynda D. Talmadge
Department of Psychology
Georgia State University
Atlanta, Georgia

William C. Talmadge
Private Practice
Atlanta, Georgia

Lyn Thaxton
William Russell Pullen Library
Georgia State University
Atlanta, Georgia

Donna Ulrici
Private Practice
New York, New York

Joan Vondra
College of Human Development
The Pennsylvania State University
University Park, Pennsylvania

Victor Wagner, Ph.D.
Suite 114
3505 Turtle Creek Boulevard
Dallas, Texas 75219

Lynn S. Walker
Department of Pediatrics
School of Medicine
Institute for Public Policy Studies
Vanderbilt University
Nashville, Tennessee

Janet Warburton
Western States Family Institution
Salt Lake City, Utah

Donald J. Wendorf
Family Therapy Associates
Birmingham, Alabama

Edward Zigler
Department of Psychology
Yale University
New Haven, Connecticut

Irla L. Zimmerman
Family Styles Project
Neuropsychiatric Institute
Center for the Health Sciences
Los Angeles, California

Contents

Section Two
Individual and Family Life Cycles

Section Five
Parenthood and Parenting

Volume II

Section Six
Nontraditional Family Styles and Groups

Section Seven
Psychopathology and the Family

Section Eight
Methods of Evaluation

exchange conceptions of marital and family behavior and clinical evaluation. Additional considerations.

Section Nine
Therapeutic and Preventive Interventions

Section Ten
Issues in Training

Section Six

Nontraditional Family Styles and Groups

Chapter 22

A Historical Perspective on Black Family Research*

RUSSELL W. IRVINE
JOSEPH H. STEVENS, JR.

Research on black families has engaged the interest of scholars for a considerable period of time, approaching a century of study. Both in interest and in pace, however, research focusing on African-American families has quickened most dramatically in the past 20 years. Such intense concern for conceptualizing and analyzing family life among African-Americans is attributable to the convergence of the following tightly interrelated factors: *(a)* the Black Power protest movement of the 1950s and 1960s; *(b)* the increased reliance on social-behavioral science research for social policy formulations; *(c)* the often-questioned status of existing black family research as a guide in such social policy determination; and *(d)* the increased level of participation of blacks and other culturally sensitive scholars committed to the study of black family life (Smith & Killian, 1974; Staples, 1971).

The decades of the 1960s and 1970s produced five times more black family research articles than had been produced during the preceding century (Johnson, 1981). An even more dramatic expression of interest in this area of research is noted by the fact that articles produced between 1975 and 1980 matched the total number produced prior to 1974.

Notwithstanding this meteoric rise in scholarly attention devoted to black family research, the field's growth had not kept pace with concomitant growth in theory and methodology. In this sense, the flurry of research activity portended a threat to the scientific legitimacy of this fledgling subspeciality (Allen, 1978). In Allen's view, the major impediment confronting the advancement of quality research on black

---

families centered, among other things, on differences among black family researchers on ideological grounds.

Allen (1978) identified three basic ideological orientations employed in the study of black families: (1) the "cultural equivalent" perspective, (2) the "cultural deviant" perspective, and (3) the "cultural variant" perspective. Each perspective is guided by a common set of assumptions about the nature of black life and the forces which create and sustain its patterned features of group life. In the nature of competing conceptualizations, attention is focused selectively on one set of conditions and dimensions of group life to the exclusion of others.

Researchers assuming the cultural-equivalent perspective deny or fail to acknowledge the existence of a distinct cultural base underlying black family structure, function, or member behavior. Black families share equivalent values, structural characteristics, and functions in fundamental ways compared to white families. The cultural-deviant perspective views black families as exhibiting distinctive traits, but sees such traits as serving to distinguish black families from other family types in ways that attest to their deviation from what is normatively prescribed. Moreover, such cultural traits in a modern technological society are problematic and/or dysfunctional. Families of this type do not instill in children, as an example, values and dominant cultural norms necessary for their adaptation in an advanced and complex society. In the extreme, these families are viewed as pathological. In the third view, cultural-variant, acknowledgment is explicitly made of the distinctive qualities and characteristics of black family life. This perspective recognizes differences in history and social experience of African people in America (Allen, 1978). Because of these differences between black and white people in social and historical experiences. Observable family variation is attributable to the unique position black people face and have faced in accommodating their corporate survival.

In a recent study investigating the utilization of the various ideological orientations among black family researchers, Johnson (1981) found that by the close of the 1970s, more authors publishing in family journals used the cultural-variant perspective than the cultural-equivalent perspective. In her review of the major family sociology journals for the period under study, no evidence was found (to any appreciable extent) that authors view black family behavior as deviant.

Recent advances in terms of its popularity and theoretical, ideological, and methodological refinement indicate that black family research has reached near-complete maturity and has been catapulted to its present status of development in a comparatively short period of time. Its development in the past 20 years, moreover, is significantly the result of the four factors suggested at the outset. These factors, however, might accurately be considered the more immediate precipitating conditions that provided the impetus for renewed interest in black family research.

Of equal significance, as suggested by Johnson (1981) and clearly indicated by the position taken by a widely diverse group of analysts, is the observation that the field is now broadly in agreement as to the most effective form of analysis. That is to say, black family analysis is best approached in terms of its own internal dynamics, order, and adaptational responses to the social and economic condition of the family environment.

Given the phenomenal growth of the field, its struggle for legitimacy, and the focus on the pressing problems and issues at hand, it might be expected, as is the case, that scant attention has been given to other forms of contribution which impinge on the current analysis and study of black family life. Specifically, reference is made to assessments of the field that seek to place in broader historical sweep the evolutionary processes that connect the past to the present.

There exist few historical reviews of sociological black family research which examine inclusively, if not exhaustively, the major contributions to the field. More generally, much of black family research proceeds without a conscious recognition of its past. In a word, analyses in this area are ahistorical. Advancement in any field of endeavor is predicated upon the debt one period of its development owes to the one immediately preceding it. This, of course, is not to say that there exists in the case of black family analysis one continual body of research work building and extending on the other. Rather, it is suggested that a historical account is needed that would clearly demonstrate significant continuities in research effort and, perhaps equally important, significant forms of discontinuities in conceptualizing black families as well.

This chapter has two objectives in light of the two primary features that characterize the field of black family research as suggested to this point. First, we attempt to set in developmental terms the emergence of the field with particular attention given to the pioneering work of W. E. B. DuBois, who might legitimately be called its founding father. Second, we shall review the role and contribution made to the field by E. Franklin Frazier, considered by some (Billingsley, 1968) as the individual who has made the greatest contribution to the study of black family life. We should hasten to point out, however, that while Frazier's work has perhaps had the greatest impact in contributing to our understanding of family dynamics, this fact should not be permitted to overshadow the initial groundbreaking work of DuBois.

There are three distinct historical periods into which the sociological study of black families might be conveniently classified: (a) the Nascent Period, 1890–1930; (b) the Middle Period, 1930–1960; and (c) the Contemporary–Culturally Conscious Period, 1960 to the present. Other classificatory schemes have been advanced, notably by Billingsley (1968) and Allen (1978). However, neither Billingsley nor Allen were concerned with establishing the connections between the periods, nor were they concerned with tracing the evolutionary development of the research field per se. We offer that these three time frames are sufficiently broad in scope, yet distinct enough from each other in intellectual and social climate as to gauge the impact of conceptualizing the dynamics of black life.

Additionally, each period (and more particularly the first two) bears the imprint of single individuals as the driving intellectual force behind analyses of black group and family life. Accordingly, the Nascent Period was championed by DuBois. The Middle Period was dominated by Frazier. While no single individual stands out as the dominant personality in the Contemporary–Culturally Conscious Period, the present period has witnessed the greatest proliferation of research and scholarly activity on the family. This is to be accounted for by three factors. The first factor is related to changes in the nature of social and behavioral science research. In these disciplinary areas, there has been a shift in emphasis from macro to micro levels of research analysis. Secondly, the sheer number of individual scholars engaged in some facet of study of black family life has dramatically increased. Thirdly, the conceptual boundaries within which black family analysis takes place has, to a greater or lesser extent, been agreed upon. That is to say, emphasis has been placed variously on culture or class as the relevant dimension maintaining and/or sustaining patterned features of group life among African-Americans.

THE NASCENT PERIOD: 1890–1930

Among contemporary black family researchers, Billingsley (1968) was the first to attempt to place the treatment of the study of the black family in American scholarship into a historical context. He notes that family sociology, beginning in the late 19th century and extending through the 1920s, had completely ignored the study of black families. Family sociology, as a field of study, grew rapidly and was marked by three distinct phases in its earlier development.

The first phase was characterized by the preoccupation of social scientists at the time in finding validation for the Darwinistic hypothesis. The nature of these studies was not analysis of the contemporary family but of "earlier more primitive forms." "The idea," Billingsley (1968) writes, "was to search among primitive peoples for the earlier forms of family life, so that the evolutionary process could be traced and the sources of such perfection (European family forms) established" (p. 202).

The second phase focused on the contemporary family. Here, however, attention was focused on the effects poverty conditions had on family life. Many such studies were conducted both in America and in Europe.

The third phase of family sociological study began in the 1920s. The primary emphasis of family study shifted from poverty conditions to problems facing middle-class families. The problems of family adjustment, individual happiness, and a search for meaning characterized this "psychological phase." The theoretical works of Freud and Mead served as the psychological bases of interpretation and analysis for these family problems.

The 1930s and 1940s were the "golden age" for the study of black life and for black family research, as Billingsley (1968) observed. The most notable family research works were the 1932 *The Negro Family in Chicago* and the 1939 *The Negro Family in the United States* by Frazier. Two points of observation can be noted regarding Billingsley's historical assessment of black family study to that point. The first was the evaluation of family sociology. Billingsley correctly recognized the complete absence of concern for the study of black families in their own right. However, equally glaring is Billingsley's omission of two earlier sociological treatments of black families by DuBois.

What makes Billingsley's (1968) "historical context" of black family study substantively incomplete turns roughly on the following order of issues. He was either unaware of, or failed to acknowledge, the work of DuBois as having made a contribution to the study of black families; if he was aware of DuBois' work, he did not view it as significant enough to mention. Billingsley's failure is compounded, moreover, because his historical assessment of black family research gives an incomplete accounting of those few studies that did exist prior to the 1930s. At another level, this historical assessment fails to show necessary continuity of black scholarly interests and thoughts over time.

In other words, the impression is given that the golden age of study of black life and family study had no antecedent base. More accurately, the golden age represented in some sense a further extension and refinement on the prior period of scholarly concerns (Apthaker, 1976, p. 193); but as it shall be indicated later, this period also represented, at least in the works of Frazier, a radical departure from the prior period.

Whether as a function of Billingsley's lack of awareness of DuBois's work on the black family or of Billingsley's judgment as to the merit and value of DuBois's work, scant attention is given to his earlier works.

In part, this oversight stems from the fact that DuBois is not yet properly positioned in the contemporary analyses of black family dynamics. Understanding DuBois's role and contribution to black family behavior must be appreciated, not simply in his early family study (though meritorious) but rather in his broader, deeply penetrating analyses of the paradoxes and contradictions faced by blacks in the American social, economic, and political structure. Tied dependently to these anomalies of American life are a host of conditioned behaviors, which DuBois called "symptoms," in black life. The black family is but one primary institutions most dramatically and immediately affected by these endemic features of America's racially based character.

While, as indicated, DuBois's primary contributions to black family research lie beyond his study of black families, it is necessary in the interest of accuracy to summarize at least briefly two of his black family studies.

The first is *The Philadelphia Negro* (1899) that had its origin in an initiative taken by Susan P. Wharton, then a member of the Executive Committee of the Philadelphia College Settlement, an eleemosynary agency whose objective was assisting the adjustment of blacks in the city of Philadelphia. The Seventh Ward held the largest concentration of blacks during the 1890s. Susan Wharton approached the provost of the University of Pennsylvania, Charles Curtis Harrison, to determine the university's interest in undertaking a thorough and systematic sociological inquiry into the social status conditions of its black population. DuBois, a recently minted Harvard Ph.D., was tapped for this investigation.

As he was later to reflect on this study, DuBois (1968) wrote:

> I counted my task here as simple and clear-cut; I proposed to find out what was the matter with this area and why. I started with no "research method" and I asked little advice as to procedure. The problem lay before me. Study it. I studied personally and not by proxy. I sent out no canvassers. I went myself. Personally I visited and talked with 5,000 persons. (pp. 197–198)

The Philadelphia Negro was a herculean undertaking requiring its author to labor day and night for over 15 months. DuBois mapped the district, obtained biographical histories of the residents, gathered pertinent library data, and successfully compiled a two-century history on the people of the Seventh Ward. The study sought to ascertain: *(a)* the geographical distribution of the race, *(b)* their occupations and daily life, *(c)* their homes, *(d)* their organizations, and *(e)* their relation to their million white fellow citizens (DuBois, 1899).

The study consisted of 18 chapters, two of which he devoted to family conditions: chapter 6, "Conjugal Conditions," and chapter 5,

"The Negro Family." The former dealt with the factors necessary, in the first instance, for the establishment of family; the latter was concerned with factors sustaining or, conversely, disruptive of family life.

The Philadelphia Negro was conducted during the time of an exodus after Emancipation of massive numbers of blacks from the rural areas of Virginia, Maryland, North Carolina, and South Carolina into the city of Philadelphia. What confronted DuBois in his study was a population of rural migrants inhabiting a city not more than one generation removed from slavery. As he lamented, no reliable method of sociological research and no theory were available. At the time, DuBois, the consummate scholar, forged a mode of sociology adequate to explain the underlying feature of the emerging pattern of behavior of his subjects, notably those factors affecting the nature of their family life.

Conjugality of the black population of Philadelphia, prior to the close of the 19th century, was most significantly affected by the complex interplay of the following conditions: urbanization, residual of the slave regime, the peculiar sex ratio characteristics of the migrating group, and employment opportunities in the city. These factors affected conjugality, as DuBois's statistical profile data indicated, in several ways.

His statistical tabulation revealed the total male population, age 15 and above, was 4,504. The total female population was 5,174. The percent of single males compared to the percent of single females was 41.4 to 30.5. In the population, the percentage of married males was 52.5; female married was 47.1. For the categories of "widowed" or "permanently separated," percentages were 6.1 for males and 22.4 for females.

A larger than expected number of black single men and women were found to exist compared to the total population of the city. The larger than expected number of "singles" among the black population of the Seventh Ward was further corroborated by comparative data which was obtained from Great Britain, France, and Germany. Of this large number of single men and women, DuBois (1899) wrote, "Away from home and oppressed by the peculiar lonesomeness of a great city, they form chance acquaintance here and there, thoughtlessly marry and soon find that the husband's income cannot alone support a family. [Such realities] result in desertion or voluntary separation." The penchant for causal over more-stable marriage relationships was fostered, DuBois asserted, and sustained *by* residual effects of the slave regime. This factor contributed dramatically to high rates of desertion and family breakdown as well. The statistical data tabulated by DuBois revealed other interesting points of observation. For instance, there was a tendency toward later marriages, a tendency for the young to enter marriage before economic conditions warrant, and a tendency for those over 40 to remain single.

In the chapter entitled "The Negro Family," DuBois developed more fully additional factors impacting on selected dynamics and the structure of family life among Philadelphia's black Seventh Ward population. This chapter was divided into four sections: size of the family, income, property, and family life. We shall concentrate attention only on the section on family life. Family life in the Seventh Ward, DuBois revealed, was roughly but not evenly divided into two types: the type of family characteristics exhibited by the newest migrants to the city and the type of families, largely a free population, who were indigenous to the state of Pennsylvania.

Each family type exhibited a unique and discernible set of characteristics and features which added to the diversity of observed family structures among Seventh Ward blacks. The former family type was associated most immediately in time with prevailing family plantation life in organization and values. DuBois characterized families of this variety as those which were more prone toward sexual promiscuity and cohabitation and, for the women of this group, inclined to "support men."

This former family type made up the slum district of the ward and represented from 10 to 25 percent of the total number of families. Among the other 75 to 90 percent of the families, the second type, were families struggling with varying degrees of success to adapt to the dual condition of racial oppression, low wages, limited occupational opportunity for men, and housing and rental exploitation. Families comprising this category were what we might call "working poor," "laboring class," and "lower middle" class. The dual conditions of oppression placed unique forms of economic, social, and moral stress on these families. These conditions of racial oppression brought about manifest secondary family problems. Emerging as an adaptable response to high rent, for example, was the "lodging system." Thirty-eight percent of the family households in the ward admitted "unknown strangers" to the home. One problem this system posed was the protecting of young children and young women when parents were out of the home. Examining the lodging system in these terms is to suggest one of the variety of adaptative responses black families were forced to make to the economic conditions that confronted them in their new urban environment. DuBois's analysis reveals his unique sociological insight, suggesting, as he did, the deterministic relationship of economic conditions to family responses.

The other segment of the second family type that made up the Seventh Ward was what DuBois termed the "better-class families." Such families traced their origin to the free population of blacks living in the state of Pennsylvania prior to the Civil War. DuBois's views on these families turned less on a sociological analysis and more on what he viewed as this class's "moral duties" to the masses of the race. Chastising this class for their conspicuous display of consumption, he felt they had an obligation to the masses of black people of the ward. The masses needed to be taught, by example, respect for the sanctity of the home and the making of home and family life the center of social and moral life. One senses in the position DuBois took toward this class of families an adumbration of his famous "talented tenth" concept.

One additional point might be made about DuBois and his sociological treatment of family life among Philadelphians of the Seventh Ward. He was the first sociologist to identify the differentiation of family types among blacks. More important, however, was his observation that this differentiation of the two segments was a function of the differential social experiences that were tied to the slave regime. What is noteworthy about this observation was that the identical point was made by Frazier some 30 years after DuBois's *The Philadelphia Negro* was published.

It is almost certain, or arguably so, that given Frazier's familiarity with DuBois's work and Frazier's strikingly similar conceptual premise and argument of a dual class structure among blacks, Frazier owed much to DuBois on this point of dualism.

To conclude briefly, *The Philadelphia Negro* was undertaken under the auspices of the University of Pennsylvania to be a systematic sociological inquiry into the social conditions of blacks in Philadelphia's Seventh Ward. It was a massive study conducted single-handedly by DuBois. This study represented the first systematic communitywide sociological treatise (Allen, 1978). The two chapters in which DuBois treats the family status of blacks in the Seventh Ward are examples of carefully derived analyses of the underlying conditions and factors impacting family life. This is but one aspect of DuBois's work that, as suggested, has been omitted from the body of family sociology literature and reviews.

Yet, there is another aspect of *The Philadelphia Negro* that is rarely acknowledged even by students of DuBois. This point relates to the emergence of DuBois's thinking concerning the peculiar situation that Africans in America face compared to other groups. In the final pages of this volume, a chapter entitled "The Meaning of All This," one sees a growing suspicion in DuBois's mind that Africans in America will never participate in the "common humanity" of America that other groups enjoy. DuBois anticipated by five years his now-famous "double consciousness" thought. He wrote:

> We grant full citizenship in the World-Commonwealth to the "Anglo-Saxon," the Teuton and the Latin; then with just a shade of reluctance

we extend it to the Celt and Slav. We half deny it to the yellow races of Asia, admit the brown Indians to the anteroom only on the strength of an undeniable past; but with the Negroes of Africa we come to full stop. (1899, p. 387)

This clearly articulates the peculiar situation with which African-Americans in America are confronted. In this quote, one senses in embryonic form a caste position in the analysis of black-white relations. In 1903, DuBois set forth his point in these terms:

It is a peculiar sensation, this double-consciousness, this sense of always looking at one's self through the eyes of others, of measuring one's soul by the tape of a world that looks on in amused contempt and pity. One ever feels his twoness, as American, a Negro; two souls, two thoughts, two unreconciled strivings; two warring ideals in one dark body; whose dogged strength alone keeps it from being torn asunder. (p. 45)

This quote is interpreted by many contemporary analysts of black life to mean the duality of the black experience. It is the embodiment of the American dilemma, but also the undergirding foundation for the claim of biculturalism of blacks. As we shall see later, DuBois moved beyond the concept of caste and added to it the companion notion of culture. DuBois, unlike Frazier, was clear: It was not class that impeded the progress of blacks in America; color alone was the criterion for group disbarment.

DuBois acknowledged in his third autobiography, written some 60 years after the publication of *The Philadelphia Negro*, that few persons ever read his Philadelphia research. This statement by DuBois seems appropriately correct in view of the fact that it is never cited in family sociology literature. His other work, *The Negro American Family* (the volume to be reviewed next), is also frequently omitted.

DuBois, as it seems from the quote above, was keenly aware of the caste status African-Americans were subjected to in America. An event in 1906 forced DuBois to come to grips with the African past of blacks, that is, with their African heritage. In 1906, the anthropologist Boas was the commencement speaker at Atlanta University. DuBois was in attendance. Boas said to the graduating class, "You need not be ashamed of your African past"; and then he recounted the history of the black kingdoms south of the Sahara for a thousand years. DuBois was astonished. "All of this I had never heard and I came then and afterwards to realize how the silence and neglect of science can let truth utterly disappear or even be unconsciously distorted" (1938, p. VII).

His first occasion to correct the distortions of history was reflected in his book *The Negro American Family* (1908). What is perhaps the

most-noteworthy aspect of this volume is DuBois's insistence on connecting the African past to the present family conditions. He wrote,
"In each case an attempt has been made to connect present conditions
with the African past. This is not because Negro Americans are African,
or can trace an unbroken social history from Africa, but because there
is a distinct nexus between African and America which, though broken
and perverted, is nevertheless not to be neglected by the careful student" (DuBois, 1908). DuBois anticipated by some 60 years the central
argument now being advanced by contemporary black family analysts
stressing the cultural foundation for black people's behavior as well
as their family behavior.

His black family study can best be described as a somewhat crude
and mechanistic attempt to demonstrate those African carryovers. His
case is overdrawn, for example, in his attempt to show how home
design and structure in Africa show parallel design features to home
construction at the turn of the century. However, in other parts of
the book, his work deserves some attention because of the striking
similarities between, for example, marriage ceremonies as practiced
in parts of Africa and marriage ceremonies practiced among blacks
in the southern part of the United States. A description of a Zulu
marriage ceremony is given. After the groom gives his gift of cattle,
water is thrown over the head of the bride and groom, the bride
breaks a spear and makes a run for the exit of the kraal; the groom
is the only person permitted to catch her, though others try. If the
groom catches her, the ceremony is completed. DuBois noted a similar
practice in Lowndes County, Alabama, in 1892 which he called "chas-
ing the bride." He admitted that such practices are not widespread,
in part because slavery had effectively wiped out many such customs
and practices; but as in this example, not all marriage customs had
been crushed by the slave regime. In the area of religion, DuBois
asserted, one finds the greatest expression of African retention. The
church is the center of the community social life around which all
other festive activity is carried out.

In *The Negro American Family,* an attempt was made to gather
data on a wide range of family conditions, such as conjugal conditions,
descriptions of the homes and home life of a representative sample
of urban and rural populations, property value and wealth of black
families, income and expenditures, and literacy rates. DuBois, in his
1908 volume, sought to demonstrate, where possible, the African-
American nexus. The extent to which he was successful might be questioned. Notwithstanding the volume's defects, which DuBois protested
was due to a lack of financial backing, it stands out as the seminal
work on black family research—the first of its kind.

THE MIDDLE PERIOD: 1930–1960

The undisputed giant in the field of black family study from the 1930s through the early 1960s was Frazier. His work took place, in both time and space, in a different America than when DuBois wrote about the conditions affecting black family life. In other respects, these were vastly differently men, due in part to their temperament, personality, academic training, and influences. While both were trained in the field of sociology (DuBois's training was in philosophy, economics, and history as well as in sociology) their differences, as we shall indicate later, extended beyond the superficial level of disciplinary orientation. Frazier was some 37 years DuBois's junior, but Frazier admired and respected DuBois and, in fact, saw his own work on the black family as an extension of DuBois's work (Aptheker, 1976, pp. 193–194). Frazier's terminal degree work was done at the University of Chicago in the department of sociology. His two mentors at the university were Ernest W. Burgess and Robert E. Park. The influence of these two men on the development of Frazier's view regarding the issue of "African retentions" is not altogether clear; however, for Herskovitz (1941), one of Frazier's earlier critics, their influence was considerable, more particularly in the case of Park. The significance and bearing of this point will be discussed at the end of our review of Frazier's two books.

Frazier (1966) begins his examination of the black family by first extensively reviewing the prevailing social and "scientific" literature on black family life of the late 19th and early 20th centuries. This literature largely focused on the characterization of the moral status and sexual behavior of blacks in the context of family relations.

Scientific or otherwise, the literature of the period (1890–1930) seemed unanimously in agreement that the masses of black people significantly deviated in family behavior patterns and development as compared to white families and that black families were farthest behind modern "civilization" in morality and sexual behavior. The following excerpts are typical of the climate of opinion and sentiment reflected in the literature Frazier reviewed:

> In his home life the negro is filthy, careless and indescent. He is as destitute of morals as any of the lower animals. . . . It is quite apparent that in manner of life, general morality, and observance of obligation of the marital state, the negro . . . is greatly lacking. . . . So lacking in moral rectitude are the men of the negro race that we have known them to take strange women into their homes and cohabit with them with the knowledge, but without the protest, from their wives and children. (1966, pp. 3–6)

The scientific community, as Billingsley (1968) noted, was thoroughly and philosophically wedded to the precepts embodied in social Darwinism. Expectedly, social scientists of this era attempted to account for the differences of moral and sexual turpitude of blacks in classic Darwinistic—that is, evolutionary—terms. Accordingly, theories advanced to account for observed variations between blacks and whites in family life and general morality sought to explain the origins of black behavior from his "African past." The general conditions necessary for survival on the continent of Africa in climate, hostile environs, and other life conditions, developed within Africans discernible behavioral dispositions among which were strong sexual impulses, the tendency to act on instinct stimulation, and the predisposition generally to view the world in simplistic, childlike terms. Africans were viewed, as the expression goes, as "children of nature."

This was the inescapable and undeniable legacy of the "Negro's African past." His aberrant sexual conduct was in a generally low state of moral development, was conditioned by the centuries of his African heritage, and as such was fixed by the laws of social evolutionary development. Underlying the message of Darwinism of this period was that blacks were by the nature of evolutionary principles and dynamics permanently disbarred from any but the most-marginal forms of participation in the common humanity of civilized man. These were not matters which man's hand engineered or fashioned, but God Himself had ordained this in His wisdom.

By at least the second decade of the 20th century, the sway of social Darwinism began to wane. There were other competing and challenging conceptions of the basis for determining group behavior. There was the growing recognition among anthropologists and sociologists that significant dimensions and aspects of group life were fundamentally conditioned culturally rather than biologically.

Frazier's task in establishing an explanation for the demoralization of black family life was twofold: first, to loosen from the grip of social Darwinism those conceptions of black behavior that sought to explain black life as a carryover from the African past. Then, in dismissing the notion of "carryovers," Frazier sought to redirect black family life analyses, particularly the issue of the demoralized family life as a manifestation of the peculiarly cultural and historical effects of the processes of enslavement and the conditioning influence of the slavery itself.

Frazier maintained that it was highly improbable, "because of the conditions under which slavery was introduced into America" (1932, p. 23), that any coherent set of values, traditions, or African customs could have survived. The diversity of the slave trade, Frazier believed, precluded a culturally homogeneous group of Africans from coming to America. Slaves, Frazier argued, came from various parts of Africa, spoke different languages and dialects, and had variously different cultural traditions. Consequently, Frazier believed that little if any African culture survived the journey across the Atlantic.

Group and family life grew out of the human levels of individual need fulfillment. The basis of family life developed as a "natural organization." Family life under slavery, Frazier maintained, was a natural occurrence primarily centering on the bonding relationship of mother and offspring. The particular pattern of family life organization, whether adhering to monogamic patterns or deviating from the normative family patterns, was almost entirely shaped by the peculiar conditions and forces inherent in the system of slavery and by the extent of interest slave owners took in the family life of their slaves. As Blasingame (1972) notes, slave owners' interest in maintaining stable family life increased their leverage over slaves, since males with family attachments would be less likely to attempt escape and, more practically speaking, stable family life was functionally important to their general labor productivity.

In either case, black family life, Frazier argued, grew out of, and was an "accomodation" to, the slave regime. Stability of the family system and the degree of compliance to normative patterns of such family forms were a function of the controls imposed by the system of slavery.

Emancipation from slavery loosened the controls plantation life imposed. The slave communal system of plantation life exercised virtually total control over vital dimensions of slave life. Freedom from the constraints of the institutional life of the slave system loosened the cohesive base which maintained family unity. Lacking the undergirding institutional support structure established under slavery, family unity for newly freed slaves began to disintegrate.

For a considerable time after emancipation, blacks of the rural South continued to live under a modified plantation system (sharecropping) which exerted some degree of social and family stability, but this "version of slavery" did not reach the level of social control that had existed under the older, more formalized plantation system.

The demoralization of family life was most severely manifest among blacks as significant numbers of them, largely illiterate, unskilled, and lacking sustaining cultural moorings, began migrating out of their communal pockets of the rural South into urban centers of southern and northern cities. Between 1900 and 1910, the urban population of blacks increased by 34.1 percent while the rural population increased by only 4.6 percent (Frazier, 1966, p. 69). Prior to World War I, southern cities received the greatest number of migrants; however, after the war, northern cities began to attract the greatest number of rural southern blacks.

The influx of significant numbers of rural blacks into northern cities, as Frazier observed in the case of Chicago, had a disorganizing and demoralizing effect on black family life. There was first the loss of the constraining influence of the church, which in the rural South was the center of communal life. Moreover, as Frazier argued, there were the attraction and temptations of city life, "and freed from every form of group control, he is prey of vagrant impulses and lawless desires" (1966, p. 76). Demoralization is measured to the extent which individual disillusionment and cynicism set in upon individuals who aimlessly wandered through the city, unprepared to effectively cope with the demands and requirements of the urban environment. The urban environment transformed black life, transformed how blacks would view themselves and their fellows, and indeed transformed how they would view the world.

In this later sense, Frazier alludes not only to the process of disorganization of black life resulting from urbanization but to how black group life itself was changed. The challenges of reorganization revolved on the degree of family stability which, as Frazier viewed it, was the primary building block of community institutional structure and solidarity.

Not all segments of the black urban population were equally susceptible to the disorganizing effects of urbanization. Two segments of the population remained fairly insulated from the generally demoralizing influences of urbanization. Prominent among such segments were the free class of blacks who were never enslaved and those who were manumitted prior to emancipation. The prior segment was largely comprised of mulattoes. The other segment was ex-slaves who, while enslaved, had acquired normative family values and customs consistent with dominant family values. Frazier argued that these two segments of the black population secured education, property, and other economic and social advantages sufficient to sustain them from the ravages of pauperism that gripped the mass of blacks after emancipation.

Incipient forms of class differentiation centered on the growing distinctions between these latter two segments and the mass of inarticulate and resigned blacks. Frazier believed variation in family stability between these segments—as measured by rates of desertion, divorce, domestic violence, delinquency, crime and so forth—were clearly observable in urban areas. Frazier attempted to demonstrate empirically that the degree of demoralization in family life fell along a geographical continuum which corresponded to zones of settlement in Chicago. Park (1922) had advanced that natural areas of selected and specialized activity existed within urban communities. At the core of the urban community (Zone 1) exist certain enterprises and activities; in Zone 1, one finds office buildings, banking, retail shops, and wholesale houses. Toward the periphery of the city, different kinds of activities and enterprises take place; for example, in Zones 6 and 7, one finds higher-status residential communities, industrial parks, and other forms of social activities.

Each "natural area" of a city attracts a select population or collection of individuals. Areas immediately outside the downtown business district, because of natural growth in city size, face upward pressure on land value. In land lying, say, in Zones 2 and 3, land is held for speculative purposes and is without immediate utility. Such land and the buildings on it are permitted to deteriorate, since the value of the land exceeds the return value of improvements.

It is to these deteriorated areas that immigrant and/or migrant populations are first attracted because of their relatively low rent value. As Park (1967) observed, "These areas easily assume(s) the character of a slum; . . . areas of casual and transient population, an area of dirt and disorder" (p. 58). Park further noted with regard to zone succession that:

> Within these immigrant colonies and racial ghettoes, however, other processes of selection inevitably take place, which bring about segregation based upon vocational interests, upon intelligence, and personal ambition. The result is that the keener, the more energetic, and the more ambitious very soon emerge from their ghettoes and immigrant colonies and move into an area of second immigrant settlement, or perhaps into a cosmopolitan area in which the members of several immigrant and racial groups meet and live side by side. More and more, as the ties of race, of language, and of culture are weakened, successful individuals move out and eventually find their places in business and in professions, among the older population group which has ceased to be identified with any language or racial group. (p. 60)

Frazier adopted Park's conceptualization of "natural social areas" of the city with its concomitant moral order as his bases of analyses for distinguishing the degree of family disorganization and, conversely, the processes of family group life reorganization. For instance, Frazier demonstrated that in each of the seven zones into which Chicago was divided, family stability and organization progressed respectively from the areas of most disorganization to greatest family stability. In Zones 2 and 3, one finds the greatest amount of illegitimacy, divorce, and desertion. Within Zones 6 and 7, one finds a marked increase in home ownership and few numbers of families per dwelling.

After World War I, because Chicago offered prospects for industrial opportunity, many more men were attracted to the city than women. These men concentrated chiefly in areas of deterioration, in close proximity to earlier migrant centers of southside Chicago. "Many of the men," Frazier wrote, "who were concentrated in areas of deterioration were unmarried or had broken family ties. The proportion of men who were reported as single in the first two zones was more than one and a half times as great as in the seventh zone" (1966, p. 118).

One detects no reservation on Frazier's part in wholeheartedly endorsing Park's belief that blacks would, as other immigrants had, eventually assimilate into mainstream American culture. Moreover, Frazier believed (as Park had) that each of the natural social areas of the city exercised an independent moral force over the inhabitants of its respective area and, as such, acted to constrain or facilitate the movement of its members from one zone to another. The impediment for the advancement of blacks, for Frazier, centered on the constraint imposed by the moral order of the least desirable zone and the lack of the necessary family orientation, which perpetuated a sort of vicious cycle of disorganization and demoralization.

Frazier's 1932 study, *The Negro Family in Chicago,* was a study of the socially and culturally conditioned bases which determined the emergence of the black family system and which contributed over time to its stability and/or disorganization. The study focused on one city, Chicago, and concerned the effects city and urban life exerted on family life behavior of blacks.

Frazier's prominence as a sociologist and analyst of the American black family gained wider recognition following the publication of his second book in 1939. This book was entitled *The Negro Family in the United States.* The bulk of the data for this book had been gathered two years after the publication of his first. This second book was, however, roughly parallel to the first in both theory and argument; it was a logical outgrowth of the former. As its title suggests, it attempted to view black family analysis from a macrocosmic level. The patterns and influences of urbanization and its impact of family structure are extended to a national level. Frazier observed that blacks were increasingly migrating to the great northern cities such as Washington, D.C., Philadelphia, Detroit, New York, and Chicago. He argued that one finds the same or similar family disorganization problems in these urban centers as he had noted in his 1932 study of Chicago.

Between the two works, two relatively distinct differences appear which deserve mention. The first is that in *The Negro Family in the United States,* Frazier placed greater emphases on the central role of black womenhood and black motherhood as a stabilizing influence in black community and family life. As he argued in his first family study, the origin of the black family was rooted in the bond and natural attachment of the mother to her children. Even during slavery, the importance of the mother-child relationship was recognized, and seldom were mother and children separated. These relationships were sustaining and necessary for the most rudimentary form of family life. During the period immediately after emancipation and through the waves of urbanization, black mothers gained significance and importance as the most reliable stabilizing influence in the family unit. Frazier devoted three chapters to an analysis of the role of the black woman/mother.

Secondly, Frazier devoted considerably more attention in his second book to those segments of black family life which exhibit "conventional" family norms. Edwards, one of Frazier's chief biographers, noted that Frazier gave full attention to "stable and conforming family units," as suggested by such chapter headings as "Sons of the Free" and "Black Puritans" (1972, p. 95).

Finally, one notes with interest two other aspects of Frazier's study. The first observation is that Frazier believed in the inevitability of black assimilation into mainstream American life. One suspects Frazier was caught on the horns of a dilemma. As indicated above, out of necessity he had to dismiss the previous perjorative characterization of the nature of black family life which was part of the social Darwinism of the period which immediately preceded his study. To have argued the existence of African retention among blacks would have been untenable given the vilificatious nature of biological determinism in the late 19th and early 20th centuries. In a sense, Frazier had nowhere else to go philosophically or sociologically. In his insistence on the nonexistence of any African retention, his class-based analysis was the only avenue available to him to account adequately for the variations in family behavior between white and black populations.

Given the prominence of the Chicago school of sociology, of which he was a product, and his personal and intellectual influence during the succeeding three decades, conceptualizing black families as essentially a matter of class variation and deviation was a foregone conclusion. Since there were no other individuals of his stature who could effectively challenge his work or (more appropriately put) advance a contending paradigm for black analysis, Frazier's conceptualization was widely accepted. It was not until the appearance of the Moynihan Report (1965) and the aftermath of the controversy it engendered, that Frazier's "perjorative tradition" as Valentine (1968) describes it, was seriously challenged.

THE CONTEMPORARY–CULTURALLY CONSCIOUS PERIOD: 1960–PRESENT

Assessment of the pertinent issues in the current study of black families requires a two-pronged approach in that the relevant issues turn on different types of considerations. The first consideration centers on the situationally specific series of events precipitating the renewal of interest in the study of black family life. The second consideration focuses on the underlying features of these events, which afford the opportunity to abstract a sociologically based interpretation of the research efforts of those involved in studying black family dynamics. In terms of this latter consideration, what is proposed by way of interpretation profitably derives from the specialty area in sociology known as the sociology of knowledge. The perspectives from this area of investigation attempt to locate and/or demonstrate the linkages between existentially conditioned bases of group life and the correspondence of these bases with mental production—for example, ideology (Merton, 1955).

The 1960s were a decade of tremendous social change, and nowhere in American life was change more profoundly evident than in the arena of race relations. In one sense, the conditions effecting change in race relations in the 1960s might be considered as a product of a long series of struggles blacks mounted during the prior decade and earlier. The most-notable aspect of these struggles was the successful effort at overturning the reigning Jim Crow doctrine of "separate but equal." The 1954 Supreme Court decision in *Brown* v. *The Board of Education* outlawed de jure school segregation. The ramification of the decision, however, extended beyond the rights of black children to attend school on a nonsegregated basis. The Court's decision had ramifications for, among other things, public transportation and accommodations, housing, employment opportunity, and voting rights.

The series of civil rights victories in the mid-1950s and early 1960s resulted in what might be described as incipient crystallization of black consciousness. Each successful challenge to one segregation law, policy, or practice infused confidence in blacks that other such laws or statutes could be successfully challenged. From such struggles and victories were the source and substance of black assertiveness and group efficacy derived. An important corollary of group efficacy was the demand for self-determination. The claim and demand for self-determination— translated self-definitions—marked more urgently and more precisely than before, the criteria of evaluations for subsequent directions and activities of the group. It also set the criteria and basis of legitimacy by which even well-intended initiatives by others on their behalf would be judged.

Set against this emergence of collective consciousness was a series of actions being taken and being proposed by the federal government in the area of civil rights within the same time frame. In the early part of the 1960s, the federal government had established a broad range of domestic race policy. It was, however, during the middle part of the decade that the federal government policy initiative shifted toward a more-aggressive stance in civil rights, in that efforts were put forth for establishing policy specifically focusing on the black family.

This effort by the Johnson administration to establish a black family policy as an extension of its civil rights concerns sparked the controversy surrounding the role, use, and nature of social science research in the area of black family life. The use and even the role of social science research per se was not the issue of contention. Rather, the storm center of the debate extended more deeply, toward issues such as assumptions, design, and value premises.

The government document which ignited the controversy was entitled "The Negro Family: The Case for National Action;" its principle author was Daniel Patrick Moynihan (1965). The report is too well known to fully recount here, except to point out that Moynihan (like Frazier at an earlier time) viewed the black family as a disorganized-disintegrated structure, in Moynihan's terms as a "tangle of pathology."

Perhaps the most relevant facet of the Moynihan Report might be viewed less for what it proposed about the nature of black family life than for the fact that it emerged at a time when blacks were questioning old definitions and conceptions of them by others. The report emerged at a singular moment in the psychosocial climate in American life that represented a repudiation of those intellectual models which viewed blacks as cultural deviants either as it pertained to the structure of dynamic quality of their family life or as it pertained to other features of their corporate life.

That America witnessed change in the nature of race relations is, viewed from one perspective, a common-place observation. At another level, however, this observation offers a profound insight which helps explain deeper levels of changes in the nature of intergroup relations. Whether viewed symbolically or empirically, changes in the position of blacks vis-à-vis whites in the spheres of economic, political, and social relations engendered, in its wake, cleavages in the "domain of the intellect" (Merton, 1972). Structural realignment of group relationships signaled realignments in their respective ideologies and in the theories and models which guide scientific inquiry.

The central dynamic process occurring among blacks during the mid-1960s was the crystallization of consciousness. A heightened sense of consciousness made imperative at least a more-critical examination of the concepts, models, and theories which purported to explain aspects of their behavior. Among academics of the group, underpinning this thrust for its reexamination process is the intent to ferret out and discard those perspectives which appear to buttress or serve as ideological justification for the maintenance of status quo group relations.

The emergence of black family research is a special mechanism of the larger forces at work in the maintenance of group integrity whereby group life conditions are affirmatively advanced in ways consistent with group consciousness. The first phase of activity in the process of cultural affirmation was necessarily reactive in the sense that no culturally based paradigm had been articulated in the early stage of black family study. As was suggested at the outset of this chapter, the field of black family study has progressed toward greater conceptual and methodological refinement. Intimately tied to this development has been a cultural awakening that is useful in accounting for the variant aspect of black family functioning. Such a cultural base relies heavily upon the notion of Africanity. Authors in more recent years try to demonstrate the linkages and connections between the behavior of blacks in America with cultural antecedents traceable to certain retentive features of their African past. Since the middle of the 1970s, Afro-American scholars in various fields of endeavor greatly stress the centrality of Africanity to their explanatory paradigm—that is, the point of departure for their analyses of black behavior. The field of black family study has likewise followed in this direction. What remains is to point out, in rather specific research terms, the current status of black family research in light of this Afrocentric orientation.

One of the foremost proponents of such a view was Nobles (1974) though others have made significant, important contributions (Herskovitz, 1941; Hilliard, 1976; Hale, 1982; Billingsley, 1968).

THE IMPORTANCE OF FAMILY AND OTHER SOCIAL TIES FOR BLACK INDIVIDUALS

A major focus of recent research on black families has been the description of the function of the black individual's social ties to the extended family, to friends, and to community institutions. Billingsley (1968) and Nobles (1974) were among the first contemporary black family scholars who identified extended family relations as an important and salient characteristic of black family life and one with clear links to blacks' African heritage. Gutman (1976) found that the typical parent-child unit among blacks was closely tied to a supportive kinship network as early as the 1850s. Some argued that the extended family served a more-important function for black individuals than for whites (Nobles, 1974; Sudarkasa, 1981). Not only were blood ties more salient than conjugal ties, but the very definition of family for black Americans went beyond the nuclear family members to include cousins, aunts, uncles, and grandparents (Dodson, 1981; Sudarkasa, 1981). McAdoo (1978) has argued that the modal family type among blacks is not the nuclear family but a neolocal extended family—one comprised by different households which maintain close contact, interaction, and an exchange system.

Moreover, Billingsley (1968) argued that the mutual-aid system provided by an extended family enabled one to cope and survive in a hostile world. McAdoo (1981, 1982) found that family assistance in money, transportation, decision making, and crisis as well as in-kind help (furniture, food, clothing) was exchanged in the black families interviewed. Rainwater (1970) and Stack (1974) also have documented how the mutual aid and exchange systems bound extended family members together and that important services exchanged were child care, advice, counseling, help to the aged and to those migrating to other parts of the country, and assistance during crisis.

There is substantial evidence that individual migration patterns appear to be influenced by kinship and friendship (i.e., social network) ties, (Lee, 1979). It is not uncommon to find that blacks from a given community or from a set of families within a community have moved to the same city in the North or West during the middle part of this century. A relative who migrated first may later be followed by siblings, cousins, and family friends. The established individual often provided monetary, emotional, and informational assistance in acculturation to the new environment. Undoubtedly, such ties and support not only enabled the newcomer to secure stable employment but also to adapt to the new environment.

Much-needed evidence about the prevalence of social linkages to extended family members and the degree to which such ties provide social support to individuals has been provided by the National Survey of Black Families (Taylor, Jackson, & Quick, 1982). This sample of 2,107 individuals was a multistage probability sample. Sixty-two percent were female; 41 percent were between 18 and 34 years, 31 percent between 35 and 54 years of age, and 28 percent were over 54 years old. More than half resided in the southern region, 22 percent in the north central region, 18 percent in the Northeast, and 7 percent lived in the West. Forty-four percent had not completed high school, 31 percent were high school graduates, with 25 percent having completed at least some college or graduated. Approximately one quarter of the sample fell into each of four income groups: less than $5,000, $5,000–10,000, $10,000–20,000, and over $20,000.

Most were well integrated into a close, supportive kinship network. And most saw or were in touch with relatives not living in their household at least once a week (37 percent daily and 28 percent at least once weekly). In contrast, only 6 percent were isolated; they reported seeing relatives hardly ever or never. Six percent were in contact with relatives only a few times a year, and 7 percent had contact about once per month. The majority of the respondents saw their families as being close-knit; 60 percent felt they were very close, 31 percent fairly close, and only 9 percent felt they were not close. Few reported never receiving support or help from relatives and in-laws (16 percent said they never received such help, and 10 percent said they never needed such help). Twenty-five percent reported receiving such help very often, 22 percent fairly often, and 27 percent not too often.

As one might predict, individuals who received more family help had more contact with relatives and felt their families were close. Younger respondents received more assistance than older blacks— those over 55 were much more likely to report never receiving assistance from their families. However, the age categories used (55 and over, rather than 55–64 years and 65 and over) may mask somewhat higher rates of help to the aged. Lee (1979) has reported that while the flow of help is age related, it tends to flow from middle-aged individuals to older and to younger individuals. However, the data from the national survey would seem to support a linear relationship for blacks between age and frequency of support.

Males and females reported equal levels of support, yet income was negatively related to frequency of support. Individuals with the lowest incomes were more likely to report they never received support than were individuals who were better off economically. Similarly, individuals with the lowest levels of education were more likely to indicate they never received family support. Poor and poorly educated black Americans were the group most isolated from family support. While some researchers (Rainwater, 1970; Stack, 1974) have argued that family help systems may be an adaptation or a survival mechanism adopted by the black family due to the vicissitudes of poverty (one advantaged blacks do not need), these data would not seem to support such an interpretation. On the contrary, most blacks at all levels of income and education reported that some support was available to them, though more of the poorest and least well educated were likely to be isolated.

Interestingly, support availability was related to the region of the country in which the respondent resided. More blacks in the South reported they received help very often; while more in the northeast and north central United States reported they never or seldom received support. Recall that over half of black Americans were found in the South, even in 1980; it was here that ties to extended family members appeared to be somewhat stronger.

Other research supports the findings from the National Survey of Black Families with respect to the availability of social support from ties to extended family and friends (McAdoo, 1980; Stack, 1974). McAdoo demonstrated that the kin help system continued to be important for blacks who did not live in poverty. She interviewed single and married middle-class black adult women with dependent children. Half of the families were suburban and half urban, though all lived in the mid-Atlantic region; one fourth were single parents, and the balance were married. Virtually equal proportions of the women either had completed some college, were college graduates, or had done some graduate work. Ninety percent of the mothers received help from a kinship and/or friendship network. Fifty-three percent received more help from family, 27 percent more from friends, and 10 percent received equal amounts from family or friends. The most frequent type of help exchanged was child care; next was financial assistance and then emotional support; few parents (less than 10 percent) exchanged either repairs or clothing. While all mothers appeared to receive more help than they gave, there were no differences here between single and married mothers.

McAdoo did find, however, that married mothers were more likely to report that family help had remained constant; in contrast, single mothers were more likely than were married ones to report that family help had increased (23 percent versus 7 percent). Still, 55 percent of the single women and 74 percent of the marrieds indicated the amount of family help had remained constant.

Most women lived within 50 miles of close relatives, though 40 percent lived more than 150 miles away. Virtually all, however, saw such relatives at least several times a year. Single women were much more likely either to see or to maintain contact with such relatives on a daily basis than were married mothers, who maintained weekly or monthly contact. Most (68 percent) were satisfied with their level of interaction with close family members.

The phenomenon of fictive kin was widely discussed by sociologists and anthropologists but largely documented anecdotally. McAdoo found that 76 percent of the 175 women interviewed had close friends either now or when they were growing up who "passed for" cousins, aunts, uncles, or close relatives. Such designation moves friendship to a different plane. And friends also provided significant support to the women McAdoo interviewed, though such help was related to marital status. Single women were more likely than married women to receive help from friends. But there were also differences in the type of help provided. For married women, such help from friends tended to be emotional; for single women, it was often financial.

Thus substantial empirical evidence corroborates that ties to extended family members and to friends are present for many blacks, that such ties are functional for blacks representing a variety of income levels. Thus, social integration of the individual with an informal support system made up of family and friends appears typical rather than atypical for black Americans. Let us examine the function and benefits for the individual which derive from the construction and maintenance of such ties.

Social ties, individual well-being, and role performance

The absence of social support appears related to both increased disease and mental health problems among blacks. Carter and Glick (1970) reported that death rates for nonwhite males and females who were single, divorced, or widowed were significantly higher than for married nonwhites. Death rates were higher when due to heart disease, stroke, cancer, cirrhosis, hypertension, homicide, tuberculosis, suicide, and motor vehicle accidents. Widowed, single, and divorced nonwhite individuals also experienced higher rates of hospitalization for mental illness.

The relationship between morbidity and the absence of social support were corroborated in the National Survey of Black Americans (Neighbors, Jackson, Bowman, & Guren, in press). Lower-income blacks were more likely to have a severe personal problem (such as a nervous breakdown) than were higher-income individuals. Income was unrelated, however, to the percentage of blacks reporting mild versus moderate personal problems. Poor people were more likely to report health as a problem and less likely to report interpersonal difficulties as a problem. Thus, from this data set, lower-income individuals were more likely to experience a severe problem which was health related; this group was also less likely to receive help from others.

While family and network ties among poverty blacks many be viewed as providing significant economic benefits besides the emotional and informational benefits, others have questioned such a view. Ball's (1981) study of 300 southern black poverty women has suggested that living with relatives did not increase these single mothers' standard of living. Increased income was offset by more dependents. These data appear to corroborate Stack's (1974) observation that strong reciprocal ties between network members, while enabling them to survive, also seemed to keep the women in her study in poverty. One can readily speculate about the impact of affirmative action programs on members of the new employee's personal social network. As a consequence, network members have access to examples of effective achievement behavior and to increased resources in the network, but also to contacts with extra-network agencies and with individuals who might enable them to secure jobs and job training. Though living with another adult may not have economic advantages, certainly there are other likely advantages.

Other data indicate that network ties may facilitate upward mobility. McAdoo (1980) found that women who had moved from a working-class background to the middle class were more likely to indicate they had received financial help from their extended family. In contrast, women whose family origin was middle class were more likely to indicate they had received emotional support from their families.

In a subsequent report, McAdoo (1982) found a relationship between stress and social integration patterns. Families with the highest levels of life stress were in frequent contact with their relatives and received more and a greater variety of help. Perhaps support from the extended family was critical during times of stress, though certainly other interpretations are possible. Greater life stress also was associated with intergenerational mobility patterns and with the degree of social integration of families in their ethnic communities. Among these quite advantaged black families, those who experienced the highest levels of stress were those whose families had been middle class for three generations. However, adults whose grandparents had been in poverty, whose parents had moved up to the working class, and who had moved in their generation to the middle or upper class reported the lowest levels of life stress. And those families which participated in integrated or predominantly white social and work structures also reported much higher levels of stress than those who participated in predominantly black social structures. This positive relationship between social integration in one's ethnic community and greater social well-being has been substantiated in research about other ethnic groups.

Social integration also appears related to effective coping and problem-solving strategies. Mitchell, Barbarin, and Hurley (1981) found that black and white citizens who were active in community groups and civic affairs were more aware of both strengths and deficits in their communities, generated a greater number of alternative solutions to problem situations, and manifested greater, flexibility in the types of resources utilized to solve problems, compared to less active citizens. Active citizens were more likely than inactive citizens to call upon professionals as well as family and friends in solving problems. Individuals who reported that they used more channels (i.e., friends, relatives, TV, radio, newspapers) to get information about the community, also generated more alternative solutions to problems.

Black citizens also were more likely to utilize informal resources like family, friends, and civic associations than were whites, while whites were more likely to use formal services and professionals. And blacks were more likely to report the lack of community services and to see these missing services as critical problems.

Social ties, social integration, and parenting

Social connectedness to others is likely to be strongly related to a black parent's childrearing skill and strategies. One can readily extrapolate how observing a friend distract her child from a potentially dangerous activity with a toy, play hiding games, or sing simple songs might add to any parent's repertoire. Yet not only are parenting strategies influenced (either positively or negatively) but information is also acquired about children's characteristics and about the influence of environmental processes on children's development. Ford (1978) has suggested another type of influence of the extended family on the young black mother:

> Adult female relatives serve as role models of strong resourceful womanhood because they, too, have had major responsibility for the support of a family. Thus, they are able to offer empathy and understanding to the younger woman. The older women are constant reminders that it is possible to cope with the strains of being head of a household, and they give them the faith to believe it is not an impossible task. (p. 8–9)

Among middle-income families, Allen (1981) found that black women were more likely to seek advice on childrearing than were their husbands. The largest percentage sought such advice first from their own mothers; the next largest percentage contacted their spouse. In contrast to black women, more of the middle-income white women that Allen studied named their spouse as their first consultant. Whites also were much more likely to seek advice from professionals than were black mothers; the latter group more often sought the help of other relatives and friends. Sparling & Lewis (1981) also found that for information about children's problems, parents preferred information to come first from family and friends and subsequently from professionals. Female relatives were the preferred source of information when mothers wanted information about how children learn, and unless the infant was ill, female relatives were preferred over physicians for help about a problem with the baby.

The influence of extended family members, particularly key female members, becomes particularly salient when one considers young black parents. There is growing evidence that the knowledge and skill of older females in the young black teenage mother's social network are related to the teenager's own parenting skill and knowledge. In examining the child development knowledge of teenage mothers who lived at home and that of their own mothers, Stevens (in press) found significant positive correlations. Teenage mothers who had more accurate information about early infant normative development lived with mothers who were also more knowledgeable. And less knowledgeable teen mothers had mothers who tended to score lower on such a test. As a total group, the mothers of teenagers knew significantly more about early infant normative development than did their daughters. However, among a group of teenagers who were not yet parents, correlations between their knowledge scores and their mother's scores were not significant. These findings suggest that some exchange of information about normative infant development occurs in three-generation households when the teenager becomes a parent. Moreover, these black grandmothers were better parenting models than were their daughters: they were more emotionally and verbally responsive with infants and were less punitive.

The same teenagers were asked to whom they would turn first for help if they encountered a typical childrearing problem (Stevens, in press). Most indicated this would be their own mother. However, with personal problems, teenagers were no more likely to contact their own mother than extended family members, friends, professionals or others. Clearly, their own mothers were viewed as potent resources of information about children. Therefore, among both very young black mothers and older black mothers, there appears to be considerable reliance on one's own mother for information about childrearing.

Stevens (1984) has provided additional evidence about the relationship between parents' parenting skill and their social integration with extended family members and with others. In this study, 69 low-income women were interviewed. Their mean age was 26.7 years. They had completed an average of 10.8 years of school. Their median yearly income was $3,032, and 68 percent received aid to dependent children. They had 3.0 children on the average, and 50 percent had been in their teens when their first child was born. Sixty-two percent were single women living alone with their children, 19 percent lived with a spouse, 15 percent with another relative, 3 percent lived with a spouse and another relative, and 1 percent lived in other household types.

Black mothers who were knowledgeable about developmental processes, who lived in households with another adult, who were more likely to utilize general community services (i.e. banks, post office, and drug stores), and who contacted their own mother or other extended family members for help with childrearing problems provided more support for cognitive and language development. This support was reflected in their likelihood to read to their infants, to provide stimulating toys, and to play with their infants.

It was expected that mothers whose networks were more supportive and less tight would evidence more optimal parenting skill, because they would have more information and assistance available to them. However, the amount of network support available to the mother and how closely knit the network was were unrelated to parenting skill. On the contrary, a different facet of the mother's connectedness to others was related. Black mothers' *instrumental use* of the resources available to them was more important; general supportiveness of the network was not directly associated with parenting skill. Mothers more functionally isolated from relatives with respect to childrearing issues and problems (but not more isolated from general social support) were less able to provide their infants with instrumental support for language and cognitive development. Stevens (1984) argued that maintenance and use of such linkages with other female relatives increased the flow of information, support, and parenting strategies to the mother, which then resulted in enhancement of her parenting behavior.

Kellam et al. (1975) reported that low-income black first-graders who manifested higher levels of social adjustment in school were more likely to come from mother-father households and mother-grand-mother households than from single female-headed households. The presence of the second adult may have provided the help and support with parenting which enhanced children's social development. It is not clear whether the second adult brings additional economic re-sources as well as information, help, support, and respite. The critical dimensions of such availability to mothers need to be carefully deli-neated.

A revisionist perspective on black childrearing

Until recently, research about black parenting was focused on black-white differences and often confounded cultural differences with social-class differences (Baratz & Baratz, 1970; Sroufe, 1970). Such research also tended to focus solely on low-income blacks. In the past decade, there has been a decided shift towards studying black parents without comparing them to whites and greater emphasis on examining how such variability within black families is related to developmental out-comes in children. This has led to the identification of socialization goals and strategies which distinguish black Americans as a ethnic group, and of others which may overlap considerably with different groups (Hale, 1982; Peters, 1981; Shade, 1983).

One such model has been outlined by Ogbu (1981), who has de-scribed how childrearing strategies in general are a function of broader societal variables: the economic opportunity structure, the social roles available to a group, and consequently, subsistence tasks within a soci-ety. His argument is that societal subsistence tasks dictate adult roles and competencies and define in turn the native theories parents con-struct to guide the generation of appropriate childrearing strategies which shape appropriate competencies in their offspring.

In applying this model to American low-income blacks, Ogbu (1981) identified several subsistence tasks which enable survival. One set of tasks was the conventional job; others included activities like hustling, acting as broker, and preaching. Examples of entrepreneurial and brokerage activities would be odd jobs or hiring others to perform such jobs. Brokers serve as intermediaries for a variety of services: machine repair, painting, electrical work, plumbing, and yard work. Schooling and educational achievement may be a route to success in the conventional economy, but may be less salient for success in the street economy. Moreover, blacks have less access to the conventional economy due to a number of factors: transportation difficulties, discrimination, few or no network linkages to the white business structure.

Street competencies, according to Ogbu (1981), include a mistrust of authority, the ability to fight back, skill in warding off attacks, resourcefulness, self-reliance, and the ability to manipulate others. Certainly some of these may be adaptive for minority children's survival and functioning in quite a wide variety of contexts, including mainstream settings. Morgan (1980) assembled family stories, told across four generations, which illustrate some of these values as they were inculcated in the young within one black family. While we do not argue that these are normative or typical, the stories illustrate some of the socialization strategies used to enable youngsters to acquire such competencies. This family mythology illustrates another mechanism for the transmission of appropriate socialization goals for the young as well as transmission of appropriate socialization strategies. Each story is a striking illustration of a particular trait that these black parents saw as essential to instill in their children—for example, "resourcefulness":

How Caddy Made Marjorie Find a Way to Walk Over the Bridge

Marjorie had to walk over the bridge every day to get to school and every day she would meet this "trash" boy who would make her get off the bridge and walk in the street where the horses walked. She did this every day. He would wait for her on the bridge and when she got ready to walk across he would push her off into the street. Caddy found out what was happening. I don't know who told her but she called Marjorie in the kitchen and she said, "Maggie, you will have to find a way to walk on the bridge. . . . It's up to you to find your own way to walk across the bridge."

Now when Caddy told you you had to find your own way, you had better find it. Marjorie went to her room to think up a way. The only way she could think of was her mama's old rusty hatpin. She put it in her handbag the next day so nobody would see it and she went off to school as usual. Sure enough after school there he was waiting on the bridge, and when he went to push her she took the hatpin and stuck it clean through his arm. Then she ran home and told Caddy what she had done. Well, Caddy said she had found a way but it was the wrong way, but she wouldn't let anybody bother Marjorie because she had told her to find a way and Marjorie had found the only way she could. (Morgan, 1980, p. 30)

Shade (1982) also has argued that wariness and distrust of others is an Afro-American world view. Parents socialize their children to be independent, cautious, skilled in manipulating the system, and doing the white man one better within his own rules to avoid becoming a "victim." "Putting on Mr. Charlie" and other techniques are strategies used to avoid victimization and to control one's environment. Competencies necessary to manipulate the environment successfully, according to Shade, are careful attention to social cues, searching explicit messages for their hidden meaning, preference for social distance, and reliance on nonverbal communication.

These "alternative" socialization outcomes would require a divergent pattern of childrearing practices. One of those which may well fit in this fabric is the arbitrary use of physical punishment. Shade argued that parents' use of power assertion helped to assure that black children maintain their wariness and vigilance of others at all times— even of those with whom they have strong attachment bonds. The task of the black parent is complicated by the need to rear a child who is dually competent: skillful in the black culture and in the white subculture.

There is growing evidence that black mothers' relationships with extended family members are related to their ability to parent well. Black women who are socially integrated with family members provided more support for their children's development. Family members are viewed as potent resources for information and help with childrearing. Many black women make use of such help. We are just beginning to investigate systematically these processes and relationships around the socialization of parenting within black families. Other female relatives, including older, more experienced childrearers, appear to play an important role in this. What is not clear is whether there is simply a transmission of new information from one network or family member to another or whether the process of exchange of information and discussion facilitates restructuring of information and knowledge the parent already has, in addition to adding new information and skill. It is likely both processes operate. What is absent is documentation and description of these processes and of their relationship to learning to be an effective parent. What is becoming increasingly apparent is that among many black families, the extended family is a potent influence on this aspect of adult role performance.

CONCLUSION

This admittedly brief and restrictive overview of the major features in the evolutionary development of black family research and study poses the challenge of comprehensively drawing the periods together in terms of analytical coherence. Wallace (1974), perhaps one of the most incisive black sociological theoreticians, offers such an encompassing paradigm for an analysis of the problems confronted in this respect.

Wallace argues that the central problem in studies of black Americans revolves around the tendency to blur the theoretic distinction that otherwise ought to be maintained between social organizations and cultures. Social organization refers to the patterns and regularities of group life that are external and observable: that is, "who-does-what-to-whom." As such, social organization necessarily involves the physical actions between people. Culture, on the other hand, refers to patterns and regularities of group life that are concerned with the subjective dispositions of individuals: that is, "who-thinks-or-feels-with-whom." As such, culture necessarily involves internal psychical behavior of members of a group who invest meaning to symbols, beliefs, perception, loyalities, and so forth.

While social organization and culture are logically independent in terms of content, each acts in ways that mutually modify the other. However, heuristic assumptions are ascribed to one or the other, thus giving causal primacy to one or the other. In this connection, it might be noted that in his conceptualization of the dynamics of black family structure and function, Frazier emphasized black social organization as a causal influence on culture. In other words, Frazier gave causal primacy to social organization over culture, which lead him to devalue the role of culture and ultimately to view black culture in pathological terms.

DuBois, on the other hand, tended to view culture as causally primary to social organization; in fact, he came to view black social organization as a perversion of black cultural orientation. For DuBois, certain externally imposed forces, "color-caste constraints," operated to prevent the maturing of black social organization. Grasping this distinction, as Wallace (1974) insists, it might be asserted that in the current period, Black family analysts tend to emphasize the cultural features of black family dynamics and as such are more consonant with a DuBoisian rather than a Frazierian analysis of black family life.

However, emphases on social organization or culture are not merely mechanical processes in the sense that they are individual volitional issues. Rather, as Wallace points out, social organization and culture correspond significantly with each other. The emphasis upon culture increases during periods of heightened consciousness, on the one hand,

and recedes during periods of diminished consciousness. This ebb-and-flow process is functionally tied to forces external to the group, that is, exogenous influences. It should be expected, accordingly, that the current status in black family research will continue to evolve and change in light of sociological and other exigencies of American life.

REFERENCES

Abernathy, V. Social network and the response to the maternal role. *International Journal of Sociology of the Family*, 1973, *3*, 86–92.

Allen, W. The search for applicable theories of black family life. *Journal of Marriage and the Family*, 1978, *40*(1), 111–129.

Aptheker, H. (Ed.). *The correspondence of W. E. B. DuBois* (Vol. II): *Selections 1934–1944*. Amherst: University of Massachusetts Press, 1976.

Ball, R. E. *Black family structure and income disparity*. Paper presented at the annual meeting of the National Council on Family Relations, Milwaukee, October 1981.

Baratz, S. S., & Baratz, J. C. Early childhood intervention: The social science base of institutional racism. *Harvard Educational Review*, 1970, *40*, 29–50.

Belle, D. H. (Ed.). *Lives in stress: Women and depression*. Beverly Hills, Calif.: Sage Publications, 1982.

Billingsley, A. *Black families in white America*. Englewood Cliffs, N.J.: Prentice-Hall, 1968.

Blassingame, J. W. *The slave community: Plantation life in the ante-bellum South*. New York: Oxford University Press, 1972.

Bronfenbrenner, U. *The ecology of human development*. Cambridge, Mass.: Harvard University Press, 1979.

Carter, H., & Glick, P. *Marriage and divorce: A social and economic study*. American Public Health Association, Vital and Health Statistics Monograph. Cambridge, Mass.: Harvard University Press, 1970.

Dodson, J. Conceptualizations of black families. In H. P. McAdoo (Ed.), *Black families*. Beverly Hills, Calif.: Sage Publications, 1981.

DuBois, W. E. B. *The Philadelphia Negro: A social study*. Boston: Ginn, 1899.

DuBois, W. E. B. *The Negro American family*. Atlanta: Atlanta University Press, 1908.

DuBois, W. E. B. *The autobiography of W. E. B. DuBois: A soliloquy on viewing my life from the last decade of its first century*. New York: International Publishers, 1968.

DuBois, W. E. B. *The souls of black folks*. New York: New American Library, 1969.

Edwards, G. F., & Frazier, E. F. In J. E. Blackwell & M. Janowitz (Eds.), *Black sociologists: Historical and contemporary perspectives*. Chicago: University of Chicago Press, 1974.

Ford, B. O. *Supportive structures for black single parent families: A contemporary kinship system*. Paper presented at the University of Notre Dame Black Studies Program, "Support for single parent families through extended family networks," May 1978.

Frazier, E. F. *The Negro family in the United States*. Chicago: University of Chicago Press, 1966.

Gutman, H. *The Black family in slavery and freedom: 1750–1925.* New York: Random House, 1976.

Gottlieb, B. H. Social support as a focus for integrative research in psychology. *American Psychologist,* 1983, *38,* 278–287.

Hale, J. E. *Black children, their roots, culture and learning styles.* Provo, Utah: Brigham Young University Press, 1982.

Herskovits, M. J. *The myth of the Negro past.* Boston: Beacon Press, 1941.

Hilliard, A. Alternatives to IQ testing: An approach to the assessment of gifted children. Sacramento, Calif.: Final Report, Special Education Support Unit. California State Department of Education. Eric no. ED 147009.

Johnson, L. B. Perspectives on Black family empirical research: 1965–1978. In H. McAdoo (Ed.), *Black families.* Beverly Hills, Calif.: Sage Publications, 1981. Pp. 87–102.

Kellam, S. G., Branch, J. D., Agrawal, K. C., & Ensminger, M. E. *Mental health and going to school: The Woodlawn program of assessment, early intervention and evaluation.* Chicago: University of Chicago Press, 1975.

Lee, G. R. The effects of social networks on the family. In W. R. Burr, R. Hill, F. I. Nye, & I. L. Reiss (Eds.), *Contemporary theories about the family* (Vol. 1): *Research-based theories.* New York: Free Press, 1979.

McAdoo, H. P. Minority families. In J. H. Stevens, Jr. & M. Mathews (Eds.), *Mother/Child, Father/Child Relationships.* Washington, D. C.: NAEYC, 1978.

McAdoo, H. P. Patterns of upward mobility in black families. In H. P. McAdoo (Ed.), *Black families.* Beverly Hills, Calif.: Sage Publications, 1981.

McAdoo, H. P. Stress absorbing systems in black families. *Family Relations,* 1982, *31,* 479–488.

Merton, R. A paradigm for the study of the sociology of knowledge. In P. Lazarsfeld & M. Rosenberg (Eds.), *The language of social research.* New York: Free Press, Pp. 498–510, 1955.

Merton, R. Insiders and outsiders: A chapter in the sociology of knowledge. *American Journal of Sociology.* July, 1972, *78* (1), 11.

Moynihan, D. P. The Negro family: The case for national action. In L. Rainwater & W. L. Yancey, *The Moynihan report and the politics of controversy.* Cambridge, Mass.: MIT Press, 1965. Pp. 47–94.

Mitchell, R. E., Barbarin, O. A., & Hurley, D. J., Jr. Problem-solving, resource utilization, and community involvement in a black and a white community. *American Journal of Community Psychology,* 1981, *9,* 233–246.

Morgan, K. L. *Children of strangers: The stories of a black family.* Philadelphia: Temple University Press, 1980.

Neighbors, H. W., Jackson, J. S., Bowman, P. J., & Guren, G. Stress, coping and black mental health. *Prevention in Human Services,* in press.

Nobles, W. African root and American fruit: The black family. *Journal of Social and Behavioral Sciences,* 1974, *20,* 52–64.

Nobles, W. Toward an empirical and theoretical framework for defining black families. *Journal of Marriage and the Family,* 1978, *40,* 679–688.

Ogbu, J. U. Origins of human competence: A cultural-ecological perspective. *Child Development,* 1981, *52,* 413–429.

Park, R. E. The urban community as a spatial pattern and a moral order. In R. H. Turner (Ed.), *Robert E. Park: On special control and collective behavior.* Chicago: University of Chicago Press, 1967. Pp. 58–60.

Peters, M. F. Parenting in black families with young children: A historical perspective. In H. McAdoo (Ed.), *Black families.* Beverly Hills, Calif.: Sage Publications, 1981.

Rainwater, L. *Behind ghetto walls.* Chicago: Aldine, 1970.

Rainwater, L., & Yancey, W. L. *The Moynihan report and the politics of controversy.* Cambridge, Mass.: MIT Press, 1965.

Shade, B. J. Afro-American cognitive style: A variable in school success. *Review of Educational Research,* 1982, *52,* 219–244.

Smith, C. U., & Killian, L. Black sociologists and social protest. In J. E. Blackwell & M. Janowitz (Eds.), *Black sociologists: Historical and contemporary perspectives.* Chicago: University of Chicago Press, 1974.

Sroufe, L. A. A methodological and philosophical critique of intervention-oriented research. *Developmental Psychology,* 1970, *2,* 140–145.

Sparling, J. & Lewis, I. *Information needs of parents with young children.* Washington, D.C.: Administration for Children, Youth, and Families, 1981.

Stack, C. *All our kin.* New York: Harper & Row, 1974.

Staples, R. Toward a sociology of the black family: A decade of theory and research. *Journal of Marriage and the Family,* 1971, *33,* 19–38.

Stevens, J. H., Jr. *Social integration, social support and parenting among black and white mothers.* Paper presented at the annual meeting of the American Educational Research Association, New Orleans, April 1984.

Stevens, J. H., Jr. Black grandmothers' and black adolescent mothers' knowledge about parenting. *Developmental Psychology,* in press.

Sudarkasa, N. Interpreting the African heritage in Afro-American family organization. In H. McAdoo (Ed.), *Black families.* Beverly Hills, Calif.: Sage Publications, 1981.

Taylor, R. J., Jackson, J. S., & Quick, A. D. The frequency of social support among black Americans: Preliminary findings from the National Survey of Black Americans. *Urban Research Review,* 1982, *8*(2), 1–4; 11.

Valentine, C. A. *Culture and poverty: Critique and counter-proposals.* Chicago: University of Chicago Press, 1968.

Wallace, W. L. Sociological theory in studies of black Americans. In J. E. Blackwell and M. Janowitz (Eds.), *Black sociologists: Historical and contemporary perspectives.* Chicago: University of Chicago Press, 1974.

Chapter 23

Social Adaptation: A Review of Dual-Earner Family Literature*

LYNN S. WALKER
BARBARA STRUDLER WALLSTON

INTRODUCTION AND CONCEPTUAL FRAMEWORK

When married women left home to work in factories and offices during World War II, social scientists began to study the link between work and family processes. Of course, wives had always played a productive role in the family (Aldous, 1982; Hesse, 1979; Turner, 1971). In preindustrial agrarian societies, the couple worked together in the home to form the core economic unit. Industrialization and unionization led men to work in factories as sole breadwinners of a "family wage" (Pleck, 1983). Wives worked at home as before, but both their unpaid labor and their earnings from goods such as eggs and services such as sewing were ignored in the new conception of work. This segregation of domestic and occupational activities was reflected in sociology and psychology, which for many years treated work and the family as independent areas of investigation.

As it became clear that married women's role in the workplace was not merely a wartime phenomenon, studies of "working wives" were designed to investigate the impact that a wife's work outside the home might have on children and marriage. Underlying these studies was the assumption that the viability of the family depended on sex-typed division of roles. This literature had an absolute view of family structure, failing to appreciate that family structure has evolved

* We wish to thank Joseph Pleck and Jeylan Mortimer for leads to the literature. Christy Edgin's speedy typing, ability to read twisted inserts, and willingness to do it again when the word processor failed have greatly enhanced our ability to produce this chapter. We appreciate the comments of Michael Berger, Ruth Czirr, Lucia Gilbert, Kathleen Hoover-Dempsey, George Howe, Chaya Piotrkowski, and Sally Robinson on previous drafts of the chapter.

in relation to a changing environmental context. Families with employed wives were viewed, at best, as an anomaly. At worst, it was implied that families were developing a deviant lifestyle which threatened the well-being of society.

The Rapoports turned this perspective on end when they described the dual-career couple as a "variant pattern"—an adaptive response to industrial society (Rapoport & Rapoport, 1969). By switching from the language of deviance to that of evolutionary biology, the Rapoports rejected the stigma that had been attached to the new family lifestyle. The dual-career literature, now using the broader term *dual-earner family*,[1] badly needs a conceptual framework to integrate the diverse areas that comprise the field. The social ecological model, which is rooted in biology, is one fertile theoretical framework. Three characteristics of this model make it particularly useful for studies of the dual-earner family:

1. Level of analysis. Studies of the dual-earner family require a level of analysis that moves beyond the individual to consider relationships among family members and the interface between the family and the work world. In social ecology, the level of analysis extends from the individual to the progressively broader series of contexts (family, community, culture) surrounding the individual (Bronfenbrenner, 1977).

2. Causality. Nonlinear causality is essential if one is to examine both the effects of family members on each other and the mutual influences of family and work. Within the social ecological framework, human adaptation is viewed as a feedback process in which environmental changes require new human responses and human initiatives change the environment (Melson, 1980).

3. Time. The modern family is in a rapid process of change which cannot be captured by static theoretical models. Social ecology recognizes the dynamic, changing nature of the relationship between an individual and the surrounding contexts.

Although this review includes few studies framed in social ecological terms, it is possible to integrate the results of diverse studies within that framework, thus enabling us to identify areas in which research is lacking and relationships which have yet to be examined. We describe the social ecological model in more detail before reviewing the literature on dual-earner families.[2]

---

[1] Dual earner is more inclusive than dual career, eliminates the class bias inherent in the other term (Benenson, 1983), and negates the notion inherent in "dual worker" that only income-producing activity should be labeled work (Aldous, 1982).

[2] For a more comprehensive discussion of the ecological model as it applies to families, the readers is referred to Melson (1980).

Social ecological model

Adaptation is a central construct in social ecology. In the ongoing process of daily life, individuals both respond to environmental demands and become actively involved in the creation of their world (Melson, 1980). Figure 1 applies the process of adaptation to dual-earner families. The individual characteristics of each family member interact with those of the family, workplace, and environment, yielding the family's adaptational strategies. These strategies are the techniques the family uses to perform the functions necessary for its maintenance and development (Cohen & Lazarus, 1983).

Figure 1

Social ecological model of the process of social adaptation in dual-earner families

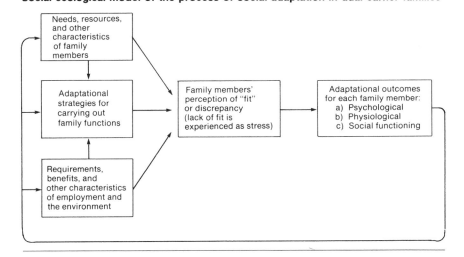

An individual's adaptation to a particular situation at a particular time has been conceptualized in terms of "person-environment fit" (French, Rodgers, & Cobb, 1974). Fit is good when there is a balance between the demands and expectations of a situation and the individual's capacities. Poor fit is a state of discrepancy between demands and capabilities; the individual experiences this state as stress. The quality of fit is subjective: Circumstances that produce stress for one person may be innocuous for another.

The general quality of a person's adaptation may be assessed in three outcome domains: psychological, physiological, and social functioning (Cohen & Lazarus, 1983). These domains may be independent of each other. For example, overtime work may meet an employer's expectations and thus be adaptive in the social domain, while also having maladaptive consequences such as high blood pressure in the physiological domain. Individual outcomes in any domain affect the family system and its adaptational processes. For example, negative individual outcomes may lead that person to make a smaller contribution to family resources, such as providing less emotional support to family members or being less efficient in household work, and also increase demands on other family members for support.

The process of adaptation and specific adaptational strategies, including coping,[3] are most obvious when some change affects the fit between demands on the family and resources available to meet them (Melson, 1980). This change may originate in the environment, as when inflation outpaces family income, or within the family, as when a daughter graduates from high school and wishes to go to college. In either case, families direct their efforts toward reducing the discrepancy between demands and resources. Such a discrepancy might develop when a housewife returns to work and housework is neglected. If the quality of housekeeping does not meet family members' needs, the change at home is stressful. A better fit between the family's need for a clean house and the wife's reduced resources of time and energy could be achieved via a variety of adaptational strategies: Other family members could share in the housework, increased income could be used to hire a housekeeper, the wife could work harder, or the standards for housekeeping could be lowered. Of course, any of these resolutions might be unsatisfactory for some family members, and thus the situation would continue to be stressful. Consequences of this stress might be seen in individual health problems, depression, or family conflict.

Human ecosystems are made up of individual members who are active and goal directed. The quality of adaptation must be measured in terms of their individual perceptions and aspirations. Rather than asking whether the dual-earner family is better or worse than the traditional family, this perspective raises a more basic issue of identifying the various adaptational strategies of dual-earner families and tying these adaptations to effects on family members.

Overview of the literature review

This review focuses on published empirical data collected since 1970 in the United States, omitting some small areas of research such as decision making and marital power in dual-earner families. Articles on the effects of maternal employment on individual children are

---

[3] Adaptation is a superordinate category which subsumes coping processes (Cohen & Lazarus, 1983; White, 1974). Coping, however, is generally used to refer to adaptational processes in unusually difficult situations—i.e., those which tend to be perceived as stressful.

omitted because they have been thoroughly reviewed elsewhere (e.g., Bowman, Quarm, & Gideonse, 1983; Wallston, 1973).

The review is organized into two major sections. The first, on current adaptational strategies of the dual-earner family, examines how dual-earner families organize their lives and what social factors limit their choice of adaptational strategies. The second section examines the outcomes of these various adaptational strategies in three domains (Cohen & Lazarus, 1983): (a) psychological outcomes, measured in terms of individual variables such as marital satisfaction and self-esteem; (b) physiological outcomes, measured in terms of health status; and (c) social outcomes, measured in terms of the quality of family relationships and the success of individual members in fulfilling social roles. The chapter concludes with suggested directions for research.

ADAPTATIONAL STRATEGIES

The literature reviewed in this section rarely uses terminology or theory relating to adaptation. Much work uses sociological or economic theories of family functioning, such as resource theory, role theory, and household production function. Even more common are atheoretical attempts to describe some variant of dual-earner couple functioning. This literature can be organized within an ecological framework, however, since the ways the family carries out its functions may be thought of as its adaptational strategies.

This section reviews literature relevant to adaptational strategies used in household and family functioning and in employment role functioning. Social structural factors which help determine the feasibility of various strategies are also discussed.

Household and family functioning

Certain necessary tasks must be negotiated, "whether implicitly or explicitly, once, regularly or continuously" (Weingarten, 1978, p. 45), to meet the family's requirements. Studies have focused on mechanics of living and childrearing—"family work" in Pleck's (1979) terms. The division of labor within the family has been a particular focus. Table 1 details studies in this area and summarizes conclusions relevant to the effect of the wife's employment on men's family work.

It is still the case that wives have the primary responsibility for family work and spend more time on household and family functions than do husbands. Women's entry into employment has proceeded far more rapidly than men's involvement in family work (e.g., Miller & Garrison, 1982; Mortimer & London, 1982). With the exception of a few couples consciously struggling toward egalitarian divisions of household labor (e.g., Haas, 1980), the early finding of nonegalitarian division of labor still tends to be true even among families of professional women. The amount of husband contributions does not appear to have increased over the past decade. Nonetheless, most studies in Table 1 do show that husbands of employed wives do more family work than husbands whose wives are not employed. Summing employment and family work hours, dual-earner husbands and wives worked an equal number of total hours in one study (Nickols & Metzen, 1982); but in others, wives put in more total work time (see Pleck, 1979).

Despite some conflicting evidence, several structural factors appear to increase husbands' participation in family work: lower income (Berk & Berk, 1978; Ericksen, Yancey, & Ericksen, 1979; Model, 1982), more education (Farkas, 1976; Lopata, Bamewolt, & Norv, 1980; Perrucci, Potter, & Rhoads, 1978), working fewer hours (Nickols & Fox, 1983), being black (Ericksen et al., 1979; Farkas), and husband's positive attitude toward involvement (Model; Perrucci et al.). Job factors such as shiftwork may influence the husband's role in childrearing more than does his attitude (Hood & Golden, 1979).

In studies comparing spouses' reports about household work, the reporter generally gives a higher estimate of his or her own household work than the spouse gives of the same work (e.g., Albrecht, Bahr, & Chadwick, 1979; Condran & Bode, 1982). There is greater agreement for tasks which are stereotypically masculine or feminine and when measures of overall work rather than individual tasks are used (Berk & Shih, 1980). These data indicate the importance of obtaining data from both spouses, although it should also be noted that spouses' perceptions may be more important than actual hours of family work in determining outcomes. Finally, in addition to focusing on relative equality of family work, broader perceptions of equity should be considered.

Pleck (1977, cited in Ericksen et al., 1979) notes the importance of distinguishing between absolute time and proportion of time in family work. Women's employment typically decreases their total hours of family work, resulting in an increase in husband's proportional time but not necessarily an increase in his actual time in family work. Thus, discrepant findings in this area may be accounted for by differential measurement.

There is a lack of uniformity in the definitions of family work and disagreement on the best measurement strategy. Berk and Shih (1980) argue for the use of specific tasks, while Bohen and Viveros-Long (1981) argue that aggregating tasks done on a regular and uniform basis provides the most-reliable data. Berk and Berk (1978) suggest that task rather than time units are meaningful to household members. They also point out that childrearing differs greatly from other housework,

Table 1

Studies of division of family work

Authors (article date): Data collection date	Theory	Sample nature and size	Information source and style	Tasks included	Dependent measure and type of questions	Other variables	Wife employment influence on husband family work	Comments
Perruci, Potter, & Rhoads (1978): 1972	Relative resources versus time available versus socialization.	98 couples: stratified-area probability sample of Lafayette and West Lafayette, Indiana.	Husband interview.	12 specific tasks (e.g., grocery shop, shovel sidewalk, buy children's clothes, straighten up for company).	Husband or wife always, greater or equal for each task; proportion husband equal or more as dependent variable.	8 ideology attitude items; husband's mother work; marital happiness; desire to engage in leisure with wife; spouse education; husband occupation; wife employment; no. of children at home; length of marriage; husband age; husband expect wife full-time	Husbands of employed wives do 12 percent more tasks than those with wives not employed.	Interviewed spouses independently but used husband data for major analyses.

Study	Theory	Sample	Method	Definition	Measures	Predictors	Findings	Comments
Farkas (1976): 1969–1973—data recall about previous year; predicted to data about 1972.	Relative education resources versus economic view (comparative wage) versus subcultural hypothesis.	University of Michigan Survey Research Center panel study of income dynamics; 1,500 couples; only about 800 met criteria of wife employed in 1981.	Interviews.	Housework—cleaning, cooking, and other work around the house.	Reported annual hours at housework and market labor; percent of years wife some marketwork and husband some housework as sharing measure; also husband annual housework as criterion.	employed next 10 years. Husband / wife wage ratio; previous hours worked; education; race; number and age of children; relative education.	Husbands of employed wives did twice as much annual housework (about 3 more minutes per week) for both younger and older couples.	For all analyses, divide into younger couples (wife <35) and older couples (wife 35–60 in 1972); excellent analyses and controls; prospective analysis; author notes life-cycle importance; different older, younger prediction may reflect change in sex role attitudes.

Table 1 (continued)

Authors (article date): Data collection date	Theory	Sample nature and size	Information source and style	Tasks included	Dependent measure and type of questions	Other variables	Wife employment influence on husband family work	Comments
Nickols & Metzen (1982): 1968–1973		University of Michigan Survey Research Center panel study of income dynamics; 1,156 intact families under 65 with no disabilities.	Interviews usually with husband; 4 years were face-to-face; 2 years were telephone.	Meal preparation and cleanup; housecleaning; laundry; record keeping.	Recall of hours per week.	Wife and husband market work and housework; numerous demographic data provided but not analyzed.	Wife employment had minimal effect on husband housework; for wives whose time in paid work increased from 1972 to 1973, husband's housework increased about 18 minutes per week.	Noted equality of total hours worked for both spouses when employment and family work added.
Weingarten (1978): 1973	Adaptation perspective; couples negotiate to meet family needs	Boston professional couples; N = 32.	Couples interviewed together; asked to resolve disagreements;	20 questions each covering meeting each other's sexual and psychological	1 point for more involvement of husband or wife; each gets a point if	Age; similar or different spouse work histories; interaction mode:	When wives work full-time versus part-time, husbands do proportionally	Notes the importance of historical context and psychological meaning of

706

Study & date	Theoretical framework	Sample	Data collection	Activities measured	Measurement	Other variables	Findings	Comments
	implicitly or explicitly.		60 questions orally and 20 paper and pencil.	needs; mechanics of daily living; maintaining relations with community; raising children.	equal involvement.	interdependence and participation.	more family work.	family division of labor.
Johnson & Johnson (1977): ?	Role strain and adaptation.	28 dual-career families with young children in upstate New York.	2-hour separate interviews with husband and wife.	Marketing, home maintenance, food preparation, cleaning, quantitative child care, child-care responsibility, child-care stress, etc.	Work load distribution; open-ended and forced-choice questions.	Career activities; power; pattern of family activities; childrearing attitudes and behavior; role strain.	While all husbands participated in domestic functions, wives retained major childrearing responsibility.	
Albrecht, Bahr, & Chadwick (1979): 1974		Phone directory random sample of Utah adults; $N = 759$ couples; 4 age groups: ≤ 29, 30–44, 45–64, ≥ 65.	Mail questionnaire with 4 follow-ups; husband and wife complete independently.	Four roles—provider, housekeeper, kinship, child care—assessed with total of 7 questions (3 on child care).	Who usually does each task? husband, $h > w$, $h = w$, $w > h$, wife.	Preferences regarding each task; marital decision making; agreement with hypothetical alternative lifestyles; age.	Data not analyzed for role interrelationships.	Used generational differences to approximate change over time with younger groups representing new patterns expected to emerge.

Table 1 *(continued)*

Authors (article date): Data collection date	Theory	Sample nature and size	Information source and style	Tasks included	Dependent measure and type of questions	Other variables	Wife employment influence on husband family work	Comments
Berk & Berk (1978): 1975	Chicago school household production function.	Evanston, Ill., N = 184 people from larger random sample (N = 304) who met criteria.	Phone survey of married women with children.	60 tasks *not* including child care; (e.g., cooks meals, makes beds, does laundry).	Proportion of tasks done by each family member; whether each task is done, and who generally does it.	Years of marriage; employment status of each spouse; spouse income; children by age; husband education; husband / child decided to do more housework.	Indirect evidence that professional women have husbands who do more tasks, but employment of wife per se little effect on increase in husband household effort.	Unusual in inclusion of child family work; good or problems with economic theory and on measure issues.
Ericksen, Yancey, & Ericksen (1979): 1975	Networks support segregated roles versus power perspecive.	Probability sample of adults in Philadelphia under 65; N = 1,212 intact couples; for child dependent	Survey— husband and wife responses.	Shopping, cooking, cleaning, laundry, and household repair; child care.	Work role sharing; housework sharing; child-care sharing; define as share or not.	Social network; marital power (measured by wife education, husband income); race; children under 12.	If wife works full time, but not if she works part time, husband is more likely to share housework; husband more likely to	Recognize a very liberal definition of sharing.

	variable $N = 534$.					share child care if wife works part time, but not full time.
Robinson (1980): 1975	University of Michigan Survey Research Center on Americans' use of time; $N = 438$ women from larger national probability sample; 18–65; nonrural; at least one adult employed.	Diary of activities in 24 hours; women sampled.	Specific activities in categories of housework, child care, and shopping = family care.	Minutes per day in family care.	Demographic variables; satisfaction with household cleanliness, meal quality, etc.; data for women 1965–66.	Analyses not computed by employment status in terms of husband family care.
Zinn (1980): 1975	8 Chicano families in urban New Mexico.	Interviews and participant observation over 10 months.	Qualitative description based on self-report and observation.	Conjugal power; ethnicity; decision making; social class.	Husbands of employed wives assist with some housework.	Move to go beyond simple acculturation theories.

Table 1 *(continued)*

Author (article date): Data collection date	Theory	Sample nature and size	Information source and style	Tasks included	Dependent measure and type of questions	Other variables	Wife employment influence on husband family work	Comments
Berk (1979): ?		From national probability sample of 748 intact urban households; randomly sampled 50 percent husbands, $N = 348$.	Husband's structured interview to provide retrospective diary; also wife 24-hour diaries for full sample.	81 household activities, coded from wife open-ended diaries (e.g., friends visit, ate breakfast, made beds).	Order of activities for previous evening on return from work and morning before leave for work.	Children.	Little or no difference in morning activities; in the evening, slight increase (5 more activities) for husbands of employed wives.	No information on weekends requested; husbands with employed wives compared to employed wives.
Lopata (1980): ?	Symbolic interactionist construction of reality and role theory.	Chicago women married and employed, aged 25–54.	Wife.		Wife perception of husband occupational, husband, and homemaking roles.	Education; occupational characteristics.	Men are rarely seen as involved in household management.	
Pleck (1979): 1977	Social and historical context important;	From 1977 quality of employment survey,	Personal interviews.		Time estimates for average work and	Children present.	Husbands of employed wives reported 1.8	

men's changing family roles.	national representative sample of 1,575 people, selected 270 married women and 757 married men.		nonworkday converted to hours per week of child care and housework.	Low or high egalitarian role structure for each factor.	more hours per week in housework and 2.7 more hours per week in child care than those with wives not employed.	
Ybarra (1982): 1977	N = 100 Chicano families in Fresno, Calif., using stratified random sample.	Open-ended interviews separately with both spouses in English and Spanish.	Decision making, household work, childrearing; housekeeping scale included 10 specific tasks (e.g., dish washing, laundry, home repairs).	Economic class, occupation; age; education; level of acculturation; attitudes toward female employment, male family work.	More egalitarian housekeeping and childrearing when wife employed.	Study developed from dissertation, and information on measures is scanty.

Table 1 (continued)

Authors (article date): Data collection date	Theory	Sample nature and size	Information source and style	Tasks included	Dependent measure and type of questions	Other variables	Wife employment influence on husband family work	Comments
Berk & Shih (1980): ?		From national probability sample of 748 intact households; randomly selected 350 husbands, so $N = 700$.	Husband and wife independent card sorts.	45 routine household tasks (e.g., cleaning oven, weeding, setting table, talking with children).	Activity frequency, who generally does task, task importance & pleasantness; proportion husband-wife agreement on who does task.	Stereotypic nature of task.	Wife employment in interaction with wife perception does not predict husband's household task involvement on most tasks.	Focus is methodological testing husband versus wife reports.
Bohen & Viveros-Long (1981): 1978	Ecological and family systems theory.	$N = 706$ employees in two agencies; Washington, D.C.: tabled data for 350–425 people.	Male and female employees; questionnaires hand delivered and picked up.	Estimate of time spent daily on home chores (things like cooking, cleaning, repairs, yardwork) and childrearing (e.g., feeding, dressing, going places,	Aggregated to weekly time spent on home chores and on child-rearing for respondent and spouse; family equity.	Family earning structure; family life-cycle stage (number and age of children); occupational level; hours worked and commuted;	Fathers with employed wives spent more weekly hours on home chores than fathers with wives not employed, but no differences for men	Focus of study is on influence of flextime (limited to half-hour deviations in start and leave time).

Study	Theory	Sample	Method	Tasks	Scale	Variables	Findings
				disciplining, reading, chauffeuring).		outside help with home responsibilities; living alone or with others; flextime versus standard time.	without children; more equity when wives employed (40 percent male activity) versus not employed (25 percent male activity).
Huber & Spitze (1981): 1978	Cognitive dissonance; adaptation.	National probability sample of 682 couples.	Telephone interviews; both spouses.	Meal preparation; food shopping; child/aged care; daily housework; meal cleanup.	1 to 5 scale on each task from wife always to husband always.	Perceptions of household decision making; age; education; race; spouse earnings; age of youngest child; attitudes toward women's employment; other related attitudes (e.g., ERA, abortion); work attachment (wife employment indexed over 10 years).	Wife's current employment is the best predictor of both spouses' perceptions of husband family work involvement.

Table 1 *(concluded)*

Authors (article date): Data collection date	Theory	Sample nature and size	Information source and style	Tasks included	Dependent measure and type of questions	Other variables	Wife employment influence on husband family work	Comments
Model (1982): 1978		650 married women in Detroit.	Interviews with wives.	Grocery, laundry, dinner, dishes, and vacuuming.	Percent husband work on household tasks.	Wife sharing attitude; husband income; life cycle; newly wed; retired; teen children; latency children; education.	Wife employment is a significant predictor of husband housework.	With equal husband/wife income ($N = 55$), there was more husband participation.
Malson (1981): ?	Role adaptation overload.	54 urban black women in Boston with at least one child under 12.	2–4 hour interviews in the home with women.			Employment; marital status; role models.	Husbands provided little help with family work.	At this point, a more qualitative initial data report.
Condran & Bode (1982): 1980	Relative resources versus socialization and social class versus time available versus	Random sample of 316 married adults in Middletown.	10-minute interview with husband or wife but *not* both by telephone.	Disciplining children; taking children to M.D.; preparing meals; paying bills, minor	Likelihood of wife performing task; recoded to usually performed by wife versus all others (i.e.,	Sex of respondent; education, age, family income, religious involvement, wife's mother	Small effect of wife employment on meals (primarily) but also M.D. visits and home repairs;	Method comparison of male versus female respondents found differences.

714

economic efficiency.	repair (to represent traditionally male, female, and neutral tasks).	share, husband, or another person).	employed, perception of relative economic status.	wife *more* likely to discipline child if employed.	Women saw themselves as doing more, while men said household work shared.
Stahl, Wheeler, Edwards, & Vicks (1983): ?	80 professional couples in Southeast; women were doctoral-level college professors or administrators; actual *N* = 100; half of couples black.	Questionnaires to both spouses.	25 items on household responsibilities (e.g., shopping, car maintenance, housecleaning).	Percent family responsibility they assume.	Androgyny; how should family responsibility be shared? Race; age; children.	Since all women employed, no analysis by wife employment.

Note: The table is ordered by date of data collection, using an estimate where this information could not be ascertained from the article.

particularly in terms of its psychic rewards, which may give some child care a recreational component (Nickols & Metzen, 1982).

These few studies with a limited focus are only a beginning to our understanding of strategies used to distribute family work. The literature does not address the strategies for division of labor in blue-collar families, which may differ significantly from those of professional couples. Another omission is strategies used by ethnic minority families, even though wives' employment in these families has a long history (e.g., Ybarra, 1982; Zinn, 1980). Basic descriptive literature needed to understand processes of family work is becoming available (e.g., Berk, 1979). Research on decision making in relation to family work, acceptability of various adaptational strategies, and relation of these strategies to outcome is needed to broaden our understanding of family work, as are longitudinal studies of almost any of the questions mentioned.

Employment Role Functioning

In addition to household and family functions in dual-earner families, spouses have employment role functions. The literature on job seeking and mobility reveals some strategies related to coordination of employment. The degree of involvement in employment is also discussed in this section, since seeing employment as secondary to family is a major strategy for coordinating the two careers.

Mobility and job seeking.   Job-related geographic mobility is a major problem for white-collar and professional dual-earner couples. Although nearly all research and discussion on this topic focuses on dual-career couples or those where at least one member is a professional, the issue can be important at all socioeconomic levels, with migrant farm workers a prime example (Mortimer, Hall, & Hill, 1978).

Many employers require or expect geographic mobility. Dual-earner couples must develop strategies not only for finding two initial jobs (Berger, Foster, Wallston, & Wright, 1977) but for finding employment for one spouse when the other moves. It is clear from the literature that for the majority of couples, the husband's career takes precedence when a move is made for employment (Bryson & Bryson, 1980; Bryson, Bryson, Licht, & Licht, 1976; Duncan, 1975; Erkut & Fields, 1983; Haemmerlie & Montgomery, 1981; Matthews & Matthews, 1980b; Poloma, Pendleton, & Garland, 1981; Taylor, 1980). However, the wife's occupation has some effect on migration (Duncan, 1975), and husbands may be less mobile than unmarried men (Long, 1974, cited in Miller & Garrison, 1982). Even studies which find that husbands' careers take precedence tend to find some effect of wives' careers on husbands' attitudes toward job changes (Bryson & Bryson; Haemmerlie & Mont-gomery; Matthews & Matthews) and their actual moves (Erkut & Fields; Taylor). Couples' moves were unrelated to wives' career oppor-tunities in only one study, a follow-up of couples first investigated in 1969 (Poloma et al., 1981). These data may reflect a cohort effect, with couples holding different assumptions about women's careers than couples in the last decade have held.

In fact, recent work suggests that couples prefer egalitarian job-seeking strategies, but that situational constraints may prevent egali-tarian choices (Berger, 1980; Wallston, Foster, & Berger, 1978). Little is known about individual or institutional factors that affect job mobility. In one study, self-reports of feminism were related to nontraditional choices on hypothetical job-seeking situations without institutional con-straints. A hypothetical tight job market and time pressure eliminated the effect of feminism. The egalitarianism in actual job choices did not relate to feminism, probably because such constraints did exist (Foster, Wallston, & Berger, 1980). Such constraints are seen in a study of psychology couples, where those in the same specialty and at the same type of institution had the most problems of job mobility (Butler & Paisley, 1980).

More research is clearly needed on the influence of family member characteristics and institutional characteristics on job mobility. Better descriptions are needed of strategies such as taking turns or trying to maximize joint options. The dominance of male careers is often explained by the societal expectation that the man is the breadwinner, and there is evidence that women as well as men have internalized this belief (e.g., Bryson & Bryson, 1980). As assumptions catch up with the reality that most families need two earners, strategies may change. Thus, longitudinal research which considers the developmental cohort and the cultural context is particularly important to understanding changing mobility strategies.

Involvement in employment.   Bailyn (1978) provides a framework for considering the coordination of functions related to employment and family roles. She introduces the term *accommodation,* defined as "the degree to which work [sic] demands are fitted into family requirements" (p. 159). Accommodation can be seen as one adapta-tional strategy. The accommodation of each spouse in a dual-earner family could range from an exclusive focus on employment (nonaccom-modation) to a primary or exclusive focus on family. Discrepant accom-modation by the spouses may cause long-term negative effects on the spouse who feels cut off from the family or the one who resents lack of employment success (Bailyn, 1978).

The limited literature in this area suggests that the most typical family strategy is for the wife to be accommodating and the husband nonaccommodating, with his career taking precedence over family. For example, among married attorneys, the women were involved in ancillary work such as library research while the men were more likely to see clients or appear in court (Epstein, 1970); women psychologists expressed less personal involvement in careers and less full-time employment by choice (Matthews & Matthews, 1980b). Similar deductions can be made from data that married female psychologists were more willing to make sacrifices for husbands' careers than husbands were willing to make for theirs (Bryson et al., 1976). Women's perceptions of employment assistance they give to, and receive from, their husbands also suggest that the male career is primary (Lopata et al., 1980). Finally, there is consistent evidence that parenthood requires employment demands be fit into family requirements and that the wife is usually the one who makes this accommodation (e.g., Broscart, 1978; Poloma et al., 1981; Yohalem, 1979, cited in Poloma et al., 1981).

When wives accommodate their careers to family needs, their degree of involvement in employment is decreased. This lesser involvement has often been treated as an individual-difference variable of lesser "career commitment." But work involvement is negotiated within the family and social context and does not necessarily reflect individual traits or preferences. A dual-*career* couple has been defined as two persons for whom jobs are highly salient, with a developmental career sequence (Rapoport & Rapoport, 1969). But from a broader perspective, a spouse can be committed to employment that does not meet such a strict definition; part-time work or other adaptations need not be seen as lack of employment commitment (Walshok, 1979).

As norms change, it is becoming more common for dual-earner spouses to maintain equal involvement in employment by trying to share responsibility equally. Equal sharing is complex, has few guidelines, requires more energy to manage, and may produce overload. It may be implemented in several ways: (*a*) limiting involvement in either family or employment by *both* partners—as when family demands are lessened for those who are child-free or work demands are lessened by lower career aspirations; (*b*) scheduling work and family events to peak at different times, as with delayed childrearing or later career entry; (*c*) compartmentalizing activities so that work is left at the office (Bailyn, 1978).

Although a number of adaptational strategies have been identified by researchers, strategies have seldom been put in a theoretical framework. Some progress has been made by Elman and Gilbert (in press). Drawing on role theory and a general stress and coping model (Lazarus & Launier, 1978), they classify strategies as problem-focused (changing the situation itself) or emotion-focused (alleviating one's emotional reaction to the situation). This conceptual framework is consistent with a social ecological model and promises to stimulate research on the adaptational strategies of dual-earner families.

Social structural influences on adaptation

The adaptational strategies discussed to this point assume a continuous interplay of factors related both to individual family members and to their social context. But studies of dual-earner families tend to present these strategies as if they were derived from individual characteristics and preferences, ignoring the influence of social structure. It is important to highlight existing research on social structural factors that shape adaptational strategies.

In many employment settings, work is structured in a way that assumes the contribution of both the employee and a spouse to a "two-person career" (Papanek, 1973). Success in these settings is difficult for any man or woman who does not have a wife in the traditional sense. Even in less extreme cases, employer expectations about overtime, job mobility, entertaining, and other aspects of performance constrain the choices available to dual-earner families.

Certainly shiftwork and inflexible hours influence adaptations (e.g., Mortimer & London, 1983; Pleck, Staines, & Lang, 1980). Flextime is a policy with important potential for increasing options, but there is limited research on its consequences. Bohen and Viveros-Long's (1981) excellent study found that men and women on flextime spent more time on home chores. Persons reported liking flextime and using it to spend more time with their families. But only cautious generalizations can be made, since the flextime options in this study were quite limited—eight-hour days were required, with half-hour variations in beginning and ending time. Other alternatives such as 10-hour days might have different implications. The authors suggest that the continued expectation that women are responsible for family work may lead flextime to put an added burden on employed married women. This somewhat unexpected suggestion reminds us of the need for conducting research on changing societal structures before their benefits are assumed.

Discrimination against women in the workplace also limits family adaptation. Because of unequal pay, giving the wife's career significant consideration generally reduces family income (Steil, 1983). The job market, particularly the lack of jobs for women, has consequences for job seeking (Berger et al., 1977; Foster et al., 1980; Wallston et al., 1978). Antinepotism rules also tend to limit women's options more than men's (Berger et al.; Matthews & Matthews, 1980b). Managers' skepticism about women's ability to balance work and family demands leads to subtle discrimination that influences married women's careers (Rosen, Jerdee, & Prestwich, 1975). Data from executives (Wright, 1978) and from dual-earner couples (Wallston et al.) show negative attitudes of employers toward married women in particular, but also toward dual-earner couples (Wright, 1978). Even structural solutions to discrimination may create problems in other areas. For example, affirmative action may at times protect equality of opportunity for women and minorities, but it also may work against the dual-earner couple by limiting the husband's ability to find a second job in the same location (Moore, 1980).

In addition to the structure of employment, other societal institutions have important consequences for adaptation. Options may be limited drastically by public policy issues, such as tax structure, or availability of services during off-hours (ranging from doctors to supermarkets to repair persons who expect someone to wait at home) (Mortimer & London, 1983). Child-care availability certainly is a major factor affecting the adaptation of dual-earner families, as the vast literature on child care and its effect on families implies (e.g., Dunlop, 1981; Hobbs, Dokecki, Hoover-Dempsey, Moroney, Shayne, & Weeks, in press; Kamerman, 1980).

Research on dual-earner families must move away from the individual perspective, which "blames the victim" or sees the solutions as the individual adapting to current reality (see Wallston, 1980). An ecological model provides a framework for recognizing the linkages between macroscopic social processes and the functioning of dual-earner families. Research in this area is the key to understanding the ways in which adaptational strategies are formulated out of daily experience.

ADAPTATIONAL OUTCOMES

The study of adaptation requires evaluating the outcomes of an individual's behavior (Cohen & Lazarus, 1983). This undertaking inevitably leads to controversy, since behavior can be judged adaptive or maladaptive depending on the evaluator's values and choice of outcome measures.

Many studies examine possible negative consequences of the dual-earner family pattern, reflecting the assumption that this lifestyle is stressful. Some studies test this assumption by measuring the individual's subjective experience of stress. In others, the presence or absence of stress is only inferred, using measures of depression, marital satisfaction, self-esteem, and so on.

This section considers literature on the outcomes of the dual-earner family pattern. Discussion is organized into the three outcome domains described earlier: psychological, physiological, and social. Within each domain, we consider family and social structural variables which influence the outcomes studied.

Psychological outcome domain

Much of the research on the psychological impact of the dual-earner family pattern has been done within the framework of role theory, using the construct of role conflict. Two types of role conflict have been studied in dual-earner families: (a) interrole conflict, in which demands of one role are incompatible with those of another; and (b) role overload, in which role demands occur in too short a period of time for effective role performance. Role conflict is assumed to be stressful and to have a negative impact on the individual's well-being. In the social ecological model (see Figure 1), role conflict is analogous to poor person-environment fit—a discrepancy between environmental demands and individual resources. Members of dual-earner families have multiple roles with diverse and sometimes competing obligations; to the extent that they find it difficult to meet these obligations, we may say that there is role conflict or that there is a discrepancy between role demands and individual resources.

It seems important to test the assumption of role conflict prior to examining its effects. Do all members of dual-earner families always experience role conflict? Under what circumstances are some individuals able to manage family and employment roles without experiencing role conflict? We would expect that the discrepancy between role demands and the individual's resources to meet them would vary with individual characteristics, particular roles, and the stage in the family life cycle of that individual. At times of more limited resources (e.g., less available time due to the presence of preschoolers) or heightened role demands (e.g., pressure due to a promotion decision), one would expect a greater discrepancy between role demands and ability to meet them.

Yogev and Vierra (1982) provide evidence that role overload is a subjective matter. The number of hours dual-earner wives worked was unrelated to their feeling of being overworked. She concludes that (a) women may not feel overworked by certain activities, such as childcare, which they enjoy; or (b) women may deny feeling overworked in order to protect themselves from a sense of inadequacy. Another hypothesis is that childhood socialization leads women to accept higher levels of stress as normal (Bebbington, 1973).

Family, individual, and employment characteristics can moderate perceived role conflict. Among married professional women with children, both personal and situational resources (i.e., self-esteem, career engagement, spouse and social support) are associated with lower role conflict (Elman & Gilbert, in press). Robison (1978) found that the presence of preschoolers and financial dissatisfaction made the most important contribution to the role strain[4] felt by employed married women. Lack of control over decisions related to one's work and its scheduling is also central to the role strain of employed mothers (Katz & Piotrkowski, in press). Since lower-income jobs typically offer less autonomy, we might expect women in these jobs to suffer more role strain than those in the professions.

One of the few studies using the framework of person-environment fit examined the relationship between androgyny and stress in several settings. For dual-earner spouses, androgyny was related to stress in the work setting but not in one's personal life or at home (Rotheram & Weiner, 1983). The authors hypothesized that androgynous persons may be caught between their desire for flexible sex role behavior and the demands of the work setting, which typically rewards male sex-typed behavior. This study shows how individual traits may conflict with role demands, creating stress.

There is a popular notion that women in dual-earner families experience greater role conflict and stress than their husbands because more roles are simultaneously salient for women. However, researchers have found no relation between role conflict and gender (Haemmerlie & Montgomery, 1981; Herman & Gyllstrom, 1977; Holahan & Gilbert, 1979). In one study, while lower role conflict was correlated with working fewer hours, higher spouse support, and higher career commitment for both sexes, career aspirations were negatively correlated with role conflict for men and positively correlated with role conflict for women (Holahan & Gilbert, 1979). This finding supports a role conflict model: Men with high career aspirations are meeting society's expectations, but their female counterparts are adding a nontraditional role that competes with their traditional role.

Self-esteem and self-concept.   If multiple roles present competing demands, there is a chance that the individual will perform some or all roles inadequately, leading to negative self-evaluation. Higher perceived role conflict is associated with lower self-esteem for both men and women in dual-earner marriages (Holahan & Gilbert, 1979). Self-esteem of women in dual-earner families may not differ according to their strategy for dealing with role conflict; women who cope by trying to meet all role demands and those who cope by redefining role expec-

---

[4] In the sociological literature, the term *strain* is frequently used as we would use stress, while stress is used where we would use stressor. We use stressor to refer to an external force, while stress is the individual's experience.

tations have reported similar levels of self-esteem (Gilbert, Holahan, & Manning, 1981).

Comparisons of women in dual-earners and traditional families indicate that the multiple roles of dual-earners do not diminish their self-esteem (Barnett, 1982) or their self-regard and self-acceptance (Huser & Grant, 1978). Reduced self-esteem is not necessarily a consequence of the dual-earner family pattern. However, we do not know whether the families studied had resources which might have enabled them to manage multiple roles without increased risk of negative self-evaluation. All of the samples have been from the professional classes and may have employed others to assist with performance of their multiple roles. Many jobs are drudgery; self-evaluation based on these jobs might be more negative. Finally, use of global measures of self-esteem can not rule out the possibility that self-esteem of dual-earners suffers in some areas of role functioning. For example, it has been suggested that dual-earner wives feel inadequate in the maternal role (Johnson & Johnson, 1977; Nye, 1974a).

Psychiatric impairment. There is consistent evidence that marriage is associated with higher rates of mental disorder for women than for men (Gove, 1972), leading to speculation that the housewife role is an inadequate source of esteem and fulfillment for women and that employment may provide married women with an alternate source of gratification (Bernard, 1972).

Depression was reported to be lower for employed wives than for housewives when happiness with job and marriage were held constant (Radloff, 1975). Similarly, wives employed full time for more than a year reported less psychiatric impairment than did never-employed housewives (Welch & Booth, 1977). Most research suggests that employed wives enjoy better mental health overall than housewives (Gove & Geerken, 1977; Kessler & McRae, 1982; Powell, 1977). While two studies found no difference in the mental health of employed and nonemployed wives (Brocki, 1979, cited in Gove & Peterson, 1980; Pearlin, 1975, cited in Gove & Peterson, 1980), none reported poorer mental health among employed wives. Adding the employment role does not seem to detract from women's mental health and, in fact, may enhance it.

Moderating characteristics help explain the relationship between wives' employment status and their mental health. Women with more traditional beliefs about female roles, for example, experience greater anxiety about working outside the home (Lashuk & Kurian, 1977). A woman's desire to work or not work may also affect the mental health outcome of her employment status. Full-time housewives who desired employment were in much poorer mental health than working wives (Brocki, 1979, cited in Gove & Peterson, 1980). The family life cycle also affects the relationship between wives' employment and their mental health: Among mothers of grown children, employment was associated with better mental health; but for women with children at home, employment did not improve mental health (Powell, 1977). However, employment was associated with improved mental health even for women with children at home, *if* their husbands shared child care (Kessler & McRae, 1982). The moderating influence of other family characteristics, such as marital conflict about the wife's employment, remain to be investigated. Finally, there is a need for research examining how particular job characteristics (e.g., flexibility, responsibility, scheduling) affect the relationship between wives' employment status and psychiatric impairment.

The literature provides conflicting information on the psychiatric impairment of husbands in dual-earner families. Involvement in "feminine" household tasks has been linked to depression in men whose wives are employed (Keith & Schafer, 1980). Burke and Weir (1976) reported poorer mental health in the husbands of employed wives, but a replication of their work failed to validate this finding (Booth, 1977). Using data from a representative national survey, Kessler and McRae (1982) attempted to resolve this inconsistency. They found more depression and low self-esteem in husbands with employed wives. This impairment was *not* due to husbands' increased child-care responsibilities nor to husbands' feeling a threat to their competence nor to overt conflict over responsibilities to family and job, although it appeared possible that the husband's distress was inversely related to his approval of his wife's employment. Other factors responsible for an association between wives' employment and husbands' distress remain to be identified.

Marital satisfaction. Reviews of the literature on marital satisfaction of dual-earner spouses have yielded mixed results (Gove & Peterson, 1980; Moore & Hofferth, 1979; Nye, 1974b; Yogev, 1982). This may be due to changes in sample characteristics over the years, to changes in research paradigms (Yogev, 1982) and to methodological difficulties in the measurement of marital satisfaction (Laws, 1971; Spanier & Lewis, 1980). This section is limited to studies operationalizing marital satisfaction as a subjective, general rating of affect about the marital relationship—typically, ratings of satisfaction or happiness. (Literature dealing with specific marital behaviors such as reports of arguments will be reviewed in the section on social functioning outcomes).

The wife's employment alone seems unlikely to be responsible for differences in marital satisfaction between dual-earner and traditional marriages, since the two types of couples differ in many ways other than the wife's employment status (Nye, 1974b). Studies have controlled for very few such differences.

A number of studies have considered the effect of social class. Literature before the mid-1970s suggested that among lower-class families, marital satisfaction was slightly higher if the wife was not employed, while the wife's employment did not affect marital satisfaction in the middle classes (Nye, 1974b). This trend was later reported by Staines, Pleck, Shepard, and O'Conner (1978), but Ferree (1975) found no difference in the marital satisfaction of housewives and employed wives in the working classes. Wright (1978) found somewhat greater marital satisfaction for employed wives in the working class and no difference in the middle class. In a study of men in the professions and their wives, both spouses reported greater relationship satisfaction if the wife was employed (Rotheram & Weiner, 1983). The employed wives of professionals in another study also reported greater marital satisfaction than housewives; their husbands, however, reported less marital satisfaction than those whose wives were not employed (Burke & Weir, 1976).

There is evidence that wives' employment is positively associated with marital satisfaction when there are no children in the home and negatively associated with marital satisfaction when there are (Geerken, 1979, cited in Gove & Peterson, 1980; Richardson, 1979; Staines et al., 1978). It seems reasonable that during parenting, dual-earner spouses might have difficulty meeting each other's needs in addition to those of job and children and consequently would feel less satisfied with their marriage.

What about the nature of the relationships among family members? We would expect that when family relationships are emotionally and instrumentally supportive, the wife's employment would be less likely to be associated with lower marital satisfaction. This hypothesis has not been tested. Richardson (1979), however, found no support for the notion that competition and marital unhappiness would result if the wife was equal or higher in occupational prestige than her husband. In his conclusion, he emphasized the fallacy of deriving a psychological consequence from a structural arrangement, since the individual characteristics of the spouses moderate the effects of any family structure. For example, it is people with high concerns about status achievement who tend to report less marital satisfaction if their spouse's occupational status is inconsistent with their own (Hornung & McCullough, 1981).

Few studies focus on how personal qualities of the spouses affect the relationship between wife's employment and marital satisfaction. Bailyn (1970) reported that men who emphasize career are not very happy if they are married to employed women who get personal satisfaction from their own careers. She concluded, "A husband's mode of integrating family and work in his own life is crucial for the success— at least in terms of marital satisfaction—of any attempt of his wife to include a career in her life" (p. 108).

The processes which link a woman's job to family relationships have rarely been studied. For women in both high- and low-status jobs, work features such as job satisfaction, job-related mood, time spent at work, and occupational rewards account for a significant proportion of variance in their satisfaction with family relations and in their mood at home (Piotrkowski, 1981; Piotrkowski & Crits-Christopher, 1981; Piotrkowski & Katz, 1982). This appears to be a fruitful area for investigation.

Work role satisfaction. Women in dual-earner families have two work roles: an employment role and a household role. Ferree (1976) challenged the assumption that working-class women prefer to be full-time housewives. She predicted that these women would be no different from men, who have been found to value even dead-end jobs as a source of social contact and personal satisfaction. She found that working-class housewives were more likely than employed wives to be dissatisfied with the way they are spending their lives, to perceive their husband's day as more interesting than their own, and to feel that they have not had a fair opportunity in life. The majority of both housewives and employed wives reported little subjective competence as homemakers. Since none of the employed women felt incompetent in their jobs, Ferree concluded that outside employment is important as an alternate source of esteem and gratification for married working-class women.

A replication of Ferree's study (Wright, 1978), using a much larger sample drawn from several national surveys, found no consistent, substantial differences in the reported happiness of employed women and housewives. Among middle-class wives, however, housewives perceived their lives as substantially *easier* than did employed wives. Among the working class, housewives viewed their lives as less *free* than did employed wives. Wright concluded that both types of work roles have their costs and benefits, but that homemakers as a group are just as happy as employed wives. Whether a wife's work is limited to the home or also includes outside employment seems to make little difference in her reported role satisfaction (Barnett, 1982; Spreitzer, Snyder, & Larson, 1975).

Variation in women's employment satisfaction is influenced by individual characteristics and strategies for managing home and employment demands. Coping strategies positively related to role satisfaction include family members sharing household tasks, reduction in some work standards, and careful scheduling and organizing of activities; strategies negatively related to role satisfaction include having no conscious strategies for dealing with role conflict, attempting to meet all role demands, and keeping all roles totally separate (Gray, 1983).

There are significant gaps in the literature regarding the work role satisfaction of dual-earner families. Family variables such as family attitudes, division of labor, and the presence of children have been studied in relation to the work satisfaction of employed wives. The role of specific job characteristics should also be considered. Finally, work role satisfaction of husbands has been neglected. In one study, husbands of employed wives had less job satisfaction than husbands of housewives (Burke & Weir, 1976). This may indicate that the husband loses support for his own work role when his wife is also employed; perhaps, as Hunt and Hunt (1978) have suggested, families are not able to support adequately the work roles of both spouses. If so, support from outside the family is extremely important for dual-earner spouses.

Physiological health outcome domain

The relationship between lifestyle, stress, and health outcomes has been a focus of much recent research. Given the popular assumption that a dual-earner family lifestyle is stressful, it is curious that the physical health of dual-earner families has rarely been examined.

The first researchers to consider health outcome used a self-report measure of mental and physical well-being in a study of the effects of wives' employment. Men with employed wives reported poorer health than those whose wives were not employed. Employed wives themselves, in contrast, reported better health than housewives (Burke & Weir, 1976).

Replications of this study with more diverse samples and improved methodologies yielded different results. Booth (1977) reported that the wife's employment had little effect on her husband's health, as measured by physical exam, reports of alcohol and sedative use, and an inventory of psychiatric impairment. In a similar study, unemployment and transitional employment, rather than full-time employment, were associated with decrements in blue-collar wives' health. Employment seemed to make little difference in the health of white-collar women (Welch & Booth, 1977). Finally, on indexes of physical health, wives' employment had no effect for husbands, but had a positive effect for the wives themselves (Kessler & McRae, 1981).

A particularly interesting study considered health in relation to work-related variables, rather than merely grouping married women by their employment status. There was no difference in blood pressure by employment status or by perceived workload. Among housewives, tension about, and poor self-evaluation of, housework were associated with high blood pressure. Among employed women, high commitment to their work role was related to high blood pressure (Hauenstein, Kasl, & Harburg, 1977). These results highlight the importance of considering individual differences within each category of employment status. Family variables should also be considered in determining the impact of a woman's employment on her health.

Social functioning outcome domain

Marital and family functioning outcomes. Behavioral assessment of family functioning is relatively new (Spanier & Lewis, 1980), so this section primarily reviews subjective reports of family members about their interaction. These studies have focused almost exclusively on marital functioning, neglecting parent-child interaction. (Piotrkowski & Repetti, in press, review studies of parent-child relations in dual-earner families.)

A frequent concern is that the marital bond might be weaker in dual-earner families. Occupational activities of the spouses may insulate them from each other in time, space, and socialization patterns, decreasing the structural constraints reinforcing the marriage; the relationship becomes a matter of choice rather than necessity (Turner, 1971). From an economic perspective, the wife's income allows her to consider alternatives to her marriage, and marital dissolution is more likely for women whose potential wages compare favorably to that of their husbands (Cherlin, 1979). We believe the quality of the marital and family relationships are as important as the spouses' financial independence from each other. Early studies of dual-earner marriages found more conflict, arguing, living apart, and consideration of divorces than for traditional marriages, although divorces were no more frequent (Nye, 1974b). Recent studies found no differences between dual-earner couples and traditional couples in marital adjustment and companionship (Locksley, 1980) and in marital discord (Booth, 1977). Dual-earner couples were superior in mutuality, commitment, and satisfaction (Simpson & England, 1982) and communication (Burke & Weir, 1976).

The mere fact of the wife's employment does not lead to poor marital relations. Houseknecht and Macke (1981) found that the extent to which the family accommodated the wife's career was important in determining marital adjustment. Association between job satisfaction and marital adjustment has been shown for husbands but not for wives (Ridley, 1973).

Turner (1971) has suggested particular adaptational strategies that may increase the likelihood of divorce for dual-earner couples: lack of home-centered activities, low degree of resource control and management at the household level, and a division of labor which maximizes the independence of the spouses. Spouses who maximize interdependence between occupational and domestic spheres may increase the likelihood of maintaining their marital bond. These hypotheses have yet to be tested.

Commuter couples are a subgroup of dual-earner families for whom some outcome information exists. These couples live apart for periods of time so both can pursue careers. They have developed an adaptational strategy which allows them to maintain their relationship and maximize their career development in the face of structural constraints such as lack of jobs in the same city or antinepotism rules. Most couples view the situation as a forced choice (Gerstel & Gross, 1982) which benefits their personal autonomy and work achievement but which generates considerable new tensions in the marital relationship (Bunker & Vanderslice, 1982). These tensions are easier to manage for couples who have a more established relationship, are older, are free from childrearing, and have material resources to mitigate the impact of living apart (Gerstel & Gross, 1983; Gross, 1980; Gross, Thomas, & Van Gemert, 1982).

These commuter couples provide a stringent test of the notion that the separateness of dual-earner couples inevitably weakens the marital bond. Their arrangement reduces the structures that help maintain a marriage, such as an interdependent division of household labor. There has been concern that spouses' personal commitment to each other depends on these structural constraints. But in a study of extramarital affairs in commuter couples, the increased opportunity to have affairs was not associated with an increased frequency of affairs (Gerstel, 1979). It was suggested that the changing structure of marriage does not necessarily change behavior, since spouses internalize norms.

In most studies, the relationship between the family and employment is presented as unidirectional. An exception is work based on indexes of penetration of jobs into the family setting (as by talking about the job or doing job activities at home), and penetration of family into the workplace (as by doing errands during work hours) (Rossi, 1980). The relationship between work and family life has been organized into five categories by Evans and Bartolome (1980): (a) spillover, where work and family life affect each other positively or negatively; (b) independent, where they exist side by side without obvious interaction; (c) conflict, where they cannot easily be reconciled; (d) instrumental, where one is primarily a means to obtain something desired in the other sphere; and (e) compensation, where one is a way of making up for what is missing in the other. This framework could broaden the usual focus on the impact of wives' employment on the family to consideration of the reciprocal influence of family and employment roles.

Social network outcomes. The workplace is often a hub for a person's social networks. For dual-earner couples, this means that there may be two social networks with little overlap. Separation of social activities may pull the spouses away from each other (Turner, 1971). Or, on the other hand, the squeeze between available time and the demands of home and work may force the spouses to become an efficient team with socially restricted lives.

Knowledge about the social networks of dual-earner families is based primarily on open-ended interview data. It appears that dual-earner families are likely to become isolated from their extended family because members tend to turn to spouses rather than relatives to meet emotional needs (Johnson & Johnson, 1980). Loosening of kinship ties is exacerbated by a frequent inability to meet traditional social obligations (John-Parsons, 1978); juggling of two work schedules, child care, and household tasks leave less time to be attentive to the extended family. It is also possible, however, that ties are strengthened in circumstances where extended family members can provide resources and support not available within the nuclear family.

Families with unconventional lifestyles may find themselves particularly isolated. Commuter couples, for example, report difficulties with disapproval from relatives or others who fear a breakup or assume they are having marital difficulties (Gerstel & Gross, 1982). Couples who have successfully broken out of conventional lifestyles and sex roles are likely to report that they have had the benefit of social support. Many egalitarian, role-sharing couples have found similar friends who make them feel less deviant (Haas, 1982). These couples may also report parental support (frequently based on parents' misperception of the situation as temporary or less egalitarian than it actually is).

Employment outcomes. Most literature on the occupational success of dual-earner women has focused on professionals. Marriage to another professional seems to facilitate professional women's careers. Dual-career women in psychology (Bryson & Bryson, 1980; Bryson et al., 1976) and in sociology (Martin, Berry, & Jacobsen, 1975) were more productive than single women in those fields. Among dual-career psychologist couples, similarity of specialty area and type of work setting was related to similar number of publications by husband and wife (Butler & Paisley, 1980). Taken together, these studies support the notion of "professional-marital endogamy": that the wife's professional success is facilitated by the close marital interaction with a professional husband (Martin et al.).

Although married professional women tend to be more productive than their single female counterparts, they are still less productive than their husbands (Bryson & Bryson, 1980; Bryson et al., 1976), and do less prestigious work (Epstein, 1971). A woman with a Ph.D. is less likely to be in the labor force if she is married to another Ph.D. (Ferber & Huber, 1979). Apparently, marriage to a highly educated wife has a negative effect on men's careers. Male Ph.D.s married to Ph.D.s publish fewer articles and hold fewer offices than single male Ph.D.s (Ferber & Huber, 1979).

What underlying processes are responsible for the difference in occupational success by dual-earner wives and their husbands? To what extent can the wife's lesser productivity be explained by her personal preferences and by structural constraints of family and workplace? After marriage, women are less likely than men to further their education (Sharda & Nangle, 1982), and families are less likely to further the wife's career (Poloma et al., 1981). Such findings could be explained by traditional sex role orientations of the spouses or by lack of opportunities for the wives.

Dual-earner wives with high career aspirations are likely to experience role conflict, while for their husbands, career aspirations appear to be negatively related to role conflict (Holahan & Gilbert, 1979). Women may be more sensitive to the impact of their career pursuits on the family. When dual-earner wives experience such a conflict, cultural prescriptions encourage a resolution favoring the family (Coser & Rokoff, 1971). This is a clear example of an outcome that is adaptive in one domain and may be maladaptive in another, with family functioning reducing job functioning. The wife's resolution of these conflicts will be influenced by her personal characteristics. For example, wives with conservative attitudes about women's roles expect themselves to adjust when there is role tension, while others expect their husbands to make more of the adjustments (Holahan & Gilbert, 1979).

CONCLUSIONS

Research on dual-earner families has drawn attention to the relationship between work and the family that affects all families. There is increasing recognition that family members' employment affects family life. With changing employment patterns, it has become likely that at some time during their life cycles, most families will have two earners. In fact, the term *dual-earner family* is now so inclusive that it is of minimal value in describing a distinct family structure. We expect that the dual-earner literature will cease to be a self-contained area of investigation. Instead, we anticipate that researchers will focus on specific features of the family and the workplace and on the ways in which these affect each other.

We have already begun to see emphasis shift from comparisons of traditional and dual-earner families toward the recognition of differences within the broad category of dual-earner families. For example, commuters have been studied as a distinct subgroup with particular adaptational strategies, and some researchers have begun to focus on dual-earner families at particular stages in the life cycle, relating their adaptations to various outcomes. With such perceptual shifts, the literature departs from the use of the male-breadwinner family as the single standard against which to evaluate the adaptation of dual-earner families and recognizes that dual-earner families are a heterogeneous group.

A number of gaps must be addressed by future research on the interface between employment and the family. Important adaptational strategies have been described in the areas of household functioning and job mobility. However, we know little about how family members negotiate these strategies with each other and even less about how social structures influence their options. The relationship of these adaptational strategies to various outcomes has been even less well addressed. To take one example, we do not know how a husband's increased involvement in household tasks affects individual family members or the overall quality of family functioning.

The impact of dual-earner family patterns has been measured almost exclusively in terms of individual psychological variables, ignoring other outcomes. Despite their potential threats to health, adaptational strategies have not been evaluated for their physiological consequences. Studies using the family-level measures which are becoming available (e.g., Olson, McCubbin, Barnes, Larsen, Muxen, & Wilson, 1982) could contribute to our understanding of how family life is affected by adaptations to employment situations. There is also a need to examine the long-term outcomes of these adaptations. Ideally, studies should consider outcomes in several domains and for several family members simultaneously, since what is adaptive in one domain may not be in another and what is adaptive for one individual may harm or frustrate another.

Research on the interface between the family and the workplace will be strongly influenced by theoretical development in the broader field of family research. Too little consideration has been given to the interplay between family and society that is central to the continuing evolution of new family forms. When unidirectional causal models predominate, the family tends to be viewed as the victim of social change. From a social ecological perspective, however, it is clear that the family is active in the process of adaptation. Dual-earner family members integrate social roles in new ways, often without role models from their families of origin or society at large. We can assume that when dual-earner families reach situations characterized by lack of fit between their needs and resources, they invent strategies for dealing with these situations, mobilize resources from new sources, and attempt to change the environment to meet their needs. By studying their initiatives, we will learn more about what Boulding (1983) calls "familia faber"—the family's role as creator of the future order. At the same time, the study of the family's efforts to modify the environment should lead to the identification of social structures that stand in the way of their successful adaptation. This information will better prepare us to contribute to the development of social policies that allow families to achieve a better fit between their needs, the demands of employment, and environmental resources.

REFERENCES

Albrecht, S. L., Bahr, H. M., & Chadwick, B. A. Changing family and sex roles: An assessment of age differences. *Journal of Marriage and the Family,* 1979, *41,* 41–50.

Aldous, J. From dual-earner to dual-career families and back again. In J. Aldous (Ed.), *Two paychecks: Life in dual-earner families.* Beverly Hills, Calif.: Sage Publications, 1982. Pp. 1–26.

Bailyn, L. Career and family orientation of husbands and wives in relation to marital happiness. *Human Relations,* 1970, *23,* 97–113.

Bailyn, L. Accommodation of work to family. In R. Rapoport & R. N. Rapoport (Eds.), *Working couples.* London: Routledge & Kegan Paul, 1978. Pp. 159–174.

Barnett, R. C. Multiple roles and well-being: A study of mothers of preschool age children. *Psychology of Women Quarterly,* 1982, *7,* 175–178.

Bebbington, A. C. The function of stress in the establishment of the dual-career family. *Journal of Marriage and the Family,* 1973, *35,* 530–537.

Beneson, H. Women's occupational and family achievement in the U.S. class system: A critique of the dual-career family analysis. *British Journal of Sociology,* 1984, *35,* 19–41.

Berger, M. *The integration of work and family life in dual-career couples: A follow-up study.* Unpublished manuscript, Georgia State University, 1980.

Berger, M., Foster, M., & Wallston, B. S. Finding two jobs. In R. Rapoport & R. N. Rapoport (Eds.), *Working couples.* London: Routledge & Kegan Paul, 1978. Pp. 23–35.

Berger, M., Foster, M., Wallston, B. S., & Wright, L. You and me against the world: Dual-career couples and joint job seeking. *Journal of Research and Development in Education,* 1977, *10,* 30–37.

Berk, R. A., & Berk, S. F. A simultaneous equation model for the division of household labor. *Sociological Methods and Research,* 1978, *6,* 431–468.

Berk, S. F. Husbands at home: Organization of the husband's household day. In K. W. Feinstein (Ed.), *Working women and families.* Beverly Hills, Calif.: Sage Publications, 1979. Pp. 125–158.

Berk, S. F., & Shih, A. Contributions to household labor: Comparing wives' and husbands' reports. In S. F. Berk (Ed.), *Women and household labor.* Beverly Hills, Calif.: Sage Publications, 1980. Pp. 191–227.

Bernard, J. *The future of marriage.* New York: Bantum Books, 1973.

Bohen, H. H., & Viveros-Long, A. *Balancing job and family life: Do flexible work schedules help?* Philadelphia: Temple University Press, 1981.

Booth, A. Wife's employment and husband's stress: A replication and refutation. *Journal of Marriage and the Family,* 1977, *39,* 645–650.

Boulding, E. Familia faber: The family as maker of the future. *Journal of Marriage and the Family,* 1983, *45,* 257–266.

Bowman, K. M., Quarm, D., & Gideonse, S. (Eds.). Women in the workplace: Effects on families. Norwood, N.J.: Ablex Publishing, 1983.

Bronfenbrenner, V. Toward an experimental ecology of human development. *American Psychologist,* 1977, *32,* 513–531.

Broscart, K. R. Family status and professional achievement: A study of women doctorates. *Journal of Marriage and Family,* 1978, *40,* 71–76.

Bryson, J. B., & Bryson, R. Salary and job performance differences in dual-career couples. In F. Pepitone-Rockwell (Ed.), *Dual-career couples.* Beverly Hills, Calif.: Sage Publications, 1980. Pp. 241–259.

Bryson, R. B., Bryson, J. B., Licht, M. H., & Licht, B. G. The professional pair: Husband and wife psychologists. *American Psychologist,* 1976, *31,* 10–16.

Bunker, B., & Vanderslice, V. J. *Tradeoffs: Individual gains and relational losses of commuting couples.* Presented at the annual meeting of the American Psychological Association, Washington, D.C., 1982.

Burke, R., & Weir, T. Relationship of wives' employment status to husband, wife and pair satisfaction and performance. *Journal of Marriage and the Family,* 1976, *38,* 279–287.

Butler, M., & Paisley, W. Coordinated-career couples: Convergence and divergence. In F. Pepitone-Rockwell (Ed.), *Dual-career couples.* Beverly Hills, Calif.: Sage Publications, 1980. Pp. 207–228.

Cherlin, A. Work life and marital dissolution. In G. Levinger & O. C. Moles (Eds.), *Divorce and separation.* New York: Basic Books, 1979.

Cohen, F., & Lazarus, R. S. Coping and adaptation in health and illness. In D. Mechanic (Ed.), *Handbook of health, health care, and the health professions.* New York: Free Press, 1983.

Condran, J. G., & Bode, J. G. Rashomon, working wives, and family division of labor: Middletown, 1980. *Journal of Marriage and the Family,* 1982, *44,* 421–426.

Coser, R. L., & Rokoff, G. Women in the occupational world: Social disruption and conflict. *Social Problems,* 1971, *18,* 537–555.

Duncan, R. P. Dual occupational participation and migration. *Dissertation Abtracts International,* 1975, *36,* 1115A.

Dunlop, K. H. Maternal employment and child care. *Professional Psychology,* 1981, *12,* 67–75.

Elman, M. R., & Gilbert, L. A. Coping strategies for role conflict in professional married women with children. *Family Relations,* in press.

Epstein, C. Law partners and marital partners: Strains and solutions in the dual career family enterprise. *Human Relations,* 1970, *24,* 549–563.

Ericksen, J. A., Yancey, W. L., & Ericksen, E. P. The division of family roles. *Journal of Marriage and the Family,* 1979, *41,* 301–313.

Erkut, S., & Fields, J. P. *Relocation: Black and white dual career couples on the move.* Paper presented at the annual meeting of the American Psychological Association, 1983.

Evans, P. A. L., & Bartolome, F. The relationship between professional life and private life. In C. B. Derr (Ed.), *Work, family and the career.* New York: Praeger Publishers, 1980.

Farkas, G. Education, wage rates, and the division of labor between husband and wife. *Journal of Marriage and the Family* 1976, *38,* 473–483.

Ferber, M., & Huber, J. Husbands, wives, and careers. *Journal of Marriage and the Family,* 1979, *41,* 315–325.

Ferree, M. M. Working class jobs: Housework and paid work as sources of satisfaction. *Social Problems,* 1976, *23,* 431–441.

Foster, M. A., Wallston, B. S., & Berger, M. Feminist orientation and job seeking behavior among dual-career couples. *Sex Roles,* 1980, *6,* 59–65.

French, J. R. P., Rodgers, W., & Cobb, S. Adjustment as person-environment fit. In G. V. Coelho, D. A. Hamburg, & J. E. Adams (Eds.), *Coping and adaptation.* New York: Basic Books, 1974.

Gerstel, N. R. Marital alternatives and the regulation of sex: Commuter couples as a test case. *Alternative Lifestyles,* 1979, *2,* 145–176.

Gerstel, N. R., & Gross, H. E. Commuter marriages: A review. *Marriage and Family Review,* 1982, *5,* 71–93.

Gerstel, N. R., & Gross, H. Commuter marriage: Couples who live apart. In E. Macklin & R. Rubin (Eds.), *Contemporary families and alternative lifestyles.* Beverly Hills, Calif.: Sage Publications, 1983.

Gilbert, L. A., Holahan, C. K., & Manning, L. Coping with conflict between professional and maternal roles. *Family Relations,* 1981, *30,* 419–426.

Gove, W. The relationship between sex roles, marital status, and mental illness. *Social Forces,* 1972, *51,* 34–44.

Gove, W. R., & Geerken, M. The effect of children and employment on the mental health of married men and women. *Social Forces,* 1977, *56,* 66–76.

Gove, W. R., & Peterson, C. An update of the literature on personal and marital adjustment: The effect of children and the employment of wives. *Marriage and Family Review,* 1980, *3,* 63–96.

Gray, J. D. The married professional woman: An examination of her role conflicts and coping strategies. *Psychology of Women Quarterly,* 1983, *7, 235–243.*

Gross, H. E. Dual-career couples who live apart: Two types. *Journal of Marriage and the Family,* 1980, *42,* 567–576.

Gross, H. E., Thomas, C., & Van Gemert, M. *Merchant marine and commuter families: A comparison of couples who live apart.* Paper presented at the annual meeting of the American Sociological Association, San Francisco, September 1982.

Haas, L. Determinants of role-sharing behavior: A study of egalitarian couples. *Sex Roles,* 1982, *8,* 747–760.

Haemmerlie, F. M., & Montgomery, R. L. *A survey of dual career couples in engineering.* Paper presented at the meeting of the Southwestern Psychological Association, Houston, 1981.

Harrison, A. O., & Minor, J. Interrole conflict, coping strategies and satisfaction among working wives. *Journal of Marriage and the Family,* 1978, *40,* 799–805.

Hauenstein, L. S., Kasl, S. V., & Harburg, E. Work status, work satisfaction, and blood pressure among married black and white women. *Psychology of Women Quarterly,* 1977, *1,* 334–349.

Herman, J. B., & Gyllstrom, K. K. Working men and women: Inter- and intra-role conflict. *Psychology of Women Quarterly,* 1977, *1,* 319–333.

Hesse, S. J. Women working: Historical trends. In K. W. Feinstein (Ed.), *Working women and families.* Beverly Hills, Calif.: Sage Publications, 1979.

Hobbs, N., Dokecki, P. R., Hoover-Dempsey, K. V., Moroney, B., Shayne, M., & Weeks, K. *To strengthen families: The challenge of child care and parent education.* San Francisco: Jossey-Bass, in press.

Holahan, C. K., & Gilbert, L. A. Conflict between major life roles: The women and men in dual-career couples. *Human Relations,* 1979, *32,* 451–467.

Hood, J., & Golden, S. Beating time/making time: The impact of work scheduling on men's family roles. *Family Coordinator,* 1979, *28,* 575–582.

Hornung, C. A., & McCullough, B. C. Status relationships in dual-employment marriages: Consequences for psychological well-being. *Journal of Marriage and the Family,* 1981, *43,* 125–141.

Houseknecht, S. K., & Macke, A. S. Combining marriage and career: The marital adjustment of professional women. *Journal of Marriage and the Family,* 1981, *43,* 651–661.

Huber, J., & Spitze, G. Wives' employment, household behaviors and sex-role attitudes. *Social Forces,* 1981, *60,* 159–169.

Hunt, J. G., & Hunt, L. L. Dual-career families: Vanguard of the future or residue of the past? In J. Aldous (Ed.), *Two paychecks: Life in dual-earner families.* Beverly Hills, Calif.: Sage Publications, 1982.

Huser, W. R., & Grant, C. W. A study of husbands and wives from dual-career and traditional-career families. *Psychology of Women Quarterly,* 1978, *3,* 78–89.

John-Parsons, D. S. Continuous dual-career families: A case study. *Psychology of Women Quarterly,* 1978, *3,* 30–42.

Johnson, C. L., & Johnson, F. A. Attitudes toward parenting in dual-career families. *American Journal of Psychiatry,* 1977, *134,* 391–395.

Johnson, C. L., & Johnson, F. A. Parenthood, marriage, and careers: Situational constraints and role strain. In F. Pepitone-Rockwell (Ed.), *Dual-career couples.* Beverly Hills, Calif.: Sage Publications, 1980. Pp. 143–161.

Kamerman, S. B. *Parenting in an unresponsive society.* New York: Free Press, 1980.

Katz, M. H., & Piotrkowski, C. S. Correlates of family role strain among employed black women. *Family Relations,* in press.

Keith, P. M., & Schafer, R. B. Role strain and depression in two-job families. *Family Relations,* 1980, *29,* 483–488.

Kessler, R. C., & McRae, J. A. The effect of wives' employment on the mental health of married men and women. *American Sociological Review,* 1982, *47,* 216–227.

Lashuk, M. W., & Kurian, G. Employment status, feminism, and symptoms of stress. *Canadian Journal of Sociology*, 1977, *2*, 195–204.

Laws, J. L. A feminist review of marital adjustment literature: The rape of the locke. *Journal of Marriage and the Family*, 1971, *33*, 485–516.

Locksley, A. On the effects of wives' employment on marital adjustment and companionship. *Journal of Marriage and the Family*, 1980, *42*, 337–346.

Lopata, H. Z., Bamewolt, D., & Norr, K. Spouses' contributions to each other's roles. In F. Pepitone-Rockwell (Ed.), *Dual-career couples*. Beverly Hills, Calif.: Sage Publications, 1980.

Madell, T. O., & Madell, C. M. A professional pair at the job market: A reply. *American Psychologist*, 1979, *34*, 275–276.

Malson, M. R. *Black women's sex role integration and behavior (Working Paper 87)*. Wellesley, Mass.: Wellesley College Center for Research on Women, 1981.

Martin, T. W., Berry, K. J., & Jacobsen, R. B. The impact of dual-career marriages on female professional careers: An empirical test of a Parsonian hypothesis. *Journal of Marriage and the Family*, 1975, *37*, 734–742.

Matthews, J. R., & Matthews, L. H. A professional pair at the job market. *American Psychologist*, 1978, *33*, 780–782.

Matthews, J. R., & Matthews, L. H. Going shopping: The professional couple in the job market. In F. Pepitone-Rockwell (Ed.), *Dual-career couples*. Beverly Hills, Calif.: Sage Publications, 1980. Pp. 261–281. (a)

Matthews, J. R., & Matthews, L. H. A survey of dual-career couples in psychology. Paper presented at the meeting of the Southwestern Psychological Association, Oklahoma City, 1980. (b)

Melson, G. F. *Family and environment: An ecosystem perspective*. Minneapolis: Burgess, 1980.

Miller, J., & Garrison, H. H. Sex roles: The division of labor at home and in the workplace. *Annual Review of Psychology*, 1982, *8*, 237–262.

Model, D. Housework by husbands. In J. Aldous (Ed.), *Two paychecks: Life in dual-earner families*. Beverly Hills, Calif.: Sage Publications, 1982. Pp. 193–205.

Moore, D. M. Equal opportunity laws and dual-career couples. In F. Pepitone-Rockwell (Ed.), *Dual-career couples*. Beverly Hills, Calif.: Sage Publications, 1980.

Moore, K. A., & Hofferth, S. L. Effects of women's employment on marriage: Formation, stability, and roles. *Marriage and Family Review*, 1979, *2*, 1+.

Mortimer, J., Hall, R., & Hill, R. Husbands' occupational attributes as constraints on wives' employment. *Sociology of Work and Occupation*, 1978, *5*, 285–313.

Mortimer, J. T., & London, J. The varying linkages of work and family. In P. Voydanoff (Ed.), *Work and family: Changing roles of men and women*. Palo Alto, Calif. : Mayfield, 1983.

Nickols, S. Y., & Fox, K. D. Buying time and saving time: Strategies for managing household production. *Journal of Consumer Research*, 1983, *10*.

Nickols, S. Y., & Metzen, E. J. Impact of wife's employment upon husband's housework. *Journal of Family Issues*, 1982, *3*, 199–216.

Nye, F. I. Effects on mother. In L. N. Hofman & F. I. Nye (Eds.), *Working mothers*. San Francisco: Jossey-Bass, 1974. (a)

Nye, F. I. Husband-wife relationship. In L. W. Hoffman & F. I. Nye (Eds.), *Working mothers.* San Francisco: Jossey-Bass, 1974. (b)

Olson, D. H., McCubbin, H. I., Barnes, H., Larsen, A., Muxen, M., & Wilson, M. *Family inventories.* St. Paul: Family Social Science, University of Minnesota, 1982.

Papanek, H. Men, women, and work: Reflections on the two-person career. *American Journal of Sociology,* 1973, *78,* 852–872.

Perrucci, C. C., Potter, H. R., & Rhoads, D. L. Determinants of male family-role performance. *Psychology of Women Quarterly,* 1978, *3,* 53–66.

Piotrkowski, C. S. *Impact of women's work on family health.* Paper presented at the NIOSH Conference on Occupational Health Issues Affecting Clerical and Secretarial Personnel, Cincinnati, Ohio, July 1981.

Piotrkowski, C. S., & Crits-Christoph, P. Women's jobs and family adjustment. *Journal of Family Issues,* 1981, *2,* 126–147.

Piotrkowski, C. S., & Katz, M. H. Women's work and personal relations in the family. In P. W. Berman & E. R. Ramey (Eds.), *Women: A developmental perspective* (NIH Publication No. 82–2298). April 1982.

Piotrkowski, C. S., & Katz, M. H. Work experience and family relations among working-class and lower middle-class families. In H. Z. Lopata & J. H. Pleck (Eds.), *Research in the interweave of social roles* (Vol. 3): *Families and jobs.* Greenwich, Conn.: JAI Press, 1983.

Piotrkowski, C. S., & Repetti, R. L. Dual-earner families. *Marriage and Family Review,* in press.

Pleck, J. H. Men's family work: Three perspectives and some new data. *Family Coordinator,* 1979, *28,* 481–488.

Pleck, J. H. Husbands' paid work and family roles: Current research issues. In H. Lopata & J. Pleck (Eds.), *Research in the interweave of social roles* (Vol. 3): *Families and jobs.* Greenwich, Conn. JAI Press, 1983. Pp. 130–177.

Pleck, J. H., Staines, G. L., & Lang, L. Conflicts between work and family life. *Monthly Labor Review,* 1980, *103*(3), 29–32.

Poloma, M. M., & Garland, T. N. The myth of the egalitarian family: Familial roles and the professionally employed wife. In A. Theodore (Ed.), *The professional woman* Cambridge, Mass.: Shenkman, 1971. Pp. 741–761.

Poloma, M. M., Pendleton, B. F., & Garland, T. N. Reconsidering the dual-career marriage: A longitudinal approach. *Journal of Family Issues,* 1981, *2,* 205–224.

Powell, B. The empty nest: Employment and psychiatric symptoms in college educated women. *Psychology of Women Quarterly,* 1977, *2,* 35–43.

Radloff, L. Sex differences in depression: The effect of occupation and marital status. *Sex Roles* 1975, *1,* 249–265.

Rapoport, R., & Rapoport, R. N. The dual career family: A variant family and social change. *Human Relations,* 1969, *22,* 3–30.

Rapoport, R., & Rapoport, R. N. The next generation in dual-earner family research. In J. Aldous (Ed.), *Two paychecks: Life in dual-earner families.* Beverly Hills, Calif.: Sage Publications, 1982.

Richardson, J. G. Wife occupational superiority and marital troubles: An examination of the hypothesis. *Journal of Marriage and the Family,* 1979, *41,* 63–72.

Ridley, C. A. Exploring the impact of work satisfaction and involvement on marital interaction when both partners are employed. *Journal of Marriage and the Family,* 1973, *35,* 229–237.

Riger, S., & Galligan, P. Women in management: An exploration of competing paradigms. *American Psychologist,* 1980, *35,* 902–910.

Robinson, J. P. Housework technology and household work. In S. G. Berk (Ed.), *Women and household labor.* Beverly Hills, Calif.: Sage Publications, 1980. Pp. 53–68.

Robison, E. *Strain and dual role occupation.* Paper presented at the annual meeting of the Society for the Study of Social Problems, 1978.

Rosen, B., Jerdee, T. H., & Prestivich, T. L. Dual-career marital adjustment: Potential effects of discriminating managerial attitudes. *Journal of Marriage and the Family,* 1975, *37,* 565–572.

Rossi, A. S. Life-span theories and women's lives. *Signs,* 1980, *5,* 4–32.

Rotheram, M. J., & Weiner, N. Androgyny, stress, and satisfaction: Dual-career and traditional relationships. *Sex Roles,* 1983, *9,* 151–163.

Scanzoni, J., & Fox, G. L. Sex roles, family and society: The seventies and beyond. *Journal of Marriage and the Family,* 1980, *42,* 743–756.

Sharda, B. D., & Nangle, B. N. *Status attainments of couples: The reciprocal effects of postmarital education and occupation.* Paper presented at the meeting of the American Sociological Association, Toronto, Canada, 1981.

Simpson, I. H., & England, P. Conjugal work roles and marital solidarity. In J. Aldous (Ed.), *Two paychecks: Life in dual-earner families.* Beverly Hills, Calif.: Sage Publications, 1982.

Spanier, G. B., & Lewis, R. A. Marital quality: A review of the seventies. *Journal of Marriage and the Family,* 1980, *42,* 825–839.

Spreitzer, E., Snyder, E. E., & Larson, D. Age, marital status, and labor force participation as related to life satisfaction. *Psychology of Women Quarterly,* 1975, *1,* 235–247.

Stahl, J. M., Wheeler, A., Edwards, B. L., & Vicks, T. D. *Psychological androgyny, role perceptions and actual sharing of household responsibilities among married women college professors and their husbands.* Paper presented at the meeting of the South-eastern Psychological Association, Atlanta, 1983.

Staines, G. L., Pleck, J. H., Shepard, L. J., & O'Conner, P. Wives' employment status and marital adjustment: Yet another look. *Psychology of Women Quarterly,* 1978, *3,* 90–120.

Steil, J. M. Marital relationships and mental health: The psychic costs of inequality. In J. Freeman (Ed.), *Women: A feminist perspective* (ed ed.). Palo Alto, Calif.: Mayfield, 1983.

Taylor, J. E. C. Satisfactions, management skills, and attitudes of dual-career couples. *Dissertation Abstracts International,* 1980, *40*(12), 640A.

Turner, C. Dual work households and marital dissolution. *Human Relations ,* 1971, *24,* 535–548.

Vanek, J. Household work, wage work, and sexual equality. In S. F. Berk (Ed.), *Women and household labor.* Beverly Hills, Calif.: Sage Publications, 1980. Pp. 275–291.

Wallston, B. S. Effects of maternal employment on children. *Journal of Child Psychology and Psychiatry,* 1973, *14,* 81–95.

Wallston, B. S., Foster, M. A., & Berger, M. I will follow him: Myth, reality or forced choice—job seeking experiences of dual-career couples. *Psychology of Women Quarterly,* 1978, *3,* 9–21.

Walshok, M. L. Occupational values and family roles: Women in blue-collar and service occupations. In K. W. Feinstein (Ed.), *Working women and families.* Beverly Hills, Calif.: Sage Publications, 1979. Pp. 63–83.

Weingarten, K. The employment pattern of professional couples and their distribution of involvement in the family. *Psychology of Women Quarterly,* 1978, *3,* 43–52.

Welch, S., & Booth, A. Employment and health among married women with children. *Sex Roles,* 1977, *3,* 385–397.

White, R. W. Strategies of adaptation: An attempt at systematic description. In G. V. Coelho, D. A. Hamburg, & J. E. Adams (Eds.), *Coping and adaptation.* New York: Basic Books, 1974.

Wright, J. D. Are working women really more satisified? Evidence from several national surveys. *Journal of Marriage and the Family,* 1978, *40,* 301–314.

Ybarra, L. When wives work: The impact on the Chicano family. *Journal of Marriage and the Family,* 1982, *44,* 169–179.

Yogev, S. Happiness in dual-career couples: Changing research, changing values. *Sex Roles,* 1982, *8,* 593–605.

Yogev, S., & Vierra, A. Are professional women overworked? *Journal of Occupational Psychology,* 1981, *55,* 165–169.

Zinn, M. B. Employment and education of Mexican-American women: The interplay of modernity and ethnicity in eight families. *Harvard Educational Review,* 1980, *50,* 47–62.

Chapter 24

Research with Families with Handicapped Children: A Multilevel Systemic Perspective

MARTHA FOSTER
MICHAEL BERGER

The diagnosis of a handicapping condition in a child is a major event in a family that has implications at two very broad dimensions of family functioning. In terms of task demands, a child whose development is atypical generally needs special services, unique learning environments, additional health care, and an alteration in routine parenting patterns. Because they are ongoing, these task demands are likely to have a pervasive effect on family functioning, roles, and structure. Unlike a family that reorganizes temporarily to accommodate an acute illness in a child, the family with a handicapped child must evolve a pattern of living as a family that incorporates these continual additional tasks. At an emotional level, the family with a handicapped child is challenged in some way to "make sense" out of the fact that one of the members of the family carries the label of a devalued status in our society. Certainly, most families have at some point a member or members whose behavior or values are labeled by someone as deviant. However, the judgment of a significant handicap in a child, because of its stigma and chronic nature, challenges a family's core values and stresses its emotional equilibrium and usual means of functioning (Goffman, 1963; Reiss, 1980).

The study of families with a handicapped child is relevant to the emerging field of family psychology for two reasons. First, the study of such families can provide information relevant to our understanding of families in general—for example, the exploration of questions such as the impact of significant and chronic stressors on families, or questions related to variations in family structure across the "family life cycle." To elaborate, the concept of the family life cycle (Duvall, 1971) is based in large measure on the predictability with which children develop increasingly greater degrees of independence and autonomous activity beyond the nuclear family. To what extent does the presence of a child whose disability limits his or her autonomy alter a family's passage through these stages? Is the temporal course of families determined primarily by changes in the child, or are other factors (such as parents' career patterns or changes in the grandparent generation) equally powerful forces effecting transition to the next life-cycle stage (Berger & Berger, Chapter 5 of this *Handbook*)? For the investigator of generic family processes, the study of families with a handicapped child provides one avenue for examining such questions.[1]

Secondly, studies of families with a handicapped child provide the descriptive and comparative data necessary for intelligent intervention. Research with this population often has immediate applicability to the intelligent development and evaluation of services for handicapped children and their families, services which ideally ought to be specifically tailored to the needs of such families (Berger & Foster, 1976, Berger & Foster, 1983; Foster, Berger, & McLean, 1981; Turnbull, Brotherson, & Summers, in press; Wolfensberger & Menolascino, 1970).[2]

It is the aim of this chapter to consider the literature on families with handicapped children from a multilevel systemic perspective. To a great degree, we shall have to impose this framework upon the existing literature, since there are very few published family studies using methodologies appropriate to a family-level analysis (Keeney, 1983). A number of studies, however, contribute to an understanding of such families by examining processes, relationships, or issues in one or more subsystems of the family. Drawing from family systems theory, we will attempt to construct a view of the family with a handicapped child based upon the available data. We will examine the major subsystems in the family and the impact of life-cycle changes and consider the tasks and resources of such families. Our intention is not to present an exhaustive review of the literature, but rather to develop a scaffolding on which to place available data about these families. We hope that the scaffolding itself will provide an intriguing guide for the researcher or clinician studying or intervening with this population.

We will draw most heavily from studies of families with retarded children, since these comprise the most extensive published literature in the area, but will also include research with families with children

---

[1] Furthermore, a careful reading of the nonsignificant findings of comparative studies of families with handicapped and nonhandicapped children may provide information about family characteristics and behaviors generic to families in general.

[2] The reader is referred to a recent paper by the authors (Berger & Foster, 1983) which details the implications of this literature and the applications of family systems theory for interventions with families with handicapped children.

with sensory or physical handicaps, including chronic illnesses, as they seem relevant to our organizing framework. Findings directly related to a specific type of disability or level of severity will be noted as such. In a number of studies in the area, children with different diagnoses, including mental, motoric, health, and sensory handicaps, are treated as one group. Such mixed groupings may be a function of the difficulty in obtaining a large enough sample of children with low-incidence conditions such as sensory impairments or in being able to reliably categorize multiply handicapped children whose disabilities impair functioning in more than one area. We would guess that what may be crucial, rather than the label itself, is the family's idiosyncratic interpretation of the label plus factors related to the extent to which a child's disability is disruptive to family functions and expectations.

A SYSTEMIC FRAMEWORK FOR UNDERSTANDING FAMILIES WITH A HANDICAPPED CHILD

We view all families, including the families of developmentally disabled persons, as being mutually interactive systems. This aspect of family life has been beautifully described by Minuchin (1974), who writes:

> The individual influences his context and is influenced by it in constantly recurring sequences of interaction. The individual who lives within a family is a member of a social system to which he must adapt. His actions are governed by the characteristics of the system, and these characteristics include the effects of his own past actions. The individual responds to stresses in other parts of the system to which he adapts; and he may contribute significantly to stressing other members of the system. The individual can be approached as a subsystem, or part, of the system, but the whole must be taken into account. (p. 9)

Families, as well as individuals, should be viewed in their own ecological context. Families are connected to, and influenced by, other systems in the environment. Some of the systems are internal to the family, some external. Families are influenced by changes in the developmental capacities and needs of different family members or subsystems (Carter & McGoldrick, 1980; Haley, 1973; Hughes, Berger, & Wright, 1978; Minuchin, 1974). For example, some parents who respond successfully to the needs of young children have difficulty changing to meet the new tasks of parenting adolescents. Family functioning is influenced also by systems outside the family—such as changes in the extended family system of one or both spouses (Bowen, 1978), the positive or negative interaction of a family member with external social institutions (for example, a promotion at work or the loss of a job, the inability to obtain needed services for a disabled family member, or prolonged academic difficulties for a school-aged child), or difficulties experienced by the entire family in coping with a stressor that is external to the family (for example, the disruption in family functioning caused by war, economic depression, or migration).

Nuclear family functioning is also affected by the availability of supports within the family or external to it. An example of an internal support would be the presence of an older child to help in parenting efforts when a biological parent is unavailable for younger children. Examples of external supports would include the availability of extended family members to help with child care, or access to adequate day-care facilities. An adequate understanding of the family system of the developmentally disabled individual, therefore, means understanding that family system in its ecological context, including its cultural context and its social network of extended family, friends, neighbors, and service agencies (Attneave, 1976; Bott, 1971).

Needed also is a precise description of the structure of families. Much recent work has been done in terms of describing family structure (for example, Haley, 1976, 1980; Madanes, 1981; Minuchin, 1974; Minuchin, Rosman, & Baker, 1978) and mapping the changes in family structure over the course of the family life cycle (Carter & McGoldrick, 1980; Haley, 1973).

Every family has a structure, the pattern of roles and alliances used to make decisions and carry out family tasks. Also, every family can be conceptualized both as a total system and as a collection of smaller subsystems organized in a patterned relationship to one another. Examples of important family subsystems are the spouse subsystem, the parental subsystem which includes all persons in the family who have responsibility for taking care of children, the sibling subsystem, and the individual subsystem (Minuchin & Fishman, 1981). Since different kinds of competencies are called for in the various subsystems, it is to the advantage of family members that all of the subsystems be able to function. In order for this to happen, subsystem boundaries (the rules defining who participates in a subsystem and how) must be sufficiently clear to allow subsystem members to carry out their functions without undue interference—to permit, for example, spouses to resolve a marital dispute without the input of grandparents or children, or siblings to end a quarrel without parental interference. Subsystem boundaries must also be flexible enough to allow contact between the members of the subsystem and others (Aponte, 1976; Minuchin, 1974).

Hierarchy is the second key concept used to describe family structure. Families, like other living systems, are organized hierarchically (Haley, 1976, 1980; Madanes, 1981). Family hierarchies tend to be age graded, with parents occupying the upper levels of the hierarchy and children the lower levels. Attention to the hierarchy in the family has, thus far, proved important because the presence and severity of family dysfunction has been linked to the presence of coalitions across hierarchical levels, between, for example, a symptomatic child and one parent against another parent or between a young adult and her grandparents against her parents (Haley, 1976, 1980; Madanes; Minuchin et al., 1978). However, since little information exists about adaptive family structure in families with a developmentally disabled member, generalizations to this population must proceed cautiously.

The notion of family structure implies, erroneously, that families are static entities. Rather, families are continually pressed to change their patterns of organization. Demands for family change come both from outside the family (as when professionals indicate that a developmentally disabled person is now able to live independently outside the family and the parental subsystem must change to acknowledge this independence and increasing competence) and from inside (when, for example, changes in the developmental competence of family members require alterations of family rules and subsystem boundaries to allow adolescents more autonomy). Recognition that the family is a changing organization has focused attention on the family life cycle, a schema designed to take account of the predictable developmental changes in families—changes in membership, in family roles, and in family tasks—that are likely to require important changes in family organization (Carter & McGoldrick, 1980; Haley, 1973; Kearns & Berger, 1980). Indeed, recent studies have suggested that the onset of symptoms in a family member is likely to be associated with the failure of the family to negotiate a life-cycle transition (Hadley, Jacob, Milliones, Caplan, & Spitz, 1974; Haley, 1973, 1980; Hughes et al., 1978; Walsh, 1978).

Attention to predictable developmental changes in the family is particularly relevant to families with a developmentally disabled person for several reasons. First, there is some data suggesting that the diagnosis of a disabling condition in one family member is often so upsetting to the family that the family "freezes" at the stage of organization it had at the time of diagnosis (Berger & Foster, 1976; Berger & Fowlkes, 1980; Farber, 1968). Kearns (1978), for example, in a study of families with a retarded member who ranged in age from 12 months to 40 years, found that the parents talked of the retarded person as if he or she were a young child, regardless of the person's age. Analogously, Hollister (1978), studying families with an adolescent who had died accidentally, described these families as having frozen in time, unable to evolve beyond the death of the child.

Second, when the nature of the disabling condition is such that the disabled individual progresses much more slowly than usual (for example, when a disabled child does not walk until age four), family members, in order to make sense of the individual's developmental delay, may come to think of the individual as being permanently younger than he or she is. Thus, when the individual does change developmentally, this change may not be seen or accepted by the family. It is not uncommon, for example, in programs for young handicapped children, for parents of slowly developing children to have become so used to taking more care of these children than they would of normally developing children, that they fail to notice when the child becomes more capable of independent behavior and may inhibit this independent behavior (Foster & Berger, 1979; Foster et al., 1981).

Finally, attention to family life-cycle stages is important because the needs of families at different life-cycle stages differ. Family tasks are different at different life-cycle stages, the social institutions with which family members are involved differ, and relevant supports and barriers to family development differ (Kearns & Berger, 1980; Turnbull, Summers, & Brotherson, 1983).

In summary then, a comprehensive view of families with a handicapped child (in fact, we would contend, of any family) takes into consideration the family's ecological context, its organizational structure including the subsystems comprising the family and their pattern of organization (hierarchy), and the family's life cycle. This is the perspective from which we consider the literature on families with a handicapped child.

OVERVIEW OF THE LITERATURE

The published literature on families with a handicapped child is an extensive though disappointing one. The early work in the area dating from the 1940s was dominated by personal opinion, armchair speculation, and clinical reports of family dynamics and treatment approaches. This body of literature was important in that it focused professional attention on this population and served to raise hypotheses about these families that could be evaluated more systematically. The early, nonempirical work has been followed by a large number of descriptive studies assessing various dimensions of family life, parental or sibling adjustment, or parent-child relationships. It is from this second literature that this article will draw. However, the reader should be aware that the bulk of these descriptive studies are characterized by a number of methodological and conceptual problems that both weaken the studies and contribute to the many inconsistencies in the results that are apparent when the work is considered as a whole.

Methodological and conceptual weaknesses

Methodologically, design, sampling, and measurement problems are common. Designs tend to be retrospective in nature with prospective longitudinal studies virtually nonexistent. Cross-sectional designs examining families at different life-cycle stages or with children of different developmental levels have also been rare. Therefore, there is a limited perspective in the literature as to how the circumstances of families with handicapped children may change across time or differ as a function of the child's age or of the family's life-cycle stage. In addition, many of the studies lack control groups or appropriate contrast groups. The absence of control groups makes interpretation of results difficult and has contributed to a tendency to attribute the finding of any sort of problems to the presence of the handicapped child. For example, a finding of marital discord or poor adjustment in the siblings can only be interpreted accurately if information is known about the relative frequency of these difficulties among families with children who are not handicapped. Selection of an adequate control group requires specification of the relevant control variables; the heterogeneity of families with a handicapped child makes this a difficult task, one which many researchers have chosen to avoid (Bailey & Simeonsson, 1983). Further, the majority of the research in the area has used interview and questionnaire methodologies. While these self-report methods are generally appropriate to many of the questions being posed, questionnaires and interview techniques have often not been clearly specified and reliability assured. Therefore, the effects of observer bias in both the collection and interpretation of the data is unclear. In addition, the minimal number of researchers that have employed norm-referenced instruments or direct observational methods is striking.

Perhaps the most pervasive methodological difficulty, particularly in earlier studies, is the nonrepresentativeness of the samples (Kelman, 1964; Wolfensberger, 1967). The participants most often were middle to upper socioeconomic class white families who were consumers of outpatient services. Families with younger and lower-functioning children were also overly represented. And though the unit of interest was the family, the mother was often the only informant. Thus, for example, information about marital functioning or sibling adjustment was most often determined through maternal interview with no information obtained from fathers or other family members directly; much of this literature, therefore, primarily reflects mother's *perceptions* of family life. The limitations of such data are clearly described in Keeney (1983).

At a conceptual level, research with families with handicapped children is often flawed by some faulty assumptions and questionable logic. First, much of the work is essentially atheoretical in nature, consisting of descriptive studies whose questions seem to have been derived from clinical observation. Notably lacking is evidence in most of the studies that the researcher was guided by a coherent theoretical framework for understanding the family. Secondly, most of the research seems to carry an implicit assumption that families are homogeneous units; little recognition is made of differences in family structures (e.g., single-parent, multigenerational, dual-career) and how these structural differences among families might be important. In addition, ethnic and racial differences are virtually ignored. These failings seem more than sampling limitations; they seems to reflect a restriction in how families are conceptualized.

Third, much of the work rests on an implicit assumption of pathology in families. Studies focus more on the problems and difficulties families face, no doubt following from a presumption of the inevitably devastating effects of having a disabled child. While this is more characteristic of the early literature in the area, it is not uncommon in more recent studies. Finally, many studies imply that any differences found in families with a disabled child are solely or primarily attributable to the child's handicapping condition. For example, research on family adjustment most often focuses on the effects of the handicapped child upon parents or siblings. The reciprocal influence of family members upon one another, and particularly upon the handicapped child, receives little recognition. Clearly, family behavior depends upon a variety of mutually interactive forces, some within the family unit, some external to it. Assumptions of univariate and unidirectional causation are inconsistent both with contemporary family theory and with contemporary developmental theory (e.g., Bell, 1968).

The reader is cautioned to keep in mind the above methodological and conceptual limitations when evaluating this literature.

A MULTILEVEL ANALYSIS OF THE LITERATURE

Theoretically, families with handicapped children can be studied from several different levels of analysis. By level of analysis is meant the unit of observation or interpretation: family members as individuals, various subsystems within the nuclear family (sibling, marital, parental), the nuclear family as a whole, the nuclear family plus its social network, or the nuclear family and the service system(s) with which it interacts. Systems thinking holds that these levels are interconnected, that change at one level can affect processes at other levels, and that the most-accurate perspective on families is one that recognizes the interplay among the different levels. Systems theory, however, does not require that the same variables and laws be operative at each level (Berger & Jurkovic, 1984; Scheflen, 1980; Spiegel, 1971).

Individual level

The most common level of analysis chosen by researchers studying families of disabled children is the individual level. There is a vast body of literature describing the individual parent's (most commonly the mother's) emotional reaction to the diagnosis of a handicap in a child and her long-range adjustment (see Wolfensberger, 1967, for a review of this literature). Much of the data on parental emotional status is impressionistic and, if experimental, poorly controlled and character-ized by the sampling biases and retrospective research designs noted earlier. In terms of parents' initial reaction to the disability, no consis-tent patterns of emotional reaction have been described, though re-sponses such as guilt, fear, anger, anguish, denial, depression, hopeless-ness, and embarassment figure frequently in the reports. Though the intensity of these reactions varies from mild to severe, what seems most characteristic is a period of negative emotional reaction and, often, disruption in functioning at some point around the time the handicapped condition is identified. Wolfensberger (1967) describes this intense, crisis-type reaction as "novelty shock" in that it is precipi-tated by the sudden violation of the parents' expectation for, and antici-pation of, a normal child. He notes, though, that articles on parents of the more severely retarded are numerically and proportionally over-represented in the literature and that less is known about the initial reactions of parents of mildly retarded or otherwise mildly impaired children.

The continuity of parental reactions to the handicapped child, in-cluding coping skills, personality functioning, and perception of family adjustment, past the initial crisis phase has also been studied exten-sively. Again, the bulk of the work has been with mothers (but see the excellent review paper on fathers by Bristol & Gallagher, 1983). The consensus of the early research and impressionistic reports in this area was that parents showed recurrent crises and abnormally high emotionality and conflicts (Wolfensberger, 1967). Later research, which has been somewhat better designed, reveals a more positive picture of parents and their perceptions of family life, with a number of studies reporting satisfactory adjustment in terms of the parents' acceptance and integration of the handicapped child into family routines, and positive affect on the part of the parent toward the handicapped child as well as acknowledgment of the benefits to the family of having to adjust to a handicapped child (e.g., Birenbaum, 1970, 1971; Caldwell & Guze, 1960; Darling, 1979; Salk, 1972; Voysey, 1975). Thus, while the majority of parents probably experience a period of intense upheaval and emotional distress in the beginning, the continuity of this reaction cannot be assumed for all families. More precise information as to factors related to good and poor parental adjustments is still needed.

Though reports by parents often indicate good adjustments and positive reactions toward their children, rearing a handicapped child presents to families a number of practical and logistical problems that have been well documented for some time. Commonly cited difficulties include increased child-care tasks (Dunlop & Hollingsworth, 1977; Holt, 1958; Schonnel & Watts, 1956), financial difficulties (Dunlop & Hollingsworth; Gumz & Gubrium, 1972; Holt; Salk, 1972), problems in finding adequate educational or treatment programs (Schonnel & Watts), and lack of time for relaxation and restrictions on freedom of movement (Holt; Schonnel & Watts; Wortis & Margolies, 1955). After the point of initial crisis, it is around such reality concerns that parents generally report their greatest distress, and there is some evidence that the level of such stressors or the availability of mechanisms to alleviate them (e.g., social-support system, adequate treatment programs) are directly related to parents' reports of overall family adjustment as well as indicators of their individual emotional reaction (Farber, 1959; Friederich, 1979; Friederich & Friederich, 1981; Schonnel & Rorke, 1960; Wortis & Margolies).

However, though reality issues have been described since the 1950s by parents as having a major impact on both individual and family functioning, investigators have clung for the most part to intrapsychic explanations of adjustment in parents until fairly recently. For example, constructs such as idealization or overprotection, presumed to be mediated by parental guilt and inadequate "acceptance" of the handicapped child, have been used to explain many of the difficulties experienced by parents. Darling (1979) notes that this pattern of explanation is presumptive and is an example of what Ryan (1971) has called "blaming the victim." For example, if a mother has difficulty managing her retarded child, one interpretation is that she is experiencing difficulty "accepting her child and is in need of counseling. An alternative assessment might be that a different type of service is needed for the child, one that will relieve the parents of some of the burden of child care. "The former method implies that the mother's behavior is pathological and needs changing; the latter suggests that she is responding normally to a difficult situation, which needs alleviating" (Darling, p. 70).

The area of parental emotional adjustment and coping, both during the initial period of learning about the handicap and particularly throughout parents' pattern of adjustment across the life course of raising a disabled child, is an important topic of investigation. The adults in the family "set the stage" and determine much of the emotional climate of the family for other family members. For families with a handicapped child, the reaction of the parents to the disabled child is a key determinant of how the siblings will adjust to their handicapped brother or sister and define for themselves the experience of being in a family of this type (Graliker, Fishler, & Koch, 1962; Grossman, 1972). Furthermore, a number of studies have demonstrated a correlation between parental adaptation, attitudes, and behavior and the adjustment of their handicapped children (Denhoff & Holden, 1971; Grebler, 1952; Heilman, 1950; Kolin, 1971). Therefore, research on parental adjustment and coping can be related readily to intervention. However, the question of an individual parent's emotional reaction or of his or her perception of family life must be examined in context in order to be meaningfully understood. Drawing from family systems thinking, we would argue that investigations of functioning in an individual family member must be made in combination with attention to the impact of other factors at the dyadic, family system, and community levels. Though questions of parental emotional adjustment may be studied by individual self-report, the meaning of obtained responses must be interpreted in the light of contextual factors from all levels. To illustrate, we will describe possible factors that likely affect reported individual adjustment in parents at different levels.

The nature, duration, and degree of parental responses are mediated in part by factors attributable to the handicapped child. A parent does not raise the generic category "handicapped child," but is involved in daily transactions with a specific child with particular characteristics and attributes. Diagnostic category (Cummings, 1976; Cummings, Bayley, & Rie, 1966; Holroyd & McArthur, 1976), child's age and sex (Bristol, 1979; Farber, 1959), and care-giving demands of the child (Shere & Kastenbaum, 1966) have all been shown to have an impact on parents' level of reported stress and overall adjustment. In a recent study, Beckman (1983) found that in a sample of mothers with handicapped infants, the strongest predictors of stress in the mother were care-giving demands, child responsiveness, and self-stimulatory behavior in the child. Care-giving demands alone accounted for 66 percent of the variance in amount of stress reported.

The quality of parents' relationships in other family subsystems (marital, parent/normal child) as well as relationships with extended family members affect parental emotional reaction and coping and may influence their descriptions of family life in general. An example of this type of linkage is Friedrich's (1977) finding that the coping skills of handicapped infants' mothers who had a satisfactory relationship with their husbands were better than those of mothers who did not. In addition, patterns of relationship in the family as a whole and particular structural or organizational dimensions of families influence individual reports of personal or family adjustment. In a family organized around the avoidance of conflict, a mother may minimize her presentation of problems or personal pain.

At a community level, the availability of necessary services for the handicapped child can have an impact on parents' adjustment and reports of coping. Conceivably, without adequate services, the ongoing process of rearing a handicapped child may become an overwhelming problem that pervades parents' day-to-day living, creating intensely negative emotional reactions and deficits in coping skills. However, given the availability of reasonably adequate community services, the presence of a disabled child may assume for most parents the proportion of other problems which the family handles adequately. Similarly, either the presence of other types of support from a family's social network or perhaps simply the absence of sanction and stigma may be mediating factors in parental reaction (Bristol & Gallagher, 1983; Darling, 1979). Many of the studies on parental adjustment were conducted at a time when handicapping conditions were less discussed in the media and when the acceptance of diversity among people was less valued; therefore, it is possible that parents, themselves products of this culture, were less able to cope positively with their child's stigmatized condition. As our culture shifts toward more awareness of disabilities and possibly greater acceptance of them, parental reactions may also be moderated. The above analysis hopefully lays to rest the assumption that questions of parental adjustment and coping can be meaningfully investigated solely at the individual level.

Related to the issue of adjustment, it is important to note that most of the research has focused on descriptions of parental outcomes. The processes of coping also need to be studied that mediate successful or unsuccessful adjustment in family members. While there are no longitudinal studies of coping in families with a handicapped child, cross-sectional investigations such as Darling's (1979) point to many parents actively redefining their situation in order to derive positive meaning from the experience of rearing a handicapped child ("reframing"), as well as their utilization of spiritual and social supports (see also Reiss, 1980). The ability of family members to use resources both within and outside of themselves to cope deserves further investigation both in research and in intervention.

Family subsystems

In this section we will examine the literature on families with handicapped children in terms of the functioning of the other three major subsystems within the family—marital, parental, sibling. While each of these subsystems by definition involves interaction among or between the persons comprising the particular unit of the family, few investigators have used methodologies that tap these interactions. Rather than interactional analyses of subsystem participants, the pervasive focus has been an assessment of the functioning or a description of the issues faced by individuals who are members of one of these subsystems. The limitations of such analysis are well described in Keeney's (1983) paper.

Marital system. Information about the marital system is based on investigations which document the divorce rate, marital satisfaction or integration, and fertility patterns among families of the handicapped. A number of studies have reported cases of marital breakdown that are attributable, at least in part, to the handicapped child (Freeston, 1971; Hare, 1966; Kolin, 1971; Tew, Lawrence, Payne, & Rawnsely, 1977). The latter study reported a divorce rate twice that of matched controls in a sample of families with physically handicapped children. Based on his work with families with retarded children, Love (1973) concluded that their divorce rate was three times that of families with normal children. On the other hand, Dorner (1975) and Martin (1975) present data showing no difference between divorce rates of parents with children with spina bifida and the rest of the population. And Wikler (1981) reports that the divorce rate in families of mentally retarded children, when matched for social class, does not differ significantly from that of families with nonretarded children. Finally, in a comparative study with low-income families with a mildly retarded child, Meyerowitz and Farber (1966) reported a greater amount of remarriage (with the retarded child more often predating the divorce) among families with the retarded child. In contrast to the above studies which seem to be assessing the frequency of marital breakdown as a sequalae to the birth of a more severely handicapped child, the latter study finds marital instability to be but one of a constellation of negative social and demographic factors characteristic of the life pattern of many families with a mildly retarded child. Mild (educable) retardation is disproportionately more prevalent among persons of lower-class status, and considerable research and discussion has been devoted to its social and environmental determinants (Maloney & Ward, 1979). Rather than marital instability being a consequence of a mildly retarded child's entrance into the family, it is more likely that marital problems and mild retardation are but two of the many risks of the "culture of poverty."

The second approach to understanding the nature of the marital subsystem is through indexes of marital satisfaction or distress. Here many researchers have relied on self-report (often again, only from the mothers), and the data are mixed. For example, D'Arcy (1968), in a study of 90 mothers of Down's syndrome children, found that over 80 percent report their marriage happy and unchanged. McAndrew (1976) noted that all but 17 of his 116 mothers of cerebral palsy children reported good marital relationships. Dunlop and Hollingsworth (1977), in a survey study of rural families with a handicapped member, note that only 7 percent of the respondents indicated that there had been any effect on the marriage, and 42 percent of these saw the effect as positive. Gath (1977), on the other hand, reported severe disharmony or marital breakdown in one third of his sample; earlier, Gath (1972) had found that in the two years following the birth of a Down Syndrome child, two thirds of the families had either had a parent with a depressive psychiatric illness or displayed significant marital conflict.

Two recent studies, both using the Locke-Wallace marital adjustment inventory (Locke & Wallace, 1959), report conflicting results with samples of parents of retarded children. Friedrich and Friedrich (1981) found that mothers of school-aged retarded children showed a lower level of marital satisfaction than a matched sample of mothers of nonhandicapped children. In contrast, Waisbren (1980) found no differences in marital satisfaction between matched samples of couples who were parents of normal or handicapped infants. If the sample differences account for the variation in finding, marital satisfaction may decrease as children get older.

Farber (1959), studying 240 families with a severely retarded child living at home or in an institution, assessed the impact on "marital integration" of the child's age, sex, and degree of dependence. His index of marital integration consisted of (1) a consensus index (the extent to which the husband and wife agreed in their ranking of 10 domestic values) and (2) a measure of marital role tension. This composite index correlated positively with parents' self-reports of marital satisfaction. Retarded males living at home affected marital integration, especially in lower-class families, more than did retarded girls; this effect was stronger the older the child and tended to diminish if he were institutionalized. However, Fowle (1968), using the same measurements as Farber, found little difference in marital integration whether the child was at home or residing in an institution.

Farber (1960) also classified the family organizational strategies used by families with a severely retarded child as falling into one of four types: parent-oriented, child-oriented, home-oriented, or residual (no consistent or crystallized strategy, or disagreement between parents about the family strategy). He found that parents who used a consistent strategy, whether it be parent-oriented, child-oriented, or home-oriented, were found to have a higher marital integration than those who did not. Farber's work can be faulted methodologically, and his assumption that good marital functioning can be equated with consensus between spouses might be questioned. Indeed, Farber himself has recently questioned this assumption (in a personal communication). However flawed, his studies with families are commendable for their theoretical basis and for their attempt to identify mediating processes and assess multivariate relationships at a time when much more conceptually simplistic research was the norm with this population.

In a recent preliminary report of a sample of 24 families with "developmentally delayed" children, Corrales and his colleagues (Corrales, Kostoryz, Ro-Trock, & Smith, 1983) assessed the marital relationship, using multiple measures including interview, direct observation, and self-report. They found significant marital distress in two thirds of the sample. Interestingly, almost all the families with high marital distress were rated as families in which one parent had formed a coalition with the handicapped child. Marital separation was noted in a quarter of the sample. Though their sample size, at this point, is very small and quite possibly nonrepresentative, the report does corroborate family therapy theory linking cross-generational coalitions to marital disturbance (e.g., Napier & Whitaker, 1978). The age of the handicapped children in the study (one to eight years) also may be significant. Gath (1972) also found high rates of marital disturbance in families with young children, although Waisbren (1980) did not. Moreover, a high degree of marital distress and divorce also characterizes the at-large population of families with young children (Aldous, 1979).

Decisions regarding procreation are also within the purview of the marital relationship. A number of investigators have explored the question of whether the presence of a handicapped child has resulted in a decision to limit family size. Both Tips (1963, cited in Carr, 1974) and Holt (1958) argue it does. Holt reports that nearly two thirds of the mothers in his sample did not want more children, either because of their fear of giving birth to another child or because of the difficulty of child-care tasks; however, mothers' age (under 30) and birth order of the handicapped child (firstborn) mitigated this somewhat. On the other hand, Sigler, Cohen, Lilienfeld, Westlake, and Hetznecker (1967) studying families with children with Down Syndrome and cleft palate and Fraser and Latour (1968) studying families with children with Down Syndrome both found no difference in parity either before or after the birth of the handicapped child, in comparison to a control group. Carr (1974) notes that age of mother, size of family at the time of the handicapped child's birth, and intended family size are important determinants and should be considered in further research. Again, all the published reports are based on information obtained from mothers. Exploration of this question with couples may well reveal data of a different order. In addition, given the wider availability of genetic counseling, increased use of prenatal diagnostic techniques such as amniocentesis, and trends in society toward postponement of child-bearing by many women and toward smaller family size, the topic deserves further scrutiny.

In summary, more research is needed before we can assert that families with handicapped children suffer substantially poorer marriages or are at greater risk for divorce or marital distress, particularly in light of the increasing acceptability of divorce in the culture at large. In addition, longitudinal studies and well-controlled cross-sectional studies are needed to chart marital relationships across the course of the family life cycle. In particular, the question whether the marital relationship of parents of a handicapped child is at unusual risk at certain points in time deserves more study. Lastly, methodologies and measures are needed which assess the interactional nature of the marital relationship and examine it in the context of other family relationships. An individual spouse's perception of her or his marriage is an insufficient and possibly distorted measure of the marital subsystem.

Lastly, there are two questions related to the interpretation of the findings in this area. First, Farber (1959) notes that the dominant factor determining marital integration in his sample was simply the degree of integration achieved prior to the introduction of the handicapped child. Without documentation of prior marital adjustment as well as sources of concurrent stress in families, the implication of many researchers that the handicapped child is the sole or primary determinant of marital distress or dissolution can be disputed. Second, what is the meaning placed on "good" or "poor" marital outcomes? A degree of stress and some symptomatic behavior characterize the majority of families at one point or another in the course of the life cycle (Lewis, Beavers, Gossett, & Phillips, 1976). It is not simply the presence of problems that characterize a dysfunctional family, but rather a family's inability to resolve them (Napier & Whitaker, 1978; Reiss, 1980; Stuart, 1980). A couple's ability to resolve marital conflicts, therefore, may be a better index of the functionality of the marital subsystem than is a static description of the level of marital distress. Some family therapists (Bowen, 1978; Guerin, 1976) contend that family dysfunction may crystallize in marital problems, dysfunction in a spouse, or dysfunction in a child, but the locus of the symptom is idiosyncratic for individual families. A "good" marriage at one point in time may be maintained at the cost of symptoms in a child or in one spouse. And, for some families, the ability to contain problems at the level of the marriage at a given point in time without involving the children may be a sign of strength in coping.

Parental subsystem. The parental subsystem includes those individuals in the family charged with nurturing and socializing the children, typically mother and father. However, it can include other family members such as a grandparent or a sibling who plays the role of a "parental child." As a subsystem, it includes the transactions between the caretaking individuals in the discharge of parental functions as well as their interactions with the child (children). Therefore, investigations of this subsystem seem to call for at least a dyadic, if not a triadic, perspective (see the lucid discussion in Bristol & Gallagher, 1983). However, most of the research concerned with parenting has explored the perceptions or attitudes of individual parents toward childrearing. More recently, though, observational studies of mother-child interaction have provided more direct information about how parents actually behave in interaction with their children.

The attitudes of parents of handicapped children have received a considerable amount of research attention, but the nearly total focus on maternal as opposed to parental attitudes, the inadequacies in the measurement instruments, and the lack of control groups are all significant limitations in the research. In addition, as in all attitudinal research, the question of congruence with actual behavior must be raised.

Much of the attitudinal research has been focused on dimensions and characteristics of parenting attitudes as assessed by the parent attitude research instrument (PARI) (Schaefer & Bell, 1958), an instrument which has been faulted for a number of deficiencies limiting its validity for research purposes (Becker & Krug, 1965). Using the PARI, Dingman, Eyman, and Windle (1963) and Klebanoff (1959) both found mothers of handicapped children to be "overprotective" and "authoritarian" in their childrearing attitudes. Cook (1963) studied mothers of children in four disability categories (blind, deaf, mentally retarded, and cerebral palsied) and found all but the mothers of the deaf children were strongly authoritarian in attitudes. Degee of handicap was also important in that mothers of mildly handicapped children were more likely to be categorized as rejecting, while mothers of the severely handicapped were more overprotective. In addition, Shere (1955) and Shere and Kastenbaum (1966) interpreted the responses of the mothers in their studies as indicating overprotection, infantilization, and extended mutual interdependence of mother and child. Cummings et al. (1966) found mothers of mentally retarded children, in contrast to mothers of nonhandicapped children, to show more preoccupation with the handicapped child and feelings of greater possessiveness toward the child. In a later study of the personality functioning of fathers, Cummings (1976) found that fathers of retarded children also showed more preoccupation with their child as well as more depression and low self-esteem.

Parental expectations and concerns, and parents' ability to accurately assess their child's level of disability have also been studied. Minde (1977, cited in Harvard, 1978; Minde, Hackett, Killov, & Silver, 1972) found through interviewing parents of physically handicapped children that almost half of his sample of 41 parents were unwilling to contemplate the long-range development of their children and an even larger percentage felt that their children would eventually be normal. On follow-up eight years later, one third continued to hold to this expectation of normalcy. Without a control group of parents of nonhandicapped children, it is impossible to say whether it is unusual for parents to avoid thinking of their child's future or to hold unlikely expectations for the child. Inflated expectations for the future, however unlikely, do not necessarily mean that parents are unable to accurately assess their children's current level of functioning or type of disability. Indeed, Schopler (in a personal communication) has suggested that this form of "denial" which permits parents to maintain hope is often, for short periods of time, adaptive. The findings of Strom, Rees, Slaughter, and Wurster (1981) are consistent with this position. After dividing parents of retarded children into groups with high or low expectations for their child, they found that parents with higher expectations complied more fully with a home-based intervention program focused toward training parents to teach their children. A number of investigators have also studied the accuracy of parental judgments of child ability level. Ewert and Green and Boles, Shulman, and Stern (reviewed in Wolfensberger, 1967) found that when parents were asked to estimate their handicapped child's intelligence or social functioning, their judgments correlated reasonably well with that of professionals (correlations in the neighborhood of .65–.85). Korn, Chess, and Ferndeg (1978) also report that over 90 percent of their sample of parents of children with birth defects were able to identify their child's disabilities with reasonable accuracy.

Parental attitudes or expectations, however, may or may not correlate with actual parenting practices. Self-report methods are not adequate to assess the actual behavior of the parental system; observational methods are necessary. Recent observational investigations of the interactions between mothers and their handicapped children all report findings of greater directiveness and controlling behavior among the mothers of the handicapped children. Marshall, Hegrenes, and Goldstein (1973), observing mothers of mentally retarded children and mothers of "normal" children (3–5 years), found that the mothers of the retarded children were more demanding and were commanding in their verbal exchanges with their children. Kogan (1980) and her associates studied the interactions of preschool-aged children with cerebral palsy with their mothers during free play and physical therapy sessions. They found that both the mothers and the children displayed more negative behaviors when the mothers were performing therapy than when playing and that the mothers became "excessively controlling." In addition, over repeated observations, though the actual amount of interaction remained high and primarily "mother-directed," there was a progressive reduction in warm and positive behaviors in both play and therapy sessions. This decrease in behaviors such as smiling, positive verbalizations, and physical closeness (termed "affect turnoff") was interpreted as a shift in the quality of the interaction over time.

Terdal, Jackson, and Garner (1976) compared mother-child interactions of preschool-aged "normal" and mentally retarded children, matched on mental age, during both structured tasks and in a free-play situation. Mothers of the retarded children showed more directiveness, while the retarded children were less responsive than were the nonhandicapped children. Mothers tended to respond to inadequate responding on the part of their children by increased structuring. Moreover, while the normal children were at least four times as likely to receive positive feedback for compliant rather than noncompliant behavior (and similarly more negative feedback for noncompliant behavior), the retarded children received about as much negative feedback for compliant behavior as they did for noncompliant behavior. The authors interpret this as relating to the "blurred input" provided by retarded children; that is, "their behavior may be more difficult to evaluate as representing compliance or approximation to compliance on the one hand, or as representing refusal or inability to comprehend instruction or inability to perform the task on the other hand. The mothers, not sure of what the children's behavior represents, respond somewhat diffusely to them" (p. 260).

Cunningham, Reuler, Blackwell, and Deck (1981) examined the verbal and behavioral interactions of young retarded and "normal" children with their mothers during free-play and task situations. Retarded children initiated fewer social interactions, were less responsive to their mother's interactions, and engaged in more solitary play than "normal" peers. Mothers of retarded children were more directive during both play and task situations and initiated fewer social interactions. Although the retarded children proved no less compliant than normal children, their mothers used more commands and were less likely to respond positively to cooperative behavior. In addition, consistent with other investigators, the authors report that the retarded children with higher mental ages, in comparison to those with lower mental age, showed a greater deficit in expressive language skills and link this in part to the more-directive pattern of interaction shown by the mothers. "Retarded children appear to elicit a pattern of maternal responses which contributes to difficulties in the child's interactions and expressive language development" (p. 69).

Lastly, in a unique study, Stoneman, Brody, and Abbott (1983) observed 16 mothers, fathers, and their four- to seven-year-old children interacting in their homes in three family groupings: (a) mother and child, (b) father and child, and (c) mother, father, and child. Half the children had Down Syndrome, and half were nonhandicapped. The two groups were matched on a number of demographic variables. Observations were conducted during play sessions in which standard sets of toys were used. The study is notable in that it assessed reciprocal interactions between parents and children, father-child interaction, and the effects of the presence of one parent on the interactions of the other parent with his or her child. Consistent with previous research, parents of the retarded children structured their interactions with their offspring by assuming "manager and teacher roles" more often than did parents of nonhandicapped children. The children with Down Syndrome were less contingently responsive to both parents than were the controls. While the two parents were more similar than diff⌐ ᵔent in the play situation, the mothers of the Down Syndrome chilⅆᵤᵢen did assume the teacher role twice as often as did the fathers. Finally, in the triadic grouping, fathers of both groups of children interacted less with their children, while the level of interaction of the mothers remained high across both the dyadic and the triadic groups.

These recent observational studies of mother-child interaction represent a clear step forward in our understanding of the parental subsystem in families where a child is disabled. The finding of a directive, controlling pattern in the mother's behavior in all of these studies is consistent with earlier findings of authoritarian parenting attitudes in mothers of handicapped children. The literature on parental attitudes, as well as several clinical reports, also points to overprotectiveness as a characteristic of parental behavior. Overprotectiveness implies a discrepancy between the perceived required amount of parental intervention and the child's capabilities. However, what is labeled by clinicians as overprotective behavior on the part of parents may, in fact, be the persistence of a parenting pattern that develops out of the controlling, directive style documented with younger handicapped children, a pattern that occurs in response to the handicapped child's behavioral deficits. Bell and Harper (1977) described "lower limit control strategies" as a pattern in which adults respond to unresponsive behavior with increasing directive behavior aimed at increasing the child's level of interaction. As Cunningham et al. (1981) note, this pattern is similar to that found in their and prior studies of mother–handicapped child interaction. The extent to which lower-limit controls, established in response to younger, less responsive handicapped children, persist despite developmental improvements in the child awaits further longitudinal investigation. That is, a parental pattern of response that may have been quite appropriate to the relatively unresponsive behavior of a less mature child may become overprotective if the pattern persists rigidly even if the child becomes more responsive.

Despite the advances of the recent observational studies, information about the parental subsystem remains very incomplete. To date, the research focus has been on younger children and their mothers. More information is needed about the parenting patterns of fathers and of parents of older children, and these studies need to take into account both direct and indirect parental inputs (Bristol & Gallagher, 1983). Moreover, parenting cannot be understood independent of the characteristics of the child which organize and modify the parent. More studies are needed which portray the reciprocal nature of parent-child relationships, such as those by Cunningham et al. (1981), Stoneman et al. (1983), and Vietze, Abernathy, Ashe, and Faulstich (1978). In addition, although parenting occurs in a broader family context that includes the marital, sibling, and extrafamilial subsystems, the impact of these on parenting patterns has not been empirically investigated with this population. Minde (1977, cited in Howard, 1978) reported from his interviews that parents of adolescents with physical handicaps were emotionally distancing themselves from their handicapped child. Parents attributed this to their wanting to give more attention to their nonhandicapped children or to their marital relationship. Minde's finding points to the importance of considering parenting practices against the evolving context of the family as a whole. Levy (1970) commented on the high incidence of maternal overprotection of retarded children but argued that, in his experience, the strength of the husband-wife relationship is inversely related to overprotection. A good marriage can operate against the mother-child monopoly. Family therapy theorists argue that this would be true for most families as well. Case reports (Foster & Berger, 1979; Foster et al., 1981; Harris, 1982) also point to the interconnection between the parental and the marital subsystems. In a sense, then, research on parenting practices in families with handicapped children needs to go in two different directions simultaneously. The lens needs to be narrowed toward additional observational studies of parents and children of different developmental levels in transaction. At the same time, the lens must be widened to consider the potential influence of other relational contexts such as the marriage or the life-cycle stage of the family on parenting practices.

Sibling subsystem. Research on the siblings in families with a handicapped child has been focused primarily on the impact of the disabled child on the adjustment, attitudes, or behavior of the non-handicapped siblings. Until more recently, reflecting the "pathology bias" of this literature, the majority of investigators assessed only the presence of problems or difficulties in the nonhandicapped sibling, largely ignoring prosocial behaviors or other positive outcomes. More-over, like the rest of the research related to families of the handicapped, studies of siblings have been predominately based on parent report of child behavior, have not employed adequate controls, and have focused on siblings only at the individual level of analysis. Although there recently have been a number of studies examining the effect of the nonhandicapped sibling on the handicapped child, these have all been studies of the efficacy of using the sibling as an agent of inter-vention (e.g., Colletti & Harris, 1977; Laviguer, 1976; Schreibman, O'Neill, & Koegel, 1983; Weinrott, 1974). In these intervention studies, the sibling relationship itself was not the focus of investigation; more-over, the research again considered the siblings from an orientation of the handicapped child's pathology.

Determining the effect of the handicapped child on the "normal" sibling is difficult because of the interactive effects of independent variables such as social class, birth order, and gender. As a whole, research results in this area are highly variable, if not inconsistent. Simeonsson and McHale (1981), however, do note three findings which have been identified across several studies, suggesting some degree of robustness. The first is a finding of detrimental effects on the develop-ment of the "normal" sibling's sense of identity (Cleveland & Miller, 1977; Grossman, 1972; Kaplan, 1969). Such concerns include worry by the "normal" children that they may also be handicapped, feelings of guilt for not being handicapped, and fears about having children themselves.

A second theme is that of stress or frustration experienced by the sibling as a result of perceived or actual demands imposed by the parents. A number of investigators (Cleveland & Miller, 1977; Gath, 1974; Holt, 1958; Skrtic, Summers, Brotherson, & Turnbull, in press) report increased caretaking responsibilities by the siblings of handi-capped children, most especially by the oldest female sibling. Siblings may also perceive demands by their parents that they "overachieve" or succeed in some ways to compensate for the limitations of their less-able sibling (Simeonsson & McHale, 1981). While this is an intrigu-ing question, it has not been empirically investigated to date.

The third theme, and one that is in apparent contrast to the above findings, is that a number of investigators have reported that rather than being harmed by their experiences, siblings of handicapped children are often quite well-adjusted (Caldwell & Guze, 1960; Cleveland & Miller, 1977; Gralicker et al., 1962; Grossman, 1972). Findings of greater maturity and responsibility and increased altruistic concerns and tolerance toward others have also been reported (Cleveland & Miller; Farber & Jenne, 1963; Grossman). Since findings of both positive and negative outcomes often occur in the same studies, these general findings must be considered with caution until mediating factors are clearly explicated. For example, parents' demands on their nonhandicapped children, whether the demands be in the realm of increased chores and responsibilities or expectations of accomplishment, may well show a curvilinear relationship with child outcome.

As noted above, a number of independent variables appear to mediate the effects of one child on another (Simeonsson & McHale, 1981). Differential adaptation of the "normal" sibling has been found as a function of socioeconomic status, probably because of greater caregiving responsibilities expected of siblings, particularly the oldest female, from lower-class homes (Gath, 1974). Gender of the handicapped child also appears to be a factor in the adaptation of the "normal" siblings. Younger children are more affected when the handicapped child is of their own gender; however, as the handicapped child grows older, both males and females are more negatively affected by a male handicapped child (Farber & Jenne, 1963).

Other factors that have been demonstrated to mediate sibling adjustment are birth order and family size. Older siblings are less adversely affected than are younger siblings (Gralicker et al., 1962; Grossman, 1972), except when the handicapped child and the older sibs are both adults (Cleveland & Miller, 1977). The effects of family size are not clear, probably because family size is compounded with socioeconomic status. Severity of the handicap has also not been systematically investigated, though there is some evidence that when the handicapping condition is severe, the sibling is more adversely affected (Simeonsson & McHale, 1981).

Based on the research to date, all of these subject and family variables can be expected to account for some of the variance in studies of sibling adjustment and need to be considered in future research on this topic. Moreover, research on the actual nature of the sibling relationship is needed. Currently, there is a paucity of studies which address the interactive relationship between nonhandicapped and handicapped siblings, or relationships between siblings and parents. The available descriptive studies raise a number of questions about the sibling subsystem in families with a handicapped child that merit further study with methods appropriate to the study of relational systems. The observational research of Brody and Stoneman (1983) is one example of the direction work in this area should follow.

Nuclear family as a whole

In this section, interactional research on the family as a whole unit will be discussed. In contrast to the rather extensive literature on whole-family interaction in families with an emotionally disturbed member (Jacob, 1975), there are very few observational studies of families with a handicapped child that have been conducted from this level of analysis.

O'Connor and Stachowiak (1973) compared family interactions in three groups: families with a nonhandicapped child with low adjustment prior to formal clinic contact (LA group), families with a nonhandicapped child with high adjustment (HA group), and families with an educable mentally retarded child (MR group). Level of adjustment was determined by ratings of school personnel. The target child in each of the 24 families was an oldest male between 10 and 12 years; each family also had a younger male sibling of school age. Groups were roughly equated on family size, income, and parents' education levels. The families were observed discussing eight different topics on which they had been individually assessed as showing disagreement; they were instructed to attempt to reach consensus (Strodbeck's revealed-difference task). Among the strongest findings were differences among the groups in amount and specificity of communications, amount of expressed conflict, and degree of "cohesion" (defined as resolution of conflict). The communications of the LA group were characterized by a number of relatively long speeches directed to the family as a whole rather than to persons in particular. Both cohesion and conflict scores were significantly lower than the other two groups. The HA group, in contrast, was characterized by highly specific and effective communications, a higher degree of expressed conflict, and high scores on cohesion. Thus, the HA group appeared to be able "to tolerate a great deal of disagreement in a basically cohesive unit with clear communication resources" (p. 239). The MR group was similar to the HA group except for lower scores on amount of expressed conflict and more-accentuated parental control in the face of conflict. One distinctive feature of the MR families was that the older retarded child in these families was comparable on family structure variables to the youngest child in the other groups.

Byassee and Murrell (1975) assessed the interaction patterns of three groups: six families with an autistic child, six families with a child with behavioral problems, and six families with a normal child. Observations were made in the home, with the mother, father, and normal sibling (average age 11 years) interacting on the Ferreira and Winter unrevealed-differences task, which entailed completing a questionnaire about family life, first as individuals and then as a family as a whole. The families were matched on socioeconomic status, age, sex, and IQ of the normal siblings. Results indicated only one significant finding: The families with a child with behavior problems showed lower spontaneous agreement between parents than did either the normal or autistic families. On all other measures including degree of spontaneous agreement in other dyads, choice fulfillment, decision-making time, and the "index of normality," there were no differences between groups.

Kucia and her colleagues (Kucia, Drotar, Doershuk, Stern, Boat, & Matthews, 1979) assessed the family interaction patterns of 15 well-adjusted and 15 poorly adjusted children between 6 and 17 years with cystic fibrosis. Maladjustment was determined by physician rating and confirmed by independent measures of psychological functioning. Observations were made in each family's home as they interacted around two structured tasks, the unrevealed-differences technique and a motoric game where they were required to work together to discover the rules of the game. The two tasks yielded measures of (a) openness of communication, (b) successful problem solving, (c) creativity (number of attempted solutions to the game), and (d) support (positive and negative). Families of the well-adjusted children showed significantly more creative solutions, but less successful problem solving than the families of maladjusted children. No significant differences were found in total family openness of communication or support. The association of creativity with positive adjustment is consistent with previous observations that well-adjusted families are more able to consider alternative solutions to problems than are poorly adjusted families (Lewis et al., 1976; Odom, Seeman, & Newbrough, 1971). The finding of higher scores in problem solving among families of the less well adjusted children is intriguing. Problem solving referred to the numbers of times the family followed a rule of the game. As the authors seem to imply, this "greater orientation to rules" on the part of the family may lead to the low-adjusted children's behavior problems. On the other hand, rather than leading to behavior problems, it might reflect a more-structured pattern of family interaction resulting from parent's experiences with a difficult-to-discipline child. The answer would require longitudinal investigation.

Most recently, Corrales et al. (1983) reported preliminary results with a partial sample of 24 families with "profoundly handicapped" children between one and eight years. Most of the children were deaf and blind. No other demographic data about the families was provided except that all family members were residing in the home. Families participated in an extensive interview and were observed during three tasks designed to promote family interaction. The Timberlawn family evaluation scales (Lewis et al., 1976) were used to rate family processes. The clearest findings were that three quarters of the families were judged as having either a weak parental subsystem or a parent-child coalition, almost two thirds reported marital stress, and more than three quarters exhibited varying degrees of reality distortion in reference to their handicapped child. The most dysfunctional families tended to have the most-incongruent mythologies about the child. In addition, half the sample was rated as depressed or pessimistic in mood, as having unresolved conflicts, or as showing difficulty in expressing feelings. The results of this study, however, must be interpreted with caution in light of the incomplete sample size, lack of a control group, and minimal specification of sample characteristics. For example, it is not known to what extent this sample of 24 families represents a clinical population of families; reference is made to a number of families "continuing in family therapy" but the context from which families were drawn is not known.

The above four descriptive studies represent initial efforts to examine families with handicapped children at the whole-family level of analysis. It is interesting that in the two studies employing nonhandicapped controls, families with handicapped children either did not differ or differed only slightly from the controls.

To generalize from these few studies, it appears that "whole-family research" may be proceeding in two directions: normative studies comparing families with handicapped children with appropriate control and contrast groups, and within-group studies to identify particular patterns of family interaction associated with specific outcomes. The latter would appear to offer information potentially more useful to intervention planning; however, more normative studies at this level of analysis are also needed in order to provide data against which within-group comparisons can be interpreted.

The family and the larger society

Up to this point, we have been considering the research literature on families with handicapped children at the level of the nuclear family and its subsystems. In the following section, we shall discuss research on the family's relationship to the larger society. Two topics will be discussed at this level of analysis: the relationship between families of handicapped children and their social networks, and the relationships between families and service providers.

Social networks. From a theoretical standpoint, the family social network, (e.g., family members, friends, and neighbors) is important because as Berger and Fowlkes (1980) argue:

> [They] are the largest group of persons easily accessible to the family of the handicapped child. Further, the social network is the group of people with whom family members have the most contact and who have the greatest importance for family members. Most importantly, network members know family members and care for family members as people rather than as "the family of the handicapped child." Finally, the network is the group most likely to offer the family the resources it needs, both in terms of direct assistance (e.g., money, babysitting, emotional support) and of indirect assistance (obtaining contacts with persons or institutions known to network members). (p. 23)

The empirical literature on the social network involvements of families with a handicapped child has, thus far, focused upon two issues: (1) the question of network contraction, or family isolation from the social network, and (2) the relationship between network involvement and family adjustment. Methodologically, this literature suffers from flaws previously enumerated: characteristically, network descriptions are obtained only from mothers of handicapped children, are obtained at only one point in time, and are global in character (that is, questions such as "Do you feel supported by your social network?" are asked).

Several authors have reported that many families reduce or curtail contact with members of their social network after the diagnosis of a handicapping condition in their child (Davis, 1967; Farber, 1968; Holt, 1958); similar findings have also been hypothesized by theorists (e.g., Goffman, 1963) and reported by clinicians (Berger & Fowlkes, 1980). Other studies, however, fail to find this network contraction. Moran (1982), for example, found an increase in network size in a sample of families with handicapped children aged 39 months to 5 years. However, in his definition of social network membership, Moran includes kin, friends, and professionals who deal with the handicapped child or with other family members around issues related to the care of the handicapped child. It is possible, therefore, that his findings conceal a process of reduced contact with the initial social network at the time of diagnosis followed by increased contact with professionals or with other parents of handicapped children, a process noted by several clinicians (Berger & Fowlkes, 1980; Foster et al., 1981; Wolfensberger, 1967).

On a related issue, Carr (1974), reviewing British literature on whether the presence of a handicapped child in the family increases family isolation, concludes that the presence of a handicapped child does not result in these families feeling more socially isolated than parents of normal children, at least for families with preschool-aged handicapped children. Nor are parents in these families less likely to go out socially without their children. However, Carr notes contrary findings from a study by Tizard and Grad (1961) which included a large proportion (40 percent) of families with adolescent children. Kearns (1978) reports a similar finding in his cross-sectional study of families with a mentally retarded child ranging in age from 1 to 40 years. Dividing his sample into five groups based on the mentally retarded person's chronological age, Kearns found that while the mean number both of family outings and of parental outings without the child increased slightly with the age of the child, parents of older children were significantly more likely to report that they were unable to go out alone without the child as much as they would like.

With regard to the other major issue addressed in the social network literature, namely the relationship between social network involvement and family adjustment, two findings are consistently reported. First, "better-adjusted" families are those who are involved with, and feel supported by, their social networks (Bristol, 1979, in press; Darling, 1979; Wortis and Margolies, 1955). Secondly, parents of handicapped children who feel supported by their social networks report that the difficulties involved in parenting the handicapped child are more manageable than do parents who feel unsupported by their social networks (Bristol, 1979, in press; Darling; Meyerowitz & Kaplan, 1967; Wortis & Margolies, 1955).

We have only been able to locate one study, Kearns's (1978) master's thesis, which describes the kinds of resources exchanged between network members and families of handicapped children. Using Weiss's (1968) schema for classifying the kinds of resources characteristically exchanged by families with children at different ages, Kearns found no differences in the kinds of resources characteristically exchanged by families with children at different ages. All the families were most likely to report assistance exchanges (that is, instances of instrumental help) with their network members. Families were also likely to report social exchanges (transactions in which family and network members did some pleasant activity together). By contrast, families were very unlikely to report exchanges with network members which Weiss would describe as providing reassurance of worth, nurturance (taking care of someone), and emotional integration (obtaining emotional support).

To summarize, as noted earlier, the kinds of data obtained by the studies described in this section do not permit an understanding of the kinds of resources exchanged between network and family members or of the interactions which characteristically occur between family and network members. Thus, at this stage, while the data suggest that better-adjusted families are more involved with, and feel more supported by, their social networks and that families which feel supported by their networks report the difficulties of childrearing as being more manageable, we do not know what families and network members do or do not do that results in family members feeling supported. Nor can we delineate the processes through which family members come to view the issues involved in parenting these handicapped children as being relatively manageable (Darling, 1979). These serious omissions need to be rectified in order both to increase our understanding of family and social network transactions and to provide the necessary information to guide sensible interventions aimed at repairing or improving the relationships between family members and their social networks.

The family and service systems. Krauss (1983) has delineated two levels at which this relationship can be investigated: the macro level at which one investigates institutional-level outcomes of the relationship between families and professionals and the micro level at which one looks at the ways in which families and individual professionals perceive and interact with one another.

At the first level, it is important to distinguish between studies which merely describe the outcomes of the relationship between professionals and family members: studies which, for example, look at the fit between the kinds of services family members request or utilize and the kinds of services offered, and studies which take into account that these outcomes occur within a given social context in which optimal choices may not be available. Tizard (quoted in Moroney, 1983) puts the latter perspective succinctly when he notes that "you can say that a family has a choice between keeping their handicapped child at home or putting him in an institution only if the family has a choice between excellent supportive services if they keep the child at home and an excellent institution. Anything else is not a real choice" (p. 16).

In terms of what family members (at least mothers) want from service systems, the research findings are consistent. Families want help with pragmatic issues: obtaining and paying for medical and educational services, home assistance, respite care, etc. (Gorham, Des Jardins, Page, Pettis, & Scheiber, 1975; Minnesota State Planning Agency, 1975; Wolfensberger, 1967). Also consistent is the finding that services are often fragmented and that agencies have different eligibility criteria, lack institutional means of coordinating with other relevant services, and often even lack knowledge of relevant services (Gorham et al.; Schwartz, 1970; Wolfensberger). Reading this literature, one could reasonably conclude that locating and obtaining optimal services for one's handicapped child, especially if the child has multiple handicaps, is a full-time job.

Using a 1977 national survey conducted by the U.S. Childrens' Bureau, MacEachron and Krauss (1983) studied the kinds of services offered to four groups of children (nonhandicapped, emotionally disturbed, physically handicapped, or mentally retarded) by generic service systems. Generic service systems are those which serve children in general rather than only special categories of children. MacEachron and Krauss looked at two broad issues: (1) whether services were provided to both families and children or only to children; and (2) when categorizing services as supportive (designed to use the family's own resources to reduce strain in the parent-child system), supplemental (designed to be used when part of the parental role is in jeopardy but can be restored with additional services such as financial assistance), and substitute (services used when there is a temporary or permanent need to sever the parent-child relationship), whether the kinds of services provided to the different types of families were similar or different.

With regard to their first issue, with the exception of the mentally retarded group, all types of families generally received both family and child services; the mentally retarded group generally received only child services. With regard to the second question, except for the mentally retarded group, more than half the families received supportive or supplemental services; the mentally retarded group, by contrast, was most likely to receive substitute services—that is, these children were most likely to be placed outside the home and, if placed outside the home, were likely to remain outside the home longer that the other three groups of children.

Insofar as these findings are typical, they suggest some fit between the services desired by parents of emotionally and physically handicapped children and the services offered to these families by the generic service system. For families of retarded children, however, the service system was likely to provide services only to the child and was more likely to remove the child from the home.

Another of MacEachron and Krauss's (1983) findings, namely the fact that the most common supportive service offered was counseling, is consistent with the literature on what categorical service systems offer parents of handicapped children. That is, parents ask for pragmatic supportive or supplemental services, while professionals offer therapy (Gorham et al., 1975; Wolfensberger, 1967).

Finally, it must be noted that the bulk of therapeutic or educational services provided to "families" are not actually provided to families; they are provided to mothers. This practice carries two important implications. First, it may overfocus mothers on their role as the primary caretaker of the handicapped child, possibly taking away from the needs of other siblings, their spouses, or themselves (Foster et al., 1981; Turnbull et al., 1983). Secondly, it means that we have little idea of the kinds of services fathers want and the kinds of roles it may be useful to ask fathers to play in families with handicapped children (Bristol & Gallagher, 1983).

At the micro level, findings about the perceptions of professionals with regard to families of handicapped children are relatively consistent. Wolfensberger (1967) reviews a large number of studies suggesting that professionals lack knowledge; make confident, authoritative pronouncements to parents about how they should care for their children; and label parents as "good" if they comply with the pronouncements and as "pathological" if they do not. Similar findings are put forth by Krauss (1983), Gorham et al. (1975), and Schwartz (1970). Krauss reports that the current version of this situation has professionals viewing "good" parents as parents who either play the sick role (Parsons, 1955) consistently or who function well as case managers for their children. Both of these roles, Krauss notes, are prescribed for parents by professionals. We would add that, in our experience, professionals who value either of these roles for parents fairly rapidly move to characterizing parents as "pathological" when they do not play whichever of the two roles the professional wants them to (see also Turnbull & Turnbull, 1982).

It is also relatively clear what parents want. They want the kinds of services noted earlier, offered to them with courtesy and with the right to make their own choices about when and how to use the services (Gorham et al., 1975; Wolfensberger, 1967). In this regard, the English experience with thalidomide children (reported in Moroney, 1983) is instructive by its lack of correspondence with American practice. Basically, the government of Great Britain gave money to a private foundation with only the instruction to meet the needs of families of thalidomide children. The foundation did so by asking the families what they wanted (families wanted dishwashers, respite care, etc.—a range of pragmatic services) and then giving it to them. Moroney indicates that families were highly satisfied with the services provided and suggests, though he does not present data for this, that the services were quite cost-efficient.

Lacking in this area are detailed studies of the way in which parent-professional contacts alter both parents' views and expectations for their handicapped child and their behavior with regard to their handicapped child and with professionals. Also lacking are studies of the interrelationship between parent-professional contacts and parent–social network contacts. Darling (1979, p. 78) provides an interesting chart hypothesizing the relative salience of different groups to the families of handicapped children over time; research testing her hypotheses would be most useful. Needed also are studies detailing and comparing the effects of different kinds of professional interactions with families—for example, comparing the effects of interventions involving only mothers with those involving both mothers and fathers, or the effects of programs designed by professionals with programs that asked families what they wanted and then tried to meet the needs as family members defined them. Finally, research also seems required on methods to improve the behavior of professionals toward families of handicapped children.

CONCLUSION

The research literature on families of handicapped children is characterized by a number of serious shortcomings, including the small number of adequately controlled comparative studies; the absence of prospective, longitudinal designs; an overreliance on the use of only one type of measure (e.g., questionnaire, interview) in a given study; the frequent use of measures with poor or undetermined reliability and validity; and an almost singular focus on analyses at the individual level.

As noted earlier, we do not see family research as necessarily limited to methods that allow for the assessment of whole-family interaction. Many questions are best addressed by examining the behavior of individuals or dyads. But the family researcher conceptualizes individual or dyadic behavior as imbedded within a family context and will accordingly assess at more than one level. The bulk of the available research, however, because it examines only individual functioning, cannot stand conceptually as family research.

An additional limitation of the present body of research is its focus on families at only one point in time. Both longitudinal and cross-sectional designs which examine families at different points in the family life cycle are needed to explicate the ways in which the presence of a handicapped child affects and perhaps alters a family's interaction at different points in time. For example, the available research on marital satisfaction has yielded contradictory results, with some investigators indicating lower satisfaction when the children are older and others finding greater marital distress when the handicapped child is very young. No study, however, has assessed marital satisfaction adequately in families with children at different age levels or at different stages of the family life cycle to determine whether marital satisfaction, in fact, fluctuates with life-cycle stage as it does in nonhandicapped samples.

Despite these significant limitations in the body of research as a whole, there are, in the more recent research, indications of changes portending positive trends. Though these hardly characterize the field as a whole, they are glimmers worth highlighting. First, the use of more-sophisticated designs and observational and multivariate methods is becoming slightly more common among researchers in the field. Secondly, some investigators seem to be more clearly reflecting a theoretical perspective or to be conceptualizing their work within current traditions with child development or family research. Examples include the work of Brody and Stoneman (1983) on siblings and parent-child interaction and the family systems perspectives of Turnbull et al. (in press) and Corrales et al. (1983). Given the transactional and ecological viewpoints of family systems researchers and many contemporary child developmentalists, these perspectives should begin to be reflected more in the research on families with handicapped children. Third, while much of the work still seems "pathology-oriented," focusing on the stresses, problems, and presumed negative outcomes for families rearing a handicapped child, some researchers are calling for studies of adaptive processes and coping strategies in families of disabled persons. Findings of positive outcomes in many of the studies of siblings of handicapped children (Simeonsson & McHale, 1981) are consistent with this direction. Lastly, and related to the previous two points, the field seems to be moving toward more research on processes within families that lead to positive and negative outcomes, and somewhat away from purely descriptive studies of the ways this population differs from families with nonhandicapped children. If these trends continue, it is possible that the literature will come to represent fairly the complexities of life faced by families with handicapped children.

REFERENCES

Aldous, J. *Family careers*. New York: John Wiley & Sons, 1979.

Aponte, H. The family-school intervention: An eco-structural approach. *Family Process*, 1976, *15*, 303–311.

Attneave, C. Social networks as the unit of intervention. In P. Guerin (Ed.), *Family therapy: Theory and practice*. New York: Gardner Press, 1976.

Bailey, D., & Simeonsson, R. J. *Evaluating the impact of early intervention on families with young severely handicapped children: Design issues*. Paper presented at the Conference on Evaluating Early Intervention, Vanderbilt University, Nashville, Tenn., March 1983.

Becker, W. C., & Krug, R. S. The parent attitude research instrument: A research review. *Child Development*, 1965, *36*, 329–365.

Beckman, P. J. The influence of selected child characteristics on stress in families of handicapped infants. *American Journal of Mental Deficiency,* 1983, *88,* 150–156.

Bell, R. Q. A reinterpretation of the direction of efforts in studies of socialization. *Psychological Review,* 1968, *75,* 81–95.

Bell, R. Q., & Harper, L. V. *Child effects on adults.* Hillsdale, N.J.: Lawrence Erlbaum Associates, 1977.

Berger, M., & Foster, M. Family-level interventions for retarded children: A multivariate approach to issues and strategies. *Multivariate Experimental Clinical Research,* 1976, *2*(1), 1–21.

Berger, M., & Foster, M. *Application of family therapy theory to research and intervention with families with mentally retarded children.* Paper presented at the NICHD Conference on Research on Families with Mentally Retarded Persons, Rougemont, N.C., September 1983.

Berger, M., & Fowlkes, M. The family intervention project: A family network approach to early intervention. *Young Children,* 1980, *35,* 22–32.

Berger, M., & Jurkovic, G. J. (Eds.). *Family therapy in context: Practicing systemic therapy in community settings.* San Francisco: Jossey-Bass, 1984.

Birenbaum, A. On managing a courtesy stigma. *Journal of Health and Social Behavior,* 1970, *11,* 196–206.

Birenbaum, A. The mentally retarded child in the home and the family cycle. *Journal of Health and Social Behavior,* 1971, *12,* 55–65.

Bott, E. *Family and social network.* London: Tavistock Publications, 1957.

Bowen, M. *Family therapy and clinical practice: The collected papers of Murray Bowen, M.D.* New York: Jason Aronson, 1978.

Bristol, M. *Maternal coping with autistic children: The effect of child characteristics and interpersonal support.* Unpublished doctoral dissertation, University of North Carolina at Chapel Hill, 1979.

Bristol, M. The home care of developmentally disabled children: Some empirical support for a conceptual model of successful coping with family stress. In S. Landesman-Dwyer & P. Vietze (Eds.), *Environments for developmentally disabled persons.* Baltimore: University Park Press, in press.

Bristol, M., & Gallagher, J. *Psychological research on fathers of young handicapped children: Evolution, review, and some future directions.* Paper presented at the NICHD Conference on Research on Families with Mentally Retarded Persons, Rougemont, N.C., September 1983.

Brody, G. H., & Stoneman, Z. *Contextual issues in the study of sibling socialization.* Paper presented at the NICHD Conference on Research on Families with Mentally Retarded Persons, Rougemont, N.C., September 1983.

Byassee, J., & Murrell, S. Interaction patterns in families' of autistic, disturbed, and normal child. *American Journal of Orthopsychiatry,* 1975, *45,* 473–478.

Caldwell, B. M., & Guze, S. B. A study of the adjustment of parents and siblings of institutionalized and non-institutionalized retarded children. *American Journal of Mental Deficiency,* 1960, *64,* 845–861.

Carr, J. The effect of the severely subnormal on their families. In A. M. Clark & A. D. B. Clark (Eds.), *Mental deficiency: The changing outlook.* New York: Free Press, 1974.

Carter, E., & McGoldrick, M. (Eds.). *The family life cycle.* New York: Gardner Press, 1980.

Cleveland, D., & Miller, N. Attitudes and life commitments of older siblings of mentally retarded adults: An exploratory study. *Mental Retardation,* 1977, *15*(3) 38–41.

Colletti, G., & Harris, S. L. Behavior modification in the home: Siblings as behavior modifiers, parents as observers. *Journal of Abnormal Child Psychology,* 1977, *5,* 21–30.

Cook, J. J. Dimensional analysis of child-rearing attitudes of parents of handicapped children. *American Journal of Mental Deficiency,* 1963, *68,* 354–361.

Corrales, R. G., Kostoryz, J., Ro-Trock, L., & Smith, B. Family therapy with developmentally delayed children: An ecosystemic approach. In D. Bagarozzi, A. Jurich, & R. Jackson (Eds.), *Marital and family therapy: New perspectives in theory, research, and practice.* New York: Human Sciences Press, 1983.

Cummings, S. T. The impact of the child's deficiency on the father: A study of fathers of mentally retarded and chronically ill children. *American Journal of Orthopsychiatry,* 1976, *46,* 246–255.

Cummings, S. T., Bayley, H., & Rie, H. Effects of child's deficiency on the mother: A study of mothers of mentally retarded, chronically ill, and neurotic children. *American Journal of Orthopsychiatry,* 1966, *36,* 595–608.

Cunningham, O. E., Reuler, E., Blackwell, J., & Deck, J. Behavioral and linguistic developments in the interaction of normal and retarded children with their mothers. *Child Development,* 1981, *52*(1) 62–70.

Davis, D. R. Family processes in mental retardation. *American Journal of Psychiatry,* 1967, *124,* 340–350.

Darling, R. *Families against society.* New York: Russell Sage Foundation 1979.

D'Arcy, E. Congenital defects: Mother's reactions to first information. *British Medical Journal,* 1968, *3,* 796–798.

Denhoff, E., & Holden, R. H. Understanding parents: One need in cerebral palsy. In R. L. Noland (Ed.), *Counseling parents of the ill and the handicapped.* Springfield, Ill.: Charles C Thomas, 1971.

Dingman, H. F., Eyman, R. K., & Windle, C. D. An investigation of some childrearing attitudes of mothers with retarded children. *American Journal of Mental Deficiency,* 1963, *67,* 899–908.

Dorner, S. The relationship of physical handicap to stress in families with an adolescent with spina bifida. *Developmental Medicine and Child Neurology,* 1975, *17,* 765–776.

Dunlop, W. R., & Hollingsworth, J. S. How does a handicapped child affect the family? Implications for practitioners. *Family Coordinator,* July 1977, 286–293.

Duvall, E. *Family development.* Philadelphia: J. B. Lippincott, 1971.

Farber, B. Effects of a severely mentally retarded child on family integration. *Monographs of the Society for Research in Child Development,* 1959, 24(2), 1–112.

Farber, B. Family organization and crisis: Maintenance of integration in families with a severely mentally retarded child. *Monographs of the Society for Research in Child Development,* 1960, *25*(1), 1–95.

Farber, B. *Mental retardation: Its social context and social consequences.* Boston: Houghton Mifflin, 1968.

Farber, B., & Jenne, W. Family organization and parent-child communication: Parents and siblings of a retarded child. *Monographs of the Society for Research in Child Development,* 1963, *28:7,* 1–78.

Foster, M., & Berger, M. Structural family therapy: Applications in programs for preschool handicapped children. *Journal of the Division of Early Childhood,* 1979, *1,* 52–58.

Foster, M., Berger, M., & McLean, M. Rethinking a good idea: A reassessment of parent involvement. *Topics in Early Childhood Special Education,* 1981, *1,* 55–65.

Fowle, C. The effect of the severely mentally retarded child in his family. *American Journal of Mental Deficiency,* 1968, *75*(3), 468–473.

Fraser, F. C., and Latour, A. Birth rates in families following birth of a child with mongolism. *American Journal of Mental Deficiency,* 1968, *72,* 883–886.

Freeston, B. M. An inquiry into the effects of a spina bifida child upon family life. *Developmental Medicine and Child Neurology,* 1971, *13,* 456–461.

Friedrich, W. N. Predictors of the coping behavior of mothers of handicapped children. *Journal of Consulting and Clinical Psychology,* 1979, *47,* 1140–1141.

Friederich, W. N., & Friederich, W. L. Comparison of psychosocial assets of parents with a handicapped child and their normal controls. *American Journal of Mental Deficiency,* 1981, *85,* 551–553.

Gath, A. The mental health of siblings of congenitally abnormal children. *Journal of Child Psychology and Psychiatry,* 1972, *13,* 211–218.

Gath, A. Sibling reactions to mental handicap: A comparison of brothers and sisters of mongol children. *Journal of Child Psychology and Psychiatry,* 1974, *15,* 187–198.

Gath, A. The impact of an abnormal child upon the parents. *British Journal of Psychiatry,* 1977, *130,* 405–410.

German, M. L., & Maisto, A. A. The relationship of a perceived family support system to the institutional placement of mentally retarded children. *Education and Training of the Mentally Retarded,* 1982, *17*(1), 17–23.

Goffman, I. *Stigma.* Englewood Cliffs, N.J.; Prentice-Hall, 1963.

Gorham, K., Des Jardins, C., Page, R., Pettis, E., & Scheiber, B. Effect on parents. In N. Hobbs (Ed.), *Issues in the classification of children* (Vol. 2). San Francisco: Jossey-Bass, 1975.

Graliker, B. V., Fishler, K., & Koch, R. Teenage reactions to a mentally retarded sibling. *American Journal of Mental Deficiency,* 1962, *66,* 838–843.

Grebler, A. M. Parental attitudes toward mentally retarded children. *American Journal of Mental Deficiency,* 1952, *56,* 475–483.

Grossman, F. K. *Brothers and sisters of retarded children: An exploratory study.* Syracuse, N.Y.: Syracuse University Press, 1972.

Gumz, E., & Gubrium, J. Comparative parental perceptions of a mentally retarded child. *American Journal of Mental Deficiency,* 1972, *77*(2), 175–180.

Hadley, T. R., Jacob, T., Milliones, J., Caplan, J., & Spitz, D. The relationship between family developmental crises and the appearance of symptoms in a family member. *Family Process,* 1974, *13*(2), 207–214.

Haley, J. *Uncommon therapy.* New York: W. W. Norton, 1973.

Haley, J. *Problem-solving therapy.* San Francisco: Jossey-Bass, 1976.

Haley, J. *Leaving home.* New York: McGraw-Hill, 1980.

Hare, E. H. Spina bifida cystica and family stress. *British Medical Journal,* 1966, *2,* 757–760.

Harris, S. L. A family systems approach to behavioral training with parents of autistic children. *Child and Family Behavior Therapy,* 1982, *4*(1), 21–35.

Heilman, A. E. Parental adjustment to the dull handicapped child. *American Journal of Mental Deficiency,* 1950, *54,* 556–562.

Hollister, M. Families who experience the loss of a child. In R. Sagar (Ed.), *Georgetown family symposia* (Vol. II). Washington, D.C.: Georgetown University, 1978.

Holroyd, J., & McArthur, D. Mental retardation and stress on the parents: A contrast between Down's syndrome and childhood autism. *American Journal of Mental Deficiency,* 1976, *80,* 431–436.

Holt, K. Home care of severely retarded children. *Pediatrics,* 1958, *22,* 744–754.

Howard, J. The influence of children's developmental dysfunctions on marital quality and family interaction. In R. M. Lerner & G. B. Spanier (Eds.), *Child influences on marital and family interaction: A life-span perspective.* New York: Academic Press, 1978.

Hughes, S. F., Berger, M., & Wright, L. The family life cycle and clinical intervention. *Journal of Marriage and Family Counseling,* 1978, *44,* 33–40.

Jacob, T. Family interaction in disturbed and normal families: A methodological and substantive review. *Psychological Bulletin,* 1975, *82*(1), 33–65.

Kaplan, F. Siblings of the retarded. In S. Sarason & J. Doris (Eds.), *Psychological problems in mental deficiency.* New York: Harper & Row, 1969.

Kearns, D. *Social networks of parents of the mentally retarded: Characteristics and influences on family functioning.* Master's thesis, Department of Psychology, Wichita State University, 1978.

Kearns, D., & Berger, M. Family response to change. *Dimensions,* 1980, *9*(1), 20–23.

Keeney, B. Ecological assessment. In B. Keeney (Ed.), *Diagnosis and assessment in family therapy.* Rockville, Md.: Aspen, 1983.

Kelman, H. R. The effect of a brain-damaged child on the family. In H. G. Birch (Ed.), *Brain damage in children: The biological and social aspects.* Baltimore: Williams & Wilkins, 1964.

Klebanoff, L. B. Parents of schizophrenic children. I: Parental attitudes of mothers of schizophrenic, brain-injured, and retarded and normal children. *American Journal of Orthopsychiatry,* 1959, *29,* 445–454.

Kogan, K. L. Interaction systems between preschool handicapped or developmentally delayed children and their parents. In T. M. Field, S. Goldberg, D. Stern, & A. Sostek (Eds.), *High risk infants and children: Adult and peer interactions.* New York: Academic Press, 1980.

Kolin, I. S. Studies of the school-aged child with meningomyelocele: Social and emotional adaptation. *Journal of Pediatrics,* 1971, *78,* 1013–1019.

Korn, S. J., Chess, S., & Ferndeg, P. The impact of children's physical handicaps on marital quality and family interaction. In R. M. Lerner & G. B. Spanier (Eds.), *Child influences on marital and family interaction: A life span perspective.* New York: Academic Press, 1978.1

Krauss, M. *Social policy consideration: Macro and micro-level considerations.* Paper presented at the NICHD Conference on Research on Families with Mentally Retarded Persons, Rougemont, N.C., September 1983.

Kucia, C., Drotar, D., Doershuk, C. F., Stern, R. C., Boat, T. F., & Matthews, L. Home observation of family interaction and childhood adjustment to cystic fibrosis. *Journal of Pediatric Psychology,* 1979, *4*(2), 189–195.

Lamb, M. E. The role of the father: An overview. In M. E. Lamb (Ed.), *The role of the father in child development*. New York: John Wiley & Sons, 1976.

Laviguer, H. The use of siblings as an adjunct to the behavioral treatment of children in the home with parents as therapists. *Behavior Therapy*, 1976, *7*, 602–613.

Levy, D. Maternal overprotection. In E. J. Anthony & T. Benedek (Eds.), *Parenthood*. Boston: Little, Brown, 1970.

Lewis, J. M., Beavers, W. R., Gossett, J. T., & Phillips, V. A. *No single thread: Psychological health in family systems*. New York: Brunner/Mazel, 1976.

Locke, H. J., & Wallace, K. M. Short marital adjustment and prediction tests: Their reliability and validity. *Marriage and Family Living*, 1959, *21*, 251–255.

Love, H. *The mentally retarded child and his family*. Springfield, Ill.: Charles C Thomas, 1973.

Madanes, C. *Strategic family therapy*. San Francisco: Jossey-Bass, 1981.

Maloney, M. P., & Ward, M. P. *Mental retardation and modern society*. New York: Oxford University Press, 1979.

Marshall, N., Hegrenes, J., & Goldstein, S. Verbal interactions: Mothers and their retarded children versus mothers and their nonretarded children. *American Journal of Mental Deficiency*, 1973, *77*(4), 415–419.

Martin, P. Marital breakdown in families of patients with spina bifida cystica. *Developmental Medicine and Child Neurology*, 1975, *17*, 757–764.

McAllister, R., Butler, E., Lei, T. J. Patterns of social interaction among families of behaviorally retarded children. *Journal of Marriage and the Family*, 1973, *36*, 93–100.

McAndrew, I. Children with a handicap and their families. *Child: Care, health, and development*, 1976, *2*, 213–237.

MacEachron, A., & Krauss, M. A national survey of handicapped children receiving public service: Prevalence rates and service patterns in 1977. *Children and Youth Services Review*, 1983, *5*, 117–134.

Meyerowitz, J. H., & Farber, B. Family background of educable mentally retarded children. In B. Farber (Ed.), *Kinship and family organization*. New York: John Wiley & Sons, 1966.

Meyerowitz, J., & Kaplan, H. Familial responses to stress: The case of cystic fibrosis. *Social Science and Medicine*, 1967, *1*, 249–266.

Minde, K. K., Hackett, J. D., Killov, D., & Silver, S. How they grow up: 41 physically handicapped children and their families. *American Journal of Psychiatry*, 1972, *128*(12), 1554–1560.

Minnesota State Planning Agency. *CAIR: Community Alternatives and Institutional Reform*. St. Paul: State Planning Agency, Developmental Disabilities Program, 1975.

Minuchin, S. *Families and family therapy*. Cambridge, Mass.: Harvard University Press, 1974.

Minuchin, S., & Fishman, C. *Techniques of family therapy*. Cambridge, Mass.: Harvard University Press, 1981.

Minuchin, S., Rosman, B., & Baker, L. *Psychosomatic families*. Cambridge, Mass.: Harvard University Press, 1978.

Moran, M. A. *Living with a handicapped child: Findings on families and early intervention*. Paper presented at the Annual International Conference of the Council for Exceptional Children, Houston, April 1982.

Moroney, R. *Some considerations in arriving at social policy implications.* Paper presented at the NICHD Conference on Research on Families with Mentally Retarded Persons, Rougemont, N.C., September 1983.

Napier, A. Y., & Whitaker, C. A. *The family crucible,* New York: Harper & Row, 1978.

O'Connor, W. D., & Stachkowiak, J. Patterns of interaction in families with low-adjusted, high-adjusted, and mentally retarded members. *Family Process,* 1971, *10,* 229–241.

Odum, L., Seeman, J., & Newbrough, J. R. A study of family communication patterns and personality integration in children. *Child Psychiatry and Human Development,* 1971, *1,* 275–285.

Parsons, T. *The social system.* New York: The Free Press, 1955.

Price-Bonham, S., & Addison, S. Families and mentally retarded children: Emphasis on the father. *Family Coordinator,* 1978, *27,* 221–229.

Reiss, D. *The family construction of reality.* Cambridge, Mass.: Harvard University Press, 1980.

Ryan, I. W. *Blaming the victim.* New York: Random House, 1971.

Salk, L. The psychosocial impact of hemophilia on the patient and his family. *Social Science and Medicine,* 1972, *6,* 491–505.

Schaeffer, E. S., & Bell, R. Q. Development of a parent attitude research instrument. *Child Development,* 1958, *29,* 339–361.

Scheflen, A. *Levels of schizophrenia.* New York: Brunner/Mazel, 1980.

Schonnel, F. J., & Rorke, M. A second survey of the effects of a subnormal child on the family unit. *American Journal of Mental Deficiency,* 1960, *64,* 862–868.

Schonnel, F. J., and Watts, B. H. A first survey of the effects of a subnormal child on the family unit. *American Journal of Mental Deficiency,* 1956, *61,* 210–219.

Schreibman, L., O'Neill, R. E., & Koegel, R. L. Behavioral training for siblings of autistic children. *Journal of Applied Behavioral Analysis,* 1983, *16,* 129–138.

Schwartz, C. Strategies and tactics of mothers of mentally retarded children for dealing with the medical care system. In N. Bernstein (Ed.), *Diminished people.* Boston: Little, Brown, 1970.

Shere, E., & Kastenbaum, R. Mother-child interaction in cerebral palsy: Environmental and psychosocial obstacles to cognitive development. *Genetic Psychology Monographs,* 1966, *73,* 255–335.

Shere, M. Social-emotional factors with families of twins with cerebral palsy. *Exceptional Children,* 1955, *22*(5), 197–199.

Sigler, A. T., Cohen, B. H., Lilienfeld, A. M., Westlake, J. E., & Hetznecker, W. H., Reproductive and marital experience of parents of children with Down's syndrome (mongolism). *Journal of Pediatrics,* 1967, *70,* 608–614.

Simeonssen, R. J., and McHale, S. M. Research on handicapped children: Sibling relationships. *Child: Care, health, and development,* 1981, *7,* 153–171.

Skrtic, T. M., Summers, J. A., Brotherson, M. J., & Turnbull, A. P. Severely handicapped children and their brothers and sisters. In J. Blacher (Ed.), *Young severely handicapped children and their families: Research in review.* New York: Academic Press, in press.

Spiegel, J. *Transactions.* New York: Science House, 1971.

Stoneman, Z., Brody, G. H., & Abbott, D. In home observations of young Down's syndrome children with their mothers and fathers. *American Journal of Mental Deficiency,* 1983, *87*(6), 591–600.

Strom, R., Rees, R., Slaughter, H., & Wurster, S. Childrearing expectations of families with atypical children. *American Journal of Orthopsychiatry,* 1981, *51,* 285–296.

Stuart, R. *Helping couples change.* New York: Guilford Press, 1980.

Suelze, M., & Keenan, V. Changes in family support networks over the life cycle of mentally retarded persons. *American Journal of Mental Deficiency,* 1981, *86,* 267–274.

Terdal, L., Jackson, R., & Garner, A. Mother-child interactions: A comparison between normal and developmentally delayed groups. In E. J. Mash, L. A. Hamerlynck, & L. C. Handry (Eds.), *Behavior modification and families.* New York: Brunner/Mazel, 1976.

Tew, B., & Lawrence, K. M. Some sources of stress found in mothers of spina bifida children. *British Journal of Preventive and Social Medicine,* 1975, *29,* 27–30.

Tew, B. J., Lawrence, K. M., Payne, H., & Rawnsley, K. Marital stability following the birth of a child with spina bifida. *British Journal of Psychiatry,* 1977, *131,* 79–82.

Tizard, J., & Grad, J. *The mentally handicapped and their families.* London: Oxford University Press, 1961.

Turnbull, A. P., Brotherson, M. J., & Summers, J. A. The impact of deinstitutionalization on families: A family systems approach. In R. H. Bruininks (Ed.), *Living and learning in the least restrictive environment.* Baltimore: P. H. Brooks, in press.

Turnbull, A. P., Summers, J., & Brotherson, M. *Family life cycle: Theoretical and empirical implications and future directions for families with mentally retarded members.* Paper presented at the NICHD Conference on Research on Families with Mentally Retarded Persons, Rougemont, N.C., September 1983.

Turnbull, H. R., & Turnbull, A. P. Parent involvement in the education of handicapped children: A critique. *Mental Retardation,* 1982, *20*(3), 115–122.

Vietze, P. M., Abernathy, S. R., Ashe, M. L., & Faulstich, G. Contingency interaction between mothers and their developmentally delayed infants. In G. P. Sackett (Ed.), *Observing behavior: Theory and applications in mental retardation.* Baltimore: University Park Press, 1978.

Voysey, M. *A constant burden: The reconstitution of family life.* London: Routledge & Kegan Paul, 1975.

Waisbren, S. E. Parents' reactions after the birth of a developmentally disabled child. *American Journal of Mental Deficiency,* 1980, *84,* 345–351.

Walsh, F. (Ed.). *Normal family processes.* New York: Guilford Press, 1982.

Weinrott, M. R. A training program in behavior modification for siblings of the retarded. *American Journal of Orthopsychiatry,* 1974, *44,* 362–375.

Weiss, R. Materials for a theory of social relationships. In W. Bennis, E. Schein, K. Steele, & W. Barlow (Eds.), *Interpersonal dynamics* (2d ed.). Homewood Ill.: Dorsey Press, 1968.

Wikler, L. Chronic stresses of families of mentally retarded children. *Family Relations,* 1981, *30,* 281–288.

Wolfensberger, W. Counseling parents of the retarded. In A. Baumeister (Ed.), *Mental retardation: Appraisal, education, rehabilitation.* Hawthorne, N.Y.: Aldine Publishing, 1967.

Wolfensberger, W., & Menolascino, F. A. A theoretical framework for the management of parents of the mentally retarded. In F. Menolascino (Ed.), *Psychiatric approaches to mental retardation.* New York: Basic Books, 1970.

Wortis, H. Z., & Margolies, J. Parents of children with cerebral palsy. *Medical Social Work,* 1955, *4,* 110–120.

Chapter 25

Families of Gifted Children

JOSEPH FREY III
DONALD J. WENDORF

Research on gifted children (IQ of 130 or higher) has traditionally focused on the identification of gifted students, determination of their educational and intellectual needs, assessment of their individual personality formation and adjustment, and tracking the course of their lives. However, behavioral patterns and interactions in the families of gifted children ("gifted families") have been neglected. What has been written on behavioral patterns in gifted families pertains to demographic data, history of achievement in family members, effects of family relationships on development of giftedness, and pathological patterns contributing to mental illness, underachievement, and poor adjustment in gifted individuals. This work is highly pertinent to the study of gifted children; however, it contributes little to an understanding of gifted families as systems. It provides little insight into how gifted family members relate among each other; how giftedness affects family functioning; what triggers, exacerbates, or perpetuates dysfunctional patterns in gifted families, and what kinds of personal, educational, and transitional issues are important to them. This chapter reviews the studies on families with gifted children and presents the results of a research project on interactional patterns in these families.

TRADITIONAL APPROACHES

Family factors influencing gifted children

A variety of family variables influencing gifted children have been investigated. For the most part, such studies focus on the effects that demographic characteristics, parental achievement, and birth order have on the development and maturation of gifted children, especially with respect to intellect and later achievement. The most-ambitious study undertaken on gifted children was begun in 1921 by Terman (1925–1959). Terman and his associates followed 1,500 gifted children throughout their life span, collecting data on their social, emotional, and academic growth, vocational achievement, and the maintenance of their intellectual functioning. The purposes of Terman's longitudinal study were to gain a better understanding of gifted children so that their future educational needs would be properly met, to find out what intellectually superior children are like, and to see how well they turn out as adults (Terman & Oden, 1959). Terman shared Galton's view of the inheritability of intelligence (Gear, 1982); thus, his primary interest in the family background of his gifted subjects was evidence regarding the achievement and intelligence of their parents. In summarizing the parental background of his gifted subjects, Terman and Oden stated: "The typical gifted child is the product of superior parentage— superior not only in cultural and educational background, but apparently also in heredity. As a result of the combined influence of heredity and environment, such children are superior physically to the average child of the general population" (Terman & Oden, 1976, pp. 65–66).

With respect to family composition, Terman (1940) reported that gifted children had, on the average, two siblings. Also, after almost 20 years of follow-up, 20 percent of the parents of his gifted subjects had been divorced. Both these findings were below what would have been expected for the general population in 1940 (Barbe, 1956).

In a similar manner, Hollingworth (1926) collected exhaustive data during the 1920s on gifted children, including family origins and background, family circumstances, and psychological characteristics. Among her data pertaining to family characteristics, she found that the educational level of the parents of gifted children is far above average for their generation. She reported that more than 50 percent of her subjects testing above 140 IQ had fathers who were in professional or managerial occupations. Hollingworth also corroborated Terman's data regarding size of family, finding that a larger than expected number of gifted subjects were only children or had only one sibling. Barbe (1956) came to similar conclusions, finding that 22 percent of gifted children in his study had no siblings, while 43 percent had only one.

Several studies have indicated that gifted children tend to be firstborns. Goddard (1928) found that roughly 25 percent of his gifted subjects were firstborns, and 75 percent were either firstborn or secondborn. He also reported that of the firstborn, 18 percent were only children. This is consistent with findings by Hollingworth that one half of her subjects were firstborn and by Barbe that 52 percent of his subjects were firstborn.

More recently, Groth (1975) investigated characteristics of mothers of gifted children. She found that, as a group, they had small families and a low percentage of divorce. Mothers who were not identified as gifted themselves more often reported being housewives than the mothers identified as gifted.

Pulvino (1978) tested the "confluence model" of the development of intellectual potential. This model assigns scores for birth order and family size, and postulates that since firstborns and children from small families obtain higher scores, they thus develop a higher intellectual potential. Pulvino, using 380 gifted students, found that those from small families performed better on a test of concept mastery than students from large and medium-size families. He also found that first-borns from medium and large families (but not from small families) performed better than later-borns.

Hayes and Bronzaft (1979) analyzed 529 questionnaires given to members of a Phi Beta Kappa association. They found, contrary to Pulvino (1978), that birth order, family size, and spacing of children did not appear critical to intellectual endowment, but this finding was true only in families who placed high value on education. However, the data this study presents are more practically useful than methodologically sound. The authors do not report any quantitative data which allow a direct assessment of birth order and family size on specific abilities related to intellectual potential.

These studies provide an excellent example of how family factors relating to gifted children have been investigated. The focus is on the linear nature of the relationships between subjects and family variables. The approach yields little that is directly applicable to the family psychology of gifted children, especially with respect to contextual and relational issues. To look at one particular child in a family, even if gifted, gives a poor picture of the family in which that child develops and matures. Quantities of data about the social, personal, and achievement atmosphere of families with gifted children is of immense value in identifying them, planning their educational curricula, and understanding their particular needs. But this data is uninformative on issues concerning the quality of sibling relationships, expectation levels of parents toward children (and vice versa), the impact of gifted education programs on family life, and cross-generational patterns of family achievement—just to list a few of the questions relative to the family psychology of gifted children. Nevertheless, a number of studies have purported to investigate specific relationship patterns of gifted children and their parents.

Acontextual relationship factors influencing gifted children

The studies we review in this section isolated the relationship between parents and gifted child from all other relationships in the family. Hence, they are termed "acontextual."

Datta and Parloff (1967) attempted to determine the type of family which is most likely to produce a creative individual. "Creative young scientists" were compared to less gifted colleagues, and both groups described their parents as moderately affectionate, nonrejecting, and high in encouraging intellectual independence. However, the authors also found that subjects in the creative group were more likely to have perceived both parents as providing a "no rules" situation in which integrity and responsibility were assumed rather than one in which expectations were enforced by authoritarian controls and punishments. Thus, the authors indicate that family relationships which foster autonomy are more likely to produce creative and gifted individuals.

Groth (1971) tested the related hypothesis that a "warm" opposite-sex parent during the first seven years of life is a positive contributing factor toward achievement of degrees. She collected data from 400 members of the Mensa organization and found that warmth from the opposite-sex parent appears important for inspiring achievement among males. For females to achieve, however, warmth from both same- and opposite-sex parents is needed.

Albert (1976) described the childhood of unusually gifted children in terms of relationships to mother, father, and companions. He concluded that the extremely gifted individual is emotionally estranged from his family and others of his age by his preoccupation with the richness of his mind.

These studies do address issues related to the quality of family life in gifted families and do offer insight into their functioning, despite the readily apparent methodological flaws inherent in retrospective, self-report, uncontrolled research. However, depending upon the study, the authors viewed parental characteristics either as nurturant of a bright child's giftedness or as destructive. None of the studies postulated that a gifted child can affect parenting attitudes directly. Thus, they assumed a unidirectional, cause-effect posture with respect to the parents and the gifted subjects. This is quite different from the more circular causal model assumed by a systems orientation.

Underachievement problems in gifted children

Although some authors have commented on the struggles of gifted children with their perfectionistic traits, supersensitivity, and social isolation (e.g., see Whitmore, 1980), the bulk of the concern on problems of the intellectually superior has centered on academic underachievement, including difficulties at home, at school, or within the child. This section reviews research on the role of the family and how it has been studied. We first examine individual case studies, both as research projects and as clinical reports. We then turn our attention to large-group research including studies obtaining data from the children, those using the parents as sources, and finally, projects correlating data from parents and children.

Case studies. *Research projects.* One of the classic works on gifted underachievement was the longitudinal study of Hollingworth (1926), cited above, who described numerous problems such as the social difficulties highly intelligent (IQ over 180) children experience due to their confusing mixture of superior intellect and immaturity. She believed underachievement to be related to emotional disturbance stemming from conflicts around adjusting to being very bright intellectually but immature emotionally. At home, these children learned to manipulate their less-intelligent parents, lost respect for them, and rebelled against their expectations, including their academic demands.

In her studies of gifted adolescent boys, Kimball (1952, 1953) found poor father-son relationships in a high number of cases. The fathers tended to be distant or domineering. The sons did not feel close to their fathers, and their identification seemed feminine. They inhibited their anger and felt anxious and guilty. This interfered with their learning. However, this conclusion came from interviews only with the boys and data of questionable validity from projective instruments such as the sentence completion.

Sears and Sherman (1964), in their case studies on self-esteem, also suggested "unconscious hostility" and resistance to adult pressures as dynamics of gifted underachievement. They felt underachieving gifted students often worked only for external adult evaluation rather than internalized self-motivation.

Using data from longitudinal case histories, Schneidman (1981) suggested that the absent fathers of gifted adults started the adult's life course that eventuated in suicide. Chronic feelings of inferiority and helplessness compounded this course, while the mother could either effect rescue from this progressive situation or play a sustaining or participating role in it. As will be seen later, this finding parallels some of the conclusions of the authors' research on interactions of gifted families with an underachievement problem.

Clinical reports. Several clinicians reported findings from cases they had seen in treatment for underachievement. For example, Kelly (1970) concluded that her five-year-old patient's failure in kindergarten was the "pathological outcome of the interaction of her high capacities with the extreme demands of her environment" (p. 144), especially her school and parents. This conclusion was made solely on the basis of psychodynamically oriented treatment interviews of the child by herself.

Similarly, Colarusso (1980) found from his psychoanalysis of a gifted adolescent with a "neurotic learning disturbance" that the causes of the underachievement were family related. The patient had linked learning with an oedipal conflict with the father, homosexual submission, passive identification with father, a passive aggressive way to punish his parents, and identification with a bright but "defective" uncle. Colarusso, like Kelly, never saw the child in the context of his family and could make no observations of the circular relationship patterns they shared.

Group studies.   Many large-group research studies have examined the family as a variable involved in the underachievement of the gifted. We group these according to the source of the data, whether from the children themselves, their parents, or both. None of them took a systemic view.

Data obtained from children.   Gowan (1955) surveyed several research projects that had students give their views of their parents' behaviors toward them. The gifted underachievers felt either indifference or outright rejection from their parents and even viewed parental support and helpfulness negatively. Furthermore, he found that there were often disagreements between parents over childrearing issues, "transference problems" of parents to the child, parental overprotectiveness, and divorce among families of gifted underachievers. He also reported that the underachieving gifted child tends to be self-sufficient and unsociable, identifies less with parents than do achievers, and is less secure than his achieving counterparts.

Similarly, McClelland (1953) had boys' trait ratings of their parents which he correlated with several variables intended to measure achievement motivation. The high school–aged boys with high motivation saw their fathers as being "friendlier" to them than did the low-motivation students. This tendency then reversed for the college-level students.

Shaw and Brown (1957) studied gifted achieving and underachieving college freshmen. They did not find their results as discriminating between the two groups as have other investigators, perhaps due to their assessment instrument (a social behavior inventory). Nevertheless, their findings were that underachievement in the gifted was related to "the basic personality matrix of the individual." They specifically hypothesized that the major personality characteristic operating was unconscious hostility toward authority. Shaw and Brown did suggest that researching the underachiever's family milieu would be "fruitful."

Horall (1957) compared achieving and nonachieving gifted and nongifted college freshmen on a variety of projective test variables from the Rorschach and Thematic Apperception Test. Her findings indicated that "it seems certain that academic underachievement for brilliant students is a symptom of deep-seated personality problems" (p. 77). Specifically, she stated that underachieving gifted students showed poor overall adjustment, conflicted parent-child relationships (especially with fathers), and lack of emotional responsiveness.

Haggard (1957) studied gifted students from the Laboratory School of the University of Chicago over the course of six years in order to consider academic learning "in relation to the totality of the individual's personality and experience" (p. 389). In particular, Haggard and his colleagues investigated patterns of socialization, developing personality structures, achievement, and the interrelationships among these variables in achieving and nonachieving gifted students. As in Horall's (1957) study, Haggard collected extensive data on the individuals he used, including measures of parental pressures on the child to achieve, projective test data, behavioral observations during school activities, mental ability tests, and teachers' ratings of classroom behavior.

Besides finding differences in personality makeup among achieving gifted students who excelled across different subjects, Haggard found differences between achieving and nonachieving students. Haggard started from the general assumption that the level and pattern of academic achievement are related to how an individual perceives and operates in his world. He found that by third grade, high achievers were different from low achievers in that they were more responsive to socialization pressures from their parents and more accepting of adult values. He also found that they had better relationships with their parents, better work habits, and were more aggressive and competitive than underachieving students.

Haggard's investigation is notable in that it clearly typifies the linear, personality-in-a-vacuum approach common to most research on gifted children and their families. Although he implicated the role of parental pressures to achieve, he also very explicitly localized the "cause" of learning difficulties with the child. In fact, Haggard maintained in his research that an academic problem in a gifted student "results from conflicts in the pattern of socialization pressures imposed upon him, or is a symptom of rebellion against excessive pressures to acquire the valued linguistic skills or against related pressures which have become intolerable, *or is caused by inner conflicts resulting from pressures*" (pp. 402–403; authors' italics).

Luby (1981) investigated a number of variables that might differentiate his samples of successful (grade point $\geq$ 3.2) versus unsuccessful (g.p.a. $\leq$ 2.8) gifted high school students. One of his conclusions was that there was less family closeness among the unsuccessful group. Yet, typical of these linearly conceived studies, this was based solely on the self-reports of the students.

Data obtained from parents. The typical approach of studies reviewed in this section was to examine the effects of various parental traits and attitudes on underachievement by directly testing the parents of achieving versus underachieving gifted children. For example, Norman (1966) administered the Gordon survey of interpersonal values to parents of these two groups. Supposedly, this instrument measured critical values involving the individual's relationship with other people as if these were consistent, unitary traits affecting all situations (assumptions unacceptable to systemic thinkers). Norman found the like-sexed parents (i.e., the one with whom the child would "identify") of achievers showed higher independence and lower conformity scores.

Drews and Teahan (1957) adapted three subscales from Shoben's parent attitude survey: the dominating, possessive, and ignoring scales. They administered these to only the mothers of high and low achievers of both gifted and "moderately able" junior high groups. The mothers of the high achievers were more authoritarian in the way they treated their children. The authors concluded that the successful student has a rigidly designed place in his family that he is expected to accept passively.

Pierce (1961), on the other hand, found mothers of successful, gifted high school boys to be lower on authoritarian control and strictness measures. The mothers of high-achieving girls held stronger opinions on equality values than those of low achievers.

Strang (1951) identified several conditions contributing to maladjustment in the gifted, including parental pressure and exploitation in overemphasizing their child's intellectual development, and parental indifference and neglect toward their children's needs.

Studies correlating data from parents and children. Several investigators attempted to look at parent-child relationship factors in gifted underachievement by testing both parents and children of achievers and underachievers and correlating the results. Ziv, Rimon, and Doni (1977) examined children's self-concepts and their parents' evaluations of their child's self-concept and compared the results of their fifth- to eighth-grade gifted and average achievers and underachievers ($n =$ 134). The average-achievers sample had higher self-concepts than underachievers; yet, the gifted underachievers had higher self-concepts than the achievers. The parents' evaluations of their children seemed unrelated to the school performance.

Schneyer (1981) administered the Tennessee self-concept scale and the Maryland parent attitude survey (MPAS) to the parents of gifted achievers and underachievers. He gave the Piers-Harris children's self-concept scale to the students and then did correlational studies within and between groups. He found no differences in either group in the parents' or children's self-concept scores or on the MPAS rejecting, indulgent, or protective scores; nor was there a significant relationship in either group between the parents' and children's self-concepts. Underachievers' fathers were higher only on the discipline scale. Schneyer concluded that there were few significant differences in parent-child relationships between families of achieving versus underachieving gifted children. Furthermore, he felt the relationship between parents' and children's self-concepts and parental attitudes was much less significant than self-concept theories suggest.

The research on gifted underachievement can be criticized on several grounds. None of the research reviewed for this section approached the question of family role in underachievement from a family systems viewpoint, and none used observational data other than the nonempirical clinical treatment observations. More specifically, it purported to investigate parent-child relationships, yet assessed this with individual measures of questionable validity—usually self-report, trait-oriented instruments. In fact, all but a few studies looked at only one side of this dyadic relationship. Most used no "here and now" observational data at all, and none viewed the relationship as circular or enlarged their perspective to include siblings and the school system.

Contextual relationship factors influencing gifted children

This section reviews the small literature on work that has approximated a more-circular view of gifted families. The studies used observational and/or interactional methodologies rather than individual testing or self-report, or they reported results from a multidirectional standpoint. Also, two clinical cases using family therapy approaches for problems of gifted underachievement are summarized.

Research studies. *Interactional studies.* Fisher (1978) sought as one objective of his study to learn how the family was affected by the child's "gifted" label. Fisher interviewed the parents of first-graders who were tested and either made or failed to make the 130 IQ score to be labeled gifted. Of interest were the effects of childrearing practices, time-related issues, sibling relationships, and parents' concepts of intelligence and giftedness. The main finding was that the important label was the parents', not the school's. Where parents and school agreed, the label justified more demands on the school, parental expectations and demands on the children increased, and parental tolerance increased. Where parents disagreed with the school's "gifted" label, they saw it as a burden, questioned their own parenting role, and felt the label had a disruptive effect on nongifted siblings.

While this study was not observational and measured only one part of the several relationships it addressed, it did deal with the relationships as at least interactional, if not quite systemic. It also dealt with effects going in the child to parent to school directions. The themes of labeling effects on siblings and parental expectations of children and school are similar to those studied by the present authors, although their conclusions were quite different.

Several other articles have described what they term "family interaction patterns" in gifted families; yet, they are seen under closer scrutiny to actually involve very linear assumptions. For example, Fine (1977) discussed family interaction patterns, parents' emotional needs, and the need for parental counseling when gifted children are involved. Actually, the assumption here was that parents' behavior affects gifted children and parent education is needed. This conclusion, while probably valid to some extent, was unidirectional rather than interactional, circular, or systemic.

Thiel and Thiel (1977) analyzed gifted family interaction patterns based on Heider's balance theory. This theory involves triangles of people describing relationships with alegebraic summation rules using positive or negative valences. Thiel and Thiel administered to parents the general abilities section of Michigan State University's self-concept of ability test, the SRA "Being Me" kit (an experimental classroom self-rating instrument), and another experimental scale based on Cattell's scientific analysis of personality. The gifted children themselves took an experimental child-family system survey and the Coopersmith self-esteem inventory. These researchers found that the underachieving children had weak self-concepts and that the perceptions between child and mother on most personality variables were closer than between father and child.

Thus, while Thiel and Thiel claimed to be looking at relationships, their approach more closely resembled the other linear studies cited above. They were merely using individually oriented self-reports on personal and others' self-concepts and correlating these data. They used no direct observations of actual interactions to transcend the limitations of individuals' biased perceptions.

A study using a more-interactional view was reported by Gurman (1970), although the method was not observational. Gurman identified several themes from transcripts of group counseling sessions with underachieving nongifted children in one group and their parents in another. For example, the children thought they had too much self-determination and that this meant their parents were indifferent toward them. The parents felt they themselves were poor and inconsistent in discipline. Gurman proposed that ineffective discipline was perceived by the children as rejection. They then responded with poor grades as a means to call attention to their unhappiness. Several similar factors such as a lack of adequate parental role models, too little parental time, an absence of mutual trust, and an overemphasis on grades established a relationship in which underachievement served a rebellious "cry for help" function. Gurman found the children and parents to be wrestling with similar issues but with no real communication between them. He recommended counseling for the children and parent training. He did not, however, see the benefits of working with the family system in conjoint sessions.

Observational methods. Surprisingly few studies have actually made direct observations of gifted families' behavior as a way of investigating family interaction patterns. Newman, Dember, and Krug (1973) used observational data on 15 underachieving gifted boys to assess variables related to development, psychodynamic processes, and family interactions. Their results suggested that marital unhappiness and intellectual frustration in the mothers play an important role in their son's failure to achieve. From their traditional psychoanalytic thinking, they maintained that the boys' mothers had "eroticized" general intellectual functions due to "intellectualized relationships with their own fathers" and subsequently displaced their academic ambitions onto their sons. Furthermore, Newman et al. discovered that most of the fathers had histories of school problems and occupational difficulties. According to the authors, the resulting patterns foster excessive emotional investment by the mother onto the son and hostility by the father toward the son. In return, the sons typically are seen as passive-aggressive, covertly resistant, hostile, and depressed.

Bradshaw (1981) observed parents attempting to provide helpful messages to their bright achieving or underachieving children in completing a problem-solving (puzzle) task. She found "stylistic" differences in that the achievers' parents gave more relevant and specific instructions. This study was observational and slightly interactional in that it examined the reciprocity in whether parents gave help when requested. However, Bradshaw was primarily interested in seeing how parents helped their children, without considering any circular patterns such as effects of children's responses to assistance on parents' subsequent help and how parents might encourage or discourage asking for aid.

Clinical case studies. There are only two reports of gifted under-achievers being treated with a family therapy approach. Taichert (1979) provided an interactional, systemic analysis of two gifted adolescent stepbrothers, both of whom were performing poorly at school and had neurodevelopmental problems with sensory-motor integration and coordination. One boy seemed in a reversible stage of "early adolescent psychosis" while the other was more advanced in a psychotic process. Taichert described the family system as a "pseudo-democracy with no one person in authority." The boys were allowed to do as they pleased and then criticized for it. They reacted with anger, which led to their parents backing off even more. The parents each had an "immobilizing fear" that kept them from being effective parents. Each parent-son dyad shared an "insightless idea or myth" based on these fears. More specifically, the mother (a linguist by training) could not set limits, as she feared the power of the spoken word. The father had a "seemingly life-threatening fear of being unfair." The mother was in an enmeshed relationship with her son and in a disengaged relationship with her husband.

Unfortunately, Taichert (1979) did not really describe a family systems approach to intervention nor did she relate the problem to the giftedness of the parents or children. She did, however, provide an excellent portrayal of the family dynamics from an interactional perspective.

The other case study of family therapy with a gifted family is that of Araoz (1977). From his counseling perspective, Araoz seemed to view the problems of his 11-year-old, highly gifted (IQ = 173) client as developing in a step-wise interactional sequence rather than in a self-recursive cycle. Her unexpected giftedness led to behavioral problems which her parents, ignorant of how to handle her and not helped by the "experts," mishandled. They then blamed the child and each other, leading to significant marital problems and scapegoating of the child. This furthered their mishandling of the child's problems.

Araoz proposed a step-wise approach to counseling, beginning with a didactic-supportive stage and then moving to an exploration of the "unconscious psychodynamic" involved. He recommended a parents' group to further insight and mutual tolerance and then conjoint family counseling sessions. The goals would be to improve communication, facilitate expression of feelings, clarify family members' perceptions and expectations of each other, and allow new behaviors to be planned. The couple might also need to spend additional time in marital counseling. Thus, Araoz saw the role of each family member in this dysfunctional sequence, treated the whole family directly, and included the child's giftedness in his formulation.

Conclusion

The often contradictory research on the role of the family in underachievement problems of gifted children can be criticized on many conceptual and methodological grounds, as mentioned above. However, several themes do seem to emerge from this literature. In general, there appears to be a lack of good, helpful communication between parents and children, yet the parents' values, expectations, and demands heavily influence academic performance. In particular, fathers of underachievers tended to be seen as absent, authoritarian, or hostile. Highly intelligent but emotionally immature children reacted to the parental pressures with passive-aggressive resistance or did poorly in school due to the low self-concept engendered by the parent-child relationship.

These trends are mirrored to some extent in the research presented below. Yet, this linear, individually focused literature reveals little as to how gifted children get along with their siblings, how nongifted siblings adjust to having a gifted sibling, whether parents change their expectations of a gifted child relative to their nongifted child(ren), the parents' adjustment to having a gifted child, the impact of gifted education on marital and family relationships, and cross-generational patterns in achievement and affiliation. It is our belief that a family systems viewpoint can greatly expand the perspective provided by the research reviewed above.

A SYSTEMS APPROACH TO GIFTED FAMILIES

In order to explore adequately the interactional patterns of families of gifted children, we designed the present study to assess family functioning at a systems, or circular, level as opposed to the intrapsychic or interpersonal level typical of the linear approach of individual psychology. At issue was how all members of a gifted family affect one another—not just how a child is affected, for example, by socialization pressures or lack of intellectual support from his parents. Analysis of family interactional patterns is typically associated with a systems orientation towards the family (e.g., Bowen, 1976; Haley, 1975; L'Abate, 1976; Minuchin, 1974; Minuchin & Fishman, 1981; Watzlawick, Beavin, & Jackson, 1967), and it was from this literature that we drew our assessment instruments.

Conflict resolution tasks have been productive research tools in assessing interactional patterns in families. Minuchin and his colleagues have used conflict tasks with normal, psychosomatic, and delinquent families (Minuchin, Montalvo, Guerney, Rosman, & Schumer, 1967; Minuchin, Rosman, & Baker, 1978). The Timberlawn group (Lewis,

Beavers, Gossett, & Phillips, 1976) has also used conflict situations to assess nonclinical families and has developed a rating scale to discriminate between optimal, midrange, and dysfunctional patterns of interaction. Furthermore, Watzlawick (1966) described a detailed family interview which used a variety of conflict-inducing tasks to gather information about the family.

As discussed below, three tasks were used to assess families in this study, plus the rating scales from the Timberlawn group. In addition, a structured interview was developed to obtain a three-generational family history with respect to achievement/success and patterns of family closeness. The interview also contained questions relevant to having a gifted child in a family and reflected our main purpose in this project.

Method

Subjects. Subjects were 24 gifted families in which at least one child had a tested IQ score ≥ 130 (Binet or WISC–R). An IQ score of 130 or higher is the typical criterion for acceptance into a gifted class. For the study, only intact families of mother, father, and children were used, although step-parents were accepted ($n = 1$). Subjects were divided into nonclinical, problem, and clinical groups ($n = 14, 7,$ and 3, respectively; this was later changed to 13, 7, and 4 as described below). Problem families were identified by personnel in the gifted programs on the basis of known school problems (i.e., underachievement). Clinical families were those who had actually sought professional treatment for a child-related problem in a gifted child. Three had begun treatment at the time of the study.

The gifted child was of school age (range $\times$ 6–18 years). Most were in gifted programs at the time of the study, although several had ceased their program participation. Several families included more than one gifted child, while others had nongifted siblings, too. Of the children, 19 were male and 13 female. The families' socioeconomic status (SES) ranged from lower-middle to lower-upper class, with most in the upper middle-class range. The three groups did not differ appreciably in gender or SES composition. The range of other children in the family was from infancy to adulthood with most grown children not able to participate in the study.

Tasks. Each family began the two-hour assessment with three interactional tasks that lasted a total of 20 minutes. In the first task, they were asked to "plan something they could do together as a family" (Minuchin et al., 1978). The second task involved their choosing and discussing a recent family argument (Minuchin et al., 1967). The third task had the parents discuss the meaning of a proverb (i.e., "A rolling stone gathers no moss") with the children out of the room and then "teach the meaning" to their children (Watzlawick, 1966). All tasks were given a maximum of five minutes and were videotaped by the interviewer from behind a one-way mirror.

Interview. The rest of the session consisted of a structured family interview designed by the authors to assess demographic data and the education levels, occupations, relationship patterns, marital and family issues, and outstanding accomplishments of the children's grandparents, aunts, and uncles. The parents then rated their own parents and families of origin as to their degree of success and family, marital, and individual relationship styles (from enmeshed to disengaged). Finally, the family answered questions relating to the gifted child, his or her discipline, benefits or problems with their gifted schooling, effects of labeling on the family, and family interest patterns.

Measures. The authors, both experienced family therapists, reviewed the tapes of the interactional tasks and independently filled out the Beavers-Timberlawn scale. This scale includes a family global health-pathology rating as well as scores on empathy, clarity of expression, power relationships, mood and tone, strength of the marital coalition, etc. The authors then rated the families on their adaptiveness and cohesion in a number of specific areas (e.g., discipline, roles, coalitions, rules, system feedback, emotional bonding) by using behavioral descriptions of Olson's (1978) FACES dimensions. Adaptiveness variables ranged from "chaotic" through "flexible" and "structured" to "rigid" on the other extreme. Cohesion ranged from "disengaged" through "separated" and "connected" to "enmeshed."

Results and discussion

Although our sample was small and divided into groups by the criteria of being in treatment, having a history of underachievement, or having no problems, there are strong suggestions that these are separate groups. The means on the Timberlawn global health-pathology rating were all significantly different from each other statistically (t-test, $p < .01$), and the groups were observed to interact differently.

Nonproblem families. We found the nonproblem families to be truly "gifted." They displayed a variety of resources and used them consistently and creatively. They handled the conflict tasks with aplomb and relished the interview session. Their interactions were both humorous and serious, and conveyed a sense of genuine family warmth and openness even while they openly disagreed with each other.

Marital/parental subsystem. With respect to the conflict resolution tasks, we found a fairly consistent pattern among the nonproblem families. One parent, typically the father, started off the negotiation procedures by enlisting the opinions of the other family members. Resolution was typically accomplished by the parent through a procedure we have termed "participatory exploration." The parents made sure each member offered his/her own position—which was highly valued and generally incorporated by the other family members into their discussion. The parents typically used the tasks as teaching devices which they tied to current family issues. Parents adapted their approach according to children's ages, usually using more Socratic or lecture methods with younger children. In the majority of cases, the proverb elicited two opposing interpretations within the maternal/parental subsystem. The differences were handled easily and the couples were not threatened by them; in fact, they seemed to enjoy them. The overall style was democratic but with strong leadership from the parents, with the father usually at the top of the hierarchy.

Sibling subsystem. In families with more than one child, the sibling interactions were congruent with the marital/parental interactions. There was little or no competition for parental approval, and no jealousy was observed. There were instances of teasing or mutual antagonism, but these behaviors were under parental control. Parental support was readily shifted to younger siblings when the discussion was at too difficult a level, and older siblings frequently participated in this. In families with teenage children, a great deal of sibling comaraderie was evident, even when only one of the children was gifted.

Family system. On the Beavers-Timberlawn family evaluation scale, this nonproblem group scored in the extremely healthy range on the global family rating ($\bar{x} = 1.77$). Their range was 1 (the highest) to 4 (mildly healthy). In general, they were seen as displaying an appropriate level of closeness, without significant conflict detouring, domination/submission, or invasiveness. They were flexible, emotionally open, and unthreatened. As a result, they easily resolved the tasks in ways that benefited all family members.

On the behavioral FACES ratings, these families were also seen as high functioning. Although interrater agreement between the two middle (optimal-range) categories of the adaptability and cohesion dimensions ("structured" and "flexible" for adaptability and "separated" and "connected" for cohesion) was low, the ratings were consistently in the "healthy" range as opposed to the dysfunctional extremes ("rigid" and "chaotic" for adaptability and "enmeshed" and "disengaged" for cohesion).

There was one nonproblem family who, although not reporting significant problems, received ratings of their interactions suggesting they were experiencing difficulties in the areas of leadership, parental coalitions, and triangling. They had difficulty in negotiating the conflict tasks and were frequently observed to "mind read" other family members. In fact, this family several months later admitted to trying to cover up some serious problems during the research, and they then entered therapy. Thus, they were reclassified as a clinical family for discussion purposes and data from their staged interview was not included in the analysis. This left numbers of 13, 7, and 4 for the nonproblem, problem, and clinical groups, respectively.

Interview family history. The family histories of these families were marked by a high degree of success and achievement in previous generations. The success was not predicated on financial, educational, or material accomplishment alone but also on personal accomplishment and fulfillment. In all but two cases, success ratings for the previous generation were average or greater; and in 6 of the 14 cases, all grandparents received ratings of moderately to highly successful. One family gave "generally unsuccessful" ratings to two of four grandparents; this family was also the same family who received an "adequate" score (4) on the Beavers scale. However, this family also has shown an established pattern of success and achievement in the present generation above and beyond that of the previous generation.

The second major focus of the interview was a family's history of "affiliation," or the significant interactional patterns recalled by the parents in their families of origin. Basically, we cannot draw any conclusions from these data. The families came from a wide variety of patterns of closeness/distance and adaptability. Three of the 13 families (23 percent) in this group reported problems with alcohol abuse, physical abuse, legal problems, and/or long-standing family/marital problems (e.g., sexual affairs, divorce, separations, intense conflict) in the previous generation. However, these families were functioning in the optimal range on the Beavers scale, suggesting they have made a more than adequate adjustment in their own families.

Family interview: Present situation. This part of the interview focused on the family's adjustment to having a gifted child and the interactions among the school, family, and gifted child or children. These families expected their children to be bright and were not surprised that they qualified for gifted placement. As to placement, these families reported feeling unusually dependent on the school system. The families fell into two groups with respect to their attitudes about the school system. One group of families found that the school took pressure off of them by providing their child with adequate educational resources and intellectual stimulation. They were involved with their child's education process and spoke with respect for teachers and school. Their children also reported satisfaction with their placement. They liked the work, felt challenged and stimulated, and found more-satisfactory peer relationships in the gifted program. Name-calling incidents had been frequently reported, and gifted children felt singled out by nongifted peers. A gifted program reduced their sense of isolation and raised their level of self-esteem.

The second group of families were displeased with the gifted education program and reported a significant amount of conflict between the school and the family. Their teachers were often resentful of gifted children and made little attempt to understand them. Their school systems provided for gifted education primarily through a "resource room" used once a day for an hour. The children felt isolated from peers and regular teachers. These families reported increased family conflict over school issues, with parents taking opposing sides at times against the child versus the school. These families typically circumvented the school's shortcomings by compensating for them at home with their own educational activities.

The nonproblem group reported no major repercussions at home from having a child identified as gifted. Sibling interaction was described as normal. In families with gifted and nongifted children, parents reported making efforts to emphasize strengths in all their children. Nongifted siblings did not appear resentful of their gifted sibling's label.

These families reported some differences in discipline as they felt obligated to provide their children with reasons and explanations. They saw their children's "whys" not as resistance but as real questions and attempted to turn discipline into learning experiences. One of the hallmarks of these families was their emphasis on teaching in all phases of family life.

These families reported no changes in expectation levels as a result of the gifted label. The parents expected their children, gifted or not, to do the best they could regardless of intellectual potential. Some families became more involved in their children's education, but this did not change expectation levels.

Conclusions.   These families were impressive. Their problem solving contained frequent metacommunications and was indistinguishable from other interactions. Subsystem boundaries were clearly demarcated and respected, and leadership functions were carried out effectively and democratically. They were truly "gifted" in displaying a variety of personal and familial resources and using them consistently and creatively.

Nonclinical problem families.   As a group, these families displayed more variable patterns of interactions than did the nonproblem group.

Two of these families functioned at the same level as the extremely healthy nonproblem families, while the remaining five functioned in the mildly to moderately healthy range. They did not display interactions suggestive of pathological functioning.

Marital/parental subsystem. On the conflict resolution tasks, the two extremely healthy families functioned as did the families in the nonproblem group. The remaining five families displayed patterns which suggested some weaknesses in the parental subsystem. These parents were not seen as highly supportive of each other, as only one was typically involved in the conflict resolution tasks when the directions explicitly called for this behavior (i.e., discussion in the proverb task).

Otherwise, these families were seen as functioning much like the extremely healthy families. They tended to use the tasks in an educational fashion and were able to adapt their teaching style according to their children's ages.

Sibling subsystem. Siblings in these families appeared to get along well; in fact, they displayed interactions similar to those siblings in the extremely healthy families.

Family subsystem. On the Beavers scale, this group of families obtained a mean global health-pathology rating of 3.2 (moderately healthy range). Except for the two families in the optimal range, these families were seen as exhibiting tendencies to dominate in leadership and had problems negotiating. With one parent functioning as a "switchboard," negotiations tended to become confusing and communication vague. There were incidents of one family member answering questions directed to another, as well as efforts at avoiding answering questions. Conflict was usually honestly acknowledged, but at times it was handled ineffectively.

The five mild-moderate families were observed to have some liabilities on the conflict resolution tasks. The liabilities were limited to the parental subsystem and were not judged to be pathological or dysfunctional. Though they did falter on the conflict tasks, they accomplished the objectives and displayed an overall sense of family warmth and unity in the process.

The family history of these families was similar to that of the optimally functioning families. Members of the previous generation tended to be highly successful, and in all but two families, the success ratings for all members of the previous generation were average or greater. In three of the seven families, all grandparents received ratings of moderately to highly successful. In two families, paternal grandmothers were given "generally unsuccessful" ratings.

As with the extremely healthy families, we cannot draw any conclusions as to definite patterns of closeness and distance in these families; however, their histories contain more instances of problems in previous generations than the extremely healthy families. Four of the five (80 percent) mild-to-moderate families in this group indicated problems with alcoholism, criminal activity, and parental conflict and separation in the previous generation. This compares with 23 percent for the optimally healthy group. Nevertheless, given such problematic backgrounds, these families were functioning in an adequate and healthy fashion and appeared to be making a more satisfactory adjustment than their families of origin.

Family interview: Present situation.   Like the extremely healthy families, these families expected their children to be bright. However, unlike the extremely healthy, they were generally pleased with the gifted education program, as it relieved family pressure. In particular, most families mentioned that their child was no longer bored in school and long-standing child/family/school conflicts had abated with the gifted labeling. For example, one family had only found out two weeks prior to their interview that their child was gifted and that this may have been the reason for his school problems. They reported that their interactions with the school had significantly affected them as a couple, producing numerous disagreements about handling the situation. They reported experiencing tremendous relief at the prospect of having the problems dealt with effectively.

This group of mildly-moderately healthy families had less direct praise for the schools than the satisfied extremely healthy group. Their satisfaction seemed to be predicated more on how the gifted label and/or program had taken pressure off of them and placed it on the school rather than on the great job the school was doing. This was also evident in that several sets of parents reported being more pleased with the friends their children associated with in a gifted program as opposed to a regular program.

The children in this group of families reported more interest and satisfaction in school as a result of the gifted placement. Like their extremely healthy counterparts, they felt more secure in their peer interactions and intellectual ability. In general, they appeared to have a better relationship with their parents following the gifted education placement. No nongifted children in this group reported any jealousy toward gifted siblings. As in the extremely healthy group, however, it was not unusual for all the children in a family to be gifted.

Discipline or limit setting did not occur as smoothly in these families as in the extremely healthy families. The families described inconsistent discipline patterns, with the bulk of the disciplining falling on one parent. This was consistent with the observations of the conflict tasks which revealed a tendency in these families to have one peripheral parent. In general, discipline in these families tended toward rigidity or a power struggle rather than the teaching experience reported by the extremely healthy families.

Five of these families reported no change in academic expectations from either the gifted child or his/her siblings as a result of the gifted label. They simply expected all their children to do their best. Two families, however, had explicit expectations. One family (who had just found out about their child's giftedness) expected a large increase in academic performance from their child along with a decrease in family tension secondary to school problems. The second family was also candid about increased expectations of their gifted child. They reported increasing the pressure for him to go to college and to achieve and did not hide their disappointment that an older sibling had not gone on to college.

Conclusions. These families were distinguishable from the extremely healthy families on several counts. First, observations of their interactions in resolving conflict indicated they did not handle such situations as easily as the extremely healthy families. Second, they typically came from family backgrounds which, despite high achievement and success, were marred by issues of alcoholism, legal problems, and parental divorce and/or family separations. Third, they seemed more pleased on the whole with the gifted education program in which their child was enrolled than the extremely healthy group. This appeared to be related to the relief of pressure these families experienced by the gifted education placement. And fourth, within the parental subsystem, one parent tended to be more peripheral than the other with respect to discipline and/or school achievement.

This group of families is more properly termed "mildly to moderately healthy" as opposed to "problem." This more-positive label highlights their functional interactions and effectiveness in dealing with problems of underachievement. Also, these families are functioning without major issues interfering in their lives at present; this represents an achievement in itself, as the majority came from disrupted family backgrounds.

Clinical families. Four families were evaluated who had problems with a gifted child and entered family therapy for that problem. As a group, these families displayed moderately dysfunctional patterns of interaction which appeared to play a significant role in the presenting problems.[1] In one family, the presenting problem was amnesic episodes in a 17-year-old girl who was president of her class and the class valedictorian. A second family complained of bulimia and scholastic underachievement in their 15-year-old daughter. The other two families presented with oppositional behavior, temper tantrums, and academic underachievement in the gifted children (age 9 and 15).

---

[1] As noted above, one family was not included in the statistical analysis, as they admitted to faking their interview.

Most of these gifted identified patients were females, which is unusual in that the prevalence of psychiatric disorders in children is usually at least 2:1 for boys versus girls (Rutter, 1970).

Marital/parental subsystem. These families performed poorly on the conflict resolution tasks. The parents were typically polarized with respect to the solution of the task. Such impasses were generally resolved through dominant-submissive means (i.e., one parent imposing his/her solution, with the other parent passively accepting it). The tasks were not used in educating the children, but more as a power struggle between the parents.

Sibling subsystem. Siblings did not display the camaraderie of the other two groups. They were fairly polite with each other without showing a great deal of warmth or openness. They reported placing more value on outside relationships than on family relationships. Some overt hostility was also seen.

Family subsystem. On the Beavers scale, this group of families received a mean global health-pathology rating of 7.83 (range = 7–8.5), placing them in the moderately dysfunctional range. As a family group, each of these families displayed poor problem-solving skills. While one parent typically remained peripheral, aloof, and emotionally unavailable, the other parent overcompensated for this with intrusive behavior indicative of enmeshment. In resolving the tasks, these families displayed thinly veiled hostility, covert undercutting, and inappropriate parent-child coalitions. On the behavioral FACES rating, these families were observed to function in the extreme ranges of adaptability (rigidity-chaotic) and cohesiveness (enmeshment-disengagement).

Interview: Family history. These families' families of origin tended to be less successful on the whole than the other two groups' families of origin. However, a clear-cut trend could not be defined on their success or affiliation patterns. The parents in all four families mentioned serious problems during their formative years. However, conclusions remain speculative since the sample was small.

Family interview: Present. For the most part, the problems these families were experiencing at the time of the interview diminished the focus on having a gifted child. Although three identified gifted patients presented with school problems, their parents were more concerned with behaviors at home than at school. It was as if these families did not have the time or energy to show interest in their child's giftedness because of the problems. In fact, the 17-year-old girl with amnesic episodes had hidden her school successes from her parents and felt more accepted at school than at home. After several therapy sessions, the amnesic episodes ceased, but neither the girl nor her family wanted to continue therapy. The other three families have shown stronger motivation to continue in therapy. In all cases, there were fairly quick remissions in presenting problems, with the families subsequently requesting therapy on relational or marital difficulties.

The therapy sessions further illustrated some of the findings of the current and past research, such as the parents' immobilizing fear or insightless myth noted by Taichert (1979). In one case, for example, the father strongly resisted requiring his son to achieve at the high level he expected, as he rigidly believed the boy had to *want* to achieve. This stemmed from his own boyhood conflicts with his mother, who totally structured his adolescent social life. His wife, a teacher in the boy's gifted program, also strongly wanted her son to achieve but feared disagreeing with her husband. Instead, she tried to "help" the son by almost totally structuring his studying, but backing off at the point of making any demands. Thus, there was serious unresolved parental-marital conflict which their son used to his advantage in gaining attention that distracted his parents from fighting. This same sort of fear was evident in another case in which the mother feared "forcing her influence" on anyone. She tried to be her child's friend and rear her "democratically." The resulting relationship was one of verbal battles and aggressive play that was a substitute for, and a metaphor of, her lack of relationship with her husband. He avoided the criticism and competition of his wife for fear that she would again become manic. Thus he escaped to his work, leaving his wife unsupported in disciplining their rebellious, underachieving daughter.

In conclusion, the highly dysfunctional patterns of these gifted families seemed to be readily identified in the FACES observational ratings, Beavers-Timberlawn scores, success and relationship ratings, and the manner in which they handled the interactional tasks. The problems in the present generation were clearly reflected in the families of origin. Although the family members were well educated, they did not show as high a success picture as our other families, especially in relationships, where we found more divorces, psychiatric problems, and extreme scores. The gifted programs helped, but only to a limited extent. All four cases showed covert coalitions, poor problem solving, and unresolved parental-marital conflict.

Summary and conclusion

Present study. Several limitations are evident in this study, and the conclusions should be interpreted in this context. Our referral system picks up only high IQ children who have been identified and placed in gifted classes. We only used intact families, (father, mother, children), which may not be the most-common situation for gifted children (these are minority families for the general population). Also, we used only the principal researchers as nonblind raters and used primarily descriptive statistics in our analysis.

The sample size was small, and we did not have a control group of bright but nongifted children. Obviously this would be essential to make firm conclusions. Another problem we encountered is with global family ratings. Although reliable, we found the scales to be too restrictive in describing family patterns. Several conclusions can be drawn on the basis of the data we collected. First of all, it appears that families dealing with underachieving gifted children may experience a reduction in family discord following identification and enrollment in a gifted program. This would appear to be an important benefit arising from gifted programs. However, our preliminary findings suggest there are some important issues to be considered regarding these families and their gifted children. Primary among these issues are the family dynamics.

These families may be more vulnerable to the stress of having a child whose needs are not being met by the school. The dynamics of these families indicated the presence of cross-generational triangles with one parent peripheral to the family (usually the father) and the other parent compensating for this peripheralness with excessive involvement with the children. These patterns are not uncommon and not dysfunctional per se. However, they do limit a family's resources; and we often found the underachievement served to reinvolve the distant parent in family matters. Involvement in a gifted education program would appear to help these families to return to their previous level of adaptation, which is typically appropriate and functional, if not optimal.

This finding also appears to be important for child and adolescent clinicians. Academic underachievement can be indicative of a wide range of underlying difficulties, such as learning disorders, emotional problems, or attentional/behavioral disorders. However, our findings suggest that less than optimally functioning families may also present with an underachieving child. Although such problems in gifted children can represent boredom and lack of stimulation in regular classroom placement, we feel it is important to be attentive to the family dynamics in such situations. We are not necessarily advocating treating such a family, but feel the child can benefit from the clinician's awareness of the family's interactional patterns.

The impact of the school system's gifted education program can also be negative. We found the negative impact to be more common in our healthiest families, although we are not sure why. We did draw subjects from several school systems with programs quite vulnerable to criticism. The most common negative impact was that the family felt a lack of understanding by the school toward their gifted child.

Although not usually sufficient to cause underachievement problems, both parents were involved in home-school conflict. Parents typically reported taking extra time during the evenings to make up for deficits in the school's program. One family even developed their own entire program. These families had the resources to devote to such problems, although it was not uncommon for a parent to admit life had been easier prior to the placement.

In general, our findings tended to parallel those of the Timberlawn research with normal families (Lewis et al., 1976). Our nonproblem nonclinical families closely resembled their "optimal families." They showed strong parental coalitions, a creative spontaneity in interactions, a growth or teaching orientation to problem solving, a lack of inappropriate child-parent coalitions, and a high degree of individual initiative and success. They were truly "gifted" families.

Our problem nonclinical families were similar to the Timberlawn "adequate" families in being efficient and functional, but with less closeness in the parental coalition, a tendency toward peripheral fathers and overinvolved mothers, and some evidence of problems with school achievement (the characteristic defining this group). Thus, they clearly showed the kinds of patterns seen in our obviously dysfunctional "clinical" group, yet in a substantially attenuated fashion. In fact, they still functioned overall at a very high or "gifted" level, perhaps due to the influence of one unusually strong parent.

The clinical families were comparable to the Timberlawn "moderately pathological" or "midrange" families, with simmering conflicts, negative affects, inappropriate behaviors, problems in the family of origin, rigidity in patterns, control struggles, parent-child coalitions, and inappropriate family boundaries. These families evidenced less success in relationships, growth, careers, and school achievements.

To conclude, we generally found "gifted families" to be creative, engaging, growth oriented, and fascinating to work with. Just as the Timberlawn researchers found that "the family is alive and well," we found that gifted families are alive, well, and "super" in almost every respect.

Relationship of findings to previous studies. This investigation offers an alternative, nontraditional approach to studying the family psychology of gifted children. The interactional methodology presents an added dimension to gifted families by observing the members functioning as a family unit. The current data do not refute the more traditional studies reported earlier; moreover, these studies are enhanced by our findings.

In the first place, this investigation found that there are differences in behavior patterns between families in which there is an underachieving gifted child and those with an appropriately achieving gifted child. Since they describe only part of a circular relationship, the dynamics earlier investigators reported (hostility, parental rejection, etc.) are not addressed in a systems approach. However, we did find that fathers in underachieving gifted families tended toward disengagement from the family, while the mother apparently compensated for this with some degree of enmeshment. Furthermore, systemically and circularly speaking, the gifted child's underachievement could be viewed as a mechanism to decrease father's disengaged position. This viewpoint takes the onus for the underachievement off the parental subsystem and makes it a family issue. Also, the achievement or underachievement is explained in the context of relationships, not just in terms of individual psychodynamics or inadequacies of the school system.

Secondly, the data reported here emphasize what researchers in the 1920s found out about most families with gifted children: they were the "best and the brightest." What this investigation adds to these studies is that the optimal functioning of these families goes beyond demographics, questionnaires, and birth order. These families tend to function optimally in vivo and convey a sense of depth and commitment to their children's potential not captured on paper or in routine history-gathering interviews.

Third, this investigation accounts for the group of gifted families in the literature who do not function optimally. These families are typically glossed over because they do not fit with the majority of healthy families. These are the gifted families with histories of divorce, mental illness, alcoholism, and chronic conflict. The interactional methodology of this study provides a more complete picture of these families and the relationship of their family patterns to giftedness and achievement. These families apparently have few resources left to devote to development of intellectual potential, having to place higher priorities on personal and family issues.

Last, by conceptualizing academic problems in a gifted population as occurring in the context of family relationships, more and varied treatment options become available. Viewing problems in relationship and system terms creates a range of intervention strategies not available through linear, individualistic treatment strategies.

CONCLUSION

This chapter has reported on the lack of meaningful family interaction research with families of gifted children and presented the results of a project designed to address this neglected area. Using well-documented family assessment techniques, we have shown that it is both practical and useful to evaluate the interactional patterns of gifted families. Our results also emphasize the importance of family assessment when a gifted child has a significant history of underachieving in school.

Moreover, assessing the entire family leads to a contextual understanding, and hence a systems-oriented framework, of the gifted child's needs, motivations, and behaviors. This framework provides a mechanism through which it is possible to integrate more meaningful data from different systems in which the gifted child operates, as well as to perceive more accurately the impact on the gifted child of events occurring in these systems. In this respect, we believe a family/systems approach to gifted children provides educators, counselors, therapists, parents, and teachers with many more alternatives in meeting the needs of this very special population.

REFERENCES

Albert, R. S. A composite portrait: The unusually gifted child. *Creative Child & Adult Quarterly,* 1976, *1,* 214–217.

Araoz, D. C. Marital problems and the exceptional child. *International Journal of Family Counseling,* 1977, *5*(1), 64–69.

Barbe, W. B. A study of the family background of the gifted. In Barbe, W. B. (Ed.) *Psychology and Education of the Gifted: Selected Readings.* New York: Appleton-Century-Crofts, 1956.

Bowen, M. Theory in the practice of psychotherapy. In P. Guerin (Ed.), *Family therapy: Theory and practice.* New York: Gardner Press, 1976.

Bradshaw, R. V. A comparative study of styles of communication between two groups of triads: Parents and their bright underachieving child and parents and their achieving child. *Dissertation Abstracts International,* 1981, *42*(2), 857A.

Chopra, S. L. A comparative study of achieving and underachieving students of high intellectual ability. *Exceptional Children,* 1967, *33*(9), 631–634.

Colarusso, C. A. Psychoanalysis of a severe neurotic learning disturbance in a gifted adolescent boy. *Bulletin of the Menninger Clinic,* 1980, *44*(6), 585–602.

Datta, L. E., & Parloff, M. B. On the relevance of autonomy: Parent-child relationships and early scientific creativity. *Proceedings of the American Psychological Association,* 1957, *2,* 149–150.

Drews, E. M., & Teahan, J. E. Parental attitudes and academic achievers. *Journal of Clinical Psychology,* 1957, *13,* 328–332.

Fine, M. J. Facilitating parent-child relationships for creativity. *Gifted Child Quarterly,* 1977, *21,* 487–500.

Fisher, E. An investigation into the effects of positive labeling on the families of gifted children. *Dissertation Abstracts International,* 1978, *39*(6), 3317A–3318A.

Gear, G. *Gifted education in the 1980s: The future in retrospect.* Unpublished manuscript, University of Alabama in Birmingham, 1982.

Goddard, H. H. *School training of gifted children.* New York: World, 1928.

Gowan, J. C. The underachieving gifted child—a problem for everyone. *Exceptional Children,* 1955, *21,* 247–249; 270–271.

Grotberg, E. H. Adjustment problems of the gifted. In W. B. Barbe (ed.), *Psychology and education of the gifted: Selected readings.* New York: Appleton-Century-Crofts, 1965.

Groth, N. J. Mothers of gifted. *Gifted Child Quarterly,* 1975, *19,* 217–222.

Gurman, A. S. The role of the family in underachievement. *Journal of School Psychology,* 1970, *8*(1), 48–53.

Haggard, E. A. Socialization, personality, and academic achievement in gifted children. *School Review,* 1957, *65,* 388–414.

Haley, J. *Problem-solving therapy.* San Francisco: Jossey-Bass, 1976.

Hayes, R. F., & Bronzaft, A. L. Birth order and related variables in an academically elite sample. *Journal of Individual Psychology,* 1979, *35,* 214–224.

Hollingworth, L. S. *Gifted children: Their nature and nurture.* New York: Macmillan, 1929.

Horall, B. M. Academic performance and personality adjustments of highly intelligent college students. *Genetic Psychology Monographs,* 1957, 3–83.

Kelly, K. A precocious child in analysis. *Psychoanalytic Study of the Child,* 1970, *25,* 122–145.

Kimball, B. Case studies in educational failure during adolescence. *American Journal of Orthopsychiatry,* 1953, *23,* 406–415.

Kimball, B. The sentence completion technique in a study of scholastic underachievement. *Journal of Consulting Psychology,* 1952, *16,* 353–358.

L'Abate, L. *Understanding and helping the individual in the family.* New York: Grune & Stratton, 1976.

Lewis, J. M., Beavers, W. R., Gossett, J. T., & Phillips, V. A. *No single thread: Psychological health in family systems.* New York: Brunner/Mazel, 1976.

Luby, L. W. A longitudinal comparison of IQ in academically successful and unsuccessful mentally gifted high school students and an analysis of personal, family and school differences. *Dissertation Abstracts International,* 1981, *41*(8), 3161B–3162B.

McClelland, D. C., Atkinson, J. W., Clark, R. A., & Lowell, E. L. *The achievement motive.* New York: Appleton-Century-Crofts, 1953.

Minuchin, S. *Families and family therapy.* Cambridge, Mass.: Harvard University Press, 1974.

Minuchin, S., & Fishman, H. C. *Family therapy techniques.* Cambridge, Mass.: Harvard University Press 1981.

Minuchin, S., Rosman, B. L., & Baker, L. *Psychosomatic families: Anorexia nervosa in context.* Cambridge, Mass.: Harvard University Press, 1978.

Minuchin, S., Montalvo, B., Guerney, B. G., Rosman, B. L., & Schumer, F. *Families of the slums.* New York: Basic Books, 1967.

Newman, C. J., Dember, C. F., & Krug, O. "He can but he won't": A psychodynamic study of so-called "gifted underachievers." *Psychoanalytic Study of the Child,* 1973, *28,* 83–129.

Norman, R. D. The interpersonal values of parents of achieving and nonachieving gifted children. *Journal of Psychology,* 1966, *64,* 49–57.

Olson, D., Bell, R., & Portner, J. *FACES: Family adaptability and cohesion evaluation scales.* Unpublished manuscript, University of Minnesota, 1978.

Olson, D., Russell, C., & Sprenkle, D. H. Circumplex model of marital and family systems. II: Empirical studies and clinical interventions. In J. P. Vincent (Ed.), *Advances in family intervention, assessment and theory.* Greenwich, Conn.: JAI Press, 1979.

Pierce, J. V. Sex differences in achievement motivation of able high school students. Quincy, Ill.: University of Chicago Quincy Youth Development Project, December 1961 (mimeographed).

Pulvino, C. J., & Lupton, P. E. Superior students: Family size, birth order, and intellectual ability. *Gifted Child Quarterly,* 1978, *22,* 212–216.

Raph, J. B., Goldberg, M. L., & Passow, A. H. *Bright underachievers.* New York: Teachers College Press, 1966.

Rutter, M. *A neuropsychiatric study in childhood.* Philadelphia: J. B. Lippincott, 1970.

Schneidman, E. S. Suicide among the gifted. *Suicide and life threatening behavior,* 1981, *11*(4), 254–281.

Schneyer, L. C. A comparison of the parent-child relationship in gifted children and children with academic problems. *Dissertation Abstracts International,* 1981, *42*(4), 1496A.

Sears, P. S., & Sherman, V. S. *In pursuit of self-esteem.* Belmont, Calif.: Wadsworth, 1964.

Shaw, M. C., & Brown, D. J. Scholastic underachievement of bright college students. *Personnel and Guidance Journal,* 1957, *36,* 195–199.

Strang, R. Mental hygiene of gifted children. In P. Witty (Ed.), *The gifted child.* Lexington, Mass.: D.C. Heath, 1951.

Taichert, L. C. Two adolescents at risk for schizophrenia: A family case study. *International Journal of Family Therapy,* 1979, *1*(2) 152–162.

Terman, L. M., & Oden, M. H. *Genetic studies of genius* (5 vols.). Stanford, Calif.: Stanford University Press, 1925–1959.

Terman, L. M. & Oden, M. H. The Terman Study of Intellectually Gifted Children. In Dennis, W., and Dennis, M. W. (Eds.). *The Intellectually Gifted: An Overview.* New York: Grune and Stratton, 1976.

Thiel, R., & Thiel, A. F. A structural analysis of family interaction patterns, and the underachieving gifted child. *Gifted Child Quarterly,* 1977, *21*(2), 267–275.

Watzlawick, P. A structured family interview. *Family Process,* 1966, *5,* 256–271.

Watzlawick, P., Beavin, J. H., & Jackson, D. D. *Pragmatics of human communication.* New York: W. W. Norton, 1967.

Whitmore, J. R. *Giftedness, conflict and underachievement.* Boston: Allyn & Bacon, 1980.

Zilli, M. G. Reasons why the gifted child underachievers and some of the implications of guidance and counseling to this problem. *Gifted Child Quarterly,* 1971, *15,* 279–292.

Ziv, A., Rimon, J., and Doni, M. Parental perception and self-concept of gifted and average underachievers. *Perceptual and Motor Skills,* 1977, *44,* 563–568.

Chapter 26

Nontraditional Families*

BERNICE T. EIDUSON
IRLA LEE ZIMMERMAN

In contemporary American society, families are structured in a variety of forms. The traditional two-parent nuclear unit which was the model family form in America for many decades is now the format for no more than 70 percent of families (Masnick & Bane, 1980). There are, in addition, 8.7 percent of families which are single-parent, usually mother (Glick, 1979). It is estimated that a fourth of young children will be raised by single parents in the 1980s and that one half of all children born in the 1980s will spend part of their childhood with one parent (Thomson & Gongola, 1982). The proportion of children being reared for at least part of their lives in never-married or unmarried households in which two parents reside reflects one of the most rapidly growing lifestyles, and this is occurring at the same time that the two-parent families undergo a small but notable (4 percent) decrease. In addition, from 3 to 6 percent of Americans live in extended family units, communes, or living groups (Brudenell, 1982). Thus, in the last two decades, America has become a "melting pot" of family forms which have just begun to be conceptualized in terms of their norms, internal processes, and implications for parents and offspring.

CONCEPT OF ALTERNATIVENESS

The definition of an alternative family is frequently based on structural features that are conveyed by the family descriptor (Thompson & Gongola, 1982). Blended, restructured, or reconstituted families are

* This work was supported in part by USPH Grant No. MH24947 and Carnegie Corporation Grant No. B4198.

families in which remarriage has brought into one unit segments of two previously existing families, usually adults and young children. One-parent families often include the divorced and the widowed as well as the never-married household.

However, not all nonnuclear families are alternative in values and perspectives. In fact, those arising through default tend to be derivations of the traditional family despite differences in their structural appearance. Their values are not the same as those of the alternatives, who have opted for a nontraditional lifestyle and in so doing are consciously rejecting mainstream values and identifications. It is this segment of alternatives that is the focus of the present chapter: the alternatives who questioned the values of the mainstream culture and their implementation as affected in existing institutions, and who *chose* a nontraditional lifestyle. Although reared in traditional homes, by the 1960s, the young adults saw their parents' contemporary values as outmoded, anachronistic to their current perspectives, and illustrative of the archaism and unresponsiveness of institutions to changing needs of Americans. Thus, in a visible and even exhibitionistic way, they sought to recast the primary institution of society, the family. This involved looking for new households forms, new definitions of who constitutes a family, and ways of implementing changed values so that they would have tangible expression in the setting in which everyday living takes place.

The alternative movement has frequently been described as a culture (Kanter, 1972). Such an assignation presumes a fairly standard body of norms, values, concepts, laws and behaviors, and limits for tolerating deviancy (Havighurst, 1973). This line of thinking suggests that a substantial body of values, attitudes, and practices would be found in alternative lifestyle adherents.

Rocheford (1978) found that the alternative ideology can be conceptualized in eight dimensions: (1) the desire for humanism or strong interpersonal relationships, with the aim of building a sense of generalized trust in others; (2) a striving to break away from conventional achievement goals, in favor of achievement which is more creative and personally fulfilling; (3) sex egalitarianism, a recasting of traditionally stereotyped roles and responsibilities; (4) a preference for natural-organic ways, thus making man's existence more in line with those of the natural environment of which he is a part; (5) an orientation toward, and desire for, gratification in the "here and now" as compared to "planning ahead" and an orientation toward the future; (6) antimaterialism; (7) an antiauthority perspective which goes along with the desire for less dependence on medical, social, and educational institutions in society and an interest in self-help and taking control of one's own fate; (8) an antiscience, antiintellectual bent in which sensory and intuitive data and mystical sources of knowledge are regarded as worthy supplements to objective, rational ways of problem solving and knowing.

The extent to which alternatively living persons affiliate with alternative value systems varies (Weisner, 1976). However, alternatives are vividly and predictably distinguishable from persons who have chosen a traditional lifestyle (Weisner & Project Staff, 1976). Clear associations exist between type of alternative lifestyle and extent of identification: The unwed couples are at the extreme alternative end point of the traditional/alternative distribution on each dimension; the single mother shows the most vacillation, sometimes exhibiting alternative leanings and sometimes traditional ones depending on the dimension; and living groups split on the basis of whether or not they are creedal, leader-directed groups or loosely structured domestic (often rural) units living together as friends who share common interests and philosophies. The former, although in a family form that is visibly nontraditional, reveal traditional positions on some dimensions such as orientation toward authority and sex role egalitarianism, while the latter lean toward positions taken by the most clearly alternative family group, the social contracts. Thus, alternatives as a group proved to be heterogeneous in ideology, even revealing some overlap with members of the more-conventional family groups.

The differences between values of alternatives and traditionals can be summarized in two dimensions: (a) affiliation with conventional achievement-orientation, and (b) extent of their planning ahead or antiauthority attitudes, sex egalitarianism, and natural-organic leanings (Eiduson, Weisner, & Project Staff, 1980). Traditional lifestyle adults tend to be grouped in the high-authority/high-achievement cluster. The high antiauthority, sex egalitarian, low-achievement orientation group was mainly composed of unwed couples, single mothers, and some members in living groups. The high-authority/low-achievement cluster characterized single mothers and living-group members, most of whom were creedal; while the moderate-achievement/moderate-authority cluster contained mainly unwed couples and single mothers. Studies have indicated that affiliation with these values persist over time, even when families have changed from one form of alternative lifestyle to another or moved into a traditional two-parent nuclear relationship (Mickey & Eiduson, n.d.). Thus, alternativeness appears to be less of a cultural system, with cohesive cultural specificity, than a body of perspectives, attitudes, and behaviors that vary depending on the kind of family grouping and on certain differences such as size, philosophical orientation, and whether a group is leader directed.

The intensity of commitment to these values within families can be assessed from the extent to which they influence everyday life: their implementation in experiences and relationships, their expression in internal family dynamics, and—even more telling—the extent to which they are transmitted to their offspring and thus perpetuated from one generation to another. Particularly when contrasted with traditional families with children, the strategy in one longitudinal interdisciplinary effort (Alexander & Kornfein, 1983), the ways in which alternative values tend to restructure family strategies and family behaviors become evident.

On the basis of studies of sizable samples, this chapter describes some of the most-prototypic behaviors of three of the alternative family groupings that young adults have adopted and which have remained viable structures over the last two decades. Comparative data on traditional and alternative-by-choice families suggest the ways their perspectives have been translated into ecological niches, relationships, strategies for handling stress, and childrearing practices. While it is easier to evaluate the way alternativeness shapes adult experiences, the impact on children is particularly of interest, since effects on the child who has grown up in a one-parent, group, or unwed family (many of which admittedly developed by default from once-traditional families) have been discussed as having negative or at least problematic consequences (Biller, 1971; Deutsch, 1967; Herzog & Sudia, 1970). Space limitations do not permit discussion of findings on intellectual and socioemotional growth, but longitudinal data on children born into voluntary alternative families and studied from birth through the first eight years of life, along with cross-sectional data, are beginning to question the saliency of the family structure as the critical variable for early child outcome. This chapter concludes with a discussion of the psychotherapeutic issues that arise in diagnosing and treating alternative families.

ALTERNATIVE FAMILY STYLES

Social contract or unmarried couple families

Some alternatives express interest in developing strong, humanistically oriented relationships between individuals, where commitment to a husband-wife relationship rests on emotional rather than legal bonds. "A relationship should endure only so long as it meets the emotional needs of the individuals involved" was frequently expressed during the heyday of the counterculture and became the tenet on which some young families based their conjugal experience. The notion of commitment to one another became a common expression and contrasted with the existential immediacy in gratification and the lack of long-range planning that were also valued by these same young people (Coffins, 1972; Macklin, 1972, 1977).

Five types of nonmarital cohabiting have been identified: *(a)* the short-term relationships, usually based on convenience; *(b)* the couples who are going together steadily, and who decide to move in together; *(c)* the trial marriage, embarked upon with the intention of following up with marriage; *(d)* the temporary alternative to marriage, with a commitment made to marriage; and *(e)* the permanent alternative to marriage. (Macklin, 1983).

The social contract families that are identified with alternative values and have a child usually fall into the last category. They are cohabiting in order to live out their alternative values. They want to break down stereotyped sex role family arrangements and maximize individual needs in a loosely structured but psychologically important relationship. Some had been so sensitive to the unhappiness of parents through divorce and separation experiences that they were "running scared." Though some women particularly expressed a desire for legal marriage to protect the status of their offspring, they were able to tolerate the uncertainty in this arrangement because the quality of interaction made them feel both secure and free at the same time (Kornfein, Weisner, & Martin, 1976).

Among the unmarried couple families are those who could not wed because of legalistic complications. Committed to each other emotionally, many of these would have preferred being married. Unlike couples who are expressing their views about the "pure" *raison d'être* for a relationship, these couples are less able to assume personal responsibility for their lives; rather, they have been prohibited from being able to make a free choice. Yet, interestingly, these differences in overt motivations for being unmarried have not significantly influenced identification with the values found in committed unmarried couples. Social contract couples put a premium on a more-egalitarian role for both marital parents, are interested in achievement for its own sake rather than for materialistic goals, and value interpersonal relationships and the intuitive subjective bases for decision making.

Nontraditional single-mother households

The single-mother household reflects the change in attitude among contemporary single Caucasian mothers, who are able to keep their children and raise them without the guilt (characteristic of previous generations) associated with having an out-of-wedlock child. These women have glibly identified themselves with the characterization of the modern liberated woman. However, when motivations for having a child are explored, there appear to be a number of categories of women within the group who differ both in motivations for seeking single parenthood and in the structure and dynamics of their lifestyle. (Kornfein et al., 1976).

1. The single mother who is a professional. Some professionally trained, capable, and ambitious women desire "the total female experience," an expression common in the women's movement. To them, this means fulfilling goals involving motherhood as well as career. Thus, they proceed to get pregnant, often choosing a biologically preferred man as the father. For these women, marriage is not in the immediate offing, although not ruled out. Pioneering in their orientation, buoyed up by educated talents and tested competencies in the world of work, they perceive a child as enhancing an already full and vital life. They consciously plan to start a new family unit, to "build a nest." Many express a preference for a baby girl; and in one study, the single mothers did have a slightly higher proportion of girls than did the other alternative comparison groups, although the numbers in the total population were about equally divided between sexes (Eiduson, 1981a).

Although some of the career mothers are determinedly identified with aspects of the alternative philosophy, such as sex role egalitarianism and humanism, their values are traditional in other respects: they value material gains, are achievement oriented, and have long-range goals. They are economically and psychologically self-sufficient, and become active and creative in developing and maintaining social relations that would provide enough personal contact and support to keep them engaged in the community (Caplan & Killilea, 1976).

Most of these women live by themselves in apartments that reflect sophisticated tastes and interests. They have friends through both professional and neighborhood contacts. A few are active members in professional or social groups, but they find that work and child caretaking occupy their lives, especially when the children are small. However, they are conscious of making time for social contacts so they can go out on weekends or in the evenings. Once the child is older, with regular caretaking activities, the women become conscious of being lonely. They desire more male companionship and want to get married despite the active pace of their lives.

The child's life is shaped by the mother's. During infancy and early years, there are regular day-care arrangements (usually in private homes) lasting the entire day, until the working mother picks up the child enroute to home. Relatives occasionally assist, as when children are ill or the day-care parent is away. Once home, mother and child are invariably alone together. An unusually intense emotional attachment and dependency grows up between mother and child, despite the fact that both spend large parts of their days with others (Eiduson, 1983). Weekends find their intimacy reinforced by errands and activities which they do together: visiting relatives, going to the park, or seeing the mother's friends (some of whom also have a child). In some families, a "fox hole" intimacy has been observed (Thompson & Gongola, 1982); in others, the proximal intimacy appears to mask a real distantness between mother and child (Eiduson, 1983). However, there is no question that the mother's attitudes and activities serve as the primary model for the child. Some children show unusual competencies that are like those of the mother—skills in art, singing, and dancing that are beyond their years. Mothers serve as a focal and anchoring point for the children, some of whom report even at six years that they are lonesome when the mother is away and admit jealousy of mother's friends (Eiduson, 1983).

2. Single mother managing on her own. Two other groups of women who have decided to head family units find the antiauthority stance of the alternative movement an ego-syntonic rationale for keeping their babies. In these groups, women become pregnant without planning to do so and then opt to become like the single women who are setting up new families and ostensibly managing on their own. One type of woman tries to manage a family on her own resources; the other moves in with her own parents.

The single mother who lives alone and who has less educational and financial resources than the professional single mother leads an existence that is less goal directed and future oriented than her professional sister. She moves among work, welfare, and school in order to make ends meet, develop skills, and make an interesting life for herself (Klein, 1973). Sometimes she shares quarters with female friends (those with small children find each other) or, for a few, with male friends. Sometimes the men are boy friends who may or may not be interested in, or attentive to, the child. While mothers welcome the assistance or the response of their man to their child, they often are so psychologically needy that they seek to fill their lives with adult relationships in which the child plays a secondary role (Eiduson, 1981a).

A child is important to these women as one tangible evidence of permanency in their lives, but the child is likely to be regarded with ambivalence when his or her needs interfere with the parent's.

3. Single mother who lives with her family. These single mothers become pregnant while living at home or close to home, returning during trying times. This subset of single mothers is (in personality, psychological resources, and lifestyle) reminiscent of the unwed young mother of earlier times, whose fate was often identified with economic and emotional deprivation (Furstenberg, 1976; Gershenson, 1972). They are younger than the other single-mother groups, are more naive, have more-limited educational and vocational competencies, and are psychologically and economically dependent on their families of origin (Kornfein et al., 1976).

The internal dynamics of this mother-child family unit are integrated with that of the grandparent family (Eiduson, 1978b). While the mother takes care of the baby and often shares sleeping quarters, mother and baby become merely two other family members so far as other family functions. The mother is usually treated much as she was when part of the family originally, motherhood giving her no special status. The baby, however, takes the role of youngest and is enjoyed by all. Few of these mothers have trouble using all the affection and assistance with the baby that the family gives; only "advice" causes problems.

A child left with its grandparents is usually the only child in the household. He or she is brought up as an only child of older "parents" and is frequently fawned over and given many advantages. The stay with the grandparents is, however, usually temporary (ranging from a few weeks to as long as two years in one case) because of the mobility, the impulsiveness, and the rebelliousness of the young mother.

Such behaviors on the mother's part might have occured without the support given by the youth rebellion of the 1960s, but the ease of finding confreres who share their views gives new credence to the developmental battle against parents.

Economically (mainly through welfare), the mothers contribute to board and room, and some get part-time jobs; but since few want to release parenting to grandparents or sisters completely, they take care of the child during the daytime hours. The mothers remain eager to have personal and social lives of their own.

Communes

The living groups, intentional communes, or (more appropriately today) communities are variable along a number of dimensions that prove to be relevant for their ways of functioning as a family (Ramey, 1976). They can be small or large, rural or urban, creedal or espousing an ideological commitment, or social, political, or geographically proximal domestic units.

It has been found useful to distinguish between the creedal, or religious, groups and the domestic groups (Berger, 1971; Blois, 1971; Cavan, 1971). The former are based mainly upon either Eastern philosophies and culture or on the "Jesus movement," which seeks a new way to live out traditional Judeo-Christian convictions. A smaller number of creedal groups are derived from allegiance to a charismatic leader who may espouse a personalized philosophical system. The domestic group, by contrast, tends to be a less formally organized unit, developing spontaneously around shared crafts, political convictions, or identification with the natural rural environment or the small contemporary farm. In the latter, people who like each other decide to live in a small household or in close proximity and to share some quarters and tasks and some social and domestic activities, often child care. Differences emerge in their family composition, structure, roles, and responsibilities (Greenfield, 1974; Kaslow & Sussman, 1982; Minturn & Lambert, 1964; Weisner & Martin, 1979).

1. The Christian religious family groups. The fundamentalist Christian groups found a new impetus from young people who joined them during the late 1960s and early 1970s in order to find a way back from a drug-ridden, unstructured, and meaningless counterculture life (Kaslow & Sussman, 1982). The Christian groups that attracted them were energized by contemporary young people who sought ways of giving new meaning to their lives in pledging themselves to Jesus.

Group cohesion and identity is served by the philosophy as well as by shared daily practices. Members may live in individual nuclear family units to afford some private areas of family existence; however, functions of everyday life are more determined by common practices of the group. When people arise, times of prayer, nature of work activities, and eating practices are group decisions. Members demonstrate concern for each other, share knowledge and skills, work toward common ends which reinforce shared values (Zablocki, 1980).

Children have a special place when reared in these Christian homes. They are the future evangelists, tomorrow's truth-sayers. Their own activities, growth, and development are governed with this in mind. They pledge themselves to the Lord at an early age, already having regularly participated in prayer service. Parents expect that children will assume some group-assigned responsibilities from age two or three.

Group philosophy determines the parental role. The Lord's will is perceived as dictating the child's personality and his response to parenting practices. The parent must work with the child to make him responsive to the Lord's teachings, often spanking the child. This form of discipline is followed by hugging to show the child that the real purpose was teaching the child, with the parent as God's representative of love and care.

Family life, then, is rigorous, scheduled, and rationalized by goals larger and more important than any individual aims. As parents live by certain group decisions, so children learn that lives will be regulated from the outside. Even when the children go to public school (since church schools are not always viable alternatives), scheduled chores and activities at home are also adhered to before and after school. "Proper" behaviors are sex-stereotypic, with both adults and children in traditional roles (Eiduson, 1980b).

2. Eastern religious family groups. Doctrines of various Eastern religions differ, rituals differ, and relationships and involvement with the outside community vary. However, they share common family structures (Judah, 1974; Ornstein, 1973).

Like the Christian families, Eastern religious families have a family life that is private and apart from the group experience, as well as a domain that is group-shared. A child's family structure begins as a nuclear unit—father, mother, child(ren)—but if families separate, one parent then remains in the group. In most communities, nuclear families have separate quarters or some private space (an apartment, a duplex, or a bedroom upon occasion) while sharing public spaces. Meals assume ritualistic features, sometimes around dietary restrictions, or convictions about prayer or interpersonal communication.

The parents are usually expected to nurture their own young, with supports from group members who may baby-sit, run a preschool program, or carry out those activities that make it possible for the mother to play a role in the common activities of the group. Parents find all manner of personal and social assistance and resources from group members.

Children are given some opportunity to partake of what the community environment offers: public schools, companions, family friends and relatives, grandparents. Eastern religions offer few definite principles to guide young parents in childrearing (Kornfein, 1975). In those religions in which the children are isolated alone with the mother for days following the birth in order to protect the newborn from unwanted influences, creedal rules do not cover the later, less-ritualistic aspects of mother-child interactions or childrearing practices in regard to discipline or toilet training. At many intervention points, the parents make their own decisions; thus, a child sees a model in which the belief system provides the general outlines for life and the parent gives it his or her interpretation.

As the child moves out of infancy, special schooling oriented toward religious beliefs is initiated. The spontaneity and creativity of the young, impulsive child are highly valued; thus, in a rigorous and ritualized family, the young child may be unfettered by most conventions as long as this does not conflict with movement toward the roles children must assume as young adults. Invariably, early orientation toward religious roles follows sex-stereotyped lines.

3. The leader-directed communal family. Religious family groups are, in a sense, leader directed. However, there are also family groups in which the leader is a tangible and charismatic figure (Weisner & Martin, 1979). Leader-directed families are usually distinguished by their devotion to specified goals and aims and are often considered religious (Brudenell, 1982) with members as devotees, but their allegiance is to a belief system that is not structured around the concept of God. Instead, tenets of the leader show "The Way," with a search for self through goals shared in a hierarchically structured family organization with proscribed relationships within and outside the immediate family (Blanton, 1980; Eiduson, 1978b).

The development of personal but shared philosophical views encourages the development and practice of cult-like rituals (Singer, 1978). Practices may be polyandrous relationships, in which a few powerful men in the group sire offspring with various women, or practices in which parents allow children to be separated from them and placed with group or infant-school caretakers who will see that the child's special powers, or "energies," are used to group advantage. In a commune that believes that children are too age-graded in mainstream life, sensual group activities may involve children or teenagers. Such sexual activities are rationalized as in the psychological interests of healthy child adjustment. While the ideology of the group may more or less direct childrearing philosophy and practice, strategies for reshaping child development may turn out to be experimental, erratic, and radical (Brudenell, 1982).

For the children, the group experience provides companionship, allies, models for learning, and the social competencies that come with having to find ways to live with many other children and various caretakers. Children are usually expected to find their own ways of using the social and cognitive environment. As with brothers and sisters in one very large biological family, the children learn to make their ways with each other and have personal attachments, rivalries, and toy exchanges.

4. The family in the semirural domestic group. The desire to return to the land and a more-simple, traditional rural existence brings this family group to the small, almost-hidden community in remote areas (Diamond, 1971; Gross, 1968; Steiner & Maran, 1971). Their simple houses show a mixture of minimum conveniences with sophisticated books and electronic equipment. The family has usually gathered a group of interested friends to live in close proximity and thus share companionship, some meals, and some activities while maintaining the privacy of the private dwelling.

The process of building up one's own wherewithal for existence becomes the sum and substance around which family life proceeds. As in the farm family in the 1800s, there is little time or energy left for less-mundane, more-sophisticated activities (Kinkade, 1972; Mungo, 1970; Roberts, 1971). Pleasures include simple respites from hard work, often drudgery; but the greatest gratifications rest with the fact that the family is constantly renewing its vitality and viability by its own hands.

Children have the freedom that has always been provided by farms, busy parents, and an almost-exclusive concern with the basics of life.

They participate in the parent's activities and play with makeshift toys and spontaneously thought-up games. Lives are regulated by the needs of an early-to-rise, early-to-bed family. Eating, toileting, and discipline have the same up-front, immediate character. School initiates the combination of home freedom and outside-family structure for the child; both usually serve as complements to each other.

There is little ceremony in these families. Informal games and get-togethers are as taken for granted as the slaughtering of animals for food or the continual rebuilding and improvising of homes. As these families find less need to prove their self-sufficiency in this self-selected life pattern, they venture with their child into the nearby small town, go to classes and lectures, see friends and shop, and move toward the life of the small, urbanized community.

5. The urban domestic family. The child in this family also is constantly with parents and their friends (Eiduson, 1978b). Life has an informal, relaxed quality, with living as easy and flexible as possible. When the parents work away from home during all or part of the day, the child's day is shaped by the caretaking arrangements that the parents have made: day care, neighborhood nursery group, or baby-sitter. The parents place minimal demands on themselves, trying mainly to do the things they like to do, seeing the people they like to see, and interacting openly and without ceremony. The parent's demands on their children for behavior or conformity are light. The parents see themselves as supportive and meeting minimal needs without pressure; the children adapt accordingly. They relate to their parents in a casual way, seeing other adults and children as important persons in their environment. Childrearing has a casual, spontaneous, sometimes-impulsive quality about it in contrast to the planned, scheduled milieu found in many traditional homes. Sharing is an important principle, so decision making, homemaking jobs, and baby-sitting are shared.

By contrast to the religious and charismatic-leader groups, there is less stability in these last two domestic communities. In the UCLA study, these communities lost most of their members by the time the child (studied since birth) was 6 years of age, for families lacked the explicit goal, philosophy, charismatic leadership, formal organizational characteristics that, along with economic effectiveness, might have made them viable (Eiduson, Cohen, & Alexander, 1973).

CHARACTERISTICS OF NONCONVENTIONAL FAMILIES

Demographic characteristics

Some general population characteristics suggest that alternative men and women are in the middle and late 20s and early 30s. Most live in urban settings, but about a sixth are in semirural areas. The socioeconomic status (SES) of several samples studied suggests the middle-class status of the contemporary Caucasian nontraditionals (Cohen & Eiduson, 1975; Macklin, 1983). The alternative parents have more frequently interrupted their education than have traditionals, in line with the "dropout" alienation of the original countercultural adherents. While most have completed high school, women in emergent family variations are underrepresented as achieving college-level degrees, and men have completed one less year in college compared to men who had more-traditional career experiences.

Few background variables and attitudes seem to differentiate nonalternative family participants from traditional family members (Cohen & Eiduson, 1975). However, the factors that were significant suggested family instabilities in childhood years, for parents of alternative family participants had moved from one residence to another more frequently than had those in the traditional lifestyles and their own parents had remarried significantly more often. As a group, alternatives view their early childhoods as unhappy; traditional mothers have maintained better relationships with their own mothers during adolescence than have those who chose to live in an alternative lifestyle. Women in living groups and in social contract marriages appeared to have had the most difficulty with their own parents, especially in adolescent years. Among the alternatives, the single mother seemed to have related most successfully to her own parents in early years.

Adaptive strategies

1. Alternatives feel they have a wide range of options on which to draw in developing family styles.   They put a premium on being experimental and effecting changes needed to bring family styles increasingly into line with beliefs (Eiduson & Forsythe, 1983; Eiduson, Kornfein, Zimmerman, & Weisner, et al., 1981). They recast sex roles in the family and decisions about what are and are not appropriate personal and parental ways of earning livelihoods (Eiduson, 1982). Also, having been advantaged (or at least not disadvantaged) as children, they have become accustomed to a range of options and resources. They have also learned that each has a different payoff. Thus, some could choose to be "voluntary poor," the price paid for abandoning the puritan work ethic (Weisner, 1981). They are willing to take risks, to accept the stresses that come with uncertainty, and to make changes to try to make their lives more satisfying; departing from conventional ways of thinking and behaving does not make them anxious (Coles, 1978; Eiduson, 1981b).

2. Alternatives can live with norms that remain more or less ambiguous.

Some cope with the absence of positive referent groups by using the standards of the mainstream in a negative way: Alternative behaviors are valued and appropriate if they are antimainstream (Keniston, 1974). Others adopt a strategy of consciously taking on norms of a specific group (Eiduson, 1978b). When these are leader-directed or creedal groups, norms have often proved more hierarchical and authority oriented than those of the referent groups the alternatives had abandoned, but directed to more-appealing and personally meaningful goals (Kanter, 1972). Other parents adopt the values of local referent groups who, like themselves, search for the psychological grails of personal fulfillment and adjustment, with pragmatic answers to daily problems. In their roles as parents are found a certain questioning attitude toward the taken for granted, a certain disbelief in "experts," and a premium placed on independently finding out for one's self (Cohen & Eiduson, 1975).

3. Alternatives have sought insularity from the prevailing culture in various ways. Rural living, rejection of their own parents, and living and working within one's own community are examples. Diets are changed, television more or less controlled, and some attempts made to return to simple patterns of American life that were pre-Industrial Revolution (Eiduson, 1978b; Weisner, Bausano, & Kornfein, 1983). Some opt for a fairly closed system in which there is little influence or interchange with the outside world (Weisner & Martin, 1979). The aim has been to set up a more-simple life, a place of residence, size of family, kinds of contacts, activities, and demands which are sufficiently limited or able to be circumscribed, so parents might get the feeling that they are in control of their lives, a perspective regarded as important to pass on to children (Eiduson & Alexander, 1978b).

4. Peers are powerful cohorts for parents who take an alternative stance (Eiduson, 1979a; Kanter, Jaffe, & Weisberg, 1975). As alternative families are formed, relationships with peers become pivotal. Peers provide support networks, caretaking resources, and a host of the informal and formal relationships previously delegated to biologically or legally related family members. Alternatives anticipated that peers would be more compatible in attitudes and ideas than were biological relatives. Their more-tenuous commitments, however, subsequently result in frequent changes in families and households.

5. Alternatives are generally intelligent. Those who have embraced all or parts of the alternative ideology are intellectually average or above, comparable to traditionals, in verbal, quantitative, and spatial skills (Zimmerman & Bernstein, 1983). By and large, they came from intellectual homes (Weisner & Weibel, 1981). Many did not follow customary educational career lives: As a group, they have fewer degrees, less professional training or high-level skills. They hold posts that are at lower levels than traditionals on the average and may look down condescendingly on conventional education and on the focus on academic skills for the child.

Alternatives appreciate the value of self-teaching, setting personally meaningful goals, and learning "basics." Basics include the kinds of knowledge that permit one to fix things at home and survive in less technologically sophisticated environments. It also includes learning those things that extend one's natural interests and propensities, such as undersea diving that can be used in marine engineering. While in some aspects of life (such as religion, philosophy, and psychology) they retain an interest in the abstract and in symbolic content, they also have a vocational set in pragmatic, tangible activities. Both seem to give them satisfaction and a sense of self-worth, whereas more-conventional activities and interests do not. In personality, alternatives are by and large within normal limits as measured by the Minnesota Multiphasic Personality Inventory (MMPI) (Zimmerman & Bernstein, 1983). Within this range, they would be described as feisty, provocative, argumentative individuals. They tend to provoke conflict, have passive-aggressive flare-ups, and are not readily assuaged.

6. *Alternatives tend to pick and choose as appropriate from practices and behaviors that, on face, are not compatible* (Eiduson, Weisner, and Project Staff, 1980). Rather than searching for a coherence that would go under a single label such as liberal or neoconservative, they make choices and show preferences on the basis of individual situations or demands. Thus, a strong and even righteous-sounding or moralistic sense of family is found, along with an insistence on natural diets or opposition to sexually liberated behaviors (Eiduson & Weisner, 1978). The lack of synthesis or integration of behaviors is not uncomfortable for them.

In summary, the styles of adaptation of alternative parents lie in the nature of pivotal relationships, in the casting off of traditional authorities as experts, in the flexibility of norms and standards, in the willingness to take risks, in the need to draw attention to themselves, in the feeling they have many options and they are equipped to take advantage of them.

Physical and social environment of alternatives

1. *Economic consequences of being alternative are well known* (Sawhill, 1976). Income is less than in traditional homes, so the usual material appurtenances of homes are more simple, often more innovative; yet there is no dearth of personally valued possessions such as stereos and books (Weisner & Weibel, 1981). Also, total family income is frequently patched up from more personally provided, public, and private

sources; it is more variable and less able to be depended upon (Eiduson et al., 1981). Despite the search for independence from families of origin and their values through alternativeness, there is dependence on work in the mainstream for dollars and services. Also, family economic needs force parents to live in ways other than they had hoped for (i.e., working away from home) and in less than ideal jobs despite preferences to the contrary (Eiduson et al., 1980). Thus, the attitude toward work is often not one of satisfaction and pleasure but one of ambivalence and compromise forced by reality considerations (Zimmerman & Bernstein, 1983).

2. Residences and residence arrangements in nontraditional families can be unusual. Space is at a premium and quarters shared, so there is often some reduction in opportunities for privacy (Weisner & Weibel, 1981). As a result, the alternative child is often exposed to more family experiences than is the traditional family child. Since situations likely to be stressful to a child are more frequent in alternative homes (Eiduson & Forsythe, 1982), this suggests that while such exposure may on the one hand promote early maturity (or more likely, a pseudomature attitude about adults and relationships), it may also be anxiety producing and threatening to security. In close, non private quarters, the young child is more likely to be sensitized to personal pathologies of parents, such as depression in the mother (Anthony, 1975), and to conflict between mates (Eiduson, 1981b). Also, there is a greater likelihood that parent/child relations will get the spillover of such adult troubles (Eiduson, 1981b). An extensive literature points to the negative effects of home turmoil and conflict on the child's ability to use resources (Dohrenwend & Dohrenwend, 1974), on the perception of relationships (Hetherington & Morris, 1978), and on the absence of conflict-free spheres of functioning (Anthony, 1978).

3. Distinctive for alternative children is the ecological "niche" of the family unit. We have described the nesting of the immediate family in an extended group for some alternatives (Eiduson, 1978b); the attachment of some immediate families to cohorts in shared living arrangements (Weisner & Martin, 1979); the way one-parent units realign their families with grandparents, other relatives or like-minded friends. Thus, the social consequences of small family size or socially limited and lonely independent existences are offset in some ways (Eiduson, 1981a). Some studies of the child's concept of his family suggest that children frequently include "live-withs" as family members (Eiduson et al., 1980).

Further, the inevitable presence of other children in close proximity and on a more-frequent and intensive basis than usually found in traditional homes (Eiduson et al., 1980) suggests that an important trade-off in alternative structures is that peers can function as parent substitutes, teachers, goal setters, and models. As in poverty families, sibling caretaking can supplement or supplant parent caretaking and has learning and socioemotional consequences (Cicirelli, 1976; Koch, 1973).

Thus, alternative home environments are identified by different economic and personal resources in the home, inconsistency of family membership, greater or at least different kinds of social stimulation, and the likelihood of some dilution of parent involvement offset by intensification of other-adult and peer involvement.

Parent-child relationships and interactions

1. Parents are the primary caretakers in alternative families. Caretaking may be the prevailing practice in alternatives; and contrary to notions that some children do not know their biological mother, the family unit is most often structured as a unit, with the child living with mother and father. Mothers are invariably primary caretakers during infancy and early childhood. However, the extent to which fathers and other adults are secondary caretakers highlights a unique development in alternative units. Fathers spend more time with children during the first years of life, involved with both caretaking and play activities. The kind of parent-child contacts involved in nurturing, affectional exchanges, and learning are generalized to include the use of others as the child gets older (Alexander & Kornfein, 1983).

Although alternative families were not developed with children's needs primarily in mind, children are seen as important transmitters of their outlook and their ways of behaving (Eiduson et al., 1980). The effort put into parenting is not seen as a casual endeavor. During pregnancy, alternatives viewed children as changing their lives, altering personal goals, and becoming full-time preoccupations significantly more frequently than did traditionals (Eiduson & Alexander, 1978). In alternative homes where there is a high value placed on close relationships among adult family members, there is a greater range of social interactions, a high quality of involvement, and a high quality of verbal interaction with the child (Eiduson et al., 1980). In addition, those adults who seem to be the most alternative in values stress naturalness and so tend to take infants along wherever they go, to carry them physically close, and to expose them to a wide variety of experiences; they used "in-house" baby sitters but few outsiders (Weisner et al., 1983). This reflects the desire to generalize to parent and child relationships the intimate bonds prized between adults. Thus, despite the greater background of potentially available caretaking adults, the child's exposure to emotionally interactive expressions, communicative responsiveness, mutuality of affect, and frequency of child-initiated or parent-initiated behaviors show few significant differences (Eiduson

& Weisner, 1978). As the children grow older, alternatives and traditionals are indistinguishable in the kinds and amount of nurturant caretaking and stimulation. Ways of stimulating the child are similar, as
are ways of comforting the cranky, ill, or frightened child (Eiduson
et al., 1981). Greater control and direction of child behavior is shown
by traditional parents, but alternatives show considerable range in the
extent to which they are controlling or permissive (Alexander & Kornfein, 1983). In general, alternative children are exposed to richly varied
and complex kinds of stimulation, appropriately modulated by parents
(Eiduson & Weisner, 1978). As family groups, traditionals may be more
directive, but the encouragement in all families for child spontaneity,
playfulness, and a lightness of regimentation in the early years proved
to be a striking feature in relationships (Eiduson, et al., 1981).

 *2. Some alternative parents have difficulty assuming roles as parents
because they are openly against authority as defined by mainstream
mores and values.* Therefore, in taking the role of as parent, they
often assume a laissez-faire stance. For them, development is "natural,"
with children being like flowers which, given appropriate water and
sunshine, grow at their own tempo and in their own way—or as determined by "higher" powers. In an analysis of the attitudes shown by
alternatives so far as their role as parent, they could be classified as
interveners, sometime intervenors, or nonintervenors (Cohen & Eiduson, 1975). Whereas noninterveners only shaped the child's behaviors
and attitudes as necessary to meet prescribed family norms and standards, interveners attempted to adapt and time their shaping strategies
to the growth needs of the child. Unwed couples and domestic groups
who shared the most alternative values perceived themselves as noninterveners; creedal living groups thought that parents' role as interveners would prepare children for ascribed family roles. Traditional marrieds, by contrast, comprised the largest proportion of sometime
interveners. Single mothers lined up with traditional parents, although
some who appear immature assume a laissez-faire attitude. Study of
actual parental behaviors showed that fewer alternative parents assumed the laissez-faire role they had postulated they would, and more
took an authoritative role when needed by the child; of 205 parents
whose behaviors were assessed, the largest group (42 percent) were
sometime intervenors, 41 percent were intervenors, and 16 percent
parented in a laissez-faire manner. Laissez-faire parenting occurred
significantly more often in psychologically marginal alternatives.

 *3. Alternative fathers expressed a significantly stronger desire to be
home more, and more involved with their child in formative years, as
compared to traditionals.* Yet, by the time the child was aged 4½,
very few (less than 10 percent of families) had a father who could
be characterized as the primary or most-frequent parent involved in

child-parent interaction. About 15 percent of the households in our project were truly joint-activity households, i.e., families in which both parents participated equally in their involvement with the child. Very low father involvement or none was found in approximately 5 percent of families (Weisner, 1982).

Four types of fathering behavior were identified by daily routine and other behavioral data (Weisner, 1982). "Coequal managers" were primarily responsible for their child more than three hours a day for more than three days a week. They had behavioral profiles of interaction with their children which proved to be the most similar to mothers' profiles: more discipline, negative comments, and instructions. Supportive fathers, whose role was of help with child care, had behavioral profiles more typical of average American fathers: more play, positive affect, information exchange, and less need to directly change behavior. Careerist fathers were characterized by occasional involvement in child care, while intermittent parenting characterized the fourth group of fathers.

An apparent paradoxical result was observed in the relationships between fathers' availability in the home and the style of involvement in family activities. Fathers in egalitarian-oriented, unwed couple families were in the home and available for interaction and caretaking more often throughout the 4½-year period than other fathers. These same fathers, however, are least likely to follow the patterns found for the differential involvement of the father in laughing, play, and other cooperative activities, as compared to the mother who handled management-related behaviors. Increased availability, shared activities, and involvement paradoxically do not produce an interaction style that simply enhances or exaggerates what has commonly been reported for American fathers—a high proportion of play and nonmanagement time. Instead, fathers who were more child involved appeared to be taking on more sustained daylong and weeklong involvement and acted more like the conventional mothers in our sample (Weisner, 1982).

4. The parent's and child's relationships with their own parents is also significantly different in alternatives. While traditional married families remained the group most identified with their own parents during the child's first six years of life, they were also the group who felt most positively about their childhood experiences and the way they were raised (Cohen & Eiduson, 1975).

There is some improvement in the relationship between alternatives and their parents over time, usually attributable to the birth of a child. Yet, significant differences remain in the distance they live from their families and in the frequency with which they visit. The more-nonconventional parents live further from their parents and see them less frequently. This was not the case for single mothers: The women who were single were the most-likely group to live in the same city as their parents to a significant extent. The single mother appears to use her own family extensively as a resource, even though only a minority return to the physical household of their parents (Eiduson, 1983).

5. *None of the alternative lifestyles studied is free from conflict, tension, or stress.* However, the traditional married two-parent nuclear family, overall, experiences fewer of the kind of events considered likely to be stressful for the young child. Different types of stress seem to be present in different kinds of families. For the traditional family, two types of experience are particularly stressful: (1) moves and changes in the household and other reality-found or external events, and (2) conflict or tension between mates, which throughout the first six years is generally higher than in any other family group (Eiduson & Forsythe, 1982). There are fewer divorces and separations than in other types of families, suggesting that the traditional couple is likely to stay together in spite of conflict. In the social contract family and for the single-mother group, parents' psychological status events (such as maternal depression and emotional disturbance) are noteworthy. For the communal group, stresses in the parent-child relationship area stand out.

Different lifestyles resonate to stressful events differently (Eiduson, 1983). A relatively small amount of stress is likely to be extremely disruptive to the child in the traditional family. Family groups that are used to solving problems through effecting external changes, as do social contract or communal families, may experience a great deal of stressful change of the kind normally considered disruptive, but these do not prove to be as stressful to their children; in these families, change is a common way of solving problems. The single-mother family, while not necessarily experiencing the greatest amount of stress, is most susceptible when it occurs.

Family style has a bearing on whether or not conflicts and stress affect the child. The child of a single mother seems the most poorly buffered against conflict and stress. Cognitive performance as early as one year is negatively affected, and this consistently holds at two years (maternal ratings) and at three (when Stanford-Binet scores are lowered). The social competence of the social contract child is affected in a significant way by stresses during the first year. These remain high in subsequent years, although they are not associated in a statistically significant way at two and three years. Attachment to the mother, tested typically at one year, finds the social contract child who has experienced stress to be more anxiously attached than are children in any other family group (Eiduson, 1983).

Child symptomatology at four, five, and six does not differ by lifestyle (Eiduson, 1983). Nor is there any association between level of parental tension and symptom formation in the children. However, there are significant associations between children perceived as difficult or shy by parents at 18 and 24 months and the symptoms shown in early life. The UCLA study of the infancy, early childhood, preschool, and initial school adjustment of children raised in alternative families suggests that lifestyle differences interact strongly with such variables as parental stability and emotional adjustment. Few measures of child adjustment differentiated by lifestyle alone. Even the most-variant lifestyle produced its share of happy, well-adjusted, and achieving youngsters. Overall, the alternatively reared children in this study were of bright average intelligence, and their good school achievements paralleled their ability. As expected, children ranged from those school-labeled "gifted" to those at risk and requiring special interventions. Lifestyle was not the critical determinant of individual differences among children, but interacted with such variables as stress in the home, parental competence, and supporting resources in the family.

PSYCHOTHERAPY WITH ALTERNATIVE FAMILIES

Given this picture of values, preferences and behaviors, what clinical issues are raised when alternatives seek psychological assistance?

Diagnostic issues

1. Work with nontraditional families highlights some interesting issues when clients from American subcultures are compared to the traditional middle-class patient. How does one appropriately assess child behaviors and adult childrearing practices that mental health specialists believe produce deviance or pathology, when these behaviors are valued by the "family" subculture? Or, put more simply, under what conditions does "difference" becomes "deviance" or "pathology" (Eiduson, 1978b)? In recent years, research on minority populations has indicated that differences do not invariably connote deviance nor deficit (Deutsch, 1967; Reissman, Cohen, & Pearl, 1964; Ungerleider & Wellish, 1979). The clinician's perspective and that of the cultural framework providing his reference and anchoring points have been shown at times to inhibit culture-free inferences and conclusions.

Some alternatives look different, hold unpopular views, and prioritize differences in unusual ways. Also, being antimainstream in some of their attitudes and behaviors, they reject many of the values with which clinicians may identify. There is a tendency, then, for clinicians to view their behaviors (particularly the values and practices that influence childrearing patterns) as "lesser" and pathogenic rather than different (Clark, 1978; Hopkins, 1978).

The perspective of the cultural anthropologist, who tries to identify the competencies and attitudes that serve adaptive and adjustive purposes in another culture or subculture, is useful for understanding and evaluating differences that some alternatives show. Yet, the marginal individuals who come from nontraditional families challenge even an enlightened cross-cultural position, because alternatives often appear diffuse, vague, and confused in their own perspectives and identifications. The ways of compromise when one is on the cutting edge of change can be both vagarious and elusive. Such personalities may appear to reflect "one foot in two cultures" and, in the process, may seem to be poorly integrated, vacillating individuals who are torn by ambivalence and confusion.

Clinical study of the alternative adult, and particularly of the child who is reared in a nontraditional family, may turn out to be the only effective way to see how personality patterns are shaped when responding to different values and different cultural demands. What does it mean for a child to have multiple models for identification rather than nuclear models, when his alternative family specifically aims to dilute the child/parent tie in order to reduce what they see as the child's inevitable absorption of his parent's neurotic trip? Is confusion or ambiguity in identification an unrelenting consequence? Can the fact that the family fosters this kind of identification promote integration of diverse models, so that the child's development is enhanced rather than fragmented and fraught with ambivalence and manipulative behaviors?

This kind of clinical issue has been raised by the conscious changes in values and behaviors of some contemporary families (Eiduson & Alexander, 1978). A clinical or psychotherapeutic issue in the immediate sense, it also has important theoretical implications relating to drawing the line between difference and pathology and to the influence of societal acceptability as a criterion for adjustment (Eiduson & Alexander, 1978). The behaviors and attitudes of nontraditionals must be viewed in terms of the service to which their unusual or different stresses are put in their personality. A priori determination that deviant-appearing behaviors are inevitably maladjustive, destructive, or a lesser form of adjustment can be dangerously and erroneously discriminatory. Furthermore, such a view may blind the clinician to the adaptive, adjustive, and restitutive strengths that different and even unique values and perspectives may have, both for an individual and for a group (Ungerleider & Wellish, 1979).

2. This not-taken-for-granted diagnostic position is particularly important in assessing the extent of the client's disturbance. Since the development of the counterculture movement in the late 1960s, numerous questions have arisen about the psychological stability of the

individuals drawn into the nontraditional lifestyles (Appel, 1983; Clark, 1978; Hopkins, 1978). Participants have been seen as rebellious adolescents (Keniston, 1974), as sociopathic personalities (Roszak, 1969), as psychotics in search of a therapeutic community (Phillips, 1982). In general, systematic studies have shown the counterculture adults to be within the normal range and functioning adequately (Zimmerman & Bernstein, 1983). They are generally above average in intelligence, verbally adept, and often drawn to the counterculture because of its intellectual and philosophical rethinking of present-day society. The elaborate rationales which they devise for their own behaviors also attest to their verbal sophistication and personal insightfulness. If there is any pattern that particularly describes their personality structure, it is the proneness to feistiness and an acting-out of tensions and anxieties, some latent depressiveness, and suspicion and distrust of authority.

In a study of 146 women and 43 men who were living alternatively at the time they had their first or second child, only 36 percent of the mothers and 45 percent of the fathers available presented themselves on the MMPI as falling into the possibly "impaired" range. (One or more T-scores over 69 was the criterion on which this assignment was based.) Using Lashar's (1974) criteria, 10 percent of the mothers and 14 percent of the fathers had MMPI profiles which would veer toward "psychotic," 18 percent of the mothers and 30 percent of the fathers revealed characterological problems, and 8 percent and 2 percent respectively endorsed items suggesting neurosis. However, the largest percentage of the MMPI profiles, those of 64 percent of the mothers and 55 percent of the fathers, would be diagnosed as within the normal range (Zimmerman & Eiduson, n.d.). The high hypomania and psychopathic deviate scale pattern (9,4 or 4,9) characteristic of alternative men and women is the most-common one for adolescents. Such a pattern suggests behavior which would be characterized as impulsive, self-centered, manipulative yet friendly, fun-loving, and creative. Such a pattern has been considered fairly common in women in normal marriages, although in males it has been associated with poor marital adjustment and, often, poor adjustment in work and with friends (Catlin, Croske, & Keller, 1976).

These data were supported by studies of members of highly ritualized, authoritarian, religious groups in which roles and behaviors are specifically ascribed and adherence to group patterns rigidly enforced (Ross, 1983). Other clinicians have also noted that adult members who have moved into such families show strong dependency needs rather than pathogenicity. Also, some alternatives did use the social movement represented by the counterculture as a way of masking their own problems (such as conflicts with authority) or problems around their own alienation from peers. However, this is a relatively small group. Others appear genuinely experimental in the avant garde sense. A clue about how disturbed a person may be is his or her tendency and willingness to return to straight society or to live according to mainstream values in some ways, although remaining quite alternative outwardly or in some areas.

3. Studies of persons who seek out alternative families, then, point out that all alternative individuals are not alike in personality or motivations. Members within the nontraditional group are not any more homogeneous than are persons who are traditionally married. Research indicated that considerable heterogeneity exists among alternative families and even within single kinds of nontraditional families such as single mothers or living groups. Differences can be marked, both in their beliefs and in the kinds of perspectives they hold dear. They also may differ in their childrearing behaviors and attitudes. There are variations in values and behaviors within an alternative family, just as in a conventional one. However, the limits within which differences can occur without threatening the integrity and stability of the family unit may be much more restricted for the alternative family. Many of the visible bonds which make for cohesiveness and integrity in the traditional family do not exist in alternative families, and the breakup of families is more probable.

4. Looking at the other side of the coin, there are some people who do not live alternatively and who give few outward signs of being affiliated with nontraditional values, but who in fact are nonconventional in their perspectives and attitudes. These persons are often the movers and changers within mainstream society who try to inject some change into traditional ways of doing things by questioning "the system." Under a middle-class cloak, there may be a very strong antiauthority stance or a determined sex egalitarian division of household roles. Numerous political and social outlets can be found for the decision to "bore from within," or to use the mechanisms of existing institutions with which they interface to question and reexamine some of the assumptions underlying societal practices.

An accurate diagnosis of the client, then, demands a rather careful scrutiny of many facets of behavior. It is easy to assume that some of the values nonalternative-appearing clients espouse are in fact polar ends of positions seen in the widely ranging stances of traditionally structured families. The overlap and blurring of difference between alternative and nonalternative populations has always been evident and is increasingly so, as the mainstream culture has absorbed some of the once-alternative behaviors and found them consonant to its evolving positions in the face of needs for change. The person who was once instrumental in recognizing the need for, and effecting, changes in the face of opposition and the person who accepts change once it becomes more acceptable and thus institutionalized may have quite different personality structures. In one, the search for change may be central to his main personality thrust; the other reveals a dominant need to integrate rapidly all forces bearing on action. As in the case of other personality and behavioral dimensions, the identification with alternativeness must be examined in detail to determine its role in the client's psychology.

5. Thus, alternatives should be thought of as subcultures in American society: groups who seek to express their values, behaviors, and ideologies in a coherent framework through which they can live, interact, set goals, etc. Most are trying to effect social change through modeling a family life that they consider more likely to produce a healthy, self-fulfilled personality, more in line with an ascetic or a hedonistic philosophy and/or more capable of injecting meaningful goals into life experiences. Even those who take on the most overtly nontraditional lifestyles—with rituals, prescribed roles, or unusual modes of economic subsistence—can derive a sense of cohesion and purpose from their family units. The client's family environment, however odd, must therefore be viewed with this diagnostic perspective in mind.

A further diagnostic footnote to keep in mind is that choice of a family unit may for some clients be an immediate or temporary affiliation with alternativeness, rather than a permanent decision. Mobility studies show that of people who have lived alternatively, approximately 50 percent change lifestyle in a six-year period. While half of these move into traditional family units, another half change into a different nontraditional lifestyle. Thus, the temporal pattern of affiliation has some clinical meaning and needs to be explored for what light it can throw on the strategies used to resolve conflict, to provide a sense of identification and "family," and to provide new relationships, new bonds, and new goals.

Motivations for seeking help

1. It is well known that individuals take their troubles along as they move from one residence or one situation into another (Reissman et al., 1964). Therefore, the search for amelioration through environmental change (i.e., into and/or out of a nontraditional family) may be less productive than anticipated. However, because the alternative family unit may have different pressures from the traditional unit in which a client grew up, he or she is often confronted with the fact that difficulties lie within, rather than with the rest of the "family" on which blame has in the past been projected. As will be noted below, many alternatives do tend to project blame onto others—their own

parents, the "system," or various mainstream agencies or institutions. In alternative settings, however, the new "framework," with its internal dynamics, often acts to confront the individual with his inability to get along in any "family system." Such confrontation serves to motivate some persons to seek outside help.

2. Alternatives suffer, even though they often appear overtly to throw off personal despair or anxiety through their feisty, chip-on-the-shoulder attitudes or by flight, i.e., making changes. Personality studies (Ross, 1983) have shown that alternatives are just as aware of their unhappiness and dissatisfactions with their lives as traditionals are. Sometimes they are more sensitive to internal troubles because they spend so much time ruminating about personal relationships. Rather than putting relationships in the context of the larger picture of life, many alternatives feel they know life through what they get out of personal relationships. When these are less than happy, there is a diminution or even a collapse of their whole world. Thus, although the outward demeanor may appear to be contrary, the suffering and unhappiness of alternatives are real and deeply felt. Such problems bring them to seek help.

No alternative lifestyle offers a panacea for happy living. Research on stresses found in a variety of different family styles has indicated that there are certain different stressors associated with each lifestyle (Eiduson & Forsythe, 1982). Parent-child relationships are more stressful in living groups, whereas present psychological problems are found more frequently in unwed couple arrangements. Also, as noted above, the level of stress found in family life differs by lifestyle. The traditional family members are exposed to far-lower levels of stress than are alternatives. Studied longitudinal, high stress levels were most chronic in unwed couples and single-parent families. Also, research has shown that each alternative style has certain weaknesses in terms of its capability for protecting its members during crisis and stress (Eiduson & Forsythe, 1982). Living groups tend to be inured to problems; members face difficulties together and present themselves as allies under stress.

The generally fairly persistent levels of stress associated with alternative lifestyles might serve as precipating factors in motivating an alternatively living individual to seek help. However, because families have unique stresses, strengths, and vulnerabilities, each must be explored to see how the specific alternative family the individual has chosen contributes to his or her difficulty.

Psychotherapeutic issues

1. Transference issues. The development and resolution of the usual transference in psychotherapy is colored by some ambivalent attitudes alternative patients have toward psychotherapy. For many, psychotherapy is regarded as one of many change agencies, and the psychotherapist is grouped with the herbalist, the naturopath, the religious leader, or the guru. Psychotherapists are compared with a host of other change agents whose efficacy is evaluated in terms of their magical or mystical powers, their facility to resolve immediate problems, and the new meaningfulness they engender in life. Alternatives tend to test out one remedial agent against another and make commitments to treatments tentatively, until they have weighed a series of approaches to see which one is optimal. As a result, they often appear ambivalent in their help-seeking efforts, "on the fence," contentious, even disputatious. Further, their intellectual demeanor (at times arrogant and rejecting) may make them appear distant and distrustful, thus hiding their genuine desire for help.

As agents of society, clinicians generate distrust, suspicion, and fear of disclosure for many alternatives. Die-hard alternatives, or the countercultural persons as they have been called, feel they should be distrustful of doctors as representatives of mainstream mores; to do otherwise would weaken loyalties to the group with which they are identified. At the same time, viewed as persons who are experts in motivation, in the unconscious, and in dealing with personal relationships, therapists arouse admiration and interest. Since the image of clinicians is as persons who reject the obvious garments of social morality, they are also viewed as compassionate allies.

The alternative may initially balk at seeing clinicians who are too old or who appear too sex stereotypic in dress or manner. However, those are first-level or superficial objections. In the experience of one longitudinal study of alternatives, middle-aged clinicians were embraced as interviewers because they were viewed as "nonjudgmental parent figures" who respected the participants and even valued their unusual outlooks and perspectives (Eiduson, 1980). This mixture of attitudes with which alternatives may view the psychotherapist will make the alternative patients' testing out and reluctance to make commitments easier to understand. This is a strong element in their response to therapy that must be addressed in terms of both their current adjustment and their past experiences and relationships. When dropout rates are high, it is either because clinicians have not dealt with the ambivalences in the patients' attitudes or when therapy has been allowed to deviate from treating the alternatives as troubled persons who need help no matter what their lifestyle.

2. Countertransference issues. Alternatives have had a "bad press." Journalistic accounts have looked for the sensational in lifestyle behaviors. They have singled out strange and exotic beliefs, curious interpersonal relationships, and the most-unconventional behaviors that were likely to have mass appeal. Less publicized have been socially acceptable, innovative trends that have been responsive to changing values and attitudes of mainstream Americans toward commonplace features of living: Ecological concerns, a focus on physical health, natural food, and home industries are apt examples. The psychotherapist is likely to prejudge the alternative negatively in line with his mainstream identifications. The connotations of "looking for a free ride," "irresponsible hippies and flower children," and "ripping off the system" have to be consciously recognized and put aside.

More difficult for the practitioner to cope with are behaviors and attitudes that seem to conflict with his beliefs about what constitutes maturity and what behaviors are conducive to mental health and what are not. For example, some alternatives believe anxieties should not be tolerated; the ability to delay gratification and to work toward long-range goals (indexes of maturity to clinicians) are deemed inappropriate to their here-and-now perspective.

Even more alien to the practitioner's customary orientation is the attitude of some alternatives toward their parental roles and responsibilities. Although some parent as they were parented, comfortable with the conventional, more or less authoritative stance, others decry the interventionist aspect of this philosophy. They choose instead to retreat from any intervention or responsibility, feeling that a child's fate is sealed by the stars, God, or other inimitable progenitors. Thus, their role is to treat their children as individuals, providing only the necessary nutrients and conditions for growth and making them responsible for themselves from a very early age (Berger, 1971).

If this way of handling responsibility on both the parents' and the child's part were found only in alternative populations, the implications of this attitude would be limited to a subgroup who might not come into psychotherapy at all. However, there is substantive evidence that such stances are beginning to diffuse rapidly from once-counterculture populations into many young contemporary parents in "straight" society (Eiduson, 1980a). Therefore, some serious thinking about our expectancies and our prejudgments is in order for both theoretical and pragmatic reasons. Otherwise responsiveness to individual and cultural needs, an essential feature of good clinical work, may be jeopardized.

A related problem in working with alternative patients is the clinician's attempt to over-identify with and take on alternative stances in his own work. Despite the generally negative portrayal of marginals or nonmainstreamers in the media, personal contact often brings out their good intellect, verbal facility, sensitivity in recognizing social injustices, and willingness to risk censure and exclusion for the sake of ideals. The flexibility of alternative lifestyles—the willingness to experiment and to give up familiar though chronically troubled relationships for unknown but promising contacts—is appealing. The rise of divorces in established, long-married families has been in part attributed to the alternative model (Wallerstein & Kelly, 1980). Clinicians have noted that working with alternatives can unwittingly encourage their own acting-out tendencies (Phillips, 1982). When this is the case, the therapist loses sight of the client's goals and is handicapped in helping the client examine his expectations, motivations, and adaptive and defensive strategies.

3. Other therapeutic issues. How can the therapist help sort out personal from social factors that have contributed to problems for which a client seeks help? It is easy to point to the forces in the sociocultural environment that have been responsible for person's moving into alternative family developments. The times, the well-recognized peer pressure, the triggering influence of the Vietnam War are but a few of these forces.

It is not unusual to find a sociocultural phenomenon presenting itself as an acceptable way of expressing or resolving personal psychological conflict (Roszak, 1969). The counterculture, antimainstream movement proved useful to young adults who were at the psychosexual and chronological age when their adolescent wishes to be independent found them critical of parents, their affiliation with mainstream values, and the many compromises adults make in adjusting to reality. To the youth, compromises and adaptations were hypocrisies; parent's neuroses were prices paid for accepting and living with frustrations. Some added credence was given to these recriminations because they were shared by many peers.

In psychotherapy, alternatives tend to focus on the Vietnam War and related social phenomena during the 60s and 70s that gave young people cause for rebelliousness, hostility, and a breaking away from existing mores. However, all young people were not drawn into the sociocultural fray, nor was their resolution of the developmental adolescent crises shaped by it. Therefore, in therapy, the focal issues remain rooted in the psychodynamics of the individual. Why was he or she drawn into the alternative movement? What were the precursors and psychoetiological circumstances that made it a viable expression of what was going on internally? How effective is the resolution of anxieties, angers, or conflict through identification with alternative family living? Why do problems arise?

b. The adjustment of the individual in one of the more-exotic alternative lifestyles often is naively seen by the clinician as a manifestation in itself of problems and maladaptiveness. The mystical pull of a guru seems less understandable than the reliance on a priest or rabbi, even though all are authority figures. This may blind a clinician to searching for the positive, adaptive purposes that "way-out" family groups offer, as well as their conflict-stimulating or pathology-promoting aspects.

Research has shown that many of the most highly authoritative formalized family structures drew their adolescents from addicts and heavy drug and alcohol users and thus served to break seriously debilitating drug dependency problems (Eiduson & Project Staff, 1975). To do this, substitutes in the way of strong guiding and ruling figures were introduced in some cases; in others, peers became useful cohorts and models; in still others, a philosophy was relied upon which provided rules, directions, and self-enhancing beliefs with which to identify.

Alternative lifestyles offer the possibility of living with people one likes and admires, of strong social bonds, of choices among relationships. They can reinstitute a meaning and purpose into everyday life and bring goals and actual experiences into closer contact with each other. They can offer more security, more privacy, and more stimulation and diversity. They can provide protection and affection from diverse sources, as well as direct assistance in managing the complex roles in today's stressful society. It would be simplistic to see the choice of an alternative lifestyle as merely a way of not coping with the relationship problems and conditions found in traditional families; the nontraditional lifestyles offer strengths and assets in themselves that have made them psychologically attractive and able to be seen as viable alternatives to more-common ways of life.

c. Clients who are parents and who live alternatively may tend to view psychotherapy differently for themselves and their children. Studies show that alternative parents utilize traditional doctors and want traditional treatments for their children, even when they seek more alternatively oriented diagnostic treatment modes for themselves (Eiduson, Garvey, & Yale, in preparation). In the case of children about whom they are concerned, the "tried and true" approaches are usually preferred. This makes for some apparent discrepancies in their behaviors: sending a Caucasian child to a school with an East Indian philosophy, while seeking counseling at a clinic known for its traditional, even orthodox psychological views.

This ability to pigeonhole seemingly incongruent behaviors and attitudes provides useful insights into the kind of defense structure that many persons may display who operate on the threshold of change. Since new modes of family and personal living styles remain experimental for long periods of time, there is a reluctance to make a complete commitment to one position at the expense of cutting off another. A good deal of psychological energy is thus expended in maintaining an on-the-fence position, and a defensive structure is fostered which reinforces the desire to avoid complete commitment. This strategy—

plus the desire to manipulate the environment instead of reexamining one's own motivations and styles of relating, and the desire for rapid resolution of conflict rather than careful and often-painful examination of complex issues—makes the alternative client a difficult and seemingly resistive patient. Dropout rate is likely to be high (Phillips, 1982) and treatment failures to be rationalized by the client as failures of another agent and institution in mainstream society.

However, the challenge in treating alternatives lies in their excellent resourcefulness, their genuine suffering, and their *real* commitment to social and institutional change, if their potential can be appropriately liberated and directed. Society has been changed by so many issues to which they as alternatives have spoken: pluralism in family structures, fathers in delivery rooms, sex egalitarian caretaking, ecological priorities, inheritance rights of men, women, and children in nontraditional relationships, alternative schooling, parent involvement in setting educational philosophy, enhanced consumer roles, and revival of self-help endeavors. When such individuals so clearly involved in changing society and leading others can admit their need for help, therapists will find them the most potentially worthwhile and rewarding recipients.

REFERENCES

Alexander, J., & Kornfein, M. Changes in family functioning amongst nonconventional families. *American Journal of Orthopsychiatry,* 1983, *53,* 408–417.

Anthony, E. J. The influence of a manic-depressive environment in the developing child. In E. J. Anthony & T. Benedek (Eds.), *Depression & human existence.* Boston: Little, Brown, 1975.

Anthony, E. J. Theories of change and children at high risk for change. In E. J. Anthony & C. Chiland (Eds.), *The child and his family: Child and parents in a changing world.* New York: John Wiley & Sons, 1978.

Appel, W. *Cults in America—programmed for paradise.* New York: Holt, Rinehart & Winston, 1983.

Berger, B. *Child-rearing practices of the commune family* (Progress report to the National Institute of Mental Health). Bethesda, Md., 1971.

Biller, H. B. The mother-child relationship and the father-absent boy's personality development. *Merrill-Palmer Quarterly,* 1971, *117,* 227–241.

Blanton, J. Communal child rearing: The Synanon experience. *Alternative Lifestyles,* 1980, *3,* 87–116.

Blois, M. S. *Child-rearing attitudes of hippy adults* (Progress report to the National Institute of Mental Health). Bethesda, Md., 1971.

Brudenell, G. Radical community: Contemporary communes and international communities. In E. D. Macklin & R. H. Rubin, *Contemporary families and alternative life styles.* Beverly Hills, Calif.: Sage Publications, 1982.

Burns, C. W., & Brassard, M. R. A look at the single parent family: Implications for the school psychologist. *Psychology in the Schools,* 1982, *19,* 487–494.

Caplan, G., & Killilea, M. (Eds.). *Support systems and mental health.* New York: Grune & Stratton, 1976.

Catlin, N., Croske, J. W., & Keller, J. F. MMPI profiles of cohabiting college students. *Psychological Reports,* 1976, *36,* 407–410.

Cavan, P. Hippies of the redwood forest. Berkeley, Calif., l971 (Mimeographed).

Cicirelli, V. G. Siblings helping siblings. In V. L. Allen (Ed.), *Children as tutors.* New York: Academic Press, 1976.

Clark, J. C. Problems in referral of cult members. *Journal of the National Association of Private Psychiatric Hospitals,* 1978, *9,* 27–29.

Coffins, P. The young unmarrieds. In J. S. Delora & J. R. Delora (Eds.), *Intimate lifestyles: Marriage & its alternatives.* Santa Monica, Calif.: Goodyear Publishing, 1972.

Cohen, J., & Eiduson, B. T. Changing patterns of child-rearing in alternative life-styles. In A. Davids (Ed.), *Child personality and psychopathology: Current topics.* New York: John Wiley & Sons, 1975.

Coles, R. *Privileged ones: The well-off and the rich in America* (Vol. 5, Children of crisis series). Boston: Little, Brown, 1978.

Deutsch, M. *The disadvantaged child.* New York: Basic Books, 1967.

Diamond, S. *What the trees said.* New York: Dell Publishing, 1971.

Dohrenwend, B., & Dohrenwend, B. *Stressful life events: Their nature and effects.* New York: John Wiley & Sons, 1974.

Eiduson, B. T. Child development in emergent family styles: A research update. *Children Today,* 1978, *7,* 24–31. (a)

Eiduson, B. T. Emerging families of the 1970's: Values, practices, and impact on children. In D. Reiss & H. Hoffman (Eds.), *The family: Dying or developing.* New York: Plenum Press, 1978. (b)

Eiduson, B. T. Changing sex roles in alternative family styles: Implications for young children. In E. J. Anthony & C. Chiland (Eds.), *The child in his family: Changing roles of children and parents* (Vol. 6). New York: John Wiley & Sons, 1980. (a)

Eiduson, B. T. Looking at children in emergent family styles. In M. Bloom (Ed.), *Life span development.* New York: Macmillan, 1980. (b)

Eiduson, B. T. Contemporary single mothers as parents. In L. G. Katz (Ed.), *Current topics in early childhood education* (Vol. 3). Norwood, N.J.: Ablex Publishing, 1981. (a)

Eiduson, B. T. Parent-child relationship in alternative family styles. In B. T. Eiduson, *Studies of child development in alternative family styles: The child aged 1–3.* Symposium presented at the meeting of the Society for Research in Child Development, Boston, April 1981. (b)

Eiduson, B. T. *Mother-child dynamics in the alternative single mother family.* Paper presented at the Clinical Seminar on Developmental Problems of Children at the Anna Freud Clinic, London, June 1983.

Eiduson, B. T. Non nuclear families: Vulnerabilities, stresses, & implications for policy. In M. Bloom (Ed.), *Life span development* (2d ed.) New York: Macmillan, 1984.

Eiduson, B. T., & Alexander, J. The role of children in alternative family styles. In N. Feshbach & S. Feshbach (Eds.), The changing status of children: Rights, roles, and responsibilities. *Journal of Social Issues,* 1978, *34,* 149–167.

Eiduson, B. T., Cohen, J., & Alexander, J. Alternatives in child-rearing in the 1970s. *American Journal of Orthopsychiatry,* 1973, *43,* 720–731.

Eiduson, B. T., & Forsythe, A. Comparative study of parent-child stresses in non-traditional and traditional families. In M. Lamb, *Infant social development in nontraditional families.* Symposium presented at the International Conference for Infant Studies, Austin, Tex., 1982.

Eiduson, B. T., Garvey, C. S., & Yale, C. L. *Pediatric use by alternative life styles.* Paper in preparation.

Eiduson, B. T., Kornfein, M., Zimmerman, I. L., & Weisner, T. S. Comparative socialization practices in alternative family settings. In M. Lamb (Ed.), *Nontraditional families.* New York: Plenum Press, 1981.

Eiduson, B. T., & Project Staff. *Drug using parents and their children: Part 1. Anticipatory socialization behaviors* (Report to the National Institute of Drug Use). Los Angeles: UCLA Department of Psychiatry, 1975.

Eiduson, B. T., & Weisner, T. S. Alternative family styles: Effects on young children. In J. Stevens & M. Mathews (Eds.), *Mother/child, father/child relationships.* Washington, D.C.: National Association for the Education of Young Children, 1978.

Eiduson, B. T., Weisner, T. S., & Project Staff. *Child mental health in alternative family styles* (Technical report submitted to the National Institute of Mental Health). October 1980.

Furstenberg, F. F. *Unplanned parenthood: The social consequences of teenage childbearing.* New York: Free Press, 1976.

Gershenson, C. Child development, infant day care, and adolescent parents. *Sharing,* 1972, 8, 1–10.

Glick, P. Future American families. *Washington COFO Memo (Coalition of Family Organizations),* Summer/Fall 1979, *2,* pp. 2–5.

Greenfield, P. M. *What can we learn from cultural variation in child care?* Paper presented at the meeting of the American Association for the Advancement of Science. San Francisco, December 1974.

Gross, C. *The flower people.* New York: William Morrow, 1968.

Havighurst, R. J. History of developmental psychology: Socialization and personality development through the life span. In P. B. Baltes & K. W. Schaie (Eds.), *Life-span developmental psychology—personality and socialization.* New York: Academic Press, 1973.

Herzog, E., & Sudia, C. E. Boys in fatherless families. Washington, D.C.: Office of Child Development, 1970.

Hetherington, E. M., & Morris, W. N. The family and primary groups. In W. H. Holtzman (Ed.), *Introductory psychology in depth: Developmental topics.* New York: Harper & Row, 1978.

Hopkins, R. P. The hospital viewpoint: Mental illness or social maladjustment. *Journal of the National Association of Private Psychiatric Hospitals* 1978, *9,* 19–21.

Judah, J. S. *Hare Krishna and the counter-culture.* New York: John Wiley & Sons, 1974.

Kanter, R. M. *Commitment and community: Utopics and communes in sociotopical perspective.* Cambridge, Mass.: Harvard University Press, 1972.

Kanter, R. M., Jaffe, D., & Weisberg, D. K. Coupling, parenting, and the presence of others: Intimate relationships in communal households. *Family Coordinator,* 1975, *24,* 433–452.

Kaslow, F., & Sussman, M. B. (Eds.). *Cults and the family.* New York: Haworth Press, 1982.

Keniston, K. *Young radicals.* New York: John Wiley & Sons, 1974.

Kinkade, K. A. *Walden Two experiment: The first five years of Twin Oaks Community.* New York: William Morrow, 1972.

Klein, C. *The single parent experience.* New York: Walker, 1973.

Koch, H. G. The relation of certain formal attributes of siblings to attitudes held toward each other and toward their parents. *Monographs of the Society for Research in Child Development,* 1960, *25*(4, Whole No. 78).

Kornfein, M. Infancy in creedal and non-creedal communities. Los Angeles: 1975 (Mimeographed).

Kornfein, M., Weisner, T. S., & Martin, J. Women into mothers: Experimental family life styles. In J. R. Chapman & M. J. Gates (Eds.), *Women into wives* (Sage Annual Review of Women's Policy Studies, Vol. 2). Beverly Hills, Calif.: Sage Publications, 1976.

Lashar, D. *The MMPI: Clinical assessment and automated interpretation.* Los Angeles: Western Psychological Services, 1974.

Macklin, E. D. Heterosexual cohabitation among unmarried college students. *Family Coordinator,* 1972, *21,* 463–467.

Macklin, E. D. Personal communication, 1977.

Macklin, E. D. Non-marital heterosexual cohabitation: An overview. In E. D. Macklin & R. H. Rubin, *Contemporary families and alternative lifestyles.* Beverly Hills, Calif.: Sage Publications, 1983, 49–74.

Masnick, G., & Bane, M. J. *The nation's families 1960–1990.* Cambridge, Mass.: Joint Center for Urban Studies of MIT and Harvard University, 1980.

Mickey, R., & Eiduson, B. T. *The analysis of alternative families over time.* Paper in preparation.

Miniturn, L., & Lambert, W. *Mothers of six cultures.* New York: John Wiley & Sons, 1964.

Mungo, R. *Total Loss Farm.* New York: Bantam Books, 1970.

Ornstein, R. E. *The nature of human consciousness.* San Francisco: W. H. Freeman, 1973.

Phillips, R. A., Jr. Clinical issues in alternative life styles. In E. D. Macklin & R. N. Rubin, *Contemporary families and alternative lifestyles.* Beverly Hills, Calif.: Sage Publications, 1983.

Ramey, J. W. Multi-adult household: Living group of the future? *Futurist,* 1976, *10,* 78–83.

Reissman, F., Cohen, J., & Pearl, A. (Eds.). *Mental health of the poor.* New York: Free Press, 1964.

Robert, R. *The new communes: Coming together in America.* Englewood Cliffs, N. J.: Prentice-Hall, 1971.

Rocheford, E. B. Values of alternative and traditional contemporary families. In J. Alexander (chair), Alternative families of the 1970's. Symposium presented at the meetings of the American Orthopsychiatric Association, San Francisco, April, 1978.

Ross, M. W. Clinical profiles of Hare Krishna devotees. *American Journal of Psychiatry,* 1983, *140,* 416–420.

Roszak, T. *The making of a counterculture.* Garden City, N.Y.: Doubleday Publishing, 1969.

Sawhill, I. Discrimination and poverty among women who lead families. *Signs,* 1976, *1,* 201–211.

Singer, M. T. Personal communication, 1978.

Steiner, S. P., & Maran, M. *Chamisa Road with Paul and Meredith: Doing to dogs in Taos.* New York: Random House, 1971.

Thompson, E. H., & Gongola, P. Single-parent families: In the mainstream of American society. In E. D. Macklin & R. H. Rubin, *Contemporary families and alternative lifestyles.* Beverly Hills, Calif.: Sage Publications, 1982. Pp. 97–124.

Ungerleider, J. T., & Wellish, D. K. Cultism, thought control, and deprogramming: Observations on a phenomena. *Psychiatric Opinion,* 1979, *16,* 10–15.

Wallerstein, J. S., & Kelly, J. B. *Surviving the breakup.* New York: Basic Books, 1980.

Weisner, T. S. As we choose: Family life styles, social class, and compliance. In B. T. Eiduson, *Studies of child development in alternative family styles: The child aged 1–3.* Symposium presented at the annual meeting of the Society for Research in Child Development, Boston, April 1981.

Weisner, T. S. *Fathering in egalitarian American families: Shared support and co-equal management.* Paper presented at the meeting of the American Anthropology Association, Washington, D.C., December 1982.

Weisner, T. S., Bausano, M., & Kornfein, M. Pro-natural families: Attempts to socialize for emotional expressiveness in conventional and non-conventional families. *Ethos,* 1983, *9,* 278–304.

Weisner, T. S., & Martin, J. C. Learning environments for infants: Communes and conventionally married families in California. *Alternative Life Styles,* 1979, *2,* 201–291.

Weisner, T. S., & Project Staff. *Ideology, values and family lifestyles* (Technical report submitted to the National Institute of Mental Health, Applied Research Branch). June 1976.

Weisner, T. S., & Weibel, J. D. Home environment and family lifestyles in California. *Environment & Behavior,* 1981, *13,* 417–460.

West, L. J., & Allen, J. R. Three rebellions: Red, black & green. In J. Masserman (Ed.), *The dynamic of dissent.* New York: Grune & Stratton, 1968.

Zablock, B. D. *Alienation and charisma, a study of contemporary American communes.* New York: Macmillan, 1980.

Zimmerman, I. L. Intellectual competence in three year olds reared in alternative life styles. In B. T. Eiduson, *Studies of child development in alternative family styles: The child aged 1–3.* Symposium presented at the annual meeting of the Society for Research in Child Development, Boston, April 1981.

Zimmerman, I. L., & Bernstein, M. Parental work patterns in alternative families: Influence on child development. *American Journal of Orthopsychiatry,* 1983, *53,* 418–425.

Zimmerman, I. L., & Eiduson, B. T. *Personality patterns of alternatives.* Paper in preparation.

Section Seven

Psychopathology and the Family

Chapter 27

The Family and Sociocultural Factors of Psychopathology

VICTOR D. SANUA

Childrearing practices and their effects on personality development have long been of great interest to psychologists and anthropologists. Various theories have been developed to explain the intricacies of child development, among the better known of which are those of Jean Piaget, Sigmund Freud, Eric Erikson, and several learning theorists. In developing their ideas, these theorists hardly considered the variable of culture. The cultural factors in mental illness have been recognized more frequently in recent times, but not frequently enough. Culture in psychiatric research is either a complication that must be controlled or a prime variable that must be studied. Mixing subjects from different cultural backgrounds, a common research practice, makes no sense and blurs the significance of the research (Murphy, 1969). (For example, Myers and Roberts, 1959, studying the relationship between social class and mental illness, reported the family interactions of mental patients of different nationalities.)

Although the literature on the family in Western society is voluminous, little is known about the relationship between family and society (Bott, 1971). Few attempts have combined anthropological studies of the family with the psychological examination of the personalities of husband and wife. After studying a sample of families in London, Bott concluded that performing family roles depends on the personal needs and preferences of the family members relative to the tasks they must perform, on their immediate social environment, and on the norms they adhere to (p. 23). In a thought-provoking book, Keniston (1977) insisted that blaming the family for all the ills of today's children is a myth because the family cannot be separated from society: The entire social ecology defines and limits what parents can do.

Klineberg (1954) was a pioneer in considering cultural factors when studying personality and in stressing the importance of anthropology to understanding human behavior. The concept reached a milestone with the publication of the six-volume *Handbook of Cross-Cultural Psychology* (Triandis, 1980).

Clausen (1978) reviewed some of the research being performed in the United States on the family's role in socializing children. Families provide children with a matrix for developing within the larger social environment of the neighborhood, whose culture is part of the economic and political systems. Advocates of the transfer of cross-cultural and anthropological knowledge to the clinical domain include Favazza and Faheem (1982), Favazza and Oman (1977), and Kleinman (1980).

INFLUENCE OF THE CULTURAL BACKGROUND ON NORMAL PERSONALITY DEVELOPMENT

A group of psychologists, in collaboration with anthropologists, have for many years conducted a series of studies to assess how children are socialized in different cultures. Whiting and Child (1953) divided the socialization process into two parts: the period of indulgence and the period of socialization. Socialization may be gradual, abrupt, or gentle, and it may involve punishment and reward. They distinguished two kinds of reactions that might hamper a smooth growing-up process: positive fixation, which occurs when a childish habit, given up with some difficulty, still affords considerable pleasure; and negative fixation, which occurs when a child has difficulty making a transition (e.g., harsh weaning may result in anxiety associated with eating).

In 1975, Whiting and Whiting published the summary findings of their research on socialization in six cultures and the effects that the cultures had on the children's personalities. Children brought up in complex cultures tended to be more dependent-dominant and less nurturant-responsible than were children brought up in simple cultures. Children brought up in cultures in which the ideal composition of the household was nuclear were more social-intimate and less authoritarian-aggressive than were children brought up in cultures in which the ideal composition of the household was not nuclear.

The cultures of middle-class Europeans and Americans probably exert more severe pressure upon the young child than does any other culture in the world (Whiting & Child, 1953). An analysis of 47 primitive societies showed that America's middle class practices rather severe or extreme socialization. According to Montagu (1962), Western children are being trained in anomic values that lead them to become disorganized and confused individuals. In the same vein, Montagu (1961) suggested that nations can be categorized as neurotic, even psychotic.

EARLY FAMILY EXPERIENCES AND
PSYCHOLOGICAL DISTURBANCE

The rapid changes that have occured in the past few decades in the American family must affect the socialization of children. Feiring and Lewis (n.d.) listed an inventory of these changing factors: changes in parent-child interactions and the quality of them; decreased size of the average American family; increased number of single-parent families; increased geographical mobility, which cuts off close family ties; and increased number of working mothers. An attempt has been made to document the consequences of such changes, particularly the consequences to mothers and the possible deleterious effects on neonates and children (Sanua, 1981b). A recent book (Rutter, 1980) discussed how a changing society has altered the patterns of adolescent development and disorders.

There are two schools of thought on modern-day psychological maladjustment. One school (primarily psychoanalytical) believes that early experience and trauma are central in later-developing disturbances in a child and that maladaptation thus tends to be intrapsychic. The other school (primarily made up of learning theorists) believes that interpersonal problems should be examined in the present rather than as the result of growing-up difficulties. The two may not be mutually exclusive. Early traumas may make current difficulties loom larger. On the other hand, children who have some early difficulties may, because of favorable conditions, never have their vulnerabilities tested. Children at risk thus may not necessarily develop psychological problems. Rutter (1974), reassessing the effects of maternal deprivation on children, accepted as proven the idea that "bad" care of children produces bad effects (p. 128). In a review of the literature, however, Clarke and Clarke (1976) concluded that early learning is far from irreversible.

Whichever theory is used to explain child development, the process is mediated through the family; and mental health, or mental illness, is related to how family members interact. Training children to fulfill cultural norms is related to parent-child relationships, which profoundly influence the personality development of the child but which are, in turn, greatly influenced by the family's class and cultural norms. Sociocultural forces may be considered the forces that shape the individual through the family. Cultural demands may be so harsh that they inflict personal conflicts that result in "maladjustment." Sociocultural influences may also affect the symptoms of maladjusted behavior (Al-Issa, 1970, 1977)—for example, the various exotic psychoses (amok, latak, koro). By the same token, the environment may include variables, such as the availability of family support and network (Caplan & Killilea, 1976), that definitely aid the maladjusted person's recovery.

GENERAL REVIEW OF RESEARCH ON THE FAMILY'S CONTRIBUTION TO MENTAL ILLNESS

Of the studies indicating that cultural norms influence parent-child interaction, most of those included here are recent, and most are on schizophrenia, which has been frequently studied.

Interestingly, Freud (1920) was sensitive to the effects of social factors on the development of pathology, although he used them very little in developing his theories. The following hypothetical example illustrates the different consequences that early sexual experience may have on two young girls of different socioeconomic status—the daughter of a rich man and the daughter of a caretaker:

> The differences, which ensue in these two destinies in spite of the common experience undergone, arise because in one girl the ego has sustained a development absent in the other. To the caretaker's daughter sexual activity seemed as natural and harmless in later years as in childhood. The gentleman's daughter had been "well-brought-up" and had adopted the standards of her education. Thus stimulated, her ego had formed ideals of womanly purity and absence of desire that were incompatible with sexual acts; her intellectual training had caused her to depreciate the feminine role for which she is intended. This higher moral and intellectual development in her ego has brought her into conflict with the claims of her sexuality. (p. 309)

Many of the reviews of studies of the family and the family's contribution to mental illness have criticized the research methodologies.

Antecedent influences

Heilbrun (1973), Hingtgen and Bryson (1972), Howells (1971), and Roff (1972) deal with antecedent influences. The study of the specific impact of family forces on mental illness has had its critics. Frank (1965), analyzing 148 studies on the family's role in the development of psychopathology, found no unique factors in the families of schizophrenics to distinguish them from the families of neurotics or from the families of controls who had no gross pathology. Frank depicted schizophrenics as having dominant mothers and passive fathers. The mothers are overprotective, overpossessive, and overcontrolling, but unconsciously reject their children. These mothers frown on sex, are inconsistent in their methods of discipline, and introduce unrealistic modes of thinking, feeling, and behaving. Because these characteristics can be found also in the parents of neurotics, even of normals, Frank considered the findings of only limited use. He urged that human behavior, because of its complexity, not be wrenched out of the context in which it occurs. For example, a child reacts differently to strict discipline, depending on whether the child is in a "warm" or a "cold" atmosphere. Moreover, the personality of the father can compensate for the effects of the rejecting mother.

Frank (1965) appeared surprised by Gerard and Siegel's results (1950), which seem to differ markedly from those of other studies. The schizophrenic subjects apparently were adequately breast-fed, did not come from broken homes, and as far as could be ascertained, were not unduly rejected or punished. Gerard and Siegel's different findings could be attributed to the fact that 70 percent of the parents of the schizophrenics were Jewish or Italian; the family interactions may thus have been quite different from those in the other studies that Frank reviewed. Frank rejected the findings of the studies he reviewed and quoted Freud's statement, made in 1920, that no one knows why some people are affected by anxiety while others are not. Frank closed with the discouraging remark that, after 40 years of research, no one was any closer to an answer than Freud had been.

Family interactions

Studies of family interaction were initiated by Bateson, Jackson, Haley, and Weakland (1956) and include, in addition to the publications cited in this section, works and reviews by Doane (1978), Garmezy (1974a, 1974b), Leff (1976), and Olson (1972).

Wynne, Toohey, and Doane (1980) reviewed the clinical and experimental research in family relationships. Wynne has used projective techniques to study extensively the communication between parents of schizophrenics and their children (Singer, Wynne, & Toohey, 1978); the basic hypothesis (Wynne & Singer, 1963) is that abnormal communications may induce in the listener difficulties in handling the meaning of communications (see Chapter 30). Disruptions, lack of closure, irrelevance, and vagueness characterize the speech of parents whose children are predisposed to schizophrenia. Hirsch and Leff (1975) tried to replicate the study in England, but failed to find the same degree of gross communication disorder in all parents of schizophrenics. The two groups of researchers have argued about how to explain the discrepancy between the two apparently similar studies. The difference seems to be that the studies used different populations: The subjects that Wynne and his associates studied were schizophrenics who tended to chronicity; Hirsch and Leff's patients seemed to be transient schizophrenics. The question still remains whether in different cultures as closely related as those of England and the United States, culture can be a significant factor in studies conducted in societies that differ far more.

Goldstein and Rodnick (1975), in reviewing the literature on the family's contribution to the etiology of schizophrenia, indicated a relationship between disordered family relationships and schizophrenia. Like Frank, however, they did not consider such family patterns unique to schizophrenia. Most family studies have been conducted with small groups and fairly nonrepresentative samples. Goldstein and Rodnick noted that Arieti (1974) found psychopathological families that did not conform to the descriptions by Lidz, Fleck, and Cornelison (1965) and by Wynne and Singer (1963), whose subjects were from middle- and upper-class families. Goldstein and Rodnick suggested the need for large-scale epidemiological studies on the incidence of disordered family relationships.

Only two of the reviews discussed culture. Jacob (1975) quite forcefully showed the deficiencies in comparative studies in which age and socioeconomic status had not been controlled. The different degrees of intrafamily conflict and parental dominance make a comparison of such studies very difficult. Riskin and Faunce (1972) devoted only nine lines to the topic in a 90-page article. Culture as manifested in the interaction of the family should be considered an important variable, one that may affect investigators' findings and lead to contradictory results (Sanua, 1982a).

Heilbrun (1973) did not consider communication an etiologic factor in schizophrenia:

> It is most difficult to generate enthusiasm over the importance of maternal communication as an etiologic factor in schizophrenia based on this survey of relevant research. The impressive amount of work that went into the small-sample study (32 schizophrenic families and 17 normal families) of Mishler and Waxler (1968) makes it clear why better communication research is out of reach, except for those who have substantial research funding. While there may be technical barriers to human communication in research, the paucity of positive findings relevant to mother- or parent-schizophrenic child interactions certainly make this the sector of maternal behavior in which we can invest the least confidence as a source of influence in schizophrenic development. (p. 25)

During the past decade, a number of publications have appeared on the social system theory, which is an eclectic strategy for viewing an entire organization in relation to the environment. This strategy has certainly found application in psychopathology, which views the social system of the patient, the family, and outside forces as influences to be considered to effect change.

Clinicians must recognize deficiencies in family functioning, not only after a severe disturbance has emerged but early enough to take preventive measures, thus promoting a healthful family life (Fleck, 1980). Beels (1978), in the introduction to a number of papers on social networks, the family, and schizophrenic patients (Cohen & Sokolovsky,

1978; Garrison, 1978; Hammer, Makiesky-Barrow & Gutwirth, 1978), reflected on the possibility that a patient has a better chance for maintenance without relapse when flexibility and understanding characterize the relationships connecting family, friends, fellow workers, and clinic. Howells' (1979) concept of family psychiatry is to accept the family rather than an individual as the patient. Using the child as the introduction to the family, the therapist can involve the family as the patient.

Steger and Kotler (1979) reviewed the literature on the relationship between child psychopathology and the quality of family interaction. Applying the systems framework to a number of empirical studies, they found that premarital interpersonal conflict in the lives of parents may affect their psychological development. These early problems are amplified by marital conflicts and affect other family members. The authors suggested that nonfamily interactions can offer compensating support.

Sociocultural backgrounds

Dealing specifically with the sociocultural backgrounds of patients (the subject of fewer studies) are studies and reviews on the family (Sanua, 1961), migration (Sanua, 1970), and the antecedents of mental illness (Sanua, 1980) and the publications of Giordano and Giordano (1977), Murphy (1969, 1978), and Murphy and Leighton (1965).

Differences in findings about the family backgrounds of schizophrenics can be attributed to lack of control on the patients' cultural backgrounds:

> Research in this area can become effective only if a genuine, concerted, interdisciplinary effort is directed toward its solution. I suggest that an international research organization be established to coordinate research. The goals are to tackle the problems of mental health and illness on an international level . . . with intensive clinical studies. (Sanua, 1961, p. 265)

Specific suggestions for such research have been published (Sanua, 1983b). The review was updated and extended to the gamut of schizophrenic conditions (Sanua, 1969), and other reviews have explored infantile autism and childhood schizophrenia (Sanua, 1981a, 1981b, 1983a). Schizophrenics of different religious and ethnic backgrounds— Protestants, Italians, Irish, and Jews—have been the subject of a series of studies (Sanua, 1963).

The difficulties in conducting large-scale family research were recently emphasized as follows:

> Progress in the family studies area is painfully slow. . . . It appears that the special problems encountered by family researchers, . . . com-

pounded by the methodologic difficulties common to all studies of schizophrenia (e.g., sample selection, types of measures used), have held back
the accretion of reliable, replicable result. . . . Yet the impact of one
critically important part of the environment, the family, remains extraordinarily difficult to define, measure precisely, and relate to the development of schizophrenia. (Keith, Gunderson, Reifman, Bucksbaum, &
Mosher, 1976, p. 540)

Because of the difficulties in studying cause-and-effect relationships,
the trend in recent family studies has been toward longitudinal research, or the study of children who are at high risk for mental illness
(to be discussed later).

Nature versus nurture

Two schools of thought about whether culture contributes to psychopathology compose the nature versus nurture controversy. Some investigators discount cultural influences completely, particularly in more-
serious psychopathology such as psychosis. Berne (1960) considered
mental illness essentially independent of culture and believed that
the "reservoir of endogenous psychoses" (true prevalence) maintains
a constant ratio, regardless of racial, cultural, geographic, or socioeconomic conditions (p. 46), implying that all mental illness is organically
determined. Kline (1979) also seemed convinced that social factors
do not influence the incidence of schizophrenia: "Throughout the rest
of the world, . . . the incidence of schizophrenia appears to be just
the same as it is in the Western world. Poverty, oppression and minority
status are not of themselves a cause of schizophrenia" (p. 5). According
to Kline, much evidence has been accumulated to indicate that schizophrenia is related to a disturbance in brain chemistry and that the
neurotransmitter dopamine is implicated. The evidence does not, however, conclusively support this point of view.

Opler (1969) wrote of the prevalence of schizophrenia: "Those who
claim that schizophrenias (of modern type) are biogenic in origin and
therefore distributed randomly in population are simply ignorant of
the anthropological data. Variations in the form and epidemiology of
mental illness occur transculturally" (p. 102).

Bleuler (1978) pointed out that physicians assume the presence of
physical dysfunctions when physical symptoms are present and that
the medical profession is reluctant to state authoritatively that some
physical dysfunction lies concealed behind a symptom if the physical
dysfunction and the symptom cannot be related as cause and effect.
Referring specifically to schizophrenia, he wrote:

> Through the present day, many clinicians and researchers are fully convinced that primary physical disorders (functional or structural) constitute the most essential onset conditions for schizophrenia, although they are unable to identify any clear symptoms indicating such supposed physical disorders. At certain times, researchers were even in danger of being reproached for having an unscientific, uncritical mentality, of being insulted and ostracized if they did not conform by "admitting" that there were physical explanations for schizophrenia. (p. 477)

Surveying the literature on the biochemical studies of patients with autism, childhood schizophrenia, and related developmental disabilities, Ritvo (1977) concluded that *"these studies have raised more questions* [italics added] than they have answered—a sure sign that our science is young" (p. 378).

A transnational survey (Sanua, 1983c) showed that in the United States 61 percent of psychiatrists, 78 percent of psychologists, and 70 percent of social workers considered organic factors highly important in the etiology of infantile autism; most of the other respondents considered organic factors somewhat important. In Europe, professionals were less inclined to implicate organic factors: psychiatrists—22 percent; psychologists—36 percent; and social workers—29 percent. Interestingly, the differences among the disciplines on each of the two sides of the Atlantic are negligible, which indicates (as pointed out by Bleuler, 1978) that belief in organicity tends to be more an ideology than a belief based on scientific facts.

Kernberg (1979) illustrated further the problem of trying to determine the etiology of childhood psychoses in general:

> None of the biological parameters studied to date (biogenic amines, pink spot or mauve factor in the urine, bufotenine, histamine, serum factors, chromosomal abnormalities, endocrinological changes, or other metabolic factors) have been proven to be causally related to the etiology of childhood psychosis. (p. 513)

Some efforts have been made to include both mind and body in assessing pathology. Reiss (1976), who has primarily studied abnormalities of family interaction, particularly communication deviances, has suggested that the study of normal and abnormal perceptual development might be a meeting ground for researchers in the biological and the familial theories of schizophrenia. Another attempt to combine nature and nurture (Wynne, Singer, & Toohey, 1976) brought together for the first time two separate research approaches to schizophrenia: the study of the adoptive parents of schizophrenics and the study of deviant parental communication. The authors believed, with some reservations, that their study added support for both genetic and psychosocial hypotheses.

STUDIES RELATING MENTAL ILLNESS TO FAMILY PROBLEMS, WITH PARTICULAR REFERENCE TO CULTURAL FACTORS

Social psychiatrists consider both social class and culture to be important variables that may be related to the incidence of mental illness. More attention, however, has been paid to social class than to culture, as can be seen in the large-scale epidemiological investigations of the Midtown Manhattan study (Srole, Langner, Michael, Opler, & Rennie, 1962) and the New Haven study (Hollingshead & Redlich, 1958). This section emphasizes the studies that have concentrated on culture.

It is very difficult to separate cultural forces from the family's enforcement of those forces on children, and parents may differ in how strictly they enforce cultural demands. A family seems to select—according to family politics and the history of personal relationships within the family network—from a large number of potential signs of pathology (Hollenbach, 1978). Thus, neither the traditional medical assumption (mental illness is purely within the individual, a biological or a psychological matter) nor the sociological assumption (social factors are primary) should be adopted. The relative importance of individual, biological, and social factors must be studied in each case.

Cultural background and attitudes toward mental illness or psychotherapy

In a study of attitudes about seeking professional psychological help, Fischer and Cohen (1972) noted that earlier studies that had tried to relate psychological mindedness and obtaining aid for personal problems to social class had neglected the ethnic aspect. In their own study with college students, social class was less a factor than was religion (e.g., Jews at every socioeconomic level presented the most-positive attitude about seeking psychiatric help).

Perhaps, then, the prevalence of mental illness (both inpatient and outpatient) may be affected by a person's readiness to seek professional help, which is in turn influenced by ethnocultural background. This readiness was tested in the Midtown Manhattan study (Srole et al., 1962), which posed psychiatric problems in a hypothetical family and asked what action would be most appropriate. Jewish respondents (49.2 percent) were much more inclined to suggest psychiatric consultation as a solution, compared with Catholics (23.8 percent) and Protestants (31.4 percent) (p. 317). Readiness to seek professional help thus inflates the rates of outpatient treatment for Jews when they are compared with non-Jews. In the Midtown Manhattan study, the ratio was 4 to

1. Lower rates of serious impairment among Jews may be attributed to their early attempts to do something about their problems. There may, however, be another reason for the lower impairment rate: The cultural atmosphere—"historically realistic anxiety"—of a Jewish family "may function prophylactically to immunize its children against the potentially disabling sequelae of the more severe pressures and traumas of existence" (p. 306).

Andrulis (1974) sought the paths by which clients of different ethnic affiliations moved through a comprehensive mental health center. Young Mexican-Americans were most frequently referred by nonmedical professionals; young Anglo patients tended to be referred by their families. Diagnoses of the Mexican-American group typically included transient situational disorders, and many were diagnosed as mentally retarded. The diagnoses of the Anglo patients tended to be deferred, pending the collection of additional information. Mexican-American families were less inclined to refer their children for psychiatric help and withdrew them from treatment sooner.

In a comparison of Jewish and Irish attitudes about mental illness, significantly more Irish than Jewish families tolerated deviant thinking in a psychotic relative; significantly more Jewish than Irish families tolerated deviant verbal emotionality. Jewish families tend to overemphasize intellect, correct thought, and communication (Wylan & Mintz, 1976). In a study (Sanua, 1960) that compared Jewish and non-Jewish patients who had lost a limb, the Jewish patients were more likely than non-Jewish patients to cry and express deep mourning at the loss. In an Italian-Polish neighborhood in Baltimore, the extended family was considered the front-line resource for initial advice about emotional problems; priests and psychiatrists were rarely mentioned (Fandetti & Gelfand, 1978). In general, the culturally reflective attitudes toward mental illness that encourage help-seeking may have a significant impact by decreasing the incidence and prevalence of mental illness.

The need for therapists to understand and differentiate the cross-cultural, transcultural, and idiosyncratic uses of symbols as well as the patient's expressed and felt emotions has been elaborated in a number of examples (Tatara, 1980). Special problems arise in conducting psychotherapy when the patient and the therapist belong to different cultures (for example, conducting psychotherapy in the Arab world, where verbal interaction between therapist and patient is fruitless) (Sanua, 1979). Just as family therapy emerged from the intrapsychic view, the behavior of an individual cannot be understood in isolation from the family, and the behavior of the family makes sense only in the larger context of culture (McGoldrick, Pearce, & Giordano, 1982).

Generational conflicts

Papajohn and Spiegel (1975), using the transactional theoretical model to compare a psychotic group with a nonpsychotic group, analyzed the stresses felt by Greek families in the United States. In the sample of families with patients, the generations showed a high degree of discord on the question of cultural values: The children had moved toward American values; their immigrant parents had not.

Wolfenstein (1955) compared the attitudes and mother-child interactions of Jewish mothers born in Russia or Poland with those of native American Jewish mothers. The Eastern European mothers saw the children at all ages as extremely vulnerable and incapable of taking care of themselves. At the same time, the child appeared to be showing independence and to be capable of "killing the mother." The Eastern European was depicted as a suffering mother who derived emotional gratification in a narcissistic way. The American Jewish mothers did not see their children as fragile but as independent beings whom they should stop babying as quickly as possible and who should proceed to acquire skills.

Segal and Yahraes (1978) strongly defended the images of Jewish mothers as celebrated by comedians and writers:

> The Jewish mother surely produced a few ripe candidates for therapy, but she did not nurture a cohort of angry criminals or flat, schizoid personalities, empty shells incapable of recognizing or giving love. Whatever tendencies Jewish mothers and fathers have to be "super-protective" and whatever they may do in creating unusual anxieties in their children, . . . Fraiberg says, "There are worse diseases of moral conflict, which are after all curable. In contrast, there is nothing one can do to overcome the disease of non-attachment created when there is no bond to begin with."
>
> Moreover, as Fraiberg reminds us, "neurotic" reactions to the overprotective mother can often lead to some very successful adaptations. Among the products of her commitment and caring are not only the couch-riding Portnoys but the Leonard Bernsteins and John F. Kennedys of the world. She has produced the builders and leaders of civilization, not the assassins and destroyers. (p. 103)

In a study of Puerto Rican families in New York slums, the parents saw their personal relationships and values being replaced by a threatening system of interpersonal relationships and norms (Murillo-Rhode, 1976). As the children assimilate American values, they challenge parental values and judgments. In rebellion against parental authority, they reject the ways of their parents. But a price must be paid for this acculturation. In a study of lower-class psychiatric outpatients at Bellevue, an inverse relationships was found between adherence to Latin American family beliefs and the development of psychopathology

(Fernandez-Pol, 1980). When Latin American parents in the United States are willing to accept dominant values, however, conflicts tend to be reduced.

Hoppe and Leon (1977) characterized the behavioral styles of Mexican-American families as adaptive or nonadaptive and labeled two groups "copers" and "noncopers." Children of coping families were allowed to form separate identities in spite of strong feelings of family identity. These parents provided affection and expressed interest in their children. The noncoping parents, in general, displayed little warmth to their children and tended to be disorganized. The mothers in the noncoping families had grown up in deprived families; the lack of a nurturant environment and stimulating relationships with their own mothers probably prevented them from being flexible.

Problems between parents and offspring are, of course, not limited to the foreign-born or to ethnic groups in the United States. Schwartzman (1973) studied the problems caused by parental rigidity in 40 families whose members were outpatients at a mental health clinic and who suffered from many symptoms. The parents did not permit psychological distance between their children and themselves, despite the children's increasing competence. The family must be able to fit changing needs into a changing society. The family, by adapting, prepares the child to deal with change. In an evolving society of the Old or the New World, when families maintain old traditions, strife between the generations may be bound to result in personality problems. On the other hand, conflicts may be lessened in societies that tend to be static and that are not exposed to change; as a result, the incidence of mental illness may be lower.

Studies of familial and societal influences on children

The following studies illustrate the influence of the family's cultural background on the development of mental illness. Destructive forces within family dynamics are influenced by cultural values, but family attitude or structure also mediates the negative impact of societal pressures.

Most researchers who have studied mental illness in blacks have found that the rate of mental illness tends to be higher for blacks than for any other group. A combination of economic deprivation and prejudice undoubtedly affects the mental health of blacks. A comprehensive analysis of the characteristics of mental patients in the United States showed that 18.7 percent of the patients in mental institutions were nonwhite, compared with 11 percent of nonwhites in the total population (Ozarin & Taube, 1974). Many reasons—from genetics to economic deprivation—have been given for this overrepresentation in the hospital population. Blacks have suffered from less education, more unemployment, and, in general, more socially disorganized communities.

After the Midtown Manhattan study, which concentrated on an older group (19–59 years of age), Langner, Gersten, and Eisenberg (1974) compared the stresses incurred by white, black, and Puerto Rican children. Parents of more than 1,000 children were interviewed; the mental health ratings of the children were provided by psychiatrists. Among the many stressors, two important ones pertained to the family: marital discord and rejecting parental attitudes. Black and Puerto Rican children, compared with whites, experienced the highest number of such stressors. White children were more likely to be involved in extra-familial conflicts and antisocial behavior. Puerto Rican children displayed more organic-developmental problems associated with illness and social factors. In general, social class was less important than ethnicity in predicting childhood psychopathology.

A study of black schizophrenics revealed that the black patient has usually suffered from two sources of family-mediated conflict (Brody, 1967). The black mother explicitly urges her son to achieve any possible goal, whether or not the world is controlled by whites; on the other hand, she communicates to him that he cannot achieve anything because he is black (on a sociocultural level, similar to the double-bind communication of Bateson et al., 1956). The second source of conflict is the boy's desire to identify himself with black people as opposed to the unexpressed wish of his parents to abandon the devalued identity associated with the black man in a white society. Brody found that the disturbed black tended to be more hostile toward whites than did the normal black. In a comparison of disturbed adolescents—whites, blacks, and Puerto Ricans—the data suggested that black adolescents suffer more from family instability (White, 1978).

Influencing the welfare of children in general is the social class of the families who are raising them. Families who live in poverty are more vulnerable to disease, have lower prestige, and experience pervasive daily stresses that negatively influence the children (Hess, 1970); child abuse has become a national problem (see Chapter 29 of this volume). Poverty virtually ensures inadequate health care, which has noxious effects on normal development (Keniston, 1975). The social context of poverty and/or minority status creates doubts in the parents about their ability to be successful parents (David & Baldwin, 1979). An increased family income that comes when both parents work full-time without improving their education or without the community's social acceptance may not be enough to diminish rates of impairment among black children, possibly among Puerto Rican children as well (Langner, Herson, Greene, Jameson, & Goff, 1970). Although a negative relationship exists between whites' social class and their distress levels, the black middle class seems to experience more-intense stress than do blacks of higher and lower status (Derogatis, Covi, Lipman, Davis, & Rickels, 1971). Bronfenbrenner (1974) wrote about the changes in the American family that seem to be depleting family resources for the child. Two thirds of the parents seen at an outpatient clinic were moderately to severely disturbed, a proportion that must be seriously considered in possible long-term measures of prevention (Naylor, 1980).

In a study of depressed women in England, a higher level of depression was related to four specific social factors: an intimate, confiding relationship with a male; the number of children (younger than 14 years) living at home; loss of the mother before the depressed subject reached age 11; and whether or not the subject was employed before she became depressed (Harris, 1978). In Europe, the following countries have the highest number of psychiatric beds per 10,000 inhabitants: Finland, 52.3; Ireland, 49.1, Scotland, 48.9. In comparison, the number of beds is 31.9 in England and 14.2 in the United States (1976). Scheper-Hughes (1977) examined with great thoroughness a village in Ireland and administered the Thematic Apperception Test to a sample of inhabitants. She found a pattern of minimal handling and isolation of infants and an absence of maternal attachment behavior. A combination of the demands of rural Irish living, celibacy, social isolation, and relative economic deprivation leads to maladjustment, which probably affects Ireland's rate of hospitalization for mental illness.

A large-scale epidemiological comparison of the psychological adjustment of 10-year-olds and their mothers in the Inner London Borough and on the Isle of Wight revealed twice as many psychiatric disorders in the children in the big city as on the Isle of Wight (Rutter, 1977; Rutter, Tizard, Yule, Graham, & Whitmore, 1976). In both locations, mothers suffered from neurosis and depression, and criminal behavior was characteristic of the fathers. (The authors ensured that neither drift nor outmigration factors could be responsible for the results.) To compare the two areas, Rutter devised an index of family adversity which included family discord and disruption, parental illness, and social disadvantages. Family adversity was three times as high in London as on the Isle of Wight; when families were equated in the frequency of adversity, differences in psychiatric disorders disappeared. City life by itself thus had little direct adverse effect on the children; whatever effect city life did have was mediated through the family.

The remaining question was why families in the city had more marital discord than did families on the Isle of Wight. Depression in mothers on the Isle of Wight was associated with disturbed interpersonal relationships but not with social status; the depression of mothers in London was strongly associated with low social status, as measured by husbands' occupations. Rutter (1977) concluded that sufficient evidence indicates that patterns of family life, as shaped and modified by sociocultural mores and by social circumstances, should be part of the evaluation of children if a patient's difficulties are to be accurately assessed and treatment is to be appropriate (p. 129).

Family and community support and mental illness

Family influences, through the support of the family network, can sometimes reduce or even eliminate the negative effects of mental illness. The Italian schizophrenic's tendency to remain in contact with one member of the family seems to prevent chronicity: Strong family ties buffer the stresses of social isolation and economic deprivation, perhaps thus altering the course of schizophrenia (Parsons, 1960). Apparently, then, secluding patients in mental hospitals tends to lead to deterioration. Leighton, Hardin, Macklin, Macmillan, and Leighton (1963) showed that lack of social integration and lack of affectionate ties were more important as causes of psychological problems than was low social status or poor physical condition. Isolated families, even those who are financially secure, tend to have more problems. The Italian family's closeness and in-group feeling can counterbalance the consequences of poverty: More mental illness occurred among the wealthier Italians who moved out of their old neighborhood than among those who remained (Mintz & Schwartz, 1964). Rehousing may be disruptive, breaking up neighborhood friendships, altering patterns of social interaction, and lessening contact with kin (Fried, 1965); rehousing with special attention to these factors, however, may benefit mental health (Wilner, Wakeley, Pinkerton, & Tayback, 1962).

Kim and Rhi (1976) discussed the emotional ties between patient and family that are so strong that the family rejects the diagnosis and interferes with psychiatric treatment. On the other hand, this attitude is also positive: first, giving tolerance and emotional support to the patient and, second, reducing occupational and social demands on the patient, making easier the patient's reintegration with the community during rehabilitation. Waxler (1979) found that schizophrenic patients in Sri Lanka, compared with schizophrenics in the West, seemed to do very well from the prognostic point of view. In modern societies, expectations about psychiatric problems and the therapeutic system alienate schizophrenics from their normal roles, thus prolonging illness. On the other hand, beliefs and practices in traditional societies encourage short-term illness. Possibly, then, cultural differences in prognoses may engender different self-fulfilling prophecies.

In Africa, parents may take care of the patients in special villages while they are under doctor's care (Lambo, 1970). This practice would certainly reduce the isolation that patients in the United States suffer after being committed to a mental institution. A comparison of the discharge problems of mental patients in Missouri and in Turkey showed that many families in Missouri were reluctant to take patients home from the hospital, and when they did, adjustment problems caused readmissions. By contrast, doctors in Turkey had problems keeping patients in hospital. At the slightest improvement, families wanted their patients to return home (Klein, Person, Cetingok, & Itil, 1978).

Support may involve the community, in addition to the immediate family. For example, the cohesiveness of the kibbutz civilian population successfuly reduced the severity of stress reactions and lowered the incidence of psychiatric casualties among children and adult members of the kibbutzim (Kaffman, 1977). A number of Israeli families were interviewed after the Yom Kippur and the Vietnam wars about their efforts to cope with the deaths of their sons (Sanua, 1982b). Many of the bereaved parents sought out other parents whose sons had fallen on the same battlefield as their own sons, thus establishing new relationships. The parents, who got together socially, found that talking about their sons provided some solace for their tragedy.

In a comparison of Anglo-American and Mexican-American families, the Mexican-Americans were more distressed when the extended family's informal support was absent or malfunctioned (Keefe, Padilla, & Carlos, 1979). Teja (1978) argued that the American cultural emphasis on role adequacy is reflected in a much-higher incidence of adjustment reactions and personality disorders among American than among Indian patients.

Dunkas and Nikelly (1972) studied the Persephone syndrome (named for the Greek goddess who, having been abducted to the Underworld, was permitted to return for only four months of each year, her return marking the beginning of spring) in 60 Greek women who separated from their parents and married in the United States. The researchers hypothesized that the typical cohesiveness of the Greek family encourages mother-daughter loyalty; when daughters are separated from their mothers through marriage in the United States, the stress resulting from the abandonment of the mother may bring about depression. Thus, according to Dunkas and Nikelly, the mother-daughter attachment, although perhaps not recognized as a problem in the country of origin, becomes a problem upon exposure to a different culture.

After studying the treatment practices of the Yoruba in Africa, Edgerton (1980) urged the study of social and cultural phenomena to help in understanding the reasons for the rate of recovery of schizophrenics in nonindustrialized countries. In a study of 142 adults in England, a strong inverse relationship between "social bonds" and neurotic symptoms was found (Henderson, Byrne, Duncan-Jones, Adcock, Scott, & Steele, 1978). The relationship was strongest when the affectional ties were close. The findings suggest that the prevalence of minor psychiatric disorders is associated with deficiencies in social relationships, an association that strongly supports the view that neurosis is principally a social illness.

Important cross-cultural research that may shed some light on the family influence on schizophrenia is the international pilot study on schizophrenia (WHO, 1973, 1979), which was conducted in nine countries. As expected, a core group in each country was found to have similar characteristics of the schizophrenic disorder. An unexpected result from a five-year follow-up, however, was that patients from different countries had not followed the same pathways in their recoveries: Schizophrenic patients in the Western countries followed the traditional expectation that they would display residual schizophrenic qualities; non-Western patients appeared to recover completely and five years later, no longer appeared schizophrenic (Cooper & Sartorius, 1977; Sartorius, Jablonsky, & Shapiro, 1978). Further evidence of a good prognosis for schizophrenia is the report by Lo and Lo (1977), who conducted a 10-year follow-up of Chinese schizophrenics in Hong Kong: 65 percent had a full and lasting remission; females had an even better rate of recovery.

STUDIES OF HIGH RISK

In the early 60s, a different type of study—labeled "high risk"—was initiated, probably because the results from retrospective studies and studies in communication had been discouraging. High-risk studies are carried out on populations that have higher than normal risk of developing schizophrenia (Garmezy, 1975; Grunebaum, Weiss, Gallant, & Cohler, 1974; Roff, 1976). Garmezy (1974a, 1974b, 1978) has written an extensive evaluation and critique of this kind of research.

The classic effort in the study of populations at high risk was that by Mednick (1978) and Schulsinger (1976, 1980), who followed 207 children of schizophrenic mothers and compared their autonomic instability with that of 104 children of normal parents in Denmark. An early evaluation disclosed that the disturbed offspring of schizophrenics, compared with offspring who showed no deviances, had had significantly longer periods of separation from their mothers during early development, had suffered more birth complications related to deviant psychophysiological reactions, and had had more problems in school. The picture then, is quite complex, and the sequence of the factors and the importance of each are difficult to disentangle. Mednick addressed the fact that other researchers had failed to replicate his findings. Many factors, such as the severity of parental illness, intactness of the family, ages of the subjects, and personality of the nonschizophrenic parent, must be considered. For example, Mednick found that a high proportion of schizophrenic mothers had married men who had criminal tendencies.

A study by Erlenmeyer-Kimling and Cornblatt (1978) did not find important psychophysiological differences between the high-risk and the low-risk groups. Mednick (1978) most appropriately noted that intactness of the family in Copenhagen in 1962 might not have been the same thing as intactness of the family in New York in 1972. He added that the patterns of psychiatric treatment might have changed in 10 years. What seems most important is Mednick's statement (p. 450) that there might be "cultural differences" between the two countries, certainly an interesting observation but one that has played no part in any of the studies reviewed.

A sample of 138 grade school–age children from 46 families in which a parent was psychotic was evaluated on four clinically derived variables: logical thinking, reality testing, identity, and organizational competence (Anthony, 1974). Anthony showed that the measure could distinguish these children from a matched group of children whose parents were normal. Four intervention approaches were used: a compensatory program, individual and group therapy, a cathartic program emphasizing family interviews during the psychotic illness, and a corrective program of reality-testing sessions. Although there are some indications that vulnerability was lessened, only very tentative conclusions can be drawn because the study did not include an untreated group.

Commenting on a number of high-risk studies presented at the Second Rochester International Conference on Schizophrenia, Garmezy (1978) noted that "it is fair to say that only now are researchers growing more aware of methodologic uncertainties and marked logistical difficulties that characterize studies of vulnerable children" (p. 480). The Rochester group—Singer, Wynne, and Toohey—has shifted attention to families who have younger children who risk developing personality aberration (Romano, 1978). The Rochester group is testing a number of hypotheses that emerged from their earlier studies of families whose children had reached adulthood.

Bleuler (1978) systematically followed, from 1938, the life course of 184 children of 206 schizophrenic parents whom he had treated. His finding a higher rate of normality among those children than did other investigators may be attributed to two factors: differential diagnosis and the fact that Bleuler knew his subjects very well. He considered long-term exposure to a schizophrenic parent insufficient to explain the subsequent development of schizophrenia. However, the children's early suffering because of a parent's illness marked their personalities indelibly, preventing them from enjoying life fully.

High-risk research seems to have replaced the large number of interaction studies that were started about two decades ago. Although extremely cautious about whether this approach will provide the answers to the etiology of schizophrenia, Garmezy (1974a, 1974b) believed that "current investigations and the ones to follow should enhance our understanding of the disorder and provide data that will eventually have to be incorporated into the complex etiological equation this extraordinary, complex disorder will require" (1974b, p. 116).

Fisher and Jones (1978), after reviewing 70 longitudinal studies conducted during the past three decades, emphasized the methodological problems in such research, particularly the clarification of objectives and selection of the sample. They warned that unless action in this field is concerted, investigators are likely to continue indefinitely to produce research marred by the same limitations.

Garmezy, Master, Nordstrom, and Ferrarese (1979) surveyed social competence in psychological research from its emergence in 1927 to 1977. They suggested that in the past, intelligence had been assessed to indicate competence, but that more recent research had focused on social adaptation and the relationship of competence to attachment, socialization, and parenting.

As a result of these longitudinal studies, many kinds of interventions have been suggested, but the one that has received most attention is cognitive and language competence. Reporting the results of cross-cultural studies of cognitive development, Dasen (1980) noted that differences in cognitive development appear to have been strongly affected by educational practices and by the structure of a subject's daily activities, especially within the family.

CONCLUSION

The chapter has discussed the negative effects of culture on the etiology of mental illness, with specific reference to the family and, to a lesser extent, to the cultural variables that may provide support when mental illness strikes. Illustrations have shown that neglecting the patient's family background has resulted in poor assessment of the existing psychopathology. Although professionals occasionally express an awareness of cultural variables, no concerted effort has been devoted to studying the influences of culture. Kraepelin (1904/1974), well known for his work on the classification of schizophrenia, visited mental institutions around the world and was a pioneer in describing the influence of culture on mental illness.

The importance of cultural factors to mental illness has been noted by Naka and Kawakita (1964), who advocated comparative studies of the social background of each country so that cultural forces could be related to the psychiatric disorders in each country. More recently, Draguns (1980) observed that cultures can be studied through the "prism of psychopathology." The content and the style of the prevailing symptomatology are relatively easy to record. Symptoms may provide valuable clues to the preoccupations of a culture and how they are expressed. Further, Draguns pointed out, how a culture treats and conceives of its "mentally ill" may be an issue in its own right.

What are the reasons for reluctance to recognize the importance of cultural factors in mental illness? During training, psychiatrists and psychologists generally have very limited contact with social scientists in other disciplines. Familiarity with sociocultural concepts would enable them to adequately assess psychopathology and move beyond the psychodynamic interpretations typically offered in regular training (Sanua, 1978). Most researchers who have expressed some interest in sociocultural variables have been affected by their personal experiences, either as immigrants or children of immigrants, or they have become sensitive to the issue during a sabbatical or service abroad.

A second reason for slow progress could be attributed to the fact that cultural explanations for disease are not popular: "Accusing a culture of being disease-producing is like casting doubt on someone's religion. . . . Moreover, if one starts questioning someone else's religious or cultural beliefs, then one can end up by questioning the sanity of one's own" (Murphy, 1978, p. 586). Hollingshead and Redlich (1958), discussing the relationship between social class and mental illness, indicated that the idea of stratification in our society runs counter to our cherished beliefs about equality, especially when those beliefs are applied to the care of the sick. Today, social class is more frequently recognized as a factor in mental illness, but culture lags well behind.

A third explanation for the lag is that granting agencies, private and governmental, may not be geared to evaluate interdisciplinary research plans adequately. There seems to be greater safety in pursuing traditional, primarily organic, approaches.

In the past few years, the World Health Organization has taken the initiative in pursuing interdisciplinary and cross-cultural research in psychiatry, an initiative that has resulted in important publications. It is hoped that integrating data from research conducted in several countries with comparable samples, even different subcultural groups, will lead to more valid and universal findings about the ravages of mental illness in a family context.

REFERENCES

Al-Issa, I. Cross-cultural studies of symptomatology in schizophrenics. In I. Al-Issa & W. Dennis (Eds.), *Cross-cultural studies of behavior.* New York: Holt, Rinehart & Winston, 1970.

Al-Issa, I. Social and cultural aspects of hallucination. *Psychological Bulletin,* 1977, *84,* 570–587.

Andrulis, D. P. Ethnicity as a variable in the utilization and referral patterns of a comprehensive mental health center (Doctoral dissertation, University of Texas at Austin, 1973). *Dissertation Abstracts International,* 1974, *34*(11), 7034A.

Anthony, E. J. The syndrome of the psychologically vulnerable child. In E. J. Anthony & C. Koupernick (Eds.), *The child and his family: Children at psychiatric risk.* New York: John Wiley & Sons, 1974. Pp. 3–10.

Arieti, S. An overview of schizophrenia from a predominantly psychological approach. *American Journal of Psychiatry,* 1974, *131,* 241–249.

Bateson, G., Jackson, D. D., Haley, J., & Weakland, K. Towards a theory of schizophrenia. *Behavioral Science,* 1956, *1,* 251–264.

Beels, C. E. Social networks, the family and the psychiatric patient: Introduction to the issue. *Schizophrenia Bulletin,* 1978, *4,* 512–521.

Berne, E. A psychiatric census of the South Pacific. *American Journal of Psychiatry,* 1960, *117,* 44–47.

Bleuler, M. *The schizophrenic disorders: Long-term patient and family.* New Haven, Conn.: Yale University Press, 1978.

Bott, E. *Family and social networks: Roles, norms, external relationships in ordinary urban families.* New York: Free Press, 1971.

Brody, E. Socio-cultural influences on vulnerability to schizophrenic behavior. In J. Romano (Ed.), *The origin of schizophrenia.* Amsterdam: Excerpta Medica, 1967. Pp. 166–178.

Bronfenbrenner, U. Origin of alienation. *Scientific American,* 1974, *231,* 53–61.

Caplan, G., & Killilea, M. (Eds.). *Support systems and mutual help: Multidisciplinary explorations.* New York: Grune & Stratton, 1976.

Clarke, A. N., & Clarke, A. D. B. *Early experience: Myth and evidence.* New York: Free Press, 1976.

Clausen, J. American research on the family and socialization. *Children Today,* 1978, *7,* 7–10.

Cohen, C., & Sokolovsky, J. Schizophrenia and social networks: Ex-patients in the inner city. *Schizophrenia Bulletin,* 1978, *4,* 546–550.

Cooper, K. J., & Sartorius, N. Cultural and temporal variations in schizophrenia: A speculation on the importance of industrialization. *British Journal of Psychiatry,* 1977, *130,* 50–55.

Dasen, P. R. [Individual differences and cultural differences.] *Bulletin de Psychologie,* 1980, *33,* 675–683.

David, H. P., & Baldwin, W. P. Childbearing and child development: Demography and psychosocial trends. *American Psychologist,* 1979, *34,* 866–871.

Derogatis, L. R., Covis, L., Lipman, R. S., Davis, D. M., & Rickels, K. Social class and race as mediator variables in neurotic symptomatology. *Archives of General Psychiatry,* 1971, *25,* 31–40.

Doane, J. A. The role of family in psychiatric disorders: An interpretative review of family interaction and communication deviation in disturbed and normal families. *Family Process,* 1978, *17,* 357–376.

Draguns, J. Psychological disorders of clinical severity. In H. Triandis & J. Draguns (Eds.), *Handbook of cross-cultural psychology* (Vol. 6): *Psychopathology.* Boston: Allyn & Bacon, 1980. Pp. 99–174.

Dunkas, N., & Nikelly, G. The Persephone syndrome: A study of conflict in the adaptive process of married Greek female immigrants in the United States. *Social Psychiatry,* 1972, *7,* 211–216.

Edgerton, R. B. Traditional treatment for mental illness in Africa: A review. *Culture, Medicine, and Psychiatry,* 1980, *4,* 167–189.

Erlenmeyer-Kimling, L., & Cornblatt, B. Attentional measures in a study of children at high risk for schizophrenia. In L. C. Wynne, R. L. Cromwell, & S. Mathysse (Eds.), *The nature of schizophrenia: New approaches to research and treatment.* New York: John Wiley & Sons, 1978. Pp. 359–365.

Fandetti, D. V., & Gelfand, D. E. Attitudes towards symptoms and services in the ethnic family and neighborhood. *American Journal of Orthopsychiatry,* 1978, *48,* 477–486.

Favazza, A. R., & Faheem, A. D. *Themes in cultural psychiatry: An annotated bibliography 1975–1980.* Columbia: University of Missouri Press, 1982.

Favazza, A. R., & Oman, M. *Anthropological and cross-cultural themes in mental health: An annotated bibliography 1925–1974.* Columbia: University of Missouri Press, 1977.

Feiring, C., & Lewis, M. *Changing characteristics of the United States family: Implication for family relationships and child development.* Unpublished manuscript, Educational Testing Service, Princeton, N.J., no date.

Fernandez-Pol, B. Culture and psychopathology: A study of Puerto Ricans. *American Journal of Psychiatry,* 1980, *137,* 724–726.

Fischer, E. H., & Cohen, S. L. Demographic correlates of attitudes toward seeking professional help. *Journal of Consulting and Clinical Psychology,* 1972, *39,* 70–74.

Fisher, L., & Jones, F. H. Planning for the next generation of risk studies. *Schizophrenia Bulletin,* 1978, *4,* 223–236.

Fleck, S. Family functioning and family pathology. *Psychiatric Annals,* 1980, *10,* 17–35.

Frank, G. H. The role of the family in the development of psychopathology. *Psychological Bulletin,* 1965, *64,* 191–205.

Freud, S. *A general introduction to psychoanalysis.* New York: Livewright, 1920.

Fried, M. Transitional functions of working-class communities: Implications for forced relocation. In M. B. Kantor (Ed.), *Mobility and mental health.* Springfield, Ill.: Charles C Thomas, 1965. Pp. 123–165.

Garmezy, N. Children at risk: The search for the antecedents of schizophrenia: Part I. Conceptual models and research methods. *Schizophrenia Bulletin,* 1974, *8,* 14–90. (a)

Garmezy, N. Children at risk: The search for the antecedents of schizophrenia: Part II. Ongoing research programs, issues and intervention. *Schizophrenia Bulletin,* 1974, *9,* 55–125. (b)

Garmezy, N. The experimental study of children vulnerable to psychopathology. In A. Davids (Ed.), *Child personality and psychopathology* (Vol. 2): *Current topics.* New York: John Wiley & Sons, 1975. Pp. 171–220.

Garmezy, N. Observations on high-risk research and pre-morbid development in schizophrenia. Current status of a sample of other high-risk research programs. In L. C. Wynne, R. C. Cromwell, & S. Mathysse (Eds.), *The nature of schizophrenia: New approaches to research and treatment.* New York: John Wiley & Sons, 1978. Pp. 400–480.

Garmezy, N., Masten, A., Nordstrom, L., & Ferrarese, M. The nature of competence in normal and deviant children. In M. Kent (Ed.), *Social competence in children.* Hanover, N.H.: University Press of New England, 1979. Pp. 23–43.

Garrison, V. Support system of schizophrenic and nonschizophrenic Puerto Rican immigrants in New York City. *Schizophrenia Bulletin,* 1978, *4,* 561–596.

Gerard, D. L., & Siegel, L. J. The family background of schizophrenia. *Psychiatric Quarterly,* 1950, *24,* 47–73.

Giordano, J., & Giordano, G. O. *The ethno-cultural factor in mental health: A literature review and bibliography.* New York: American Jewish Committee, 1977.

Goldstein, M. J., & Rodnick, E. H. The family contribution to the etiology of schizophrenia: Current status. *Schizophrenia Bulletin,* 1975, *14,* 48–63.

Grunebaum, H., Weiss, J. L., Gallant, D., & Cohler, B. Attention in young children of psychotic mothers. *American Journal of Psychiatry,* 1974, *131,* 887–891.

Hammer, M., Makiesky-Barrow, S., & Gutwirth, L. Social network in schizophrenia. *Schizophrenia Bulletin,* 1978, *4,* 522–545.

Harris, T. Social factors in neurosis, with special reference to depression. In H. M. Van Praag (Ed.), *Research in neurosis.* New York: SP Medical and Scientific Books, 1978. Pp. 22–39.

Heilbrun, A. B. *Aversive maternal control: A theory of schizophrenic development.* New York: John Wiley & Sons, 1973.

Henderson, S., Byrne, D. G., Duncan-Jones, P., Adcock, S., Scott, R., & Steele, G. P. Social bonds in the epidemiology of neurosis: A preliminary communication. *British Journal of Psychiatry,* 1978, *132,* 463–466.

Hingtgen, J. N., & Bryson, C. L. Recent developments in the study of early childhood psychosis: Infantile autism, childhood schizophrenia and related disorders. *Schizophrenia Bulletin,* 1972, *5,* 5–54.

Hess, R. D. Social class and ethnic influences on socialization. In P. H. Mussen (Ed.), *Carmichael's manual of child psychology* (3d ed.). New York: John Wiley & Sons, 1970. Pp. 457–557.

Hirsch, S. R., & Leff, J. P. *Abnormalities in parents of schizophrenics: A review of the literature and an investigation of communication defects and deviances.* London: Oxford University Press, 1975.

Hollenbach, M. G. Culture and madness: A Colombian case study (Doctoral dissertation, University of Washington, 1978). *Dissertation Abstracts International,* 1978, *39*(2), 962A–963A.

Hollingshead, A. B., & Redlich, F. C. *Social class and mental illness: A community study.* New York: John Wiley & Sons, 1958.

Hoppe, S. K., & Leon, R. L. Coping in the barrio: Case studies of Mexican-American families. *Child Psychiatry and Human Development,* 1977, *7,* 264–275.

Howells, J. G. Family psychopathology and schizophrenia. In J. G. Howells (Ed.), *Modern perspectives in world psychiatry.* New York: Brunner/Mazel, 1971. Pp. 391–424.

Howells, J. G. Family psychiatry and child psychiatry. *Acta Paedopsychiatrica,* 1979, *44,* 179–188.

Jacob, T. Family interaction in disturbed and normal families: A methodological and substantive review. *Psychological Bulletin,* 1975, *82,* 33–65.

Kaffman, M. Kibbutz civilian population under war stress. *British Journal of Psychiatry,* 1977, *130,* 489–494.

Keefe, S. E., Padilla, A. M., & Carlos, L. M. The Mexican-American extended family as an emotional support system. *Human Organization,* 1979, *38,* 144–152.

Keith, S. J., Gundersen, J. G., Reifman, A., Bucksbaum, S., & Mosher, L. R. Special report: Schizophrenia 1976. *Schizophrenia Bulletin,* 1976, *2,* 509–565.

Keniston, K. *All our children: The American family under pressure.* New York: Harcourt Brace Jovanovich, 1977.

Kernberg, P. F. Childhood schizophrenia and autism. In L. Bellak (Ed.), *Disorders of the schizophrenic syndrome.* New York: Basic Books, 1979. Pp. 509–559.

Kim, K. I., & Rhi, B. Y. A review of Korean cultural psychiatry. *Transcultural Psychiatric Research Review,* 1976, *13,* 101–114.

Klein, H., Person, T. M., Cetingok, M., & Itil, T. M. Family and community variables in adjustment of Turkish and Missouri schizophrenics. *Comprehensive Psychiatry,* 1978, *19,* 230–233.

Kleinman, A. *Patients and healers in the context of culture: An exploration of the borderland between anthropology, medicine and psychiatry.* Berkeley: University of California Press, 1980.

Kline, N. "Schizophrenia": The causes are complex; the condition is chronic. *This Month in Mental Health,* July 1979, pp. 4–5.

Klineberg, O. *Social psychology* (2d ed.). New York: Holt, Rinehart & Winston, 1954.

Kraepelin, E. [Comparative Psychiatry.] *Centralblatt für Nervenheitkunde und Psychiatrie,* 1904, *27 Jargang Neue Folge.* 15 Bd., 433–437. (Also in *Transcultural Psychiatric Research Review,* 1974, *11,* 108–112).

Lambo, T. A. The importance of cultural factors in psychiatric treatment. In I. Al-Issa & W. Dennis (Eds.), *Cross-cultural studies of behavior.* New York: Holt, Rinehart & Winston, 1970. Pp. 548–552.

Langner, T. S., Gersten, J. C., & Eisenberg, J. C. Approaches to measurement and definitions in the epidemiology of behavior disorders: Ethnic background of child behavior. *International Journal of Health Services,* 1974, *4,* 483–501.

Langner, T. S., Herson, J. H., Greene, E. L., Jameson, J. D., & Goff, J. A. Children of the city: Affluence, poverty and mental health. In V. L. Allen (Ed.), *Psychological factors in poverty.* Chicago: Markham, 1970. Pp. 185–209.

Leff, J. P. Schizophrenia and sensitivity to the family environment. *Schizophrenia Bulletin,* 1976, *2,* 566–574.

Leighton, D. C., Harding, J. S., Macklin, D. B., Macmillan, A. M., & Leighton, A. H. *The character of danger* (Vol. 3): *The Stirling County study of psychiatric disorder and sociocultural environment.* New York: Basic Books, 1963.

Lidz, T., Fleck, S., & Cornelison, A. R. *Schizophrenia and the family.* New York: International Universities Press, 1965.

Lo, W. H., & Lo, T. A ten-year follow-up study of Chinese schizophrenics in Hong Kong. *British Journal of Psychiatry,* 1977, *131,* 63–66.

McGoldrick, M., Pearce, K. J., & Giordano, J. (Eds.). *Ethnicity and family therapy.* New York: Guilford Press, 1982.

Mednick, S. Berkson's fallacy and high-risk research. In L. C. Wynne, R. C. Cromwell, & S. Mathysse (Eds.), *The nature of schizophrenia: New approaches to research and treatment.* New York: John Wiley & Sons, 1978. Pp. 442–452.

Mintz, N. L., & Schwartz, D. T. Urban ecology and psychosis: Community factors in the incidence of schizophrenia and manic depression among Italians of Greater Boston. *International Journal of Social Psychiatry,* 1964, *10,* 101–118.

Mishler, E. G., & Waxler, N. E. *Interaction in families: An experimental study of family process and schizophrenia.* New York: John Wiley & Sons, 1968.

Montagu, A. Culture and mental illness. *American Journal of Psychiatry,* 1961, *118,* 15–23.

Montagu, A. Social and cultural forces: Their effects on social institutions and children. *Child Welfare,* 1962, *41,* 291–296.

Murphy, H. B. M. Handling the cultural dimension in psychiatric research. *Social Psychiatry,* 1969, *4,* 11–18.

Murphy, H. B. M. Cultural influences on incidence, course, and treatment response. In L. C. Wynne, R. C. Cromwell, & S. Mathysse (Eds.), *The nature of schizophrenia: New approaches to research and treatment.* New York: John Wiley & Sons, 1978. Pp. 586–594.

Murphy, J. M., & Leighton, A. H. (Eds.). *Approaches to cross-cultural psychiatry.* Ithaca, N.Y.: Cornell University Press, 1965.

Murillo-Rhode, I. Family life among mainland Puerto Ricans in New York City slums. *Perspectives in Psychiatric Care,* 1976, *14,* 174–179.

Myers, J. K., & Roberts, B. H. *Family and class dynamics in mental illness.* New York: John Wiley & Sons, 1959.

Naka, S., & Kawakita, Y. Psychiatry in Japanese culture. *Diseases of the Nervous System,* 1964, *25,* 298–303.

Naylor, A. K. Early intervention: Panacea or challenge? Characteristics of parents in a mental health clinic for young children. In E. J. Anthony & C. Chiland (Eds.), *The child in his family: Preventive child psychiatry in an age of transition.* New York: John Wiley & Sons, 1980. Pp. 455–472.

Olson, D. N. Empirically unbinding the double bind: A review of research and conceptual reformation. *Family Process,* 1972, *11,* 69–94.

Opler, M. K. Anthropological contributions to psychiatry and social psychiatry. In C. Plog & R. B. Edgerton (Eds.), *Changing perspectives in mental illness.* New York: Holt, Rinehart & Winston, 1969. Pp. 88–104.

Ozarin, L. D., & Taube, C. Psychiatric inpatients: Who, where, and the future? *American Journal of Psychiatry,* 1974, *131,* 98–101.

Papajohn, J., & Spiegel, J. *Transactions in families.* San Francisco: Jossey-Bass, 1975.

Parsons, A. Family dynamics in South Italian schizophrenics. *Archives of General Psychiatry,* 1960, *3,* 507–518.

Reiss, D. The family and schizophrenia. *American Journal of Psychiatry,* 1976, *133,* 181–185.

Riskin, J., & Faunce, E. F. An evaluation review of family interaction research. *Family Process,* 1972, *11,* 365–455.

Ritvo, E. R. Biochemical studies of children with the syndrome of autism, childhood schizophrenia and related developmental disabilities: A review. *Journal of Child Psychology and Psychiatry,* 1977, *18,* 373–379.

Roff, J. E. Peer-status and the directionality of symptomatic behavior: Prime social competence predictors of outcome for vulnerable children. *American Journal of Orthopsychiatry,* 1976, *46,* 74–88.

Romano, J. The central core of madness. In L. C. Wynne, R. L. Cromwell, & S. Mathysse (Eds.), *The nature of schizophrenia: New approaches to research and treatment.* John Wiley & Sons, 1978. Pp. 1–5.

Rutter, M. Sociocultural influences. In M. Rutter & L. Hersov (Eds.), *Child psychiatry: Modern approaches.* Oxford, GB: Blackwell Scientific, 1977. Pp. 109–135.

Rutter, M. *Changing youth in a changing society: Patterns of adolescent development and disorder.* Cambridge, Mass.: Harvard University Press, 1980.

Rutter, M. *The qualities of mothering: Maternal deprivation reassessed.* New York: Jason Arsonson, Inc., 1974.

Rutter, M., Tizard, J., Yule, W., Graham, P., & Whitmore, K. Isle of Wight studies 1964–1974. *Psychological Medicine,* 1976, *6,* 313–332.

Sanua, V. D. Sociocultural factors in response to stressful life situations: Aged amputees as an example. *Journal of Health and Human Behavior,* 1960, *1,* 1–24.

Sanua, V. D. The sociocultural factors of families of schizophrenics: A review of the literature. *Psychiatry,* 1961, *24,* 246–265.

Sanua, V. D. The sociocultural aspects of schizophrenia: A comparison of Protestant and Jewish schizophrenics. *International Journal of Social Psychiatry,* 1963, *9,* 27–36.

Sanua, V. D. The sociocultural aspects of schizophrenia: A review of the literature. In L. Bellak & L. Loeb (Eds.), *The schizophrenic syndrome.* New York: Grune & Stratton, 1969. Pp. 256–310.

Sanua, V. D. Immigration, migration, and mental illness: A review of the literature with special emphasis on schizophrenia. In E. Brody (Ed.), *Behavior in new environments: Adaptation of migrant populations.* Beverly Hills, Calif.: Sage Publications, 1970. Pp. 291–352.

Sanua, V. D. *The training of psychologists for minority groups.* New York: Clearinghouse on Urban Education, 1978. (ERIC Document Reproduction Service No. ED 469 140)

Sanua, V. D. Psychological intervention in the Arab world: A review of folk treatment. *Transcultural Psychiatry Research Review,* 1979, *16,* 205–208.

Sanua, V. D. The familial and sociocultural antecedents of psychopathology. In H. C. Triandis & J. G. Draguns (Eds.), *Handbook of cross-cultural psychology* (Vol. 6): *Psychopathology.* Boston: Allyn & Bacon, 1980. Pp. 175–236.

Sanua, V. D. Autism, childhood schizophrenia and culture: A critical review. *Transcultural Psychiatric Research Review,* 1981, *18,* 165–181. (a)

Sanua, V. D. Cultural changes and psychopathology in children, with special reference to infantile autism. *Acta Paedopsychiatrica,* 1981, *47,* 133–142. (b)

Sanua, V. D. Family studies and psychopathology: A review from the cross-cultural perspective. In I. Al-Issa (Ed.), *Culture and psychopathology.* Baltimore: University Park Press, 1982. Pp. 157–180. (a)

Sanua, V. D. Psychological effects of war bereavement in the United States and Israel. In L. L. Adler (Ed.), *Issues in cross-cultural research.* New York: Academic Press, 1982. Pp. 349–360. (b)

Sanua, V. D. Childhood schizophrenia and infantile autims: A review of the issues from the sociocultural point of view. *Social Science and Medicine,* 1983, *17,* 1633–1651. (a)

Sanua, V. D. Cross-cultural study of paranoid schizophrenia. In J. B. Calhoun (Ed.), *Perspectives on adaptation, environment and population.* New York: Praeger Publishers, 1983. Pp. 282–284. (b)

Sanua, V. D. A transnational survey on the etiology of infantile autism. In J. D. Call, E. Galenson & R. Tyson (Eds.). New York: Basic Books, 1983 (c).

Sartorius, N. S., Jablonsky, A., & Shapiro, R. Cross-cultural differences in the short-term prognosis of schizophrenic psychoses. *Schizophrenia Bulletin,* 1978, *4,* 102–113.

Scheper-Hughes, N. M. Saints, scholars and schizophrenics: Mental illness and Irish culture (Doctoral dissertation, University of California, Berkeley, 1977). *Dissertation Abstracts International,* 1977, *38*(2), 882A.

Schulsinger, R. A ten-year follow-up of children of schizophrenic mothers: The clinical assessment. *Acta Psychiatrica Scandinavica,* 1976, *53,* 371–376.

Schulsinger, R. Biological psychopathology. *Annual Review of Psychology,* 1980, *31,* 583–606.

Schwartzman, J. The American family and mental illness: An ethnography of family dysfunction (Doctoral dissertation, Northwestern University, 1973). *Dissertation Abstracts International,* 1973, *34*(6), 2435B.

Segal, J., & Yahraes, H. *A child's journey: Forces that shape the lives of our young.* New York: McGraw-Hill, 1978.

Singer, M. T., Wynne, L. C., & Toohey, M. Communication disorders and the families of schizophrenics. In L. C. Wynne, R. L. Cromwell, & S. Mathysse (Eds.), *The nature of schizophrenia: New approaches to research and treatment.* New York: John Wiley & Sons, 1978. Pp. 499–511.

Srole, L., Langner, T. S., Michael, S. T., Opler, M. K., & Rennie, T. A. C. *Mental health in the metropolis: The Midtown Manhattan study* (Vol. 1). New York: McGraw-Hill, 1962.

Steger, C., & Kotler, T. Contrasting resources in disturbed and non-disturbed family systems. *British Journal of Medical Psychology,* 1979, *52,* 241–251.

Tatara, M. Four paradigms of relatedness in cross-cultural context: Comments on Dr. Davidson's paper. *Hiroshima Forum for Psychology,* 1980, *7,* 9–12.

Teja, J. S. Mental illness and the family in America and India. *International Journal of Social Psychiatry,* 1978, *24,* 225–231.

Triandis, H. C. (Ed.). *Handbook of cross-cultural psychology* (6 vols.). Boston: Allyn & Bacon, 1980.

Waxler, N. E. Is outcome for schizophrenia better in industrial societies? The case of Sri Lanka. *Journal of Nervous and Mental Disease,* 1979, *167,* 144–158.

White, S. L. Some sociocultural determinants of academic performance among behaviorally disturbed adolescents. *Journal of Genetic Psychology,* 1978, *133,* 145–146.

Whiting, B. B., & Whiting, J. W. (in collaboration with R. Longabaugh). *Children of six cultures: A psychocultural analysis.* Cambridge, Mass.: Harvard University Press, 1975.

Whiting, J. W. & Child, I. L. *Child training and personality: A cross-cultural study.* New Haven: Yale University Press, 1953.

Wilner, D. M., Wakeley, R. P., Pinkerton, T. C., & Tayback, M. *The housing environment and family life: A longitudinal study of the effects of housing on morbidity and mental health.* Baltimore: The John Hopkins Press, 1962.

Wolfenstein, M. Two types of Jewish mothers. In M. Mead & M. Wolfenstein (Eds.), *Childhood in contemporary cultures.* Chicago: University of Chicago Press, 1955. Pp. 424–440.

World Health Organization. *Report of the international pilot study of schizophrenia: I. Results of the initial evaluation phase.* Geneva: Author, 1973.

World Health Organization. *World health statistic annual 1973–1976* (Vol. III): *Health personnel and hospital establishments.* Geneva: Author, 1976.

World Health Organization. *Schizophrenia: International follow-up study.* New York: John Wiley & Sons, 1979.

Wylan, L., & Mintz, M. Ethnic differences in family attitudes toward psychotic manifestations, with implications for treatment programmes. *International Journal of Social Psychiatry,* 1976, *22,* 86–95.

Wynne, L. C., & Singer, M. T. I. Thought disorders and family relations of schizophrenics, in a research strategy. II. A classification of form of thinking. *Archives of General Psychiatry,* 1963, *9,* 191–206.

Wynne, L. C., Singer, M. T., & Toohey, M. L. Communication of the adoptive parents of schizophrenics. In J. Jorstad & E. Ugelstad (Eds.), *Schizophrenia 1975: Psychotherapy, family studies and research.* Oslo, Norway: University Press, 1976. Pp. 413–452.

Wynne, L. E., Toohey, M. L., & Doane, J. Family studies. In L. Bellak (Ed.), *Disorders of the schizophrenic syndrome.* New York: Basic Books, 1980. Pp. 264–288.

Chapter 28

Wife Abuse

LYN THAXTON

The purpose of this chapter is to examine theories that have been advanced to explain wife abuse. In order to establish the extent and nature of the problem and provide a sociological context, historical and demographic information will be included. Based on a number of research studies, psychological profiles of the victim, the batterer, and their children will be given in an attempt to identify some potential causes and ramifications of family violence and to determine why the battered woman remains in her situation. Possible approaches to treatment will also be presented briefly. While acknowledging that the serious problems of societal violence include child abuse, parent abuse (see Chapter 9), battered husbands, and unmarried women, this chapter will be limited to situations in which the victim (female) of battering is married to the abuser.

HISTORICAL LEGACY OF WIFE BEATING

Although the outcry against wife abuse is of recent origin, the problem is as old as recorded history. Dobash and Dobash (1979) state:

> The seeds of wife beating lie in the subordination of females and in their subjection to male authority and control. The relationship between women and men has been institutionalized in the structure of the patriarchal family and is supported by the economic and political institutions and by a belief system, including a religious one, that makes such relationships seem natural, morally just, and sacred. (p. 34)

In prebiblical times, when the deity was considered to be female, there is no evidence of battering between men and women. With the biblical

876

view of creation in which the Fall of Man is attributed to Eve, a rationale is provided for chastisement of women, who are viewed as intrinsically evil. In the New Testament, this view was corroborated by the Apostle Paul, who indicated that women were created "for" men and should submit themselves to their husbands (Davidson, 1977).

The word *family* (from *familias* in Latin) originally denoted the totality of slaves belonging to an individual (Martin, 1976). Roman husbands could commit adultery with impunity but were not punished for murdering their wives for the same offense. This concept of the wife as the necessary and inseparable possession of the husband continued into the Middle Ages: Friar Cerubino in his 15th-century *Rules of Marriage* recommended scolding, bullying, and terrifying one's wife. As a last resort, she should be beaten soundly to punish the body and save the soul (Davidson, 1978).

English common law reinforced wife beating with a bizarre "catch-22": the concept that when two people marry, they become one under the law. The woman could not sue her husband because of the logical impossibility of suing oneself. In 1768, Blackstone wrote, "By marriage the husband and wife are one person in law, that is, the very being or legal existence of the woman is suspended during the marriage or at least is incorporated and consolidated into that of the husband" (Langley & Levy, 1977). Within the last two centuries, however, laws have been passed that provide wives with more protection. An 1824 law that a husband could chastise his wife provided "he . . . [use] a switch no bigger than his thumb" was overruled in 1874 by the North Carolina Supreme Court with the decision that "the husband has no right to chastise his wife under any circumstances" (Hilberman, 1980). Today, several states have enacted laws making it a felony for a husband to assault his wife. Nevertheless, the application of the law is often inconsistent and inadequate, leaving assaulted wives with little assurance that they will be protected from beating (Langley & Levy, 1977).

Not only are the legal ramifications of wife beating not known and understood by much of society, but the situation is still often considered as a source of humor. The old vaudeville joke "When did you stop beating your wife?" is generally considered as an amusing example of the fallacy of the complex question and included in many introductory logic textbooks. In the television show "The Honeymooners," Jackie Gleason became famous for the line, "One of these days . . . Pow! Right in the kisser!"

Gleason portrayed a manual laborer: Wife beating is often considered as a phenomenon restricted to the lower socioeconomic classes. A review of demographic research will indicate that this viewpoint is not justified.

THE DEMOGRAPHICS OF WIFE BEATING

Major research on aggression between husbands and wives was conducted by Gelles (1972), who interviewed 40 New Hampshire families identified by a private social work agency and the case log of a police department as being involved in domestic violence. This research indicated that 78 percent of the respondents were married at the time of the interviews, with the mean length of marriage as 11.4 years. The average number of children was three. Of the husbands, 44 percent had not completed high school, 30 percent had graduated from high school, 20 percent had some college, and 6 percent had completed college or graduate school. The wives generally had more education than the husbands: Only 30 percent had not completed high school, while 51 percent had graduated. The occupations of the husbands ranged from unemployed to professional managers, with most husbands either operatives (such as machine operators or cooks) or laborers. Over half of the wives (58 percent) did not hold jobs. Most of the wives who were employed worked as secretaries, waitresses, or domestics. Family income ranged from under $3,000 to $25,000 a year. The mean age of the husband was 37.5 and of wives, 34.7. The sample was predominantly white and either Catholic (46 percent) or Protestant (44 percent).

Other research has supported Gelles' finding that wife beating is not restricted to the lower or working classes. A survey by Pagelow (1981) of women staying at the Women's Transitional Living Center in California determined that 40 percent were middle class. About 30 percent of the husbands had some college education, and 19 percent reported husband's income over $15,000 a year. Thirty-five percent of the women had some college education. The women's occupations included teacher, nurse, and librarian, while the husbands' occupations ranged from laborer (unemployed) to doctor, lawyer, and minister. Whites represented 78 percent of the sample, and blacks 14 percent. The investigator concluded that working-class and middle-class families were about evenly represented.

A third survey was conducted through an ad in *Ms.* Of the 43 respondents who indicated a history of battering, 46 percent were between the ages of 30 and 39. Eighty-two percent of the women (as opposed to 73 percent of the batterers) had some college education. Three fourths (76 percent) were employed, with 56 percent in professional or managerial positions. Only 30 percent of the male partners were identified as being employed in similar high-level positions (Prescott & Letko, 1977). These results are in keeping with Carlson's findings (1977) on 101 victims of battering, who were generally young, white, and of low socioeconomic status, but with more education than their assailants.

Other research has focused on identifying the context and history of abuse. Hilberman (1980) studied a sample of 60 battered women. In half the cases, violence between parents, parental alcoholism, and physical and/or sexual abuse as children was found. The husbands were generally reported to have come from even more violent backgrounds. These women usually married to escape from an oppressive home environment. About 60 percent reported premarital pregnancy. Alcohol was frequently, though not invariably, associated with abuse. Hofeller (1982) interviewed a group of 50 battered women and determined through multiple regression and discriminant analysis that violence can be best predicted by violence in the backgrounds of both men and women, status inequality, and heavy alcohol use by men.

The women reported that violence took place whenever the husband did not get his way. Scratching, slapping, punching, throwing down, kicking, and sexual abuse were common modes of attack, with violence often increasing during pregnancy. Children were often also victims of physical and sexual abuse.

In order to determine approximate frequency of wife beating, Straus (1977–1978) developed a "wife-beating index," including such items as throwing things at spouse; kicking, biting, or hitting with a fist; or threatening with a knife or gun. Of a sample of 2,143 randomly selected couples, 3.8 percent reported one or more physical attacks that would constitute "beating up." About 28 percent reported at least one violent act. The researchers believe that this is an underestimate because families are hesitant to admit to incidents of violence.

Roy (1977) conducted a survey involving questionnaires and in-depth interviews from the Abused Women's Aid in Crisis (AWAIC) hotline. This study supported other research findings that husbands were abused as children; this was reported in 81.1 percent of the cases. Women, however, reported that they had been abused much less frequently, in only 33.3 percent of the cases.

A more-extensive survey by Roy (1982), based on interviews with 400 abused women, revealed the following patterns:

1. Most abusive partners are between 26 and 35 years of age.
2. Children are generally between one and 13 years of age.
3. Most partnerships are supported by joint incomes, primarily from blue-collar jobs.
4. Most abuse occurs during the first 15 years of the relationship.
5. Ninety percent of the abusive partners do not have criminal records.

6. In over 70 percent of the sample, abuse began shortly after the relationship began.
7. Most abuse was physical, without use of weapons.
8. Over 80 percent of the abusers but only 33 percent of the victims had experienced or witnessed abuse as a child.
9. About 35 percent of the abusers had alcohol problems.
10. About 16 percent of the abusers had drug-related problems.

Demographic data are not conclusive in identifying a specific socio-economic profile of batterers and their victims. It appears that the problem cuts across a wide spectrum of society. An investigation of the social context of battering, as well as psychological profiles of family members, may provide a better understanding of the phenomenon.

PSYCHOSOCIAL FACTORS RELATED TO WIFE BEATING

The social context

Sociological studies of spouse abuse have focused on the macro level (the relationship between societal violence and violence in the family) and the micro level (immediate causes of battering within the family). There is considerable evidence for a correlation between societal violence—e.g., violent crime—and intrafamily aggression. For example, rates for homicide are considerably higher in Germany, where 60 percent of parents interviewed expressed belief in beating children to discipline them, than in Florence or Copenhagen, where severe physical punishment of children was not generally advocated. It is suggested that macrolevel conditions, such as unemployment, poverty, and acceptance of violence, may affect both high crime rates and family aggression. The complexity of the data does not allow for selecting the more-plausible theory at this time (Steinmetz, 1977).

The problem with the social-violence theory is that it does not account for the fact that women are victims of battering more often than men are. The importance of socialization in the acceptance of violence by men is an alternative theory. The mother and father are the role models that have the strongest effect on the child's gender identity. The lack of an humane, loving father as a role model may be the most-important factor in a child's identifying masculinity with brutality (Martin, 1976). This viewpoint is compatible with a social-learning model, which holds that battering is not easily extinguished because it is differentially reinforced. This model states that a child may internalize traditional ideology with its acceptance of the patriarchal hierarchical order of social structure and the concept of aggressive, tough behavior as appropriate for men. If the women have also been socialized to accept traditional ideology, the primary battering incident is likely to occur without punishment. Battering continues because the man is reinforced by feeling a sense of control and power and because his wife may attempt to placate him by removing sources of irritation: thus, behavior may receive both positive and negative reinforcement (Pagelow, 1981).

The demographic data cited above add credibility to the theory that status discrepancies may contribute to family violence. A husband's anger may reflect his frustration over his failure to live up to the family's expectations of financial support. A man who is unemployed or feels dissatisfied with his job may believe that the family sphere is the only area over which he can exercise control. If his wife is more highly educated or employed in a better-paying job, this situation may exacerbate the husband's sense of failure or lack of authority. Women may in turn feel guilt over deviation from their traditional sex roles and may associate this with violence (Gelles, 1972; Prescott & Letko, 1977). Force and its threat may be seen as a resource that tends to bring about social control.

Violence can also be seen within the framework of a general systems theory in which spouse abuse can be considered within the context of the marital or family system. Violence can be seen as a response to disequilibrium resulting when one or more goals of the marital system, such as provision of ego support, is not being met. The conflict theory of violence may be viewed as related to the systems perspective. In this view, conflict is considered as basic to, and often a positive aspect of, problem solving in organizations. This viewpoint is essentially conservative in nature because violence is a means of restoring the basic social structure and hierarchy. With the rise of feminism, women no longer maintain their rightful place in the family hierarchy; beating may be seen as a means of returning wives to the "one down" position (McLeer, 1981).

The immediate causes of violence may be divided into those that precipitate the battering incidents, and causes for the women's staying in the battering situation. According to various research studies, the nine major causes leading to eruptions of violence are (a) arguments over money, (b) jealousy, (c) sexual problems, (d) alcohol, (e) disputes over children, (f) husband's unemployment, (g) wife's desire to work outside the home, (h) pregnancy, and (i) wife's use of alcohol and other drugs. Major factors preventing the wife from leaving are (a) hope that the husband will reform, (b) no place to go, (c) fear of reprisals from the husband, (d) difficulties in finding a place to live with the children, (e) financial problems based on unemployment and lack of money, (f) fear of living alone, and (g) the stigma of divorce

(Roy, 1977). Even when the wife leaves the relationship temporarily, the above-mentioned factors may draw her back. In a follow-up of 74 women two months after discharge from a battered women's shelter, 55 percent were still living with their assailants (Snyder & Scheer, 1981).

Langley and Levy (1977) cite nine basic reasons for spousal violence: *(a)* mental illness, *(b)* alcohol and drugs, *(c)* public acceptance of violence, *(d)* lack of communication between the spouses, *(e)* sexual problems, *(f)* poor self-image of the husband, *(g)* frustration, *(h)* response to threat of change, and *(i)* use of violence as a resource for solving problems. Reasons given for staying in the marriage are similar to those cited above and revolve around the wife's feeling trapped in the relationship, totally dependent on her husband and having nowhere else to go. Gelles (1976) conducted interviews with women from 41 families in which battering had occurred and found the respondents were more likely to remain in the relationship if violence was less severe, if the women had been beaten as children, and if the wife had few resources and little power. Kalmuss and Straus (1982) have studied the relationship between objective (economic) and subjective (perceived) dependency and abuse. Wives' subjective dependency was found to be related to minor violence, while objective dependency was related to severe violence.

Perhaps the most frequently mentioned "cause" of battering is the use of alcohol. It is undeniable that drinking and violence often occur together: however, many battering incidents do not involve alcohol use, and most persons who drink do not become violent. Alcohol may not, in fact, be the direct cause of battering but may be an excuse used by the families to explain what would otherwise be unacceptable behavior (Moore, 1979). Eberle (1982), from structured interviews with 390 battered women, found that only about 16 percent of the incidents were accompanied by "excessive" use of alcohol and that almost an equal number involved no alcohol use. Bard (1974), in an extensive study, found that alcohol use does not invariably exacerbate violence but may instead have a calming effect. Shapiro (1982) suggests that alcohol use and family violence should, at any rate, not be considered in terms of linear causation but should be studied and treated in light of interactional patterns, the systems view.

Psychological profile of the victim

A prevalent view of the battered woman is that she is a masochist or possesses certain undesirable traits, such as aggressiveness or frigidity, that incite the husband to violence. Psychoanalytic theory has supported the viewpoint that violence between husband and wife results from the woman's inadequacies. In particular, violence is seen as an attempt to redress the "inappropriate" imbalance between male dominance and female submission. Early research on wife beating was clearly interpreted from the psychoanalytic perspective. Schultz (1960) studied four working-class black men who had attempted to murder their wives. He alleged that each man's childhood was characterized by "a domineering, rejecting mother relationship" and that the wives were "very masculine, outspoken, domineering women [who] tended to exploit and profit from their husbands' passiveness and dependency" (p. 105). It almost appeared that the husbands were the victims in these relationships.

Snell, Rosenwald, and Robey (1964) studied 12 cases of women from a middle-class Massachusetts suburb who charged their husbands with assault and battery. A "typical" wife was described as aggressive, masculine, frigid, and masochistic, with behavior that was construed as fostering her husband's dependency needs. Therapy allowed the wife to accept responsibility for her behavior and philosophically allow an occasional beating to maintain the delicate balance in the marriage.

This stereotype is perpetuated in more-recent writing as well. Shainess (1977) states:

> It may come as a surprise that the wife almost inevitably plays a part in her own assault. . . . People pick mates responsive to their own (unrecognized) neurotic needs. . . . One partner may be overly submissive; one may be attacking, overly demanding, and sadistic. . . . Masochism here does not imply enjoyment of suffering—the women, because of low self esteem, fail to view their role as underdog and therefore do not take the necessary steps to free themselves from this kind of relationship. (pp. 215–216)

Shainess points out that healthy, assertive behavior may upset the family homeostasis and provoke a beating also; thus, the wife appears to be in a no-win situation.

Waites (1977–1978) has pointed out that what is customarily viewed as female masochism may in fact be due to the restricted choices the woman faces. That is, she remains in the situation not because of the perverse pleasure it affords her but because the alternatives, such as dire poverty or divorce, are so negatively valued. With virtually no social support for leaving the marriage, the question of internal motivation appears irrelevant.

A current psychoanalytic approach to wife beating is stated in terms of object relations theory. Prochaska and Prochaska (1978) state:

> An individual who has developed a sense of self as victim . . . has internalized pathogenic introjects that revolve around aggressive conflicts. The aggressor polarity of the pathogenic introjects tends to be repressed or

split off. The person with a sense of self as victim will have a high propensity to project the repressed or split-off aggressor dimensions of the self onto significant others, such as a spouse. The conscious and immature need for an aggressor upon which to project the repressed dimensions of the early introjects will lead to the selection of a mate who can provide optimal gratification of these unconscious and narcissistic needs. (p. 16)

Again, the wife is viewed as fundamentally masochistic and responsible, albeit unconsciously, for her fate.

If the battered wife cannot be stereotyped as masochistic, she can generally be found to support the traditional stereotype of the male as superior and female inferior, a view that, ironically, contributes to battering because the man cannot live up to his wife's expectations. Because of the traditional values and the importance of having a successful marriage, many battered women appear to be guilt-ridden, feeling that something in their behavior provokes violence. The battered woman is typically unable to express her anger and is frequently a prey to depression and psychosomatic disorders, partially because she does not exercise control over her life (Davidson, 1978). Ways in which repressed anger may surface include *(a)* passive aggression, *(b)* lack of energy, *(c)* psychosomatic complaints, *(d)* religious fanaticism, mysticism, and moral righteousness, *(e)* complaining and nagging, *(f)* crying and other emotional displays of pain, *(g)* emotional breakdown, *(h)* helplessness and fear, and *(i)* compulsive homemaking and mothering (Goldberg, 1982).

While most conclusions regarding the psychological nature of battered women are based on clinical observations, a few are derived from quantitative data. Star, Clark, Goetz, and O'Malia (1979) administered the 16 personality factors (16 PF) and the clinical analysis questionnaire to 57 battered women, the majority of whom were staying in shelters. The overall profile was that of low self-esteem, lack of self-confidence, and a tendency to withdraw. Star (1978) administered the Buss-Durkee hostility-guilt inventory and the 16 PF to 46 physically abused and 12 nonabused women at the Haven House in southern California. The results gave no evidence to support masochism theories, as the battered women scored in the normal range of the submissive-assertive continuum. These women did, however, show anger, timidity, emotional reserve, and low coping abilities—qualities consistent with passivity, an inability or unwillingness to change one's environment.

Hartik (1982) administered the 16 PF and the Tennessee self-concept scale to 30 battered and 30 nonbattered wives. Battered wives were found to be lower on ego strength, undisciplined self-conflict, integration, and self-esteem than nonbattered wives. Battered women were also found to be higher on apprehensiveness and ergic tension, less satisfied with themselves, and in general, more maladjusted than the control group.

Snyder and Fruchtman (1981) provide data to suggest that there may be homogeneous and distinct subgroups of abused women. The researchers used a multivariate qualitative taxonomic procedure to study 119 residents at a shelter for battered women. Measures considered included frequency and severity of abuse, usual precipitants, typical responses of the woman and assailant, history of violence in the family of origin, and disposition following residence in the shelter. Five basic types of relationships were identified. Type I women are involved in stable relationships, seek shelter only after a severe injury, and generally return to their assailants. On the other hand, Type II women have unstable, explosive relationships and seldom remain with the batterers. Women in the Type III group are subject to the most-severe and chronic abuse. They, however, do not report violence in their families of origin and usually leave their partners. Type IV women report a high level of child abuse but little abuse toward themselves. Type V women report extensive abuse in their families of origin and generally continue to live with the batterers.

Symonds (1979) compares the psychological profile of battered women to that of the victims of catastrophes such as floods, earthquakes, or airplane crashes. Like victims of disasters, battered women may initially experience terror that traumatically infantilizes them. Without an outside support system, they may feel isolated and hopeless and may give in to apathy, despair, and submission to the batterer. Symonds cautions against confusing submissiveness with masochism, however, stating, "When [battered women] remain in relationships where they are being degraded or mistreated it is because they feel hopelessly trapped and see no feasible way out" (p. 172).

Perhaps the most widely accepted theory about the psychology and behavior of battered women, one similar to Symonds', has been developed by Walker (1979). She states these common characteristics of battered women: (a) low self-esteem, (b) belief in myths about battering relationships, such as "she gets what she deserves," (c) traditional values in terms of family unity and traditional sex roles, (d) acceptance of responsibility for the batterer's actions, (e) passive facade, but strength to manipulate environment to some extent to avoid violence, (f) severe stress reactions, with psychosomatic symptoms, (g) use of sex to establish intimacy, and (h) belief that only she can resolve her problem. Walker believes, however, that the recounting of these traits does not explain why the vicious battering cycle continues. To explain the phenomenon, Walker expounds the theory of "learned helplessness."

This theory was originally developed by Seligman (1975), who hypothesized that dogs who were administered electrical shocks at random and varied intervals would learn that no behavior would control the shock and would soon lose motivation to respond at all. Indeed, the dogs soon ceased to make any voluntary effort to escape and became passive and submissive. Even when doors were left open for the animals to escape, they did not do so. The handlers had to drag the dogs repeatedly to the exit in order for them to respond voluntarily again. Eventually, the learned helplessness disappeared when the dogs discovered that a voluntary response could alter the environment.

The learned helplessness theory has three components: *(a)* information about what will happen, *(b)* thinking or cognitive representation about what will happen, and *(c)* behavior about what will happen. The second or cognitive component is most important; the belief about the uncontrollable outcome is more important than whether or not the outcome can in fact be controlled. Victims of learned helplessness tend to be externalizers, believing that events in their lives are basically determined by factors outside themselves. Given this cognitive set, one can see the inability of battered women to avoid incidents of battering or to escape from the relationship.

Learned helplessness can generalize across situations. In many instances, battered women witnessed or experienced instances of violence in the family as a child. At this point, they discovered that the situations could not be controlled. At any rate, they were probably socialized into the docile, submissive, nurturing, traditional female role. Acculturated to be passive and dependent upon others, they have little experience in independent decision making or in being responsible for themselves (Ball & Wyman, 1977–1978).

The consequences of learned helplessness may be depression or a developing insensitivity to violence or death. The likelihood that the victim or the batterer will kill or be killed tends to increase. In order to avoid these dire consequences, the effects of learned helplessness must be reversed, possibly by "dragging" the women from the setting of violence and certainly by reversing the negative cognitive set that contributes to passivity.

Psychological profile of the batterer

The perpetuator of violence has been studied more extensively than has the victim. Research indicates that the batterers do not fit any particular profile. Although they may be alcoholics and/or psychopaths, they frequently appear to be normal, well-adjusted people with a relatively low tolerance for frustration (Langley & Levy, 1977). In analyzing 23 men who were in custody for seriously assaulting their wives or girlfriends, five different personality types emerged: *(a)* the dependent, passive husband with a querulous, demanding wife, *(b)* the dependent, suspicious type, controlled by jealousy, *(c)* the violent bully, *(d)* the dominating husband, and *(e)* the stable, affectionate spouse. In the last instance, violence usually occurred at a time of mental disturbance, generally a depressive episode (Faulk, 1977).

The wife beater frequently presents a positive image to the outside world but is often lacking in self-esteem. Below his masculine exterior, he is often dependent, immature, needing to fuse his identity with that of his wife (Davidson, 1978). Martin (1976) indicates, "Battering husbands are described by their wives as angry, resentful, suspicious, moody, and tense. Though they may be terrifying, they often have about them an aura of helplessness, fear, inadequacy, and insecurity. The battering husband is likely to be a 'loser' in some basic way" (p. 45). Wife beaters may have doubts about their own masculinity or sexuality and may blame their wives for their lack of potency. Goldberg (1982), who also delineated characteristics of the victim, sets forth these manifestations of anger in the batterer: *(a)* withdrawal and nonresponsiveness, *(b)* paternalism, *(c)* criticalness and sarcastic humor, *(d)* intellectualization, *(e)* passive indifference, *(f)* insensitivity, *(g)* workaholism, and *(h)* self-destructiveness and impulsiveness. Abusive males are also often less assertive than nonabusive males, possibly because of their lack of good communication skills (Ponzetti, Cate, & Koval, 1982).

The batterers are usually adept at laying the blame for the violent episodes on the spouse. In a survey of 33 men seeking psychiatric assistance for conjugal violence (Coleman, 1980), the reasons given for the eruption of violence fell into three major categories: *(a)* chronic dissatisfaction with the spouse as wife and mother, *(b)* retaliation to verbal or physical aggression, and *(c)* jealousy. Loss of control was expressed by 75 percent of the cases and was often associated with alcohol use. Coleman states:

> One prominent characteristic of the men . . . was their belief that to be a man, one must be strong and dominant, superior and successful. Feelings of inadequacy in any of these areas were devastating to the men's self-esteem and self-regard. Getting fired from a job, being told what to do by a wife, or feeling unsuccessful as a breadwinner created intense anxiety and feelings of helplessness. The men expressed ambivalence about dependence on their wives. They simultaneously desired and feared intense fusions with the women. (p. 211)

Walker admits that the profile of the typical batterer is based on evaluations by women in her sample. Still, the traits generally support the findings of other research. These are: *(a)* low self-esteem, *(b)* belief in myths about the battering relationship, *(c)* belief in traditional views of male supremacy, *(d)* tendency to blame others for actions, *(e)* pathological jealousy, *(f)* dual personality, *(g)* severe stress reactions, *(h)* frequent use of sex as an act of aggression to enhance waning virility; possible bisexuality, and *(i)* refusal to admit that violent behavior should have negative consequences. Walker also points out that abusers are characterized by denial of problems and, in 90 percent of the cases, had served in the military, which may be construed as a "school of violence."

Fleming (1979) points out that the stereotype of the wife abuser (working class or poor, and mentally ill) often does not apply. The most-common trait is self-justification, or denial of responsibility. The abuser is often a weak, infantile person with a low tolerance for frustration. Having often been abused as a child, he has a split identity: the aggressor (through identification with the parent who beat him) and the frightened, powerless child. This may account for the "Jekyll and Hyde" personality of many abusers. When not being violent, the husband may seem fragile, dependent, and yearning for nurturance. These dependency needs may account in part for the extreme jealousy many abusers manifest.

Despite his desperate need of support, he is generally incapable of true intimacy. He can usually be described as one of four personality types: *(a)* the defender, who uses violence to make his wife depend on him, *(b)* the controller, who enjoys manipulating others, *(c)* the approval seeker, who has inappropriately high expectations of himself and his wife, and *(d)* the incorporator, who needs to incorporate another's ego to seem whole. In addition to the traits and characteristics mentioned above, the abuser is often preoccupied with weapons, cruel to animals, and accepting of violence as an appropriate problem-solving method.

The children of battered women

Despite the generally acknowledged importance of socialization and the evidence that both victims and batterers often come from violent homes, little research has focused on the children of women who are abused. Recently, however, special programs have been developed for the children of women in shelters, and in connection with these, characteristics of the children have been examined. Anagnost, Mallory, Modigliani, and Yinger (1981) list the following characteristics of children who have witnessed violence: *(a)* pattern of general aggressiveness or of overcompliance or fearfulness, *(b)* low self-esteem, *(c)* fear and distrust of close relationships, *(d)* conflict over taking sides with parents, *(e)* guilt over having escaped punishment, and fear for the future, *(f)* bed-wetting, nightmares, and psychosomatic complaints, and *(g)* problems relating to authority.

Gordon (1982) points out that shelter children often emulate the violent behavior patterns that have been witnessed. These children generally have short attention spans, a low level of trust, inability to delay gratification, a high level of aggressiveness, and pseudomaturity. The battered woman and one of her children may reverse roles, with the child accepting responsibility for the family's problems. It is not uncommon for children to blame themselves for the family's difficulties or even consider suicide. Davidson (1978) reports the infants from violent homes often show bad sleeping habits, poor health, and excessive screaming, while toddlers may indicate fear by yelling, hiding, shaking, or stuttering. Older children may try in various ways (primarily diversionary tactics) to halt the violence but may eventually begin to lose respect for the mother. Teenagers frequently ally with their fathers and may themselves become batterers of their mothers.

Pfouts, Schopler, and Henley (1982) reported on interviews with children who had witnessed abuse in their families. Of the 25 children who had seen their mothers abused, 53 percent acted out with parents, and 60 percent acted out with siblings. A majority (58 percent) were rated below average or failing in school. In addition, the children were often anxious and depressed.

Prescott and Letko (1977) point out that 43 percent of the women interviewed believe that the experience of violence has affected their children's attitude toward marriage. Female children especially manifest a distrust of intimate relationships. As these children are frequently also characterized by social withdrawal, they often do not learn the communication skills to resolve disagreements in a nonviolent fashion. Physical illness, hyperactivity, destructiveness, anxiety, and moodiness are other problems frequently identified in the children of battered women.

In a study of 23 violent families by the National Society for the Prevention of Cruelty to Children (NSPCC) School of Social Work (1977) in London, the researchers described the "yo-yo syndrome" in which the children were used as pawns, shuttlecocks, or yo-yos between embattled spouses. The children's living arrangements were in constant flux; many moved as often as 12 times in five months. The movements were usually not random, however. Generally, there were identifiable stages in the "game" between the parents, with the maternal grandmother often involved. The parents tended to be so concerned with their own problems that the needs of their children were overlooked. In over a third of the cases, the children were either battered themselves or threatened with violence. While some children in the study were described as coping well, the majority were viewed as nervous, frightened, withdrawn, and poor students. This study and others agree on the necessity of providing warm, supportive, and stable role models to offset the effects of the negative models that the children have experienced. Shelters are often now employing children's advocates or program directors to meet this need.

The cycle of violence

In addition to delineating the theory of learned helplessness described above, Walker (1979) has also developed a cyclical theory of violence that goes far toward explaining why battered women remain in the relationship and why they seldom seek help. The cycle includes a tension-building phase, the explosion or acute battering incident, and the calm, loving respite. The length of the various stages of the cycle varies: however, Phase 1 appears usually to be the longest and Phase 2 the shortest.

During the tension-building phase, minor incidents of violence often occur. The woman often deludes herself into thinking that her behavior will prevent violence from erupting. She denies her anger over physical and psychological mistreatment and often rationalizes that the violence is justified. As she tends to be an externalizer, she is likely to blame factors such as alcohol or job stress for her husband's behavior and hopes that changes in these situations will improve the relationship at home. Toward the end of the cycle, the woman's coping strategies no longer seem to work. She withdraws, while the batterer hovers over her oppressively.

The acute battering incident may be interpreted as a discharge of tensions built up during Phase 1. The stage is characterized by uncontrollable rage on the part of the batterer. The event is usually precipitated by some external event or the husband's internal state but may sometimes be provoked by the woman, who finds that the tension of Phase 1 is no longer bearable. Women often report a calmness, a dissociation from the experience, during the battering incident itself. Except in cases of extreme physical injury, women characteristically do not seek medical attention or counseling until at least 24 hours after an attack.

During the third phase, the batterer becomes loving, contrite, and charming. He vows that he never again will injure his spouse. As many battered women adhere to traditional values about the sanctity and permanency of marriage, she is relieved that her spouse is manifesting the behavior and personality that originally attracted her to him. A major difficulty for counselors lies in the fact that they generally see the battered woman (with or without her husband) during this phase.

At this stage, she has little motivation to leave even the most-traumatic relationship. The husband may enter counseling to humor his wife during this stage; he seldom continues after the symbiotic ties between the mates have been reestablished and the tensions of Phase 1 begin to build.

TREATMENT APPROACHES

As the major emphasis of this chapter is on theory rather than treatment, only brief coverage will be given to therapeutic approaches toward battered wives, the abusers, and couples together. The fact that battered women seldom seek mental health assistance can be discouraging to the concerned counselor. The victim's situation and personality, as well as her generally negative experience with social services, contribute to her indifference. Many of the factors that keep the victim with her husband preclude her seeking aid. She often feels guilty and believes that her own behavior, under her control, will ward off battering in the future. She may also feel shame in confiding her lot to others. The phenomenon of learned helplessness contributes to the woman's sense of apathy. Attempting to find help to escape from the situation may require more effort than she can muster. She may fear retribution from her spouse if she makes a move toward independence. Almost undoubtedly, she is emotionally and economically dependent on her husband. She may doubt that she has the internal and external resources to make it on her own.

Furthermore, the woman who has sought help from social service agencies in the past may be cynical over the lack of concern she has found. The law does not appear to be on her side; wife abuse is a felony in few states. The police appear indifferent, insulting, or concerned but helpless unless the batterer is "caught in the act." The established psychiatric attitude of "blaming the victim," of treating the battered woman as a masochist, is a major factor in discouraging women from continuing in therapy. In fact, the traditional psychoanalytic approach to psychotherapy appears to have little to offer most battered women.

The feminist counseling orientation appears more appropriate in that it stresses the long-term goal of engendering in the victim the strength to make the choice to remain in or leave the relationship. If this choice becomes hers, she ceases to be a passive victim. The goal cannot, however, be met until some of the crisis aspects of the woman's situation have been resolved. Legal aid, medical assistance, child care, and economic support are all areas of immediate concern to the woman. The counselor thus must often function in the role of advocate but can also begin to help the client develop problem-solving skills as these issues are resolved (Council on Battered Women, 1981). Support groups of peers with similar problems may be a useful adjunct to individual counseling or therapy, as may be assertiveness training.

Despite considerable writing regarding the characteristics of the wife, little information is available on therapeutic approaches for the batterer. Feminists, who have published the bulk of recent books and articles on wife abuse, are primarily oriented toward helping the victim and usually operate on the assumption that the abuser will not be receptive to aid. Many men believe that they have a right to beat their wives and that their behavior is normal. If they do agree to counseling, it may be merely a coercive technique to lure back a wife who has temporarily left. Occasionally, a judge may recommend counseling in lieu of a jail sentence for abusers. The value of counseling in these situations is debatable unless the batterer can be convinced of his problems.

The appropriate form of therapy will depend in part on the mental state of the batterer. Some abusers may be extremely disturbed, with little sense of reality, confusion over boundaries between self and others, and extremely low self-esteem. Under these circumstances, treatment with antipsychotic drugs and institutionalization may be in order (McLeer, 1981). Explosive rage may well be the result of some neurological or metabolic dysfunction, such as temporal-lobe epilepsy or hypoglycemia. In a sample of 286 patients (referred by physicians) with a history of family violence, 94 percent showed some objective evidence of developmental or acquired organic defects that could conceivably be controlled by medication or proper diet (Elliott, 1982). It is important to note, however, that violence is also partially learned behavior and that treatment with drugs will not necessarily eliminate abuse.

Psychoanalysis or another form of individual psychotherapy may be the most-suitable form of treatment for neurotics with insufficient impulse control. The goal is to replace unrealistic standards and expectations, both for self and others. Insight therapy does not appear to be useful, however, for persons who lack the mechanisms for choice delay, the ability to postpone instant gratification. Many abusers might be more receptive to a behavioral therapy model for controlling rage behavior. Koval, Ponzetti, and Cate (1982) suggest group therapy interventions focusing on stress management, alteration of rigid sex role stereotypes, appropriate expression of emotion, and development of interpersonal skills, including assertiveness.

In a review of the current psychological literature, few references to conjoint counseling of the batterer and victim can be found. When the pattern of battering is not firmly entrenched and the husband is willing to seek help, however, couple counseling may be effective.

With any conjoint marital technique, it is important for the therapist to join with the clients to communicate his or her understanding of how the spouses view themselves and their relationship (Bagarozzi & Giddings, 1983). Anger management appears to be the major issue in conjoint marital therapy. One widespread approach involves teaching the spouses to express their aggression and hostility. Bach and Wyden (1968) are probably the best-known proponents of techniques to teach couples to fight properly. Implicit in this viewpoint is the notion that verbal aggression may be a substitute for physical aggression. Research by Straus (1974) does not, however, support this catharsis view of aggression. His results indicate that physical aggression increases with verbal aggression but is incompatible with "civility" or rational problem solving.

A second approach to dealing with marital violence is based on the social-learning theory: essentially the view that violence, physical or verbal, begets violence. According to this theory, coercive tactics are used by the aggressor to elicit change in a spouse. If coercion produces compliance, the behaviors are reinforced. The victim often reciprocates the exchange of aversive behaviors, leading to an escalation of coercive interactions (Margolin, 1979). Margolin's approach to therapy treats anger as a problem in the relationship and teaches the spouses to refrain from destructive expressions of anger, primarily by identifying cues that lead to negative exchanges and interrupting the pattern.

Walker (1979) does not agree that focus on the relationship should be primary in couples therapy. Instead, she emphasizes strengthening individuals in order that they may function adequately, even if the relationship does not endure. In order to break the strong symbiotic ties, the couple temporarily separates while male and female therapists work with the spouses individually. Paradoxical techniques may be used to foster differentiation (Coleman, 1980). After a time, joint therapy begins with training to recognize the buildup of tension, which is communicated by prearranged cues. As in Margolin's training, the couples take a time-out period to allow anger to subside before resuming discussion. The couples are taught to ask directly for what they want, emphasizing natural positive reinforcers.

DISCUSSION AND EVALUATION

A major difficulty with many of the psychosocial theories about family violence lies in the research methodology. Bagarozzi and Giddings (1983) point out three major drawbacks of most sociological research: (a) limited generalizability, due to small, nonrepresentative samples, (b) statistical analyses based on correlational rather than observational methods, and *(c)* overall reliance on linear-causal rather than systems models of human behavior and societal functioning. The lists of characteristics of the "typical" victim are usually derived from clinical observations, often made at shelters for battered women. It is likely, however, that women who seek help may differ in significant ways from those who do not. Furthermore, many frequently mentioned traits (such as passivity) are certainly not unique to battered women. The research of Star and her coauthors (Star, 1978; Star et al., 1979) is a step in the right direction, as objective measures such as the 16 PF were used. More research of this nature, especially using matched control groups, is needed.

Compiling accurate information about the batterer is probably even more difficult than studying the victim, as subjects are often in custody or have been referred to counseling or therapy by the courts. Many of these subjects may be inclined to present a socially desirable, positive image in order to exonerate themselves. Information received from the victims will probably be biased in the opposite direction, as the battered women will generally present their persecutors in any unfavorable light.

Research that centers on traits of individuals involved in family violence or that examines only the social context will at any rate be limited and potentially misleading. Notably lacking has been research on family interactional patterns in violent situations. As Pittman (1982) points out in a review of five books on family violence, the systems perspective is not presented in most work published thus far. Pittman states, "Most people lose control and use violence at some time. The reactions and interactions, the alliances and loyalties, the feedback mechanisms and whatever, will determine whether the violent reaction is effective, is tolerated, is encouraged. The concept of villains and victims misses the point and can only worsen the situation" (p. 366).

The idea of systems, when employed in family violence research, often has a different meaning than that used by family therapists. Rounsaville (1978) writes of a "systems analysis" theory of family violence as a final, common pathway of multiple determinants. In his multifactorial model, psychological determinants include conflicts over dependency and autonomy, deficient impulse control, alcohol and drug abuse, and learned helplessness. Sociological determinants are pressured entry into marriage, distorted concepts of marital roles, severe social stress, and status inconsistency. Rounsaville also acknowledges the importance of society's indifference to the issue. Family process and dynamics are not considered, however. Goldberg (1982) has written one of the few articles in which the dynamics of rage, not merely the traits of the involved individuals, are considered. Weitzman and Dreen (1982) take a systemic approach to viewing the violent marital dyad, which is described in terms of inflexibility regarding sex role polarization, narrow coping responses, and a high level of enmeshment. Complementary relationships are also typical of these couples: Battering incidents may bring the participants into a more-symmetrical position. While the theories developed by Goldberg and by Weitzman and Dreen suggest important new avenues for research, neither article is based on empirical data.

Walker's cycle-of-violence theory may be interpreted systemically. From this perspective, interventions could ideally be made at any stage in the cycle. In actuality, interventions during Phase 3 (the "honeymoon" stage) have met with little success. It should be pointed out, however, that few family systems–oriented interventions have been developed and that those that have been used, such as the notion of "structured fighting," appear misguided. Studying the sequence around the symptom (focusing on Phase 2) might be a more-appropriate means of assisting the victim to change the system, whether or not the spouse is willing to participate in therapy.

Giles-Sims (1983) has developed a six-stage systems model of wife battering, primarily sociological in perspective, that utilizes principles such as homeostasis that are also relevant to family psychology. The first stage centers on how the family system was established to allow for violence. In the second stage, the sequence of interaction around the first incident of violence is examined. The homeostatic function, which stabilizes violence, is considered in Stage 3. Stage 4 examines the choice point at which the situation becomes unbearable to the battered woman. In the fifth stage, the possibility of "second-order change," the shifting of the system's boundaries, is the focus. The sixth stage examines the various options for the battered woman, from the establishing of a new, more satisfactory system to returning to the former pattern. This model provides a useful alternative to the more-widespread linear ways of considering family violence causation.

The macrosystem, society, has been considered more frequently than the microsystem, the family. Until certain widespread attitudes about men, women, and their relationships are changed, wife abuse will probably continue to be a serious problem. Carlson (1977) points out three major beliefs still held by a large segment of society: that men's status must and should be higher than women's, that men who are not physically more powerful than women are inadequate and not fully masculine, and that physical power and coercion are valid means of solving disputes in the family. Despite the positive influence of the women's movement over the last few decades, a large segment of society still shares these beliefs.

A counselor who is concerned with issues of family violence may feel the need to act as an advocate and lobbyist. Family violence is not merely a psychological issue but carries over into areas of statutory reform and governmental support for shelters and support services. Morgan (1982) points out the need for multilevel community psychology programs, including job training for abused women and peer counseling. The climate of opinion will not be easily changed, but adequate laws and services for the victims of battering will contribute to this end.

CONCLUSION

Wife abuse, prevalent in various cultures for many centuries, has become the subject of serious research interest during the past several decades. Statistics indicate that wife abuse is a widespread phenomenon in all classes of society. Sociologists have been particularly concerned with the issue of family violence and have suggested various explanations, including the social violence, social learning, and general systems theories.

Interest in wife abuse on the part of psychologists is of relatively recent origin and is closely related to the rise of the feminist counseling movement. In the past, battered women were frequently viewed as masochists, in keeping with the traditional psychoanalytic perspective. The concept of the abused woman as a victim of "learned helplessness" is now given more credence, however. The batterer has also been considered from the psychoanalytic and feminist standpoints. In addition, violence has in some instances been shown to have a psychological basis. Treatment approaches, for both the victim and the batterer, have included supportive counseling for battered women, work with both groups of women and groups of abusers, and behavioral interventions with either batterers or couples. Wife abuse has not, however, been thoroughly considered from the family systems perspective; instead, wives and husbands are usually viewed as separate entities with individual and not necessarily interrelated sets of traits. Consideration of abuse in terms of processes involved, and the development of appropriate interventions, may be seen as a challenge for the field of family psychology.

REFERENCES

Anagnost, E., Mallory, E., Modigliani, K., & Yinger, K. *Children in shelters: A resource guide for family violence programs.* Ypsilanti, Mich.: Domestic Violence Project/Safe House, 1981.

Bach, G. R., & Wyden, P. *The intimate enemy: How to fight fair in love and marriage.* New York: William Morrow, 1978.

Bagarozzi, D. A., & Giddings, C. W. Conjugal violence: A critical review of current research and clinical practices. *American Journal of Family Therapy*, 1983, *11*, 3–15.

Ball, P. G., & Wyman, E. Battered wives and powerlessness: What can counselors do? *Victimology*, 1977–1978, *2*, 545–552.

Bard, M., & Zacker, J. Assaultiveness and alcohol use in family disputes: Police perceptions. *Criminology*, 1974, *12*, 281–292.

Carlson, B. E. Battered women and their assailants. *Social Work*, 1977, *22*, 455–460.

Coleman, K. H. Conjugal violence: What 33 men report. *Journal of Marital and Family Therapy*, 1980, *6*, 207–213.

Council on Battered Women. *Orientation*. Atlanta: Author, 1981.

Davidson, T. Wifebeating: A recurrent phenomenon throughout history. In M. Roy (Ed.), *Battered women: A psychosociological study of domestic violence*. New York: Van Nostrand Reinhold, 1977.

Davidson, T. *Conjugal crime: Understanding and changing the wifebeating pattern*. New York: Hawthorn, 1978.

Dobash, R. E., & Dobash, R. *Violence against wives: A case against the patriarchy*. New York: Free Press, 1979.

Eberle, P. A. Alcohol abusers and non-users: A discriminant analysis of differences between two subgroups of batterers. *Journal of Health & Social Behavior*, 1982, *23*, 260–271.

Elliott, F. A. Biological contributions to family violence. In J. C. Hansen (Ed.), *Clinical approaches to family violence*. Rockville, Md.: Aspen, 1982.

Faulk, M. Men who assault their wives. In M. Roy (Ed.), *Battered women: A psychosociological study of domestic violence*. New York: Van Nostrand Reinhold, 1977.

Fleming, J. B. *Stopping wife abuse*. Garden City, N.Y.: Anchor Press/Doubleday, 1979.

Gelles, R. J. *The violent home: A study of physical aggression between husbands and wives*. Beverly Hills, Calif.: Sage Publications, 1972.

Gelles, R. J. Abused wives: Why do they stay? *Journal of Marriage and the Family*, 1976, *38*, 659–668.

Giles-Sims, J. *Wife-battering: A systems-theory approach*. New York: Guilford Press, 1983.

Goldberg, H. The dynamics of rage between the sexes in a bonded relationship. In J. C. Hansen (Ed.), *Clinical approaches to family violence*. Rockville, Md.: Aspen, 1982.

Gordon, J. D. *What to do with the children?* Atlanta: Council on Battered Women, 1982.

Hartik, L. M. *Identification of personality characteristics and self-concept factors of battered wives*. Palo Alto, Calif.: R & E Research Associates, 1982.

Hilberman, R. Overview: The "wife-beater's wife" reconsidered. *American Journal of Psychiatry*, 1980, *137*, 1336–1347.

Hofeller, K. H. *Social, psychological and situational factors in wife abuse*. Palo Alto, Calif.: R & E Research Associates, 1982.

Kalmuss, D. S., & Straus, M. A. Wife's marital dependency and wife abuse. *Journal of Marriage and the Family*, 1982, *44*, 277–286.

Koval, J. E., Ponzetti, J. J., & Cate, R. M. Programmatic intervention for men involved in conjugal violence. *Family Therapy*, 1982, *9*, 147–154.

Langley, R., & Levy, R. C. *Wife beating: The silent crisis*. New York: Dutton, 1977.

Margolin, G. Conjoint marital therapy to enhance anger management and reduce spouse abuse. *American Journal of Family Therapy*, 1979, *7*, 13–23.

Martin, D. *Battered wives*. San Francisco: Glide, 1976.

McLeer, S. V. Spouse abuse. In G. P. Sholevar (Ed.), *The handbook of marriage and marital therapy*. New York: Spectrum, 1981.

Moore, D. M. Editor's introduction: An overview of the problem. In D. M. Moore (Ed.), *Battered women*. Beverly Hills, Calif.: Sage Publications, 1979.

Morgan, S. M. *Conjugal terrorism: A psychological and community treatment model of wife abuse*. Palo Alto, Calif.: R & E Research Associates, 1982.

NSPCC School of Social Work. Yo-yo children: A study of 23 violent matrimonial cases. In M. Roy (Ed.), *Battered women: A psychosociological study of domestic violence*. New York: Van Nostrand Reinhold, 1977.

Pagelow, M. D. *Woman battering: Victims and their experiences*. Beverly Hills, Calif.: Sage Publications, 1981.

Pfouts, J. H., Schopler, J. H., & Henley, H. C. Forgotten victims of family violence. *Social Work*, 1982, *27*, 367–368.

Pittman, F. S. Books Review on Family Violence. *Family Process*, 1982, *21*, 363–367.

Ponzetti, J. J., Cate, R. M., & Koval, J. E. Violence between couples: Profiling the male abuser. *Personnel and Guidance Journal*, 1982, *61*, 222–224.

Prescott, S., & Letko, D. Battered women: A social psychological perspective. In M. Roy (Ed.), *Battered women: A psychosociological study of domestic violence*. New York: Van Nostrand Reinhold, 1977.

Prochaska, J., & Prochaska, J. Twentieth century trends in marriage and marital therapy. In T. J. Paolino & B. S. McCrady (Eds.), *Marriage and marital therapy: Psychoanalytic, behavioral and systems theory perspectives*. New York: Brunner/Mazel, 1978.

Rounsaville, B. J. Theories of marital violence: Evidence from a study of battered women. *Victimology*, 1978, *3*, 11–31.

Roy, M. A current survey of 150 cases. In M. Roy (Ed.), *Battered women: A psychosociological study of domestic violence*. New York: Van Nostrand Reinhold, 1977.

Roy, M. Four thousand partners in violence: A trend analysis. In M. Roy (Ed.), *The abusive partner: An analysis of domestic battering*. New York: Van Nostrand Reinhold, 1982.

Schultz, L. G. The wife assaulter. *Journal of Social Theory*, 1960, *2*, 103–112.

Seligman, M. *Helplessness: On depression, development and death*. San Francisco: W. H. Freeman, 1975.

Shainess, N. Psychological aspects of wifebattering. In M. Roy (Ed.), *Battered women: A psychosociological study of domestic violence*. New York: Van Nostrand Reinhold, 1977.

Shapiro, R. J. Alcohol and family violence. In J. C. Hansen (Ed.), *Clinical approaches to family violence*. Rockville, Md.: Aspen, 1982.

Snell, J. E., Rosenwald, R., & Robey, A. The wifebeater's wife: A study of family interaction. *Archives of General Psychiatry*, 1964, *11*, 107–112.

Snyder, D. K., & Fruchtman, L. A. Differential patterns of wife abuse: A data-based typology. *Journal of Consulting and Clinical Psychology*, 1981, *49*, 878–885.

Snyder, D. K., & Scheer, N. S. Predicting disposition following brief residence at a shelter for battered women. *American Journal of Community Psychology,* 1981, *9,* 559–566.

Star, B. Comparing battered and non-battered women. *Victimology,* 1978, *3,* 32–44.

Star, F., Clark, C. G., Goetz, K. M., & O'Malia, L. Psychosocial aspects of wife battering. *Social Casework,* 1979, *60,* 479–487.

Steinmetz, S. K. *The cycle of violence: Assertive, aggressive, and abusive family interaction.* New York: Praeger Publishers, 1977.

Straus, M. A. Leveling, civility, and violence in the family. *Journal of Marriage and the Family,* 1974, *36,* 13–29.

Straus, M. A. Wife beating: How common and why? *Victimology,* 1977–1978, *2,* 443–458.

Symonds, A. Violence against women—the myth of masochism. *American Journal of Psychotherapy,* 1979, *33,* 262–273.

Waites, E. A. Female masochism and the enforced restriction of choice. *Victimology,* 1977–1978, *2,* 535–544.

Walker, L. E. *The battered woman.* New York: Harper & Row, 1979.

Weitzman, J., & Dreen, K. Wife beating: A view of the marital dyad. *Social Casework,* 1982, *63,* 259–265.

Chapter 29

Characteristics of Abusing Families

AUDREY BERGER

Child abuse occurs in many contexts, but it most often occurs within the family. Although the family is characteristically associated with love, protection, and nurturance, for some children it can be the source of violence, fear, and pain. There is a voluminous literature on child abuse, but most of the research tends to focus on isolated aspects of the problem (e.g., personality characteristics of parent or child) and ignores the context in which child abuse occurs. Since child abuse is a problem within the family unit, it must be viewed within this context to be adequately understood, prevented, and treated.

The present chapter attempts to organize the available data on child abuse in a way that sheds some light on what abusing families are like. Due to space limitations, some of the incidence, definitional, and methodological issues will be only cursorily discussed, since they have received detailed attention in many other review articles (e.g., Berger, 1980a). Also, there will be a greater emphasis on the more-recent and more methodologically sound research than on some of the earlier research which is adequately reviewed in many other publications (e.g., Berger, 1980a, 1980b; Parke & Collmer, 1975).

INCIDENCE

The precise incidence of child abuse in the United States is difficult to estimate since it does not always come to the attention of the authorities. Furthermore, case-finding strategies and definitions of child abuse have changed over time. However, the Child Abuse Prevention and Treatment Act of 1974 (PL 93–247) provided a definition of child abuse which is now used nationwide for collecting incidence statistics. This definition of child abuse includes not only physical abuse but sexual abuse, emotional abuse, and neglect as well. The National Center on Child Abuse and Neglect (NCCAN) reports that approximately 1 million children are maltreated annually in the United States, and approximately 250,000 of those are physical abuse cases.

Some investigators have generated incidence estimates based on their own research, and their estimates generally suggest a more-widespread problem than is indicated by the national statistics, which are based on reported cases only (Egeland & Brunnquell, 1979; Gelles, 1980; Sapp & Carter, 1978; Straus, 1980a, 1980b). For example, based on a survey of a nationally representative sample of 1,146 American families, Gelles estimated that approximately 3.6 percent of American children (or 1.4–1.9 million children) are physically abused each year.

Thus, the actual magnitude of the problem remains unclear. But there is no question that child abuse is a significant problem in this society.

DEFINITIONS OF CHILD ABUSE

Different studies use different definitions of child abuse (see Berger, 1980a; Besharov, 1981; Zigler, 1979, 1980), which seriously confuses attempts to understand the problem since it renders many studies incomparable. In effect, different authors may be studying somewhat diversified populations but applying the same label to them all.

There are a number of unresolved theoretical issues involved in defining physical child abuse: how broad or narrow the definition should be, whether parental intent should be considered, and whether the cultural context should be considered (Berger, 1980a). In recent studies, these issues have been circumvented by the use of reported and/or "verified" cases of child abuse, where the definition of abuse is implicitly determined by state child abuse agencies. Although such an approach is quite practical for the researcher, it tends to further obscure definitional issues, since the criteria for "reported" and "verified" abuse are not specified.

It might be useful for researchers to attempt a standardized definition which separates physical abuse into severe, moderate, and mild categories and which specifies the parental behavior (rather than intent), and the range of consequences to the child, needed for inclusion in each category. Researchers could then examine each group separately, as well as compare the groups on various factors. Some authors argue that cultural context should be included in the definition of child abuse (Garbarino, 1976, 1977; Gelles, 1973; Gil, 1970; Korbin, 1977; Parke, 1980). But it may be more appropriate to exclude it from the definition and systematically study cultural context as an independent variable (see Berger, 1980a).

Different types of child abuse (physical abuse, neglect, and sexual abuse)

Physical abuse and neglect are sometimes combined under the rubric "child maltreatment," which may lead to misleading conclusions about physical abuse and neglect. It is imperative that physical abuse be defined and studied apart from neglect, so that the two phenomena can be compared and contrasted. Physical abuse and neglect do seem to have certain characteristics in common (Disbrow, Doerr, & Caulfield, 1977; Gaines, Sandgrund, Green, & Power, 1978; Hoffman-Plotkin & Twentyman, 1980; Kent, 1976; Larrance & Twentyman, 1982; M. Martin, 1972; Ruppenthal, Arling, Harlow, Sackett, & Suomi, 1976; Suomi, 1978; Twentyman & Plotkin, 1982; L. Young, 1964). But there also are some important differences in the variables associated with each (e.g., Bauer & Twentyman, 1983; Bousha & Twentyman, 1982; Egeland & Sroufe, 1980; Larrance & Twentyman, 1982; Twentyman & Plotkin, 1982), and in the apparent consequences of each (e.g., Bousha & Twentyman, 1982; Hoffman-Plotkin & Twentyman; Plotkin, Azar, Twentyman, & Perri, 1981; Suomi).

Although the Child Abuse Prevention and Treatment Act includes sexual abuse in its definition of child abuse, most investigators of physical abuse and/or child maltreatment do not include cases of sexual abuse in their studies. It is clearly possible for the same child to be physically and sexually abused; but in general, they do not tend to occur together (Schechter & Roberge, 1976). Sexual abuse has received little attention in the literature. Most existing reports on sexual abuse are based on case studies (e.g., Kaufman, Peck, & Tagiuri, 1980; Renshaw & Renshaw, 1980; Schechter & Roberge; Yorukoglu & Kemph, 1980), and much of the available "information" is really inference drawn from such case studies. Although some authors infer some similarities between sexual and physical abuse (e.g., Steele, 1980) it is generally agreed that they are really quite distinct in terms of etiology, associated variables, and consequences (Walters, 1975). Sexual abuse will not be further addressed, and the reader is referred to some discussions of this topic (Geiser, 1979; Henderson, 1972; Walters).

The remainder of this chapter will be exclusively focused on the physical abuse of children, although occasional comments will address child neglect. Unless otherwise noted, the term *child abuse* will hereafter always refer to the physical abuse of children.

METHODOLOGICAL ISSUES

The child abuse literature abounds with methodological inadequacies. Plotkin et al. (1981) examined the methodological quality of 270 articles on causative factors in child abuse. Only 25 percent of the articles used original data collected by the author, and few of those employed matched control groups. Only one third of this 25 percent used inferential statistics, and in many they were used inappropriately. A priori predictions were found to be lacking, thereby increasing the probability of obtaining significance by chance alone. Overall, fewer than 5 percent of the articles met all their criteria for a methodologically sound study, but they noted a recent positive trend toward more methodologically sound research.

The degree to which methodological inadequacies can distort the data is aptly demonstrated in two recent papers (Leventhal, 1981; Milner & Wimberly, 1980). In their work on the child abuse potential (CAP) inventory, Milner and Wimberly found that 13 percent of the items significantly discriminated abusers from matched nonabusers, while 38 percent of the items (almost a threefold increase) significantly discriminated abusers from nonabusers when the groups were not matched. Leventhal (1981) reviewed a number of retrospective child abuse studies that examined a few specific variables. Although the majority of reviewed studies suggested that one of the variables was significantly associated with child abuse, the importance of that factor in child abuse was not confirmed when the methodologically inadequate studies were discounted. Leventhal concluded that the use of a specific control group and of matching techniques is crucial.

CHARACTERISTICS OF ABUSING PARENTS

Among the various theoretical perspectives on child abuse, the oldest and most prominent has been the psychiatric model (Gelles, 1973; Parke & Collmer, 1975; M. Young, 1976). This viewpoint suggests that the abusing parent is always the locus of the problem and that all other variables—if they are considered at all—are secondary to the psychiatric or personality problems of the abusing parent. Six questions relevant to this perspective will be addressed in this section: (1) Do abusing parents fit into any traditional psychiatric categories? (2) Do abusing parents share particular personality traits that differentiate them from nonabusing parents? (3) Is parental age a factor in child abuse? (4) Do abusing parents have distorted perceptions of the abused child? (5) Do abusing parents have unrealistically high expectations of the abused child? (6) Are certain parental characteristics necessary or sufficient to explain child abuse?

Psychopathology and personality traits

Very few abusing parents are psychotic (Berger, 1980a; Blumberg, 1974; Cohen, Raphling, & Green, 1966; Flynn, 1970; Fontana & Bernard, 1971; Galdston, 1971; Parke & Collmer, 1975; Steele, 1970, 1980; Steele & Pollack, 1974; Wasserman, 1968). But, as a group, abusing parents seem to evidence a higher rate of social and psychiatric deviance than is found in the general population (Baldwin & Oliver, 1975; Elmer, 1967; Gil, 1970; Scott, 1980; Smith, Hanson, & Noble, 1973; Steele & Pollack, 1974). Abusing parents overall do not fit any particular diagnostic category, but rather show considerable variability in the type of psychopathology manifested (Blumberg; Boszormenyi-Nagy & Spark, 1973; Gelles, 1973; Green, Gaines, & Sandgrund, 1974; Morse, Sahler, & Friedman, 1970; Spinetta & Rigler, 1972; Steele & Pollack).

Although abusing parents constitute a diagnostically heterogeneous group, these parents could still be homogeneous with respect to certain personality traits. A plethora of personality traits have been suggested to characterize this population, and there is little consensus about these traits (Gelles, 1973).

Abusing parents have been described as narcissistic, immature, aggressive and impulsive (Bennie & Sclare, 1969; Blumberg, 1974; Galdston, 1971; Green et al., 1974; Johnson & Morse, 1968; Kempe, Silverman, Steele, Droegemueller, & Silver, 1962; Nurse, 1964; Terr, 1970; Wasserman, 1968; Zalba, 1967), rigid and compulsive (Fontana & Bernard, 1971; Milner & Wimberly, 1980), anxious, hostile and depressed (Johnson & Morse), and as having low self-esteem (Blumberg; Green, 1979; Green et al.; Milner & Wimberly; Spinetta & Rigler, 1972; Steele & Pollack, 1974). "Impulsive," "apathetic-futile" and "childish-dependent" personality styles have been reported as well (Hunter, Kilstrom, Kraybill, & Loda, 1978). Abusing parents have also been described as unable to form attachments due to lack of basic trust (Steele, 1980; Steele & Pollack). In most of the foregoing studies, inferences about personality traits were based on clinical observation alone, and few studies used control groups, standardized testing, or "blind" observers. But some studies have more systematically investigated the characteristics associated with abusing parents.

A few well-executed studies have suggested that low empathy and low self-esteem may be characteristic of many abusing parents. Abusive or neglecting parents were compared with matched control parents on parental attitudes and empathy, using an interview and questionnaire format (Disbrow et al., 1977). Abusers showed less empathy and lower self-esteem than neglecters and controls. Melnick and Hurley (1969) compared abusers and matched controls on a number of personality measures and concluded that the abusers evidenced lower self-esteem and empathy. However, Shorkey (1980) found that abusers and matched controls did not differ on feelings of personal worth independent of the evaluations of others; but the abusers did score significantly lower on feelings of personal worth based on their perceptions of others' evaluations of them. This finding supports Parke's (1980) point that the act of being labeled an abuser may produce some of the characteristics that investigators later view as etiological in the child abuse. It also raises the point that different methods of assessing the same construct may yield different findings, particularly when the measures are of questionable validity and reliability, as is the case with assessments of empathy and self-esteem. Since poor empathic ability may be a significant variable in child abuse, it is interesting to note that the inhibitory effect of pain cues on aggression may depend upon the development of empathy (Feshbach & Feshbach, 1969).

Measuring the physiological reactions of abusing parents to various stimuli has generated some intriguing results. Abusing and neglecting parents were compared with matched controls on heart rate, galvanic skin response, skin temperature, and respiration rate when exposed to videotapes of neutral, pleasant, and unpleasant family scenes (Disbrow et al., 1977). Both abusers and neglecters showed greater physiological arousal throughout the videotape presentation. They both also showed less heart rate variability between the different types of family scenes than did the controls, suggesting less differentiation in their responses to very different social stimuli. Frodi and Lamb (1978c) compared the physiological responses of abusive and matched control parents to the smiling and crying of an infant. The heart rate data suggested that abusing mothers were less responsive to changes in the infant's affect and behavior, and a self-report measure indicated that they had a more marked aversive reaction to the infant's crying and a less positive reaction to the infant's smiling. These studies suggest that abusing parents have a diminished sensitivity to changes in social stimuli and that they react more negatively and less positively to at least some social stimuli. These data also lend some support to Knutson's (1978) hypothesis that abusing parents may be hyperreactive to noxious social stimuli. Bauer and Twentyman (1983) tested Knutson's hypothesis by comparing the responses of abusing, neglecting, and matched comparison mothers to a standard set of audiotapes depicting child-related stressors and nonchild-related stressors. Abusing mothers reported more annoyance in response to both types of stressors than did mothers in either of the other two groups, supporting the presence in abusing parents of a generalized hyperreactivity to noxious social stimuli.

A statistically significant difference between two groups on a variable does not necessarily imply that the variable has clinical or predictive utility. For example, abusing parents were compared with a matched comparison group of clinically disturbed parents on the Huesmann et al. aggression scale (Plotkin & Twentyman, 1982). Although this measure showed abusing parents to be significantly more aggressive statistically, a discriminant analysis based on these scores correctly classified only 26.3 percent of the abusing parents. An important factor that impacts on the predictive utility of a variable is the base rate of that variable in the general population and its base rate in specific subgroups of interest in the population (e.g., lower socioeconomic class individuals). A methodological strategy that addresses this issue to some extent is the prospective study. Recently, a number of researchers have begun to utilize this approach in the child abuse area, and specifically, they have looked at parental characteristics associated with high risk for child abusive behavior.

A longitudinal, at-risk approach combined with a prospective methodology was used to study maternal characteristics and other variables related to child maltreatment (Brunnquell, Critchton, & Egeland, 1981; Egeland & Brunnquell, 1979). High risk was defined as low socioeconomic status (SES), and these first-time mothers were recruited from a public health infant- and child-care clinic. Personality testing was completed at three months postpartum. Based on home observations of mother and child, Egeland and Brunnquell identified an inadequate-care group (physical abuse, neglect, and failure to thrive) and an excellent-care group, and compared the results of personality testing for the two groups. Inadequate-care mothers seemed to lack an understanding of their relationship with their children, reacted negatively to the pregnancy, had less realistic expectations about the nature of being a parent, were more aggressive and suspicious, and were more likely to describe themselves negatively. Interestingly, traditional personality traits like aggression and impulsivity were not, by themselves, predictive of the parent-child relationship. The more predictive variables were broadly defined characteristics such as "psychological complexity" and "level of personal integration." The authors suggested that these predictive variables reflected factors such as level of ego functioning, intelligence, and the ability to understand and deal effectively with their own ambivalence about the child, as well as the ability to appreciate their own and their children's needs for autonomy. This study supports the notion that traditional personality variables may not contribute much to attempts to understand or predict child abuse. However, physical abuse was combined with other forms of child maltreatment in those data. Thus, variables which might have been significantly related to physical abuse could have been obscured by the inclusion of neglect and failure-to-thrive cases in the sample.

Parental age

Youthful parenthood may be associated with child abuse (Bolton, Laner, & Kane, 1980; Gelles, 1980; Lynch & Roberts, 1977; Smith, 1975), although some investigators have concluded that there is no relationship between the two variables (Earp & Ory, 1980; Elmer, 1967; Gil, 1970; Kinard & Klerman, 1980). The conflicting findings are most likely a function of the numerous methodological inadequacies that characterize studies in this area (Leventhal, 1981), along with the fact that different definitions of youth have been used (Kinard & Klerman) and each definition has led to different conclusions.

The best study to date in this area examined the relationship between parental youth and child abuse using two comparison groups: population data and a matched control group (Kinard & Klerman, 1980). Age was measured from the birth of the mother's first child. There was no difference between the abuse group and the matched control group in the mother's age at the birth of the first child, but both groups differed significantly from the general population statistics. The authors concluded that teenage mothers are not more likely to abuse their children, and that the link between child abuse and youthful parenting may be due to factors common to both, such as poverty and disturbed family state.

Distorted perceptions of the abused child

Abusing parents may have distorted perceptions of their abused child (Galdston, 1971; Green et al., 1974; Gregg & Elmer, 1969; Smith, 1975). Recently, the question of whether or not abusing parents evidence a negative bias in the way they perceive their children has been specifically examined in a series of attribution studies.

"Blind" examiners presented abusing, neglecting, and matched control mothers with pictures of their own and other children involved in various activities and asked the mothers to explain why their children would behave in a particular way (Larrance & Twentyman, 1982). Attributional research has indicated that most people show a self-serving bias and ego involvement when they make attributions about the behavior of significant others. The comparison mothers in the study showed this self-serving bias when making attributions for their children's behavior. However, the abusing mothers made attributions similar to those that people might make for the behavior of a competitor or a disliked person: They saw their children's negative behavior as reflecting highly internal and stable traits, but saw their children's positive behaviors as more externally caused and less stable. The comparison mothers showed the reverse pattern. The neglecting mothers showed an attributional pattern that fell somewhere in between the patterns shown by the other two groups; also, the attributions of neglecting mothers did not change much across different situations. Larrance, Amish, Twentyman, and Plotkin (1982) reported that the more seriously abusive the mothers were judged to be, the more internal and stable were their attributions for their children's negative behavior. They also reported that abusing and neglecting mothers were more likely than matched comparison mothers to rate their children's behavior as intentional and aversive and to interpret these behaviors as the children's attempts to annoy them.

Abusing parents may well have distorted perceptions of their children and/or unusually negative attributions for their children's behavior, but such distortions are not necessarily etiological in child abuse. It is even possible that they might be a consequence of the abusive interactions. Following aggressive behavior, an aggressor frequently will alter his or her perceptions of the victim, seemingly in order to justify the behavior (Brock & Pallak, 1969). One such distortion that has been identified is derogation of the victim by attributing negative characteristics to him or her. And even if such distortions are sometimes etiological in child abuse, it is possible that they develop from early parent-child interactions rather than necessarily being an enduring characteristic that the parent brings to the childrearing situation.

Inappropriate expectations of the abused child

Abusing parents may have inappropriate and unrealistically high expectations of their children (Dubanoski, Evans, & Higuchi, 1978; Elmer, 1977b; Galdston, 1965; Helfer, 1980; Smith & Hanson, 1975; Steele, 1970; Steele & Pollack, 1974; Wasserman, 1968). For example, Galdston reported that abusing parents spoke about their children as if they were capable of the same intentional and organized behavior as adults.

However, recent studies do not support previous conclusions about parental expectations. For one year, Hunter et al. (1978) followed 255 babies who had been hospitalized in the intensive care unit after birth and then discharged to their parents. An array of information was collected on these families while the babies were still hospitalized. Ten of the babies (3.9 percent) were confirmed as abused or neglected during the first year of life. Data collected on these families were compared with data on the families of the remaining 245 children. Unrealistic expectations of the infant was unrelated to later maltreatment. These results must be viewed cautiously because there were only 10 maltreated children in the sample, only one year had elapsed, only babies in the ICU were included, and abuse and neglect cases were combined. But this study is important because it addresses this question using a prospective methodology.

"Parental expectations" was not operationally defined and carefully measured in a methodologically appropriate manner in the foregoing studies. Some recent studies have, however, examined this construct with more attention to methodology. Twentyman and Plotkin (1982) constructed a developmental expectation questionnaire to assess the extent and direction of inappropriate parental expectations of child development. Items and normative scores based on the Vineland social maturity scale were utilized for the questionnaire, which contained descriptions of 20 developmental milestones of childhood and adolescence. Abusing, neglecting, and matched comparison parents were asked to estimate the expected age level of each developmental milestone, for their own child and for the "average child." The abusing parents expected *less* from their own children than from the average child, and they differed in this respect from both the neglecting and comparison parents. Also, abusing and neglecting parents evidenced both inappropriately high and inappropriately low expectations of their own child and of the average child. These findings may be relevant to inconsistent use of discipline, an issue which will be addressed in a later section. Twentyman and Plotkin suggested that the abusing and neglecting mothers had an informational deficit regarding child development. This hypothesis is consistent with Elmer's (1977a, 1977b) conclusion that the abusing mothers in her study lacked knowledge of child development.

Larrance and Twentyman (1982) showed abusing, neglecting, and matched comparison mothers pictures of their children involved in ambiguous, competitive, and cooperative interpersonal situations and asked the mothers to estimate their children's likelihood of success with the various tasks depicted. The abusing and neglecting mothers held significantly more negative expectations of their children's performance than was true for the comparison mothers. A chance task was also included, in which the mothers' estimates of their child's success should theoretically have been independent of their child's capabilities; once again, the abusing and neglecting mothers expected more-negative outcomes for their children. Thus, the negative bias was not necessarily based on realistic evaluations of their children's capabilities.

In summary, unrealistic expectations may be relevant to child abuse, but not in the way that has previously been assumed. Abusing parents may have an informational deficit that leads to both unrealistically high and unrealistically low expectations of child behavior, and they may expect less from their own children than from other children. Twentyman, Rohrbeck, and Amish (in press) have proposed a four-stage cognitive-behavioral model of child abuse that hypothesizes primacy of parental cognitions in the abusive process: Stage 1 involves informational deficits which lead to unrealistic expectations about appropriate child behavior; in Stage 2, the child behaves in a manner that is inconsistent with parental expectation; in Stage 3, the parent misattributes the child's behavior to willful disobedience; and then, in Stage 4, the parent aggresses against the child. The authors suggest that Stage 4 aggression could be either an instrumental response to terminate the child's behavior or a response to frustration. Although this model may provide a useful conceptualization for part of the process of child abuse, it fails to account for a number of other variables that seem relevant, and it does not really address the process by which parental misattributions are translated into abusive behavior. This model does, however, suggest a number of testable hypotheses and treatment interventions, and it does point to the interactive nature of the abusive process.

Conclusions

Of those parental characteristics which appear to be related to child abuse, none may be considered sufficient condition for child abuse, since not all parents with such characteristics abuse their children. Furthermore, none may be considered necessary since there is no evidence that all abusing parents manifest these characteristics. It is possible that particular combinations of some of these characteristics may be necessary for certain subgroups of abusing parents and not for others; but at present, there are no data relevant to this specific question.

Child abuse is far too complex, however, to be explained using a model based on parental characteristics alone. At a minimum, child abuse involves at least two individuals, and the interaction between those individuals occurs within the broader context of the family. Although factors external to the family may also contribute to child abuse and thus must be explored, these factors must filter through particular constellations of family variables to culminate in child abuse. Consequently, it is crucial to explore many different aspects of these families in order to begin to identify the combinations of factors that might lead to abuse.

THE MULTIGENERATIONAL HYPOTHESIS OF CHILD ABUSE

Many abusing parents report that they were themselves abused, neglected, or rejected in childhood (Baldwin & Oliver, 1975; Blumberg, 1974; Cohen et al., 1966; Fontana & Bernard, 1971; Gelles, 1973; Gil, 1970; Green et al., 1974; Helfer, 1980; Hunter et al., 1978; Johnson

& Morse, 1968; Justice & Justice, 1976; Kempe & Helfer, 1972; Nurse, 1964; Oliver & Taylor, 1971; Paulson & Chaleff, 1973; Scott, 1980; Silver, Dublin, & Lourie, 1969; Smith, 1975; Spinetta & Rigler, 1972; Steele, 1970, 1976, 1980; Steele & Pollack, 1974; Van Stolk, 1972; Walters, 1975; L. Young, 1964; Zalba, 1967). The idea that abusing parents were mistreated in childhood is so widely accepted that it receives almost axiomatic status. Some authors further assert that today's abused children will become tomorrow's abusing parents (Green, 1979; Helfer; Scott; Steele, 1976). In this section, two questions will be separately addressed: (1) Were abusing parents themselves abused in childhood? (2) Is a history of abuse in childhood predictive of later abusive parenting?

Childhood experiences of abusing parents

Despite widespread agreement that abusing parents were abused children, the actual data are not quite so clear-cut. The statistics are difficult to interpret since some investigators report rates of childhood physical abuse only, while others report combined rates of abuse, neglect, and rejection. Furthermore, most of the data are retrospective self-reports, so the statistics actually reflect the perceptions and personal definitions that abusing parents have of their childhood experiences. The available statistics on these self-reports vary widely. Rates for physical abuse in childhood range from 11 percent (Gil, 1970) to 47 percent (Conger, Burgess, & Barrett, 1980), while rates for maltreatment in childhood (i.e., abuse, neglect, and/or rejection) are often close to 100 percent (Blumberg, 1974). An anecdote related by de Lissovoy (1979), however, argues for cautious interpretation of these statistics. Eleven abusing parents had reported a history of abuse in their childhoods. Months later, de Lissovoy interviewed these same parents and asked them more specific questions about their childhood disciplinary experiences. They described spankings, deprivation of privileges, and other normative disciplinary experiences, and only one described a history of physical abuse.

Only a few studies have specifically been able to trace the family patterns of discipline across generations, and those studies have in fact found clear multigenerational patterns of abuse (Oliver & Taylor, 1971; Silver et al., 1969). But those were multiproblem families with severely abusive behavior. With the exception of such extreme cases, it is unfortunately necessary to rely predominantly on parental self-reports to gather these statistics, since systematic records of child abuse are a relatively recent phenomenon.

Twenty abusing parents and 20 matched controls were asked if they or a sibling had ever been severely punished as a child (Conger et al., 1980). There was a significantly higher rate of such a history in the abuse group. But more than half of the abusing parents did not report this type of history. There was also an interaction between childhood history and life stress: life stress was more frequently related to child abuse for those individuals who also had witnessed or experienced severe parental violence as a child. These findings highlight the fact that any identified attributes of abusing parents most probably must interact with other variables for child abuse to occur (Belsky, 1980).

A history of abuse in childhood is clearly not a necessary condition for abusive parenting, and it is probably not sufficient either. Furthermore, the likelihood of abused children growing up to abuse their own children cannot really be ascertained using a retrospective methodology, particularly in the absence of base-rate information on the history of childhood abuse in the general population. Longitudinal studies are best suited to address this question, although it would take years to obtain the data. But cross-sectional designs can be used to obtain some preliminary data on this issue.

Childrearing correlates of a history of abuse in childhood

Rutter (1979) points out that retrospective links are much stronger than prospective ones and that probably only a small proportion of abused children become abusing parents. But, abused children may well have an increased risk of becoming abusing parents. Learning plays an important role in the development of aggressive behavior (Bandura, 1973; Bandura, Ross, & Ross, 1961; Lefkowitz, Walder, & Eron, 1963; Owens & Straus, 1975; Sears, Maccoby, & Levin, 1974), and data will be reviewed later which show that abused children frequently are found to behave aggressively. These aggressive, abused children may be imitating an aggressive repertoire modeled by their parents, and they may later come to imitate their parents' aggressive childrearing methods as well. Abused children may also acquire other characteristics from their parents which might add to their probability of becoming abusing parents. For example, abused children show some characteristics similar to those shown by their parents (e.g., insensitivity to socioemotional contexts), which could be precursors to later abusive parents (Barahal, Waterman, & Martin, 1981). Furthermore, there are some intriguing longitudinal animal data which lend partial support to the multigenerational hypothesis (Ruppenthal et al, 1976; Suomi, 1978), but they will not be reviewed here.

Some recent studies examine the multigenerational hypothesis more directly. Hunter et al. (1978) followed 255 mother-infant dyads, where the baby had been in the intensive care unit, and found that 3.9 percent of the babies were abused or neglected within one year. At the outset of the study, they had ascertained the presence or absence of abuse or neglect in the mother's childhood. They did not provide the specific statistics, but reported that a history of abuse or neglect was related to later abusive or neglectful parenting. However, many parents with such a history did not mistreat their children. The small number of maltreated children and the rather brief follow-up period render these findings interesting but tentative.

In a study involving a nationally representative sample of 1,146 parents (Gelles, 1980; Straus, 1980a, 1980b), one parent in each household was asked about the type of disciplinary strategies used in that household, the parent's own history of physical discipline in childhood, and a number of other variables. Child abuse was defined as the utilization of severe violence such as kicking, biting, and punching with children. Having been the victim of violence in childhood was related to an increased probability of using such disciplinary strategies as a parent, but having observed violence in childhood (i.e., marital violence) was even more relevant to the probability of later abusive parenting (Gelles, 1980). For this same sample of parents, Straus looked at the rate of life stress and its interaction with other child abuse–related variables. For the subset of families with high life stress, a history of physical punishment by mothers during adolescence was associated with a *lower* rate of later abusive parenting, whereas a history of physical punishment by fathers during adolescence was associated with a higher rate. And, as with the entire sample, those in this high-stress group who had witnessed violence between their parents in childhood showed a much higher rate of abusive parenting.

A study by Berger (1981) specifically addressed the multigenerational hypothesis. Nonclinical middle-class young adults who were abused in childhood were selected, based on their self-reports of specific types of discipline experienced. Some of these individuals labeled their experiences abusive (physical abuse group), while others did not (severe physical punishment group). Three other demographically similar groups were also selected: (1) individuals who were never themselves abused but who had an abused sibling (abused-sibling group); (2) individuals who had received normative physical discipline (mild physical punishment group); and (3) individuals who received no physical discipline (no physical punishment group).

An interactive analogue disciplinary task was employed to assess and compare the disciplinary strategies utilized by the subjects in the five groups. The subjects were presented with disciplinary options and asked to discipline five separate children whose aversive behaviors were escalating and each of whom manifested some of the child characteristics frequently associated with abuse.

Although these results must be interpreted cautiously, they did not support a simplistic multigenerational hypothesis of child abuse: physical abuse in childhood was not associated with more excessive or more rapid choosing of physical discipline, with more yelling or verbally threatening strategies, or with more subjective annoyance in the face of difficult child behaviors. The pros and cons of self-report of childhood history have already been discussed. As for analogue tasks, they clearly have serious limitations. However, some data show that self-reports of disciplinary strategies utilized do discriminate abusing from nonabusing parents (Disbrow et al., 1977; Dubanoski et al., 1978; Smith, 1975), and analogue tasks sometimes provide the only method of directly assessing a particular issue. It is noteworthy that subjects in each group did choose physical discipline on some occasions despite the lack of statistically significant overall group differences.

Some possible group differences were tentatively suggested by the planned comparisons. Although such findings cannot be assumed reliable in the absence of overall group differences, some are of particular theoretical interest. It appeared that when physical discipline was used, the siblings of abused children might use it more often and choose it sooner than subjects in the other groups. Also, a significantly larger proportion of subjects in the Abused-Sibling group chose to use physical discipline at all (78 percent) than was true for the Physical Abuse group (33 percent) and the No Physical Punishment group (33 percent). These data raise the possibility that the nonabused siblings of abused children might be at greater risk of later using excessive physical discipline with their children. This hypothesis is consistent with observational learning theory and data (Bandura, 1973) and with Gelles's (1980) finding that having observed marital violence in childhood was more associated with later abusive parenting than was having been the victim of parental violence in childhood. It can be speculated that learning an aggressive repertoire without experiencing the pain involved for the victim may actually increase the probability of later imitation; or conversely, having experienced the pain and fear involved may actually decrease the likelihood of later imitation in some cases (Fraiberg, Adelson, & Shapiro, 1975).

The Berger (1981) study also suggests that adults who were abused in childhood may not be a homogeneous group. One variable which appears to distinguish between formerly abused individuals is the way in which they label and/or perceive their abusive experiences, although the clinical utility of this variable remains to be seen. There were, however, certain trends in the data which appeared consistent with Herzberger, Potts, and Dillon's (1981) hypothesis that perceiving the abuse as a legitimate strategy for conflict resolution (perhaps similar to mislabeling the experience) may increase the probability of imitation and that perceiving it as illegitimate (perhaps similar to appropriately labeling it abusive) may decrease the probability of imitation.

Knutson, Berger, and Mehm (1983) administered the Berger (1981) questionnaire on childhood upbringing to 216 parents of 119 consecutive child referrals to a mental health clinic. Parental scores on various questionnaire scales were used in a discriminant analysis to predict characteristics of their children. Neither maternal nor paternal history alone was a good predictor of rearing either an abused or an antisocial child. But when maternal and paternal history data were combined for those families where both parents participated in childrearing, the ability to predict abuse and antisocial behavior in the child's history was remarkable. In particular, 98 percent of the abuse classifications were correctly made, with only one false positive and one false negative classification. This study provides strong support for the multigenerational hypothesis, but only when *both* parents report a history of abuse in childhood.

The data reviewed in this section, while somewhat supportive of a multigenerational hypothesis, cast doubt on a simplistic model. Both experiencing and merely observing family violence in childhood may be related to an increased probability of later abusive parenting. But some percentage of abused children will grow up to become nonabusive parents, and some percentage of children from nonabusive families will become abusive parents. The presence or absence of certain contextual factors in adulthood—such as poverty and stress (e.g., Rutter, 1979; Rutter & Madge, 1976), certain constellations of family and/or personality variables, and the childhood history of the other caretaker—may interact with an individual's childhood history to increase or decrease the probability that child abuse will assume a multigenerational pattern.

CHARACTERISTICS OF THE ABUSED CHILD

Abused children appear to manifest an array of behavioral, physical, and developmental deviations, and certain of these child characteristics may play an eliciting role in the abuse. While some of these child characteristics can be conclusively identified as having existed prior to the abuse and thus might elicit or contribute to the abuse, it is more difficult to determine the onset of others. This section will be divided into two parts: (1) characteristics that are known to have existed prior to the abuse, and (2) characteristics that could have either preceded or resulted from the abuse.

Characteristics that precede the abuse

Prematurity and low birth weight have been found to be associated with child abuse (Baldwin & Oliver, 1975; Faranoff, Kennell, & Klaus, 1972; Fomufud, Sinkford, & Louy, 1975; Friedrich & Boriskin, 1976; Frodi, 1981; Herrenkohl & Herrenkohl, 1979; Hunter et al., 1978; Kennell, Voos, & Klaus, 1976; Klein & Stern, 1971; Lynch, 1976; Lynch & Roberts, 1977; H. P. Martin, 1976; Smith, 1976). However, Leventhal (1981) examined 18 of the studies in this area and concluded that only 2 were methodologically adequate. In particular, most studies had compared the abuse group with either general population statistics on prematurity and low birth weight or with an unmatched control group, both of which are methodologically inappropriate procedures. Overall, the 18 studies supported prematurity and low birth weight as risk factors for abuse, but the two methodologically sound studies did not. Leventhal concluded there is no evidence that prematurity and low birth weight constitute risk factors.

Some recent, more methodologically adequate studies support Leventhal's (1981) conclusion. Gaines et al. (1978) found that neonatal complications leading to hospitalization did not discriminate between abusing, neglecting, and control groups. In addition, some prospective studies with high-risk (i.e., low SES) families have found no evidence that premature status is related to later maltreatment (Egeland & Brunnquell, 1979; Egeland & Vaughn, 1981).

The weight of the evidence, at this point, seems to cast doubt on the importance of prematurity and low birth weight as risk factors. However, it would be overhasty to consider the issue closed, since there are some intriguing data which suggest that an infant's premature status may adversely affect parent-child interaction. Frodi and Lamb (1978a, 1978b), showed that crying by both full-term and premature infants elicited marked autonomic arousal and was perceived as irritating by normal adults and that this reaction was significantly more marked when the infant was premature. The issue must also remain open because the prospective studies, which provide the bulk of the evidence here, have not followed the infants for very long and have combined physical abuse with other forms of maltreatment.

Premarital conception and illegitimacy (Baldwin & Oliver, 1975; Cohen et al., 1966; Johnson & Morse, 1968; Kempe et al., 1962; Nurse, 1964, Smith, Hanson, & Noble, 1974; Steele, 1970; Terr, 1970) and a higher than normal frequency of congenital defects (Baldwin & Oliver; Hunter et al., 1978; Lynch, 1976; Smith, 1975) have also been reported to characterize abused children. In both cases, however, the literature is laden with methodological inadequacies and inconsistent results, so no conclusions can be drawn. But it is interesting that recent studies have not focused on the variables.

Child characteristics with unknown onset

Mental retardation (Friedrich & Boriskin, 1976; Green, 1978; M. Martin, 1972; Morse et al., 1970), physical handicaps (Elmer & Gregg, 1967; Friedrich & Boriskin, 1967; Johnson & Morse, 1968), and developmental deviations (Elmer & Gregg, 1967; Green, 1978; Johnson & Morse, 1976; Kent, 1976; M. Martin) have been found with high frequency in samples of abused children. It is usually difficult to determine whether these characteristics play an eliciting role in the abuse or whether they are consequences of the abuse. Even when the deviations are known to have existed prior to the identified abusive episode, there is no guarantee that previous, unreported abusive episodes are not responsible. In fact, in Straus's (1980) survey, as few as 6 percent of the abusive families had experienced only a single episode of abuse; the mean number of assaults per year in these families was 10.5. But even if the deviations are products of abuse, it is possible that the presence of these characteristics will serve to increase the probability that abuse will recur.

Of all the child characteristics associated with abuse, behavioral deviations have received the most attention. Since abuse is only one aspect of a more-general pattern of parent-child interaction, behavioral deviations may be seen as a product of the more general pattern rather than exclusively as a product or precipitant of the abuse. To some extent, these behavioral deviations may also involve temperamental factors in the child which impact on the parent-child interaction. But the extent to which they are necessary for abuse to occur is unknown.

Studies of abused infants have found that they sometimes seem to be less responsive to care givers, as compared with other infants (Egeland, Breitenbucher, & Rosenberg, 1980; Gaensbauer & Sands, 1979; George & Main, 1979). George & Main systematically recorded observations of 10 abused and 10 matched control infants between 12 and 36 months of age. Both groups were similar in the frequency of spontaneous approaches made toward adults. However, the abused children were much less responsive to friendly overtures made by the adults. The abused children were also much more aggressive than the control children.

Martin (1972) suggested that there may be two types of abused children: an apathetic and relatively unresponsive type and an aggressive type. Although he hypothesized that abused children are more often the former type, the literature suggests that aggressive, coercive, and provocative behaviors are actually more common (Burgess & Conger, 1977; Galdston, 1971; Green, 1978; Hoffman-Plotkin & Twentyman, in press; Johnson & Morse, 1968; Kent, 1976; Kinard, 1980, 1982; Reid & Taplin, 1976; Reidy, 1977).

Only a few studies in this area have used standardized measures of aggression. Hoffman-Plotkin and Twentyman (in press) compared matched groups of abused, neglected, and comparison children on aggressive behavior during free play and on parent and teacher ratings of aggression. Behavioral observations showed the abused children to be more aggressive than either neglected or comparison children. However, teacher and parent ratings depicted both abused and neglected children as more aggressive than the comparison children, but not different from one another. Reidy (1977) reported very similar findings for observations of free-play behavior and for teachers' ratings of abused, neglected, and comparison children. Home observational studies have also found that children in abusing families display more aggressive and coercive behavior than children in comparison families (Burgess & Conger, 1977; Reid & Taplin, 1976).

PARENT-CHILD INTERACTIONS IN ABUSING FAMILIES

It has long been recognized that parents influence their children, but only recently have the issues of children's influence on their parents' behavior (e.g., Bell, 1968) and reciprocal parent-child influences (see L'Abate & Wagner, Chapter 33 of this *Handbook*) gained much attention. Despite the fact that child abuse is an interactional occurrence that cannot really be understood by studying parent and child behavior separately, very few interactional studies are available in this area.

Some recent studies have begun to examine the dyadic interactions of abusing mothers and their infants. Hyman (1977) found that the interaction sequences in mother-infant abuse dyads were more disjointed and less reciprocal than those of the matched control dyads. Mothers and infants in the abuse dyads emitted a high proportion of behaviors to which the other member of the dyad did not respond, which was not true of the control dyads. Egeland and Brunnquell (1979) evaluated 24 mother-infant interaction variables during feeding, at three months postpartum. They later identified "adequate care" and "inadequate care" (i.e., abuse, neglect, and failure to thrive) subsamples from among the 275 high-risk mothers followed. A discriminant analysis found that "mother's caretaking skills," "mother's affect toward baby," and "baby's social behavior," as assessed at three months of age, contributed to the prediction of the later-identified group membership. An overall correct classification rate of 81.8 percent was achieved, using the observational data. Even though mother's personality characteristics, life stress, family circumstances, and baby characteristics all contributed to the prediction of maltreatment, the most important variable was the relationship between parent and child.

A few observational studies are available on older abused children and their parents (Bousha & Twentyman, 1982; Burgess & Conger, 1977; Reid & Taplin, 1976). They are basically well designed studies that have used standardized observational techniques and blind observers and have demonstrated good interrater reliability. Bousha and Twentyman (1982) observed abuse, neglect, and matched comparison mother-child dyads and found that abusing mothers evidenced significantly higher rates of verbal and physical aggression toward their children than did mothers in other groups. Neglecting mothers had a lower rate of interaction with their children than abusing mothers, who in turn interacted less with their children than the comparison mothers. The abused children were significantly more verbally aggressive toward their mothers than were children in the other groups and similar to the neglected children in being significantly more physically aggressive than the comparison children. Although both abused and neglected children engaged in high rates of aggressive behavior, the maternal response to those behaviors differed markedly between groups. The authors suggested that abusing mothers may characteristically relate to their children in an aggressive manner across situations.

Burgess and Conger (1977) examined the interactional patterns in abusing, neglecting, and matched comparison families, rather than just dyads within the families. They found high rates of coercive and noncompliant behaviors and low rates of reciprocity among all members of abusing families. The mothers in the abuse families not only initiated fewer contacts with other family members, but they also tended to behave more negatively toward their children when they did interact with them, as compared with the control mothers. The fathers in the abuse families directed slightly more contacts to their children than did the mothers, a reversal of the pattern seen in the comparison families. Also, the fathers in the abuse families directed toward their families less negative behavior than did their spouses and even less than the matched comparison fathers. Individuals in the abuse families had less physical contact of any sort with each other, as compared with individuals in the comparison families. And finally, children in the abuse families behaved more negatively and coercively toward one another than was true for the matched comparison children. Similar interactional patterns were found in the neglect families. This study did not identify any clear differences between the interactional patterns of abusing and neglecting families, contrary to the Bousha and

Twentyman (1982) study discussed above. It is not clear whether differences in the methodology utilized or differences in the unit of observation (i.e., family versus dyad) might account for some of the discrepancy. Nevertheless, both studies identified very similar patterns of interactions for the abusing families and dyads.

Reid and Taplin (1976) compared interactional patterns in abusing, distressed nonabusing, and nondistressed nonabusing families. Abusing families engaged in significantly more aversive interactions than the distressed nonabusing families and the nondistressed families. Both parents and children in the abusing families evidenced consistently higher rates of physically aggressive behaviors and verbally threatening behaviors than did parents and children in the comparison families. Despite the otherwise excellent methodology utilized in this study, the abuse group was selected in an unusual manner, and the abusing and distressed nonabusing groups were not matched. Nevertheless, these findings are consistent with the findings from the other observational studies.

Some analogue laboratory studies have demonstrated that certain child behaviors or characteristics can evoke punitive responses from adults. For example, the number of times a mother was interrupted by her child was related to the severity of punishment she chose for her child's mistakes in a learning task (Passman & Mulhern, 1977). Children's behavior has been shown capable of negatively reinforcing high levels of parental punitiveness (Mulhern & Passman, 1978). A child's persistent inability to learn can lead adults to use increasingly intense physical responses to terminate a failure feedback signal (Vasta & Copitch, 1981). And unattractive children may sometimes receive more-severe punishment than attractive children for mistakes on a learning task (Berkowitz & Frodi, 1978; Dion, 1974), underscoring the subtle nature of some of the factors that can influence interpersonal behavior.

The data reviewed in this section, together with the data on the characteristics of abused children, support the notion that children may contribute to their abuse. Further, abuse may not be an isolated event, but rather, may occur within the context of certain types of ongoing interactive patterns in the family that may escalate into abusive episodes (see L'Abate & Wagner, Chapter 33 of this *Handbook*).

PATTERNS OF CHILDREARING IN ABUSING FAMILIES

A large proportion of abusive incidents occur within the context of disciplinary action by the parents (Dubanoski et al., 1978; Gil, 1970). Abusing parents may lack child-management skills, and discipline in abusing families may tend to be both inconsistent and overly punitive

(Disbrow et al., 1977; Friedman & Morse, 1974; Morse et al., 1970; Reid & Taplin, 1976; Smith, 1975; Smith & Hanson, 1975; L. Young, 1964).

Home observations showed that children in abusing families were almost as likely to receive positive reinforcement for aversive as for prosocial behaviors, and parental interventions were more often verbally and physically aggressive than in comparison families (Reid & Taplin, 1976). Based on social worker reports, L. Young (1964) found that both abusing and neglecting families lacked consistent disciplinary strategies and provided little in the way of clear structure for their children. But abusing parents utilized more abusive language, nagging, and scolding than the neglecting parents. Disbrow et al. (1977) found that abusing parents reported using punishment (physical and nonphysical), more frequently than comparison parents. Also, mothers and fathers in these abusing families reported inconsistencies in the way they each handled the same child behaviors.

In an analogue laboratory study, inconsistent discipline for aggressive behavior in boys led to significantly more persistent aggressive behavior than did consistent discipline. (Deur & Parke, 1970). Thus, parents who utilize inconsistent discipline are apt to have more difficulty controlling their children's behavior, which could lead them to use increasingly intense punishment in an attempt to obtain control over the behavior. If abusing parents model aggressive behavior for their children and use inconsistent discipline as well, they might easily find themselves faced with a tenacious discipline problem and trapped into the type of coercion process proposed by Patterson and Reid (see L'Abate & Wagner, Chapter 33 of this *Handbook*).

Disciplinary strategy seems an important area of child abuse research, and more data are needed which overcome the methodological problems found in the foregoing studies (e.g., self-report data, lack of matched control groups). Inconsistent discipline may be characteristic of both abusing and neglecting families. The combination of inconsistent and punitive discipline could be what distinguishes abusing from neglecting families. This possibility gains support from Bousha and Twentyman's (1982) findings that abusing mothers responded aggressively to aggressive child behaviors, whereas neglecting mothers did not.

The presence of inconsistent and punitive discipline is unlikely to be a necessary condition for abuse, since abuse does not always occur within a disciplinary context. Furthermore, even when the context is a disciplinary one, the behaviors being punished may be normal child behaviors that most nonabusing parents would not consider grounds for punishment. For example, abusing parents have sometimes identified such child precipitants to abusive parental behavior as crying, soiling, not eating, splashing water, and needing love and attention (Weston, 1974). These data support the hypothesis discussed earlier, that some abusing parents react more negatively than nonabusing parents to certain aversive social stimuli.

The presence of inconsistent and punitive discipline is also unlikely to be a sufficient condition for abuse since such discipline probably occurs in nonabusive families as well. Furthermore, in some abusing families, only one child is abused, clearly indicating that factors in addition to disciplinary strategy are involved in those cases.

SIBLINGS OF THE IDENTIFIED ABUSED CHILD

Very little is known about the siblings of identified abused children, but some proportion of them are also abused (Baldwin & Oliver, 1975; Friedman & Morse, 1974; Gil, 1970; Herrenkohl & Herrenkohl, 1979; Johnson & Morse, 1968; Kempe et al., 1962; Nurse, 1964). For example, Baldwin and Oliver reported that slightly more than half of the siblings of the target abused children had also been abused. More than half of the maltreating families in Herrenkohl and Herrenkohl's (1979) study had more than one target child, and about 20 percent had more than two target children. The paucity of data renders it difficult to make even an educated guess about the percentage of abusing families with more than one target child, but the above studies suggest that it is not negligible.

Since child abuse is associated with factors that affect all the children in the family (e.g., parental characteristics, disciplinary patterns), it seems curious that there are many abusing families where only one child is abused. The number of children abused in a family may vary with the particular constellation of factors contributing to the abuse in that family. For example, in a family with only one target, that child may possess certain characteristics that are particularly aversive to the abusing parent; the child might be very irritable, very aggressive, a new financial burden, the favored child of the other parent, and so forth. Or when the abuse is a onetime occurrence, the target child might simply be at the wrong place at the wrong time, when particular stressors are impinging on the parent. Research is needed, however, to clarify these issues. In particular, there may be important differences between abusing families with only one target child versus families with more than one target of abuse.

MARITAL ISSUES IN ABUSING FAMILIES

Single-parent families appear to be disproportionately represented in the abusing population (Ebbin, Gollub, Stein, & Wilson, 1969; Egeland & Brunnquell, 1979; Elmer, 1977a; Gil, 1970; Nurse, 1964; Smith et al., 1974; L. Young, 1964). However, in one prospective study of infants in the ICU, marital status was unrelated to the occurrence of physical abuse and neglect as measured within 20 months after birth (Hunter et al., 1978). Thus, the findings on marital status are conflicting, although the weight of the evidence seems to support the presence of this variable.

When the marital relationship is intact in abusing families, it may frequently be plagued by conflict (Bennie & Sclare, 1969; Blumberg, 1974; Flynn, 1970; Galdston, 1971; Gelles, 1973; Green et al., 1974; Hunter et al., 1978; Johnson & Morse, 1968; Smith, 1975; Steele & Pollack, 1974; Straus, 1980b; L. Young, 1964). For example, abusing parents reported more recent quarrels with their spouses than did matched control parents, and more mothers in the abuse group reported a lack of spouse cooperation with childrearing (Smith, 1975). Similarly, in a one-year prospective study of high-risk infants, marital maladjustment was significantly related to abuse and neglect of the infants (Hunter et al., 1978).

The above studies on marital conflict have not utilized standardized measures to assess marital distress. Butler and Crane (1980) administered the Locke-Wallace marital adjustment test, the marital status inventory, and the areas of change questionnaire to 14 abuse and 29 demographically similar control parents. The controls were parents seeking assistance for child management problems. The groups did not differ on the amount of marital distress reported. Furthermore, parents in both groups reported only mild marital distress, according to the norms utilized for these scales. These results may differ from previous findings because of the use of standardized assessment tools and also because of the use of a clinical control group. The seeming relationship between child abuse and marital conflict could actually be a function of a relationship between child behavioral problems and marital conflict, since it is known that child psychiatric problems and marital discord are related (e.g., Rutter, 1979) and since abused children frequently do manifest behavioral difficulties. Marital discord might discriminate abusing from nonabusing nonclinical families, but not from nonabusing clinical families. To better assess these possibilities, Butler and Crane's findings must be replicated with a matched nonclinical control group as well as a matched clinical control group. It would be premature to dismiss marital discord as specifically relevant to child abuse because spouse abuse and child abuse may be related (Bennie & Sclare, 1969; Black & Mayer, 1980; Gelles, 1980; Green et al., 1974; Nurse, 1964; Straus, 1980a, 1980b; L. Young, 1964). If marital discord and child abuse are specifically related, it must be recognized that such correlational data do not imply causality—a common mistake made in this literature.

The issue of marital conflict aside, certain interactional patterns may characterize the marital relationship in abusing families. For example, dominant-submissive patterns have been inferred to exist in the marital relationships in some abusing families (Boszormenyi-Nagy & Spark, 1973; Kempe & Helfer, 1972; Terr, 1970; L. Young, 1964). In a survey of a nationally representative sample of 1,146 families, violence toward children was twice as common in families where one spouse dominated the other (Gelles, 1980). It has also been hypothesized that the nonabusing parent plays an important role (passive or active) in the child abuse (Parke, 1980; Steele, 1980; Steele & Pollack, 1974). For example, nonabusing parents may contribute to the abuse by not reacting to it, which could function as a reinforcer of the abuse (Parke, 1980). Steele (1980) and Steele and Pollack even propose that the nonabusing parent may actively encourage the abuse.

ENVIRONMENTAL FACTORS AND THE ABUSING FAMILY

Isolation

Abusing families may be socially isolated (Elmer, 1977a; Hunter et al., 1978; Morris & Gould, 1963; Nurse, 1964; Parke & Collmer, 1975; Smith & Hanson, 1963; Smith et al., 1974; Spinetta & Rigler, 1972; Steele & Pollack, 1974; Straus, 1980a; L. Young, 1964). L. Young found that most of the abusing families in her study had no ongoing relationships with individuals outside the family. When abusing parents did make friends outside the family, the relationships were very brief and usually ended in a violent quarrel. Only 15 percent of the abusing families belonged to some sort of social organization. In Hunter et al.'s (1978) one-year prospective study of high-risk infants, social isolation of the mother was significantly related to child abuse and neglect. In the high-stress subsample of a nationally representative sample of parents, the rate of child abuse was substantially higher for those who did not belong to a social or religious organization (Straus, 1980a, 1980b).

Social isolation could be induced by an uninterested or hostile community (Parke, 1980), but it could also be self-induced. Parents who eventually mistreated their children showed little interest in utilizing the support services offered to them while their children were still in the hospital (Hunter et al., 1978). Mothers under high stress but who did not mistreat their children were more seeking of support than were high-stress mothers who mistreated their children (Egeland et al., 1980). A large proportion of abusing families actively prevented their children from becoming attached to anyone outside the family (L. Young, 1964).

Abusing families may also be alienated from their own extended families (Bennie & Sclare, 1969; Green et al., 1974; Johnson & Morse,

1968; Nurse, 1964; Parke & Collmer, 1975; Smith et al., 1974; Spinetta & Rigler, 1972). But Straus (1980a, 1980b) found that individuals with many relatives within a one-hour driving distance had a higher rate of child abuse than those with few relatives in the vicinity. Relatives may have been suggesting and supporting the use of punitive discipline. However, physical proximity and emotional attachment are quite separate, and the parents in Straus' study may have had little contact with their relatives despite physical proximity.

When social isolation exists, it could contribute to child abuse by increasing stress within the family and by decreasing the likelihood that stress will be handled effectively (Belsky, 1980).

Environmental stress

Stress may play an important role in child abuse (Conger et al., 1980; Erlanger, 1974; Garbarino, 1976, 1977; Gelles, 1973, 1980; Gil, 1970; Justice & Justice, 1976; Kempe & Helfer, 1972; Parke, 1978; Parke & Collmer, 1975). However, the issue of stress is confounded with the issue of socioeconomic status, since a disproportionate number of families reported for child abuse are low-income families. But child abuse does occur at all socioeconomic levels (Berger, 1981; Daniel, Newberger, Reed, & Kotelchuck, 1978; Steele & Pollack, 1974; Straus, 1980b; Von Stolk, 1972; Walters, 1975; Zalba, 1971). The overrepresentation of lower-class families in the abuse statistics may be partly, although probably not completely (e.g., Pelton, 1978), a function of sampling bias. Consequently, it is necessary to examine the role of stress in child abuse apart from socioeconomic status.

Some recent studies have found environmental stress to be important in child abuse, independent of social class. The schedule of recent events showed abusing families to have experienced more recent life changes than the neglecting or matched control families (Burgess & Conger, 1977). Justice and Justice (1976) administered the Holmes and Rahe social readjustment rating scale (SRRS) to abusing and nonabusing parents from varying economic groups. The abuse group reported significantly more, and more serious, recent life changes than the nonabusing group, and these changes were not a function of socioeconomic status.

In a prospective study of high-risk (low-SES) mothers and their children, 38 percent of the mothers who abused or neglected their children during the first 20 months of life had experienced severe life stress, as compared with 13 percent of the high-risk mothers who provided their children with adequate care (Egeland et al., 1980). However, if the life event scores had been used to predict maltreatment in this sample, 15 percent would have been false positives.

A modified version of the SRRS was administered to a nationally representative sample of 1,146 families (Gelles, 1980). The more stress the parents had experienced during the previous year, the more likely they were to have been seriously violent toward their children. However, this relationship held only for families earning between $6,000 and $20,000 per year; for the very poor and the well-to-do, stress was unrelated to the probability of child abuse. Further, the very poor had the highest rate of family violence, while the well-off had the lowest rate.

Some researchers have begun to examine possible interactions between stress and other factors and have found that the role of stress in child abuse is rather complex. For example, stress may interact with parental personality variables. Maltreating mothers under high stress were more aggressive, anxious and suspicious, and less seeking of support and had less-appropriate expectations about child care, poorer caretaking skills, and less sensitivity to the infant's cues than adequate-care mothers under high stress (Egeland et al., 1980). Stress may also interact with childhood history and with present attitudes and social circumstances. A childhood history of experiencing or observing family violence, current approval of hitting a spouse, social isolation, and a combined index of occupational level, educational level, and income, mediated the impact of stress on the use of violence with children (Straus, 1980a, 1980b). Life crises had the most-significant impact, in terms of abusive parenting, on those individuals who had experienced punitive discipline in childhood (Conger et al., 1980). And stress was more highly related to child abuse in communities with fewer child-care facilities and resources (Garbarino, 1976).

The foregoing data must be interpreted cautiously since, in most cases, only descriptive statistics were used. Further, most life change scales include numerous items which refer to events that could easily be self-induced, e.g. getting fired from a job. Thus, higher life event scores could actually reflect a tendency for abusing parents to cause themselves problems or could reflect fewer coping skills. There are a number of important issues an methodological problems involved in the assessment of stress (Brown, Harris, & Birley, 1973; Rabkin & Struening, 1976) which deserve closer attention in the child abuse literature.

HETEROGENEITY OF ABUSING FAMILIES AND WAYS TO REDUCE THE HETEROGENEITY

A number of variables are involved in child abuse, but it seems unlikely that any one of them is either necessary or sufficient for abuse to occur. Rather, it is likely that constellations of interacting variables are involved in child abuse, although precisely which variables are included in any given constellation and how many such constellations exist is unknown. Abusing families constitute a heterogeneous population, and to continue treating them as homogeneous may interfere with efforts at prediction, prevention, and treatment.

One way to reduce the heterogeneity would be to focus on the family as a unit and then search for clusters of factors that characterize different types of abusing families. A given cluster of factors would probably include certain child, parent, family interactional, and social/ecological variables. Ideally, a typology of abusing families would utilize polythetic classification (Sokal, 1974), in which the individuals in a group share many characteristics but not necessarily all. In other words, no single characteristic is required for group inclusion, nor is any specific combination of the defining characteristics necessary for group inclusion. An example of a polythetic classification system is the *Diagnostic and Statistical Manual (DSM III)*.

A typology can be developed on an a priori basis by hypothesizing the variables that might belong to particular groups of abusing families and then by testing the typology empirically to determine its validity and utility. Or a typology can be developed empirically by first identifying the characteristics associated with abusing families and then cluster analyzing them to determine which clusters of variables characterize different types of abusing families (see, for example, Frederiksen, 1972). The latter approach seems the more fruitful of the two, since it would be difficult to predict which variables belong together on the basis of the presently available child abuse literature. However, a number of authors have suggested typologies, utilizing an a priori strategy (Dubanoski et al., 1978; Gil, 1970; Walters, 1975; Zalba, 1967). Only Dubanoski et al.'s and Zalba's typologies are specifically concerned with types of abusing families.

Dubanoski et al.'s (1978) typology involves five classes, with inclusion in any given class based on a single criterion: (1) parental lack of child management skills; (2) parental use of deliberately punitive childrearing practices; (3) impulsive acts by the parent, triggered by the child; (4) high levels of stress; (5) negative attitude toward the child. Zalba's (1967) classification system includes six categories: (1) families with a psychotic parent; (2) families with a pervasively angry and abusive parent; (3) families with a depressive, passive-aggressive parent; (4) families with a cold, compulsive, disciplinarian parent; (5) families with an impulsive but generally adequate parent, and where there is marital conflict; (6) families where there is a role crisis for a parent. Zalba hypothesizes that the first three types of families cannot be helped and the children must be removed, whereas the latter three types of families have better prognoses.

Both classification systems offer opportunities for hypothesis testing, but neither seems to provide a comprehensive classification of abusing families. Again, a polythetic classification system of abusing families would be best suited to the complexity of child abuse. But a new classification system should include many of the variables specified in the above typologies, along with other variables such as the abuser's own upbringing, child characteristics, parental expectations, and social isolation.

CONCLUSIONS

The quality of the research on child abuse may be improving. Much of the earlier research in this area was methodologically inadequate and lacked control groups (or matched control groups), hypothesis testing, blind observers, standardized assessment techniques, and appropriate statistics. Some of the recent contributions have paid more attention to experimental design in an attempt to empirically evaluate what was previously inferred. Furthermore, a number of recent studies have tried to address the complex nature of child abuse by examining the interactions between variables and by studying more than one individual at a time. Also, a few researchers have begun to utilize prospective methodologies, a sorely needed approach in this area of inquiry.

Many problems still remain, however. Among the most-serious problems is the fact that causation is often implied on the basis of correlational data. Also, it must be recognized that retrospective data are not equivalent to prospective data and that a variable which is significant in a retrospective study is not necessarily predictive of child abuse. More attention should also be given to the ways in which the variables associated with child abuse interact. A standardized operational definition of child abuse is sorely lacking; many different definitions are presently utilized, rendering meaningful comparisons between studies rather difficult. A standardized definition might be adopted which specifies severe, moderate, and mild forms of physical abuse and delineates the range of parent behaviors and child injuries included in each category.

The research reviewed in this chapter underscores the fact that abusing families are a heterogeneous population. A typology of abusing families would reduce this heterogeneity and would help point out patterns of variables that may presently be obscured by treating child-abusing families as a homogeneous group.

REFERENCES

Baldwin, J. A., & Oliver, J. E. Epidemiology and family characteristics of severely abused children. *British Journal of Preventive Social Medicine*, 1975, *29*, 205–221.

Bandura, A. Social learning theory of aggression. In J. F. Knutson (Ed.), *Control of aggression: Implications from basic research.* New York: Aldine-Atherton, 1973.

Bandura, A., Ross, D., & Ross, S. A. Transmission of aggression through imitation of aggressive models. *Journal of Abnormal and Social Psychology,* 1961, *63*(3), 575–582.

Barahal, R. M., Waterman, J., & Martin, H. P. The social cognitive development of abused children. *Journal of Consulting and Clinical Psychology,* 1981, *49*(4), 508–516.

Bauer, W. D., & Twentyman, C. T. *Abusing, neglectful and comparison mothers' responses to child and non-child stressors: Situational specificity, annoyance ratings and attributional style.* Unpublished manuscript, University of Rochester, 1983.

Bell, R. Q. A reinterpretation of the direction of effects in studies of socialization. *Psychological Review,* 1968, *75,* 81–95.

Belsky, J. Child maltreatment: An ecological integration. *American Psychologist,* 1980, *35*(4), 320–335.

Bennie, E. H., & Sclare, A. B. The battered child syndrome. *American Journal of Psychiatry,* 1969, *125*(7), 975–979.

Berger, A. M. The child abusing family: I. Methodological issues and parent-related characteristics of abusing families. *American Journal of Family Therapy,* 1980, *8*(3), 53–66. (a)

Berger, A. M. The child abusing family: II. Child and child-rearing variables, environmental factors and typologies of abusing families. *American Journal of Family Therapy,* 1980, *8*(4), 52–68. (b)

Berger, A. M. *An examination of the relationship between harsh discipline in childhood, later punitiveness toward children and later ratings of adjustment.* Unpublished doctoral dissertation, University of Iowa, 1981.

Berkowitz, L., & Frodi, A. *Reactions to a child's mistakes as affected by his/her looks and speech.* Unpublished manuscript, 1978.

Besharov, D. J. Toward better research on child abuse and neglect: Making definitional issues an explicit methdological concern. *Child Abuse and Neglect,* 1981, *5,* 383–390.

Black, R., & Mayer, J. Parents with special problems: Alcoholism and opiate addiction. In C. H. Kempe & R. E. Helfer (Eds.), *The battered child* (3d ed.). Chicago: University of Chicago Press, 1980.

Blumberg, M. L. Psychopathology of the abusing parent. *American Journal of Psychotherapy,* 1974, *28,* 21–29.

Bolton, F. G., Laner, R. H., & Kane, S. Child maltreatment risk among adolescent mothers: A study of reported cases. *American Journal of Orthopsychiatry,* 1980, *50*(3), 489–504.

Boszormenyi-Nagy, I., & Spark, G. M. *Invisible loyalties.* New York: Harper & Row, 1973.

Bousha, D. M., & Twentyman, C. T. *Abusing, neglectful and comparison mother-child interactional style: Naturalistic observations in the home setting.* Unpublished manuscript, University of Rochester, 1982.

Brock, T. C., & Pallak, M. S. The consequences of choosing to be aggressive: An analysis of the dissonance model and review of relevant research. In P. G. Zimbardo (Ed.), *The cognitive control of motivation.* Glenview, Ill.: Scott, Foresman, 1969.

Brown, G. W., Harris, T., & Birley, J. L. T. Life-events and psychiatric disorders: Part I. Some methodological issues. *Psychological Medicine,* 1973, *3,* 74–87.

Brunnquell, D., Crichton, L., & Egeland, B. Maternal personality and attitude in disturbances of child rearing. *American Journal of Orthopsychiatry,* 1981, *5*(4), 680–691.

Burgess, R. S., & Conger, R. D. Family interaction patterns related to child abuse and neglect: Some preliminary findings. *Child Abuse and Neglect,* 1977, *1,* 269–277.

Butler, J. F., & Crane, D. R. Self-report schedules for use in assessing the marital adjustment of abusive and nonabusive parents. *American Journal of Family Therapy,* 1980, *8*(4), 29–34.

Cohen, M. I., Raphling, D. L., & Green, P. E. Psychological aspects of the maltreatment syndrome in childhood. *Journal of Pediatrics,* 1966, *69,* 279–284.

Conger, R. D., Burgess, R. L., & Barrett, C. Child abuse related to life change and perceptions of illness: Some preliminary findings. In J. V. Cook & R. T. Bowles (Eds.), *Child abuse: Commission and omission.* Toronto: Butterworths, 1980.

Daniel, J. H., Newberger, E. H., Reed, R. B., & Kotelchuck, M. Child abuse screening: Implications of the limited predictive power of abuse discriminants from a controlled family study of pediatric social illness. *Child Abuse and Neglect,* 1978, *2,* 247–259.

de Lissovoy, V. Toward the definition of "abuse provoking child." *Child Abuse and Neglect,* 1979, *3,* 341–350.

Deur, J. L., & Parke, R. D. Effects of inconsistent punishment on aggression in children. *Developmental Psychology,* 1970, *2*(3), 403–411.

Dion, K. K. Children's physical attractiveness and sex as determinants of adult punitiveness. *Developmental Psychology,* 1974, *10*(5), 772–778.

Disbrow, M. A., Doerr, H., & Caulfield, C. Measuring the components of parents' potential for child abuse and neglect. *Child Abuse and Neglect,* 1977, *1,* 279–296.

Dubanoski, R. A., Evans, E. M., & Higuchi, A. A. Analysis and treatment of child abuse: A set of behavioral propositions. *Child Abuse and Neglect,* 1978, *2,* 153–172.

Earp, J., & Ory, J. G. The influence of early parenting on child maltreatment. *Child Abuse and Neglect,* 1980, *4,* 237–245.

Ebbin, A. J., Gollub, M. H., Stein, A. M., & Wilson, M. G. Battered child syndrome at the Los Angeles County General Hospital. *American Journal of Diseases of Children,* 1969, *118,* 660–667.

Egeland, B., Breitenbucher, M., & Rosenberg, D. Prospective study of the significance of life stress in the etiology of child abuse. *Journal of Consulting and Clinical Psychology,* 1980, *48*(2), 195–205.

Egeland, B., & Brunnquell, D. An at-risk approach to the study of child abuse. *Journal of Child Psychiatry,* 1979, *18*(2), 219–235.

Egeland, B., & Sroufe, L. A. Attachment and early maltreatment. *Child Development,* 1981, *52,* 44–52.

Egeland, B., & Vaughn, B. Failure of "bond formation" as a cause of abuse, neglect, and maltreatment. *American Journal of Orthopsychiatry,* 1981, *51*(1), 78–84.

Elmer, E. *Children in jeopardy.* Pittsburgh: University of Pittsburgh Press, 1967.

Elmer, E. A follow-up study of traumatized children. *Pediatrics,* 1977, *59*(2), 273–279. (a)

Elmer, E. *Fragile families, troubled children.* Pittsburgh: University of Pittsburgh Press, 1977. (b)

Elmer, E., & Gregg, G. S. Developmental characteristics of abused children. *Pediatrics,* 1967, *49*(4), 596–602.

Erlanger, H. S. Social class differences in parents' use of physical punishment. In S. K. Steinmetz & M. A. Straus (Eds.), *Violence in the family.* New York: Dodd, Mead, 1974.

Faranoff, A., Kennell, J., & Klaus, M. Follow-up of low birth weight infants—the predictive value of maternal visiting patterns. *Pediatrics,* 1972, *49,* 287–290.

Feshbach, N., & Feshbach, S. The relationship between empathy and aggression in two age groups. *Developmental Psychology,* 1969, *1,* 102–107.

Flynn, W. R. Frontier justice: A contribution to the theory of child battery. *American Journal of Psychiatry,* 1970, *127*(3), 375–379.

Fomufod, A. K., Sinkford, S. M., & Louy, V. E. A mother-child separation at birth: A contributing factor in child abuse. *Lancet,* 1975, *2,* 549–550.

Fontana, V. J., & Bernard, M. L. *The maltreated child.* Springfield, Ill.: Charles C Thomas, 1971.

Fraiberg, S., Adelson, E., & Shapiro, V. Ghosts in the nursery. *Journal of Child Psychiatry,* 1975, *14*(3), 387–421.

Fredericksen, N. Toward a taxonomy of situations. *American Psychologist,* 1972, *27,* 114–123.

Friedman, S. B., & Morse, C. W. Child abuse: A 5-year follow-up of early case finding in the emergency department. *Pediatrics,* 1974, *54*(4), 404–410.

Friedrich, W. N., & Boriskin, J. A. The role of the child in abuse: A review of the literature. *American Journal of Orthopsychiatry,* 1976, *46*(4), 580–590.

Frodi, A. M. Contribution of infant characteristics to child abuse. *American Journal of Mental Deficiency,* 1981, *85*(4), 341–349.

Frodi, A. M., & Lamb, M. E. Fathers' and mothers' responses to the faces and cries of normal and premature infants. *Developmental Psychology,* 1978, *14,* 190–198. (a)

Frodi, A. M., & Lamb, M. E. *Fathers' and mothers' responses to the signals and characteristics of young infants.* Paper presented at the International Conference on Infant Studies. Providence, R.I., 1978. (b)

Frodi, A. M., & Lamb, M. E. *Psychophysiological responses to infant signals in abusive mothers and mothers of premature infants.* Paper presented to the Society for Psychophysiological Research. Madison, Wis., 1978. (c)

Galdston, R. Violence begins at home. *Journal of the American Academy of Child Psychiatry,* 1971, *10,* 336–350.

Gaensbauer, T. J., & Sands, K. Distorted affective communications in abused/neglected infants and their potential impact on caretakers. *Journal of Child Psychiatry,* 1979, *18*(2), 236–250.

Gaines, R., Sandgrund, A., Green, A. H., & Power, E. Etiological factors in child maltreatment: A multivariate study of abusing, neglecting and normal mothers. *Journal of Abnormal Psychology,* 1978, *87*(5), 531–540.

Garbarino, J. A preliminary study of some ecological correlates of child abuse: The impact of socioeconomic stress on mothers. *Child Development,* 1976, *47,* 178–185.

Garbarino, J. The human ecology of child maltreatment: A conceptual model for research. *Journal of Marriage and the Family,* 1977, *39*(4), 721–735.

Geiser, R. L. *Hidden victims: The sexual abuse of children.* Boston: Beacon Press, 1979.

Gelles, R. J. Child abuse as psychopathology: A sociological critique and reformulation. *American Journal of Orthopsychiatry,* 1973, *43*(4), 611–621.

Gelles, R. J. A profile of violence toward children in the United States. In G. Gerbner, C. J. Ross, & E. Zigler (Eds.), *Child abuse: An agenda for action.* New York: Oxford University Press, 1980.

George, C., & Main, M. Social interactions of young abused children: Approach, avoidance and aggression. *Child Development,* 1979, *50,* 306–318.

Gil, D. G. Physical abuse of children. *Pediatrics,* 1969, *44,* 857–864.

Gil, D. G. *Violence against children.* Cambridge, Mass.: Harvard University Press, 1970.

Green, A. H. Psychopathology of abused children. *Journal of Child Psychiatry,* 1978, *17*(1), 92–103.

Green, A. H. Child-abusing fathers. *Journal of Child Psychiatry,* 1979, *18*(2), 270–282.

Green, A. H., Gaines, R. W., & Sandgrund, D. Child abuse: Pathological syndrome of family interaction. *American Journal of Psychiatry,* 1874, *131*(8), 882–886.

Gregg, G. S., & Elmer, E. Infant injuries: Accident or abuse? *Pediatrics,* 1969, *44*(3), 434–439.

Helfer, R. E. Developmental deficits which limit interpersonal skills. In C. H. Kempe & R. E. Helfer (Eds.), *The battered child* (3d ed.). Chicago: University of Chicago Press, 1980.

Henderson, D. J. Incest: A synthesis of data. In G. J. Williams & J. Money (Eds.), *Traumatic abuse and neglect of children at home.* Baltimore: The Johns Hopkins Press, 1980.

Herrenkohl, E. C., & Herrenkohl, R. C. A comparison of abused children and their nonabused siblings. *Journal of Child Psychiatry,* 1979, *18*(2), 260–269.

Herzberger, S. D., Potts, D. A., & Dillon, M. Abusive and nonabusive parental treatment from the child's perspective. *Journal of Consulting and Clinical Psychology,* 1981, *49*(1), 81–89.

Hoffman-Plotkin, D., & Twentyman, C. T. A multimodal assessment of behavioral and cognitive deficits in abused and neglected pre-schoolers. *Child Development,* in press.

Hunter, R. S., Kilstrom, N., Kraybill, E. N., & Loda, F. Antecedents of child abuse and neglect in premature infants: A prospective study in a newborn intensive care unit. *Pediatrics,* 1978, *61*(4), 629–635.

Hyman, C. A. Preliminary study of mother/infant interaction. *Child Abuse and Neglect,* 1977, *1,* 315–320.

Johnson, B., & Morse, H. A. Injured children and their parents. *Children,* 1968, *15*(4), 147–152.

Justice, B., & Justice, R. *The abusing family.* New York: Human Services Press, 1976.

Kaufman, I., Peck, A. L., & Tagiuri, C. K. The family constellation and overt incestuous relations between father and daughter. In G. J. Williams & J. Money (Eds.), *Traumatic abuse and neglect of children at home.* Baltimore: The Johns Hopkins Press, 1980.

Kempe, C. H., & Helfer, R. E. *Helping the battered child and his family.* Philadelphia: J. B. Lippincott, 1972.

Kempe, C. H., Silverman, F. N., Steele, B. F., Droegemueller, W., & Silver, H. K. The battered child syndrome. *Journal of the American Medical Association,* 1962, *181*(1), 17–24.

Kennel, J., Voos, D., & Klaus, M. Parent-infant bonding. In R. E. Helfer & C. H. Kempe (Eds.), *Child abuse and neglect: The family and the community.* Cambridge, Mass.: Ballinger Publishing, 1976.

Kent, J. T. A follow-up study of abused children. *Journal of Pediatric Psychology*, 1976, *1*(2), 25–31.

Kinard, E. M. Emotional development in physically abused children. *American Journal of Orthopsychiatry*, 1980, *50*(4), 686–696.

Kinard, E. M. Experiencing child abuse: Effects on emotional adjustment. *American Journal of Orthopsychiatry*, 1982, *52*(1), 82–91.

Kinard, E. M., & Klerman, L. V. Teenage parenting and child abuse: Are they related? *American Journal of Orthopsychiatry*, 1980, *50*(3), 481–488.

Klein, M., & Stern, L. Low birth weight and the battered child syndrome. *American Journal of Diseases of Children*, 1971, *122*, 15–18.

Knutson, J. F. Child abuse research as an area of aggression research. *Pediatric Psychology*, 1978, *3*(1), 20–27.

Knutson, J. F., Berger, A. M., & Mehm, J. G. Correlates of the self-report of abusive childhood experiences in clinic and non-clinic populations. Presented at the 1983 North American Meeting of the International Society for Research on Aggression. Victoria, British Columbia, June 29–July 2, 1983.

Korbin, J. Anthropological contributions to the study of child abuse. *Child Abuse and Neglect*, 1977, *1*, 7–24.

Larrance, D. T., Amish, P., Twentyman, C. T., & Plotkin, R. C. Attribution theory and child abuse. *Selected Proceedings of the Third International Congress on Child Abuse and Neglect*. Amsterdam: Frie University Press, 1982.

Larrance, D. T., & Twentyman, C. T. *Maternal attributions and child abuse*. Unpublished manuscript, University of Rochester, 1982.

Lefkowitz, M. M., Walder, L. O., & Eron, L. D. Punishment, identification and aggression. *Merrill-Palmer Quarterly*, 1963, *9*, 159–174.

Leventhal, M. A. Risk factors in the child: A study of abused children and their siblings. In H. P. Martin (Ed.), *The abused child: A multidisciplinary approach to developmental issues and treatment*. Cambridge, Mass.: Ballinger Publishing, 1976.

Lynch, M. A., & Roberts, J. Predicting child abuse: Signs of bonding failure in the maternity hospital. *Child Abuse and Neglect*, 1977, *1*, 491–492.

Martin, H. P. Which children get abused: High risk factors in the child. In H. P. Martin (Ed.), *The abused child: A multidisciplinary approach to developmental issues and treatment*. Cambridge, Mass.: Ballinger Publishing, 1976.

Martin, M. The child and his development. In C. H. Kempe & R. E. Helfer (Eds.), *Helping the battered child and his family*. Philadelphia: J. B. Lippincott, 1972.

Melnick, B., & Hurley, J. R. Distinctive personality attributes of child-abusing mothers. *Journal of Consulting and Clinical Psychology*, 1969, *33*(6), 746–749.

Milner, J. S., & Wimberly, R. C. Prediction and explanation of child abuse. *Journal of Clinical Psychology*, 1980, *36*(4), 875–884.

Morris, M. G., & Gould, R. W. Role-reversal: A necessary concept in dealing with the "battered child syndrome." *American Journal of Orthopsychiatry*, 1963, *33*(6), 746–749.

Morse, C. W., Sahler, O. J. Z., & Friedman, S. B. A three-year follow-up study of abused and neglected children. *American Journal of Diseases of Children*, 1970, *120*, 439–446.

Mulhern, R. K., & Passman, R. H. *Children's behaviors affect their mother's selection of punishment intensities: Child abuse may be under reinforcement control.* Paper presented at the meeting of the Midwestern Psychological Association, Chicago, May 1978.

Nurse, S. M. Familial patterns of parents who abuse their children. *Smith College Studies in Social Work,* 1964, *32,* 11–25.

Oliver, J. E., & Taylor, A. Five generations of ill-treated children in one family pedigree. *British Journal of Psychiatry,* 1971, *119,* 473–480.

Owens, D. J., & Straus, M. A. The social structure of violence in childhood and approval of violence as an adult. *Aggressive Behavior,* 1975, *1,* 193–211.

Parke, R. D. Child abuse: An overview of alternative models. *Journal of Pediatric Psychology,* 1978, *3*(1), 9–13.

Parke, R. D. Socialization into child abuse: A social interactional perspective. In J. V. Cook & R. T. Bowles (Eds.), *Child abuse: Commission and omission.* Toronto: Butterworths, 1980.

Parke, R. D., & Collmer, C. W. *Child abuse: An interdisciplinary analysis.* Chicago: University of Chicago Press, 1975.

Passman, R. H., & Mulhern, R. K. Maternal punitiveness as affected by situational stress: An experimental analogue of child abuse. *Journal of Abnormal Psychology,* 1977, *86*(5), 565–569.

Paulson, M. J., & Chaleff, A. Parent surrogate roles: A dynamic concept in understanding and treating abusive parents. *Journal of Clinical Child Psychology,* 1973, *2,* 38–40.

Pelton, L. H. Child abuse and neglect: The myth of classlessness. *American Journal of Orthopsychiatry,* 1978, *43*(4), 608–617.

Plotkin, R. C., Azar, S., Twentyman, C. T., & Perri, M. G. A critical evaluation of the research methodology employed in the investigation of causative factors in child abuse and neglect. *International Journal of Child Abuse and Neglect,* 1981, *1*(5), 449–455.

Plotkin, R. C., & Twentyman, C. T. The utility of a measure of aggression in differentiating abusing parents from other parents who are experiencing familial disturbance. *Journal of Clinical Psychology,* 1982, *38*(3), 608–610.

Rabkin, J. G., & Struening, E. L. Life events, stress and illness. *Science,* 1976, *194,* 1013–1020.

Reid, J. B., & Taplin, P. S. *A social interactional approach to the treatment of abusive families.* Paper presented to the American Psychological Association, Washington, D.C., 1976.

Reidy, T. J. The aggressive characteristics of abused and neglected children. *Journal of Clinical Psychology,* 1977, *33,* 1140–1145.

Renshaw, D. C., & Renshaw, R. H. Incest. In G. J. Williams and J. Money (Eds.), *Traumatic abuse and neglect of children at home.* Baltimore: The Johns Hopkins Press, 1980.

Ruppenthal, G. C., Arling, G. L., Harlow, H. F., Sackett, G. P., & Suomi, S. J. A ten-year perspective of motherless-mother monkey behavior. *Journal of Abnormal Psychology,* 1976, *85*(4), 341–349.

Rutter, M. Maternal deprivation, 1972–1978: New findings, new concepts, new approaches. *Child Development,* 1979, *50,* 283–305.

Rutter, M., & Madge, N. *Cycles of disadvantage: A review of research.* London: Heinemann Medical Books, 1976.

Sapp, A. D., & Carter, D. L. *Child abuse in Texas: A descriptive survey of Texas residents' attitudes* (Survey Research Program). College of Criminal Justice, Sam Houston State University, 1978.

Schechter, M. D., & Roberge, L. Sexual exploitation. In Ray E. Helfer & C. H. Kempe (Eds.), *Child abuse and neglect: The family and the community.* Cambridge, Mass.: Ballinger Publishing, 1976.

Scott, W. J. Attachment and child abuse: A study of social history indicators among mothers of abused children. In G. J. Williams & J. Money (Eds.), *Traumatic abuse and neglect of children at home.* Baltimore: The Johns Hopkins Press, 1980.

Sears, R. R., Maccoby, E. E., & Levin, H. The sources of aggression in the home. In S. K. Steinmetz & M. A. Straus (Eds.), *Violence in the family.* New York: Dodd, Mead, 1974.

Shorkey, C. T. Sense of personal worth, self-esteem and anomie of child-abusing mothers and controls. *Journal of Clinical Psychology,* 1980, *36*(3), 817–820.

Silver, L. B., Dublin, C. C., & Lourie, R. S. Does violence breed violence? Contributions from a study of the child abuse syndrome. *American Journal of Psychiatry,* 1969, *126*(3), 404–407.

Smith, S. M. *The battered child syndrome.* Toronto: Butterworths, 1975.

Smith, S. M., & Hanson, R. Interpersonal relationships and child-rearing practices in 214 parents of battered children. *British Journal of Psychiatry,* 1975, *125,* 513–525.

Smith, S. M., Hanson, R., & Noble, S. Parents of battered babies: A controlled study. *British Medical Journal,* 1973, *4,* 388–391.

Smith, S. M., Hanson, R., & Noble, S. Social aspects of the battered baby syndrome. *British Journal of Psychiatry,* 1974, *125,* 568–582.

Sokal, R. R. Classification: Purposes, principles, progress, prospects. *Science,* 1974, *185*(4157), 1115–1123.

Spinetta, J. J., & Rigler, D. The child abusing parent. *Psychological Bulletin,* 1972, *77,* 296–304.

Steele, B. F. Parental abuse of infants and small children. In E. J. Anthony & T. Benedick (Eds.), *Parenthood: Its psychology and psychopathology.* Boston: Little, Brown, 1970.

Steele, B. F. Violence within the family. In R. E. Helfer & C. H. Kempe (Eds.), *Child abuse and neglect: The family and the community.* Cambridge, Mass.: Ballinger Publishing, 1976.

Steele, B. F. Psychodynamic factors in child abuse. In C. H. Kempe & R. E. Helfer (Eds.), *The battered child* (3d ed.). Chicago: University of Chicago Press, 1980.

Steele, B. F., & Pollack, C. B. A psychiatric study of parents who abuse infants and small children. In R. E. Helfer & C. H. Kempe (Eds.), *The battered child* (2d ed.). Chicago: University of Chicago Press, 1974.

Straus, M. A. Stress and child abuse. In C. H. Kempe & R. E. Helfer (Eds.), *The battered child* (3rd ed.).Chicago: University of Chicago Press, 1980. (a)

Straus, M. A. Stress and physical child abuse. *Child Abuse and Neglect,* 1980, *4,* 75–88. (b)

Suomi, S. J. Maternal behavior by socially incompetent monkeys: Neglect and abuse of offspring. *Journal of Pediatric Psychology,* 1978, *3*(1), 28–34.

Terr, L. C. A family study of child abuse. *American Journal of Psychiatry,* 1970, *127*(5), 665–671.

Twentyman, C. T., & Plotkin, R. C. Unrealistic expectations of parents who maltreat their children: An educational deficit that pertains to child development. *Journal of Clinical Psychology,* 1982, *38*(3), 497–503.

Twentyman, C. T., Rohrbeck, C. A., & Amish, P. L. A cognitive-behavioral model of child abuse. In S. Saunders (Ed.), *Violent individuals and families: A practitioners handbook.* Springfield, Ill.: Charles C Thomas, in press.

Vasta, R., & Copitch, P. Simulating conditions of child abuse in the laboratory. *Child Development,* 1981, *52,* 64–170.

Van Stolk, M. *The battered child in Canada.* Toronto: McClelland & Stewart, 1972.

Walters, D. R. *Physical and sexual abuse of children: Causes and treatment.* Bloomington: Indiana University Press, 1975.

Wasserman, S. The abused parent of the abused child. *Children,* 1968, *14*(5), 175–179.

Weston, J. T. A summary of neglect and traumatic cases (pathology). In R. E. Helfer & C. H. Kempe (Eds.), *The battered child* (2d ed.). Chicago: University of Chicago Press, 1974.

Yorukoglu, A., & Kemph, J. P. Children not severely damaged by incest with a parent. In G. J. Williams & J. Money (Eds.), *Traumatic abuse and neglect of children at home.* Baltimore: The Johns Hopkins Press, 1980.

Young, L. *Wednesday's children: A study of child neglect and abuse.* New York: McGraw-Hill, 1964.

Young, M. Multiple correlates of abuse: A systems approach to the etiology of child abuse. *Journal of Pediatric Psychology,* 1976, *1*(2), 57–61.

Zalba, S. R. The abused child: II. A typology for classification and treatment. *Social Work,* 1967, *12,* 70–79.

Zigler, E. Controlling child abuse in America: An effort doomed to failure? In R. Bourne & E. H. Newberger (Eds.), *Critical perspectives on child abuse.* Lexington, Mass.: Lexington Books, 1979.

Zigler, E. Controlling child abuse: Do we have the knowledge and/or the will? In G. Gerbner, C. J. Ross, & E. Zigler (Eds.), *Child abuse: An agenda for action.* New York: Oxford University Press, 1980.

Chapter 30

Parental Communication Deviance and Offspring Psychopathology

JERI A. DOANE

Over the past three decades, investigators have persisted in their efforts to study the role of the nuclear family in the etiology and maintenance of schizophrenic disorders. Various theories, too numerous to elaborate upon here, were developed and have been studied systematically in a variety of research settings with different patient populations. One attribute of the family that has been extensively studied is the role of disturbed intrafamilial communication in families with a psychiatrically ill member.

Disturbed communication can be conceptualized in a myriad of ways. Families in which there is a real paucity of any kind of verbal communication could be construed as deviant, as are families in which blatant hostility and conflict are pervasive. This chapter will discuss one particular type of disturbed communication—*communication deviance,* a construct developed by Singer and Wynne (1965) that refers to a set of defects and deviances in the communication of parents of schizophrenics. This particular attribute has been extensively studied since the mid-1960s, and the evidence for its association with offspring psychopathology continues to accumulate.

The purpose of this chapter is to acquaint the reader with this measure and its theoretical roots and to examine issues and unanswered questions that arise when one considers the impact of this family attribute on the onset and course of psychopathology, particularly schizophrenia.

The term *communication deviance* (CD) was originated by Singer and Wynne (1965), who found that disordered styles of verbal exchanges were distinguishing features of families containing a schizophrenic or borderline schizophrenic member. In their view, CD in the parent(s) is related to disturbed thinking in the preschizophrenic offspring, and this linkage can be conceptualized as resulting from the child's gradual internalization of disturbed styles of parental communication.

Singer and Wynne have stressed that if the efforts of two or more people to focus their attention in a conversation fail or become confused, the consequences for the rest of the communication process are profound (Wynne, Singer, Bartko, & Toohey, 1977). They believe that the communication in families of schizophrenics is disturbed at this attentional level, in the early stages of a communication sequence, while that of neurotics or normals is disturbed later on after an attentional focus has been shared. Rather than being a subclinical manifestation of schizophrenia itself, CD has been shown to be a distinct measure that differs from clinical psychopathology, one which reflects the *impact* of the communication upon the listener (Wynne, Singer, & Toohey, 1975). Theoretically, the extent to which parents fail to communicate effectively reflects the extent to which the child, who is dependent upon transactions with them, will become muddled and distressed (Singer, 1967).

The operating concept underlying this work assumes that the ways in which people learn to share foci of attention and derive meaning from external stimuli is related to basic, repeated parent-child exchanges during the formative years of a child's development. As growth and development proceed, this learning experience could, it was hypothesized, contribute to disturbed thinking and communication of children who were attempting to relate to parents with highly deviant styles of communication.

CD measures the manner in which family members focus their attention and that of others on a task at hand. A projective test, usually the Rorschach or the TAT, is used to elicit communications from the parent to the examiner in a standard situation. In this task, parents "name" and "explain" percepts, which is analogous to everyday parent-child communications. The form or style of the person's speech is emphasized rather than content. When the speaker manifests communication deviance, the listener has difficulty following and comprehending a line of thought and visualizing what the person is trying to say. The essence of the importance of CD occurs at this point, when the listener finds himself confused and puzzled about what s/he is hearing and doesn't know how to evaluate what is being said.

It is important to emphasize that CD is a structural or formal quality of verbal interaction and has little to do with the actual content of what is said. Bad grammar, informal styles of speaking, or bizarre content, for example, are not scored as CD unless their occurrence obscures meaning or disrupts the listener's focus of attention.

Manuals have been developed for scoring numerous types of deviance on the Rorschach (Singer, 1973) and the TAT (Jones & Doane, 1979). Singer (1973) grouped these deviance items into the following five problem areas:

1. *Commitment problems.* The impact of the items in this section is to cause a listener to wonder whether the speaker is really committed to his idea. Does he really mean what he is saying?
2. *Referent problems.* When referent problems occur, the listener cannot be sure he is sharing the proper referent point.
3. *Language anomalies.* Here the speaker may use words peculiarly and place them in odd order, play with their sounds, and even invent words.
4. *Contradictory, arbitrary sequences.* Here the speaker contradicts himself or violates logic in a variety of ways.
5. *Disruptions.* Here several types of occurrences are noted which have a distracting, disrupting effect upon the listener.

Examples of CD on the Rorschach would include statements such as:

> (Card I) The whole sort of a, the insects, and the two on the outer look like wings. Nothing like that in this. (Examiner: You mean the wings of the insect?) Wings of the insect, yes, wings the whole, all I can, all it means to me is a, it's a, it's a complete picture, and I would think sort of ah, ah. At first I thought it was a bat, but then I saw these two things out here and it, I sort of went off that and it might be a sort of flying insect. (This passage includes fragmentation, commitment problems, peculiar set, vagueness.)
>
> (Card I) That could be a broken mirror or a bat. (Incompatible images.)

Communication deviance in TAT stories includes things such as lack of commitment to ideas or percepts, unclear communication of themes or ideas, language anomalies, disruptive speech, and closure problems. Examples:

> (Card I) He's contemplating something he's not really seeing because he's got on earphones. (Peculiar reasoning and a misperception of the card.)
>
> (Card 3GF) If she—umm, the essence is to denote finality, the obviously she's come to a closing phase in her life. (Lack of commitment, peculiar set, and unintelligible meaning.)

Reviewers of the family research literature have pointed to studies of communication clarity and unclarity as having the greatest degree of replicability (Doane, 1978; Goldstein & Rodnick, 1975; Jacob, 1975). In the remaining sections of this chapter, a number of issues and questions regarding communication deviance will be addressed, and empirical evidence related to these issues will be discussed. This report is not intended as an exhaustive review of all relevant studies, but rather attempts to focus the reader on some of the more-salient issues surrounding the uses and misuses of this measure and to suggest areas worthy of further study.

REPLICATION STUDIES

In 1963, Singer and Wynne published results from a study showing that their Rorschach and TAT CD measures could discriminate accurately among parental pairs of autistic, withdrawn, acting-out, and young-adult schizophrenic offspring. Results from a study carried out in 1965 showed that parents of "frank schizophrenics" and "schizophrenics" could be differentiated reliably from both parents of borderlines and parents of nonschizophrenic neurotic patients. Further, predictions of form of thinking (amorphous versus fragmented) were made, as were predictions of severity of index symptomatology. In yet another study, 80 percent of parents of schizophrenics were discriminated from parents of normal offspring on a different type of task, the object sorting test (Wild, Singer, Rosman, Ricci, & Lidz, 1965). Using still a different source of material, Morris and Wynne (1965) were able to predict diagnosis of offspring and forms of thinking (amorphousness, fragmentation) by comparing parental communication styles from recorded excerpts from family therapy sessions.

More recently, Wynne et al., (1977) compared CD in 114 parental pairs with offspring ranging from normal to severely schizophrenic. They found that parental CD correlated with severity of offspring disturbance. Behrens, Rosenthal, and Chodoff (1968) used Loveland's (1967) Rorschach technique in a study of schizophrenics and normals. Using a modification of her criteria for scoring communicative content (clarity, grasp of the nature of the task and of other family members' comments, and family cooperation and coordination), they were able to correctly identify 80 percent of the parents of schizophrenics. They found parents of schizophrenics to be deficient on a measure of ability to maintain a shared focus of attention.

Hirsch and Leff (1971) attempted to replicate Singer and Wynne's National Institute of Mental Health study but admit to irregularities in their method of Rorschach inquiry. Nevertheless, they were able to significantly differentiate parents of schizophrenics from nonschizophrenics, although the separation was not as accurate as that found in Singer and Wynne's work. Hirsch and Leff found a correlation between word count and CD and concluded, therefore, that CD was an artifact of increased responding by parents of schizophrenics. This explanation seems highly unlikely, however, inasmuch as a number of independent studies have since found that CD continues to predict accurately, even with word count partialed out (Glaser, 1976; Wild, Shapiro, & Goldenberg, 1975; Wynne et al., 1977).

CONCURRENT VALIDITY

In addition to the Singer-Wynne type of CD studies, several other investigators have also measured disturbed communicative styles. These studies assessed such dimensions as acknowledgment and clarity and offered support for the construct validity of the CD construct.

Acknowledgment is a measure that reflects the degree to which a family member responds to the content and intent of a statement by another family member. The code ranges from total ignoring to full acknowledgment of the other's speech. One would hypothesize that schizophrenic families would exhibit much less direct acknowledgment of each another. Mishler and Waxler (1968), as already reviewed by Johnson and Notarius (Chapter 12 of this *Handbook*), in a large, well-controlled study, found that families of normals were higher on this measure than were families of poor premorbid schizophrenics. Families of good premorbids were in between. Solvberg and Blakar (1975) found that parents of schizophrenics tended to ignore the other's active utterances more than normal couples. Stabenau, Tupin, Werner, and Pollin (1965), in a study of families of schizophrenics, juvenile delinquents, and normals, found that schizophrenic families failed to acknowledge important themes.

Herman and Jones (1976) discovered that families at high risk for schizophrenia (defined as presence of marked CD in the parents) used significantly fewer acknowledging responses in their interactions with one another in a family Rorschach task than did low-CD families.

Finally, Hassan (1974) found that normal couples had maximal transactional validation between them, while parents of juvenile delinquents and schizophrenics had the least. She discovered that scales assessing disqualifications of the interactional context differentiated parents of juvenile delinquents and schizophrenics from the rest (ulcerative colitis, underachievement, and normal). Finally, a scale measuring closure and coordination (ability to share the other's focus of attention and to participate together) in the couple's interaction allowed separation of the groups of parents of juvenile delinquents and parents of schizophrenics. While parents of delinquents were marked by "disconnectedness" (parallel messages), parents of schizophrenics showed mostly "contextual blurring" (dubious logic, recurring tangentializations, obliteration of the sense of meaningfulness, and lack of closure and coordination). Hence, in the families of schizophrenics, a total interactional context is often invalidated.

These studies provide further support for Singer and Wynne's argument that CD is related to schizophrenia in the offspring. Studies, such as that by Hassan, that isolate different styles of communication deficits in different diagnostic groups, are particularly valuable for determining which types of disturbed communication are associated with specific offspring outcomes.

To summarize, there are many studies that support the notion that offspring schizophrenic disorders are associated with increased communication deviance in the parents. Nearly all of these studies are cross-sectional, however, involving samples of families with an already-diagnosed psychiatrically ill offspring. This state of affairs has raised a number of issues about the nature of communication deviance, such as its origins, how it relates to other known characteristics of parents of schizophrenics, and whether it is etiologically linked to the development of schizophrenia or is a parental response to living with a severely disturbed son or daughter.

CD AS A MANIFESTATION OF PARENTAL PSYCHOPATHOLOGY

One of the criticisms of Singer and Wynne's concept of CD is that it merely reflects an underlying, subclinical form of schizophrenia in the parent. In one study by Wynne et al. (1977), parental CD was compared for 114 offspring with diagnoses ranging from normal to severe schizophrenia. The authors found that both severity of psychopathology in the parent(s) and parental CD correlated independently with severity of offspring disturbance. Severity of parental psychiatric illness, however, accounted for less of the variance in the illness of the offspring than did parental CD. Parents of schizophrenics were correctly identified on the basis of amount of CD, even in cases where neither parent had a diagnosis of schizophrenia or borderline symptomatology. One interesting finding from this study was that frequency of CD was higher in the nonschizophrenic parents than in their overtly schizophrenic offspring. This finding has been interpreted to mean that CD is not merely a subclinical manifestation of the psychosis itself. In a recent study by Doane and colleagues (Doane, Jones, Fisher, Ritzler, Singer, & Wynne, 1982), the highest amounts of CD were found in nonschizophrenic, psychiatrically disturbed parents as compared with parents diagnosed as schizophrenic. These studies suggest that CD is not merely a reflection of schizophrenia in the parent. However, the relation of CD to other, perhaps more subtle forms of psychopathology in the parent has not been ruled out.

Wynne has pointed out that although parental psychopathology and CD are conceptually linked and are statistically correlated to some degree, they can be differentiated both conceptually and statistically.

CD and psychopathology ratings overlap to some extent, but they are not identical. When multivariate statistical methods are used, holding one of the two variables constant, the other remains significantly predictive of severity of offspring psychopathology (Wynne et al., 1977).

RELATIONSHIP OF CD TO GENETIC FACTORS

Another question regarding CD and schizophrenia concerns the issue of whether CD is an indicator of a genetic endowment for schizophrenia in the parent. If this were the case, then CD itself might be construed as an epiphenomenon, and any role it has in the etiology of the disorder would be confounded by causes due to genetic transmission.

Wynne et al. (1975) carried out a study of CD in the biological and adoptive parents of schizophrenics in order to address this question. They discovered that biologic and adoptive parents of schizophrenics were indistinguishable on the CD measure. All parental pairs with a schizophrenic offspring (regardless of biologic or adoptive parental status) and those with nonschizophrenics were perfectly separated during prediction on the basis of total amount of CD on the Rorschach. This finding argues strongly against a purely genetic explanation of schizophrenia. The authors conclude that their results support an interactionist view that CD may be a necessary but not sufficient condition for schizophrenia. One limitation of this study, however, is that the psychiatric histories and diagnoses of the adoptive and biologic parents were not available for study or diagnosis. A study which used the biologic and adoptive parents of the same schizophrenic offspring would allow for a more-direct test of the role of CD versus biologic/genetic factors.

A related question, not yet studied, is whether parents with a positive family history for schizophrenia have more CD than parents without this history. Cognitive and attentional deficits may be viewed as components of schizophrenia which might be more tightly linked to genetic endowment than to overt clinical schizophrenia. Perhaps CD is higher in individuals with noticeable deficits on cognitive and attentional laboratory tasks than in parents without these deficits. Conceptually, the two kinds of deviances are logically linked, as both reflect a deficiency on the part of the individual to adequately establish and maintain a clear focus of attention. If an association were found between verbal parental CD and parental attentional deficit on laboratory tasks, this would be consistent with the theory that CD may be an indicator of some underlying biologic (perhaps genetically transmitted) diathesis in the parents of schizophrenics. Currently, a collaborative study which is testing this question is underway in Los Angeles and Pittsburgh.

Preliminary findings suggest that there may be an intra-individual relationship between these two sets of measures in a sample of parents of schizophrenics.

It should be noted that if empirical evidence were found to support a link between CD and any kind of biologic/genetic schizophrenogenic endowment, such findings would not be inconsistent with the theoretical propositions expressed by Singer and Wynne. On the contrary, they have argued that CD in the parents is a necessary but not sufficient condition for the development of schizophrenia. Thus, theoretically at least, CD can interact with other factors such as genetic predisposition in the offspring to increase the vulnerability to schizophrenia (Wynne, 1978). Thus, CD is viewed as an "intermediate," component part of the diathesis for schizophrenia. Given this theoretical assumption, it would not be inconsistent to hypothesize that a coexisting biologic-attentional deficit, genetically common to parent and child, could be manifested in the form of CD in the parent and more overt disturbed thinking in the vulnerable offspring.

RESPONSIVITY VERSUS ETIOLOGY

If one accepts the cross-sectional evidence that CD is associated with having a schizophrenic son or daughter, the question still remains whether high-CD parents contribute (in a causal fashion) to the development of schizophrenia or whether parental CD develops *because of* living with a schizophrenic child.

There are some studies in literature that shed light on this important issue, but the results from these investigations raise as many questions as they answer. Historically, most studies have addressed this issue of causality as if it were a linear process in which one of two one-way processes explained the relationship of parental CD to offspring schizophrenia: (1) "CD causes schizophrenia"—a purely etiologic interpretation, in which parental CD and concomitant family patterns of interaction are presumed to have existed prior to the development of schizophrenia; or (2) a "responsive" interpretation, in which it is assumed that deviant behaviors appeared first in the identified patient, and family members develop CD as an "adaptive" coping response to the patient's schizophrenic behavior.

One approach to addressing this question of direction of causality has involved laboratory studies in which "artificial family" situations have been set up, involving family members participating in CD-type tasks with and without their own schizophrenic offspring. To the extent that one views parental CD as a state rather than a trait, this approach is legitimate. Waxler (1971) constructed "artificial" families in order to study short-term direction of effects. The twenty questions task, a conceptual task, was given to these artificial families, each consisting of a parents-offspring triad. The parents were unacquainted with the adolescent or young adult offspring, some of whom were schizophrenic and some normal. The key finding was that the "normal" parents facilitated improved cognitive performance of the schizophrenic offspring. This report underlined the importance of studying corrective aspects of family interaction and fits with much clinical and experimental data that suggest that schizophrenic performance can be "normalized" under appropriate conditions. However, it is important to note that all hypotheses about the possible effects of parents on an offspring or the impact of schizophrenic offspring upon the parents, have specified that the effects should be expected only within the context of long-term, repetitious relationships. It would seem unreasonable to expect that schizophrenia or schizophrenia-like functioning could be induced in one-hour experimental sessions such as were used in this study.

In another artificial family study using tape-recorded exchanges of communication rather than the actual family interaction of Waxler's study, Liem (1974, 1976) reported that schizophrenic sons, compared with normal sons, were harder for all parents to understand. Although she interpreted this finding as supporting a responsive versus an etiologic hypothesis about family variables, it is not reasonable to regard this experiment as relevant to the long-term developmental issue of etiology. She did not find that parents of schizophrenics communicate with their own sons more adequately than they do with strangers' sons. This finding supports the view that transactional or reciprocal learning may have occurred within the family, but it can throw no light on the precursors of the schizophrenic disorder.

Another approach to the etiological versus responsive question using cross-sectional family data was carried out by Wild and Shapiro (1977). These authors used the twenty questions task, first individually with each family member and then with the family as a unit. Performance of each individual and family unit was compared for problem-solving efficiency and conceptual level. In contrast with the control sons, far more of the schizophrenic sons performed better individually than they did subsequently with their families. When such deterioration took place, it also was found that the parents had difficulty attending to, and making use of, "competent" information from the schizophrenic son, even though this information would have improved the effectiveness of the family performance. Also, the fathers of the schizophrenics typically dominated the family task and closed off discussion without appearing to grasp corrective or alternative strategies of problem solving offered by other family members. Wild and Shapiro acknowledged that their study could not answer the question of whether this current behavior of families was etiological or responsive, but the evidence did suggest that the current impact of the family context was to impair competencies of the offspring that were apparent outside the family.

Studies of this type do not adequately address this very important issue of direction of causality. Throughout their writings, Singer and Wynne have stressed the importance of the developmental aspect embedded in their theoretical explanation of how parental CD might exert its deleterious effects. As with many other theories introduced in the study of schizophrenia, subtle, perhaps less-exciting, nevertheless-important components of the theory have been overlooked or downplayed by the research community. From the start, CD has been consistently cast in the framework of a cognitive-developmental etiological model. In short, CD is thought to exert its deleterious effects on the developing child, over time, such that normal stages of cognitive mastery are not adequately established. Presumably, this period of mastery takes years. The idea that one could demonstrate the impact of such a long-term process upon a developing child in one or two laboratory sessions seems unlikely at best. Differences observed between strangers and relatives in a brief laboratory setting cannot be assumed to be analogous to, or reflective of, a lifetime of interaction between family members.

Inferences about causality are limited at best when they are based upon cross-sectional and/or experimental studies. Rather, prospective, longitudinal studies are needed to assess responsive/etiologic issues. One recent study by researchers at UCLA provides support for the contributory role of parental CD to the development of schizophrenia-spectrum disorders in the offspring. A cohort of 65 nonpsychotically disturbed adolescents and their families participated in this prospective, longitudinal study. At the time of the first five-year follow-up, a measure of CD obtained five years earlier, and defined and measured by the Singer-Wynne criteria, predicted the presence of disorders on the extended schizophrenia spectrum (Doane, West, Goldstein, Jones, & Rodnick, 1981). Very briefly, a measure of parental CD developed by Jones (1977) was obtained from Thematic Apperception Test data obtained at the time of the original assessment. These investigators found that, when a measure of the family's emotional climate (affective style) was coupled with the CD measure, remarkably precise identification occurred of offspring who subsequently developed schizophrenia-spectrum disorders. Only cases whose parents exhibited both high CD and this negative affective style manifested schizophrenia-spectrum disorders at the five-year follow-up. It should be emphasized that while both of these parental characteristics were measured at least five years before the onset of overt schizophrenic symptomatology and were, therefore, clearly not reactive to the presence of psychosis in the offspring, one cannot assume from these results that CD plays an etiologic role in the development of schizophrenia. The 15-year follow-up of this sample is nearing completion, and preliminary results are consistent with the findings regarding CD and the family's affective style at the five-year follow-up. That is, it appears that individuals who develop a schizophrenia-spectrum disorder come from families in which there is a high level of CD and a negative style of emotional relating on the part of the parent(s).

Another prospective, longitudinal study of family characteristics of schizophrenics is under way at the University of Rochester Child and Family Study. This group of investigators uses genetic risk as its criterion for defining vulnerability in the offspring. In this study, a sample of 4-, 7-, and 10-year-old male offspring of rigorously diagnosed DSM–III schizophrenics are contrasted with offspring of parents with a history of psychiatric hospitalization for other diagnoses such as unipolar and bipolar affective disorders or neurotic depression. Various measures of family functioning are collected, such as parental CD and measures of the family's affective climate. Ultimately, these data will be used to predict which offspring suffer a schizophrenic break in young adulthood.

Data on the psychosocial status of the index offspring for the first three-year follow-up are being collected now, and preliminary results will be available in the near future. However, one study recently carried out by the Rochester group indicates that a measure of parental CD is significantly associated with concurrently measured ratings of reduced psychosocial competence in the index offspring, as related by teachers and peers in the school setting (Doane et al., 1982).

TRAIT OR STATE

It is usually assumed that CD is a trait, reflective of an individual's usual style of communicating with a listener. Several studies clearly indicate that parents of schizophrenics exhibit CD in a task when alone with an examiner; however, it is important for the theory that CD also be exhibited when parents actually interact with their offspring. A study by Doane and colleagues (Doane et al., 1982) reported that not all parents show a consistent amount of CD across measurement contexts (individual, spouse, and whole family consensus Rorschachs). However, there was a group of mothers who had consistently high CD across settings. The psychosocial competence ratings of their 7- or 10-year-old sons were significantly lower than for children of low-CD mothers. This finding suggests that CD may be more of a stable trait in some individuals than it is in others. Furthermore, the data suggest that offspring of mothers whose CD is high in multiple measurement contexts are at more of a disadvantage than are children of parents whose CD is confined to certain contexts.

A related issue concerns the question of whether CD is a trait which remains relatively stable across time within the individual. This question can be answered only with prospective, longitudinal studies. Such a study is currently underway by the author. In this study, CD obtained at adolescence is being correlated with CD measured 15 years later.

CROSS-CULTURAL VALIDITY

Another important issue concerning the role of parental CD in schizophrenia is the question of whether findings from studies using primarily Anglo cohorts are equally valid for other cultural or subcultural groups. Cross-cultural reports on CD are few. However, the findings to date suggest that the cross-sectional relation between CD and schizophrenia is found in other cultural and subcultural groups.

Behrens et al. (1968) used the consensus family Rorschach in the home setting with families, all of lower socioeconomic status, divided into three groups: those with (a) black schizophrenic offspring; (b) white schizophrenic offspring; and (c) a black control. The authors found that several methods of scoring family Rorschachs blindly from tape recordings enabled them to differentiate with high statistical significance between the schizophrenic families, both black and white, and the black control families. These findings are contrary to a frequently expressed speculation that disturbed patterns of communication may be an undifferentiated aspect of disadvantaged socioeconomic status. In the same study, 46 percent of the families were not intact and had no biologic father present, but did have a variety of other adult males in the home. Factors such as broken homes and differences in educational achievement and in social mobility failed to show significant differences in the scores of family attentional communication disorder; for example, these factors were not related to the family's ability or inability to maintain and share a focus of attention on the designated task.

Wynne and colleagues (Wynne, Caudill, Kasahara, Kuromaru, Singer, & Higa, 1971) carried out a study of CD in parents of Japanese schizophrenics. They found comparable amounts and types of CD in these parents, and the predicted relation of CD to offspring schizophrenia versus other psychiatric disorders was observed. Interestingly, however, some modifications in the coding categories were necessary because of differences in the way language is used in this population.

Doane and Karno are currently studying CD in a sample of unacculturated Mexican-American families of schizophrenics in Los Angeles. This study is still in progress. However, preliminary results suggest that the amounts and types of CD in this cohort are comparable to that found in samples of Anglo families.

THE QUESTION OF SPECIFICITY

One of the most-important issues concerning CD is the extent to which its link to schizophrenia (be it etiologic or reactive) is specific to that particular disorder. Several studies have shed light on this question, but a definitive answer has not yet been established.

Before discussing the empirical findings regarding this question, it is useful to point out some factors that pose additional problems to studying this already-difficult issue. The first issue concerns the lack of norms for various populations. One contributing factor to this state of affairs is the fact that different investigators use different measurement contexts (e.g., the Rorschach versus the TAT) to elicit samples of CD. Usually these different ways of eliciting CD have different coding methods and data reduction systems, which makes comparisons across studies and samples difficult at best.

Another problem concerns the continually evolving state of the art in differential diagnosis among schizophrenic syndromes, affective psychoses, and related disorders. There is currently, for example, a lack of consensus among researchers with regard to the role of thought disorder in the affective psychoses. There is some question as to whether CD is associated with thought disorder, schizophrenia disorders, or merely with psychosis per se. A crucial test for the specificity of CD to schizophrenia would be a study of CD in parents of rigorously diagnosed schizophrenics and bipolar patients. Such a study is currently underway at UCLA, in which the relative amounts and types of parental CD in those two groups will be examined.

If CD is specific to schizophrenia, one would expect to find markedly more in the parents of schizophrenics than in the parents of affective psychotics. If no differences were observed, it would suggest that it is related to psychosis in general or perhaps even to severity of illness, rather than specifically to clinical schizophrenia.

A recent study by Greene (1982) suggests that CD is higher in mothers of schizophrenics than in mothers of patients with affective disorders. She included in this latter group patients with bipolar illness. Unfortunately, however, no differentiation was made between psychotic and nonpsychotic affective disordered families.

In a study by Doane et al. (1981), it was found that while most offspring who subsequently developed schizophrenia-spectrum disorders had high-CD parents, not all high-CD parents had offspring with schizophrenia-spectrum disorders. Interestingly, the high-CD cases who did develop spectrum disorders, came from homes in which the emotional climate (affective style) of the family, as assessed during a direct interaction task, was critical or intrusive. In contrast, the high-CD cases with a more-benign emotional family climate did not develop spectrum disorders. This finding raises the intriguing notion that for CD to have a deleterious impact on the child, it must perhaps occur in the context of an emotionally stressful relationship with the parents.

Goldstein (1981) reported on a sample of families of 11 anorectics and found that half of them had levels of parental CD similar to that found in parents of offspring with schizophrenia-spectrum disorders. Only one of the families had a negative affective style, however, and this case did not have high CD. This finding is consistent with the idea that *both* CD and a negative affective style are important components in the development of schizophrenia-spectrum disorders.

An issue somewhat related to the question of specificity concerns the relation of parental CD to schizophrenics with different symptomatic pictures. Singer and Wynne have emphasized from the very beginning that CD is not a unidimensional construct. Rather, it is an umbrella term that encompasses many different types of deviances. In their original work, Wynne and Singer classified parental CD into two types: (1) an amorphous style which reflects a global, predominantly undifferentiated form of thinking in which attention drifts, perception is uncertain and blurred, and communication is vague, indefinite, and poorly focused right from the start; and (2) fragmentation, which is thought to be a form of CD that is of a higher order than the amorphous style. Here, differentiation of the idea or percept is initially established, but communication breaks down later on in the sequence when disturbances occur that distract or disrupt the listener. Singer and Wynne reported that the fragmented style is more often found in parents of good premorbid schizophrenics, while amorphousness often characterizes the style of parents of poor premorbids (Singer & Wynne, 1965).

More recently, Singer, Wynne, and Toohey (1978) carried out a factor analysis of CD data from 72 parents of remitting and nonremitting schizophrenics. They found that all parents had very high amounts of total deviances. Interestingly, however, they reported that there were differences between the two groups on some of the factors (Wynne, 1978). Patients who had remissions had parents whose communication style was distressing but often clear enough to permit differentiation of the percept or idea. The sample size for this study was small, and this finding would certainly need to be replicated. Nevertheless, it supports the notion that substyles of CD do indeed exist and that perhaps these substyles have implications for the form or severity of the offspring's illness. Wynne and Singer (Wynne et al., 1977) have in fact reported that amount of CD is related to severity of illness in the offspring. Additional research is needed that addresses the relation of substyles of CD to different types and levels of severity of illness.

A study recently completed by Sass (1979) found that two forms of parental CD could be qualitatively distinguished—the "disorganized" type and the "evasive" type. The disorganized style includes such things as peculiar reasoning, referent problems, idiosyncratic word usage and syntax, and a tendency to jump about confusingly among different topics. The evasive style, in contrast, is characterized by attempts to avoid making a statement or to withhold commitment to what has been said. Examples include disqualifications of what one has said, retractions and denials, responses in subjunctive form, and vacillations between several different interpretations. He found that parents of schizophrenics with definite and severe formal thought disorder had more CD (especially of the disorganized type) than parents of constricted schizophrenics with low levels of thought disorder. This finding suggests that parental CD may be associated more with the degree of disorganization in cognitive functioning than with a diagnosis of schizophrenia per se.

CD AS A TRANSACTIONAL PROCESS

By definition, the term *CD* implies a transactional process between persons. That is, the importance of its influence lies in the *impact* it has on the listener. This fact necessitates taking into account the individual characteristics of the listener. The theory states that CD contributes to disturbed cognitive functioning in the developing child because it occurs repeatedly, over a long period of time, and in fact is characteristic of the speaker's attempts to communicate. The response of the listener in these dialogues can vary. And, theoretically, the way in which the listener reacts to, and copes with, the speaker's CD may influence the degree to which it has a detrimental effect upon him. An example would best illustrate this point.

In the popular television situation comedy "All in the Family," both Edith and Archie Bunker periodically display various types of CD. Archie is best known for using "big" words in the wrong way, while Edith is famous for non sequiter replies to questions or for peculiar reasoning. For adults with a reasonable degree of ego intactness, these "deviances" (as it were) add to the humor and enjoyment of the program. In this setting, the deviances are occasional, not constant, and because of the context, the listener "knows" what is really going on and is therefore not bewildered or confused.

In contrast to this kind of situation is one in which a child lives with a parent whose speech is *continuously* deviant. Presumably, many instances arise in which the child feels it is important to get the message, but cannot because s/he has become distracted, muddled, or stressed. In an ideal situation, the child could interrupt the parent and seek clarification. For a variety of possible reasons, however, s/he may not be able to do this. Perhaps his cognitive/attentional functioning is somewhat impaired; perhaps s/he is typically punished for challenging parental statements; or perhaps the constant, day-to-day effort to seek clarification becomes tiresome, and the child "gives up."

Despite the fact that many people assume parental CD is something that happens *to* the child, the theory does not require that this be the case. In fact, it may be that the presence of a child with a constitutional, cognitive/attentional deficit of some sort actually serves as a releasing stimulus for parental CD. Similarly, such a child might help to exacerbate preexisting but lower levels of CD in the parent. One can only speculate about how CD might exert its impact. Only prospective, longitudinal research with high-risk samples can address questions such as this. There is no evidence to date that parental CD exerts a one-way influence on the child. Further studies are needed to understand this issue of CD's "mechanism of action."

Another important issue that deserves further study is why one offspring is affected by CD (i.e., the person is or becomes symptomatic) while the siblings are not. Little work has been done in this area. The possible reasons are numerous for why one child is affected (presumably by CD) and the others not. Examples of possible explanations include the following: (*a*) perhaps the familial role of the affected offspring is different somehow, or (*b*) perhaps he or she has a qualitatively different emotional relationship with the parents. If one adopts the view of a stress-vulnerability model of schizophrenia in which the targeted offspring is genetically/biologically predisposed and he or she is then overloaded with environmental stress, parental CD might be conceived of as a necessary but not sufficient environmental stressor that increases an individual's vulnerability to clinical schizophrenia. Such an explanation makes common sense in that one might expect that the children in a high-CD family could vary in terms of temperament, personality, ego strength, biologic/genetic endownment, and so on.

CD AND OTHER FAMILY ATTRIBUTES

Another issue concerns the relation of CD to other intrafamilial attributes. It is reasonable to expect that if CD has such an important association with offspring schizophrenia, then other intrafamilial attributes or dimensions of family functioning ought to be different for high- and low-CD families.

A recent study by Lewis and colleagues at UCLA (Lewis, Rodnick, & Goldstein, 1981) explored this very issue. Lewis studied measures of parental CD derived from parental projective test data and compared these with independent observations of interactions among family members. She found that high-CD families differed from low-CD families on a number of interactional variables. High-CD families had unusual parental role structures (e.g., in low-CD families, fathers were more active, while mothers were more active in the high-CD cases), a poorly focused communication style, and a rigid, avoidant, nonverbal style of interaction (low-CD parents were nonavoidant and relaxed).

Other investigators from the UCLA group have reported other interactional correlates of CD. As mentioned previously, Herman and Jones (1976) found that parents high in CD on the TAT were less acknowledging of other family members' responses on a family Rorschach task than were low-CD parents. The fact that Mishler and Waxler (1968), among others, have found decreased acknowledgment characteristic of families of diagnosed schizophrenics makes this result even more interesting. Lieber (1977) found that these same high-CD parents, when observed in a structured discussion of videotapes of their own triadic interaction, were less likely than low-CD parents to use task-focusing comments when the family discussion began to drift away from the requested structure.

All of the above studies suggest that high- and low-CD families differ, particularly on the dimension of ability to maintain an effective focus of discussion. Further research is needed to determine whether high- and low-CD families differ with regard to other family attributes. The author, for example, is currently studying whether CD is related to Vaughn and Leff's (1976) measure of expressed emotion (EE), a variable shown to predict course of illness in recently hospitalized schizophrenics (see also Johnson & Notarius, Chapter 12 of this *Handbook*).

NEW DIRECTIONS

Earlier work on CD and schizophrenia has concentrated on establishing its link to offspring schizophrenia-spectrum disorders. As discussed earlier in this chapter, this work has included cross-sectional studies of parents with offspring with other, nonpsychotic diagnoses as well as studies examining a possible etiological role of CD in the development of schizophrenia.

Currently, a number of new areas of exploration are under way. One area concerns the relation of parental CD to the genetic/biologic endowment of the individual parent. This pursuit concrns the relation of these two variables within individuals. Thus, this line of inquiry is concerned with the origins and development of CD per se, without regard necessarily to its already established association with schizophrenia in the next generation. The previously mentioned work with parental CD and parental attentional deficits is an example of this kind of endeavor. It would also be useful to document whether or not CD is related to an increased incidence of schizophrenia in the family histories of high-CD individuals.

A second area of concern currently being studied by the author and her colleagues is whether the amount of CD in the relatives influences the course of schizophrenia once it has already developed. One hypothesis would be that schizophrenics from high-CD families would have an increased risk for clinical relapse or an unremitting course of the illness. The logic behind this hypothesis is twofold: (a) if CD is a genetic marker of schizophrenia in the parent, then schizophrenic offspring of parents with very high levels of CD would presumably have a relatively larger genetic/biologic component to their disease; or (b) alternatively, high levels of parental CD could (theoretically at least) be conceived of as psychosocial stressers which serve to exacerbate disturbed thinking in vulnerable individuals.

A related question is whether the combination of high CD and other familial attributes (such as a hostile or overinvolved family emotional climate) acts in a synergistic fashion to overstress the recent-onset schizophrenic, resulting in early relapse or deterioration. This question is currently being studied by the author and her colleagues at the Mental Health Clinical Research Center for the Study of Schizophrenia in Los Angeles.

Another promising new direction of research concerns the relation of CD to psychosocial family intervention. This area is just beginning to be studied. Family therapists have long been aware of the countertransference problems or sense of exhaustion that comes from working with families of schizophrenics. It is likely that an important contributory factor to this is that therapists must work in the context of family interaction characterized by high CD. Families with severely disturbed members are difficult enough to work with. The added difficulty introduced by high levels of CD in family members makes the task even more formidable. If one could classify families of schizophrenics as to type and level of CD before treatment was begun, perhaps intervention programs could be planned ahead of time that were designed to correct (or at least offset) the potentially interfering effects of high CD. Work in this area is just beginning, and the empirical studies of this issue are lacking, but needed.

SOME METHODOLOGICAL CONSIDERATIONS FOR FUTURE RESEARCH

For investigators studying CD and its relation to other variables, some procedural/methodological considerations should be noted.

1. It has already been mentioned that different investigators use different instruments to serve as stimuli for CD. This is perfectly legitimate, since CD theoretically (as well as empirically) occurs in a wide

variety of measurement contexts. Nevertheless, this practice results in some problems and confusion that can be difficult to disentangle. When investigators use different procedures and/or stimuli, it then becomes difficult to make comparisons across studies, such as cross-validation. With the TAT, for example, one investigator may use five cards, while another uses seven. If findings from the two studies conflict, then one doesn't know whether it might be due merely to the fact that the subjects in the seven-card study produced more CD because they had greater opportunity to do so. With the Rorschach, one investigator may choose Cards I, II, III, and IV and administer the task individually. A second person may administer Card II only to an individual, while yet a third could administer Card II to an entire family in the context of a consensus task. How does one make comparisons among these three sets of data? It is recommended, therefore, that standardization of instruments be a high priority in order to facilitate cross-validation comparisons.

2. A related precaution is that the procedure chosen be administered in a standardized way for all subjects in a given sample. What the examiner says and does, and how he presents the task, answers questions, and so on, very much influence the subjects' responses and the subsequent scoring of CD.

3. A third important area concerns accurate, standardized transcription of the subject's responses. Audio recording is absolutely essential to get verbatim transcription. When using consensus procedures, videotaping is recommended in addition to audio recording since it is often difficult to ascertain from the audiotape who is actually speaking. CD coding from the TAT and Rorschach is very precise, and extremely accurate transcription is a necessity. Careless transcription can result in distortions in the data, which render it virtually useless.

4. Establishing interrater reliability is essential. Training usually requires extensive supervision and practice. This is particularly important if one wants to look at dimensions of CD, rather than a global, overall estimate of the level of disturbed communication.

5. A final recommendation is that the investigator think through what it is he or she wants to do with a measure of CD. Often, people neglect to remember that there are many different kinds of deviances subsumed under the term *CD*. A total amount of CD may be appropriate for one research question, while factor scores or substyles may be more appropriate for another.

REFERENCES

Behrens, M. I., Rosenthal, A. J., & Chodoff, P. Communication in lower-class families of schizophrenics: II. Observations and findings. *Archives of General Psychiatry*, 1968, *18*, 689–696.

Doane, J. A. Family interaction and communication deviance in disturbed and normal families: A review of research. *Family Process,* 1978, *17,* 357–376.

Doane, J. A., & Jones, J. E. *Communication deviance scoring manual for TAT.* Unpublished coding manual, 1979.

Doane, J. A., Jones, J. E., Fisher, L., Ritzler, B., Singer, M. T., & Wynne, L. C. Parental communication deviance as a predictor of competence in children at risk for adult psychiatric disorder. *Family Process,* 1982, *21,* 211–223.

Doane, J. A., West, K. L., Goldstein, M. J., Jones, J. E., & Rodnick, E. H. Parental communication deviance and affective style: Predictors of subsequent schizophrenia spectrum disorders in vulnerable adolescents. *Archives of General Psychiatry,* 1981, *38,* 679–685.

Glaser, R. *Family, spouse and individual Rorschach responses of families with and without young adult schizophrenic offspring.* Unpublished doctoral dissertation, University of California (Berkeley), 1976.

Goldstein, M. J. Family factors associated with schizophrenia and anorexia nervosa. *Journal of Youth and Adolescence,* 1981, *10*(5), 385–405.

Goldstein, M. J., & Rodnick, E. H. The family's contribution to the etiology of schizophrenia: Current status. *Schizophrenia Bulletin,* 1975, *1,* 48–63.

Greene, R. *The relation of family communication deviance and attentional dysfunction in schizophrenia.* Unpublished doctoral dissertation, Florida Institute of Technology, 1982.

Hassan, S. Transactional and contextual invalidation between the parents of disturbed families: A comparative study. *Family Process,* 1974, *13,* 53–76.

Herman, B., & Jones, J. E. Lack of acknowledgment in the family Rorschachs of families with a child at risk for schizophrenia. *Family Process,* 1976, *15,* 289–302.

Hirsch, S., & Leff, J. Parental abnormalities of verbal communication in the transmission of schizophrenia. *Psychological Medicine,* 1971, *1,* 118–127.

Jacob, T. Family interaction in disturbed and normal families: A methodological and substantive review. *Psychological Bulletin,* 1975, *82,* 33–65.

Jones, J. E. Patterns of transactional deviance in the TAT's of parents of schizophrenics. *Family Process,* 1977, *16,* 327–337.

Lewis, J. M., Rodnick, E. H., & Goldstein, M. J. Intrafamilial interactive behavior, parental communication deviance, and risk for schizophrenia. *Journal of Abnormal Psychology,* 1981, *90,* 448–457.

Lieber, D. J. Parental focus of attention in a videotape feedback task as a function of hypothesized risk for offspring schizophrenia. *Family Process,* 1977, *16,* 467–475.

Loveland, N. The relation Rorschach: A technique for studying interaction. *Journal of Nervous Mental Disease,* 1967, *145,* 93–105.

Liem, J. H. Effects of verbal communications of parents and children: A comparison of normal and schizophrenic families. *Journal of Consulting and Clinical Psychology,* 1974, *42,* 438–450.

Liem, J. H. Intrafamily communication and schizophrenic thought disorder: An etiological or responsive relationship? *Clinical Psychologist,* 1976, *29,* 28–30.

Mishler, E., & Waxler, N. *Interaction in families: An experimental study of family processes and schizophrenia.* New York, John Wiley & Sons, 1968.

Morris, G., & Wynne, L. Schizophrenic offspring and parental styles of communication. *Psychiatry,* 1965, *28,* 19–44.

Sass, L. *Styles of communication deviance in the parents of thought-disordered and non-thought-disordered schizophrenics.* Unpublished doctoral dissertation, University of California (Berkeley), 1979.

Singer, M. Family transactions and schizophrenia: I. Recent research findings. In J. Romano (Ed.), The origins of schizophrenia. *Proceedings of the First Rochester International Conference of Schizophrenia.* Amsterdam: Excerpta Medica Foundation, 1967.

Singer, M. Scoring manual for communication deviances seen in individually administered Rorschach. Unpublished manuscript, University of California (Berkeley) 1973.

Singer, M., & Wynne, L. Differentiating characteristics of parents of childhood schizophrenics, childhood neurotics, and young adult schizophrenics. *American Journal of Psychiatry,* 1963, *120,* 234–243.

Singer, M., & Wynne, L. Thought disorder and family relations of schizophrenics: IV. Results and implications. *Archives of General Psychiatry,* 1965, *12,* 201–212.

Singer, M. T., Wynne, L. C., & Toohey, M. L. Communication disorders and the families of schizophrenics. In L. C. Wynne, R. Cromwell, & S. Matthysse (Eds.), *The nature of schizophrenia: New approaches to research and treatment.* New York: John Wiley & Sons, 1978. Pp. 499–511.

Solvberg, H., & Blakar, R. Communication efficiency in couples with and without a schizophrenic offspring. *Family Process,* 1975, *14,* 515–534.

Stabenau, J., Tupin, J., Werner, M., & Pollin, W. A comparative study of families of schizophrenics, delinquents and normals, *Psychiatry,* 1965, *28,* 45–59.

Vaughn, C. E., & Leff, J. P. The influence of family and social factors on the course of psychiatric illness. *British Journal of Psychiatry,* 1976, *129,* 125–137.

Waxler, N. Parent and child effects on cognitive performance: An experimental approach to the etiological and responsive theories of schizophrenia. *Family Process,* 1974, *13,* 1–22.

Wild, C. M., & Shapiro, L. Mechanisms of change from individual to family performance in male schizophrenics and their parents. *Journal of Nervous and Mental Disease,* 1977, *165,* 41–56.

Wild, C., Shapiro, L., & Goldenberg, L. Transactional communication disturbance in families of male schizophrenics. *Family Process,* 1975, *14,* 131–160.

Wild, C., Singer, M., Rosman, B., Ricci, J., & Lidz, T. Measuring disordered styles of thinking. *Archives of General Psychiatry,* 1965, *13,* 471–476.

Wynne, L. C. From symptoms to vulnerability and beyond: An overview. In L. C. Wynne, R. L. Cromwell, & S. Matthysse (Eds.), *The nature of schizophrenia: New Approaches to Research and Treatment.* New York: John Wiley & Sons, 1978.

Wynne, L. C., Caudill, M., Kasahara, Y., Kuromaru, S., Singer, M. T., & Higa, M. *Translation problems in the cross-cultural study of psychopathology: A comparison of Japanese and American communication disorders.* Paper presented at the Conference on Mental Health Research in Asia and the Pacific, Honolulu, March 15–19, 1971.

Wynne, L. C., & Singer, M. Thought disorder and family relations of schizophrenics: II. A classification of forms of thinking. *Archives of General Psychiatry,* 1963, *9,* 199–206.

Wynne, L. C., Singer, M., Bartko, J., & Toohey, M. Schizophrenics and their families: Recent research on parental communication. In J. M. Tanner (Ed.), *Developments in psychiatric research.* London: Hodder & Stoughton, 1977. Pp. 254–286.

Wynne, L. C., Singer, M., & Toohey, M. Communication of the adoptive parents of schizophrenics. In J. Jorstad & E. Ugelstad (Eds.), *Schizophrenia 1975: psychotherapy, family studies, and research.* Oslo, Norway: University Press, 1976. Pp. 413–451.

Section Eight

Methods of Evaluation

Chapter 31

Observational Assessment of Marital and Family Interaction: Methodological Considerations

RICHARD GILBERT
ANDREW CHRISTENSEN

Current interest in observational assessment of marital and family interaction stems from both theoretical and methodological considerations. On a theoretical level, there is increasing recognition for the role of nuclear family interactional processes in the etiology, development, and maintenance of various psychobehavioral disorders. This emphasis reflects an important conceptual shift from viewing intrapsychic and biological factors as *the* primary causal conditions. Historically, Fromm-Reichmann's (1948) concept of the "schizophrenegenic" mother, the double-bind hypothesis advanced by Bateson, Jackson, Haley, and Weakland (1956), and Wynne, Ryckoff, Day, and Hirsch's (1958) discussion of transactional thought disorder have been influential in defining and advancing the family interactional perspective.

With respect to methodology, observational assessments of nuclear family interaction processes have been fueled by the empirical inadequacies of alternate forms of measurement. Specifically, the validity of questionnaires, psychological tests, individual psychiatric interviews, and case history analyses rests on the tenuous assumption that "people are able and/or willing to accurately report events and feelings of the past and present and that such reports are minimally affected by forgetting, defensive distortion or inaccurate elaboration as a justification of actions." (Jacob, 1975, p. 33). In contrast, it can be argued *(a)* that direct observation methodologies require fewer assumptions or inferences about behavior and *(b)* that their own inherent sources of bias (e.g., reactivity to observation) can be minimized such that confidence in the validity of obtained data is not severely compromised.

In this chapter, methodological considerations in conducting direct observational assessments of family interaction will be discussed. While the issues to be raised are generally applicable to all family subsystems (i.e., marital, parent-child, sibling, triads, whole family), the primary focus of the present review involves *direct* assessments of the marital dyad, either alone (marital interaction) or with one or more children (family interaction). Studies involving other family subsystems (e.g., parent-child interaction) will only be cited when they significantly add to the discussion of an important issue. In addition, the present paper will focus on comparisons of interaction in distressed and nondistressed family systems, although the points raised are also applicable to other comparisons (e.g., cross-ethnic groups).

Direct observational assessments are characterized by the use of trained observers who are not also members of the interpersonal system under investigation. Thus, studies employing methods of indirect observation, such as parent or spouse observation data (Eyberg & Johnson, 1974; Peterson, 1979), will not be discussed. The review of methodological issues in direct observation studies will be divided into three major areas: sampling and design, observational methods, and dependent measures.

ISSUES OF SAMPLING AND DESIGN

Group designs

Observational studies of marital and family interaction have generally employed group rather than single-case designs. These group designs have involved either distressed-nondistressed comparisons, comparisons of multiple types of distressed systems, or single-group studies in which samples of distressed or nondistressed systems have been investigated without a comparison group. While both comparative and single-group designs can generate findings which contribute to our understanding of interactive differences between distressed and nondistressed systems, comparative studies have the advantage of minimizing between-group variance associated with experimenter effects as well as historical and geographical factors. Thus, by reducing sources of variance between groups, comparative designs can generate less-ambiguous conclusions than those derived by comparing findings across single-group distressed and single-group nondistressed studies.

When employing a group design to investigate interaction in distressed and/or nondistressed systems, three central issues need to be considered: sample specification, demographic matching, and procedural comparability.

Sample specification.   The first issue, equally applicable to comparative and single-group designs, pertains to the method employed to classify interpersonal systems as either distressed or nondistressed. Specifically, in order to permit valid generalizations from the data and to compare findings across studies, it is essential to accurately locate the research sample(s) along the normal-deviant continuum. To date, however, the methods of classification have generally been imprecise. For example, Haley (1972) notes that a widely used definition of a normal family is one in which "no member has ever been arrested or in therapy." In addition to providing relatively little information about the sample, such global screening criteria exclude only a portion of distressed families. The resulting failure to restrict sample heterogeneity increases the possibility of obscuring meaningful differences among groups.

Similar though less extreme problems are associated with the use of "current involvement in psychotherapy" or "the presence of a particular symptom" as methods for classifying a system as distressed. Specifically, the degree of system distress associated with involvement in psychotherapy or the presence of particular symptomatology is highly variable. Thus, the dual problems of imprecise sample specification and inadequate restriction of sample heterogeneity also apply to these qualitative designations of system distress. Of course, these problems can be reduced somewhat through the use of multiple qualitative measures. For example, Henggeler, Borduin, Rodick, and Tavormina (1979) classified families as favorably adjusted if the nuclear family was intact for at least the past five years, there was no history of psychiatric referral or felony conviction, and the family was referred as well adjusted by a mental health professional who knew the family personally.

An alternative approach to sample specification involves the use of quantitative methods. Marital interaction researchers, for example, have specified system distress or satisfaction in terms of cutoff scores on either the Locke-Wallace (1959) marital adjustment scale or a similar measure, the dyadic adjustment scale (Spanier, 1976). The use of cutoff scores on self-report measures has a number of advantages. First, it enables the investigator to report sample heterogeneity and severity level along a clinically relevant dimension (e.g., perceived satisfaction). Second, it allows the researcher to draw clear comparisons with other studies which have employed the same criterion measure.

At the same time, the use of quantitative designation procedures is not without potential problems. For one, the investigator must be cautious only to employ those measures whose reliability and validity have been adequately demonstrated. Secondly, as Margolin (1978) indicates, the correlations between some indexes of marital adjustment are low. Margolin suggests that the correlations are reduced because the various measures seem to assess somewhat independent aspects of marital adjustment (e.g., perceived satisfaction versus specific desires for behavior change). However, these problems concerning the potential unreliability and modest intercorrelation of self-report measures of system distress can be minimized. The investigator can achieve this end by *(a)* employing multimethod quantitative designation procedures (e.g., the use of two self-report measures of distress or the combined use of self-report measures and independent ratings of distress), and *(b)* employing only those self-report measures with adequate psychometric properties.

It is interesting to note that in research currently in progress (Christensen & Margolin, 1979), over one half of those families who would be classified as nondistressed by global qualitative criteria (e.g., self-definition as nondistressed, no history or current involvement in psychotherapy) fail to meet multimethod empirical criteria of this status. In sum, studies which employ a global qualitative screening criteria (and to a lesser extent, studies which employ single-method quantitative screening) are likely to have fairly heterogeneous samples which *(a)* are not sharply distinct from their logical comparison group, and *(b)* which promote the finding of small or insignificant interactive differences between contrast groups. The attainment of distinct comparison samples with low within-group variability can be facilitated by multicriteria specification involving quantitative and/or qualitative measures.

Demographic matching. A second central design issue in studies of interaction in family systems pertains to demographic matching. Certainly, in the interests of defining the population to which results may be generalized and in order to compare findings across studies, it is important to specify the demographic characteristics of the systems under study. The matter becomes less clear, however, when defining which demographic factors, if any, it is essential to match for when conducting a comparison group design. To date, there has been considerable support by interaction researchers for the careful matching of demographic variables across comparison groups. Jacob (1975), for example, has urged researchers conducting comparative studies of family interaction to match those demographic variables which have been "found to be (or strongly suggested to be) related to different patterns of family interaction" (p. 33) (i.e., age, sex, and birth order of child; family size, socioeconomic status (SES), religion and ethnicity, and parents' ages).

Consistent with this position, there are two advantages to careful matching on demographic variables. First, matching procedures help approximate experimental conditions, given the inevitability of using intact (i.e., nonrandomly assigned) groups in comparative studies of system interaction. In the present case, for example, matching would reduce the likelihood that factors other than the "distressedness" of the systems accounted for interactive differences. Second, careful demographic matching reduces sources of between-group variance and thus makes potentially important group differences easier to identify.

At the same time, it should be noted that there are occasions when the careful matching of demographic variables across intact groups can significantly compromise external validity. For example, Meehl (1971) points out that case-matching of intellectual, academic achievement, and social-class variables in archival studies of preschizophrenics and nonpsychotic samples could result in comparing extremely nonrepresentative samples of preschizophrenics, nonpsychotics, or both. Preschizophrenics more often come from lower-socioeconomic backgrounds and are deficient on indexes of academic and intellectual achievement relative to nonpsychotics.

This important observation suggests a general guideline to researchers conducting comparative investigations of marital or family interaction: If demographic matching results in sampling outliers from the population of systems under study, it is advisable to do a careful descriptive study rather than severely compromise external validity. However, if careful matching does not significantly reduce external validity, there are meaningful advantages to demographic controls. In sum, decisions pertaining to demographic matching, rather than being "reflexive" or automatically positive, should be based upon preexisting knowledge and descriptive data concerning the relationship between demographic variables and the populations under study (see also Christensen & Arrington, in press).

Procedural comparability.   The final central design issue in group studies of marital and family interaction may be labeled procedural comparability. Specifically, it is necessary to equate those research procedures which are likely to intensify existing group differences in expectancies, motivation, and set. A large body of literature has demonstrated that such mediating variables often have a meaningful effect on observable behavior (Mischel, 1973). In particular, it is ideal to equate renumeration procedures across groups. Numerous studies (e.g., Becker & Iwakami, 1967; Leighton, Stollak, & Fergusson, 1971) have increased initial group differences in set by only paying subjects in nondistressed systems for their participation in the assessment. In fairness, it should be noted that *(a)* nonmonetary recruitment of nondistressed systems can be problematic, and *(b)* paying already motivated, distressed subjects adds additional cost with little direct benefit in an expensive research area. Nevertheless, every effort should be made to remunerate either both or neither group for their involvement in the observational assessment.

Secondly, in order to avoid the potential impact of initial treatment sessions on system interaction, the assessment phase should completely precede the introduction of treatment for distressed systems. Finally, in recognition of the discriminant influence of environmental context on interpersonal interaction (O'Rourke, 1963), it is essential that comparison groups be assessed in similar situations (home, laboratory, etc.). For example, a number of interaction researchers (Haley, 1972; Riskin & Faunce, 1972) have discussed the various confounding factors which are introduced when assessing two groups not equated for current hospitalization status.

Longitudinal and single-case designs

Carefully conducted, single-assessment group designs can generate valuable information about interaction in distressed and/or nondistressed systems. At the same time, such studies are limited in their ability to address a number of theoretical assumptions which are fundamental to the field of marital and family interaction. In particular, central questions concerning the relationship between system interaction variables and individual symptomatology over time and questions pertaining to the direction of these effects require longitudinal methods. However, a number of difficult pragmatic and conceptual problems have limited the use of longitudinal designs in systems interaction research. On a pragmatic level, problems with subject recruitment and attrition, organizational and personnel changes which reduce research efficiency, and the financial costs involved all serve as inhibitors. On a conceptual level, the researcher is confronted with the fact that variability associated with situational factors (e.g., illness, job changes) may mask all but highly significant trends (Baldwin, 1960). In addition, the possibility always exists that the target systems will be altered in some meaningful way by repeated assessments, such that over time they no longer represent the population from which they were originally drawn (Hill, 1964). For example, couples who are repeatedly asked to discuss and negotiate solutions to relationship problems may reflect upon and change their communication in a manner somewhat different from its natural development.

To an extent, the benefits of longitudinal research can be approached, and its problems moderated, through the use of single-case designs. Such methods can be viewed as the simplest, most-manageable form of a longitudinal design. For example, Straker and Jacobson (1979) intensively studied five families with an encopretic child in order to investigate the relationship between family interaction and child symptomatology over time. Specifically, these researchers correlated family interaction variables from 20 family therapy sessions with parent report data on the between-session frequency of child encopresis. The results indicated that symptom frequency was more highly correlated with the preceding rather than the subsequent week's family therapy interaction. This suggests that changes in family interaction relate more strongly to changes in symptom frequency than vice versa. While not without problems, this study illustrates how single-case designs can provide a cost-efficient method of addressing central theoretical assumptions which cannot be adequately investigated with single-assessment group designs.

In addition, the restricted scope of single-case designs should enable researchers to monitor and report major situational changes in the system under study (illness, starting school, etc.). Reporting major instances of situational variability provides a global means of assessing the extent to which situational influences may be accounting for, or masking, hypothesized systemic trends. In sum, the use and refinement of single-case methods in studies of interaction in systems represents a virtually unexplored and potentially valuable research direction.

ISSUES PERTAINING TO OBSERVATIONAL METHODS

Classification of methods

A variety of dimensions can be employed to classify the range of observational procedures used in assessments of system interaction[1] (Cromwell, Olson, & Fournier, 1976; O'Neill & Alexander, 1970). In the present discussion, major observational procedures will be conceptualized as falling within one of four cells in a 2×2 (structure $\times$ assessment setting) matrix.

Degree of task structure is a primary classification dimension for two related reasons. First, task structure can have an important impact on interactive content. Specifically, detailed instructional guidelines are often necessary to elicit theoretically important, low base-rate processes such as problem-solving or decision-making discussions. Weick (1968) has referred to this process of eliciting meaningful low base-rate responses as "amplification." Conversely, the investigator whose primary goal is the collection of a minimally obtrusive sample of interaction should avoid the imposition of structure. In this case, higher

---

[1] In this chapter, the term *system interaction* will be used to denote both marital and family interaction. The typical generic term *family interaction* will not be used, in order to avoid confusing the general meaning of family interaction (i.e., marital with or without children) with its specific meaning (i.e., both parents and at least one child).

base-rate processes and heterogeneity of interactive content would be more likely to occur.

Secondly, the modulation of task structure can expand or restrict the number of theoretically relevant variables operative in the assessment context. For example, time-limited laboratory assessments of alcohol consumption rates have generally failed to discriminate between solitary and social drinkers. However, later naturalistic (i.e., unstructured) investigations revealed that while solitary and social drinkers cannot be differentiated on rate measures, the latter group drinks longer (Sommer, 1977). Thus, the use of a relatively structured, time-limited assessment of alcohol consumption patterns rendered the critical duration variable inoperative and obscured existing group differences. Similarly, explicit instructions for family members to verbally resolve conflictual situations reduces the possibility that one or more individuals will choose to be silent or withdraw. In this case, the investigator is less likely to discriminate family or marital systems in terms of the use of withdrawal as a coping mechanism, when this may actually be a crucial discriminator in less-structured situations.

At the same time, it should be noted that when relevant variables have been clearly articulated in a research area or when particular variables are the subject of study, the careful use of structure can maximize their operation in a given situation. In sum, the operation and effect of task structure is analogous to a zoom lens on a camera: It can be employed to heighten attention to particular aspects of system process (thus narrowing the observational field as a whole), or it can be minimized, enabling the viewer to scan the full range and complexity of the system under study.

The choice of assessment setting as a primary classification dimension is supported by *(a)* personality research implicating context as an important influence on emergent behavior (Mischel, 1968), and *(b)* a number of studies which specifically demonstrate low cross-situational generality of system interaction. These latter findings are consistent across a variety of family subsystems and task contents (Dysart, 1973; O'Rourke, 1963).

Description of observational methods

At this time, major types of observational procedures falling within each of the four cells of the 2×2 classification matrix will be described.

Structured laboratory assessments of system interaction have been the most-common methods used to date. In general, there are four types of structured laboratory tasks distinguished by the particularly low base-rate process(es) they amplify: Game playing, decision making, conflict resolution and stimulus interpretation.

Game-playing situations enable the investigator to observe the system's ability to establish and comply with rules, the capacity of system members to enjoy and have fun with each other, and/or the extent to which system members adopt competitive or cooperative stances with respect to each other. Two common game-playing tasks are the SIMFAM technique (i.e., simulated family activity measurement) employed by Straus and his colleagues (e.g., Straus & Tallman, 1971) and the prisoner's dilemma game, which has been adapted for the study of marital interaction by Speer (1972). Ravich (1969) argues that the innocuous quality and nonverbal nature of game techniques like SIMFAM or the prisoner's dilemma permits clear observation of marital and family patterns that might otherwise be obscured due to anxiety-related reactive effects or a lack of interpersonal insight and verbal proficiency.

Decision-making tasks amplify the process through which systems attempt to arrive at mutually agreeable points of view or plans for action. The two most commonly used decision-making procedures are Ferriera and Winters' (1965) unrevealed differences technique and the plan something together task from the Mental Research Institute's structured family interview (Watzlawick, 1966). In the unrevealed differences technique, family members attempt to reach consensus on preferences initially made in private. In the plan something together task, system members are simply instructed to plan an event together, such as a special meal or a family outing.

In conflict resolution tasks, interaction data is generated under conditions of disagreement, allowing observation of the system's ability to restore equilibrium, of its acceptance or intolerance of differences, and of the negotiation strategies of individual system members. The most-common procedure for generating interactional data under conditions of conflict is Strodbeck's (1951) revealed differences technique. In this technique, system members discuss disagreements over preferred solutions to standardized marital or family problems. This procedure is distinct from the unrevealed differences technique in the uniformly high affective loading of the discussion topics and in the initiation of discussion under conditions of explicit disagreement. A popular derivative of the revealed differences technique is Olson and Ryder's (1970) inventory of marital conflicts procedure. This task asks couples to discuss a series of short vignettes depicting various types of marital conflict and to come to a joint resolution concerning the relative responsibility of the husband or the wife in each vignette. Both the revealed differences techniques and the inventory of marital conflicts are similar in that the conflict areas which system members discuss are not necessarily those which the system itself is currently experiencing. In contrast, the problem-solving assessments employed by behavioral family researchers enable marital partners or family members to discuss a conflict which is of particular salience to them (Hops, Wills, Patterson, & Weiss, 1972, Patterson & Hops, 1971). In this procedure, system members work with the investigator to select a salient conflict area. Subsequently, system members are instructed to discuss the area of conflict, try and understand it better, and work toward a resolution. The lack of complete standardization introduces a new source of variance while increasing the relevance of the conflict discussion to the system.

Finally, stimulus interpretation tasks assess the degree to which system members exhibit formal communication deficits characterized by blurred or distorted meanings, inconsistent or fragmented messages, denials of the obvious, lack of acknowledgment, nonsequiturs, etc. (see Jones, Rodnick, Goldstein, McPherson, & West, 1977; Singer & Wynne, 1966). Such transactional disturbances have been consistently found in families with a schizophrenic offspring, and their presence defines a system as at risk for later serious disturbance. Loveland, Wynne, and Singer (1963) have asked system members to attempt to reach consensus on the meaning of a Rorschach card in order to assess formal communication deficits. Other researchers (e.g., Jones, 1974) have employed TAT cards as the stimuli to interpret.

In contrast to structured laboratory tasks, unstructured laboratory assessments have been a rarity. An excellent example, however, is provided by Snyder (1977) in his investigation of reinforcement contingency across distressed and nondistressed families. In this study, family members were videotaped through a one-way mirror for 45 minutes in a room set up to be a combined living room and playroom. Appropriate furnishings, toys, and magazines helped achieve this effect. Family members were given a general rationale for the study and instructed only to remain inside the room for the entire 45 minutes. In addition, Birchler, Weiss, and Vincent (1975) videotaped and coded four-minute segments of free-marital interaction. Couples were instructed to "talk about anything" while the investigators prepared for subsequent structured assessments.

There have been two varieties of structured home assessments. First, in order to assess the possible impact of setting familiarity on system interaction, a number of researchers have taken structured laboratory tasks and employed them in subjects' homes (Gottman, 1979; O'Rourke, 1963). Second, following the work of Patterson and his colleagues (Patterson, Ray, Shaw, & Cobb, 1969), a number of researchers (e.g., Lobitz & Johnson, 1972) have employed trained observers to code home interaction under a number of restrictive conditions: *(a)* all family members must be present in two adjoining rooms, *(b)* no interactions with the observer are permitted, *(c)* the television set may not be on, and *(d)* no visitors or extended telephone calls are permitted.

Finally, increasing attention is being directed toward assessing system behavior in the home with minimal restrictions. These unstructured home assessment procedures are distinguished according to whether they sample behavior in single versus multiple situations and whether interaction is directly coded by observers or audiorecorded without observers present and later coded. Dreyer and Dreyer's (1973) observations of family dinnertime behavior is an example of nonrestrictive single-situation assessment with observers present. Jacob (personal communication) has also focused on dinnertime as an assessment situation; however, he has employed audiotape equipment to collect the interaction data rather than have it directly coded by observers. The latter procedure enables the investigator to employ more-complex coding systems and to conduct secondary analyses of the data. Steinglass (1980) has introduced the home observation assessment method (HOAM) in which an observer is assigned to each marital partner. Rather than restrict the mobility of family members, as in the Patterson system, the observers move throughout the home according to the whim and needs of their assigned family member. Observation sessions last between two and four hours. Finally, Christensen and his colleagues (Christensen, 1979; Christensen & Hazzard, 1983) have described the development of an automated recording system capable of sampling family interaction in multiple situations. In this system of observation, family interaction is randomly sampled during typical high-interaction periods in the home (e.g., dinnertime).

The generalizability of observational assessments of marital and family interaction

Foster and Cone (1980) note that the adequacy of observational systems has traditionally been discussed in terms of reliability and validity. More recently, however, these concerns have been subsumed under the broader rubric of generalizability theory (Cronbach, Gleser, Nanda, & Rajaratnam, 1972). From the perspective of generalizability theory, the adequacy of observational data is determined by the ways in which it can be generalized rather than by its ability to meet certain fixed standards of reliability and validity. For example, the classical categories of test-retest and interrater reliability have been reconceptualized in terms of generalizability across time and observers, respectively.

In considering the utility of marital and family observational data, three central aspects of generalizability should be mentioned: *(a)* generalizability to diagnostic or evaluative judgments (discriminativeness); *(b)* generalizability to naturally occurring instances of the process under study (representativeness); and *(c)* generalizability across conditions when observers are present or absent (nonreactiveness). It should be noted that reactivity and representativeness are distinct though interrelated concepts. Observational data which is highly reactive cannot be representative; however, nonreactive data is not necessarily representative. For example, interaction during laboratory decision-making tasks may not be influenced by the presence of observers (nonreactive), while bearing little resemblance to the manner in which marital or family systems typically make decisions (nonrepresentative). Each of the three aspects of data generalizability will be considered in turn. In addition, given the fundamental importance of nonreactive measurement, a more-detailed discussion of this issue will be undertaken.

First, the observational method employed should produce data which are generalizable to diagnostic or evaluative judgments about the systems comprising the research sample (discriminativeness). Most useful theoretically and practically are procedures which generate data capable of discriminating between distressed and nondistressed systems or categories of distressed or nondistressed systems, or in general which produce a range of scores permitting some meaningful discrimination among systems. In contrast, procedures which do not highlight either individual-system or group differences provide more information about method attributes than meaningful characteristics of systems. For example, Speer (1972) indicates that the results of the prisoner's dilemma game with married couples shows poor convergence with Navran's (1967) self-report measure of marital communication and the Locke-Wallace (1959) marital adjustment scale. Clearly, additional work is needed to assess the generalizability of data from game-playing and other observational procedures to theoretically relevant assessment dimensions (e.g., perceived satisfaction).

Second, the observational method should generate data which is generalizable to naturally occurring instances of the interactive process under investigation (representativeness). For example, problem-solving interaction during laboratory assessments should generalize to those instances when the family or marital couple attempts to solve problems on their own initiative. Typically, nonnaturalistic assessments of system interaction have been criticized in that the observed interaction is often unrelated to the day-to-day interaction of the system—the relevance criterion. In support of this position, Steinglass (1979) reports that the large majority of naturalistic family data can be classified as "maintenance" (as opposed to problem-solving) behavior. Similarly, preliminary data obtained via random in-home audio recordings (Christensen & Hazzard, 1983) indicate that the bulk of home interaction is neutral rather than affectively loaded. Thus, based upon existing naturalistic data, it is apparent that those interactive processes which are theoretically prominent and typically assessed in research investigations (i.e., decision-making, problem-solving, conflict-resolution, etc.) constitute low base-rate behaviors in the natural setting. At the same time, a lack of daily relevance does not in and of itself mitigate the importance of such tasks. Laboratory assessment of low base rate processes remains valuable if it can be demonstrated that *(a)* the process under investigation occurs, in at least some systems, in the natural environment; *(b)* the relevant process has an important impact on the systems in which it occurs; and *(c)* the laboratory assessment is representative of those infrequent occasions when systems self-initiate the relevant process. In order to establish the representativeness of laboratory observational procedures, additional information is needed concerning the manner in which families typically arrive at decisions, discuss problems and resolve conflict. One hypothetical outcome of such information might be that conflict resolution in families is often a dyadic process. If this were the case, whole-family assessments of conflict resolution would be nonrepresentative or deficient in ecological validity.

Finally, it is always desired that the interaction generated by an observational procedure is nonreactive (i.e., it can be generalized to situations in which observers or recording apparatus are not present). Despite such hopes, the presence of significant reactive effects is almost ubiquitously assumed in the area of observational research (Jones, Reid, & Patterson, 1975).

Four theoretical positions can be advanced to account for reactive effects. First, subjects may behave in either socially desirable or socially undesirable ways depending on the demand characteristics of the setting (Orne, 1962). Members of systems volunteering for research participation may attempt to impress the investigator with their level of adjustment. Conversely, members of systems seeking treatment may accentuate areas of difficulty in order *(a)* to guarantee that they will receive services and/or *(b)* to clearly demonstrate the behavior problems of a particular system member. Secondly, knowledge of observation may lead to increases in behavioral variability, perhaps due to heightened anxiety in subjects (Schalock, 1958). Some observational studies of parent-child interaction (Paul, 1963; White, 1973), however, have not provided empirical support for this plausible assumption. Third, ambiguity concerning being a subject under observation could lead to changes in behavior. Since there are relatively few norms or social scripts (see Schank & Abelson, 1977) governing the role of an observee, subjects may adopt roles inconsistent with the researchers' goals (e.g., host, actor, etc.). Finally, it is plausible that knowledge of observation by others may lead to heightened self-monitoring which may in turn reduce the variability of emitted responses.

A variety of research strategies have been employed to gather information on reactivity to observation. These include *(a)* anecdotal reports from observers and subjects of observation (Patterson & Cobb, 1971; Wood, 1978); *(b)* habituation studies which look at changes in behavior over time in the presence of observers (Foster & Cone, 1980); *(c)* awareness studies in which the degree of conspicuousness of the observational procedure is manipulated (Christensen & Hazzard, 1983; Johnson & Bolstad, 1975); and *(d)* "fakeability" studies which look at the degree to which parents are capable of manipulating child behavior according to experimental instructions (Lobitz & Johnson, 1972). A good review of reactivity studies is provided by Baum, Forehand, and Zegiob (1979).

The empirical evidence in support of significant reactive effects is less than definitive. Nevertheless, the number of studies which do report positive findings advises the conservative researcher to consider procedural variables that could serve to intensify or mitigate potential reactive effects. A number of guidelines are offered in this regard. First, investigators can benefit by systematically assessing subjects' perceptions of their behavior while being observed. For instance, it is doubtful that the reactive effects of any procedure are invariant across systems or across individuals within systems. This could be assessed through global ratings of interaction representativeness by individual system members directly following the observation session. Subsequently, individuals or systems failing to indicate some minimal degree of representativeness could be eliminated from the analysis, thus decreasing the possibility of obscuring genuine effects. Second, in order to minimize potential response sets (e.g., social desirability), to reduce anxiety and/or guardedness, and to clarify expectations, subjects should be provided with a rationale and explanation for the observation procedure and their role in it. As one aspect of this introduction, system members might discuss the issue of relaxing, being themselves, and acting as naturally as possible. If, as Lobitz and Johnson (1972) have demonstrated, parents comply with task instructions to systematically alter family behavior, perhaps similar instructional guidelines can enhance the attainment of a representative sample of interaction. Third, the literature suggests that significant variations in the obtrusiveness of observational procedures influences reactivity. While practical and ethical constraints inhibit the routine use of observation under conditions of unawareness, assessments which minimize the salience of observers or recording apparatus (e.g., through the use of one-way mirrors) are preferable. A number of investigators have employed automated recording equipment in the home as a means of minimizing subject awareness and procedural obtrusiveness (e.g., Bernal, Gibson, William, & Pesses, 1971; Christensen, 1979). Fourth, in laboratory assessments, reactivity to observation is often confounded with alterations in behavior owing to the unfamiliarity and discomfort of the observation room. Similar assessment procedures conducted in the laboratory versus the home have consistently found differences (Gottman, 1979; O'Rourke, 1963). As a result, the investigator employing laboratory assessments should attend to salient features of the environment (other than the fact of observation) which may be contributing to behavioral differences. Studies by White (1973) and Snyder (1977) have attempted to design laboratory assessment contexts of maximum comfort and familiarity. The relative contributions of physical setting features and knowledge of observation in laboratory assessments has yet to be investigated.

ISSUES PERTAINING TO DEPENDENT MEASURES

Methods of approaching the data

Prior to the measurement and analysis of interaction variables, the investigator must decide whether to code the data or to employ rating scales, how to unitize the stream of interaction, and whether to employ real-time or repeat-scan methods of study (e.g., audiotapes, transcripts). Each of these fundamental choices of orientation will be considered in turn.

As Cairns (1979) notes, it is not unusual for ratings of an interaction to be negligibly associated with direct observations of the same interaction. Because of this discrepancy, recent attention has been directed toward considering the relative virtues of coding and rating procedures for the evaluation of social interaction data (Bakeman & Brown, 1980; Cairns & Green, 1979; Christensen & Arrington, in press, Prinz & Kent, 1978). The result of these considerations has been the specification of differences between the two approaches with respect to *(a)* underlying assumptions about the observers doing the rating or coding, *(b)* the type of data the two methods generate, and *(c)* the research questions which the respective methods can best address.

Underlying the use of behavior ratings are the assumptions that observers share a common conception of the quality or attribute under investigation (e.g., aggression, alliance) and that they are aware of, and can detect in a stream of interaction, behavior which is reflective of this quality or attribute. In addition, rating methods assume that observers evaluate the relevant variable on the same internal scale. Ideally, raters have similar conceptions as to what constitutes average or extreme levels of the relevant quality. However, two observers whose lives are sharply distinct in their level of independence may vary when making judgments of dependency, for example. In general, major differences in rater "experiences in living" and/or in knowledge of the population under investigation may result in highly variable evaluations. Finally, it is assumed that the observers are thoroughly insulated from knowledge of the research hypotheses and detailed information about the systems to be rated. Because of the subjective judgment involved, observer bias is a serious concern whenever global ratings are employed (Kent, O'Leary, Diament, & Dietz, 1974; Shuller & McNamara, 1976).

In contrast to rating methods, behavioral coding requires fewer assumptions about the information-processing abilities of observers. It is assumed that, with training, observers have the ability to record the acts of others consistent with defined coding categories. No preexisting knowledge of constructs (e.g., dependency) is assumed, nor are similar internal scales necessary for evaluating the interaction. In addition, while the problem of observer bias cannot be dismissed when employing behavioral coding, high interobserver agreement scores usually imply that its operation is not pronounced (Johnson & Bolstad, 1973).

Ratings and coding methods also differ in the type of data they generate and the research questions they best address. Coding methods generate more specific information which is able to reflect a wider range of variability in the phenomena under study. For example, rating methods can help "locate" family systems on the dimension of distress. Coding systems, however, have the potential to specify differences in systems which are rated equivalently on the relevant dimension (e.g., either high or low on distress). The specificity of the information derived from coding and rating is related to the research questions most suited to the two approaches. In general, systematic coding is uniquely valuable for studying the specific mechanisms through which behavior is regulated with respect to temporary sources of variability such as the situation (e.g., assessment setting and tasks), the interpersonal context (e.g., the ages and sexes of the agents present), and the communication sequence (e.g., prior communications in the interactive stream). With respect to the last point, while many hypotheses about system interaction are expressed in terms of interaction sequences (reciprocity, coercion, etc.), empirical findings are often reported in terms of single variables (e.g., fairness, parental demands). Coded data offer the opportunity to capture interaction sequences either through data analytic methods such as sequential analysis (Gottman, 1979) or through direct coding of relevant sequences (e.g., the number of times parental demands are followed by child deviant behavior).

In contrast, ratings are best suited to capturing relatively stable properties or qualities of behavior or interaction (e.g., spouse satisfaction). As such, ratings have been somewhat more useful than have coding systems in capturing cross-situational regularities in such behavior (correlations of about .50) (Yarrow & Waxler, 1979) and in predicting behavior patterns later in development (Bakeman & Brown, 1977). The distinction between the two methods on the basis of their applicability to the study of interactive mechanisms (coding) and interactive properties (rating) has an important exception. In cases when the constituent behaviors of an interactive property can be specified, one should expect a meaningful association between ratings of the property and scores reflecting a summary of the operational codes. In such cases, coding methods have the advantage of generating data relevant to both interaction mechanisms and properties. However, it has yet to be finally determined whether the behavioral grammar and subtle affective components of complex interaction properties such as empathy or responsiveness are amenable to discrete behavioral description (Prinz & Kent, 1978).

If the investigator chooses to code interaction, the issue of how to unitize the stream of interaction is an important one. Two basic methods of unitization are available—interval and event. The interval method (e.g., coding in units of 10 seconds) has the important advantage of precision. At the same time, unitization on the basis of precisely defined intervals is undoubtedly discrepant with the manner in which the interactants naturally segment the stream of behavior. Conversely, segmentation on the basis of interaction events (units of speech or meaning) is probably more congruent with the phenomenology of the interactants while suffering from problems of subjective interpretation and potential unreliability.

Another basic issue facing the investigator concerns whether to code interaction directly or to employ repeat-scan methods of study such as audiotapes, videotapes, and transcriptions. The use of direct coding methods has two central problems. First, in order to permit immediate, accurate recording, the coding distinctions need to be few and simple. Secondly, it is difficult for a single observer to code multiple dimensions of interaction simultaneously (e.g., affect, communication content). Thus, in order to address more-complex and more-interesting processes, most research investigations employ repeat-scan methods. It should be noted, however, that repeat-scan methods are more costly and time consuming (e.g., equipment, transcripts, and time to do complex coding).

Operationalizing interaction constructs

Many investigators of marital and family interaction have attempted to operationalize aspects of system interaction which have been proposed to distinguish between meaningful contrast groups (dominance, conflict, alliances, transactional style, reciprocity, etc.). However, due to the complexity of such constructs, it is a significant methodological challenge to satisfy requirements for empirical specificity while retaining some of the conceptual richness of the initial theoretical notion. Nevertheless, the simultaneous realization of both objectives is important. In the absence of empirical specification, theoretically prominent constructs cannot make the transition from heuristic to scientific value. In the absence of maintaining conceptual richness, the relationship between systems-oriented clinicians and researchers will continue to be characterized more by division than by collaboration. To date, empirical specificity has often been achieved at the expense of conceptual richness. Frequently, systems interaction researchers have operationalized complex constructs using single measures derived from a single dimension of interaction. For example, family conflict has been evaluated in terms of the frequency of simultaneous speech and/or interruptions (e.g., Ferriera, Winter, & Poindexter, 1966; Stabenau, Turpin, Werner, & Pollin, 1965). Similarly, dominance patterns have been assessed by frequency counts of successful interruptions, talking time, statement length and to whom acts are directed (e.g., Mishler & Waxler, 1968). While these "pure process" (Doane, 1978) or "quantitative process" measures (Jacob, 1975) are logically related to the relevant constructs and require relatively little inference to record, exclusive reliance on such variables to operationalize complex ideas like conflict or dominance is necessarily at the expense of construct validity. In addition, Jacob (1975) indicates that measures of quantitative process do not consistently discriminate comparison systems.

In order to enhance the construct validity and discriminative adequacy of coding systems of marital and family interaction, a number of researchers have advocated the use of multiple indicators of a construct drawn from multiple dimensions of interaction (Gilbert, Christensen, & Margolin, 1984; Jacob, 1975; Lewis & Goldstein, 1978, Riskin & Faunce, 1972). In this regard, system interaction can be viewed as operating on three conceptually distinct dimensions: the dimension of process (who talks, how much, to whom, about whom, how often are they interrupted, etc.), the dimension of content (whether the interactant agrees, disagrees, defends, protects, attacks, etc.), and the dimension of nonverbal behavior (posture, gaze, tone of voice, etc.). To the extent that a construct is operationalized after considering possible indexes from each dimension of interaction, it is more likely that the eventual definition will at least address many of the sources of information from which the clinician derives synthetic judgments of interaction process.

Evaluating the stability of observations

A basic requirement of any scientific inquiry of social interaction is the demonstration that observations of that interaction have some stability and are not a function of the idiosyncratic perceptions of a single individual. Traditionally, this requirement has been translated into the necessity of demonstrating that observations can be generalized across two independent observers (interobserver agreement). Recently, however, when relatively complex aspects of interaction are the focus of investigation, efforts have been directed toward demonstrating that the majority of a team of observers have equivalent perceptions (consensual agreement). In this section, observer agreement and consensual methods of evaluating the generalizability of coded observations will be discussed. In addition, methods of evaluating the generalizability of rating-scale data will be presented. Finally, a discussion of the generalizability of observer agreement and consensual agreement data will be undertaken.

Johnson and Bolstad (1973) point out that calculations of observer agreement should be made after considering the dependent variable for which an index of accuracy is required. In general, the investigator must decide whether an index of accuracy is needed for total-score data (e.g., total deviant behavior scores) or with respect to individual events or intervals (point-by-point agreement). If the investigator is interested only in scores for total deviant behavior, analysis of agreement on individual components of that score (e.g., criticisms) is unnecessary. Different methods of analysis are available for obtaining indexes of agreement on total or individual scores. Indexes based on total scores include correlational analyses (i.e., correlating the total scores recorded by the independent observers) and overall percent agreement analyses. According to Johnson and Bolstad, the correlational method may be superior in that it is computed over an array of subjects or observation sessions.

It is important to note that high estimates of observer agreement on total-score data, using either method, do not necessarily imply any agreement on specific events. For example, two observers may record the total frequency of Behavior X as 9 and 10, respectively, over a single observation session. In this case, the overall percent agreement score would be 90. While it would be tempting to infer at least moderate agreement on specific occurrences of Behavior X, it is conceivable that the target response occurred 19 or more times with absolutely no agreements on specific events. As a result, total-score estimates of observer agreement do not provide support for conducting sequential analysis or any analyses which focus on individual scores.

A variety of indexes are available for calculating observer agreement on individual scores: percent agreement, occurrence/nonoccurrence agreement, and kappa. Percent agreement may be calculated by dividing the number of agreements by the number of disagreements. However, when using this index, the investigator must be cognizant of the base-rate problem (Johnson & Bolstad, 1973). When high-probability behaviors are being coded, two observers coding at random can obtain high agreement scores. Chance agreement can be computed by squaring the base rate of each code and summing these values (Hartmann, cited in Johnson & Bolstad, 1973). For example, in a simple binary code (Behavior X, not Behavior X), where X occurs 90 percent of the time, the agreement expected by chance alone would be given by $(.90)^2 + (.10)^2 = .82$. One common way of handling this problem is to employ nonoccurrence and occurrence agreement indexes when there is a high base-rate probability of occurrence or nonoccurrence respectively. In our previous example, the probability that two observers would both code nonoccurrence given a probability of occurrence of .90 would be $(.10)^2$ or only 1 percent. However, indexes of occurrence or nonoccurrence agreement may be overly stringent in that no credit is given to agreements on occurrence and nonoccurrence when high- and low-probability codes, respectively, are being monitored. As a result, many investigators have employed Cohen's (1960) kappa as a measure of agreement. Essentially, kappa adjusts the percent occurrence or nonoccurrence index according to the expected index of agreement given each observer's coding base rates (Hartmann, 1977).

While high individual-score observer agreement permits analyses to be performed on specific events, there can be costs associated with obtaining these indexes of accuracy. Most importantly, when complex interaction processes are the focus of investigation, it is often extremely difficult to obtain an acceptable level of agreement using the methods previously discussed. In this case, the investigator is faced with three basic options. First, the investigator can dismiss individual-score analyses and compute agreement using less-demanding total-score indexes. Second, the investigator could conclude that such complex processes are not amenable to scientific inquiry and (a) focus on simpler processes or (b) redefine the complex process in terms of simpler, more easily coded variables. In the latter case, however, it is often questionable whether the essential meaning of the target process or construct is retained in the process of redefinition and simplification. In cases where constructs, such as conflict or alliances, are exclusively defined according to the frequency of simultaneous speech (conflict) or the pattern of who talks to whom (alliances), it can be argued that validity has been sacrificed for operational precision.

A third option open to the researcher involves the use of a consensual agreement format. In consensus agreement, an odd number of observers (three, five, etc.) independently code each event, and majority judgments are selected as a best estimate of the content of the specific event. Recent applications of consensual agreement have found that consensual judgments occur between 85 and 97 percent of the time, even with complex coding systems (Cohen & Christensen, 1980; Gilbert et al., 1984). Because majority judgments are used to determine the content of each event, it can be argued that a consensus agreement format could be used to support analyses on individual scores (e.g., sequential analysis) as well as providing a means of ensuring stability of the overall coding (e.g., total scores). In those infrequent instances when there is no consensus among the original observers, the investigator can either choose a code at random or add additional observers until consensus is achieved on each event. In sum, consensus agreement is a novel and interesting approach to demonstrating the stability of observations using complex coding systems. It stands at a compromise point between rigorous point-by-point indexes of observer agreement and unchecked subjective judgment and inference.

When evaluating the stability of rating-scale data, measures of interrater agreement and interrater reliability are available. According to Tinsley and Weiss (1975), interrater agreement represents the extent to which different observers tend to make exactly the same judgments about the rated subject. Interrater reliability means that the relationship of one rated individual to other rated individuals is the same although judges vary in the absolute numbers used to express this relationship. Both types of information are valid ways of evaluating the stability of rating data. Tinsley and Weiss critique a variety of measures of interrater agreement (the proportion of agreement (P), various chi square indexes, pairwise correlations between raters, and Kendell's coefficient of concordance) and recommend the chi square test of significance proposed by Lawlis and Lu (1972).

With respect to the evaluation of interrater reliability, Tinsley and Weiss (1975) suggest the use of the intraclass correlation (R). According to these authors, the intraclass correlation can be viewed as the proportion of the total variance in ratings attributable to the persons being rated as opposed to random error or between-rater variance.

A final topic in this section concerns the generalizability of observer agreement indexes over time. A number of studies have clearly indicated that single evaluations of interobserver or interrater agreement obtained at the outset of the coding or rating process are rarely generalizable to the remainder of the observer's data (Reid, 1970; Talpin & Reid, 1973). Three mediators of this phenomenon have been discussed. First, Johnson and Bolstad (1973) point out that both the interaction data and the context of evaluation may be nonrepresentative during the initial tests of accuracy. With respect to the data, the selected segments of interaction may not be representative of other observation sessions or segments the observer will be required to evaluate later in the study. With respect to context, observers may be highly enthusiastic to begin coding at the outset of the study, and the coding process may be experienced as highly novel and interesting. This enthusiasm and novelty might be translated into "heightened vigilance for critical behaviors or for the coding peculiarities of the calibrator" (Johnson & Bolstad, 1973, p. 19).

Secondly, coders are likely to perform more carefully when they are aware that they are under evaluation. Finally, over time, observers may decrease in efficiency due to the processes of forgetting, fatigue, etc. This process has been variously labeled "instrument decay" (Campbell & Stanley, 1966) or "observer drift" (Johnson & Bolstad, 1973). In order to attenuate these difficulties, most investigators agree that it is necessary to provide consistent training, accuracy checks, and performance feedback throughout the process of observation (Browning & Stover, 1971).

One final point deserves attention. When observers are placed in fixed and unchanging pairs or groups, high intraobserver or intragroup agreement does not always reflect proper use of the coding system. An alternate hypothesis is that the observers have accommodated to each other's idiosyncratic methods of coding. Baer, Wolf, and Risley (1968) and Bijou, Peterson, and Ault (1968) have labeled this possibility "consensual observer drift." In order to avoid or monitor this possibility, observers should be calibrated with multiple observers, code in different groups, and/or be carefully monitored with respect to conformity to some external criterion of coding accuracy.

CONCLUSION

An implicit theme in the preceding discussion has been that methodology should be in the service of theory and the exploration of hypotheses. That is, methodological decisions should be made after considering whether the procedures employed enhance or detract from the ability of the researcher to investigate relevant theoretical issues or hypotheses. For example, in the area of sampling and design, it was noted that many investigations of system interaction have sought to specify interactive correlates of system distress and satisfaction. Given this objective, it becomes important to employ methods which ensure that the systems which are investigated are representative of the comparison populations (i.e., distressed and satisfied systems). As such, attention was directed toward considering the relative benefits of various approaches to sample selection and specification. It was argued that multimethod quantitative and/or qualitative selection procedures most efficiently partition the samples into distinct comparison groups. A second threat to studying representative distressed and nondistressed systems pertains to demographic controls. It was suggested that, if demographic equation results in sampling outliers from the population of systems under investigation (i.e., nonrepresentative systems), then a careful, descriptive study might prove most useful. If, however, demographic controls do not significantly compromise external validity (representative systems), then there are meaningful advantages to such controls (e.g., increased internal validity, reduced sources of between-group variance). Finally, in the area of sampling and design, a number of researchers have investigated the relationship of system interaction and individual symptomatology over time rather than explore interactive correlates of distress and satisfaction. In this case, single-subject or multiple-case longitudinal designs more directly address the area of interest than do single-assessment group designs.

After selecting the appropriate design for an investigation and demonstrating that the system(s) have been sampled from the intended population, the researcher must ensure that the responses which are studied adequately capture the interaction process under investigation. These issues were discussed in the sections on observational methods and dependent measures. With respect to observational methods, this implies that (a) the investigator takes all reasonable steps to reduce reactivity to observation (e.g., habituation time, instructional controls, comfortable or natural settings, unobtrusive measurement), and (b) the obtained interaction is representative of those instances when the relevant process (e.g., decision-making, problem-solving) occurs in the natural environment. With respect to dependent measures, it was argued that valid investigations of complex interaction processes necessitate operationalizations beyond the level of single-variable, single-dimension coding (e.g., defining conflict on the basis of a frequency analysis of simultaneous speech). The use of coding systems tapping process, content, and affective dimensions of interaction was suggested as an alternative. It was noted that the increased complexity of coding systems (in the service of enhanced construct validity) makes the attainment of high point-by-point observer agreement scores more difficult. As such, the use of new indexes of event reliability such as consensus agreement may become more popular. In sum, choices regarding sampling, design, observational context, and coding systems should be carefully geared to the particular questions under investigation rather than automatically following procedures which have become convention.

REFERENCES

Baer, D. M., Wolf, W. M., & Risley, T. R. Some current dimensions of applied behavior analysis. *Journal of Applied Behavior Analysis*, 196, *1*, 91–97.

Bakeman, R., & Brown, J. V. *Mother-infant interactions during the first months of life: Differences between preterm and fullterm infant-mother dyads from a low income population* (Tech. Rep. No. 5). Atlanta: Georgia State University, 1977.

Bakeman, R., & Brown, J. V. Early interaction: Consequences for social and mental development at three years. *Child Development*, 1980, *51*, 437–447.

Baldwin, A. L. The study of child behavior and development. In P. Mussen (Ed.), *Handbook of research methods in child development*. John Wiley & Sons, 1960.

Bateson, G., Jackson, D., Haley, J., & Weakland, J. Toward a theory of schizophrenia. *Behavioral Science*, 1956, *1*, 251–264.

Baum, C. G., Forehand, R., & Zegiob, L. E. A review of observer reactivity in adult-child interactions. *Journal of Behavioral Assessment*, 1979, *1*, 167–178.

Becker, J., & Iwakami, E. Conflict and dominance within families of disturbed children. *Journal of Abnormal Psychology*, 1969, *74*, 330–335.

Bernal, M. E., Gibson, D. M., William, D. E., & Pesses, D. I. A device for recording automatic audio tape recording. *Journal of Applied Behavior Analysis*, 1971, *4*, 151–156.

Bijou, S. W., Peterson, R. F., & Ault, M. H. A method to integrate descriptive and experimental field studies at the level of data and empirical concepts. *Journal of Applied Behavior Analysis*, 1968, *1*, 175–191.

Birchler, G. R., Weiss, R. L., & Vincent, S. P. Multimethod analysis of social reinforcement exchange between maritally distressed and non-distressed spouse and stranger dyads. *Journal of Personality and Social Psychology*, 1975, *31*, 349–360.

Browning, R. M., & Stover, D. O. *Behavior modification in child treatment: An experimental and clinical approach.* Hawthorne, N.Y.: Aldine Publishing, 1971.

Cairns, R. B., & Green, S. A. How to assess personality and social patterns: Observations or ratings? In Robert B. Cairns (Ed.), *The analysis of social interactions: Methods, issues and illustrations.* Hillsdale, N.J.: Lawrence Erlbaum Associates, 1979.

Campbell, D. T., & Stanley, S. C. *Experimental and quasi-experimental designs for research.* Skokie, Ill.: Rand McNally, 1966.

Christensen, A. Naturalistic observation of families: A system for random· audio recordings in the home. *Behavior Therapy*, 1979, *10*, 418–422.

Christensen, A., & Arrington, A. Research issues and strategies. In T. Jacob (Ed.), *Family interaction and psychopathology: Theories, methods and findings.* New York: Plenum Press, in press.

Christensen, A., & Hazzard, A. Reactive effects during naturalistic observation of families. *Behavioral Assessment*, 1983, *5*, 349–362.

Christensen, A., & Margolin, G. *Investigation and treatment of multiproblem families.* NIMH Grant No. 32616. 1979–1983. (Available from A. Christensen, UCLA, Department of Psychology, Los Angeles.)

Cohen, J. A coefficient of agreement for normal scales. *Educational and Psychological Measurement*, 1960, *20*, 37–46.

Cohen, R. S., & Christensen, A. Further examination of demand characteristics in marital interaction. *Journal of Consulting and Clinical Psychology*, 1980, *48*, 121–123.

Cromwell, R. E., Olson, O. D., & Fournier, D. G. Tools and techniques for diagnosis and evaluation in marital and family therapy. *Family Process*, 1976, *15*, 312–354.

Cronbach, L. S., Gleser, G. C., Nanda, H., & Rajaratnam, N. *The dependability of behavioral measures.* New York: John Wiley & Sons, 1972.

Doane, J. A Family interaction and communication deviance in disturbed and normal families: A review of the research. *Family Process*, 1978, *17*, 357–376.

Dreyer, C. A., & Dreyer, A. S. Family dinner-time as a unique behavior habitat. *Family Process*, 1973, *12*, 291–301.

Dysart, R. R. A behavioral description of family interactions in the home and the clinic: Inter and intra setting analysis (Doctoral dissertation, University of Houston, 1973). *Dissertation Abstracts International*, 1973–74, *34*, 1744B. (University Microfilms No. 73-22, 901)

Eyberg, S. M., & Johnson, S. M. Multiple assessment of behavior modification with families: Effectiveness of contingency contracting and order of treated problems. *Journal of Consulting and Clinical Psychology*, 1974, *42*, 594–606.

Ferriera, A. J., & Winter, W. D. Family interaction and decision-making. *Archives of General Psychiatry*, 1965, *13*, 214–223.

Ferriera, A. J., Winter, W., & Poindexter, E. Some interactional variables in normal and abnormal families. *Family Process*, 1966, *5*, 60–75.

Foster, S. L., & Cone, J. D. Current issues in direct observation. *Behavioral Assessment*, 1980, *2*, 313–338.

Fromm-Reichmann, F. Notes on the development of treatment of schizophrenics by psychoanalytic psychotherapy. *Psychiatry*, 1948, *11*, 263–272.

Gilbert, R., Christensen, A., & Margolin, G. Patterns of alliances in nondistressed and multiproblem families. *Family Process*, 1984, *23*, 75–87.

Gottman, J. M. *Marital interaction: Experimental investigations*. New York: Academic Press, 1979.

Haley, J. Critical overview of present status of family interaction research. In J. Framo (Ed.), *Family interaction: A dialogue between family researchers and family therapists*. New York: Springer Publishing, 1972.

Hartmann, D. P. Considerations in the choice of interobserver reliability estimates. *Journal of Applied Behavior Analysis*, 1977, *10*, 105–116.

Henggeler, S. W., Borduin, C. M., Rodick, J. D., & Tavormina, J. B. Importance of task content for family interaction research. *Developmental Psychology*, 1979, *15*, 660–661.

Hill, R. Methodological issues in family development research. *Family Process*, 1964, *3*, 186–206.

Hops, W., Wills, T. A., Patterson, G. R., & Weiss, R. L. *The marital interaction coding system (MICS)*. Unpublished manuscript, University of Oregon, 1972.

Jacob, T. Family interaction in disturbed and normal families: A methodological and substantive review. *Psychological Bulletin*, 1975, *82*, 33–65.

Jacob, T. (Personal communication, 1981.)

Johnson, S. M., & Bolstad, O. D. Methodological issues in naturalistic observation: Some problems and solutions for field research. In L. A. Hamerlynck, L. C. Handy, & E. J. Mash (Eds.), *Behavior change: Methodology, concepts and practice*. Champaign, Ill.: Research Press, 1973.

Johnson, S. M., & Bolstad, O. D. Reactivity to home observation, a comparison of audio recorded behavior with observers present or absent. *Journal of Applied Behavior Analysis*, 1975, *8*, 181–185.

Jones, J. *Transactional style deviance in families of disturbed adolescents*. Unpublished doctoral dissertation, University of California (Los Angeles), 1974.

Jones, J., Rodnick, E., Goldstein, M., McPherson, S., & West, K. Parental transactional style deviance as a possible indicator of risk for schizophrenia. *Archives of General Psychiatry,* 1977, *34,* 71–74.

Jones, R. R., Reid, J. B., & Patterson, G. R. Naturalistic observation in clinical assessment. In P. McReynolds (Ed.), *Advances in psychological assessment* (Vol. 3). San Francisco: Jossey-Bass, 1975.

Kent, R. N., O'Leary, K. D., Diament, C., & Dietz, A. Expectation biases in observational evaluation of therapeutic change. *Journal of Consulting and Clinical Psychology,* 1974, *42,* 774–780.

Lawlis, G. F., & Lu, E. Judgement of counseling process: Reliability, agreement and error. *Psychological Bulletin,* 1972, *49,* 270–273.

Leighton, L., Stollak, G., & Fergusson, L. Patterns of communication in normal and clinic families. *Journal of Consulting and Clinical Psychology,* 1971, *36,* 252–256.

Lewis, J. M., & Goldstein, M. J. *A review of the family interaction research literature in regard to its applicability to analyses of family therapy process.* Unpublished manuscript, University of California (Los Angeles), 1978.

Lobitz, G., & Johnson, S. M. *Normal versus deviant—fact or fantasy?* Paper presented at the convention of the Western Psychological Association, Portland, Ore., April 1972.

Locke, H. J., & Wallace, K. M. Short term marital adjustment and prediction tests: Their reliability and prediction. *Marriage and Family Living,* 1959, *21,* 251–255.

Loveland, N. T., Wynne, L. C., & Singer, M. T. The family Rorschach: A new method for studying family interaction. *Family Process,* 1963, *2,* 187–215.

Margolin, G. Relationships among marital assessment procedures: A correlational study. *Journal of Consulting and Clinical Psychology,* 1978, *48,* 1556.

Meehl, Paul E. High school yearbooks: A reply to Schwartz. *Journal of Abnormal Psychology,* 1971, *77,* 143–148.

Mischel, W. *Personality and assessment.* New York: John Wiley & Sons, 1968.

Mischel, W. Toward a cognitive social learning reconceptualization of personality. *Psychological Review,* 1973, *80,* 252–283.

Mishler, E., & Waxler, N. *Interaction in families: An experimental study of family process and schizophrenia.* New York: John Wiley & Sons, 1968.

Navran, L. Communication and adjustment in marriage. *Family Process,* 1967, *6,* 173–184.

Olson, D. H., & Ryder, R. G. Inventory of marital conflicts (IMC): An experimental interaction procedure. *Journal of Marriage and the Family,* 1970, *32,* 443–448.

O'Neill, M. S., & Alexander, J. F. *Family interaction patterns as a function of task characteristics.* Paper presented at the meeting of the Rocky Mountain Psychological Association, Salt Lake City, Utah, 1970.

Orne, M. T. On the social psychology of the psychological experiment with particular reference to demand characteristics and their implications. *American Psychologist,* 1962, *17,* 776–783.

O'Rourke, J. F. Field and laboratory: The decision-making behavior of family groups in two experimental conditions. *Sociometry,* 1963, *26,* 131–145.

Patterson, G. R., & Cobb, J. A. A dyadic analysis of "aggressive" behaviors. In J. P. Hill (Ed.), *Proceedings of the Fifth Annual Minnesota Symposia on Child Psychology* (Vol. V). Minneapolis: University of Minnesota, 1971.

Patterson, G. R., & Hops, H. Coercion, a game for two: Intervention techniques for marital conflict. In R. E. Ulrich and P. Mountjoy (Eds.), *The experimental analysis of social behavior.* New York: Appleton-Century-Crofts, 1971.

Patterson, G. R., Ray, R. S., Shaw, D. A., & Cobb, J. A. *Manual for coding family interactions* (6th revision Document No. 01234, available from ASIS National Auxiliary Publications, 1969.

Paul, J. S. *Observer influence on the interactive behavior of a mother and a single child in the home.* Unpublished master's thesis, Oregon State University, 1963.

Peterson, D. R. Assessing interpersonal relationships by means of interaction records. *Behavior Assessment,* 1979, *1,* 221–236.

Prinz, R. J., & Kent, R. N. Recording parent-adolescent interactions without the use of frequency or interval-by-interval coding. *Behavior Therapy,* 1978, *9,* 602–604.

Ravitch, R. A. The use of an interpersonal game-test in conjoint marital psychotherapy. *American Journal of Psychotherapy,* 1969, *23,* 217–229.

Reid, J. B. Reliability assessment of observation data: A possible methodological problem. *Child Development,* 1970, *41,* 1143–1150.

Riskin, J., & Faunce, E. E. An evaluative review of family interaction research. *Family Process,* 1972, *11,* 365–455.

Schalock, H. D. *Observer influence on mother-child interaction in the home: A preliminary report.* Paper presented at the meeting of the Western Psychological Association, Carmel, Calif., 1958.

Shank, R., & Abelson, R. *Scripts, plans, goals and understanding: An inquiry into human knowledge structures.* Hillsdale, N.J.: Lawrence Erlbaum Associates, 1977.

Shuller, D. Y., & McNamara, J. R. Expectancy factors in behavioral observation. *Behavior Therapy,* 1976, *7,* 519–527.

Singer, M. T., & Wynne, L. C. Principles of scoring communication defects and deviances in parents of schizophrenics: Rorschach and TAT scoring manuals. *Psychiatry,* 1966, *29,* 260–288.

Snyder, J. J. Reinforcement analysis of interaction in problem and nonproblem families. *Journal of Abnormal Psychology,* 1977, *86,* 528–535.

Sommer, R. Toward a psychology of natural behavior. *APA Monitor,* 1977, *8,* 528–535.

Spanier, G. B. Measuring dyadic adjustment: New scales for assessing the quality of marriage and similar dyads. *Journal of Marriage and the Family,* 1976, *38,* 15–28.

Speer, D. C. Marital dysfunctionality and two-person run–zero sum game behavior: Cumulative monadic measures. *Journal of Personality and Social Psychology,* 1972, *21,* 18–24.

Stabenau, J., Turpin, J., Werner, M., & Pollin, W. A comparative study of families of schizophrenics, delinquents and normals. *Psychiatry,* 1965, *28,* 45–59.

Steinglass, P. The home observation assessment method (HOAM): Real-time naturalistic observation of families in their homes. *Family Process,* 1979, *18,* 337–354.

Straker, G., & Jacobson, R. A study of the relationship between family interaction and individual symptomatology over time. *Family Process,* 1979, *18,* 443–450.

Straus, M. A., & Tallman, I. SIMFAM: A technique for observational measurement and experimental study of families. In J. Aldous (Ed.), *Family Problem-Solving.* Hinsdale, Ill.: Dryden Press, 1971.

Strodbeck, F. L. Husband-wife interaction over revealed differences. *American Sociological Review,* 1951, *16,* 468–473.

Talpin, P. S., & Reid, J. B. Effects of instrumental set and experimenter influence on observer reliability. *Child Development,* 1973, *44,* 547–554.

Tinsley, H. E. A., & Weiss, D. J. Interrater reliability and agreement of subjective judgements. *Journal of Counseling Psychology,* 1975, *22,* 358–376.

Watzlawick, P. A structured family interview. *Family Process,* 1966, *5,* 256–271.

Weick, K. E. Systematic observational methods. In G. Lindsey & E. Aronson (Eds.), *The handbook of social psychology,* 1968, *2,* 357–451.

White, G. The effects of observer presence on mother and child behavior (Doctoral dissertation, University of Oregon, 1973). *Dissertation Abstracts International,* 1973–74, *34,* 2957B. (University Microfilms No. 73–28, 642)

Wood, S. M. The relationship between observer and observed. *Humanistic Psychology Institute Review,* 1978, *1,* 11–30.

Wynne, L., Ryckoff, I., Day, J., & Hirsch, S. Pseudomutuality in the family relations of schizophrenics. *Psychiatry,* 1958, *21,* 205–220.

Yarrow, M. R., & Waxler, C. Z. Observing interaction: A confrontation with methodology. In Robert D. Cairns (Ed.), *The analysis of social interactions: Methods, issues and illustrations.* Hillsdale, N. J.: Lawrence Erlbaum Associates, 1979.

Chapter 32

Dimensions of Family Evaluation

DENNIS A. BAGAROZZI

INTRODUCTION

This chapter will focus on assessment and evaluation of families for the purpose of planned intervention by clinical practitioners. Having no intention to duplicate the work done by Straus and Brown (1977) by presenting a compilation of family measurement techniques and assessment instruments, it will, however, offer some examples of how selected instruments and procedures can be used to develop a multifaceted, multidimensional "family profile" which can serve as a guide for outlining treatment goals, devising treatment strategies, and evaluating treatment outcome. Before doing this, some introductory comments about the various dimensions of family assessment are necessary.

A number of clinicians (Cromwell, Olson, & Fournier, 1976; Gurman & Kniskern, 1981; Kniskern & Gurman, 1983; Olson, 1974) have stressed the importance of gaining both an "insider's" (family member's) and an "outsider's" (therapist's) perspective of family process and functioning in order to evaluate the effects of family therapy. It is the contention of this chapter that the "insider-outsider" perspectives are equally important for developing treatment goals and for devising treatment strategies. The "insider-outsider" continuum can be subdivided even further. For example, both perspectives can be analyzed in terms of the degree to which inference and subjectivity color the evaluation process. Similarly, both perspectives can be judged according to the degree of behavioral specificity they require. One may be tempted to assume that the more an assessment tool or procedure requires behavioral specificity, the less subjective and inferential the evaluation will tend to be. However, this assumption is not valid, because behavioral self-reports are subject to bias, distortion, and idiosyncratic interpretation by family members. Similarly, behavioral coding procedures are subjective in that coding and classification systems include some behaviors while they exclude others. Although behaviorally focused evaluation procedures can be said to be less subjective than more traditional self-reports and nonbehavioral rating systems, it would be naive to assume that they are totally objective and without bias.

In this writer's opinion, it is not fruitful to debate the merits of each approach. Each provides the clinician with different data, and both sources of data can be used to develop family profiles. A more important issue to consider when selecting an assessment instrument is the extent to which an instrument or procedure requires specialized training or expertise on the part of the test administrator. Several issues must be considered before using any assessment tools. For example, does the test require administration and/or interpretation by a highly trained professional? To what extent does an assessment procedure require the use of trained coders or raters? To what extent does evaluation of certain family process variables and characteristics necessitate that judgments be made by seasoned family therapists and family experts?

One additional issue deserves consideration. Gurman and Kniskern (1981) and Kniskern and Gurman (1983) have suggested that since most family therapy approaches are concerned with improved functioning of entire family systems, it is essential that change be assessed at all levels of system functioning—at the individual, dyadic, and family systems levels. Following this line of reasoning, one might say that in order for family evaluation to be complete, it should include assessments of each constituent member; all combinations of dyads, triads, coalitions, etc.; and the family system as a whole. Obviously, time, energy, and financial factors make such comprehensive evaluation difficult for most practicing family therapists to undertake. When trained coders, raters, experts, etc., are required for consultation and evaluation, time and cost considerations become prohibitive. The question then becomes: What guidelines can clinicians use to select instruments and assessment procedures that will enable them to make accurate and useful evaluations of families seen in their day-to-day clinical practice? This issue will be discussed at length in the following sections.

THE ROLE OF THEORY IN INSTRUMENT SELECTION

The selection of instruments and assessment procedures should follow logically from the therapist's theoretical orientation concerning the nature of human behavior, family functioning-dysfunctioning, and family treatment. For example, a family therapist who conceptualizes family process and treatment according to systems theory would be expected to select evaluation instruments and procedures that provide valuable information about how the family functions as a system. More specifically, the therapist might choose the following instruments and procedures to develop a family systems profile:

1. For an insider's view of the two major dimensions of overall systems functioning—adaptability and cohesion—the therapist might ask all family members to make nonbehavioral ratings of the family's adaptability and cohesiveness using the family adaptability and cohesion scales (FACES II) (Olson, Portner, & Bell, 1982). For an outsider's view of family adaptability and cohesion, the clinician can use the therapist's version of FACES II.

2. For an outsider's evaluation of overall systems functioning which focuses specifically on certain process variables (e.g., task efficiency, negotiation, clarity of expression, invasiveness, feelings, empathy, mood, and tone) and structural characteristics (e.g., power, coalitions, closeness, boundary permeability), the therapist can use the Beavers-Timberlawn Family Evaluation Scales (Lewis, Beavers, Gossett, & Phillips, 1976). For family members' perspectives of these same phenomena, the self-report version of the scales can be administered (Bagarozzi, 1983a).

3. In order to obtain each family member's perspective of his/her relational-communication style (e.g., complementary, symmetrical, and parallel) vis-à-vis all other family members, the therapist can administer the Relationship Styles Inventory (Scoresby, 1975). This instrument can provide the therapist with valuable insights into the power dynamics and functioning of all combinations of dyads that make up the family system.[1]

4. Finally, in order to get a family group portrait of the various dyads, triads, coalitions, cyclical patterns, and redundant sequences, the systems therapist can conduct an initial, problem-focused interview according to the guidelines for circular questioning outlined by Penn (1982). This model of circular questioning, developed by the Milan group (Selvini-Palazzoli, Bascolo, Cecchin, & Prata, 1980), requires that the therapist interview the family by using the feedback received from family members in response to questions about family relationships. For a more graphic representation of the processes reported by family members during circular questioning, the therapist may ask family members to enact selected sequences and have each member sculpt

---

[1] For a behaviorally oriented, less subjective outsider's view of these phenomena, one must resort to using the Relational Communication Coding System (Ericson & Rogers, 1973; L. E. Rogers, 1972; Rogers & Bagarozzi, 1983), which requires the utilization of trained coders. Time, cost, and personnel considerations make this highly complex evaluation procedure impractical for use by the practitioner.

(Papp, Silverstein, & Carter, 1973) his/her perception of how the family has tried to resolve the presenting problems.

The instruments and procedures outlined in the above example are those which relate to family process as conceptualized by systems therapists. They provide the therapist with information about relationship dynamics, interaction sequences, patterns, redundant cycles, hierarchies, feedback processes, homeostatic mechanisms, coalitions, etc. However, they offer little information about the functioning of individual components of the system—the family members themselves. While it can be argued that evaluation and assessment of an individual's behavior, personality traits, characteristics, moods, etc., belong to a totally different (if not incorrect) clinical epistemology (Dell, 1983), assessment of individual functioning (especially that of the identified patient) still remains an essential component of family evaluation. Evaluating individual functioning does not mean that the therapist must abandon the systems orientation, because measures of individual functioning can be used to gain valuable information about how the family functions as a system. Systems theorists (Bateson, 1935, 1936, 1972; Haley, 1963; Watzlawick, Beavin, & Jackson, 1967) postulate that all behavior is communication and all communicational interchanges are either symmetrical (based upon equality between and among interactants who reciprocate similar or identical behaviors) or complementary (based upon the maximization of difference between and among interactants who exhibit behaviors which are logically opposite). If one accepts this premise, then assessment of a family member's behavior, personality traits, cognitions, affects, etc., is meaningful only if all other family members also are evaluated along the same dimensions. Then, the therapist can gain some understanding of the complementary and symmetrical functions that specific behaviors, characteristics, affects, etc., serve in maintaining a family's equilibrium. Some examples are offered below:

1. The depressed behavior of an identified patient, as measured by Beck's Depression Inventory (Beck, 1970), may be the logical complement to another family member's vivaciousness, elation, etc.

2. The symptoms reported by a depressed person on the Depressive Behavior Survey (Cautela, 1977)—such as isolation, inadequacy, helplessness, worthlessness, sadness, hopelessness, and suicidal ideation—may, however, in a different family system be complementary to all other family members' feelings of cohesion, competence mastery, importance, optimism, and zest for life.

3. In a family where no one person is singled out as the identified patient, one may discover that all family members have similar levels of anxiety or some other trait measured by the 16 PF (Cattell & Stice,

1957). These levels may remain relatively stable, indicating relational symmetry, or they may fluctuate to create a complementary balance.

In order to understand the systemic nature of a family member's behavior, one must try to discover how it complements or is symmetrical to the behavior of other family members. This statement is true also for understanding family systems when more than one person is symptomatic. For example, in the case of one family where *all* family members exhibited symptomatic behavior, the complementary nature of these symptoms became apparent over the course of treatment. A brief example of how these symptoms were woven together to maintain family stability is outlined in Table 1.

In this family, physical illness was the central theme. Numerous family myths and attendant rituals associated with illness were used to maintain homeostasis (Anderson & Bagarozzi, 1983; Bagarozzi & Anderson, 1982; Ferriera, 1963). In this particular example, the family came for treatment by order of the juvenile court. The identified patient was the 16-year-old son, who had used a stolen credit card to purchase over $300 worth of merchandise. In addition to using the instruments described above, the therapist used the Genogram (Guerin & Pendergast, 1976) to discover the pervasive theme of illness. *Circular questioning* (Penn, 1982) was employed to gain an understanding of family organization and process around each symptom. At the time this family presented itself for treatment, it had stabilized around the son's presenting problem. A brief description of the interlocking nature of symptoms is presented below.

In this family, mother had major responsibility for discipline and upbringing of the three children. She was in a one-down complementary position vis-à-vis her husband, but she was in a one-up complementary position in relationship to her children. The daughters were "model children." They had been expected to achieve careers and goals that their mother had been unable to realize because of her out-of-wedlock pregnancy, which resulted in the birth of the identified

Table 1

The L family

Family member	Age	Symptom
Father	37	Ulcers, high blood pressure
Mother	36	Anxiety, obsessive compulsive behavior
Son (identified patient)	16	Stealing
Daughter	14	Asthma
Daughter	12	Accident proneness

patient. The youngest daughter was expected to excel in sports, but recurring injuries and accidents prevented her from continuing to compete in track and field events. The oldest daughter was being groomed for a professional singing career. However, asthma attacks frequently interfered with her ability to sing in the church choir. The identified patient had a history of poor academic performance and was considered to be a discipline problem by school personnel and his parents. Even though he was one of the better wrestlers on his high school team and sang with a rock band from time to time, these accomplishments were not acknowledged by his mother as having much merit. She was "obsessed" with his conduct at school and his grades. As the children grew older, mother found it increasingly difficult to exert control over them, especially her son. As their relationship to her became more symmetrical, she turned to her husband for assistance. However, her incessant requests for help with the children were experienced as "nagging" and "demanding," (i.e., they were perceived by the husband as a bid for a more-symmetrical conjugal relationship). As a response to this, the husband's ulcers would "flare up," and his blood pressure would rise. He claimed that his wife "gives me ulcers." These "attacks" enabled him to maintain his one-up position. As the daughters began to gain more independence, their symptoms subsided. However, mother became more symptomatic—e.g., she engaged in compulsive house cleaning, obsessed about her son's school performance, increased her community activities, and "nagged" all family members. It was at this time that the credit card incident occurred. As a result of the son's arrest, mother "fell apart" and became "hysterical," and a pseudocomplementary pattern was established between the husband and wife: the husband was forced to take control of his spouse and the children. The identified patient responded positively to his father's increased interest and attention. He said he did not want to give him ulcers or cause his father to have a stroke. With father taking more responsibility for the son, mother was able to regain her influence over the daughters, and their symptoms reappeared.

This example shows the seesaw pattern of symptoms in family systems and how the amplification of one member's deviant behavior can produce family stability at a different level of organization (Hoffman, 1971). Although it may be unusual to find a family where all members exhibit psychiatric symptoms, this family graphically demonstrates the interlocking nature of behavior between and among family members. Conceptualizing individual behavior in this fashion allows one to utilize measures of individual functioning to gain a better understanding of the entire family system.

Thus far this chapter has focused on the selection of instruments and evaluation procedures which are philosophically compatible with a family systems orientation. Now, attention will be given to family assessments and evaluations which reflect social exchange and sociobehavioral conceptions of family behavior.

SOCIAL EXCHANGE CONCEPTIONS OF MARITAL AND FAMILY BEHAVIOR AND CLINICAL EVALUATION

Principles of equity and social exchange have been used to explain the internal dynamics of marital and family behavior (Blood & Wolfe, 1960; Carson, 1969; Edwards, 1969; Homans, 1974; Levinger, 1976; Thibant & Kelley, 1959; Waller & Hill, 1951), and behaviorally oriented practitioners have devised treatment approaches derived from social exchange theory to treat distressed couples (Azrin, Naster, & Jones, 1973; Gottman, Notarius, Bank, Yoppi, & Rubin, 1976; Jacobson & Margolin, 1979; Patterson & Hops, 1972; Patterson, Hops, & Weiss, 1975; Patterson & Reid, 1970; Patterson, Weiss, & Hops, 1976; Rappaport & Harrell, 1972; Stuart, 1976; Weiss, 1978; Weiss, Birchler, & Vincent, 1974). Recently, there has been a movement to incorporate social exchange conceptions of family behavior into a more comprehensive family systems relationship–oriented model of marital and family behavior which takes into account the symbolic meaning of behaviors exchanged between and among family members (Alexander & Parson, 1982; Bagarozzi, 1982b, 1983b; Bagarozzi & Giddings, 1983; Bagarozzi & Wodarski, 1977, 1978; Birchler & Spinks, 1980; Gurman, 1980; Strong, 1975). Although there has been movement in the direction of an integrated sociobehavioral systems approach to family behavior and intervention, this author is unaware of any instruments which have been developed for evaluating the exchange dynamics of the entire family system. However, numerous measures of behavioral reciprocity and social exchanges between spouses are available. Some of the most frequently used behavioral self-report instruments developed by exchange-oriented clinicians include: Marital Pre-Counseling Inventory (Stuart & Stuart, 1973), Spouse Observation Checklist (Patterson, 1976), Marital Interaction Inventory (Patterson, 1976), Areas of Change Questionnaire (Patterson, 1976), Marital Status Inventory (Weiss & Cerreto, 1975), the Conflict Tactics Scale (Straus, 1979), and the Spousal Inventory of Desired Changes and Relationship Barriers (Bagarozzi, 1983b; Bagarozzi & Pollane, 1984), which helps spouses identify specific areas of the relationship where exchange inequities are perceived. SIDCARB offers the therapist an insider's view of each spouse's commitment to the marriage and the strength of the barriers that will prevent a spouse from terminating an unsatisfactory marriage.

At this point in time, no measures of parent-child exchange and reciprocity exist. Typically, parents are asked to make behavioral reports of their children's behavior. The following instruments are frequently used by sociobehavioral clinicians: the Referral Problems Checklist (Patterson, Reid, Jones, & Conger, 1975), the Child Behavior Profile (Achenbach, 1978), Becker Adjective Checklist (Becker, 1960), the Kohn Social Competence Scale (Kohn 1977), the Kohn Symptom Checklist for Parents, Teachers, & Clinicians (Kohn), and the Behavior Problems Checklist (Quay, 1977).

There are several behaviorally oriented questionnaires which ask children to report on, and evaluate, their parents' behavior toward them. These include: the Parent Perception Inventory (Hazzard, Christensen, & Margolin, 1984), Bronfenbrenner's Parental Behavior Questionnaire (Siegelman, 1965), and the Child Report Questionnaire (Schaefer, 1965).

Finally, behaviorally oriented interviews have been developed which attempt to outline redundant behavior patterns and interaction sequences in order to help clinicians discover the functional relationship outcomes they produce for each family member (Alexander & Barton, 1980; Barton & Alexander, 1982).

If one were to conduct a family evaluation using the available instruments and procedures derived from sociobehavioral and exchange conceptions of family behavior, a different family profile would emerge. For example, in treating domestic violence, the following instruments and procedures have been used to evaluate family functioning once the family has been stabilized and violence has been discontinued.[2]

1. *Spousal inventory of desired changes and relationship barriers (SIDCARB)* (Bagarozzi, 1983b; Bagarozzi & Pollane, 1984). This instrument measures spouses' perceptions of the fairness of the conjugal exchange system in 10 areas of exchange. SIDCARB is comprised of three empirically derived factors: *(a)* areas of desired change, dissatisfaction with the equity of exchange, and commitment to the marriage; *(b)* willingness to separate/divorce and internal-psychological barriers to separation/divorce; and *(c)* external-circumstantial barriers to separation/divorce.

In addition to gaining each spouse's perception of the fairness of the conjugal exchange system and his/her satisfaction with this exchange, SIDCARB also helps the therapist identify which spouse has more power and influence over the other by virtue of perceiving fewer barriers to separation and divorce (Waller & Hill, 1951). In many families where husbands physically assault their wives, the wife often feels compelled to remain in the relationship because she perceives insurmountable barriers to separation or divorce. SIDCARB allows the ther-

---

[2] For a detailed discussion of treating marital and family violence, the reader may wish to consult Bagarozzi (1982a) and Bagarozzi and Giddings (1982, 1983).

apist to assess the degree to which a spouse perceives his/her relationship as nonvoluntary (Bagarozzi & Wodarski, 1977).

2. *Conflict tactics scale* (Straus, 1979). This self-report measure enables the therapist to assess the degree to which family members use various tactics to resolve interpersonal difference. The scale is comprised of four empirically derived factors: reasoning, verbal aggression, violence, and lethal violence. Each family member can be asked to rate how he/she resolves conflicts with all other family members, and each family member can be asked to report his/her perceptions of how other family members resolve their conflicts.

3. *Irrational beliefs test* (Jones, 1968). This self-report instrument consists of 10 empirically derived factors which measure the extent to which a family member holds irrational beliefs in the following areas: *(a)* demand for approval, *(b)* high self-expectation *(c)* blame proneness, *(d)* frustration reaction, *(e)* emotional irresponsibility, *(f)* anxious overconcern, *(g)* problem avoidance, *(h)* dependency, *(i)* helplessness, and *(j)* perfectionism. Irrational beliefs and expectations about one's spouse often serve as antecedent cues which ignite a negative response chain that may lead to violence (Ellis, 1976). The irrational beliefs test can be very helpful in aiding the therapist plan cognitive intervention strategies (Bagarozzi, 1982a; Bagarozzi & Giddings, 1982, 1983) in violence-prone families.

4. *Conflict negotiation task assignments.* There are a variety of tasks that can be assigned to families which allow the therapist to assess a family's ability to negotiate and successfully resolve conflict (Cromwell et al., 1976). Some of the most frequently used tasks include the Revealed-Difference Technique (Strodbeck, 1951; Titchener & Golden, 1963) and the Blame Technique (Watzlawick, 1966). Once a task has been assigned, the therapist who has the time, equipment, and personnel available to employ observational coding systems can use the Marital Interaction Coding System III (Weiss & Summers, 1983) or the Couple Interaction Scoring System (Gottman, 1979; Notarius, Markham, & Gottman, 1983) to assess the degree to which family members use punishment, negative reinforcement, coercion, etc., in their attempts to strike more-equitable bargains and negotiate conflicts.

Since such coding procedures are impractical for everyday use by most practicing therapists, the clinician should focus on those molar aspects of a couple's or family's conflict negotiation attempts which are most relevant for devising an intervention plan. For example, the therapist can focus on family communication styles, coercive behavior change strategies, the type of conflict negotiation orientation held by each family member (i.e., zero-sum game, nonzero-sum game), the degree to which family members are able to negotiate equitable quid pro quo exchanges, the extent to which family members behave in a cooperative manner as opposed to taking a competitive stance in the negotiation process, etc.

This molar approach to family process can be used by family therapists when molecular analysis is not feasible. Identifying those aspects of family behavior which serve to escalate conflict and impede successful resolution is the goal of molar assessment and evaluation.

5. *Tennessee self-concept scale* (Fitts, 1965). This instrument is a self-administered questionnaire. Each family member is asked to respond to 100 five-point, Likert-type questions ranging from "strongly agree" to "strongly disagree." The Tennessee self-concept scale yields 10 subscale scores: total self-concept, self-criticism, identity, self-satisfaction, behavior, physical self, moral-ethical self, personal self, family self, and social self.

This measure is used because of the important role played by self-esteem in domestic violence. Husbands who assault their wives frequently lack the verbal skills necessary to "win" in arguments with their spouses (Bagarozzi & Giddings, 1983). This holds true especially for husbands who lack valued resources which they can use to influence their mates (Nye, 1978). In such instances, the husband's willingness and ability to inflict costs (in the form of physical assaults) may be the only way for him to increase his self-esteem and gain some leverage in a relationship where he seems to have little control. This "ultimate resource" explanation of interpersonal violence has been proposed by a number of exchange theorists (Goode, 1971; Rodman, 1972; Rogers, 1974) and has received some empirical support (Allen & Straus, 1980).

Viewed in concert, these instruments and procedures provide one with an appreciation of the major aspects of family process as conceptualized by sociobehavioral-exchange theorists. Specific treatment goals and intervention strategies which are consistent with this approach can then be implemented to bring about desired changes.[3]

ADDITIONAL CONSIDERATIONS

The major sections of this chapter have been devoted to instrument selection based upon one's theoretical orientation concerning the nature of family behavior. The implicit assumption throughout this presentation has been that therapists will choose only those instruments that have been proven to be reliable and valid measures of the various theoretical constructs that are thought to be central to a particular theory of family process and functioning. However, no time has been spent discussing issues of reliability and validity.

---

[3] To devise a sociobehavioral systems family profile, one would have to select instruments and procedures from both theoretical camps. Meaningful integration and interpretation of such a battery would require in-depth knowledge and understanding of both schools of thought. Such a discussion goes far beyond the scope of this chapter.

The importance of using empirically tested instruments for diagnostic purposes cannot be underestimated, and the clinician should take time to conduct a thorough investigation of an instrument's empirical status before adopting it for use. One should guard against selecting instruments simply because they can be administered easily and scored quickly. Similarly, one should not select a measure because it has a long history of use by family practitioners. Ease of administration and tradition are not substitutes for reliability and validity. For example, Bienvenu (1970) developed a paper and pencil questionnaire designed to assess the quality of communication between spouses. This instrument has been accepted as a valid indicator of marital communication and has been used in countless studies since it was introduced over a decade ago. Although the Marital Communication Inventory (Bienvenu, 1970) has a long history of use, it should not be considered a valid indicator of couples' actual behavior. At best, nonbehavioral self-reports can offer only each spouse's perceptions. Recently, research undertaken by Schumm, Anderson, Race, Morris, Griffin, McCutchen, and Benegas (1983) has shown that the marital communication inventory is not even an accurate assessment of spouses' perceptions of their communication. Schumm et al. assert that this instrument more accurately measures spouses' perceptions of positive regard rather than spousal communication. Similarly, the Family Environment Scale (Moos & Moos, 1981) was designed to profile various types of family environments, and this measure has been used in a number of studies by Moos and his colleagues (see Billings & Moos, 1982). Although the subscales of this instrument have been shown to be internally consistent and discriminant validity has been established, certain issues must be addressed before the family environment scale is considered appropriate for use by family therapists. First, the items chosen for inclusion on this scale do not seem to have been derived from any recognizable theory of family functioning or family development. Second, the validity of one of the major subscales, family cohesion, has been criticized by Russell and Olson (1983). These researchers, in discussing the development of the circumplex model of marital and family systems, show that the family environment scale failed to receive support for convergent validity for cohesion when compared with two other indicators of that construct. Russell (1980) contends that the Moos scale may actually be a measure of "support" rather than family cohesion.

CONCLUSION

This chapter has focused on family evaluation from both theoretical and practical perspectives. One cannot separate theory from practice, and evaluation is an essential component of clinical practice. The instruments chosen and the procedures used to evaluate families should be selected because they validly and reliably assess those aspects of family process that are considered to be central to a coherent theory of family functioning-dysfunctioning. Systematic and thoughtful evaluation is a sine qua non for designing effective treatment strategies. However, the plight of clinicians who do not have the time and resources to conduct lengthy and extensive evaluations needs consideration. Therefore, this chapter has concentrated on presenting instruments and assessment procedures that can be used in everyday practice. Interview methods such as Circular Questioning and Sculpting should not be subjected to the same procedures for establishing reliability and validity as one would use to standardize paper and pencil tests, questionnaires, and experimental procedures. Interviews of the first type provide the therapist with different and complementary information about family processes. The difference between these two approaches can be conceptualized as the difference between analogic and digital information. Both types of information are necessary to conduct a thorough evaluation.

REFERENCES

Achenbach, T. M. The child behavior profile: I. Boys aged 6 through 12. *Journal of Consulting and Clinical Psychology,* 1978, *46,* 478–488.

Allen, C. M., & Straus, M. A. Resource power and husband-wife violence. In M. A. Straus & C. T. Hotaling (Eds.), *The social causes of husband-wife violence.* Minneapolis: University of Minnesota Press, 1980.

Alexander, J. F., & Barton, C. Intervention with delinquents and their families: Clinical, methodological and conceptual issues. In J. P. Vincent (Ed.), *Advances in family intervention, assessment and theory.* Greenwich, Conn.: JAI Press, 1980.

Alexander, J., & Parsons, B. V. *Functional family therapy.* Monterey, Calif. Brooks/Cole Publishing, 1982.

Anderson, S. A., & Bagarozzi, D. A. The use of family myths as an aid to strategic therapy. *Journal of Family Therapy,* 1983, *5,* 145–164.

Azrin, N. H., Naster, B. J., & Jones, R. Reciprocity counseling: A rapid learning based procedure for marital counseling. *Behavior, Research and Therapy,* 1973, *11,* 365–382.

Bagarozzi, D. A. Family therapy with violent families. *American Journal of Family Therapy,* 1982, *10,* 69–72. (a)

Bagarozzi, D. A. The symbolic meaning of behavior exchanges in marital therapy. In A. S. Gurman (Ed.), *Questions and answers in the practice of family therapy.* New York: Brunner/Mazel, 1982. (b)

Bagarozzi, D. A. *Beavers-Timberlawn family evaluation scales: self report version.* Unpublished instrument, 1983. (a)

Bagarozzi, D. A. Methodological developments in measuring social exchange perceptions in marital dyads (SIDCARB): A new tool for clinical intervention. In D. A. Bagarozzi,

A. P. Jurich, & R. W. Jackson (Eds.), *New perspectives in marital and family therapy: Issues in theory, research and practice.* New York: Human Sciences Press, 1983. (b)

Bagarozzi, D. A., & Anderson, S. A. The evaluation of family mythological systems: Considerations for meaning, assessment and treatment. *Journal of Psychoanalytic Anthropology,* 1982, *5,* 71–90.

Bagarozzi, D. A., & Giddings, C. W. A conceptual model for understanding and treating marital violence. *Arete,* 1982, *7,* 49–59.

Bagarozzi, D. A., & Giddings, C. W. Conjugal violence: A critical review of current research and clinical practices. *American Journal of Family Therapy,* 1983, *11,* 3–15.

Bagarozzi, D. A., & Giddings, C. W. Behavioral marital therapy: Empirical status, current practices, trends and future directions. *Clinical Social Work Journal,* 1983, *11,* 263–279.

Bagarozzi, D. A., & Pollane, L. A replication and validation of the spousal inventory of desired changes and relationship barriers (SIDCARB): Elaborations on diagnostic and clinical utilization. *Journal of Sex and Marital Therapy,* 1983, *9,* 303–315.

Bagarozzi, D. A., & Wodarski, J. S. A social exchange typology of conjugal relationships and conflict development. *Journal of Marriage and Family Counseling,* 1977, *3,* 53–60.

Bagarozzi, D. A., & Wodarski, J. S. Behavioral treatment of marital discord. *Clinical Social Work Journal,* 1978, *6,* 135–154.

Barton, C., & Alexander, J. F. Functional family therapy. In A. S. Gurman & D. P. Kniskern (Eds.), *Handbook of family therapy.* New York: Brunner/Mazel, 1982.

Bateson, G. Culture contact and schismogenesis. *Man,* 1935, *35,* 148–183.

Bateson, G. *Naven.* Cambridge: Cambridge University Press, 1936.

Bateson, G. *Steps to an ecology of the mind.* New York: Ballantine Books, 1972.

Beck, A. T. *Depression: Causes and treatment.* Philadelphia: University of Pennsylvania Press, 1970.

Becker, W. C. The relationship of factors in parental ratings of self and each other to the behavior of kindergarten children as rated by mothers. *Journal of Counseling Psychology,* 1960, *24,* 507–527.

Bienvenu, M. J., Sr. Measurement of marital communication. *Family Coordinator,* 1970, *19,* 26–31.

Billings, A. G., & Moos, R. H. Family environment and adaptation: A clinically applicable typology. *American Journal of Family Therapy,* 1982, *10,* 26–38.

Birchler, G. R., & Spinks, S. H. Behavioral systems marital and family therapy: Integration and clinical application. *American Journal of Family Therapy,* 1980, *8,* 6–28.

Blood, R. O., & Wolfe, D. M. *Husbands and wives.* New York: Free Press, 1960.

Carson, R. *Interaction concepts of personality.* Hawthorne, N.Y.: Aldine Publishing, 1969.

Cattell, R. B., & Stice, G. F. *Sixteen personality factor questionnaire* (Rev. ed.). Champaign, Ill.: Institute for Personality and Abilities Testing, 1957.

Cautela, J. R. *Behavior analysis forms for clinical intervention.* Champaign, Ill.: Research Press, 1977.

Cromwell, R. E., Olson, D. H., & Fournier, D. G. Diagnosis and evaluation in marital and family counseling. In D. H. Olson (Ed.), *Treating relationships.* Lake Mills, Iowa: Graphic Publishing, 1976.

Dell, P. F. Researching the family theories of schizophrenia: An exercise in epistemological confusion. In D. A. Bagarozzi, A. P. Jurich, & R. W. Jackson (Eds.), *Marital and family therapy: New perspectives in theory, research and practice.* New York: Human Sciences Press, 1982.

Edwards, J. M. Familial behavior as social exchange. *Journal of Marriage and the Family,* 1969, *31,* 518–527.

Ellis, A. Techniques for handling anger in marriage. *Journal of Marriage and Family Counseling,* 1976, *2,* 305–315.

Ericson, P. M., & Rogers, L. E. New procedures for analyzing relational communication. *Family Process,* 1973, *12,* 244–267.

Ferriera, A. J. Family myths and homeostasis. *Archives of General Psychiatry,* 1963, *9,* 457–463.

Fitts, W. H. *Tennessee self-concept scale.* Nashville, Tenn.: Counselor Recordings & Tests, 1965.

Goode, W. J. Force and violence in the family. *Journal of Marriage and the Family,* 1971, *33,* 624–636.

Gottman, J. M. *Marital interaction: Experimental investigations.* New York: Academic Press, 1979.

Gottman, L., Notarius, C., Markham, R., Bank, S., Yoppi, B., & Rubin, N. E. Behavior exchange theory and marital decision making. *Journal of Personality and Social Psychology,* 1976, *34,* 14–23.

Guerin, P., & Pendergast, E. Evaluation of family system and genogram. In P. Guerin (Ed.), *Family therapy: Theory and practice.* New York: Gardner Press, 1976.

Gurman, A. S. Behavioral marriage therapy in the 1980's: The challenge of integration. *American Journal of Family Therapy,* 1980, *8,* 86–96.

Gurman, A. S., & Kniskern, D. P. Family therapy outcome research: Knowns and unknowns. In A. S. Gurman & D. P. Kniskern (Eds.), *Handbook of family therapy.* New York: Brunner/Mazel, 1981.

Haley, J. *Strategies of psychotherapy.* New York: Grune & Stratton, 1963.

Hazzard, A., Christensen, A., & Margolin, G. Children's perceptions of parental behaviors. *Journal of Abnormal Child Psychology,* in press.

Hoffman, L. Deviation-amplifying processes in normal groups. In J. Haley (Ed.), *Changing families.* New York: Grune & Stratton, 1971.

Homans, G. *Social behavior: Its elementary forms* (2d ed.). New York: Harcourt Brace Jovanovich, 1974.

Jacobson, N. S., & Margolin, G. *Marital therapy: Strategies based on social learning and behavior exchange principles.* New York: Brunner/Mazel, 1979.

Jones, R. G. *A factoral measure of Ellis' irrational beliefs system, with personality and maladjustment correlates.* Unpublished doctoral dissertation, Texas Technological College, 1968.

Kohn, M. The Kohn social competence scale and Kohn symptom checklist for the preschool child: A follow up report. *Journal of Abnormal Child Psychology,* 1977, *5,* 249–263.

Kniskern, D. P., & Gurman, A. S. Future directions for family therapy research. In D. A.

Bagarozzi, A. P. Jurich, & R. M. Jackson (Eds.), *New perspectives in marital and family therapy: Issues in theory, research and practice.* New York: Human Sciences Press, 1983.

Levinger, G. A social psychological perspective on marital dissolution. *Journal of Social Issues,* 1976, *32,* 21–47.

Lewis, J. M., Beavers, W. R., Gossett, J. T., & Phillips, V. A. *No single thread: Psychological health in family systems.* New York: Brunner/Mazel, 1976.

Moos, R. H., & Moos, B. S. *Family environment scale manual.* Palo Alto, Calif.: Consulting Psychologists Press, 1981.

Notarius, C. I., Markham, H. J., & Gottman, J. M. Couples interaction scoring system: Clinical implications. In E. E. Felsinger (Ed.), *Marriage and family assessment: A sourcebook for family therapy.* Beverly Hills, Calif.: Sage Publications, 1983.

Nye, F. I. Is choice and exchange theory the key. *Journal of Marriage and the Family,* 1978, *33,* 692–698.

Olson, D. H. *Insiders and outsiders view of relationships: Research strategies.* Paper presented at the Symposium on Close Relationships. University of Massachusetts, 1974.

Olson, D. H., Portner, J., & Bell, R. *Faces II: Family adaptability and cohesion evaluation scales.* St. Paul: Family Social Science, University of Minnesota, 1982.

Papp, P., Silverstein, O., & Carter, E. Family sculpting in preventive work with well families. *Family Process,* 1973, *12,* 197–212.

Patterson, G. R. *Some procedures for assessing change in marital interaction patterns.* Eugene, Ore.: Oregon Research Institute, 1976.

Patterson, G. R., & Hops, H. Coercion, a game for two: Intervention techniques for marital conflict. In R. C. Ulrich & P. Mountjoy (Eds.), *Behavior modification in clinical psychology.* New York: Appleton-Century-Crofts, 1972.

Patterson, G. R., Hops, H., & Weiss, R. L. Interpersonal skills training for couples in early stages of conflict. *Journal of Marriage and the Family,* 1975, *37,* 295–303.

Patterson, G. R., & Reid, J. B. Reciprocity and coercion: Two facets of social systems. In C. Neuringer & J. L. Michael (Eds.), *Behavior modification in clinical psychology.* New York: Appleton-Century-Crofts, 1970.

Patterson, G. R., Reid, J. B., Jones, R. R., & Conger, R. E. *Families with aggressive children* (Vol. I). Eugene, Ore.: Castalia Publishing, 1975.

Patterson, G. R., Weiss, R. L., & Hops, H. Training of marital skills: Some problems and concepts. In H. Leitenberg (Ed.), *Handbook of behavior modification.* Englewood Cliffs, N. J.: Prentice-Hall, 1976.

Penn, P. Circular questioning. *Family Process,* 1982, *21,* 267–280.

Quay, H. C. Measuring dimensions of deviant behavior: The behavior problems checklist. *Journal of Abnormal Child Psychology,* 1977, *5,* 277–287.

Rappaport, A., & Harrell, J. A behavioral exchange model for marital counseling. *Family Coordinator,* 1972, *21,* 203–212.

Rodman, H. Marital power and the theory of resources in cultural context. *Journal of Comparative Family Studies,* 1972, *3,* 50–69.

Rogers, L. E. Dyadic systems and transactional communication in a family context. Unpublished doctoral dissertation, Michigan State University, 1972.

Rogers, L. E., & Bagarozzi, D. A. An overview of relational communication and implications for therapy. In D. A. Bagarozzi, A. P. Jurich, & R. W. Jackson (Eds.), *New perspectives in marital and family therapy: Issues in theory, research and practice*. New York: Human Sciences Press, 1983.

Rogers, M. F. Instrumental and infra-resources: The bases of power. *American Journal of Sociology*, 1974, *79*, 1418–1433.

Russell, C. R. A methodological study of family cohesion and adaptability. *Journal of Marital and Family Therapy*, 1980, *6*, 459–470.

Russell, C. R., & Olson, D. H. Circumplex model of marital and family systems: Review of empirical support and elaboration of therapeutic process. In D. A. Bagarozzi, A. P. Jurich, & R. W. Jackson (Eds.), *Marital and family therapy: New perspectives in theory, research and practice*. New York: Human Sciences Press, 1983.

Schaefer, E. S. Children's reports of parental behavior: An inventory. *Child Development*, 1965, *36*, 413–424.

Schumm, W. R., Anderson, S. A., Race, G. S., Morris, J. E., Griffin, C. L., McCutchen, M. B., & Benegas, J. E. Construct validity of the marital communication inventory. *Journal of Sex and Marital Therapy*, 1983, *9*, 153–162.

Scoresby, L. *Relationship styles inventory* (Rev. ed.). Provo, Utah: Brigham Young University Press, 1975.

Selvini-Palazzoli, M., Boscolo, L., Cecchin, G., & Prata, G. Hypothesizing-circularity-neutrality: The guidelines for the conductor of the session. *Family Process*, 1980, *19*, 3–12.

Siegelman, M. Evaluation of Bronfenbrenner's questionnaire for children concerning parental behavior. *Child Development*, 1965, *36*, 163–174.

Straus, M. A. Measuring intrafamily conflict and violence. The conflict tactics (CT) scales. *Journal of Marriage and the Family*, 1979, *41*, 75–88.

Straus, M. A., & Brown, B. W. *Family measurement techniques*. Minneapolis: University of Minnesota Press, 1977.

Strodbeck, F. L. Husband-wife interaction over revealed differences. *American Sociological Reviews*, 1951, *16*, 468–473.

Strong, J. R. A marital conflict resolution model: Redefining conflict to achieve intimacy. *Journal of Marriage and Family Counseling*, 1975, *1*, 269–276.

Stuart, R. B. An operant interpersonal program for couples. In D. H. L. Olson (Ed.), *Treating relationships*. Lake Mills, Iowa: Graphic Publishing, 1976.

Stuart, R. B., & Stuart, F. *Marital pre-counseling inventory*. Champaign, Ill.: Research Press, 1973.

Thibaut, J., & Kelley, H. H. *The social psychology of groups*. New York: John Wiley & Sons, 1959.

Titchener, J. L., & Golden, M. Prediction of therapeutic themes from observation of family interaction evoked by the "revealed differences" technique. *Journal of Nervous and Mental Diseases*, 1963, *136*, 464–474.

Waller, W., & Hill, R. *The family: A dynamic interpretation*. Hinsdale, Ill.: Dryden Press, 1951.

Watzlawick, P. A structured family interview. *Family Process*, 1966, *12*, 127–144.

Watzlawick, P., Beavin, J. H., & Jackson, D. D. *Pragmatics of human communication*. New York: W. W. Norton, 1967.

Weiss, R. L. The conceptualization of marriage from a behavioral perspective. In T. J. Paolino, Jr., and B. S. McCrady (Eds.), *Marriage and family therapy: Psychoanalytic, behavioral and systems theory perspectives.* New York: Brunner/Mazel, 1978.

Weiss, R. L., Birchler, G. R., & Vincent, J. Contractual models for negotiation on training in marital dyads. *Journal of Marriage and the Family,* 1974, *36,* 321–331.

Weiss, R. L., & Cerreto, M. *Marital status inventory.* Unpublished manuscript, University of Oregon, 1975.

Weiss, R. L., & Summers, K. J. Marital interaction coding system-III. In E. E. Filsinger (Ed.), *Marriage and family assessment: A sourcebook for family therapy.* Beverly Hills, Calif.: Sage Publications, 1983.

Chapter 33

Theory-Derived, Family-Oriented Test Batteries

LUCIANO L'ABATE
VICTOR WAGNER

Some of the concerns about family assessment were voiced years ago (L'Abate, 1983): *(a)* uselessness of individually oriented measures to evaluate families; *(b)* limited scope of verbally worded statements that do not allow children full participation in the evaluation process; *(c)* need for stimuli that will allow families to evaluate themselves in terms of their give and take and *(d)* that will take into account their phenomenological perceptions of themselves and each other; *(e)* need for multidimensional batteries (more than one test) rather than single-test approaches; *(f)* importance of consistent pre/post evaluations as a standard modus operandi that continuously links intervention with evaluation and theory with research.

Other concerns that entered into the construction of theory-derived batteries were: *(g)* ease of administration, possibly in the hands of clerical-level personnel; *(h)* ease of scoring, possibly by computer; and *(i)* objective scoring, with potential for ultimate computer-written interpretations. All of these concerns have been satisfied except the last, which is to be postponed for the distant future. These and other concerns are part of what has been called the laboratory method, which has been applied in the past to individual psychodiagnoses of children (L'Abate, 1979) and structured enrichment with couples and families (L'Abate, in press; L'Abate & Rupp, 1981).

THE THEORY IN BRIEF

A theory of personality development in the family (L'Abate, 1976, 1983) comprises two assumptions of space and time, three postulates concerning differentiation, priorities, and congruence, and seven models. An outline of this theory is summarized in Table 1.

ble 1

ﬡtline of a theory of personality development in the family

Assumptions	Postulates	Models
Space: Levels of behavior Self-presentational Phenotypical: Approach- avoidance Genotypical: Thinking and feelings	1. Continuum of likeness Abusive: A (symbiosis-alienation) Reactive: R (sameness-oppositeness) Conductive: C (similarity-differentness)	1. Bell-shaped curve over continuum of likeness 2. Triangles of self and parents 3. Multiplicative, summative, sub- tractive, and divisive dyadic self-expression
Time: Aspects of behavior Reception Control: Discharge- delay Expression Feedback History	2. Family priorities Self Marriage Children Others	4. Overlapping circles 5. Spokes 6. Wheel
	3. Congruence and incongruent stances* Blaming (B) Computing (C) Distracting (D) Placating (P)	7. Orthogonal structure (cross) D B————†————P C

te: From L'Abate, L., *Understanding and Helping the Individual in the Family* (New York: Grune & Stratton, 1976); and
ﬡbate, L., *Family Psychology: Theory, Therapy, and Training* (Washington, D.C.: University Press of America, 1983).
his postulate has been changed to one of negotiation (Chapter 46).

Briefly, this theory postulates that healthy individual adjustment within the family context is a function of three variables: differentiation, priorities, and congruence. Optimal levels of functioning are associated with a high degree of differentiation, an appropriate ranking of priorities, and congruent communication patterns. Differentiation is defined as a dynamic, lifelong process of developing clear boundaries between self and others. A likeness continuum, on which the opposite extremes of symbiosis and autism represent equal levels of nondifferentiation, was conceptualized. Both extremes are pathological, indicative of a failure to differentiate from one's interpersonal system: Whether symbiotically merged or autistically isolated, the individual defines him/ herself by external rather than internal referents. Optimal levels of differentiation are represented by the middle range of the likeness continuum, where the individual perceives both similarity and differentness from significant others. This range provides the most flexibility and complexity, based on internally guided choices. Two middle ranges of sameness-oppositeness define a middle ground between functionality and dysfunctionality.

The postulate of priorities states that a healthy structuring of priorities in marital and family life follows this order: self, marriage, children,

Table 2

Testing theory of personality development in the family through family evaluation batteries

Visual battery*		Verbal marital evaluation battery	
Bell-Fagan symbols	*Postulates*	*Marital questionnaire*	*Other tests*
(1 and 2)	1	Likeness scale†	Self-concept grid
Feelings (3)	2	Priorities scale	Priorities rating list
Situations (3)	3	Incongruent stances	What would you do?
Animals (1, 2, and 3)		Blaming	—
		Placating	
		Distracting	
		Compulsion	

* Numbers in parentheses indicates number(s) of postulates from Table 1.
† Each scale in the marital questionnaire consists of 20 true-false statements.

parents and in-laws, work, leisure, and friends. Several authors concur that dysfunctional families are characterized by confusion in priorities, such as giving more priority to parent-child relations than to the marital relationship (Boszormenyi-Nagy & Spark, 1973; Lewis, 1980; Minuchin, 1974).

Both L'Abate and Satir (1972) concurred that dysfunctional families exhibit incongruent communication patterns (i.e., they lack clarity and consistency between verbal and nonverbal messages). Satir identified four discrete incongruent patterns labeled blaming, placating, computing, and distracting. The theory postulates two dimensions, related to direction of punitiveness and degree of control. In this postulate, punitiveness directed inward is labeled placating; outwardly directed punitiveness is labeled blaming. Excessive emotional control is computing; insufficient control is distracting. To test this theory, two theory-derived, family-oriented test batteries—one composed of pictorial (nonverbal) drawings and one consisting of verbal statements—were created. The relationship between the theory and these test batteries is schematically shown in Table 2. Since these batteries were derived and designed from the theory, it follows that the validity of the theory hinges in part on the validities and reliabilities of both test batteries. Studies on the construct, concurrent, and clinical validity of both batteries will be reported.

VISUAL BATTERY

This battery has been described in a variety of sources (L'Abate, 1976, 1977) and has been subjected to two doctoral dissertation studies, one by Golden (1974) and one by Gallope (1979). It is composed of, four tests.

Bell-Fagan family symbol (B–F) test

This instrument was developed from the graphic representation of emotions index (GEI) (Bell, 1972). Bell found that certain symbols tend to be correlated with certain emotions, which in turn can be grouped into six dimensions, or scales: Anxious-afraid, angry, sad, loving, quiet, and happy. L'Abate then modified the GEI by transferring 52 symbols to cards and instructing each person in the family to sort a complete set of cards into separate piles, describing each person in the family including the sorter.

After recording the number of each card on the individual scoring sheet for the various family members, these numbers are transformed into "feelings" through the use of the scoring manual. The feeling value of each card is converted through the manual and recorded in the appropriate cell in the column on the right of the individual scoring sheet. For instance, Card 7 has a value of 5 points on loving (column 4). This score is recorded in the appropriate cell on the right of the card number recorded. Note that for some cards (e.g., 6, 11, 12, 16, 20), the values are split into various columns. For instance, Card 6 receives 4 points on loving (column 4) and 1 point for quiet (column 5). The numbers are then summed within each cell for each family member. It should be noted that the feeling scales are orthogonal; that is, the higher the score on the feeling, the more the particular family member is associated with that feeling.

Once the conversion from cards to feelings is done for each individual record, all of the numbers in each cell are totaled across individuals, and this value is entered in the appropriate row of the family record sheet. For instance, if Father gave himself 15 points on the afraid-anxious scale (column 1), this value is reported in the appropriate cell of the family record sheet under "Father" (column 1). In the same cell are reported all of the values for Father gathered by the other family members—i.e., what Mother chose for Father, what children said about Father, cell by cell. The same process is followed for each family member. The family record sheet records whatever feelings have been expressed through the choice of cards. Once each cell of the family record sheet is filled with the numbers gathered from all family members, the numbers in each cell are totaled, representing the "feeling" value that each family member received from himself and the other family members. Comparisons among intra- and interindividual scores become possible.

The B–F test, then, is a measure of family perceptions in terms of the feelings each member has toward every other member in the family; consensus scores are reported for analysis. It is used as an ice-breaker in the battery, as the family usually has fun taking it and sees it as nonthreatening. Containing the most ambiguous stimuli, the B–F may also be viewed as the most "projective" of the four tests in the battery.

Description of feelings in the family (DFF) test

This test consists of 72 cards, each card depicting a member of the family in one of four feeling states: sad, mad, distracting, or smug. Intensity of feeling is represented by weighted scores (low, medium, or high) given to each card.

In the administration, each family member is asked to choose those cards which remind him/her of the family and to circle the number of each card selected on the individual answer sheet. The scores from the individual answer sheets are then transferred to the family score sheet through appropriate weights. Cards in the low intensity are scored 1, cards in the medium intensity are scored 2, and cards in the high intensity are scored 3 points. These scores are transferred to the family score sheet by columns. Father's ratings are placed in column 1 under "Father," Mother's ratings are placed in column 2 under "Mother," Sibling 1's in column 3 under "Sibling 1." If Father had picked up, for instance, Cards 2, 5, 6, 7, 8, and 12 for Father (on the left on both scoring sheets), Father receives, respectively, 2 points under Sad, 5 points under Distracted, 3 points under Smug, and 3 points under Mad. All the other cards picked by Father for the other members of the family are scored accordingly under the same column, following the same rows of the individual answer sheet, on the family score sheet: Father, Mother, Teenage Son, etc.

After transferring all of the individual scores to the family score sheet, the scores of the four scales (sad, distracting, smug, and mad) are totaled at the bottom for each member of the family (totals). These scores are used in the analysis. Then, each score is totaled horizontally (rows) toward the right for each picture. The scores in the right column (totals) are then totaled downward by each individual feeling. Consequently, the scores obtained by totaling vertically on the right should equal the scores obtained by totaling horizontally across the bottom (totals) in the last four cells in the lower right side of the sheet. These totals are divided by the number of family members and transferred into the bottom right scoring rectangle.

Individual and family scores are then drawn in a 2 × 2 space (on graph paper), using two polarities of Mad to the left and Sad to the right of the horizontal line (Mad scores–Sad scores). On the vertical axis, Smug goes at the top, using the subtraction of scores (Smug — Distracting). In this way, it is possible to demonstrate visually how each member compares with the rest of the family in his/her perception of the family.

Another comparison involves the scores at the bottom (totals) of each individual against the scores on the right of the picture for that individual (totals), representing how the picture of that individual (e.g., Father) compares with how that individual is seen by the total family (including himself). A further comparison consists of comparing individual scores with the scores of other individuals in the family for each picture; e.g., how Father is described by Father compared with how Father is described by Mother and the other members. Also, one may plot the manner in which the individual is viewed by the entire family. This is done by utilizing the scores in the Totals column on the right. Thus, if "Young Son" receives a total score of 17 on distracting and 9 on smug, we conclude that the family perceives him as toward the distracting end of that continuum. The DFF is a free-choice test, and the number of cards selected may be viewed as an index of openness or expressiveness in the family (L'Abate & Wildman, 1973).

Family situations pictures series (FSPS) test

This test consists of 264 cards depicting one or two family members in combinations of postures akin to Satir's (1972) dysfunctional response patterns: blaming, placating, distracting, and computing. Members are allowed to pick as many as they wish of the cards that remind them of the family. The scores are based on the postures and the number of family members on each card. After scoring by each family member (preferably crossing each number or letter of each card with two horizontal lines), transfer from individual to family score sheet is accomplished by doing one member at a time. The scores from the father go under the column marked Father, scores from the mother under the column marked Mother, etc. The transfer is done on the basis of 1 point for each of the first 24 cards and 2 points for the rest of the cards (25 to 264). The letters above each abbreviation for an individual on the individual answer sheet show where the point should be given. For instance, if Father chooses Card 7, 1 point should be given in the row marked F and D. If he chooses Card 18, 1 point is given to Younger Daughter (row YD under "Father" column) in the bottom row under "F."

The points for Cards 25 through 264 are double, according to the letters on the top of each card. For instance, Card 45 is scored 1 point for B for Younger Sister and 1 point for D for F. Card 96 would give 1 point for B for Older Son and 1 point to M for C.

After conversion from individual to family record sheet for each member of the family, the same procedures illustrated in the previous test (feelings) are followed. Scores are totaled individually (vertically, downward) and by family (horizontally, left to right). Total at the bottom for the four categories (blaming, distracting, placating, and computing) totaled horizontally should be the same as the totals obtained in the right column (totals) totaled downward in the right-bottom cells of the second sheet. The numbers in these four cells are then divided by the number of family members and recorded in the box at the bottom right of the second sheet. The scores in these cells are used in the analysis.

The individual scores for the four scales (blaming, placating, distracting, and computing) are charted on graph paper, the horizontal axis defined by "blaming" to the left and "placating" to the right. The vertical axis is defined by "computing" at the bottom and "distracting" at the top. Each score for the two axes is obtained by subtracting P from B (B − P) and D from C (C − D). In this way, each family member can be compared visually with the others. A second comparison is through individual scores at the bottom with the scores in the right column (how each member sees the family compared with how the family sees a member through each picture). As with the DFF, this test is a free-choice format, and the number of cards selected is a response measure.

Animal concepts pictures series (ACPS) test

In this instrument, 90 pictures of different animals are assigned a stimulus value based on semantic differential ratings. Each animal picture is rated on 10 bipolar scales: strong/weak, powerless/powerful, small/big, helpless/helpful, bad/good, slow/fast, quiet/noisy, dangerous/harmless, pleasant/unpleasant, and aggressive/passive. Each member is asked to make four sortings: two for family members as they are and two for members as one would like to see them.

After finishing the administration, scoring from individual answer sheets to family scoring sheets is done separately on two scoring sheets, one for the first two scorings (actual scores) and another for sortings 3 and 4 (ideal). Conversion from individual to family scores involves looking up each picture in the scoring manual. The horizontal numbers 1 through 10 represent the 10 scales on the left of the scoring sheet (strong-weak, powerless-powerful, etc.). Each picture receives 10 different weights which are transferred into the scoring sheet through the manual. These weights are obtained by asking subjects to rate each animal on each scale as to where that animal falls on that particular dimension. The most frequently occurring score (1–7) is then taken as the weight for that animal on that scale. For instance, if Father picks up Card 20 for Father in the first sorting, he receives a score of 2 in the column marked Father for strong-weak, 6 for powerless-powerful, 6 for small-big, 5 for helpless-helpful, etc. If Father picks Card 35 in the second sorting, all the values for the 10 scales for that card are added to the values already recorded for card 20. The highest score that may be obtained on any dimension for a single picture is 7. The higher the score, the closer it is to the second pole in each dimension. For example, Card 90, which depicts a fish, is given a weight of 7 on the dangerous/harmless scale, indicating that it is seen as relatively harmless. The cards picked by each individual for each individual go in the appropriate columns; that is, values for Father picked by Father go into the "Father" column; cards picked by Mother for Father go into the "Father" column; cards picked by Mother for Sib 2 go under "Sib 2;" cards picked by Father for Mother go into the "Mother" column; etc. The same process, of course, applies to the siblings. In other words, each member of the family receives all of the weights for the cards picked for that member. The scores in each cell are totaled and written into the little box at the right bottom of each cell.

The same procedure for "actual" sortings 1 and 2 is followed for "ideal" scorings 3 and 4. The scores in the little boxes allow comparisons among family members and between actual and ideal.

Another comparison within individuals is totaling the absolute difference between actual-ideal scores for each individual downward for the 10 scales. Any score below 30 represents "Normality" (i.e., no great discrepancy between actual and ideal). Scores above 30 to 40 represent some deviation. Discrepancy scores above 60 represent significant deviation.

Comparisons could be made among family members in each scale and within each member among the 10 scales. Comparisons among family members according to discrepancy (actual-ideal) totaled scores could also be made. Intuitively, this test is a good indicator of family perceptions in relation to the two dimensions described. It also gives an estimate of the degree to which family members are satisfied with their present state.

The main purpose of Golden's (1974) study was to provide a preliminary evaluation of the validity of this battery. This battery seems to promise a convenient, economical, and objective technique for assessing family functioning through the analysis of intrafamily perceptions.

This battery was administered to 37 families, ranging from those who reported few problems in the members to those who reported multiple problems. The level of reported problems was used as a criterion measure, and analyses were directed to the basic question: How and to what extent do the tests discriminate among families with different levels of problems? Because of the small sample size and the relatively large number of test variables, a series of separate analyses were performed on each test.

In general, the findings indicated that: (a) although several of the variables yielded significant discriminations between families with few reported problems and families with multiple problems, the test scales accounted for a minimal amount of the variance in the criterion; (b) the individual-level scores tended to be more sensitive discriminators than the family mean scores; and (c) there was a relatively high degree of interscale correlation within three of the four tests, indicating redundancy in the battery.

Although the findings generally did not provide evidence to support the validity of the battery, they did suggest some interesting trends. Differences between the parents in the low-problem and the high-problem families were more striking than were differences between the children in these families. The members of families with a high number of reported problems were generally more variable in their test responses, as compared with members of families who had a low number of reported problems. Among all the families studied, there was a significant tendency to describe male and female members in a relatively conventional, stereotyped fashion.

A minor part of the study investigated the relationship between conjugate lateral eye movements and selected family variables. The results indicated that there was no more than a chance relationship between direction of eye movement, sex, position in the family, level of problems in the family and most of the test scales.

On the basis of these findings, which admittedly must be viewed as preliminary and provisional, the visual family evaluation battery (VFEB) appears to need some modification. Suggestions for future research included: (a) selection of more valid criteria measures; (b) investigation of the reliability of the tests; (c) factor analysis of the complete battery; (d) analysis of the differential effects of free versus forced choice procedures; and (e) investigation of the effects of the order of test administration.

Lalor (1975) used one test of the Visual Family Evaluation Battery— the Family Situations Pictures Series (FSPS)—and one test of the Verbal Marital Evaluation Battery, to be described later—the Who Would Say This? (WWST).

Two groups of subjects—9 with essential hypertension and 10 with active stomach ulcers—were given a battery of tests, once at the beginning of medical treatment and again after three weeks of treatment for their illnesses. A group of control subjects who received no treatment were given the tests on two occasions at least three weeks apart.

Two of the tests—the FSPS and WWST—were designed to evaluate subjects' communication styles. Subjects also took the social reaction inventory, designed to measure locus of control, and the Myers-Briggs type indicator, which was used to evaluate personality development from a Jungian standpoint.

The results indicated that ulcer subjects, as measured by the FSPS, placated significantly more than hypertensive and control subjects, computed significantly more than hypertensive subjects, and used the distracting style significantly more than hypertensive and control subjects. The results from the WWST indicated that ulcer subjects used the blaming and computing styles significantly more than did the control subjects. However, in view of the questions raised about the validity of these instruments, any conclusions about the communication styles used by the subjects in this study must be qualified. Most of the results on the other tests used by Lalor were not significant.

Gallope (1979) essentially replicated Golden's study with a few additions. His study investigated interindividual variability in the family, using profiles of test responses and the relationship to the degree of family disturbance as judged by independent agency criteria. The Visual Family Evaluation Battery (VFEB), consisting of four separate tests—the Bell-Fagan Symbols Test, the Family Situations Pictures Series, Description of Feelings in the Family, and Animal Concepts Pictures Series—was administered to three groups of 20 families. Group 1 was considered normal, Group 2 moderately disturbed, and Group 3 severely disturbed. Results showed that the predicted relationship of greater family variability with greater disturbance was not found across the three groups of families. Moreover, the VFEB did not generally discriminate among families, using family mean scores as an indicator of the degree of disturbance. Some scales (blaming, placating, and sad) showed greater variability in severely disturbed families, and the DFF test did discriminate these families from others. Raters familiar with the battery but blind to the family's diagnosis were able to find, without error, the identified patient in a family.

An area of future research should include the determination of norms for both scale scores and profile variabilities. Such norms for both individual members and families would permit determination of degrees of difference, in terms of both variability and actual scores, from standard or population expected levels. One could speak to what differences in variability or scores actually mean and how much difference would normally be expected. These norms would add to the usefulness of the battery.

Future research should employ, as also recommended by Golden (1974), stricter criteria for division of families according to the level of disturbance. In Gallope's study, agency criteria were used to group families. However, it is questionable whether these criteria are them-selves valid and reliable. Are families who ask for enrichment more disturbed than those who keep problems within the family? Seeking help may be, and often is, viewed by many as a sign of strength and health in a family. What defines a healthy family has only recently been explored (Lewis, Beavers, Gossett, & Phillips, 1976), and the crite-ria have yet to be tested fully. Gallope's study found no consistent significant differences between those families considered normal and those considered mildly disturbed. Perhaps future studies should em-ploy multiple convergent criteria, such as those used by Lewis et al., Golden (1974), and Gallope (1979). In addition, multiple raters could assign families to groups to add further to the validity of the criteria.

Results from Gallope's study suggest that future research into the question of variability in the family employ only the DFF and FSPS tests of the family evaluation battery until the others can be modified as previously suggested. When one uses the battery to discriminate among families, the DFF and the ACPS tests would appear to be the best suited as they are presently constituted. With suggested scoring and procedural changes, the validity and reliability of these tests could be enhanced. The battery as presently constituted does not appear to hold much promise to assess quantitatively disturbance in families but could, with modifications, yield results that an experienced tester could use to locate an identified patient or to describe patterns and tendencies in any one family.

Future research in the variability of families could yield clearer, more meaningful results if the number of family members was held constant in comparison families. Although no significant differences between groups in terms of the number of members per family were found in Gallope's study, trends appeared to indicate that scores and variability would increase across groups for some scales. The mean number of family members also showed an increasing trend across groups. Although not significant, it does cause one to hesitate in inter-preting trends for any scale. Controlling for the number of family members would eliminate this concern.

Finally, the question of the relationship between the variability of a family unit and the judged level of disturbance remains to be an-swered. Gallope's study suggested some relationship between profile variability, as reflected in the response scores on some scale, and distur-bance in severely impaired families. However, only three scales (blam-ing, placating, sad) of 34 were significant in the predicted direction. If it were not for the convergent evidence from both types of profile variability, which lends more credence to the validity of these results, one could attribute this much significance, without replication, to chance alone. Even with the convergent evidence from this study, the results from these scales must be replicated before they may be viewed as reflective of a relationship between family variability and family disturbance. It must be considered that these scales may have been salient for the sample of families used in this study but offer little support for the general thesis that variability is important in family disturbance. Investigations in this area could take several directions. Future research could determine how much of a factor such variability is across families with different degrees of disturbance, using several different measures of variability. The correlation or convergence between behavioral and paper and pencil response measures would help to determine whether variability is indeed a true and significant descriptor of families. In addition, measuring the variability of response scores of positions in families (i.e., variability of fathers, mothers, first children, etc.) and comparing these member groupings across types of families could further indicate whether variability is more a member (or individual) factor as opposed to a unit (or system) factor. For example, it may be that the high variability of fathers in severely disturbed families, rather than the variability of the family as a system, is the significant correlate with family disturbance. A further method of measuring validity (i.e., of individual members across time) could also provide evidence for an individual versus a system determination. Such research could employ the Visual Family Evaluation Battery if, as suggested, the scales were more consistent in their ranges. In this manner, one could determine how significant each member's variability is in relation to the system variability. In the view of these authors, further study is required to determine the significance of variability as a descriptor in families. Such research could add further credence and acceptance to the system orientation in family therapy and assessment.

Work is continuing in the gathering of data on a larger sample of functional and dysfunctional families; the data supporting the use of this battery to assess results from structured enrichment are reported elsewhere (L'Abate, 1977).

VERBAL BATTERY

Various tests of this battery have been subjected to a medley of theses and dissertations, most of them to be reviewed here. This is essentially a Marital Evaluation Battery (MEB) because it is administered solely to the parents, not to the children. It comprises four instruments: the Marital Questionnaire (MQ), the Likeness Grid (LG), the Priorities Inventory (PI), and the What Would You Do? (WWYD) test. Each instrument is designed to measure properties related to L'Abate's (1976) theory of personality development in the family. The theory, which was described in detail in preceding sections, proposes that differentiation, priorities, and congruence are key factors in evaluating the functionality of individuals in marriage and family life. The instruments utilized in Wagner's (1980) study were designed to assess one or more of these areas.

The Marital Questionnaire is an experimental assessment device derived from the theoretical notions of L'Abate (1976) and Satir (1972). In its present form, the instrument is composed of six scales of 20 items each. Each scale on the questionnaire is related to one of the three postulates of L'Abate's (1976) theory of personality development in the family. The postulates of the theory, explained earlier, concern differentiation, priorities, and congruence. Hence, this questionnaire includes scales that measure degree of likeness (used for differentiation), ordering of priorities, and congruence in terms of Satir's (1972) four modes—blaming, placating,.computing, and distracting. Questions are true-false, and participants are given 1 point for each response they make, in concordance with the more functional response as defined by the theory from which the questionnaire is drawn. Participants can thus score between 0 and 20 for each scale. The higher the score, the more functional the participant's attitude is purported to be for the trait being measured. The individual taking the test is given 1 point on the relevant scale for indicating agreement with a statement that, from a theoretical point of view, is indicative of a healthy attitude. An individual is also given 1 point for rejecting a statement suggestive of an unhealthy attitude. Thus, the higher the score on a particular scale, the stronger is the indication that the respondent possess psychologically healthy attitudes in that area (L'Abate, 1976).

An earlier version of the questionnaire, which included seven other scales that related to tasks of marital enhancement but that did not stem directly from the theory of personality development in the family, has received some empirical study (Soper & L'Abate, 1976). A sample of 446 subjects, drawn over a two-year period, was used to provide some preliminary normative data for the Marital Questionnaire. The subjects were drawn from a variety of populations, including Girl Scouts aged 15 or less ($n = 99$), Girl Scouts 16 or over ($n = 114$), psychiatric inpatients ($n = 6$), Georgia State University undergraduates ($n = 50$), parent study group ($n = 23$), and pregnant women ($n = 80$). Means and standard deviations were calculated for the entire sample and for each subgroup, thus providing some preliminary normative data. Pearson product-moment correlations were calculated between the 13 scales and the total score. The intercorrelations between the subscales were all positive but tended to be low, thus providing some evidence for the independence of the subscales.

The described study suffered from several shortcomings. Since the test was designed to assess functionality in marriage, the utility of drawing roughly half the sample from a Girl Scout population is questionable. In addition, it would appear that this study tried to accomplish too much too fast. Rather than assessing the reliability and validity of the MQ (a necessary first step in the development of an assessment tool), the study gathered normative data for a variety of groups (a necessary second step in the development of an assessment tool). Wagner's (1980) study was designed to provide the needed data on the reliability and validity of the MQ as well as for the other instruments that together compose the Marital Evaluation Battery.

The Likeness Grid was developed by L'Abate (L'Abate & Wildman, 1973) as a measure of self-differentiation and is derived from Kelly's (1955) test of Personal Constructs. The Likeness Grid consists of a list of 24 persons related in some way to the subject. For each of the 24 persons, participants rate themselves as "completely the same as," "the same as," "similar" and/or "different from," "opposite from," or "completely the opposite of" that person. In keeping with the theoretical notions of the continuum of likeness (L'Abate, 1976), ratings of "completely the same" (symbiosis) or "completely opposite" (autism and alienation) are considered equivalent and are scored 1. Ratings of "same" or "opposite" are likewise considered equivalent and are scored 2. Ratings of "similar/different" are scored 3. The ratings of the 24 items are then summed to provide a total differentiation score.

The Priorities Inventory was developed (Wagner, 1980) to assess the individual's functionality in his/her ordering of priorities inside and outside the family. The test comprises all 56 possible permutations of the categories of self, spouse, children, parents and/or in-laws, brothers and sisters, work, leisure, and friends. The individual's task in taking this test is to rate the items in a given triad as to their relative importance to that individual. For each triad that the individual rates, the individual is given a point. Therefore, the higher the total score that the individual receives on the Priorities Inventory, the more functional the individual's ordering of priorities inside and outside the family is considered. (Wagner used this approach to score this test. However, since the scoring was based on a priori theoretical assumptions, it is questionable.)

The original WWYD test (L'Abate & Wildman, 1973) was composed of 26 multiple-choice problem situations in which the subject was asked to choose the response that most closely resembled how the subject would behave in similar situations. For each situation described, there were four alternatives, each corresponding to one of Satir's (1972) four response styles—blaming, placating, distracting, or computing. This instrument was developed primarily for use with adolescents and their families. Wagner's (1980) study employed a revision of this test to reflect situations more relevant to a general adult population. The WWYD in its present form consists of 20 hypothetical situations in which the individual is asked to rate each alternative response as to the likelihood that s/he would respond in a manner similar to that described by the alternative. In this fashion, a composite score is obtained for each individual on each of the Satir response styles through computation of the individual's ratings of the alternative responses to all 20 situations. Thus, through a comparison of the total ratings for each Satir category, the individual's propensity can be determined for responding in one particular manner as opposed to another.

The Marital Evaluation Battery would appear to satisfy most of the criteria that Reiss (1980) and Olson (1976) cited in determining the utility of an assessment device (one major criterion, of course, is the reliability and validity of the instrument, which is the subject of Wagner's study). The MEB provides assessment in three areas related to personality functioning in marriage and can thus be conceptualized as multidimensional, a characteristic of assessment devices that Olson, Sprenkle, and Russell (1979) stressed. The MEB is derived from a theory of personality development in the family and thus satisfies Olson's criterion of limiting assessment to theory, as well as avoiding the pitfall of being grounded in nonsystem thinking. Both Reiss (1980) and Olson (1976) stressed the role that a useful assessment device can play in the evaluation of therapy and in treatment planning. The multidimensionality of the MEB as well as its foundation in a theory of personality development in marriage and the family result in its being useful in both the development of treatment planning and in the evaluation of treatment progress.

Hutton (1974) attempted to relate the concept of self-differentiation to the process of mate selection. She employed two measures of differentiation in her study—the likeness scale of the Marital Questionnaire and the Likeness Grid (L'Abate & Wildman, 1973). Hutton hypothesized that dating and engaged couples would evidence similar degrees of differentiation through similar scores on both the Likeness Scale of the MQ and the Likeness Grid. The hypothesis was supported, as indicated by significant correlations between couples on the two measures of differentiation utilized. This result lends support to the premise that similarity in degree of differentiation is a significant factor in mate selection, since the tests were designed to measure differentiation and mates obtained similar scores on the two measures.

The Hutton study offers some evidence for the utility of the Likeness Scale and the Likeness Grid for the evaluation of differentiation in the marriage and the family, since both measures resulted in similar scores between mates. These results are open to some question, however, since the likeness scale and the likeness grid scores correlated significantly only for men in the sample. Since both of these measures were intended to measure differentiation, significant correlations were to be expected for both men and women on these scales. On the basis of this study, it is not possible to conclude with any certainty that the two scales are in fact measuring the same construct.

Another finding of Hutton (1974), relevant to the present review, was that self-esteem scores of men as measured by the Leary interpersonal checklist were significantly related to their likeness questionnaire scores and that the self-esteem scores of women were significantly related to the likeness scale scores of their male partners. These findings may be interpreted as providing support for the concept of differentiation as an indication of functionality, as well as evidence for the validity of the likeness scale as an assessment tool.

Cohen (1975) studied sex differences in level of differentiation by employing the draw-a-person test, the embedded figures test (Witkin & Goodenough, 1977), and the 13-scale version of the marital questionnaire (L'Abate, 1976).

The embedded figures test (EFT) requires subjects to find simple geometric figures embedded in more-complex geometric figures. The number of figures that the subject correctly identifies determines the score. Since this test requires the subject to separate figure from ground, an ability that Witkins attributes to high differentiation, the higher the score on this test, the more differentiated the individual is considered. The Draw-A-Person (DAP) Test has been used by Witkin and Goodenough (1977), as well as others, to measure differentiation. According to Witkin and Goodenough, the more differentiated individual has a more articulated body concept, and this can be seen in human figure drawings. He has developed a five-point, sophistication-of-body-concept scale to rate the level of differentiation an individual exhibits in his/her drawing.

Cohen's (1975) results indicated that on visual-spatial means of measuring differentiation (Embedded Figures Test), males appear to be more differentiated; on verbal measures (Marital Questionnaire), females tend to be more differentiated. No significant difference between males and females was found on the DAP. Cohen argued that females' higher scores on the verbal measure need not be interpreted in terms of Witkin and Goodenough's (1977) contention that undifferentiated people with a global field approach are more heavily invested in verbal skills. Cohen contended that the difference in scores on these two measures of differentiation are a function of their measuring differing aspects of differentiation. These results point to possible sex differences related to the instruments used to measure differentiation and suggest that we not rely solely on verbal scales or, if we do, that we interpret them with caution. Thus, Cohen's study underlined the importance of fostering more normative data before a scale specific to measuring differentiation in marriage can be used meaningfully.

Wright (1976), in a study on the relationship between self-differentiation and marital happiness over two stages of the family life cycle, used the Likeness Scale, the Embedded Figures Test (Witkin & Goodenough, 1977), and the Titchner Circles Test (Wapner & Werner, 1957) as measures of differentiation. The Titchner Circles Test (TCT) is a perceptual measure based on the articulation of relationships between parts; since it is based on embeddedness determinants, it is structurally similar to the EFT. The Revised Marital Happiness Scale (Azrin, 1973), a 10-item rating sheet of areas relevant to marriage, was used to measure marital satisfaction.

The study was undertaken to provide some rationale for the reported, subjectively rated decrease in marital satisfaction during the childbearing and childrearing years of the family life cycle. Wright hypothesized that this difference in marital happiness could stem from lack of concordance in level of differentiation between spouses in the childbearing, childrearing years, as contrasted to similar levels of differentiation in spouses who are not in that stage of the family life cycle.

The results of Wright's study do not lend support to his hypotheses, nor do they offer much support for the similarity among the three measures of differentiation. Although Wright did find significant correlations between male scores on the EFT and the Likeness Scale and between females scores on the TCT and the Likeness Scale, other correlations among the three measures were not significant. Thus, virtually no support for the validity of the likeness scale as a measure of differentiation can be found in this study. The major implication from the results of this study is the likelihood that the three measures, although related to some degree, may be measuring different constructs.

A study by Del Monte (1976) provided evidence that directly linked L'Abate's (1976) concept of differentiation to Rotter's (1966) theory of internal-external control and to Harvey, Hunt, and Schroder's (1961) four conceptual systems of personality functioning. Del Monte administered Rotter's (1966) I–E Scale (which measures internal versus external locus of control), Harvey et al.'s (1961) This I Believe Test (which classifies individuals into one of Harvey's four systems), and L'Abate's Likeness Grid and Likeness Scale.

Del Monte's results indicated significant relationships between: L'Abate's concept of sameness and Harvey's System I, characterized by cognitive simplicity and conventional conforming behavior; L'Abate's concept of oppositeness and Harvey's System II, characterized by cognitive simplicity and rebellious behavior; L'Abate's concept of similarity and Harvey's System III, characterized by individuals who are cognitively complex and attuned to proper social behavior; and L'Abate's concept of differentness and Harvey's System IV individuals, who are characterized as being cognitively complex and autonomous. Del Monte also found that less differentiated individuals had an external locus of control, whereas more differentiated individuals had an internal locus of control. These results are in line with both L'Abate's and Witkin's notions of differentiation.

The results of tests using L'Abate's measures of differentiation in Del Monte's (1976) study correlate at a significant level with both Harvey's and Rotter's instruments. Thus, support is found for the validity of the Likeness Scale and the Likeness Grid as assessment tools. In addition, Del Monte found significant correlations between scores on the Likeness Grid and the Likeness Scale, which suggests that they are measuring similar constructs. When Del Monte's results are looked at in the light of a study done by Harvey (1966) (who examined the relationship between the Embedded Figures Test and his conceptual systems), a link between L'Abate's and Witkin's theories can be inferred. Harvey found that individuals who scored lowest on the Embedded Figures Test were in System IV. Harvey's results using Witkin's measures of differentiation are quite similar to those obtained by Del Monte using L'Abate's measures. Thus, indirect support exists both for L'Abate's theory and for its assessment tools.

Jessee (1978) examined the relationship between self-differentiation and separation of college students from their families of origin. Two perceptual measures of differentiation that had been employed in earlier studies—the Embedded Figures Test (Witkin & Goodenough, 1977) and the Titchner Circles Test (Wapner & Werner, 1957)—as well as L'Abate's Likeness Scale, were used to measure differentiation.

Jessee hypothesized that individuals living away from home would be more highly differentiated and that this would be reflected in higher scores on the TCT, EFT, and the Likeness questionnaire. It was thus proposed that, since all three instruments were measures of differentiation, significant positive correlations would obtain across the three measures. The results of the study were that the Likeness Scale and the Embedded Figures Test, but not the Titchner Circles Test, significantly discriminated the level of differentiation of groups of students living at home and away from home. The computed correlation coefficients indicated that there was an overall significant correlation between scores for subjects on all three tests but that the main effect was in terms of the correlations of test scores of the students still living at home. Jessee contended that the differences in the strength of correlations could be the result of undifferentiated individuals scoring low on all cognitive-style measures of differentiation while more differentiated individuals might reflect a development of one cognitive style as opposed to another. Thus, more differentiated individuals might score high on one measure, such as the Likeness Scale, and low on another; undifferentiated individuals would score consistently low.

The results of this study offer some support for the validity of the Likeness Scale as a measure of self-differentiation. Since both the Embedded Figures Test and the Likeness questionnaire discriminated between the two experimental groups and the correlations obtained among the three instruments on individuals living at home were significant, the notion that they are measuring similar constructs is supported. This provides suggestive evidence for the validity of the Likeness Scale. Since, however, scores on the Likeness questionnaire did not correlate with the other two measures on the subjects who live away from home, the three scales are probably, in part, measuring different constructs.

Bryson (1978) conducted a study to investigate the relationship between personality differentiation and the verbal communication patterns in dyadic interaction. It was his hypothesis that the verbal communication of less differentiated individuals would be different on a variety of dimensions from the verbal communication of more differentiated individuals. Bryson used the Likeness Scale (L'Abate, 1976), the Embedded Figures Test (Witkin & Goodenough, 1977), and the Draw-A-Person Test (Witkin & Goodenough) as measures of differentiation and Thomas's (1977) procedure of content analysis to gather the data on communication patterns.

Bryson found only very limited support for his hypothesis that patterns of communication are related to level of differentiation. It is important to note that although Bryson summed individual differentiation scores across the three measures of differentiation to get a sum score for each individual on differentiation, correlation among the measures was not significant. The fact that there were not significant correlations among the measures of differentiation suggests that these scales may in fact be measuring different traits or different components of differentiation. If these scales are measuring different traits, the utility of summing them is questionable. It would appear from this study that these scales are either measuring different constructs, that differentiation is not a unitary construct, or that the scales themselves are unreliable or invalid. Bryson's study suggests the need for further research on the Likeness Scale itself to determine its utility.

One can see from the results of these studies that the evidence is somewhat contradictory. Several studies (Del Monte, 1976; Hutton, 1974; Jessee, 1978) have found strong relationships between L'Abate's constructs and instruments, and similar constructs with differing assessment techniques. Other studies (Bryson, 1978; Cohen, 1975; Wright, 1976), however, have found results that are less impressive but nonetheless intriguing because of their lack of concordance with studies employing the same instruments of evaluation. It would seem that the research suggests the utility of L'Abate's techniques for evaluating differentiation as well as indicating the need for further work on the evaluation of the reliability and validity of the measures.

In a study (Goglia, 1982) designed to examine some of the potential long-term effects of parental role assignments in childhood, 100 college students were administered a specially designed parentification questionnaire derived from the literature on this topic. Subjects also completed the Socialization, Responsibility, Self-Control, and Social Presence Scales of the California Personality Inventory, the Likeness Scale (L'Abate), and Ego Identity Scales. Scores on these measures were expected to covary with the degree and kind (expressive, instrumental) of parental responsibilities that subjects reported having been assigned as children. Higher scores on the expressive components of the Parentification Questionnaire were found to correlate negatively with L'Abate's Likeness questionnaire ($r = -.18$, $p < .05$), suggesting that parentification interferes with differentiation from one's family of origin. Parentified subjects also obtained lower scores on socialization and self-control, suggesting possible deviant patterns of socialization. Additional findings suggest that parentification may be especially detrimental for females.

In marital and family life, every individual is faced with the task of structuring his/her priorities. The manner in which priorities are structured by the individual plays an important role in determining the quality of marital and family life. Until the present, only one study (Cohen, 1975) included the Priorities Scale. Cohen reported a significant positive correlation between the subscales of priorities and likeness (differentiation) for women, which is in keeping with the idea that there must be separation from parents (hence, differentiation) if priorities are to be ordered accurately. The postulate has not otherwise been put through empirical study, nor has the Priorities Inventory or the Priorities Scale of the Marital Questionnaire (L'Abate & Wildman, 1973) been tested for validity and reliability. There is suggestive theoretical support for the postulate, but empirical verification is needed. This verification would entail, initially, gathering empirical data for those instruments derived from L'Abate's (1976) theory which deal with priorities, and subsequently testing those instruments with nontheory-derived techniques that measure similar constructs.

A family which is operating in a functional manner is characterized by communication patterns that are clear, consistent, and congruent. L'Abate (1976) contends that the manner in which affect and emotions are handled in relation to thinking and action are vital to the welfare of the individual in the family. Both L'Abate's (1976) and Satir's (1972) patterns of incongruent behavior are the reflection of clinical observations.

The Marital Questionnaire, described previously, was utilized in a study by Cohen (1975) on sex differences in differentiation (already cited in this review). Although not central to her investigation, in computing correlation coefficients between the various scales of the Marital Questionnaire, Cohen found negative correlations between the Blaming and the Placating Scales and between the Computing and the Distracting Scales. These findings are relevant to the orthogonal model of Blaming-Placating and Distracting-Computing suggested by L'Abate (1976). Cohen's findings thus provide some evidence for the validity of the instrument derived from the model and suggest that further empirical study of the instrument could be beneficial.

Bryson (1973) used the following instruments: the WWYD to measure individual response styles; the Zuckerman and Lubin Multiple Affect Adjective Check List to measure dimensions of the subject's affect; and the Cortes and Gatti Self-Description Test to measure self-report evaluations of self and physical traits in a study designed to explore the relationship between physique, self-description of personality, and the behavioral styles of blaming, placating, distracting, and computing. The hypotheses advanced by Bryson in terms of the relation of a particular physical type to a specific affective state and to a predominant incongruent style were not completely supported.

The lack of hypothesized correlations between instruments can be taken as evidence against the validity of the WWYD. Although this possibility cannot be denied, it is plausible that Bryson's hypotheses were off the mark or that his choice of instruments to assess the other variables was inappropriate. Despite the lack of the hypothesized correlations between measures, the findings pertaining to the WWYD are relevant to Wagner's (1980) study since they offer some evidence that this instrument differentiates individuals on the hypothesized orthogonal dimensions of blaming-placating and distracting-computing.

Bryson found negative correlations between blaming and placating and between computing and distracting on individuals' scores on the WWYD. The consistent negative intercorrelations indicate that these are two bipolar dimensions, thus providing some support for the model proposed by L'Abate (1976). The majority of individuals in the study fell in the placator-computer quadrant of the orthogonal model. Since the subjects were drawn from a college population, in which these two behaviors seem most appropriate for survival, some concurrent validity for the instrument is provided. Similarly, more men scored highest in the computer dimension and more women in the placating dimension. These findings are also in keeping with sterotyped sex-role patterns and again offer some evidence for the validity of the instrument. Thus, Bryson's study provides some mixed results concerning the WWYD. He suggested that additional study of the instrument, using other instruments that measure similar factors, is needed, which in turn is in part the purpose of Wagner's (1980) study.

McNatt (1973) studied the following: the relationship between Satir's patterns of communication, using the WWYD; self-esteem, using the global self-esteem scale and the Revised Interpersonal Checklist; and nonverbal behavior, using a scale based on Smith's (1972) postural and gestural ratings. McNatt was concerned with the ways in which opposite-sexed computers and placators interacted, the kinds of nonverbal messages communicated, and the effects of the patterns of communication on the responses to these nonverbal messages. Results of her study suggested that there is no consistent relationship between Satir types (as identified by the WWYD) and nonverbal behavior. Nevertheless, a multiple comparison of means on the global self-esteem score indicated that higher self-esteem was associated with leveling (defined in this study as a difference of no more than four points between computing and placating), which offers some evidence in the appropriate direction.

The results obtained by McNatt offer only a small degree of support for the effectiveness of the WWYD. McNatt suggested that some of the items in the test need revision and also that more than one instrument may be needed to assess the four styles of Satir. The intent of Wagner's study was to take heed of this issue, employing two methods to measure these constructs.

Although there is some evidence that supports the WWYD as useful for differentiating dysfunctional styles, the evidence for the utility of this test is limited. There are only limited data, as well, on the scales of blaming, placating, computing, and distracting on the Marital Questionnaire. It is apparent that more research on these scales is necessary before a definitive statement can be made about them.

In Wagner's (1980) study, partially reported here, participants were 138 undergraduates at Georgia State University: 77 males (56 percent) and 61 females (44 percent). The vast majority of participants were white (73 percent), between the ages of 17 and 35 (95 percent). There were 40 individuals (29 percent) in the sample who were currently married. Few of the individuals in the sample had children ($n = 30$, 21 percent). The interested reader can consult the original manuscript for greater detail.

Wagner used six assessment instruments in the study. Two instruments were employed to measure each of the three postulates—differentiation, priorities, and congruence (blaming, computing, distracting, and placating). Table 3 indicates which instruments were used to measure the three postulates and is a more specific derivation of Table 2.

Table 3

Postulates of the theory

Postulates	Instrument
1. Differentiation (likeness)	Marital questionnaire—likeness scale Likeness grid
2. Priorities	Marital questionnaire—priorities scale Priorities inventory
3. Congruence	
Blaming	Marital questionnaire—blaming scale What would you do?—blaming scale
Computing	Marital questionnaire—computing scale What would you do?—computing scale
Distracting	Marital questionnaire—distracting scale What would you do?—distracting scale
Placating	Marital questionnaire—placating sale What would you do?—placating scale

Wagner hypothesized that each instrument being evaluated would evidence reliability. The reliability of each instrument was assessed by two separate methodologies of reliability estimation: (a) stability/test-retest reliability, and (b) internal stability/consistency reliability. One shortcoming of Wagner's study, as relevant and important as it is, lay in his a priori scoring of the Priorities Inventory according to the predictions of the theory rather than on the basis of strictly normative results. This shortcoming is being corrected by a reanalysis of the original data (L'Abate & Wagner, manuscript in preparation) and by Karan's (1982) study which found that in a test of the Priorities Inventory, undergraduates and their parents ranked the self much lower than the theory predicted.

This discrepancy between theoretical prediction and normative results concerning the position of the self vis-à-vis other priorities is not unusual. In their comparison of rankings of family members' and therapists' descriptive statements about family functioning, Fisher, Giblin, and Hoopes (1982) found a similar discrepancy: Therapists ranked self-related messages 1st; family members ranked them 12th. This discrepancy indicates that although therapists (and theorists!) may stress the importance of the self in regard to various priorities, this expectation is not shared by the population at large. As Fisher et al. concluded, therapists and families define "healthy family functioning" differently.

CONCLUSION

We have reviewed the creation and initial validation of two theory-derived couples- and family-oriented batteries. The major issue posed by the review of the evidence lies more in the psychometric validity of the test batteries than in the validity of the theory. However, a theory is only as valid as the instruments designed to test it. Consequently, we shall continue to refine these batteries to achieve a better fit between the theory and the instruments purporting to test it.

REFERENCES

Bell, G. L. *Graphic representation of emotion: The development of indices of reception and expression.* Unpublished doctoral dissertation, Georgia State University, 1972.

Boszormenyi-Nagy, I., & Spark, G. *Invisible loyalties.* New York: Harper & Row, 1973.

Bryson, C. H. *A study of the reliability of relationships between self-description and family dysfunction.* Unpublished master's thesis, Georgia State University, 1973.

Bryson, C. H. Personality, differentiation, and communication (Doctoral dissertation, Georgia State University, 1978). *Dissertation Abstracts International,* 1978, *40,* 442B.

Cohen, J. *Sex differences in differentiation.* Unpublished master's thesis, Georgia State University, 1975.

Del Monte, R. *Locus of control and conceptual systems in personality differentiation.* Unpublished master's thesis, Georgia State University, 1976.

Fisher, B. L., Giblin, P. R., & Hoopes, M. H. Healthy family functioning: What therapists say and what families want. *Journal of Marital and Family Therapy,* 1982, *8,* 273–284.

Gallope, R. A. *Test profile variabilities within families and their relationship to family disturbance.* Unpublished doctoral dissertation, Georgia State University, 1979.

Goglia, L. *An exploration of the long-term effects of parentification.* Unpublished master's thesis, Georgia State University, 1982.

Golden, R. P. *A validation study of the family assessment battery.* Unpublished doctoral dissertation, Georgia State University, 1974.

Harvey, O. J. System structure, flexibility, and creativity. In O. J. Harvey (Ed.), *Experience, structure, and adaptability.* New York: Springer Publishing, 1966.

Harvey, O. J., Hunt, D. E., & Schroder, H. M. *Conceptual systems and personality organization.* New York: John Wiley & Sons, 1961.

Hutton, S. P. Self-esteem, values, and self-differentiation in pre-marital dyads (Doctoral dissertation, Georgia State University, 1974). *Dissertation Abstracts International,* 1974, *36,* 888B.

Jessee, E. *Separation and differentiation in the college individual.* Unpublished master's thesis, Georgia State University, 1978.

Karan, D. N. *Leaving home/launching children.* Unpublished master's thesis, Georgia State University, 1982.

Kelly, G. *Psychology of personal constructs.* New York: W. W. Norton, 1955.

L'Abate, L. *Understanding and helping the individual in the family.* New York: Grune & Stratton, 1976.

L'Abate, L. *Enrichment: Structured interventions with couples, families, and groups.* Washington, D.C.: University Press of America, 1977.

L'Abate, L. Aggression and construction in children's monitored play therapy. *Journal of Counseling and Psychotherapy,* 1979, *2,* 137–158.

L'Abate, L. *Family psychology: Theory, therapy, and training.* Washington, D.C.: University Press of America, 1983.

L'Abate, L. Structured enrichment (SE) with couples and families. *Family Relations,* in press.

L'Abate, L., & Rupp, G. *Enrichment: Skills training for family life.* Washington, D.C.: University Press of America, 1981.

L'Abate, L., & Wagner, V. *Testing a theory of personality development in the family.* Manuscript in preparation.

L'Abate, L., & Wildman, R. *Parental questionnaire.* Unpublished manuscript, Georgia State University, 1973.

Lalor, K. M. *An application of Virginia Satir's communication theory, locus of control, and Jungian theory to psychosomatic illness.* Unpublished master's thesis, Georgia State University, 1975.

Lewis, S. The family matrix in health and diseases. In S. Lewis & C. Hofling (Eds.), *The family: Evaluation and treatment.* New York: Brunner/Mazel, 1980.

Lewis, S. M., Beavers, W. R., Gossett, S. T., & Phillips, U. A. *No single thread: Psychological health in family systems.* New York: Brunner/Mazel, 1976.

McNatt, V. *Non-verbal communication: A study of Satir typology, interpersonal attraction, and self-esteem.* Unpublished doctoral dissertation, Georgia State University, 1973.

Minuchin, S. *Families and family therapy.* New York: Basic Books, 1974.

Olson, D. H. *Treating relationships.* Lake Mills, Iowa: Graphic Publishing, 1976.

Olson, D. H., Sprenkle, D., & Russell, C. Circumplex model of marital and family systems: 1. Cohesion and adaptability dimensions, family types, and clinical applications. *Family Process,* 1979, *18,* 1; 3–28.

Reiss, E. Pathways to assessing the family: Some choice points and a sample route. In S. Lewis & C. Hofling (Eds.), *The family: Evaluation and treatment.* New York: Brunner/Mazel, 1980.

Rotter, J. B. Generalized expectancies for internal versus external control of reinforcement. *Psychological Monographs,* 1966, *80* (1, Whole No. 609).

Satir, V. *People making.* Palo Alto, Calif.: Science and Behavior Books, 1972.

Smith, D. K. *Induction/sensitization: A model for examining teaching styles of classroom management.* Unpublished doctoral dissertation, Georgia State University, 1972.

Soper, P., & L'Abate, L. *A theory-derived experimental marital questionnaire.* Unpublished manuscript, Georgia State University, 1976.

Thomas, E. J. *Marital communication and decision making: Analysis, assessment, and change.* New York: Free Press, 1977.

Wagner, V. *An evaluation study of a theory-based marital assessment battery.* Unpublished doctoral dissertation, Georgia State University, 1980.

Wapner, S., & Werner, H. *Perceptual development.* Worcester, Mass.: Clark University Press, 1957.

Witkin, H. A., & Goodenough, D. R. Field dependence and interpersonal behavior. *Psychological Bulletin,* 1977, *84*(4), 661–689.

Wright, L. *Self-differentiation and marital happiness over two stages of the family life cycle.* Unpublished master's thesis, Georgia State University, 1976.

Section Nine

Therapeutic and Preventive Interventions*

---
*This work was supported in part by National Institute of Mental Health Grant MH 35340.

Chapter 34

Current Status of Outcome Research in Marital Therapy

STEVEN R. H. BEACH
K. DANIEL O'LEARY

Marital discord is very frequent, and it has widespread mental health and industrial implications. Based on national projections, approximately 40 percent of couples who married in 1980 will divorce (Glick & Norton, 1978). Following the death of a close family member, divorce and marital separation are the most-important stressors in an adult's life (Holmes & Rahe, 1967). Marital discord increases the likelihood of physical and psychological disorders such as alcoholism and coronary disease (Bloom, Asher, & White, 1978). Almost half of first admissions to state hospitals have marital stress as a major participant (Beisser & Glasser, 1968). Suicide often follows marital discord, separation, and divorce (Schniedman, Farberow, & Litman, 1970).

Marital discord and fights regarding passion are the fabric of literature and history, but treatment of marital discord has not received serious research attention until recently. Further, despite the evident seriousness of marital distress from a mental health view, marital discord is not a diagnostic classification for which one can receive insurance reimbursement from most companies in the United States, even when the therapy is provided by licensed practitioners. Apart from financial considerations, this restriction on insurance reimbursement reflects in part a view of mental health problems as individual psychopathology. Marital problems require dyadic models, and such models are more complicated than individual-psychopathology models both in terms of general conceptualization and in terms of a research methodological basis. While individual-psychopathology models do have some

important role in the understanding and treatment of marital problems, dyadic models ultimately are needed to account for the interactions between a husband and wife, and these models are clearly in
their formative stages.

Why do we need outcome research?

Outcome studies provide evidence of effectiveness which readily
can be made understood to members of the psychological community,
to members of the allied health professions, to the educated lay public,
and to members of Congress and other potentially regulatory bodies.
Well-conducted outcome studies make the dissemination of effective
therapeutic techniques and approaches easier by providing compelling
documentation of effectiveness and by forcing increased precision in
the specification of the techniques being used. The type of documentation provided for by well-conducted outcome studies also addresses
potential consumer concerns such as issues of safety and cost effectiveness. In the process of addressing these concerns, well-conducted outcome studies help to enhance the status of the field of marital therapy
in the public arena. There is also the potential of receiving insurance
reimbursement if evidence can be produced documenting the efficacy
of marital therapy; with such evidence, marital therapy could be a
reimbursable expense in a comprehensive mental health care plan.
In many ways, the future of the field of marital therapy rests on a
foundation which is only as solid as the outcome work which demonstrates its usefulness in helping couples achieve more satisfying marital
relationships. Hence, it is difficult to overestimate the importance of
well-conducted outcome research in establishing the scientific basis
and future growth of the marital therapy movement.

Issues in the measurement of marital outcome

Outcome research has been revolutionized since Eysenck's (1952)
pronouncement that there was no compelling evidence that existing
forms of psychotherapy were effective. Issues relating to internal and
external validity in marital outcome research have been widely addressed (Gurman & Kniskern, 1978; O'Leary & Turkewitz, 1978). Fortunately, marital therapy outcome research has increased in quantity
and quality in the past 10 years. This is a great boon to the marital
therapist because, although poorly controlled studies can be useful
for initial demonstrations or for hypothesis generation, they cannot
provide unequivocal evidence about the effectiveness of the various
treatment approaches available to us.

Of primary importance for documenting effectiveness in group design research is the existence of a control group and the procedure of random assignment to conditions. For group designs, only these attributes allow us to safely argue that something about the treatment itself accounted for differences between the groups and that this difference represents a gain over no treatment at all. That is to say, these attributes provide a major safeguard against bias and consequent lack of internal validity (Shapiro & Shapiro, 1983). In the absence of a control group, we simply have no way of knowing how many of the couples in this particular sample would have gotten better with minimal or no therapeutic contact. Consequently, we have no way of clearly assessing the impact of the treatment. On the other hand, in the absence of random assignment to conditions, we cannot exclude the competing hypothesis that any observed differences were due to sampling differences between the two groups. Consequently, we cannot appropriately infer that the intervention is responsible for the observed differences.

In view of these very basic considerations, it is appropriate for us to examine research on the effectiveness of the available therapeutic approaches in marital therapy by systematically reviewing only those studies which meet the basic criteria of having a control group and having random assignment to groups. We will accordingly not be reviewing the very large literature documenting success rates in the absence of a control group. Nor will we be reviewing the single-subject design studies which have appeared in the marital literature. While this literature has played a central role in the development of marital techniques (e.g., Stuart, 1969), there are grave problems in generalizing from treated individuals to the larger population of maritally distressed couples. In addition, single-subject designs are not well suited to evaluating therapeutic procedures which may have generalized and/or non-reversible effects (e.g., communication therapy).

Because we are interested in documenting the effectiveness of therapy, we will not be including studies which have only a brief intervention followed by assessment. While these analogue therapy studies do play an important role in investigating the effects of specific techniques, they cannot be considered actual therapy trials. Accordingly, studies having four or fewer sessions will not be included. Our aim in restricting the studies to be reviewed is to assure ourselves that the studies which remain meet the minimal criteria for internal validity (Campbell & Stanley, 1966) in experimental design. We are certainly not claiming that only experimental designs provide valuable insight into the process of marital therapy. However, only studies meeting the minimal criteria for internal validity in experimental design are useful in conclusively answering the specific question, "Does marital therapy help alleviate marital distress?"

INCLUSION AND EXCLUSION CRITERIA

Recently the importance of explicitly specifying inclusion and exclusion criteria for a review of the literature has been elaborated in the context of metaanalytic studies (Glass & Kliegel, 1983; Wilson & Rachman, 1983). Strube and Hartman (1982) have also called for reliable and defensible rules for inclusion and exclusion of studies for a review of the literature in general. But, as Wilson and Rachman point out, none currently exist. Any rule will be subject to question; accordingly, we prefer a rule which provides for highly reliable judgments regarding the inclusion of studies in the review and a reasonable level of protection against individual reviewer bias.

Consequently, we propose to confine this review to studies which have gone through standard peer review procedures provided for by any of the English-language journals publishing marital outcome work.[1] No attempt has been made to include studies which appear only in dissertation reports, book chapters, unpublished manuscripts, convention presentations, other nonreferred sources, or sources with highly restricted availability. While this limits the scope of the review, it also limits the amount of idiosyncratic bias introduced in the literature selection process and accordingly increases the confidence which can be placed in the conclusions drawn. In addition, it ensures that certain minimal standards of quality are met by the studies included in the review—i.e., those standards provided by the existing scientific journals. While different journals may apply different criteria in making acceptance decisions, those journals which provide for external peer review provide a stamp of professional approval for the studies they publish. This stamp of professional approval cannot be provided by the individual reviewer who rates large numbers of unpublished studies on an idiosyncratic scale of "methodological adequacy." Conversely, it is difficult in a major review of the literature to provide sufficient methodological detail to allow the reader to draw his or her own conclusions regarding the overall scientific adequacy of the study. In the absence of a restriction which requires some external review process, the reader of a literature review is often left wondering how thoroughly the studies were examined. In many cases, the reader will find that the only readily available additional information which can be obtained

---

[1] Our strategy in locating studies was twofold. First, we located those journals which had been identified in earlier reviews as publishing outcome studies. These journals were searched by hand for additional outcome studies meeting the criteria of group design, untreated/minimal contact control group, and random assignment to conditions. Second, the entire data base of over 700 journals covered by the psychological abstracts was searched via computer. The 40 studies yielded in this manner were again examined with regard to meeting the methodological requirements necessary for the purposes of this review.

is a one-paragraph abstract. This material is hardly the basis for a well-considered rating of methodological adequacy.

We are sure that the debate over inclusion and exclusion criteria will continue, as indeed it should. The growing popularity of meta-analytic techniques in summarizing the literature in an area is one force favoring the acceptance of large numbers of studies, and there have been articulate arguments presented in favor of such a strategy (e.g., Glass & Kliegel; 1983). However, if a review can be characterized as the study of a population of research reports (where the individual reports are rather like the individual observations made in our usual research practices), then consider the likely impact on one's confidence in one's conclusions of including a large number of potentially unsound observations. Even if including extra, unsound observations does not actually change one's conclusions, the fact that it *might* change the conclusions must be disquieting. On the other hand, if including the potentially unsound observations does change one's conclusions, surely this cannot be taken unequivocally as an advance to greater accuracy and understanding. Accordingly, in this review, we find ourselves guided by Strube and Hartman's (1982) observation that "if inappropriate studies are included in the analysis, ambiguous or misleading interpretations will follow." And we take the necessary steps to avoid being misled.

Focus on effectiveness per se

We entirely agree with Rachman and Wilson (1980) and Gurman (1979) that there has been too much emphasis on comparative studies and insufficient attention to studies which have an untreated control group or a minimal-treatment control group. Looking only at the outcome of "horse race" comparisons could lead us to inappropriately discard therapeutic approaches which are valuable for some subgroup of couples. Nevertheless, a therapeutic approach which cannot demonstrate its superiority to no treatment or minimal treatment for some population must be viewed as having questionable or no value. Accordingly, we will include all studies which address the issue of the effectiveness of any marital therapy program whether or not a comparison group other than the control group is included. Our primary purpose is to review what has been established about the effectiveness of particular approaches to marital therapy, not to make statements about the relative effectiveness of treatments which have been shown to be effective. When more than one group is compared in a study, we will focus on the effectiveness of each treatment individually relative to the control group. This is not to argue that comparative studies which do not include a minimal therapy or wait-list control group have nothing to offer. In fact, we believe such studies can play an important role in providing a basis for treatment decisions. However, they cannot provide the initial evidence of a treatment approach's value. That is, they can not provide the evidence which is required before we can confidently add a treatment approach to our clinical repertoire.

INSIGHT-ORIENTED MARITAL THERAPY

Insight-oriented marital therapy represents an important influence on the marital therapy scene today (e.g., Gurman, 1981; Sager, 1976). These approaches typically emphasize the unconscious factors which are held to determine both one's choice of a mate and the conflicts which later develop in the marriage. Unfortunately, there is a dearth of research documenting the effectiveness of this approach either in combination with other approaches or on its own. This is especially unfortunate in the context of the rather striking claims of effectiveness which have been put forward by some representatives of this approach (see L'Abate, 1985). In our own search for controlled-outcome studies, we were able to locate three studies which included an insight-oriented therapy as one of their groups (Boelens, Emmelkamp, MacGillavry, & Markvoort, 1980; Crowe, 1978; Epstein & Jackson, 1978). None of the 11 studies discussed by Gurman and Kniskern (1978) in their review of the marital therapy literature proved helpful in this regard. Six are unpublished; one consisted of only one trial of video feedback with minimal therapist contact and so is not a test of any type of marital therapy program; one study did not have random assignment to conditions; and two studies were applications of marital therapy to treatment of other problems such as alcoholism. One study (Hickman & Baldwin, 1971) is reviewed later.

The earliest controlled study testing the efficacy of nonbehaviorally oriented insight therapy was conducted by Crowe (1978). Crowe randomly assigned 42 couples with marital problems to one of three therapy conditions: (1) a directive therapy based on the work of Stuart (1969) and Liberman (1970) (primarily contracting), (2) an interpretative approach based on the work of Skynner (1969, 1976) (insight-oriented marital therapy), and (3) a control condition in which couples met with a therapist who avoided giving either advice or interpretation as much as possible. For the purposes of this section, we will focus on the contrast between the insight-oriented group and the control group only.

On the global measure of marital adjustment used (a 16-question self-report measure), the insight group was significantly superior to the control group at nine month follow-up but not at posttherapy, 3-month follow-up, or 18-month follow-up. No differences between the insight group and the control group were found on improvement in sexual adjustment, general individual adjustment, or specific target problems. Thus, the Crowe study found the insight group to be weaker than predicted by the authors. Indeed, the one difference found (at the .05 probability level) out of the 20 posttherapy comparisons is not different than a result which would be expected by chance alone and cannot be taken as evidence that the insight group fared any better than the control group.

It should be pointed out, however, that the therapists in the interpretative condition were limited to interpretation and not allowed to be directive. Skynner (1981) regards this as a critical deviation from his own preferred mode of therapy, and it may in fact account for the observed weakness of the therapeutic effects. Indeed, a study by Boelens, Emmelkamp, MacGillavry, and Markvoort (1980) suggests that insight-oriented marital therapy can be more effective in resolving marital problems than no therapy.

Boelens et al. (1980) randomly assigned 21 couples to one of three therapy conditions: (1) a behavioral contracting approach based on the work of Azrin, Naster, and Jones (1973), (2) an insight-oriented approach based on the work of Watzlawick, Weakland, and Fisch (1974) among others, and (3) a wait-list control condition. Outcome was assessed using (1) the Maudsley marital questionnaire (MMQ), which was based upon the marital adjustment scale used by Crowe (1978); (2) the marital deprivation scale (MDS) (Frenken, 1976), which was adapted from the marital attitude evaluation scale of Schutz (1967); (3) partner ratings of severity of their three main marital problems; (4) therapist ratings of the couple's relationship; and (5) an observational rating scale measure of rates of positive and negative verbal behavior (MICS) (Hops, Wills, Patterson, & Weiss, 1972).

Pre-post analyses indicated than the two treatments considered together were significantly better than a wait-list control in improving scores on the MMQ, the MDS, the partner ratings of problem severity, the therapist ratings, and the observed level of positive social reinforcement. Only the level of negative social reinforcement failed to change more for the treated groups than for the wait-list. While analyses were not presented which contrasted each treatment separately with the control group, it was possible to compute Fisher exact probabilities based on the number of couples showing improvement or showing no improvement in treated versus control conditions. (For the purposes of these computations, couples who had separated or divorced were considered unimproved.) Immediately posttherapy, the group receiving insight-oriented treatment was significantly better off than the untreated group $(p = .0435)$. However, at one-month follow-up and six-month follow-up, there was no significant difference between the group receiving insight-oriented treatment and the untreated group. Out of eight couples treated with insight-oriented therapy, at one-month follow-up, two were separated, three remained together but showed no improvement, and three showed improvement. This represented a deterioration from results obtained immediately posttherapy.

It is interesting to speculate that the strength exhibited at posttherapy by the insight-oriented approach used in the Boelens et al. (1980) study was due to its being more structured and directive than the insight-oriented approach used by Crowe (1978). Certainly, it appears that clear messages were given regarding which marital behaviors were considered helpful in producing marital satisfaction and which were not. However, no data were presented on therapist activity, and it is difficult to tell from the description presented how directive the therapists actually were in instigating change. More clearly discernible from these data is the deterioration of positive changes in the insight-oriented condition. This highlights the importance in future research of focusing on strategies to help couples maintain gains derived from insight-oriented approaches.

Epstein and Jackson (1978) conducted a controlled-outcome study which included an interaction insight group which might fairly be described as a behaviorally oriented insight group. Epstein and Jackson (1978) randomly assigned 16 couples (mean age not reported) to one of three conditions: (1) a communication group based on the work of Alberti and Emmons (1974), (2) an interaction insight group, or (3) a no-treatment waiting-list group. Subjects in the treatment group met for five sessions of one and one-half hour each over a three-week period. The communication treatment emphasized assertion training and clear communication. The insight treatment involved instruction in the observation of verbal and nonverbal messages that exacerbate conflict. The major goal was to increase each subject's awareness of the impact of his/her behavior on the spouse's feelings and behavior. However, in the insight condition, directive interventions regarding alternative behaviors were kept to a minimum.

An analysis of variance on the pretest scores showed no difference between groups. Dependent measures used were ratings of communication by trained raters on 11 categories of verbal behavior (no reference given) and three scales from the Barrett-Lennard relationship inventory (Barrett-Lennard, 1962) yielding scale scores for degree of empathy, congruence, and unconditional positive regard generally received from the spouse. For our present purposes, we will focus on the planned t-test comparisons between the insight group and the control group.

Of the 11 coding categories, only one (disagreement) showed a significant change for the insight group relative to the control group. None of the three scales derived from the Barrett-Lennard showed a significant change for the insight group relative to the control group. Since 1 of 14 variables showing a significant change is not different from a result which could be anticipated on the basis of chance variability, behaviorally oriented insight therapy was not demonstrated to be an effective treatment of marital distress.

The Crowe (1978) and the Epstein and Jackson (1978) studies both investigated the impact of awareness alone on marital difficulties. Unfortunately, neither represents insight-oriented marital therapy as it is commonly described by prominent writers in the field (such as Skynner, Sager, and Gurman). In both cases, insight was used without any directive techniques being used. Accordingly, these two studies suggest that insight alone is not a valuable approach to marital therapy in the absence of a clearly specified direction of desirable change. On the other hand, the Boelens et al. (1980) study suggests that when a direction of desirable change is clearly specified, insight-oriented approaches can be effective in helping couples change. However, future tests of insight-oriented marital therapies may do well to focus on how to maintain these gains. An alternative avenue of research would be to integrate the use of insight-oriented strategies with the use of directive approaches to which we now turn.

CONTRACTING APPROACHES

Perhaps the simplest of the directive interventions is the contracting approach for increasing positive behavior. The origins of this approach can be traced to the work of Stuart (1969), Liberman (1970), Azrin, Naster, and Jones (1973), Patterson and Hops (1972), and Weiss, Hops, and Patterson (1973). In this approach, couples are seen as suffering from a low rate of exchange of reinforcers. The goal of therapy is to increase the frequency of behaviors the spouses desire in one another. Typically, therapists help spouses construct written behavior change agreements.

Often the contracting approach is combined with other approaches. However, it has been tested three times alone in the context of a controlled-outcome study. The first study of this type was the Crowe (1978) study discussed earlier. Crowe (1978) found that contracting was effective on a number of outcome measures relative to a control group. On the 16-item self-report measure of marital adjustment used, couples in the contracting approach were significantly less maritally distressed than couples in the control group at 9 months and 18 months following therapy. On sexual adjustment, the contracting group was significantly superior to the control group at posttreatment, at 9-month follow-up, and at 18-month follow-up. On general individual adjustment, the contracting approach was significantly superior to the control group at posttreatment assessment and nine-month follow-up. Similarly, the interpersonal and the intrapersonal target problems selected for therapy each showed significantly greater improvement for the contracting than for the control group at posttreatment and at nine-month follow-up. Thus, out of 20 opportunities to differ from the control condition following therapy, the contracting group differed 11 times in the direction of being superior and no times in the direction of being inferior. In the absence of an omnibus, multivariate F, submitting these differences to a sign test indicates the superiority of the contracting condition.

Boelens et al. (1980) included a contracting-only condition in their study which was discussed earlier. Improvement was found for the treated groups relative to the control group on all self-report measures of the marital relationship and on positive verbal behavior as judged by an observer using the MICS. No significant difference between treated and untreated couples was found for level of marital functioning as rated by an independent assessor, nor was any effect found on rate of negative verbal behavior using the MICS. Change was also rated in terms of overall improvement for each couple. Improvement was defined in terms of the amount of change on target problem scores. Changes of 25 percent or more were counted as improved, while changes of less than 25 percent were counted as unimproved. Using this scheme, it is possible to separately contrast the group receiving training in contracting with the control group at posttherapy, one-month follow-up, and six-month follow-up. Although not conducted by the authors, using the Fisher exact-probability test, it is possible to determine the superiority of contracting to no treatment at each point in time with $p = .0435$, $p = .0046$, $p = .0046$ at post, one month, and six month respectively. Thus, contracting proved superior to no treatment and maintained this superiority over time.

A more recent investigation of the use of contracting in marital therapy in the context of a controlled-outcome study was performed by Baucom (1982). Baucom randomly assigned 72 maritally distressed couples (mean age 32) to one of four treatment conditions: *(a)* quid pro quo contracting only, *(b)* communication training plus contracting, *(c)* communication training only, or *(d)* wait-list control. Outcome was assessed using trained observer ratings of positive and negative behavior (MICS) (Marital Studies Center, 1975) and two self-report inventories of global marital satisfaction: (1) areas of change (Weiss et al., 1973) and (2) Locke-Wallace marital adjustment scale (Locke & Wallace, 1959). Comparisons of the contracting-only condition to the wait-list control group showed that contracting was superior at posttreatment on both self-report measures and on negative behavior as coded by the trained raters. Thus, contracting alone was superior to no treatment on three or four measures used. No significant changes in any of the measures were found from posttherapy to 3-month follow-up, indicating maintenance of treatment effects. These results indicate that the contracting was effective in helping alleviate marital distress.

Thus, all three tests of the contracting approach demonstrate its superiority to control conditions. In addition, the three trials complement each other nicely in that one assesses the impact of treatment on the individual as well as the couple and two use both trained raters and self-report to assess the impact of treatment on marital behavior and satisfaction. Overall then, the available evidence suggests that contracting approaches used alone can be effective in alleviating marital difficulties.

CONTRACTING WITH COMMUNICATION TRAINING

Contracting has been coupled with problem-solving communication training in a number of studies. In many ways, contracting would appear to require certain problem-solving skills, such as carefully defining what is wanted. Indeed, in some therapy programs, communication training is a precursor to actual contracting (Weiss et al., 1973). The earliest study to evaluate the effectiveness of a combination of problem solving and contracting as a marital intervention in the context of a controlled-outcome study was done by Jacobson (1977). Jacobson (1977) randomly assigned 10 married couples (mean age 31) to either a problem-solving and contingency contracting approach or a minimal contact/wait-list control group. Outcome was assessed using trained raters' observations of positive and negative verbal behavior (MICS) (Hops et al., 1972) and a self-report inventory of marital satisfaction (Locke-Wallace marital adjustment scale). Univariate t-tests at posttest revealed significant differences on both positive and negative couple interactions and for self-report of marital satisfaction. In all cases, the couples receiving communication and contracting training performed better than the control group. Thus, all three outcome measures showed the superiority of contracting with communication training to no treatment. At one-year follow-up, couples were asked to complete self-report marital inventories. Gains on global marital adjustment were maintained at this time.

In a subsequent study, Jacobson (1978) assessed two different types of problem-solving/contracting aproaches to marital therapy. Jacobson randomly assigned 32 couples (mean age 32) to one of four conditions: (1) problem solving and good-faith contracts, (2) problem solving and quid pro quo contracts, (3) a wait-list control, or (4) a placebo control group. Outcome was assessed using trained observers' ratings of positive, negative, and neutral verbal behavior (MICS) (Hops, Wills, Patterson, & Weiss, 1971), as well as through two self-report indexes of global marital adjustment (the Locke-Wallace, and Stuart and Stuart's (1973) marital happiness scale. Both of the problem-solving/contracting groups showed significant pre-post change in rate of negative verbal behavior and performed significantly better than wait-list controls at posttest. Similarly, both treatment groups showed significant pre-post changes in rate of positive verbal behavior and performed significantly better than wait-list controls at posttest. The two self-report inventories also showed both treatment groups improving significantly and performing significantly better than the wait-list control at postassessment. Thus, both approaches to problem-solving/contracting therapy demonstrated their effectiveness relative to no treatment on all four outcome measures used. Couples were assessed on the Locke-Wallace at one-year follow-up. Gains in global marital adjustment were maintained at this assessment.

Turkewitz and O'Leary (1981) randomly assigned 30 couples (mean age 35.4 years) to one of three conditions: (1) a problem-solving/contracting condition, (2) a problem-solving/supportive-communication training condition, or (3) a wait-list control. Outcome measures used included the MAT, the primary communication inventory (PCI) (Navran, 1967), the positive feeling questionnaire (PFQ) (O'Leary, Fincham, & Turkewitz, 1983), individual ratings of change, and behavioral ratings of communication behavior by trained raters (no reference given). Change scores on the three primary self-report inventories (MAT, PCI, PFQ) were highly intercorrelated. A multivariate analysis of variance simultaneously considering the MAT, PCI, and PFQ found significant differences between groups, with the two treated groups performing better than the wait-list control group. Taken as a group, the standardized self-report measures of change differentiated the treated from the untreated groups although, due to the large variability in response to treatment, two of these measures (MAT, PFQ) did not differentiate treated and untreated groups when considered alone. Treated couples also performed significantly better than untreated couples on ratings of positive change regarding their most important presenting marital problems. Finally, observational measures failed to show change as a function of therapy. Analyses of maintenance data indicated that gains were maintained at four-month follow-up. No significant differences between the two groups were found.

The Turkewitz and O'Leary (1981) sample included a wide range of ages (from 25 to 61). Accordingly, their finding that age was a predictor of success in therapy $(r = -.76$ to $-.52)$ and moderated the effect of two therapy conditions is especially interesting. T-tests revealed that on the MAT, the young couples (mean age 29.4) in the problem-solving/contracting condition did better than the young control group. The Mann-Whitney U test, used because of heterogeneity of variances in the older sample, revealed that the older couples (mean age 40.9) in the problem-solving/contracting condition did not change significantly more on the MAT than the older control group. This pattern of results was replicated for the PCI.

In a study by Hahlweg, Revenstorf, and Schindler (1982), 85 couples (mean age 33.7 years) were randomly assigned to one of five conditions: (1) problem-solving/contracting, (2) supportive-communication training, (3) problem-solving/contractting in a group format, (4) supportive-communication training in a group format, or (5) a wait-list control group. All couples were between the ages of 25 and 40. Outcome measures included the partnership questionnaire (Halweg, 1979), the conflict score (Hahlweg, Kraemer, Schindler, & Revenstorf, 1980), a five-point rating scale of happiness in the marriage, and a behavioral rating of positive and negative communication behaviors using trained raters (MICS) (Hops et al., 1972).

Although specific contrasts were not reported, it is possible to reconstruct them from the information provided. Since there were no significant differences between groups at pretherapy assessment, we will present the results of t-tests conducted by us on the differences between posttherapy and postwait scores. With the exception of the quarreling subscale of the partnership questionnaire, all comparisons between the problem-solving/contracting groups and the wait-list control group were significant. More specifically, both problem-solving/contracting groups showed significantly higher scores at posttherapy than the control group showed at postwait on the tenderness and communication subscales of the partnership questionnaire, on the conflict score, on the single-item general happiness score, and on positive communication behavior rated by trained observers. Both groups also showed significantly less negative communication behavior as rated by trained observers. The quarreling subscale scores were significantly lower for the couples in the problem-solving/contracting condition who received therapy in the group format than for couples in the wait-list control group, but missed significance for those in the couple format. Thus, out of 14 possible comparisons, the two problem-solving/contracting groups performed better than the wait-list control group on 13 occasions.

In the Baucom (1982) study discussed earlier, comparisons of the problem-solving/contracting condition with the waiting-list condition indicated that the therapy group was superior on all four dependent measures following therapy. That is, couples in the contracting/communication-training condition showed significantly greater gains in positive communication behavior as rated by trained observers, significantly greater reductions in negative communication behavior as rated by trained observers, and significantly more improvement on global marital satisfaction as measured by the areas of change questionnaire and the Locke-Wallace MAT. Follow-up data for the 13 of 17 couples who returned forms indicated no significant loss of gains from posttest to three-month follow-up. Thus, Baucom (1982) found contracting with communication training to be clearly superior to no treatment.

In a subsequent study, Melman, Baucom, and Anderson (1983) assigned 30 couples (mean age 35 years) to one of six treatment conditions (a) immediate treatment by Therapist A, (b) immediate treatment by Therapist B (the 10 couples who received immediate treatment by a single therapist also had their data included in the Baucom, 1982, report), (c) immediate treatment by Therapists A and B as a cotherapy team, (d) delayed treatment by Therapist A, (e) delayed treatment by Therapist B, and (f) delayed treatment by the cotherapy team. Treatment for all couples consisted of contracting and communication training. Outcome was assessed by the same measures used in Baucom's (1982) study. No differences were found on the immediate treatment versus delayed treatment comparison or the single therapist versus cotherapy team comparison. However, it was found that treated couples improved more than couples in the wait-list control group on the areas of change questionnaire, the Locke-Wallace marital adjustment test, and on the frequency of negative communication behavior as rated by trained observers. Frequency of positive communication behavior did not change differentially for the treated and wait-list control group. Thus, three of four measures showed the superiority of the contracting and communication-training group to the control group.

Contracting in conjunction with communication training has shown its effectiveness as a treatment package in a number of trials. Contracting with communication training has been found to be effective when the effect is measured from the perspective of trained observers and when rated by the spouses themselves. It has been found to be effective across a number of areas of marriage and across a number of facets of the marital relationship. There is also some evidence that this approach might be more effective with younger couples than with older couples, although this finding needs to be replicated.

COMMUNICATION MARITAL THERAPY

Between marital therapists across many different schools of therapy, there is a high level of agreement that effective communication is critically important for a well-functioning marriage. A randomly sampled group of marital therapists (Geiss & O'Leary, 1981) rated poor communication as the most frequent and destructive problem presented by couples entering therapy. Not surprisingly then, various programs have developed for treating communication problems. The programs which have been the focus of controlled-outcome studies can roughly be characterized either as (1) nonbehavioral programs which focus on training couples in the listening skills Rogerian client-centered therapy has emphasized as important for therapists, or (2) behavioral communication-training programs which have emphasized training couples in problem-solving communication strategies. Although derived from different traditions, the two approaches overlap in practice, and they target conceptually overlapping behaviors for change. Accordingly, we will review them together in this section.

The earliest controlled-outcome study assessing the impact of communication training on marital difficulties was performed by Hickman and Baldwin (1971). They randomly assigned 30 couples (mean age not reported), who had been referred to the conciliation court, to one of three conditions: (1) communication training in a couples format, (2) communication training using a programmed text format, or (3) a wait-list control group. Outcome was assessed using a semantic differential measure (no reference given) and by comparing the number of spouses in each group willing to sign reconciliation agreements. It was found that communication training in a couples format produced significantly more reconciliation agreements than the wait list and that couples in this condition also improved significantly more on the semantic differential measure than did the wait-list control group. Thus, communication training in the couple format demonstrated effectiveness on both outcome measures used. Interestingly, communication training in the programmed text format did not produce significantly better results than the wait-list control group on either measure.

Ely, Guerney, and Stover (1973) assigned 23 couples randomly to one of two conditions: (1) a communication-training condition, or (2) a wait-list control group. The mean age of the couples was 32.6 years. Outcome was assessed using: the primary communication inventory (Navran, 1967); trained observers' ratings of two categories of communication behavior during role-play conditions (no reference given), *(a)* feeling expression and *(b)* feeling clarification; and trained observers' ratings of feeling expression and feeling clarification in response to the situations presented in the Ely feeling questionnaire (no reference given) under two sets of instructions, *(a)* What would you say if you were in this situation? and *(b)* What should you say in this situation? In addition, each couple was assessed using the conjugal life questionnaire, a global self-report measure of marital harmony. In all, eight outcome measures were generated.

Comparisons of the group receiving treatment with the wait-list control were made using analysis of covariance, with the pretreatment scores as the covariate. It was found that couples in treatment increased their communication skills significantly as measured by the observational measures and by the PCI. However, the treated couples did not change significantly more than the control group on the global measure of marital satisfaction. Unfortunately, since no reference is given for the measure of global change used, it is difficult to tell whether the failure to find significant differences as a result of therapy represents a failure of the treatment to have an impact on couples' satisfaction, or a failure of an unvalidated measure to be responsive to such change. However, communication therapy did demonstrate significantly greater gains than the wait-list group on six of the eight outcome measures used in this study, indicating its superiority to no treatment.

In the study described earlier by Epstein and Jackson (1978), one of the conditions included was a communication-training condition which emphasized the ability to communicate in a precise, clear, and assertive manner. Of the 11 communication categories rated by trained observers, there were significant improvements for the communication group relative to the control group on frequency of three categories: assertive requests, rate of disagreement, and rate of attacks. While there were trends $(p < .10)$ toward decreases in the use of self-justification and trends toward an increase in the use of requests for feedback, these results did not reach traditionally accepted levels of significance. In addition to the changes on observational measures of communication behavior, there were also significant changes on spouse-perceived empathy in the communication group relative to the control group. Thus, the communication group improved on 4 of 14 possible comparisons, which provides only moderate evidence of treatment efficacy.

Hahlweg et al. (1982), whose study was discussed earlier in the communication/contracting section, also included two communication-training conditions in their study. Both communication-training conditions emphasized stating feelings in a clear, direct, and open way without accusing or blaming the spouse, active listening, and appropriate metacommunication for clarifying ambiguous statements. The two conditions differed in that one was a group format while the other was a couple format. Analyses of covariance indicated significant differences between groups on all measures except the observational ratings of positive communication behavior. The couple format condition produced significant changes across all the measures used except the ratings of positive communication behavior. The group format failed to produce changes on a number of measures including the quarreling, tenderness, and communication subscales of the partnership questionnaire, the conflict score, and the general happiness question. Indeed, the group format produced significant change relative to the control group only on the observational measure of negative communication behavior.

Hahlweg et al. (1982) report follow-up analyses. However, these analyses combine the data for the group format and the couple format. In light of the differences between the two groups which were manifest at posttherapy, the conclusions drawn from this follow-up analysis are highly questionable. Hahlweg et al. report that couples in communication therapy returned to pretreatment levels on the subscales of the partnership questionnaire. However, since couples in the group format condition never showed significant change in therapy on these scales, their presence in the follow-up analyses may be masking the performance of the couple format condition. Lack of maintenance would only be interesting if demonstrated for the couple format condition when analyzed separately. Since the data required for this analysis are not provided, we limit our conclusions to the effect of communication therapy at posttherapy assessment. Thus, while communication training in a couple format produced changes on 6 of 7 possible comparisons posttherapy, lending strong support to its efficacy as a marital intervention, communication training in a group format produced change on only 1 of 7 possible comparisons, which must be considered as particularly weak evidence of effectiveness.

The Turkewitz and O'Leary (1981) study discussed earlier included a communication-training–only group. A multivariate analysis of variance considering the MAT, PCI, and PFQ (the three major marital inventories used) found a significant effect of treatment condition, indicating the superiority of treatment to no treatment. Age was found to have a strong effect on response to treatment. Older couples (mean age = 40.9) improved significantly more than did couples in the older control group on the Locke-Wallace marital adjustment test as well as on the primary communication inventory. Younger couples (mean age = 29.4) did not show more improvement on these measures than the younger control group. Thus, Turkewitz and O'Leary (1981) found support for the effectiveness of communication therapy alone, but found that this effect was moderated by the age of the couple. It is important to note that Turkewitz and O'Leary (1981) did not find any significant changes on their observational measure of communication behavior. Unfortunately, the scoring system used was poorly validated, rendering the null result particularly difficult to interpret in light of the significant effects obtained on other measures.

The Baucom (1982) study discussed earlier included a communication-training–only condition. Couples in this group received training in problem-solving skills including stating problems clearly, discussing possible alternatives, and coming to an agreement on a mutually acceptable solution. In addition, couples were taught to avoid using guilt and to avoid becoming sidetracked. It was found that the communication training was superior to the wait-list control group on all dependent measures except positive communication behavior rated by trained observers. That is, self-report of problems, overall marital satisfaction, and trained observers' ratings of negative communication behavior all showed significant improvements relative to the control group. Thus, Baucom (1982) found strong support for the efficacy of communication training alone in the treatment of marital distress.

Trials of the communication-training approach have resulted in some evidence that it is an effective treatment approach. Some studies have shown that couples' communication patterns change both as measured by trained raters and as measured by the spouses' reports. In addition, most studies have shown an impact of communication training on the couples' marital satisfaction. However, several studies in this section presented serious problems in interpretation: The Hickman and Baldwin (1971) study used no standardized measures; the Ely et al. (1973) study found no effect of treatment on their criterion measure of marital satisfaction, but as no references were given for validation work, this finding is difficult to interpret; the Epstein and Jackson (1978) study found changes on only 4 of 14 disparate change measures (note that 11 of these are observer ratings of communication behavior on a measure for which no validation work is reported); and the Turkewitz and O'Leary (1981) study found change on their standardized measures of marital satisfaction and communication, but no change on their nonstandardized observational measure of communication behavior. Perhaps the most-important lesson to be learned from these studies is that poorly standardized or poorly validated measures are unlikely to show change, and do more to confuse than to clarify the interpretation of one's results.

In a more substantive vein, it is interesting to note that the studies of group approaches (i.e., Ely et al., 1973; Epstein & Jackson, 1978; and the group condition in Hahlweg et al., 1982) all showed relatively weak outcomes relative to the control group, while the couples format approaches (i.e., Baucom, 1982; Hahlweg et al., 1982; Hickman & Baldwin, 1971; Turkewitz & O'Leary, 1981) tended to make stronger showings. It is particularly tempting to conclude that the couple format is superior to the group format for communication training in light of Hahlweg et al.'s (1982) direct comparison which found the couple format superior. However, this hypothesis is not established by one study only and bears further scrutiny.

EVALUATION OF THE FINDINGS: METHODOLOGICAL CONSIDERATIONS

Although all the studies reviewed in this chapter have met minimal criteria of internal validity sufficiently well to allow them to be a part of the empirical justification of the practice of marital therapy, they vary in their methodological adequacy on other counts. (For a complete discussion of methodological errors in marital outcome research, see O'Leary & Turkewitz, 1978.) We will review these methodological considerations and explore their potential ramifications in this section.

Small sample size. "Obtaining significant results with a small sample may be a compelling testimony to treatment effects, since small n's decrease power or the ability to detect treatment differences. However, the smaller the sample, the greater the probability of sampling error and artifacts that would limit the generalizability of the results" (O'Leary & Turkewitz, 1978). In addition, with small samples, negative results become almost impossible to interpret.

Certainly this consideration looms large as we examine several of the studies under review here. For both the Epstein and Jackson (1978) study and the Jacobson (1977) study, the number of couples in each cell was five. Because of the low power associated with this sample size, it is particularly difficult to interpret the null results obtained for the insight-oriented therapy (Epstein & Jackson) with any confidence. We are left wondering if a slightly larger number of couples in each treatment condition would have provided sufficient power to produce significant differences between the behavioral interaction, insight-oriented therapy, and the control condition. It is not a foregone conclusion that a larger n would have made this difference, but at the same time, the possibility can not be entirely discounted.

On the other hand, a small sample can also raise some questions even when significant differences are found, as in the Jacobson (1977) report. Some statistical tests are prone to a higher rate of false positives under the condition of small n's. This concern must be raised regarding Jacobson's (1977) use of the Hoetelling T^2 statistic to test the difference between the treatment group and the control group on his two observational measures of communication. This seemingly paradoxical concern is raised by the fact that the Hoetelling T^2 statistic has a substantially inflated Type 1 error rate when the degrees of freedom for the error term are less than $10 \times n$ dependent variables $\times$ degrees of freedom in hypothesis (Olson, 1976). Accordingly, because of his small sample size, Jacobson (1977) could have rejected the null hypothesis of no difference between conditions at a nominal .05 probability level when, in fact, his true Type 1 error rate was well above this. Fortunately, Jacobson (1978) quickly provided a replication of his previous results with a larger sample, showing that the observed changes in both positive and negative communication behavior need not be interpreted as artifactual results of the small sample size.

Although not suffering initially from overly small cell size, the Turkewitz and O'Leary (1981) study should be mentioned here also because of their decision to split their groups into older and younger couple subsamples. This decision left them with only 5 couples in each of four groups and 10 couples in their control group. While they report significant results using acceptable statistical procedures, the need is obvious for replication with a larger sample of the observed moderating effect of age. In addition, the decision to split groups according to age was post hoc and so may have capitalized on chance effects.

YAVIS samples. Hahlweg et al. (1982) actively restricted their sample to persons below the age of 40, and there is a tendency in the studies reviewed for the subjects to be young. Whether or not they are also attractive, intelligent, and successful (i.e., YAVIS) (Williams, 1956) is difficult to ascertain from the reported demographics. However, given the potential moderating effects of these variables (e.g., Turkewitz & O'Leary, 1981), samples should be selected to include a wide age range or else conclusions should be restricted to the particular age group involved in the study.

Unspecified subject characteristics. Most although not all the studies reviewed here specified the method of subject recruitment, inclusion and exclusion criteria, age, and number of years married. More sporadically reported were number of children, educational level, length of distress, and specific problem areas. No study except for Turkewitz and O'Leary (1981) reported on the variables of previous therapy experience and previous marriage. Particularly noteworthy for poor performance in this area was the Hickman and Baldwin (1971) study, in which it was reported only that there was "variability on demographic measures." Specification of these variables is important so that other researchers can attempt replications of the research and practicing clinicians can judge if the treatment program described is likely to have similar effects for the population with whom they are working.

Small therapist samples. "A minimum of three-four therapists per experimental condition is strongly advised" (O'Leary & Turkewitz, 1978). The studies we have reviewed vary widely with regard to the number of therapists used (from one to six). This issue is important due to its impact on the likely generalizability of the results. Of more importance, perhaps, is the extent to which therapist characteristics are reported. For example, while no study reviewed here reported on the marital status of the therapists, most studies provided at least some information regarding therapists' training, educational and professional background, sex, age, and previous experience. This type of information is important both for future replication of the findings and to give some guidelines to practicing clinicians about the potentially necessary prerequisites to conducting the therapy.

Multiple outcome criteria. The inclusion of well-validated measures which assess change through different methods represents an important step toward better understanding of the effects of marital therapy programs. When this step is taken, as when communication change is measured through both self-report and observational measures, the converging evidence of effectiveness across measurement methods increases our confidence that the changes detected by both measures are assessing the variables intended (see Campbell & Fiske, 1959). While all studies reviewed here included more than one measure of change, not all used multiple methods of assessment, nor did all use well-validated and standardized measures. For example, Hickman and Baldwin (1971) included a semantic differential measure as their only measure of marital satisfaction despite the measure's lack of associated validity data. Ely et al. (1973) used the conjugal life questionnaire as their only global measure of marital satisfaction although no validity work is referenced. Turkewitz and O'Leary (1981) used a poorly validated observational measure of communication behavior. This lack of associated validity data becomes a particular problem when changes on the measure are nonsignificant, as they were in the latter two cases, but it presents serious problems for comparison across studies even when the findings are positive.

Comprehensive assessment. While the issue of providing for a comprehensive assessment must be faced in any outcome study, it should be recognized that the measurement issues faced by the marital outcome researcher are particularly complex. Marital therapy outcome is inherently composed of three relatively distinct outcomes: the outcome for the husband, the outcome for the wife, and the outcome for the relationship. Assessment of each of these outcomes may provide information which is clinically important and distinct from the information provided by assessments of the other two outcomes. For example, a therapy which typically increases husbands' satisfaction but not wives' would be interestingly different than a therapy which typically increases the satisfaction of the spouse who is initially less satisfied. In turn, such a therapy would be interestingly different from a therapy which typically increases the satisfaction of both spouses. Nevertheless, these possibilities would be indistinguishable for the most part in the outcome studies reviewed here, because all the studies focused on the combined data of both spouses in conducting their analyses. Of course, the investigator who decides to examine changes for each member of the couple and for the couple as a unit is faced with a statistical problem of analyses which are somewhat redundant. For an excellent discussion of these issues and some possible solutions, the reader is referred to Baucom (in press).

Of the studies reviewed here, only Crowe (1978) and Turkewitz and O'Leary (1981) made an attempt to investigate the impact of therapy on the individual well-being of spouses. Interestingly, however, both Crowe and Turkewitz and O'Leary found some positive effects of marital therapy on individual functioning. This finding suggests that further assessment of the effects of marital therapy on "individual" problems is promising.

Finally, completing the complexity of ensuring that a comprehensive assessment of marital outcome has been accomplished, it must be noted that marital quality is only conceptualized with difficulty as a single, undifferentiated construct. Indeed, Spanier (1976) proposes that four distinct facets of marital adjustment are tapped by his measure (the dyadic adjustment scale), while factor analysis of the Locke-Wallace suggests that it also taps multiple dimensions of marital satisfaction (Kimmel & Van der Veen, 1974). In addition, marital adjustment/happiness is not the only variable of intrinsic interest to the clinician attempting to increase marital quality. Given the high rates of divorce found in our society as a whole—now over 1 million per year (Spanier & Glick, 1981)—and the finding that over 50 percent of couples completing marital therapy may be divorced at long-term follow-up (Cookerly, 1980), long-term marital stability and commitment to marriage deserve increased attention as variables of importance in marital outcome research. In addition, while we may agree that increased marital happiness is an appropriate goal for marital therapy, we certainly cannot agree that increases on this variable constitute the sine qua non of successful marital therapy. Accordingly, we propose that the discussion of marital health and the properties which constitute marital quality receive serious attention.

Treatment specification. Failure to specify the therapeutic procedures used and the training received by therapists represents a serious obstacle to the replication of the treatment in future research or by therapists interested in using methods of proven value. Indeed, a treatment which cannot be described and disseminated to others is of little value to the field of marital therapy even if the author of the treatment can show that he/she can make it effective. Accordingly, for any therapy which is past the preliminary stages of outcome work, it becomes increasingly important to specify the treatment in detailed manuals. Useful in this regard are general guidelines and principles as well as more-detailed descriptions of techniques and their appropriate application. Ideally these manuals should be available on request from the author of the study or some equally accessible source. Of course, an initial outcome study of a previously untested therapy may be of interest even in the absence of a detailed treatment manual because of the potential it suggests for a powerful new technology. However, development of a treatment manual should receive high priority thereafter.

Measurement of the independent variable.   For approaches which have received substantial empirical support, it becomes more important to examine the assumptions which guide the treatment and to scrutinize the evidence upon which they are based. We suggest that outcome studies on these therapies assess two levels of the independent variable: (1) the extent to which therapists actually implemented the procedures described in the therapy manual, and (2) the extent to which the targeted mediating goals (Parloff, 1976) for the couple were attained. Of the studies reviewed here, several assessed both (Crowe, 1978; Jacobson, 1978; Turkewitz & O'Leary, 1981). However, both Jacobson and Turkewitz and O'Leary found that they had difficulty differentiating the treatment groups on the measures of therapist activity they used. While Crowe was able to differentiate his groups, the measure he used was a global judgment by a rater on the basis of therapy tapes rather than a detailed coding of the activities therapists engaged in. Consequently, the measure does not give us much information about exactly what the therapists were doing in each condition. Because demonstrating that therapists are engaging in the behaviors described in the manual is important for confidence that the manual can be used effectively in other settings, this lack of useful measures for documenting relevant therapist behavior deserves considerable attention in the marital therapy area, and development of these measures deserves high priority. Once developed, measures of the therapist outcome would be invaluable in helping train new therapists as well as in assuring quality control in therapy settings.

INAPPROPRIATENESS OF PLACEBO GROUPS IN MARITAL THERAPY

Placebo groups involving the use of substances that are chemically inactive for the condition being treated have enjoyed a highly esteemed role in psychopharmacological research. Unfortunately, the placebo model was borrowed by researchers evaluating psychological treatments, and placebo groups were held by some to be necessary to any adequate test of the efficacy of psychological therapies. Placebo groups in long-term psychological treatment research are ethically inappropriate and conceptually inadequate (O'Leary & Borkovec, 1978). More specifically, it seems ethically indefensible to apply some procedure which theoretically seems unrelated to the target problem, in this case marital discord. Marital problems, unlike many developmental problems such as fears in children or adult problems such as anxiety, do not characteristically improve without treatment over a four-six month period. Just as important, it is impossible to devise a treatment with which experienced therapists feel comfortable that has no theoretical likelihood of aiding the clients in ameliorating their problems.

In brief, it is impossible to devise a good "psychologically inert" treatment for marital problems that can be used comfortably by therapists and that is credible to clients. Consequently, we suggest that the concept be dropped from use in marital therapy outcome research.

An alternative to placebo groups: TOD

One reason for the popularity of placebo treatments in psychotherapy outcome research is that they involve the client couple immediately in some type of therapeutic activity. This could reasonably be expected to lower the likelihood that couples will refuse random assignment to condition, drop out of the research project after assignment to condition, or seek out other "helpers" in the community such as clergy, friend, or even other nonstudy mental health professionals. High rates of refusal to participate in the research may limit the generalizability of the results, especially if those couples with more-severe problems are the most likely to refuse to participate. Differential dropout rates between treated and untreated couples and high levels of uncontrolled, unreported interventions from other helpers in the community can introduce biases of unknown and unspecified proportions into the comparison of treatment with no treatment. While differential dropout from treated and untreated groups has not been a problem in the studies reviewed here, unreported contacts with community helpers represents a possible variable of some potential importance. Indeed, it has been cogently argued that no waiting-list group is a pure no-treatment group (Gurman & Kniskern, 1981).

To help deal with these difficulties, we would suggest that researchers consider using a treatment on demand (TOD) condition as a control group. In this condition, couples are told that while they are awaiting therapy, they may request therapeutic consultation. This consultation is presented as crisis intervention only and is limited in time and frequency of contact. This procedure has the advantage of allowing for recorded and specifiable amounts of contact between patients awaiting treatment and therapist. It also provides reassurance to more severely distressed couples that they are not to be left strictly "on their own" for the next three to four months. Finally, it reduces the likelihood that a transient crisis will cause a couple to drop out of the waiting-list control group and introduce a problem of "differential mortality." In addition, it is comparable to treatment at many clinics, where three-month waiting lists are not unheard of but some emergency coverage is typically offered. Accordingly, we see the inclusion of TOD conditions as potentially superior to both placebo and standard wait-list controls in terms of acceptability to client couples, ethical considerations, and methodological concerns.

ARE THERE CRITICAL DEPENDENT MEASURES?

This review provided an evaluation of marital therapy accepting the measures used by the investigators. No a priori judgments were made regarding the importance of the various measures, as the importance of one's dependent measures hinges upon one's theory or orientation to therapy. However, independent observations of the critical phenomena of interest have long been seen as critical in the evaluation of therapeutic effectiveness (Wolf, 1978). Interestingly, with marital problems and adult disorders or problems which are not easily observed by independent observers, it has become especially problematic to collect observational data of the phenomena in question. Unlike observations of children in schools and homes, which have been typically collected for many days during a baseline period (O'Leary, 1982), observations of marital interactions have been collected on one occasion, in a marital clinic (e.g., Baucom, 1982; Ely et al., 1973; Jacobsen, 1978; Turkewitz & O'Leary, 1982). It is interesting that independent observations of marital interactions have not been especially supportive of the efficacy of behavioral marital therapy. Turkewitz & O'Leary (1978) did not obtain changes in independent observations of marital therapy, but they did obtain significant improvements on self-reported changes during marital therapy. In addition, others such as Hahlweg et al. (1982) and Epstein and Jackson (1978) did not find evidence of consistent differences in their observational measures. It has become apparent that differences in therapy are much more difficult to detect with independent observations than they were with rating data and self-reports (O'Leary, 1982). Further, it has become apparent that behavioral observations are plagued with their own set of methodological problems and that sampling of many units of behavior across time is generally critical to such methodology (O'Leary, 1979, 1982). Interestingly, all of the studies of marital therapy have included only *one* observation of marital interaction. Methodological variations which may be attempted in future studies could include the use of voice-activated recorders in the home (Weiss & Margolin, 1977) to achieve less reactive measurement with a larger number of observations, and refinements of the coding scheme used (Jacobsen, Elwood, & Dallas, 1981). However, at this point, it would appear that behavioral observations are simply not developed well enough to allow reliable detection of differences resulting from treatment in a fashion that the codes can be used *and* analyzed readily by various research teams (see Snyder, 1981). Nevertheless, the observational coding system performing the best would appear to a modification of the MICS (Hops et al., 1972) in which categories are collapsed to produce positive and negative communication categories.

CONSUMER SATISFACTION MEASURES

One type of measure that is relatively independent of one's theory of marital discord and treatment is a consumer satisfaction evaluation. Some analytic theorists may believe that client reports are not to be highly regarded as useful barometers (Auerbach & Luborsky, 1968); but before the year 2000, consumer evaluations of mental health services are likely to be fairly routine. In fact, legislation now dictates the need for such evaluations (Bornstein & Rychtarik, 1983). Our own treatment evaluation in behavioral marital therapy and communication therapy indeed suggests that clients are satisfied with their therapists and their therapy program (Turkewitz & O'Leary, 1981). The clients' ratings of their therapists were very high: Using a 7-point scale, wives' ratings averaged 6.83 and the husbands' mean was 6.71 across the four personal characteristics of empathy, concern, likableness, and competence. Ninety percent of the clients indicated that they would recommend the treatment to a friend. Similarly, Hahlweg et al. (1982) found that clients highly evaluated both communication training and behavioral marital therapy. Approximately 91 percent of the clients saw the therapy as a "worthwhile experience," and 94 percent would recommend the treatment to a friend. (In both cases, there were no differences across treatment modalities.)

As has been indicated in a recent series in *Behavior Therapy* on consumer satisfaction such satisfaction ratings should be seen in a more-general framework of attitude formation and change. It is to be hoped that such a framework would be grounded in cognitive theory, and methodological issues not yet addressed in such research are important to note. In fact, as noted by Kiesler (1983), "The quality of the research literature on consumer satisfaction with behavior therapy is poor." More specifically, Kiesler argues that generally positive attitudes clients have about treatment before receiving any particular treatment must be separated from the client evaluation of treatment. Alternatively stated, Kiesler argues that preexisting attitudes about therapy should be covaried in order to attribute the remaining variance to the effect of the therapy per se. This argument by Kiesler certainly makes sense when the concern is why certain evaluations occur and when one is evaluating the impact of various therapies. Kiesler also cogently argues that variables that are theoretically irrelevant to the particular treatment under scrutiny deserve attention as potentially important in determining consumer satisfaction. For example, in marital therapy evaluations, it would be possible that clients would find therapists' comments about the normalcy of their problems comforting (e.g., "most of our patients or clients have serious communication problems"; "recent evidence indicates that about half of all married persons have affairs and cope with them in a fashion that does not seriously harm their marriage"). Accordingly, such comments could influence clients' ratings of therapist warmth or their own satisfaction with therapy. However such comments could be made by therapists of almost any theoretical persuasion. Accordingly, if one wishes to know why consumer evaluations change, it is important to relate such changes to various components of the therapeutic process.

In summary, consumer satisfaction evaluations are here to stay, and research on such measures has only begun. In an era of consumer power and accountability, it is wise that marital therapists enter the satisfaction area and take their self-scrutiny very seriously. The success or failure of marital therapy can often affect the lives of a family in very important ways, and if clients feel that they are not served well by their therapists, such information should be considered important.

CLINICAL VERSUS STATISTICAL SIGNIFICANCE

It is clear from our own research (Turkewitz & O'Leary, 1981; O'Leary & Arias, 1983) as well as that of others (see Jacobson, Follette, & Elwood, in press) in the field of marital therapy, that we often attain significant improvements in clients' evaluation of their marriage without leaving them with fully satisfying marriages. We find that, on the average, our clients move from an extremely dissatisfied rating of their marriage at pretherapy to a just-satisfactory rating of their marriage at posttherapy (O'Leary & Arias). This result is similar to that of our colleagues at Stony Brook in the sex therapy area with low-desire clients (Schover & LoPiccolo, 1982).

While it is clear that communication training and contracting approaches are associated with improvements in couples' evaluations of their marriages it is also clear that these treatments have not been shown to be so powerful that they regularly help unhappy couples become very happy with their marriage. We must be concerned with the issue of whether couples can care for, or love, each other after therapy, as well as change significantly in certain ratings of their marital satisfaction (O'Leary et al., 1983). We have only begun to understand who can be helped by marital therapy and who may need to consider alternatives to the marriage (e.g., separation or divorce). We must also seriously consider the comments often made by our clients at pretherapy assessment—namely, "I would like to remain in this marriage if my spouse changes, but I doubt whether he/she can change enough to make it worthwhile." We as therapists must admit that while we may want to help our clients change so that they could stay together, we may not always be able to do so.

EVALUATION OF THE FINDINGS: SUBSTANTIVE CONSIDERATIONS

The evidence reviewed here establishes that communication skills training and contingency contracting approaches taken alone or in combination can provide effective approaches to alleviating marital distress. Nondirective, insight-oriented approaches, whether of a behavioral or nonbehavioral variety, have not generated evidence of therapeutic utility. However, an insight-oriented approach which clearly specified the type of changes which would be desirable has proven more effective than no treatment in producing positive change (Boelens et al., 1980). This result suggests that further attention is warranted in investigating insight-oriented procedures, although satisfactory maintenance of gains remains to be demonstrated. While the evidence is not clear-cut, some results also speak to the issues of optimal format for therapy and moderators of the effectiveness of therapy. These are important applied issues speaking to the optimal delivery of marital therapy. The results reviewed here suggest that couple format marital therapy may be more effective than group format work and that older couples may do better with communication training while younger couples may do better with contracting approaches.

Some methodological shortcomings in the data base reviewed here constrain the generalizations which can legitimately be drawn. However, it is clear from the data available to us at the time of this review that couples *can* be trained in some types of marital skills and that therapies emphasizing the training of couples in these skills *do* improve couples' satisfaction. In particular, contracting and communication skills appear to be reasonable targets of intervention in marital therapy.

The success of some types of marital therapy in documenting their effectiveness in increasing marital satisfaction allows the field to address more-advanced issues. We believe that the field of marital therapy outcome research now needs to address four major issues:

1. Increased scope of assessment of marital quality.
2. Assessment of other areas of family functioning.
3. Increased specification of change models.
4. Aggressive testing of previously untested forms of marital therapy.

We now will consider each of these four issues.

Increased scope of assessment of marital quality. While available outcome research establishes some forms of marital therapy as effective in producing increases in marital happiness, there are other aspects of marital quality which have received no attention. It would be unfortunate if marital therapy outcome researchers allowed this state of affairs to continue. In a study of what aspects of marriage were considered important by community couples, Broderick (1981) found that a number of aspects of marital quality were considered as important as marital happiness. Six categories were rated as being in the extremely important range: trust and commitment, love, fidelity, understanding, honesty, and respect. Unfortunately, we have little way of knowing whether the therapies which have fared well in producing increases in marital happiness for distressed couples would also be able to produce increases in these other aspects of marital quality. Currently, it appears unwise to assume that all aspects of marital quality necessarily covary as a single factor. Factor analysis of the dyadic adjustment scale (Spanier, 1976) suggests that it is composed of several distinct factors: consensus, satisfaction, cohesion, and affective expression. Factor analysis of the marital adjustment test (Locke & Wallace, 1959) reveals two relatively distinct factors (Kimmel & Van der Veen, 1974). In addition, Broderick & O'Leary (1983), Beach & Broderick (1983), and Dean & Spanier (1974), found only moderate correlations between a measure of commitment to marriage and global marital adjustment according to the Locke-Wallace. Thus, commitment and marital satisfaction appear to be relatively distinct aspects of marital quality. Accordingly, converging evidence suggests that marital quality may not be a unitary construct and will not be accurately reflected by a single-outcome measure of marital happiness.

We suggest that attention be paid to developing psychometrically sound measures of a variety of aspects of marital quality. Such measures would allow increased precision and flexibility in our outcome assessments and stimulate the development of new techniques which have their primary impact on specific aspects of marital quality other than global marital happiness. Given the success marital therapists have had in improving marital happiness, advances in facilitating improvement in other areas of marital quality constitute a viable goal for the future. In addition, outcomes measures with increased specificity are likely to have increased sensitivity in detecting changes already being produced in therapy.

Assessment of other areas of family functioning.   While the effects of marital therapy on individual adjustment and satisfaction have been looked at occasionally (e.g., Crowe, 1978; Turkewitz & O'Leary, 1981), the effect of marital therapy on parental feelings toward children, on childrearing practices, and on the presence of child problems has been entirely overlooked. Nevertheless, some relationship between marital problems and childhood difficulties has been hypothesized to exist for the last several decades (e.g., Baruch & Wilcox, 1944). Currently, psychodynamic therapists, family systems therapists, and behavior therapists all emphasize marital distress as a determinant and/or maintainer of childhood problems. The avoidance of looking at the impact of marital therapy on the broader family context can be considered a residual symptom of the exclusively individual and intraindividual perspective from which the field of psychology is now moving away (L'Abate, 1983).

Recently, a body of empirical evidence has linked marital distress and childhood behavior problems (e.g., Emery and O'Leary, 1982; Johnson & Lobitz, 1974; Porter & O'Leary, 1980; Rutter, 1978). In light of this strong current of theory and research, it would be interesting to know if resolving marital disharmony can have a positive effect on children for at least some types of marriages. The available literature suggests that the negative effects of marital discord are likely to be strongest for families where there are stressors in addition to the marital discord, such as behavior problems in the child, severe job stress, or psychological problems of either parent. Also, the association between marital discord and childhood problems appears strongest for aggression in boys (see O'Leary & Emery, 1982). Accordingly, it would be interesting for outcome research to focus on the effect of marital therapy in couples who have aggressive boys.

Increased specification of change models. There are a number of models of change in marital therapy which suggest viable interventions. Change in patterns of communication (e.g., Guerney, 1977), change in patterns of cognition (e.g., Baucom, 1981; Epstein, Pretzer, & Fleming, 1982; Jacobson, in press), change in level of insight into the origins of one's problems (e.g., Skynner, 1969, 1978), change in marital contracts from unrealistic to realistic contracts (e.g., Sager, 1981), change in rate of behavior exchange (e.g., Azrin, Naster, & Jones, 1973; Stuart, 1969), and change in perceptual processes (e.g., Arias & O'Leary, 1981; Morrison & Bellack, 1981) have all been suggested as models which can explain the presence and alleviation of marital distress. In each case, it is hypothesized that changes in the variable(s) specified in the model should lead to changes in marital satisfaction.

The variables specified by each model may be considered potential "mediating goals of therapy" (Parloff, 1976). That is, the therapist may work directly to produce change in these variables because they are hypothesized to produce the desired changes in the marital relationship. Unfortunately, we know very little about the actual impact of changes in any of the potential "mediating goals of therapy" on changes in marital happiness or other aspects of marital quality. Even when change in a mediating goal has been assessed, as when communication skill has been evaluated, its ability to account for the observed changes in marital satisfaction has not been investigated.

For those therapies which have received some initial support for their claims to effectiveness, we believe it is time to explicate and test directly the models of marital change which guide the therapies. Gottman's (1979) discussion of empirical program development is instructive in this regard. There may be considerable variability in response to treatment. This variability could either be entirely consistent with the proposed change model or suggestive of the presence of other crucial factors which have been left out of the change model. Certainly, if the later possibility is suggested by the pattern of results, the researcher must begin to amend his/her model of change in therapy. By doing so, components may be added to the therapy or greater attention directed to unspecified aspects of the intervention process. On the other hand, if the variability is consistent with the proposed change model, then the researcher may more confidently focus on identifying those variables which influence attainment of the "mediating goals" specified by the model and work toward enhancing the power of the intervention by enhancing change on these mediating goals. Without careful assessment of the variables identified in one's change model, real progress in clarifying and amending the basic model that guides a particular therapy program is difficult to imagine.

A multiple correlational analytic strategy can be used to relate hypothesized mediating variables to outcome measures such as marital happiness or other aspects of marital quality. If most of the variance in outcome measures is accounted for by changes in the mediating variables, then the researcher is given a mandate to try new techniques aimed at enhancing effectiveness in producing changes on the hypothesized mediating variables. On the other hand, if most of the variance in outcome measures is unrelated to the proposed mediating variables, then the researcher is given a mandate to investigate other competing change models and potentially to come to a different understanding of the kinds of processes which need to be enhanced to increase the effectiveness of marital therapy. In either case, the researcher gains valuable information related to program enhancement.

Recently, researchers (e.g., Jacobson et al., in press) have begun to notice that a substantial minority of couples do not appear to be significantly aided by the same technology which is successful in aiding other client couples. One explanation for this result is that different change models may best account for successful change in therapy for the two groups. This possibility should be born in mind as researchers attempt the valuable goals of greater specification and testing of change models. If the group being examined is heterogeneous with regard to the change model which best accounts for their gains in therapy, any correlation between attainment of particular "mediating goals" and attainment of successful outcome of therapy will be diminished. To attain best results, researchers will wish to identify subgroups of the population of marital distressed couples who are likely to fit different change models. The extent to which this "differential diagnosis" is successful can then be directly examined by assessing the power of each model to account for observed changes. If the researcher has been successful, each model should account for most of the variance in successful outcome of therapy for one group of client couples but not the other(s). Problematic, uninformative results may be avoided if researchers pay attention to the presence of possible subtypes of marital distress. In addition, if diagnostic interviews are successful in identifying homogeneous subtypes of marital distress which are responsive to therapy according to different models of change, this will constitute a valuable advance in the field of marital therapy. Such an advance would make it possible to work on tailoring treatment to fit the particular subtype of marital distress presented. This fit would, in our view, represent a giant step toward differential diagnosis and differential treatment of subtypes of marital distress, by providing empirically tested guidelines for predicting which particular treatment technique(s) are likely to be most useful with which particular client couples.

We would suggest that the most useful approach to classifying couples is to carefully construct alternative models of marital distress and generate guidelines for their differential application to subgroups of the population of maritally distressed client couples. In order to be useful, these models would need to be explicit enough that they would fit only some subgroup of couples. To be a useful addition to clinical practice, each model must supply one or more variables which can be influenced through clinical activity and which are related to some specified desirable outcome (e.g., increased marital happiness). The variables and their hypothesized relationship to each other and to outcome constitute the change model and provide points of intervention for the clinician (see Beach, Abramson, & Levine, 1981). We would suggest that this approach to typologizing client couples has the advantages of increasing the clarity of the results we will obtain as we begin to scrutinize more closely the change models which guide our interventions and of staying close to treatment issues. Thus, we would recommend this approach as potentially increasing both the rigor and the relevance of future process/outcome work in marital therapy.

Aggressive testing of previously untested forms of marital therapy.   Most forms of marital therapy have not yet received outcome trials with adequate internal validity and appropriate external review. In part, this no doubt reflects the arduous nature of carrying out this type of research and seeing it through to completion. However, it may also reflect an inappropriate undervaluation of outcome research. Marital therapy is currently receiving ever broader acceptance in the general population, but this acceptance may be tarnished by excessive or unrealistic claims on the part of some practitioners, by unsubstantiated attacks by members of one orientation on the effectiveness of other orientations, or by a perception that marital therapy is not really scientifically based. Outcome research directly addresses each of these three major threats to the integrity of the field of marital therapy.

As a methodological stance, the emphasis on the documentation of therapeutic effectiveness directly undercuts any who would package their therapy as a panacea for all ills, while supporting documented claims of efficacy. The presence of data can also have a salutory effect on the tendency toward backbiting recriminations between members of differing orientations and provides a climate which is conducive to the borrowing and sharing of technologies between effective approaches. In addition, well-conducted experimental research reviewed by peers in the scientific community provides a scientific basis for the field of marital therapy which is inherently more stable and more trustworthy than competing claims based on personal experience. Currently, we feel there is a need for outcome work aimed at assessing promising intervention strategies such as cognitively oriented interventions, directive insight-oriented interventions, and interventions which focus on altering perceptual processes in the marital dyad.

CONCLUSION

Marital discord is a serious problem which only relatively recently has begun to receive the direct attention it deserves. While there are many studies of marital outcome which fail to meet standard criteria for internal validity or have never received external peer review, these studies are not well suited to provide answers to a basic question: Does receiving any form of marital therapy help alleviate marital distress? Studies which are internally valid and have received external peer review allow us to answer this question affirmatively. Nevertheless, the question is not as straightforward as it seems, and outcome research in the marital area should be considered as in its infancy. Future research efforts should continue adhering to methodological guidelines which allow for replication and dissemination of effective therapeutic approaches, but also should attend to certain broader substantive issues. Future marital outcome research should broaden the scope of assessment of marital quality to include more aspects of marital quality than can be inferred from measures of global marital adjustment. In addition, we would call for increased attention to the effects of marital therapy on other areas of family functioning, increased attention to specifying and directly testing the change model that guides a particular change program, and an aggressive policy of testing the broad array of exciting technologies which promise increases in flexibility and power to marital therapy intervention programs.

REFERENCES

Alberti, R. E., & Emmons, M. L. *Your perfect right* (2d ed.). San Luis Obispo, Calif.: Impact, 1974.

Auerbach, H. H., & Luborsky, L. Accuracy of judgments of the "good hour." In J. M. Shlein (Ed.), *Research in psychotherapy* (Vol. 3). Washington, D.C.: American Psychological Association, 1968.

Azrin, N. H., Naster, B. J., & Jones, R. Reciprocity counseling: A rapid learning based procedure for marital counseling. *Behavior Research and Therapy*, 1973, *11*, 365–382.

Barrett-Lennard, G. T. Dimensions of therapist response as causal factors in therapeutic change. *Psychological Monographs*, 1962, *76*(43, Whole No. 562).

Baruch, D. W., & Wilcox, J. A. A study of sex differences in preschool children's adjustment coexistent with interpersonal tensions. *Journal of Genetic Psychology*, 1944, *64*, 281–303.

Baucom, D. H. *Cognitive behavioral strategies in the treatment of marital discord.* Paper presented at the 15th annual convention of the Association for the Advancement of Behavior Therapy, Toronto, November 1981.

Baucom, D. H. A comparison of behavioral contracting and problem solving/communications training in behavioral marital therapy. *Behavior Therapy*, 1982, *13*, 162–174.

Baucom, D. H. Conceptual and psychometric issues in evaluating the effectiveness of behavioral marital therapy. In J. P. Vincent (Ed.), *Advances in family intervention, assessment and theory: A research annual* (Vol. 3). In press.

Beach, S. R. H., Abramson, L. Y., & Levine, F. M. Attributional reformulation of learned helplessness and depression: Therapeutic implications. In J. F. Clarkin & H. I. Glazer (Eds.), *Depression: Behavioral and directive intervention strategies.* New York: Garland, 1981.

Beach, S. R. H., & Broderick, J. E. Commitment: A variable in women's response to marital therapy. *American Journal of Family Therapy*, 1983, *11*, 16–24.

Beisser, A. R., & Glasser, N. The precipitating stress leading to psychiatric hospitalization. *Comprehensive Psychiatry*, 1968, *9*, 50–61.

Bloom, B. L., Asher, S. J., & White, S. W. Marital disruption as a stressor: A review and analysis. *Psychological Bulletin*, 1978, *85*, 867–894.

Boelens, W., Emmelkamp, P., MacGillavry, D., & Markvoort, M. A clinical evaluation of marital treatment: Reciprocity counseling versus system-theoretic counseling. *Behavioral Analysis and Modification*, 1980, *4* 85–96.

Bornstein, P. H., & Rychtarik, R. G. Consumer satisfaction in adult behavior therapy: Procedures, problems and future perspectives. *Behavior Therapy*, 1983, *14*, 191–208.

Broderick, J. E. A method for derivation of areas for assessment in marital relationships. *American Journal of Family Therapy*, 1981, *9*, 25–34.

Broderick, J. E., & O'Leary, K. D. *Contributions of behavior, affect, and attitudes to marital satisfaction.* Unpublished manuscript.

Campbell, D. T., & Fiske, D. W. Convergent and discriminant validation by the multitrait-multimethod matrix. *Psychological Bulletin*, 1959.

Campbell, D. T., & Stanley, J. C. *Experimental and quasi-experimental designs for research.* Chicago: Rand McNally, 1966.

Cookerly, J. R. Does marital therapy do any lasting good? *Journal of Marital and Family Therapy*, 1980, *6*, 393–397.

Crowe, M. J. Conjoint marital therapy: A controlled outcome study. *Psychological Medicine*, 1978, *8*, 623–636.

Dean, P. G., & Spanier, G. B. Commitment: An overlooked variable in marital adjustment? *Sociological Focus*, 1974, *1*, 113–118.

Ely, A. L., Guerney, B. G., & Stover, L. Efficacy of the training phase of conjugal therapy. *Psychotherapy: Theory, Research and Practice*, 1973, *10*, 201–207.

Emery, R. E., & O'Leary, K. D. Children's perceptions of marital discord and behavior of boys and girls. *Journal of Abnormal Child Psychology*, 1982, *10*, 11–24.

Epstein, N., & Jackson, E. An outcome study of short-term communication training with married couples. *Journal of Consulting and Clinical Psychology*, 1978, *46*, 207–212.

Epstein, N., Pretzer, J., & Fleming, B. *Cognitive therapy and communication training: Comparison of effects with distressed couples.* Paper presented at the annual meeting of the Association for the Advancement of Behavior Therapy, Los Angeles, November 1982.

Frenken, J. *Afkeer van Sexualiteit.* Deventer: Van Loghumd Slaterus, 1976.

Geiss, S. K., & O'Leary, K. D. Therapist ratings of frequency and severity of marital problems: Implications for research. *Journal of Marriage and Family Therapy*, 1981, *7*, 515–520.

Glass, G. V., & Kliegel, R. M. An apology for research integration in the study of psychotherapy. *Journal of Consulting and Clinical Psychology*, 1983, *51*, 28–41.

Glick, P. G., & Norton, A. J. Marrying, divorcing, and living together in the United States today. *Population Bulletin*, 1978, *32*, 3–38.

Gottman, J. M. *Marital interaction: Experimental investigations.* New York: Academic Press, 1979.

Guerney, B. G., Jr. *Relationship enhancement: Skill training programs for therapy, problem prevention, and enrichment.* San Francisco: Jossey-Bass, 1977.

Gurman, A. S. Dimensions of marital therapy: A comparative analysis. *Journal of Marital and Family Therapy*, 1979, *5*, 5–18.

Gurman, A. S. Integrative marital therapy: Toward the development of an interpersonal approach. In S. H. Budman (Ed.), *Forms of brief therapy.* New York: Guilford Press, 1981.

Gurman, A. S., & Kniskern, D. P. Research on marital and family therapy: Progress, perspective and prospect. In S. L. Garfield & A. E. Bergin (Eds.), *Handbook of psychotherapy and behavior change: An empirical analysis* (2d ed.). New York: John Wiley & Sons, 1978.

Gurman, A. S., & Kniskern, D. P. Family therapy outcome research: Knowns and unknowns. In A. S. Gurman & D. P. Kniskern (Eds.), *Handbook of family therapy.* New York: Brunner/Mazel, 1981.

Hahlweg, K. Konstruktion und Validierung des Partnerschaftsfragebogens. *PFB. Z. Klin. Psychol.,* 1979, *8,* 17–40.

Hahlweg, K., Kraemer, M., Schindler, L., & Revenstorf, D. Partnerschaftsprobleme: Eine empirische analyse. *Z. Klin. Psychol.,* 1980, *9,* 159–169.

Hahlweg, K., Revenstorf, D., & Schindler, L. Treatment of marital distress: Comparing formats and modalities. *Advances in Behavior Research and Therapy,* 1982, *4,* 57–74.

Hickman, M. E., & Baldwin, B. A. Use of programmed instruction to improve communication in marriage. *Family Coordinator,* 1971, 121–125.

Holmes, T. H., & Rahe, R. H. The social readjustment rating scale. *Journal of Psychosomatic Research,* 1967, *11,* 123–128.

Hops, H., Wills, T. A., Patterson, G. R., & Weiss, R. L. Marital interaction coding system. Eugene: University of Oregon and Oregon Research Institute, 1971. (Order from ASIS/NAPS, c/o Microfiche Publications, 305 E. 46th Street, New York, N.Y. 10017.)

Hops, H., Wills, T. A., Patterson, G. R., & Weiss, R. L. Marital interaction coding system. Unpublished manuscript, University of Oregon and Oregon Research Institute, 1972. (See NAPS Document 02077 for 29 pages of supplementary material. Order from ASIS/NAPS, c/o Microfiche Publications, 440 Park Avenue South, New York, N.Y. 10016.)

Jacobson, N. S. Problem solving and contingency contracting in the treatment of marital discord. *Journal of Consulting and Clinical Psychology,* 1977, *45,* 92–100.

Jacobson, N. S. Specific and non-specific factors in the effectiveness of a behavioral approach to the treatment of marital discord. *Journal of Consulting and Clinical Psychology,* 1978, *46,* 442–452.

Jacobson, N. S. The modification of cognitive processes in behavioral marital therapy: Integrating cognitive and behavioral intervention strategies. In K. Halweg & N. S. Jacobson (Eds.), *Marital interaction: Analysis and modification.* New York: Guilford Press, in press.

Johnson, S. M., & Lobitz, C. K. The personal and marital adjustment of parents as related to observed child deviance and parenting behavior. *Journal of Abnormal Child Psychology,* 1974, *2,* 193–207.

Jacobson, N. S., Elwood, R., & Dallas, M. The behavioral assessment of marital dysfunction. In D. H. Barlow (Ed.), *Behavioral assessment of adult disorders.* New York: Guilford Press, 1981.

Jacobson, N. S., Follette, W. C., & Elwood, R. W. Outcome research on behavioral marital therapy: A methodological and conceptual reappraisal. In K. Hahlweg & N. S. Jacobson (Eds.), *Marital interaction: Analysis and modification.* New York: Guilford Press, in press.

Kiesler, G. A. Social psychological issues in studying consumer satisfaction with behavior therapy. *Behavior Therapy,* 1983, *14,* 226–236.

Kimmel, D., & Van der Veen, F. Factors of marital adjustment in Locke's marital adjustment test. *Journal of Marriage and the Family,* 1974, *36,* 57–63.

L'Abate, L. The family as a unit of psychological study and practice. In L. L'Abate, *Family Psychology: Theory, therapy, and training.* Washington, D.C.: University Press of America, 1983.

L'Abate, L. *Systematic family therapy.* New York: Brunner/Mazel, 1985.

Liberman, R. P. Behavioral approaches in family and couple therapy. *American Journal of Orthopsychiatry,* 1970, *40,* 106–118.

Locke, H., & Wallace, K. Short marital adjustment and prediction tests: Their reliability and validity. *Marriage and Family Living*, 1959, *21*, 251–255.

Marital Studies Center. *Marital interaction coding system.* Unpublished manuscript, University of Oregon, 1975.

Melman, S. K., Baucom, D. H., & Anderson, D. Effectiveness of cotherapists versus single therapists and immediate versus delayed treatment in behavioral marital therapy. *Journal of Consulting and Clinical Psychology*, 1983, *51*, 258–266.

Morrison, R. L., & Bellack, A. S. The role of social perception in social skill. *Behavior Therapy*, 1981, *12*, 69–79.

O'Leary, K. D. Assessment of hyperactivity: Observational and rating methodologies. In S. A. Miller (Ed.), *Nutrition and behavior.* Philadelphia: Franklin Institute Press, 1981. Pp 291–297.

O'Leary, K. D., & Arias, I. The influence of marital therapy on sexual satisfaction. *Journal of Sex and Marital Therapy*, 1983, *9*, 171–181.

O'Leary, K. D., & Borkovec, T. D. Conceptual, methodological, and ethical problems of placebo groups in psychotherapy research. *American Psychologist*, 1978, *33*, 821–830.

O'Leary, K. D., & Emery, R. *Marital discord and child behavior problems.* Paper presented at the Middle Childhood Symposium, New Orleans, January 1982.

O'Leary, K. D., Fincham, F., & Turkewitz, H. Assessment of positive feelings toward spouse. *Journal of Consulting and Clinical Psychology*, 1983, *31*, 949–951.

O'Leary, K. D., & Turkewitz, H. Methodological errors in marital and child treatment research. *Journal of Consulting and Clinical Psychology*, 1978, *46*, 747–758.

Olson, C. L. On choosing a test of significance in multivariate analysis of variance. *Psychological Bulletin*, 1976, *83*, 579–586.

Parloff, M. B. The narcissism of small differences and some big ones. *International Journal of Group Psychotherapy*, 1976, *26*, 311–319.

Patterson, G. R., & Hops, H. Coercion, a game for two: Intervention techniques for marital conflict. In R. E. Ulrich & P. Mountjoy (Eds.), *The experimental analysis of social behavior.* New York: Appleton-Century-Crofts, 1972.

Porter, B., & O'Leary, K. D. Types of marital discord and child behavior problems. *Journal of Abnormal Child Psychology*, 1980, *8*, 287–295.

Rachman, S., & Wilson, G. T. *The effects of psychological therapy.* Elmsford, N.Y.: Pergamon Press, 1980.

Rutter, M. Family, area and school influences in the genesis of conduct disorders. In L. A. Hersov, M. Berger, & D. Shafer (Eds.), *Aggression and antisocial behavior in childhood and adolescence.* Elmsford, N.Y.: Pergamon Press, 1978.

Sager, C. J. *Marriage contracts and couple therapy.* New York: Brunner/Mazel, 1976.

Sager, C. J. Couples therapy and marriage contracts. In A. S. Gurman & D. P. Kniskern (Eds.), *Handbook of family therapy.* New York: Brunner/Mazel, 1981.

Schniedman, E. S., Farberow, N. L., & Litman, R. E. *The psychology of suicide.* New York: Science House, 1970.

Schover, L., & LoPiccolo, J. Treatment effectiveness for dysfunctions of low sexual desire. *Journal of Sex and Marital Therapy*, 1982, *8*, 179–197.

Schutz, W. C. *Mate, a Firo scale; husband's form, wife's form.* Palo Alto, Calif.: 1967.

Shapiro, D. A., & Shapiro, D. Comparative therapy outcome research: Methodological implications of meta-analysis. *Journal of Consulting and Clinical Psychology,* 1983, *51,* 42–53.

Skynner, A. C. R. A group analytic approach to conjoint family therapy. *Journal of Child Psychology and Psychiatry,* 1969, *10,* 81–106.

Skynner, A. C. R. *One flesh, separate persons: A systems approach to family therapy.* New York: Grune & Stratton, 1976.

Skynner, A. C. R. An open-systems, group-analytic approach to family therapy. In A. S. Gurman & D. P. Kniskern (Eds.), *Handbook of family therapy.* New York: Brunner/ Mazel, 1981.

Snyder, D. K. Advances in marital assessment: Behavioral, communications, and psychometric approaches. In C. D. Spielberger & T. N. Butcher (Eds.), *Advances in personality assessment* (Vol. 1). Hillsdale, N.J.: Lawrence Erlbaum Associates, 1981.

Spanier, G. B. Measuring dyadic adjustment: New scales for assessing the quality of marriage and similar dyads. *Journal of Marriage and the Family,* 1976, *38,* 15–28.

Spanier, G. B., & Glick, P. C. Marital instability in the United States: Some correlates and recent changes. *Family Relations,* 1981, *31,* 329–338.

Strube, M. J., & Hartman, D. P. Meta-analysis: Techniques, applications, and functions. *Journal of Consulting and Clinical Psychology,* 1983, *51,* 14–27.

Stuart, R. B. Operant-interpersonal treatment for marital discord. *Journal of Consulting and Clinical Psychology,* 1969, *33,* 675–682.

Stuart, R. B., & Stuart, F. *Marital pre-counseling inventory.* Champaign, Ill.: Research Press, 1973.

Turkewitz, H., & O'Leary, K. D. A comparative outcome study of behavioral marital therapy and communication therapy. *Journal of Marital and Family Therapy,* 1981, *7,* 159–169.

Watzlawick, P., Weakland, J., & Fisch, R. *Change: Principles of problem formation and problem resolution.* New York: W. W. Norton, 1974.

Weiss, R. L., Hops, H., & Patterson, G. R. A framework for conceptualizing marital conflict, a technology for altering it, some data for evaluating it. In L. A. Hamerlynck, L. C Handy, & J. Mash (Eds.), *Behavior change: Methodology, concepts, and practice.* Champaign, Ill.: Research Press, 1973.

Weiss, R. L., & Margolin, G. Marital conflict and accord. In A. R. Ciminero, K. S. Calhoun, & H. E. Adams (Eds.), *Handbook for behavioral assessment.* New York: John Wiley & Sons, 1977.

Williams, W. S. Class differences in the attitudes of psychiatric patients. *Social Problems,* 1956, *4,* 240–244.

Wilson, G. T., & Rachman, S. J. Meta-analysis and the evaluation of psychotherapy outcome: Limitations and liabilities. *Journal of Consulting and Clinical Psychology,* 1983, *51,* 54–64.

Wolf, M. M. Social validity: The case for subjective measurement of how applied behavior analysis is finding its heart. *Journal of Applied Behavior Analysis,* 1978, *11,* 203–214.

Chapter 35

Research in Family Therapy

COLE BARTON
JAMES F. ALEXANDER
JILL D. SANDERS

In his contemporary novel *The Delta Star*, Joseph Wambaugh draws parallels between police detective work and scientific inquiry. It is not enough to know that someone has been murdered, for the conventions of justice and detective work require that the detective reconstruct the critical motivations, causes, and details of evidence that allow for public scrutiny and create a compelling argument that indeed the crime was committed as the detective asserts. Outcomes alone are not sufficiently informative for either scientist or detective; both must understand process and mechanisms.

Contemporary reviewers of the family therapy literature will note that a similar challenge exists for them. Reviews of the outcomes of family therapy proliferate, drawing the substantive conclusion that family therapy produces sufficiently worthwhile clinical results to justify it as a beneficial and professionally responsible practice (Gurman & Kniskern, 1978; Wells & Dezen, 1978), even though early reviews of family therapy theory alleged that there was no convincing evidence that aspects of family life caused abnormal behavior (Fontana, 1965; Frank, 1967; Handel, 1965). An all-inclusive review of prior studies would be redundant with other excellent reviews, and reiterations of promising clinical outcomes will not serve to advance knowledge about families and their therapy. In fact, Gurman and Kniskern's review of family therapy research calls for an end to reviews, citing their ready availability and the trend to review rather than research (e.g., Gurman & Kniskern, 1981; Masten, 1979; Patterson & Fleischmann, 1979; Pinsof, 1981).

Despite their availability, these scholarly discourses seem to have had disappointingly little impact on the progress of either family therapy research or practice. Clinicians interested in how to do family therapy usually skip research material, presuming it to be irrelevant to their needs and interests.

As a contrasting form of influence, clinical disseminations of technique frequently sway the practice of family therapy. Family therapy books, training manuals, models of intervention, and training centers are rapidly increasing in number and scope. This information proliferates despite a lack of support provided by research findings, and this state of affairs may merely point out that the creativity and intuition of clinicians have outstripped the tools and technology of family therapy researchers. As a professional issue, however, the inattention to research or the cynical dismissal of its findings creates professional divergence between researcher-practitioners and practitioners. Consumers of the family therapy clinical literature and consumers of family therapy research are often two different and noncommunicating groups of professionals. This professional chasm is widened by training programs which emphasize either a research or clinical training focus but ignore or communicate cynicism about the other focus.

Fortunately, recent advances in methodology, statistics, and family theory can serve to lessen the gap between researchers and clinicians. Forward movement in family therapy research and practice can now be stimulated by contemporary developments in statistics and research methodologies. Researchers are being compelled by new methods and statistics which allow them to better characterize phenomena of interest and relevance to family therapists (Cairns, 1979; Galligan, 1982; Gottman, 1982). The more challenging professional persuasion task remains to convince the clinician that these research developments are not merely esoteric tools for sifting through meaningless information, but rather that these are vehicles to enhance not only the overall quality of the family therapy field but the personal clinical growth of family therapists as well. This assertion is prompted by the appraisal that new procedures and models are coming increasingly closer to the richness and subtlety of clinical work with families.

WHY CLINICIANS AND RESEARCHERS NEED FAMILIARITY WITH ONE ANOTHER

Though clinicians and researchers share some common goals of understanding, they have some important differences in how they operate on clinical problems. In contrast to researchers, clinicians can impact interaction processes as they unfold and as the family responds to the intervention, meaning that clinicians need only study the family for short periods of time, or in a relatively short and discrete time frame. A therapeutic intervention can be hypothesized, applied, and evaluated relatively quickly. If need be, hypotheses can be developed, revised, and discarded several times within the same therapy hour. Because this process of formulation, rejection, and revision is not carefully articulated, it can seem fickle to the researcher. If family therapists could articulate this process in research terms, they could help researchers better understand and scrutinize the therapy endeavor.

Researchers operate within a more formal set of rules, which compromises spontaneous activity. Researchers must operate less flexibly and within much longer time frames. Unlike clinicians, researchers cannot directly control or manipulate families in an ongoing and responsive fashion. Rather, researchers try to demonstrate control by predicting how family members and therapists are likely to behave, with the additional stipulation that families and therapists will not vary appreciably from this prediction. Family therapy researchers must manipulate and/or predict some important contexts for family behavior at the outset and then passively observe families and therapists to test whether or not the situation arranged by the research rules has been sufficiently well designed to shed light on the phenomenon of interest. They cannot respond to changes in family therapy process as they occur or have the clinical luxury of changing tactics "midstream." Researchers must commit themselves to a particular strategy and technology for assessment and intervention well in advance of a research endeavor. Coding systems and other assessment devices must be developed early on and research questions formulated and observers trained before observation of therapy can even begin. Researchers must therefore not only have a sense for how families and therapists are likely to behave but must also have a sense that substantial properties of family therapy are both predictable and controllable. The struggle for the family therapy researcher is to describe and understand those properties as they emerge over time and to do so in an a priori fashion.

Despite these differences in operating constraints, clinicians and researchers share some fundamental concerns in trying to understand what is important about changing families. Thus, it is our contention that the field of family therapy will be enhanced by a conjoint literacy in research conventions. Both researchers and clinicians struggle to identify those features of families which are problematic or to discriminate that which is meaningful from those properties of families and therapists which in no way influence their feelings and behavior. Researchers try to do this by identifying and describing meaningful research variables, which is conceptually akin to the therapist's assessment function. Both therapists and therapy researchers seem compelled to identify things which will create change or a more efficient therapy.

Unfortunately, clinicians often use terminologies that seem to the researcher to be either unclear or subject to dramatically different interpretations. For example, the "reframing" technique is presented in a variety of family therapy models (Alexander & Parsons, 1982; Bandler & Grinder, 1979; Barton & Alexander, 1980; Minuchin & Fishman, 1981), though there are differences in timing and execution for each model, with differing interpretations as to how or why reframing works. The specific components of a reframe, the therapist's skills necessary to utilize the technique, and the criteria for successful versus unsuccessful reframes have been poorly delineated by these descriptions in the literature to date. A researcher would characterize these disparities within a framework allowing for systematic definitions of the technique and formal scrutiny of the technique to determine the adequacy of the definition (reliability), as well as investigate the efficiency or effectiveness (validity) of the reframe. Research guidelines constrain therapists to be descriptively precise and help clarify precisely what is intended by descriptions of technical operations. These guidelines have obvious utility for the training and supervision of therapists and can reduce the aura of "magic" which surrounds clinical work and impedes its legitimacy.

Yet another advantage of bringing together research and clinical concepts exists because the literature asserts that most people in Western culture still think about human behavior in global, imprecise, individualistic terms. It appears that our language for describing relationship phenomena is inadequate and doesn't capture the "relationship meaning" to which family therapy models ascribe. The precision and rigor of research terminology can force a clarity of thinking and recognition of relationship properties of human behavior, such as competition (Boyle & Bonacich, 1967), coalitions (Strodtbeck, 1951), and interpersonal exchange (Thibaut & Kelley, 1959).

To the extent that family therapists are compelled or required to base their practices in material disseminated in technical professional journals, a pragmatic advantage to familiarizing with research strategies is that family therapists must consume substantial amounts of professional literature to keep abreast of developments in the field. In many situations, preliminary description and discussion of new techniques takes place in research journals. Whether or not family therapists perform research themselves, they need to decode technical information, have some basis for critical and informed consumption of the data, and recognize whether the findings are a challenge or confirmation of their clinical work. It must be remembered, too, that there is a promotional bias which operates in the clinical dissemination literature. Most clinical accounts of family therapy do not include tedium, humdrum events, or failures. The descriptions of family therapy as characterized in therapy textbooks or manuals rarely describe more than a few minutes of therapy, and the examples are usually carefully chosen. To create persuasive examples, advocates of a given family therapy logically include and focus upon powerful and successful interventions. To the researcher, this is selectively sampling phenomena in unrepresentative ways, creating a serious bias. Highlighting exemplary segments of intervention obscures several naturally occurring but important components of family therapy: How many relabels or paradoxes "fall flat" before families register a positive reaction? How much conversation is off the subject or otherwise resistant to the change effort? How much conversation is just "filler" as the therapist struggles to understand the family? Formal data or even just informal reports of such phenomena rarely appear in the clinical dissemination or training literature, wherein clinicians seem to have more license to report selectively than do researchers. Most research publications require that researchers make public statements of theory, methods (techniques and procedures), results and how they are measured, and finally, the implications of the results.

Thus, despite the overstated stereotype that researchers and clinicians rarely communicate, the two can learn much from each other. As suggested earlier, family therapists perform research-like operations of observation, unitizing, coding, and data analysis all the time, but do it more spontaneously and label it as clinical work rather than research. To the extent that this clinical artistry can be made more systematic, family therapists will have enhanced their own and others' well-being and effectiveness. Aside from the information provided by any particular research report, the process of formulating clinical problems in research terms can make our assumptions about family therapists and the ingredients and effectiveness of family therapy more explicit. Research need not inhibit clinical growth or development nor rule out any particular content area of theory and therapy. Rather, conducting research makes explicit those dimensions of families and therapies with a degree of rigor, descriptiveness, and clarity which renders ideas more accessible to all practicing therapists.

The family therapists' mandate: Understand and change

To be useful, research material must serve as a plausible metaphor for family therapists' professional activities. It therefore behooves researchers to consider the task characteristics of the family therapist's role.

Family therapists have a clear social and professional mandate to help families change ("Ethical Principles," 1981). To fulfill this mandate, therapists must first have a sense of how families work and what the targets and limits of change ought to be (Watzlawick, 1978). Therapists must process formidable amounts of information to understand family interaction. Some families talk quickly, loudly, and frequently in therapy, while others say relatively little but are rich in nonverbal cues. From what they are presented by the family, therapists must derive the clinically important elements in a very short period of time (Falicov, Constantine, & Breunlin, 1981; Haley, 1976; Minuchin & Fishman, 1981). Further, these elements must then be organized into a coherent picture of family behavior. While having different targets of information, all family therapies begin change from an evaluation of the family's initial state.

Meaningful clinical information comes in several varieties. The *content* of behavior and communication represents *what* people do and say to themselves and each other. Examples include marital pleases or displeases (Wills, Weiss, & Patterson, 1974) and defensive and supportive messages (Alexander, 1973). Clinicians and researchers find certain kinds of content to be meaningful reflections of family life, and they make inferences about families based on their presence or absence. The *process* of behavior represents *how* people behave and communicate, and this can be consistent or inconsistent with the content. Clinicians and researchers sometimes ignore content, finding processes—such as who speaks most often (Mishler & Waxler, 1968)—to be more accurate reflections of family life (such as who is in charge, in this case) than content. Clinicians and researchers may examine content and process together. A classic example is the "double bind" (Bateson, Jackson, Haley, & Weakland, 1956), which is defined both by content which is contradictory and by process which is sequential.

Content and process are analyzed at two levels (Falicov et al., 1981). The first level is organized around overt family behavior. Therapists observe family behavior and begin to specify the clinically relevant elements of the interaction as filtered through an observational framework. Different therapy models dictate attention to different features of the interaction. While a structural family therapist would concentrate on between-generation events (Minuchin, 1974), Bowenian therapists might direct attention to instances of self-differentiation (Bowen, 1974). One of the key values of a therapy model is providing the therapist with parameters for discriminating relevant family behavior from the irrelevant. At a second level of analysis, therapists must also be able to abstract important concepts from their first-level observations (Falicov et al., 1981). Conceptually, therapists must pattern the observations into clinically meaningful phenomena. Clinical significance is dictated by the therapy orientation, such as triangles (Bowen, 1978), coalitions (Minuchin & Fishman, 1981), or functions (Barton & Alexander, 1981). These are not tangible properties of families, but rather must be inferred from some organization of observations the clinician has made.

Nonetheless, researchers and clinicians scrutinize abstract concepts in different ways. While the clinician is likely to test immediately the veracity of an abstraction by asking a question, structuring a comment to create a process, or calling attention to a family member's vulnerability, the researcher faces a more rigorous series of criteria for describing and demonstrating the presence of an abstraction. Guided by the principles of a theoretical orientation, the researcher has a systematic observational framework for describing the family.

Relatedness, association, relative magnitude, and temporal sequencing

So far, we have argued that researchers and therapists share some common problems of understanding and observation. Recognizing these joint concerns, a next important consideration is to identify some conventions or a language system which allow therapists and researchers to identify, label, and evaluate phenomena of mutual interest.

In family therapy, a basic premise is that the important phenomena are related to each other: Talk of divorce is related to acting-out children, drug use elicits concern, parents who ignore quiet play routinely reward tantrums, and so forth. It is not clear what causes what in these circumstances, though the relationship between the phenomena may be obvious. Within the family, the question of who caused the relationship may be irrelevant or even nontherapeutic. Nonetheless, the therapy paradigm is one wherein there is a strong presumption of influence or linear causality, or more concretely, an expectation that therapists change the behavior, feelings, or perceptions of family members. As a communication issue, it is incumbent on researchers to adopt conventions about describing relatedness and cause-effect relationships in ways which are replicable, are verifiable, and can be demonstrated to occur with meaningful regularity. Researchers can be described as using stringent criteria to characterize clinical work. No small part of this stringency is separating out components of *relatedness* that are typically lumped together. Clinical judgments of relatedness usually include one, some, or all of the following components: association, magnitude, and temporal sequencing.

Association refers to how often events occur together. Clinicians observe meaningful cooccurrences of events, such as every time parents dispute each other, a child acts out. Without clearly understanding its causes, it is still possible for therapists to recognize this association as a meaningful ritual in a family. Minuchin and colleagues (Minuchin, Rosman, & Baker, 1978) demonstrated that biological properties of children's blood changed as a function of parental conflict in verbal exchanges in families. This demonstration represented a measure of association that confirmed clinical speculation and verified the appropriateness of family therapy.

Other times, clinicians may have a sense that someone is doing too much of something, while others are doing too little. Lidz et al. (Lidz, Cornelison, Fleck, & Terry, 1957) hypothesized that families of schizophrenics had one parent who talked too much, another who talked too little (in his vocabulary, 'skewed' families). When clinicians evaluate this "too much or too little" dimension of family life, then they are interested in the *relative magnitude* of family behavior. Therapists usually have a sense of what kinds of behavior constitute an excess versus what kinds represent a deficit in effective human functioning. One way of categorizing the relatedness of family members is to rank order their performance on some important excess or deficit and then evaluate whether differences in rank constitute something clinically meaningful. For example when estimating the adaptability of a family system, the therapist may be more interested in whether distressed families do as many "appropriate" things as nondistressed families. Do delinquent families talk enough? Does a schizophrenogenic parent talk too much? The point is to recognize that important differences are usually detected and described as a phenomenon of "relative magnitude."

Yet a third means of identifying the relatedness of family members is to recognize regularities in the *temporal sequencing* of family behavior. The order (or lack of it) in which family communications occur paints a descriptive picture of family life. Many important clinical phenomena such as double binds, coalitions, functions, or coercion require that therapists recognize a systematic ordering of family behavior. Many interaction phenomena (such as power) are defined by temporal relationships (such as who initiates conversation), while behavioral phenomena (such as social reinforcers) are defined by those events which follow a given behavior. Most clinicians see meaningful differences between families who talk in chaotic fashion and those which appear to be ritualistically ordered (Alexander, 1973; Haley, 1967). There are new technologies available for evaluating temporal sequencing (described in subsequent portions of the chapter) which make the clinically rich, temporally sequenced phenomena available to the researcher.

In summary, we assert that family therapists make a host of complex information decisions and that similar information is processed by family therapy researchers, albeit with more rigorous criteria. Regardless of theoretical orientation, all family therapists observe families, conceptually organize the behavior of family members, and make decisions about which elements of families are targets for change. These activities implicitly require the family therapist to have some scheme for inferring relatedness and for hypothesizing causes and effects (both of families' behavior and of ingredients for change). In turn, relatedness and cause-effect relationships are established by understanding one or more of three properties of events: their association, relative magnitude, and temporal sequencing. Lack of progress, inefficiencies in dissemination and training, confusion, and poor therapy may reflect ineffective or unsystematic appraisals of families and the change process. Family therapists cannot afford the license of treating each therapy session as a series of random events, to say nothing of treating their clients' problems as capricious and unsystematic. It is up to the family therapist as researcher to demonstrate the orderliness, coherence, and critical elements of family therapy. Researchers have made progress in generating the technology to examine clinical elements of family therapy, and these developments represent the focus of the next portions of the chapter.

RESEARCH STRATEGIES FOR CLINICAL PROBLEMS

Like the clinician, the researcher identifies relatedness and the cause-effect nature of phenomena by evaluating their association, relative magnitude, and sequencing. Unlike the clinician, however, the researcher cannot formally rely on clinical judgment, intuition, implicit assumptions, and a set of flexible decision rules to perform this evaluation. Instead, researchers use consistent decision rules to define, recognize, and count clinical phenomena by following *coding schemes* (Bakeman, Cairns, & Appelbaum, 1979; Pinsof, 1981). Then, researchers appraise the phenomena they investigate with *quantitative analyses.* These analyses, like coding schemes, are based on a set of formal assumptions and consistent internal relationships that do not change over time (Cairns, 1979; Winer, 1971). As described in the first section of this chapter, the inflexibility that results from this consistency can interfere with the spontaneity demanded of the clinician (Cook & Reichardt, 1979). At the same time, however, this consistency allows the researcher to identify clinically important regularities which can escape the clinician. Particularly with tape recordings which can be repeatedly replayed and with computers that can store and process large amounts of information, researchers can provide considerable information that the clinician simply does not have the time or capacity to develop and evaluate. This section of the chapter will discuss the nature of coding schemes, the decision rules they involve, and the ways they can help clarify a family clinician's task demands and implicit assumptions. The next section will describe several types of quantitative analyses, again relating them to the clinician.

Coding schemes

All coding schemes relevant to family therapy process research involve, in one form or another, three major elements: *roles, boundaries,* and *content.* Roles tell us who or what instigated or received a phenomenon of interest, boundaries tell us how to identify the occurrence of a phenomenon of interest, and content tells us what that phenomenon of interest is.

Roles. The operations of therapy ultimately involve changing phenomena that are experienced by people, expressed by people, or occur between people. Even purely transactional theories (Fisher, 1982) identify people in a *certain context* at a certain *time.* Thus, most if not all of the problems and transactions that clinicians identify as meaningful imply the importance of family roles. Clinical issues such as sex differences in therapy, coalitions across generations, and the relatedness of children's problems to marital dysfunction are all phenonema which require that clinicians and researchers be able to distinguish family members from each other and to tie to people's roles the units of information that are worthwhile (Achenbach, 1979; O'Leary & Turkewitz, 1978).

Though identifying roles rarely creates a major concern for researchers, it can sometimes be difficult. As an instrumentation problem, family therapy researchers should ensure that the format by which they gather raw data is able to distinguish family members from each other (Gelfand & Hartmann, 1975). Audiotape recording equipment and tape is less expensive than videotape recording equipment and tape. However, many adolescents and one of their parents sound the same, making it difficult to distinguish identities, particularly if someone mumbles or the sound quality is uneven. Family therapy researchers must therefore ensure that the data constituting their therapy process sample can be identified and tied to the appropriate therapist and family member. Further, if a researcher feels it is important to relate communication or behavior to both their *sources* and *objects* (or receivers), then the researcher must occasionally rely on sophisticated recording equipment to discern the direction of eye gazing or must otherwise be able to discern which family member is being referred to in such statements as "You never . . ." and "You always . . ." (Bakeman et al., 1979). Research with dyads doesn't encounter this problem to a great extent, but it is common with families of three or more (Strodtbeck, 1954). Often, in fact, the clinician in the room is unclear as to the object of some statement or gestures, as reflected in the often-heard phrase "Who are you referring to when you say that?"

In sum, for researchers, the identification of roles is usually fairly straightforward, at least conceptually, but it can represent more than a perfunctory or trivial process.

Boundaries. Boundaries are those physical properties of an event, phenomenon, person, or thing which allow us to identify it as meaningful. Practically speaking, in family therapy process research, boundaries are usually the starting and stopping points for phenomena embedded in family process. Decision rules about when somebody starts a conversation or behavior and when somebody ends it are important to the researcher who wishes to organize family behavior in a meaningful way (Pinsof, 1981). Unfortunately, people do not speak in discrete units: they ramble, they change the subject, they include several thoughts in a paragraph, they are interrupted, they often talk at once. In a complicated interpersonal situation such as a family therapy session, different people often respond to different parts of complex messages. Many times, the nature of the response is qualitatively different than the original act, or the respondent reacts to an "unintended" part of the message. The ways in which senders and receivers "scramble" messages can make it difficult to articulate when and how someone is responding to a message. Therefore, family therapists and researchers need ways to identify the boundaries of the verbal or physical behavior we wish to measure and understand.

In interaction research, boundaries are defined by units. Units are generally represented as temporal units, speeches, and thoughts or acts (Pinsof, 1979). Each of these procedures has advantages and disadvantages.

Temporal units usually create the simplest case. In temporal unitizing, the researcher decides what lengths of time generate a reasonable sample of behavior. For example, a time period of six seconds provides a reasonable density of many verbal phenomena and, at the same time, allows for contributions of that phenomenon from each member of the family (Barton, 1982). To the extent that the researcher can identify a meaningful time period like this, the researcher then punctuates a data sample (i.e., an audiotape or a videotape) with a signal occurring at the predesignated time interval. In a similar manner, observers coding in vivo therapy can receive an unobtrusive signal through earphones or behind a one-way mirror.

When researchers are interested in the density of phenomena or in a phenomenon that has a high rate of occurrence, temporal unitizing can create a straightforward decision rule for how to create both a starting point and ending point for a unit. This information can, in turn, have relevance for the clinician. For example, it can be useful for the clinician to know that, compared to normal families, delinquent families have a higher proportion of temporal units which are defensive in nature. The clinician may also find it relevant that the associations between family members' roles of defensiveness differ in normal and delinquent families (Alexander, 1973). This latter finding, though it might be "sensed" by the clinician, probably requires the researcher's technology to be demonstrated, and it can translate into therapeutic or prevention strategies.

Practically speaking, the researcher should do two things to enhance the quality of the coded material. First, the data should be numbered by intervals. This will ensure that in discussions of the data or in checks on the accuracy of the coding, people can readily identify the same intervals in the data set. Second, depending on the nature of the coding scheme, the researcher may want to include a short coding interval associated with the time interval in addition to the sampling unit. Coders usually need at least one second between intervals to make the appropriate mark or recognition on their coding forms.

Though temporal unitizing is the simplest form of unitizing, it has several drawbacks. It completely confounds time and the importance, or "weight," of a phenomenon. For example, if a behavior such as yelling extends over three temporal units, it receives three times as many counts as does a yelling episode that occurs in only one interval. Clinicians often feel events are not simply weighted by their duration and may want (in this case) to argue that each episode of yelling simply be counted as one event.

A second major drawback to temporal unitizing is its inability to identify the order in which events occur, in that two or more events can occur in one unit but their order is not identified. In order to capture the importance of interpersonal sequencing (who follows whom, what type of speech or behavior follows another type), the researcher may want to use a unitizing rule based on *speeches* (Pinsof, 1979). Speeches are usually defined as one person's verbalizations bounded by another. When using speeches as the unit, researchers generally use a descriptive word or phrase which characterizes a speaker's entire series of verbalizations, be they long or short. This can create a problem because people many times "hold the floor" and talk for two to three paragraphs. Many times, people's long speeches are complex arrays of several qualitative components of conversation. It is not unusual for people to blame and, at the same time, praise another in one conversation (familiar as the "yes-but" message). Thus, researchers using the speeches to unitize their interaction sample may have a clear sense of sequencing (i.e., who follows whom), but the forced global coding of what appears to be a complex configuration of different contents may obscure the clinical complexity of speeches, reducing its relevance for the clinician. Clinicians rarely think in terms of large global units such as speeches. Instead, they usually target specific phrases or behaviors which are embedded in a larger stream of behavior or interaction.

To make a finer-grained distinction about the content of what people actually say, as well as identify the smaller units targeted by clinicians, many researchers use an *act* or *thought unit* coding rule. These two unitizing strategies utilize the rules of language and syntax as the boundaries of verbal behaviors. An act or thought unit is any single act or word or series of acts or words which expresses a complete behavior or thought (Gottman, Markman, & Notarius, 1977). Act and thought coding schemes recognize distinct transitions in meaning as defined by the speaker's content; thus, a single individual can produce a series of acts or thought units. Obviously, acts and thought units are among the most molecular unitizing rules. These unitizing rules create substantial information, in terms of both quantity and making the qualitative decoding of these dimensions almost infinite. However, they can be difficult systems in which to train raters, and they also pose some interesting nuance questions for interpersonal research. For example, consider the situation when one person emits a stream of thought units or acts. When another person follows this complicated stream with one or more acts or thought units, it is difficult to know which particular act or thought unit the respondent is responding to. Though the lag analyses described below can sometimes clarify this situation, researchers must still use considerable creativity to capture accurately the essence of interaction.

Content. Much of the meaning or relatedness of units in family therapy interaction is defined by the actual content. Ultimately, much of the qualitative evaluation of therapy and research boils down to a critical discussion of the content of the coding scheme. The content of the coding scheme is that part of reality which we are trying to understand and manipulate in either clinical or research settings. A researcher's ability to describe the phenomenon in question and to communicate clearly that understanding is a critical component for both clinical and research work. Content coding schemes may utilize response topographies and qualitative judgments (Kiesler, 1973). Each of these types of content coding schemes involves a set of decision rules and implications.

Researchers may opt to code on the basis of recognition of a defined *response*. In this case, the researcher merely recognizes the presence of some response within a coding unit. Examples might be the mere act of talking, a physical activity such as a physical strike, or moving from one place to another. The researcher presumes that the overt activity has some meaning common to all people and situations, allowing for a high degree of data generalization. The value of the code depends on the degree to which this is so. To make the point, physically striking somebody in the nose with sufficient force to make them bleed is an overt codable response that has fairly uniform meaning in most cultures. However, other behaviors do not have uniform meaning. A nuance like smiling, for example, is a recognizable behavior, but may sometimes be an expression of affection and at other times be more an indication of sarcasm or snideness. Further, it is difficult to assert directly who the target or stimulus antecedent of a smile might be.

An additional problem with coding systems based on a certain response configuration is conceptual, since many family therapists have long argued that the function and context of behavior may be more important than its form (Alexander & Parsons, 1982; Watzlawick, Beavin, & Jackson, 1967). Much of family therapy theory argues that behavior only assumes meaning within the particular context of a relationship, which is one argument for asserting that a response topography or recognition type of content coding method may not capture the actual intent, meaning, or function of a behavior in a particular event. Researchers using this coding scheme must therefore give substantial thought to whether or not the regularity in response topography is sufficient to be counted frequently in the occurrence of a family therapy session and, secondly, to whether or not the overt behavior has any useful clinical meaning associated with it.

As opposed to having decoders merely recognize the presence or absence of certain phenomena, the researcher or clinician may choose to decode the data with inferences derived from clinical or otherwise useful meaning (Cairns & Green, 1979; Haberman, 1979). This procedure makes the coder arrive at a *qualitative judgment* or meaning about the importance of a given unit. This kind of coding scheme can be particularly useful when some sort of clinical judgment is an efficient way of organizing much of family members' behavior. For family therapy researchers, the most relevant qualitative judgments are those which make relationship inferences. Here, the researcher defines a behavior as essentially interactional in nature, meaning, and impact. Relationship inference types of coding methods require researchers to have a decision rule not only for what initiates the phenomenon in question but also for a relatively hard and fast decision rule about what ends it.

Consider the phenomenon of agreements, as an example. Because family therapy sessions involve triads and even larger groups, it is often the case that a person who makes a bid for an agreement is not always immediately agreed with. Further, if he or she is agreed with, there have often been several intervening events between the initial bid and agreement. Finally, when the agreement finally occurs, it often simultaneously represents a disagreement with someone else. The following example serves to highlight the problem:

> **Father:** Yeah, I could use some help here.
> **Therapist:** In what way?
> **Adolescent:** [interrupting]: Bullshit.
> **Therapist:** What's that?
> **Adolescent:** He never accepted anything from anybody.
> **Mother:** Oh, yes . . . he's asked for help just like he is now. You just never listened.

This example demonstrates how the researcher faces the complex task of identifying what constitutes a meaningful response to, or end point of, an agreement bid. It also demonstrates that a single response (e.g., mother's) can have very different meaning in different relationships. In this instance, her single speech represented an agreement with father and a disagreement (or accusation) with adolescent.

Additionally, researchers and clinicians alike should make sure that they do not compound or confuse the form of a response with its functions or impact. The phenomenon of sexual abuse makes the point. It is difficult to define abuse in purely overt terms, because the same form of a behavior has different emotional, psychological, or interpersonal impact depending on the situation. A tender massaging of the buttocks if directed at a spouse may constitute an acceptable relationship behavior to that spouse, while if directed toward a child, the same behavior may constitute unacceptable sexual abuse. The point is that relationship inference coding schemes require not only a recognition task but also a contextual description or qualitative judgment about the flavor (qualitatively defined) of the act itself and its relationship meaning. Such systems can be useful to the clinician because of their ability to capture clinical complexity and meaning, but they also tend to suffer from problems of bias and unreliability. While the qualitative judgment type of coding scheme can globally summarize much of the complexity of family interaction, the expenditure and costs can be great in creating hard and fast decision rules about the qualitative dimension used in the code. After creating these rules, it is incumbent upon the researcher to assert in some meaningful way that these judgments have been systematically and accurately made. Using such a coding scheme requires that the researcher can communicate to other coders the nature of the qualitative judgment and provide some evidence of reliability. The relevant form of reliability is a statistical indication that raters are able to agree on the qualitative judgment (Walizer

& Wienir, 1978). Consumers of research are always interested in the degree to which a qualitative judgment type of coding scheme can be replicated.

DESCRIBING FAMILY THERAPY QUANTITATIVELY

This section of the chapter will discuss how family therapy phenomena can be described with statistics. This discussion will not have a technical focus but rather will portray how statistics can describe and test assumptions about family therapy.

In general, statistics describe three properties of variables (as described or obtained with a coding scheme). These properties are association, relative magnitude, and temporal sequencing. In the most straightforward case, some statistics quantify the amount of difference or the magnitude of effect between two or more variables. The mean of a group of variables is compared to that of another group, with allowances for how the scores in each group are distributed (computed as variance). Following statistical assumptions, the means are then presumed to differ from each other at some level of confidence. The most common examples of difference statistics are the Z-test, T-test, and F-test. All of these tests model data on a normal distribution, and they differ only in the means by which they are computed. (Hays, 1963).

The second general quantification of variables describes the degree to which two or more variables have a measured association (McNemar, 1969). Rather than asserting that one variable is necessarily greater than another, a measure of association describes how two or more variables covary over time or appear to influence each other or are part of the same thing. (To contrast, a magnitude-of-effect statistic might describe if a group of fathers were higher than mothers on some dimension; while a measure of association would describe whether fathers' and mothers' scores were complementary or symmetrical.) Measures of association are computed with variations of the correlation coefficient, where the rank ordering of variables is as important as the mean and variability of variables to the quantitative derivation of the measure. To meaningfully covary or be related by a measure of association, the rank ordering of sets of scores (or numbers assigned to variables) must remain basically the same across people, time, or situations.

The appropriateness of magnitude-of-effect statistics or measure-of-association statistics for establishing cause-effect relationships is related to the design of a research project, the nature of the coding scheme, and the sequencing of data in a study (Campbell & Stanley, 1963; Kirk, 1982). Causality cannot be inferred from the type of statistics that is used. Rather, it must be inferred from the contextual configuration of experimental variables.

Historically, magnitude-of-effect statistics have been applied to true experiments. True experiments are those in which the researcher manipulates a certain set of variables (independent variables) and identifies the effect of this manipulation on some other measure (dependent variables). The difference in dependent variables of interest (such as, does therapeutic reframing reduce defensiveness?) can be asserted with the use of a magnitude-of-effect statistic. Historically, behavioral science researchers were pushed to develop experimental situations where they could demonstrate that they had control of a given variable. A probability statement was made about the degree to which researchers could influence variables, and then the robustness of this assertion was quantified and tested with the magnitude-of-effect kind of statistic.

Unfortunately, many phenomena of interest to clinicians and behavioral science researchers are not amenable to experimental manipulations. In doing preliminary descriptive research, it is often more worthwhile for researchers to understand whether or not two or more variables are appreciably related to each other. That is to say, for example, do some characteristics of fathers covary with those of mothers? Do some characteristics of parents as a set covary with their children? Do some properties of therapists covary with some properties of their clients? The historical caveat associated with measure-of-association statistics has been to say that a covariation does not imply causality. For example, while it can be shown that height and weight generally covary, it cannot be shown that weight causes height or that height necessarily causes weight. Problems of causality are problems both of direction and of the possibility that a third variable may be causing an influence on two that covary (for example, it may be that a construct such as growth causes both height and weight). However, contemporary advances in statistics are making it possible for researchers to configure variables in such a way that notions of causality can be inferred from measure-of-association statistics.

Two developments have yielded more isomorphism between magnitude-of-effect and measure-of-association statistics. First, multiple regression procedures have been developed wherein correlation coefficients are significance tested in ways similar to the F-test in the analysis of variance. The point of these developments has been to assert that both magnitude-of-effect statistics and measure-of-association statistics are ratios of true-score variability to error variability, making them conceptually analogous in certain situations. Second, the crossed and lagged panel analysis quasi-experimental methodology (to be described below) has made it possible to configure correlations in ways which allow the researcher to make causal inferences. If it can be shown that measures of association between people either increase or decay over time, for example, then the researcher is in a position to interpret the changes in measures of correlation in ways which allow a causal statement.

In describing some statistics and methodologies below, we will assert that consumers should evaluate statistics for their ability to describe a magnitude of effect or a measure of association and how they can help researchers make assertions about what causes what. In so doing, we recognize that we are reducing much of the richness, circularity, and complexity of family therapy into more discrete examples of cause and effect phenomena. We think that this enterprise is worthwhile insofar as it becomes more descriptive and predictive of the events that are interesting and clinically relevant for family therapy researchers. A major characteristic which distinguishes family therapy research from basic family research is the presumption that therapists somehow cause differences in family behavior. For this reason, the notion of causality and establishing cause and effect relationships between the behavior of therapists and family members is an important feature of family therapy research. As readers review the statistical models described below, they will recognize some discussion of magnitude of effect, measure of association, and notion of causality as being important characteristics of both their clinical and research assumptions.

ANOVA or MANOVA

A useful analytic procedure is estimating the magnitude of effect for a given effect in the analysis of variance (Hays, 1963; Winer, 1971). Basically, a magnitude-of-effect statistic compares the variance associated with a particular effect to the overall variance obtained in the study. This statistic is a proportion of the variance accounted for by that particular effect (Cronbach, Gleser, Nanda, & Rajaratnam, 1972). For example, it is the case that even though a researcher detects a significant difference between family members or some variable, it may also be the case that this statistically significant difference accounts for only 5 percent of the variability in family member scores. Some separate feature of family status or the nature of an experimental task may account for more variability in family behavior than their roles. The magnitude-of-effect statistic (Omega square, interclass correlation coefficient, generalizability coefficient) can be used to describe not only the significance of the effect but a proportion of variance accounted for in an experiment by that particular effect. This statistic can therefore be very useful if researchers want to identify, for example, the relative importance of such phenomena as family roles, the normal versus abnormal status of family members, or the difference in family members' behavior between first and last therapy sessions.

The analysis of variance has a serious requirement associated with it, namely that data points analyzed do not have an appreciable amount of relatedness between them. Obviously, family therapy researchers are interested in phenomena wherein the behavior of family members is meaningfully and, it follows, quantitatively related. To accommodate this potentially problematic situation, researchers may opt to perform a more elaborate multivariate analysis of variance. Briefly stated, the multivariate analysis of variance (MANOVA) creates error terms which do not depend on the independence of data points, and can in fact meaningfully describe the degree of relatedness between these same data points. The MANOVA can therefore describe not only the meaningful differences within a data set but the meaningful points of relatedness as well. At any rate, family therapy researchers can use MANOVA with assurances that problematic sources of relatedness are appropriately accommodated.

Another procedure discussed extensively by Kirk (1981) is that of having the researcher identify a priori contrasts between specific means in an experiment. For example in the analysis of variance, it is not uncommon for researchers to describe family members by roles. When a researcher detects a role effect, if there are more than two roles in families (e.g., husband, wife, and child), the researcher cannot be clear on which family member differs from the others or if there is a consistent difference between the family members. One way to address this problem is for the researcher to hypothesize in advance that family roles will be different, then do the permitted number of role contrasts. The researcher can identify in advance which scores ought to be different from which other scores and multiply those scores by a series of coefficients which make the comparison of interest. For example, a researcher may want to compare whether or not parents and children respond differently to therapy intervention on a specific variable for which scores are available. To do so, the therapist could sum both parent scores, divide by two, and subtract childrens' scores from this total. Such a series of algebraic operations on the data create comparisons of particular interest to the researcher. In general, the effects of interest to many interaction researchers are within-subject effects as described in models of the analysis of variance (Alexander & Barton, 1980; Hays, 1963; Winer, 1971). These within-subject effects can be partitioned in ways which allow the researcher to make specific comparisons within families. The important point is to recognize that multivariate and contrast analyses can greatly enhance the descriptive power and utility of the analysis of variance for the family therapy researcher.

Conditional probabilities

For the family therapy researcher, one of the most meaningful concerns is what events covary with other events and how often (Patterson,

1979). One way of characterizing rituals, for example, is to identify how frequently an event occurs relative to other events: A family therapy researcher might be interested in how often family members express positive statements in a session, or in the more restricted case of how often family members express positives when the therapist expresses positives. In family therapy research, it is often worthwhile to depict one family member's behavior relative to another's. Social-learning theorists, for example, have pointed out that certain family types can be distinguished from other family types by the probability with which one class of responses follows another.

Conditional probabilities provide this information as ratios of one event compared to another (Fleiss, 1981; Hays, 1963) In simplest form, a probability is a proportion of occurrences relative to a larger set of possible occurrences. For example, in the case of a coin flip, we would expect a two-headed coin to come up heads 50 out of 100 times. This is expressed as a probability of .50. Conditional probabilities can also be reflected as joint probabilities or the product of two conditional probabilities. For example, given that mother responds quickly to problem behavior 40 percent (or a probability of .40) of the time, what is the joint probability that the child again behaves negatively in the interval immediately succeeding mother's reaction? The joint probability is established by figuring out the percentage of the time that a child behaves negatively immediately following attention from mother and multiplying the two together. The interpretation of the two multiplied together ($.50 \times .40 = .20$) is, "given that mother attends to a problem behavior, the likelihood that the son will follow attention with more negative behavior is X."

Conditional probabilities can therefore describe some aspects of interpersonal relatedness very well when the question of interest is, "given that therapist does X, how likely is it that Family Member 1 will respond with Y" or that "Family Member 2 will respond with Z?" etc. The conditional probability is based on data derived from a process phenomenon, since its computation requires the researcher to code some orderly sequence in which the phenomenon can be said to occur. In this sense, the conditional probability is more descriptive than mere rates and can be computed to capture a variety of relevant family therapy processes. The probability can be established, for example, of how each family member responds to a therapist, how family members respond to each other, how likely it is that somebody in the family will be negative, and so forth. The same data can be sliced in a variety of ways, and several conditional probability statistics can be computed.

Conditional probabilities can also be built into "decision trees," or Markov chains (Hawes & Foley, 1973; Stuart, 1971). A family therapy researcher can construct a series of hierarchical "if-then" statements which progressively build upon proportions derived from the data. Consider the following example:

	Therapist	Family member		
		Mother	Father	Adolescent
Positive comment	.50a	.25b	.15c	.10d
Direct positive to therapist	—	.125e	.075f	.05g

Statistic a represents a reasonably favorable case for the therapist, wherein half the time, some member of the family follows the therapist's comments with a positive comment. If mother makes half of the entire family's favorable comments, then the probability she will make a positive comment after a therapist's favorable comment is probability a times .5, the proportion of mother's positive comments, or b. If mother talks to the therapist twice as much as she talks to the other two family members, then at a minimum, she again has a .5 probability of responding positively and directly to the therapist, times the .5 likelihood she responds positively after the therapist, times the .5 probability that a family member responds positively after a therapist's positive comment. The probability of e is therefore relatively small, even if therapists elicit positive responses half the time, mothers are positively reciprocal half the time, and mothers talk twice as much as the other two family members.

The derivation and array of conditional probabilities can therefore be illuminating in describing the likelihood of events, given a particular situation. Conditional probabilities are usually computed within a particular family, and the numbers assume meaning only to the extent that they represent phenomena derived from a particular family.

Contingency tables

Family therapy researchers often have questions about whether or not there is a significant relatedness between the sequential ordering of events. When researchers have coded the behaviors or speeches of family members and the therapist and these speeches are temporally sequenced, then the family therapy researcher can use contingency table analyses to investigate the systematic relatedness of different classes of events (Fleiss, 1981; Kelley & Thibaut, 1978). The relatedness of interest is how often the behavior (or speech properties) of one family member are followed by the behavioral patterns of another family member. This focus requires the researcher to have a coding scheme which has sequentially ordered the data. Assume, for example, that the therapy researcher was interested in the number of occasions when the family therapist emitted a positive statement and it was followed by a positive statement from a family member as compared to the number of times that the family therapist emitted a negative comment and it was followed by a negative comment from a family member. The researcher could create a two-by-two table. On the horizontal axis (or rows) the researcher could put therapist positive comments versus therapist negative comments. On the vertical axis (or columns), the family therapy researcher could array family positive comments versus family negative comments. Rows and columns therefore form four distinct cells in the two-by-two table. The family therapy researcher then counts those occasions on which the therapist emits a positive-column comment and goes to his or her coded data to see if a family member follows that comment with a positive or negative comment. The entry is made accordingly in the proper cell of the two-by-two table. Similarly, when a therapist makes a negative comment, the researcher goes to the coded data to identify whether or not a family member followed that comment with a positive or negative comment. Following the chi square computational procedure, the quantitative analysis compares the frequency of events in each of the cells to the frequency of events that one would expect to be there as a proportion determined by the row and column sums. To the extent that the number of positives, for example, exceeds the number of positives that would be expected by chance, the computations would reveal something about the distribution of positive or negative comments as emitted by family members.

It is also the case that the two-by-two table then be expanded to include as many cells as are of interest to the researcher (Castellan, 1979). For example, the family therapy researcher may want to partition family members into roles. In this case, both axes would read family therapist positive, family therapist negative, child positive, child negative, and so on. Thus, the researcher can identify whether the father or the mother or the child followed the therapist's positive or negative comments with a positive or negative comment of their own. Similarly, the researcher could identify who follows each family member and whether that comment is positive or negative as well. The computational procedures for contingency tables allow the researcher to hypothesize in advance which cells or rows or columns constitute an interaction question of interest. For example, a therapy researcher interested in same-sex dyads as a therapy question could compare whether or not a female family therapist was followed more or less often by positive comments from female family members than by male family members. To do so, the family therapy researcher merely identifies those rows or columns identified with the people of interest and tests the proportions accordingly.

Contingency tables provide a strategy to both array and meaningfully quantify sequentially ordered data. Note that in coding these data, the researcher is required to have a constraint about a uniform and meaningful set of intervals in which to code the data. It is also the case that the researcher should have a coding scheme wherein people emit a relatively high rate of the behavior in order to be accurately encoded in the table and to generate enough data points for the subsequent analysis, which basically consists of comparing how many observations are actually in the cell versus how many should be there just by the chance distribution of events. The question is similar to a conditional probability notion. For example, given that dad was a negative consequator one third of the time, does he consequate mother or son more than 16½ percent of the time. If the answer were "no," it would be reflected in a nonsignificant chi square type of statistic. If, however, father negatively consequated son more than mother, for example, then over one half of his distribution of negatives would be directed towards son. In this case, that cell would have appreciably more data points than would be expected by an randomly spaced distribution. The contingency table analysis, therefore, identifies not only measures of association but also the degree to which those measures of association depart from an equivalent distribution.

Similar to conditional probabilities, the contingency table can be sliced in a variety of ways. For example, a researcher can ask a question of whether or not the role distributions of who makes preliminary comments are appreciably different from each other. Similarly, the researcher could ask a column distribution question such as, "Does one family member get followed by aversive consequences more than another?" Specific cells can be independently summed, as in the case of a researcher trying to identify whether parents are followed more frequently than are their children. It is also the case that rather than using actual distributions of entries in a cell for a basis of comparison, the researcher can have a hypothesized notion about how often, for example, someone ought to be followed by negative events and use this as the basis of constructing the summary chi square statistic ratio.

In summary, contingency tables offer a way not only to tabulate data but also to systematically make a meaningful statistical statement about both the measure of association and the magnitude of effect. They provide a useful quantitative tool in those circumstances where the family therapy researcher is interested in the sequential ordering of family members' behavior. There are a variety of computational procedures available, and creative slicing of the contingency table allows the researcher to test a variety of hypotheses. However, it is worthwhile to note that as the researcher conducts tests, he or she may in fact be increasing the likelihood of detecting chance effects, so probability levels should be adjusted for the number of tests being performed (Cairns, 1979; Castellan, 1979).

Cross-lagged panel and path analyses

Ordinarily, a measure of association or a correlation statistic cannot in and of itself describe causality. However, if a family therapy process researcher has a sense of the sequential ordering of events in family therapy processes, then he or she can array correlation coefficients in ways which allow for more powerful causal inferences.

Cross-lagged panel and path analyses are similar in that they use measure-of-association statistics configured in a way that allows the researcher to make some assertions about causality (Jones, 1974; Kenney, 1979; Markus, 1979). The notion is that the researcher arrays his or her data in ways which create a sequence of events. For example, different measures of families and therapists can be taken at different points in time. At Time 1, a therapist's scores on defensiveness can be related to a family member's scores on defensiveness. At Time 2, a family member's score and a therapist's score can again be related to each other with a measure of association. Just as these measures (at Time 1 and Time 2) reflect a measure of association *between* the therapist and family member, we can also create a measure of *within-* therapist's and within–family member's scores. To do so, we would correlate a therapist's scores at Time 1 with the therapist's scores at Time 2. The relatedness of a person' scores at Time 1 and Time 2 is asserted as reliability. In essence then, the researcher has created in these two manipulations a measure of the relatedness of therapist's and family's scores at two different points in time, and has also indicated whether or not therapist's and family member's scores have remained relatively stable over time (i.e., whether or not the same relative rank order and covariation have maintained over time; note that this is different from saying that they have remained the same). The cross-lag wrinkle comes in when a therapist's score at Time 1 is correlated with the family member's at Time 2 and vice versa (family member's score at Time 1 correlated with therapist's score at Time 2). From these correlations or measures of association, it can be established whether or not (in a comparative sense) family member's scores at Time 2 are more like therapist's at Time 1 or whether therapist's at Time 2 are more similar to family member's at Time 1. *If the reliabilities are equivalent,* then the comparison of therapist (1)–family member (2) versus therapist (2)–family member (1) can be a basis on which to assert who is influencing whom the most. Note that causality is inferred from the temporal sequencing of the data, but again the reader is reminded that this temporal sequencing is also relative to the stability (reliability) of both therapist's and family member's scores over time. If there is an appreciable difference between the reliability of therapist's and family member's scores, then one cannot assert that the differential correlation between Therapist (1)–Family Member (2) and Family Member (1)–Therapist (2) are indeed related to their systematic relationship to each other (rather, the difference in relationships may be an artifact of instability of measurement) (Markus, 1979). The value of this design for the family therapy researcher-clinician is not only that it conveys a sense of the relatedness of family therapist's and family member's scores, but the temporal sequencing of this relatedness can address issues such as whether or not the therapist is being responsive to family members or is indeed guiding or influencing their behavior in certain ways. In order both to create the stabilty of data points and to generate the between-person correlatons, the researcher should use a coding scheme which creates a substantial number of data points for computing the correlations. Both the reliability and the validity of the assertions in this design depend on the number of data points sampled by the coding scheme. While the researcher may not need to have as great an appreciation for the order of events at Time 1 and Time 2, the researcher's coding scheme should nonetheless capture a substantial frequency of data points at both Time 1 and Time 2.

Similar in strategy to the cross-lagged panel analysis, path analyses utilize a more complicated analytic technique to make similar kinds of assertions. Multiple regression is a strategy of intercorrelating variables in ways such that it is possible to isolate the true-score and error variance components of each variable. Similarly it is possible to examine the extent to which variables covary with each other, have independent sources of variance, or are composed of error (Kenny, 1979). In this design, the relative importance of a relationship can be systematically compared to the relative scores of people as individuals and/or the random and capricious variance associated with error. Rather than merely compare the magnitude of correlations as in the cross-lagged panel analysis, the researcher goes through the more elaborate multiple regression, partial and semipartial correlation procedures to identify what amounts of variance are due to overlap in variables. Again utilizing some quasi-experimental criterion to establish an order effect (usually temporal order), the researcher computes the overalp in therapist and family member at Time 1 and therapist and family member at Time 2. The family therapy researcher can then estimate (with multiple regression procedures) the overlap between therapist at Time 1–family member at Time 2, and family member at Time 1–therapist at Time 2. The relative comparisons of these overlaps can be done simultaneously with the multiple regression procedure. An additional advantage of these multiple comparisons with the multiple regression procedure is that the researcher can make some inferences as to whether or not there is an appreciable difference in the magnitude of effect between the overlap of each variable. In essence then, the family therapy researcher is comparing proportions of overlap in scores between therapists and themselves, family members and themselves, family therapists and family members with each other, and family therapists and family members with each other at different points in time. Similar to the analysis of variance, each of these comparisons can be constructed as main effects associated with family therapists, family members, for Time 1 versus Time 2. In addition, the analysis of variance metaphor as used in multiple regression allows the family therapist researcher to compare the interaction of the overlap between family therapist and family member at Time 1 versus the overlap between family therapist and family member at Time 2. These interaction comparisons thus become the strategy by which the family therapist can assert causality. The analytic strategy is one of deciding whether or not the prediction of family members' scores at Time 2, for example, is enhanced not only by knowledge of their scores at Time 1 but by therapist's scores at Time 1 as well.

The path analysis procedure therefore utilizes multiple regression analytic methods to construct an equation which comprises scores of people as they interact with each other. In a quantifiable way, people's behavior can be characterized as properties of themselves, stability over time, and most importantly for the family therapy researcher, as a function of their covariation with somebody else.

Structural equations

Multiple regression estimates of measures of association can provide an estimate of what part of a score is associated with a variable, versus that part of a score which is associated with overlap of other variables, versus that part of a score which is associated with error (Kerlinger & Pedhazur, 1973). Similar to the cross-lag panel equation, rather than array correlations, the researcher can do a multiple regression and array variables by that portion of variance which is associated with a single variable versus that portion of the variance which is associated with the overalp between variables. Similar to the path analysis mentality, the researcher can then decide whether certain variables predict overlap better than overlap predicts certain variables. For example, it may be noteworthy to know if father's scores on a measure of therapeutic obnoxiousness are related to his first-session scores, or if we can predict his scores better by knowing something about the obnoxiousness of other family members or the therapist, or both. To form a structural equation analysis, the researcher uses a strategy similar to the cross-lagged panel development analysis. Rather than using only the raw correlations, the researcher uses the partial and semipartial correlations obtained from a multiple regression: Stated nontechnically, the researcher is using that part of scores which are associated with a single person versus their overlap with other people. If the researcher has a clear model of the sources of influence in family therapy, then the degree to which the scores of family members can be measured allows him or her to use the structural equation technique. In general, in order to use the structural equation technique, the researcher must have some sense that the scores are coded in some meaningful continuous fashion. The structural equation analysis requires the researcher, then, to use measures of association to identify which portions of scores are associated with which variables. The temporal sequencing of the variables is similar to the path analysis or cross-lagged panel analysis, where inferences of causality are derived from the ordering of the variables. A further advantage to the structural equation is the multiple regression analysis of the data, which allows the researcher to test the magnitude of the effect or the significant difference between the components of the structural equation. While complicated, the structural analysis equation can be a very powerful tool if the researcher has a very clear model of how the variables in question are related to each other and can build a plausible model of how the variables ought to be ordered.

Lag and time series analyses. Lag and time series analyses are descriptive analytic strategies for molecular elements of process over time (Cook & Campbell, 1979; Glass, Willson, & Gottman, 1975; McCleary & Hay, 1980). If a family therapy researcher had many molecular data points taken over a substantial period of time, the time series and lag analyses will describe some important characteristics of the pattern of these data points.

Before understanding the between-person similarities or differences in time series, it is probably important to understand first the descriptive character of lag and time series analyses. The researcher must have a coding scheme which encodes a frequency or binary data point at a discreet point in time. For example, a family therapy researcher may be interested in the number of words used by a therapist in each three-minute segment of therapy sessions over a long number of sessions. To develop 200 intervals the researcher would need to have 10 sessions of one hour each. Within each of these intervals, the number of words that a family therapist used would be counted. A first question might be whether or not what a therapist says in one unit is related to what he said in the last unit as reflected in the number of words spoken. In a lag 1, the therapist would correlate the number of words spoken in Unit 1 with the number of words spoken in Unit 2, the number in Unit 2 with the number in Unit 3, . . . the number of words in Unit 199 with the number of words in Unit 200. A lag 1 analysis of this type would reflect the lag 1 sequential dependency or order in the data. The meaning of this correlation would be in identifying whether or not the best prediction of the number of words the therapist will speak is best related to the number of words he or she spoke in the previous unit. However, in family process, it is likely the case that the therapist might pause to allow family members to speak. Assuming for a moment that the therapist speaks for three minutes and then allows family members to speak for three minutes, then the best predictor of the therapist's rate of speech would not be reflected in a lag 1 analysis, but might be better reflected in a lag 2 analysis. In this instance, the family therapy researcher would code the number of words spoken in Unit 1 with the number of words coded in Unit 3, the number of words in Unit 2 with the number of words in Unit 4, . . . and the number of units in Unit 198 with the number of words in Unit 200. This lag 2 relationship can therefore characterize something different about the pattern of the therapist's speech. As a first characteristic of lag or time series analyses, then, researchers identify the relatedness between units as a function of their time or distance apart. The measure of association between these data points becomes a property of an equation which predicts the form of the process over time. This equation tells the researcher whether or not there is an appreciable relatedness between the data points.

A second feature of the time series analysis is that it can tell something about the rate of a given expression of behavior or feelings over time. A slope can be computed for the properties of a time series analysis that describes the degree to which a rate of a given behavior increases or decreases over time. For example, it may be worthwhile for the family therapist to know if a family member's rate of negative comments decreases over the course of therapy. From the model of time series that we have developed so far, it may be the case that the family member's expressions of negatives occur at a lag 4 (because there is an orderly progression of speech of therapist, father, mother, and then the Identified Patient), and it may also be the case that the *slope,* or rate, of the behavior decreases over time. Finally, the time series analysis can describe the degree to which there is a sudden versus gradual change in the slope of (or rate of change of) behavior. The time series analysis can describe not only the extent to which the slope changes but if this change is sudden versus gradual and if the influence of the change leaves the system quickly or slowly (Ostrom, 1978).

It is also possible for the researcher to compare time series between two or more people. Similar to the path analysis or structural equation model, the researcher is using a time series analysis to build a quantifiable structural model which describes the flow of process over time. The family therapy researcher can compare differences in the sequential dependency (or lags), slope (or rate of change), or form of influence (or shock) between people as well. This is accomplished by comparing those elements of the structural equation of the time series of a given person to those structural elements of the time series of another person. This requires the researcher to compute a separate time series for each family member, the implication being that the researcher cannot do a sequential form of coding (McDowall, McCleary, Meidinger, & Hay, 1980). Rather, the researcher must be able to capture data points for each family member within the same coding interval to be able to do this parallel, or between-person, type of time series analysis.

In summary, time series and lag sequential analyses are the most descriptive means for capturing formal properties of substantial process data. There are appreciable costs associated with gathering time series data, not the least of which is the need to capture an extraordinarily large number of data points over a long period of time. The researcher also faces substantial technical problems of coding the data, conspicuously the problem of a time interval which allows the researcher to capture a substantial number of data points for more than one person at a time. The "micro" flavor of this coding scheme poses substantial technical difficulties to coders. The researcher also should probably be guided by some model of the important characteristics of processes over time.

Summary of statistical procedures

In summary, we have described how a series of statistical procedures can be used to quantify the phenomena of interest to researchers. In so doing, we have tried to convey some of the descriptive richness which can come about through a thoughtful application of statistical techniques. The reader no doubt recognizes that the efficacy of these statistical techniques is tied to the data points generated by the clinician's coding scheme. As in the development of a coding scheme, the researcher implicitly conveys in the application of statistical technique some of his or her assumptions about what is important about family therapy.

In addition, the family clinician who becomes a family researcher recognizes that he or she is in a more passive mode and is "making some bets." An important part of the development of statistical theory has been the relationship of statistics and empirical method to the hypothesis test. The probability notions underlying statistics and hypothesis testing are forcing the researcher to make a commitment to *experimental* control of phenomena of interest. In many ways, this is less direct than the reflexive and responsive kind of control of phenomena that clinicians can exert in clinical settings. However the trade-off to using a statistical method is that researchers can use quantifiable indexes of their judgment to document phenomena that they cannot monitor on a momentary basis. Seminal thinkers in family therapy argued that the process of family intervention and family life is more important than issues of content (Haley, 1963). In analogous fashion, we are arguing that the process of research is a descriptive, vigorous, and rigorous process for advancing the field of family therapy. Just as therapists seek to improve the channels, reduce confusion, increase efficiency, and clarify communication in families, we argue that research is a paradigm and language system that can enhance the dialogue between family therapists, model builders, and trainers. Within the structured process of research dialogue, the meaningful content issues between therapies should become more clear, as should the important areas of lack of information.

We herein propose the conservative position that research training should be an important component of the development of the family therapist. A central function of science has been to serve as a language system that is relatively rule governed, clear, and an effective means of disseminating new information. This is to overlook the difficulties inherent in learning a new language and to recognize that sometimes the methods of science do lag clumsily behind the creativity and intuition of the clinician. The integrity of the clinician's activity can only be enhanced by rigorous translation and scrutiny within the research arena.

REFERENCES

Achenbach, T. M. Psychopathology of childhood research problems and issues. *Journal of Consulting and Clinical Psychology,* 1978, *46,* 759–776.

Alexander, J. F. Defensive and supportive communications in normal and deviant families. *Journal of Consulting and Clinical Psychology,* 1973, *40,* 223–231.

Alexander, J. F., & Barton, C. Systems-behavioral intervention with delinquent families: Clinical, methodological, and conceptual considerations. In J. Vincent (Ed.), *Advances in family intervention* (Vol. 1): *Assessment and theory.* Greenwich, Conn.: JAI Press, 1980.

Alexander, J. F., & Parsons, B. Short-term behavioral intervention with delinquent families: Impact on family process and recidivism. *Journal of Abnormal Psychology,* 1973, *81,* 219–225.

Alexander, J. F., & Parsons, B. V. *Functional family therapy.* Monterey, Calif.: Brooks/ Cole Publishing, 1982.

Bakeman, R., Cairns, R. B., & Appelbaum, M. Note on describing and analyzing interactional data: Some first steps and common pitfalls. In R. B. Cairns (Ed.), *The analysis of social interactions: Methods, issues, and illustrations.* Hillsdale, N.J.: Lawrence Erlbaum Associates, 1979.

Bandler, R., & Grinder, J. *Frogs into princes: Neuro linquistic programming.* Moab, Utah: Real People Press, 1979.

Barton, C. *Communication, cognitions, and contingencies in delinquent and control families.* Unpublished doctoral dissertation, University of Utah, 1982.

Bateson, G., Jackson, D., Haley, J., & Weakland, J. Toward a theory of schizophrenia. *Behavioral Science,* 1956, *1,* 251–264.

Bowen, M. Toward the differentiation of self in one's family of origin. In F. Andres & J. Lorrio (Eds.), *Georgetown family symposium papers I.* Washington, D.C.: Georgetown University Press, 1974.

Bowen, M. *Family therapy in clinical practice.* New York: Jason Aronson, 1978.

Boyle, J. T., & Bonacich, M. Strategies of competition in mixed-motive games. *Journal of Conflict Resolution,* 1967, *12,* 26–32.

Cairns, R. B. Toward guidelines for interactional research. In R. B. Cairns (Ed.), *The analysis of social interactions: Methods, issues, and illustrations.* Hillsdale, N.J.: Lawrence Erlbaum Associates, 1979.

Cairns, R. B., & Green, J. A. How to assess personality and social patterns: Observations or ratings? In R. B. Cairns (Ed.), *The analysis of social interactions: Methods, issues, and illustrations.* Hillsdale, N.J.: Lawrence Erlbaum Associates, 1979.

Campbell, D. T., & Stanley, J. C. *Experimental and quasi-experimental designs for research.* Skokie, Ill.: Rand McNally, 1963.

Castellan, N. J. The analysis of behavior sequences. In R. B., Cairns (Ed.), *The analysis of social interactions: Methods, issues, and illustrations.* Hillsdale, N.J.: Lawrence Erlbaum Associates, 1979.

Cook, T. D., & Campbell, D. T. *Quasi-experimentation: Design and analysis issues for field settings.* Skokie, Ill.: Rand McNally, 1979.

Cook, T. D., & Reichardt, C. S. (Eds.). *Sage Research Progress Series in Evaluation,* (Vol. 1): *Qualitative and quantitative methods in evaluation research.* Beverly Hills, Calif.: Sage Publications, 1979.

Cronbach, L. J., Gleser, G. C., Nanda, H., Rajaratnam, N. *The dependability of behavioral measurements: Theory of generalizability for scores and profiles.* New York: John Wiley & Sons, 1972.

Ethical principles of psychologists. *American Psychologist,* 1981, *36,* 633–638.

Falicov, C. J., Constantine, J. A., & Breunlin, D. C. Teaching family therapy: A program based on training objectives. *Journal of Marital and Family Therapy,* 1981, *7,* 497–505.

Fisher, B. L., Giblin, P. R., & Hoopes, M. H. Healthy family functioning: What therapists say and what families want. *Journal of Marital and Family Therapy,* 1982, *8,* 273–284.

Fisher, B. L. Transactional theories but individual assessment: A frequent discrepancy in family research. *Family Process,* 1982, *21,* 313–320.

Fleiss, J. L. *Statistical methods for rates and proportions* (2d ed.). New York: John Wiley & Sons, 1981

Fontana, A. F. Familial ideology of schizophrenia: Is a scientific methodology possible? *Psychological Bulletin,* 1966, *66,* 214–227.

Framo, J. L. Symptoms from a family transactional viewpoint. In D. J. Sago & H. S. Kaplan (Eds.), *Progress in group and family therapy.* New York: Brunner/Mazel, 1972

Frank, G. H. The role of the family in the development of psychopathology. *Psychological Bulletin,* 1965, *64,* 191–205.

Galligan, R. J. Innovative techniques: Siren or rose. *Journal of Marriage and the Family,* November 1982, 875–886.

Gardiner, W., Hartmann, D. P., & Mitchell, C. The effects of serial dependence on the use of chi square for analyzing sequential data in dyadic interactions. *Behavior Assessment,* 1982, *4,* 75–82.

Garrigan, J., & Bambrick, A. Family therapy for disturbed children: Some experimental results in special education. *Journal of Marriage and Family Counseling,* 1977, *3,* 83–93.

Gelfand, D., & Hartmann, D. *Child behavior analysis and therapy.* Elmsford, N.Y.: Pergamon Press, 1975.

Glass, G. V., Willson, V. L., & Gottman, J. M. *Design and analysis of time-series experiments.* Boulder: Colorado Associated University Press, 1975.

Gottman, J. M. Temporal form: Toward a new language for describing relationships. *Journal of Marriage and the Family,* November 1982, 943–962.

Gottman, J., Markman, H., & Notarius, C. The topography of marital conflict: A sequential analysis of verbal and non-verbal behavior. *Journal of Marriage and the Family,* 1977, *39,* 461–477.

Gurman, A. S., & Kniskern, D. P. Research on marital and family therapy: Progress, perspective, and prospect. In S. L. Garfield & A. E. Bergin (Eds.), *Handbook of psychotherapy and behavior change: An empirical analysis* (2d ed.). New York: John Wiley & Sons, 1978.

Gurman, A. S., & Kniskern, D. P. Family therapy outcome research: Knowns and unknowns. In A. S. Gurman & D. P. Kniskern (Eds.), *Handbook of family therapy.* New York: Brunner/Mazel, 1981.

Haberman, S. J. *Analysis of qualitative data* (Vol. 2). New York: Academic Press, 1979.

Haley, J. Critical overview of present status of family interaction research. In J. Framo (Ed.), *Family interaction: A dialogue between family researchers and family therapists.* New York: Springer Publishing 1972.

Haley, J. *Problem solving therapy.* San Francisco: Jossey-Bass, 1976.

Handel, G. Psychological study of whole families. *Psychological Bulletin,* 1965, *63,* 19–41.

Hawes, L. C., & Foley, J. M. A Markov analysis of interview communication. *Speech Monographs,* 1973, *40,* 208–219.

Hays, W. L. *Statistics for the social sciences.* New York: Holt, Rinehart & Winston, 1963.

Jackson, D. The study of the family. *Family Process,* 1965, *4,* 1–20.

Jones, R. R. Design and analysis problems in program evaluation. In P. O. Davidson, F. W. Clark, & L. A. Hamerlynck (Eds.), *Evaluation of behavioral programs in community, residential and school settings.* Champaign, Ill.: Research Press, 1974.

Katz, A., Kransinski, M., Philip, E., & Wieser, C. Change in interactions as a measure of effectiveness in short term family therapy. *Family Therapy,* 1975, *2,* 31–56.

Kelley, H. H., & Thibaut, J. W. *Inter-personal relations: A theory of interdependence.* New York: John Wiley & Sons, 1978.

Kenny, D. A. *Correlation and causality.* New York: John Wiley & Sons, 1979.

Kerlinger, F. N., & Pedhazur, E. J. *Multiple regression in behavioral research.* New York: Holt, Rinehart & Winston, 1973.

Kiesler, D. J. *The process of psychotherapy: Empirical foundations and systems of analysis.* Hawthorne, N.Y.: Aldine Publishing, 1973.

Kirk, R. E. *Experimental design: Procedures for the behavioral sciences* (2d ed.). Monterey, Calif.: Brooks/Cole Publishing, 1982.

L'Abate, L. Issues of reductionism: Can circular models be reduced to linearity? *Zeitschrift fur Systemische Therapie,* in press.

Lidz, T., Cornelison, A., Fleck, S., & Terry, D. The intrafamilial environment of schizophrenic patients: II Marital Schism and Marital Skew, *American Journal of Psychiatry,* 1957, *114,* 241–248.

Markus, G. B. Analyzing panel data. In J. L. Sullivan (Ed.), *Quantitative applications in the social sciences.* Beverly Hills, Calif.: Sage Publications, 1979.

Masten, A. S. Family therapy as a treatment for children: A critical review of outcome research. *Family Process,* 1979, *18,* 323–336.

McCleary, R., & Hay, R. A. *Applied time series analysis for the social sciences.* Beverly Hills, Calif.: Sage Publications, 1980.

McDowall, D., McCleary, R., Meidinger, E. E., & Hay, R. A. Interrupted time series analysis. In J. L. Sullivan (Ed.), *Quantitative applications in the social sciences.* Beverly Hills, Calif.: Sage Publications, 1980.

McNemar, Q. *Psychological statistics* (4th ed.). New York: John Wiley & Sons, 1969.

Miller, B. C., Rollins, B. C., & Thomas, D. L. On methods of studying marriages and families. *Journal of Marriage and the Family,* November 1982, 851–873.

Minuchin, S. *Families and family therapy.* Cambridge, Mass.: Harvard University Press, 1974.

Minuchin, S., & Fishman, H. C. *Family therapy techniques.* Cambridge, Mass.: Harvard University Press, 1981.

Minuchin, S., Montalvo, B., Guerney, B. G., Rosman, B. L., & Schumer, F. *Families of the slums.* New York: Basic Books, 1967.

Minuchin, S., Rosman, B., & Baker, L. *Psychosomatic families: Anorexia nervosa in context.* Cambridge, Mass.: Harvard University Press, 1978.

Mishler, E. G., & Waxler, N. E. *Interaction in families: An experimental study of family processes and schizophrenia.* New York: John Wiley & Sons, 1968.

O'Leary, K. D., & Turkewitz, H. Methodological errors in marital and child treatment research. *Journal of Consulting and Clinical Psychology,* 1978, *46,* 747–758.

Olson, D., Sprenkle, D., & Russell, C. Circumplex model of marital and family systems I: Cohesion and adaptability dimensions, family types, and clinical applications. *Family Process,* 1979, *18,* 3–28.

Ostrom, C. W. Time series analysis: Regression techniques. In J. L. Sullivan (Ed.), *Quantitative applications in the social sciences.* Beverly Hills, Calif.: Sage Publications, 1978.

Parsons, B. V., & Alexander, J. F. Short-term family intervention: A therapy outcome study. *Journal of Consulting and Clinical Psychology,* 1973, *41,* 195–201.

Patterson, G. R. A performance theory for coercive family interaction. In R. B. Cairns (Ed.), *The analysis of social interactions: Methods, issues, and illustrations.* Hillsdale, N.J.: Lawrence Erlbaum Associates, 1979.

Patterson, G. R., & Fleischman, M. Maintenance of treatment effects: Some considerations concerning family systems and follow-up data. *Behavior Therapy*, 1979, *10*, 168–173.

Patterson, G. R., & Reid, J. F. Reciprocity and coercion: Two facets of social systems. In C. H. Neuringer (Ed.), *Advances in behavior therapy. New York: John Wiley & Sons, 1970.*

Pinsof, W. M. The Family Therapist Behavior Scale (FTBS): Development and evaluation of a coding system. *Family Process*, 1979, *18*, 451–461.

Pinsof, W. M. Family therapy process research. In A. S. Gurman & D. P. Kniskern (Eds.), *Handbook of family therapy.* New York: Brunner/Mazel, 1981.

Poor, D. S. CANOVA: An extension of the MANOVA program. Philadelphia: Temple University Measurement and Research Center, 1973.

Reiter, G. F., & Kilmann, P. R. Mothers as family change agents. *Journal of Counseling Psychology*, 1975, *22*, 61–65.

Snedecor, G. W. *Statistical methods: Applied to experiments in agriculture and biology.* Ames: Iowa State College Press, 1946.

Strodtbeck, F. L. The family as a three-person group. *American Sociological Review*, 1954, *19*, 23–29.

Stuart, R. B. Behavioral contracting within the families of delinquents. *Journal of Behavior Therapy and Experimental Psychiatry*, 1971, *2*, 1–11.

Thibaut, J. W., & Kelley, H. H. *The social psychology of groups.* New York: John Wiley & Sons, 1959.

Walizer, M. H., & Wienir, P. L. *Research methods and analysis: Searching for relationships.* New York: Harper & Row, 1978.

Wampold, B. E., & Margolin, G. Nonparametric strategies to test the independence of behavioral states in sequential data. *Psychological Bulletin*, 1982, *92*, 755–765.

Watzlawick, P. *The language of change.* New York: Basic Books, 1978.

Watzlawick, P., Beavin, J., & Jackson, D. *Pragmatics of human communication: A study of interactional patterns, pathologies and paradoxes.* New York: W. W. Norton, 1967.

Wells, R. A., & Dezen, A. E. The results of family therapy revisited: The non-behavioral methods. *Family Process*, 1978, *17*, 251–274.

Wells, R. A., Dilkes, T. C., & Trivelli, N. The results of family therapy: A critical review of the literature. *Family Process*, 1972, *11*, 189–208.

Wills, T. A., Weiss, R. L., & Patterson, G. R. A behavioral analysis of the determinants of marital satisfaction. *Journal of Consulting and Clinical Psychology*, 1974, *42*, 802–811.

Winer, B. J. *Statistical principles in experimental design* (2d ed.). New York: McGraw-Hill, 1971.

Chapter 36

A Transactional Perspective on the Treatment of Sexual Dysfunctions

WILLIAM C. TALMADGE
LYNDA D. TALMADGE

Sexual expression in the life of a committed couple can be a haven of delight and renewing or an arena of struggle and frustration. For most couples, their sexuality runs the continuum from frustration to delight. At no other time in the life of a couple do they confront themselves and each other more vulnerably than when they engage in sexual pleasuring. It is for this very reason that so many couples experience difficulty in marriage and sex.

In a committed relationship, sexuality is a physical expression of primary emotional bonds and is best understood in the context of the relationships which govern it, primarily the family of origin and marriage. The experience of giving and receiving—one of the most enjoyable pleasures in life that is acted out time after time in the life of a couple—is a constant, unconscious symbolic reawakening of early child-parent interactions and all that they were or were not. Through the marital sexual relationship, a couple is given the opportunity to rework these early life interactions.

Sexual interaction of a committed and loving married couple is one of the most highly intimate forms of relating. The purely physical act of sexual intercourse between a couple places each partner in a vulnerable and dependent position. For the sexual relating between a committed couple to be satisfactory and enjoyable over time, each partner must bring to that interaction love, power, passion, dependency, neediness, strength, openness, and affection. When couples can bring these types of affectional qualities to their sexual relating, their relationship is intimate.

However, the sexual relationship of a couple is an ongoing process needing continual work from both partners if it is to be successful and satisfactory. This type of intimate relationship does not come easily, yet is highly desired by many. Freedman (1978) concluded, in his study of happiness, that the marital sexual relationship is still one of the most highly valued sources of happiness. From his surveys, he stated:

> There is no simple recipe for producing happiness, but all of the research indicates that for almost everyone one necessary ingredient is some kind of satisfying, intimate relationship. Sex is not far behind in importance, and marriage, that venerable institution that is to some extent a combination of the two, is still, despite all the changes in our attitudes, a crucial factor in many people's happiness. People who are lucky enough to be happy in love, sex, and marriage are more likely to be happy with life in general than any other people. (p. 48)

Sex therapy has focused primarily at the behavioral and technical levels (Annon, 1974; Barbach, 1975; Heiman, LoPiccolo, & LoPiccolo, 1976; LoPiccolo & LoPiccolo, 1978; McCarthy, Ryan, & Johnson, 1975; Zilbergeld, 1976). These formulations of diagnosis and treatment of sexual dysfunctions have been very useful, especially in the early development of sex therapy. Kaplan (1974, 1979, 1983) has added greatly to our understanding and resolution of sexual problems, especially in the area of the interaction of the intrapsychic with sexual behavior. Sex therapists will forever be indebted to Masters and Johnson (1966, 1970), the grandparents of sex therapy, for their discoveries and formulations of human sexuality and pleasuring. They have brought human sexuality out of the closet around the world in a most professional manner.

PURPOSE

The purpose of this chapter is to describe the important role of the relationship in the understanding and treatment of sexual dysfunctions. The relationship of the couple is one of the most important avenues in the diagnosis and treatment of sexual dysfunctions. The model of sexual relationships formulated in this chapter is based on object relations theory, systems theory, and Gestalt and experiential psychotherapy. This chapter is concerned solely with married couples who have psychogenic sexual problems and, for emphasis, only discusses one level of intervention, the relationship.

UNDERSTANDING THE PATTERN OF THE PROBLEM

Understanding the emotional relatedness in the marital system is crucial for both diagnostic and treatment purposes of sexual dysfunctions (Messersmith, 1976). Sex therapy needs to integrate the work of couples psychotherapists and scientific psychological research on close relationships, such as the work of the Atlanta Experiential Psychotherapy Group of Whitaker, Warkentin, Malone, and Felder, the work of Henry Dicks (1967), John Bowlby (1969) at Tavistock, and the early systems work of Bateson, Jackson, Haley, Watzlawick, and Weakland, the transactional view of Framo and the close relationships research by Kelly, Berscheid, Christensen, Harvey, Huston, Levinger, McClintock, Peplau, and Peterson (1983). The work of Wile (1981), Segraves (1982), and Scharff (1982) is encouraging in the integration of some of these theoretical formulations.

Five levels of evaluation are important for successful diagnosis and treatment of sexual problems: (1) physical state, (2) overt sexual behavior, (3) interpersonal relationship issues of the pair, (4) intrapsychic issues of the individual, and (5) sexual attitudes, values, and knowledge.[1] For the sake of emphasis, the interpersonal relationship of the pair is the most salient factor in our discussion. However, all five factors are important in the intervention for sexual dysfunctions.

Treating sexual dysfunctions has become increasingly more difficult, complex, and less successful (Chapman, 1982). Many couples now are treating themselves successfully for their sexual dysfunctions. Magazines such as *Redbook, Playboy, Ladies Home Journal*, and *Reader's Digest* have been helpful to the public in enabling them to understand and resolve their sexual difficulties. Part of the failures in sex therapy can be attributed to improper handling of the relationship and/or attempting to do sex therapy with a couple whose relationship is really the primary source of difficulty (Chapman). In evaluating a sexual complaint, it is critical that one consider the various interacting variables which may be supporting this problem. A differential diagnosis is in order. However, we must now think of differential diagnosis not as focusing on a restrictive cause but as delineating the multiplicity and complexity of the variables involved as well as the pattern they produce. This type of evaluation is an interactional model which Fagan (1970) describes as patterning:

> While diagnosis is a more common term it has the disadvantage of provoking the analogy of the medical model in implying that the purpose of the process is arriving at a specific label. A better analogy for the process of patterning is that of artistic creation involving sometimes cognitive sometimes perceptual and intuitive skills in interaction with the material

---

[1] Individual and couples therapists have largely neglected the physical state in their treatment of sexual dysfunctions. Such things as prolactin-secreting pituitary tumor, the use of hypertensive medications, blood flow, and disease states are examples of specific areas to be addressed in the physical evaluation of sexual dysfunctions. The new works of Wagner and Green (1981) and Kaplan (1983) are useful volumes in this area of evaluation.

and demands of the environment as, for example, in the creation of the mobile in which a variety of pieces or systems are interconnected into an overall unity and balance. (p. 89)

TREATING THE RELATIONSHIP OR THE SEXUAL DYSFUNCTION

Sager (1976b) has stated that about 75 percent of the couples who, present with the primary complaint of either the marriage or sex, have a combination of significant marital and sexual problems regardless of which is the primary complaint. Framo (1982) has stated that about 90 percent of the couples he sees for marital therapy have significant sexual problems. With this in mind, the therapist must then decide which problem to treat, the marriage or the sexual dysfunction—an issue of debate in sex therapy. Different approaches have been used in resolving this dilemma. At the sexual clinic at the State University of New York at Stony Brook, LoPiccolo (1983) has reported that cutoff scores on the Locke-Wallace Marital Adjustment Test are used to discriminate maritally distressed couples from sexually distressed ones. Anyone with a score below 90 is not treated for sexual dysfunctions, because a score at this level is indicative of marital distress.

Berg and Snyder (1981) have proposed using a multidimensional approach in the differential diagnosis of marital and sexual distress. In their study, the Marital Satisfaction Inventory (Snyder, 1979) was found as a useful instrument in being able to discriminate between two treatment groups, one of marital distress and the other of sexual dysfunctions. Berg and Snyder stated, "There has emerged a growing consensus that treatment of sexual dysfunctions using a short-term behaviorally oriented directive approach without carefully examining the role of marital conflict in other dimensions of the relationship is both incomplete and shortsighted" (p. 290).

These researchers suggest that in using the Marital Satisfaction Inventory, two criteria stand out which indicate when brief, direct sex therapy is not the treatment of choice. These criteria are: (1) when the absolute global marital distress score is greater than 65, or (2) when the nonsexual clinical scales, such as those that deal with communication or intimacy, are elevated higher in relationship to the sex scale. More specifically, comparing sexually distressed males and maritally distressed males, it was found that there were significant differences in three areas. Sexually distressed males reported greater sexual dissatisfaction, less global marital distress, and less discontentment with the problem-solving communication in their marriage. The significant differences between the sexually and maritally distressed females were that the sexually distressed females reported greater sexual dissatisfaction, a level of less discontentment with leisure time together, and a less frequent history of family distress. No significant differences were found between the sexually distressed males and females. However, significant differences existed between the maritally distressed males and females: The males were more sexually dissatisfied, less conflicted about parenting, and had less family distress.

Frank, Anderson, and Kupfer (1976) looked at differences between couples seeking marital therapy and sexual therapy at the Western Psychiatric Institute and Clinic. All couples were given the KDS–15, which is an extensive self-report questionnaire that covers many variables involved in the marital relationship, such as attitudes about marriage, individual development, courtship, current living situation, premarital and marital sexual activity, and the role of children in the marriage. There were 29 couples seeking marriage therapy and 25 who sought sexual therapy at two different clinics at the same institution. Results were analyzed using chi square. Results indicated that the marital therapy group, as compared to the sexual therapy group, complained significantly more about their spouse not understanding them, too frequent arguments, financial disagreements, disagreements about the division of responsibilities, and different social needs or desires. The sex therapy patients had significantly more sexual dissatisfaction than the marital therapy patients.

However, in terms of specific sexual difficulties, the two groups were very similar. In fact, in some areas, the marital therapy patients were having more difficulty than the sex therapy patients. For example, those men in marital therapy were having greater difficulty getting an erection, difficulty in ejaculating, and disinterest. Many of the marital therapy female patients complained of similar sexual difficulties as that of the sex therapy female patients. The authors found that "in general the sex therapy patients were happy with their spouse and involved in basically affectionate relationships whereas the relationships of the marital therapy couples were characterized by antagonism" (p. 561). The preliminary evidence in this discrimination between these two groups appears to suggest that the sex therapy patients were less impulsive and more mature than the marital therapy group. Frank et al. note that this is just one step in the direction of finding out who comes to which type of therapy. They suggest that the next step is to evaluate the treatment outcome of the two groups, which would assist in making some judgment as to the correctness of fit between patient and treatment.

In a more recent study by Chapman (1982), criteria for determining when to do sex therapy has been developed based on 30 couples who were seen in sex therapy. Charts of these 30 patients were retrospectively reexamined to discriminate the critical factors which accounted for treatment success or failure. The author found six criteria which were helpful in diagnosing when one should conduct sex therapy instead of some other type of relationship or individual intervention.

The first criteria was an absence of a physical problem such as that of a specific disease, physiological disability, or drug side effect. The next criteria was an absence of other primary problems, such as severe relationship issues, depression, alcohol abuse, or drug abuse. The author states that it does not seem appropriate that one would deal primarily with the sex therapy approach to such problems. The third criteria was the presence of a bona fide sexual dysfunction such as those classified in DSM III. The fourth is the presence of therapy-positive factors such as the patient's motivation for sex therapy and belief that it is the appropriate treatment and one that will be successful. The fifth criteria is an absence of interfering situational events such as lengthy visits by relatives, work schedules, family distress such as death, and other situational events which would give the couple difficulty in doing their homework assignments. The final criteria was the presence of basic relationship requirements. This meant that the couple functioned at some minimal level within their relationship and that there was no serious psychopathology. Secondly, it meant that the couple appeared to be committed and had a basic level of communication skills.

In a study by Hartman (1980), 20 couples who were referred to an outpatient family therapy unit were assessed using the Marital Happiness Scale, a self-report measure of marital satisfaction. These patients were then assigned to four categories based upon subscales of the Marital Happiness Scale. The subscales that were used in defining the categories were sexual satisfaction, communication or general happiness, and marital conflict. The author was addressing the question of whether couples differ who are sexually dysfunctional as opposed to maritally dysfunctional, or a combination of the two.

Each couple engaged in three structured interactions which were videotaped. These discussions were: (1) a conversation on problems within the relationship; (2) the early history of their marriage; and (3) the planning of a joint task. Independent raters, who were not aware of the category into which the patients had been divided, judged the structured interaction videotapes and completed the couple evaluation scale which is a modified version of the Beavers-Timberlawn Evaluation Scale. This study is of significance because of this observational mode of investigation. Significant differences were observed between the control, sexual dysfunction, marital conflict, and combined sexual dysfunction and marital conflict, and combined sexual dysfunction and marital conflict. It was found that the control and sexual dysfunction couples were more likely to show a structure of shared leadership with flexibility and respectful negotiation. The sexual dysfunction group demonstrated more skill in negotiation, more interpersonal congruence in their self-appraisals, greater acceptance of responsibility for their actions, more acknowledgement of their own and their spouse's stated feelings, thoughts, and behavior, they showed less invasiveness and a greater overall adequacy and autonomy and tended to encourage more open expression of affect, optimism, and empathy.

Hartman (1980) concludes "that competence in couple functioning may be preserved in the presence of an unsatisfactory sexual relationship" (p. 579). However, a criticism of this study is that clinical patients who were seen in therapy were used as the control group. Thus, if the sexual dysfunction group had been compared to a population of couples who declared more general happiness and satisfaction within their relationship, they may not have looked as good as they did in this research.

Sager (1976b) discusses the interrelatedness of marital and sexual therapy and the difficulty in distinguishing when to do one or the other. Due to the complexity of the multiplicity of interacting variables, simply deciding to do sex therapy or marital therapy is shortsighted and fails to acknowledge the interactional quality within marital relationships. Sager states:

> In my first published opinion on this issue, I stated definitely that the therapist who is qualified to use both marital and sex therapy should keep the two sharply separated. With additional experience I have become less rigid. The interplay between immediate and remote causes often requires a frequent shift of therapeutic emphasis. (pp. 556–557)

The whole idea of being able to differentially diagnose whether sex therapy or marital therapy is to be the treatment of choice with the couple is an assumption based on the medical model. This model holds that if one can simply define the cause, then one automatically knows the prescribed treatment. However, this approach to human relationships fails to acknowledge an interdependence and relatedness of two individuals who bring a unique set of history and development to bear in their coupling. A more reasonable approach is to consider the relationship more globally and the sexuality of the couple as a highly significant interlocking dimension within the coupling. Any movement within any area of the relationship is likely to vibrate throughout the whole. Therefore, in treating couples who present with a primary sexual complaint, it is crucial that the relationship be seen as one of the patients involved. The odds are greatly against any sex therapy treatment which does not deal with the relationship of the couple. Typically with couples in sex therapy, we tell them of the five levels of intervention and emphasize the importance of dealing with all of these. The relationship is one of the primary levels of sexual intervention.

There are factors to consider when deciding which level needs attention and at which level there will be the least disruption to the total relationship. First is the availability of the couple. Such questions need to be raised within the mind of the therapist as to how the couple defines their problem and whether they are amenable for direct sexual intervention. However, when the patients' and therapist's definitions of the problem are not the same, this does not necessarily mean that the therapist proceeds with the patients' definition. Often a reframing of the problem is in order. Secondly, the impasses within the relationship must be recognized. For example, it would be foolish with a rapid-ejaculation couple to start them on the squeeze technique or stop-start when the levels of hostility and hurt are so high as to block significantly the perception and cooperation of the couple. A third consideration is the quality of relationship between the therapist and the couple. Often when the relationship is positive, nurturing, and healing, the therapist can persuade and encourage the couple into new forms of relating. This usually allows a couple to proceed in their work with one another with a more optimistic outlook (Frank, 1976; Whitaker & Warkentin, 1967). This whole area of therapeutic process is one which needs more attention in sex therapy. A fourth consideration is the distance within the couple's relationship. In this area, we consider such variables as openness, trust, honesty, self-disclosure, and affectional quality. Often, the level of distance between a couple must be attended to before any direct intervention can be made into the overt sexual behavior of the couple. The final consideration is the quality of communication of the couple. The perceptual set and expectations that the couple bring to bear on each other can have an inhibiting effect upon their communication. The whole sexual arena for a couple is often a place where old, unconscious messages are provoked and thus distort the couple's ability to hear one another.

THE MARITAL RELATIONSHIP

Human beings have strong needs to be connected to one another in mutual dependency. This assumption derives from an ethological tradition of research: Observations of the phylogenetically lower primates as well as human infants and children reveal strong evidence supporting the social nature of humans (Bowlby, 1969, 1973; Harlow, 1958). Berscheid and Peplau (1983) have stated:

> Relationships with others lie at the very core of human existence. Humans are conceived within relationships, born into relationships and live their lives within relationships with others. Each individual's dependency on other people—for the realization of life itself, for survival during one of the longest gestation periods in the animal kingdom, for food and shelter and aid and comfort throughout the life cycle—is a fundamental fact of the human condition. (p. 1)

Marriage is an attempt to address this primary need to be related. Next to the parent-child relationship, the marital relationship is the most intense example of the social-emotional-physical interdependence of humans (Dicks, 1967). Most couples who seek sex therapy are having difficulties in this interdependent relationship. The relational and transactional problems within the connectedness of the couple have provided an environment for the development of a sexual difficulty which has become functional within the perceptual set of the couple. Often the couple can deny, collude, and distort their perception in such a way as to avoid seeing the relational difficulty until they are confronted with a sexual problem (Framo, 1970). Masters and Johnson (1976) state that the relationship of a sexually dysfunctioning couple must be the primary focus:

> A sexual problem may represent an isolated facet of an otherwise healthy relationship, but sexual distress usually arises from hostility, poor communication, maintenance of a double standard, unrealistic expectations, deception, differences in reproductive goals, or a host of other factors. Unless therapy focuses primarily on the relationship as a whole rather than being restricted to the sexual component, important treatment dynamics may be overlooked. (p. 551)

The following are several assumptions we make about marriage which influence the goals and the process of sex therapy:

1. Coupling is an organic process, not a product or an end. This process also proceeds through predictable developmental phases with each couple handling each particular phase in their own unique way. Marriage does not magically happen, but requires dedication, work, and commitment (Barnett, 1981). It requires that each partner monitor where they see themselves within the relationship, what their needs are, what they are willing to give. Marriage is, at its best, a living system progressing through developmental stages toward a goal of shared intimacy (Talmadge & Talmadge, 1984).

2. Marriage can serve a long-term curative function for the individuals (Wile, 1980). This may be in the form of healing old wounds or working through unfinished or interpersonal struggles. Marriage is an interpersonal approach to personhood. Choosing a partner for his or her curative potential is almost entirely an unconscious process (Dicks, 1967).

3. Spouses often respond to one another transferentially, especially in times of distress. Thus, couples perceive and respond to one another in a way that is an aberration of who they really are. This transference not only includes the family of origin but also significant others who are in the developmental history of the individual, such as an old hurt with a former lover (Segraves, 1982).

4. There is a basic ambivalence in interdependency. There is the fear that in being too independent, we will lose our connection with

the beloved, and in being too dependent, we will lose ourselves. The paradox in relating within this interdependency is that too much closeness brings the fear of merger, and too much distance brings the fear of separateness. Health within marital relating requires both interdependence and individuation. Thus, marriage is the arena wherein the maturity of the personality is most fully challenged, for only the emotionally mature can negotiate closeness without merger.

5. Individuals joining together in the marital bond are ill prepared for the task of marriage and bring with them many unrealistic expectations of each other. The basis for these expectations is in each partner's unique perceptual set, which originates in their families of origin, personality structure, and social context (Segraves, 1982). The lack of preparation and the fantasy expectations soon lead to disappointment within the marriage, thus requiring that the couple make adjustments within each perceptual set as well as in their expectations of each other. This adjusting must be done in such a way that it fits their overall system of relating. As the partners adjust to one another's representational sets, they begin to form a new one together, which is often a negotiated combination of the two they brought to the relationship. In short, each couple constructs its own reality (Berger & Kellner, 1964).

6. The whole range of powerful feelings is elicited within marital relating. Couples typically try to avoid those feelings which have negative connotations, because they seem to threaten their connection. If they are to become intimate, they need to express these strong negative feelings. In order for issues to be resolved, they must be incorporated within the relationship, not excluded from it (Braiker & Kelley, 1979; Douvan, 1977; Gurman, 1978; Raush, Barry, Hertel, & Swain, 1974; Wile, 1981).

RELATIONAL SEXUALITY

1. Each partner has an enormous effect on the other's experience and expression of his or her own sexuality. Spouses' character structures and internalizations of the family of origin and social context shape and guide the emerging and developing sexuality of the couple. The sexuality of the couple is dependent upon their interaction. The powerful influence which each partner exerts on the other's sexuality is described vividly in a study by Marshall and Neill (1977). They conducted an investigation of the effects on the marriages of 12 patients who underwent intestinal bypass surgery for extreme obesity. The most striking changes occurred in the sexuality and dependence/independence of the partners. While the surgery patients generally reported a renewed interest in sex, arousability, and sexual self-image and desire, the spouses generally felt threatened by the weight loss. Some began

to lose their sexual desire and to become impotent, and it was revealed that a few of the participants had been hiding their homosexuality within the context of a sexless marriage. Only two spouses reported being pleased with the increase in sexual desire and change in sexual self-image in their partners. A more positive change can be seen in a couple where the husband becomes more intimate with his wife through affectual expression, and the wife's sexual desire increases (Framo, 1970; Haley, 1977; Jackson, 1957; Watzlawick, Weakland, & Fisch, 1974).

2. The relational sexuality of the couple is the formation of the sexual values, behavior, and affect of the personality of the marital relationship. The marital relationship develops a distinct character or personality through the bonding of the couple. The values, behavior, and affect of the couple are formed through the transactions of the personalities of the individuals, their families of origin, their physical health, and their social context. Dicks (1967) emphasizes the importance of the social context so often neglected by psychotherapists:

> It is at its broadest a contract by two persons ("with their central egos") to play certain social roles in ways which not only satisfy the needs of the other as far as they can perceive but also to varying degrees fulfill the requirements of the culture. . . . Clearly there is a top level at which a couple have a common purpose, a need to be seen as a harmonious unit. (pp. 126–127)

3. The sexual dysfunction is assumed to serve a function within the couple's system, much as any symptom can be viewed. The sexual problem helps to maintain the couple's definition of their relationship (Jackson, 1957). Partners elicit behavior from one another that confirms their perceptions of themselves and the world. An example of this can be seen with a couple who came with the presenting problem of vaginismus. As the couple had defined their problem, it was all the woman's fault, and in their perception, the husband had no participation in this problem. However, from the sexual history that was taken from the husband, it was strongly suspected that he had had numerous questions about his sexual self-image and his adequacies as a sexual partner. These feelings were not exposed until the female became receptive to intercourse, at which time her husband began to experience secondary impotence. For this couple, the way they had originally defined their relationship was functional in keeping their perception of the marriage at status quo, a collusion to protect the husband from his own painful feelings. As long as the wife was willing to carry the symptom within the relationship, her husband could avoid his negative sexual self-image and his inadequacies.

4. Sexual expression between a couple has a special power for elicit-

ing the unconscious to participate in the relating. Sexual expression within a committed relationship is one of the most intimate forms of expression that a couple may share—a powerful interaction involving body, mind, and soul wherein the unconscious is easily provoked to interact within the relationship at the symbolic level. Scharff (1982) has stated that those forms of relating which involve the body have a stronger, potent poignancy which nonbody relationships lack. The couple's sexual expressiveness brings forth from the unconscious mind that original give-and-take bonding that was established in the mother-infant interaction, reviving both the old feelings of gratification and the disappointments. Thus, old messages from early parent-child bonding are put into play within the context of the marital relationship.

5.   Psychogenic sexual problems of a couple are often an indicator of the difficulty with intimacy within the relationship. Both partners are involved. The lack of connectedness within the relationship supports the sexual dysfunction, which is an acting out and/or symptom of the lack of intimacy within the marital relationship. Intimacy within marriage requires ego strength, power, vulnerability, interdependency, trust, mutuality, and the knowing and seeking of self. Waring (1981) describes intimacy as being a composite of (1) affection, (2) expressiveness, (3) compatibility, (4) cohesion, (5) sexuality, (6) conflict resolution, (7) autonomy, and (8) identity. Thus, in marriage, intimacy is especially difficult to negotiate in that it requires "an established sense of personal identity and ego strength with a preservation of the capacity for dependency" (Dicks, 1967, p. 29).

6.   The affectional quality of the marital pair can be a healing and growth-inducing force in marital sexuality and relating. In a marital relationship in which there is open expression of nonsexual physical affection, there is likely to be heightened sexual excitement, satisfaction, and pleasure. The physical body contact of affection is a special force which can reawaken old body sensations from the early child-parent bonding (Bowlby, 1979; Harlow, 1962; Hollender, Luborsky, & Harvey, 1970; Montagu, 1978; Wallace, 1981). Through bodily contact, our first forms of communication are made. The present-day contact of skin between husband and wife is a means of conscious and unconscious emotional feeding which can touch the innermost parts of the self. Physical affection between two marital partners has a positive association in sexual desire and expression (Wallace, 1981).

THERAPY

Sex therapists have designed specific sexual treatment techniques for various sexual dysfunctions. Some of these techniques are the use of vaginal dilators, sensate focus, squeeze technique, and stop-start, relaxation, and masturbatory exercises (Barbach, 1975; Heiman et al., 1976; Kaplan, 1974; Masters & Johnson, 1970; Zilbergeld, 1978). These various techniques are very helpful in the treatment of sexual dysfunctions. Since they are so well documented elsewhere, the focus in this section will be purely on relational considerations, which have been less understood in sex therapy.

1. History-taking from both partners. All successful sex therapy approaches begin with a sex history of the two individuals and the relationship. In these early interviews, the relationship of the therapist and patients is being shaped. The interaction of therapist and patients is as important as the information obtained. This interaction can often tell a therapist about the styles of interaction of the couple and the various impasses of relating. In the history-taking, the therapist sends messages to the patients through the way in which he/she asks questions, about what, and how he/she responds to the information given.[2] In this phase of therapy, the therapist establishes himself/herself as an open sexual expert with whom one is free to discuss sexual issues.

2. Three patients are involved in sexual therapy—the two individuals and the marriage (Warkentin & Whitaker, 1966). In the structure of the therapy, all three patients need attention. Thus, spouses are worked with individually as well as together. The individual focus is particularly useful in assisting the person to take charge of himself or herself in the interdependence, thereby interrupting the blaming of the partner for one's unfulfilled sexual needs. This approach emphasizes that both spouses are responsible for the sexual relationship which they have developed. Thus, in treating a female patient with a primary orgasmic difficulty, her husband would participate fully in the therapy because he plays a significant role in the development and maintenance of this sexual dysfunction for the couple.

This approach of working with couples broadens Masters and Johnson's (1976) focus, which is purely upon the couple, to include the individuals as well. Kaplan (1983) supports this approach, stating that "most frequently both factors play a role and the therapist must be prepared to shift the therapeutic emphasis as resistance arises sometimes confronting the partners with their destructive interactions and at other times working with the intrinsic anxieties of one or the other" (p. 60). Cole, Blakeney, Chan, Chesney, and Creson (1979) investigated the differences between symptomatic and asymptomatic partners who came for sex therapy. The results of this study indicated few significant

---

[2] In the sexual history-taking, some questions may need to be avoided. A good example of a question that is often better left to later stages of therapy is one which has to do with incest. Sometimes, the issue of incest can be raised too early in therapy and can precipitate difficulties within the patient and between the therapist and the patient.

differences between the two groups. The authors state in conclusion, "that in general the couple's ongoing relationship (rather than the individual characteristics) appears responsible for establishing satisfactory levels of sexual intimacy" (p. 79).

3. No one is to blame. Within this format of therapy, the couple soon learns that there aren't any good guys or bad guys within their marriage. This nofault approach to sexual dysfunction is especially important when one partner is carrying the symptom within the relationship. In the feedback interview, when the therapist gives his/her assessment of the two individuals and the relationship, marriage is discussed as an organic system in which both partners have a hand at guiding and influencing each other. The couple is told that the way that they have been responding as individuals was probably functional at some earlier time, but is no longer. The sexual dysfunction is interpreted to the couple as a result of difficulty in their satisfying some personal need(s) in the relationship (Wile, 1981).

4. Reframing. In the feedback session, the therapist discusses the five levels of evaluation: (a) physical state, (b) overt sexual behavior, (c) interpersonal relationship issues of the pair, (d) intrapsychic issues of the individual, and (e) sexual attitudes, values, and knowledge. All relevant levels of evaluation are discussed with the couple as it relates to their situation. The overt sexual behavior of the symptomatic partner is deemphasized. Emphasis is placed upon how the relationship supports the sexual problem which the couple presents. In the reframing, the problem is defined as relational, and examples are given of how both partners participate in the difficulty presented.

An example of this reframing is again with a couple in which the female was experiencing vaginismus. In the reframing with this couple, the husband was helped to see how his lack of pursuit with his wife in the sexual arena encouraged and supported the vaginismus of the couple. Later in therapy, this was once again brought home to the husband when they were beginning the initial phases of intercourse and he fell asleep. At this point in the therapy, it was suggested to the couple that they were seriously and very wisely considering all the repercussions which would take place within their marital relationship if they were to become consistently sexually active with one another. Thus, the husband's falling asleep was interpreted within a positive tone as being one of wisdom in trying to decide if they really wanted to change their sexual relationship. The reframing of the couple's problem as relational tends to defuse the blaming generally accompanying marital sexual discord.

However, in the feedback interview, not all observations, assessments, and interpretations of the therapist are presented. The importance of this interview and the reframing is to help the couple see their difficulty as relational without raising impasses or resistance prematurely.

5. Acting out of internal struggles of the parent-child interaction within the marital relationship. Because of the powerful nature of sexual interaction between married partners, unconscious struggles of the early parent-child relationship are easily awakened. These early object relations begin to be acted out within the sexual relationship of the couple. The spouses begin to act transferentially to each other as if they were parents or other significant others with whom they had difficulty in the past. It is explained to the couple that each partner has a perception and that their perception is neither right nor wrong, it simply is based upon their way of seeing the world, a way which was formed in their early development. Each member within the couple is assisted in seeing their perceptual set which is being acted out within the sexual relationship.

An example of this is with a couple which presented with low sexual desire and secondary impotence. The female had grown up in a family in which she was the middle child, having an older sister and a younger sister. The elder sister was the golden one who was highly successful at everything she undertook. The younger sister was sickly from birth and required a great deal of attention. The middle child was constantly asked why she couldn't be like her older sister and make good grades, look beautiful, and be successful, while, on the other hand, receiving messages that she was getting in the way of the care of the younger child. This female basically grew up with a highly critical attitude toward herself and constantly feeling as though she were unimportant. In the relationship with her husband, with her critical perceptual set of being unwanted, she perceived almost anything he said as expressing her lack of significance. As the years went on in this couple's marriage, she began to feel less and less important to her husband, and as this occurred, her sexual desire declined. In therapy, her perceptual set was uncovered for her so that she could see how she had been experiencing her husband's comments.

6. Experiential interaction and modeling. The interaction between the couple and the therapist within the experiential psychotherapy framework becomes the agent of change in the therapy. The therapist teaches the couple about emotional intimacy and its inclusion of negativity by his or her willingness to confront and share feelings. The therapist's ability to disclose himself/herself in a disciplined manner to the couple assists them in becoming more intimate with one another. Within the therapeutic relationship, the therapist demonstrates basic parental qualities with the couple, such as limit setting, nurturing, protection, affection, support, and guidance. Through these interac-

tions, spouses are taught to perform these functions for one another within the marriage.

7.   Spouses' regression of each other. In the reframing of the problem, the interpretation is given that the problem is really an unmet need on each partner's part. Each spouse is told that they should view their marital partner as a needy little child and are encouraged to meet the needs of the spouse. Within this framework, each partner is encouraged to reparent their spouse. This approach assists in reworking those early parent-child interactions which left unfulfilled needs. In one interview, a husband was told that his wife was a needy little child who needed to be constantly told how wonderful she was and how important she was to him. The same wife was told that her husband, who was a needy little child, wanted her constant attention and involvement through all manner of little things. It was suggested to the couple that there will be times which arise in which both partners are feeling extremely needy. In these times, it is encouraged that the partners comfort one another and not take on any major tasks. It is often recommended to couples when their neediness collides at the same time to simply lie together and hold one another.

8.   Interdependence. As previously mentioned, interdependence is an ambivalent state. If we are too interdependent, we fear losing ourselves; if we are not interdependent enough, we fear losing our partner. Within the sexual therapy, couples are assisted in seeing their efforts at becoming connected and separate and how these movements sometimes are expressions of their ambivalence concerning their intimacy. Couples presenting with sexual problems are frequently acting out independence (care-giving) and dependency (care-receiving) struggles. The sexual interaction of a couple frequently revives early childhood struggles with each of these.

For example, a husband who grew up in a family in which he was the oldest son was constantly trying to make his parent's marriage last and care for his two younger siblings. In his family of origin, he learned quickly that he was valued for his care-giving. Thus, in his sexual relationship, he is constantly giving to his wife and this overattention to her needs interrupts and distracts him from his experience of his passion. This lack of passion then interacts within the sexual relationship of the pair to deaden their sexuality. In dealing with interdependency with couples, another common issue which arises is control. Control is not interpreted negatively. All persons enjoy and desire to be in control of themselves (Wile, 1981). However, couples are assisted in seeing how their control may sometimes get in the way of their receiving care.

9.   Extreme hostility. Often, with couples who have been experiencing a sexual difficulty over a period of time, one of the partners usually

has extreme forms of hostility and blame for the other partner. This extreme form of anger can severely interfere with the therapeutic process if it is not attended to properly in the early phase of therapy. One way in which to deal with this negative affect is to interpret to both spouses this hostility as a form of deep hurt, unmet need, and anxiety. This often helps assist the couple in moving to deeper levels of intimacy with one another.

10.   Balancing the relationship. Frequently, within couples' sexual therapy, it is common to see one partner expressing most of the need, most of the affect, most of the support, or most of the power. Couples are assisted in seeing their imbalances within these areas. When a couple becomes imbalanced in these areas, they fail to give each other perspective, and the relationship is in serious danger. When imbalances are noted, the therapist reports these to the couple. For example, when a husband is expressing all the anger within the relationship, it is suggested that the wife might switch roles with her husband and do the same type of expressing by simply role playing him. Often this role playing leads the wife to finding her own form of anger within the relationship. Another means of dealing with this imbalance is to exaggerate it. For example, when a wife is expressing most of the need within a relationship, she is encouraged to be more and more needy with her husband. Eventually this gross exaggeration leads him to discover his need.

11.   Lighting the passion. Often, with couples experiencing sexual difficulties, a lack of passion within the relationship at both the personal and sexual levels is noted. Usually this lack of passion is a result of the partners colluding with one another to keep the marriage smooth and exclude their powerful negative feelings which end up blunting their intense positive feelings, their passion. This expenditure of energy to keep the relationship smooth drains the life from the marriage and the personal and sexual passion of the pair. This bound-up energy may also result in physical, emotional, or psychosomatic symptoms in a partner or in their children. Couples are encouraged to express their intense emotional feelings to the therapist as a means of rediscovering their passion. The therapist's experience of his or her passion and expression of it in the interviews with the couple is a helpful means of encouraging the couple to find theirs.

12.   Affection and touching. Sex therapists have emphasized the importance of touch through such techniques as sensate focus (Masters & Johnson, 1976). Many couples who come to sex therapy have lost their appetites for affection and touching. Commonly, most of their expressiveness with one another is being acted out verbally. Within this relational framework, it is encouraged that couples simply try at various times within their interactions with one another to physically

act out a statement to one another instead of talking with one another. For example, a husband who was feeling particularly saddened by a recent sexual encounter with his wife attempted to physically express this sadness to her through his touch. As he spoke of this recent sexual encounter, tears came to his eyes. He wiped his tears and placed them on his wife's cheeks. This expression was a turning point within this couple's sexual relationship.

CONCLUSION

This chapter has emphasized the importance of the role of the relationship in both understanding and resolving sexual issues with couples. The transactions of the couple emerge from the personalities of the individuals, their families of origin, their physical health, and the social context. The relational sexuality of the couple is the product of the sexual values, behavior, and affect of the personality of the marital relationship. The emotional relatedness of the couple is the core of relational sexuality.

REFERENCES

Abramowitz, S. I., & Sewell, H. H. Marital adjustment and sex therapy outcome. *Journal of Sex Research,* 1980, *16*(4), 325–337.

Annon, J. *The behavioral treatment of sexual problems* (Vols. 1–2). Honolulu: Enabling Systems, 1974.

Barbach, L. G. *For yourself: The fulfillment of female sexuality.* New York: New American Library, 1975.

Barnett, J. E. Natural history of marriage. *Pilgrimage,* 1981, *9,* 5–19.

Berg, P., & Snyder, D. K. Differential diagnosis of marital and sexual distress: A multidimensional approach. *Journal of Sex and Marital Therapy,* 1981, *7*(4), 290–295.

Berger, P., & Kellner, H. Marriage and the construction of reality. *Diogenes,* 1964, *46,* 1–24.

Berscheid, E., & Peplau, L. A. The emerging science of relationships. In H. H. Kelley, E. Berscheid, A. Christensen, J. H. Harvey, T. L. Huston, G. Levinger, E. McClintock, L. A. Peplau, & D. R. Peterson (Eds.), *Close relationships.* San Francisco: W. H. Freeman, 1983.

Bowlby, J. *Attachment and loss (Vol. I).* New York: Basic Books, 1969.

Bowlby, J. *Attachment and loss (Vol. II).* New York: Basic Books, 1973.

Braiker, H. B., & Kelley, H. H. Conflict in the development of close relationships. In R. Burgess & T. Huston (Eds.), *Social exchange in developing relationships.* New York: Academic Press, 1979.

Chapman, R. Criteria for diagnosing when to do sex therapy in the primary relationship. *Psychotherapy: Theory, research and practice,* 1982, *19*(3), 359–367.

Chesney, A. T., Blakeney, P. E., Cole, C. M., & Chan, F. A. A comparison of couples who have sought sex therapy with couples who have not. *Journal of Sex and Marital Therapy,* 1981, *7,* 131–140.

Cole, C. M., Blakeney, P. E., Chan, F. A., Chesney, A. T., & Creson, D. L. The myth of symptomatic versus asymptomatic partners in the conjoint treatment of sexual dysfunc-tion. *Journal of Sex and Marital Therapy,* 1979, *5*(2), 79–89.

Dicks, H. V. Experiences with marital tension in the psychological clinic. *British Journal of Medical Psychology,* 1953, *26,* 181–196.

Dicks, H. V. Object relations theory in marital studies. *British Journal of Medical Psychology,* 1963, *36,* 125–129.

Dicks, H. V. *Marital tensions.* New York: Basic Books, 1967.

Douvan, E. Interpersonal relationships: Some questions and observations. In G. Levinger and H. Raush (Eds.), *Close relationships: Perspectives on the meaning of intimacy.* Amherst: Univ. of Mass. Press, 1977.

Fagan, J. The task of the therapist. In J. Fagan & I. L. Shepherd (Eds.), *Gestalt therapy now.* New York: Harper & Row, 1970. 88–106.

Framo, J. L. Symptoms from a family transactional viewpoint. In N. Ackerman (Ed.), *Family therapy in transition.* Boston: Little, Brown, 1970. Pp. 125–171.

Frank, E., Anderson, C., & Kupfer, D. J. Profiles of couples seeking sex therapy and marital therapy. *American Journal of Psychiatry,* 1976, *133*(5), 559–562.

Frank, E., & Kupfer, D. J. In every marriage there are two marriages. *Journal of Sex and Marital Therapy,* 1976, *2*(2), 137–142.

Freedman, J. *Happy people: What happiness is, and why.* New York: Harcourt Brace Jovano-vich, 1978.

Greene, B. L., Lustig, N., & Lee, R. L. Clinical observations of sex as a reverberation of the total relationship. *Journal of Sex and Marital Therapy,* 1976, *2*(4), 284–288.

Gurman, A. S. Contemporary marital therapies: A critique and comparative analysis of psychoanalytic, behavioral, and systems theory perspectives. In T. J. Paolino and B. S. McGrady (Eds.), *Marriage and marital therapy: Psychoanalytic, behavioral, and systems theory perspectives.* New York: Brunner/Mazel, Inc., 1978.

Haley, J. Toward a theory of pathological systems. In P. Watzlawick & J. H. Weakland (Eds.), *The interactional view.* New York: W. W. Norton, 1977.

Harlow, H. F. The nature of love. *American Psychologist, 13,* 1958, 673–685.

Harlow, H. F. Social deprivation in monkeys. *Scientific American,* 1962, *207,* 136.

Hartman, L. M. The interface between sexual dysfunction and marital conflict. *American Journal of Psychiatry,* 1980, *137*(5), 576–579.

Heiman, J., LoPiccolo, L., & LoPiccolo, J. *Becoming orgasmic: A sexual growth program for women.* Englewood Cliffs, N.J.: Prentice-Hall, 1976.

Hollender, M. H., Luborsky, L., & Harvey, R. B. Correlates of the desire to be held in women. *Journal of Psychosomatic Research,* 1970, *14,* 387–390.

Jackson, D. D. The question of family homeostasis. *Psychiatric Quarterly Supplement,* 1957, *31*(1), 69–70.

Kaplan, H. S. *The new sex therapy: An active treatment of sexual dysfunctions.* New York: Brunner/Mazel, 1974.

Kaplan, H. S. *The new sex therapy (vol. 2): Disorders of sexual desire: And other new concepts and techniques in sex therapy.* New York: Brunner/Mazel, 1979.

Kaplan, H. S. *The evaluation of sexual disorders: Psychological and medical aspects.* New York: Brunner/Mazel, 1983.

Kelley, H. H. Berscheid, E., Christensen, A., Harvey, J. H., Huston, T. L., Levinger, G., McClintock, E., Peplau, L. A., & Peterson, D. R. (Eds.), *Close Relationships.* San Francisco: W. H. Freeman, 1983.

Kinder, B. N., & Blakeney, P. Treatment of sexual dysfunction: A review of outcome studies. *Journal of Clinical Psychology,* 1977, *33*(2), 523–530.

Levay, A. N., & Kagle, A. Ego deficiencies in the areas of pleasure, intimacy, and cooperation: Guidelines in the diagnosis and treatment of sexual dysfunctions. *Journal of Sex and Marital Therapy,* 1977, *3*(1), 10–18.

LoPiccolo, J. Direct treatment of sexual dysfunction. In J. LoPiccolo & L. LoPiccolo (Eds.), *Handbook of sex therapy.* New York: Plenum Press, 1978. Pp. 1–18.

Marshall, J. R., & Neill, J. The removal of a psychosomatic symptom: Effects on the marriage. *Family Process,* 1977, *16*(3), 273–280.

Masters, W. H., & Johnson, V. E. *Human sexual inadequacy.* Boston: Little, Brown, 1970.

Masters, W. H., & Johnson, V. E. Principles of the new sex therapy. *American Journal of Psychiatry,* 1976, *133*(5), 548–554.

McCarthy, B. W., Ryan, M., & Johnson, F. A. *Sexual awareness: A practical approach.* San Francisco: Boyd & Fraser, 1975.

Messersmith, C. E. Sex therapy and the marital system. In D. Olson (Ed.), *Treating relationships.* Lake Mills, Iowa: Graphic Publishing, 1976. Pp. 339–353.

Montagu, A. *Touching: The human significance of the skin* (2d ed.). New York: Harper & Row, 1978.

O'Leary, K. D., & Arias, I. The influence of marital therapy on sexual satisfaction. *Journal of Sex and Marital Therapy,* 1983, *9*(3), 171–181.

Rausch, H. L., Barry, W. A., Hertel, R. K., and Swain, M. A. *Communication, conflict and marriage.* San Francisco: Jossey-Bass, 1974.

Roffe, M. W., & Britt, B. C. A typology of marital interaction for sexually dysfunctional couples. *Journal of Sex and Marital Therapy,* 1981, *7*(3), 207–222.

Sager, C. J. Editorial: Sex as a reflection of the total relationship. *Journal of Sex and Marital Therapy,* 1976, *2*(1), 3–5. (a)

Sager, C. J. The role of sex therapy in marital therapy. *American Journal of Psychiatry,* 1976, *133*(5), 555–558. (b)

Scharff, D. E. *The sexual relationship: An object relations view of sex and the family.* Boston: Routledge & Kegan Paul, 1982.

Schover, L. R., & LoPiccolo, J. Treatment effectiveness for dysfunctions of sexual desire. *Journal of Sex and Marital Therapy,* 1982, *8*(3), 179–197.

Segraves, R. T. *Marital therapy: A combined psychodynamic-behavioral approach.* New York: Plenum Press, 1982.

Talmadge, L. D., & Talmadge, W. C. Relational sexuality: An understanding of sexual desire. Manuscript submitted for publication, 1984.

Wagner, G., & Green, R. *Impotence: Physiological, psychological and surgical diagnosis and treatment.* New York: Plenum Press, 1981.

Wallace, D. H. Affectional climate in the family of origin and the experience of subsequent sexual-affectional behaviors. *Journal of Sex and Marital Therapy,* 1981, *7*(4), 296–306.

Waring, E. M. Facilitating marital intimacy through self-disclosure. *American Journal of Family Therapy,* 1981, *9*(4), 33–42.

Warkentin, J., & Whitaker, C. Serial impasses in marriage. *Psychiatric Research Report,* 1966, *20,* American Psychiatric Association.

Watzlawick, P., Weakland, J., & Fisch, R. *Change: Principles of problem formation and problem resolution.* New York: W. W. Norton, 1974.

Whitaker, C. & Warkentin, J. The therapist as a prototype. In J. F. T. Bugental (Ed.), *Challenges of humanistic psychology.* New York: McGraw-Hill, 1967. Pp. 241–245.

Wile, D. B. *Couples therapy: A non-traditional approach.* New York: John Wiley & Sons, 1981.

Zilbergeld, B. *Male sexuality: A guide to sexual fulfillment.* Boston: Little, Brown, 1978.

Chapter 37

Paradoxical Treatment of Depression in Married Couples *

EDGAR H. JESSEE
LUCIANO L'ABATE

Depression is today the common cold of mental health. Cole, Schatzberg, and Frazier (1978), writing in what they have labeled "the age of depression," stated that depression is the most commonly experienced psychiatric disorder. Whether the frequent occurrence of depression is due to increasingly isolated nuclear families, more dual-career couples, or other social and biological factors, almost everyone experiences feelings of depression at some time. Approximately 1 in 5 clinically depressed persons receive treatment, and 1 in 50 is hospitalized (Lehmann, 1971). Women, in particular, appear to be seriously afflicted, comprising two thirds of all depressed patients treated by psychiatrists (Wing & Hailey, 1972).

Despite the alarming incidence of depression, very few attempts have been made to examine and treat depression systematically. The traditional view of depression as primarily an intrapsychic difficulty still predominates with lay person and professional alike. This chapter presents a systematic treatment model for understanding and treating depression paradoxically in married couples.

MARRIAGE AND DEPRESSION

It is probably no accident that more has been written about depression in marriage than in any other specific context. Depression and

---

* This review is part of a doctoral dissertation by Jessee (1984), under the direction of Dr. L'Abate.

marriage appear to have formed a natural partnership. Failure to meet the difficult demands apparently made by the roles in this stage of the family life cycle often contributes to depression. Hinchliffe, Hooper, and Roberts (1978) described marriage as "a social system which requires a certain kind of initial structure and a continuous input to the system which not only sustains it but also remains appropriate to the emergent needs of the system" (p. 26). Many questions are inherent in such a definition. What kind of initial structure results in depression? What kind of input must occur? How must a marriage change to meet emerging needs?

One essential prerequisite for a successful marriage is that the individuals develop to a state in which they are individuated enough to relate to one another from positions of tested autonomy (Allman & Jaffe, 1978), or what L'Abate (see Chapter 40 of this *Handbook*) has labeled "autonomous interdependence." In addition to individual differentiation, many background factors influence the initial marital structure (Barry, 1970). The most important factors appear related to the husband. Barry found that the marital happiness of the husband's parents and the husband's close attachment to his father were highly correlated with marital happiness. Also, the higher the husband's socioeconomic status and educational level, the more marital happiness. Barry, using personality inventories showing that increased marital happiness related to stable male personality, concluded that all of these factors relate to the crucial factor of a stable male identity.

Yet, the fact that the male feels adequate is apparently not the only factor. Barry found that the higher the wife rated the husband on emotional maturity and role fulfillment, the happier the marriage. In addition, the more the wife came to resemble her husband on attitude and personality, the happier the marriage. Additional evidence for the importance of the husband comes from Uhr's (1957) conclusions that happily married husbands' and wives' values became more alike after 18 years of marriage and that wives moved in the direction of their husbands' values.

Barry maintained that women have more difficulty establishing their roles because of their greater dependence on their husbands, again indicating that the husband's stability appears to affect the happiness of the marriage. This finding has devastating repercussions for the woman when Parson and Bales' (1955) instrumental and expressive role functions are considered. The implication is that when marital unhappiness occurs, the expressive wife is more likely than is the husband to show evidence of the disorder. The contention about inexpressive males and overexpressive females appears to be supported in recent work (Balswick, 1979; Sattel, 1976). Although some might argue that Barry's findings may be somewhat outdated because of cultural and familial changes, many authors, such as Hinchliffe et al. (1978), still believe the husband's role to be vital in depression and marital happiness.

The relationship between marriage and depression is well documented. Depressed women are most likely to report that marital difficulties preceded the depression, indicating that depressed women are less likely to have well-functioning marriages (Paykel, Myers, Diendelt, Klerman, Lindenthal, & Pepper, 1969). In fact, Kreitman, Collins, Nelson, and Troop (1971) found that marital interactions between depressives and their spouses were pathogenic. Weissman and Paykel (1974) found that depressed women were more likely to have marital relationships typified by friction and hostility. Overall (1971), who examined the relationship between symptom patterns and marital status in more than 2,000 subjects, found that depressive moods and guilt were much more likely to be found in the married and once-divorced group. Rounsaville, Weissman, Prusoff, and Herceg-Baron (1979) reported that women involved in active marital disputes had a poorer prognosis than did those without mates or those who were happily married. Yet, women who were able to improve their marriages were also more likely to recover from their depression. Depressed women, then, most often report marital difficulties and appear to have a good chance of recovering from the depression only if their marital relationships are treated.

The nature of the depressive marital relationship has been commented on by various authors. Overall (1971) stated that depressive symptoms in married persons have to do with dependency relationships that are burdened by stressful events. Hinchliffe et al. (1978) delineated several factors which may relate to marital dysfunction that ultimately manifests as depression. In addition to the importance of the male role, they maintained that the marital system must be flexible enough to respond effectively to stress. A relationship prone to depression is inflexible, they contended, because of a dependent mode of functioning. Neither partner has achieved a proper sense of mastery in the situation; consequently, both are vulnerable to actual or threatened loss because they tend to increase their dependency demands during stress. Hinchliffe et al. maintained that this relationship pattern is counterproductive because it does not allow the couple to support each other successfully in threatening situations and ultimately results in one spouse's depression.

Rubinstein and Timmins (1978) stressed the interactional nature of depression, maintaining that whatever the cause of the original depression, the partnership ensures the continuance of the depressive behavior. In severe depression, a pattern of cycling behavioral responses repeats every few minutes. This "microcycling" consists of a set of responses generally initiated, either verbally or nonverbally, by the patient. Verbally, the voice is exemplified by a very slow tempo and low pitch, hesitation, a whining quality, and an absence of inflections. The overall number of verbalizations by the patient is small, and the partner exhibits a very similar pattern, using the same speed, pitch, and number of verbalizations. Nonverbally, the partners' body movements and positions are similar, with a marked scarcity of total body movement. The partners tend to sit in fixed, symmetrical positions, essentially forming mirror images of one another. Often, one partner will exhibit the other's exact movements at the same speed a few seconds later. Eye contact is infrequent and brief.

Rubinstein and Timmins (1978) described the partner of a depressed patient as a "caretaker." Compliant caretakers reassure, explain, and support in their dialogue. Conversations between partners are brief and focus on the patient's immediate thoughts. The aggressive caretaker attempts to "talk sense" to the depressive. This type of caretaker talks most of the time and attempts to force the partner out of the depression. Compliant and aggressive caretakers express a critical attitude toward the patient's depressive behavior and, in so doing, tend to perpetuate the depression. Rubinstein and Timmins speculated that a depressed mother or father may have provided the caretaking pattern in the family of origin. Ironically, such a marriage is often an attempt to leave a depressed ingrained, the new marriage repeats the depressive patterns.

The depressed marital dyad has several specific characteristics (Rubinstein & Timmins, 1978). Even during symptom-free periods, the marital relationship is not healthy, as shown by the lack of shared interests and activities and the absence of emotional growth in the relationship. Closeness and warmth are distorted and manifested in possessiveness and dependency. Whenever one partner feels autonomous, the other is threatened by fears of abandonment. The marriage in essence reflects a too-close, symbiotic-like emotional union.

The most comprehensive empirical analysis of marital depression was conducted by Hinchliffe et al. (1978). In an attempt to understand depression in terms of disturbed communication, they inadvertently tested many of Rubinstein and Timmins' clinical observations. Videotaping of the revealed-difference technique provided verbal and nonverbal data on 20 depressed and 20 nondepressed couples. After recording each marital pair, a recording was made of the same discussion between the identified patient and a stranger of the opposite sex, thus providing data on whether the communication pattern was specific to the married pair. Next, each couple was compared at two different times: The first recording was made a couple of days after admission to the hospital; the second was made after discharge (time lapses varied from 3 to 12 months). The depressed couples were selected from locally hospitalized individuals who had been diagnosed as depressed. To repeat the separation and hospitalization experience of these couples, the researchers drew the "normal" couples from patients admitted for minor surgical procedures. The nonpsychiatric couples were screened for history of psychiatric disturbance or major marital conflict.

Hinchliffe et al. (1978), using the system that Mishler and Waxler (1968) developed to study schizophrenic communication, divided each recorded session into communicative acts (a communicative act was defined as the smallest unit of meaningful speech). For each couple, 400 acts were coded from the last section of each tape. The emotional tone of the words used for each act was coded for positive, negative, or neutral affect. In addition, the acts were categorized by expressiveness, responsiveness, disruptions, and power. Nonverbal measurements included hand movements, posture, and eye gaze. Couple and individual comparisons were made within and across sessions.

The most important finding was that depressed couples showed considerably more expressiveness, both as individuals and as a couple, than did normals. Most of the expressiveness, however, was negative. By recovery, the expressiveness of depressed couples had fallen to the level of expressiveness of the surgical couples. Interestingly, there was a marked difference between couples with a depressed male and couples with a depressed female partner. The difference between the depressed-male marriages and the depressed-female marriages lies in the role change necessitated by the depression. The authors maintained that when the male is depressed, the shift in his behavior, from the instrumental to the expressive mode, is much greater. In comparison, when the female is depressed, the husband becomes expressive and supportive to handle her disturbances and has difficulty assuming his old instrumental role at recovery. Role change is especially difficult for the male if the wife enjoys her newfound dependent role and her husband's expressiveness. The conclusion is that because the woman is already functioning in the expressive role mode, the wife of a depressed man makes the necessary role adjustments more easily than does the husband of a depressed wife.

Focus on interaction content revealed the following: Depressed couples used their own experience in a more self-centered way, one that distorted reality; depressed individuals tended to act more like "normals" when conversing with a stranger; depressed couples displayed more tension in their speech than did normals; the spouse of the depressed patient adapted behaviorally to the patient, exhibiting a symmetrical style and, often, the same nonverbal behavior; depressed couples spoke more slowly than did normals; and the women in depressed couples made more control attempts than did normal women.

In a family systems model of depression and marital interaction, Feldman (1976) attempted to integrate the intrapsychic concept of cognitive schema and the interpersonal concepts of social stimulus and social reinforcement with a systems theory framework. He maintained that the depressed person's current patterns of reciprocal interaction with intimate others, especially the spouse, have a powerful effect in triggering and maintaining the depression. In this pattern, each behavior of each spouse is simultaneously a stimulus, a response, and a reinforcer. Thus, the process (because of its mutual causality) is circular rather than linear. Feldman illustrated the depressive process in the following:

> The non-depressed spouse's undermining behavior is generally an "innocent" remark or act that "just happens" to strike at a particularly sensitive spot in the depressed spouse's shaky sense of self-worth. This leads to a depressive response (e.g., sadness, dysphoria, self-depreciation, guilt), which stimulates in the non-depressed spouse a cognitive schema of over-protectiveness and omnipotence, leading to depression-reinforcing behavior (e.g., attention, overconcern). That part of the depressed person's personality that wishes to be autonomous and competent is repeatedly frustrated by the spouse's oversolicitousness, leading to feelings of helplessness and resentment. The depressed spouse may respond by withdrawal (passive-aggressivity), overt hostility, or by making a move toward independent self-assertion. Each of these potential responses triggers cognitive schemata of self-depreciation in the non-depressed spouse. This, in turn, leads to depression-inducing behavior by the non-depressed spouse. and the cycle has come one full turn. (p. 391)

Although the depressed spouse vacillates between self-depreciation and other-directed hostility, the nondepressed spouse seldom experiences self-depreciation. Instead, the nondepressed spouse moves into the role of rescuer, which reestablishes the depressive homeostatic cycle and triggers further depressive reaction from the spouse.

Overall, ample evidence—theoretical and practical—links marriage and depression. One half of all patients who seek psychotherapy do so because of marital problems (Sager, Gundlach, & Kremer, 1968); and in at least 30 percent of marital problems, one spouse is clinically depressed (Rush, Shaw, & Khatami, 1980). Therefore, as a practical matter, therapists frequently confront depression in married persons. A couples format allows the therapist to see and treat the system that maintains the depression. The spouse's role, feelings, and actions can be dealt with individually and as a part of the depressive transaction in the marriage, thus creating a positive rather than a negative influence in the marriage. In addition, during treatment, the spouse can help by collecting data and giving information about the depressed partner's experience. Involving the depressed partner's spouse in therapy makes sense, theoretically and practically.

TREATMENT OF MARITAL DEPRESSION

Difficulties in treating depression as an intrapsychic problem can be traced to the systemic nature of the disorder. As is true with various other problems, treating only the symptomatic member is often ineffective because it does not alter the context of the problem (Feldman, 1976; Hinchliffe et al., 1978; Hogan & Hogan, 1975; Rubinstein & Timmins, 1978). Although treating depression in the context of the marriage is relatively new and lacks sufficient outcome data, empirical results to date indicate the need to treat the marital context as well as the depression.

Friedman (1975) compared drug therapy and marital therapy, alone and in combination, offering 196 patients a drug or a placebo and either minimal contact therapy (30 minutes twice weekly) or marital therapy (1 hour weekly). After 12 weeks, 89 percent in the drug/marital therapy group had improved versus 75 percent in the placebo/marital therapy group, 68 percent in the drug/minimum therapy group, and 67 percent in the placebo/minimum therapy group. Additionally, he found that marital therapy sometimes worsened the marital relationship initially; in the drug and minimal therapy condition, the reverse was true. Initially, as the symptoms subsided, the depressed person exhibited a more positive view of the spouse, but this perspective did not last for the 12 weeks of the study. Friedman concluded that the patients treated with marital therapy were more likely to have gained some assurance against future relapses into depression.

Various other studies (Rounsaville et al., 1979; Weissman & Paykel, 1974) have found that antidepressant drug therapy coupled with intrapsychic individual psychotherapy can reduce unpleasant physical symptoms but has little effect on interpersonal difficulties. Weissman (1979) reviewed the literature on the treatment of depression and also found that antidepressants effectively relieved symptoms but generally affected social adjustment only minimally.

Hinchliffe et al. (1978) emphasized the need to understand the marital situation during treatment. In their small sample of depressed couples, disturbances in the marriage invariably seemed to perpetuate the depression. The researchers treated couples conjointly with cognitive couples therapy, including (a) attempting to make the nondepressed spouse feel more helpful, sometimes beginning paradoxically with the admission of his or her own feelings of helplessness; (b) analyzing for the couple the systemic dynamics of their situation, emphasizing their rigid role structure and lack of adaptiveness; (c) interpreting the couple's needs to each spouse and clarifying the dynamics of hostility and resentment; and (d) working toward increased autonomy and intimacy in the marriage. Specific intervention strategies varied according to each couple's needs, but treatment based on these principles was generally effective in reducing individual depressive symptoms and changing depressive interactions.

Rounsaville et al. (1979) attempted to provide evidence that depression related to marital difficulties could be treated by relationship-focused individual therapy. Although therapy focused on interpersonal rather than intrapsychic issues, treatment effectiveness was virtually the same for those who received medication only and those who received medication and psychotherapy. More than 50 percent of the women in the study had severe marital disputes, but the treatment groups were equally ineffective in decreasing the amount of marital difficulty. From a systemic point of view, working with both spouses makes it easier to change the marital relationship. Interpersonal therapy of this kind with only one spouse appears to be no more effective than traditional intrapsychic therapy.

Rubinstein and Timmins (1978) advocated therapy for the individual's pathological dynamics as well as therapy for the partners' relationship. They believed in dealing with the individual dynamics of rationalization, intellectualization, anger, dependency, and hostility in addition to altering the relationship. The first step in the treatment was to treat the relationship by (a) evaluating and recognizing the microcycling behavior in the relationship; (b) using videotapes to demonstrate the cycling patterns to the clients; and (c) understanding the dynamics, both interpersonal and individual, of the cycling.

If the goals of treatment are to promote autonomy and differentiation, the authors reasoned, increasing autonomy would decrease the couple's dependency needs and therefore allow the relationship to change. Furthermore, establishing a dyadic relationship with each partner would weaken their former symbiotic union. The authors intimated that the risk in performing individual therapy is that the therapist may become an active participant in the pathological system.

Rush et al. (1980) successfully treated three cases of depression by involving the spouse. Cognitive therapy (Beck, 1967) was used to help each spouse identify the maladaptive interactions and cognitive distortions that had led to depressive reactions. Although the case number was very small, objective measures and clinical observation indicated dramatic improvement. The authors stated that including the nondepressed spouse in sessions gave needed practical support during treatment and avoided systemic resistance.

Marital treatment has a pragmatic therapeutic rationale in addition to empirical and theoretical justification. Therapists who work solely with the depressed client are especially vulnerable to becoming part of the pathological relationship system. Cohen, Baker, Cohen, Fromm-Reichmann, and Weigert (1954) observed that therapists tend to give unrealistic reassurance and promises, which are followed by hostility and rejection. The same caretaking pattern has been observed in spouses (Rubinstein & Timmins, 1978). The therapist or the spouse seeks, by exhibiting empathy, to provide some immediate relief for the depressed client. Empathy quickly turns into reassurances because of the depressive's minimal response. Apparently, "the more you give, the more they want." The interactional game, in which attempts to help repeatedly fail, often culminates in the caretaker's hostility and rejection. Such behavior only recreates the depressive cycle and perpetuates the depression. Conjoint treatment certainly does not ensure that the therapist will not fall prey to the depressive behavior. Treatment that makes the spouse an active participant can, however, enable the therapist to feel less pressured and responsible for the client's improvement.

Apparently, then, several different treatment approaches to interpersonal depression may prove effective. Individual psychotherapy, pharmacotherapy, or a combination of the two has been effective in some cases (Weissman, 1979). Social problems often persist, however, unless the marital relationship is treated (Friedman, 1975). Weissman and Klerman (1973) found that despite symptom improvement, marital problems were the problems discussed most frequently by depressed individuals in maintenance therapy. Bothwell and Weissman (1977) confirmed this finding in a four-year follow-up of depressed patients who had received eight months of maintenance treatment. Marital disputes continued to be an enduring problem, even when the patient was asymptomatic. Treatment of the marital system thus appears indicated to achieve symptom relief and social adjustment.

PARADOXICAL PSYCHOTHERAPY

In recent years, family therapists have become fascinated with therapeutic paradoxes (Haley, 1973; Hare-Mustin, 1975; Selvini-Palazzoli, Boscolo, Cecchin, & Prata, 1978; Weeks & L'Abate, 1982). Alfred Adler is generally acknowledged as the first person in Western civilization to use paradoxical strategies (Mozdzierz, Macchitelli, & Lisiecki, 1976). Although many therapists have used paradoxical techniques (Dunlap, 1946; Farrelly & Brandsma, 1974; Frankl, 1939; Rosen, 1953), perhaps the most influential contributors in the family therapy field have been the Palo Alto group (Bateson, Jackson, Haley, & Weakland, 1956). This group, in studying the double bind, recognized the pathological aspects of paradoxical communication and defined a paradox as a "contradiction that follows correct deduction from consistent premises" (Watzlawick, Beavin, & Jackson, 1967). The Palo Alto group's work resulted in the development of a therapeutic double bind to mirror the pathological double-binding communication. Essentially, the therapeutic double bind is implemented by asking the client to change by remaining unchanged. The demand characteristics of the therapy context suggest and value change; yet, the therapeutic injunction values no change.

The variety of paradoxical techniques, such as prescribing (De Shazer, 1978), positioning (Watzlawick, Weakland, & Fisch, 1974), reframing (Watzlawick et al., 1974), restraining (Rohrbaugh, Tennen, Press, & White, 1981), and declaring hopelessness (Selvini-Palazzoli et al., 1978), have been the subject of diligent clinical study during the past couple of years. Less attention has been directed to the types of disorders for which paradoxical intervention may be most appropriate. The emphasis on particular paradoxically inclined disorders appears to have waned in favor of a more generalized study of the concept of paradox (Dell, 1981; Weeks & L'Abate, 1982). Certainly, all behavior involves some paradoxical elements. It is equally plausible, however, that certain problems (e.g.; depression) manifest these paradoxical elements and therefore may be more suitable for paradoxical intervention (L'Abate, in press-a).

Paradoxes of depression

"Depression may someday be understood in terms of its paradoxes" (Beck, 1967, p. 3). Any clinician who has worked extensively with depressed clients has a working knowledge of the incongruencies in the disorder. For example, how many times has a depressed client asked for support from the spouse, only to reject it when received? Jessee and L'Abate (1983b) attempted to identify these inherent paradoxes in depression.

Perhaps the most apparent paradox is that the depressed individual seeks support and reassurances from others but does not respond well when the support is received. Depressed persons, because they rely so heavily on the opinions of others for their own self-concepts, are unable to benefit substantially from the reassurances offered by loved ones. To accept the reassurances of others—"It will be fine"—is to discount one's own feelings of hurt. Paradoxically, the person who relies on others for self-concept can only get in touch with the self through the hurt and thus becomes caught in a vicious approach-avoidance cycle—needing others but unable to accept them because acceptance equals loss of autonomy (Jessee & L'Abate, 1983a, 1983b).

A second, related paradox is our tendency to seek comfort and be comforted by those we hurt and who have hurt us most (L'Abate & L'Abate, 1979), a task that is almost impossible for the depressed person. Coyne (1976) demonstrated that alienation and loneliness usually result when a depressed person tries to elicit support from others. Thus, when a depressed individual seeks intimacy by increasing the depressed behavior, the result is an alienation from loved ones, which ultimately increases the depression. The nondepressed spouse typically responds to the depressive behavior for a short while but soon distances physically or emotionally as ineffectiveness increases. Consequently, when intimacy is desired, it is often more unlikely to occur.

A third paradox is based on the depressed person's ambivalence toward loved ones. The depressed person must grapple with the unsolvable dilemma of whether support from others is based on genuine concern or on manipulation. As the caretaking spouse becomes more frustrated in trying to help, the depressed spouse sees the efforts as manipulation. Accordingly, the more perceived manipulation, the more depression, and vice versa. The approach-avoidance cycle allows nothing more than temporary closeness between partners because the depressed person is doomed to oscillate between feeling that the partner cares somewhat and feeling that the partner is simply manipulating.

Watzlawick (1978) presented a final paradoxical element: Depression is maintained by the individual's efforts to resist it. No one enjoys feeling depressed; the natural response is to fight it. The more a person fights depression, however, the more depressed the person becomes. As mentioned, the normal, logical procedures for alleviating the depression only make it worse. Often, the dilemma increases as the depressed person internalizes the injunction from significant others, particularly the spouse, not to feel unhappy. The more the person tries not to be depressed, the greater the depression.

Paradoxical marital treatment

Several clinicians have reported isolated successes with the paradoxical treatment of depression (Adler, 1956; Madanes, 1981; Watzlawick & Coyne, 1980; Weeks & L'Abate, 1982). A paradoxical model for treating depression in couples has been proposed (L'Abate, 1985) and needs to be tested. Because of the marital and paradoxical links with depression, a paradoxical marital treatment approach may prove effective.

The proposed treatment approach comprises sequential stages: *(a)* positive reframing of the depression, *(b)* prescribing the depression ritualistically, *(c)* prescribing the caretaking spouse's help in keeping the identified patient depressed, *(d)* restraining the couple from more-optimal functioning, and *(e)* resolving the underlying conflict.

Stage 1: positive reframing. The first stage of treatment is the positive reframing of the depression. Reframing the depression as a positive function for the individual and for the couple has several purposes. The positive reframing is a message to the couple that the therapist will not proffer the usual reassurances and negativity about the depression. Therapists are often manipulated into an adversarial relationship with the depression, to the point that they provide false reassurances about overcoming it (Cohen et al., 1954). Reframing the depression in positive terms circumvents much of this process by implying that the condition has positive aspects. Depression becomes something to value rather than to avoid at all costs, and the therapist is the one who can encourage this process. L'Abate (in press-a, in press-b) proposed at least nine different ways of positively reframing depression.

A second purpose of reframing is to help the client begin to see a cognitive rationale for not fighting the depression. In Watzlawick's (1978) terms, a rationale is created to allow the problem-maintaining solution (i.e., fighting the depression) to change. If the problem can be seen differently, perhaps the solution is different. Surprisingly, very few depressed clients report positive aspects of depression or attempts to accept depression.

The third purpose of reframing is to establish the interactional nature of the difficulty. Positive reframing of how the depression works in the relationship can be a powerful cognitive restructuring tool:

> I think you are to be congratulated for being depressed to help your husband. It is obvious that you have become depressed in an attempt to take his mind off being unemployed. I cannot think of anything else you could have done that would have demonstrated your caring and loyalty to him so convincingly.

Because the depression's specific function in the relationship is, unfortunately, not always clear at the beginning of treatment, initial reframings are usually limited to the individual. Clumsy, inaccurate systemic reframings can do more harm than good.

A fourth purpose for giving the depression positive connotations is to "save face" for the depressed person, who often understands for the first time that there may be some "good" reason for being depressed. Attaching an adaptive function to the depression is consistent with viewing the individual as competent rather than sick and deeply disturbed. The positive reframing forces the spouse to view the depressed person's behavior as more functional, which correspondingly often improves the depressive's self-concept.

Many generic positive reframing statements have been found useful with clients:

Statement 1: "I am glad to hear that you are depressed because if you were not, I doubt that you would have sought professional help." This statement reframes positively the reason for having asked for help (L'Abate, 1975).

Statement 2: "I am glad to hear that you are depressed. Lots of people are unwilling or unable to recognize or accept their depressions. These people, who are unable or unwilling to ask for help, end up in hospitals, jails, morgues, and cemeteries." This statement differentiates between people who ask for help and those who do not and makes depression a positive and constructive motivation for therapy.

Statement 3: "We are all depressed individuals. We only vary in the degree to which we are willing or able to recognize and accept depression in ourselves. We cannot live and not be depressed, because all of us, as fallible human beings, are vulnerable to hurts" (L'Abate & L'Abate, 1979).

Statement 4: "I am glad to hear that you are depressed, because now we can do something about it. If you were depressed and did not admit it, you might be doing something destructive, such as drinking, gambling, or driving fast cars." Although this statement may seem to repeat preceding statements, especially Number 2, it is a somewhat different refrain, or a variation on the same theme. Further, this statement is hopeful.

Statement 5: "Depression can be used; eventually, if you use it right, you may even learn to enjoy it." This rather startling reframing of the symptom is perhaps one of the best attention getters of all the statements.

Statement 6: "Up to now, you have considered depression an enemy, a foe to fight and avoid: the Black Hole of Calcutta, something to run away from. I suggest instead that you start thinking of depression as a friend, something you want to join, use well, and eventually learn to live with and enjoy." This statement is also a rather useful attention getter and reflects in many ways our convictions.

Statement 7: "Depression is your body's natural way of slowing you down to take a look at yourself. Otherwise, you'd probably keep right on going—in an uncomfortable rut." The idea of this statement is that depression is a natural, adaptive experience.

Statement 8: "Depression is the royal road to selfhood." A person can learn most about himself or herself and can improve most by looking at the "ugly," darker sides of the self.

Statement 9: "All of us deal with depression when we face death. You are lucky enough to deal with it now so that you will be ready later." This statement encourages the person to see that depression is inevitable and that learning to deal with it now can be beneficial.

None of the positive reframings were designed as a universal intervention. Each reframing must be tailored to each client and each couple so that it will be meaningful (i.e., using their language, values, and beliefs). It is also helpful for the therapist to believe in the value of the reframing statement. Often, many positive statements, not just one, must be used to help clients begin to accept the reframing.

Stage 2: Prescription of the depression. Once the depression has been labeled a positive feeling state that is to be encouraged, it follows that the therapist's function is to help the client reach the desired state. The therapist encourages through ritualized prescription of the depression.

The prescription of the depression serves three purposes. First, it interdicts the normal problem-maintaining solution (i.e., fight and avoid the depression). The person's usual attempts at avoiding the depression are now shut off because the objective is to encourage the depressive feelings. The idea is for the individual to stop exhibiting the behaviors that perpetuate the depression.

A second purpose of prescription is for the depressed person to experience the depression more fully in the hope that if the person deals with it once and for all, it can be resolved. This concept parallels the Gestalt concept of "exaggeration," in which a movement or a gesture is repeated or amplified until it reaches cessation (Levitsky & Perls, 1970). The behavioral technique of stimulus satiation (Ayllon, 1963) reflects the same concept. Clients who comply with the request to be more depressed frequently report that the experience is the most valuable one in therapy.

A client who does not comply with the request to be more depressed usually reacts to it. The defiant reaction (Rohrbaugh et al., 1981) usually results when the depression is seen as too ominous or too overwhelming to deal with or when the client rebels against the controlling quality of the assignment. Thus, the prescription may encourage fuller experience (compliance-based paradox) or help the person avoid the depressive mood and behavior (defiance-based paradox). In either event, the client ultimately ceases the depressive behavior.

The depression is prescribed for a specified space and time. The client is asked what time of day is normally the most difficult. The depression is prescribed for 30 minutes or 1 hour during the identified time period. The task is assigned for every day or for alternating days (Tuesday, Thursday, and Saturday, or Monday, Wednesday, and Friday), at the same time, to stress the importance of the endeavor and to create either an order that is difficult to follow for long (Madanes, 1981) or a sense of control over the symptom (L'Abate, 1983a). The prescription allows the client some control over what the client normally perceives as an uncontrollable state. The client exercises control either by being depressed during the specified time or by refusing to be depressed. If the client is afraid of being unable to get out of the depression after one hour, the client is told to call a friend or arrange an activity to begin after the hour.

Stage 3: Paradoxically prescribing the spouse's help. The systemic link to the individual's prescription is to enlist the caretaking spouse's help in keeping the identified patient depressed ("Make sure that he [she] is depressed and does what he [she] is supposed to do during the time he [she] is depressed"). The mate is to remind the patient of the assignment and see to it that no disturbances (children, phone, etc.) interrupt the assigned task. Caretakers are involved, feel helpless, and need to feel helpful (Hinchliffe et al., 1978). Giving the mate a task acknowledges the mate's situation and implies that the mate can help solve the problem. The systemic linkage changes the interactional pattern around the depression and the direction of it. Typically, when one person in a system changes, the rest of the system resists the change. If the normal forces of resistance can be changed, however, the chance is greater that the change will last and become incorporated into the normal behavioral pattern.

The spouse is asked to perform exactly those behaviors that have been identified as upsetting and depressing to the mate. The therapist explains that this is crucial because the depressed mate will undoubtedly have a difficult time with the assignment and will need help to be and stay depressed. Spouses rarely refuse this assignment when they become convinced that it will be helpful.

Prescription of the depressive helping pattern places the caretaking spouse in an untenable position. The spouse wants to be helpful but not helpful in making the depressed spouse more depressed. The typical reaction or solution is for the spouse to attempt the task halfheartedly, once or twice. Even when the task is carried out, it now has the new, positive connotation of helping. With the caretaker's approach, insight into the problems may or may not occur, but insight is not necessary for behavioral change. The focus is strictly on changing the behavioral pattern around the depressive behavior.

Stage 4: Restraining the couple. The earlier stages of treatment focus on changing the behavior and the interactional pattern of the identified patient and the spouse. Obviously some new behavior must emerge to replace the depression. One option is for the clinician to let the couple replace the depression with whatever they wish. Clinical experience, however, has revealed very few chronically depressed couples who spontaneously began to have more intimacy and fulfillment in their lives after the depression improved. The common response is an improved mood and more comfortableness with each other.

A second (and preferred) option is to restrain the couple from optimal functioning. If a couple rebels against the directives and stops the dysfunctional sequences, the restraining message gives a direction for their rebellion. The therapist attempts to channel the couple's reactance to depression in a more positive direction. The couple is already defying the therapist, so why not use the engendered reactance to push the couple in a positive direction?

The actual restraining has two steps. First, the couple is asked to talk about a time in their life together (e.g., courtship) when they enjoyed each other and felt close. The therapist carefully draws out details about what they did, where they were, and how they felt. In effect, the mood and the situation of the earlier period are briefly recreated in the remembrances. If the couple cannot recall any happy times, they are asked to talk about an ideal evening together. Revitalizing these experiences is important because many chronically depressed couples have forgotten how to have an enjoyable time together and feel extremely awkward being together in a nondepressed state.

When the positive information has been gathered, the therapist can begin to restrain their more optimal functioning. The general restraint-from-change message is "Go slow." The specific form of this communication depends on the particular couple and the therapist, but a typical restraining message might be as follows:

> I know there will be a natural urge to engage in enjoyable, intimate activities together, such as going out to eat together and dancing afterwards. However, you must stifle those urges because you could not possibly enjoy yourselves while you're attending to the depression.

A couple's normal response to a restraining message is to rebel against the restraint, but frequently the rebellion takes an unexpected turn. For example, after the restraining message, a couple might take a weekend vacation together rather than going out on the town. Perhaps the variations on the theme are the couple's way of assuming some control and responsibility for success. Nevertheless, the chances of positive behavior appear to be enhanced by a restraint message. Ideally, the restraint should be given before the depression lifts completely to prevent an uncomfortable vacuum after relief from the depression. Some couples will become depressed again if being nondepressed is uncomfortable enough.

Stage 5: Resolution of conflictual issues. Our experience with depression is that it frequently serves a protective, symptomatic function, much like that delineated by Madanes (1981). The depression itself is an adaptive attempt to resolve some other conflict in the relationship. Although the underlying issues vary for each couple, Feldman's (1976) concept of depression as a distance-regulating phenomenon guides much of our work. Often we have found that depression in couples originates as an attempt to regulate intimacy (see Chapter 13 of this *Handbook*). Depression and intimacy rarely coexist (Brown & Harris, 1978; Jessee & L'Abate, 1983a). In fact, depression appears to replace or supplant intimacy. Generally, couples who are depressed are unable to be intimate. All issues of causation aside, the major underlying theme for depressed couples appears to be tolerating or creating intimacy.

Further therapy after the successful completion of Stages 1–4 should not be forced on clients. Many clients will spontaneously exhibit improved functioning and have no desire for further treatment. Perhaps the underlying, or initial, issues have been resolved during treatment. The therapist definitely should not pressure the clients at this point; but if the couple is visibly struggling with other aspects of the relationship, the therapist should certainly offer help.

Underlying issues are usually resolved much more effectively after the depression has lifted. Not only has the symptom been removed, but the balance of power in the couple's relationship inevitably changes. The depressed partner is no longer seen as weak, incompetent, and able to influence only through manipulation. Instead, the previously depressed person is a hero who has loyally made sacrifices, finally battled the villain face-to-face, and won. In Madanes' (1981) terms, the incongruous hierarchy has been altered, and issues between the couples can now be dealt with from more equal positions of power and authority.

At times during this stage of treatment, one spouse (sometimes the previously nondepressed spouse) will become depressed. When this occurs, refocusing on the depression in much the same way as before (only making more of an ordeal of it) is helpful. Usually, the therapist's prediction that depression will recur is powerful enough to forestall recurrence.

Case example

Bill, a 28-year-old black male, had been unemployed and depressed for one year before treatment. Jill, a 26-year-old black female, was employed as a telephone operator and lived with their 14-month-old son at her mother's home. The couple, married for six years but separated for six months before treatment, were living with their respective families when therapy began. Neither had been in therapy before. The husband's chief complaint was depression about the loss of his job, financial pressures, and separation from his wife. The couple reported that the depression began when the husband lost his job. The specific symptoms that they cited were lack of self-confidence, lack of motivation, irresponsible behavior, sleeping more than usual, and marital conflict. The wife maintained that her husband was "too jealous" and acted "like a gorilla" when angry. The couple reported that the separation had been a mutual decision based on disharmony and financial problems.

The couple's interactional pattern was characterized by frequent reassurances from the wife. The husband would act discouraged and his wife would attempt to reassure him, physically and verbally, that everything would be fine. The husband either shrugged off her reassurances or ignored them completely. Increased depression would follow, which only pushed the wife to be more reassuring. The cycle would escalate until the husband would explode in a fit of anger at the wife, which would result in physical and emotional distancing.

The therapist explained that the depression was a "blessing in disguise" in that it allowed the husband to focus on all the aspects of his personality that he did not like. Certainly, he did not have time for this when he was working. He was encouraged to get to the bottom of the depression because "it looks like years before it could possibly improve." The husband was also told that he might as well learn to control the depression rather than being controlled by it. He was asked to be as depressed as possible every day between 9 and 10 A.M. (the time he usually awakened and was most depressed). His wife was asked to help make him depressed by calling him on the phone and attempting to reassure him. The husband agreed, assuring the therapist that the assignment would be easy. The wife agreed but said that she was uncomfortable with the idea of making her husband depressed. The last part of the session was devoted to restraining the couple. The couple, who had been very close before the depression, was told not to try to be close or intimate in any way because it would only "interfere" with the husband's assignment.

The following week the couple came in smiling and looking very pleased. When asked about the assignment, the husband sheepishly admitted that he hadn't done very well—"It's hard to be depressed, to turn that depression on and off." He said that he had tried several times but had been unable to stay depressed for very long because he was feeling better. The wife had called the husband once to help him be depressed but had "forgotten" after that. The couple had not only been out together several times but, the day before, they had decided to move back in together. The therapist responded that he was glad that they were feeling better but was disappointed that they had not completed the task. The therapist also warned that the depression would probably recur: "You know how it is. There are periods of ups and downs. Don't be too encouraged." The husband assured the therapist that a relapse would not occur. The task was reassigned "in case you feel the need to be depressed."

The final three sessions of therapy dealt with the couple's enmeshing relationship, symbolized by the husband's jealousy. For the first time the husband was able to deal effectively with his verbally superior wife about issues of closeness and distance. Able to allow each other more individual freedom, they discovered a new intimacy in their relationship. By the final session, the couple had moved back in together and were very happy. The wife reported that her husband no longer acted like a gorilla. The husband verified that he was no longer depressed and was now comfortable letting his wife be with her girlfriends. Both reported increased marital happiness and satisfaction. The change was sealed by the therapist's request that they pretend to be as they were before—the husband was to be depressed and the wife was to cheer him up. The couple attempted the assignment but broke into laughter as the wife tried to console the husband. The therapist explained that if the couple ever worried about slipping back into the old pattern, one of them could test the other by acting out his or her part. At six-month follow-up the couple reported no depression and continued marital satisfaction. Also, the husband had started a painting business with a friend and was doing quite well financially.

CURRENT RESEARCH

The paradoxical treatment model for depression was developed from our experiences with depressed clients. Initially, we used a trial-and-error approach to discover effective components of the program. The current program, which appears effective, is now being empirically tested.

A single-case analysis of the treatment was conducted with five marital couples, in which one partner of each couple was clinically depressed (Jessee, 1984). A multiple baseline treatment design was used to assess self-report of depression and depressive interactional behavior. Couples were screened by the University of Illinois Affective Disorders Clinic in Chicago for family history of depression, evidence of a major affective disorder, suicide potential, and partner's willingness to be involved. All accepted subjects had been clinically depressed for one year or longer, had no family history of severe depression, no evidence of a major affective disorder, and were married. Self-report of depression was assessed by the Beck Depression Inventory and the interactional coding of videotaped interactions. All but one person reported clinically significant improvement in depression after the paradoxical treatment phase began. The one person who did not report clinically significant improvement did show a nonsignificant decrease in the depression score. Also discovered was a significant positive correlation between couples' depression scores and their dysfunctional interactions. Follow-up analysis revealed that treatment effects (including increased marital satisfaction) were being maintained. These findings were replicated by Buzas (1983), who studied three other subjects and their spouses and who used the same kind of single-subject design, adding a few refinements in the technique.

PROFESSIONAL AND ETHICAL ISSUES

The treatment approach described is not for every depressed client nor for every therapist. The described paradoxical approach requires the clinician to make certain implicit and explicit professional and value judgments.

Perhaps the most obvious concern is the types of depressed clients with whom this approach will work. We have used this approach in clinical practice with all types of depressive disorders, including manic-depressive. Empirically, however, the usefulness of the approach has been demonstrated only with the dysthymic type of depressive disorder.

Clinical experience has revealed that the two most difficult kinds of patients are the suicidal depressive and the manic-depressive. Obviously no one wants to prescribe depression in a way that may precipitate a suicide attempt; the wisest course is not to use this approach with suicidal patients. If the patient becomes suicidal, that threat must be alleviated before treatment can continue. Interestingly, in dozens of cases, no one has yet attempted suicide after being asked to be more depressed.

The manic-depressive patient is somewhat more difficult to control. Typically, the patient responds well to the paradox but has more difficulty stabilizing in a nondepressed state. The spouse, tending not to trust the improvement, thus has greater difficulty changing behavior directed toward the depressed mate and, by behaving in the same old ways, inadvertently encourages the patient to stay depressed. The therapist can usually help by insisting that the spouse not change or begin to hope. Using the treatment in conjunction with medication has not been addressed but may be appropriate with manic-depressives, for whom labeling the depressive phase "good" and the hypermanic phase "bad" ("because you are avoiding being depressed") is completely open to further clinical and empirical study.

The requirements for the therapist are just as important as the requirements for the patient. Extensive experience with depression (in self and in patients) helps the therapist understand the patient's reactions and believe in the approach. The treatment cannot be used merely as a technique. The therapist must be willing to let clients become more depressed if they follow the therapist's directive. If the therapist becomes uncomfortable, clients will surely be affected adversely. Clients cannot comfortably change behavior if they are afraid the therapist will not be able to handle it. The therapist must truly believe that the approach is paradoxical only to the client, not to the therapist. Sincerely encouraging more pain and discomfort is difficult for most therapists, who have been trained to help people out of their suffering.

Another difficult professional issue is choosing the unit of treatment. A systemic approach is implicit. The question then becomes how many of the persons in the context should be included in the treatment.

We recommend, in general, that only the couple be included in the first phase of treatment; the extended family can be dealt with in a second phase. Working only with the couple allows the therapist to draw a boundary around the marital relationship and accent it as a focal element in the depression (for families with very diffuse boundaries, this procedure is especially helpful). Including the family is sometimes appropriate: For example, when the depressed individual has a strong cross-generational alliance with a family member, it is often useful to have that family member try but fail to help the patient, then help the mate succeed in a paradoxical way. The major focus, however, should be to strengthen the marital subsystem as the depression is taken care of.

CONCLUSION

As is true with any treatment approach, a paradoxical strategy is not a panacea for all the ills of depressed couples. Used appropriately, however, it can be a powerful and effective tool for reducing depression and improving marital satisfaction. Perhaps this treatment approach can provide the symptom-reducing function of medication and the social adjustment function of long-term interpersonal therapy. Certainly the time has come for a more systematic therapy model that addresses the paradoxical elements of depression in the marital context (L'Abate, 1983b). Only further empirical evaluation can determine how useful this approach will ultimately be.

REFERENCES

Adler, A. *The individual psychology of Alfred Adler* (H. L. Ansbacher & R. R. Ansbacher, Eds. and trans.). New York: Harper & Row, 1956.

Allman, L. R., & Jaffe, D. T. *Abnormal psychology in the life cycle.* New York: Harper & Row, 1978.

Ayllon, T. Intensive treatment of psychotic behavior by stimulus satiation and food reinforcement. *Behaviour Research and Therapy,* 1963, *1,* 53–62.

Balswick, J. The inexpressive male: Functional conflict and role theory as contrasting explanations. *Family Coordinator,* 1979, *28,* 330–336.

Barry, W. A. Marriage research and conflict: An integrative review. *Psychology Bulletin,* 1970, *73,* 41–54.

Bateson, G., Jackson, D. D., Haley, J., & Weakland, J. Toward a theory of schizophrenia. *Behavioral Science,* 1956, *1,* 251–264.

Beck, A. T. *Depression: Clinical, experimental, and theoretical aspects.* New York: Harper & Row, 1967.

Bothwell, S., & Weissman, M. Social impairments four years after an acute depressive episode. *American Journal of Orthopsychiatry*, 1977, *47*, 231–237.

Brown, G. W., & Harris, T. *Social origins of depression*. New York: Free Press, 1978.

Buzas, H. P. *A systemic approach for treating depression in a spouse*. Unpublished doctoral dissertation, Georgia State University, 1983.

Cohen, M. B., Baker, G., Cohen, R. A., Fromm-Reichmann, F., & Weigert, E. B. An intensive study of twelve cases of manic-depressive psychosis. *Psychiatry*, 1954, *17*, 103–137.

Cole, J. O., Schatzberg, A. F., & Frazier, S. H. *Depression: Biology, psychodynamics, and treatment*. New York: Plenum Press, 1978.

Coyne, J. C. Depression and the response of others. *Journal of Abnormal Psychology*, 1976, *85*, 186–193.

Dell, P. Some irrelevant thoughts on paradox. *Family Process*, 1981, *20*, 37–41.

De Shazer, S. Brief therapy with couples. *American Journal of Family Therapy*, 1978, *6*, 17–30.

Dunlap, K. *Personal adjustment*. New York: McGraw-Hill, 1946.

Farrelly, F., & Brandsma, J. *Provocative therapy*. Fort Collins, Colo.: Shields Publishing, 1974.

Feldman, L. Depression and marital interaction. *Family Process*, 1976, *15*, 389–395.

Frankl, V. Sur medikamentosen unterstutzung der psychotherapie bei neurosen. *Schweizer Arshio fur Neurologie und Psychiatrie*, 1939, *43*, 26–31.

Friedman, A. S. Interaction of drug therapy with marital therapy in depressive patients. *Archives of General Psychiatry*, 1975, *32*, 619–637.

Haley, J. *Uncommon therapy*. New York: Ballantine Books, 1973.

Hare-Mustin, R. Treatment of temper tantrums by paradoxical intervention. *Family Process*, 1975, *14*, 481–486.

Hinchliffe, M., Hooper, D., & Roberts, F. J. *The melancholy marriage*. New York: John Wiley & Sons, 1978.

Hogan, P., & Hogan, B. K. The family treatment of depression. In F. F. Flach & S. Draghi (Eds.), *The nature and treatment of depression*. New York: John Wiley & Sons, 1975.

Jessee, E. H. *Paradoxical treatment of depression in married couples*. Unpublished doctoral dissertation, Georgia State University, 1984.

Jessee, E. H., & L'Abate, L. Depression and intimacy: Interactional partners. *International Journal of Family Therapy*, 1983, *5*, 39–53. (a)

Jessee, E. H., & L'Abate, L. The paradoxes of depression. *International Journal of Family Psychiatry*, 1983, (b), *3*, 175–187.

Kreitman, N., Collins, J., Nelson, B., & Troop, J. Manifest psychological interaction. *British Journal of Psychiatry*, 1971, *119*, 243–252.

L'Abate, L. A positive approach to marital and familial intervention. In L. R. Wolberg & M. L. Aronson (Eds.), *Group therapy 1975: An overview*. New York: Stratton Intercontinental, 1975. Pp. 63–75.

L'Abate, L. *Systematic family therapy*. New York: Brunner/Mazel, 1985.

L'Abate, L. Paradoxical techniques: One level of abstraction in family therapy. In G. Weeks (Ed.), *Promoting change through paradoxical techniques*. Homewood, Ill.: Dow Jones-Irwin, in press. (a)

L'Abate, L., & L'Abate, B. The paradoxes of intimacy. *Family Therapy,* 1979, *6,* 175–184.

Lehmann, H. Epidemiology of depressive disorders. In R. R. Fieve (Ed.), *Depression in the seventies.* Princeton: Excerpta Medical Foundation, 1971.

Levitsky, A., & Perls, F. The rules and games of Gestalt therapy. In J. Fagan & I. Shepherd (Eds.), *Gestalt therapy now.* New York: Harper & Row, 1970.

Madanes, C. *Strategic family therapy.* San Francisco: Jossey-Bass, 1981.

Mishler, E. G., & Waxler, N. *Interaction of families.* New York: John Wiley & Sons, 1968.

Mozdzierz, G., Macchitelli, F., & Lisiecki, J. The paradox in psychotherapy: An Adlerian perspective. *Journal of Individual Psychology,* 1976, *32,* 169–184.

Overall, J. Associations between marital history and the nature of manifest psychopathology. *Journal of Abnormal Psychology,* 1971, *78,* 213–221.

Parson, T., & Bales, R. F. *Family, socialization and interaction process.* New York: Free Press, 1955.

Paykel, E. S., Myers, J. K., Diendelt, M. N., Klerman, G. L., Lindenthal, J. J., & Pepper, M. P. Life events and depression: A controlled study. *Archives of General Psychiatry,* 1969, *21,* 753–760.

Rohrbaugh, M., Tennen, H., Press, S., & White, L. Compliance, defiance, and therapeutic paradox. *American Journal of Orthopsychiatry,* 1981, *51,* 454–467.

Rosen, J. *Direct psychoanalysis.* New York: Grune & Stratton, 1953.

Rounsaville, B. J., Weissman, M. M., Prusoff, B. A., & Herceg-Baron, R. L. Process of psychotherapy among depressed women with marital disputes. *American Journal of Orthopsychiatry,* 1979, *49,* 505–510.

Rubinstein, D., & Timmins, J. F. Depressive dyadic and triadic relationships. *Journal of Marriage and Family Counseling,* 1978, *4,* 13–23.

Rush, A. J., Shaw, B., & Khatami, M. Cognitive therapy of depression: Utilizing the couples system. *Cognitive Therapy and Research,* 1980, *4,* 103–113.

Sager, C. J., Gundlach, R., & Kremer, M. The married in treatment. *Archives of General Psychiatry,* 1968, *19,* 205–217.

Sattel, J. W. The inexpressive male: Tragedy or sexual politics? *Social Problems,* 1976, *23,* 469–477.

Selvini-Palazzoli, M., Boscolo, L., Cecchin, G., & Prata, G. *Paradox and counterparadox.* New York: Jason Aronson, 1978.

Uhr, L. M. *Personality changes during marriage.* Unpublished doctoral dissertation, University of Michigan, 1957.

Watzlawick, P. *Language of change: Elements of therapeutic communication.* New York: Basic Books, 1978.

Watzlawick, P., Beavin, J., & Jackson, D. *Pragmatics of human communication.* New York: W. W. Norton, 1967.

Watzlawick, P., & Coyne, J. Depression following stroke: Brief problem-focused family treatment. *Family Process,* 1980, *19,* 13–18.

Watzlawick, P., Weakland, J., & Fisch, R. *Change: Principles of problem formation and problem resolution.* New York: W. W. Norton, 1974.

Weeks, G., & L'Abate, L. *Paradoxical psychotherapy.* New York: Brunner/Mazel, 1982.

Weissman, M. M. The psychological treatment of depression. *Archives of General Psychiatry,* 1979, *36,* 1261–1269.

Weissman, M. M., & Klerman, G. L. Psychotherapy with depressed women: An empirical study of content themes and reflection. *British Journal of Psychiatry,* 1973, *123,* 55–61.

Weissman, M. M., & Paykel, E. S. *The depressed woman: A study of social relationships.* Chicago: University of Chicago Press, 1974.

Wing, J. K., & Hailey, A. M. *Evaluating a community psychiatric service.* London: Oxford University Press, 1972.

Chapter 38

Systems Interventions with Hyperactive Children: An Interdisciplinary Perspective

MICHAEL T. SMITH
MONTA P. SMITH
LUCIANO L'ABATE

Hyperactivity is quickly becoming an American institution. Not only are children in this country diagnosed as hyperactive at a rate as high as any other industrialized country (Wunsch-Hitzig, Gould, & Dohrenwend, 1980), but concern for hyperactivity permeates PTAs, popular magazines, and TV talk shows. Professional interest in hyperactivity has also been high, as numerous treatment modalities (each with its own conceptions of etiology and intervention) have arisen in the last two decades. The three most prevalent points of view may be described as: *(a)* the constitutional view, where there is a deficit in the child; *(b)* the educational view, where there is a deficit in the child's social and academic learning; and *(c)* the family view, where there is a deficit in the interactions of the family. The purpose of this chapter is to review the literature on hyperactivity and to recommend an interdisciplinary, systemic treatment approach to this syndrome.

In a book by one of the principal advocates of constitutional theories of hyperactivity (Wender, 1971), one hyperactive child was described by his parents as follows:

> Mark was a premature baby, had jaundice after he was born, was a bit slow developing, a bit clumsy and awkward, and our doctor always felt that he might have a little bit of cerebral palsy. He's been a very nice boy. He's very affectionate—if anything, he hangs on you too much for attention and love. He's very immature and it's hard for him to do his chores. He's eight now and he really can't tie his shoelaces. He doesn't

take care of his room, he just forgets to do what you tell him to. He had to repeat first grade and is having trouble now in the second. They said his I.Q. was low-normal and that he should be able to learn but he still seems to be having a great deal of difficulty. He has a lot of trouble writing and he has very messy handwriting. I've tried to help him with that and with reading. He reverses a lot of letters and words and just can't stick with it. You try to get him to sit down and five minutes after you start he's up again. (p. 11)

Wender viewed the problem as a result of minimal brain dysfunction; therefore, the treatment of choice was medication and individual therapy for the "problem child." Other variants of the constitutional view include the genetic and biochemical theories of hyperactivity (McMahon, 1981), nutritional therapies (Feingold, 1975), and child play therapy (Axline, 1947), to name but a few.

The second major thrust of work with hyperactivity has focused on the child's performance in the classroom. Hewett (1968) described one hyperactive child as follows:

Blair . . . was a ten-year-old mentally retarded boy with an IQ of 75 and was capable of acquiring certain basic academic skills in school. But his impulsivity and unwillingness to follow directions were constant limiting factors in his learning. While most of the other children functioning at the same intellectual level in his class could participate in a number-counting lesson using disc counters, Blair quickly and carelessly sorted out his discs with little attention to teacher directions and as a result often made errors. (p. 5)

Hewett viewed the problem as a lack of impulse control and of sustained attention, thereby interfering with the child's ability to complete assignments. These problems can become chronic in the form of academic underachievement, failure to exhibit appropriate classroom behavior, and difficulty in establishing relationships with teachers and peers. Due to this assortment of problems, a number of interventions have been used. For example, classroom environments were restructured to reduce overstimulation (Cruickshank, Bentzen, Ratzeburg, & Tannhauser, 1961); behavioral techniques were used to shape appropriate classroom behaviors and increase academic achievement (Ayllon, Layman, & Kandell, 1975; Backman & Firestone, 1979; Jones & Kazdin, 1981); verbal mediation was used to reduce impulsiveness (Camp, 1980); and social skills training has also been applied in the classroom (Michelson & Wood, 1980; Stephens, 1978). This second thrust, while congruent with the concept of the "problem child," represented the initial steps in providing the child treatment in the setting where the child typically exhibits the problem behavior.

The next step in the development of theories related to hyperactivity occurred in the 1970s, as investigators became interested in the relationship between hyperactivity and the home environment (Paternite & Loney, 1980). Studies of psychopathology in parents were undertaken (Cantwell, 1972; Morrison & Stewart, 1971) to see whether psychopathology occurred across generations in families. In addition, the style of parenting was examined to determine its relationship to hyperactivity. The social-learning model (Becker, 1971) was proposed as an explanation for how negative, coercive parenting reinforces the child's inappropriate behaviors. An advocate of this theory (Barkley, 1981) described one hyperactive child as follows:

> Greg was 11 years and 8 months old and had a history of hyperactive behavior since the age of 2. He was referred for evaluation of difficult behavior at both home and school. The interview with his parents and his teacher, as well as the behavior rating scales, were all consistent with the diagnosis of hyperactivity. The parents were also concerned about his poor grades on his report card and his apparent problems with and aversion to reading and spelling. Greg was in the fourth and final quarter of his sixth-grade year at a public school, and there was some question as to whether he would be passed to a seventh-grade program. Both the parents and the teacher felt that Greg could achieve at grade level if he would simply pay attention and complete his assignments. (p. 177)

Barkley has recommended parent training to teach parents the principles of behavior exchange, thereby reducing coercive sequences of behavior.

These three similar case examples with highly dissimilar interventions indicate the lack of consensus among professionals regarding the treatment of choice for hyperactivity. What was once considered a single etiological syndrome resulting from minimal brain dysfunction is now viewed as a heterogeneous group of disorders of attention and impulsivity (Loney, 1980). Major secondary symptoms of high activity level, aggression, noncompliance, social isolation and academic underachievement have also been identified. Meanwhile, the disorder is now considered most acute in specific situations, rather than across all settings and situations (Schachar, Rutter, & Smith, 1981). This consideration has encouraged clearer distinctions regarding symptom clusters and the ecology of hyperactivity, placing more diagnostic emphasis on description rather than etiology. However, the rapid changes in research and treatment have made it difficult for all but the specialists to keep abreast of changes in the conceptualization of hyperactivity. Thus, the temptation is to see hyperactivity exclusively as an individual-child problem, a problem in learning (academically or socially), or a family problem.

Unequivocally, each approach has its merit. One cannot dispute that some children respond to medication, that some modified classroom procedures have improved academic performance, or that parent training has reduced some problem behaviors. However, the hetero geneity of the disorder in question requires that all of these modalities be equipotent treatment alternatives. Furthermore, a larger scheme is essential for organizing the clinician's decision rules about the nature of the problem and the treatment of choice.

The recent call for multimodal treatment with hyperactive children (Satterfield, Cantwell, & Satterfield, 1979) reflects the need to enlarge the treatment repertoire and redefine who constitutes the treatment team. Yet, even in cases where the doctor, teacher, and parent all agreed on the problem and the desired treatment, poor coordination of these three agents of change has prohibited the intended changes from occurring (Robin & Bosco, 1981). Regardless of the nature and severity of a particular child's hyperactivity, the most important prognostic indicator is the degree to which the agents of change are able to cooperate with one another. It is imperative that clinicians, who are charged with the responsibility to change behavior, equip themselves with strategies that provide them leverage vis-à-vis these change agents. Systems theory provides a contextual view of hyperactivity, which helps the clinician develop a set of decision rules regarding both the nature of the hyperactive symptoms and the best means for organizing the treatment team.

SYSTEMS THEORY AND THE INTERDISCIPLINARY APPROACH

In addition to helping the clinician make sense of the discrepant information from various change agents, systems theory also provides a vehicle for integrating apparently contradictory research on hyperactivity. Perhaps the major reason for such contradictions relates to the epistemology of the researchers. Representatives from each school (e.g., organic, learning, family) stress their etiological framework and treatment approach, to the exclusion of others. A systemic approach to the question of etiology is to acknowledge how each level of the child's ecology contributes to the current problem (Salzinger, Antrobus, & Glick, 1980). This approach includes genetic, organic, and temperamental features of the child, the developmental and learning history of the child, the family history, and the current organization of the social network, including agents of change. For the clinician, this last item is the most important, as hyperactive behavior can be best understood in relation to the context in which it occurs (Conrad, 1977; Salzinger et al.; Whalen & Henker, 1980). In addition, change in the behavior will only be maintained if the social network is organized to support the change.

Often, consensus is never achieved regarding the best course of action; thus, a coordinated treatment plan is not implemented. The presence of contradictory professional opinions provides an escape route for parents who are not satisfied with the treatment approach. This is a major contributing factor in premature termination from treatment. Such early termination generally takes the form of dropping out of parenting classes (Firestone & Witt, 1982) or discontinuing medication against the doctor's advice (Firestone, 1982). Robin and Bosco (1981) were one of the first to note that although treatment procedures worked in research settings, they did not always produce desired effects in clinical settings. They discovered that the lack of coordination of the agents of change (e.g., doctor, teacher, parents) related to a lack of consensus on who had the power and authority to institute treatment. Thus, the most significant goal from the outset is to establish a hierarchy in the agents of change. Therefore, a treatment plan for hyperactivity must include not only goals related to the child's behavior, but also goals related to the family and the larger social, academic, and medical contexts.

FAMILIAL INFLUENCES ON HYPERACTIVITY

Numerous family studies have shown response to medication (Conrad & Insel, 1967; Loney, Comly, & Simon, 1975; Minde, Weiss, & Mendelson, 1972), rate of delinquency (Mendelson, Johnson, & Stewart, 1971; Minde et al.), and academic performance (Minde et al.) to be related to "poor family environment." Based on this, Paternite and Loney (1980) undertook a factor analysis of 135 subjects who had been treated for hyperactivity during a five-year period. Although they could not isolate a specific factor in the home environment (e.g., parental psychopathology, mother-father relationship, parent-child relationship) that is primarily responsible for the emergence of hyperactivity, they did conclude that home influences are related both to the development and expression of hyperactive symptoms.

One of the major hypotheses in family research related to hyperactivity has been the assumption that a pattern of psychopathology (including a hyperactive component) can be traced through families. Simultaneous psychopathology in family members of hyperactive children has been documented (Cantwell, 1972; Idol-Maestas, 1981; Morrison & Stewart, 1971), with the most common forms being paternal alcoholism, paternal sociopathy, and maternal hysteria. Nevertheless, parental psychopathology generally accounts for a smaller proportion of the variance in children's school behavior disorders than does marital discord (Emery, Weintraub, & Neale, 1982).

Behavior problems have also been related to temperament styles (Thomas & Chess, 1977.) For example, Lambert (1982) noted that children with a difficult temperament are more at risk for behavior problems, generally due to restlessness, difficulty with scheduling, and tension between mother and child. However, Thomas and Chess noted that parent-child interactions mediate the degree to which behavior problems emerge in temperamentally difficult children. As a corollary to this position, Paternite, Loney, and Langhorne (1976) indicated that it is unlikely that "adverse parental behavior is solely the result of frustrations with a constitutionally difficult child" (p. 300). When viewed as a whole, these conclusions suggest that the child's temperament and inappropriate parenting interact to create behavioral sequences supportive of hyperactivity.

Predominantly negative parent-child interactions in families with hyperactive children have been widely reported (Barkley, 1981; Kozloff, 1979; Paternite & Loney, 1980; Wahler, 1980). These repetitive, coercive sequences generally revolve around a series of escalating attempts by the child and parents to gain power. The assumption is that the parents are functioning as a unit. However, Barkley (1981) notes that most parents have different disciplinary abilities and styles. It is very likely that these differences emerge in trying to provide structure for the hyperactive child. As a consequence, marital conflict also plays a role in hyperactivity.

In a thorough investigation of marital interaction and conflict resolution, Gottman (1979) identified two major forms of negotiation deficits in marital dyads: validation deficits and contracting deficits. Validation deficits occur when the partners fail to view the problem in the same terms, preventing movement toward a solution. Contracting deficits occur after a dyad has agreed on the problem but failed to devise and execute a workable strategy. It is due to deficits like these that parents tend to engage in power struggles with each other regarding how to manage the child's behavior, and the child learns this conflictual style from them. Parents defeat each other and the child learns to defeat both. This defeating behavior eventually generalizes to the school and the doctor's office.

Not only do marital discord and parent-child conflict contribute to hyperactivity, but the extended family also influences the presence of hyperactivity. As Wahler (1980) has noted, a family ecosystem of "negative mands" is created. Whereas the child exhibits "negative mands" when relating to parents, the parents often receive the same from extended family, which further undercuts the ability of the parents to work as a unit. In fact, those parents who do reduce coercive behavior are not supported by extended family (Wahler, 1980), which adds a multigenerational aspect (Bowen, 1978) to the transmission of hyperactivity.

In a sense, it is as if the "defeat or be defeated" view of the world permeates the family. This is consistent with the research of Reiss (1981) that families develop a shared perception of reality. Furthermore, the interactional patterns of hyperactive children and their parents are different from those in families where the children are normal (Alabiso & Hansen, 1977). However, the parents have a stake in appearing "normal" and united, strongly denying any indication of conflict between themselves. Since Reiss argued that the family's view of the internal and external social environments is stored in interaction, their style of defeat and hostility reflects the family's pattern of conflict with each other and with the agents of change.

CONTEXTUAL INFLUENCES ON HYPERACTIVITY

Studies of the way that the setting influences behavioral problems and behavior change is the newest area in hyperactivity research. The work of Wahler (1980) suggests that social and extended family contexts do not necessarily support increases in desired behavior by parents. As a result, parents generally terminate the new behavior, which is indicative of the power of contexts. This conclusion echoes the remarks of Conrad (1977), who contends that hyperactivity is an adaptive response to a crazy context—the family.

Although Conrad's comments were not empirically tested, recent studies of the "kenosystem" of the hyperactive child by Robin and Bosco (1980, 1981) support this argument. They found that the failure to organize the medical, educational, and family systems regarding how to conduct treatment with the hyperactive child led to the disarray which constitutes a nonsystem, or "kenosystem." This is reflective of the unpredictable, chaotic, and often hostile environment of the child. Robin and Bosco conclude, therefore, that the child's behavior is a metaphor for the social system, a conclusion we strongly endorse.

Sandoval, Lambert, and Sassone (1980) also endorse an "interactive view" of the process of labeling and treating hyperactivity. They suggest that characteristics of the child interact with characteristics of the child's social ecology (i.e., home and school). Like Robin and Bosco (1980), they identify parents, teachers, and doctors as agents of identification and intervention. Their results indicate that these three agents do not always agree on the presence of hyperactivity. These inconsistencies in identification lead to irregularity in treatment regime. Sandoval et al. view this treatment irregularity as an indication of the parents' willingness to utilize several treatment alternatives. However, Bosco and Robin (1980) did not find multimodal treatment to be the norm. Instead, they found that medication was the most prevalent form of treatment, rather than an adjunct to a more comprehensive psychoeducational intervention. In fact, Robin and Bosco (1980) note that most families experience frustration in trying to establish a comprehensive, multimodal treatment program involving all three change agents. Only those parents who are able to organize the change agent "interface" are able to bring about an orderly multimodal treatment plan.

Thus, both the family context and the larger social context appear to be disorganized in a fashion analogous to the symptom cluster of hyperactivity. This defeating confusion is consistent with the clinical theories of strategic therapy (Haley, 1976; Madanes, 1981), where the problem is a metaphor for the disorder in the social system, or kenosystem as Robin and Bosco (1981) refer to it. Such disorganization—both within the family system, due to poor parental conflict resolution and to intergenerational boundary and hierarchy violations, and within the kenosystem, due to poor interface—undercuts the parents as they attempt to fulfill their role as executives in the family system. Thus, the treatment of choice is an interdisciplinary systemic intervention that reorganizes the internal hierarchy of the family while assisting the parents in resuming control of the disordered kenosystem. Consequently, the actors in the hyperactive child's family and social networks are both targets for change and agents of change (Salzinger et al., 1980).

AN INTERDISCIPLINARY, SYSTEMIC TREATMENT MODEL

As an alternative to conventional psychotherapeutic approaches to handicapped children, an ecological assessment and treatment plan coordinated by a "case manager" has been recommended (Hobbs, 1980). The effective case manager will organize the kenosystem in a new way, enabling each of the change agents to do what they do best, thereby working productively as a team. The liaison function of the case manager is crucial, as there is less possibility for the triangulation of the family and two agents when all of the change agents have agreed on a joint plan. A reduction in triangulation is necessary to prevent premature termination from medical, educational, or psychological treatment programs. Often the family leaves one "expert" due to a disagreement, only to hire a new "expert" and begin the cycle of defeat anew. If all three systems are coordinated, then many premature terminations may be prevented, and those that are not prevented will still have continuity in the remaining two systems. Failure to coordinate a plan across systems will lead to coalitions, triangles, and violations of hierarchy that are symptomatic of the cycle of defeat, which we see as the common denominator of hyperactivity.

The degree to which the cycle of defeat is blocked will relate directly to the leadership of the case manager. Just as Robin and Bosco (1981) indicated that the physician, teacher, and parents generally disagreed on who possessed the legitimacy to direct interventions with hyperactive children, the mere presence of a psychologist or other mental health clinician will not automatically create cohesion in the treatment group. In fact, mental health professionals should not assume that the role of case manager is automatically theirs. Flexibility here is important. Although it is generally preferable for a mental health professional who understands human relations and the function of systems to take the responsibilities of case manager, an energetic teacher, doctor, or parent can function admirably in this role. What is more important than who assumes this role is the unanimity of support for the person designated as case manager. It is also important to remember that the goal is for parents to ultimately assume this role and thereby resume their control of the family hierarchy. If someone other than the parent is the initial case manager, an implicit goal is to prepare the parents to assume this function as soon as they are ready.

In addition to establishing a cohesive, interdisciplinary treatment team, other general goals include providing parents a sense of mastery in the management of their child's behavior, providing the child opportunities to acquire developmentally appropriate academic and social skills, and controlling the various health factors (e.g., diet) that may contribute to the problem behavior. Obviously, no one person can do all this. What is needed is an integration of relevant information from each system, so that all the appropriate goals for a family may be met under the umbrella of one treatment team.

The first contact

The way in which the first interview with the family is conducted will set the tone for treatment. When the family member (generally the mother) first calls for help, it is important not only to obtain her point of view but to inquire as to the impression of her husband and other adults with significant child-care responsibility, including relatives, teachers, doctors, and other professionals. This information will immediately communicate that these other adults are considered to be important resources. A time and setting should be selected for the first appointment that will allow the following, if possible: (1) the presence of both parents and/or other adults in a child-care function; (2) the contribution of teachers, counselors, school psychologists, and the principal; (3) observation of the child in the social setting where the hyperactivity is manifest (e.g., classroom, home); and (4) the contribution of the family physician. Based on the above, the school is often the best site for an initial consultation.

Some problems with this procedure will occur, and it is best to try to anticipate them. First, the family may not want the change agents from the three systems to work together for a variety of reasons, including fear that the parents will be scapegoated, denial that the problem is serious, concern about confidentiality, or resistance to change. The first two examples of these barriers will be alleviated by a firm team approach which realistically assesses the problems and the resources available. An interview style adapted from the Mental Research Institute approach to brief therapy (Fisch, Weakland, & Segal, 1982)—which focuses on how each party sees the problem, what other parties (not present at the meeting) have advised, and what solutions to date have been tried—will matter-of-factly lead to a treatment contract that specifies the treatment objectives and each person's responsibility for change.

The issue of confidentiality may be resolved by having the family sign release forms at the beginning of the meeting. Not all families will be willing to sign this release. To allay their fears, the parent may be told during the first phone conversation that this information will be essential to a full understanding of the problem behavior. They may complain that they do not trust the school. One may note that this is often the case but that an effective intervention will only be possible if improvement occurs at school also. Improvement at school will only be possible by getting the school's view of the problem first-hand. Thus, the therapist must frame the release as a way of gathering more information that will confirm their view of the problem. If the first interview with the family is held at a clinic rather than at the school, release forms will have to be signed in advance (i.e., by mail) in order for this information to be obtained before the first interview. The time which is required to mail, sign, and mail back the release forms and then to contact the other professionals can be used in negotiating with a family that wants services immediately but does not want to conduct the first interview at the school.

The most complicated problems are encountered when the family wants to change the behavior problem but not the ecology that supports it. Many families, in fact, come to therapy not to change but to stay the same (Andolfi, Angelo, Menghi, & Nicolo-Corigliano, 1983). Thus, if the therapist uses language suggesting that the parents should behave differently, the parent will generally list all the things that have already been tried, unsuccessfully. The implication is "fix the kid and leave us alone!" Other indications of this position are a history of jumping from one "helper" to another and difficulty in arranging a time that is convenient for everyone. Their behavior is designed to defeat the therapist, which is the name of the game in these families. Thus, the therapist must work very slowly, giving the parent credit for improvements and staying with the presenting symptom as the focus of treatment.

An absenteeism problem may develop when the other parent or the other child-care figure (e.g., aunt, uncle, grandparent, roommate, baby-sitter) is invited to the intake. The parent who calls will rightfully become anxious about asking other adults to come if they believe the family or the ecosystem is going to be treated. Since they have called about a hyperactive child, it is best to ask about these others only in relation to the child's behavior. For example, one may express interest in the additional adult resources and invite their help as follows: "So your mother helps out by watching Johnny in the afternoon? How does that usually work out? Can you arrange to get her here so she can help me understand the problem?" At each subsequent session, the membership may be renegotiated, but it is crucial that the parent is put in charge of getting other family resources in. On the other hand, at least at the beginning, it is important for the case manager to assume responsibility for contacting the school and the physician. Otherwise, the parent may do this in a way that will block their attendance. In general, it is important to proceed cautiously as you introduce new elements into the treatment team, keeping in mind that parents of hyperactive children have an investment in *(a)* saving face and *(b)* appearing normal.

One member of the treatment team who is generally hard to involve and therefore is often overlooked is the family physician. Since few doctors are available to actually attend team treatment meetings, the best approximation of this involvement is a regularly scheduled phone consult. It is particularly important that the physician and case manager consult before each medication evaluation to prevent the family from triangulating them. Although physicians may be reluctant to invest this time on the phone at first, they may be willing to do so after it is evident to them that such coordination will reduce their time dealing with irate and frustrated parents. As a case manager, it is important to remember that the task is not to make decisions for the physician but to organize the context so that the physician will coordinate decisions with the team. It is surprising how many physicians respond favorably to this interest from other professionals, regardless of their status.

Finally, problems may emerge because of misinformation (e.g., the family does not accurately describe school performance), resistance by the family to a school-initiated referral or a medication regime, or unrealistically high or low expectations for treatment. The interdisciplinary intake addresses these problems by defining the problem behavior, the setting and time of the problem behavior, previous evaluation data, previous interventions, current choice of evaluation and treatment alternatives, realistic targets of change, the tasks of each change agent, and the outcome measures. It is sometimes helpful to write a summary of this initial meeting, furnish a copy to all present, and set a date for the evaluation of this plan.

The evaluation phase

Haley (1976) describes intervention and assessment as inseparable processes. Generally, this is an argument used by family therapists to avoid formal assessment. However, Hobbs (1980) has noted that ecological treatment requires a comprehensive evaluation of all resources available to the treatment team. There is no doubt that a complete assessment of the child and the available treatment resources is a lengthy process. However, given the heterogeneity of the hyperactive population and the great number of referrals for apparent hyperactivity, the possibility of misdiagnosis is high. Thus, in the case of hyperactivity, early assessment is essential.

In addition to establishing the nature of the child's social, academic, medical, and behavioral problems, the evaluation allows for the exchange of information across the three systems. Although some would argue that extensive assessment will scapegoat the child, the evaluation phase is an important intervention designed to create more order in the kenosystem by regulating the flow of information. The first task of the case manager is to serve as liaison, filtering the flow of information through him. The goal of this phase is a team diagnostic summary, which will serve to differentiate between different forms of hyperactivity and between hyperactive and nonhyperactive referrals.

In conjunction with the family physician, the following are important components of the medical evaluation: (1) history of the pregnancy and delivery; (2) developmental history; (3) history of allergies; (4) nutrition and exposure to toxins; (5) history of injuries and illnesses; and (6) medication history. Any information not available from the family doctor may be pursued with the parents, who may complete a developmental checklist.

When the case manager contacts the school, the following types of information are crucial: (1) academic history; (2) classroom and social behavior; (3) evaluation data; (4) previous interventions; and (5) relationship with the family. The academic history is primarily used to document both current and past levels of academic achievement. A note should be made regarding whether a child has repeated a grade and, if so, whether the retention helped increase the child's ability to complete grade-level assignments. Additionally, valuable diagnostic information can be learned from reviewing school records. Often, the hyperactive child will already be receiving special education (e.g., behavior disorders or learning disabilities classes) or related services (e.g., Title I classes or tutoring). Parents should have personal copies of the child's individual educational plan as required by Public Law 94–142 (1975). Generally included in the individual educational plan is a report of previous psychological testing, hearing and vision evaluations, and classroom observations as a part of the screening for behavior disorders and learning disabilities. Obtaining copies of this information from the parents can save valuable time during the evaluation phase of treatment.

After determining whether the child is in a self-contained or resource special education class, then assessment may take place regarding on-task and social behavior across classroom settings and across structured versus unstructured periods. The appropriateness of the child's behavior may be measured at various times of the school day and during a variety of activities (e.g., on the bus, at meals, during recess or free time). The assessment of these behaviors may be conducted informally through anecdotal records and incident reports or formally with published checklists and behavior rating scales. Two commonly used instruments are the Connors Teacher Questionnaire (Goyette, Connors, & Ulrich, 1978) and the Werry-Weiss-Peters Activity Rating Scale (Routh, Schroeder, & O'Tauma, 1974).

The school psychologist is an important member of the interdisciplinary treatment team. Not only can this professional serve as the case manager, but the school psychologist's analysis of standardized intelligence tests can provide information regarding the behavioral and cognitive style of the child. The most commonly used intelligence test is the Wechsler Intelligence Scale for Children-Revised (WISC–R) constructed by Wechsler (1974). In addition to providing a cognitive profile of intellectual abilities, the WISC–R has recently been factor analyzed by Kaufman (1979). He identified a third dimension (beyond the verbal and performance IQ) which he termed the distractibility factor. Although this third factor need not be routinely computed for all children, there are some children for whom the distractibility factor holds the key for competent WISC–R interpretation. This group includes children described as reading disabled, anxious, distractible, learning disabled, or hyperactive (Kaufman, 1979). The computation of this factor, which is described in Kaufman (1979), is an important determinant in the decision regarding the appropriateness of a referral for medication evaluation.

In addition to the analysis of testing results, the school psychologist can also provide information regarding the effects of previous behavior management plans. For example, the history of previous interventions is important in identifying what "solutions" might presently be supporting the problem behavior. Finally, the frequency and nature of parent-teacher contact (e.g., Who calls whom? When? Do they usually agree?) provides information on the degree of parent-school cooperation.

The mental health professional is responsible for evaluating the child and the family. The child assessment should address constitutional features of the child which interact with the social context, the nature of which is depicted in the family assessment. Included in the child assessment is an intellectual evaluation (if not conducted already at school) with emphasis on cognitive and organic features. For example, Kinsbourne and Caplan (1979) distinguish between problems associated with cognitive power (innate intellectual ability) and problems associated with cognitive style (attention deficits due to impulsivity or compulsivity). Therefore, beyond simply administering the tests to screen out learning disabilities or behavior disorders, the response style and subtest patterns may be analyzed, as these yield information regarding the child's cognitive style. For this reason, the analyses of the McCarthy Scales of Children's Abilities (Kaufman & Kaufman, 1977) and the WISC–R (Kaufman, 1979) are valuable aids when interpreting the test profile. Other measures of cognitive style are the Matching Familiar Figures Test, the Jumbled Numbers Game, and the Porteus Mazes (Homatidis & Konstantareas, 1981), which provide opportunities to observe the child's information-processing style, problem-solving style, problem-solving capacity, and reflectiveness. An additional assessment based on psychophysiological research (and thereby pertinent to the question of medication appropriateness) would include the child's EEG, skin conductance levels, or heart rate and heart rate variability. For a complete discussion of this subject, see Porges and Smith (1980) and Hastings and Barkley (1978).

The mental health professional's family assessment must capture the family context at the time of referral, in addition to multigenerational influences on the presenting problem. Completing a genogram provides preliminary information on both levels. The form for drawing the genogram may be found in *The Family Lifecycle* (Carter & McGoldrick, 1980). Questions to be asked include the health, occupation/school status, household makeup, and frequency of contact with other relatives for all family members in the last three generations. By exploring what each member says about the problem, one discovers the family context of the problem. This discovery may give some indication of the levels of cohesion and adaptability in the family, the degree to which extended family members interfere in the responsibilities of the parents, and the degree to which symptoms occur across generations in a family. In addition to this information regarding the family network, one may also assess the amount of support available to the family from outside forces (Wahler, 1980).

Within the nuclear family, four levels of analysis are important: (1) parent-child, (2) marital, (3) sibling, and (4) family. The parent-child level may be assessed using the Connors Parent Questionnaire (Goyette et al., 1978). In lieu of this, the Behavior Problem Checklist (Quay,

1967) or Walker Problem Behavior Identification Checklist (Walker, 1976) provide an index of the parent's view of the child's behavior. One may also observe the parent and child in structured and unstructured situations (e.g., giving commands versus playing together) to see whether a coercive and defeating interaction pattern exists (Barkley, 1981; Wolfe, St. Lawrence, Graves, Brehony, Bradlyn, & Kelly, 1982).

The next level of analysis is marital interaction, with an interest in validation and contracting deficits. This is possible by using the revealed-differences technique (Strodtbeck, 1954), where parents have to discuss their differing views of an issue. Generally, this is done by having them negotiate their disagreement regarding an item on a questionnaire. A discussion of different scores on the questionnaires listed above is appropriate. Other studies have employed the Thematic Apperception Test (TAT), Rorschach, and Wechsler Adult Intelligence Scale (WAIS) (Ferreira & Winter, 1968; Singer & Wynne, 1966).

The third level of analysis, sibling, may also use the revealed-differences technique or structured problem-solving exercises (e.g., the Means-Ends Problem Solving Test by Spivack, Platt, & Shure, 1976). Dimensions of interest are sibling hierarchy, cohesion, and cooperation.

The fourth level of analysis is the nuclear family at present. This analysis includes the level of stress in the family, common interaction patterns, and the structure of the family. The Schedule of Events (Holmes & Rahe, 1967) and the Family Inventory of Life Events (McCubbin & Patterson, 1981) are measures of family stress. The Family Inventory of Resources for Management (McCubbin & Patterson, 1981) also provides a measure of family coping with stress. Family interactions may be observed by having the family make up a story together from three TAT cards or by completing a series of structured tasks (Minuchin, Montalvo, Guerney, Rosman, & Shumer, 1967). Various observational methods exist, but the most frequent analyses relate to who talks the most, who talks to whom, who interrupts whom, the quality of speech (vague or fragmented), the degree of agreement, and the time to solution. These are, admittedly, gross measures of family cohesion and problem solving. Finally, family structure relates to the degree of differentiation between various subsystems of the family and the hierarchical arrangement of these subsystems. The degree to which each family member is fulfilling appropriate developmental tasks is critical. One method for assessing family structure is the family behavioral snapshot (Meyerstein, 1979). The goal of the family analysis is to determine what stresses are currently affecting the family, how the family distributes power and responsibility, how conflicts are resolved, how boundaries are observed, and how well the hierarchy is maintained.

The diagnostic summary

Once the case manager has solicited input from all change agents regarding the child's behavior in each system, the case manager integrates all of this information in the form of a diagnostic summary. This is generally the opportunity for reconvening all the change agents and the family. The goal of such a meeting is to construct a framework which defines the problem in such a way that it is subject to change. Thus, a child who might previously have been diagnosed as having minimal brain dysfunction might instead be described as a child who fails to concentrate and follow directions. The emphasis is on observable behaviors which will serve as the target for the intervention plan. Rather than emphasizing the child's "condition," which has an ominously permanent sound to it, a focus on target behaviors provides the family and the change agents clear goals with the expectation that they will be reached. This is critical to parents who have become hopeless and often appear helpless to control the behavior of their child.

Each member of the team, including the parents, identifies what their responsibilities will be and a time frame for completion. A system for communicating progress periodically is established, with the case manager serving as the "switchboard." It is important for the agents to communicate through the case manager, in order to control the flow of information and to support the leadership position of the case manager in the treatment system. Thus, the diagnostic summary pools the information from all sources into a realistic and optimistic assessment of the behaviors to be changed, specifying each person's responsibilities and a means for evaluating progress. At this stage in treatment, the case manager must function as a chairman of the board, extracting useful information in an orderly way from each member of the treatment team. It is imperative that the case manager assume control of the case, so that this authority may then be transferred to the parents once change is instituted. In a sense, this is an intermediate phase of treatment, in which the case manager better organizes the ecosystem, provides the family hope that the behavior may be altered, and gradually allows the parents to assume more control.

The progressive treatment plan

The following progression of treatment alternatives is designed to meet two needs: (a) the need of therapists who seek specific ideas regarding the management of hyperactivity, and (b) the need for a staged set of interventions which reflect the highly diverse characteristics of families of hyperactive children. The treatment plan ranges from the support of parents who are presently working well with their child, but need reassurance, to families where the hyperactive behavior is a critical dimension around which family life is organized. Thus, the most basic approaches are educational and supportive in nature, the moderate-intensity approaches are based on linear concepts of behavior management, while the most intense approaches are based on the notions of circularity and family homeostasis. Although the techniques progress from the most basic to the most complex, they are suggested as guides to the therapist, who may use whatever elements appear to be appropriate.

The first treatment domain to be considered is medical. The use of medication is the most frequently employed treatment approach and, unfortunately, often the sole treatment (Robin & Bosco, 1980). However, in this interdisciplinary approach, medication alone is insufficient. Based on the physician's evaluation of the child, the decision to use medication is examined. The least intrusive approach is to not prescribe medication or other environmental changes. If medication does not appear appropriate but nutrition or exposure to toxins might contribute to the problem behavior, then a diet and vitamin regimen may be prescribed. The next step would be the use of psychostimulants. If the child is not responsive to these, then trials on small doses of antianxiety medication, antidepressants, or tranquilizers may be tried. If possible, the treatment plan of choice would begin with no intervention and proceed through diet and vitamin treatment to medication, depending upon the child's response. If this stepwise approach is used, many children may be stabilized without the use of medication.

While the physician is evaluating a "no medication" intervention, classroom or home behavior (depending upon the site of the problem) may become the target of intervention. The classroom teacher may first examine when and where the child has the most problems. For example, some children perform well in a structured classroom, but they have difficulty in unstructured play situations. Thus, the teacher may look at what minor environmental changes could be made without disrupting the classroom context. This might include keeping the child in small-group and individual instruction, moving the child into a study carrel to reduce distractions, or changing the child's daily schedule to reduce the number of transitions from one activity or setting to another.

The teaching team should carefully examine the diagnostic testing to determine how the child processes information best, to identify the child's instructional level, and to identify and teach to both strengths and weaknesses. In particular, the child's attentional capabilities may be examined. A distinction should be made between overfocused and underfocused attention and between deficits in selective attention and sustained attention. Specific academic interventions might include using programs like the Specific Skill Series (Boning, 1976) to develop appropriate study skills. Other self-paced instructional programs available to the teacher may be implemented. If more intensive intervention is needed academically and behaviorally, the teacher may begin with reminding the child about the target behaviors from the diagnostic summary. Some children will need more structure than this, such that point systems can be useful. The teacher may use points for time periods of on-task behavior, or may simply mark a star on an index card attached to the child's desk when the child is on task. The teacher may also set up a system where the child monitors his own on-task behavior, which is then checked by the teacher. All of these may be sent home for the family to check, and this often leads to more cooperative home-school relations.

Other educational interventions require more time and often special preparation by the teacher. One example is to set up a contract with the child related to the target behavior. These contracts are generally more effective when the family also supports the contract. Skills training can also be implemented, but it is usually more cost effective when the teacher can serve a small group of children rather than just one. The skills can range from verbal mediation and problem solving to reduce impulsiveness and aggressiveness, to social skills training, which covers a wide range of behaviors. Training in verbal mediation is fully elaborated in Camp (1980), Douglas (1980), and Spivack and Shure (1974), while the best social skills curriculum for teachers is by Stephens (1978).

Many of these programs are in use in resource classrooms for children with learning and behavior problems. Thus, children may receive these interventions if they are in a resource or self-contained special education classroom. However, it would be most effective if these programs could first be used experimentally in the regular classroom, which might help them interact more appropriately with their peers and thereby reduce their social isolation. Special education placement, either on a resource or self-contained basis, may also have certain academic advantages (e.g., smaller class size, individual educational plan). However, research suggests that the social and academic problems of some hyperactive children persist into adulthood despite special education services (Hechtman, Weiss, & Perlman, 1980). Thus, removal from the regular classroom should be the treatment of last resort. For a more exhaustive list of interventions that can be used in a variety of school settings, see Alabiso and Hansen (1977), Barkley (1981), Jones and Kazdin (1981), and Kozloff (1979).

Just as the educational interventions range from simple to complex, so too do the family interventions. Some families have hyperactive children whose behavior is entirely unrelated to family dynamics. It would be a mistake not to be able to identify this immediately. Typically, these parents noticed the hyperactivity of their child at an early age, often related to an organic impairment. They have shown resolve as a parental dyad in finding or developing services for their child. In these cases, the parent's support for each other and the lack of symptomatology in other siblings are characteristic. These families fit the description of families who are able to organize the social network to support their efforts to help their child (Robin & Bosco, 1981). When it is clear that they are effectively managing their child's behavior overall, then the therapist's job is to point this out, provide encouragement, and find them a network of similar parents who can help them persevere. Generally, these parents respond well to education about the nature of hyperactivity, as it helps them make sense of their child's behavior without being too self-critical. It is tempting to place such parents in a parenting group or in multiple-family therapy because they tend to respond to suggestions from the leader. However, the dissimilarity in the ability of these families to organize the kenosystem and the correspondingly poor executive ability of parents of less experience leads to a poor match for such groups. Thus, the therapist should allay the anxieties of the parents regarding their parental functioning and refer them to existing, mainstream support groups.

Other parents who are less sophisticated than the above families, yet not so organized by the hyperactivity as to require family therapy, may respond to psychoeducational treatment approaches. These approaches are based on training in behavior management, in order to reduce coercive parent-child interactions. This training can be done individually or in groups, and two excellent guides to this approach are available (Barkley, 1981; Kozloff, 1979). Two advantages of the group format are peer support and cost efficiency.

The most intensive form of treatment of families of hyperactive children combines medical and educational interventions with family therapy. The family therapy option may be exercised when the family evaluation indicates that family interactions are supporting the hyperactive behavior. Without an alteration of these interactions, no significant reduction in hyperactivity may be maintained. Family therapy is also indicated when families do not respond favorably to the less intensive interventions described above.

The task of the family therapist is to determine why the family is seeking treatment now. This information should be supplemented with what advice the family has been given about the problem and what they have elected to do. An inclusion of how they have worked with other change agents is critical. This composite of the presenting problem may then be examined in regard to the life-cycle shift that may be blocked in the family. For example, a child whose hyperactivity did not emerge until kindergarten, the first structured social experience away from home, may be indicative of a binding quality in the home that prohibits age-appropriate differentiation and initiative. The focus of treatment, therefore, would be not simply the reduction of hyperactive behavior but also the development of interpersonal boundaries that allow the child to form social relationships outside the family. Thus, the child will be able to establish his own sense of initiative if boundaries within the family are made more clear by blocking parent-child coalitions and if the boundary with the outside world is made more permeable. Tactics to encourage such a strategy might include having the parents select a mutually agreeable after-school activity in which the child might participate. While the aid of the more peripheral parent could be enlisted to arrange for this activity, the more central parent (probably in a coalition with the child up to this point) could be put in charge of preventing interference from extended family that might sabotage the child's new interest.

As the above example indicates, intervention in the family system will require a series of therapeutic moves. While formulating the strategy, it will be useful to keep in mind the family evaluation, indicating whether the family is consensus sensitive, distance sensitive, or achievement sensitive (Reiss, 1981). The first type of family is characterized by enmeshment and fear of open disagreement, the second type is characterized by disengagement and alienation, and the third type is characterized by competition. The quality of the hyperactivity will often serve as a metaphor for the interactional patterns in the family. One child, for instance, may exhibit concentration difficulties due to "daydreaming" as a way of trying to insulate himself in an enmeshed emotional field. His failure to follow instructions may be primarily due to an inability to execute a sequence of acts, similar to the parents' inability to coordinate a joint behavior management plan. On the other hand, a child from a distance-sensitive family, whose parents do not even agree on the existence of a problem, may appear more unpredictable, distractible, and oppositional. Therefore, the form of the hyperactivity must be considered when conceptualizing a strategy for family intervention.

An appreciation of the nature of the family system will be crucial if the problem behavior is to be reframed effectively. The way in which the behavior is characterized or framed will determine whether the therapist will use compliance-based or defiance-based directives (Schwartz, 1982). In families where cooperation is still possible between the adults, compliance-based directives are generally successful. The frame used will often label the child's behavior in negative terms (i.e., disobedience) with the goal of uniting the parents to follow the directives of the therapist. If successful, the parents would have gained control of their child, restoring their position at the top of the hierarchy and reducing marital conflict related to the child.

If unsuccessful, the therapist may utilize circular, defiance-based techniques designed to capitalize on the family's resistance. In these cases, the therapist will retract earlier, negative statements about the behavior and frame it in positive terms (e.g., "he's just all boy"). This includes a full range of paradoxical techniques, elaborated elsewhere (Weeks & L'Abate, 1982), that seek system change by encouraging the family to stay the same. Therapists have, for example, suggested to the family that change will threaten the family's stability; therefore, they should continue as they have. Sometimes, it is useful to encourage the family to do even more of the same by prescribing the problem sequence. These techniques often appear very magical and therefore attractive to therapists; however, they require a thorough understanding of the family organization. Only then can the reframing and paradoxical directive fit the system. Due to this proviso, therapists are encouraged to resist this approach unless more linear, compliance-based approaches have consistently failed.

In most families, the compliance-based approaches are successful, basically because most families of hyperactive children have a disrupted internal hierarchy, while their interface with other systems is disorganized. A common sequence occurs as follows: The parent who most frequently structures the hyperactive child appears to be overwhelmed by the child's behavior, at which point the other parent (or relative, or other change agent) senses the defeat and intervenes; however, the central parent does not agree with the tactic of the peripheral adult, thereby sabotaging that intervention. This form of within-family disorganization is often reported as mother cannot control the child, father tries to help, but mother sees him as too harsh and protects the child from the punishment. The between-systems scenario is often that the teacher senses that the child lacks sufficient structure, so she calls a parent conference where the parents deny the problem and attack the teacher.

This sequence establishes a coalition between the child and central adult(s) as they defeat the peripheral adult and maintain the distance between change agents. The immediate goals of treatment will therefore be as follows: (1) establishing agreement among the adults on what constitutes problem behavior; (2) defining the behavior management techniques to be employed with each behavior; (3) clarifying who may employ these techniques; and (4) blocking coalitions between the child and any adults in the nuclear family, extended family, or other systems. One may expect that if the parental schism is reduced and the kenosystem is organized by Steps 1 through 3, then the child will attempt to depict the new hierarchy as unjust, thus triangulating a "rescuer" adult against the "persecuting" hierarchy. Often, the hyperactivity will increase as proof of the "misguided intervention." Thus, it is important to prepare the change agents for this exacerbation by predicting this "regression." A common frame is, "When things start to get worse, this represents the recognition by the child that the adults are gaining control of the situation." They will then find it easier to maintain their resolve.

If the system cannot be organized as outlined above, then a defiance-based directive appears appropriate. Each of these paradoxical prescriptions indirectly encourages the parents to prove the therapist wrong by taking charge of the child, thereby assuming their desired position in the hierarchy. Again, it is critical to realize that these techniques are very complicated and should only be used as a last resort. Nevertheless, in both linear, compliance-based approaches and circular, defiance-based approaches, data from the family assessment and subsequent interviews must be used strategically to create a frame that matches the family system. From this frame, the therapist may devise a sequence of tactics that will master the resistance of the family during each stage of the family's reorganization.

CONCLUSION

Just as hyperactivity represents a diverse set of problems, so the therapist who seeks to treat hyperactivity must possess a diverse fund of knowledge and skills. It is no longer satisfactory to treat hyperactivity from an office. Instead, active outreach and liaison are required with the systems that label and treat the hyperactive child. In such a treatment approach, a systemic epistemology allows for the appreciation of the individual, family, and environmental contributions to both the presence and the management of hyperactivity. A systemic view of hyperactivity is based on the following premises (Salzinger et al., 1975):

A. Hyperactive behavior can best be understood in relation to the context in which it occurs, especially since most hyperactive children do not display maladaptive behavior across all settings.
B. Compliance with interventions is often affected by family circumstances, as concomitant family problems are often found in families with hyperactive children.
C. The family, teacher, and doctor often disagree on the targets of change and who is responsible for making the intervention.
D. Thus, the ecosystem must be both the target of change and the agent of change.

Although some broad categories have been used here to try to demarcate general groups of families with hyperactive children, each family presents unique challenges. It is for this reason that a stepwise, progressive treatment plan is recommended. An interdisciplinary, systemic treatment model includes the following components:

A. The first contact: Framing the problem and defining the treatment goals.
B. The evaluation phase: Examining medical, academic, behavioral, and familial factors.
C. The diagnostic summary: Defining the treatment responsibility of each change agent.
D. The progressive treatment plan.
   1. Medical interventions:
      a. No medication.
      b. Diet and vitamin regimen.
      c. Psychostimulants.
      d. Tricyclics and antianxiety medications.
      e. Small doses of major tranquilizers.
   2. Educational interventions:
      a. Restructuring the classroom environment.
      b. Curriculum modifications.
      c. Behavioral tactics to increase on-task behavior and social skills.
      d. Cognitive training.
   3. Familial interventions:
      a. Support for effective parenting.
      b. Education to increase positive behavior exchanges.
      c. Parent education group to create a network of parents.
      d. Parent counseling to improve marital interaction and problem solving.
      e. Family therapy.
      f. Paradoxical family therapy.

At this time, the primary need is for the application of an ecological, multimodal treatment approach to hyperactivity, in conjunction with stringent outcome research. Given that the population of hyperactive children is heterogeneous, single-case methodology may be most appropriate. Some of the questions to be answered include the following: *(a)* Will a progressive treatment plan improve the matching between client needs and treatment approach? *(b)* Will improved client-treatment matching lead to better long-term social and vocational adjustment? *(c)* Will helping parents organize the kenosystem of the hyperactive child not only improve the child's adjustment but also reduce the frustration common in these families? These questions will not be easy to answer; but without these findings, psychotherapeutic practice with hyperactive children will itself become a kenosystem.

REFERENCES

Alabiso, F., & Hansen, J. *The hyperactive child in the classroom.* Springfield, Ill.: Charles C Thomas, 1977.

Andolfi, M., Angelo, C., Menghi, P., & Nicolo-Corigliano, A. *Behind the family mask: Therapeutic change in rigid family systems.* New York: Brunner/Mazel, 1983.

Axline, V. *Play therapy.* Boston: Houghton Mifflin, 1947.

Ayllon, T., Layman, D., & Kandel, H. A behavioral-educational alternative to drug control of hyperactive children. *Journal of Applied Behavior Analysis,* 1975, *8,* 137–146.

Backman, J., & Firestone, P. A review of psychopharmacological and behavioral approaches to the treatment of hyperactive children. *American Journal of Orthopsychiatry,* 1979, *49,* 500–504.

Barkley, R. *Hyperactive children: A handbook for diagnosis and treatment.* New York: Guilford Press, 1981.

Becker, W. *Parents are teachers: A child management program.* Champaign, Ill.: Research Press, 1971.

Boning, R. *Specific skill series.* Baldwin, N.Y.: Barnell-Loft, 1976.

Bowen, M. *Family therapy in clinical practice.* New York: Jason Aronson, 1978.

Camp, B. Two psychoeducational treatment programs for young aggressive boys. In C. Whalen & B. Henker (Eds.), *Hyperactive children: The social ecology of identification and treatment.* New York: Academic Press, 1980.

Cantwell, D. Psychiatric illness in families of hyperactive children. *Archives of General Psychiatry,* 1972, *27,* 414–417.

Carter, E., & McGoldrick, M. *The family lifecycle: A framework for family therapy.* New York: Gardner Press, 1980.

Conrad, P. Situational hyperactivity: A social system approach. *Journal of School Health,* 1977, *47*(5), 280–285.

Conrad, W., & Insel, J. Anticipating the response to amphetamine therapy in the treatment of hyperkinetic children. *Pediatrics,* 1967, *40,* 96–98.

Cruickshank, W., Bentzen, F., Ratzeburg, F., & Tannhauser, M. *A teaching method for brain injured and hyperactive children.* Syracuse, N.Y.: Syracuse University Press, 1961.

Douglas, V. Treatment and training approaches to hyperactivity: Establishing internal or external control. In C. Whalen & B. Henker (Eds.), *Hyperactive children: The social ecology of identification and treatment.* New York: Academic Press, 1980.

Emery, R., Weintraub, S., & Neale, J. Effects of marital discord on the school behavior of children of schizophrenic, affectively disordered, and normal parents. *Journal of Abnormal Child Psychology,* 1982, *10*(2), 215–228.

Feingold, B. F. *Why your child is hyperactive.* New York: Random House, 1975.

Ferreira, A., & Winter, W. Decision-making in normal and abnormal two-child families. *Family Process,* 1968, *7,* 17–36.

Firestone, G. Factors associated with children's adherence to stimulant medication. *American Journal of Orthopsychiatry,* 1982, *52*(3), 447–457.

Firestone, P., & Witt, J. Characteristics of families completing and prematurely discontinuing a behavioral parent-training program. *Journal of Pediatric Psychology,* 1982, *7*(2), 209–222.

Fisch, R., Weakland, J., & Segal, L. *The tactics of change.* San Francisco: Jossey-Bass, 1982.

Gottman, J. *Marital interaction: Experimental investigations.* New York: Academic Press, 1979.

Goyette, C., Connors, C., & Ulrich, R. Normative data on revised Connors parent and teacher rating scales. *Journal of Abnormal Child Psychology,* 1978, *6,* 221–236.

Haley, J. *Problem solving therapy.* San Francisco: Jossey-Bass, 1976.

Hastings, J., & Barkley, R. A review of psychophysiological research with hyperkinetic children. *Journal of Abnormal Child Psychology,* 1978, *6*(4), 413–447.

Hechtman, L., Weiss, G., & Perlman, T. Hyperactives as young adults: Self-esteem and social skills. *Canadian Journal of Psychiatry,* 1980, *25*(6), 478–483.

Hewett, F. *The emotionally disturbed child in the classroom: A developmental strategy for educating children with maladaptive behavior.* Boston: Allyn & Bacon, 1968.

Hobbs, N. An ecologically oriented, service-based system for the classification of handicapped children. In S. Salzinger, J. Antrobus, & J. Glick (Eds.), *The ecosystem of the "sick" child.* New York: Academic Press, 1980.

Holmes, T., & Rahe, R. The social readjustment scale. *Journal of Psychosomatic Research,* 1967, *11,* 213–218.

Homatidis, S., & Konstantareas, M. Assessment of hyperactivity: Isolating measures of high discriminant ability. *Journal of Consulting and Clinical Psychology,* 1981, *49*(4), 533–541.

Idol-Maestas, L. Behavior patterns in families of boys with learning and behavior problems. *Journal of Learning Disabilities,* 1981, *14*(6), 347–349.

Jones, R., & Kazdin, A. Childhood behavior problems in the school. In S. Turner, K. Calhoun, & H. Adams (Eds.), *Handbook of clinical behavior therapy.* New York: John Wiley & Sons, 1981.

Kaufman, A. *Intelligent testing with the WISC–R.* New York: Wiley-Interscience, 1979.

Kaufman, A., & Kaufman, N. *Clinical evaluation of young children with the McCarthy scales.* New York: Grune & Stratton, 1977.

Kinsbourne, M., & Caplan, P. *Children's learning and attention problems.* Boston: Little, Brown, 1979.

Kozloff, M. *A program for families of children with learning and behavior problems.* New York: Wiley-Interscience, 1979.

Lambert, N. Temperament profiles of hyperactive children. *American Journal of Orthopsychiatry,* 1982, *52*(3), 458–467.

Loney, J. Hyperactivity comes of age: What do we know and where should we go? *American Journal of Orthopsychiatry,* 1980, *50*(1), 28–42.

Loney, J., Comly, H., & Simon, B. Parental management, self-concept, and drug response in minimal brain dysfunction. *Journal of Learning Disabilities,* 1975, *8,* 187–190.

Madanes, C. *Strategic family therapy.* San Francisco: Jossey-Bass, 1981.

McCubbin, H., & Patterson, J. *Systematic assessment of family stress, resources and coping: Tools for research, education, and clinical intervention.* Minneapolis: University of Minnesota Press, 1981.

McMahon, R. Biological factors in childhood hyperkinesis: A review of genetic and biochemical hypotheses. *Journal of Clinical Psychology,* 1981, *37*(1), 12–21.

Mendelson, W., Johnson, N., & Stewart, M. Hyperactive children as teenagers: A follow-up study. *Journal of Nervous and Mental Disease,* 1971, *153,* 273–279.

Michelson, L., & Wood, R. Behavioral assessment and training of children's social skills. In M. Hersen, R. Eisler, & P. Miller (Eds.), *Progress in behavior modification* (Vol. 9). New York: Academic Press, 1980.

Minde, K., Weiss, G., & Mendelson, N. A 5-year follow-up study of 91 hyperactive school children. *Journal of the American Academy of Child Psychiatry,* 1972, *11,* 595–610.

Minuchin, S., Montalvo, B., Guerney, B., Rosman, B., & Shumer, F. *Families of the slums.* New York: Basic Books, 1967.

Morrison, J., & Stewart, M. A family study of the hyperactive child syndrome. *Biological Psychiatry,* 1971, *3,* 189–195.

Myerstein, I. The family behavioral snapshot: A tool for teaching family assessment. *American Journal of Family Therapy,* 1979, *7*(1), 48–56.

Paternite, C., & Loney, J. Childhood hyperkinesis: Relationships between symptomatology and home environment. In C. Whalen & B. Henker (Eds.), *Hyperactive children: The social ecology of identification and treatment.* New York: Academic Press, 1980.

Paternite, C., Loney, J., & Langhorne, J. Relationships between symptomatology and SES-related factors in hyperkinetic/MBD boys. *American Journal of Orthopsychiatry,* 1976, *46,* 291–301.

Porges, S., & Smith, K. Defining hyperactivity: Psychophysiological and behavioral strategies. In C. Whalen & B. Henker (Eds.), *Hyperactive children: The social ecology of identification and treatment.* New York: Academic Press, 1980.

Quay, H., & Peterson, D. *Manual for the Behavior Problem Checklist.* Champaign-Urbana, Ill.: University of Illinois Press, 1967.

Public Law 94–142. *Education For All Handicapped Children Act.* 94th Congress, 1975.

Reiss, D. *The family's construction of reality.* Cambridge, Mass.: Harvard University Press, 1981.

Robin, S., & Bosco, J. Hyperkinesis as a pathology and as a social metaphor: Life within a kenosystem. In S. Salzinger, J. Antrobus, & J. Glick (Eds.), *The ecosystem of the "sick" child.* New York: Academic Press, 1980.

Robin, S., & Bosco, J. *Parent, teacher, and physician in the life of the hyperactive child: The incoherence of the social environment.* Springfield, Ill.: Charles C Thomas, 1981.

Routh, D., Schroeder, C., & O'Tauma, L. Development of activity level in children. *Developmental Psychology,* 1974, *10,* 163–168.

Salzinger, S., Antrobus, J., & Glick, J. The ecosystem of the "sick" kid. In S. Salzinger, J. Antrobus, & J. Glick (Eds.), *The ecosystem of the "sick" child.* New York: Academic Press, 1980.

Sandoval, J., Lambert, N., & Sassone, D. The identification and labeling of hyperactivity in children: An interactive model. In C. Whalen & B. Henker (Eds.), *Hyperactive children: The social ecology of identification and treatment.* New York: Academic Press, 1980.

Satterfield, J., Cantwell, D., & Satterfield, B. Multimodality treatment: A one-year follow-up of 84 hyperactive boys. *Archives of General Psychiatry,* 1979, *36*(9), 965–974.

Schachar, R., Rutter, M., & Smith, A. The characteristics of situationally and pervasively hyperactive children: Implications for syndrome definition. *Journal of Child Psychology and Psychiatry and Applied Disciplines,* 1981, *22,* 375–392.

Schwartz, R. Parental reversals: A framework for conceptualizing and implementing a class of paradoxical prescriptions. *Journal of Marital and Family Therapy*, 1982, *8*(1), 41–50.

Singer, M., & Wynne, L. Principles for scoring defects and deviances in parents of schizophrenics: Rorschach and TAT scoring manuals. *Psychiatry*, 1966, *29*, 260–288.

Spivack, G., Platt, J., & Shure, M. *The problem-solving approach to adjustment: A guide to research and intervention.* San Francisco: Jossey-Bass, 1976.

Spivack, G., & Shure, M. *Social adjustment of young children: A cognitive approach to solving real-life problems.* San Francisco: Jossey-Bass, 1974.

Stephens, T. *Social skills in the classroom.* Columbus, Ohio: Cedars Press, 1978.

Strodtbeck, F. The family as a three person group. *American Sociological Review*, 1954, *11*, 23–29.

Thomas, A., & Chess, S. *Temperament and development.* New York: Brunner/Mazel, 1977.

Wahler, R. Parent insularity as a determinant of generalization success in family treatment. In S. Salzinger, J. Antrobus, & J. Glick (Eds.), *The ecosystem of the "sick" child.* New York: Academic Press, 1980.

Walker, H. *The Walker Problem Behavior Identification Checklist Manual.* Los Angeles: Manson Western, 1976.

Wechsler, D. *Manual for the Wechsler Intelligence Scale for Children-Revised.* New York: Psychological Corporation, 1974.

Weeks, G., & L'Abate, L. *Paradoxical psychotherapy: Theory and practice with individuals, couples, and families.* New York: Brunner/Mazel, 1982.

Wender, P. *Minimal brain dysfunction in children.* New York: Wiley-Interscience, 1971.

Whalen, C., & Henker, B. *Hyperactive children: The social ecology of identification and treatment.* New York: Academic Press, 1980.

Wolfe, D., St. Lawrence, J., Graves, K., Brehony, K., Bradlyn, D., & Kelly, J. Intensive behavioral parent training for a child abusive mother. *Behavior Therapy*, 1982, *13*, 438–451.

Wunsch-Hitzig, R., Gould, M., & Dohrenwend, B. Hypotheses about the prevalence of clinical maladjustment in children in the United States. In S. Salzinger, J. Antrobus, & J. Glick (Eds.), *The ecosystem of the "sick" child.* New York: Academic Press, 1980.

Chapter 39

Marital and Family Problem Prevention and Enrichment Programs

BERNARD G. GUERNEY, JR.
LOUISE GUERNEY
TERESA COONEY

Definitions of the various types of prevention most widely accepted among mental health professionals were provided by Caplan (1964), who adapted them from general medicine to psychiatry. Caplan distinguished among three types of prevention. *Primary prevention* "involves lowering the rate of new cases of mental disorder . . . by counteracting harmful circumstances before they have had a chance to produce illness" (p. 26). *Secondary prevention* programs reduce the number of cases among those "at risk" (that is, those who might come to suffer from an illness). Such reduction is accomplished either through primary prevention or by shortening the duration of the illness in existing cases by early diagnosis and effective treatment. However, Caplan explains that by custom the term *secondary prevention* is used only in the latter way: i.e., for efficient and effective diagnosis and treatment on a large scale (p. 28). *Tertiary prevention* programs aim to reduce defective functioning due to a disorder. It encompasses both primary and secondary prevention. But in practice, Caplan explains, the term is restricted to programs which reduce the *residual* defect remaining after the disorder has ended. What is rehabilitation on an individual level is tertiary prevention on the community level (p. 113).

What this means is that when one is concerned with prevention, one is concerned with dealing with problems on a communitywide basis rather than an individual basis. It does *not* mean one works only with people who have no problems—that concept is but one of the three types of prevention, as Caplan explains. Early and efficient treatment programs and programs dealing with the aftermath of problems also may be prevention programs.

A major implication of all these developments for the mental health professional concerned with prevention is that programs—whether they be before, during, or after a problem arises—should be designed in such a way as to make them applicable to large numbers of people. The impact must be broad enough to make a substantial difference when one looks not at individuals but at the rate of the problems on a communitywide basis.

Enrichment programs might be defined as programs designed to strengthen families not at risk. However, in today's world, when drugs are easily available in all social strata and divorces after 20 years of marriage are not uncommon, who would be so bold as to say, "Here is a family that is *not* at risk"? Therefore, *enrichment* programs probably should not be sharply distinguished from prevention programs but rather viewed as belonging at the lower end of the at-risk continuum, not off the continuum entirely. Types of interventions need not be sharply segregated with respect to whether they are prevention versus enrichment versus therapy. Rather, any particular program may define as its target population families anywhere or everywhere on a continuum of risk or on a continuum of strength or satisfaction. Also, all intervention programs (whether they be prevention, enrichment, or therapy programs) may be viewed as having a common purpose: improving the family as a system and improving the psychosocial well-being of each member of that family system.

If virtually all families, then, are worthy candidates for being strengthened and if prevention/enrichment/therapy programs share the common purpose of providing such strengthening, what is left as the special feature of a program that would warrant calling it a prevention/enrichment program as distinct from a nonprevention/enrichment program? In our view, the special feature is that it would have high potential for broad impact. Such a program would have characteristics enabling it to impact relatively large numbers of families within its targeted population group. It would have characteristics that permit it to have the kind of scope, scale, and community impact Caplan (1964) indicates as the essence of prevention. What are these characteristics? In our view, the special characteristics of a prevention/enrichment program which allow it to have potential for such scope, scale, and community impact are as follows:

1. It is programmatic and systematic. The goals, content, procedures are clear and specific.

2. The procedures and processes employed in the program are truly replicable and teachable, so that a large number of professionals

and/or paraprofessionals and/or volunteers may be taught to conduct it. Programs which depend heavily on charisma or brilliant flashes of insight on the part of the leader do not qualify.

3. The standard procedures are flexible enough to accommodate a wide variety of personality traits among potential leaders and a wide variety of personality traits and educational and intellectual levels within the group intended to benefit from it. Hence, the program's *essential* nature or procedures do not change depending on which individual is leading the group or the particular individuals taking part in it.

4. The objectives of the program, when achieved, are ones important enough to make a substantial difference in the participants' ability to more effectively meet their needs and those of society.

5. It is relatively fast and efficient in dealing with individual family units, and/or it is applicable for groups of families. Often, this would mean the program can take advantage of teaching aids such as books, manuals, and audio- or videotapes or films (and in the future, we would guess, such things as biofeedback machinery and computers).

6. It is potentially attractive, marketable to the population for which is it intended. For mental health programs, this implies that those taking advantage of it will be relatively free of feeling socially stigmatized.

7. It may have the special advantage of ripple or chain-reaction effects, wherein those whom the program has reached will actively spread the effects or advantages to others and/or encourage others to participate in it.

Looking for these characteristics helped us to decide what intervention programs to cover here. But with space limited to a single chapter, the application of further criteria was necessary. These will be discussed later.

ISSUES AND CHOICES IN PROGRAM DESIGN

Four of the major issues or choices which confront those who design family-oriented prevention/enrichment programs will be considered. These are the questions of (1) timing/marketing—the phase of the family development cycle to target; (2) the choice or mix of methods to use in working with the targeted group; (3) the choice of topics to be discussed in the program—who chooses them and what they are; and (4) leadership—who will run the program?

Timing/marketing

Common sense suggests that if you want to prevent marital and family problems, the time to start is as early as possible in the family development cycle. As an example, let's consider premarital versus marital programs. Common sense suggests that engaged couples are a more efficient population to target than married couples. However, there is another possible viewpoint. It may be, for example, that engaged couples are not ready—not sufficiently motivated—to undertake the task of learning what they need to know to prevent marital difficulties. Most premarital couples are riding very high on romantic waves. It may be that a few waves have to break against the rocks before the couples are ready to think any program could make their relationships any richer than they already are or before they will take seriously the idea that they will ever encounter any major problems. Using another metaphor: Maybe, like the proverbial mule, couples will not come to a program or will not be ready to learn until they have been emotionally "hit on the head" really hard once or twice by their spouse.

On the other hand, a program designed for already-married couples will be too late to reach the large percentage of couples who divorce during their first three years. And couples coming after several years of marriage may already be slightly punch-drunk, making it more difficult for them to learn from the program.

Perhaps, therefore, the most auspicious time for presenting marital problems or enriching relationships, the time that has the best cost-effectiveness ratio, would be during the first year of marriage. We are not saying this is so—although there is some evidence for it (Bader, Riddle, & Sinclair, 1980)—but merely illustrating the nature of the problem. Unfortunately, research has scarcely begun concerning recruitment or cost effectiveness of programs at different stages of individual and family development.

It seems safe to say, though, that programs should be designed to fit the motivations of the group for which they are intended. For example, while it is possible to teach nonengaged, even nondating, adolescents concepts and skills which would be highly useful to them when they do get married, such a program would best be presented, in our judgment, not as a *marital* relationship–building course but simply as a *relationship*-building course. The examples, topics, and situations discussed would best be centered not around the marital situation but around the types of relationship concerns which are of immediate interest to that group. Similarly, in our view, if one wanted to teach parenting skills to high school students, it would be best to approach the issue from another direction: how they as teenagers might skillfully communicate with their own parents. The lessons about their own future parenting would derive, secondarily, from that primary focus. We think that programs designed primarily around roles which will be fulfilled only in the far distant future are not likely to have a good cost-benefit ratio. And they will be difficult to market—that is, it will be difficult to attract participants to them.

Very likely, in most instances, family programs should be designed to attract and to meet the needs of those who are already attempting to make a marriage or family work better and are *concerned* about their ability to be as successful as they would like to be in that effort. At present, it seems that the people most likely to attend a prevention/ enrichment program are those already experiencing some frustration or disappointment (Powell & Wampler, 1982).

This may change, and probably already is changing, as more people attend problem-prevention/enrichment programs and as such programs get more publicity. An observation about a different area of instruction may be pertinent in that regard: At first, that portion of the public which knew the most about nutrition and about skills related to proper food intake were persons who had a weight problem. Now, many people who are interested in *positive* health and prevention are just as knowledgeable and skillful about controlling their eating habits.

The segments of the population now most advanced in seeking positive marital/family education, without first experiencing some degree of problem, are those that have been educated about such programs by organizations. Many religious organizations, some colleges, and some private organizations now actively promote programs designed to enhance marital/family satisfaction. Particularly noteworthy in this regard is ACME, the Association of Couples for Marriage Enrichment (Mace, 1975; Mace & Mace, 1976). Perhaps the work of these organizations will allow prevention/enrichment programs to reach people before they experience even a modest degree of failure.

Methods

Reading/lecture/discussion.   This is the first of the three methods used, singly or in combination, in problem-prevention/enrichment programs. In this approach, transmission of information is considered primary. Central goals here are: to give information the absence of which might cause problems; to describe the kinds of difficulties and problems which are encountered; and to tell about methods and procedures that might be used to avoid or overcome such problems. The kinds of shared activities and experiences that tend to enrich a marriage or family might also be described. Discussion is used to ensure that the participants are actively involved in considering the concepts and that they see how the information provided is pertinent to their own lives.

Experiential teaching.   Here, experience is primary. The couples are given exercises designed to make the points emotionally meaningful to them. For example, to better understand and promote trust, one member of the pair may be asked to fall backwards, trusting the other to catch him/her. Or, one may be blindfolded and then walked around obstacles by a partner. Or, to experience the importance of differences in perspective and of difficulties in communication, one member of a pair may be asked to assemble a small jigsaw puzzle depending solely on verbal instructions from the other, who alone can see what the finished product looks like.

Skill training. The idea here is to teach specific skills deemed important to prevent and solve problems or to enrich the marriage or family. An example of a skill would be how to negotiate or resolve a conflict in such a way as to best meet the needs of all concerned. The instructor explains the skill, demonstrates its execution, and supervises the couples in their practice of the skill in much the same way as an instructor teaches a language, piano playing, or skiing.

Topic selection

Who chooses? Topics that are discussed may be chosen by the program originators, by the participants themselves, or by a combination of both. Examples of the combination methods would be for the instructor to list topics and have the participants choose one that interests them, or to have participants choose topics according to guidelines set forth by the instructor, perhaps also requiring the instructor's approval before a topic is discussed. A questionnaire might be used to help participants make selections for topics to discuss. Examples of these are PREPARE (Olson, Fournier, & Druckman, 1979) and the View Sharing Inventory (Cavanaugh, 1982).

What topics? Naturally, the specific topics will vary with the type of group. But it is possible to construct a list of topics which is phrased broadly enough to cover most of the specific topics discussed in prevention/enrichment groups regardless of whether they are premarital, marital, or family groups. The following, in no special order, is a fairly comprehensive list of the types of things generally discussed in marital/family groups: *(a)* love/trust/fidelity/loyality; *(b)* responsibility/discipline/privileges; *(c)* time usage and priorities; *(d)* intimacy/togetherness; *(e)* financial issues and priorities; *(f)* honesty/integrity/openness; *(g)* power/decision making/control/dependence versus independence; *(h)* fairness/jealousy/rivalry; *(i)* competitiveness versus cooperation; *(j)* values/religion/aesthetics/lifestyles; *(k)* sexual attitudes and behaviors; *(l)* personal habits: grooming/neatness/cleanliness/manners; *(m)* questionable habits: work or school performance/

gambling/alcohol, etc.; *(n)* living conditions: area/dwelling type/ neighborhood, *(o)* relationships with relatives; *(p)* parenthood: e.g., number and spacing of children/discipline/privileges.

Providers of service

Prevention/enrichment programs may be conducted by professionals such as psychiatrists, clinical psychologists, social workers, or counselors, or they may be led by volunteers or paraprofessionals. A few programs have special requirements (e.g., leaders of marital enrichment groups being themselves married couples). Some of the programs provide training for people wishing to learn to lead groups and will certify the leaders.[1]

PROGRAM SELECTION CRITERIA

The programs covered here have three broad target populations: family, marital, and premarital groups. (The family-marital-premarital order of presentation was used rather than a chronological order because some of the programs covered more than one population and these were best and most parsimoniously explained in the order used.)

Describing all such marital/family, prevention/enrichment programs, in a manner full enough to give the reader a flavor of what they are like, and summarizing the research done on them would require a monograph if not a book. Rather than sacrifice meaningful descriptions of programs or the research on them, it was decided not to attempt covering all such programs here. In choosing which programs to cover, we used the following criteria:

1. The extent to which a program fit the characteristics of a preventative or enrichment program outlined in the introduction.
2. The extent to which the program had actually been used and researched using populations on the low-distress (i.e., for prevention) and low-risk (i.e., for enrichment) halves of the distress and risk continua instead of, or in addition to, the high ends of these continua.
3. The inclusion of the key target person(s) in the training program. (This excluded most parent skill training programs, since most do not include the child.)

---

[1] We are aware of nationwide leader training/certification for two of the programs detailed in this chapter. Interpersonal Communications Programs Inc., 1925 Nicollet Avenue, Minneapolis, MN 55403, trains leaders for the Minnesota couples communication program. The Institute for the Development of Emotional And Life Skills (IDEALS) Inc., P.O. Box 391, State College, PA 16801, trains leaders for the relationship enhancement programs.

4. A description of the program in a *published* book, manual, or professional journal, which was complete and detailed enough to provide a good picture of all the procedures and methods employed in the program,
5. The quality of the research assessing the effectiveness of the program. Generally, this meant:
    a. Minimally, the use of a control group, or better, use of an alternate treatment group.
    b. Random assignment (or at least quasi-random assignment) of subjects to these groups.
    c. The appropriate use of tests of statistical significance.
    d. The quality of the published report of the research design and procedure in the research, so that one could get a clear picture of such things as the quality of the measures and the number of significant results compared to the number of significance tests conducted.
    e. The results of such high-quality research and reporting showed in a fairly clear-cut manner that the program was an effective one.
6. The degree to which the program has been disseminated.
7. Number of unique qualities or features.

Our purpose was to exemplify the types of programs existing in each of the three areas. Therefore, a program was not chosen for description in detail if it was similar in nature to one already selected for its superior match with the criteria.

We do not claim perfection in applying these standards, especially since it often was difficult to know how to weigh and balance the various criteria against one another. Also, we would like to point out that some of the programs not detailed here could well be better programs or may better fit a particular need than those which are included. But some of these nondetailed programs may be simply too new or too specialized to have established a record of research and dissemination at this time.

For these reasons, we have included a reference section which contains a reasonably comprehensive list of family problem-prevention/enrichment programs not described in the text. We urge readers who are interested in application or research in family prevention/enrichment to consult all references relevant to their interest rather than relying only on the programs described in detail in this chapter. We particularly want to call attention to certain of these references. Our inability to explicate the programs/research of the following programs was especially painful:

In the *family* area: the Functional Therapy of Alexander and Barton

(1976); the Family Game approach of Blechman and Olson (1976); the Communication–Problem Solving program of Robin (1979, 1980, 1981); Robin, Kent, O'Leary, Foster, and Prinz (1977); the Family Cluster approach of Sawin (1979, 1980); and Kahn and Kamerman's (1982) review of family services.

In the *marital* area: the mass media (television) approach used by Burka (1978); the marriage enrichment approach of Hof and Miller (1981); the Behavioral Communication Training approach of Jacobson (1977, 1982); the Marital Exercise and Contracting approaches of Knox (1974) and Knox and Knox (1974); the ACME methods described by Mace and Mace (1976); the Choice-Awareness program of Nelson and Friest (1980); the Conflict Resolution and Interpersonal Skill Training methods of Patterson and Hops (1972), Patterson Hops, and Weiss (1975), and Weiss, Hops and Patterson (1973); the Operant Interpersonal program of Stuart (1969, 1976); and the Pairing Enrichment Program of Travis and Travis (1975, 1976a, 1976b, 1979).

In the *premarital* area: the Learning to Live Together program described by Bader et al. (1980) and the Mutual Problem Solving program described by Ridley, Avery, Harrell, Haynes-Clements, and McCunney (1981) and Ridley, Avery, Harrell, Leslie, and Dent (1981).

FAMILY PROGRAMS

Family structured enrichment (SE)

L'Abate and collaborators have developed many programs for family problem-prevention/enrichment (L'Abate, 1977, 1982; L'Abate & Rupp, 1981). Collectively, these didactic programs are now called structured enrichment programs. The goals of SE programs are to build personal skills into daily living. Sometimes, the goals may also include the elimination of dysfunctional living patterns. However, L'Abate and Weeks (1976) point out that when families exhibit long-standing patterns of dysfunction and deeply rooted problems, SE may not work. Uncooperative behavior and resistance to change, they say, are not easily handled in the programs; and when clients exhibit denial and externalization of their problems, SE may be inappropriate.

Several historical antecedents are responsible for the birth of SE, according to L'Abate (1974; L'Abate & Associates, 1975b): (1) programmed interpersonal relations—which promoted use of materials developed for programmed instruction, such as tapes, packaged programs, and other techniques using systematic, stepwise presentation of material; (2) the human potentials movement—techniques developed in such perspectives as the psychodynamic, humanistic, or existential movements, such as role playing, psychodrama, Gestalt therapy, sensitivity training, and group and family therapy; (3) games and play behavior—the use of play behavior to express oneself; and (4) family life education—which emphasized informing families of problem-solving and other issues.

L'Abate views SE programs as the application of programmed instruction to couples and families. Hence, SE can be used in applying a wide range of theories. L'Abate says, "We have borrowed, appropriated, and used any major theory, notion or model that can be applied to families" (1982, p. 4). The process, L'Abate points out, remains the same for all programs. A description of that process follows.

Each program proceeds through a structured series of events. The participants (whether they are a premarital couple, a marital couple, or a family) are interviewed, and the leader gives them a program overview and establishes the contract. The next step involves the administration of pretest measures, and the clients are offered suggestions as to the appropriate programs to use. The participants then undergo the enrichment sessions with the leader. That is followed by administration of posttest measures and an evaluation of the participants' progress. At this point, the leader determines whether to recommend additional assistance. A follow-up evaluation is routinely conducted six months later.

The SE programs are presented in 3 to 10 (usually 6) structured sessions. The basic unit of these sessions is the exercise. Exercise instructions from the manual for a program are read aloud by the leader, who then assists the participants in carrying out the exercise. The exercise instructions proceed from the simple to the complex. Five or six exercises, each of which is structured around a specific family issue, comprise each session (L'Abate & Rupp, 1981; L'Abate, 1982).

The three manuals L'Abate and his associates have developed differ in their presentation structure. The first manual (L'Abate et al., 1975b) is designed to cover a range of structural viewpoints. Depending on the family's education level, a program may be simple or complex; depending on the communication style of the family, the selected program can be cognitively or affectively oriented; and depending on the issues relevant to the particular family, the specificity of the program may vary, addressing either general enrichment needs, such as feeling awareness and problem solving, or more specific problems, such as alcoholism or adoption. The family's strengths and skills are of primary importance in the program selection. Examples of particular theories which have served as a basis for exercises are Adler's "practical matters," Satir's "dysfunctions," and Spiegel's "transactional approaches" (L'Abate & Rupp, 1981).

The second manual (L'Abate & Associates, 1975a) is structured on a developmental framework. It focuses on particular stages in the family life cycle and contains 27 different programs "ranging from court-ship and premarital problem solving to sexuality and sensuality, man-woman relationships, becoming parents, the family as a whole, family breakdowns, widow- or widowerhood, and death" (L'Abate, 1982, p. 7).

The most recent manual (L'Abate & Sloane, 1981) consists of 16 programs which are divided into three sections: family development, family needs, and special families. Family development programs are for different stages in the family life cycle, such as for newlyweds, new parents, and the recently widowed. Family needs programs train participants in different areas of functioning, such as problem solving, health needs, and coping with depression. The special-families programs are for families who have a variety of difficult situations to deal with, such as divorce and dual careers. Examples of programs for the family as a whole are problem solving, communication, three-generation families, the meaning of adolescence, between parents and teenagers, and separating parents from their teenagers.

L'Abate reports on a study involving 217 participants from 55 families (L'Abate, 1977). There were four groups: (1) clinical families who received SE; (2) clinical families who served as no-treatment controls; (3) nonclinical families who received SE; and (4) nonclinical families who were no-treatment controls. There were a great many dependent variables (based on four different picture tests) designed to reveal variables related to family functioning and affective states of family members. There were differences related to treatment versus notreatment on the number of cards selected on one of the measures, but the interpretations to be given to the finding could not be clear-cut. L'Abate's major point in the discussion of the results was that although most of the measures were sensitive to differences between the clinical versus the nonclinical groups, generally they were not appropriate or sensitive enough for revealing possible differences in the effectiveness of treatment versus no treatment.

Family Relationship Enhancement (FRE)

Relationship Enhancement (RE) methods were developed by Guerney and colleagues. A broader overview than space allows here can be found elsewhere (B. Guerney, 1982b, 1983, 1984). Two books provide how-to-do-it descriptions and readings and forms that may be used with clients (B. Guerney, 1977; Preston & Guerney, 1982). Videotapes demonstrating certain formats are available (Figley & Guerney, 1976; Vogelsong & Guerney, 1977). Audiotapes to use in the instruction of clients also are available (Guerney & Vogelsong, 1981). Although major emphasis in RE programs is on marital/family relationships, a program for individuals also has been developed and field tested (Preston & Guerney, 1982).

RE programs (including FRE) integrate psychodynamic, humanistic, and behavioral orientations. The theoretical base for RE includes elements of the theories of Freud, Adler, Rogers, Skinner, Bandura, Dollard and Miller, and Harry Stack Sullivan as his work was further developed by Timothy Leary. The FRE problem-prevention/enrichment program is derived from Relationship Enhancement therapy. It differs from therapy mainly in terms of recruitment procedures, length, meeting format, the topics clients are likely to bring up, and the lesser frequency with which the leader and clients are likely to use those techniques designed to overcome resistance or uncover unconscious motives and conflicts. Also, in problem-prevention/enrichment, a time-limited format is usually used, as distinct from the time-designated format usually used in RE therapy. A time-limited format might be intensive (e.g., one or two weekends) or extensive (e.g., 10 or 20, two and one-half hour meetings). FRE can be used with an individual family member, a subgroup from a family, an entire family, or with groups comprised of any of these units from different families.

The method used is skill training and practice. Lecture/discussion methods are used only to establish and maintain the attitudinal and motivational foundation on which the skill training rests. No experiential exercises are used. Nine skill sets (modes) are taught in a full-length program:

1. The Expresser mode enables participants to attain greater awareness of their own feelings, perceptions, and desires, especially as they pertain to family relationships. The guidelines for this mode are designed to maximize empathy and understanding on the part of the person(s) being addressed.

2. The Empathic mode is used to show appreciation and understanding of the other person(s), thereby encouraging the other person(s) to reach a deeper level of understanding, to clarify values, feelings, and conflicts, and to bring unconscious aspects of the self and the relationship to awareness.

3. Discussion/Negotiation (mode-switching) skill involves knowing when and how to use Empathic and Expressive modes in the service of advancing understanding and problem/conflict resolution.

4. The Teaching (facilitative) mode is used to encourage and train others to behave in growth-enhancing ways, that is, with openness, empathy, and compassion.

5. The Problem/Conflict Resolution skills are designed to assure that the work in problem/conflict resolution takes place at the deepest level, that it is done at an appropriate time and place, that the solutions

sought maximize satisfaction of the needs of all concerned, that operationally defined agreements are reached, that difficulties which arise in such contracting are anticipated and potential sources of trouble are eliminated, and that agreements for change are properly evaluated and modified at a later time if necessary.

6. Self-changing skills are designed to help an individual change his/her habit patterns in accord with agreements reached in the problem-solving/conflict-resolution process.

7. Other-changing skills are designed to be of assistance to intimates who are attempting to change old or develop new habitual patterns of behavior.

8. Transfer/Generalization skills are designed to help individuals to make the transition from in-session behavior to using the skills in their daily interactions.

9. Maintenance skills are designed to help individuals maintain their skills over long periods of time.

With the help of a simple Relationship Questionnaire, the leader guides the clients to choose topics in a gradually increasing order of difficulty. First, clients discuss a topic which they have strong feelings about but which does not involve other family members. Soon, after they have achieved some mastery of Empathic skill in this manner, they move on to discuss positive attitudes, feelings, and opinions toward other family members (positive attitudes and feelings continue to be discussed frequently throughout the program). Next, clients discuss enhancement issues—that is, suggestions they want to make to other family members for improving the level of satisfaction within the family in ways which they believe those others are not likely to find objectionable. Next, clients are helped to choose mild problems and conflicts for discussion. Then they discuss moderate problems. Finally, they discuss their most serious and fundamental problems and conflicts.

Usually beginning with the very first session, clients are given home assignments to complete. Home assignments include reading about the skills, listening to tapes which demonstrate the skills, practicing the skills in dyadic or familywide meetings (sometimes tape-recorded), choosing or revising topics on the Relationship Questionnaire for discussion in the sessions, completion of a Home Practice Form for recording reactions to the practice sessions conducted at home, and a Generalization Log which tracks skill usage (and the failure to use skills) in everyday situations.

There have been a number of studies on RE with groups that would be considered by professionals as clinically deviant and studies with groups in which some members would be classified as distressed and others not. An empirical but uncontrolled study on FRE was conducted with five families (17 participants) each of which included an adolescent who was a juvenile offender. The program was conducted by probation officers who had had one week of training in RE methods and received professional supervision. Significant improvement was found in participants' perceptions of family harmony, family satisfaction, and family members' ability to handle problems (Guerney, Vogelsong, & Glynn, 1977). In the absence of a control group, this study could not rule out the possibility that these findings resulted from generic treatment factors (e.g., attention placebo, thank you, and experimenter demand) rather than from treatment-specific factors or, indeed, other growth-inducing factors entirely unrelated to treatment.

A study by Ginsberg (1977) did control growth factors unrelated to treatment. He used random assignment to compare 14 father-son pairs in an FRE program (then called PARD) to 15 father-son pairs waiting for treatment. He used a time-limited format of 10 sessions lasting two hours each. In discussing emotionally significant topics, the FRE participants showed more improvement in *(a)* empathic acceptance and *(b)* the expression of their views and feelings in ways deemed both to reflect greater sensitivity and self-awareness and to be less psychologically threatening to others. Unobtrusively observed natural interactions between the fathers and sons as well as more standardized interactions showed that the FRE participants gained significantly on those variables, while the participants not receiving treatment showed no such gains. A hypothesis that the FRE-trained fathers and sons would show greater improvement than the controls in their patterns of general communication also was confirmed. Here, greater improvement was shown in: *(a)* transmission processes in communication *(b)* feedback processes and *(c)* satisfaction with communication. Also confirmed was an hypothesis that the general quality of the relationship between the fathers and sons would show greater improvement in FRE participants than in control-group participants. A quasi-replication study comparing the control groups' gains during the time it received no treatment with their later equivalent time in treatment generally confirmed the results reported above. The quasi replication also showed significant improvement in the self-concept of both the fathers and the sons who had been trained in RE. These studies suggest that nontreatment growth factors do not account for the improvement shown with RE treatment. However, these studies did not rule out generic treatment factors being responsible for the positive findings. The following studies were designed to do so.

Guerney, Coufal, and Vogelsong (1981) compared group FRE (again called PARD) to a traditional (discussion-based) group treatment and to a nontreatment control group. The traditional and FRE methods were carefully equated with respect to such variables as meeting times, amount of homework, and topic selection. In addition, the therapists/ leaders were the same for both groups, and they were perceived by the client as being virtually identical in their administration of both treatments in terms of their empathy, warmth, genuineness, enthusiasm, and competence. The 54 pairs of mothers and daughters were randomly assigned to the three conditions. In the two treatment conditions, the subgroups of two or three pairs met for two hours weekly, approximately 13 times. Three general hypotheses were confirmed, using a wide variety of measures. The FRE participants were superior both to traditional-treatment participants and to the notreatment participants in: *(a)* specific empathic and expressive communication skills as measured both behaviorally and with paper and pencil measures, *(b)* general patterns of communication, and *(c)* the general quality of the relationship between the mothers and daughters. This study virtually rules out the possibility that generic factors rather than treatment-specific factors could account for all of the improvement found in FRE programs.

Maintenance of gains was investigated (Guerney, Vogelsong, & Coufal, 1983) in a follow-up to the above-mentioned study. Six months after termination, participants in FRE showed significantly greater improvement relative to both the traditionally treated group and the control group in *(a)* specific communication skills, *(b)* general communication patterns, and *(c)* the quality of their relationships. In addition to demonstrating more long-term superiority of FRE to a traditional, discussion-oriented approach, this study indicates that such long-term gains of FRE programs, like the short-term ones, are not attributable solely to generic treatment factors.

Parent-Child Relationship Enhancement (PCRE)

The PCRE program was developed by Coufal and Brock (1983). They modeled PCRE after filial therapy (B. Guerney, 1964; L. Guerney, 1976). (In filial therapy, parents serve as primary change agents under the supervision of professionals after being trained in play therapy and child-socializing skills.) PCRE is designed primarily for families with 3- to 10-year-old children on the low-risk, low-distress halves of the risk and distress continua. Unlike other parenting skills programs, PCRE is interactive—that is, children are involved in the weekly sessions. The goals of PCRE are to create a more harmonious and mutually satisfying relationship between parent and child.

The parenting skills emphasized in PCRE are relationship-building ones, primarily empathic responding and nonverbal attention combined with skills that help parents to express their needs and to set limits. An instructor's manual for PCRE group leaders (Coufal & Brock, 1983) explicates the 10 lessons in detail. The manual includes a guide for "special times" or "quality times" (as the home sessions are referred to) which was written by Stollak and Kallman (1978). (Stollak has long been an advocate of parents conducting play sessions, but his manual previously was not used in the context of a short-term, systematic parent-training course.) Groups of 6 to 10 parents meet for two hours per week for 10 weeks. Both parents participate whenever feasible. PCRE is described by Coufal and Brock as having three stages.

The first stage involves presentation of the rationale and demonstration by the leader of the basic skills: reflection of the child's feelings, parent expression, limit setting, and allowing the child self-direction. The parents role-play under supervision to learn the skills. Beginning with the third session, with supervision and reinforcement by the leader, parents take turns conducting play sessions with their children, one at a time. (The other parents in the group observe the sessions and participate in the supervision.)

In the second stage, usually at Session 5 or 6, parents begin to conduct similar sessions at home—up to three per week. In each group session, two of the stage parents conduct 15–20 minute play sessions with one of their children. These play sessions are supervised. Also, home sessions are reported on and supervised.

The third stage usually begins at the eighth session. In this stage, much greater emphasis is given to how the skills may be generalized to everyday parent-child interaction and childrearing issues and to other special times devoted to the child.

A study on the effectiveness of PCRE involved 93 parents who were randomly assigned to three different groups—29 parents to PCRE, 43 to a similar skills training program without play sessions (skills only) and 22 parents to a no-treatment group (Coufal, 1982). The skills-only group was significantly higher than the control group, indicating that skills training without children was effective in improving verbally expressed acceptance. Both the skills-only and the PCRE were superior to no-training groups in relation to scores on nonacceptance measures. Parents in the PCRE group scored significantly higher than both the other groups on behavioral interaction measures of empathy and warmth. They also produced significantly more responses indicating acceptance of the child on quasi-behavioral measures than did the other two groups. The superiority of the parents in the PCRE program across all of the dependent measures indicates that its effectiveness cannot be attributed to generic factors and may be attributed to the inclusion of the play sessions.

MARITAL PROGRAMS

Marriage Encounter (ME)

Marriage Encounter, which was developed in Spain in 1958 by Father Gabriel Calvo, was first presented in this country in 1967 (Durkin, 1974). Although ME originated in the Roman Catholic Church, it has been altered to fit both Protestant and Jewish faiths. Hundreds of thousands of couples have participated in the program (Otto, 1976). ME uses lecture and experiential methods designed to develop unity between the couple through mutual expression and understanding of feelings.

A theoretical rationale for Marriage Encounter has been presented by Regula (1975). He discusses the concept of "central person" (p. 154), which Redl proposed, as being the major conceptual basis of the program. The participants are to identify with a leader couple as their central persons. According to Regula, participants experience a struggle with anxiety when resolving their inner conflicts, and this resolution is facilitated by the modeling ("infectiousness") of the central persons' self-awareness, self-disclosure, and the affirmation of one another. The growth process is also aided when the leader couple(s) discuss the positive effects ME had on them. Regula points out that ME provides for solitary reflection (as Maslow suggested was necessary for actualized people) and a time for mutual dialogue (which fulfills the aspect of interaction stressed by Erich Fromm). Whitaker's belief—that a couple reaches a point in interpersonal relating where fear prevents them from growing closer and weakens marital growth and intimacy—is accepted by Regula, but he believes self-disclosure dissolves this block. Unconditional positive regard, part of Rogerian methods, is encouraged also.

ME is a 44-hour retreat in which very large numbers of couples may be involved. The topics may vary somewhat depending on the leadership. This summary is based mainly on the reports of Demarest, Sexton, and Sexton (1978), Durkin (1974), and Genovese (1975). The program, which begins on a Friday evening and goes through Sunday afternoon, is divided into four stages: "I," "We," "We-God," and "We-God-World." Beginning on Friday night, following a brief acquainting period, the team couple and/or clergy present the first topic—the methods of communication. This instructional presentation discusses the difference between thoughts and feelings and the importance of expressing feelings. Understanding and appreciation of others' feelings is also encouraged. Dialogue is initiated by giving open-ended questions to participants. In dialogue, each person goes off separately and writes answers to those questions in a book. Each couple then reunites. The pair read each others' writings and then talk about them.

Saturday opens with the I-phase presentation, which focuses on getting in touch with one's true self. This requires that all participants write in their books their feelings about self (virtues and faults, etc.). These written expressions are the only ones which are not shared through dialogue with the spouse.

The We phase follows, with the presentation centering on marriage and love. Specific presentations that Durkin (1974) mentions include: "levels of toleration," which deals with how couples differ in acceptance of, and toleration of, various aspects of the partner (p. 36); the three stages of love (romance, disillusionment, and true joy); and marriage in the modern world. The We-God phase emphasizes how marital unity and sharing of spirituality brings couples closer to God.

Sunday focuses primarily on the We-God-World phase. Discussion here involves issues like the marital sacrament. An example of a dialogue issue in this area is: "planning expression of love for one another in the future." A religious ceremony and renewal of marriage vows ends the weekend.

Hof and Miller (1981) cite an unpublished study by J. W. Huber in which Marriage Encounter couples, who were compared with a waiting-list control group, completed a Caring Relationship Inventory at pre- and post-encounter. The ME men's scores improved significantly, but not womens'. The men's gains were maintained at a six-week follow-up.

Louise Costa (1981) compared 51 Marriage Encounter couples with 29 waiting-list control couples. Experimental couples achieved significant gains in marital communication, adjustment, and in the quality of their relationships. Maintenance of gains was demonstrated at a two-month follow-up.

Marital Structured Enrichment (SE)

We have given an overview of the general nature of SE programs earlier. Here we will provide a list of the types of SE programs that might be used with marital couples. We will illustrate one of the SE programs in some detail and then review SE research with married couples.

Programs described in *Manual: Enrichment Programs for the Family Life Cycle* (L'Abate et al., 1975a) and which are used for married couples include the following titles: Assertiveness, Equality, Reciprocity, Negotiation, Conflict Resolution, Working Through, and Expecting Couples. We will illustrate one of the programs—Expecting Couples—by quoting the last exercise and homework assignment (if any) for the first, third and last sessions. Examples can be found in L'Abate and McHenry (1983):

Lesson 1 ("Looking Inside"), Exercise 6: NOW THAT WE'VE TALKED ABOUT WHAT A PARENT IS IN THIS FAMILY, CAN YOU SEE SOME THINGS ABOUT THE TWO ROLES, MOTHER AND FATHER, THAT ARE ALIKE. WHAT THINGS ARE DIFFERENT? Pause for answers. HOW DO YOU FEEL ABOUT YOURSELF AS THE MOTHER OR FATHER YOU DESCRIBED? Let them answer and then say: HOW DO YOU FEEL ABOUT (NAME) AS A MOTHER/FATHER? Pause for answer.

Homework

BEFORE WE MEET AGAIN, I'D LIKE YOU TO LOOK AT SOME PARENTS ON TELEVISION. JUST PICK ANY SET OF PARENTS TO STUDY. NOTICE THE SITUATION, THE KIND OF PEOPLE THEY ARE, AND WHAT HAPPENS TO THEM. KEEP TWO SETS OF PARENTS IN MIND, AND WE WILL TALK ABOUT THEM NEXT TIME. THEY CAN BE ON COMMERCIALS, SOAP OPERAS, NEWS REPORTS, ANYWHERE ON TELEVISION. DO YOU UNDERSTAND? WELL, WE HAVE COME TO THE END OF OUR FIRST LESSON. WHAT DID YOU THINK OF IT? I APPRECIATE WORKING WITH YOU.

Lesson 3 ("Closeness"), Exercise 5: FOR THE LAST EXERCISE TODAY, WE WILL USE PENCIL AND PAPER. Pass them each several sheets of paper and a drawing pencil. FIRST, I WANT YOU TO DRAW YOURSELF. DO THE BEST SELF PORTRAIT YOU CAN IN ABOUT FIVE MINUTES. When time is up, say: NOW LET'S GO ON TO THE NEXT PICTURE. THIS TIME DRAW BOTH OF YOU AS A COUPLE. YOU HAVE FIVE MINUTES TO DO THIS. Pause. NOW, LET'S DO ONE MORE. THIS TIME, DRAW YOURSELVES AND YOUR BABY AS YOU THINK IT WILL BE A FEW MONTHS FROM NOW. Allow slightly more time on this one. NOW, LET'S LOOK AT YOUR PICTURES. VERY NICE. Praise their work for imagination if not artistic ability. Place the pairs of pictures side by side and compare them. WHAT IS DIFFERENT IN THE WAYS YOU SEE YOURSELVES? WHAT THINGS DID YOU DRAW THE SAME ABOUT THIS FAMILY? HOW DO YOU FEEL ABOUT THESE DRAWINGS? Pause. WHICH IS YOUR FAVORITE? Pause. WHY? Let each answer.

Closing:

THAT IS THE END OF THE THIRD LESSON. WHAT DID YOU THINK OF IT? Pause for answers. THANKS, AND I'LL SEE YOU NEXT TIME.

Lesson 6 ("The Baby in the Family"), Exercise 5: FOR THE LAST EXERCISE TODAY, YOU WILL GO TO AN IMAGINARY MOVIE. CLOSE YOUR EYES AND IMAGINE A MOVIE SCREEN. THE PICTURE FLICKERS ON. NOW IT BECOMES CLEARER, AND YOU SEE THAT IT IS A CHILD. YOU THINK ABOUT WHAT YOU ARE WATCHING AND REALIZE THAT IT IS THE CHILD YOU HAVE ALWAYS WANTED: IT IS YOUR IDEAL CHILD. LOOK AT THE CHILD AND

NOTE HOW OLD IT IS, ITS SEX, ITS BUILD, HOW IT LOOKS. NO-
TICE WHAT IT IS THAT YOU LIKE ABOUT HOW IT LOOKS. WHAT
KIND OF CHILD IS IT? WHAT IS THE CHILD LIKE? WHAT IS IT
DOING? THINK ABOUT THE PERSONALITY OF THIS CHILD.
WHAT THIS IDEAL CHILD AND THINK ABOUT WHY YOU LIKE
IT. Let them continue this silently for a few minutes, then say: IF THE
CHILD WERE REAL, WHAT WOULD YOU SAY TO HIM? THINK
ABOUT HOW YOU WOULD ACT TOWARDS THIS CHILD. NOW
OPEN YOUR EYES. WHO WOULD LIKE TO SHARE THEIR IMAGE
OF THE IDEAL CHILD? Let them freely discuss their child, making
sure that they include sex, looks, resemblance to anyone they know and
how they would react to the child. DO YOU THINK YOU LEARNED
ANYTHING IN THIS EXERCISE? HOW DID YOU LIKE IT?

Closing:
THIS IS THE END OF THE PROGRAM. WHAT DID YOU THINK
OF IT AS A WHOLE? Pause for answers. WHAT PARTS DID YOU
FIND THE MOST HELPFUL TO YOU? Pause. WHICH PARTS DO
YOU WISH COULD BE DIFFERENT? Pause. THANK YOU SO MUCH
FOR YOUR HELP.

We now turn to research on marital SE. One study (L'Abate &
Rupp, 1981) used 46 volunteer couples drawn from introductory psychology courses. The study compared four groups: a no-treatment control, and three six-session SE marital enrichment groups, one which
did not receive a letter and two of which received a letter (maximum
length, one page) after the fourth session. One of the letter groups
received a "linear" letter and the other received a "paradoxical" letter.
The linear letters were written in an easy-to-understand way and provided "direct feedback . . . much like the verbal feedback given in
insight-oriented therapies." The paradoxical letters were obscure and
designed to "raise more questions than . . . answers." They cryptically
focused on issues which occur at the underlying "genotypical" level.

There were three dependent variables: marital happiness (an inventory), marital happiness (self-rating), and satisfaction with communication (self-rating on 10 dimensions). Mean changes were larger in size
for the intervention groups than for the control group, but no significant differences were found favoring the treatment groups over the
control group or one treatment group over another.

L'Abate (1982; L'Abate & McHenry, 1983) has summarized results
of a dissertation by Ganahl (1981) which used marital couples. We
will paraphrase L'Abate's summary here. The 127 couples were mainly
students who volunteered for the project for research credit. Ganahl
compared (1) a no-treatment group, (2) a group receiving written
homework in communication, (3) an SE group with homework assignments, and (4) an SE group comprised of couples with marital difficulties and contrasted only with Group 5, and (5) a clinical sample receiv-

ing marital therapy. The dependent variables were questionnaires covering *(a)* marital adjustment, *(b)* communication, *(c)* marital happiness, and *(d)* marital satisfaction. Results indicated that the SE program was effective in improving marital satisfaction and adjustment. Results were mixed for communication. The enrichment and homework group produced positive results in satisfaction and communication and demonstrated a trend in adjustment. The homework group showed positive results only in marital satisfaction (L'Abate, 1982, p. 15; L'Abate & McHenry, 1983, p. 90). There were no significant differences between the groups in the amount of gains they achieved. Because of insufficient data, the two clinical groups were not evaluated on the measures of adjustment or communication. The clinical enrichment group showed significant improvement in marital satisfaction, marital happiness, and in a communication item within that measure. The clinical enrichment group was found to be "inferior" to the therapy group on marital satisfaction and on a communication item within the marital happiness measure (L'Abate, 1982, p. 15; L'Abate & McHenry, 1983, p. 90).

The Minnesota Couples Communication Program (MCCP)

Developed in 1968 by Miller, Wackman, and Nunnally (Miller, Nunnally, & Wackman, 1976), the Minnesota Couples Communication Program has become one of the most widely used and extensively researched marital enrichment programs (Wampler, 1982b). MCCP is based on the theory of growth-oriented systems, in which a family or marital system is considered to have a number of potential structures and patterns. Therefore, couples are trained in a group setting to develop interactional strategies that will allow them to experience better levels of interaction, both within and outside of the marital setting. This is accomplished by instructing them in ways of monitoring and changing ineffective communication patterns (Miller, Nunnally, & Wackman, 1971).

There are program goals for each partner as well as for the marital relationship. The first goal of MCCP is the development of each partner's ability to accurately perceive him/herself, in addition to recognizing the contribution s/he makes to the relationship. The second goal calls for the improvement of each couple's communication skills in order to promote more clear, direct, and open communication (Miller et al., 1976). The objective is to build into a couple's behavior repertoire certain skills which will act as a strengthening agent for the couple currently and in the future as well (Miller et al., 1971). The program emphasizes flexibility in interactional styles; it is assumed that in possessing a collection of alternative communication patterns, a couple is better prepared to adjust to a variety of situational constraints (Miller, Nunnally, & Wackman, 1975). The skills emphasized in the program are specific and are directed at both the exploration and awareness of self-information and the elicitation of information from the spouse.

Prior to the onset of skills training in the group, each of the participating five to seven couples meet with the leader for contracting purposes. All responsibilities the couple assumes in signing a "maxicontract" (Miller et al., 1976, p. 28) are made explicit. The couple agrees to: attend all sessions together, specify the skills they choose to acquire, practice these skills in the group, and rehearse the skills outside the group. Another contract, the "minicontract" (p. 28), is part of the group process. It provides couples with a choice of whether or not to participate in particular group tasks as they occur (Miller et al., 1971).

Couples meet for three hours once a week for four weeks (Miller et al., 1971). The approach taken is reading/lecture/discussion and skill practice assisted by feedback from the leaders and group members. The instructional component consists of brief lectures, discussions, and homework assignments, all three of which are based on *Alive and Aware: Improving Communication in Relationships* (Miller et al., 1975). Each of the four group meetings deals specifically with one of the four conceptual frameworks of MCCP. Session 1 introduces the awareness wheel, which consists of the five dimensions through which individuals experience self. It is suggested that the examination of one's sensing, thinking, feeling, wanting, and doing enables individuals to be more aware of who they really are. Individuals can then alter themselves, if desired, and more easily decide just what they do and do not want to expose to others (Miller et al., 1975). The exercises used to develop skills in this phase emphasize speaking for *self* and then applying those "I" expressions to disclosure of information from each of the five dimensions (Miller et al., 1976).

Session 2 goes beyond self-awareness by adding the aspect of *the other*. Through *shared meaning* (Miller et al., 1971, p. 116), individuals start to witness how their dimensions of self are received by others. The communication processes here involve sending of the initial message, the receiver's restatement of the communication, followed by the sender's confirmation or clarification. This process assures accurate message transmission.

The framework for Session 3 is a modified version of the Hill Interaction Matrix, used to examine the different intentions and behaviors which are part of four types of *communication styles*. Special attention is devoted to work on what is referred to as the "committed style." This style consists of a direct, complete approach to dealing with a situation in a manner free from blame, self-defensiveness, demands, and reticence (Miller et al., 1975). The skills practiced in this segment focus on the interdependence of communication.

The final phase of the course to be presented is similar to Transactional Analysis' "I'm OK, You're OK" (Miller et al., 1976). Self- and other-esteem is developed through mutually expressing oneself and trusting the other's self-disclosure. Skills employed here may lead to mutually congruent solutions (Miller et al., 1975).

Emphasized throughout training is a communication process which Miller (1975) and associates refer to as work-pattern communication. This process involves specification of an issue, agreement to work on it (minicontract), and then dealing with it, using the committed style and tentative style—both of which are highly receptive and self-disclosing, with the committed style being more affective (Miller et al., 1975).

Group skills practice may be between nonpartners or partners. Either way, the group provides a supportive environment for couples to work on their personal interactions. The other couples serve as models and also provide feedback to the working couple (Miller et al., 1971).

Wampler (1982b) presents a review of 19 studies which assessed the effect of MCCP. She discussed results on both self-report and behavioral measures: For self-report instruments, she found that participating couples were better able to recall prior communication with their spouses after an MCCP program, which suggests a greater awareness of the communication occurring in the relationship. On measures of self-disclosure, couples showed no posttest improvement. One of three studies found an effect on ability to accurately perceive their partner's feelings and thoughts as measured by predicting their responses to a questionnaire. Although only two of nine studies revealed self-reports of improved communication quality, both of those studies showed maintenance of gains at follow-up three and five months later. Positive effects on immediate measures of satisfaction were found in seven of 13 studies. Wampler accounts for these mixed results by recognizing the mixed quality of studies. Eight studies used behavioral measurements, and all reported posttest improvement in communication work style.

Wampler notes the need for better controls in future research work and also discusses looking at the use of MCCP with distressed couples, which has not yet been done. She also encourages study into format types, use of MCCP with nonmiddle-class populations, and the need to examine components of the program to determine their effect and necessity.

Marital Relationship Enhancement (MRE)

MRE may be used for problem prevention, enrichment, or therapy. Problem-prevention/enrichment RE programs generally are in a group format and last 16–20 hours. Therapy group programs may be either in a single-dyad format or a group format. They are generally "time-designated" (B. Guerney, 1977, p. 72), lasting until the problems are resolved. The theoretical background, the skills taught, and the methods used for topic selection have been discussed in the Family Programs section of this chapter. Here we will briefly discuss the leadership techniques used, the general instructional paradigm, and the research on MRE.

In teaching RE skills, the leader attempts to be genuine, honest, and compassionate and to convey warmth, enthusiasm, competence, impartiality, and fairness. The leader motivates and inspires clients to acquire the attitudes and skills s/he is teaching by linking those skills to the important goals for family relationships and for self-satisfaction which the clients have revealed. Instilling and maintaining confidence among the participants in their ability to learn and to change is also an important part of the leaders's task. To accomplish this, the leader elicits and then resolves clients' doubts through discussion and paces the skill practice and problem solving in such a way as to promote successful experiences. The leader also uses encouragement and praise very liberally in the instructional process.

To accomplish the objective of teaching the clients the skills, the leader uses seven types of responses:

1. Administrative (to ensure that the session proceeds smoothly).
2. Praise (to provide motivation, encouragement, and reinforcement).
3. Demonstration (to illustrate and clarify the skills).
4. Modeling:
   a. Behaving in a same way as the leader is advocating for the clients.
   b. Providing specific statements for the clients to "copy."
5. Encouraging and prompting (eliciting the use of appropriate skills).
6. Doubling (saying skillfully what the clients would say for themselves at times when they are unwilling or unable to do so themselves).
7. Troubleshooting (a rarely used response the leader may employ to deal with sharply differing values between the leader and the client or to overcome strong resistance by expressing his/her own opinion; by offering interpretations, making suggestions, and discussing his/her own feelings; and/or by directly providing empathy, nurturance, reassurance, and support).

Once the clients have achieved basic mastery of the skills, the typical sequence in an RE session is as follows. First, the leader supervises the homework assignment and provides appropriate reinforcement. Second, the leader follows up on any previously reached problem-solving agreements that may be due for reevaluation. The leader reinforces the clients for successes in living up to the agreement or for appropriately renewing problem-solving efforts if difficulties have been encountered in implementing the agreement. Third, clients usually share positive attitudes/behaviors/feelings which they have for one another. Fourth, areas for which some change is desirable for the relationship (listed in advance on the Relationship Questionnaire) are reviewed by the leader and client, and one is chosen. Fifth, the leader supervises the clients in their use of skills as they work to reach a mutually acceptable agreement for change. Each issue is followed directly through to an agreement within the session or at home. In the closing minutes of each session, the therapist prepares the clients for their home assignments.

Group MRE was first studied with distressed couples and referred to as "conjugal" therapy. This first study (Ely, Guerney, & Stover, 1973) sought mainly to discover whether the couples were able to learn the skills. It was found that trained couples did gain more in specific skills than did a control group. In a later quasi-replication portion of this study, RE clients gained more during the treatment time period than they had gained in a comparable time period before treatment began. Significant gains also were found in their patterns of general communication and in the general quality of their marital relationships. Collins (1977) later studied a full-length program and found that the RE couples showed greater improvement in marital communication and marital adjustment than did a control group of couples.

An intensive group-MRE format was studied by Rappaport (1976) who used subjects as their own controls. On all of the variables studied, the marital couples showed significantly greater gains during the treatment period than they had during the waiting period. In discussions of emotionally significant topics, the couples gained more during the treatment period in sensitivity to their own feelings, in expressing themselves in ways deemed less likely to induce argument, and in showing empathic acceptance of their partners. Over the treatment interval, as contrasted to the control period, clients also experienced greater improvement in marital communication and in marital harmony. They showed greater gains in trust and intimacy and a greater rate of change in the overall quality of the marital relationships. They also showed more improvement in marital satisfaction and in their perceptions of their ability to resolve problems in their relationships satisfactorily.

A later series of studies shed light on the question of whether MRE effects were treatment-specific rather than due to generic factors. These studies compared group marital RE to other programs which seemed equally credible and competently administered. Wieman (1973) compared group MRE with his Reciprocal Reinforcement program which drew heavily upon principles and techniques used by Knox (1971), Rappaport and Harrell (1972), and especially Stuart (1969). The MRE program Wieman used was an abbreviated, time-limited one. Both treatments showed equally greater improvement on measures of marital communication, marital adjustment, and cooperativeness than did a waiting-list control group. Ratings on 16 semantic differential scales were generally positive for both of the active treatment conditions. However, there were also many significant differences between the treatments on these measures. Clients in the Reciprocal Reinforcement program viewed their treatment as being more light, safe, easy, cold, and calm than did the clients in the MRE programs. Clients in the marital RE program viewed their experience as being significantly more deep, good, worthwhile, exciting, strong, fair, important, comfortable, and professional than the Reciprocal Reinforcement clients viewed their program.

Jessee and Guerney (1981) compared group MRE to Jessee's Group Gestalt Relationship Facilitation program. Both treatment groups gained significantly on all variables that were studied: marital adjustment, communication, trust and harmony, rate of positive change in relationship satisfaction, and ability to handle problems. Participants in the MRE program showed greater gains than those in the Gestalt Relationship Facilitation program in communication, in relationship satisfaction, and in ability to handle problems.

MRE was compared to a discussion treatment of equal length by Ridley, Jorgensen, Morgan, and Avery (1982). Participants in the MRE program showed significantly greater improvement on a measure assessing satisfaction, sensitivity, communication, intimacy, openness, and understanding in their marital relationship.

Ross (1981) did a study in a mental health center in which the five therapists involved averaged six years in marital and family therapy experience. These therapists had had a three-day training program in marital relationship enhancement. By random assignment, they used their own preferred modes of marital therapy (ranging from psychodynamic through client-centered to behavioral preferences) with half the marital therapy couples assigned to them and used MRE with the other half. Ten weeks later at posttesting, the clients in MRE showed greater improvement than the clients treated with the therapists' preferred marital treatment method. This was true on all three variables studied: (a) marital adjustment, (b) the quality of their relationship, and (c) the quality of their communication.

Maintenance of gains in group MRE was demonstrated in the Wieman study mentioned earlier. As was true also for the couples in the Reciprocal Reinforcement treatment, MRE participants had maintained their gains very well 10 weeks after the close of treatment.

PREMARITAL PROGRAMS

Premarital couples communication program

The couples communication program described in the marital program section can be used with premarital couples as well. Miller et al. (1976) report on dissertation studies by Miller (1971) and Nunnally (1971) using the same premarital sample. They randomly assigned 17 couples to four weeks of MCCP and 15 to a no-treatment control group.

Pretesting, involving seven questionnaires and taped interactions between the dyads, was administered to all the couples. The treatment group then participated in four weekly sessions of MCCP. One week following the termination of treatment, all couples were posttested on the same measures used in the initial testing.

There were no significant differences on the questionnaire measures, but behavioral measures did reveal two significant effects. Nunnally's dissertation examined the recall accuracy of the couples. This was done by each couple taking five minutes to plan some activity with their partner. Then, each partner answered a 12-item questionnaire which required them to remember the pattern of interaction which took place—who performed which communication behaviors (expressing feelings, making suggestions, etc.). These interactions were all taped and scored by raters who compared the actual interactions with the partners' recalls. Results showed that at pretest the two groups scored at a similar accuracy level. At posttest, the MCCP-treated group had significantly increased their accuracy in communication observation over the control group.

Miller's dissertation reported the effect of MCCP on a couple's work-pattern communication (Miller et al., 1976). As mentioned in the marital section, "work" (p. 33) refers to a couple's agreeing to discuss a particular topic and then openly discussing on that issue. To measure this, couples were to discuss behaviors their partners exhibit which annoyed them. This five-minute interaction was taped and scored using the interaction-styles framework. Desirable work patterns were scored by timing the sequence of exchanges and totaling those for the five minutes. Results revealed that at pretest, the controls had a higher mean work-pattern communication than did the experimental couples. At posttest, the control couples had decreased their work-style communication while the MCCP-treated couples had increased theirs. The difference was significant.

Premarital Relationship Enhancement (PRE)

Since we have summarized the nature of RE programs in other sections and referred readers elsewhere for the guidelines which determine specific types of leader responses, here we need deal only with the research in PRE. PRE (then called PRIMES) was first investigated by Schlein (1971), whose study was also reported by Ginsberg and Vogelsong (1977). Schlein used a small-group format in which three or four couples met for two and one-half hours per week for, on average, 10 weeks. Random assignment was used to place couples either in the PRE group or in a waiting-list control group. In behavioral interaction while discussing emotionally important topics, PRE participants showed significantly greater gains in (a) empathic skill, and (b) expressive skill (i.e., nonthreatening openness, appropriate self-disclosure, etc.). As determined by questionnaires, significantly greater gains were made by the PRE couples in their ability to handle problems, satisfaction with the relationship, and the general quality of their relationship.

The couples evaluated by Schlein were reevaluated by D'Augelli, Deyss, Guerney, Hershenberg, and Sborofsy (1974), using a different set of behavioral measures: Carkhuff's scales of Empathic Understanding and Self-Exploration. The PRE couples were found to have gained significantly more than the control couples. In fact, the PRE couples changed from levels typical of college students to levels typical of professional counselors in their use of these skills.

Most and Guerney (1983) used pretest-posttest comparisons on a variety of measures to assess whether volunteer lay couples could be trained in two weekends to competently lead a weekend-format PRE program: The study was to determine whether, after such training, they were skilled enough to: (a) produce favorable assessments of their leadership by PRE participants they trained, and (b) produce significant changes in the PRE participants. That the lay volunteer leader trainees learned the program well in their two-weekend training program was revealed by significant pre- to posttesting gains on all the measures used: an assessment of their understanding of the concepts, behavioral measures of their empathic skills and expressive skills, and quasi-behavioral measures of their ability to use constructive problem-solving responses.

After training, these lay volunteer couples led PRE groups. Their ability to lead these groups effectively was assessed by: (a) the judgment of experts, (b) ratings made by the premarital participants, and (c) whether or not they would be able to produce significant changes in pre- to posttesting of the premarital participants. Experts and participants alike rated the volunteer leaders very highly on a wide variety of measures. The PRE participants trained by the volunteers showed significant pre- to posttesting gains in their own self-assessed skill levels and in confidence in their ability to successfully resolve future marital problems. The participants also showed significant gains in behaviorally assessed empathic skills and expressive skills as they role-played attempts to resolve hypothetical conflicts and problems. And they showed significant gains in their quasi-behaviorally assessed use of constructive problem-solving responses.

The PRE program has been compared to an alternate program in a number of studies. Avery, Ridley, Leslie, and Milholland (1980) compared group premarital RE with a Relationship Discussion (RD) program designed to improve premarital attitudes and functioning through supervised discussion. Each program was conducted for three hours per week for eight weeks. The subjects, except if it conflicted with class schedules, were randomly assigned. The PRE participants improved significantly more than the RD participants on behaviorally assessed measures of empathic skill and appropriate self-disclosure (expressive skill).

In comparing PRE to the RD program, Ridley et al. (1982) also found differences on four questionnaires measuring other variables. The couples who participated in the PRE program made significantly greater gains than RD couples in four questionnaire measures reflecting general relationship adjustment; empathy, warmth and genuineness; trust; and communication.

Another study (Ridley, Avery, Dent, & Harrell, 1981) involved a three-way comparison between RD (with 26 couples, a mutal problem-solving program (Ridley, Avery, Harrell, Haynes-Clements, & McCunney, 1981; Ridley, Avery, Harrell, Leslie, & Dent, 1981) with 24 couples, and a PRE program with 24 couples. (The PRE program involved only four skills: Expressive, Empathic, Mode-switching and Facilitative.) Participants were randomly assigned to the three treatments. All programs ran for three hours per week for eight weeks. The dependent variable was perception of confidence in heterosexual relationships. Analysis of covariance yielded one significant difference: Couples in the PRE program showed greater gains than the couples in the RD program.

A study by Sams (1983) compared couples participating in an intensive PRE program with couples who participated in the widely used engaged encounter (EE) program. The EE program closely follows the model of the Marriage Encounter program described in the marital section of this chapter. It was developed by Betsy and Jim Carr (Demarest, Sexton, & Sexton, 1978). Father Calvo's original manual for the encounter experience was partially translated and modified by them to fit its application to couples preparing for marriage. Some of the adaptations which have been made involve the content of the lecture/discussion/dialogue include an examination of weaknesses in the couple's relationships, roles in marriage, and potential conflicts the couple may experience. The couples also have the opportunity to plan the liturgy for their wedding day.

The married couple(s) who lead EE are viewed as providing a strong, influential model for premarrieds. To serve as models, they openly share the marital joys and obstacles they have experienced. Both the EE and the PRE programs were led by the same lay volunteer leaders. As a group, they had had extensive experience in leading EE groups. They were then trained in the two-weekend program mentioned earlier (Most & Guerney, 1983) to conduct PRE.

The premarital participants were measured on two dependent variables. The EE group showed no significant gains in communications skills (empathic/expressive) as measured behaviorally from pre- and posttest role-plays of hypothetical problem situations. They also showed no significant change in constructive problem-solving skills measured quasi-behaviorally from their written responses in attempting to deal with hypothetical problem situations. The PRE participants showed significant gains—and significantly greater gains than the EE participants—in both communication and problem solving.

Maintenance over time of gains resulting from the PRE program was studied in the earlier-mentioned research by Avery et al. (1980). Despite a decline from the levels attained at immediate posttesting to the follow-up testing six months later, the PRE couples maintained their superiority on the variables assessed over the couples who had been seen in the RD program. These were behaviorally assessed empathy and expressive skill. The RD was a carefully developed program implemented by leaders of the same caliber as the PRE program. The previously mentioned alternate treatment comparisons had indicated that for the variables on which RE proved superior, generic treatment variables (placebo, attention, experimenter demand, etc.) could be ruled out as accounting for the significant gains found in PRE programs. This study demonstrated that *maintenance* of RE gains also cannot be due solely to such generic treatment factors.

FUTURE POSSIBILITIES

A significant segment of the public has already participated in problem-prevention/enrichment programs, and an even larger percentage probably is aware of their existence. The number, scope, and types of such programs are expanding rapidly. Programs involving actual interaction, not only between marital couples, adolescents, and their parents but young children and their parents, have begun to receive serious attention.

In the future, we expect to see more application of interactive programs to improving relationships between adults and their midlife or elderly parents. This seems of special importance because of the increase in the average lifespan and also because of an apparent trend for more young adults, even couples, to live with their parents. We also expect to see more active use of the many applicable programs described here, and new ones as well, for two other rapidly growing segments of the population: single-parent families and "blended" families—those composed of previously married couples and their children.

The quantity and quality of research on family problem-prevention/enrichment is no worse than might be expected in a recently developed area of service. Problem-prevention/enrichment programs are easier to perfect through well-controlled research than many other types of psychosocial intervention (B. Guerney, 1982a). Therefore, we predict explosive growth in such research over this coming decade.

We believe that the major problems which need to be solved are: (1) how to increase the public's awareness of family problem-prevention/enrichment programs, and (2) how to make intensive, small-group, problem-prevention/enrichment programs available and affordable to a large part of the population. On the other end of the size continuum, the development of truly mass programs through the use of television ought to receive much greater attention. Two-way television and computer/video programs which interact with the learner offer particularly exciting opportunities for program development, if not in this decade then in the next.

Traditional psychotherapeutic approaches cannot make a dent in the mental health problems of the nation. Perhaps the day is beginning to dawn when replicable, programmatic, community-scale primary, secondary, and tertiary problem-prevention programs for the family will improve the way family members behave toward one another. If so, it is bound to improve our mental health.

REFERENCES

Alexander, J. F., & Barton, C. Behavioral systems therapy for families. In D. H. L. Olson (Ed.), *Treating relationships*. Lake Mills, Iowa: Graphic Publishing, 1976.

Avery, A. W., Ridley, C. A., Leslie, L. A., & Milholland, T. Relationship enhancement with premarital dyads: A six-month follow-up. *American Journal of Family Therapy*, 1980, *8*, 23–30.

Avery, A. W., & Thilssen, J. D. Communication skills training for divorce. *Journal of Counseling Psychology*, 1982, *29*(2), 203–205.

Bader, E., Riddle, R., & Sinclair, C. Do marriage preparation programs really work?: A Canadian experiment. *Journal of Marital and Family Therapy*, 1980, *6*, 171–179.

Bader, E., & Sinclair, C. *The critical first year of marriage*. Unpublished manuscript, 1983. (Mimeographed)

Bagarozzi, D. A., & Rauen, P. Premarital counseling: Appraisal and status. *American Journal of Family Therapy*, 1981, *9*, 13–30.

Barton, C., & Alexander, J. F. Functional family therapy. In A. S. Gurman & D. P. Kniskern (Eds.), *Handbook of family therapy*. New York: Brunner/Mazel, 1981.

Blechman, E. A., & Olson, D. H. L. The family conflict game: Description and effectiveness. In D. H. L. Olson (Ed.), *Treating relationships*. Lake Mills, Iowa: Graphic Publishing, 1976.

Boike, D. E. The impact of a premarital program on communication process, communication facilitativeness, and personality trait variables of engaged couples. Unpublished doctoral dissertation, Florida State University, 1977.

Bosco, A. *Marriage encounter*. St. Meinrad, Ind.: Abbey Press, 1973.

Bowman, T. Developing strengths in families. *Family Coordinator*, 1976, *25*(2), 169–174.

Brown, D. L. *A comparative study of the effects of two foster parent training methods on attitudes of parental acceptance, sensitivity to children, and general foster parent attitudes*. Unpublished doctoral dissertation, Michigan State University, 1980.

Burka, J. B. *Correlates of participation of husbands and wives in a televised marital enrichment workshop*. Unpublished doctoral dissertation, Columbia University, 1978.

Caplan, G. *Principles of preventive psychiatry*. New York: Basic Books, 1964.

Carnes, P. J. *Family development I: Understanding us*. Minneapolis: Interpersonal Communication Programs, 1981.

Cavanaugh, J. *The development of a view sharing survey*. Unpublished doctoral dissertation, Pennsylvania State University, 1982.

Collett, C. S. A comparison of the effects of marital and family enrichment programs on self-concept and conflict resolution ability. Ph.D., Purdue University, 1979.

Collins, J. D. Experimental evaluation of a six month conjugal therapy program. In B. Guerney, Jr. (Ed.), *Relationship enhancement: Skill training programs for therapy, problem prevention, and enrichment*. San Francisco: Jossey-Bass, 1977.

Confer, H. P. The effects of a marital enrichment program upon spousal perception of the dyadic relationship. Doctorate of Education, Southwestern Baptist Theological Seminary, 1979.

Costa, L. A. The effects of a marriage encounter program on marital communication, dyadic adjustment and the quality of the interpersonal relationship. Ph.D., University of Colorado at Boulder, 1981.

Coufal, J. *An experimental evaluation of two approaches to parent skills training: Parent-child participation versus parents only*. Paper presented at the annual meeting of the National Council on Family Relations, Washington, D.C., October 1982.

Coufal, J., & Brock, G. *Parent-child relationship enhancement: A ten week education program*. Menomonie, Wis.: Department of Human and Family Living, 1983.

Creswell-Betsch, C. Comparison of a family microtraining program and a reading program to enhance empathic communications by black parents with young children. Doctorate of Education, University of Massachusetts, 1979.

D'Augelli, A. R., Deyss, C. S., Guerney, B. G., Jr., Hershenberg, B., & Sborofsky, S. L. Interpersonal skill training for dating couple: An evaluation of an educational mental health service. *Journal of Counseling Psychology*, 1974, *21*(5), 385–389.

David, J. R. *The effects of a structured family enrichment program upon selected dimensions of psychosocial functioning of intact families*. Unpublished doctoral dissertation, Florida State University, 1981.

Demarest, D., Sexton, J., & Sexton, M. *Marriage Encounter: A guide for sharing.* St. Paul: Carillon Books, 1978.

DeYoung, A. J. Marriage encounter: A critical examination. *Journal of Marital and Family Therapy,* 1979, *5*(2), 27–34.

Durkin, H. P. *Forty-four hours to change your life: Marriage Encounter.* New York: Paulist Press, 1974.

Elkin, M. Premarital counseling for minors: The Los Angeles experience. *Family Coordinator,* 1977, *26,* 429–443.

Ely, A. L., Guerney, B., Jr., & Stover, L. Efficacy of the training phase of conjugal therapy. *Psychotherapy: Theory, Research and Practice,* 1973, *10,* 201–207.

Evenson, M. L. An Adlerian activity approach to family enrichment. Ph.D., University of Arizona, 1980.

Fenell, D. L. The effects of a choice awareness marriage enrichment program on participants' marital satisfaction, self-concepts, accuracy of perception of spouses, and choosing awareness. Ph.D., Purdue University, 1979.

Figley, C., & Guerney, B., Jr. *The conjugal relationship enhancement program* (thirty-four minutes, 16 mm film, or 3/4- or 1/2-inch video). University Park, Penn.: Individual & Family Consultation Center, 1976.

Ganahl, G. F. *Effects of client, treatment, and therapist variables on the outcome of structured marital enrichment.* Unpublished doctoral dissertation, Georgia State University, 1981.

Garland, D. R. The effects of active listening skills training upon interaction behavior, perceptual accuracy, and marital adjustment of couples participating in a marriage enrichment program. Unpublished doctoral dissertation, University of Louisville, 1979.

Gaydosh, L. R. Socialization for role-taking in marriage: A study of the Pre-Cana Conference in Newark, New Jersey archdiocese. Unpublished doctoral dissertation, Fordham University, 1975.

Genovese, R. J. Marriage encounter. *Small Group Behavior,* 1975, *6*(1), 45–56.

Ginsberg, B. G. Parent-adolescent relationship development program. In B. G. Guerney, Jr. (Ed.), *Relationship enhancement.* San Francisco: Jossey-Bass, 1977.

Ginsberg, B. G., & Vogelsong, E. Premarital relationship improvement by maximizing empathy and self-disclosure: The PRIMES program. In B. G. Guerney, Jr. (Ed.), *Relationship enhancement.* San Francisco: Jossey-Bass, 1977.

Gleason, J., & Prescott, M. R. Group techniques for pre-marital preparation. *Family Coordinator,* 1977, *26,* 277–280.

Guerney, B., Jr. Filial therapy: Description and rationale. *Journal of Consulting Psychology,* 1964, *28,* 303–310.

Guerney, B., Jr. *Relationship enhancement: Skill training programs for therapy, problem prevention and enrichment.* San Francisco: Jossey-Bass, 1977.

Guerney, B., Jr. The delivery of mental health services: Spiritual versus medial versus educational models. In T. R. Vallance & R. M. Sabre (Eds.), *Mental health services in transition: A policy sourcebook.* New York: Human Sciences Press, 1982. (a)

Guerney, B., Jr. Relationship enhancement. In E. K. Marshall & P. D. Kurtz (Eds.), *Interpersonal helping skills.* San Francisco: Jossey-Bass, 1982. (b)

Guerney, B., Jr. Marital and family relationship enhancement therapy. In P. A. Keller &

L. G. Ritt (Eds.), *Innovations in clinical practive: A source book* (Vol. 2). Sarasota, Fla.: Professional Resource Exchange, 1983.

Guerney, B., Jr. Relationship enhancement therapy and training. In D. Larson (Ed.), *Giving psychology away through skills training.* Monterey, Calif.: Brooks/Cole Publishing, 1984.

Guerney, B., Jr., Coufal, J., & Vogelsong, E. Relationship enhancement versus a traditional approach to therapeutic/preventative/enrichment parent-adolescent programs. *Journal of Consulting and Clinical Psychology,* 1981, *49,* 927–939.

Guerney, B., Jr., & Vogelsong, E. *Relationship enhancement demonstration dialogs, 1981.* (Audiotapes available from: Individual and Family Consultation Center, University Park, PA 16802.)

Guerney, B., Jr., Vogelsong, E., & Coufal, J. Relationship enhancement versus a traditional treatment: Follow-up and booster effects. In D. H. Olson & B. C. Miller (Eds.), *Family studies review yearbook.* Beverly Hills, Calif.: Sage Publications, 1983.

Guerney, B., Jr., Vogelsong, E. L., & Glynn, S. *Evaluation of the Family Counseling Unit of the Cambria County Probation Bureau.* State College, Penn.: Ideals, 1977. (Mimeographed, 45 pages)

Guerney, L. F. Filial therapy program. In D. H. L. Olson (Ed.), *Treating relationships.* Lake Mills, Iowa: Graphic Publishing, 1976.

Guldner, C. A. Marriage preparation and marriage enrichment: The preventive approach. *Pastoral Psychology,* 1977, *25*(4), 248–259.

Gurman, A. S., & Kniskern, D. P. Enriching research in marital enrichment programs. *Journal of Marriage and Family Counseling,* 1977, *3,* 3–11.

Harrell, J., & Guerney, B., Jr. Training married couples in conflict negotiation skills. In D. H. L. Olson (Ed.), *Treating relationships.* Lake Mills, Iowa: Graphic Publishing, 1976.

Hof, L., & Miller, W. R. *Marriage enrichment: Philosophy, process and program.* Bowie, Md.: Robert J. Brady, 1981.

Hopkins, L., Hopkins, P., Mace, D., & Mace, V. *Toward better marriages: The handbook of the Association of Couples for Marriage Enrichment (ACME).* Winston-Salem, N.C.: ACME, 1978.

Horejsi, C. R. Small-group sex education for engaged couples. *Journal of Family Counseling,* 1974, *2*(2), 23–27.

Humphreys, L. Sibling, setting, and behavioral generality of treatment effects of a training program for parents of noncompliant children. Ph.D., Univ. of Georgia, 1977.

Jacobson, N. S. Problem solving and contingency contracting in the treatment of marital discord. *Journal of Consulting and Clinical Psychology,* 1977, *45,* 92–100.

Jacobson, N. S. Communication skills training for married couples. In J. P. Curran & P. M. Monti (Eds.), *Social skills training.* New York: Guilford Press, 1982.

Jessee, R., & Guerney, B., Jr. A comparison of Gestalt and relationship enhancement treatments with married couples. *American Journal of Family Therapy,* 1981, *9,* 31–41.

Kahn, A. J., & Kamerman, S. B. *Helping America's families.* Philadelphia: Temple University Press, 1982.

Kearns, W. P. *The development of a marriage enrichment program on conflict management for recently married couples.* Unpublished doctorate of ministry dissertation. Eastern Baptist Theological Seminary, 1980.

Klock, E. M. The development and testing of a microtraining program to enhance empathic communication by parents of young children. Unpublished doctoral dissertation, University of Massachusetts, 1977.

Knox, D. *Marriage happiness: A behavioral approach to counseling.* Champaign, Ill.: Research Press, 1971.

Knox, D. Behavior contracts in marriage counseling. *Journal of Family Counseling,* 1974, *2,* 23–27.

Knox, D. *Dr. Knox's marital exercise book.* New York: David McKay, 1975.

Knox, D., & Knox, F. Preparation for marriage: Beyond the classroom. *Journal of Family Counseling,* 1974, *2*(2), 16–22.

L'Abate, L. Family enrichment programs. *Journal of Family Counseling,* 1974, *2*(1), 32–38.

L'Abate, L. *Structure enrichment (SE) with couples and families.* Paper presented at the Third Annual Family Enrichment Conference at Weber State College, Ogden, Utah, September 1982.

L'Abate, L., & Associates. *Manual: Enrichment programs for the family life cycle.* Atlanta: Georgia State University, 1975. (a)

L'Abate, L., & Associates. *Manual: Family enrichment programs.* Atlanta, Ga.: Social Research Laboratories, 1975. (b)

L'Abate, L., & McHenry, S. *Handbook of marital interventions.* New York: Grune & Stratton, 1983.

L'Abate, L., & Sloane, S. Z. (Eds.). *Workbook for family enrichment: Developmental and structural dimensions.* Atlanta: Georgia State University, 1981.

L'Abate, L., & Rupp, G. *Enrichment: Skills training for family life.* Washington, D.C.: University Press of America, 1981.

L'Abate, L., & Weeks, G. Testing the limits of enrichment: When enrichment is not enough. *Journal of Family Counseling,* 1976, *4*(1), 70–74.

Latham, N. V. The effect on marital adjustment of teaching basic marital communication in a conjoint couples' group using videotape feedback. Ph.D., North Texas State University, 1979.

Lipson, J. W. Training parents as therapists of their own children. Unpublished doctoral dissertation, The University of Wisconsin—Milwaukee, 1976.

Luecke, D. L. *The relationship manual.* Columbia, Md.: Relationship Institute, 1981.

Lutz, W. J. Marriage enrichment with and without bibliotherapy. Unpublished doctoral dissertation, New Mexico State University, 1979.

Mace, D. We call it ACME. *Small Group Behavior,* 1975, *6*(1), 31–44.

Mace, D., & Mace, V. Marriage enrichment—a preventive group approach for couples. In D. H. L. Olson (Ed.), *Treating relationships.* Lake Mills, Iowa: Graphic Publishing, 1976.

Maddock, J. W. Sexual health: An enrichment and treatment program. In D. H. L. Olson (Ed.), *Treating relationships.* Lake Mills, Iowa: Graphic Publishing, 1976.

McRae, B. C. A comparison of a behavioral and a lecture-discussion approach to premarital counseling. Unpublished doctoral dissertation, University of British Columbia, 1975.

Miller, S. *The effects of communication training in small groups upon self-disclosure and openness in engaged couples' system of interaction: A field experiment.* Unpublished doctoral dissertation, University of Minnesota, 1971.

Miller, S., Nunnally, E. W., & Wackman, D. B. *The Minnesota couples communication training program* (instructor's manual), 1971.

Miller, S., Nunnally, E. W., & Wackman, D. B. *Alive and aware.* Minneapolis: Interpersonal Communication Programs, 1975.

Miller, S., Nunnally, E. W., & Wackman, D. B. Minnesota couples communication program (MCCP): Premarital and marital groups. In D. H. L. Olson (Ed.), *Treating relationships.* Lake Mills, Iowa: Graphic Publishing, 1976.

Most, R., & Guerney, B., Jr. An empirical evaluation of the training of lay volunteer leaders for premarital relationship enhancement. *Family Relations,* 1983, *32,* 239–251.

Nelson, R. C., & Friest, W. P. Marriage enrichment through choice awareness. *Journal of Marital and Family Therapy,* 1980, *6,* 399–407.

Nunnally, E. *The effects of communication training upon interaction awareness and empathic accuracy of engaged couples: A field experiment.* Unpublished doctoral dissertation, University of Minnesota, 1971.

Olson, D. H., Fournier, D. G., & Druckman, J. M. *PREPARE II.* Minneapolis: Prepare, 1979.

Otto, H. A. Marriage and family enrichment programs in North America—report and analysis. *Family Coordinator,* 1975, *24,* 137–142.

Otto, H. A. (Ed.). *Marriage and family enrichment: New perspectives and programs.* Nashville, Tenn.: Abingdon, 1976.

Patterson, G. R. Parents and teachers as change agents: A social learning approach. In D. H. L. Olson (Ed.), *Treating relationships.* Lake Mills, Iowa: Graphic Publishing, 1976.

Patterson, G. R., & Hops, H. Coercion, a game for two: Intervention techniques for marital conflict. In R. E. Ulrich & P. Mounjoy (Eds.), *The experimental analysis of social behavior.* New York: Appleton-Century-Crofts, 1972.

Patterson, G. R., Hops, H., & Weiss, R. L. Interpersonal skills training for couples in early stages of conflict. *Journal of Marriage and the Family,* 1975, *37,* 295–302.

Pearson, C. J. An experimental marriage enrichment program for navy personnel and dependents using Transactional Analysis. *Dissertation Abstracts International,* 1975, *35,* 3097A.

Peed, S., Roberts, M., & Forehand, R. Evaluation of the effectiveness of a standardized parent training program in altering the interaction of mothers and their noncompliant children. *Behavior Modification,* 1977, *1,* 323–349.

Preston, J., & Guerney, B., Jr. Relationship enhancement skill training. Unpublished manuscript, 1982. (Mimeographed, 614 pages)

Powell, G. S., & Wampler, K. Marriage enrichment participants. *Family Relations,* 1982, *31,* 389–393.

Rappaport, A. F. Conjugal relationship enhancement program. In D. H. L. Olson (Ed.), *Treating relationships.* Lake Mills, Iowa: Graphic Publishing, 1976.

Rappaport, A. F., & Harrell, J. A behavioral exchange model for marital counseling. *Family Coordinator,* 1972, *21,* 203–212.

Regula, R. R. Marriage Encounter: What makes it work? *Family Coordinator,* 1975, *24,* 153–159.

Ridley, C. A., Avery, A. W., Dent, J., & Harrell, J. E. The effects of relationship enhancement and problem solving programs on perceived heterosexual competence. *Family Therapy*, 1981, *8*, 59–66.

Ridley, C. A., Avery, A. W., Harrell, J. E., Haynes-Clements, L. A., & McCunney, N. Mutural problem-solving skills training for premarital couples: A six-month follow-up. *Journal of Applied Developmental Psychology*, 1981, *2*, 179–188.

Ridley, C. A., Avery, A. W., Harrell, J. E., Leslie, L. A., & Dent, J. Conflict management: A premarital training program in mutual problem solving. *American Journal of Family Therapy*, 1981, *9*(4), 23–32.

Ridley, C. A., Jorgensen, S. R., Morgan, A. G., & Avery, A. W. Relationship enhancement with premarital couples: An assessment of effects on relationship quality. *American Journal of Family Therapy*, 1982, *10*, 41–48.

Robin, A. L. Problem solving communication training: A behavioral approach to the treatment of parent-adolescent conflict. *American Journal of Family Therapy*, 1979, *7*, 69–82.

Robin, A. L. Parent-adolescent conflict: A skill training approach. In D. P. Rathjen & J. P. Foreyet (Eds.), *Social competence: Interventions for children and adults*. Elmsford, N.Y.: Pergamon Press, 1980.

Robin, A. L. A controlled evaluation of problem-solving communication training with parent-adolescent conflict. *Behavior Therapy*, 1981, *12*, 593–609.

Robin, A. L., Kent, R. N., O'Leary, K. D., Foster, S., & Prinz, R. J. An approach to teaching parents and adolescents problem solving skills: A preliminary report. *Behavior Therapy*, 1977, *8*, 639–643.

Rolfe, D. J. Pre-marriage contracts: An aid to couples living with parents. *Family Coordinator*, 1977, *26*, 281–285. (a)

Rolfe, D. J. Techniques with pre-marriage groups. *British Journal of Guidance and Counseling*, 1977, *5*(1), 89–97. (b)

Ross, E. R. *Comparative effectiveness of relationship enhancement and therapist-preferred therapy on marital adjustment*. Unpublished doctoral dissertation, Pennsylvania State University, 1981.

Ryan, P. R., Warren, B. L., & McFadden, E. J. *Training foster parents to serve dependent children: Summary progress report*. Ypsilanti: Eastern Michigan University, 1977.

Sams, W. *An experimental comparison of two premarital programs: Relationship enhancement and engaged encounter*. Unpublished doctoral dissertation, Pennsylvania State University, 1983.

Sawin, M. *Family enrichment with family clusters*. Valley Forge, Penn.: Judson Press, 1979.

Sawin, M. Family enrichment—the challenge which unites us. *Religious Education*, 1980, *75*(3), 342–353.

Schlein, S. *Training dating couples in empathic and open communication: An experimental evaluation of a potential preventive mental health program*. Unpublished doctoral dissertation, Pennsylvania State University, 1971.

Sensuée, M. Filial therapy follow-up study: Effects on parental acceptance and child adjustment. Unpublished doctoral dissertation, The Pennsylvania State University, 1981.

Shonick, H. Premarital counseling: Three years' experience of a unique service. *Family Coordinator*, 1975, *24*, 321–324.

Smith, A., & Smith, L. Marriage communication lab: A brief description. Unpublished manuscript, 1981 (Mimeographed; available from authors, 1605 Otter Creek Road, Nashville, TN 37215.

Smith, R. M., Shaffner, S. M., & Scott, J. P. Marriage and family enrichment: A new professional area. *Family Coordinator,* 1979, *28*(1), 87–93.

Stein, E. V. MARDILAB: An experiment in marriage enrichment. *Family Coordinator,* 1975, *24,* 167–170.

Stollak, G. E., & Kallman, J. R. Instructions for special play sessions between adults and young children. In G. E. Stollak (Ed.), *Until we are six.* (Available from: P. O. Box 9542, Melbourne, Fla., 32901. 1978.

Stuart, R. B. Operant interpersonal treatment for marital discord. *Journal of Consulting and Clinical Psychology,* 1969, *33,* 675–682.

Stuart, R. B. An operant interpersonal program for couples. In D. H. L. Olson (Ed.), *Treating relationships.* Lake Mills, Iowa: Graphic Publishing, 1976.

Sywulak, A. E. *The effect of filial therapy on parental acceptance and child adjustment.* Unpublished doctoral dissertation, Pennsylvania State University, 1977.

Taylor, G. M. Marriage enrichment: A strategy for strengthening relationships. Unpublished doctoral dissertation, The University of Utah, 1980.

Trainer, J. B. Pre-marital counseling and examination. *Journal of Marital and Family Therapy,* 1979, *5,* 61–78.

Travis, R. P., & Travis, P. Y. The pairing enrichment program: Actualizing the marriage. *Family Coordinator,* 1975, *24,* 161–165.

Travis, R. P., & Travis, P. Y. A note on changes in the caring relationship following a marriage enrichment program and some preliminary findings. *Journal of Marriage and Family Counseling,* 1976, *2,* 81–83. (a)

Travis, R. P., & Travis, P. Y. Self actualization in marital enrichment. *Journal of Marriage and Family Counseling,* 1976, *2,* 73–79. (b)

Travis, R. P., & Travis, P. Y. *Vitalizing intimacy in marriage.* Chicago: Nelson-Hall, 1979.

Vogelsong, E., & Guerney, B., Jr. *The relationship enhancement program for family therapy and enrichment.* (45 minutes, 16 mm film, sound, ¾- or ½-inch video). University Park, Penn.: Individual and Family Consultation Center, 1977.

Vogelsong, E., & Guerney, B. *Filial therapy.* (34 minutes, 16 mm film and ½- or ¾-inch videotape). University Park, Penn.: Individual and Family Consultation Center, 1978.

Wagner, V., & L'Abate, L. Written enrichment and written homework assignments with couples. In L. L'Abate (Ed.), *Enrichment: Structured intervention with couples, families, and groups.* Washington, D.C.: University Press of America, 1977.

Wampler, K. S. Bringing the review of literature into the age of quantification: Meta-analysis as a strategy for integrating research findings in family studies. *Journal of Marriage and the Family,* 1982, *44*(4) 1009–1023. (a)

Wampler, K. S. The effectiveness of the Minnesota Couple Communication Program: A review of research. *Journal of Marital and Family Therapy,* 1982, *8,* 345–355. (b)

Weiss, R. L., Hops, H., & Patterson, G. R. A framework for conceptualizing marital conflict, a technology for altering it, some data for evaluating it. In L. A. Hamerlynck, L. C. Handy, & E. Mash (Eds.), *Behavior change: Methodology, concepts, and practice.* Champaign, Ill.: Research Press, 1973.

Weissman, S., & Montgomery, G. Techniques for group family enrichment. *Personnel and Guidance Journal,* 1980, *59,* 113–119.

Wellisch, D. K., Vincent, J., & Ro-Trock, G. K. Family therapy versus individual therapy: A study of adolescents and their parents. In D. H. L. Olson (Ed.), *Treating relationships.* Lake Mills, Iowa: Graphic Publishing, 1976.

Wieman, R. J. *Conjugal relationship modification and reciprocal reinforcement: A comparison of treatments for marital dischord.* Unpublished doctoral dissertation, Pennsylvania State University, 1973.

Wildman, R., II. Structured versus unstructured marital intervention. In L. L'Abate (Ed.), *Enrichment: Structured intervention with couples, families, and groups.* Washington, D.C.: University Press of America, 1977.

Wilson, D. A. The effects of a partially structured Christian marriage enrichment program upon marital communications, general marital adjustment, and purpose in life. Ph.D., North Texas State University, 1980.

Wittrup, R. G. Marriage enrichment: A preventive counseling program designed to attain marriage potential. Unpublished doctoral dissertation, Western Michigan University, 1973.

Wolfe, D. A., Sandler, J., & Kaufman, K. A competency based parent training program for child abusers. *Journal of Consulting and Clinical Psychology,* 1981, *49,* 633–640.

Chapter 40

Descriptive and Explanatory Levels in Family Therapy: Distance, Defeats, and Dependence

LUCIANO L'ABATE

This chapter describes three major psychological concepts and relates them to family functionality/dysfunctionality. Two of these concepts are very much alive in psychology: *Distance* has been well researched in social psychology, and *dependence* is important in developmental psychology. The concept of *defeats*, although at first blush new, covers a variety of constructs used in abnormal and clinical psychology. All three concepts, however, are relevant to family psychology and therapy. Whether the concepts are explanatory rather than descriptive remains to be seen. Even considered descriptive, however, they do span such a wide range of behavior that they are useful in relating family psychology to other areas of psychology.

The thesis of this chapter is that *(a)* distance among members in dysfunctional families is regulated by defeats, and *(b)* through these defeats, family members remain dependent upon each other. By the same token, distance in functional families is regulated mostly by victories. Each concept will be reviewed separately to show how all three concepts, and the behaviors that they subsume, are intrinsically interwoven in family functioning and dysfunctioning.

LEVELS OF DESCRIPTION AND EXPLANATION

One of the most difficult issues that this chapter discusses is that of differentiating between levels of description and levels of explanation. Distance, for instance, can be measured fairly objectively (i.e., how far a person is or stays from another person). Nevertheless, what internal (explanatory) concepts define that distance between two persons? Liking? Disliking? Boredom? Hatred? We can assess the intensity, the frequency, and the number of defeating behaviors. Yet, how do these behaviors relate to more internal variables, such as body percept and self-esteem? In assessing the degree of attachment or dependence between two persons, we can fairly objectively measure how often they make contact with each other, how often they gaze at each other, and how much time they spend with each other. The descriptive observations, even the measurements, tell us nothing, however, about how the persons feel about each other.

In psychology, we have traditionally used internal states and traits as explanations for external behavior. The tradition arose from a consideration of behavior in a vacuum—that is, without an interpersonal, intimate context. Here, instead, it is assumed that behavior occurs, most of the time, in a context of intimates as a result of close and prolonged interpersonal processes (i.e., transactions). Once we become aware of the history of such transactions, antecedents, and correlates, do we need to rely on internal, intrapsychic states, attributes, or traits to explain behavior?

Levels of description and explanation have been discussed at length by L'Abate (1964, 1976), who presented at least two explanatory (internal) levels: genotypical and historical. Because a dogmatic either/or position is difficult, a vacillation between the two levels will be evident in this chapter. If the ambivalence seems confusing, consider that family psychology is pulled by two traditions: the psychological tradition, which uses internal states and traits as explanatory, and the family systems tradition, which tries to avoid internal variables and concentrates instead on observable, external transactions. As psychologists, we can opt for both traditions.

SPACE AND DISTANCE IN THE FAMILY

"Conceptions of space are culturally determined in many ways and therefore receive a great variety of linguistic expression" (Henry, 1971, p. 179). Space, according to Henry, encompasses extension, distance, direction, size, height, depth, motion, and position, which is central to order and orderliness. Unfortunately, Henry elaborated less on the conception of distance than on the other conceptions.

Distance and nonverbal behavior

A spatial metaphor for distance is nonverbal communication, or those bodily and facial cues that accompany verbalizations (Knapp, 1972; Weitz, 1974). (This metaphor, however, would bring us to consider a field that has been sufficiently reviewed by L'Abate, 1964, 1976.)

Waxer (1978) traced the early scientific thought of nonverbal behavior to Charles Darwin, William James, Carl G. Lange, Sigmund Freud, Theodore Reik, and Wilhelm Reich. In contemporary therapy systems, nonverbal behavior has been the focus of therapists whose bent is chiefly humanistic—Virginia Satir, Fritz Perls, Ira Rolf, and Alexander Lowen (bioenergetics). The experimental studies of nonverbal behavior that Waxer reviewed included those by Karl Lewin, Albert Scheflen, Paul Ekman, and Wallace Friesen's work on the facial expression of emotion.

Heslin and Patterson (1982), on the other hand, related nonverbal behavior to social psychology and the processes of attraction, social influence, and emotions, and to individual and group differences in nonverbal behavior. They focused especially on how nonverbal behavior regulates everyday life. In this regard, one needs to consider Sundstrom and Altman's (1976) theoretical model of personal space as a function of interpersonal relationships and expectations for interaction. They hypothesized an almost U-shaped curve whose vertical axis is comfort-discomfort and whose horizontal axis includes three levels of interpersonal distance—close, intermediate, and far (an intermediate level of distance equals the greatest degree of comfort).

The management of distance

We need to distinguish among the task demands in at least three kinds of interpersonal situations: *(a)* private—close and prolonged relationships (e.g., at home); *(b)* public—prolonged but not close relationships (e.g., at work); and *(c)* fleeting, superficial interactions (e.g., in a store, on an airplane, or at the theater). Each situation has peculiar task demands that may well be not only different from, but inconsistent with, the demands of the other two situations. Although most of the social psychological research on distance covers fleeting and superficial interactions, such as in contrived and artificial laboratory experiments, this very information may give us clues to the most prolonged private and public interactions.

Distance by similarity

Similarity in family relations has been reviewed by Acock, Barker, and Bergston (1982), who differentiated similarity from associational and affective solidarity, a differentiation that should be kept in mind as relevant to the metaphor of distance. Hinde (1979) discussed similarity in interpersonal relationships, and L'Abate (1976) postulated a dimension of likeness that deals with how we define ourselves vis-à-vis our caretakers and intimates. Originally, the likeness dimension was also equated to distance between and among family members, including extremes of symbiosis at one end and autism and alienation at the other end, two intermediate ranges of sameness-oppositeness, and two central ranges of similarity-differentness. This six-range continuum has more recently been reduced to a three-step continuum ranging from apathetic-abusive (A) to reactive-repetitive (R) and to conductive-changing (C) (to be presented later in this chapter).

In addition to equating identification with similarity (an equation also used by L'Abate, 1976), Lynn (1969) used the concept of distance in hypothesizing the existence of a curvilinear relationship between children's distance from their parents and the children's cognitive styles. Unfortunately, he defined distance only in its polar extremes (close-distant) and neglected to consider distance between the parents an additional independent variable in predicting cognitive style in children. He also linked the parent-child distance to field dependence-independence but not to emotional dependence. In other words, he neglected the consideration of the family as a system.

Distance in social psychology

Druckman, Rozella, and Baxter (1982) distinguished five channels along which nonverbal communication occurs: *(a)* paralanguage (e.g., pitch, pauses, hesitations, fluency, interruptions), *(b)* facial expressions, *(c)* kinesis, *(d)* visual behavior, and *(e)* various combinations and permutations of the preceding. They assigned interpersonal distance (i.e., face-to-face interactions) to the area of proximus, or what they called "interpersonal spacing," the physical distance that separates interacting persons. Unfortunately, much of the research reviewed by Druckman et al. had little to do with family members but was concerned instead with contrived, short-lived interactions between adventitious partners. Fortunately, however, the research has yielded a classification of 46 nonverbal categories with consistent reliability and a strong similarity to those originally developed by Birdwhistle (1970). Beginning family research in this area has been reported by Reiss (1981).

Despite the quantity of research on distance that social and developmental psychologists have performed, one is forced to conclude that *(a)* most of the research on distance has been conducted in contrived, short-lived situations that often are almost completely irrelevant to family life; *(b)* despite these shortcomings, some extrapolations to family functioning and nonfunctioning are relevant; *(c)* a great deal of clinical lore (e.g., seating arrangements among family members, exchange of gazes, paralinguistic cues, territorial or power struggles) finds support in much of the social psychological research on distance; *(d)* much of this research is not used by most family theorists or therapists because it has not been conducted with family members in natural settings.

Body percepts and interpersonal distance (IPD)

Much of the research on body percepts and interpersonal distance has been done with individuals outside the family context. Consequently, some of the contributions included here and in the next section are cited because they may be individual antecedents of IPD. Fisher and Cleveland (1968) studied body percepts through their Rorschach barrier and penetration scores. Unfortunately, they neglected to provide family antecedents and correlates for these scores.

Distance and personal space

IPD can be defined as the distance assumed by two persons during interaction. This phenomenon has been investigated under a number of names: proxemics (Hall, 1966), personal space (Little, 1965; Sommer, 1969), and body buffer zone (Horowitz, Duff, & Stratton, 1964). Ardrey's (1966) investigations of territoriality in animals were forerunners of research on IPD. Ardrey maintained that each organism establishes its own fixed geographical area. This establishment of territory helps the organism in protecting itself from predators, securing its food supply, and sexual selection. Intraspecies aggression, then, results from territorial intrusion; likewise, human aggression may result from the individual's need to defend one's territory.

An organism defends not only a fixed geographical territory but a certain space around its body (Hediger, 1950). Thus, territory represents a fixed geographical locale, but an organism's personal space is a moving area. According to Hediger, an organism maintains different zones of space around the self, depending on the nature of the interaction between self and another organism. Hediger's conceptualization of zones of space immediately surrounding the organism has been the basis for several models of IPD in humans. For example, Hall (1966) suggested that an individual's personal space consists of concentric circles within which varying levels of interaction occur. He posited the existence of four zones, each with a near and a far phase:

1. Intimate distance (touching to 1½ feet): Activities in the near phase include lovemaking, fighting, and other direct physical contact. The far phase involves touching (i.e., with the hands) and whispered conversations.
2. Personal distance (1½ feet to 4 feet): The near phase includes normal interaction distance between spouses or close friends. The far phase includes conversations between acquaintances.
3. Social distance (4 feet to 12 feet): The near phase includes business transactions that are somewhat impersonal but not particularly formal (e.g., conferring with a supervisor). The far phase is used for more formal business interactions (e.g., an employment interview).

4. Public distance (12 feet to 25 feet): The near phase is used for formal, primarily one-way communications (e.g., a lecture). The far phase is appropriate only for formal appearances (e.g., a play) in which two-way interaction is inappropriate.

Sommer (1969) emphasized the dynamic qualities of personal space by defining it as an area that surrounds and moves about with an individual, expanding and contracting as situations dictate. Little (1965) also emphasized the dynamic qualities of personal space, conceptualizing it as a series of fluctuating, concentric globes, each defining a region for certain kinds of interaction.

Duke and Nowicki (1972) proposed a conceptual IPD model based on Rotter's (1954) social-learning theory, specifically, his internal versus external locus of control. Using their model of IPD, they discovered differences in the spatial behaviors of internals and externals. Apparently, the work of Duke and Nowicki is the first attempt to relate human spatial behavior to a comprehensive personality theory.

Using direct behavioral measurement, several researchers have found that children's IPD preferences increase as they grow older (e.g., Jones & Aiello, 1973; Tennis & Dabbs, 1975). The relationship between IPD and age in adults has also been investigated. For example, Baxter (1970) found that adults (older than 20 years) maintained larger IPDs than did adolescents (10–20 years old). Heshka and Nelson (1972) discovered from observations in natural settings that IPD tends to increase until a person reaches age 40, after which the IPD begins to decrease.

Race and IPD. Considerable research has been conducted on the effect of race on IPD. In general, black dyads tend to stand closer together than do white dyads (e.g., Connolly, 1974), although this result has not always obtained. For example, Baxter (1970), observing white, black, and Mexican-American dyads at the Houston Zoo, found that Mexican-Americans stood closest together, followed by whites; black assumed the largest IPDs.

Gender and IPD. Tennis and Dabbs (1975) used a direct behavioral approach to assess the IPD preferences of 1st, 5th, 9th, and 12th graders as well as college sophomores. The data for all grades except the first showed that female-female dyads assumed smaller IPDs than did male-male dyads (male-female dyads were not tested). The researchers concluded that IPD preferences may reflect sex role normative behavior that first graders have not yet acquired. Observing adult subjects, Baxter (1970) found that male-female dyads assumed the smallest IPDs, followed by female-female dyads and, finally, male-male dyads.

Several investigators have looked at the effect that the gender of the interactants has on IPD and how this factor interacts with other factors. For instance, Heshka and Nelson (1972) examined the relationship between gender and the degree of the interactants' acquaintance. Male dyads stood at approximately the same distance, regardless of their relationship; female dyads assumed smaller IPDs than did males when the two females were friends but assumed greater distances when they were strangers. The IPD preferences of women are thus more influenced by the relationship of the interactants.

In general, the research on the relationship between gender and IPD has shown that female dyads stand closer together than do male dyads and that, in adults, the smallest distances are found with male-female dyads. These results have not universally obtained, however, and these effects tend to interact with other factors.

Situational factors and IPD.   IPD is affected by many situational factors, one of which is the instructions given to subjects. For example, subjects who were instructed to make friends with a confederate in an experiment chose significantly smaller IPDs than did subjects who were instructed to avoid making friends (Rosenfeld, 1965).

Another important situational factor is the characteristics of the stimulus person. For example, Mehrabian (1969) discovered that persons tend to assume a large IPD when the stimulus person is one of high status.

Physical characteristics and IPD.   The physical characteristics of the stimulus person can also influence IPD. Using an indirect technique, Lerner (1973) discovered that children preferred greater IPDs when the stimulus person's body was endomorphic (heavyset) rather than ecto- or mesomorphic. Depending on the situation, a highly attractive stimulus person can cause the subject either to approach more closely (Powell & Dabbs, 1976) or stay farther away (Dabbs & Stokes, 1975).

Personality factors and IPD.   Several investigators have explored the relationship between various personality factors and IPD. Some of the characteristics that have been studied are internal versus external locus of control, self-esteem, authoritarianism, leadership, and heterosexuality.

Duke and Nowicki (1972) studied the relationship between locus of control and IPD. They hypothesized that when the stimulus person was a stranger, externals would assume a greater IPD than would internals. Externals would generally expect nonreinforcement in such a situation and would keep their distance. When the stimulus person was a friend, internals and externals would not differ in IPD. The hypotheses were confirmed.

Frankel and Barrett (1971) studied the relationships among self-esteem, authoritarianism, and IPD. As hypothesized, subjects high in authoritarianism and subjects low in self-esteem assumed the greatest distances.

The effect that heterosexuality (as measured by the Edwards Personal Preference Test) has on IPD was studied by Hartnett, Bailey, and Gibson (1970). Subjects high in heterosexuality tended to allow smaller IPDs while interacting with opposite-sex experimenters (especially true of high-heterosexual males approached by female experimenters).

Psychopathology and IPD.   A few researchers have examined the relationship between psychopathology and IPD. In a study in which the IPDs of schizophrenics and nonschizophrenics were compared, schizophrenics assumed relatively larger IPDs, but the IPD tended to decrease gradually as a patient's condition improved (Horowitz et al., 1964). An indirect measurement technique was used to compare the IPD preferences of normal and emotionally disturbed elementary school boys (Fisher, 1967). The disturbed boys placed figures at greater distances than did the normal boys. In addition, the IPD correlated positively with the level of hostility (as measured by the Buss-Durkee Hostility Scale) in the subjects' mothers. Apparently, the boys whose mothers were hostile tended to need greater IPDs. Kinzel (1970) compared the IPDs of violent and nonviolent prison inmates. As had been predicted, inmates who were prone to violence required greater IPDs than did the nonviolent inmates.

Some preliminary evidence indicates that IPD can be affected by certain therapeutic procedures. After 12 hours of assertiveness training, subjects showed smaller IPDs compared with untrained controls (Booraem & Flowers, 1972).

Although most of the research reviewed was done with individuals, it does provide empirical support for the importance of distance among family members.

Distance in family systems

Hess and Handel (1959), in proposing five processes that together constitute family life, called the first process "a pattern of separateness and connectedness" (p. 12). Kantor and Lehr (1975) made distance a central theme in their theory, in which they considered distance regulation (a) an access-mechanism that varies among families, (b) a feature of an imaginary memory bank, (c) part of a feedback process model, *(d)* part of a four-player interaction (bystander, mover, follower, and opposer), *(e)* an information-processing issue that has various functions in the family. Their conviction that "space is the key variable in the investigation of families" (p. 7) is shared by L'Abate (1976). Nevertheless, having differentiated between psychological and actual distance, Kantor and Lehr neglected to specify what distance consists of. Distance, then, is a concept that encompasses a variety of spatial metaphors, including Hess and Handel's separateness and connectedness.

Two theoretical trends are important in a consideration of distance: *(a)* object relations theory, and *(b)* Mahler's (Mahler, Pine, & Bergman, 1975) autism-symbiosis theory. In the autism-symbiosis theory, distance is considered especially in the toddler's visual and auditory experience of being in contact with the mother when physically distant from her (Edward, Ruskin, & Turrini, 1981).

Another example of distance is cohesion, or cohesiveness, which plays a primary part in a model by Olson and his associates (Olson, Sprenkle, & Russell, 1979; Sprenkle & Olson, 1978). Olson and his co-workers, after reviewing the literature, devised an orthogonal circumplex model that has two dimensions—cohesion (referring to how close or how far apart family members are, implying distance or contiguity) and adaptability. In the model, one extreme—closeness—means symbiotic enmeshment; the other extreme—too little closeness—means disengagement. According to another model, which is shared by Stierlin (1974) and Beavers (1982), two different forces are viewed as propelling family members toward too much closeness (centripetal) or too little closeness (centrifugal).

Olson's circumplex model accounts for various degrees of cohesion (i.e., flexible separateness, flexible connectedness, structural connectedness, and structural separateness), which make up the middle of the bell-shaped distribution. L'Abate (1976) and Olson have devised similar models—circumplex, with bell-shaped distributions (Olson's cohesiveness equals L'Abate's likeness).

Rosenblatt, Titus, and Cunningham (1979) studied togetherness and apartness in 136 couples. Using a questionnaire, they paid special attention to disrespect, which they thought might be an abrasive element in marriage. Couples who scored above average on disrespect spent more time apart on days when there had been a big fight, considerable annoyance, or anger. Couples who scored below average on disrespect spent more time together on such days. The researchers commented that "privacy and interpersonal distance are, of course, necessary in close relationships."

Farley (1979) used the polarities of symbiotic union and individuation on a continuum that he saw as a continual process of development through self-other differentiation. He used a model of individual tolerance based on a doughnut-shaped figure for which a scale measured degrees of fusion (symbiosis) at one end and intimacy tolerance at the other.

Reiss (1981) borrowed from Kantor and Lehr (1975) in attributing functions to space-distance regulation, by establishing boundaries between the family and the outside world and within family members. Citing Steinglass's work in measuring distance between any two family members, Reiss found extremes that varied from 4 feet to 9 feet:

> The organization of spatial arrangements within the family, however, goes well beyond simple distances between interacting individuals. For example, families differ in how they use the space within their homes. In some families, individuals are accorded their own private and inviolate space. . . . Other families are less systematic in assigning priority use of specialized areas. (p. 235)

The regulation of distance within the family may well be representative of how the family negotiates privacy.

In addition, Reiss assumed that family ceremonials play "a central role in the family's experience of space," in terms of the sites where they take place and the boundaries incorporated in the conduct of them. Rituals also connect the family to, and protect the family from, the immediate surroundings. Rituals make demands on family resources (e.g., at Christmas), strengthening the family's historical identity and solidarity (pp. 240–243).

Anderson and Russell (1982) considered four modal themes central to the identification of family rules: *(a)* symptoms, *(b)* myths, *(c)* secrets, and *(d)* boundaries. These themes regulate the distance among family members according to a cycle of withdrawal/pursuit that occurs in space and that relates to the whole issue of intimacy (see Sloan & L'Abate, Chapter 13 of this *Handbook*).

Distance in family therapy

In proposing an integrative approach to resolving conflicts in regulating family distance, Byng-Hall and Campbell (1981) postulated as follows: "Interpersonal distance and its vicissitudes provide a major focus for psychotherapists of all hues. The abundant use of terms such as enmeshment, attachment, detachment, binding, expelling, oedipal conflicts, blurred boundaries, and many others bear witness to this" (p. 321). Byng-Hall and Campbell thus made distance regulation "the central core of the[ir] conceptual formulation." Although they failed to define distance, they did define conflicts in distance regulation as the result of "simultaneous fears of both separation and intimacy within a dyad—a so-called too far/too close system—which is stabilized through a systematic third person" (p. 322). Dysfunctional distance regulation occurs whenever the boundaries of the two involved persons are either unduly restricted or too far/too close. The boundaries may relate to fantasy as well as to behavior. In fact, the authors wrote of the "symbolic use of space" and advocated integrating space and time contexts in a way that is similar to L'Abate's (1964, 1976) conception, in which space and time are considered the two most fundamental assumptions that can be made about behavior.

Barton and Alexander (1981) proposed a tripartite model of distance, ranging from going-away ("avoidance," L'Abate, 1976) to come-here (L'Abate's "approach") behavior, with distance regulation in the intermediate position. Ferber (1972) described the "lone wolf" position of therapists who maintain distance from their clients, a position he attributed to many therapists regardless of their claimed therapeutic allegiances (p. 396). Among the lone wolves, the Milan group (Hansen & L'Abate, 1982) represents the maximum use of distance, which they rationalized as *neutrality.*

Boss and Whitaker (1979), in discussing closeness and separation, concluded:

> The more we find separateness, the more it's possible for us to be close and intimate. . . . Perhaps if we could accept the dialectical nature of separation-togetherness rather than viewing them as either/or situations, we could live life more easily and view more acute forms of separation as natural and less traumatic. (pp. 396–397)

Napier (1978) referred to the rejection-intrusion pattern as one of the central patterns in family dynamics. By intrusion, he meant closeness, reassurance, and support; by rejection, he meant separateness, independence, and autonomy. Either of the polarities was considered a type of "distance regulation" and had different historical antecedents in the family of origin. Closeness seekers have a history of *(a)* established dependence, *(b)* parental deprivation and rejection, *(c)* forced parentification, and *(d)* symbiosis and abandonment. On the other hand, distance in marriage may replicate patterns of *(a)* restricted individuation, *(b)* aggressive intrusion, *(c)* sexualized enthusiasm, and *(d)* infantilization and engulfment. Napier concluded, "The struggle over interpersonal distance is one of the most important dimensions in marriage" (p. 12).

At least seven different dimensions can be subsumed under the rubric of distance. Many of these dimensions may overlap; however, they are not isomorphic. Thus, distance can be assessed through these and assuredly through additional dimensions. We need to analyze distance as an important metaphor for family functioning and dysfunctioning. What does distance mean, and what does the term mean when it is used in the family therapy literature? (Table 1).

Table 1

Polar opposites of various dimensions used to define distance among family members

Separation .... Individuation*
Separateness .... Closeness†
Distance .... Intimacy
Symbiosis .... Autism‡
Fusion .... Alienation
Cohesiveness .... Chaos
Togetherness .... Apartness§

* See Farley, J. E., "Family Separation—Individuation Tolerance—Developmental Conceptualization of the Nuclear Family," *Journal of Marital and Family Therapy* 5 (1979), pp. 61–67.
† See Napier, A. Y., "The Rejection-Intrusion Pattern: A Central Family Dynamic," *Journal of Marriage and Family Counseling* 4 (1978), pp. 5–12.
‡ See L'Abate, L., *Understanding and Helping the Individual in the Family* (New York: Grune & Stratton, 1976).
§ See Rosenblatt, P. C., Titus, S. L., and Cunningham, M. R., "Disrespect, Tension, and Togetherness—a Partner in Marriage," *Journal of Marital and Family Therapy* 5 (1979), pp. 47–54.

DEFEATS

What is a defeat? Any transaction, including incomplete or unfinished transactions, that has adverse, painful, destructive consequences on the process and outcome of a relationship may be viewed as a defeat. Defeats refer to transactions that result in a loss or lowering of individual functioning, whether at intrapsychic/genotypic levels (such as self-esteem) or at descriptive levels (such as lowering the ability to negotiate and to conduct transactions successfully). Any loss or lowering of individual functioning affects the whole system. Even when a loss seems to be another person's victory, the victory is bound to be short-lived. Whoever has been defeated will seek revenge or will try to balance the account reactively (Boszormenyi-Nagy & Spark, 1973).

Defeats are the outcome of an interpersonal process based on mutually frustrating, reciprocally hurtful, and self-other–demeaning interactions. Defeats encompass behaviors that range from avoidance, abuse, and put-downs to coercive acts, neglect, not caring, and violence. Individual defeats become systemic defeats: That is, defeats lower functioning at all levels of the system—individual, dyadic, and family.

It is important, however, to consider the hypothesis that defeats regulate distance among family members, correcting the system's distancing processes by bringing some of the members together through the defeat. Without defeats, the system would distance itself even more and would ultimately come apart. Thus, defeats are necessary to maintain the equilibrium of the family system. Defeats demonstrate that the family is still alive and kicking—struggling and fighting. They demonstrate that the family has not given up and that the members care enough to expend energy in correction. The correction may be negative and coercive, but defeat is better than giving up and being indifferent.

An analysis of interpersonal behavior in terms of defeats and victories allows us to evaluate patterns of successes and failures that relate quantitatively as well as qualitatively to functionality and dysfunctionality in families. The qualitative aspect of an apparent defeat includes considerations of the inner feelings of the persons involved and the context of the event. The terms used to describe defeats (i.e., failures, losses/victories, successes, gains, rewards) may be irrelevant; what is relevant is the process, the outcome, and the effect on future transactions in the family. The greater the frequency, the intensity, and the duration of these defeats, the greater the degree of intra- and extrafamilial dependence.

DEPENDENCE

Dependence is a behavior by which a person remains attached to, is forced to rely on, cannot cope or survive without, external support— economic, emotional, or physical. From the preceding sections, we can conclude that defeats in the family system reduce the level of autonomy and increase the dependence of the persons involved. The more functional the system, the greater the members' degree of autonomy and the greater the members' awareness of interdependence. The less functional the system, the more the members rely on each other and on external sources (Lewis, Beavers, Gossett, & Phillips, 1976). Of course, dependence can be and often is ignored (Wortman, 1981). For instance, criminals deny dependence on anybody; however, when incarcerated, they become totally dependent on the setting of which they are a part.

Sigmund Freud associated dependence with the oral stage of development, during which an infant, to survive, must be dependent on a caretaker. Anna Freud focused on dependence as the first of eight phases ranging from dependence to emotional self-reliance: *(a)* biological dependence on caretaker, *(b)* need fulfillment, *(c)* object-constancy of mother, *(d)* preoedipal clinging, *(e)* phallic-oedipal phase, *(f)* latency, *(g)* preadolescence, and *(h)* adolescence.

Kelly (1955) postulated that each child forms dependency constructs from being inconsistently and contradictorily indulged, overindulged, frustrated, and punished. Perhaps because of these inconsistencies, most children grow up to develop fairly permeable and flexible dependency constructs, relying on different people for different objectives.

Dependence-interdependence thus becomes a dimension along which many family transactions can be explained. Dependence may be expressed in different ways and at different levels; independence is seen as a denial of dependence. Both are dysfunctional. Interdependence means minimal reliance on external sources and the realistic recognition that all persons are *(a)* interdependent, but *(b)* clearly dependent on some occasions, certainly in crisis or in sickness. In a more realistic continuum, dependence and independence are superseded by a higher construct—interdependence.

Dependence has not received the attention it deserves in the family therapy literature. In fact, almost no references to it can be found in encyclopedic treatises, past (Howells, 1971) or present (Gurman & Kniskern, 1981).

Dependence as a systemic concept

Dependence, more than any other concept in traditional psychology, is systemic by its very nature, implying reliance on someone else. The rationale for using the concept of dependence is as follows: First, there is a large body of literature, empirical (Gevitz, 1976) and clinical (Bowlby, 1969, 1973, 1980), on dependence. Second, the dependence concept can easily be grasped by most families. Third, dependence as a concept is developmentally valid throughout the life cycle. Fourth, dependence need not be used overtly and verbally with families but can be used as an explanatory construct (L'Abate, 1964, 1976) that can help us understand families. Defeats are visible at the presentational and phenotypical levels (that is, at descriptive levels); dependence is an inferred concept that can also be used at the genotypical (or explanatory) level. Fifth, dependence—an emotional, supposedly irrational process—can be reduced to an approach-avoidance, spatial dimension, as postulated by L'Abate (1976). It is, therefore, an affective process that is easily observable and assuredly measurable. Dependence is based on need, liking, or whatever intrapsychic constructs one may want to use. Because dependence can be used as overt behavior or as inferred construct, it must be differentiated at various levels of description and explanation.

Dependence can, of course, be considered on a structured continuum, ranging from extreme symbiosis at one polarity to extreme independence, or alienation, at the other, with interdependence—the most functional—in the middle. Alternatively, as will be discussed later, dependence may be considered on a developmental continuum, from attachment to autonomy.

Dependence and attachment

Bowlby's three-volume series on attachment and loss, which stresses the importance of attachment in human development, is a contribution so monumental that it defies summary. Attachment is now considered as important as mating and parental behaviors. The behavioral system develops as a result of interactions with the environment and with the principal attachment figures in the environment.

Recognition of attachment in humans has come slowly, probably because the human infant (in comparison with other animals) is so immature at birth and because attachment behavior appears more slowly in humans. Attachment is easily recognized in other animals; attachment in humans has not been considered in the same category as attachment in other species.

Bowlby (1969) described an attachment behavior continuum from the lowest primate to advanced man. In the least advanced species, the infant does most of the clinging; in the most advanced, the mother initially maintains the contact. Attachment aids survival in protecting the infant from predators. According to Bowlby, this idea does not contradict theories that attachment is necessary before the child can learn from the mother. Nevertheless, protection from predators is, he contended, the primary reason for attachment behavior.

Bowlby (1982) updated the historical background of attachment theory and reviewed the accumulation of empirical evidence that separation, loss, mourning, and maternal deprivation during the early years adversely influence personality development. He defined attachment behavior as:

> any form of behavior that results in a person attaining or maintaining *proximity* [my italics] to some other clearly identified individual who is conceived as better able to cope with the world. . . . Whilst attachment behavior is at its most obvious in early childhood, it can be observed throughout the life cycle, especially in emergencies. . . . By conceptualizing attachment in this way, as a fundamental form of behavior, with its own internal motivation distinct from feeding and sex, and of no less importance for survival, the behavior and motivation are accorded a theoretical status never before given them. (pp. 668–669)

Bowlby proceeded to equate attachment and dependence/dependency needs. He did note, however, that equating the terms has "serious disadvantages": *(a)* dependence has a negative ("pejorative") connotation; *(b)* dependence does not imply what the term *attachment* does—that is, an "emotionally charged relationship with one or a very few clearly preferred individuals" (p. 669); and *(c)* dependence performs no worthwhile biological function.

Murray-Parkes and Stevenson-Hinde (1982) and Ende and Harmon (1982) considered various implications that attachment and attachment disorders have for the etiology of personality and personality disorders. Huntington (1982) related attachment and object relations theory to divorce and remarriage.

Dependence and social-learning theory

Dependence is an important variable for those who have attempted to integrate the hard-nosed orientation of learning theory with the intuitive and clinical insights of psychoanalytic thinking (e.g., O. H. Mower, R. R. Sears, N. Miller, J. Dollard, and, more recently, A. Bandura). Dependence, according to this school, is manifested through attention-seeking behavior (clinging and efforts to be physically close to the adult). Giving in to this behavior through attention and affection makes these contingent behaviors become reinforcers for the child's attention-seeking and ego-dependence. Fears (of the dark, of being alone, of strangers) can also be considered signs of dependence that produce reinforcing responses from the caretaker. The mother, of course, is likely to be the first adult to promote, provoke, and promulgate such behaviors.

An additional feature in the development of dependent behaviors is their generalization to other persons after they have been reinforced by the mother. Because the need to be dependent may run counter to adult expectations for independence and self-reliance, conflict between the child and the adult caretaker may ensue. Dependence soon becomes related to inconsistent and contradictory practices that eventually produce conflicts about dependence in the growing child. Dependence may be rewarded, as in many Latin cultures, or it may be punished, as in many WASP cultures.

A social-learning theorist, Sears (1963) paid a great deal of attention to dependence, distinguishing five different dependence patterns: *(a)* negative attention seeking, mainly through acting-out behaviors and negativism; *(b)* reassurance seeking, through apologies, asking unnecessary permissions, or seeking protection, comfort, consolation, and guidance; *(c)* positive attention seeking, through cooperation and compliance; *(d)* touching and holding; and *(e)* physical closeness.

Under the rubric of social approach-avoidance, Maccoby and Jacklin (1974) reviewed most of the research on touching and proximity to parents, resistance to separation from parents, and touching and proximity to nonfamily adults. From their review, they concluded:

> The tendency to seek close contact with attachment objects or their surrogates does not appear to be differentiated by sex during the childhood years when this kind of behavior is most apparent—as children grow older, they less and less often seek comfort or protection through closeness to an adult. (p. 201)

Under attachment behaviors, Maccoby and Jacklin listed proximity seeking and clinging behavior (i.e., distance!).

Bee (1971) showed how social-class variables influence the problem solving that mothers directly or indirectly foster in their children. Middle-class mothers provide all the verbal techniques that allow children to learn independent problem solving (p. 209): *(a)* asking questions rather than making statements, *(b)* making very few specific suggestions (so that children can find out for themselves), *(c)* giving positive feedback, and *(d)* having little physical involvement with the children. These findings support those of Hertzig, Birch, Thomas, and Mendez (1968), who also showed how cultural factors provide training for dependence or independence. According to their study, American children are better trained for independence than are Puerto Rican children, who are trained to stay dependent upon their families. It is clear from the work of Bee (1971), as well as that of Hertzig et al., that dependence-independence cannot be separated from problem solving. Most of the evidence suggests that functional families have better problem-solving skills than do dysfunctional families (Klein & Hill, 1979).

Dependence and intimate styles

We can postulate a progression of three stages: *(a)* symbiosis-autism, *(b)* dependence-independence, and *(c)* autonomy-interdependence. The three stages converge to some degree with the A–R–C model described in Table 2.

Support for the validity of a conception of apathy, abuse, and autism (A) comes from Polanski and his associates' (Polanski, Chalmers, Butterwieser, & Williams, 1981) work with neglectful parents. Their key construct is the "apathy-futility syndrome." Neglectful parents are enmeshed in a long-lasting style of social isolation that reaches back to childhood or adolescence. They have few or no friends and are not involved in neighborhood or civic groups. The isolation seems to stem from a personal philosophy of life and a style of relating to the world that sets them apart from normal social relations.

The isolation escalates, multiplying their feelings of social and interpersonal inadequacy. All these factors tend to render the parents extremely infantile in interpersonal relationships, unable to fulfill even simple social relationships. The outcome is extreme dependence on external sources; the parents have underlying feelings of hopelessness, helplessness, and frustration, which Polanski called apathy-futility and which make it very difficult for social agencies to help in any way. The cycle is repeated in the children of such parents: Emotional deprivation in early childhood leads to impaired intellectual functioning, social detachment, and withdrawal.

Table 2

Dependence and styles in intimate relationships*

Styles	A Apathetic-abusive Symbiosis-alienation	R Reactive-repetitive Sameness-oppositeness	C Conductive-creative Similarity-differentness
Amount of change	Least	Same	Most
Locus of control	External	Contradictory, internal-external	Internal
Field-dependence (perceptual)	Dependent	Ambivalent	Independent
Amount of dependence	Extreme or extremely denied	Inconsistent	Autonomously interdependent
Degree of functionality	Minimal to nonexistent	Variable interpersonal conflicts, "psychoneuroses," divorces, litigations, etc.	Consistently higher depression and situational crises
Representative pathologies	Schizophrenia, murder, physical and chemical abuse		

* Source: L'Abate, L., "Styles in Intimate Relationships: The A–R–C Model," *Personnel and Guidance Journal* 63 (1983), pp. 277–83.

Polanski's conception of apathy-futility is also supported by clinical evidence on poor, black, single parents, for whom four major characteristics were reported (Wortman, 1981): depression, danger (of ever-present violence), dependence, and denial of dependence. The conception includes physical and pharmacological abuse, along with a pattern of giving up and feelings of uselessness, worthlessness, and hopelessness.

Dependence and autonomy

A cross-cultural core problem for individuals and for the social systems of which they are part is autonomy and dependence. An individual in any society must learn to function both as an autonomous whole, or self, and as part of the social group, for both individual and group to survive. (Schwartzman, 1982b, p. 285)

Beavers (1982) differentiated between healthy and midrange families according to intimacy seeking in the healthy families versus control seeking in midrange families. Healthy families encourage autonomy; midrange families foster dependence. Essentially the same findings had been shown in Riskin's (1980) work with "nonlabeled" families.

Midrange implies a reactive orientation (R); healthy implies a conductive orientation (C) (Table 2).

Schwartzman (1982a, 1982b) noted that one of the most pervasive themes in the incongruent messages in the families of schizophrenics relate to autonomy and dependence (Litz, 1963; Lu, 1962; Weakland & Jackson, 1958):

> Often, parental demands for autonomy, to which the adolescent responds, are then redefined as demands for dependence, and vice versa, so that the adolescent's responses are always defined as the result of wrong perceptions. . . . A result is that the transformation from a dependent to a more autonomous relationship vis-à-vis the environment, the "core" problem for successful adaptation, is never achieved. (Schwartzman, 1982b, pp. 118–119)

Summers and Walsh (1981) broke down the process of symbiotic enmeshment into six variables: *(a)* undifferentiation, *(b)* dependence, *(c)* intervention, *(d)* disapproval of other relationships, *(e)* separation difficulty, and *(f)* injunctions. Using projective techniques (Thematic Apperception Test and Make-A-Picture Story) with parents of schizophrenics ($n = 17$), parents of nonschizophrenic hospitalized patients ($n = 14$), and parents of normals ($n = 55$), they found that mothers of schizophrenics tended to be symbiotically attached to their husbands and viewed their husbands as having the same kind of attachment to them. The fathers of schizophrenics did not tend to be symbiotically involved with their wives, but they failed to affirm them.

Although the term *autonomous interdependence* evolved in the writing of this chapter, concordance and convergence can be found in a chapter by Cohler and Geyer (1982), who focused on the continuous struggle between autonomy/interdependence and the need to be taken care of and to be dependent within the family. Much of their conception is based on the works of Boszormenyi-Nagy and Spark (1973) and of Mahler and her associates (Mahler et al., 1975) on separation and individuation. They also presented data to support the conclusion that despite widespread mobility, most families tend to stay close to the wives' families; husbands usually become more distant from their families of origin. Cohler and Geyer called such closeness "affectional dependence."

> Conflict over the issues of dependency and mutual obligations between adults and their parents is one of the most important of the interpersonal conflicts that adults in our society confront. It is generally expected the adults in this society will strive to become autonomous and self-reliant, remaining independent of their own parents and expressing little continuing need for their own parents' assistance and affection. (Cohler & Geyer, p. 205)

Parens and Saul (1971) differentiated two kinds of dependence: *(a)* libidinal, or affectional, dependence based on the need to be taken care of, to feel supported and protected; and *(b)* ego-developmental, or informational, dependence based on the need to master an uncertain and uncontrollable reality. They also borrowed from Goldfarb (1965) an important concept that needs to be elaborated: pseudoindependence—that is, ego-developmental dependence that is used to mask the need for libidinal and affectional dependence. Another important meaning strictly specific to the ambivalence is waving the flag of independence ("I can take care of myself") while dependent ("Can you give me some money?").

> Interdependence rather than total independence characterizes family relationships, and adults must be able to feel comfortable depending upon others for support and assistance. Some balance must be struck between the attainment of appropriate autonomy and the continuing need that all adults have for help from others, including such important family members as adults' own parents, or, as a result of aging, adult offspring. (Cohler & Geyer, 1982, p. 374)

Feldman (1982) wrote of "mature dependency" (p. 359) as "interdependency" (p. 374). Bach and Wyden (1968) recognized the interdependence of intimates even (or especially) when they fight (p. 154). The interdependence concept has also been considered by Goldsmith (1982) in the context of the postdivorce family system.

Discussion

The review of the literature leads to the following conclusions: (1) Dependence is a pervasive, relevant concept that researchers and theorists of many different schools have considered important enough to include in their studies and their theories. (2) Dependence is so pervasive a behavior that it cuts across gender differences, ages, socioeconomic backgrounds, education, and ethnic and cultural differences. (3) Dependence is visible at a descriptive level in many behaviors, but can also be considered at a more genotypical level as representing internal "needs" or "drive" states. (4) One might reject an intrapsychic, or internal, view of dependence (as a drive state) because dependence implies an interpersonal and transactional perspective. (5) To talk about dependence, one must describe under what conditions and on whom one is relying. (6) Dependence, then, is also a systemic concept that allows transition from an individual viewpoint to a multiperson, contextual (i.e., familial) perspective. (7) Other issues arise in using the dependence concept, such as distinguishing nurturance from instrumentality. Nurturance is symbolic dependence; instrumentality is the physical expression of dependence (e.g., food, money, room and board, college expenses). Nurturance connotes the verbal and nonverbal expression of love and caring (e.g., "I love you," hugs and kisses, touching).

AN INTEGRATIVE MODEL

Table 3 is an attempt to show the integration of the three concepts: distance, defeats, and dependence.

In this model, distance and attachment are inversely related, defeats follow an inverted, U-shaped curve, with many of the extremes at the ends and fewer in the middle. L'Abate's (1976) dialectical model of differentiation predicts autism and alienation at the extreme of disengagement and symbiosis at the extreme of enmeshment. Beavers' (1982) centrifugality and centripetality fit into this model, the middle of which is accounted for by factors such as differentiation, individuation, and eventually, autonomous interdependence.

Explanation versus description

As discussed at the beginning of the chapter, the issue of explanation raises the issue of description. Can we describe without explaining? Will a specific description explain sufficiently? These questions are, of course, too important and too complex to be dealt with in one chapter. The significant point here is that description can be immense, using a veritable mass of concepts, ideas, and dimensions. Explanation, on the other hand, encompasses fewer concepts and reduces descriptions, however detailed, to a few manageable dimensions (e.g., differentiation, mastery, control, self-esteem). Such unitary explanatory concepts are usually inferred from detailed descriptions; consequently, they become hypothetical entities rather than measurable constructs. If measurable, their relationships to observable behaviors will be tenuous. Explanation, then, is a logical level different from description: Description may rely on observations, measurements, and controls; explanation may be more intuitively theoretical and attributionally vaguer than description.

Any pat explanation may become limited by repetitive generality (Scheflen, 1980). An explanation must fit a family's specific situation. Admittedly, explanation for distance, defeats, and dependence may be used as a pat answer to all the problems of family dysfunctions; but in using any explanation, one must tread gently between too much generality and too much specificity.

Therapeutic implications

Therapeutically, distance, defeats, and dependence should be reframed as *(a)* the expression of passion that is not otherwise expressed

Table 3

A model of distance, defeats, and dependence

Stages in the development of dependence

DISTANCE	ATTACHMENT	DEFEATS	Process	Disengagement	Extreme
Maximal	A **Minimal**	**Many**	⎰ Autism	Denial of	independence
D	T	D	⎱ Centrifugal / Acting out	dependence	(isolation)
I	T	E			
S	T	F			
T	A	E (Relatively	⎰ Differentia-	Balanced	Intimacy
A	C (Optimal)	A fewer)	⎱ tion	dependence	Autonomous
N	H	T			interdependence
C	M	S	⎰ Obsessive	Enmeshment	Extreme
E	E	**Many**	⎱ Symbiosis / Centripetal	Overdependence	dependence
Minimal	N				(folie à deux)
	T **Maximal**				

constructively; *(b)* the link—the glue—that keeps the family together (After all, what would the family do without defeats? The family members might drift apart, and eventually the whole family would break down.) (L'Abate & Farr, 1981); *(c)* the expression of love, caring, and protectiveness that each member feels for the rest of the family ("As long as each of you defeats the rest, there is no fear that the family will change—and change is a very threatening process."); *(d)* the avoidance of closeness and intimacy ("because intimacy is scary and to be avoided, it is better that the family go on defeating itself").

If positively reframed, defeats can be prescribed: "I like the way you keep defeating each other. The more you defeat each other, the more dependent you are on each other. I want you to keep on defeating each other until you think of something else to do." Or, "As long as you defeat each other, you will need to depend on each other. Consequently, I feel that it is important that you go on defeating each other to stay dependent."

Dependence also should be portrayed positively rather than negatively; otherwise, families will reject it as they will reject any other negative construct (even though dependence may be the major characteristic of dysfunctional families).

If the therapist is loath to prescribe positively reframed behaviors or is afraid of being too paradoxical or circular, a more linear approach can be followed. Have all family members list (possibly in writing) how they defeat other family members and how other members defeat them. After each member has discussed his or her list, all members revise their lists to reflect the new information received. Throughout the process, the therapist should ask the family to continue defeating itself—for the reasons already listed and also because they may enjoy it. If they enjoy defeating, why give it up? After all, winning may be boring, or "The devil we have is better than the devil we may get."

Inevitably, the family will split between those who want to win and those who want to keep on defeating. This split is the first step in change because the issue of closeness and separation becomes paramount. How can those who want to win differentiate themselves from those who do not? Now the process is to train members to become conductors and nonreactors (Table 2). One way of working toward this goal is to help all the members *(a)* develop individual mantras, which are to be repeated silently whenever they are confronted by defeating behaviors (e.g., "Because you rob banks, I do not have to rob banks"); *(b)* assign a routine of positive chores to avoid saluting the negative flags hoisted by the defeating member (e.g., taking out the garbage, vacuuming, making a bed); *(c)* develop the use of "I" statements that may explain how one feels about another family member's defeating behavior but that allow one to be close to the defeating person, without ignoring or making him or her feel rejected and in need of further defeating escalations.

Defeats are necessary: They are grist for the therapeutic mill. Without them, the therapist becomes defeated. Defeats attest to the aliveness and reactivity of the family system. In fact, this is another positive reframing that can be made to the family: "I prefer to see you defeat one another than to see you indifferent or uncaring toward one another. Defeats mean that you are actively struggling and passionately involved with one another. I would be concerned, and I would not know what to do without your defeats. Defeats bring you together. What would happen if you failed to defeat each other?"

In working with issues of dependence, a therapist needs to be sensitive to cultural factors. As mentioned earlier, American children are socialized toward independence and denial of dependence, in contrast to Puerto Rican children, who exemplify the opposite process of Latin cultures—that is, the valuing of dependence and the avoidance of independence. In general, dependence seems to be a dirty word in the American culture. One needs only to use the term with adolescents to see their negative reactions to it. Consequently, one must reframe dependence as the positive opposite—interpreting defeats and dependence as "attempts at independence" and ways of achieving distance.

CONCLUSION

This chapter has introduced three psychological concepts—distance, defeats, and dependence—that have systemic meaning: that is, they have meaning in relationships rather than in a vacuum. These concepts have been linked with one another and with other systemic processes and intimate styles. An integrative model for all three concepts has been introduced, and therapeutic implications have been discussed.

REFERENCES

Acock, A. C., Barker, D., & Bergston, V. L. Mother employment and parent-youth similarity. *Journal of Marriage and the Family,* 1982, *44,* 441–455.

Anderson, S. H., & Russell, C. S. Utilizing process and content in designing paradoxical interventions. *American Journal of Family Therapy,* 1982, *10,* 48–60.

Ardrey, R. *The territorial imperative.* New York: Atheneum Publishers, 1966.

Bach, G. R., & Wyden, P. *The intimate enemy: How to fight fair in love and marriage.* New York: Morrow, 1968.

Barton, C., & Alexander, J. B. Functional family therapy. In A. S. Gurman & D. P. Kniskern (Eds.), *Handbook of family therapy.* New York: Brunner/Mazel, 1981.

Baxter, J. C. Interpersonal spacing in natural settings. *Sociometry,* 1970, *33,* 444–445.

Beavers, W. R. Healthy, midrange, and severely dysfunctional families. In F. Walsh (Ed.), *Normal family processes.* New York: Guilford Press, 1982.

Bee, H. L. Socialization for problem solving. In J. Aldous, T. Coudou, K. Hill, M. Strauss, & I. Tallman (Eds.), *Family problem solving.* Hinsdale, Ill.: Dryden Press, 1971.

Birdwhistle, R. L. *Kinesics and context.* Philadelphia: University of Pennsylvania Press, 1970.

Booraem, C. D., & Flowers, J. V. Reduction of anxiety and personal space as a function of assertion training with severely disturbed neuropsychiatric patients. *Psychological Reports,* 1972, *30,* 923–929.

Boss, P. O., & Whitaker, C. Dialogue on separation: Clinicians as educators. *Family Relations,* 1979, *21,* 391–398.

Boszormenyi-Nagy, I., & Spark, G. M. *Invisible loyalties.* New York: Harper & Row, 1973.

Bowlby, J. *Attachment and loss* (Vol. I): *Attachment.* New York: Basic Books, 1969.

Bowlby, J. *Attachment and loss* (Vol. II):*Separation, anxiety and anger.* New York: Basic Books, 1973.

Bowlby, J. *Attachment and loss* (Vol. III): *Loss, sadness and depression.* New York: Basic Books, 1980.

Bowlby, J. Attachment and loss: Retrospect and prospect. *American Journal of Orthopsychiatry,* 1982, *52,* 213–222.

Byng-Hall, J., & Campbell, D. Resolving conflicts in family distance regulation: An integrative approach. *Journal of Marital and Family Therapy,* 1981, *8,* 321–330.

Cohler, B. J., & Geyer, S. Psychological autonomy and interdependence within the family. In F. Walsh (Ed.), *Normal family processes.* New York: Guilford Press, 1982.

Connolly, P. R. *An investigation of the perception of personal space and its meaning among black and white Americans.* Unpublished doctoral dissertation, University of Iowa, 1974.

Dabbs, J. M., & Stokes, N. A. Beauty is power: The use of space on the sidewalk. *Sociometry,* 1975, *38,* 551–557.

Druckman, D., Rozella, R. M., & Baxter, J. C. *Nonverbal communication: Survēy, theory, and research.* Beverly Hills, Calif.: Sage Publications, 1982.

Duke, M. P., & Nowicki, S. A new measure and social learning model for interpersonal distance. *Journal of Experimental Research in Personality,* 1972, *6,* 119–132.

Edward, J., Ruskin, N., & Turrini, P. *Separation-individuation: Theory and application.* New York: Gardner Press, 1981.

Ende, R. N., & Harmon, R. J. (Eds.). *The development of attachment and affiliative systems.* New York: Plenum Press, 1982.

Farley, J. E. Family separation-individuation tolerance—a developmental conceptualization of the nuclear family. *Journal of Marital and Family Therapy,* 1979, *5,* 61–67.

Feldman, L. B. Sex roles and family dynamics. In F. Walsh (Ed.), *Normal family processes.* New York: Guilford Press, 1982.

Ferber, A. Introduction: Teachers and learners. In A. Ferber, M. Mendelsohn, & A. Napier (Eds.), *The book of family therapy.* New York: Science House, 1972.

Fisher, S. Motivation for patient delay. *Archives of General Psychiatry,* 1967, *16,* 676–678.

Fisher, S., & Cleveland, S. E. *Body image and personality* (2d ed.). New York: Dover, 1968.

Frankel, A. S., & Barrett, J. Variations in personal space as a function of authoritarianism, self-esteem, and racial characteristics of a stimulus situation. *Journal of Consulting and Clinical Psychology,* 1971, *37*(1) 95–98.

Freud, A. *The writings of Anna Freud.* New York: International Universities Press, 1965–1974.

Gevitz, J. L. The attachment organization process as evidenced in the maternal conditioning of an infant responding (particularly crying). *Human Development,* 1976, *19,* 143–155.

Goldfarb, A. Psychodynamics and the three-generation family. In E. Thomas & G. Streig (Eds.), *Social structure and the family: Generational relations.* Englewood Cliffs, N.J.: Prentice-Hall, 1965.

Goldsmith, J. The postdivorce family system. In F. Walsh (Ed.), *Normal family processes.* New York: Guilford Press, 1982.

Gurman, A. S., & Kniskern, D. P. (Eds.). *Handbook of family therapy.* New York: Brunner/Mazel, 1981.

Hall, E. T. *The hidden dimension.* Garden City, N.Y.: Doubleday Publishing, 1966.

Hansen, J. C., & L'Abate, L. *Approaches to family therapy.* New York: Macmillan, 1982.

Hartnett, J. J., Bailey, K. G., & Gibson, W. F. Personal space as influenced by sex and type of movement. *Journal of Psychology,* 1970, *76,* 139–144.

Hediger, H. *Wild animals in captivity.* London: Butterworth, 1950.

Henry, J. *Pathways to madness.* New York: Random House, 1971.

Hertzig, M. E., Birch, H. G., Thomas, A., & Mendez, O. A. Clan and ethnic differences in the responsiveness of preschool children to cognitive demands. *Monographs of the Society for Research in Child Development,* 1968, *33*(1).

Heshka, S., & Nelson, Y. Interpersonal speaking distance as a function of age, sex and relationship. *Sociometry,* 1972, *35,* 491–498.

Heslin, R., & Patterson, M. L. *Nonverbal behavior and social psychology.* New York: Plenum Press, 1982.

Hess, R. D., & Handel, G. *Family worlds.* Chicago: University of Chicago Press, 1969.

Hinde, R. *Toward understanding relationships.* New York: Academic Press, 1979.

Horowitz, M. J., Duff, D. F., & Stratton, L. S. Body buffer zone. *Archives of General Psychiatry,* 1964, *11,* 651–656.

Howells, J. J. *Theory and practice of family psychiatry.* New York: Brunner/Mazel, 1971.

Huntington, D. S. Attachment, loss and divorce: A reconsideration of the concepts. In L. Messinger (Ed.), *Therapy with remarriage families.* Rockville, Md.: Aspen, 1982.

Jones, S. E., & Aiello, J. R. Proxemic behavior of black and white first- and third- and fifth-grade children. *Journal of Personality and Social Psychology,* 1973, *25*(1), 21–27.

Kantor, E., & Lehr, W. *Inside the family: Toward a theory of family process.* San Francisco: Jossey-Bass, 1975.

Kelly, G. A. *The psychology of personal constructs* (Vols. 1–2). New York: W. W. Norton, 1955.

Kinzel, A. F. Body-buffer zone in violent prisoners. *American Journal of Psychiatry,* 1970, *127,* 99–104.

Klein, D. M., & Hill, R. Determinants of family problem-solving effectiveness. In W. R. Burr, R. Hill, F. I. Nye, & I. L. Reiss (Eds.), *Contemporary theories about the family* (Vol. 1): *Research-based theories.* New York: Free Press, 1979.

Knapp, M. L. *Nonverbal communication in human interaction.* New York: Holt, Rinehart & Winston, 1972.

L'Abate, L. *Principles of clinical psychology.* New York: Grune & Stratton, 1964.

L'Abate, L. *Understanding and helping the individual in the family.* New York: Grune & Stratton, 1976.

L'Abate, L. Styles in intimate relationships: The A–R–C model. *Personnel and Guidance Journal,* 1983, *63,* 277–283.

L'Abate, L., & Farr, L. Coping with defeating patterns in family therapy. *Family Therapy,* 1981, *8,* 91–103.

Lerner, R. M. The development of personal space schemata toward body build. *Journal of Psychology,* 1973, *84,* 229–235.

Lewis, J. M., Beavers, W. R., Gossett, J. T., & Phillips, V. A. *No single thread: Psychological health in family systems.* New York: Brunner/Mazel, 1976.

Little, K. B. Personal space. *Journal of Experimental Social Psychology,* 1965, *1,* 237–247.

Litz, T. *The family and human adaptations.* New York: International Universities Press, 1963.

Lu, Y. Contradictory parental expectations in schizophrenia. *Archives of General Psychiatry,* 1962, *6,* 219–234.

Lynn, D. B. *Parental and sex role identifications: A theoretical formulation.* Berkeley, Calif.: McCutcheon, 1969.

Maccoby, E. E., & Jacklin, C. N. *The psychology of sex differences.* Stanford, Calif.: Stanford University Press, 1974.

Madanes, C. *Strategic psychotherapy.* San Francisco: Jossey-Bass, 1981.

Mahler, M., Pine, F., & Bergman, A. *The psychological birth of the human infant—symbiosis and individuation.* New York: Basic Books, 1975.

Mehrabian, A. Significance of posture and position in the communication of attitude and status relationships. *Psychological Bulletin,* 1969, *71,* 359–372.

Murray-Parkes, C., & Stevenson-Hinde, J. (Eds.). *The place of attachment in human behavior.* New York: Basic Books, 1982.

Napier, A. Y. The rejection-intrusion pattern: A central family dynamic. *Journal of Marriage and Family Counseling,* 1978, *4,* 5–12.

Olson, D. H., Sprenkle, D. H., & Russell, C. Circumplex model of marital and family systems: I. Cohesion and adaptability dimensions, family type, and clinical applications. *Family Process,* 1979, *18,* 3–28.

Parens, H., & Saul, L. *Dependence in man: A psychoanalytic study.* New York: International Universities Press, 1971.

Polanski, N. A., Chalmers, M. A., Butterwieser, E., & Williams, D. P. *Damaged parents: An anatomy of neglect.* Chicago: University of Chicago Press, 1981.

Powell, P. H., & Dabbs, J. M. Physical attractiveness and personal space. *Journal of Social Psychology,* 1976, *100,* 59–64.

Reiss, D. *The family's construction of reality.* Cambridge, Mass.: Harvard University Press, 1981.

Riskin, J. Research on "nonlabeled" families: A computudinal study. In F. Walsh (Ed.), *Normal family processes.* New York: Guilford Press, 1982.

Rosenblatt, P. C., Titus, S. L., & Cunningham, M. R. Disrespect, tension, and togetherness— a partner in marriage. *Journal of Marital and Family Therapy,* 1979, *5,* 47–54.

Rosenfeld, H. Effect of approval-seeking induction on interpersonal proximity. *Psychology Reports,* 1965, *17,* 120–122.

Rotter, J. *Social learning and clinical psychology.* Englewood Cliffs, N.J.: Prentice-Hall, 1954.

Scheflen, A. E. Susan smiled, or explanation in family therapy. In J. G. Howells (Ed.), *Advances in family psychiatry* (Vol. 2). New York: International Universities Press, 1980.

Schwartzman, J. Creativity, pathology, and family structure: A cybernetic metaphor. *Family Process,* 1982, *21,* 113–127. (a)

Schwartzman, J. Normality from a cross-cultural perspective. In F. Walsh (Ed.), *Normal family processes.* New York: Guilford Press, 1982. (b)

Sears, R. R. Dependency motivation. In M. R. Jones (Ed.), *Nebraska Symposium on Motivation.* Lincoln: University of Nebraska Press, 1963. Pp. 25–64.

Sommer, R. *Personal space.* Englewood Cliffs, N.J.: Prentice-Hall, 1969.

Sprenkle, D. H., & Olson, D. H. Circumplex model of marital systems: An empirical study of clinic and non-clinic couples. *Journal of Marriage and Family Counseling,* 1978, *4,* 59–74.

Stierlin, H. *Separating parents and adolescents: A perspective on running away, schizophrenia, and waywardness.* New York: Quadrangle–New York Times, 1974.

Summers, F., & Walsh, F. Symbiosis and confirmation between the parents of the schizophrenic. *Family Process,* 1981, *20,* 319–330.

Sundstrom, E., & Altman, I. Interpersonal relationships and personal space: Research review and theoretical model. *Human Ecology,* 1976, *4,* 47–67.

Tennis, G., & Dabbs, J. M. Sex, setting and personal space: First grade through college. *Sociometry,* 1975, *28,* 385–394.

Waxer, P. H. *Nonverbal aspects of psychotherapy.* New York: Praeger Publishers, 1978.

Weakland, J., & Jackson, D. D. Patient and therapist observations on the circumstances of a schizophrenic episode. *Archives of Neurology and Psychiatry,* 1958, *79,* 554–574.

Weitz, S. *Nonverbal communication: Readings and commentary.* New York: Oxford University Press, 1974.

Wortman, R. A. Depression, danger, dependency, denial: Work with poor, black, single parents. *American Journal of Orthopsychiatry,* 1981, *51,* 662–671.

Section Ten

Issues in Training

Chapter 41

Training in Family Psychology

GARY F. GANAHL
LUCY RAU FERGUSON
LUCIANO L'ABATE

LIMITATIONS OF MONADIC PSYCHOLOGY

The American Psychological Association (APA) has divisions for environment and population psychology, community psychology, and a Society for the Study of Social Issues, but no division devoted to the family. To our knowledge, the only specialty programs for training family psychologists are those at Georgia State University and Michigan State University (see Appendixes A & B of this *Handbook*). In other schools, family therapy may be taught as a special topic or treatment modality, but family courses are rarely required. Family approaches, unattached to programs, are stepchildren. They show up in child course sequences in one institution, in adult development in another, in general clinical in others. In some institutions, family courses are offered as electives for all areas; they are tangential to the program as a whole, and no single division is responsible for their development. Of the practicing professionals surveyed by Smith (1982), fewer than 5 percent of the respondents from the clinical and counseling subdivisions of APA identified family systems as their major area. Surprisingly, however, Jay Haley, a prominent family theorist, was ranked by respondents as 1 of the 10 most influential theorists. One source has reported that 34 percent of practicing psychologists were using family therapy in their work but that few had formal training other than workshops. This figure is in line with the 1965–1966 survey by the Group for the Advancement of Psychiatry (1970), which found that 40 percent of family therapy practitioners were social workers and another 40

percent were psychiatrists and psychologists. Master's-level professionals are much more likely to practice family therapy, and a number
of professional schools train marriage and family therapists—not marriage and family psychologists.

In recent surveys of psychology internship programs (Cooper, Rampage, & Soucy, 1981; Ganahl & L'Abate, 1983), a disproportionate
number cited psychiatrists as influential theorists; no psychologists were
cited as significant influences. The relative lack of family emphasis is
reminiscent of the early atomistic phases in the history of psychology,
when Lewin (1931) warned against the dangers of irrelevancy, narrow
empiricism, and the reductionistic fallacies that might arise from overlooking context and thus losing social reality.

The need to research individuals in context, as systems, call for
new methods and different thinking. The family situation may not
lend itself to the easily controlled variables and the specificity of the
S–R or S–O–R models of reality, but will avoid the problem of creating
a research environment that is too sterile to provide useful answers.
Although methodological and statistical rigor is to be valued for its
obvious benefits to the scientific endeavor, rigor without regard for
context will lead only to experimentally elegant irrelevancies. Atomistic research tendencies, which lead to deadlocked research and theory
development (Capra, 1982), are present elsewhere as well. Social psychologists still study the group and generalize to the family context
despite the minimal overlap between group and family situations (Bodin, 1966; Strodtbeck, 1954). Indeed, little overlap exists between the
family in the laboratory and the family engaged in identical tasks in
their natural environment (O'Rourke, 1963).

FAMILY PHOBIA

Why have psychologists been so hesitant to address systemic, contextual, and social concerns at the marital and family levels? Medicine
is noting the family's effects on the physical systems of the family
members (Huygen, 1982), and at least one journal *(Family Systems
Medicine)* is devoted to this topic. Psychologists, however, are just
beginning to make the more-obvious connections between the family
and psychological development and stability (L'Abate, 1983). Despite
the tradition of contextual versus trait explanations of behavior (Mischel, 1968), the family, by and large, has been left out of research
and theory. Rausch, Barry, Hertel, and Swain (1974) went even further,
suggesting that not only should psychologists make these connections
but that any layman can and does make them. Nevertheless, psychological explanations for human experience often are based solely on inter-

pretations of intrapsychic phenomena. In defense of such interpretations, it must be said that the contextual interpretation of behavior is not as easy as it is sometimes made to appear.

Psychologists may be deterred from family approaches by current theoretical models. A change in theoretical orientation requires more than a change in one's perspective; it may call for a whole new theoretical orientation, a paradigmatic shift (Kuhn, 1972). This may have contributed, more than anything else, to the estrangement between family therapy and psychology, particularly in clinical psychology training programs. The theoretical orientations that have proven most used and most useful in family therapy, such as communications theory and systems theory, are derived from disciplines other than psychology. They are interpersonal in focus and require a shift from the reactional to the transactional understanding of behavior. Theoretical models that are based on circular causality and the Batesonian concept that mind is the total circuit of decision (Bateson, 1979, p. 102) are alien to the lineal, cause-effect, actor-reactor model in most psychological research (Bateson, 1971). Liddle (1978) and Beels and Ferber (1969) felt that this conceptual shock is the primary reason for the lack of acceptance of family psychology.

Training programs have emphasized psychology's medical, biological, and philosophical roots but have neglected the sociological and anthropological connections. Choosing to see man *in context* rather than *in vacuum* threatens one of psychology's most cherished and powerful functions—individual testing—and, along with it, the professional identity of psychologists. From a contextual view, current testing strategies may be inadequate, obsolete, or irrelevant (Byles, Bishop, & Horn, 1983; Caille, 1982; GAP, 1970; Keeney, 1979; Minuchin, 1974). The basic assessment of families consists of seeing how the family responds to the therapist's interventions rather than a separate, preliminary data-gathering phase directed by an objective, uninvolved professional. Jackson (1967) summed up the conceptual shift well:

> We will move from individual assessment to analysis of the contexts, or more precisely, the *system*, from which individual conduct is inseparable. We view symptoms, defenses, character structure and personality as terms describing the individual's typical interactions which occur in response to a particular interpersonal context rather than as intrapsychic entities. Since the family is the most influential learning context, surely a more detailed study of family process will yield valuable clues to the etiology of such typical modes of interaction. (pp. 139–140)

The preceding statement still conveys clear indications of lineal causality which, given the structure of our language, are hard to avoid. Bateson (1979) wrote a more-careful statement of the same point:

> It is nonsense to talk about "dependency" or "aggressiveness" or "pride" and so on. All such words have their roots in what happens between persons, not in some something-or-other inside a person.
> No doubt there is learning in the more particular sense. There are changes in A and changes in B which correspond to the dependency—succorance—of the relationship. But the relationship comes first. It *precedes.*
> Only if you hold on tight to the primacy and priority of relationship can you avoid dormitive explanations. The opium does not contain a dormitive principle, and the man does not contain an aggressive instinct. (p. 147)

Of course, everyone does not see family treatment as necessitating a new epistemological orientation. Some see family treatment simply as a new technique for achieving old (individual) goals. However, without the new orientation, psychologists find it difficult to use the method correctly (Hare-Musten, 1976). Framo's (1975) comments are instructive:

> It's very difficult to change individuals solely through the one-to-one relationship with a professional; it is necessary to change contexts, especially intimate ones. . . . Symptoms come to be viewed as by-products of pathological relationship events . . . , as epiphenomena of relationship struggles, and the focus is on the human context rather that psychopathology. (p. 16)

On the other hand, some family theorists need to appreciate more fully the reality of the individual. In general, there is an overriding need for a better understanding of the mutuality of the effects of various facts of life on the individual, a knowledge of how systems (e.g., job, home, family, and leisure), interact and affect the individual and how the individual in turn affects these systems or contexts. Just because the suprareality and the causality of the system are accepted, it does not follow that the individual should be ignored. Engel's (1977, 1980) model of systemic hierarchies and Koestler's (1978) model of holons are good starting points. Family psychologists must build bridges to the large data base that is the legacy of psychology, rather than toss it aside, in the eagerness of family psychology's adolescence, to create a new order.

Psychologists' avoidance of the family may also be due to the lack of a research base, but current empirical efforts are meeting that need (Gurman & Kniskern, 1981a; Pinsof, 1981). A tremendous amount of information is also available from other fields. Sociology, for example, has paid attention to the family life cycle, support systems, and many other areas that are relevant to psychological functioning.

Although research in family psychology is difficult, perhaps demanding new designs and conceptualizations, Gurman (1983) argued that the methods and designs that are familiar to psychologists have already advanced our knowledge of families and can continue to do so. In general, to justify a lack of involvement in family work on the basis of insufficient empirical findings is similar to arguing against involvement because of insufficient training. The justification is self-reflexive and self-perpetuating. As long as the interest in, and the demand for, training or data are lacking, neither will come easily.

A simpler explanation for the lack of family involvement may be that psychologists are not trained in family approaches and thus are uninterested because they are relatively ignorant of them (Liddle, Vance, & Pastushak, 1979). This explanation is related to, and interacts with, Stanton's (1975) belief that a natural conservativism exists in a discipline that is so young and whose members so recently achieved the opportunity to practice psychotherapy. Psychologists do not wish to risk a hard-won image of competence and professionalism on untested approaches.

In addition, psychologists may be reluctant to enter an area not claimed by one discipline. Although the involvement of many disciplines is an asset, perhaps psychologists (so recently free to practice independently) may prefer an area in which the role definitions are clear-cut. Hobbs (1964) suggested that psychologists had been avoiding interdisciplinary practice and agreed with Bauer (1971) that this avoidance has a negative impact on psychologists' social relevance and usefulness.

Whatever the reason for psychology's recalcitrance, the best course is probably to push for increased competence and to consider later the historical reasons for the delay. The change may be considerably eased, however, by better understanding of the position of those who oppose family theories and by sensitivity to the political realities of the situation (Liddle, 1978, 1982).

CLINICAL PSYCHOLOGY AND CLINICAL FAMILY PSYCHOLOGY

Although clinical psychologists have been among the pioneers in the family therapy movement and are currently prominent in such professional associations as American Family Therapy Association (AFTA), American Association of Marriage and Family Therapy (AAMFT), and the American Association of Orthopsychiatry, clinical work with families has developed largely outside traditional academic settings. The university training programs in family therapy have usually been in medical schools, schools of home economics, departments of family ecology or human development, or clinical sociology programs. Family training programs have also tended to be *interdisciplinary* rather than identified with any one discipline such as clinical psychology. The family therapy movement has been slow to infiltrate clinical psychology training programs, and even clinical child psychologists have traditionally focused on the individual child, viewing parents only as the causative agents in the development of pathology, as adjuncts to treatment, or as sources of assessment information.

A number of developments on the national scene suggest, however, that the pace of incorporating family work into clinical and professional training is accelerating. The National Institute of Mental Health (NIMH) has decided to withdraw support from traditional generic clinical training programs, which have focused mainly on work with individuals, and to support training only in special areas (including child and family mental health) considered to have national priority. The sites and the patterns of professional training in psychology have broadened and diversified. There are now programs in health psychology, pediatric psychology, and applied developmental psychology. Particularly in health psychology, psychologists (in collaboration with other health care professionals, including family physicians) are learning new professional roles. Expertise in family psychology is likely to be important, even predominant, in these newer professional roles and activities.

The patterns of community practice in agencies that deal with the mental health problems of children and youth, including pediatric care settings, exhibit an emphasis on family work. The changes that have already taken place may lead to the justifiable conclusion that the traditional emphasis on individual psychotherapy as the primary modality of intervention is becoming more and more obsolete.

Given the changes in the professional scene, what models for training will be best? Three different models seem useful:

1. The training of "transdisciplinary" family clinicians, not in departments of psychology or any other traditional academic or mental health discipline, but in special family institutes or professional schools that may gradually be incorporated into universities and other academic institutions. The training and expertise of the family clinicians would include elements of the traditional mental health specialties, family sociology, developmental psychology, organizational psychology and sociology, systems biology, communication theory. The prevailing perspective would be that of family systems theory.

2. The training of "family clinical psychologists." The Georgia State program is an example of such training in a university setting (see Appendix A). The California Graduate School of Marital and Family Therapy, which has recently developed a doctoral program in family clinical psychology, offers such training in an independent professional training institution.

3. The integration of *systematic* training in family work into more general clinical and professional psychology graduate programs. This

model is illustrated by the Child/Family Clinical Psychology Program at Michigan State University (see Appendix B). This program requires much more than one or two courses or even practica in family therapy.

Indications of change

A number of changes indicate that the neglect of family psychology is lessening. More and more psychologists are devoting attention to marriage and the family. Behaviorists have increasingly adapted their individualistic treatment strategies to units made up of more than one client and are including marriage and family interventions (see Patterson, Chapter 44 of this *Handbook*). The AAMFT's most recent poll of approved supervisors for marital and family work showed that psychology was the discipline of most of these supervisors. In a review of personality theory, Gilmore (1974) devoted 36 of 291 pages to a discussion and review of the family as a factor in personality formation. More and more family presentations are being made at psychological conventions, and more and more psychologists are engaging in marital and family therapy, theorizing, and research. Although at least one article (Smith, 1982) has suggested that family therapists are few, that conclusion may be an artifact of the ages and positions of the psychologists surveyed and the request that they identify only one area of interest (the predominant response was a nonspecific area—eclecticism). One interest group is pushing the APA to create a division for family, marital, and sex therapy and to grant diplomate status for expertise in these areas.

Need for family psychology

One of the indicators that a greater emphasis on family psychology training is needed derives from the experience of the many psychologists who are now engaged in clinical work. Even the clinicians who wish to work primarily in individual therapy find it hard to avoid working with families. An apparently individual issue often broadens into a family issue, or a child problem may turn out to involve adults in the family.

Although one can refer such problems to other clinicians, all practitioners will, in one way or another, be faced with family or larger systemic issues and will need training to identify these issues when they arise. One may not wish to refer cases when good rapport and a working relationship have developed, or one may not wish to refer a family or patient with whom one has tenuous contact because of fear that the family may not choose to follow up another referral, particularly if the clinician was not the first to see the patient. One may also prefer not to refer clients or relatives of clients in order to avoid the complications that may arise when more than one therapist works on a case. A clinician may worry that such referrals will contribute iatrogenically to the patient's problems (Selig, 1976). An important consideration for private practitioners is the loss of revenue and the disruption of practice that may result from referring too many cases.

Cases that broaden from the individual to the family have led increasing numbers of clinicians to seek training in family treatment. Sager, Grundlach, Kremer, Lenz, and Royce (1968), in their survey of the married in treatment, found that 50 percent of the patients who were in individual therapy but whose chief complaint and symptomatology were not related to their marriages eventually revealed indications of serious marital problems. Guerin, Veroff, and Feld (1960), in an investigation of treatment requests, found that 59 percent of the patients complained of some form of marital or family problems; an additional 6 percent presented problems having to do with a death of a relative or a loved one. In the widely used Holmes and Rahe Social Readjustment Rating Scale, which is designed to evaluate stressful life events, 26 of the 40 items are intrafamilial (Ransom, 1981), including 6 of the top 10 stressors. Beck and Jones (1974), in their assessment of the need for mental health services, reported the increased likelihood of having to work with problems concerning internal family relations, marriage, and childrearing. Similarly, the Florida Department of Health and Rehabilitative Services determined a need to encourage caseworkers to increase their use of family counseling (Anderson, Amatea, Munson, & Rudner, 1979). For example, children placed in foster care could have returned home more quickly or need not have been removed at all had family treatment been used before or after the removal.

VandenBos and Stapp (1983), who evaluated services provided by psychologists, reported that 66 percent of the providers of treatment were involved in some form of marital or family treatment. The psychologists who work primarily in educational settings reported that 42 percent of their time was spent in family-related treatment activities (second only to motivational and attitudinal problems, which they dealt with 46 percent of the time). By contrast, learning disabilities required 31 percent of their time. Such data are strong evidence of the need for training in family psychology and a reminder of the often-repeated criticism of training in traditional academic programs for clinical psychology: The programs do not pay enough attention to the needs of the persons and the agencies whom they are preparing students to serve (Pottharst, 1970).

Additional needs (for treatment) are indicated by the number of psychologists who currently supervise marital and family therapy. According to an analysis of AAMFT supervisors, 26 percent of the organization's approved supervisors were psychologists, the greatest number in any one discipline (Everett, 1980). In a survey of recently graduated clinical and counseling psychologists (McColley & Baker, 1982), 55 percent were reported to be supervising marital work and 51 percent supervising family work in a university within the first two years after their graduations. Of the psychologists who were working in internship sites, only 28 percent were offering supervision in marital and family therapy. The discrepancy between graduate school preparation and postdoctoral services was clear. Of the new professionals who offered marital and family supervision, only 56 percent had had supervised experience in such supervision, and fewer than 10 percent had received formal course work in such supervision. Further training in marital and family supervision was a need expressed by 88 percent of the group.

ETHICAL ISSUES

The lag in family conceptualization and training implies that many psychologists who practice family and marital therapy are violating Ethical Principles 2 and 4 of the APA (1963/1972): They are practicing a therapy for which their education and supervision have not sufficiently or specifically prepared them. Although this outcome may be largely due to the lack of available supervisors and training programs, the situation is of considerable importance and concern to our profession. How to evaluate competence in psychotherapy and supervision and whether academic training is even of benefit are debatable questions. Nevertheless, the offering of services by those not specifically prepared to deliver them, notwithstanding the service needs, is a problem. Singled out as a primary problem in services related to child and developmental issues (APA, 1973), the problem will continue until psychology develops a coherent body of family theory and data and offers systematic training in family assessment and intervention.

A larger but related ethical problem is that individual training shirks the obligation to assess the impact that individual intervention has on other family members. For example, case studies have been reported in which an improvement in child behavior was accompanied by a deterioration of the husband-wife relationship (Engelin, Knutson, Laugh, & Garlington, 1968).

To family therapists, theorists, and researchers, improvement in one family member obviously should not be gained at the cost of adverse effects on another. Family research is designed to assess the impact of individual change on the larger system (Gurman & Kniskern, 1978a). Although some individual therapists are concerned with that impact

(Fagan, 1970), such concern is rarely evident in practice or outcome. Individual therapy for marital discord may lead to problems for the spouse who is not seen in treatment (Gurman & Kniskern, 1978b; Hurvitz, 1967). As Boszormenyi-Nagy (1983) has noted, clients are not only those whom you see but also those whom you affect. Furthermore, choosing individual rather than conjoint therapy for marital problems may double the likelihood of divorce after therapy (Kniskern & Gurman, 1979). Similar questions arise about the impact that the individual treatment of a parent has on the children and the spouse or the impact that the individual treatment of a child has on siblings and the parents. The most important question was raised by Fox (1968) more than 15 years ago: Is it ethical to treat one person, ignoring the possible adverse effects on the spouse or other family members? This question, which has perhaps even greater relevance today, has been reintroduced by Margolin (1982).

Even if family psychology could be avoided altogether by the more traditional, individually oriented groups in psychology, they may for good reasons not wish to avoid it. Chief among the reasons are the priorities set by our national health governing bodies and the accumulating research that, in many instances, a family rather than an individual treatment orientation is preferable. The health policymakers at the national (APA, 1973; Beck & Jones, 1974; Joint Commission, 1970) and at the local (Anderson et al., 1979) levels are recognizing the need for family interventions. The consumers of mental health services, the market for the graduates of our schools, are seeking more family practitioners (e.g., see Byles et al., 1983). Other observers of the development of science and profession of psychology, particularly clinical psychology (Bauer, 1971; Capra, 1982), have also pointed to the pressing need to deal with mental illness and human suffering from a broader perspective, one that involves more interdisciplinary knowledge of social systems and context, if not interdisciplinary cooperation. The danger in avoiding a broader perspective is that we, as professionals, may contribute to the problems that we seek to eliminate, iatrogenically augmenting them by monadic, fragmented, Procrustean, and often self-serving approaches to service delivery (Selig, 1976).

CONCEPTUAL ISSUES

Conjoint family sessions, which are the best way of gaining accurate information about spouses' or children's behavior, may be an important basis for treatment decisions. Certainly, a therapist wishes to know whether the traits and the pathology attributed to significant others do indeed exist: Descriptions of patients do not necessarily match reality (Gordon, 1983; Lobitz & Johnson, 1975; Margolin, 1982). Miyoshi and Liebman (1969) report that as a result of their family training sessions, students perceived the development of a client's psychopathology earlier and more clearly because the client found it harder to deny, withhold, or distort information when the family was present. Students also learned to handle better the family's resistance to treatment and to involve the family in active helping roles. Further, they found that family approval of the treatment enhanced the patient's motivation for treatment.

Family approval is particularly important: The family often serves as an important part of the health delivery system and may pull the patient in or out of treatment as well as serving as a great enhancer or inhibitor of treatment depending upon how it is involved. Family involvement contradicts the tradition of avoiding families in analytic treatment but is more in keeping with the spirit of original analytic treatment, in which the analyst frequently knew much—firsthand or through the reports of others—about the patient's family background.

The family approach is reinforced by evidence that links family involvement to lower dropout rates in treatment (Gurman & Kniskern, 1978b). Another group of trainers in a predominantly individually oriented setting reported similar results: Observing families led to a better understanding of the individual and a more realistic appraisal of problems (Abel, Bruzzese, & Wilson, 1974). Schopler, Fox, and Cochrane (1967), in exposing medical students to families, found that observations of parents and children enabled the students to better appreciate family roles and attitudes, which are crucial in intensifying or minimizing pathology. Such exposure also helped to distinguish reactions to external features of the case and reactions to intrapsychic conflict. Interrater agreement concerning the child was better when the interpretations were based on a family interaction test than when the interpretations were based on an individual interview.

Others have noted a blurring of the roles of treatment, crisis intervention, and prevention in family approaches and have particularly pointed out that family approaches are useful in identifying other treatment candidates or helping other sick family members and in stopping pathological patterns before other family members develop disorders (Miyoshi & Liebman, 1969; Spiegel, 1974). Miyoshi and Liebman identified one final benefit of the family approach for the individually oriented therapist: The family was better able than the therapist to sense when the patient was ready to change.

When therapists begin observing family members, they often find themselves wishing to treat more than just the identified patient in the family. Treatment becomes inefficient when two, three, or more family members are being seen simultaneously in individual treatment or when members of two or three generations come in sequentially for treatment over the years (e.g., in delinquency cases in which each child is seen at adolescence after involvement in delinquency, rather than having been seen preventively before the delinquent acts occurred). At this point, the shift in paradigm—from intrapsychic to interactional—is likely to occur, and the greatest benefits of family psychology are likely to be found.

Viewing the family as a nonreducible biosocial unit of treatment may make some formerly problematic phenomena easier to conceptualize; as a result, new ideas for intervention can arise, and problems that were overlooked may be easier to spot and to focus on. Jackson and Satir (1970), for example, singled out the phenomenon of the presenting patient who˜is not the sickest member of the family, but a scout sent in search of treatment. Another phenomenon noted was that of the family changes created by treatment, one member of the family may worsen as the patient improves (Hafner, 1977; Marshall & Neill, 1977). Treatment gains may dissipate during family visits or when the patient is discharged to the family. (Interestingly, the struggles among the therapists who are seeing the members of one family often strikingly mimic the conflicts of the family members themselves.)

Family psychology can also offer some ideas about the etiology of problems for which linear causality seems inappropriate. A larger causal focus can show how chance fluctuations in personal behavior and illness can be augmented and maintained because they serve a function for the family. Applying this model of stochastic processes to seemingly individual phenomena (Bateson, 1979) has led to the effective treatment of some previously resistant forms of severe psychosomatic illnesses (Minuchin, Rosman, & Baker, 1978).

Evidence has accumulated to validate the usefulness of the family model in understanding seemingly individual problems. Variations in individual symptoms are often better explained by mediating family variables than by the individual variables of the identified patients. In cases of alcohol abuse, the "healthy" spouse may account for more of the variation in drinking behavior does than the alcoholic spouse (Jacob, 1982). In treating behavior disorders, parents' views may be more pertinent to treatment status than are the child behaviors that are the diagnostic focus (Gordon, 1983; Lobitz & Johnson, 1975; Margolin, 1982). In schizophrenic populations, prognoses have been better predicted by the family variable of "expressed critical emotion" than by premorbid adjustment, severity of symptomatology, or even medication regimens (see Doane, Chapter 30 of this *Handbook;* Vaughn & Leff, 1976). Some child problems also predict problem areas for the parents (Gassner & Murray, 1969).

Evidence also supports the position that family and marital approaches in many instances are equal to individual approaches and in some instances are the treatment of choice (Gurman & Kniskern, 1981b). Family treatment should be chosen, for example, to reduce hospital recidivism and enhance the independent living of chronic schizophrenics (Falloon, Liberman, Lillie, & Vaughn, 1981; Langsley, Flomenhaft, & Machotka, 1969; Langsley, Pittman, Machotka, & Flomenhaft, 1968), to decrease hospital dependence in superlabile diabetics and severe asthmatics (Minuchin, 1975), and to treat marital problems so as to minimize the likelihood of divorce (Gurman & Kniskern, 1978a, 1978b). The family method is the treatment of choice for clients whose problems concern family conflict.

Note that when individual intrapsychic treatment applied to several family members achieves treatment outcome that is equivalent to that of family approaches (treatment applied to all members in the same session), the family methods are superior in efficiency and cost effectiveness. That superiority is also evident in some forms of drug rehabilitation (Stanton, Todd, & Associates, 1982).

NEED FOR PSYCHOLOGICAL KNOWLEDGE

The usual indicators for the growth of a new area in psychology clearly show that the recent growth of interest in family therapy and general family concerns has been exponential. Many articles on this topic, written by psychologists, are appearing in psychological journals and elsewhere. More and more presentations about the family are being made at conferences. Independent training programs and professional workshops have increased, and a number of journals exclusively address this area, one published by APA. A final indicator is the establishment of a professional society, the Academy of Family Psychology.

Unfortunately, institutional support within psychology, particularly in academic institutions, has not kept pace with the growth in interest. Although AAMFT has been working diligently to provide guidelines for acceptable training courses and for criteria for therapist competence, academic psychology has devoted relatively little energy to these issues.

The field of marital and family therapy, on the other hand, has done too little toward comprehensive and balanced development. Critics point out the overemphasis of treatment and underemphasis of theory, prevention, and basic research. Of these, theory is the most neglected (Gurman & Kniskern, 1981a; Liddle & Halpin, 1978; Pinsof, 1981). Some have called for the expertise traditionally associated with psychology (Gurman & Kniskern, 1981b; Olson, 1970) referring in particular to the preeminence of psychology in psychotherapy research. Other equally important areas are evaluation, prevention, and a focus on healthy functioning, treatment program development, and training specificity. Psychology has the potential to contribute much in each of these areas, but its greatest contribution can be to combine theory with practice and evaluation with intervention and to integrate research into all of these.

RESEARCH

Research by clinical psychologists is very underscribed; those who devote their time to practice far outnumber those who devote their time to research. In general, practice far exceeds the research base in support of the current clinical trends, and family therapy is no exception. Interventions in family psychology have gone far beyond the knowledge of how to guide and correct them. Research is lacking, too many claims remain unsubstantiated, and too much of family psychology is faddish—methods are rejected or accepted because of emotional identification with a movement (Russell, 1976). First (1975), who admitted a psychoanalytic bias, referred (in a review of family therapy books) to the "not so convincing solutions of family therapy." Malcom (1978), reviewing for the *New Yorker,* was also skeptical about family therapy.

To convince our colleagues and the insurance providers, we must do more than refer to the well-known difficulties in family therapy research. We need to accept the fact that despite systemically oriented protesters, behavioral research is providing much useful data and some very useful techniques. Gurman (1983) pointed to the usefulness of already-developed research designs and commented on the impact that they have had on third-party reimbursements in Canada.

A source of optimism is that research on social development is regaining popularity and attention among developmental psychologists after an era dominated by Piagetian theory and an exclusive interest in cognitive development. Bowlby and his followers invoked the concepts of systems and communication theory to account for the development of normal attachment relations and the disruption of them in pathological situations (see L'Abate, Chapter 40 of this *Handbook*).

As developmental psychologists turn increasingly to applied problems (e.g., the impact of divorce or training in effective parenting), their data and methods become more directly relevant to family psychology. Research on divorce (e.g., see Hetherington, 1983; Hetherington, Cox, & Cox, 1979) exemplifies the heightened relevance and the increasing use of interactional and longitudinal research designs, which can be transferred to intervention studies and to many other problem areas in family psychology.

Rapprochement between developmental psychology and family intervention does not alter the basic lack of directed research in family psychology. With the average (and the modal) number of publications for clinical psychologists hovering around zero, the imbalance is unlikely to be redressed, even by that 10 percent of psychologists who account for the bulk of the research being done (Rickard & Siegel, 1976). The research that is being conducted is too often flawed by design problems (Gurman & Kniskern, 1978b; Lambert, 1980; Wells & Dezen, 1978) and limited in conception and scope.

There is little programmatic research (Gurman & Kniskern, 1978a, 1981b) and too little replication, cross-validation, and elaboration on the work of others (Holloway & Hosford, 1983). The research seems to subscribe to the uniformity myth that one kind of client, therapist, treatment, or problem is much like any other (Kiesler, 1971). Often, research is based upon data from novice therapists (Gurman & Kniskern, 1978b) or novice trainees (Holloway & Hosford; Lambert, 1980). Basic research in family interaction, which flourished in the late 1950s, (Framo, 1972; Winter & Ferreira, 1969; Wynne, 1983) has diminished considerably, despite the fact that the results have been more challenged now than ever before (see Doane, Chapter 30 of this *Handbook*). A cadre of researchers has remained in basic family research, and some new research groups (Walsh, 1982; Wynne, 1983) have formed; but their numbers are small, and they receive too little attention for the value of their work. Process research is also greatly underrepresented (Pinsof, 1981), and research on training has been nonexistent.

The most basic current need is to involve more clinicians in research. Beyond that need are a number of other goals. Obviously, if clinical research is to be of value, it must move beyond the "new schoolism" to cooperation and broader, more collaborative studies. On the other hand, we need to study the specifics of each school and to ask questions more detailed than "Does family treatment work?" "Does training help?" "Do we do it better than you?" We must answer the specificity question of Gurman (1983) and Paul (1967): What works best with whom, when administered by whom, in what situation, for what types of problems? Kniskern and Gurman (1980) have prepared a sample list of research questions for the area of training.

New research tools and methodologies must be developed to stand alongside the more traditional and effective forms of research (Bray, Colapinto, Stanton, Gurman, & Dell, 1982; Colapinto, 1979; Merkel, Phelps, Harvey, & Pollack, 1983). In addition, there is a pressing need to develop research that is more relevant to clinical practice, more informed by clinical needs, and more adaptable to clinical settings as opposed to academic research, which has been divorced from pragmatic concerns and too large-scale to be attempted in clinical settings. A great need exists for lower-level constructs that can be tied to observable behavior, connecting theory directly with therapist and family behavior and bridging the current gap between the two. Evaluation, too, needs to be informed by current needs and to be based on clearly observable phenomena (Pinsof, 1981).

We believe, as do Lanyon and Brokowski (1969), in the phase of psychological inquiry that Hobbs (1964) referred to as the engineering phase (i.e., when basic research is tailored to fit clinical needs). This phase, in which psychologists are intermediaries between the researchers at one extreme and the clinicians-technicians-artists at the other, is a viable alternative to the Boulder model of psychology (Raimy, 1950), in which one person both applies existing knowledge and adds to the empirical base of psychology. The research and development model espoused by Lanyon and Brokowski fits the development of professional schools but does not fill the current gulf between academic departments and professional schools.

Our first recommendation is to maintain a strong scientific component in clinical training. The emphasis on science has traditionally been the strength of psychology, and we must see that it remains so. Students should take courses in the philosophy of science and the history of psychology to ensure their understanding of the place of research in psychology and its potential for clinical activities (Pottharst, 1970). The results of interaction, process, and outcome research in the empirical literature, as well as their implications for practice and training, should be considered carefully. This consideration should be required in all programs, including professional schools, so that we create good consumers of research. If we fail in this task, researchers will not be encouraged to live up to the standards of their consumers. Special attention should be given to long-term research projects such as the McMasters (Epstein & Bishop, 1981; Santa-Barbara, Woodward, Levin, Streiner, Goodman, & Epstein, 1979; Woodward, Santa-Barbara, Streiner, Goodman, Levin, & Epstein, 1981), Utah, and Oregon groups (see Barton, Alexander, & Sanders, Chapter 35, and Patterson, Chapter 44 of this *Handbook*), models for the combination of research and practice. The research centers that are currently combining theory and practice—the Milan group (Selvini-Palazzoli, Cecchin, Prata, & Boscolo, 1978), DeShazer's group in Milwaukee (DeShazer, 1982), and the Ackerman Institute in New York—should also be noted.

Awareness of the research tools available for use with couples and families should also be required, particularly the designs that are easily incorporated in, and relevant to, clinical practice. Those who will be encouraged to do research must be aware of the special problems in family research design and implementation (Framo, 1965; LeBow, 1981; Rabkin, 1965) and of the methods that are continually being developed to solve them (Fetterman, 1982; Holloway & Hosford, 1983; Wampold & Margolin, 1982). The implications of systemic epistemologies for research design will require specific attention. Early theorists (Jackson, 1959; Laszlo, 1972) pointed out a flaw in traditional research designs: In studying a theory in which all elements are believed to interact mutually, to hold all but one aspect constant is to artificially constrain the one free variable and destroy the generalizability of the results. More recently, interest has been renewed in the problem of researching systems theories. Gurman (1983) has argued that traditional designs have indeed added valuable information but that their contribution does not preclude the usefulness of nontraditional designs.

Realistically, we understand that progress is unlikely without faculty or adjunct faculty role modeling. We cannot accept Haley's (1974) extreme view that research leads to skeptical attitudes that are antithetical to the role of therapist. The work of the Mental Research Institute of Palo Alto, the Milan group, the Ackerman group, and other great research-treatment centers proves otherwise. Liddle et al. (1979) looked at programs in clinical and counseling psychology to determine the amount of research being done in 1976. In counseling programs, 75 percent of the faculty were conducting research, compared with 54 percent of the faculty in clinical psychology departments. These numbers are sufficient, if family and marital researchers have the spare time (an unlikely proposition, given the other demands placed upon them) to develop a useful research apprenticeship program. At the University of Alabama, Rickard and Siegel (1976) developed a research program that has significantly increased the research and publication activity of the graduates, well past the mean publication rates of postdegree clinical psychologists. This goal was attained by assigning new students to faculty researchers, with whom the students served research apprenticeships.

Another solution to the research deficit is, as Pottharst (1970) suggested, to scale down research (so that people will start doing it) and to make it more clinically relevant. Rather than monolithic research enterprises for students, such as dissertations and master's theses, he suggested smaller-scale projects that can be briefly presented or written but whose aggregate significance will exceed their length. He particularly recommended projects that relate theory to clinical innovations or that test theory in a clinically relevant manner. Another recommendation was to involve as trainers researchers who are active in practice and who are thus better able than full-time academic researchers to encourage feasible and relevant research. Although he was writing about professional psychology programs, his recommendations are relevant to all programs for clinical training. Littenberg (1974) similarly recommended a number of small-scale projects that would be started during graduate training, would involve more clinically relevant research, and would be conducted in clinical settings. The University of Vermont model, which he was discussing, spreads a three-year internship over several placements. The intern conducts clinically relevant research at each location, or at least presents a researchable proposal appropriate to that setting. The department hopes not only to encourage learning about clinically relevant research and the accompanying administrative and pragmatic difficulties but to get students started in research at a time when they will receive active support for their projects.

EVALUATION

Myriad measures evaluate the variables that are relevant to family interaction, family structures, and family rules (see in this *Handbook* the following chapters: Gilbert & Christensen, Chapter 31; Bagarozzi, Chapter 32; L'Abate & Wagner, Chapter 33). However, there is no standard or even widely accepted set of assessment devices for research and treatment, with the possible exception of the Locke-Wallace Short Marital Adjustment Test (Locke & Wallace, 1959) or the Dyadic Adjustment Inventory (Spanier, 1976). Measures are not linked by a comprehensive theoretical structure nor by a series of cross-validation and comparison studies (Frank, 1965; Turk & Bell, 1972). Despite the importance of a common body of clinical research data (one whose measures are comparable or identical across a variety of cases and treatment approaches) and despite the warnings of early reviewers that disconnected research efforts would result from the use of disparate measures (Mishler & Waxler, 1968; Spiegel & Bell, 1959), comparing one study with another continues to be difficult because of the lack of replication and because, even when studies are similar, researchers use different measures.

Psychological assessment has addressed, almost solely, the definition of the self, and the theory has been of reactive rather than interactive behavior. The evaluation of total systems, although lacking in the past (Fisher 1982; Hodgson & Lewis, 1979), is becoming more evident in the works of Moos (1974), Patterson (1974), L'Abate (1983), Olson, Sprenkle, and Russell (1979), and others. Fisher (1982), Reiss (1983), and Cromwell and Peterson (1983) have written useful discussions about the measurements of family systems.

Systemic family theorists have generally eschewed traditional testing approaches and have considered treatment and evaluation so interwoven that they cannot be separated (Cromwell & Keeney, 1979; Furniss, Bentovim, & Kinston, 1983; Keeney, 1979; Minuchin, 1974). Even the systemic theorists who believe that evaluation can and should precede treatment do not advise traditional testing approaches (Caille, 1982). Traditional approaches are faulted in three areas: (1) They emphasize the evaluation of individuals rather than the relationship between individuals. (2) They rely on linear epistemology, which underemphasizes context and overemphasizes the supposedly inherent and relatively immutable characteristics of families or individuals. (3) They ignore the systems principle of nonsummativity, which implies that one's knowledge of the system comes only from direct interaction or observation of the system and cannot be achieved by separately summing individual evaluations of family members without overlooking emergent properties observable only in the whole family.

Clearly, mainstream psychology has much to offer family evaluation, but more comprehensive testing is needed to assess both the individual and the systemic levels. Attempts to evaluate the outcome of family treatment are equivalent to the development of outcome assessment in individual therapy (Gurman & Kniskern, 1978b), but attempts to evaluate the outcome of training and supervision have been rare (Byles et al., 1983; Kniskern & Gurman, 1979; Liddle & Halpin, 1978). Trainees are rarely assessed by any method other than the traditional academic one; that is, a general impression leads to a grade assignment for practicum, leaving both practicum directors and trainees at a loss concerning accurate assessment. The technology exists to correct this assessment procedure, and notable exceptions to the traditional academic assessment have emerged (Breunlin, Schwartz, Krause, & Selby, 1983; Byles et al., 1983; Liddle & Saba, 1982). We suggest that evaluation include (1) conceptual and perceptual knowledge based on a pre-post written exam; (2) perceptual knowledge based on a response to a standard tape of a therapy session or other situation involving family interaction; (3) executive skills based on both role-play responses to standard video situations and *in vivo* behavior with both clinical and normal families; (4) personal life adjustment of the student, as suggested by Kniskern and Gurman (1980), particularly in relation to their spouse and immediate family; (5) the outcome or results of the student's professional behavior as a trainer, therapist, researcher, or whatever other professional roles he or she has acted in.

Improved evaluation of systems and context is needed to balance the overemphasis in psychology on the monadic individual. Moos (1974) has developed an instrument for evaluating social contexts; similar instruments could be useful in clarifying, for example, family types, life-cycle factors, and relevant social-class factors. Also worthy of consideration are comprehensive evaluation schemes such as Gurman and Kniskern's (1978b) or Cromwell and Keeney's (1979) and Cromwell and Peterson's (1983) proposal for testing system levels (individual, dyadic, family, extended family) and for evaluating deterioration as well as improvement at all levels. Multimethod, multisource, multitrait analysis (Campbell & Fiske, 1959) models for comprehensive testing, as indicated by Cromwell and Peterson's (1983) work, would also be useful. It is of note that they attempted to integrate psychology's well-developed individual testing with more systemic-level informaton. Models concerning the impact that the testing context has on family systems and individuals could be expanded by psychology's sensibleness about testing and the pragmatic effects of testing (Reiss, 1983). Haley (1963) emphasized the paramount importance of developing schemes of and assessment for family typologies two decades ago, and several theorists (Hoffman, 1981) have addressed the problem, but it has not yet been solved. The answer may grow out of the multilevel, multitrait analysis that Cromwell and Peterson suggested rather than the more primitive approaches used in the past.

A common test battery such as that proposed by Cromwell and Keeney (1979) or that developed for outcome research in individual psychotherapy (Waskow & Parloff, 1975) would also be very useful. Short of a common test battery, a common conceptual scheme—a pragmatic guide for collecting and arranging data (Caille, 1982)—would be helpful. This test battery would be similar to the mental-status exam in psychiatry (maligned as it has been). Such a scheme, once established, might help to develop theoretical sharpness, or it might lead to new measures that would aid assessment in specific areas of interest. A useful mix of nomothetic and idiographic data might result—the nomothetic to help set general goals and cautions for the therapist and the idiographic to tailor the treatment approach to the family and set specific goals for the family. Goal setting is particularly important for family therapy because of the multiple treatment consumers. Goal attainment scales have been useful in several outcome studies (Kiresuk & Sherman, 1968; Woodward, Santa-Barbara, Levin, & Epstein, 1978), as well as in evaluating training; they exemplify the scaled-down testing that is needed to assess the unique treatment needs of clients while maintaining clinical data collection that is useful to the researcher and to the field at large.

Because assessment, among mental health professionals, has traditionally been a specialty of psychologists and a major feature of professional self-identity, good training in assessment must be available to students. Assessment training is particularly important because assessment has been increasingly deemphasized at training sites outside the academic settings, and service demands have led to a decrease in assessment activity. In the internships that Cooper et al. (1981) surveyed, formal diagnostics were used at 64 percent of the sites, but only 24 percent had formal family diagnostics. Clearly, assessment and evaluation can be developed and strengthened by trained family psychologists. We recommend that all students be formally trained to construct tests, to evaluate the usefulness and the limits of tests, to interpret tests, and to use test-derived information. We also recommend a thorough survey of current assessment instruments (Cromwell, Olson, & Fournier, 1976; Straus, 1978), including clinical and structured family interviews and coding for observational data, paper and pencil tests, and other structured evaluative instruments.

Students need training in the ethical use of tests and in the interactive effects of the testing format, the tester, and the family (Reiss, 1983). Family assessment raises, of course, special issues about confidentiality. The training should be elaborated by a comprehensive assessment package to be used by trainees or a comprehensive outline of the information to be gained from an assessment interview (Caille, 1982; Cromwell & Keeney, 1979; Epstein, Bishop, & Levin, 1978; Furniss et al., 1983; Garrigan & Bambrick, 1977; Lange & van der Hart, 1983; Liddle & Saba, 1982; Resnikoff, 1981). Training in one of the formal approaches to introductory interviews (Andolfi, 1979; Haley, 1976; Napier & Whitaker, 1973; Penn, 1982; Selvini-Palazzoli, Boscolo, Cecchin, & Prata 1980) should be a supplement but is no substitute for a formal conceptual structure that relates treatment to observable and inferable family data.

We strongly recommend that learning objectives be specified and the specific skills put into operation in each component of the training program. Such specification highlights and verifies the students' natural abilities, areas of weakness, and competencies (Cleghorn & Levin, 1973; Falicov, Constantine, & Breunlin, 1981; Kaslow, 1977). Because progress is easier to follow and verification is enhanced, this approach is also useful for peer and insurance reviews. Learning objectives lend themselves to contracting (Cleghorn & Levin, 1973; Kaslow, 1977), freeing students to act responsibly and creatively within the limits imposed by their skills and by their contracts.

Learning objectives can also serve as a more general model for evaluation, one which follows a pattern of identifying skills, training others (e.g., families, supervisees) to demonstrate these skills, practicing the skills through role playing and in vivo situations, observing to determine the level of skill performance, and relating the skill performance to outcome in targeted as well as nontargeted change areas. This general model can serve as a useful foundation for an evaluation of family psychology training programs as well as evaluation of therapy and supervision.

PREVENTION AND HEALTH

As a profession, clinical psychology is no longer concerned with just one end of the health-dysfunction spectrum but can continue to look at pathology while beginning to develop a psychology of optimal (as opposed to average) functioning or a psychology of competence in the face of stress and high-risk factors for pathology (Fisher, Kokes, Weintraub, Worland, & Goldstein, 1983; Watt, Anthony, Wynne, & Rolf, in press). The emphasis on psychotherapy as a learning process (Rioch, 1970) leads easily to a focus on growth, development, and prevention; psychologists may use that focus to augment family therapy and transform it into the more encompassing field of family psychology.

The primary need is a psychology of healthy functioning and development within the family rather than, as has been true in clinical psychology, a psychology based exclusively on the study of pathological behavior and disrupted development. The results of research on health would be valuable to psychology in its efforts to educate the public in ways of relating designed to promote health.

Excellent beginnings have already been made by the Timberlawn group of Dallas (Beavers, 1977; Lewis, 1979; Lewis, Beavers, Gossett, & Phillips, 1976), who have worked not only on the distinction between normal and pathological but also on a framework of unhealthy-average-optimal functioning. Their work has opened new areas for theorizing, data gathering, and practice. Gurman and Kniskern (1981b) have noted the promise that enrichment programs hold for preventive work and recommended, from their review of psychotherapy outcome studies, that enrichment programs be included in training. L'Abate (1977) has combined enrichment and skill training packages with more traditional treatment approaches, and impressive research results have been obtained by comparing enrichment and skill training with unstructured treatment approaches (Ganahl, 1982). The details of further work by a number of groups have been published by Walsh (1982), and Westley and Epstein (1969) presented an impressive body of work by the McMaster group of Canada.

The importance of prevention through building strong family units and teaching positive family coping skills (e.g., problem resolution) for the crises that inevitably arise is recognized by all. Although such endeavors are neither readily funded nor given high priority in clinical psychology programs, other areas in psychology may help to correct this imbalance. Preventing problems is not as glamorous as rescuing families in need, nor is prevention considered as essential as treatment. But, as Vincent (1958) pointed out, more lives are saved at sea by accurate navigational aids than by the best lifeboats and rescue operations. Birchler (1979), for example, could only discriminate healthy and unhealthy families according to their problem-solving skills, *not* by their kinds presenting problems.

Enrichment and skill training approaches for normal families can develop into good preventive models. They can be used to teach skills that will minimize the likelihood of problems and be directed toward foreseeable life crises. They can become the family navigational charts during the turbulent times (see Guerney, Guerney, & Cooney, Chapter 39 of this *Handbook*). Survey responses from 20 clinical psychology programs indicated that 35 percent (7) offered enrichment as part of their usual psychological services; of the programs at 102 internship sites, 29 percent (28) offered enrichment (Ganahl & L'Abate, 1983). Although encouraging, the percentages could be better and perhaps will need to be in the near future. Shifts in attitudes are indicated by new Senate bills (S. 772–3, Hatch–R, Utah) that call for a new position—assistant director of prevention—in 10 of 11 national health institutes.

Our training will, we hope, train students to be observers not only of pathology but also of health, not only of individuals and individual families but also of the social networks that exist in the natural environments of individuals and families. So far, we know of few programs that encourage interviews with normal families or exploration of the family ecology, but we commend the programs that do include these important areas. Piercy, Hovestadt, Fernell, Franklin, and McKeon (1982) have developed a training program that takes seriously the usefulness of knowing the individual's environment and commits the program to placing students in the service delivery environment so that they know it firsthand. The Boston Family Institute also recommends an anthropological stance (Duhl & Duhl, 1979) and includes, as part of training, the interviewing of normal families, as does the family psychology specialization at Georgia State University (Kochalka & L'Abate, 1983; L'Abate, 1983). Others rely on a more-vague general systems belief that the form of one system is like another and that one needs only to learn the properties of system functioning, then—without further study—to apply them. Although the idea has some merit, Russell (1976) and Caille (1982) have pointed out that general systems theory does not provide the conceptual basis for interventions or the information that is necessary to fine-tune them. Networking (Attneave, 1969; Speck & Attneave, 1974; Speck & Reuveni, 1969), a useful approach because one gets to see the larger system in action before determining how to proceed, is a method of intervening in systems that we believe should be taught. In our survey of 22 clinical psychology programs, only 1 mentioned training in networking.

CONCLUSION

When we survey the field of academic psychology and find that the modal number of courses related to family is one, as are the mean and the median, we are not exactly sure what is being taught as family psychology. For the most part, schools offer a survey course in treatment techniques related to the pathological family or the family and the couple. Rarely are preventive or healthy aspects taught; if taught, they are squeezed into the treatment course. Some programs also offer an examination of the family and the marital pair in the development of the individual as a total personality, not just as a unit of pathology. Others, even more advanced, also offer courses on the family's potential to positively affect the individual, rather than offering the typical, exclusively negative potential of the family for the individual's growth and development. This has led to increasing use of family concepts in the treatment of medical illness, as the family has begun to be seen more and more as a source of health care and an ally rather than as an irrelevancy or a competitor to physicians, a carryover from Fruedian times. In this respect, change has paralleled the modern perspective on health and prevention and the tendency to see the unconscious as a positive force rather than just a cesspool of unsavory wishes and instinctual strivings.

Any family psychology must at least give attention to the family as *(a)* the arena for the individual's growth and continued development; *(b)* a mediator between the individual and society, particularly when services such as medical or psychological services are concerned, as the family is a major part (often overlooked) of the health delivery system; *(c)* a potentially powerful source of resources and assistance to the individual and the therapist; *(d)* a potential etiological agent in individual disturbances, either in terms of stress-induced problems or problem-maintaining solutions, or as a force that may augment and maintain chance fluctuations in individual health; and finally, *(e)* a biosocial unit of health and pathology that is irreducible to the sum of its parts. To offer any less than these areas may be enlightening and may add to a therapist's treatment repertoire, but it would not be a true family psychology.

To be a clinical family psychologist will require a clearer definition of self, as an individual and as a professional. It will also require a clear sense of priorities (i.e., "I am a clinical psychologist first, and I am a family therapist second"). The order of these priorities is crucial to the individual and collective assertion that clinical family psychology can no longer consist of an occasional seminar in family therapy. More than one seminar will be necessary for the competence and proficiency that this new profession requires. There will, of course, be compromises. There will, of course, be detours and sabotages. This new profession will challenge—indeed, will threaten—established and entrenched values ("What—you do not teach the Rorschach to your students?"). To acquire new habits, some old ones must be abandoned. Change will inevitably occur, whether it is sought or opposed.

REFERENCES

Abel, R., Bruzzese, D., & Wilson, J. Short-term hospitalized patients: A vehicle for training as well as treatment. In L. R. Wolberg & M. L. Aronson (Eds.), *Group therapy 1974: An overview*. New York: Stratton Intercontinental, 1974.

American Psychological Association. *Ethical standards of psychologists*. Washington, D.C.: Author, 1972. (Originally published, *American Psychologist*, January 1963.)

American Psychological Association. National Conference on Levels and Patterns of Training in Professional Psychology, Vail, Colorado, July 24–31, 1973.

Anderson, L., Amatea, E., Munson, T., & Rudner, B. Training in family treatment: Needs and objectives. *Social Casework*, 1979, *60*, 323–329.

Andolfi, M. *Family therapy*. New York: Plenum Press, 1979.

Attneave, C. Therapy in tribal and urban settings. *Family Process*, 1969, *8*, 192–210.

Bateson, G. A systems approach. *International Journal of Psychiatry*, 1971, *9*, 242–244.

Bateson, G. *Mind and nature: A necessary unit*. New York: Bantam Books, 1979.

Bauer, R. Can psychologists be socially relevant? *Professional Psychology*, 1971, *2*, 111–117.

Beavers, R. *Psychotherapy and growth: A family systems perspective*. New York: Brunner/Mazel, 1977.

Beck, D., & Jones, M. A new look at clientele and services of family agencies. *Social Casework*, 1974, *55*, 589–599.

Beels, C. C., & Ferber, A. Family therapy: A view. *Family Process*, 1969, *8*, 280–318.

Birchler, G. Communication skills in married couples. In A. Bellack & M. Hersen (Eds.), *Research and practice in social skills training*. New York: Plenum Press, 1979.

Bodin, A. *Family interaction, coalition, disagreement, and compromise in problem, normal, and synthetic triads*. Unpublished doctoral dissertation, State University of New York at Buffalo, 1966.

Boszormenyi-Nagy, I. Interviews in G. Robbins, Constructive entitlement: Bringing justice and fairness to families. *Family Therapy News*, 1983, *4*, 3; 15.

Bray, J., Colapinto, J., Stanton, D., Gurman, A., & Dell, P. *Research in light of the "new" epistemologies*. Panel presented at the annual conference of the American Association of Marriage and Family Therapy, Dallas, October 29, 1982.

Breunlin, D., Schwartz, R., Krause, M., & Selby, L. Evaluating family therapy training: The development of a rating instrument. *Journal of Marital and Family Therapy*, 1983, *9*, 37–47.

Byles, J., Bishop, D., & Horn, D. Evaluation of a family therapy training program. *Journal of Marital and Family Therapy*, 1983, *9*, 299–304.

Caille, P. The evaluative phase of systemic family therapy. *Journal of Marital and Family Therapy*, 1982, *8*, 29–39.

Campbell, D., & Fiske, D. Convergent and discriminant validation by the multitrait-multimethod matrix. *Psychological Bulletin*, 1959, *56*, 81–105.

Capra, F. *The turning point*. New York: Simon & Schuster, 1982.

Cleghorn, J., & Levin, S. Training family therapists by setting learning objectives. *American Journal of Orthopsychiatry*, 1973, *43*, 439–446.

Colapinto, J. The relative value of empirical evidence. *Family Process*, 1979, *18*, 427–441.

Cooper, A., Rampage, C., & Soucy, G. Family therapy training in clinical psychology programs. *Family Process*, 1981, *20*, 155–166.

Cromwell, R., & Keeney, B. Diagnosing marital and family systems: A training model. *Family Coordinator*, 1979, *28*, 101–108.

Cromwell, R., Olson, D. H. L., & Fournier, D. G. Diagnosis and evaluation in marital and family counseling. In D. H. L. Olson (Ed.), *Treating relationships*. Lake Mills, Iowa: Graphic Publishing, 1976.

Cromwell, R., & Peterson, G. Multisystem-multimethod family assessment in clinical contexts. *Family Process*, 1983, *22*, 147–163.

De Shazer, S. *Patterns of brief family therapy: An ecosystemic approach*. New York: Guilford Press, 1982.

Duhl, F., & Duhl, B. Structured spontaneity: The thoughtful art of integrative family therapy at BFI. *Journal of Marital and Family Therapy*, 1979, *5*, 59–75.

Engel, G. L. The need for a new medical model: A challenge for biomedicine. *Science*, 1977, *196*, 129–136.

Engel, G. L. The clinical application of a bio-psycho-social model. *American Journal of Psychiatry*, 1980, *137*, 535–544.

Engelin, R., Knutson, J., Laugh, L., & Garlington, W. Behavior modification techniques applied to a family unit—a case study. *Journal of Child Psychology and Psychiatry and Allied Disciplines*, 1968, *9*, 245–252.

Epstein, N., & Bishop, D. Problem-centered systems therapy of the family. In A. Gurman & D. Kniskern (Eds.), *Handbook of family therapy*. New York: Brunner/Mazel, 1981.

Epstein, N., Bishop, D., & Levin, S. The McMaster model of family functioning. *Journal of Marriage and Family Counseling*, 1978, *6*, 19–31.

Everett, C. A. An analysis of AAMFT supervisors: Their identities, roles, and resources. *Journal of Marital and Family Therapy*, 1980, *6*, 215–236.

Fagan, J. The tasks of the therapist. In J. Fagan & I. Shepherd (Eds.), *Gestalt therapy now*. Palo Alto, Calif.: Science & Behavior Books, 1970.

Falicov, C., Constantine, J., & Breunlin, D. Teaching family therapy: A program based on learning objectives. *Journal of Marital and Family Therapy*, 1981, *7*, 497–506.

Falloon, I., Liberman, R., Lillie, F., & Vaughn, C. Family therapy of schizophrenics with high rate of relapse. *Family Process*, 1981, *20*, 211–222.

Fetterman, D. Ethnography in educational research: The dynamics of diffusion. *Educational Researcher*, 1982, *11*, 17–22.

First, E. Family therapy: The new wave in psychiatry. *New York Review of Books*, February 20, 1975, pp. 37–38.

Fisher, L. Transactional theories but individual assessment: A frequent discrepancy in family research. *Family Process*, 1982, *21*, 313–320.

Fisher, L., Kokes, R., Weintraub, S., Worland, J., & Goldstein, M. *Competent children of disturbed parents: Studies of invulnerability*. Symposium presented at the 91st Annual Convention of the American Psychological Association, Anaheim, California, August 30, 1983.

Fox, R. The effects of psychotherapy on the spouse. *Family Process*, 1968, *7*, 7–16.

Framo, J. Systematic research on family dynamics. In I. Boszormenyi-Nagy & J. Framo, *Intensive family therapy*. New York: Harper & Row, 1965.

Framo, J. Personal reflections of a family therapy. *Journal of Marriage and Family Couneling*, 1975, *1*, 15–28.

Framo, J. *Family interaction: A dialogue between family researchers and family therapists*. New York: Springer Publishing, 1972.

Frank, G. The role of the family in the development of psychopathology. *Psychological Bulletin*, 1965, *64*, 191–205.

Furniss, T., Bentovim, A., & Kinston, W. Clinical process recording in focal family therapy. *Journal of Marital and Family Therapy*, 1983, *9*, 147–170.

Ganahl, G. F. Effects of client, treatment, and therapist variables on the outcome of structured marital enrichment (Unpublished doctoral dissertation, Georgia State University, 1981). *Dissertation Abstracts International*, 1982, *42*(11), 4576B.

Ganahl, G., & L'Abate, L. *Survey of graduate training in family psychology*. Unpublished manuscript, West Virginia University, 1983.

Garrigan, J., & Bambrick, A. Introducing novice therapists to "go-between" techniques of family therapy. *Family Process*, 1977, *16*, 237–246.

Gassner, S., & Murray, E. Dominance and conflict in interactions between parents of normal and neurotic children. *Journal of Abnormal Psychology*, 1969, *74*, 33–41.

Gilmore, J. V. *The productive personality*. San Francisco: Albion Publishing, 1974.

Gordon, B. Maternal perception of child temperament and observed mother-child interaction. *Child Psychiatry and Human Development*, 1983, *13*, 153–167.

Group for the Advancement of Psychiatry. *The field of family therapy*. New York: Author, 1970.

Guerin, G., Veroff, J., & Feld, T. *Americans view their mental health*. New York: Basic Books, 1960.

Gurman, A. Family therapy research and the "new epistemology." *Journal of Marital and Family Therapy*, 1983, *9*, 227–234.

Gurman, A., & Kniskern, D. Deteriorization in marital and family therapy: Empirical, clinical, and conceptual issues. *Family Process*, 1978, *17*, 817–901. (a)

Gurman, A., & Kniskern, D. Research on marital and family therapy: Progress, perspective, and prospect. In S. Garfield & A. Bergin (Eds.), *Handbook of psychotherapy and behavior change* (2d ed.). New York: John Wiley & Sons, 1978. (b)

Gurman, A., & Kniskern, D. *Handbook of family therapy*. New York: Brunner/Mazel, 1981. (a)

Gurman, A., & Kniskern, D. The outcomes of family therapy: Implications for practice and training. In G. Berenson & H. White (Eds.), *Annual review of family therapy*. New York: Human Sciences Press, 1981. (b)

Hafner, R. The husbands of agoraphobic women and their influence on treatment outcome. *British Journal of Psychiatry*, 1977, *131*, 289–294.

Haley, J. Family experiments: A new type of experimentation. *Family Process*, 1963, *1*, 265–293.

Haley, J. Fourteen ways to fail as a teacher of family therapy. *Family Therapy*, 1974, *1*, 1–8.

Haley, J. *Problem-solving therapy*. San Francisco: Jossey-Bass, 1976.

Hare-Mustin, R. Live supervision in psychotherapy. *Voices,* 1976, *12,* 21–24.

Hetherington, E. M. *Modes of adaptation to divorce and single parenthood which enhance healthy family functioning: Implications for preventive programs.* Paper presented at the NIMH-sponsored Conference on Healthy Family Functioning, Anaheim, California, May 18, 1983.

Hetherington, E. M., Cox, M., & Cox, R. Play and social interaction in children following divorce. *Journal of Social Issues,* 1979, *35,* 26–49.

Hobbs, N. Mental health's third revolution. *American Journal of Orthopsychiatry,* 1964, *34,* 822–833.

Hodgson, J., & Lewis, R. Pilgrim's progress III: A trend analysis of family therapy, theory, and methodology. *Family Process,* 1979, *18,* 163–173.2

Hoffman, L. *Foundations of family therapy.* New York: Basic Books, 1981.

Holloway, E., & Hosford, R. Towards developing a prescriptive technology of counselor supervision. *Counseling Psychologist,* 1983, *11,* 73–77.

Hurvitz, N. Marital problems following psychotherapy with one spouse. *Journal of Consulting Psychology,* 1967, *31,* 38–47.

Huygen, F. *Family medicine: The medical life history of families.* New York: Brunner/Mazel, 1982.

Jackson, D. Family interaction, family homeostasis, and some implications for conjoint family psychotherapy. In J. Masserman (Ed.), *Individual and familial dynamics.* New York: Grune & Stratton, 1959.

Jackson, D. The individual and the larger context. *Family Process,* 1967, *6,* 139–147.

Jackson, D., & Satir, V. A review of psychiatric developments in family diagnoses and family therapy. In D. Jackson (Ed.), *Therapy, communication, and change: Human communication* (Vol. 2). Palo Alto, Calif.: Science & Behavior Books, 1970.

Jacob, T. *Alcoholism and family interaction.* Paper presented during panel on understanding and treating the married alcoholic at the annual meeting of the American Psychological Association Washington, D. C., August 25, 1982.

Joint Commission on the Mental Health of Children. *Crisis in child mental health: Challenge for the 1970's.* New York: Harper & Row, 1970.

Kaslow, F. Training of marital and family therapists. In F. Kaslow (Ed.), *Supervision, consultation, and staff training in the helping professions.* San Francisco: Jossey-Bass, 1977.

Keeney, B. Ecosystemic epistemology: An alternative paradigm for diagnosis. *Family Process,* 1979, *18,* 117–129.

Kiesler, D. Experimental designs in psychotherapeutic research. In A. Bergin & S. Garfield (Eds.), *Handbook of psychotherapy and behavior change: An empirical analysis.* New York: John Wiley & Sons, 1971.

Kiresuk, T., & Sherman, R. Goal attainment scaling: A general method for evaluating community mental health programs. *Community Mental Health Journal,* 1968, *4,* 443–453.

Kniskern, D., & Gurman, A. Research on training in marriage and family therapy: Status, issues, and directions. *Journal of Marital and Family Therapy,* 1979, *5,* 83–94.

Kniskern, D., & Gurman, A. Research on training in marriage and family therapy. In M. Andolfi & I. Zwerling (Eds.), *Dimensions of family therapy.* New York: Guilford Press, 1980.

Kochalka, J., & L'Abate, L. Structure and gradualness in the clinical training of family psychologists. In L. L'Abate (Ed.), *Family psychology: Theory, therapy, and training.* Washington, D.C.: University Press of America, 1983.

Koestler, A. *Janus, a summing up.* New York: Random House, 1978.

Kuhn, T. S. *The structure of scientific revolutions.* Chicago: University of Chicago Press, 1972.

L'Abate, L. *Structured interventions with couples, families, and groups.* Washington, D.C.: University Press of America, 1977.

L'Abate, L. (Ed.). *Family psychology: Theory, therapy, and training.* Washington, D.C.: University Press of America, 1983.

Lambert, M. Research and the supervisory process. In K. Hess (Ed.), *Psychotherapy supervision.* New York: John Wiley & Sons, 1980.

Lange, A., & van der Hart, O. *Directive family therapy.* New York: Brunner/Mazel, 1983.

Langsley, D., Flomenhaft, K., & Machotka, P. Follow-up evaluation of family crisis therapy. *American Journal of Orthopsychiatry,* 1969, *39,* 753–759.

Langsley, D., Pittman, F., Machotka, P., & Flomenhaft, K. Family crisis therapy: Results and implications. *Family Process,* 1968, *7,* 145–158.

Lanyon, R., & Brokowski, A. An engineering model for clinical psychology. *Clinical Psychologist,* 1969, *22,* 140–141.

Laszlo, E. *The systems view of the world.* New York: Braziller, 1972.

LeBow, J. Issues in the assessment of outcome in family therapy. *Family Process,* 1981, *20,* 167–188.

Lewin, K. The conflict between Aristotelian and Galilean modes of thinking in contemporary psychology. *Journal of Genetic Psychology,* 1931, *5,* 141–177.

Lewis, J. *How's your family?* New York: Brunner/Mazel, 1979.

Lewis, J., Beavers, R., Gossett, J., & Phillips, V. *No single thread: Psychological health in family systems.* New York: Brunner/Mazel, 1976.

Liddle, H. A. The emotional and political hazards of teaching and learning family therapy. *Family Therapy,* 1978, *5,* 1–12.

Liddle, H. A. On the problem of eclecticism: A call for epistemologic clarification and human scale theories. *Family Process,* 1982, *21,* 243–250.

Liddle, H. A., & Halpin, R. Family therapy training and supervision literature: A comparative review. *Journal of Marriage and Family Counseling,* 1978, *4,* 77–98.

Liddle, H. A., & Saba, G. W. On teaching family therapy at the introductory level: A conceptual model emphasizing a pattern which connects training and therapy. *Journal of Marital and Family Therapy,* 1982, *8,* 63–73.

Liddle, H. A., Vance, S., & Pastushak, R. Family therapy training opportunities in psychology and counselor education. *Professional Psychology,* 1979, *10,* 760–765.

Littenberg, H. Training clinical researchers in psychology. *Professional Psychology,* 1974, *5,* 59–69.

Lobitz, G., & Johnson, S. Normal versus deviant children: A multimethod comparison. (University of Oregon, 1974.) *Dissertation Abstracts International,* 1975, *35,* 4185B.

Locke, H., & Wallace, K. Short marital adjustment prediction tests: Their reliability and validity. *Journal of Marriage and the Family,* 1959, *21,* 251–255.

Malcom, J. A reporter at large (family therapy). *New Yorker,* May 15, 1978, p. 39.

Margolin, G. Ethical and legal considerations in marital and family therapy. *American Psychologist,* 1982, *37,* 788–801.

Marshall, J., & Neill, J. The removal of a psychosomatic symptom: Effects on the marriage. *Family Process,* 1977, *16,* 273–280.

McColley, S., & Baker, E. Training activities and styles of beginning supervisors: A survey. *Professional Psychology,* 1982, *13,* 283–292.

Merkel, W., Phelps, R., Harvey, D., & Pollack, S. *Research implications of the new epistemologies: A highly speculative, pragmatically reprehensible, aesthetically noxious leap into the future.* Panel presented at the annual conference of the American Association of Marriage and Family Therapy, Washington, D.C., October 6, 1983.

Minuchin, S. *Families and family therapy.* Cambridge, Mass.: Harvard University Press, 1974.

Minuchin, S. A conceptual model of psychosomatic illness in children. *Archives of General Psychiatry,* 1975, *32,* 1031–1038.

Minuchin, S., Rosman, B., & Baker, L. *Psychosomatic families: Anorexia nervosa in context.* Cambridge, Mass.: Harvard University Press, 1978.

Mischel, W. *Personality and assessment.* New York: John Wiley & Sons, 1968.

Mishler, E., & Waxler, N. *Family process and schizophrenia.* New York: Science House, 1968.

Miyoshi, N., & Liebman, R. Training psychiatric residents in family therapy. *Family Process,* 1969, *8,* 97–105.

Moos, R. H. The assessment and impact of social climate. In P. M. Reynolds (Ed.), *Advances in psychological assessment III.* San Francisco: Jossey-Bass, 1974.

Napier, A., & Whitaker, C. Problems of the beginning family therapist. In D. Bloch (Ed.), *Techniques of family psychotherapy: A primer.* New York: Grune & Stratton, 1973.

Olson, D. Marital and family therapy: Integrative review and critique. *Journal of Marriage and the Family,* 1970, *32,* 501–538.

Olson, D., Sprenkle, D., & Russell, C. Circumplex model of marital and family systems: I. Cohesion and adaptability dimensions, family types, and clinical applications. *Family Process,* 1979, *18,* 3–28.

O'Rourke, V. Field and laboratory: The decision making behavior of family groups in two experimental conditions. *Sociometry,* 1963, *26,* 422–435.

Patterson, G. R. Interventions for boys with conduct problems: Multiple settings, treatments and criteria. *Journal of Consulting and Clinical Psychology,* 1974, *43,* 471–481.

Paul, G. Strategy of outcome research in psychotherapy. *Journal of Consulting Psychology,* 1967, *31,* 109–118.

Penn, P. Circular questioning. *Family Process,* 1982, *21,* 267–280.

Piercy, F., Hovestadt, A., Fernell, D., Franklin, G., & McKeon, D. A comprehensive training model for family therapists serving rural populations. *Family Therapy,* 1982, *9,* 239–249.

Pinsof, W. Family therapy process research. In A. Gurman & D. Kniskern (Eds.), *Handbook of family therapy.* New York: Brunner/Mazel, 1981.

Pottharst, K. To renew vitality and provide a challenge in training—the California School of Professional Psychology. *Professional Psychology,* 1970, *1,* 123–130.

Rabkin, L. The patient's family: Research methods. *Family Process,* 1965, *4,* 105–132.

Raimy, V. C. (Ed.). *Training in clinical psychology.* Englewood Cliffs, N.J.: Prentice-Hall, 1950.

Ransom, D. The rise of family medicine: New roles for behavioral science. *Marriage and Family Review,* 1981, *4,* 31–72.

Rausch, H. L., Barry, W. A., Hertel, R. K., & Swain, M. A. *Communication, conflict, and marriage.* San Francisco: Jossey-Bass, 1974.

Reiss, D. *The family's construction of reality.* Cambridge, Mass.: Harvard University Press, 1981.

Reiss, D. Critique: Sensory extenders versus meters and predictors: Clarifying strategies for the use of objective tests in family therapy. *Family Process,* 1983, *22,* 165–171.

Resnikoff, R. Teaching family therapy: Ten key questions for understanding the family as patient. *Journal of Marital and Family Therapy,* 1981, *7,* 135–142.

Rickard, H., & Siegel, P. The importance of research apprenticeships in training. *Professional Psychology,* 1976, *7,* 359–363.

Rioch, M. Should psychotherapists do therapy? *Professional Psychology,* 1970, *2,* 139–142.

Russell, A. Contemporary concerns in family therapy. *Journal of Marriage and Family Counseling,* 1976, *2,* 243–250.

Sager, C., Grundlach, J., Kremer, J., Lenz, R., & Royce, J. The married in treatment. *Archives of General Psychiatry,* 1968, *19,* 206–217.

Santa-Barbara, J., Woodward, C., Levin, S., Streiner, D., Goodman, J., & Epstein, N. The McMaster family therapy outcome study: I. An overview of methods and results. *International Journal of Family Therapy,* 1979, *1,* 304–323.

Schopler, E., Fox, R., & Cochrane, C. Teaching family dynamics to medical students. *American Journal of Orthopsychiatry,* 1967, *37,* 906–911.

Selig, A. The myth of the multiproblem family. *American Journal of Orthopsychiatry,* 1976, *46,* 526–531.

Selvini-Palazzoli, M., Cecchin, G., Prata, G., & Boscolo, L. *Paradox and counterparadox.* New York: Jason Aronson, 1978.

Selvini-Palazzoli, M., Boscolo, L., Cecchin, G., & Prata, G. Hypothesizing-circularity-neutrality: Three guidelines for the conductor of the session. *Family Process,* 1980, *19,* 3–12.

Smith, D. Trends in counseling and psychotherapy. *American Psychologist,* 1982, *37,* 802–809.

Spanier, G. Measuring dyadic adjustment: New scales for assessing the quality of marriage and similar dyads. *Journal of Marriage and the Family,* 1976, *38,* 15–28.

Speck, R., & Attneave, C. *Family networks.* New York: Random House, 1974. (Vintage Books).

Speck, R., & Reuveni, U. Network therapy, a developing concept. *Family Process,* 1969, *8,* 182–191.

Spiegel, J. The family: The channel of primary care. *Hospital and Community Psychiatry,* 1974, *25,* 785–788.

Spiegel, J., & Bell, N. The family of the psychiatric patient. In S. Arieti (Ed.), *American handbook of psychiatry* (Vol. 1). New York: Basic Books, 1959.

Stanton, M. Psychology and family therapy. *Professional Psychology,* 1975, *6,* 45–49.

Stanton, M., Todd, T., & Associates. *The family therapy of drug abuse and addiction.* New York: Guilford Press, 1982.

Straus, M. A. *Family measurement techniques.* Minneapolis: University of Minnesota Press, 1978.

Strodtbeck, F. The family as a three-person group. *American Sociological Review,* 1954, *19,* 23–29.

Turk, J., & Bell, N. Measuring power in families. *Journal of Marriage and the Family,* 1972, *23,* 215–222.

VandenBos, G., & Stapp, J. Service providers in psychology: Results of the 1982 APA human resources survey. *American Psychologist,* 1983, *38,* 1330–1352.

Vaughn, C., & Leff, J. The influence of family and social factors on the course of psychiatric illness. *British Journal of Psychiatry,* 1976, *129,* 124–137.

Vincent, C. *Human sexuality in medical education and practice.* Springfield, Ill.: Charles C Thomas, 1958.

Walsh, F. (Ed.). *Normal family processes.* New York: Guilford Press, 1982.

Wampold, B., & Margolin, G. Nonparametric strategies to test the inclusion of behavioral states in sequential data. *Psychological Bulletin,* 1982, *92,* 755–765.

Waskow, I., & Parloff, M. *Psychotherapy change measures* (Department of Health, Education, and Welfare Publication No. ADM 74–120). Washington, D.C.: U.S. Government Printing Office, 1975.

Watt, N., Anthony, E., Wynne, L., & Rolf, J. (Eds.). *Children at risk for schizophrenia: A longitudinal perspective.* New York: Cambridge University Press, in press.

Wells, R., & Dezen, A. The results of family therapy revisited: The nonbehavioral methods. *Family Process,* 1978, *17,* 251–274.

Westley, W., & Epstein, N. *The silent majority.* San Francisco: Jossey-Bass, 1969.

Winter, W., & Ferreira, A. *Research in family interaction: Readings and commentaries.* Palo Alto, Calif.: Science & Behavior Books, 1969.

Woodward, C., Santa-Barbara, J., Levin, S., & Epstein, N. The role of goal attainment scaling in evaluating family therapy outcome. *American Journal of Orthopsychiatry,* 1978, *48,* 464–476.

Woodward, C., Santa-Barbara, J., Streiner, D., Goodman, J., Levin, S., & Epstein, N. Client, treatment and therapy variables related to outcome in brief, systems-oriented family therapy. *Family Process,* 1981, *20,* 189–197.

Wynne, L. Family research and family therapy: A reunion? *Journal of Marital and Family Therapy,* 1983, *9,* 113–117.

Chapter 42

Training in Family Therapy

GARY F. GANAHL
LUCY RAU FERGUSON
LUCIANO L'ABATE

THEORETICAL NEEDS AND TRAINING PERSPECTIVE

Whether the field of family therapy has too much or too little theory is difficult to determine. Most observers of the field agree that there is too little systematic theory building. However, most also note the proliferation of "part-theories" or "part-interventions" (Zuk, 1976), which cover only a small part of observable data that need to be incorporated into a comprehensive theory. Many have referred to family therapy as existing in a conceptual wilderness where methods of intervention vary widely, each practitioner espouses a separate theory, and interventions depend as much upon individual style and personality as they do upon specific theories (Ackerman, 1972; Bloch, 1974; Russell, 1976; Yogev, 1982a). Although the situation has improved somewhat during the past five years as several schools of family therapy have achieved prominence, Gurman & Kniskern's (1981a) general text on family therapy schools indicated a continuing proliferation of theory. Both von Trommel (1982) and Skynner and Skynner (1979) considered the poor integration of theories a peculiarly American phenomenon resulting from the high value that is placed on competition and independence and leading to the highlighting of differences rather than a search for common effective factors. Von Trommel stated his opinion that the intensity of competition in America leads to an inflated allegiance to particular schools, hindering cooperative work and the integration of different concepts and methods. This situation is similar to that in early family interaction research: Each pioneer created methods from scratch and paid scant attention to replicating the methods of others (Frank, 1965; Mishler & Waxler, 1968; Spiegel & Bell, 1959).

Another problem is that theorizing may overemphasize the pathological end of the spectrum of human behavior, unbalancing the normal, or optimally healthy, end. Although warnings about such an imbalance have been carried over from psychiatry to clinical psychology, the warnings have not always been heeded (Kantor & Lehr, 1976; Ruesch & Bateson, 1968). Theory building is taking place in family psychology on a broader spectrum of human interaction (Walsh, 1982; Westley & Epstein, 1969) though sometimes at too abstract a level, in that theory is not tied closely enough to observable behavior. Until lower-level constructs are created, connecting current theory to behaviors that can be observed in therapy rooms, efficient training in therapeutic activities will be greatly hampered (Pinsof, 1981), and the empirical verification of theories will continue to be difficult.

Currently, the most pressing need is for a more comprehensive theory, not just of family therapy but of family psychology. We need a better understanding of family processes and better ways of conceptualizing and specifying those processes so that we agree sufficiently for research to follow. Unfortunately, even to agree upon standard definitions of family therapy (Gurman & Kniskern, 1978; Wells & Dezen, 1978) or of systems is difficult (Russell, 1976). We must work toward a theory that is comprehensive enough to include the range of family functioning, from wellness to pathology. Although pragmatically oriented therapists may be satisfied to stop at a theory of change, as suggested by the strategic school of therapy (Haley, 1976; Rohrbaugh, Tennen, Press, & White, 1981), we consider a theory of change insufficient for a psychology of the family, which must also include a theory of the maintenance of normal functioning, which we hope will in turn broaden into a theory of prevention, wellness, and growth. To deal with the theoretical disarticulation in family therapy and to bring together information on diverse populations, a conceptual superstructure or an integrated link with other theories of human behavior must be developed (Bagarozzi, 1980; Russell, 1976).

One specific need is for more goal-oriented theory in family system theories that place high value on nonlinear causality. As Caille (1982) and Russell (1976) have noted, unless the goals and values of the family are central, the model will be circular, more representative of the simple self-regulating mechanism of a closed system than of a complex, open-system, goal-oriented human family. Goals and values are central for the simple reason that they affect the system's structure and rules. The alternative to such theorizing is that of Aronovich (1982) and Elkhaim, Prigogine, Guattori, Stengers, and Denenbourg (1982), who drew on biological, ecological, and physical system models to create an explanatory circular causality that needs no reference to teleological principles such as cause, purpose, or goal.

Despite Haley's objections, it is possible to develop a comprehensive theory of human behavior, one that subsumes many of the divergent theories. In fact, significant efforts have already been made in this direction (Abroms, 1983; Engel, 1977, 1980; Pearce & Cronen, 1980; Pinsof, 1983). Abroms has promoted a general theory of human behavior, but the theory is limited because, in its lineal causality, physical causes precede "mental" causes (as if the two were separable and not involved in mutual causality). The Palo Alto group has provided a potential link between divergent theories—the theory of Type I and Type II changes (Watzlawick, Weakland, & Fisch, 1974). Type I changes can occur within a system without changes in the basic rules or the structure; Type II changes require a change in the basic rules or the structure of the system. These concepts may be further developed to create an integrative structure in conjunction with the cybernetic principles of positive and negative causality. Negative causality refers to situations in which a particular pattern of interaction reoccurs because other, potential patterns of interaction have been blocked. Positive causality refers to the family's choosing the potential pattern of interaction that the family believes will serve it best. Type I changes may be linked with positive causality and Type II changes linked with negative causality; particular interventions or treatment approaches may be categorized according to whether they enhance Type I or Type II changes. Skills training, for example, would be categorized a Type I change, adding to family complexity and increasing the possibility of positive choices. A sufficient amount of Type I change could lead to restructuring at the systemic level, though it may be simpler at this point to keep separate the different theoretical approaches to change.

It is particularly important in this early stage of theoretical and empirical development that we look for useful contributions wherever we find them rather than limiting ourselves to system-based approaches or to behaviorally based approaches. Barton and Alexander (1977), for example, demonstrated some of the necessary and beneficial results of a more eclectic, behaviorally based theory of family functioning. Liddle and others (Kolevzon & Green, 1983; Liddle, 1982; Pinsof, 1983) have suggested that we must be careful to avoid creating an eclectic grab bag rather than a more integrated model. Liddle (1982) suggested beginning with the "clarification, specification, and verification" of individual theories, followed then—but only then—by work on integration. Referring to a structural theory of systems, he suggested that we want most to achieve interconnections between theories, with boundaries that are neither too rigid nor too diffuse. Rigid boundaries lead to the current situation in which theories overlap little or not at all; diffuse boundaries lead to a confusing, unstructured eclecticism that leaves one at a loss about how to proceed with therapy.

A primary task of an integrative theory of family psychology is to link the structure and the function of the family to the subsystem and the suprasystem levels. With the exception of the theories reviewed in this *Handbook* (see L'Abate, Chapters 40 & 46) no current comprehensive theory links family process with individual development (Russell, 1976). Family psychology, if it is to be developed and accepted by psychology at large, must incorporate and value the experience, behavior, values, motivation, health, and many other facets of the individual personality. The comprehensiveness need not, as some have claimed (Haley, 1974), damage an understanding of the impact that members of the individual's family have upon one another; rather, the comprehensiveness should enrich our understanding. Liddle's (1978) discussion about the hazards of family therapy in academic situations highlights the absurdity of the extreme position that the individual is either real or not real, critical or not critical, rather than an independent and an interdependent system that must be dealt with at two levels. Nascent theories are attempting to do justice to both system levels at once (Engel, 1980; Koestler, 1978; Minuchin & Fishman, 1981; Pearce & Cronan, 1980). The effect of the suprafamily level, or the context in which the family is embedded, must also be addressed in any comprehensive theory. More attention needs to be paid to extended family networks, neighborhoods, self-help groups and social networks, ethnicity and subculture, and larger contextural issues such as society, work, and leisure, as well as smaller contextual issues such as the therapist-family interaction with the referring person (Selvini-Palazzoli, Boscolo, Cecchin, & Prata, 1978). Consideration should also be given to the impact that the treatment setting has on treatment effectiveness and training.

We must also be concerned with incorporating psychological knowledge about teaching, learning, motivation, and behavior change into our own teaching and supervision as well as into theories about why families change or maintain satisfactory or unsatisfactory states. Often, we pay too little attention to ourselves as teachers and supervisors, as if we somehow stand outside the total system of teacher/client/student. Too rarely do we apply our knowledge of psychology to ourselves and our job performance.

Finally, theories of family process and family functioning must be upgraded and tied to a larger understanding of human behavior. We must pay particular attention to systematizing and categorizing family process and structure, putting these terms into operation in meaningful, observable ways. We must create theories that connect process and structure to each other and to other levels of human interaction. Two decades ago, Haley (1963) called for these advances in research and theory; today, we still have not developed workable categories of families or therapies. Such development, by simplifying, would aid both theory and research and might enhance agreement and cooperation among researchers and theorists. The task we have laid out will take many years; it will not be completed by the current generation of family theorists. Encumbent upon us as trainers is the development in our students of the willingness and the ability to meet the theoretical needs of the field. Fortunately, responses to these needs are already being made, providing the groundwork for further developments.

At the Galveston Family Institute, the birthplace of several currently active theorists of note, students are expected to learn, but not necessarily practice, several conceptual approaches to family therapy and family functioning. The intention of director Harry Goolishian, an active theorist and a student of the philosophy of science, is to teach trainees to evaluate clinical assumptions and learn to create and evaluate family approaches at the theoretical and the pragmatic levels. This program goes a step beyond Haley's often repeated statement about the need to assess treatment effectiveness, a step much needed in a field that is top-heavy with practitioners balanced on a very narrow conceptual base.

A similar emphasis is placed on the development of personal theories of therapy and critical evaluative skills at the Boston Family Institute and its spin-off centers (Constantine, 1976; Duhl & Duhl, 1979). The training is experiential: All first-year students participate in a theory lab that is designed to "explore, review, shake-up, and integrate those attitudes, hypotheses and operational constructs by which trainees already function" (Duhl & Duhl, p. 60). The students explore the relationship between their theories and their function in therapy; they also study the important theories, the personalities of the theorists who developed them, and the basic data from which the theories were derived. Students are explicitly required to use their personal experiences to develop their own hypotheses and build their own theories. This requirement fits well with the research on theory development indicating that therapists' implicit theories of human nature guide their behavior (Goodyear & Bradley, 1983) and that the choice of theoretical models in any field depends upon the life histories and personality characteristics of those creating the theory (Elms, 1981).

In supervision theory, supervisors' goals and values, possibly even their personal constructions of reality, have an impact on how theories are formed (Lionels, 1967 (cited in Sunderland, 1977); Peterson & Bradley, 1980). It is important, then, to note the impact that the students' personalities have upon the adoption and implementation of theories and to help the students explore, as in the Boston group, their personal assumptions and theories. Introducing students to developmental theories about the family (Carter & McGoldrick, 1980; Ferguson, 1979) may be especially important, in that most therapists in training are young adults who will be working with families at life-cycle stages that they themselves have not yet experienced (a point that is discussed in the supervision section). Students should be encouraged to research the mesh between specific personality orientation and the theories and methods of intervention. Liddle (1982) suggested a periodic "Epistemological Declaration" of what we think we know, how we know it, and how we make clinical decisions.

Wynne (1983) commented on the importance of combining therapy and research in the development of theory. A brief look at the major innovators in family therapy indicates the importance of clinical training and experience. Pioneer programs that actively emphasized practice, research, and theory (e.g., those of the Bateson group, which produced Haley, Satir, Watzlawick, Weakland, Fisch, and Bodin, among others; the Ackerman and Milan groups; the Oregon and McMaster groups) have produced important theorists who have shown up in studies of prominence in the marital and family field (Textor, 1983; Thaxton & L'Abate, 1982). What distinguishes these teaching centers is their active commitment to theoretical exploration and development, not merely to producing outcome statistics but to making the statistics more meaningful by tying low-level observation to higher-level theorizing.

Theorizing by future family psychologists can be fostered in several ways by the programs in which they are trained. One way is continue throughout training and supervision to ask students their hypotheses about the information available to their eyes and ears. They should be continually questioned about what they see and what sense they make of their perceptions as well as what higher-level theories guide their actions. Cleghorn and Levin (1973) and Tomm and Wright (1979) have developed an exhaustive list of perceptual and conceptual skills that is of great value to trainers. The Milan group (Selvini-Palazzoli, Boscolo, Cecchin, & Prata, 1980) has offered a model for interviewing that emphasizes creating and confirming hypotheses during the clinical interview and linking them to the behavior observed. Also useful are questions about the students' theories of change and learning and how the theories relate to the way they do therapy. When presenting students with demonstration tapes of master therapists, it is important to realize that learning will not occur by imitation alone, and that trainees must clearly distinguish between the charisma of these outstanding family therapists and the theoretical assumptions that underlie their actions on screen (Bloch, 1974; Russell, 1976; Yogev, 1982a).

One particularly effective way to help students develop their abilities to theorize and to discriminate among theories is to present them with more than one model of supervision. This method was used at the family therapy internship in psychology at the Harlem Valley Psychiatric Center in New York and has been advocated by Tucker & Liddle (1978) and McDaniel, Weber, & McKeever (1983). Such teaching uses confusion positively to develop in the students a thoughtfulness that will lead them to select from, or integrate, divergent points of view and will encourage them to evaluate the usefulness of theories, develop rationales for action, and observe data that support one intervention rather than another. Maximal learning will occur when supervisors freely discuss their differences and the rationales for their approaches, supporting their actions by the data observed in the family interaction. Further help may come from exposure to anthropology and sociology, fields whose theoretical traditions are divergent enough to require (as does the method already described) thoughtfulness and integration that are accompanied by a period of confusion for the student.

In summary, we can encourage students and trainees to develop as theorists in family therapy by exposing them to disciplines in which theorizing is actively pursued, for example, sociology and anthropology, where contextual concerns and the impact of social context are seriously considered. If to this knowledge is added knowledge of developments in psychology, useful links can be forged. But the links will be forged only if the students have some interest in theory and some practice in theory development, which allows them to see themselves as potential theorists. A step toward this process is to let students see their supervisors and teachers as role models in this capacity. Co-supervisors can help by presenting divergent models which, by generating confusion, demand that the students think and integrate. Supervisors who will publicly challenge, debate, and resolve their differing points of view can help students to think more analytically. Also useful is pushing students to identify personal materials that may lead to their own theories and to see how the theories of prominent theorists have developed from their personal views. Students can be further encouraged to apply theories to their day-to-day lives and to evaluate their usefulness (Constantine, 1976; Lange & van der Hart, 1983). Finally, students can be urged in supervision to continually form hypotheses about families, to articulate the hypotheses in testable forms, and to refine them according to the evidence presented in sessions (Selvini-Palazzoli et al., 1980).

At another, more formal level, students can be exposed to the philosophy of science and to theories about what makes a "good" theory, a theory that contributes to the development of science. They can be exposed to the natural history of science and how it works, rather than to a description of how it should work (Angyal, 1939; Barzun, 1964; Bateson, 1972; Hanson, 1961; Kuhn, 1972; Popper, 1959, 1963a, 1963b). Students should know examples of successful theory development, such as the progress made by the Utah group (see Barton, Alexander, & Sanders, Chapter 35 of this *Handbook*).

Of extreme importance is the application of learning theories to teaching modes. Constantine (1976) and Duhl and Duhl (1979) have paid close attention to this application and have required their trainees to do so, first as they consider their own preferences and later as they consider the preferences of their clients. Theorizing about the necessary components for learning or change thus becomes more organic. Constantine, for example, considered preferences for setting (group, individual), for cognitive representational systems (affective, intellectual, imagistic), and for orderliness. He mentioned the usefulness of a rich mixture of the various possibilities in each teaching setting, so that students with a variety of learning styles will profit from the instruction and learn to use a variety of teaching possibilities with their own clients and to be open to information from more than one channel. Rioch (1970), discussing the training of psychotherapists, highlighted the importance of a theory about how clients and trainees learn, emphasizing theory that differentiates the kinds of education or learning needed at different stages of development and for different kinds of learning deficits. Within psychology are a number of developmental theories that can be added to the life-cycle focus of family therapists and formed into a more comprehensive theory of learning stages and cognitive receptivity. Such training would be a welcome addition to the current training models, which are based on intuition and experience rather than on explicit theory about what is and is not essential in training (Andolfi, 1979; Kniskern & Gurman, 1980). The differences in such approaches to designing teaching may account for the zest that the Duhls and Constantine have noticed in their students when they approached a task of theory building. Lambert (1980, p. 443) and Holloway and Hosford (1983) have also noted the importance of a theory about learning and training and have highlighted the important variables in learning styles that should be attended to in training.

In theory training, development is an important consideration. At first, students want answers; they may not welcome Socratic questions. Anxiety about their roles and their limited knowledge calls for a supportive educative stance that limits the field of vision while reducing anxiety and adding structure. Initially, training may teach students to simplify by categorizing or fitting information into a preordained structure. This process differs from that of the open-minded theoretician, who sees more broadly and hypothesizes, rejects, and rehypothesizes many times before achieving a testable theory that relates to the data base. It is also alien to the breadth of vision initially needed to select the variables that are important for theory. When such variables are handed to the students on a platter, preselected by their instructors, development to the level of theorizing may be slower. The Boston Family Institute has an attractive way of teaching theory in a more organic way without an initial simplified theory (Duhl & Duhl, 1979), though we believe that complicating the picture later, after initial simplification, is also viable. It is a rare student who will not begin noticing new aspects of a situation and asking a different set of questions if not deterred by an overly dogmatic belief in one approach. Those who do not ask such questions are perhaps better suited for paraprofessional training than for full preparation as professional family therapists. Their knowledge runs the risk of obsolescence if they do not have the means to renew it constantly or cannot be constantly supervised by someone who is closer to the development of the profession (Wildman & Wildman, 1974). Presumably the development of the psychotherapist is cyclical; it has been likened to tightening the nuts on the hub of a wheel (Schultz, 1971). The same issues come around again at higher levels, and needs are returned to for new attention after others have been dealt with. Engaging students in theory development will, we hope, be surety against obsolescence. The ability to renew one's knowledge from the ashes of one's disconfirmed theory should offer to psychologists, as it did to the phoenix, the promise of eternal vitality.

Because part of our theory of change is that people do not change only, or even primarily, through understanding or good intentions, we believe it important for students to engage in theory building. With proper guidance, students should then more frequently pursue theory development in their professional lives. Our suggestion (analogous to the research apprenticeship described by Rickard & Siegel, 1976) is that students, after some initial instruction in theory building and exposure to faculty role models, construct their own theories. An alternative has been described by Bateson (1979, p. 6), who required advanced students from several backgrounds to develop theories based on a problem he presented to them; they could not simply apply, in rote fashion, their own formal training, and they had to rely on their own observational, deductive, and inductive processes.

ACADEMIC TRAINING

As noted in the preceding chapter, academic training in family therapy has been minimal, but we have seen improvement in the past decade. Many universities and internship sites now offer seminars and courses in family therapy (Cooper, Rampage, & Soucy, 1981; Ganahl & L'Abate, 1983; Liddle, Vance, & Pastushak, 1979), but few offer additional courses that would provide a more comprehensive understanding of family psychology. In a survey of academic training programs and internship sites (Ganahl & L'Abate, 1983), 84 percent and 66 percent, respectively, offered courses in family therapy, the modal number being one. Very few programs offered courses beyond those, though four universities (Georgia State University, Michigan State University, University of Rhode Island, and University of Kansas) offer subspecialities in this area, and other programs offer more specialized approaches or applications as advanced seminars. Of the 22 academic programs in clinical and counseling psychology that answered the survey, only 37 percent offered more than one course in the marital and family area or recommended that coursework in this area be taken from other departments.

For those wishing to offer training in this area, textbooks in family psychology have been nonexistent; even a comprehensive textbook on family therapy training has been difficult to find. Now, however, texts are available: for example, the Goldbergs' (Goldberg & Goldberg, 1980) introduction to family therapy and Hoffman's (1981) excellent text on the development of family therapy from the theoretical and conceptual beginnings to the current, growing edges. For more sophisticated students, the Gurman and Kniskern (1981a) *Handbook of Family Therapy* offers a very useful study guide with an organizing conceptual framework which, like Ford and Urban's (1963) classic text on psychotherapy, makes theory comparison quick and efficient, highlighting the most important features of each theory.

For those wishing to offer a more comprehensive approach to family therapy, no comprehensive texts yet provide a theory for joining what is known about individual psychology to systems and family theory, though works in this area are beginning to appear (L'Abate, 1983). Although useful texts deal with the family life cycle (e.g., Carter & McGoldrick, 1980), an important perspective for family psychologists, nothing currently meets the standards of such integrative theorists as Pinsof (1983) or Alexander, Barton, Waldron, & Mas (1983), who have taken a broad approach in their family therapy. Until more comprehensive texts and more useful data collection and theorizing have been developed, teaching a comprehensive family therapy will continue to be difficult. There is still no agreement about what basic skills and techniques are necessary for family therapists or what areas of knowledge are sufficiently substantive to justify specialized training. Clearly, there are those who believe that there is a relevant body of literature, and efforts have been made to create a standard training package in family and marital therapy (Nichols, 1979; Winkle, Piercy,

& Hovestadt, 1981); but no general agreement has been reached about the necessary and sufficient components of training, either in family therapy or in the much broader area of family psychology.

For those who are interested, there are a number of descriptions of family therapy training programs in academic institutions (Garfield, 1979; Jessee & L'Abate, 1981; L'Abate, Berger, Wright, & O'Shea, 1979; Liddle, 1980; Liddle & Saba, 1982; Piercy, Hovestadt, Fernell, Franklin, & McKeon, 1982; Rosenbaum & Serrano, 1979); in community mental health centers that have professionals and paraprofessionals as well as trainees (Flomenhaft & Carter, 1977; Garrigan & Bambrick, 1977; Hare & Frankena, 1972; Kaslow, 1977; Lange & van der Hart, 1983; Meyerstein, 1977); in medical centers and internship training sites (Abel, Bruzzese, & Wilson, 1974; Cleghorn & Levin, 1973; Dell, Sheely, Pulliam, & Goolishian, 1977; Epstein & Levin, 1973; Ferber & Mendelsohn, 1969; Mendelsohn & Ferber, 1972; Miyoshi & Liebman, 1969; Sander & Beels, 1970; Schopler, Fox, & Cochrane, 1967; Shapiro, 1975; Stier & Goldenberg, 1975); and in free-standing institutes (Andolfi & Menghi, 1980, Constantine, 1976; Dillon, 1976; Duhl & Duhl, 1979; Falicov, Constantine, & Breunlin, 1981; Luthman & Kirschenbaum, 1974). Examples of training programs in family psychology are fewer— the subspecialties at Georgia State University (see Appendix A) and at Michigan State University (see Appendix B) and a special graduate program for rural psychology, which is taught from a systems perspective (Winkle et al., 1981).

The program and course descriptions referred to have been criticized for insufficient detail concerning content and the components and techniques of training, as well as for lack of information about the effectiveness of training programs in general (Byles, Bishop, & Horn, 1983; Kniskern & Gurman, 1979; Liddle & Halpin, 1978; Stedman & Gaines, 1978). Kniskern and Gurman (1979) were justified in commenting that "almost without exception the credibility of these programs has depended on the reputation of the provider" (p. 299). That situation has been changing recently because of improved evaluation of training courses and programs (see Ganahl, Ferguson, & L'Abate, Chapter 41 of this *Handbook*). Von Trommell (1982) noted that programs that had clear goals and aims also had an enhanced ability to measure the progress of training and that, in general, these programs were housed in departments of psychology. These programs emphasized technical skill development for change facilitation and generally used live observation of the trainees' therapy behavior.

As attested to by the number of current articles, such skill training, tied to learning objectives, is becoming increasingly important in training for psychotherapy. In family therapy, this development is both recent and welcome, but it is just beginning to get under way. Meyerstein (1977) commented on the lack of agreement about necessary skills, standards for specifying those skills, and the materials and procedures for teaching them but also noted the steps being taken in this direction. Most of the work in this area has been devoted to learning objectives and skill training for family therapy, though Anderson, Amatea, Munson, and Rudner (1979) have commented on training objectives for a broader program. Those who have created lists of skills and objectives for family therapy (Alexander, Barton, Shiavo, & Parsons, 1976; Alexander et al., 1983; Allred & Kersey, 1977; Cleghorn & Levin, 1973; Erickson, 1973; Falicov et al., 1981; Garrigan & Bambrick, 1977; Jessee & L'Abate, 1981; Pinsof, 1983; Street & Treacher, 1980; Tomm & Wright, 1979), as discussed in this *Handbook* by Warburton and Alexander (Chapter 43) and by Patterson (Chapter 44), have generally divided skills into perceptual, conceptual, and executive skills. Others (Alexander et al., 1983; Alexander & Parsons, 1982; Barton & Alexander, 1983) have also discussed relationship skills, which can be seen as connected to the counseling tradition in training in microskills (Forsyth & Ivey, 1980) but are based on explicit research on the impact that these skills have on family treatment.

The concreteness and the behavioral specificity of the skills and programs mentioned vary widely. Falicov et al. (1981) noted the need to address the implementation of such skills in therapy as well as the need to create increased specificity and definition in teaching the skills. The Utah group (Alexander et al., 1983; Alexander & Parsons, 1982; Barton & Alexander, 1983) and the Chicago Family Institute (Pinsof, 1983) have added greatly to the literature in this area: Their stage-specific models of therapy help put skills in perspective and make it easier to determine which skills are appropriate where. Several of the teachers who use such methods (Cleghorn & Levin, 1973; Falicov et al.; Lange & van der Hart, 1983) have pointed out that different skills should be taught and polished in different settings. For Falicov, perceptual and conceptual skills are best learned through live observation of families and video replay; Lange and van der Hart (1983) and Tomm and Wright (1979) believe that perceptual and conceptual skills can also be taught through didactic instruction, a contention to which Tomm and Leahey (1980) have added some empirical support. Resnikoff (1981) and Caille (1982) have developed a conceptual structure of evaluation questions to help shape perceptual and conceptual understanding. Green and Saeger (1982) offered a series of five written assignments that lead to the development of perceptual and conceptual skills by asking students to pay attention to, and integrate, specific types of information. One task involves observing communication in a videotaped family interview; another involves a structured family assessment report; and others involve writing family treatment plans for executive skills and analyzing both a therapist-family interaction observed on video and one's own family of origin. The latter technique was originated by Bowen (1972) and frequently used by trainers in this field.

Ferguson (1979) has argued for the use of methods such as reviewing the genogram and history of one's own family of origin, partly to build a sense of the family as developing through the stages of the life cycle as well as to heighten awareness of cultural and individual differences in family styles. The power of each of these assignments is that specific questions or outlines are provided, thus aiding the student's ability to attend to important information and undertake the task of conceptual integration. Constantine (1976) also gives observers individual assignments, as does Bagarozzi (1980). There is general agreement that executive or interventive skills can be shaped only by practice in role playing or live situations, though they can be preconditioned by observation of a model exhibiting such skills. This is because students must not only be cognizant of the range of skills but must also choose appropriate skills in specific therapeutic situations. Live observation increases the involvement of the students behind the mirror and makes the training experience more useful. The Milan group (Boscolo & Cecchin, 1982) routinely expect all members of the training group to be responsible for creating a workable intervention for the family. Garrigan and Bambrick (1977) described a technique used by many family therapy trainers: Using a videotape of an experienced therapist working with a family, they mark points where the tape will be stopped and ask students to suggest interventions before they see what the therapist did. This method can be extended and made more useful by requiring students to describe how they will decide whether their suggestions have been helpful to the family and how they will use any corrective feedback they obtain.

Another time-honored method of teaching conceptual skills has been to ask students to prepare papers or workshops on topics in family therapy, thus requiring students to conceptualize and integrate ideas better so that they can transmit them to others. Workshops and oral presentations offer an opportunity for students to see clearly the areas in which they are making sense and those in which they are confusing the audience; they also allow corrective feedback from the audience. We also recognize the value of learning to write one's ideas in traditional scientific form. Constantine (1976) extended this push for conceptualization and integration even further by asking students to recognize and articulate their personal theories of family functioning and present them rather than the theories of someone else.

Relationship skills are not as easy to teach at this point because fewer training models have been developed, though research (Alexander et al., 1976; Kniskern & Gurman, 1980) clearly indicates which skills are useful. Weiss and Bodin (Bodin, 1969), for example, referred to the positive reinforcement of clients' behaviors as a useful and effective component of an experienced therapist's style. There has also been a good deal of research on relationship skills in counseling psychology, research on relationship skills is represented by the work of Carkhuff and Truax (1965) and the microskills training of Ivey (Forsyth & Ivey, 1980).

SUPERVISION

Supervision of family therapy is the area most widely covered in the literature on the training of family therapists. Most of the literature has developed since 1975 (according to McColley & Baker, 1982, only nine articles on the supervision of psychotherapy appeared between 1950 and 1975). Considering its recency, the literature is quite good, though it is limited in several respects. The primary weaknesses are those of the field in general—too little theory, research, and delineation of specific goals and techniques.

Holloway and Hosford (1983) listed several basic design flaws in supervision research: global or imprecise variables, lack of specificity in design procedures and treatment conditions, and more basic problems such as nonrandom assignments to groups and inadequate sample sizes. Kniskern and Gurman (1979) have also commented on the poor research to date but noted that some knowledge of the effective factors in supervision has been developed. Supervision research has overemphasized the supervision of beginning therapists and neglected research on advanced supervision skills, trainee variables, training-context variables, and the generalization of training effects to actual practice, as well as the maintenance of those effects (Holloway & Hosford; Lambert, 1980). Research on the deterioration effects that may result from supervision has also been neglected; only one study, to our knowledge, has been conducted (Pierce, Carkhuff, & Berenson, 1967).

Meyerstein (1977) and others have suggested that too much emphasis is placed on skill training and not enough on basic theory or research. Although we agree about the need to specify theoretical assumptions, therapeutic procedures, and evaluative methods and the need to make explicit the connections between these, much room still exists for the specification of supervision techniques as well as the specification of goals, models, and purposes of various approaches to supervision (Liddle & Saba, 1982). This is true of supervision models that are tied to specific intervention theories as well as to the more general models for family therapy or psychotherapy. With increased specificity will come more useful research, and from the resulting data base, more effective practice and preparation for practice will follow. Kagan's (1983) demonstration that supervisors' self-descriptions do not match supervisor behaviors reminds us of the importance of including observational data in research designs.

Training for supervision has been, until recently, relatively unavailable, despite the obvious needs. A sample of clinical psychologists, who ranked 12 professional activities according to the time devoted to each, ranked supervision 5th, ahead of research (Garfield & Kurtz, 1976). Training for supervision in academic or postdoctoral settings, however, has been relatively rare and has in no way approached the time spent on training for research. McColley and Baker's (1982) survey revealed that, although supervision of supervision was available in some academic and internship sites, formal course work in this area was offered at only 20 percent of the sites, and 30 percent of the sites offered no training other than experience. In another survey of training sites (Ganahl & L'Abate, 1983), only 14 percent of the internships and 10 percent of the clinical psychology programs offered training in supervision. Although trainers might have been excused in the past for believing that being a competent therapist was sufficient training for the role of supervisor, that belief is no longer valid (Kagan, 1983; Liddle & Saba, 1982).

A major debate in the current supervision literature is whether the skills and goals of supervision are specific and/or isomorphic to those of the therapy one is supervising or whether guiding supervision requires a different set of skills and a different theory, one that is unique to supervision and not based on the therapy being supervised (Loganbill & Hardy, 1983). There is no debate about the necessity for a theory of supervision and a set of supervisory skills that are based on the developmental stage of supervision and the special characteristics of the supervisees. Where such skills should be taught is the focus of current debate and speculation. McColley and Baker (1982) considered supervision of psychotherapy as complex and difficult as therapy itself (if not more difficult) and contended that it can be learned neither vicariously (by being supervised) nor before therapy skills have been mastered. This position would limit training in supervision to postdoctoral training at the earliest and probably to supervision of one's supervision in the workplace. We agree with Russell (1976) that mandatory supervision to ensure postdegree competence and the maintenance of treatment standards is important and that examination of supervision techniques and competence would also be valuable at this level.

Although the above position is well taken, we believe that learning supervision can and should begin earlier than it does in most programs. Piercy et al. (1982) reported training their advanced graduate students in the supervision of lower-level students. Jessee and L'Abate (1981) reported the benefits of training graduate students in the supervision of lower-level students who are performing enrichment, a more structured treatment approach and one that a graduate student can be assumed to master and be able to model and supervise while developing skills in more complicated family treatment. The specification of supervisor skills (Liddle & Schwartz, 1983) may make it increasingly feasible to train graduate students in some aspects of supervision while deferring others until later stages in their professional development.

Even a cursory look at the literature on supervision reveals a variety of training formats, supervisory goals, and training models. Although we cannot yet determine which should stay and which should go, we certainly can begin to look at the benefits of each and consider how they may be usefully combined.

Supervisors of family therapy do not agree on the necessary or sufficient activities of supervision, though consistency is high within specific theoretical orientations. In these the practice of supervision is based on the same theory of change which guides the practice of therapy. For example, therapies that stress personal growth and experiential approaches tend to stress those features in the supervision format. Likewise, models more closely tied to observable behaviors and the competency of family members tend to emphasize those same factors in supervision. What has been lacking is a more general model of the stages of learning, matching supervisory techniques to the stage-specific needs of the trainee. Such models have been developed for the supervision of counseling (Goodyear, 1982; Loganbill, Hardy, & Delworth, 1982; Sansbury, 1981) and may generalize to family supervision. One initial integrative model (Berger & Dammann, 1982), which matches the supervision orientations from various schools of family therapy and the trainees' developmental stage, is a significant development and should be followed by more specific delineations of supervisory techniques based on trainee variables. Stoltenberg (1981) has suggested that, in addition to developmental stages of trainees, theorists and researchers should also pay attention to the conceptual styles, cognitive levels, motivational sources, and value systems of trainees, as well as variables related to the learning environment and the kinds of reinforcers offered to students to encourage their development. Kagan (1983) suggested attention to the learning assumptions of the supervisor as well.

Although supervision has been discussed as if it were a known quantity, there is no specific agreement about what supervision entails. Most authors agree that supervision is primarily an enterprise aimed at teaching trainees competence as therapists while protecting the welfare of the clients in treatment, but there the agreement ends. Some see supervision as primarily a didactic endeavor (Bagarozzi, 1980;

Kaslow, 1977); others see it as primarily experiential (Whitaker, 1976). Some focus on the person of the therapist (Johnson, 1961; Nichols, 1975; Wolberg, 1954); others focus on skill development (Falicov et al., 1981; Pinsof, 1983). Some focus primarily on the client, others on the student's behavior (Sansbury, 1981); and some try to balance the clients' need to receive competent treatment against the students' needs to take risks and to experiment (Kagan, 1983). Some seek to maintain a hierarchical relationship with student-trainees (Haley, 1976); others seek an egalitarian relationship (Cohen, Gross, & Turner, 1976; Whitaker, 1976). Some do their supervision almost exclusively on a one-to-one basis (Loganbill et al., 1982; Nichols), others almost exclusively in group settings (Haley, 1976; Heath, 1982; Sansbury; Tucker, Hart, & Liddle, 1976). Some see the trainee as a technician in training, some as an apprenticed artisan, and others as a fellow traveler who has not crossed the same terrain that the trainer has. Some see themselves as coaches or consultants; others see themselves as directors. Some try to help the student's capability as a healer to emerge (Whitaker, 1976); others attempt to train the student what to do to be helpful (Haley, 1976). One supervisor's intrusion is another's stock in trade. Those who prefer skill training often consider exploration of the student's personal life too intrusive; experiential advocates consider directives sent into student therapy sessions too intrusive. All the goals mentioned are sought through a variety of training formats, including group, individual, live observation, instant feedback, peer supervision, cotherapy, team treatment, family-of-origin exploration, personal therapy, skill training role-plays, sculpting.

Some approaches to training are chosen specifically because they fit the techniques of the therapy being taught, some are chosen on the basis of theory, and some seem to emerge more from the training setting than because of any underlying theory of usefulness. Most important, some focus only on the student's in-session behavior (Haley, 1976); others use an all-encompassing approach that includes the roles of teacher, therapist, consultant, evaluator, and confessor (Bartlett, 1982). Given the poor preparation students often receive for psychotherapy, the broader approach is understandable. Psychotherapy supervision then becomes a miniature training institution because it has to correct lapses in earlier training. This kind of supervision is inefficient because it detracts from the supervisors' ability to teach the advanced skills they have prepared to impart (Rice & Gurman, 1973). Kagan (1983) noted that modeling, support, skill training, evaluative feedback on behaviors in treatment sessions, and other aspects of supervision in inclusive forms could also be provided by tapes of experienced therapists, tapes of the trainees themselves, peer supervision groups, better didactic instruction, and other well-thought-out training components.

Everett (1980) expressed similar sentiments and noted that the major component in supervision impasses is the poor or nonexistent instructional preparation of students. Clearly, there are more efficient ways to train in supervision (Tomm & Leahey, 1980; Waltz & Johnston, 1963), though they are frequently not used or researched.

There seems to be general agreement that one should put some focus on the behavior and the skills of the therapist (technical competence), some on conceptual skills (the ability to tie learning to practice), and some on the person of the therapist insofar as the person affects the implementation of the abilities already mentioned (Goodyear, 1982). No consensus exists on which areas should be emphasized, and they are emphasized differently in different forms of supervision. All approaches to supervision cannot be evaluated here, but good summary descriptions have been presented by Liddle and Halpin (1978). We have limited ourselves here to making recommendations for supervision and touching on some controversial issues about which we feel strongly.

Our choice of a supervision/training model derives from several considerations and goals. First, our main contract is with the students; focus should thus be on them rather than on clients. This attitude decreases the number of complications in the supervisor-therapist-client relationship, minimizes the therapist's temptation to violate generational boundaries (bypassing the student to work directly with the family), and lessens (we hope) any tendency to triangulate one member of the treatment triad.

Concerned with protecting the family's right to optimal treatment, we must weigh the first goal against the needs of the family and the level of development of the student. Obviously, the more inexperienced the student, the more likely the need for the supervisor's intervention. We fully recognize the trainee's need for experience and increased responsibility for treatment but wish to make supervision consistent with the trainee's development (Berger & Dammann, 1982; Blount, 1982; Cleghorn & Levin, 1973; Loganbill et al., 1982; Garrigan & Bambrick, 1977; Sansbury, 1981; Simon & Brewster, 1983; Stoltenberg, 1981; Yogev, 1982a, 1982b). Chief among the novice therapists' needs are the need for support and encouragement, clear expectations from trainers, realistic self-expectations, and gradually increasing responsibility. We like to give trainees as much experience as possible without overloading them, leaving room for their personal growth despite their early wishes for direction and structure from trainers. We wish the training experience to include a fair number of families and a broad range of clients, despite the sometimes low censuses in clinics. All these goals should be accomplished efficiently; trainers cannot devote their time entirely to training.

Trainees should expect and value accurate feedback about their assets and deficits as therapists; evaluation should be empirical rather than intuitive. Specific learning objectives and skills lend themselves well to such evaluation (Cleghorn & Levin, 1973; Falicov et al., 1981), but we also believe that self-evaluation by students is crucial, as is some form of feedback from clients (Kagan, 1983). We do not want supervision focused on technical matters to the exclusion of what the student is trying to accomplish and how the student and the clients perceive that attempt. In general, we wish the learning experience not only to consist of experience in doing therapy but to be based on similarities between the training structure and the family or treatment structures.

Given all these considerations, a combination of supervision approaches appears best, including live observation and treatment in a group setting, with team responsibility for treatment at later stages, live supervision during earlier stages, and cotherapy with the supervisor if called for. Opportunities to see experienced therapists at work are also valuable.

Live supervision

Live supervision is initially the method of choice because it allows accurate assessment of family needs and student performance, undistorted by student needs to look good, please the supervisor, conform to the supervisor's theories, or by selective inattention and forgetfulness. Live supervision allows improved perceptions of nonverbal behaviors and transference and countertransference phenomena in the treatment room. It uses supervisor time efficiently: Supervisors do not have to ask trainees for diagnostic information because they see for themselves. It also minimizes the supervisors' tendency, which emerges in other forms of supervision, to underestimate client pathology (Stein, Karasu, Charles, & Buckley, 1975). Behaviors that are important in therapist-family impasses but outside the therapists' awareness are available for inspection and intervention by the supervisors, who can also instruct observers behind the mirror while supervising. The unique and most powerful benefit of live supervision is the immediate reinforcement and correction of the trainee's therapeutic activities, providing better teaching for the student and better service to the clients.

The live-supervision format fits well with what we know about learning principles, in that learning occurs in the context in which the student will need to recall it and reinforcement is immediate. The student can learn more quickly in this situation (Kempster & Savitsky, 1967) and also learns how to recover control in a difficult session. The learning format is isomorphic to treatment, in that it is a model of competence (Haley, 1976; Rickert & Turner, 1978) which teaches the student to act competently rather than to talk competently about what could or should be done in treatment. The supervisor, rather than viewing the family as foreground (as is usual in verbal-recall supervision), can view the therapist as foreground. Therapist-family interaction can be observed directly, an impossibility for the therapist who cannot be both inside and outside the therapist-family system. Direct observation minimizes avoidance of therapist-focused supervision, blaming the family, triangulation of the. family by therapist and supervisor, and feelings that the supervisor does not really understand the treatment situation with a particular family (which may be true with other forms of supervision). This method provides high-quality, efficient training: Students supported by live supervisors can begin to treat families earlier in their careers and can see a range of more difficult cases.

Those who oppose this approach to treatment (Eckstein & Wallerstein, 1958; Nichols, 1975; Whitaker, 1976) and those who caution its users (Birchler, 1975; Russell, 1976) have pointed out the potential of this approach to foster excessive dependency, to lead to excessive therapist anxiety, and to neglect the development of a personal and intense supervisory relationship. Whitaker, for example, stated that "the experience of working with the supervisor is more valuable than technical indoctrination of a particular methodology" (p. 24). Although some critics have mentioned that live supervision may distract the student from the family, presumably in a negative way, the potential for positive distraction also exists.

The first response to such criticisms must be to direct detractors to the extensive literature on the successful use of such approaches (Berger & Dammann, 1982; Boylton & Tuma, 1972; Bullock & Kobayashi, 1978; Dillon, 1976; Haley, 1976; Heath, 1982; Liddle & Schwartz, 1983; Montalvo, 1973). Boylton and Tuma, for example, found that live supervision reduced trainees' anxiety, leaving them freer to focus on the family—a family that, incidentally, the therapist might not see without live supervision. Meyerstein (1977) and Ferber and Mendelsohn (1969) noted students' self-consciousness, fear of exposure, and other reluctances; but Ferber and Mendelsohn also reported that students who had been in front of the mirror were more confident, perhaps because they had come to see and accept themselves realistically as therapists. Our experience has been that students accommodate quickly and learn to accept their need for help and their lack of omniscience, both of which will continue to be part of their careers.

Dependency is the least of concerns when this method is handled well. Beroza (1983) reported confusions about where a student's work ends and the supervisor's begins, but this should not be a continuing problem. Supervisors can become less and less specific in their directions as time passes (Rickert & Turner, 1978), or, like the Milan trainers (Boscolo & Cecchin, 1982), they can agree to make no intervention for the first 30 minutes of a session, thus assuring students that they are on their own. Independent work can also be phased into training with students by having them see some cases on their own, present others on videotape, and bring in some clients for live consultation with the supervisor.

We do not consider the preceding objections serious, nor do we believe that any other method has equivalent potential for the development of therapist skills in a context that allows both student growth and client protection. Live supervision should not, however, be the only method of supervision training. Useful alternatives may be based on supervisor preference or skills, or on situational demands (Whiffen & Byng-Hall, 1982). We must be genuinely cognizant that we do not yet know what constitutes effective therapist skills. There is a great need for research relating therapist behavior to effective outcomes, such as Alexander's work (see Barton et al., Chapter 35 of this *Handbook*). When therapist behavior can be related to outcome, training therapists through live supervision and skill training will be greatly enhanced. One could then make a case for evaluating the outcomes of student cases as indicators of their development and growth, rather than observing their in-session behavior.

Group supervision

The second training format that we recommend is group supervision. The obvious benefits, described by several authors (Ard, 1973; Bardill, 1976; Dillon, 1976; Ferber & Mendelsohn, 1969; Heath, 1982; Meyerstein, 1977; O'Hare, Heinrich, Kirschnor, Oberstone, & Ritz, 1975; Sansbury, 1981; Steir & Goldenberg, 1975; Tucker & Liddle, 1978; Yogev, 1982a), have led to American Psychological Association and American Personnel and Guidance Association (APGA) recommendations of this approach in counseling internships. Most authors have found group supervision highly efficient and a method that allows maximal support for students. Because cases were seen by all, even small case-populations constituted fairly broad training; trainer time was saved by going over therapeutic situations with all trainees at once rather than repeating the same didactic material to different students.

Group supervision offers the opportunity to learn from, and to teach, others and assists the members by providing *(a)* emotional support and validation of their skills, *(b)* normalization of their weaknesses through observation of common difficulties, and *(c)* information such as cultural and ethnic material or material based on having grown up in a particular family structure. Trainees may consult with and advise, one another as auxilliary supervisors, thus improving their potential as future supervisors and increasing the number of useful ideas and viewpoints available to the group. The group process also affords an opportunity for instruction in family structure, process, and formation, as the group behavior frequently mimicks that of the family or the therapist-trainer dyad (Hare-Mustin, 1976; Meyerstein, 1977). Finally, the group offers opportunities for observational learning, which some consider the equal of direct experience (Bandura, 1969), and for both active and passive learning, benefiting learners of both styles (Bardill, 1976). Kempster and Savitsky (1967) also noted a good deal of active learning as students behind the mirror absorbed support for their current levels of ability and technical information. The model is also an opportunity for interdisciplinary cooperation when several disciplines are represented. Steir and Goldenberg (1975) noted that group members quickly got over fears of embarrassment and exposure and functioned effectively in the group.

Concerns have been voiced that group supervision would prove unmanageable because of trainee competiveness or secretiveness, but group supervision (despite valid concerns and difficulties) also presents a very positive opportunity for experiential learning. Groups demand more personal growth (Heath, 1982), and can be valuable when trainers using this format become knowledgeable about group process. Of the authors mentioned above, only Heath, (1982) and Ferber & Mendelsohn, (1969) referred to group process literature.

The major drawback to group supervision seems to be that supervisors, because of the diffuse responsibility and emotional neutrality dictated by the group situation, occasionally fail to come to grips with issues that are significant to the trainees (Kempster & Savitsky, 1967). This drawback supports the need for supplemental individual supervision. Peer supervision, without a recognized group leader and supervisor, remains of questionable benefit (Hare & Frankena, 1972; Meyerstein, 1977), though its usefulness may depend upon the group members' level of experience or the intermittent presence of a supervisor (Wendorf, 1984). An additional benefit seems to accrue to group supervision when the group members function as a team. Sharing the responsibility for treatment effectiveness (Berger & Dammann, 1982; Boscolo & Cecchin, 1982; Cromwell & Peterson, 1983; Heath, 1982) involves all members more fully and leads to a groupwide feeling of responsibility. Although perhaps not appropriate for beginning trainees, the model may be developed over the course of work with a group of supervisees.

Observational learning has been mentioned as one of the key components of group supervision. Although several authors have mentioned observation as a useful tool in teaching skills and relieving anxieties for beginning trainees (Lange & van der Hart, 1983; Lambert, 1980;

Yogev, 1982a), Nichols (1975, 1979) feared that students who observed a skilled therapist or the supervisor might not develop their own styles afterwards. Kagan (1983) also expressed reservations about observational learning, noting that students need to study and improve their own styles, not to imitate the styles of others. He considered observational learning appropriate for technicians engaged in regimented tasks but inappropriate for those who must develop their own styles and become self-regulated. We believe that students benefit greatly from observing supervisors or other experienced therapists, because they can see in practice the techniques that fit the theory they have been learning. Seeing several master therapists enables them to try out different styles to see which fits them best. Observation of cases involves trainees more fully than verbal description can. Trainees who see therapists in moments of triumph and of failure will have more realistic expectations about themselves, reducing their anxiety and increasing their competence (Koch, Leiderman, Mann, Ross, & Starr, 1982).

Simon and Brewster (1983) surveyed several well-known trainers concerning the observation of supervisor-therapists at work; the majority indicated that they favored the technique. Some considered imitation a relatively harmless form of flattery or believed that it may help the trainees by allowing them to identify with the supervisors' ability and competence. One trainer considered imitation positive because it gave him feedback on what the students were really receiving from his teaching. Another believed it beneficial for students to model his work but not his personal characteristics. Only one supervisor believed that modeling and imitation do not aid creativity. We believe that observation may lead to a lifelong internalization of beneficial attitudes, as described by Whitaker (1981), who said that in his head are the voices of several former supervisors to whom he can refer for help in his therapy.

Cotherapy has been mentioned as having potential for modeling or learning by example, but no current evidence indicates its superiority to individual therapy (Gurman & Kniskern, 1981b) or its effectiveness as a training device. Cotherapy is more time consuming and less cost-efficient, though it may be useful when relatively scarce cases need to be shared or when a trainer needs to join a trainee to treat a more difficult case. The model also allows experiential learning about dyadic interaction and relationship development, though we believe there may be better ways of focusing on such information.

Finally, we recommend that supervision be based on some empirical foundation, such as the empirical process recommended by Mead and Crane (1978) or therapists' behavior coding schemes such as those presented by Alexander and Parsons, (1982), Allred and Kersey (1977), Piercy, Laird, and Mohammed (1983), or Pinsof (1979). (See also Patterson Chapter 44 of this *Handbook*.) Such models, although they can greatly enhance training as well as knowledge about effective and ineffective forms of treatment and training, are not the final answer to all areas of development. Some areas are too complex to be specified by skills, and skill training cannot address the necessary spontaneity, the use of skills, or the understanding of when skills should be applied. Further, such models do not incorporate the importance of therapists' personal growth. Kagan (1983) noted that we are not yet sophisticated enough to observe relevant internal growth in therapists and pointed to Kingdon's (1975) research in which changes in the supervisor's behavior were related to changes in the client's behavior but concomitant changes were not observed in the therapist's behavior.

We are concerned, too, about the excessive emphasis in some programs on technical skills to the exclusion of an important area of supervision—focus on the person of the therapist. Although Sansbury (1981) noted correctly that supervision is not therapy and that the evaluative component keeps it from being therapy, significant personal development may still take place as a planned part of supervision. Skynner (1981) considered skill training useless without the concomitant development of the person of the therapist and expressed his opinion that technical skills in such a case would be used merely to hide the inadequacies of trainees and, applied rigidly and without feeling, would fail to benefit families. Yogev (1982a), in the following, spoke for many: "No matter how well therapists assess, diagnose, theoretically understand, and use effective techniques to deal with client problems, they also have to look for self-understanding and use their own feelings and behaviors as therapeutic tools" (p. 236). She, like others, believes that excursions into personal issues should be made but that they should be limited to areas that directly affect a trainee's therapeutic competence. Simon and Brewster (1983) concluded by quoting Haley: "You can train people in special techniques but how do you give them the wisdom to use them well?" (p. 66). Skills and data will not give direction or values; direction and values must come from within the person. Walton's (1983) answer to Haley's question is that the best way of ensuring such wisdom is to focus on the development of the person therapist so that he or she reaches the fullest and deepest personal differentiation and appreciation of the human condition, presumably as represented in oneself. We consider this issue partly a developmental issue in the supervision process and believe that focus on personal growth best follows some initial skill development.

Didactic preparation for supervision

With regard to didactic preparation for supervision, our recommendations are simple. First, we believe that early in their training, all trainees should be made aware of the group supervision literature (according to our scheme, they will be auxillary supervisors within training groups). We also believe that at some point, students need an extensive course covering the current material on the supervision of psychotherapy, particularly the supervision of family therapy. Although lack of material would have been a problem in the past, more high-quality articles and several books (Liddle & Saba, in press; Whiffen & Byng-Hall, 1982) on supervision for the family field are now available. Such training will help students clarify their goals as supervisors and stimulate theory and research on supervision, which will in turn improve supervisory techniques.

CONCLUSIONS

The future of the art and the promise of the method

The future of family therapy is completely open. The paradigm shift from individual to the family is under way; more and more people are being trained and are defining themselves as family therapists. The increasing number of publications, journals, and professional organizations will raise questions about competence, skills, professional differences, and status. There is no question, however, that the field is open to unbounded progress and growth. The question will not concern quantity; the question will concern quality. At what level will the profession be content to remain, and at what speed will the profession wish progress to take place? A way of ensuring progress in the profession is to carefully consider the requirements of evaluation and accountability. As old-fashioned and as rigid as these requirements may be, they remain the criteria that will assure high standards of practice as well as the regulation of the quacks and charlatans that plague any profession that receives public exposure and attention. The emphasis on peer review evaluation, which is required by many insurance companies, may force individual practitioners to account for the methods used.

We cannot overemphasize the importance of evaluation by the therapist rather than evaluation by external judges. However, the individual therapist who does not fulfill these requirements will have to yield that responsibility to external judges, who will be much more objective about a therapist's level of performance. In spite of the issues that such a review may raise, we favor any method that will ensure the delivery of the highest level of services to the public. Even if a few professionals should be unjustly or unfairly reviewed, this evaluation is preferable to a completely unchecked field of specialty. If the profession does not regulate itself, society will regulate it. It can regulate itself only if it accounts for its methods and its procedures. The more the profession can rely on methods, the better able it will be to select the methods that are effective and efficient.

Training

So far, a great deal of the training of family therapists has taken place in clinical settings: mental health clinics, hospitals, and private practice. In the recent past, in fact, no specific training programs have been related to family therapy except for marriage and family counselors in academic departments of home economics and child and family development. A few psychiatric social work and clinical psychology programs offer courses in family therapy, but the curriculum for most family therapists either has been traditional and individually oriented. There is not, then, a speciality of family therapy. There is a conglomeration of family therapists who belong to a variety of disciplines. The disciplines have different curricula, different departments, and different backgrounds. In a way, the variety is appropriate in a pluralistic society; the variety of backgrounds of those who call themselves family therapists is a promising state of affairs. On the other hand, the variety makes it more difficult to set standards of practice or definitions for licensing.

Is a curriculum necessary? We contend, of course, that clinical experience should go hand in hand with academic training and that the academic training of those who aspire to become family therapists should be as relevant as possible to family therapy (see Ganahl, Ferguson, & L'Abate, Chapter 41 of this *Handbook*). This training should be a consistent and relevant combination of academic and clinical material. The congruence of training and experience would, we hope, increase the effectiveness of family therapy. This aspiration—the setting up of a special curriculum—is difficult because each specialty and each profession has its own requirements, which have been designed by professionals who are not particularly interested in the family. For instance, many clinical psychology students who work with families still have to take courses in neuropsychology, learning, perception, motivation, individual psychodiagnostics, and psychotherapy before they can spend their time on a curriculum specifically devoted to the family. Clearly, an ideal curriculum would encompass both paradigms—the individual and the family-oriented—so that the student is aware of both paradigms, knows the pros and cons of each, and can choose to develop in one or both areas.

Lessening the irrelevance and waste in the training of family therapists is also important. As is now true in psychiatry, for example, the required four or five years of medical training seems a tremendous length of time before one can go into family therapy. However, as long as individuals are willing to undergo such training, there will be no other way of achieving it. At this point, we leave open the question of what curriculum is necessary for family therapists: Each profession will have to get its training in whatever way it can. It is especially unfortunate, though, that the gulf between family sociology and family therapy exists. As a result neither field can profit maximally from advances in the other.

Academic or experiential learning?

Training in family therapy should, ideally, include both academic and experiential learning. The latter would focus on the person of the therapist as relevant to the therapist as a professional. We favor personal and experiential training in the person of the therapist as well as academic training specific to the therapist's professional discipline. Diversity in training should contribute to family therapy as a pluralistic approach.

Technical training. We must separate technical skills from other clinical research and professional skills. Technical training can and should be differentiated from more global, more abstract, experiential clinical training. That is, technical training should ideally take place in a protected environment (i.e., with nonclinical families, nonclinical couples) where colleagues, graduate students, and supervisors would emphasize the basic knowledge underlying various methods. Technical training is still, in a way, book learning and, in some ways, is applied to invariant situations. Technical training should precede clinical applications: The student who has not mastered technical skills should not be exposed to families defined as clinical.

Clinical training. Clinical training consists of the direct application of techniques to clinically defined families (families who ask for help). At this point, trainees can, under supervision, apply the techniques that they have learned thus far. Clinical training can and should take place as a practicum during academic training and also in an internship in a full-time clinical exposure outside the academic base. This training means exposure to a variety of supervisors and a variety of supervision modes (e.g., videotapes, personal supervision, and in vivo supervision). Once trainees have experienced a broad range of clinical training, they can then be expected to choose their own course of professional development.

Scientific training. Scientific training refers to the research orientation of the trainee and is dependent on the specialty as well as on the trainee's interest in exposure to research experiences. It encompasses both knowledge of a variety of research and statistical techniques and on-the-job-training performance of a variety of research studies. This experience should and will be emphasized differently by different professions. For example, clinical psychology will generally be defined as a research profession in contrast to social work, which as a whole defines itself as a service profession.

Professional training. Professional training not only refers to the acquisition of professional skills (which may concern case management, fees, ethical issues, case records, interpersonal contacts with other professions, consulting, and supervising) but also refers to the continuing education of the individūal, which fortunately is a requirement in many professions. Most therapists update their skills through attendance at workshops, scientific meetings, and professional seminars, which should in many cases be altered to more usefully serve educational needs.

Competence. The completion of the above areas of training prepares the individual to become a productive practitioner in the area of family therapy: one who is capable not only of applying current research and treatment practices, but also of correcting his or her understanding of the field and advancing the profession. We expect the areas of training to be distinct, but not exhaustive of information in the field. On the contrary, we believe that additional experience will allow trainees to transcend their arbitrary boundaries and to create a more complete understanding of the family.

It is our belief that the areas of training are necessary but not sufficient conditions for practice, and therefore that training in family therapy at the professional level should demand nothing less than a doctorate or the equivalent. The specific discipline in which the degree is obtained is of little matter compared to the breadth and quality of training. One danger to the field of family therapy is the assumption that a masters degree is sufficient training for independent practice. It is not. It cannot cover the technical, academic, scientific, and professional aspects of family therapy. While it may produce competent technicians who work well under supervision and consultation models, it will not ensure the disciplined and enquiring professional behavior necessary for such a diverse and challenging field as family therapy, a field still in its early stages of development.

REFERENCES

Abel, R., Bruzzese, D., & Wilson, J. Short-term hospitalized patients: A vehicle for training as well as treatment. In L. R. Wolberg & M. L. Aronson (Eds.), *Group therapy 1974: An overview.* New York: Stratton Intercontinental, 1974.

Abels, P. On the nature of supervision. *Child Welfare*, 1970, *49*, 304–311.

Abroms, E. Beyond eclecticism. *American Journal of Psychiatry*, 1983, *140*, 740–744.

Ackerman, N. The growing edge of family therapy. In C. Sager & H. Kaplan (Eds.), *Progress in group and family therapy*. New York: Brunner/Mazel, 1972.

Alexander, J., Barton, C., Shiavo, R., & Parsons, B. Systems-behavioral intervention with families of delinquents: Therapist characteristics, family behavior, and outcome. *Journal of Consulting and Clinical Psychology*, 1976, *44*, 656–664.

Alexander, J., Barton, C., Waldron, H., & Mas, C. Beyond the technology of family therapy: The anatomy of intervention model. In K. Craig & R. McMahon (Eds.), *Advances in clinical behavior therapy*. New York: Brunner/Mazel, 1983.

Alexander, J., & Parsons, B. *Functional family therapy*. Monterey, Calif.: Brooks/Cole Publishing, 1982.

Allred, G., & Kersey, F. The AIAC: A design for systematically analyzing marriage and family counselors: A progress report. *Journal of Marriage and Family Counseling*, 1977, *3*(2), 131–137.

Anderson, L., Amatea, E., Munson, P., & Rudner, B. Training in family treatment: Needs and objectives. *Social Casework*, 1979, *60*, 323–329.

Andolfi, M. *Family therapy*. New York: Plenum Press, 1979.

Andolfi, M., & Menghi, P. A model for training in family therapy. In M. Andolfi & I. Zwerling (Eds.), *Dimensions of family therapy*. New York: Guilford Press, 1980.

Angyal, A. The structure of wholes. *Philosophy of Science*, 1939, *6*, 115–116.

Aponte, H., & Hoffman, K. The open door: A structural approach to a family with an anorectic child. *Family Process*, 1973, *12*, 1–44.

Ard, B. Providing clinical supervision for marriage counselors: A model for supervisor and supervisee. *Family Coordinator*, 1973, *22*, 91–98.

Aronovich, J. *Life cycle: Stability and evolution in families*. Paper presented at the annual meeting of the American Orthopsychiatric Association, San Francisco, April 3, 1982.

Bagarozzi, D. Wholistic family therapy and clinical supervision: Systemic, behavioral and psychoanalytic perspectives. *Family Therapy*, 1980, *7*, 153–165.

Bandura, A. *Principles of behavior modification*. New York: Holt, Reinhart & Winston, 1969.

Bardill, D. The simulated family as an aid to learning family group treatment. *Child Welfare*, 1976, *55*, 703–709.

Bartlett, W. A multidimensional framework for the analysis of supervision of counseling. *Counseling Psychologist*, 1982, *11*, 9–17.

Barton, C., & Alexander, J. F. Therapists' skills as determinants of effective systems behavioral family therapy. *International Journal of Family Counseling*, 1977, *5*, 11–20.

Barton, C., & Alexander, J. *The anatomy of therapeutic directives: A framework for effecting change in families*. Workshop presented at the annual meeting of the American Association of Marriage and Family Counselors, Washington, D.C., October 9, 1983.

Barzun, J. *Science: The glorious entertainment*. New York: Harper & Row, 1964.

Bateson, G. Experiments in thinking about observed ethological material. In G. Bateson, *Steps to an ecology of mind*. New York: Ballantine Books, 1972.

Bateson, G. *Mind and nature: A necessary unity*. New York: Bantam Books, 1979.

Berger, M., & Dammann, C. Live supervision as context, training and treatment. *Family Process*, 1982, *21*, 337–344.

Beroza, R. The shoemaker's children. *Family Therapy Networker,* 1983, *7*(2), 31–33.

Birchler, G. Live supervision and instant feedback in marriage and family therapy. *Journal of Marriage and Family Counseling,* 1975, *1,* 331–342.

Bloch, D. The family of the psychiatric patient. In S. Arieti (Ed.), *American handbook of psychiatry* (Vol. 1, 2d ed.). New York: Basic Books, 1974.

Blount, C. Developmental model of supervision: Implications for practice and research. In A. Hess, *Psychotherapy supervision: Expanding conceptual models and clinical practices.* Symposium presented at the annual meeting of the American Psychological Association, Washington, D.C., August 24, 1982.

Bodin, A. Family training literature: A brief guide. *Family Process,* 1969, *8,* 272–279.

Boscolo, L., & Cecchin, G. Training in systemic therapy at the Milan Center. In R. Whiffen & J. Byng-Hall (Eds.), *Family therapy supervision: Recent developments in practice.* London: Academic Press, 1982.

Bowen, M. Towards the differentiation of self in one's own family. In J. Framo (Ed.), *Family interaction: A dialogue between family researchers and family therapists.* New York: Springer Publishing, 1972.

Boylton, M., & Tuma, J. Training mental health professionals through the use of the "bug in the ear." *American Journal of Psychiatry,* 1972, *129,* 92–95.

Bullock, D., & Kobayashi, K. The use of live consultation in family therapy. *Family Therapy,* 1978, *5,* 245–250.

Byles, J., Bishop, D., & Horn, D. Evaluation of a family therapy training program. *Journal of Marital and Family Therapy,* 1983, *9,* 299–304.

Caille, P. The evaluative phase of systemic family therapy. *Journal of Marital and Family Therapy,* 1982, *8,* 29–39.

Carkhuff, R., & Truax, C. Training in counseling and psychotherapy: An evaluation of an integrated didactic and experiential approach. *Journal of Counseling Psychology,* 1965, *29,* 333–336.

Carter, E., & McGoldrick, M. *The family life cycle: A framework for family therapy.* New York: Gardner Press, 1980.

Cleghorn, J., & Levin, S. Training family therapists by setting learning objectives. *American Journal of Orthopsychiatry,* 1973, *43,* 439–446.

Cohen, M. W., Gross, S. J., & Turner, M. B. A note on a developmental model for training family therapists through group supervision. *Journal of Marriage and Family Counseling,* 1976, *2,* 48.

Constantine, L. Designed experience: A multiple, goal directed training program in family therapy. *Family Process,* 1976, *15,* 373–396.

Cooper, A., Rampage, C., & Soucy, G. Family therapy training in clinical psychology programs. *Family Process,* 1981, *20,* 155–166.

Cromwell, R., & Peterson, G. Multisystem-multimethod family assessment in clinical contexts. *Family Process,* 1983, *22,* 147–163.

Dell, P., Sheely, M., Pulliam, G., & Goolishian, H. Family therapy process in a family therapy seminar. *Journal of Marriage and Family Counseling,* 1977, *3,* 43–48.

Dillon, I. Teaching models for graduate training in psychotherapy. *Family Therapy,* 1976, *3,* 151–162.

Duhl, F., & Duhl, B. Structured spontaneity: The thoughtful art of integrative family therapy at BFI. *Journal of Marital and Family Therapy,* 1979, *5,* 59–75.

Ekstein, R., & Wallerstein, R. *The teaching and learning of psychotherapy.* New York: Basic Books, 1958.

Elkhaim, M., Prigogine, I., Guattari, F., Stengers, I., & Denenbourg, J. I. Openness: A round table discussion. *Family Process,* 1982, *21,* 57–70.

Elms, A. Skinner's dark year at Walden Two. *American Psychologist,* 1981, *36,* 470–479.

Engel, G. L. The need for a new medical model: A challenge for biomedicine. *Science,* 1977, *196,* 129–136.

Engel, G. L. The clinical application of the biopsychosocial model. *American Journal of Psychiatry,* 1980, *137,* 535–544.

Epstein, N., & Levin, S. Training for family therapy within a faculty of medicine. *Canadian Psychiatric Association Journal,* 1973, *12,* 203–207.

Erickson, G. Teaching family therapy. *Journal of Education for Social Work,* 1973, *9,* 9–15.

Everett, C. Supervision of marriage and family therapy. In K. Hess (Ed.), *Psychotherapy supervision.* New York: John Wiley & Sons, 1980.

Falicov, C., Constantine, J., & Breunlin, D. Teaching family therapy: A program based on learning objectives. *Journal of Marital and Family Therapy,* 1981, *7,* 497–506.

Ferber, A., & Mendelsohn, J. Training for family therapy. *Family Process,* 1969, *8,* 25–32.

Ferguson, L. R. The family life cycle: Orientation for interdisciplinary training. *Professional Psychology,* 1979, *10,* 863–867.

Flomenhaft, K., & Carter, R. Family therapy training: Program and outcome. *Family Process,* 1977, *16,* 211–218.

Ford, D., & Urban, H. *Systems of psychotherapy.* New York: John Wiley & Sons, 1963.

Forsyth, D., & Ivey, A. Microtraining: An approach to differential supervision. In A. Hess (Ed.), *Psychotherapy supervision: Theory, research, and practice.* New York: John Wiley & Sons, 1980.

Frank, G. The role of the family in the development of psychopathology. *Psychological Bulletin,* 1965, *64,* 191–205.

Ganahl, G., & L'Abate, L. *Survey of graduate training in family psychology.* Unpublished manuscript, West Virginia University, 1983.

Garfield, R. An integrative training model for family therapists: The Hahneman master of family therapy program. *Journal of Marital and Family Therapy,* 1979, *5,* 15–22.

Garfield, S., & Kurtz, R. Clinical psychologists in the 1970s. *American Psychologist,* 1976, *31,* 1–9.

Garrigan, J., & Bambrick, A. Introducing novice therapists to "go-between" techniques of family therapy. *Family Process,* 1977, *16,* 237–246.

Goldberg, I., & Goldberg, H. *Family therapy: An overview.* Monterey, Calif.: Brooks/Cole Publishing, 1980.

Goodyear, R. A theory-based workshop for clinical supervisors. In *Sources of supervisory impact and models for training psychological supervisors.* Symposium presented at the annual convention of the American Psychological Association, Washington, D.C., August 23, 1982.

Goodyear, R., & Bradley, F. An introduction to theories of counselor supervision. *Counseling Psychologist,* 1983, *11,* 19–20.

Green, R., & Saeger, K. Learning to "think systems": Five writing assignments. *Journal of Marital and Family Therapy*, 1982, *8*, 285–294.

Gurman, A., & Kniskern, D. Technolatry, methodolatry, and the results of family therapy. *Family Process*, 1978, *17*, 275–281.

Gurman, A., & Kniskern, D. *Handbook of family therapy*. New York: Brunner/Mazel, 1981. (a)

Gurman, A., & Kniskern, D. The outcomes of family therapy: Implications for practice and training. In G. Berenson & H. White (Eds.), *Annual review of family therapy*. New York: Human Sciences Press, 1981. (b)

Haley, J. Family experiments: A new type of experimentation. *Family Process*, 1963, *1*, 265–293.

Haley, J. Fourteen ways to fail as a teacher of family therapy. *Family Therapy*, 1974, *1*, 1–8.

Haley, J. *Problem-solving therapy*. San Francisco: Jossey-Bass, 1976.

Hanson, N. *Patterns of discovery: An inquiry into the conceptual foundations of science*. London: Cambridge University Press, 1961.

Hare, R., & Frankena, S. Peer group supervision. *American Journal of Orthopsychiatry*, 1972, *42*, 527–529.

Hare-Mustin, R. Live supervision in psychotherapy. *Voices*, 1976, *12*, 21–24.

Heath, A. Team family-therapy training: Conceptual and pragmatic considerations. *Family Process*, 1982, *21*, 187–194.

Hoffman, L. *Foundations of family therapy*. New York: Basic Books, 1981.

Holloway, E., & Hosford, R. Towards developing a prescriptive technology of counselor supervision. *Counseling Psychologist*, 1983, *11*, 73–77.

Jessee, E., & L'Abate, L. Enrichment role-playing as a step in the training of family therapists. *Journal of Marital and Family Therapy*, 1981, *7*, 507–513.

Johnson, D. *Marriage counseling*. Englewood Cliffs, N.J.: Prentice-Hall, 1961.

Kagan, N. Classroom to client: Issues in supervision. *Counseling Psychologist*, 1983, *11*, 69–72.

Kantor, D., & Lehr, W. *Inside the family*. San Francisco: Jossey-Bass, 1976.

Kaslow, F. Training in marital and family therapists. In F. Kaslow (Ed.), *Supervision, consultation, and staff training in the helping professions*. San Francisco: Jossey-Bass, 1977.

Kempster, S., & Savitsky, E. Training family therapists through live supervision. In N. Ackerman (Ed.), *Expanding theory and practice in family therapy*. New York: Family Service Association of America, 1967.

Kingdon, M. A. A cost/benefit analysis of the interpersonal process recall technique. *Journal of Counseling Psychology*, 1975, *22*, 353–357.

Kniskern, D., & Gurman, A. Research on training in marriage and family therapy: Status, issues, and directions. *Journal of Marital and Family Therapy*, 1979, *5*, 83–84.

Kniskern, D., & Gurman, A. Research on training in marriage and family therapy. In M. Andolfi & I. Zwerling (Eds.), *Dimensions of family therapy*. New York: Guilford Press, 1980.

Koch, N., Leiderman, H., Mann, J., Ross, J., & Starr, S. *Family program*. Unpublished manuscript, 1982. (Available from Veterans Administration Medical Center, Palo Alto, CA 94304.)

Koestler, A. *Janus, a summing up*. New York: Random House, 1978.

Kolevzon, M., & Green, R. Practice and training in family therapy: A known group study. *Family Process*, 1983, *22*, 179–190.

Kuhn, T. S. *The structure of scientific revolutions*. Chicago: University of Chicago Press, 1972.

L'Abate, L. (Ed.). *Family psychology: Theory, therapy, and training*. Washington, D.C.: University Press of America, 1983.

L'Abate, L., Berger, J., Wright, L., & O'Shea, M. Training family psychologists: The family studies program at GSU. *Professional Psychology*, 1979, *10*, 58–64.

Lambert, M. Research and the supervisory process. In K. Hess (Ed.), *Psychotherapy supervision*. New York: John Wiley & Sons, 1980.

Lange, A., & van der Hart, O. *Directive family therapy*. New York: Brunner/Mazel, 1983.

Liddle, H. A. The emotional and political hazards of teaching and learning family therapy. *Family Therapy*, 1978, *5*, 1–12.

Liddle, H. A. On teaching a contextual or systemic therapy: Training content, goals, and methods. *American Journal of Family Therapy*, 1980, *8*, 56–69.

Liddle, H. A. On the problem of eclecticism: A call for epistemologic clarification and human scale theories. *Family Process*, 1982, *21*, 243–250.

Liddle, H. A., & Halpin, R. Family therapy training and supervision literature: A comparative review. *Journal of Marriage and Family Counseling*, 1978, *4*, 77–98.

Liddle, H. A., & Saba, G. W. On teaching family therapy at the introductory level: A conceptual model emphasizing a pattern which connects training and therapy. *Journal of Marital and Family Therapy*, 1982, *8*, 63–73.

Liddle, H. A., & Saba, G. W. *Family therapy training and supervision: Creating contexts of competence*. New York: Grune & Stratton, in press.

Liddle, H. A., & Schwartz, R. Live supervision/consultation: Conceptual and pragmatic guidelines for family therapy trainers. *Family Process*, 1983, *22*, 477–490.

Liddle, H. A., Vance, S., & Pastushak, R. Family therapy training opportunities in psychology and counselor education. *Professional Psychology*, 1979, *10*, 760–765.

Lionels, M. J. Themes of therapy: A study of the effects of personality and ideology on therapeutic style. Unpublished doctoral dissertation. University of Oregon, 1967.

Loganbill, C., & Hardy, E. In defense of eclecticism. *Counseling Psychologist*, 1983, *11*, 79.

Loganbill, C., Hardy, E., & Delworth, U. Supervision: A conceptual model. *Counseling Psychologist*, 1982, *10*(1), 3–42.

Luthman, S. G., & Kirschenbaum, M. *The dynamic family*. Palo Alto, Calif.: Science & Behavior Books, 1974.

McColley, S., & Baker, E. Training activities and styles of beginning supervisors: A survey. *Professional Psychology*, 1982, *13*, 283–292.

McDaniel, S., Weber, T., & McKeever, J. Multiple theoretical approaches to supervision: Choices in family therapy training. *Family Process*, 1983, *22*, 491–500.

Mead, E., & Crane, R. An empirical approach to supervision and training of relationship therapists. *Journal of Marriage and Family Counseling*, *4*, 1978, 67–75.

Mendelsohn, M., & Ferber, A. Is everybody watching? In A. Ferber, M. Mendelsohn, & A. Napier (Eds.), *The book of family therapy*. New York: Science House, 1972.

Meyerstein, I. Family therapy training for paraprofessionals in a community mental health center. *Family Process,* 1977, *16,* 477–493.

Minuchin, S., & Fishman, C. *Techniques of family therapy.* Cambridge, Mass.: Harvard University Press, 1981.

Mishler, E., & Waxler, N. *Family process and schizophrenia.* New York: Science House, 1968.

Miyoshi, N., & Liebman, R. Training psychiatric residents in family therapy. *Family Process,* 1969, *8,* 97–105.

Montalvo, B. Aspects of live supervision. *Family Process,* 1973, *12,* 343–359.

Nichols, W. *Training and supervision* (Audiotape No. 123). 1975. (Available from American Association of Marriage and Family Counselors, 225 Yale Ave., Claremont, CA 91711.)

Nichols, W. Education of marriage and family therapists. *Journal of Marital and Family Therapy,* 1979, *5,* 19–28.

O'Hare, C., Heinrich, A., Kirschnor, N., Oberstone, A., & Ritz, M. Group training in family therapy: The student's perspective. *Journal of Marriage and Family Counseling,* 1975, *1,* 157–162.

Pearce, W., & Cronen, V. *Communication, action and meaning.* New York: Praeger Publishers, 1980.

Peterson, G., & Bradley, R. Counselor orientation and theoretical attitudes toward counseling: Historical perspective and new data. *Journal of Counseling Psychology,* 1980, *27,* 554–560.

Pierce, R., Carkhuff, R., & Berenson, B. The effects of high and low-functioning counselors upon counselors in training. *Journal of Clinical Psychology,* 1967, *23,* 212–215.

Piercy, F., Hovestadt, A., Fernell, D., Franklin, G., & McKeon, D. A comprehensive training model for family therapists serving rural populations. *Family Therapy,* 1982, *9,* 239–249.

Piercy, F., Laird, R., & Mohammed, Z. A family therapy rating scale. *Journal of Marital and Family Therapy.* 1983, *9,* 49–59.

Pinsof, W. The Family Therapist Behavior Scale (FTBS): Development and evaluation of a coding system. *Family Process,* 1979, *18,* 451–461.

Pinsof, W. Family therapy process research. In A. Gurman & D. Kniskern (Eds.), *Handbook of family therapy.* New York: Brunner/Mazel, 1981.

Pinsof, W. Integrative problem-centered therapy: Toward the synthesis of family and individual psychotherapies. *Journal of Marital and Family Therapy,* 1983, *9,* 19–35.

Popper, K. *The logic of scientific discovery.* New York: Basic Books, 1959.

Popper, K. *Conjectures and refutations.* London: Routledge & Kegan Paul, 1963. (a)

Popper, K. Science: Problems, aims, responsibilities. *Proceedings of the American Sciences for Experimental Biology,* 1963, *22*(4), 961–972.

Resnikoff, R. Teaching family therapy: Ten key questions for understanding the family as patient. *Journal of Marital and Family Therapy,* 1981, *7,* 135–142.

Rice, D. G., & Gurman, A. S. Unresolved issues in the clinical psychology internship. *Professional Psychology,* 1973, *4,* 151–157.

Rickard, H., & Siegel, P. The importance of research apprenticeships in training. *Professional Psychology,* 1976, *7,* 359–363.

Rickert, V., & Turner, J. Through the looking glass: Supervision in family therapy. *Social Casework,* 1978, *59,* 131–137.

Rioch, M. Should psychotherapists do therapy? *Professional Psychology,* 1970, *2,* 139–142.

Rorhbaugh, M., Tennen, H., Press, S., & White, L. Compliance, defiance, and therapeutic paradox: Guidelines for the strategic use of paradoxical interventions. *American Journal of Orthopsychiatry,* 1981, *51,* 454–467.

Rosenbaum, I., & Serrano, A. A rationale and outline for a training program in family therapy. *Journal of Marital and Family Therapy,* 1979, *5,* 77–82.

Ruesch, J., & Bateson, G. *Communication: The social matrix of psychiatry.* New York: W. W. Norton, 1968.

Russell, A. Contemporary concerns in family therapy. *Journal of Marriage and Family Counseling,* 1976, *2,* 243–250.

Sander, F., & Beels, C. A didactic course for family therapy trainees. *Family Process,* 1970, *9,* 411–424.

Sansbury, D. L. Developmental supervision from a skills perspective. *Counseling Psychologist,* 1981, *10,* 53–57.

Schopler, E., Fox, R., & Cochrane, C. Teaching family dynamics to medical students. *American Journal of Orthopsychiatry,* 1967, *37,* 906–911.

Schultz, W. (Ed.). *Here comes everybody: Body, mind and encounter.* New York: Irvington Press, 1971.

Selvini-Palazzoli, M., Boscolo, L., Cecchin, G., & Prata, G. *Paradox and counterparadox.* New York: Jason Aronson, 1978.

Selvini-Palazzoli, M., Boscolo, L., Cecchin, G., & Prata, G. Hypothesizing-circularity-neutrality: Three guidelines for the conductor of the session. *Family Process,* 1980, *19,* 3–12.

Shapiro, R. Problems in teaching family therapy. *Professional Psychology,* 1975, *6,* 41–44.

Simon, R., & Brewster, F. What is training? *Family Therapy Networker,* 1983, *7*(2), 24–29; 66.

Skynner, R. An open-systems, group-analytic approach to family therapy. In A. Gurman & D. Kniskern (Eds.), *Handbook of family therapy.* New York: Brunner/Mazel, 1981.

Skynner, R., & Skynner, P. An open-systems approach to teaching family therapy. *Journal of Marital and Family Therapy,* 1979, *5,* 5–16.

Spiegel, J., & Bell, N. The family of the psychiatric patient. In S. Arieti (Ed.), *American handbook of psychiatry* (Vol. 1). New York: Basic Books, 1959.

Stedman, J., & Gaines, T. Trainee response to family therapy training. *Family Therapy,* 1978, *1,* 81–89.

Stein, S., Karasu, T., Charles, E., & Buckley, P. Supervision of the initial interview. *Archives of General Psychiatry,* 1975, *32,* 265–268.

Stier, S., & Goldenberg, I. Training issues in family therapy. *Journal of Marriage and Family Counseling,* 1975, *1,* 63–68.

Stoltenberg, C. Approaching supervision from a developmental perspective: The counselor complexity model. *Journal of Counseling Psychology,* 1981, *28,* 59–65.

Street, E., & Treacher, A. Microtraining and family therapy skills—towards a possible synthesis. *Journal of Family Therapy*, 1980, *2*, 243–257.

Sunderland, D. M. Theoretical orientation of psychotherapists. In A. Gurman & A. Razin (Eds.), *Effective psychotherapy: A handbook of research*. Elmsford, N.Y.: Pergamon Press, 1977.

Textor, M. An assessment of prominence in the family therapy field. *Journal of Marital and Family Therapy*, 1983, *9*, 317–320.

Thaxton, L., & L'Abate, L. The "second wave" and the second generation: Characteristics of new leaders in family therapy. *Family Process*, 1982, *21*, 359–362.

Tomm, K., & Leahey, M. Training in family assessment: A comparison of three methods. *Journal of Marital and Family Therapy*, 1980, *6*, 453–458.

Tomm, K., & Wright, L. Training in family therapy: Perceptual, conceptual, and executive skills. *Family Process*, 1979, *18*, 227–250.

Tucker, B., Hart, G., & Liddle, H. Supervision in family therapy: A developmental perspective. *Journal of Marriage and Family Counseling*, 1976, *2*, 269–276.

Tucker, B., & Liddle, H. Intra- and interpersonal process in the group supervision of beginning family therapists. *Family Therapy*, 1978, *5*, 13–28.

von Trommel, M. Training in marital and family therapy in Canada and the USA: A report of a study tour. *Journal of Strategic and Systemic Therapy*, 1982, *1*(3), 131–139.

Walsh, F. (Ed.). *Normal family processes*. New York: Guilford Press, 1982.

Walton, M. What is training? Letter in *Family Networker*, May–June 1983, p. 12.

Waltz, G., & Johnston, J. Counselors look at themselves on videotape. *Journal of Counseling Psychology*, 1963, *10*, 232–236.

Watzlawick, P., Weakland, J., & Fisch, R. *Change: Principles of problem formation and resolution*. New York: W. W. Norton, 1974.

Wells, R., & Dezen, A. The results of family therapy revisited: The nonbehavioral methods. *Family Process*, 1978, *17*, 251–274.

Wendorf, D. A model for training practicing professionals in family therapy. *Journal of Marital and Family Therapy*, 1984, *10*, 31–41.

Westley, W., & Epstein, M. *The silent majority*. San Francisco: Jossey-Bass, 1969.

Whiffen, R., & Byng-Hall, J. *Family therapy supervision: Recent developments in practice*. London: Academic Press, 1982.

Whitaker, C. Comment: Live supervision in psychotherapy. *Voices*, 1976, *12*, 24–25.

Whitaker, C. Personal communication. Elmcrest Psychiatric Institute, Portland, Connecticut, 1981.

Wildman, R., & Wildman, R., II. Training in Psychology. *APA Newsletter (Div. E)*, February 1, 1974, 6–7.

Winkle, C., Piercy, F., & Hovestadt, A. A curriculum for graduate level marriage and family therapy education. *Journal of Marital and Family Therapy*, 1981, *1*, 201–210.

Wolberg, L. *The technique of psychotherapy*. New York: Grune & Stratton, 1954.

Wynne, L. Family research and family therapy: A reunion? *Journal of Marital and Family Therapy*, 1983, *9*, 113–117.

Yogev, S. An eclectic model of supervision: A developmental sequence for psychotherapy students. *Professional Psychology*, 1982, *13*, 236–243. (a)

Yogev, S. Supervision of beginning psychotherapy students. In A. Hess, *Psychotherapy supervision: Expanding conceptual models and clinical practices.* Symposium presented at the annual meeting of the American Psychological Association, Washington, D.C., August 24, 1982. (b)

Zuk, G. Family therapy: Clinical hodgepodge or clinical science. *Journal of Marriage and Family Counseling,* 1976, *2,* 299–303.

Chapter 43

The Family Therapist: What Does One Do?

JANET R. WARBURTON
JAMES F. ALEXANDER

The process of family intervention occurs in a series of specific phases, each of which requires specific therapist skills. Many of the problems associated with the practice of family intervention occur because therapists fail to understand the uniqueness of these phases and the therapist skills associated with the therapeutic tasks of a particular phase. This failure to understand sometimes derives from a lack of training; other times, it derives from therapists being trained in a particular model of family therapy which fails to consider one or more of these phases. This chapter is written to describe the phases of family intervention, the therapist skills associated with each phase, and the process methods which may be employed to find solutions to particular problems likely to be encountered by the family therapist. Prior to describing the specific framework, the authors would like to posit some reasons why family therapy should be reconceptualized as a process in need of a problem-solution format before one considers a specific model of treatment.

Family therapy as magic

Family treatment used to, and still often does, seem like magic. Its origins lie in the work of a number of unrelated practitioners of individual treatment whose patients seemed to deteriorate when they returned home from hospital stays or terminated individual treatment (Ackerman, 1958; Jackson, 1960). As an attempt to find a solution to such deterioration, family therapy began as an ambiguous and magical process. This ambiguity has probably continued for a number of reasons, but was highlighted in a recent family therapy training workshop presented by one of our esteemed colleagues and attended by the senior author. When the question of termination of therapy was raised by a participant, the presenter answered honestly that the question of termination rarely came up at his clinic since most families simply stopped coming. It was assumed that when the families were cured, they would terminate themselves. For this eminent family therapist, such an attitude *may* be appropriate and realistic. However, for many less intuitively skilled practicing family therapists, as well as for all new trainees, the failure of family members to continue in treatment is often a disquieting event and continues the aura of mystique surrounding any sensible, sequential order to family treatment.

From a historical perspective, there has been utility in maintaining a magical aura to the practice of family therapy. During the time that family therapy was seen as an auxiliary, tangential, poorly respected, and even somewhat aberrant form of intervention, it was important for "gurus" to provide dramatic examples and persuasive demonstrations of the process. Such examples and demonstrations were necessary to counteract the inertia which trapped mental health professionals in more traditional and often ineffective approaches. However, such inertia no longer characterizes the field, and family therapy is now clearly accepted as a major form of intervention. In this current context, a large number of students and practicing therapists are trying to develop skills in this exciting and potentially powerful treatment modality. Unfortunately, practicing family therapists and trainees who encounter problems in family therapy and wish to learn or enhance their therapeutic skills often respond with disappointment and confusion to the confidence and apparently facile solutions offered by eminent leaders. Especially in workshops, this confusion and disappointment results because solutions often have a magical quality to them—a quality apparently attainable by the guru but not by most other family therapists. This feeling is captured in such often-heard expressions as: "I don't know how she does it," "He makes it look so easy," "How in the world could he have known that," and "If I could just think like she does . . . I just can't seem to pull it off."

For workshop leaders, particularly those who wish to maintain the aura of magic around family therapy process, such expressions can be quite gratifying. However, it is our belief that effective family therapy need not be magical to a majority of family therapists, just as "magic isn't magic to the magician." Both follow a very predictable and understandable, albeit often-unspecified, process. When therapy is divided into phases of intervention with associated therapist goals, functions, and skills, family therapy becomes not only understandable but teachable (Alexander, Barton, Waldron, & Mas, 1983; L'Abate, 1985; Tomm & Wright, 1979).

Models as solutions

Fortunately, many family therapy researchers and theorists have been working during the past decade to remove or at least decrease the magical nature of family therapy. During the 1970s, the field of family therapy spawned a number of approaches to family treatment (see summaries by Erickson & Hogan, 1972; Olson, Russell, & Sprenkle, 1980), each of which provided a conceptual framework and set of techniques for treating families. In many ways, these approaches, or models, attempted to articulate their own conceptual framework and set of techniques used to resolve the problems presented by troubled families. The models addressed family process as well as specific types of troubled families, such as delinquent, schizophrenic, and substance abuse. The dysfunctional processes of families posed certain problems for therapists, and each model of therapy advised new trainees to use certain techniques or strategies to solve the problems. For example, strategic therapists talked about the battle for power in early sessions and emphasized directives (Haley, 1971; Napier & Whittaker, 1978), while humanistically oriented therapists emphasized the need for warmth, empathy, and genuineness (Rogers, 1957).

While models developed as potential solutions to therapeutic problems, their proliferation began to create additional problems for researchers, trainees, and practicing family therapists. Rather than simply adding new techniques and perspectives as they developed, new models began proposing alternative and sometimes even competing concepts and techniques. This eventually added to the confusion of the therapist who was faced with choosing a model or combining models in order to provide better clinical service. One of the greatest sources of distraction resulted from the fact that each model dictated certain therapist behaviors or skills for maximum effectiveness. For example, the types of therapist skills involved in the structural model's "joining" (see Minuchin, 1974) would seem at first glance to be very different from the functional model's "education" (Alexander & Parsons, 1982) and strategic tactics such as "directives" (Haley, 1971; Selvini-Palazolli, Boscolo, Cecchin, & Prata, 1978). However, the nature of these and many other behaviors and skills was often either poorly described or at best only implicitly assumed (see Barton, Alexander, & Sanders, Chapter 35 of this *Handbook*) so that a therapist attempting to "join," "educate," or "direct" a family was frequently left to guess how these critical components of therapy were accomplished.

In comparison to the voluminous descriptions of theoretical constructs and techniques for treating families, therapists' skills and attributes have been almost ignored in the literature. For example, a recent review of family therapy references in the literature (Alexander et al., 1983) revealed that in five major therapy journals, only 1 of 265 family therapy articles was focused specifically on the family therapist. Instead, the vast majority of articles referred to techniques, while many others referred to various aspects of the family therapy process and/or characteristics of the families undergoing treatment. This lack of attention to therapist characteristics seems strange in a field that seems to almost worship the unique skills and attributes of its gurus. It is as if the major theorists can enjoy the benefits of their unique talents and skills, but the special skills and attributes of all other therapists are inconsequential. Most of the major family therapy books in the field, as well as most workshops, seem to create the impression that positive change will occur if a therapist simply understands the situation sufficiently, follows the appropriate model, and performs the appropriate techniques in the appropriate manner. This may be the case, but it assumes that the average family therapist has the particular blend of skills and attributes necessary to perform the techniques involved in the model or models s/he chooses. It also assumes that specific treatment models are articulated with sufficient clarity that therapists can match their skills and attributes to one of the competing family therapy models.

Unfortunately, neither of these assumptions can be assured, leaving therapists with the need for an alternative framework for making clinical decisions. Thus, in addition to a specific model of intervention and specific techniques, a therapist needs a conceptual framework with regard to functions and therapeutic skills. For the purposes of this chapter, then, models will be considered as specific conceptual guides for therapists, who in addition must have generic skills and attributes regardless of the preferred model of family treatment they chose.

Models as guides, explanations, or fantasies

When family therapy models proliferated and became a potent component of mental health service delivery during the 1970s, each of the major models was associated with one or two eminent leaders, or gurus. As authors and workshop presenters, these leaders articulated the components of various family therapy models for a myriad of interested family therapy trainees that followed. In this articulation, most of the participants have assumed or acted as though the following sequence existed: (1) philosophy of human behavior, (2) theory of change, (3) therapeutic model, (4) specific change techniques, (5) development and "fitting" of therapist attributes and skills to the change techniques. That is, it has been easy to assume that what therapists should do reflects a distillation of principles from the "top down." In this assumptive framework, future trainees need only understand and agree with a particular philosophy of human behavior, learn the theory and specific techniques of change, and develop the appropriate skills for the particular model they choose. Unfortunately, two major factors raise serious questions about this strategy. The first factor concerns the view that the order described above may more usefully be reversed. It may not be that gurus developed models that they then translated into techniques and skills. Instead, while the field was in its early stages of development, the family therapy pioneers may have *first* developed an effective set of techniques which were based on their own stylistic strengths. They then developed (from the "bottom up") models, and perhaps even theories of functioning and change, which described in a post hoc fashion what they did either naturally and/or serendipitously.

It makes a considerable difference whether therapeutic interventions developed from the top down as we generally assume (i.e., techniques and therapist styles were fitted to a model) or from the bottom up (i.e., models were developed to explain successful techniques and styles). Most likely, development occurred in both directions in a self-correcting and interconnected way. That is, good concepts led to successful techniques, and vice versa. If so, the connection between a particular model, specific techniques, and the necessary therapist's skills and attributes must be very carefully described and clearly understood. Otherwise, new family therapists will attempt to adopt models for which they are stylistically unsuited and will have no idea why the particular techniques that work so well for another therapist do not "fit" for them. Nor will they know what aspects of their style can and should be changed to fit the model they prefer. In later sections, this chapter will focus on, and clarify, this process.

The second factor that calls into question the strategy of developing therapists' skills to fit a particular model concerns the fact that the description of what actually occurs in family therapy according to the different models may not be completely descriptive or entirely accurate. Workshop videotapes are usually edited for "high points" or clear exemplars of specific maneuvers. Rarely are the rather extended "humdrum" periods emphasized, nor are the maneuvers that required repeated application before having an effect or that didn't work at all. Moreover, when it comes to complex judgments and other information-processing activities, a growing body of evidence suggests that people cannot describe the stimulus that effects a particular response or even the nature of the response they make (Nisbett & Wilson, 1977).

When asked, for example, to explain why they did what they did, subjects' explanations may be based not on "true introspection" but on "a priori" assumptions, implicit causal theories, or judgments about the extent to which a particular stimulus is a plausible cause of a given response (Nisbett & Wilson, p. 231).

With respect to the complex process of family intervention, it could be that rather than having clarifying descriptions, what we have in the literature is a growing body of commonly accepted folklore. This folklore is plausible and persuasive when taken in small pieces, but can be confusing and inconsistent when taken over all models of family therapy. Further, it may be inaccurate! We need only remember the early attempts to translate therapeutic attempts from one conceptual system to another (e.g., Dollard & Miller, 1950; Greenspoon, 1962) to understand that different models can take us in directions which can be quite disparate and/or contradictory. Thus, much of what we do—whether poorly or well—we seem to do automatically (Sheffrin & Schneider, 1977), and we may neither understand nor describe it very clearly or accurately (Nisbett & Wilson, 1977).

Are the problems in the solutions?

To this point, we have made several assertions: (1) At least some therapists' skills and attributes are uniquely tied to particular techniques used in particular models, (2) therapeutic models represent solutions to therapeutic problems, (3) though many overlap, specific therapeutic models may contradict each other at certain points, and (4) particular therapeutic models may also not be particularly descriptive nor accurate regarding what really occurs in family therapy. If left here, the combination of these assertions would undoubtedly leave students of family therapy in a state of considerable confusion and despair. Yet, despite the many difficulties listed above, we need a means to describe, understand, develop, perform, train, and evaluate the process of family therapy. Unfortunately, if the proliferation of new therapeutic models has (as suggested above) created as many problems as solutions, it will do little good to have more of the same. Thus, we need an alternative.

This chapter proposes an alternative based on the assumption that particular therapeutic models *should* provide solutions to therapeutic problems but often don't. They don't because, while they are designed to solve problems, the problems are not well understood nor articulated. Consider the analogy of some burning material which is producing smoke and fire. Only a naive person would propose that throwing water on the material would represent a solution. It *could* be a good solution if, for example, the burning material was wood. On the other hand, if the fire were electrical or phosphorous in nature, such a solution could not only be ineffective, it could in fact create additional problems.

Though this example may seem farfetched, many family therapy trainees seem to approach the process of family therapy with almost a rote-memorized list of solutions but with little other understanding of the process. We have literally heard some trainees rehearse mental checklists, sounding something like, "I've got to 'join' the family." "I've got to remember to relabel mother as benign." "I can't let the oldest sib keep focusing on the problems of the identified patient." "I need to involve grandmother less with the daughter." Such statements presumably represent solutions to problems that have been identified by the therapist or a supervisor at some previous time. However, if the therapist focuses solely on the solutions without understanding the problems, then s/he can end up with no understanding of *why* things work and, more importantly, why they do not. S/he can end up throwing water on an electrical fire!

Consequently, as the first critical step, family therapists need to articulate the problems they face. When we refer to problems, we do not mean simply a long list of specific complaints or questions comparable to what one hears in workshops (e.g., "What do you do with a father who. . . ," "Well, I tried this, but then she did that and I didn't know what to do"). Such specific complaints or questions are not considered here as problems, but rather as specific examples or expressions of general classes of problems that therapists face. It is these general classes of problems that must be addressed.

To understand these general classes of problems, a number of theorists have developed generic or "metamodels" of intervention which are designed to describe the common or ubiquitous aspects of most if not all family therapies (e.g., Alexander et al., 1983; Beavers & Voeller, 1983; L'Abate, 1983; Olson et al., 1979; Tomm & Wright, 1979). Each of these models views family therapy as an intricate process which goes through several phases. These phases are conceptually quite distinct from one another, and each phase involves a particular set of therapeutic goals and tasks. In some cases, it is apparent that not only are the goals and tasks of the specific phases quite different but the skills and attributes required of the therapist may also be quite distinct.

For example, The Analysis of Intervention Model (AIM) (Alexander et al., 1983), describes the intricacies of family therapy process in terms of five major phases of family intervention which are common to all family therapy relationships, irrespective of the particular therapeutic model used. Of course, specific models may or may not conceptualize and discuss each of these phases, but that is an issue of model adequacy, not an issue of whether or not the phase truly exists.

AIM involves several major assumptions which will be reiterated repeatedly when particular phases of intervention are described. These assumptions are:

1. Each phase has a unique and characteristic goal.
2. Though they are described as separate, some phases can occur simultaneously, and others can occur in various orders. The important issue is not the order in which phases occur, but that the therapist understand what phase the process is in and what the goals of that phase or phases are.
3. To accomplish the goals of each phase, therapists need to possess or demonstrate certain characteristics or skills. Family therapy is not a homogeneous process that involves the constant use of certain skills. Instead, it involves groupings of very different skills—skills which must be differentially utilized in particular phases and deemphasized (if not actually avoided) in others. In other words, therapists need not only have certain skills and characteristics, but they also need to understand when and how to express them.

Scanning: The requisite process

To this point in the chapter, a number of references have been made to gurus, or leaders, as being distinct from average practitioners, trainees, and the like. This distinction was at times arbitrary and may border on being demeaning, but was necessary to distinguish the contexts in which different family therapists operate. It was also necessary to make the point that no matter what labels we use, therapists do differ in their impact, the processes that seem to occur when they are a part of therapy, and the outcomes their families experience. So whether we call them "leaders," "gurus," "experienced therapists," or "pros," most of us recognize that some therapists perform at a level of effectiveness we would hope that all therapists could emulate.

Attempting to distinguish these therapists from others has been a difficult task. Some successful examples include Alexander, Barton, Schiavo, & Parsons, 1976; Cline, Coles, Mejia, & Klein, 1982; Strupp & Hadley, 1983. These studies seem to indicate that some combination of various skill categories characterize the experts. Cline et al. conclude: "The overlapping variance shared by the two sets of skills suggested that the therapists in this sample were likely to have integrated both relationship and structuring skills into their therapeutic repertoires. This integration of the two conceptually distinct skills is likely to have occurred due to the therapists' 'experience in the field' " (p. 109).

Our concern is not with the experience level of the therapist, but how therapist skills and attributes are used in therapy. We propose that the possession of these skills on the part of therapists represents only half the necessary conditions for effectiveness. Specifically, in addition to possessing the skills, the therapist must have the ability to *conceptually scan* the therapy process (Tomm & Wright, 1979) to be able to understand when and how to use those skills. This conceptual scanning of the therapy process on the part of the therapist is essential to staying unencumbered by the family system enough to operate both as part of the system and independent of it. This has been termed the ability to be alternatively "inside" and "outside" the family system (Minuchin, 1974). The AIM framework allows the therapist to get outside the therapy process by moving from concrete interactions to abstractions where problems can be identified. The therapist can then propose concrete solutions. This metalevel of conceptual analysis allows a free flow of thinking to occur in which the therapist can scan back and forth across the entire continuum of intervention phases, creating more options than might otherwise be available.

The scanning device of the therapist can focus within phase or across phases. Examples of questions therapists can ask in this error-activated process include: (1) In what phase of treatment am I? (2) What generic skills are most useful in this phase of treatment? (3) Am I using those skills to the best of my ability? (4) Do I need to change phases to correct the problem? (5) What skills are associated with the therapeutic phase I will move toward? More concrete examples will be presented in subsequent discussions of each of the phases of intervention.

Our emphasis on scanning derives from a belief that one major difference between effective and ineffective therapists is the ability to scan the therapeutic process effectively. All therapists experience awkward and/or difficult moments during family intervention, such as the sudden realization that you as the therapist have misunderstood the father's position in the family or when an adolescent family member continues to resist all your attempts to relabel or reframe her behavior. During these difficult times, successful therapists seem to be able to scan the therapeutic process as suggested in AIM and move fluidly to a new strategy. Scanning can occur rapidly so as to look like a fluid motion, but can be slowed down like the still frames of a motion picture. It is this ability to scan and move which produces the labels of flexibility, creativity, magic, or art when applied to these therapists.

In contrast to effective therapists, when faced with difficult situations, ineffective or less effective therapists tend to become less rather than more flexible. Instead of scanning, they typically revert to a preferred mode of thinking, feeling, and/or behaving. While they sometimes "get lucky" in that this preferred mode may be successful at this point in time with the family, quite often it is inappropriate, even though it might have been appropriate in a different phase of intervention. Quite often, this process of reverting to a preferred mode is done "unconsciously," or (in a language of the information-processing literature) is done "automatically" (Sheffrin & Schneider, 1977). A considerable amount of the time spent in clinical supervision focuses on such processes, with supervisors helping trainees to become aware of the stylistic responses they have to stress which create difficulties for them and/or the family. Again, in information-processing terms, the goal of such supervision is to bring this phenomenon into the realm of "controlled processing" (Sheffrin & Schneider).

In summary, we propose AIM or similar models (Alexander et al., 1983; Beavers & Voeller, 1983; Tomm & Wright, 1979), as a means whereby therapists can develop an error-activated and self-correcting system for dealing with problems in family therapy process. Like any other conceptual system, it will require considerable concentration (controlled processing) at first, but as it is applied over time, it will become more and more automatic. Just as in learning to drive a car or learning a new language, what at first is a slow and at times awkward process will with practice become smoother and more automatic. This will allow therapists to adaptively respond to problems as they occur and will leave more of their information-processing time available for creating more adaptive solutions.

THE PHASES OF INTERVENTION (AIM MODEL)

The five phases of intervention as defined in the Analysis of Intervention Model are: (1) introduction/impression; (2) assessment/understanding; (3) induction/therapy; (4) treatment/education; and (5) generalization/termination. The following sections describe these phases of intervention. Each will be introduced in the form of an outline which defines for that phase: (1) the goals, (2) the major therapist task (or function) that the goal(s) create, and (3) the generic skills and characteristics that the therapist must possess in order to successfully perform the function and attain the goal(s).

Introduction/impression phase

Goals: Create expectations of positive change.

Therapist function: Establish credibility.

Therapist skills: Expertness, appropriateness, resources.

Families and therapists come together at a first session with a number of expectations about what will happen. These initial sets can enhance or detract from successful activity, as well as produce some surprises and unexpected occurrences. For these initial sets to be as productive as possible, the therapist must present an image of one who can help move the family from its fixed, dysfunctional patterns of behavior to patterns the family sees as more positive. To begin to accomplish this frequently difficult task, the family therapist must, above all, *appear credible* as a helper to the family. The best therapist will fail at the task of moving a family toward its desired goals during subsequent phases of treatment if the family finds the therapist unconvincing as a change agent.

A number of factors constitute apparent credibility. Initially, stimulus characteristics of both therapist and family may interact to set up a chain of responses which can facilitate or inhibit the ease of movement of the therapist into the family system. Such things as sex, race, religion, physical size, age, dress, and office equipment have been noted in the literature (Strong, 1978; Warburton, Alexander, & Barton, 1980) as having some effect on initial impressions and on the interactions that follow. These stimulus qualities may appear as early in the acquaintance process as when appointments are made, (e.g., clients detect therapist gender) or when the therapist enters the room (e.g., gender is clearly observed). These visually observable characteristics tend to affect the earliest phases of therapy. For instance, a female of small size, youthful appearance, and unmarried status will most likely create a different initial set than would an older, well-established male therapist. This difference could dramatically influence the initiation of intervention (Warburton et al.).

As short-term therapies, especially marital and family therapies, become recognized as efficient modes of treatment, the initial client and therapist biases and expectations about stimulus characteristics increase in importance (Brodsky & Hare-Mustin, 1980; Collins & Sedlack, 1974; Gurman & Klein, 1980; Seiden, 1976). Because such stimulus characteristics of the therapist or the setting are *observable* in a visual sense, they are different from therapeutic skills which must be *demonstrated* as the therapist engages in the therapy process itself.

Quite some time ago, Frank (1961) identified the importance of the credible ritual as an important component of psychotherapeutic healing. A major part of establishing a credible ritual is the presentation of the person who will perform the ritual, the family therapist. With regard to credibility, a number of tactics have been used to positively influence clients' perceptions. These include matching characteristics, joining in obvious mannerisms and self-disclosures, and combating or using the family's stereotypes (see, for example, Minuchin, 1974).

In some measure, the decision about which tactics to use to establish credibility is dictated by the setting, with part of the issue being one of resources and identification of external constraints which must be dealt with by the family therapist. It is apparent that many tactics have considerable constraints attached to them. Matching—assigning families to therapists who have similar stimulus characteristics—assumes a pool of therapists from which selection could occur. Ideally, therapists would represent a broad spectrum of characteristics similar to those of families in the client population seen at the clinic. Unfortunately, such tactics as matching therapist and family characteristics may not be possible in a clinic where there either are few or a fairly homogeneous group of therapists from which to choose (e.g., therapists are all of one ethnic group).

Thus, the therapist must not only be aware of the impression being made on the family but about what resources are available or desirable in order to affect initial impressions. Whether matching is available or not, it is in this early phase of therapy that the therapist must begin use of the scanning process. Tomm & Wright (1979) have similarly identified a therapist perceptual/conceptual skill which refers to what takes place in the therapist's mind and forms the basis for later action or decision making. In AIM, the conceptual/perceptual skills take on a dynamic quality to qualify as the scanning process. In terms of stimulus characteristics as an important part of the introduction/impression phase, the therapist must be cognizant of how his/her stimulus qualities interact with those of the family. This is a clear conceptual skill. The therapist must decide, based on this information, whether to spend more or less time in this phase. This requires a scanning process because it requires that the therapist entertain the decision whether or not to move to other phases. If the stimulus characteristics are matched and effectively facilitate joining, the transition to the assessment/understanding phase may occur earlier than when therapist/family discrepancies must be dealt with more overtly.

Tactics such as matching obvious or even subtle therapist and family characteristics are sometimes impossible. Problems may emerge where no such common ground exists, and the therapist can present few if any cues to the family which suggest credibility. If so, scanning may suggest that the therapist must move very quickly to the induction/therapy phase, temporarily bypassing the assessment/understanding phase. A recent example in our office demonstrates this solution.

A young, collegiate-looking female trainee experienced an angry outburst from a young Hispanic gang member as he left an initial session saying he would not return. His mother also appeared reluctant to involve herself with an "Anglo" therapist. Because the therapist had been unsuccessful at presenting herself as a credible helper through interpersonal stimulus qualities or matching characteristics, the family's message of pain at being a pawn in a seemingly uncaring juvenile justice system was missed, primarily because the trainee was uncomfortable with the extent of cultural discrepancy between herself and the family. She had retreated to a defensive posture herself. However, during later supervision, the trainee was advised to move quickly to reflective listening skills, and with careful attention to the needs of the single-parent mother, the relationship skills the trainee did possess enabled her to reengage the young man at a successful therapeutic level in the second session. While supervision provided an option for this inexperienced trainee, moving to a different phase could have been initiated in the first session had the therapist scanned the situation accurately.

As can be seen in this example, phases of intervention do not occur in discrete, neatly packaged phases of therapy, but instead frequently overlap and occur simultaneously. While the therapist must be clear about each therapeutic phase and the skill classes necessary to accomplish the goals of each therapeutic phase, the therapist must also be able to discern when he/she needs to move to another phase requiring other skill classes. This ability to scan, and to reach a decision about moving forward or backward across the therapeutic continuum, will be continually emphasized throughout the chapter. The freedom to perform such movement releases the therapist from the pitfalls of "I've no place to go" feelings, and prevents additional feelings of therapist inadequacy and/or blaming of clients.

Assessment/understanding phase

Goals: Understand family and change parameters.

Therapist function: Elicit, structure, and analyze information.

Therapist skills: Intelligence, perceptiveness, conceptual model.

As emphasized above, the introduction/impression phase can be quite brief. The effectiveness of intervention quickly moves from relying on presenting a credible image to demonstrating actual clinical competence. Extravagant trappings, diploma-lined walls, or lushly furnished offices will rarely counteract the effects of a therapist who is poorly equipped conceptually, even though such things may give one an initial head start in establishing credibility.

Beyond establishing initial credibility, the therapist must collect enough information about a family in the first session to begin to make sense of its interactions. For instance, if a father is aloof to a female therapist, rather than becoming defensive, she may begin to make sense of why this is by checking when the aloofness occurs, how he is with his wife, whether he feels threatened by the therapist (e.g., fearing she will take his place in the family), or whether he feels helpless in the face of a seemingly hopeless problem. The tools or skills necessary to make sense of these varying explanations are intelligence, perceptiveness, and use of a clear conceptual model. These skills allow the therapist enough objectivity and distance to understand a family member's behavior within the context of the family as opposed to being engaged by it. At the same time, the therapist in the above example may register the fact that the father's behavior tended to elicit a defensive response from her, thus freeing her up to respond in a nondefensive manner. This distinction between feeling, thinking, and then responding is part of the conceptual task. L'Abate (1983) has suggested such distinctions can be used by the therapist to diagnose family interaction.

The therapeutic goal of understanding a family requires considerable cognitive skill on the part of the therapist. Taking on the identity of an investigator is a useful metaphor for having a cognitive set which leads to the unraveling of meanings. Such questions as: "Why are these people behaving, thinking, feeling the way they say or demonstrate they are?" "What is the interpersonal' payoff or end result of each person's part in the whole?" "How can I understand the symptoms which emerge from such behavior?" are cognitive processes requiring cognitive skills. Questions such as these must be well understood or the rest of intervention will fail. Only occasionally, and only through luck, can we change something we do not understand. The therapist must be able to create a context in which the family will present the therapist with the information relevant to these questions. The therapist then must know he or she is capable of generating meaningful hypotheses about what the information means, which in turn leads to the development of therapeutic solutions firmly based on the integration of assessment information.

The assessment phase is probably one of the least understood and researched phases of therapy in terms of therapist characteristics or skills. Unlike the relationship skills of the induction therapy phase and the structuring or technical skills of the treatment/education phase, assessment skills have not had entire models of intervention built around them (e.g., humanistic and behavioral models). The importance of cognitive and intellectual skills essential to the understanding of a family are thus underrepresented in the literature. This lack of research on therapist cognitive skill may stem from the fact that graduate schools screen for intelligence while they may not screen for relationship skills (Truax & Mitchell, 1971). It would follow that relationship and structuring skills would be more heavily emphasized following admission to graduate school.

In spite of the fact that a base level of intelligence is necessary to get into graduate programs, it is probable that intellectual skills vary considerably among therapists as do the relationship and structuring skills to be described later. Further, certain kinds of thinking may not necessarily be consistent with the elements most likely to lead to successful assessment and understanding of families, especially perceptiveness and an ability to synthesize and make sense of large amounts of sometimes discrepant pieces of information (i.e., the use of divergent versus convergent thinking). Problem solving or understanding usually involves two phases: examining alternative explanations and then choosing the one that seems most appropriate. The examination phase has been called *divergent thinking,* because the therapist must think along divergent paths. The use of this knowledge to then narrow the possibilities to the most probable explanation requires *convergent thinking* (Guilford & Hoepfner, 1971). A therapist may be strong or weak in one or another of these skills.

An additional problem derives from a relative lack of technical aids. There are numerous assessment and psychometric devices that have been used to assist the practitioner of individual therapy through the complex phase of assessment. While such psychometric devices as behavioral observation, checklists, supervision, and consultation have assisted both individual and family practitioners' assessment of individual members, few useful tools have been devised for the assessment of relationships (Fisher, 1982). "Cookbook manuals," like those available for the Minnesota Multiphasic Personality Inventory, are simply not there to assist a bewildered family interactionist, and the behavioral checklist used by some marriage and family therapists are reports on individual family members by themselves or other members rather than measures of the relationship itself. While supervision can often shed light on the meaning of a behavior or interaction sequence after the fact, the therapist in session must think autonomously.

Because a therapist must understand a family to begin to change it, it seems inadvisable to move out of this phase for very long when the therapist is seeking solutions to therapeutic problems. Instead, the therapist may wish to move within phase by tracking a preferred mode of family expression, be that behavioral, affective, or cognitive aspects of the family members' relationships (Alexander & Parsons, 1982). To do so effectively, a therapist chooses characteristic thoughts, feelings, or behavior sequences and then recreates the context within which they occurred, checking antecedents and consequences as well as long-term interpersonal payoffs. The therapist is then capable of beginning to posit plausible hypotheses about the development and maintenance of dysfunctional behavior (Alexander & Parsons, 1982; L'Abate, 1983).

It is clear that this phase differs from the previous phase, because here the therapist must *be* competent, where in the introduction/ impression phase, the therapist simply had to *appear* competent. There seems to be considerable literature to indicate that experience helps at this point (Luborsky, Bachrach, Graff, Pulver, & Christoph, 1980). The seasoned clinician is more likely than the novice to be skilled at deciphering the vast amounts of information presented in initial sessions. Much of the extraneous noise may be automatically screened out by the more experienced therapist, allowing attention to be focused on the relevant behavior. For less experienced therapists, it is the assessment/understanding phase which requires that the therapist have a clear conceptual model of therapy. Without a clear conceptual model as a guide, therapists may quickly find themselves mired in confusion.

There are two general classes of cognitive problems that the therapist may encounter in this phase of treatment: (1) therapist-centered and (2) family-promoted. The therapist-centered problems involve such things as lack of ability to track shifts between behavioral, affective, and cognitive modes of expression; inability to sift meaningful from unmeaningful materials; and inability to integrate and pull meaning from large amounts of information from divergent sources. The family-promoted problems include forms of resistance such as the unavailability of members, well-protected family secrets, and external demands on various family members.

This second class of problems, the family-promoted problems, may require that two phases of intervention be conducted *simultaneously.* As the assessment phase is conducted, problems of considerable resistance must be handled if they occur. Therapists may have to use the relationship skills associated with the induction/therapy phase (see below). In this case, the therapist must remember at phase interception that the relational skills of therapy cannot be used *instead of,* but rather in addition to, the cognitive skills. The scanning process helps the therapist identify which of these phases are most relevant at any point in time, and when and if simultaneous skills are needed. An example of such a choice may help clarify the simultaneous use of skill classes.

With what is called the internal blaming family, the therapist computes (a conceptual skill) that the family blames individual family members for its problems; at the *same time,* he or she may use directive or structuring skills, ("Slow down," "Can you speak one at a time?"). This use of two phases of treatment, calling into action two classes of therapist skills, is most likely to occur in the assessment/understanding phase because of its likeliness to merge with other phases. It is also a phase frequently returned to in later phases of intervention when the therapist questions previous assumptions or needs to gain new information during later phases of treatment.

Frequently, problems of assessment in the first session may simply be the result of the therapist's being bombarded with verbal information (the "we'll all tell on each other" phenomenon) or the opposite climate of silence ("we'll all protect each other"). The therapist can choose to see these statements as the first piece of stylistic information in a series of pieces of information the family will produce (e.g., this family blames within the system in order to focus attention on a member or subgroup, or this family blames the external environment to protect itself), or the therapist can get caught in each tangent of internal blaming or feel helpless or defensive in light of the external silence from the resistant family.

When experiencing such reactions, the therapist can use AIM as the problem-solution format. AIM points the therapist to the phase of intervention (assessment/understanding) and the skills necessary to unravel the meaning of the communication (conceptual skills). If additional problems persist, the therapist then looks across phases for alternative solutions such as calling upon relational skills from the induction/therapy phase. To summarize, if the problems are not *within-phase* problems, the therapist has the option of scanning *across phases* to identify problems and solutions.

This decision to move within, and then across, phase was recently used by the senior author. She had agreed to see a couple on an emergency basis during the lunch hour of our agency's annual budgetary retreat. Since there had been no plan to see patients that day, the therapist was very casually attired and saw the couple in an office where there was no evidence of license or diplomas. To worsen matters, most of the staff were milling around in shorts! The couple turned out to be a dignified, older, professional husband and wife. The therapist noticed the client couple seemed uncomfortable, but being somewhat rushed, she proceeded with the techniques involved in assessment/understanding. After experiencing a few minutes of short and very reserved answers on the part of the wife, the therapist scanned the problem as probably one of lack of credibility. When asked about this, the wife's response of "Well, who are you? I have no idea who I'm talking to," while gesturing toward the therapist and the bare walls, proved correct the assumption provided by the scanning process. The therapist then backed up and apologized for the atmosphere, repeating the information about the staff retreat which the therapist had shared with the husband by telephone but which he had failed to convey, in turn, to his wife. By doing so, the therapist reentered the introduction/impression phase, this time successfully establishing who she was via credentials as well as marital and parental status. In response, the wife "opened up" and the assessment/understanding phase was easily reentered. The therapist also gleaned some useful information about the husband and wife relationship as a result of this exchange. This example demonstrates how the therapist scanned, identified the goals, and then used the skills of three distinct phases of intervention (introduction/impression, assessment/understanding, and induction/therapy).

Induction/therapy phase

> Goals: Create context for new personal and interpersonal definitions of family.
>
> Therapist function: Contingent directiveness, interpersonal sensitivity.
>
> Therapist skills: Relationship skills.

In the induction/therapy phase of intervention, the effective family therapist must create a context for change. The requisite skills to accomplish this goal are relationship skills and interpersonal sensitivity. While therapy has been used as an all-encompassing word in the field, its use here is restricted to that phase of the intervention which creates the climate in which families are (1) willing to change, and (2) have the motivation to do so. It is assumed that it is the therapist's, not the family's, responsibility to move the clients through this phase of treatment. While therapy is an interpersonal process with the family members contributing their share of resistance, lack of motivation, or misunderstanding, it is the therapist who has the expertise to relabel, reframe, and otherwise change the attributional sets of the family members toward one another and toward the therapist in order to free all participants from restrictive roles and attributions (Alexander & Parsons, 1982; Barton & Alexander, 1980).

AIM identifies the therapist function necessary for successful treatment in the induction/therapy phase as contingent directiveness. Alexander et al. (1983) defined contingent directiveness as therapist behaviors, such as relabeling or reframing (Minuchin, 1974), which influence family members' cognitions and affects. These behaviors are *contingently* directive because they react to, and depend upon, what the family members say, do, and feel. Relabeling and reframing will not be successful if they do not "make sense" to the phenomenological reality of the family, and if they are not acceptable. For example, relabeling an internally protective or enmeshed family as "emphasizing loyalty" mirrors their reality in a benign light.

The skills used to accomplish contingent directiveness are *relationship skills* and *interpersonal sensitivity.* They have been empirically evaluated in the family therapy literature in terms such as affect-behavior integration, humor, and nonblaming (Alexander et al., 1976). They seem to be similar to relational skills identified in the individual psychotherapy literature, such as empathy, genuineness, nonpossessive warmth (Rogers, 1957, Truax & Mitchell, 1971), and interpersonal manner (Schaffer, 1982). These skills are necessary in order to provide a climate conducive to the application of techniques for change. Partially due to Rogers' (1957) emphasis on such skills as curative, considerable research has been done on the importance of relationship skills as necessary components of treatment (Alexander et al., 1976; Cline et al., 1982).

Relationship skills are necessary fairly early in the process of intervention and are essential by the second or third session (Alexander & Parsons, 1982). Recently, the Vanderbilt group noted the importance of the early phases of therapy and, given progress in the first three sessions in individual therapy, the increased predictability of outcome. They found that both first and second sessions were relatively weak in predicting outcome (O'Malley, Suh, & Strupp, 1983), while third sessions were predictive of outcome. This finding seems to underline the importance of a strong induction/therapy component to overall treatment effects, since this phase could be expected to occur by about the third session, assuming that introduction/impression and assessment/understanding generally occur during the first two sessions (Alexander & Parsons). However, it must be remembered that family therapy tends to be of shorter duration than individual therapy (Goldenberg & Goldenberg, 1982), so these skills are probably more relevant earlier in family therapy. The importance of relationship skills to positive outcome is further emphasized in the marital and family therapy literature (Alexander et al., 1976; Cline et al., 1982).

Relationship skills seem to be a necessary but not sufficient ingredient for change (Schaffer, 1982). It is this "necessary but not sufficient" clause which is the nemesis of the family therapist. Because the therapist works hard to create the context for change, to get the family reframed or relabeled, to overcome resistance, and to establish likability, the temptation to remain in this phase of treatment is seductive. There are, in fact, schools of therapy that imply that the application of relationship skills (for example, in establishing a climate of "unconditional positive regard") is enough to successfully accomplish all of intervention (Rogers, 1957). However, AIM maintains that once this climate is established, a forceful transition to the education phase must follow (see below). It is our experience in training therapists in functional family therapy (Alexander & Parsons, 1982) that it is this transition point between the therapy phase and the education phase which is most difficult for the clinician. No small part of this difficulty is the shift that therapists must make, from applying relationship skills to applying structuring skills. There is evidence that the most successful therapists have sufficient amounts of each of these skills and can combine them well enough to bridge what may otherwise seem an awkward gap (Alexander et al., 1976; Cline et al., 1982).

On the other hand, for therapists trained to believe relational skills are sufficient in and of themselves, there may need to be emphasis in training on identifying the appropriate entry point for the transition to the treatment/education phase. Since any form of treatment reaches a point of diminishing returns if it continues too long (for example, see Bloom, 1982), there may be a temptation to rely on relationship skills giving the therapist a false sense of security while giving the family an ever-increasing sense of disillusionment. If the therapy phase has been successful and the family *likes* the therapist at this point, it will come as a disappointment if the therapist becomes directionless when a shift must be made. When a therapist is strong on relationship skills but short on structuring skills, intervention is most likely to dwindle off without measurable results.

It has also been pointed out that mood, which is assumed to influence interpersonal manner or relational skills, varies considerably during a therapy hour (Gurman, 1973). Relationship skills are not a set of discrete, static behaviors, but rather fluctuating amounts of behaviors which, if factor analyzed, would probably produce several categories of interpersonal skills. Schaffer (1982) reviewed a number of factor-analytic studies of interpersonal manner and found that relationship skills are not a completely independent factor. The measures of interpersonal manner used in several studies were found to overlap with skillfulness and type of techniques used or the tactics used to accomplish the specific goals of intervention. This overlap may have been due to the ambiguity with which terms were defined, and conceptually subdividing relationship skills into the two separate categories of interpersonal sensitivity and contingent directiveness may minimize this problem.

Treatment/education phase

Goals: Produce change.
Therapist function: Linear directiveness, performance sensitivity.
Therapist skills: Structuring skills.

The therapist's goal in most marriage and family therapy approaches is to produce change in patterns of interaction by using specific techniques which focus on specific aspects of behavior, feelings, and thoughts or beliefs. To apply such techniques, the class of therapist skills necessary to actually produce change is structuring skills. Since the therapist must instruct the family in the use of new technologies (such as negotiation and/or communication skills, time-out techniques, relaxation techniques, techniques for changing "self-talk," or behavioral contracting—it must be remembered that the specific techniques will depend on the therapist's treatment model), the therapist must present these techniques in a clear, direct, understandable way or families will not be able to put them into use.

The therapist functions attained through structuring skills are *linear directiveness* and *performance sensitivity.* Linear directiveness differs from previously described contingent directiveness in that the therapist's behavior in linear directiveness is sequential and programmed (Alexander et al., 1983). The therapist "follows" a program, responding to the family only if the members seem unable or unwilling to perform the new behaviors. For example, the sequence of events for many communication packages is clear and established prior to their application to a specific family. They represent a script, the end of which is already well defined before it is attained by the family. At each step in the sequential program, the therapist must be sensitive to each family member's performance—that is to say, their compliance or noncompliance.

Problems of noncompliance may occur either from lack of clarity by the therapist or poor choice of technologies to treat particular relationships. When experiencing noncompliance, the therapist should ask questions such as: (1) "Is a problem arising? If not we're on course." (2) "If a problem is arising, is it me or them, my skill level or their resistance?" (3) "Have I chosen an appropriate technology?" (4) "Was I clear, directive, and competent in my presentation of that technology?"

If the therapist's structuring skills are not sufficiently developed at this phase, the family may fail to comply because they have not understood the directions. Thus, for example, a behavioral contract between a teenage child and the parents may not have been sufficiently specific in terms of rewards and punishments. This would reflect a therapist *skill* problem. On the other hand, if the therapist reviews the contract and perceives that the degree of specificity was adequate and both teenager and parents understood the contract, the family resistance would alert the therapist (via performance sensitivity) that earlier assessments and assumptions about the family were erroneous. When the therapist sees an error has occurred (e.g., the family did not comply with an assignment), she or he must scan to determine whether to (1) stay within phase, (e.g., tighten up the contract, be more clear about when rewards will be disbursed, or write out the steps of the communication training format), or (2) move back across phases to assessment/understanding, where the conceptual skills can be used to reevaluate assumptions made about the relationships between family members. Such reevaluations would lead to questions which could in turn suggest solutions: "Is it mother, not father, who should disperse the reward?" "Is the child's phobia a vehicle to keep parents *apart,* not *together?*" "Is this husband not wanting the degree of intimacy his wife is asking for?" These questions will lead the therapist back through the therapy/induction phase and then once again to a modified technology in the treatment/education phase.

Generalization/termination phase

Goals: Maintain change, produce independence from therapist.

Therapist function: Disengagement.

Therapist skills: Relationship, structuring, cognitive skills.

The goal of most families and therapists is a positive change in the family system, which will be maintained after the therapist ceases involvement. Just as therapists need to assess their impact on a system as they begin treatment, so they must be cognizant of the effect that their leaving will create. While most models of therapy make reference to the importance of termination, few models of therapy operationalize criteria for decision making regarding termination. It is generally assumed that some combination of problem cessation, problem-solving skills, behavior generalization, and/or the attainment of adaptive attitudes constitute indications to the therapist that the family is ready for termination. However, if the family has not understood or benefited sufficiently from the treatment/education phase of intervention or if assessment was inaccurate, generalization or maintenance of new patterns of behavior cannot be expected.

In addition, if positive behavior change has occurred, there is a possibility that the positive changes will cease as therapist involvement decreases. If such "cures" are dependent on continued therapist involvement, the therapist must help the family learn to function independently. Special attention must focus on experiences assigned to families between sessions, with understanding of where completion of assignments break down. If the therapist feels indispensable to the family, the therapist must question if this is the family's need or the therapist's need. Such transference and countertransference issues do arise in family therapy as well as individual therapy. At this stage of therapy, scanning also has to become an "as if" phenomenon. The therapist must "guess" how the family will behave without him or her and also "guess" about future contexts. This contrasts with other phases in which scanning is almost exclusively on the "here and now" process.

Therapists in this phase of treatment need to rely on a combination of skills, since termination contains a microcosm or condensation of the entire therapeutic experience. In order to answer the question of appropriateness of termination, a therapist must *summarize* the entirety of the intervention process, reviewing each phase mentally in order to understand the current situation. This summary then provides cues as to whether there is likely to be a successful termination.

Problems which may occur at the termination phase of intervention are (1) premature termination, (2) delayed termination, and (3) inappropriate termination. Premature termination may occur if the family or therapist have rushed toward an end of therapy, in the absence of sufficient activity in the induction/therapy phase. For example, if a family has agreed to passively accept therapist relabels, then receives the technology of the therapy/education phase without sufficiently believing about the relational or interactional nature of the problem behavior of the identified patient (which should have occurred in the induction/therapy phase), the termination may occur prematurely. This possibility frequently occurs in court-referred, nonvoluntary referrals where immediate problems are brought under control, but longer-term interactional changes do not begin. The therapist must carefully scan the intervention for signs of shallow compliance on the part of such families.

The second problem, that of delayed termination, may occur when either family or therapist is unwilling to terminate even when positive behavior change has been achieved. In individual therapy, there are indications that attraction and liking may lead to delayed termination (Bergin & Garfield, 1971). Again, this phase may correspond to transference or countertransference phenomena or simply be a desire to hold on to an experience which has been pleasant for both family and therapist. In order to solve either problem, the therapist must scan the entire spectrum of therapeutic activities to make an objective, asocial (Beier, 1966) decision. Primarily this phase requires therapist cognitive skills to assess, structuring skills to explain, and relational skills to provide a climate for the termination process. The therapist needs to explain and predict ways to continue successes at the same time s/he gives the family the message that termination is not rejection but belief in the family's ability to operate independently of the therapist. To do so, the therapist must often intercede with extrafamilial systems or help family members to learn to do so, to initiate changes in these extrafamily systems that will maintain the family's positive changes.

CONCLUSION

This chapter has emphasized several points considered important to family therapists: (1) specific intervention models are conceptual roadmaps for therapists derived from the strengths of their authors; 2) generic models (in this case, AIM) provide family therapists with a problem-solution format to questions raised but not answered by specific models; and (3) therapists must continually scan the therapeutic process for potential errors and the solutions to these problems. We hope these ideas are helpful and intriguing enough to capture the reader's imagination as much as the therapist is intrigued by the problems posed by a new family.

Let us imagine that the reader has scanned the chapter much as the therapist scans an initial session at the point of intervention with a family. At this point, a therapist can use a specific model of treatment much as it has been used with past families. In that same way, the reader of this chapter may read and digest what is said, as the reader has read numerous chapters before. We hope, instead, that both the therapist and reader may choose to utilize a new process when tackling a new family or a new chapter. The therapist may choose to superimpose a generic model over a specific model in order to identify and solve problems. After reading or scanning this book, if the reader is moved to go back to that point in the chapter which provides information about how to correct old problems, tries them out, and finds new methods which work for them, we have achieved our goal.

By adopting the AIM framework, therapists will have a means to identify the problems they are experiencing in a particular phase of intervention. Once the problems are identified, the therapist can undertake a two-stage process of finding solutions. In the first stage, the therapist can identify the generic skills classes that are appropriate for dealing with problems in that particular phase of intervention. The therapist then can choose to remain in that phase and utilize those skills or can attempt to move to a different phase of intervention and utilize the different skills which are characteristic of problem solution in that different phase.

The second step in the solution is dictated by the therapist's particular model of intervention. Unlike AIM, which merely identifies generic classes, specific models suggest specific techniques. A certain generic class of skills (such as directiveness) may take different forms in different models—for example, telling people to restate what has been said in one model, assigning homework tasks in another model, and presenting directives after returning to the room in yet a third model. In other words, the particular tactics used by therapists will vary from model to model, but all models will (or should) develop a set of tactics to perform the generic skill classes required of therapists. Our focus here has been on these generic skill classes.

REFERENCES

Ackerman, N. *The psychodynamics of family life.* New York: Basic Books, 1958.

Alexander, J. F., Barton, C., Schiavo, R. S., & Parsons, B. V. Systems behavioral intervention with families of delinquents: Therapist characteristics, family behavior, and outcome. *Journal of Consulting and Clinical Psychology,* 1976, *44*(4), 656–664.

Alexander, J. F., Barton, C., Waldron, H., & Mas, C. H. Beyond the technology of family therapy: The anatomy of intervention model. In K. D. Craig & R. J. McMahon (Eds.), *Advances in clinical behavior therapy.* New York: Brunner/Mazel, 1983.

Alexander, J. A., & Parsons, B. V. *Functional family therapy.* Monterey, Calif.: Brooks/Cole Publishing, 1982.

Barton, C., & Alexander, J. F. Functional family therapy. In A. S. Gurman & D. P. Kniskern (Eds.), *Handbook of family therapy.* New York: Brunner/Mazel, 1981.

Beavers, W., & Voeller, M. N. Family models: Comparing and contrasting the Olson circumplex model with the Beavers systems model. *Family Process,* 1983, *22,* 85–98.

Beier, E. G. *The silent language of psychotherapy: Social reinforcement of unconscious processes.* Hawthorne, N.Y.: Aldine Publishing, 1966.

Bergin, A., & Garfield, S. (Eds.). *Handbook of psychotherapy and behavior change: An empirical analysis.* New York: John Wiley & Sons, 1971.

Bloom, B. L. Planned short-term therapy in *Community Mental Health.* Monterey, Calif.: Brooks/Cole Publishing, 1982.

Brodsky, A. M., & Hare-Mustin, C. T. *Women and psychotherapy.* New York: Guilford Press, 1980.

Cline, V. B., Coles, J., Mejia, J. A., & Klein, N. *Marital therapy outcome: Therapist, clients, and judges evaluation.* Manuscript submitted for publication, 1983.

Collins, A. M., & Sedlack, W. E. Counselor ratings of male and female clients. *Journal of National Association for Women Deans, Administrators, and Counselors,* 1974, *37,* 128–132.

Dollard, J., & Miller, N. E. *Personality and psychotherapy.* New York: McGraw-Hill, 1950.

Erickson, G. D. & Hogan, T. P. *Family therapy: An introduction to theory and technique.* Monterey, Calif.: Brooks/Cole Publishing, 1972.

Fisher, L. Transactional theories but individual assessment: A frequent discrepancy in family research. *Family Process,* 1982, *21,* 313–320.

Frank, J. D. *Persuasion and healing: A comparative study of psychotherapy.* Baltimore: The Johns Hopkins Press.

Goldenberg, I., & Goldenberg, H. *Family therapy: An overview.* Monterey, Calif.: Brooks/Cole Publishing, 1980.

Greenspoon, J. Verbal conditioning and clinical psychology. In A. Bachrach (Ed.), *Experimental foundations of clinical psychology.* New York: Basic Books, 1962.

Guilford, J. P., & Hoepfner, R. *The analysis of intelligence.* New York: McGraw-Hill, 1971.

Gurman, A. S. Marital therapy: Emerging trends in research and practice. *Family Process,* 1973, *12,* 45–54.

Gurman, A. S., & Klein, H. H. Marital and family conflicts. In A. M. Brodsky & C. T. Hare-Mustin (Eds.), *Women and psychotherapy.* New York: Guilford Press, 1980.

Gurman, A. S., & Kniskern, D. P. *Handbook of family therapy.* New York: Brunner/Mazel, 1981.

Haley, J. (Ed.), *Changing families.* New York: Grune & Stratton, 1971.

Jackson, D. (Ed.), *The etiology of schizophrenia.* New York: Basic Books, 1960.

L'Abate, L. *Systematic family therapy.* New York: Brunner/Mazel, 1985.

L'Abate, L., Frey, J., III, & Wagner, V. Toward a classification of family therapy theories: Further elaborations and implications of the E–R–A–Aw–C model. *Family Therapy,* 1983, *9,* 251–262.

Luborsky, L., Bachrach, H., Graff, H., Pulver, S., & Christoph, P. Predicting the outcome of psychotherapy: Findings of the Penn Psychotherapy Project. *Archives of General Psychiatry,* 1980, *37,* 371–381.

Minuchin, S. *Families and family therapy.* Cambridge, Mass.: Harvard University Press, 1974.

Napier, A., & Whittaker, C. *The family crucible.* New York: Harper & Row, 1978.

Nisbett, R. E., & Wilson, T. DeC. Telling more than we know: Verbal reports on mental processes. *Psychological Review,* 1977, *84*(3), 231–259.

Olson, D., Sprenkle, C., & Russell, D. Circumplex model of marital and family systems I. *Family Process,* 1979, *18,* 3–15.

Olson, D. H., Russell, C. S., & Sprenkle, D. H. Marital and family therapy: A decade review. *Journal of Marriage and Family,* 1980, *42,* 973–993..

O'Malley, S. S., Suh, C. S., & Strupp, H. H. The Vanderbilt psychotherapy process scale: A report on the scale development and a process-outcome study. *Journal of Consulting and Clinical Psychology,* 1983, *51,* 581–586.

Rogers, C. R. The necessary and sufficient conditions of therapeutic personality change. *Journal of Consulting Psychology,* 1957, *21,* 95–103.

Schaffer, N. D. Multidimensional measures of therapist behavior as predictors of outcome. *Psychological Bulletin,* 1982, *92,* 670–682.

Seiden, A. M. Overview: Research on the psychology of women II: Women in families, work, and psychotherapy. *American Journal of Psychiatry,* 1976.

Selvini-Palazzoli, M, Boscolo, L., Cecchin, G., & Prata, G. *Paradox and counterparadox.* New York: Jason Aronson, 1978.

Sheffrin, R. M., & Schneider, W. Controlled and automatic human information processing: II. Perceptual learning, automatic attending, and a general theory. *Psychological Review,* 1977, *84,* 127–190.

Strong, S. Social psychological approaches to psychotherapy research. In S. Garfield & A. E. Bergin (Eds.), *Handbook of psychotherapy and behavior change.* New York: John Wiley & Sons, 1978.

Strupp, H. H., & Hadley, S. W. Specific versus nonspecific factors in psychotherapy: A controlled study of outcome. *Archives of General Psychiatry,* 1983, *36,* 1125–1136.

Tomm, K. M., & Wright, L. M. Training in family therapy: Perceptual, conceptual, and executive skills. *Family Process,* 1979, *18,* 227–250.

Truax, C. B., & Mitchell, K. M. Research on certain therapist interpersonal skills in relation to process and outcome. In A. E. Bergin & S. L. Garfield (Eds.), *Handbook of psychotherapy and behavior change.* New York: John Wiley & Sons, 1971.

Warburton, J., Alexander, J. F., & Barton, C. *Sex of client and sex of therapist: Variables in a family process study.* Paper presented at the annual convention of the American Psychological Association, Montreal, August 1980.

Chapter 44

Beyond Technology: The Next Stage in Developing an Empirical Base for Parent Training*

GERALD R. PATTERSON

INTRODUCTION

Treatment for families of preadolescent antisocial children requires two components, each necessary but neither sufficient in order for the treatment to be effective. From a social-learning perspective, it is assumed that the antisocial behavior is caused by a breakdown in family management practices provided by the parents (Patterson, 1982). One focus for the present report will be to examine the relation between measures of family management practices and measures of antisocial child behavior. The findings emphasize the importance of the first component in this treatment, which is to teach and supervise the parents in their use of four different areas of family management skills: monitoring, discipline, positive reinforcement, and family problem solving.

It is our assumption that a therapist's knowledge of the parent-training technology is not a sufficient basis for producing a positive outcome in working with the majority of families of antisocial boys referred for treatment. The second requirement necessary for positive outcomes is a high degree of clinical skill in working with parental resistance.

---

* An earlier version of this material was presented at the Banff International Conference, April 1981, Banff, Alberta, Canada.

The research presented in the present report has been supported by a grant from the John D. and Catherine T. MacArthur Foundation. The ideas reflect several years of discussions with my clinical colleagues John Reid, Patti Chamberlain, Marion Forgatch, and Kate Kavanagh.

The assumption is that efforts to teach the parents social-learning concepts and to change their childrearing behaviors produce parental resistance even when introduced by well-trained therapists. Presumably, it is the therapist's skill in resolving this resistance that functions as a prime determinant for successful treatment. A second focus for the present report will be upon coding of therapist and client behaviors during treatment as a means for studying resistance and its relation to treatment outcome. The assumption is that the resistance is a "countable" event that is *jointly* determined by what the client *and* the therapist bring to the therapeutic session. Studies will be presented that test these hypotheses.

Background

In the mid-1960s, investigators began experimenting with the application of operant procedures to the treatment of aggressive children (e.g., Hawkins, Peterson, Schweid, & Bijou, 1966). The key concept was to train the parents directly to alter the contingencies *they* applied to the behavior of their own child. Single case studies began appearing in the published literature, including actual observations demonstrating the effectiveness of these procedures for young antisocial children (Johnson & Brown, 1969; Patterson & Brodsky, 1966; Patterson, McNeal, Hawkins, & Phelps, 1967; Zeilberger, Sampen, & Sloane, 1968). By 1970, it seemed we were only a step away from proving that it was possible to help these children by the straightforward expedient of developing a technology for "teaching" their parents.

In the first flush of enthusiasm, this author wrote a book in which parents could study the relevant social-learning concepts, thereby (we thought) requiring less professional time from staff therapists (Patterson & Gullion, 1968). Giving such information to parents and supervising its use was perhaps a useful supplement to treatment, but it became clear very quickly that *the therapist was making a crucial contribution to the teaching process.* While some studies demonstrated that parents of normal preschool children could read a pamphlet and successfully alter child noncompliance (Forgatch & Toobert, 1979), we were convinced by the early 1970s that, for referred cases, a pamphlet or book *would not* be sufficient.

Unspecified "clinical skill" was required for effective treatment of extremely antisocial children and their families. Graduate students who came to the Oregon Social Learning Center (OSLC) to learn the treatment spent a minimum of a year in *weekly* supervision to learn what these skills were.

In the preliminary book for the therapists, written in 1973, clinical skills were assumed as a given, and no mention was made of them

(Patterson, Reid, Jones, & Conger, 1975). In the mid-1970s, a small group of contributors to family therapy (J. Alexander, E. Bleckman, E. Christoferson, R. Wahler, and others) began to meet a day or two prior to each of the annual Association for Advancement of Behavior Therapy conventions. It became apparent that while we all used similar language and concepts, the actual treatment procedures, when viewed on videotapes, differed widely. Furthermore, many of the parents were not only noncooperative but were, in fact, resistant to changing the way in which they managed their problem children. In the years that followed, several of the investigators have initiated research programs focused on the problem of measuring and defining these clinical skills (Alexander, Barton, Schiavo, & Parsons, 1976; Wahler & Dumas, 1983).

There was another sequence of events that gave further impetus to the growing emphasis on clinical skills. In treatment outcome studies, first Ferber, Keely, and Shemberg (1974), next Eyberg and Johnson (1974), and then Anchor and Thomason (1977) failed to obtain significant reductions in rates of deviant child behavior observed in the home. All used time-limited treatment and student-trainee therapists. While Karoly and Rosenthal (1977) and Peed, Roberts, and Forehand (1977) did obtain significant changes in observed behavior in treated families, it was clear that a treatment effect was *not* reliable across investigators.

Then several large-scale comparison studies evaluating parent-training procedures produced negative findings. Bernal, Klinnert, and Schultz (1980) compared client-centered therapy and parent-training procedures. Cases were randomly assigned. The parent-training strategy was time-limited (eight weeks, 10 sessions); both therapies were carried out by student therapists. Home observation data showed no treatment effects for either group. It should be noted, however, that the sample may have been a less than optimal one for demonstrating a reduction in observed rates of behavior. At baseline, nearly half of their subjects showed normal rates of observed aggression treatment.

However, this potential source of ambiguity did not apply to the recent studies by Fleischman (1979). In three community agencies, families of socially aggressive children were randomly assigned either to traditional casework or to a time-limited (10 weeks) and highly structured parent-training program also administered by agency staff. The latter had been given a week of intensive training in the components of parent training and varying amounts of supervision during the study. A multilevel approach, the core of which was pre-post home observations, was used to assess and compare the effects of treatment. Although most of the measures suggested that parent training was superior to casework, the observation data showed no significant improvement for either group.

Thus, a number of studies, including two systematic evaluations (Bernal et al., 1980; Fleischman, 1979), have failed to provide support for the efficacy of parent training for families of oppositional children. Two factors are shared by these studies. The first is the use of a time- or session-limited format. Our own original studies (Patterson, 1974a, 1974b) and replication studies (Fleischman, 1981, Fleischman & Szykula, 1981, Patterson, Chamberlain & Reid, 1982) typically involved an average of around 20 hours of therapist time. Second, the training of the therapists has typically been a short-term affair in which students have been trained to administer the program in a standardized, educative fashion. This second point is difficult to document, but it is our impression that the therapist training tended to deemphasize clinical skills.

It is conceivable that the parent-training procedures cannot be applied within a time-limited format. It may also be the case that reliable results are obtained only when the procedures are applied by experienced, broadly trained therapists (i.e., student therapists are not sufficient for treatment of extremely antisocial, school-age children). We hypothesize that both of these variables are involved, but the factor common to both is the concept of resistance. It is very difficult to work through parent resistance in 8 to 10 weeks, especially if the therapist has limited clinical skill.

We are currently conceptualizing our treatment process as having two or perhaps even three primary components. Each is required for successful treatment, but none by itself is sufficient to produce reliable change in clinical cases of antisocial behavior. As noted earlier, the first component is the well-known technology of parent training for family management skills. We believe that by itself this technology in the hands of novice therapists (especially in time-limited formats), will not reliably produce positive outcomes for most clinical referrals. Just knowing *what* to pitch (i.e., parenting techniques) constitutes only a part of effective treatment for most families. The component that requires skill is knowing *how* to pitch the technology so that resistance, inertia, or noncooperation is minimized.

Parental resistance to actually practicing in the home what they have "learned" is a problem familiar to all therapists treating such cases. Usually and understandably, parents of aggressive children are not predisposed at intake to feel hopeful or positive about the potential effectiveness of treatment. Most of these parents have repeatedly tried to change their child's troublesome behavior. Their prior failures plus the day-to-day misery of living with an aggressive or delinquent child have made these parents feel generally negative about themselves, the child, and "the problem." The child is equally negative about changing things. In addition, many of these families have been told by community agencies that they *must* seek treatment. All of these factors are probably relevant as determinants for parent resistance. Data relevant to some of these issues will be presented in a later section.

The obdurately abrasive client may change the behavior of even the best-intentioned therapist. In effect, the client "teaches" the therapist that with this parent it is expedient to remain distant, to refrain from teaching parenting skills, to "forget" to follow up on missed appointments, and eventually to bring this "hopeless" case to the weekly staff review. We have come to see the weekly meeting as a necessary component because it seems to function as an antidote to the effects produced by persistent "punishment" and nonreinforcement of therapist behavior. The staff can serve as a support group *for the therapist*. They can also provide new bursts of enthusiasm and a reframing, *for the therapist*, of the client's behavior or generate some new idea on how to cope with this particular resistance. While we have not yet tested the assumption, we believe that it may eventually serve as a third necessary component for effective outcome (i.e., effective delivery requires a support group for the behavior of the therapist).

The remainder of this chapter is concerned with three main issues. The first concerns the assumption that training in childrearing skills is central to the parent-training process. What is the empirical evidence that the lack of these skills relates to deviant child behavior? The second issue concerns the evidence for the efficacy of training parents to apply these skills in managing severely disturbed children. What is the evidence for the outcome being due to treatment effects and not some other variables? What is the evidence that the effects persist? The third and most important issue concerns the formulation and means of measurement for parent resistance, the data which relate to its determinants, and its relation to outcome. Included in this is a discussion of the contributions made by the therapist to resistance. The sections that follow briefly review the literature and data relevant to each of these issues.

FAMILY MANAGEMENT SKILLS AND ANTISOCIAL CHILDREN

Disruptions or omissions in the parents' application of family management practices have consistently been found to correlate with preadolescents' antisocial behavior (Rutter, Tizard, & Whitmore, 1979; West & Farrington, 1973). Clinical experience in treating families of preadolescent antisocial boys suggested that parents of these children were deficient in the practice of four interrelated family management skills: setting clearly specified house rules, monitoring the child's whereabouts, using effective discipline for antisocial behavior, employing effective problem-solving skills, and supporting the development of prosocial skills (Patterson, 1982).

The four family management variables emphasized here emerged as the result of two decades of clinical work with several hundred preadolescent antisocial children referred for treatment. More recently, the treatment was expanded to include adolescent chronic delinquent offenders and families of abused children (Patterson, Reid, & Weinrott, 1984). Each of these samples seemed to be characterized by disruptions in one or more of the parents' family management skills. Essentially, treatment involve teaching the parents to do what parents of normal children are already doing.

Monitoring and discipline

While each of the family management variables was grounded in clinical experience, each of them also had a prior history in the literature on studies of antisocial children. For example, the monitoring variable had been previously identified by studies employing both retrospective and longitudinal designs to study delinquents. These studies consistently found that parents of delinquent youths had limited awareness of where their children were, whom they were with, and what they were doing (Hirschi, 1969; McCord, 1979; West & Farrington, 1977). The most careful study of the relation between monitoring and delinquency was based on McCord's (1976) follow-up of the Cambridge-Sommerville sample. She found that the likelihood of a child being adequately supervised in an intact home was .70; given a home where parents were in conflict, the likelihood was .50; and given a broken home with a nonaffectionate mother, the likelihood was only .20. McCord found that inept monitoring covaried with high rates of delinquency; she also noted that inept monitoring covaried with lower ratings of mother affection and with higher rates of parental conflict.

In our treatment studies, we found that most of the parents of children who lie and steal at high rates simply had little information about where the children went, with whom, or what they did. If parents did not know what the children were doing, it follows that they could not punish them. The Oregon Social Learning Center study of several hundred normal families emphasized the key role played by monitoring in the development of antisocial behavior (Patterson & Stouthamer-Loeber, in press). That study showed a correlation of .39 ($p < .01$) between disruptions in monitoring for a sample of seventh-grade boys and the frequency of police offenses. The comparable correlation for a sample of 10th-grade boys was .68 ($p < .001$). In the same study, the comparable correlations for a measure of stealing were .52 ($p < .0001$) and .43 ($p < .001$), respectively; for lying, they were .44 ($p < .0001$) and .58 ($p < .0001$) respectively. Monitoring is a composite score measured by questionnaire items filled out by the mother and a score based upon daily telephone reports of the child's whereabouts from the child and the mother.

The relationship between discipline and antisocial child behavior has also been noted in a number of studies (Sears, Maccoby, & Levin, 1957; West & Farrington, 1973). However, Radke-Yarrow, Campbell, and Burton's (1968) review of discipline studies based on parents' interview data revealed inconsistent results and did not permit firm conclusions.

However, the decade of empirical studies, carried out in the laboratory and in field settings, that followed, demonstrated the fact that neither nonreinforcement (extinction) nor reinforcing competing (prosocial) behaviors serve as effective means for reducing antisocial child behavior. Well-controlled studies also demonstrated that such punishments as time-out, work details, point loss, and loss of privileges were an effective means for producing long-term changes in antisocial child behavior (see review in Patterson, 1982). These studies were in keeping with our clinical experience in suggesting that parents of antisocial children use a great deal of punishment, but most of it was threats and scolding with very little backup.

Parenting deficits related to overt antisocial child behaviors (such as fighting) seemed to revolve around the parents' ineffective use of discipline. This means they are unable to contain the coercive exchanges among family members. The failure to intervene effectively in these exchanges places the target child at special risk for becoming involved in extended coercive exchanges. It is here that he is also likely to become involved in escalations in amplitude of his coercive behavior (i.e., one or both members hit, shove, or throw an object).

The measures of discipline developed in the OSLC study were a composite of ratings made by observers in the home who had witnessed parental efforts to intervene in coercive exchanges among family members. The ratings described the consistency of parents' efforts to discipline as well as their effectiveness. In the Patterson and Stouthamer-Loeber (in press) study, the discipline score correlated .35 ($p < .05$) with the number of police contacts and .30 ($p < .10$) with the child's self-reported delinquency.

Problem solving and positive reinforcement

Minor crises from outside and conflicts among members are routine within any family. It is one of the responsibilities of the parents to cope with these as best they can. From a social-learning viewpoint, these coping skills usually include several steps:

1. Clearly stating the problem in neutral terms.
2. The recipient paraphrasing to show s/he has heard what the problem was.
3. Brainstorming discussion of alternative ways of proceeding.
4. Negotiating some sort of compromise that is then written down as a means of reducing future conflicts over what was agreed upon.
5. Agreeing upon a set of positive consequences for both members if the agreement is kept and punishments if it is not.

The third family management skill was problem solving. Videotapes of the parents and children discussing current family problems were scored to produce a composite rating of the quality of problem resolution. The hypothesis tested here was that families characterized by a poor quality of problem solving would also have children who were less socially skilled.

In the 1960s, a series of laboratory and field studies with younger children, published in the *Journal of Applied Behavior Analysis*, demonstrated that parental social reinforcement could be an important determinant for children's development of social skills such as cooperation and play with peers. These and other studies of this kind were based upon the influential writings of Bijou and Baer (1961). While the studies demonstrated that in principle such a relationship could exist, no studies in the decade that followed established a link between parent reinforcement and child social skill development.

A measure of parent reinforcement was developed, based upon a composite of variables from observations in the home. The composite score was based upon a summing across the standard scores for the following variables: the likelihood of mother approval given she was interacting with the target child, the proportion of time mother was *non*interactive with family members, the duration (in seconds) of mother positive affect while interacting with the target child, and the child's self-reports about receiving positive reinforcement for prosocial behavior. The data from the study by Patterson (in press) showed this score correlated with measures of both academic achievement and relations to peers (see section which follows).

Additional findings

It was assumed that monitoring and discipline disruptions would covary with the development of antisocial behavior, and disruptions in family problem-solving skills and parent positive reinforcement would covary with the failure of the child to develop academic and social skills. To test these hypotheses, data were collected for samples of families of boys in the 4th, 7th, and 10th grades (Patterson, in press).

Each of the families participated in an extensive multilevel assessment, including observations in the home, interviews, questionnaires, and ratings by teachers, peers, and the target child.

In keeping with the hypotheses, both monitoring and discipline scores correlated significantly with a composite score measuring the child's fighting. The score was based upon ratings by teachers, peers, and the mother about the frequency of physical fighting. The median correlation across the three grades was .44 ($p < .001$) for the monitoring variable and .35 ($p < .01$) for the discipline variable. The findings were consistent with the hypothesis that disruptions in parent monitoring and discipline were related to higher rates of antisocial child behavior.

The social skill hypothesis was tested by correlating scores from reading achievement and mothers' ratings of relations with peers as the criterion measures. The findings provided modest but consistent support for the assumption that parental skills in problem solving and in positive reinforcement covaried with measures of academic and social skills. The median correlation across the three grades was .29 ($p < .01$) between problem solving and reading achievement; for positive reinforcement, it was also .29 ($p < .10$. The correlations between the mothers' ratings of the child's social competence and the positive reinforcement score was .45 ($p < .01$); the comparable correlation with the problem-solving score was nonsignificant.

The next question raised concerned the generality of the family management measures. Are the four variables relevant only to antisocial problems in children, or do they relate in some fashion to a wide spectrum of child deviant behaviors? To investigate this question, the scores from the four family management variables were correlated with scores describing various types of child-deviant behavior as measured by the Child Behavior Checklist (CBC) (Achenbach & Edelbrock, 1979). The checklist was completed by both the mothers and the fathers. The correlations are summarized in Table 1. It can be seen that disruptions in the parents' use of family management skills relate to a surprising array of problem behaviors including hyperactivity, immaturity, and social withdrawal. In fact, the magnitude of the correlations is almost as high for these problem behaviors as it is for more direct measures of antisocial behavior. Notice that the measures of family practices do not covary with the parents' ratings of more internalized kinds of child problem behaviors.

The findings provide strong support for the relation between these four parent skills and the development of antisocial child behavior. The assumption would be that training the parents to use these skills should result in reductions in the child's observed antisocial behaviors.

Table 1

Correlation of inept family management with mothers' report of deviant child behavior*

Family management variables (N)	CBC measure of child deviancy							
	Delinquent	Aggressive	Hyperactive	Immature	Social withdrawn	Obsessive	Somatic	Schizoid
Monitoring (188)	.48†	.38†	.29‡	.34†	.35†	.22§	.21§	.15
Discipline (54)	.48†	.32‡	.28§	.47†	.39‡	.18	.16	.05
Support (79)	.39†	.29‡	.18	.38†	.35‡	.16	.13	.10
Problem solving (86)	.23§	.29‡	.17	.34†	.40†	.18	.07	.10

* From Patterson, G. R., "The Unattached Mother: A Process Analysis," in *Relationships: Their Role in Social and Emotional Development*, ed. H. Hartup and Z. Rubius (Cambridge, Mass.: Harvard University Press, in press).

† *p* < .001
‡ *p* < .01
§ *p* < .05

The findings relevant to this assumption are examined in the section which follows.

TREATMENT OUTCOME

Can parents of extremely antisocial children be trained to alter the behavior of their own child such that s/he functions within the normal range? There are several reasons why families of antisocial children provide a useful matrix in which to study such a question. Chief among these is the fact that recent analyses have shown that the behavior of extremely antisocial children tends to be stable over long periods of time (Loeber, 1982). The review of 16 longitudinal studies by Olweus (1979) showed a surprising consistency in the stability of a general trait of aggression in children. The average stability coefficient for these studies was .63. The magnitude of this correlation decreased with longer time intervals, but even when the interval was from 10–18 years, the test-retest correlation averaged .49. These studies used samples of children varying widely in age (1–18 years). The criterion measures ranged from peer sociometric observation data to teacher and parent ratings. Regardless of sample or psychometric procedure, the findings were consistently in favor of stability.

The stability of antisocial child behavior appears to provide a suitable baseline against which one may sensitively evaluate intervention programs. The issue of how to measure changes in oppositional or deviant child behavior is central to the development of empirically based interventions for antisocial children. While it seems reasonable simply to ask parents if their child's behavior has changed, several studies have shown that global ratings by parents of treatment outcome provide data biased toward positive outcomes (e.g., Lobitz & Johnson, 1975; Schelle, 1974).

During the past 15 years, numerous investigators have developed behavioral coding systems designed to study fine-grained family interactions (e.g., Bernal & North, 1972; Wahler, House, & Stambaugh, 1976). In the Family Interaction Coding System (FICS) (Reid, 1978) used at OSLC, 29 distinct behaviors of family members are recorded sequentially as they interact with each other. Fourteen of these describe negative behaviors (e.g., hit, humiliate, whine) and are combined to produce a cluster category: total aversive behavior (TAB). Rate per minute of TAB for the referred child has been used as one of the major outcome criteria for evaluating treatment changes. Studies of the psychometric properties have shown FICS to be a stable, valid measure of child deviancy (e.g., Patterson, 1982; Reid, 1978). We assume that treatment outcomes showing changes in observed child deviancy without accompanying changes in the parent's perception of the child's referral symptoms are not likely to produce long-lasting effects in the family. For this reason, and in line with the contemporary practice of using multiple measures of treatment, a second criterion used for evaluating outcome, parent daily telephone reports (PDR) of child symptom occurrence, was developed (Patterson, Cobb, & Ray, 1973). PDR has been shown to correlate well (.4 to .7) with observation measures of child deviancy. Changes in PDR scores are thought to be a necessary but not sufficient indication of treatment success. We consider the parents' global rating of treatment as a third highly reactive but necessary criterion measure. Taken together, these three measures of change provide a multilevel strategy for evaluation of treatment outcomes.

In the mid-1960s, it seemed reasonable to believe that parents could be trained to change the behavior of their own preadolescent children (Patterson, McNeal, Hawkins, & Phelps, 1967; Wahler, Winkle, Peterson, & Morrison, 1965). By the end of the decade, there was a general consensus among many investigators (Wahler, Bernal, Patterson, and Reid) concerning the language and concepts describing a simple technology for teaching parents to retrain their own problem children (e.g., Patterson et al., 1975). Since that time, there has been a steady development in the understanding of what is involved in successful treatment for these severely stressed families. These developments further refined the measurement of changes in families and the conceptualization of aspects of family process producing antisocial behavior. The developments also included a reformulation concerning the major components necessary for successful family intervention (e.g., Alexander & Parson, 1973; Wahler & Dumas, 1983).

How does one evaluate treatment procedures if they continue to be revised? The strategy selected by OSLC was to carry out evaluation studies ad seriatim. At each juncture, a successful outcome would signify that the investigators should proceed to the next question. Most of the studies involved samples with cases of extremely antisocial children referred for treatment because of long-standing problems. The families were allowed as much time for treatment as was required. The treatment was provided by the Oregon Social Learning Center staff, each of whom had received intensive training and participated in weekly clinical staffings. The parent-training technology has been described in a primer for therapists in Patterson et al. (1975) and in a series of books (Patterson, 1976), audiotapes (Patterson & Forgatch, 1975), and a videotape (Forgatch, Patterson, Chamberlain, & Kavanagh, 1982) for parents' and therapists' use. Currently, a book is in preparation detailing the clinical skills and parent-training procedures.

The first problem addressed concerned the ability of the staff to produce a reliable decrease in the observed rates of deviant child behavior. The second examined the persistence of the treatment effects; the third was whether or not the procedures could be taught to a new group of therapists. The fourth concerned the use of random assignment and comparison designs for evaluating outcome.

Can a well-trained and constantly supervised staff produce reliable changes in observed rates of behavior? A series of single-case studies led to the decision to begin treating consecutive referrals for antisocial behaviors (Patterson & Brodsky, 1966; Patterson et al., 1967). The outcomes from the six cases treated following that decision were sufficiently encouraging and led to a commitment to initiate further programmatic studies. For the next sample of 13 cases, the observation data showed a significant reduction from baseline to termination in behavior targeted by the parents for change. Treatment effects generalized to nontargeted behaviors. An average of 31.4 hours of therapist time was used.

Next, it seemed reasonable to determine if the same staff could replicate the treatment effects. The next 11 referrals showed significant reductions in observed rates of targeted behaviors, at an average cost of 25.7 hours of therapist time. There was also a significant pre-post reduction in parent daily reports of symptom behavior (Patterson & Reid, 1973). Later analyses of the total sample showed significant generalization of treatment effects to sibling and nontargeted deviant behaviors (Arnold, Levine, & Patterson, 1975; Patterson, 1974a).

Do the treatment effects persist? Systematic follow-up data for the ensuing studies showed significant reductions from baseline through 12-month follow-up periods in observed rates of deviant child behavior (Patterson, 1974a, 1974b; Patterson et al., 1973; Patterson et al., 1975). The systematic analyses of 50 families who participated in follow-up studies showed significant reductions from baseline to follow-up phases for the two criterion measures: TAB and PDR (Patterson & Fleischman, 1979).

Are the treatment procedures "teachable"? The treatment effects could be due to some characteristics unique to this one group of therapists; if this were true, then attempts to train new groups of therapists would probably not be successful. In a replication study using a new group of therapists, a significant treatment effect was obtained for a mixed sample of stealers and social aggressors (Fleischman, 1981). Confidence was increased by the findings from another replication study for 66 families, carried out in Helena, Montana. A report by an outside evaluator for that project showed that significant pre/post reductions were obtained for observations and PDR data. One year follow-up findings for this sample showed that the effects persisted (Fleischman & Szykula, 1981).

Comparison studies.   The next question concerns the attributions one is to attach to these outcome studies. Are the outcome effects specific to the treatment, to uncontrolled factors such as the mere passage of time, or to placebo effects? Four comparison studies were conducted to address this issue; the last three employed random assignment. The first two pilot studies were each flawed in some crucial aspect. In the first, a waiting-list control design was used (Wiltz & Patterson, 1974). In the second, a placebo-treatment control-group design was used (Walter & Gilmore, 1973). In both studies, pre- and post-observation data showed a significant decrease in observed rates of deviant child behavior for the experimental group and no change or an increase in deviant behavior for the control group. However, in both studies, differences in baseline data for the experimental and control groups suggested possible selective bias in group assignment.[1] In addition, the time interval (four to five weeks) was much shorter than that typically employed in our treatment.

A third comparison study (Patterson, Chamberlain, & Reid, 1982) was designed to correct the deficits characterizing the two pilot studies. Cases were randomly assigned to a treatment or waiting-list control group. Most of the latter asked to be referred elsewhere for treatment. At termination, both groups were reevaluated.

A two-way analysis of variance for repeated measures was performed on baseline and termination TAB scores for the two groups. The interaction of groups by phase was significant. The majority of the subjects in the experimental group functioned within the normal range. These findings are summarized in Figure 1. Both groups also showed significant reductions in PDR. Ninety percent of the parents in the experimental group and 25 percent of the parents in the comparison group rated treatment as very effective. The findings supported the hypothesis that the decrease in deviant child behavior was specific to the parent-training procedures and not just due to the passage of time or an outcome of applying for treatment at a community agency.

In the next study, young, chronic-offending delinquents were randomly assigned to parent training or to community facilities (Patterson et al., in preparation). A three-year follow-up showed that during their first year in the program there was a significantly greater reduction in police offenses for the subjects in the experimental groups than for

---

[1] The possibility of such a negative bias could have serious implications for studies in which parents felt they might be rejected for treatment unless their case was extremely severe. That is, they might fake bad behavior (at baseline) to ensure receiving treatment. If such a tendency was systematic, an artificial treatment effect might be observed.

Figure 1

Average rate per minute of child deviant behavior for two groups*

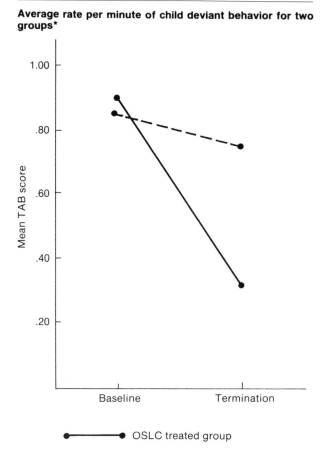

* From Patterson, G. R., Chamberlain, P., and Reid, J. B., "A Comparative Evaluation of a Parent Training Program," *Behavior Therapy* 13 (1982), pp. 638–650.

those in the comparison group. There were nonsignificant differences for the second and third years of follow-up.

Four other studies employed random assignment of families of antisocial or oppositional (less deviant) children to parent-training and comparison conditions *and* provided for pre- and post-home observation as criterion: Anchor and Thomason (1977); Bernal et al. (1980); Fleischman (1979); Karoly and Rosenthal (1977). Three of the four failed to demonstrate a significant improvement for the experimental group, and none of the control groups showed significant changes in observed rates of deviant behavior.

As noted earlier, each of these comparison studies used time-limited therapy of 8 to 10 weeks for the experimental groups. With the exception of the Fleischman (1979) study, all employed student therapists. Of the four studies, only the Karoly and Rosenthal (1977) study showed a significant reduction in observed rates of deviant behavior for the experimental group. Still, the lack of consistent replication of treatment effects for 5- to 12-year-old antisocial boys outside this center raised serious questions as to the generalizability of our findings. It led to a rethinking of what it is that is involved in the successful treatment of families of preadolescent antisocial children. Our present hypothesis is that successful intervention depends upon three components, each necessary but no one in itself sufficient for success: (1) the existence of a parent-training technology to alter ineffective family management practices, (2) the clinical skill of the therapist in dealing with parental resistance so that effective family management can be taught and practiced in the home, and (3) a therapist support system to maintain effective therapist performance. We believe that it is the ability of the skilled therapist to work through resistance that allows parents to produce changes in family management practices, and in turn, this produces changes in child deviancy. A combination of time-limited treatments provided by student therapists is probably not adequate to the task of helping these difficult families.

The question currently being investigated concerns what it is that the parent does that produces the changes in deviant child behavior. The general formulation would have it that if they began to monitor and to use effective discipline, the rates of antisocial behavior will be reduced. The current treatment studies are employing pre-post measures of family management practices to determine if this is the case.

The material presented in the next section examines the literature and the empirical findings that relate to the relation between therapist behavior and parent resistance. Is it the case that experienced therapists attempting to teach family management practices increase parental resistance during treatment?

A SOCIAL INTERACTION VIEW OF PARENT RESISTANCE

In the general model illustrated in Figure 2, it is assumed that client resistance during treatment is jointly determined by two sets of variables: On the one hand, it is partially determined by the nature of the social and psychological environment that the client brings into treatment. On the other hand, the behavior of the therapist also determines whether resistant reactions will occur and be amplified or dampened.

Figure 2

An interactional model for resistance, family management, and deviant child behavior

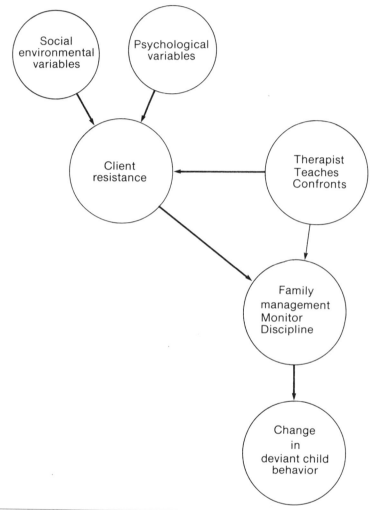

Resistance is *jointly* determined by dispositions brought to the sessions by both client and therapist. The key assumption is that if client resistance remains high, then neither the parents' family management skills nor deviant child behavior will change.

We have found it useful to measure resistance in several ways. First, there is that part of resistance that can be conceptualized in terms of specific and observable events. In the videotapes of treatment, client behavior is coded as resistance when it closely follows an effort by the therapist to introduce some new concept, including a suggestion for change in the behavior of the parent or their child. This way of defining resistance has some unique advantages; foremost among them is the fact that it permits a microsocial analysis of the functional relationships between the behavior of the client and the behavior of the therapist (e.g., is it something the therapist *does* that functions as an "elicitor"?). It is easier to study such questions if one can study interaction sequences in therapy transactions.

There is obviously more than one way of expressing resistance. For example, some parents nod their heads in agreement *during* the session and then "forget" to carry out their homework assignments. In the current studies, each session has been rated both by the therapist and independently by observers viewing videotapes as to the amount of compliance in carrying out assignments. These analyses completed thus far show that the micro and macro measures of parent resistance significantly overlap. Most parents who are resistant during the session also complete fewer homework assignments, but this is not always the case. Furthermore, there are some parents compliant during the sessions and noncompliant in carrying out their agreements at home. While the within- and between-session measures of resistance should correlate, the magnitude is bound to be a good deal less than 1.00. It is assumed that both measures tap into a common factor or construct; the proper measurement of the construct requires multiple indicators.

Wachtel's (1982) edited volume documents the clinical concerns of six major figures in the field of therapy. Coping with client resistance was a central concern of each of these writers. It was also the case that the publication was relatively innocent of empirical findings relating to these issues. The concept of resistance and the development of techniques for working with client resistance are major foci for the strategic and structural family therapy groups (Haley, 1976; Minuchin, 1974; Weakland, Fisch, Watzlavich, & Bodin, 1974). No data were presented that demonstrate that these techniques have a significant impact upon client resistance.

There are empirical studies that explicate the concept of resistance in a general way. For example, Wills (1978) notes, in his review of the therapy literature, the frequent emergence of a factor dimension analogous to client resistance. He found an across-study average of 44 percent noncompliance for patients on *medical* regimes. A survey of behavior therapists by O'Dell, Mahoney, Horton, and Turner (1979) showed that, on the average, only 27 percent of the clients were viewed as being "easy" to work with. Chamberlain, Patterson, Reid, Kavanagh, & Forgatch (in press) found that only 28 percent of the parents of antisocial children referred for treatment showed low resistance during *all* phases of the treatment process. Given the consensus about the central role of resistance, it is even more surprising that so little empirical work has been done on the subject.

One of the key assumptions in the social interactional approach taken here is that the resistance is not "in" the client; rather, it is the outcome of an interactive process involving the therapist and the client. It seems reasonable to believe that parents told by the court that they *must* seek treatment would initially be quite resistive to even the best-trained therapist. It also seems reasonable that the therapist's efforts to intervene, to interpret, to teach and confront might be followed by an increased probability that the client will resist. This would be particularly the case if the suggestions were badly presented (e.g., by an inexperienced therapist). In an intensive study of the therapy process for 25 neurotic young male patients from the Vanderbilt Psychotherapy Project, one of the seven scales that emerged was patient hostile (Strupp, 1973). In another context, Strupp (1980) goes on to make the following very significant observation: "We failed to encounter a single instance in which a difficult patient's hostility and negativism were successfully confronted or resolved. . . ." (p. 254).

Given a resistant parent, one might expect less progress in treatment. However, a social interaction implies that the effect might also be reflected in the behavior of the therapist. It is assumed here that client resistance produces long-term changes in the therapist's behavior. In general, client noncompliance and abrasive refusal to cooperate in the session function as extinction and punishment in effectively turning off even the most committed therapists. Most therapists begin their contacts with a family by viewing them in a positive light. After much resistance, the therapist may lose interest in whether or not the family keeps appointments. The therapist has been extinguished by both nonreinforcement (family not changing) and punishment for efforts to be a good therapist. We have only recently begun the study of this effect.

At the Oregon Social Learning Center, in weekly reviews of videotapes of clinical cases, it has become a practice to particularly focus upon those families about which the therapist feels deeply pessimistic. It was, in fact, a review of several dozen such tapes that led to the staff decision to study resistance as an important phenomenon. We have come to see these staff meetings as an important component for successful treatment. In these weekly meetings, the staff serves as a support group, providing new bursts of enthusiasm, new perceptions, and some alternative means for coping with resistance. In keeping with this orientation, the center arranged for one of its therapy staff to take an externship with the family therapy group at MRI in Palo Alto. Their techniques for resolving resistance are being studied here with great interest.

THE CODING OF CLIENT RESISTANCE AND THERAPIST BEHAVIOR

Fiske (1977) summarizes the problem nicely:

> It is the effects of the therapist's actions, each at its moment in time, which have any possibility of contributing to the patient's immediate benefit. When we look for relationships between two general variables, we are ignoring the fundamental questions of how one characteristic of a therapist's act may contribute to one step toward patient improvement. (p. 25)

Empirical studies of client resistance have typically relied on global ratings as measures for both process and outcome. As noted by Fiske, not only do global ratings tend to be less reliable, but they make it impossible to study resistance as a process of sequential exchanges between client and therapist.

However, the main reason for a microsocial analysis lies in its usefulness in studying functional relations between the behavior of one person and another (Gottman & Bakeman, 1979; Patterson, 1982; Sackett, 1977). If one can code resistance as an event and also code those therapist behaviors thought to be crucial in eliciting the client resistance, then it would be possible to analyze interaction sequences for such questions as: Given that the therapist did X, what is the likelihood that the client was resistant? Then knowing the general likelihood of resistance for the client, it becomes possible to compare this base rate of client resistance to the conditional likelihood of his resistance given that the therapist did X. Available statistics such as the chi square for grouped data (see Gottman & Bakeman, 1979; Sackett, 1977) are also appropriate for this type of analysis.

Sessions were videotaped with a date/time generator that dubs a running account of minutes and seconds onto the tape. Client behavior and therapist behavior were scored from these videotapes using two separate coding systems designed to interface with each other. Client behavior was scored first by one set of coders using the Client Resistance Code (CRC). CRC coders earmarked space for therapist behaviors, which were scored by a separate set of coders using the Therapist Behavior Code (TBC). Each coding protocol provides 15 minutes of scored data. Behavior was coded on 30-second timelines with 15-second intervals.

The Client Resistance Code (Kavanagh, Gabrielson, & Chamberlain, 1982) is a mutually exclusive and exhaustive seven-category code. Five categories describe resistant behavior, and two categories describe cooperative behavior. The categories and abbreviated definitions are described in Table 2. For this study, data from all five resistance categories were combined into one category, and data from the two cooperative categories were combined into another category. Client's responses

Table 2

Client Resistance Code categories

Resistant responses

1.	Interrupt/talkover:	Coded *only* when the client is obviously cutting the therapist off or talking over the therapist.
2.	Negative attitude:	Responses indicating unwillingness/inability to cooperate with therapist's suggestions (e.g., blaming others, statements of hopelessness, defeat, disagreement).
3.	Challenge/confront:	Responses challenging the therapist's qualifications and/or experience; responses that indicate that the therapist doesn't know what s/he is doing.
4.	Own agenda:	Bringing up new topics/concerns to avoid discussing or to block the issue(s) that the therapist was on.
5.	Not tracking:	Inattention, not responding, answering a question directed to another, disqualifying a previous statement.

Cooperative responses

6.	Nonresistant:	All responses that are neutral, cooperative, or following the direction set by the therapist.
7.	Facilitative:	Short utterances indicating attention or agreement.

were coded as cooperative when they seemed in accord with the direction set by the therapist's immediately previous verbalization. The result was a mutually exclusive, two-category (i.e., client cooperative or client resistant) coding system. This approach was undertaken because of the low base rate of occurrence of several of the individual resistance codes.

28 percent of the videotapes were coded independently by two observers for client resistance. The mean percent agreement (number of agreements divided by number of agreements plus disagreements) was .78 ($sd = .22$). The correlation across tapes for observer pairs was .95 ($p < .001$). The instrument meets the requirements for an adequate assessment device.

The next question concerned the stability of the resistance score. Three 15-minute segments within treatment sessions were scored for mother resistance from early, middle, and late segments were .10, .12, and .10, respectively. The analysis of variance for repeated measures produce an F value of .5 ($df = 2, 23$). These differences were not significant. Even though the tapes were separated by from two to four weeks from the first to the second sessions, the level of resistance remained stable. The mean p value for the middle 15-minute segment for the first tape was .10 and for the second tape .12. The analysis of variance for repeated measures showed this difference to be nonsignificant (F value 1.0 and df = 1, 19). Given the small samples involved in the analyses, one should accept this conclusion with some reservation. However, a similar effect was also obtained in a study by Chamberlain et al. (in press).

While the mean level for a sample may not change appreciably, it is conceivable that the rankings for individual subjects (mothers) could vary a great deal from one session to another (e.g., the scores might be unreliable in the test-retest score. A rank-order correlation was calculated for the middle segments from the first and second tapes. The rho of .79 ($p < .01$) showed that 15 minutes of sampling from a session provides a minimally stable estimate for baseline levels and client resistance.

To date, most of our analyses focused upon the mother because there were fewer fathers present in the sample. However, it is assumed that the probability-of-resistance score for the mother reflects a kind of parental "trait" (i.e., the mother and father have similar levels). In keeping with this assumption, the analyses showed a correlation of .74 ($p < .05$) for a very small sample of scores for mothers and fathers.

Client disposition

What variables external to the treatment session might covary with the client's initial level of resistance in treatment? The hypothesis is that client resistance during treatment is partially determined by (1) a matrix of social variables defining the environment in which the client lives (e.g., socioeconomic level, crises occurrence, satisfaction/dissatisfaction in marital relationship, self- or agency-referral, etc.) and (2) psychological variables (e.g., mood, level of anger).

Thus far, none of these variables have been studied systematically. But the data from pilot samples provide some promising leads. The mothers' ratings of her mood on the Lubin measure of depression correlated .72 ($p < .10$ for N of 7) with the baseline resistance score. Mothers' score on the Minnesota Multiphasic Personality Inventory scale for hostility did not correlate with her initial level of resistance (.02), but it did correlate .36 ($p > .10$ for N of 18) with the likelihood of resistance during midtreatment. There was a significant relation between self- or agency referral and initial reaction to treatment. The correlation of .45 ($p < .05$ for N of 27) showed that the mothers referred by agencies tended to be more resistant in the early phase of treatment.

The studies now under way should expand and clarify these relations further. As they stand, the fragments of data from the pilot studies suggest that factors outside of the treatment session may function as significant determinants for initial levels of client resistance.

Validity

The hypothesis is that parent resistance will covary in a meaningful way with the families' progress through treatment. To test this assumption, two sets of data were examined: changes in resistance during the treatment process and the relation between resistance at termination and successful outcome.

Chamberlain et al. (in press) studied 27 families referred because of problems in managing their preadolescent children. On a post hoc basis it seems reasonable to expect that cases that remain in treatment, show different levels of client resistance at different stages of treatment (e.g., the beginning, middle, and end of treatment). During the beginning stage, the therapist typically attempts to explore with the parents, in detail, the problems they are having with their child. Because the goals here are primarily information gathering and relationship building, relatively low levels of client resistance might occur. But as Chamberlain et al. (in press) showed, those with high levels of resistance were more likely to drop out of treatment early on. During the middle stage of treatment, the therapist probably focuses on teaching the parents strategies for directly intervening in their child's problem behaviors. Clinically, it seems that parents might have greater difficulty at this point. This might be the reason for the observed increase in the parents' level of resistance. The final stage of treatment was characterized by relatively low levels of resistance; presumably this is also the point at which they are applying their new skills. A successful case might be characterized by low levels of resistance during the final stage of treatment, high scores for family management procedures, and low scores for rates of deviant child behavior.

Figure 3 shows that the average rate per minute of observed client resistance did vary with stage of treatment with the highest rate during the midtreatment sessions, $F(2, 34) = 3.44$, $p < .05$. Differences in resistance levels from early to midtreatment were statistically significant, $F(1, 17) = 6.53$, $p < .03$; and those from midtreatment to ending treatment approached statistical significance, $F(1, 17) = 3.33$, $p < .09$.

When the relationship of the client resistance and the therapists' ratings of case outcome was analyzed, a positive correlation was found between client resistance at the end of treatment and therapists' post-treatment ratings of the success or failure of therapy. Cases rated as being more successful had lower levels of observed resistance at the end of treatment, $R(16) = .48$, p less than .05. A related finding was that therapists' ratings of successful outcome were correlated with

Figure 3

Mean levels of client resistance for three phases of treatment*

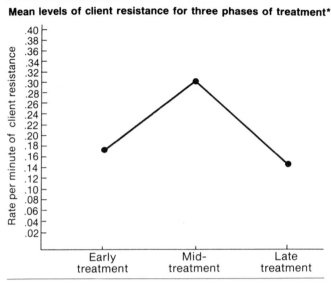

* From Chamberlain, P., Patterson, G. R., Reid, J. B., Kavanagh, K., and Forgatch, M. S., "Observation of Client Resistance," *Behavior Therapy* (in press).

drops in the rate per minute of client resistance from middle to late treatment, Rpb(16) = .68, *p* less than .01). As might be expected, there was also a correlation between therapist ratings of success in treatment and reductions in client resistance from *initial* to termination sessions, Rpb(16) = .48, *p* < .05.

MEASURE OF THERAPIST EFFECTS

Three studies have failed to demonstrate that student therapists can effectively use parent-training techniques in working with families of older antisocial children referred for treatment (Bernal et al., 1980; Eyberg & Johnson, 1974; Ferber et al., 1974). We argue that student therapists, because of their inexperience, are more likely than experienced therapists to elicit resistant reactions early in treatment and to be less effective in resolving the resistance once it occurs.

As a preliminary test of this assumption about novice therapists and clinical cases, Chamberlain analyzed videotapes from beginning, middle, and end phases of treatment for graduate student therapists treating nine families who were self-referred to the University of Oregon Psychology Clinic. These were compared to the videotapes for the 18 completers treated by experienced OSLC staff in the Chamberlain et al. (in press) study described above. The data showed that treatment by the student therapists produced significantly higher levels of client resistance during all three phases of treatment (F [1, 25] = 7.02, p < .01).

This study needs to be replicated and extended, using *random* assignment of families to therapist groups. However, it should be noted that in the Chamberlain study, a systematic attempt was made to assign the simplest cases to the student therapists.

To pursue this topic further, it is necessary to develop a reliable measure of two different aspects of the therapist's behavior. One set of categories should address the issue of what it is that the therapist does that might actually *elicit* resistant reactions. The code should also describe what it is that the therapist does that might *reduce* resistance. The Therapist Behavior Code (Forgatch & Chamberlain, 1982) is a mutually exclusive and exhaustive seven-category observation system describing therapist verbal behavior during a treatment session. The categories and abbreviated definitions are listed in Table 3. The seven therapist behavior categories are support, teach, question, challenge, reframe, talk, and facilitate.

Some of the code categories in the TBC sample aspects of the four dimensions Snyder (1961) used to score therapist behavior. For example, "reeducative responses" in the Snyder system is similar to "teach" in the TBC.

Table 3

Therapist Behavior Code categories

	Therapist behavior
1. Support:	Positive responses toward the client that show warmth, humor, understanding, and/or encouragement.
2. Teach:	Providing information about parenting, family life, or other therapy-related issues; responses that serve to structure or manage the session.
3. Question:	Responses that serve to seek information.
4. Confront:	Responses that tend to challenge the client, including disagreement, disapproval, and negative, sarcastic, or hostile comments.
5. Reframe:	Reconstructions of what another person has said, such that the result is something different from the way it was initially stated.
6. Talk:	Responses not codable with another category, including unintelligible verbalizations, conversation about the weather, scheduling, etc.
7. Facilitate:	Responses primarily indicating the therapist is listening to the client, such as: um-humm, yeah, right, sure, etc.

35 percent of the videotapes were coded independently by two observers for the therapist behaviors. The mean level of event-by-event percent agreement (number of agreements divided by number of agreements plus disagreements) for the seven categories was .75 (range .67 to .84).

The effect of therapist behavior on client resistance

The findings from the Chamberlain et al. (in press) study showed significant increases in parent resistance midway through the treatment process. We speculated that such increases were caused by an increase in the demands placed on the families by the therapist. The therapist's effort to teach parents specific child-management techniques and to convince them to use those techniques was hypothesized to be a significant determinant for increased parent resistance. To test this, videotaped sequences of therapist-client interactions were scored for six therapist-mother dyads (Patterson & Forgatch, 1984). For each dyad, the seven therapist behaviors were examined for their immediate impact on the reactions of the mother (i.e., what was the effect upon the mother's immediately following reaction?). For each dyad, the base-rate probability of mother resistance was compared to the conditional probability of mother resistance given a particular therapist behavior. It was assumed that certain therapist behaviors would be associated with significant decreases. Specifically, the therapists' efforts to teach and/or confront should produce *increases* in resistance.

It was thought that resistance patterns near termination might be altered, so the last one third of treatment sessions was not included. The tapes were randomly assigned to coders by family and by phase of treatment to prevent bias due either to familiarity with the family or to expectation based on the phase of treatment.

Given that the therapist engaged in any one of seven behavior categories, the conditional probability was calculated for the immediate and subsequent occurrence of resistance. The binomial z statistic was used to determine the level of significance for each comparison of base rate and conditional p values. An examination of the binominal z values for the effects of therapist facilitate showed that in five of the six comparisons of baseline resistance to the conditional probability values, the sign for the statistic was negative. This means that, for each therapist, facilitate was generally accompanied by a *reduced* likelihood for client resistance; the effect was significant for two of the dyads. The trend for therapist support was somewhat less reliable in eliciting lowered resistance; none was significant. While the well-trained therapist spends a good deal of time in activities that define joining, this activity is only minimally associated with *immediate* reductions in the likelihood of client resistance.

Therapist teach and therapist confront, or both together, were associated with the greatest alterations in the conditional probability values for parent resistance. The effect was consistent and significant for most dyads.

Given the behavior modifiers' traditional commitment to the educational model in training parents, it is of some interest to examine the conditional probability values that describe the outcome of efforts to teach. Given that 10 percent to 22 percent of therapist interventions are of this kind, it becomes clear that a hard-working parent trainer would encounter parent resistance *many times* during each session. For example, for one of the families, the therapist encountered an average of 14.2 resistant reactions per session; the median across families and therapists was 6.4 per session.

While some therapist behaviors were associated with increasing likelihood and others with decreasing likelihood of resistance, it does not follow that one event "caused" another. A minimal requirement in order to establish therapist behavior as a determinant would be an experimental manipulation that demonstrates that changes in therapist behaviors are followed by the predicted changes in client resistance. Therefore, the next study provided an experimental test of the causal roles of therapist behavior in client resistance (Patterson & Forgatch, 1984).

Each of seven therapist-parent dyads participated in a session characterized by an ABAB design, where the therapists increased their teach and confront behaviors during the experimental periods and refrained from their use during the baseline periods.

During the experimental (B) phase, therapists were cued to use frequent confront and teach behaviors. During the A phases, therapists were to refrain as much as possible from using either of these behaviors. The resistance means during the experimental periods were dramatically larger than the means during baseline periods. The variance (ANOVA) showed a main effect for phases, $F(1, 5) = 11.74$, $p < .02$. These findings are consistent with the hypothesis that there may be a causal relationship between these two types of therapist behavior and parent resistant behavior.

Impact of client resistance on the therapist

Within the interactional approach, it is assumed that while the therapist has an impact on the client, it is also the case that the client has an impact on the therapist. It is our general hypothesis that such interactive effects may be short- and/or long-term effects.

With short-term effects, it would be assumed that client resistance may be immediately followed by an increase in the likelihood of certain therapist behaviors including teach, confront, and support. Presumably, when the client resists, the therapist can choose simply to persist in efforts to teach/confront in the hopes of convincing the client of the utility of his/her position, or the therapist can shift alternatives and be supportive in hopes of "winning the client over."

The videotapes from early to midpoint in treatment were reexamined for the same six client-therapist dyads studied in the Patterson and Forgatch (1983) study. In descending order, the most frequent therapist behaviors demonstrated during these sessions, in terms of the average proportion of therapist statements, were: facilitate (.265); question (.171); teach (.138); and support (.132). Next was calculated the conditional probability of Therapist Behavior X_1 given client resistance. The conditional p value was then compared to the base rate for Therapist X_1; the comparison was expressed as a binomial z value. For the low-resistant clients, none of the p values were significant. Two of the highly resistant clients provided data that showed that their resistance was followed by significant increases in the likelihood that the therapist would "teach." On a short-term basis, both of these therapists tended to meet resistance by increasing the likelihood of teach and, for one of them, a significant increase in confront and decrease in support.

It is assumed that the long-range impact is for client resistance to extinguish therapist effort to help. Clinically, the client "gets to" the therapist. It is hypothesized that client resistance persisting after the midpoint of therapy will be accompanied by the following therapist behaviors: (1) a decrease in therapist weekly ratings of his/her expectancies for successful outcome, and (2) a decrease in therapist's ratings for likability for the client. Given this situation, the client is now at increasing risk for dropping out of treatment and/or having the future assessment probes indicate no significant changes in family management or child-deviant behavior scores. As noted earlier, it is here that the weekly clinical staff meetings are thought to make a significant contribution to improving treatment outcome.

Another interesting set of questions has to do with what it is that a skilled therapist does that is effective in *reducing* client resistance. The reduction does not take place in seconds, minutes, or even in a session or two. Clinically, it seems to be a slow, gradual process. What is it that the therapist does that brings this about? How is the process to be studied?

It is our subjective impression that a combination of three therapist "techniques" is most relevant to this gradual reduction. We also believe that during the course of therapy, all three of these techniques occur more frequently in sessions of well-trained therapists than is the case for sessions of novice therapists. First, there is a higher frequency of joining behaviors for the skilled therapist; we also believe that they are more subtle and better timed than is the case for the novice, but as yet we have made no effort to quantify these dimensions. In any case, joining is a construct that is part of the current code so the hypothesis can be tested that high-resistant clients working with therapists who join at a high rate are more likely to be successful in treatment than are high-resistant clients working with therapists who join at low rates. Second, it is assumed that a skilled therapist tends, *over a series of sessions,* to reframe the objectives for treatment in such a way that the parent can cooperate and carry out the prescription. It is *not* done in one brilliant maneuver—at least it is not obvious in the videotapes from OSLC. In the working-class and father-absent families we treat, the work of therapy is not carried out in a single interpretation or in a single session or enactment. It is only over a period of months that the extremely resistant client comes to trust (minimally) the therapist and then to accept the reframed objective. As noted above, reframing, although not one of the four most frequently occurring therapist codes, happens to fulfill a vital function in the overall process. The third variable simply describes the persistence of the therapist in teaching and confronting the parents.

As noted earlier, the assumption is that if no teaching of family management skills is done, then in the samples that we have been treating there will be no change in child behavior (e.g., among other things, the parent must learn to practice a more effective form of punishment). For example, efforts to utilize nondirective therapy with families of antisocial children showed that there indeed was no change in observed rates of antisocial behavior (Bernal et al., 1980) or in court-reported rates of delinquent behavior (Alexander & Parsons, 1973). As noted earlier, summaries of longitudinal studies showed that the extremely antisocial children generally do not outgrow these problems (Loeber, 1982; Olweus, 1979).

DISCUSSION

As implied in the title of this chapter, it is thought that we must now move on to a second stage in the empirical analyses of parent-training procedures for families of antisocial children. This does not mean giving up our normal insistence upon a data base for making decisions about what is to be added or deleted. A dual insistence upon the importance of a *data* base plus the importance of a *technology* for parent training is what differentiates the current form of social-learning approaches from the traditional child guidance therapies.

The last decade of studies has produced findings consistent enough to call into question certain assumptions entertained by the writer and others during the earlier stages in the development of social learning treatment for these families. One such assumption was that the development of a parent-training technology would provide a necessary and sufficient basis for helping these families to change. In retrospect, we were correct in believing that the new technology was necessary. While using the new parent training, most of us felt that we were helping more families of antisocial children than earlier in our training when we used traditional therapies. However, we were wrong in believing that the new technology was sufficient in and of itself.

It seems to be the case that treatment for the older antisocial child must include *two* components, *both necessary* and *neither sufficient* by itself: a parent-training technology component plus a clinical skill component. The latter is thought to be essential for coping with parental resistance. It may also be the case that the therapist requires a support system in order to ensure consistent therapist performance (i.e., a third component). In retrospect, it is odd that we who so fervently espoused the idea of contingency never carefully thought through the problem of what the reinforcers and punishment might be for the *therapist.*

At the present time, the most reasonable hypothesis seems to be that for older, extremely antisocial children, the therapist will often be called upon to employ a considerable degree of clinical skill in helping the family. This may itself represent the outcome of a selection process of considerable interest in its own right. Most preschool and younger elementary school-age antisocial children are eventually trained by the parents to substitute more acceptable forms of behavior. In a sense, the younger child "outgrows" the problem behaviors when the parents decide that it is no longer acceptable. Inspection of data from untreated control groups of preschool problem children suggests that at this age, high scores may show more "spontaneous remission" than is obtained for comparable groups that are eight or nine years of age. Observation data from the home of normal families (Patterson, in press) showed TAB scores of over .70 for normal two- to four-year-old children. By the time the child was of school age, the TAB scores for normals were somewhat below .40 and continued to drop thereafter. Presumably, the drop is brought about by increasing numbers of parents who decide that the time has come to reduce the frequency of these behaviors. The hypothesis is that continuity for extremely antisocial children increases with the age of the child. The 9- or 10-year-old antisocial child may have parents who wished to train him but he has long ago defeated their concerted efforts. It is our experience that the parents of chronically antisocial adolescents *can* be trained to effectively manage their problem child, but the cost to the therapist is enormous (Patterson, Weinrott, & Reid, in press). These families were so difficult that we were required to work in pairs.

The assumption is that for the older or more extreme problem child, simplistic educative efforts are likely to fail. With two- or three-year-old mild problem cases, as little as a 30-minute therapeutic contact and a brochure and tape cassette may be sufficient (Forgatch & Toobert, 1979). Four- and five-year-old problem children from middle-class families referred because of mild problems might also respond to an average of 10 hours of treatment by novice (graduate student) therapists as demonstrated in the comparison design by Peed et al. (1977).

Is it the case that time-limited (10 hours or less) treatment would not be effective for older samples of antisocial children referred for treatment? Is it also the case that the older the child and the more persistent his deviancy status, the less effective the novice therapist? We believe that both of these statements are true, but as yet, neither assumption has been systematically tested. However, it should be noted that these ideas have historical antecedents in the research literature from psychotherapy outcome studies. Here too, there has been some recognition that the experience level of the therapist may be a key variable. For example, the review of these studies by Bergin (1971) showed that only 18 percent of the studies employing inexperienced therapists produced positive outcomes. The review by Frank (1979) provides additional support for this hypothesis.

For those of us trained in the psychotherapies of the 1950s, the wheel seems to have come full circle. We find ourselves again thinking about *clinical skills.* In our training, each of the schools of therapy seemed to emphasize slightly different clinical skills (e.g., warmth, deep interpretation, reflection, unconditional positive regard). It seemed that each orginator of a school had dealt with somewhat different types of clinical problems and was shaped by this experience accordingly. But in any case, it was with a sense of relief that during the early period of behavior modification, such fuzzy and difficult-to-measure concepts such as warmth, empathy, reflection, reframing, and joining could be set aside as no longer being "relevant." The ensuing decade of work generated a parent-training technology whose varied patterns of success and failure now leads us back to the original concepts of clinical skill. There are, however, three important differences between the current perspective and that of the late 1950s, at least as it applies to the treatment of antisocial behavior in children. The most important difference lies in the development of reliable and valid criterion measures for antisocial behavior as supplements for the traditional reliance upon parent global ratings. To the extent that parent global ratings are reactive, *all* treatment efforts meet with some success, at least on a short-term basis. The emphasis upon observation data, parent daily report data, peer nomination, teacher ratings, and court records provides a multilevel assessment, which gives both a more reliable and a broader-spectrum analysis of outcome for treating antisocial children.

The development of better criterion measures leads in turn to a second shift in perspective: a clarification of the goals for treatment. The multiple goals held to be reasonable goals for traditional psychotherapy with families of aggressive children would typically include: a more positive perception of the problem child; reduction in anger and anxiety of both parents and problem child; increasing the child's ability to form relationships; helping the child to feel better about himself; and increased prosocial skills. Most or all of these remain as important outcomes for treatment with these families but they are now thought of as important secondary concomitants for intervention. The primary goal is to change the observable antisocial behavior of the problem child and the parent(s).

CONCLUSION

There are several developments of the last decade that provide a new perspective for the study of treatment process. In addition to a newfound interest in empirical studies of "soft" clinical skills (Alexander et al., 1976; Wahler & Dumas, 1983), there are the studies of social interaction, which seem to cut across the areas of child development, ethology, primatology, marital conflict, and social psychology. The recent edited volume by Cairns (1979), is a fine example. The focus for these studies is upon the structure of social interaction, the covariation between the behavior of one person and another. Typically, the data base consists of *sequences* of *behavioral events*. In the present context, such a format would make it possible to examine those behaviors of the therapist that reliably elicit client resistance. A slight shift in focus makes it possible to examine the therapist behaviors that are accompanied by significant reductions in the likelihood that client resistance will continue, given that it is already under way. The possibility exists, then, for carrying out microsocial analyses of client-therapist interchanges, which will provide an empirical base for understanding many aspects of the therapy process. This author's perception is that the wheel may have come full circle, but in doing so, it has moved forward by one small increment.

REFERENCES

Achenbach, T. M., & Edelbrock, C. S. The child behavior profile: Boys aged 12 to 16 and girls aged 6 to 11 and 12 to 16 (Vol. II). *Journal of Consulting and Clinical Psychology,* 1979, *41,* 223–233.

Alexander, J. F., Barton, C., Schiavo, R. S., & Parsons, B. V. Systems-behavioral intervention with families of delinquents: Therapist characteristics, family behavior, and outcome. *Journal of Consulting and Clinical Psychology,* 1976, *44,* 656–664.

Alexander, J. F., & Parsons, B. V. Short-term behavioral intervention with delinquent families: Impact on family process and recidivism. *Journal of Abnormal Psychology,* 1973, *81,* 219–225.

Anchor, K. N., & Thomason, T. C. A comparison of two parent-training models with educated parents. *Journal of Community Psychology,* 1977, *5,* 134–141.

Arnold, J., Levine, A., & Patterson, G. R. Changes in sibling behavior following family intervention. *Journal of Consulting and Clinical Psychology,* 1975, *43,* 683–688.

Bergin, A. E. The evaluation of therapeutic outcome. In A. E. Bergin & S. L. Garfield (Eds.), *Psychotherapy and behavior change.* New York: John Wiley & Sons, 1971.

Bernal, M. E., Klinnert, M. D., & Schultz, L. A. Outcome evaluations of behavioral parent training and client centered parent counseling for children with conduct problems. *Journal of Applied Behavioral Analysis,* 1980, *13,* 677–691.

Bernal, M. E., & North, J. D. *Scoring system for home and school* (Revision X). Unpublished manuscript, University of Denver, 1972.

Bijou, S. W., & Baer, D. M. *Child development: A systematic and empirical theory.* New York: Appleton-Century-Crofts, 1961.

Cairns, R. B. *The analysis of social interactions: Methods, issues, and illustrations.* Hillsdale, N.J.: Lawrence Erlbaum Associates, 1979.

Chamberlain, P., Patterson, G. R., Reid, J. B., Kavanagh, K., & Forgatch, M. S. Observation of client resistance. *Behavior Therapy,* in press.

Eyberg, S. M., & Johnson, S. M. Multiple assessment of behavior modification and families: Effects of contingency contracting and order of treated problems. *Journal of Consulting and Clinical Psychology,* 1974, *42*(4), 594–606.

Ferber, H., Keeley, S. M., & Shemberg, K. M. Training parents in behavior modification: Outcome of the problems encountered in a program after Patterson's work. *Behavior Therapy,* 1974, *5,* 415–419.

Fiske, D. W. Methodological issues in research on the psychotherapist. In A. S. Gurman & A. M. Razin (Eds.), *Effective psychotherapy: A handbook of research.* New York: Pergamon Press, 1977.

Fleischman, M. J. *Training and evaluation of aggressive children.* Proposal submitted to NIMH Crime and Delinquency Section, 1979.

Fleischman, M. J. A replication of Patterson's "intervention for boys with conduct problems." *Journal of Consulting and Clinical Psychology,* 1981, *49,* 342–351.

Fleischman, M. J., & Szykula, S. A community setting replication of a social learning treatment for aggressive children. *Behavior Therapy,* 1981, *12*(1), 15.

Forgatch, M. S., & Chamberlain, P. *The therapist behavior code.* Unpublished technical report, Oregon Social Learning Center, Eugene, Oregon, 1982.

Forgatch, M. S., Patterson, G. R., Chamberlain, P., Kavanagh, K., & Gabrielson, P. *Time out* (videotape). Eugene, Oreg.: Castalia Publishing, 1982.

Forgatch, M. S., & Toobert, D. J. A cost effective parent training program for use with normal preschool children. *Journal of Pediatric Psychology,* 1979, *4,* 129–145.

Frank, J. The present status of outcome studies. *Journal of Consulting and Clinical Psychology,* 1979, *47,* 310–360.

Gottman, J. M., & Bakeman, R. The sequential analysis of observation data. In S. Suomi, M. Lamb, & G. Stephenson (Eds.), *Social interaction analysis: Methodological issues.* Madison: University of Wisconsin Press, 1979.

Haley, J. *Problem-solving therapy.* San Francisco: Jossey-Bass, 1976.

Hawkins, R. P., Peterson, R. F., Schweid, E., & Bijou, S. W. Behavior therapy in the home: Amelioration of problem parent-child relations with the parent in the therapeutic role. *Journal of Experimental Child Psychology,* 1966, *4,* 99–107.

Hirschi, T. *Causes of delinquency.* Berkeley: University of California Press, 1969.

Johnson, S. M., & Brown, R. A. Producing behavior change in parents of disturbed children. *Journal of Child Psychology and Psychiatry,* 1969, *10,* 107–121.

Karoly, P., & Rosenthal, M. Training parents in behavior modification: Effects on perception of family interaction and deviant child behavior. *Behavior Therapy,* 1977, *8,* 406–410.

Kavanagh, K., Chamberlain, P., & Gabrielson, P. *Parent resistance code.* Unpublished manuscript, Oregon Social Learning Center, Eugene, Oregon, 1981.

Kavanagh, K., Gabrielson, P., & Chamberlain, P. *Manual for coding client resistance.* Unpublished manuscript, Oregon Social Learning Center, Eugene, Oregon, 1982.

Lobitz, G. K., & Johnson, S. J. Parental manipulation of the behavior of normal and deviant children. *Child Development,* 1975, *46,* 719–726.

Loeber, R. The stability of antisocial delinquent child behavior: A review. *Child Development,* 1982, *53,* 1431–1446.

McCord, J. *A thirty-year follow-up of treatment effects.* Paper presented at the meeting of the American Association of Psychiatric Services for Children, San Francisco, November 1976.

McCord, J. Some child-rearing antecedents of criminal behavior in adult men. *Journal of Personality and Social Psychology,* 1979, *9,* 1477–1486.

Minuchin, S. *Families and family therapy.* Cambridge, Mass.: Harvard University Press, 1974.

O'Dell, S., Mahoney, N., Horton, W., & Turner, P. Media assisted parent training: Alternative models. *Behavior Therapy,* 1979, *10,* 103–110.

Olweus, D. Stability of aggressive reaction patterns in males: A review. *Psychological Bulletin,* 1979, *86,* 852–875.

Patterson, G. R. Interventions for boys with conduct problems.: Multiple settings, treatments and criteria. *Journal of Consulting and Clinical Psychology,* 1974, *42,* 471–481. (a)

Patterson, G. R. Retraining of aggressive boys by their parents: Review of recent literature and follow-up evaluation. *Canadian Psychiatric Association Journal,* 1974, *19,* 142–161. (b)

Patterson, G. R. *Families: Applications of social learning to family life* (Rev. ed.). Champaign, Ill.: Research Press, 1976.

Patterson, G. R. *Coercive family process.* Eugene, Oreg.: Castalia Publishing, 1982.

Patterson, G. R. *Resistance and family therapy: A process and outcome study.* Proposal submitted to National Institute of Mental Health, March 1983.

Patterson, G. R. The unattached mother: A process analysis. In H. Hartup & Z. Rubins (Eds.), *Relationships: Their role in social and emotional development.* Cambridge, MA: Cambridge University Press, in press.

Patterson, G. R., & Brodsky, G. A behavior modification program for a child with multiple problem behaviors. *Journal of Child Psychology and Psychiatry,* 1966, *7,* 277–295.

Patterson, G. R., Chamberlain, P., & Reid, J. B. A comparative evaluation of a parent training program. *Behavior Therapy,* 1982, *13,* 638–650.

Patterson, G. R., Cobb, J. A., & Ray, R. S. A social engineering technology for retraining the families of aggressive boys. In H. E. Adams & I. P. Unikel (Eds.), *Issues and trends in behavior therapy.* Springfield, Ill.: Charles C Thomas, 1973.

Patterson, G. R., & Fleischman, M. J. Maintenance of treatment effects: Some considerations concerning family systems and follow-up data. *Behavior Therapy,* 1979, *10,* 168–185.

Patterson, G. R., & Forgatch, M. S. *Therapist behavior as a determinant for client resistance.* Manuscript submitted for publication,

Patterson, G. R., & Forgatch, M. S. *Family living series: Five cassette tapes to be used with Living with Children and Families.* Champaign, Ill.: Research Press, 1975.

Patterson, G. R., & Gullion, M. E. *Living with children: New methods for parents and teachers.* Champaign, Ill.: Research Press, 1968.

Patterson, G. R., McNeal, S., Hawkins, N., & Phelps, R. Reprogramming the social environment. *Journal of Child Psychology and Psychiatry,* 1967, *8,* 181–194.

Patterson, G. R., & Reid, J. B. Intervention for families of aggressive boys: A replication study. *Behavior Research and Therapy,* 1973, *11,* 383–394.

Patterson, G. R., Reid, J. B., Jones, R. R., & Conger, R. E. *A social learning approach to family intervention* (Vol. 1): *Families with aggressive children.* Eugene, Oreg.: Castalia Publishing, 1975.

Patterson, G. R., Reid, J. B., & Weinrott, M. R. *A comparative evaluation of a parent training program for families.* In preparation.

Patterson, G. R., & Stouthamer-Loeber, M. The correlation of family management practices and delinquency. *Child Development,* in press.

Peed, S., Roberts, M., & Forehand, R. Evaluation of the effectiveness of standardized parent training program in altering the interaction between mothers and their noncompliant children. *Behavior Modification,* 1977, *1,* 323–350.

Radke-Yarrow, M., Campbell, J. D., & Burton, R. V. *Child-rearing: An inquiry into the research and methods.* San Francisco: Jossey-Bass, 1968.

Reid, J. B. (Ed.). *A social learning approach to family intervention* (Vol. II): *Observation in home settings.* Eugene, Oreg.: Castalia Publishing, 1978.

Rutter, M., Tizard, J., & Whitmore, K. *Education, health, and behavior.* New York: John Wiley & Sons, 1979.

Sackett, G. P. The lag sequential analysis of contingency and cyclicity in behavioral interaction research. In J. Osefsky (Ed.), *Handbook of infant development.* New York: John Wiley & Sons, 1977.

Schelle, J. A brief report on invalidity of parent evaluations of behavior change. *Journal of Applied Behavior Analysis,* 1974, *7,* 341–343.

Sears, R. R., Maccoby, E. E., & Levin, H. *Patterns of child-rearing.* Evanston, Ill.: Row & Peterson, 1957.

Snyder, W. *The psychotherapy relationship.* New York: Macmillan, 1961.

Strupp, H. H. *Vanderbilt Psychotherapy Process Scale: Rater manual.* Unpublished manuscript, Vanderbilt University, 1973.

Strupp, H. H. Success and failure in time-limited psychotherapy. *Archives of General Psychiatry,* 1980, *37,* 947–954.

Walter, H. I., & Gilmore, S. K. Placebo versus social learning effects in parent training procedures designed to alter the behavior of aggressive boys. *Behavior Research and Therapy,* 1973, *4,* 361–377.2

Wachtel, P. L. (Ed.). *Resistance: Psychodynamic and behavioral approaches.* New York: Plenum Press, 1982.

Wahler, R. G., & Dumas, J. E. *Stimulus class determinants of mother-child coercive interchange in multidistressed families: Assessment and intervention.* Paper presented at the Vermont Conference on Primary Prevention, Burlington, Vermont, June 1983.

Wahler, R. G., House, A. E., & Stambaugh, E. E. *Ecological assessment of child problem behavior.* New York: Pergamon Press, 1976.

Wahler, R. G., Winkle, G. H., Peterson, R. F., & Morrison, D. C. Mothers as behavior therapists for their own children. *Behavior Research and Therapy,* 1965, *3,* 113–124.

Weakland, J., Fisch, R., Watzlavich, P., & Bodin, A. Brief therapy: Focused problem resolution. *Family Process,* 1974, *13,* 141–168.

West, D. J., & Farrington, D. P. *Who becomes delinquent?* London: Heinemann Medical Books, 1973.

West, D. J., & Farrington, D. P. *The delinquent way of life.* London: Heinemann Medical Books, 1977.

Wills, T. Perceptions of clients by professional helpers. *Psychological Bulletin,* 1978.

Wiltz, N. A., & Patterson, G. R. An evaluation of parent training procedures designed to alter inappropriate aggressive behavior in boys. *Behavior Therapy,* 1974, *5,* 215–221.

Zeilberger, J., Sampen, J., & Sloane, H. Modification of the child's problem behavior in the home with the mother as therapist. *Journal of Applied Behavior Analysis,* 1968, *1,* 47–53.

Chapter 45

Family Law

R. BARRY RUBACK

The traditional American family—composed of a working husband, a wife who stays home, and two children—is becoming less common, making up approximately 16 percent of all households in the United States today (Weitzman, 1982). Weitzman has offered several reasons why this stereotypical family is less common than it once was. These reasons include a high divorce rate, an increase in the number of never-married individuals living alone, an increasing number of working women, a rise in the number of single-parent families, an increase in nonmarital cohabitation, and a decline in fertility. Related to these changes in the family are changes in family law, although whether these changes in family law have caused or have been caused by changes in the family is not clear (Weitzman, 1982). In spite of all these factors, however, Weitzman suggests that over 90 percent of all Americans will be married at some point in their lives. When this fact is coupled with the fact that almost everyone grows up in a family, it becomes clear that the family is likely to remain one of the dominant influences in people's lives. Thus, simply because the family is such an important aspect of people's lives, mental health professionals (whether or not they work with families) need to know laws governing family relations.

In addition, mental health professionals are increasingly coming to realize that many problems traditionally defined as "family problems" involve not only counseling, psychological, and therapeutic issues but also legal questions. Indeed, most faculty teaching family studies courses believe that a course on family law should be included at the graduate level (Hicks, Hansen, & Saur, 1977). This overlap between therapy and law is particularly true for such problems as separation, divorce, child custody, adoption, and child and spouse abuse.

1380

Because of the general importance of the family and the relevance of family law to therapeutic questions, it is increasingly incumbent on family therapists to know the basics of family law. This chapter will serve as a general introduction to the field. More detailed discussions of the area include works by Clark (1968) and Krause (1977). As is true in all areas of the law, the general rules discussed here may not be true for every jurisdiction. Moreover, the specific facts of a particular case require the advice of an attorney.

This chapter will briefly review the law of domestic relations; it will consist of four sections: *(a)* establishment of marital and quasi-marital relationships, *(b)* dissolution of marital and quasi-marital relationships, *(c)* establishing the parent-child relationship, and *(d)* the parent-child relationship after divorce. In addition to summarizing the law in each of these areas, the chapter will focus on those areas of family law that most concern the family psychologist. As will be seen, these areas, for the most part, involve recent developments in the interface between family law and family psychology. Before looking at family law specifically, however, it is first necessary to have some understanding of the nature of the legal system in the United States.

The American legal system

American law comes, for the most part, from the tradition of English common law. What this tradition entails is a reliance on the past decisions of courts as authority for cases that involve similar questions of fact or law (Jacobstein & Mersky, 1981). This reliance on prior decisions developed into the doctrine of *stare decisis,* which is defined in the following way: "(T)hat when (a) court has once laid down a principle of law as applicable to a certain state of facts, it will adhere to that principle, and apply it to all future cases where facts are substantially the same" (*Moore* v. *City of Albany,* 1895). Because the law developed through court decisions rather than through a codified set of laws, the English common law also was known as the "unwritten law" (Jacobstein & Mersky, 1981).

As society became more complex, it became obvious that a legal system based on the decisions of judges could not quickly and satisfactorily provide answers to questions arising from situations that had not been encountered before. Thus, there was a need for laws that could be developed faster than through the relatively slow process of decisions by the courts. This need was met through the enactment of statutes by legislative bodies. Statutes, acts "of the legislature declaring, commanding, or prohibiting something" (*Black's Law Dictionary,* 1979), are the written law of a jurisdiction. The statutes of a jurisdiction are usually codified, so that all of the laws pertaining to a certain topic (e.g., criminal procedure, corporations, domestic relations) are arranged together, often with annotations of court cases that have interpreted the particular statute in question. The codes of the various states are fairly well indexed and are usually a good place to start finding the law of a jurisdiction. The law in common-law jurisdictions today is composed of statutes written by the legislature and decisions written by the courts.

In the United States, laws exist both at the federal level and at the state level. Whether a situation is governed by federal law, by state law, or by both depends on the nature of the legal transaction. Family law has been almost exclusively the province of the states. Recently, however, there have been several decisions by the U.S. Supreme Court that also determine the law of domestic relations.

In addition to understanding the sources of American law, it is important for the family psychologist to have some knowledge of the structure of courts in the United States. Basically, there are two levels of courts in the country: trial courts and appellate courts. Trial courts are the courts where questions of fact are decided and the rules of law are applied to the facts in the case (Jacobstein & Mersky, 1981). It is important to note that most cases, civil and criminal, are resolved at the trial level. That is, the judgment of the trial court is the final judgment in the case. This finality of judgment at the trial level is also true of family law cases, in that less that 10 percent of all family cases are appealed to a higher court.

If one party is dissatisfied with a ruling of the trial court, he or she may appeal the decision to an appeals court. In most instances, the appellate court can only make decisions regarding the law in the case; it cannot generally make decisions about questions of fact in the case. Appellate courts do not receive new evidence in the case; that is, they are limited to the evidence that was presented at the trial court (Jacobstein & Mersky, 1981). Every state has a final court of appeal, the rulings of which constitute part of the law of that state. In addition, some states have appellate courts intermediate between the trial courts and the final court of appeal. If a case tried under state law also involves a constitutional question, the case may be appealed to the Supreme Court of the United States.

The decisions of most appellate courts and of some trial courts are published in volumes (called reporters) arranged by state or region. The mechanics of legal research are too detailed to describe here, but a few basics can be mentioned. In general, a citation for a case consists of the names of the parties in the case, the volume number and name of the reporter, the beginning page number where the case can be found, and the date of the court decision. Thus, a citation for a Georgia Supreme Court case involving a dispute between a di-

vorced couple named Scherer would be as follows: *Scherer* v. *Scherer,*
249 Ga. 635, 292 S.E.2d 662. The first citation refers to reports for
decisions by the Georgia Supreme Court. The case can be found on
page 635 of volume 249 of the Georgia Reports. "S.E.2d" refers to
the second series of volumes of the South Eastern Reporter. The case
can be found beginning on page 662 of volume 292 of the South Eastern
Reporter, second series. Other cases can be found in a like manner.

THE LAW OF MARRIAGE

Because of the ambiguity of many relationships today, it is often
unclear whether a couple is in a marriage, a cotenancy, a partnership,
a joint enterprise, or something else (Weyrauch, 1980). How the relationship is defined legally has several important implications, particularly with regard to division of property after the relationship has
ended. The following discussion of family law will begin with an examination of the law of marriage, including the rights and duties of spouses,
and the emerging law concerning nonmarital cohabitation and spouse
abuse.

Marriage is, at base, a contract between a man and a woman. In
general, for a contract to be valid, several factors must be true. First,
there must be mutual assent. That is, there must be an offer (some
expression of a promise or commitment to make a contract) and an
acceptance of the offer. Second, there must be some consideration
for the contract. Consideration refers to some bargained-for change
in the legal position of the parties. Third, there cannot be any defenses
to the creation of the contract. There are two general types of defenses
to a contract: *(a)* evidence that the two parties never really formed
an agreement, because of some mistake or misunderstanding about
the nature of the contract, and *(b)* general considerations of public
policy that prohibit certain kinds of contracts from being formed. The
two most common kinds of public policy considerations are that the
contract involves something illegal and that one or both of the parties
lacked the capacity to make a contract, because of being underage,
being intoxicated, lacking mental capacity, or lacking volitional assent.

Analogously, for a marriage contract to be valid, there must be an
offer and acceptance, consideration, and no defenses to the contract.
In general, offer, acceptance, and consideration are not problems in
determining the validity of a marriage agreement. However, the public
policy considerations to a marriage, such as minority of one of the
parties or a lack of mental competency, can be a defense to the marriage.

Although marriage is a contract between two individuals, it is different from most contracts in that the state places some limitations on

who may enter into the contract and, once the contract is made, the state takes a strong interest in preserving the relationship between the two individuals. Currently, the marital contract is in a state of flux, as is the role that the state plays with regard to that contract (Shultz, 1982).

State marriage laws require that individuals be competent to make a contract and that the individuals have reached a certain minimum age (16 or 18). Moreover, some states require that the individuals must be tested for venereal disease and that they must wait for some time period (often three days) between the time the marriage license is issued and the time the marriage ceremony occurs (Clark, 1968). Strickman (1982), in his analysis of these kinds of statutes that delay marriage but do not prohibit it, indicates that they will probably withstand constitutional scrutiny. However, according to Strickman, statutes that prohibit marriage are more difficult for a state to defend against constitutional attack. For example, in *Zablocki* v. *Redhail* (1978) a male resident of Wisconsin who wanted to get married attacked a state law that required individuals subject to a court order to provide child support to prove that the children were not likely to need state funds to provide for their needs. The U.S. Supreme Court held that this law impermissibly interfered with Redhail's right to marriage.

In an earlier decision, the Supreme Court had characterized marriage as a fundamental right, since "the freedom to marry has long been recognized as one of the vital personal rights essential to the orderly pursuit of happiness by free men" (*Loving* v. *Virginia*, 1967, p. 12). Although Strickman has said that this language was not central to the Court's decision, the Court in *Loving* held unconstitutional, as a violation of the equal protection clause of the 14th Amendment, Virginia's statute prohibiting interracial marriages between whites and members of other races. According to the Court:

> Marriage is one of the "basic civil rights of man," fundamental to our very existence and survival [citations omitted]. To deny this fundamental freedom on so unsupportable a basis as the racial classification embodied in these statutes, classifications so directly subversive of the principle of equality at the very heart of the Fourteenth Amendment, is surely to deprive all the State's citizens of liberty without due process of law. The Fourteenth Amendment requires that the freedom of choice to marry not be restricted by invidious racial discrimination. Under our Constitution, the freedom to marry, or not to marry, a person of another race resides with the individual and cannot be infringed by the State. (*Loving* v. *Virginia*, 1967, p. 12)

Although a state's prohibition of interracial marriages is unconstitutional, other types of prohibitions have withstood or probably would withstand constitutional scrutiny. For example, a statute prohibiting bigamy is constitutional (*Reynolds* v. *United States,* 1879). Homosexual marriages, although usually not specifically prohibited in states' statutes, have not been upheld in any states' courts that have considered the issue (e.g., *Baker* v. *Nelson,* 1972; see Strickman, 1982). In prohibiting homosexual marriages, courts have generally relied on the traditional notion that a marriage is between a man and a woman. It is not clear whether other kinds of restrictions on marriages would withstand constitutional attack. For example, although state laws prohibiting marriage between members of a nuclear family are probably constitutional, the constitutional status is less clear for laws prohibiting marriages between family members outside the nuclear family (e.g., cousins, uncle-niece, aunt-nephew) or between individuals formerly related by marriage within a certain degree, such as a marriage between a brother- and sister-in-law (Strickman, 1982).

The most common type of marriage is a ceremonial marriage presided over by a civil official or a religious functionary. Although states usually have some requirements for ceremonial marriages (e.g., two witnesses to the ceremony, the filing of a license), the ceremony itself is usually not specified by state law. In addition to being recognized in the state where it occurred, a valid ceremonial marriage is also generally recognized as legal in all other states. Occasionally, a couple who cannot be legally married in their own state (e.g., because one or both individuals are underage) may go to another state where they can be legally married. There is some question whether this marriage should be considered valid when they return to their home state, since their only reason for getting married in the other state was to avoid the law in their own state (Clark, 1968). Recently, for example, an uncle and niece temporarily left Vermont, where their marriage was prohibited, for Canada, where they hoped their marriage could be performed ("Autumn Love," 1983).

In addition to ceremonial marriages, some states permit what is known as a common-law marriage. Common-law marriages, as their name would suggest, were marriages that were recognized by courts even though no formal marriage ceremony had occurred. Clark (1968) suggests that common-law marriages were particularly useful in places like the American frontier, where there was no one who could legally marry two individuals. Given that this problem is not as prevalent today, there is some question about whether common-law marriages are still needed. A common-law marriage is a contract between two individuals, although the contract is not written nor is there any evidence of a contract as with a marriage license. Generally, the fact that there is no written evidence of a contract is not a problem, since both individuals in the common-law marriage acknowledge that they are husband and wife. A problem can arise, however, if there is a separation and one party claims that the relationship was not a marriage. In such a case, whether or not there was a marriage would depend on which one of the two individuals was believed. To guard against the possibility that a person could fraudulently claim the existence of a common-law marriage, courts hearing the claim generally require that the couple have held themselves out to others as husband and wife. Contrary to popular belief, there is usually no minimum time period required for a common-law marriage. The effect of a common-law marriage is the same as of a ceremonial marriage; that is, the marriage is valid and requires a legal divorce to be terminated.

Antenuptial agreements

Because there has been so much uncertainty with regard to alimony and property division after divorce, a number of couples have made agreements before they were married, so as to eliminate litigation over these issues in the event of divorce. These contracts were and are common among couples in which one individual is very wealthy and among elderly couples in which the two individuals want to preserve the inheritance of their property to their children. Although couples have made antenuptial agreements for several years, many courts did not accept them until fairly recently.

One of the most important trends in recent years has been the acceptance by courts of antenuptial agreements. Until recently, these agreements were considered to be void *ab initio*. That is, they were considered to be against the state's interest in preserving marriages because they were thought to encourage divorce and separation. Although at present the majority rule is still to reject antenuptial agreements, a number of states have begun to accept these agreements as valid. For example, in Georgia, antenuptial agreements made in contemplation of divorce will be upheld unless the contesting party can show one of three things: *(a)* the agreement was obtained through fraud, duress, or mistake or through misrepresentation or nondisclosure of material facts; *(b)* the agreement is unconscionable; or *(c)* the facts and circumstances have changed so much that enforcement of the agreement is now unfair and unreasonable (*Scherer* v. *Scherer*, 1982).

Several arguments have been raised in support of enforcing antenuptial agreements. For the most part, these arguments concern providing the parties with some degree of certainty regarding their estates in the event of divorce or the death of one of the parties. In addition, it is expected that making antenuptial agreements valid should reduce the amount of litigation and the acrimony that often follows a divorce. Finally, it has been suggested that such agreements may force parties who are about to marry to realize the seriousness of marriage and may actually reduce the number of divorces, since the parties know from the beginning of their marriage what will happen if a divorce occurs (Bates, 1983).

Although less common than antenuptial agreements involving property, many couples prior to marriage are signing contracts that specify their rights and duties during the marriage, such things as responsibilities around the home and the way they expect to be treated by their partner during the marriage (e.g., Weitzman, 1981). These agreements will probably not be enforced by the courts, since judges are generally disinclined to interfere in marriages.

Nonmarital cohabitation

The purpose of antenuptial agreements is to clarify before the marriage the disposition of property in the event the couple is subsequently divorced. A related question is the status of agreements made between individuals who are not and do not plan to be married. Generally, such contracts are not written, and litigation in these cases usually involves one person's testimony contradicting that of the other. These "palimony" suits have become more common, and a number of lovers of famous individuals have sued for a division of property or for support or for both. Probably the best known case is *Marvin* v. *Marvin* (1976), in which the Supreme Court of California held that, as long as sexual relations were not part of the consideration of the agreement, a nonmarital cohabiting couple could make a contract regarding property. To reach decisions that they consider fair, courts increasingly are borrowing concepts such as implied contract, implied partnership, and constructive trust from other areas of the law (Douthwaite, 1979; Hennessey, 1980). Because, for a number of reasons, nonmarital cohabitation has been increasing in recent years (Bruch, 1976; Lavori, 1976), the problems concerning division of property when the relationship ends are likely to continue to be decided in the courts.

Spouse abuse

It has been estimated that physical assault occurs in at least one 10th of all homes in the United States annually (Straus, Gelles, & Steinmetz, 1980). The abused spouse has little legal recourse. When the abuse occurs, the abused spouse can report the assault to the police, who may or may not arrest the abuser. Their decision to arrest depends on the extent of the abuse and the desires of the abused spouse. Many times, the abuse stops when the police arrive, and the abused spouse often desires no further action. The police themselves are often reluctant to make an arrest, since the victim may later decide that he or she does not want the spouse to be prosecuted.

If the police are not called immediately, it is more difficult for the abused spouse to initiate legal action. Generally, instead of simply calling the police, she or he must instead swear out a warrant for the arrest of the abuser, in which the time and location of the assault are described. Even if the abuser is arrested and prosecuted, a court is likely to treat the offender relatively mildly, the likely outcomes being a dismissal of the charges in exchange for the abuser's promise not to beat his spouse again, a court order to stay away from the abused spouse, or a minor punishment such as a fine (State Bar of Georgia, 1981).

A fairly recent alternative in about three fourths of the states is for the abused spouse to ask a state court to issue a protective order (Schechter, 1981), which orders the abuser to stop threatening or abusing the victim. In most cases, this order is issued after a hearing during which both parties testify. In addition, many states allow this order to be issued *ex parte*, solely on the evidence offered by the abused spouse without the presence of the abuser. This *ex parte* order is only temporary, and a subsequent full hearing is necessary for a permanent order to be granted. In many states, there are limitations on who can ask for a protective order. For example, some states require that the person must be an abused spouse and that actual physical harm have occurred. A violation of the court order can lead to a contempt citation and possible jail term, although these remedies are not likely to be imposed. The state's response to spouse abuse, primarily through legislation authorizing protective orders and emergency shelters, has been characterized as an insufficient response to the problem (Schechter, 1981).

When women kill their abusers during the course of severe battering, prosecutors often look on the murder as self-defense and do not press charges (Thar, 1982). A more complex problem presents itself, however, when the women kill their abusers after the abuse has stopped, hours or days later. Under such circumstances, it is difficult to argue that the murder was in self-defense, since this defense requires that the murderer have acted with the belief that the force was necessary to protect herself from being killed or severely injured.

Because of the unsuitability of self-defense as a justification for the murder, defendants in several states have argued that the killing was justified because of a past history and expectation of future abuse from the murdered abuser. In several of these cases, they have relied on the testimony of Lenore Walker, a clinical psychologist, who argues that many women in battering relationships suffer from what she calls the "battered wife syndrome." According to Walker (1979), battering consists of three stages: *(a)* a tension-building stage during which minor abuse occurs, *(b)* an acute battering stage during which extremely violent acts occur, and *(c)* a final stage of loving during which the batterer shows affection to the woman and asks for her forgiveness. Walker argues that this cycle is part of the reason many women stay in abusing relationships. First, the third stage of the cycle indicates to the woman that the batterer's behavior has changed. Second, because the second stage of acute battering is not predictable, Walker argues that the women suffer learned helplessness, a state in which they feel unable to do anything to change their situation.

Whether or not an expert can testify on the battered wife syndrome varies among the states that have considered the question. Traditionally, an expert can testify at a trial if three criteria are met (Cleary, 1972): *(a)* the subject must be beyond the knowledge of the average layman, *(b)* the expert must be qualified in the area, based on his or her education or experience, and *(c)* the state of the scientific knowledge must be fairly well established so that the expert could make a reasonable opinion. One of the first cases to consider the question of expert testimony regarding battered wife syndrome was *Ibn-Tamas* v. *United States* (1979). There the court ruled that the testimony could be admitted. However, state supreme courts in Ohio (*State* v. *Thomas*, 1981) and Wyoming (*Buhrle* v. *State*, 1981) have declared the proffered testimony inadmissible.

ANNULMENT, SEPARATION, AND DIVORCE

This section describes the legal termination of marriage. The legal termination of a marriage most often occurs through divorce proceedings, although annulment is possible under some circumstances. Because a legal separation often occurs as a prelude to divorce proceedings, this section also contains a brief discussion of separation proceedings.

Annulment

Although less common than divorce, annulment is sometimes used to invalidate a marriage on the basis of some reason existing at the beginning of the marriage, that caused it to be invalid. Some of the reasons that can invalidate a marriage relate to whether the contract of marriage was legal: such things as insanity, underage, fraud, and duress. Other reasons that can invalidate a marriage pertain to marriages prohibited by law, such as incestuous and bigamous relationships.

Legal separation

Traditionally, courts did not approve of legal separation agreements because *(a)* common-law doctrine stated that a husband and wife's identity were merged on marriage and that a person could not contract with himself; and *(b)* the courts were reluctant to enforce agreements made "in contemplation of divorce," because it was felt that such agreements encouraged divorce (Sharp, 1981). Courts in most states have since come to accept the validity of separation agreements, with regard to such questions as child custody, child support, alimony, and property division.

Divorce

Every year there are over 1.1 million divorces in the United States, although the number of divorces seems to have leveled off in recent years (U.S. Bureau, 1983). Because the state has a strong interest in maintaining marriages, obtaining a divorce is much more difficult than is becoming married. Although the question regarding the extent to which a state can restrict divorce has not yet been considered by the Supreme Court, in the case *Boddie* v. *Connecticut* (1971) the Court did find that Connecticut's fees for court costs and service of process in divorce cases (which averaged about $50) denied indigent individuals access to divorce and therefore denied them due process.

Divorce came out of the courts of equity, and as an equitable action, there was the requirement that one party do something wrong and the other party be without fault. "Fault" originally included only adultery and physical cruelty but later came to include such other "fault" grounds as willful desertion, habitual drunkenness, and mental cruelty. Because divorce was an action in equity, it could be granted only if the party seeking the divorce was innocent of any wrongdoing, what is known as the "clean hands" doctrine. If both parties were at fault, the doctrine of recrimination prohibited the granting of a divorce. Thus, if a party did not want to be divorced, he or she could offer proof that the party seeking the divorce had committed some wrong that would bar a divorce. In addition, proof that parties colluded to obtain a divorce barred the action. Most states have abolished at least some of the traditional defenses to divorce (Freed & Foster, 1983). Because of the problems with fault divorce and the charades that were often performed to circumvent the statutes, there were a number of calls for reform of the divorce laws, the primary one being a call for the removal of fault.

No-fault divorce statutes were enacted because of the general dissatisfaction with the notion of fault in divorce proceedings. It has been suggested that the notion of fault is inappropriate for domestic relations situations, both because there is not always an indication of fault in domestic cases and because blaming one partner in a couple can be unfair, since most behaviors in a marriage are the result of interdependence (Mazur-Hart & Berman, 1977).

Initially, it was feared that the enactment of no-fault divorce laws would greatly increase the number of divorces granted. However, results from two studies indicate that there is virtually no relationship between no-fault divorce laws and the rate of divorce (Mazur-Hart & Berman, 1977; Sepler, 1981). Although no-fault divorce laws do not seem to have affected the rate of divorce, there is some evidence that they have reduced awards of alimony and child support (Weitzman & Dixon, 1980).

Because of the fears that no-fault divorce laws would greatly increase the number of divorces, several states enacted provisions requiring either a waiting period between the filing of a divorce action and the granting of a divorce, or mandatory counseling and conciliation sessions, or both a waiting period and counseling. The purpose of both of these procedures is to force the couple to reconsider their decision.

Alimony

Alimony was a concept derived from the English ecclesiastical courts, which required a husband to continue to support his wife if the divorce was such that the couple lived apart but were still legally married ("divorce from bed and board"). The notion was extended to all divorces, and the common-law rule was embodied in many states' statutes, although a gender-based classification restricting alimony to females has been declared unconstitutional (*Orr* v. *Orr,* 1979). All states but Texas permit permanent or rehabilitative alimony after divorce (Freed & Foster, 1983), although most divorces do not involve alimony. The guidelines judges have concerning the award of alimony are very general in nature and provide little guidance beyond need and ability to pay. About 30 states provide some criteria for the awarding of alimony (Connell, 1981), the major ones of which are summarized in Section 308 of the Uniform Marriage and Divorce Act (National Conference, 1971, pp. 233–234; see *Uniform Laws Annotated,* 1979b):

[T]he court may grant a maintenance order for either spouse, only if it finds that the spouse seeking maintenance:

1. Lacks sufficient property to provide for his reasonable needs; and
2. Is unable to support himself through appropriate employment or is the custodian of a child whose condition or circumstance make

it appropriate that the custodian not be required to seek employment outside the home.

(b) The maintenance order shall be in amount and for periods of time the court deems just, without regard to marital misconduct, and after considering all relevant factors including:

1. The financial resources of the party seeking maintenance, including marital property apportioned to him, his ability to meet his needs independently, and the extent to which a provision for support of a child living with the party includes a sum for that party as custodian;
2. The time necessary to acquire sufficient education or training to enable the party seeking maintenance to find appropriate employment;
3. The standard of living established during the marriage;
4. The duration of the marriage;
5. The age and the physical and emotional condition of the spouse seeking maintenance; and
6. The ability of the spouse from whom maintenance is sought to meet his needs while meeting those of the spouse seeking maintenance.

There have been several trends in the reform of alimony laws. One of these trends has been to recognize the contributions to a household of a spouse who is a homemaker and parent and who contributes to the career potential of the other spouse and to the well-being of the family. At least 31 states take one or more of these factors into account with regard to decisions about alimony or property division or both (Freed & Foster, 1983). A second trend has been to lessen the impact of marital fault (e.g., adultery or desertion). In the past, such misconduct would have been an absolute bar to receiving alimony. Today, marital misconduct is a bar in only six states (Freed & Foster, 1983). A third trend in alimony is toward rehabilitative alimony—that is, alimony granted for a limited period until the ex-spouse can be trained or educated for a new career rather than until the person remarries or dies.

Property division

How property is divided between a husband and wife after a divorce depends on the law of the state where the property was acquired. With regard to the law where the property was acquired, there are basically two types of marital property laws, common-law property states and community property states. In common-law states, property acquired during a marriage is generally that of the party in whose name it was taken. Thus, if the husband is employed outside the home and the wife takes care of the home and the children, the husband's salary in common-law property states is totally the husband's. In contrast, in community property states, property acquired during a marriage (with some exceptions) belongs to the community—that is, belongs equally to the husband and wife. The concept of community property is derived from Spanish and French law. Eight states have community property laws. In the example above, in a community property state, half of the salary the husband earned belongs to the wife. Clearly, then, property division on divorce will differ in common-law and community property states. In a common-law property state, the wage earner (usually the husband) is the legal owner of most of the couple's property since it was probably bought with his income. Because a division of property on divorce based solely on legal title would result in unfair treatment of the wife, many common-law property states have statutory or court decisional law by which property is more fairly divided. For example, the Georgia Supreme Court has recently adopted the doctrine of equitable division of property acquired during the marriage. Aside from the state law governing ownership and distribution of property, a couple may and often do negotiate their own property settlement, although such agreements often have tax consequences.

Not all property acquired by a couple during marriage is easily valued or divisible. Property in this category includes pension plans and professional degrees and licenses. Although pensions are given to the employee only, there has been a trend in the past few years to give the spouse (in most cases, the wife) a proportional interest in the pension based on the percentage of the pension earned during the marriage (Krause, 1977). When the pension is through the federal government, however, federal law controls over state law (e.g., *McCarty* v. *McCarty,* 1981).

With regard to division of the value of a professional degree or license, the typical situation arises after the couple lived primarily on the earnings of one spouse (usually the wife) while the other spouse obtained professional training. Cases on the question of whether the working spouse is entitled to an equitable interest in the professional degree or to a quasi-contractual remedy have not been consistent (Freed & Foster, 1983). According to Freed and Foster, courts have "held that a professional degree is and is not 'property' subject to equitable distribution, and that a professional license is and is not marital property" (p. 300). Remedies have included somewhat larger and longer alimony payments as reimbursements for the costs of supporting the spouse, as well as granting the working spouse a percentage interest in the projected value of the degree or license. Although the decisions have not been consistent, the trend appears to be that working spouses are entitled to some recompense for their support of their spouse obtaining a degree or license.

Divorce mediation

The traditional adversary divorce is often criticized because it is expensive and because it often engenders bitter feelings between the parties. In recent years, there has been a developing trend toward reducing the adversarial nature of divorce. Probably the best known and most controversarial is divorce mediation. Basically, the purpose of divorce mediation is to get the divorcing parties to agree to a settlement, thereby avoiding the expense and bitterness of a court suit. In addition, advocates of divorce mediation suggest that the parties are more likely to abide by an agreement that they participated in than by an order given by the court (Mnookin & Kornhauser, 1979).

According to Silberman (1982), there are presently four models of divorce mediation: (a) a single attorney acting both as a mediator and attorney for the couple, (b) a single mental health professional, (c) a two-person team composed of an attorney and a mental health professional, and (d) a mediation center with a staff of trained mediators and a panel of advisory attorneys.

There are several advantages to divorce mediation that advocates have suggested. First, proponents have argued that mediation is often cheaper than a traditional adversary divorce. Although there are problems with the research that has been conducted, there is some evidence that both mediated divorces (Bahr, 1981) and mediated postdivorce child custody disputes (Pearson & Thoennes, 1982) result in savings over the traditional adversarial method of dispute resolution. A second advantage that mediation proponents have argued for is a savings in time; that is, the disputes are settled faster when there is mediation rather than adversarial process (Pearson & Thoennes, 1982). A third advantage is that the participants are more likely to perceive a mediated settlement as fairer than a court resolution to the divorce. Unfortunately, the problems with these studies—small sample size, the fact that often only one member of the divorcing couple is interviewed, the lack of a control group, and the failure to control for the complexity of the case (Kearns, 1983)—prevent placing too much faith in these studies.

There are possible ethical problems with each of the various models of divorce mediation. With both the single-attorney model and the attorney–mental health professional team, the attorney may be in violation of Canon 5 of the A.B.A. Model Code of Professional Responsibility (American Bar Association, 1983), which proscribes the representation of two parties who have or who may have conflicting interests. The response of state bar associations to the single-attorney model of mediation has been inconsistent (Silberman, 1982).

In spite of the possible ethical problems, there have been calls for lawyers and mental health professionals to work together on such problems as divorce. For example, Steinberg (1980) has argued that an attorney-therapist team has a number of advantages. First, a client is likely to be selective in what he or she tells an attorney or therapist. When the two professionals work together, they are likely to know more about, and therefore better serve, their client. Second, a team approach is likely to lead to referrals to the other professional sooner.

THE PARENT–CHILD RELATIONSHIP

In the United States today, there are over 62 million children under the age of 18, 75 percent of whom live with both parents, 20 percent of whom live with their mothers only, 2 percent of whom live with their fathers only, and 3 percent of whom live with neither parent (U.S. Bureau, 1983). This section will discuss legal factors related to the establishment of the parent-child relationship and legal aspects of the rights and responsibilities of parents toward their children.

Establishing the parent-child relationship

The establishment of the parent-child relationship may involve five legal issues (Krause, 1977): abortion, legitimacy, paternity, adoption, and surrogate parenting. Each of these topics will be discussed below.

Abortion. The law regarding abortion changed dramatically with the Supreme Court decision *Roe* v. *Wade* (1973). In that decision, the court held that there were limits on the extent to which the state could regulate abortion. Basically, the Court established three different standards regarding the state's interest in prohibiting the termination of a pregnancy. For the first trimester of a pregnancy, the Court ruled, no state interest outweighs the mother's right to privacy and, hence, the state could not prohibit abortion during this period. For the second trimester of pregnancy, the Court held that the state does have a compelling interest in protecting the health of the mother and therefore can make reasonable regulations regarding the way abortions are conducted during this period. For the third trimester of pregnancy, the Court held that the state's interest in protecting the life of the fetus is compelling and outweighs the mother's right to privacy. According to the Court, then, abortion during the third trimester can be regulated and even prohibited. In subsequent decisions, the Court has generally limited the extent to which states can place restrictions on abortions. One such restriction that the Supreme Court has declared unconstitutional is prohibiting advertising for abortion services (*Bigelow* v. *Virginia*, 1975). The extent to which a state or municipality can require consent from a woman's husband or parent before the woman can obtain an abortion has been addressed in a series of decisions by the Supreme Court: *Planned Parenthood of Missouri* v. *Danforth* (1976); *Belloti* v. *Baird* (1979); *H. L.* v. *Matheson* (1981); *City of Akron* v. *Akron Center of Reproductive Health, Inc.* (1983); *Planned Parenthood Association of Kansas City, Mo., Inc.* v. *Ashcroft* (1983).

Legitimacy.   The legitimacy of a child is important primarily in terms of whether the child is entitled to receive support from, and to inherit from, a parent. A legitimate child, one "who has a full legal relationship with both of its parents" (Krause, 1977, p. 119), is so entitled. In most cases, if the parents are married, the child is presumed to be legitimate. Moreover, if a child is born to a married woman, the legal rebuttable presumption is that the child is the legitimate child of the mother's husband. In recent decisions, the Supreme Court appears to taking the position that the law may not discriminate between legitimate and nonlegitimate children (Krause, 1977; *Mills* v. *Habluetzel*, 1982). For example, in *Pickett* v. *Brown* (1983), the Court held that a Tennessee law that placed a two-year limitation period on paternity and child support actions for illegitimate children but not for legitimate children violated the equal protection clause of the Fourteenth Amendment and was therefore unconstitutional.

Paternity.   Within the past few years, a number of relatively sophisticated techniques have been developed that increase the confidence one can place in a determination of paternity. How evidence is heard in the courts varies from state to state. In some states, the proceeding is civil, and the standard of proof is by a preponderance of the evidence. In other states, the proceeding is criminal, and the standard of proof is beyond a reasonable doubt. If a judgment of paternity is made, the father is ordered to pay support for the child and may be obligated to pay the mother's expenses of pregnancy and birth (Krause, 1977).

Adoption.   According to Clark (1980, p. 430), "The process of adoption occurs when, pursuant to statute, a child's legal rights and responsibilities toward his natural parents are terminated and similar rights and responsibilities toward his adoptive parents are substituted." Every state has a law permitting the adoption of children (Krause, 1977).

According to Krause (1977), most adoptions are conducted through public or licensed private adoption agencies, which ensures that there is at least some scrutiny of the prospective adoptive parents, although the contact with a public child welfare agency may be only minimal. Adoptions that occur without the required involvement of an adoption agency or public child welfare agency may lead to criminal prosecution.

Nevertheless, private adoptions occur fairly frequently, simply because there is a shortage of the babies that are most desired: healthy white infants. Because of this shortage, a black market in white babies has developed (Podolski, 1975). This black market relies on payments to the biological mothers and to middlemen who arrange the transactions. For the adoptive parents, the black market allows them to become parents quicker than does adoption through adoption agencies. For the birth mothers, private adoption allows them to be reimbursed for their medical and living expenses, allows them to meet the adoptive parents, and is less demeaning than public adoptions.

Courts generally prefer adoptions by married couples rather than by single individuals, by couples of the same religious and racial group as the child rather than by couples of different ethnic backgrounds than the child (Simon & Altstein, 1977, 1981), and by couples of child-bearing age rather than by those who are older (Krause, 1977). Although courts have these preferences for adoptive parents, many times it is not in the child's best interests to wait for parents who meet all these criteria, particularly since older, handicapped, and minority group children are often difficult to place.

In recent years, nonmarital fathers have gained some rights regarding the adoption of their children. In the first case on this question, *Stanley* v. *Illinois* (1972), the Supreme Court held that the unwed father was entitled to notice and a hearing regarding the adoption of his children. However, more recent decisions by the Court indicate that unwed fathers do not have as much say about the adoption procedure as do the mothers of the children (*Caban* v. *Mohammed*, 1979; *Quilloin* v. *Walcott*, 1978).

Surrogate parenthood. As mentioned earlier, there has been a decline in the fertility of couples of childbearing age. One effect of this decline has been an increase in the number of children who are born to married couples and are the biological offspring of only one of their parents. When a mother has been artificially inseminated from a man not her husband, the child is likely to be considered legitimate since it was born to a married woman, although not all courts have reached this decision (Krause, 1977).

When the wife is infertile, some couples have turned to a surrogate mother. Although this procedure can be expensive (e.g., medical costs, psychological screening, payment to the mother for her services), probably the major problem with the procedure is that the surrogate mother may decide to keep the child. Even though lawyers have designed contracts signed by the surrogate mother and the prospective parents (e.g., Brophy, 1982), there are those who believe that these contracts are probably not enforceable (Handel & Sherwyn, 1982). In contrast to the situation where both the biological mother and the prospective parents want the child, a recent situation occurred where neither the mother nor the prospective parents wanted the child ("Surrogate Rejects," 1983).

Rights and responsibilities of parents

Under Roman law, the father had the right to do anything with his children, including selling them into slavery and killing them. Although parents' rights over their children are more limited today, they still have a great deal of discretion over their children. There are two sources of limitation on parents' decisions about, and behavior toward, their children. The first source is state statutes regarding dependency, neglect, and abuse. The second source is the growing concern with children's rights to make their own decisions.

The question of when the state should become involved with a family is not an easy one to decide. On the one hand, there is the state's concern as *parens patriae* with the welfare of children within its jurisdiction. On the other hand, there is the traditional autonomy granted the family. Goldstein, Freud, and Solnit (1979, pp. v-vii) argue that state intervention into the parent-child relationship should be confined to the following limited situations: *(a)* a "request by a parent separating from his or her spouse for the court to determine custody;" *(b)* a "request by a child's longtime caretakers to become his parents or the refusal by longtime caretakers to relinquish him to his parents or to a state agency;" *(c)* "the death or disappearance of both parents, the only parent or the custodial parent—when coupled with their failure to make provision for their child's custody;" *(d)* "conviction, or acquittal by reason of insanity, of a sexual offense against one's child;" *(e)* "serious bodily injury inflicted by parents upon their child, an attempt to inflict such injury, or the repeated failure of parents to prevent their child from suffering such injury;" *(f)* "refusal by parents to authorize medical care when (1) medical experts agree that treatment is nonexperimental and appropriate for the child, and (2) denial of that treatment would result in death, and (3) the anticipated result of treatment is what society would want for every child—a chance for normal healthy growth or a life worth living."

If the state does act to terminate a parent's rights over his or her child, proof must be by clear and convincing evidence rather than by a mere preponderance of the evidence (*Santosky* v. *Kramer*, 1982). However, the Supreme Court has also held that parents are not entitled to a lawyer if they cannot afford one, but instead the judgment must be made by the trial judge in light of all the circumstances of the case (*Lassiter* v. *Department of Social Services of Durham County,* 1981).

An issue of increasing concern and interest is the extent to which minors are competent to make decisions for themselves (Melton, 1983). Although the Supreme Court has indicated that the state may abridge the rights of minors with less justification than when it intrudes on the rights of adults (e.g., *Parham* v. *J. R.,* 1979), the scientific evidence is not generally supportive of this position. Indeed, there is evidence indicating that 14-year-olds do not differ from adults in their responses to problem solving (e.g., Grisso & Vierling, 1978) or to medical and psychological treatment decisions (Weithorn & Campbell, 1982).

CHILD CUSTODY ON DIVORCE

During the past 150 years, the law on child custody after divorce has gone through three phases. In the early part of the 19th century, custody belonged without question to the father, because it was believed (probably correctly, since men were more likely to own property) that fathers would be better able to provide for their children's needs (Weiss, 1979). In addition, following traditional English common law, children were considered the father's property. In the late 19th century, a preference for the mother developed in child custody cases. This preference, called "the tender years doctrine," was based on the idea that young children benefit most from being with their mother until they are adolescents. During adolescence, the presumption was that children need to be with the same-sex parent, although the presumption was tempered by a desire to keep siblings together (Krause, 1977). In most states today, the tender years doctrine is rejected completely or is simply one factor that may carry weight, assuming everything else is equal (Freed & Foster, 1983). Klaff (1982) has recently defended the tender years doctrine, since mothers are still more likely to be the primary caretaker.

In the past 20 years, the predominant standard for deciding child custody cases has become the "best interests of the child." This standard is summarized by Section 402 of the Uniform Marriage and Divorce Act (National Conference, 1971, p. 241; see *Uniform Laws Annotated,* 1979b):

> The court shall determine custody in accordance with the best interests of the child. The court shall consider all relevant factors including:
>
> 1. The wishes of the child's parent or parents as to his custody;
> 2. The wishes of the child as to his custodian;
> 3. The interaction and interrelationship of the child with his parents,

his siblings, and any other person who may significantly affect the child's best interests;

4. The child's adjustment to his home, school, and community; and

5. The mental and physical health of all individuals involved. The court shall not consider conduct of a proposed custodian that does not affect his relationship to the child.

These standards are not without their critics. For example, a child may not express his or her wishes out of fear of offending the nonchosen parent (Weiss, 1979). Even if the child does express a preference, it may be based on a reason that has nothing to do with proper parenting, such as which parent gave the larger gift.

The traditional custody arrangement is that one parent has sole custody of all the children in the family and the other parent has visitation rights to the children. In about 85 percent of custody decisions, it is the mother who has sole custody and the father who has visitation rights (Freed & Foster, 1983; Weitzman & Dixon, 1979). Fathers rarely challenge for custody, since they often believe the mother would be the better caretaker of the children (Slovenko, 1973, p. 38), the children often prefer the mother, and courts still have a tendency to award custody to the mother (Freed & Foster, 1983).

Joint custody

In addition to sole custody awarded to one parent and visitation rights awarded to the other, there are other possible custody arrangements (Berman & Kirsh, 1982). For example, split custody involves each parent being awarded sole custody of at least one child and visitation rights to the child or children of whom he or she does not have custody. With shared custody, the children of the marriage split their time between the parents, and the parent with whom the children are living has sole responsibility for the children at that time. The third type of custody arrangement, one that has been receiving more and more attention, is joint custody. Joint custody involves physical custody and legal custody. Physical custody refers to where the child lives and to responsibility for minor decisions. Legal custody, in contrast, refers to responsibility for major decisions. With joint custody, one parent has physical custody, but both parents have legal responsibility. As Berman and Kirsh note, however, the difference between minor day-to-day decisions and major decisions is not always clear.

There are at least 23 states that have some form of joint-custody statute (Schulman, 1982). Schulman describes four types of joint-custody statutes. The first and simplest type lists joint custody as an available alternative but does not provide guidelines for the court. The second type provides that joint custody can be ordered only when both parties agree to joint custody. The third type provides for joint custody on the request of one party. The final type provides either a preference for joint custody (i.e., that it should be considered by the court before any other type of custody arrangement) or a presumption for joint custody (i.e., that joint custody is presumed to be in the child's best interests). Some states establish the legal presumption only when both parents agree to joint custody, while other states establish the presumption in all custody cases.

In addition to these four types of joint custody statutes, Schulman describes other provisions that may be present in the statutes. One such provision, which Schulman considers to be dangerous, is the so-called friendly parent provision. According to this provision, a court should consider which parent would allow the other parent to have the most contact with the children. Generally, friendly parent provisions are used in determining which parent should get sole custody, but they may also be included in joint-custody statutes that allow courts to grant joint custody on the request of one party. Schulman argues that the parent who is least fit for custody is likely to benefit from the friendly parent provision. For example, if Parent A does not believe that Parent B would be fit to be either a sole or joint custodian of the children and Parent B requests joint custody, then Parent A is put in a very difficult position. That is, Parent A may have to agree to joint custody because, if he or she refuses, Parent B may then be granted sole custody on the basis of being the friendlier parent.

A second provision that may be included in joint-custody statutes refers to the evidentiary standard used to overcome a preference or presumption for joint custody. According to Schulman, to overcome the presumption in some states, the opposing party would have to show by clear and convincing evidence that joint custody is not in the best interests of the child. A third provision that appears in some joint-custody statutes requires the court to write its reasons for not granting joint custody. In the interests of saving time, a court may grant joint custody so that it does not have to explain its decision.

Joint custody is becoming more popular for several reasons (Gardner, 1982). First, because it is closest to the original marital household, it requires the children to make the fewest adjustments. Second, it may reduce the bitterness that often exists under sole custody arrangements, particularly among fathers who pay child support but have only limited access to their children. Third, joint custody reduces the loss that a noncustodial parent often experiences under traditional sole custody arrangements.

Although joint custody does have advantages over other types of custody arrangements, Gardner (1982) argues that it is not for every-one. He suggests that it can be workable only if three conditions are met (p. 8):

1. Both parents are reasonably capable of assuming the responsibili-ties of childrearing—their involvement with the children and affec-tion for them are approximately equal. When there is a significant difference between the parents in these areas, another custodial arrangement should be considered.
2. The parents must have demonstrated their capacity to cooperate reasonably and meaningfully in matters pertaining to raising their children. They must show the ability to communicate well and be willing to compromise when necessary to ensure the viability of the arrangment.
3. The children's moving from home to home should not disrupt their school situation. Accordingly, the arrangement generally is possible only if both parents are living in the same public school district or reasonably close to a child's private school.

Gardner goes futher to argue that parents who are actively litigating for custody should not pursue joint custody, since the adversarial pro-cess is likely to increase animosity between the parents and thus reduce the cooperation and communication necessary for joint custody to work. In addition, Gardner suggests that other poor reasons for wanting joint custody include using it *(a)* as a compromise, *(b)* to hurt the other spouse, *(c)* to reduce one parent's guilt for not wanting sole custody, and *(d)* to "dump" the children with the other parent.

Research on joint custody is still lacking, for the most part (see Clin-gempeel & Repucci, 1982). Commentators, particularly proponents of joint custody, have instead relied on findings from studies that inves-tigated other questions. For example, a fairly consistent finding from studies investigating the effects of divorce on children is that children seem to adjust better and have fewer problems if they have continued contact with their father after the divorce (Hetherington, Cox, & Cox, 1976; Wallerstein & Kelly, 1980). However, these results do not neces-sarily mean, as some have argued, that joint custody is the best place-ment for children of divorce (Maccoby, Kahn, & Everett, 1983). It should also be noted that Goldstein, Freud, and Solnit (1973) are critical of the concept of joint custody, believing that joint custody interferes with effective parenting.

Changes in child custody. Particularly when a divorce is bitter, child custody is likely to be a source of continuing conflict between the divorced couple. Since custody decrees are subject to modification, many parents bring suits to change custody. Because of the relatively high probability of continuing litigation, state laws often limit the extent to which a noncustodial parent can bring a suit asking for a change of custody. One such limitation is a minimum time period, often a year, following an unsuccessful suit for child custody, only after which can a new suit be brought. A second limitation concerns the grounds for granting a request for change of custody. Generally, the request will be granted only if there have been substantial changes in the present situation that affect the child's welfare and that have occurred since the last hearing on child custody. If there has been no substantial change in circumstances or if the change does not affect the welfare of the child, a change in custody is unlikely. Of course, what constitutes a substantial change may vary from state to state. Thus, for example, a custodial parent's sexual behavior, such as nonmarital heterosexual cohabitation or homosexuality, may be seen as a substantial change, although some courts have required a direct connection between the behavior and the child's welfare (Guernsey, 1981).

Interstate child custody conflicts

The country's population has become increasing mobile; in the past five years, almost half of the population has moved at least once (U.S. Bureau, 1983). Many of these moves have been across state lines, and given the high rate of divorce in recent years, one effect of these frequent moves has been that child custody disputes are increasingly likely to involve courts in different states. Another way in which child custody disputes may involve courts in different states is through abduction of the child by the noncustodial parent. In the past, noncustodial parents could kidnap their children, take them to a different state, and bring a suit there for change of custody. If the court in the second state granted the change, then the abducting parent now had legal custody of the child and was, in effect, rewarded for having broken the law.

To meet the problem of interstate custody disputes and of child kidnappings, 48 states have now adopted the Uniform Child Custody Jurisdiction Act (UCCJA) (Freed & Foster, 1983). The UCCJA was drafted in 1968 by the National Conference of Commissioners on Uniform State Laws to serve several purposes. These purposes are listed in the second section of the act (*Uniform Laws Annotated*, 1979a):

The general purposes of this article are to:

1. Avoid jurisdictional competition and conflict with courts of other states in matters of child custody, which competition and conflict have in the past resulted in the shifting of children from state to state with harmful effect on the children's well-being;

2. Promote cooperation with the courts of other states, to the end that a custody decree is rendered in the state which can best decide the case in the interest of the child;
3. Assure that litigation concerning the custody of a child takes place ordinarily in the state with which the child and his family have the closest connection and where significant evidence concerning his care, protection, training, and personal relationships is most readily available and also to assure that the courts of this state decline the exercise of jurisdiction when the child and his family have a closer connection with another state;
4. Discourage continuing controversies over child custody, in the interest of greater stability of home environment and secure family relationships for the child;
5. Deter abductions and other unilateral removals of children undertaken to obtain custody awards;
6. Avoid unnecessary relitigation in this state of custody decisions in other states;
7. Facilitate the enforcement of custody decrees of other states;
8. Promote and expand the exchange of information and other forms of mutual assistance between the courts of this state and those of other states concerned with the same child; and
9. Make uniform the law of those states which enact the "Uniform Child Custody Jurisdiction Act."

The most important part of the UCCJA is the section on jurisdiction (Crouch, 1981). Generally, a state has jurisdiction if *(a)* the state is the child's home state or was the home state within the previous six months, and the child was removed by a person claiming custody; *(b)* it is in the child's best interests for the state to assume jurisdiction, because the child and at least one parent are in the state and there is evidence concerning the child's care; or *(c)* the child is in the state and is either abandoned or in an emergency situation.

Although the intent of the UCCJA was to deter child snatching, these abductions still do occur. The parent from whom the child was abducted has four possible remedies: criminal sanctions by the state, tort action against the abducting parent, civil contempt charges, and habeas corpus. Each of these remedies has problems, including time and cost, and may not be effective (Katz, 1981a, 1981b). In addition to the UCCJA, there is a federal law designed to reduce child abductions, the Parental Kidnaping Prevention Act of 1980. Another federal law, the Missing Children's Act of 1982, may prove helpful in locating abducted children.

Child support

In most states, the obligation to provide child support can be imposed on both parents or apportioned between the two (Freed & Foster, 1983). Although the criteria judges use to decide the issue of child support differ from court to court and from state to state, standards provided by statutes in some states are summarized in Section 15 of the Uniform Parentage Act (*Uniform Laws Annotated*, 1979b, p. 608):

> In determining the amount to be paid by a parent for support of the child and the period during which the duty of support is owed, a court enforcing the obligation of support shall consider all relevant facts, including
>
> 1. The needs of the child;
> 2. The standard of living and circumstances of the parents;
> 3. The relative financial means of the parents;
> 4. The earning ability of the parents;
> 5. The need and capacity of the child for education, including higher education;
> 6. The age of the child;
> 7. The financial resources and earning ability of the child;
> 8. The responsibility of the parents for the support of others; and
> 9. The value of services contributed by the custodial parent.

Child support recovery

It has been estimated that less than half of all divorced women receive any payments for their children, that only about 47 percent of the 4 million women who were supposed to receive child support for their children received all they were due ("Mothers Losing Out," 1983), and that overdue child support in the United States today comes to more than $100 billion dollars (Graham, 1983).

In many of these cases of nonsupport, the obligated parent cannot be located. With regard to cases where the children are receiving welfare, the federal Office of Child Support Recovery is involved to locate the absent parent, usually through computer records such as driver license records. Even when the absent parent is found and obligated to pay by the agency, however, in about two thirds of the cases, the obligated parent does not make the required payments (Graham, 1983).

All states have adopted the Uniform Reciprocal Enforcement of Support Act (URESA), which is intended to guarantee that child support will be paid even if the obligated parent has moved to another state. URESA provides that enforcement will take place through the offices of the district attorney in the jurisdictions where the obligated parent and the custodial parent live. Under the law, a custodial parent who has not received child support payments from the obligated parent files a form with the district attorney's office where she lives. On the form, the custodial parent notes how much support is owed and, most important, where the obligated parent lives. The district attorney's office then forwards the complaint to the district attorney's office in the jurisdiction where the obligated parent lives. The district attorney there files a suit to receive the child support owed. The proceeds from the suit or from the agreement that is reached between the obligated parent and the district attorney are sent to the district attorney's office where the custodial parent lives and then on to the custodial parent.

The juvenile justice system

Although not traditionally considered as part of domestic relations law, the juvenile justice system is discussed here for several reasons: *(a)* Often juvenile delinquency and other problems are thought to be caused by, and certainly affect, the family; *(b)* the juvenile justice system is civil rather than criminal; and *(c)* in some states (e.g., New York), juvenile cases and cases involving traditional domestic relations problems such as divorce, child custody, and adoption are all heard in a family court (Mulvey, 1982).

Rationale for a juvenile justice system.

Under English common law, a child under the age of seven was conclusively presumed to lack the mental capacity required to commit a crime. A child between the ages of 7 and 14 who committed a criminal act had what was called a qualified defense. That is, the court made a determination on a case-by-case basis whether a child possessed knowledge of the wrongfulness of his or her acts. Children who were found guilty of criminal acts were usually treated in the same fashion as were adult criminals.

The similar treatment of adult and juvenile criminals was objectionable to many and helped bring about the creation of the House of Refuge in New York in 1826. The House of Refuge, modeled after a similar establishment in London, was designed to reduce the suffering and corruption of juveniles in prison (Fox, 1974). Fox suggests that the House of Refuge had what amounted to the first indeterminate sentence in the United States, in that the managers of the House of Refuge could keep the boys until they were 21 and the girls until they were 18 but could also apprentice them out at any time. According to Fox, the second major aspect of the House of Refuge was that it could accept not only children who had been convicted of serious offenses, as was true of the adult system, but also children who had been convicted of trivial offenses. The rationale for including any type of offense was that the goal of the refuge movement was rehabilitation rather than punishment; thus, a child who committed a minor offense could be as much in need of rehabilitation as was a child who committed a serious offense. That is, it was assumed that "reform, primarily effected through moral education, needed time to 'take,' and individuals progressed at different rates; similarly, the commission of crime was the opportunity to save a young life—the nature of the crime was inconsequential" (Fox, p. 378). Accordingly, it was assumed the juvenile's best interests are best served when the court looks not to the specific behavior of the child but rather to his or her disposition and environment. In other words, the state is acting as a parent *(parens patriae)* and is concerned with reforming the child. The goal of the juvenile justice system is presumably to reform delinquents rather than to punish them for their delinquent acts. Although this would seem to be a noble purpose, there have been some questions raised about whether society's concern is really reform rather than punishment and about whether juveniles really can be reformed (Fox, 1974).

Most states have established juvenile courts to handle juvenile misbehavior, both criminal and noncriminal. Juvenile courts typically can handle the cases of juveniles until they reach their 18th birthday, although a few states use 16 or 17, and a few states allow juvenile courts to retain jurisdiction over the juvenile if the criminal conduct occurred while the child was under the specified age as long as he or she is not now over a certain age (usually 20).

With regard to violations of criminal law, state laws generally provide that a juvenile may be adjudged delinquent if he or she violates a state or local law. Some states also include violations of federal law. In some states, serious felonies are processed only in the criminal justice system rather than the juvenile justice system, regardless of the age of the juvenile. Similarly, traffic offenses are often not included within the jurisdiction of the juvenile court.

Because a delinquency hearing was said to be in the child's own interest, the juvenile was typically not granted rights during the trial that would be accorded an adult in a similar proceeding. Beginning in 1967, however, the United States Supreme Court expanded the rights due a juvenile in a delinquency proceeding. In the case *In re Gault* (1967), the Court held that a juvenile in a delinquency proceeding is entitled to notice of the charges against him or her, the assistance of counsel, the right to cross-examine witnesses, and the privilege against self-incrimination. But the Court made it clear that it would not require all of the due process safeguards attendant to a criminal trial for a delinquency proceeding by quoting *Kent* v. *United States* (1966, p. 562): "We do not mean . . . to indicate that the hearing must conform with all the requirements of a criminal trial or even of the usual administrative hearing, but we do hold that the hearing must measure up to the essentials of due process and fair treatment." In a later case, the Supreme Court required that proof beyond a reasonable doubt had to be presented at the adjudicatory stage of a delinquency proceeding *(In re Winship,* 1970). However, in 1971, the Court held that a juvenile is not entitled to a trial by jury *(McKeiver* v. *Pennsylvania,* 1971).

In addition to dealing with criminal behavior, juvenile courts are also involved with noncriminal misbehavior. Indeed, one third to one half of all the cases that are heard in juvenile courts involve noncriminal misbehavior (Fox, 1977). This misbehavior usually involves behaviors that would not be illegal for adults. Included in this category are what are called "status offenses": behaviors such as running away from home, being truant from school, and being disobedient to parents (Fox, 1974).

Status offenses, which have been upheld by appellate courts as not being unconstitutionally vague, are generally easier to prosecute than are delinquency offenses. Whereas a prosecution for delinquency requires proof beyond a reasonable doubt, the right to confront witnesses, and the right to counsel, a prosecution for a status offense requires only proof by a preponderance of the evidence. In addition, evidence that would not be admissible in a delinquency proceeding may be admissible in a proceeding for a status offense. Furthermore, many states do not grant juveniles a right to counsel in these proceedings. Because it is often easier to process a juvenile as a status offender than as a juvenile delinquent, many juveniles are processed as in need of supervision rather than as delinquents.

THE MENTAL HEALTH PROFESSIONAL AND THE LAW: CONCLUSION

This brief overview of family law is simply an introduction to some of the legal issues that families face. Some knowledge of the law is important for several reasons. First, mental health professionals are often called to testify regarding family issues, particularly child custody after divorce. Familiarity with the law and the legal process may help the mental health professional in his or her role as an expert witness. Brodsky and Robey (1972) suggest several factors that the mental health professional should consider when acting as an expert witness. According to Brodsky and Robey, the courtroom-oriented witness has some knowledge of the law in the case, enters the case early, keeps thorough records of contact with the client, writes reports clearly, testifies in spoken English rather than professional jargon, advises the attorney during the trial, accepts cross-examination as a normal part of the courtroom process, and charges fees based on his or her fees in private practice.

A second way that knowledge of family law may be useful to a mental health professional is to help the client understand the problems that he or she faces (Bernstein, 1982). Finally, mental health professionals should know something about family law so that they can contribute to the operation of justice, both criticizing the way it is now and making suggestions about how it can be improved.

REFERENCES

American Bar Association, *Model Code of professional responsibility.* Chicago: American Bar Association, 1983.

Autumn love. *Atlanta Constitution,* May 10, 1983, p. 5A.

Bahr, S. J. An evaluation of court mediation for divorce cases with children. *Journal of Family Issues,* 1981, *2,* 34–41.

Baker v. *Nelson,* 291 Minn. 310, 191 N.W. 2d 185 (1971); appeal dismissed, 409 U.S. 810 (1972).

Bates, E. E. Antenuptial agreements. *First annual family law institute.* Athens, Ga.: State Bar of Georgia, 1983.

Bellotti v. *Baird,* 443 U.S. 622 (1979).

Berman, A. M., & Kirsh, D. F. Definitions of joint custody. *Family Advocate,* 1982, *5*(2), 2–4.

Bernstein, B. E. Ignorance of the law is no excuse. In L. L'Abate (Ed.), *The family therapy collections* (Vol. 1). Rockville, Md.: Aspen, 1982.

Besharov, D. J. Representing abused and neglected children: When protecting children means seeking the dismissal of court proceedings. *Journal of Family Law,* 1982, *20,* 217–239.

Bigelow v. *Virginia,* 421 U.S. 809 (1975).

Black's Law Dictionary (5th ed.). St. Paul: West Publishing, 1979.

Boddie v. *Connecticut,* 401 U.S. 371 (1971).

Brodsky, S. L., & Robey, A. On becoming an expert witness: Issues of orientation and effectiveness. *Professional Psychology,* 1973, *3,* 173–176.

Brophy, K. M. A surrogate mother contract to bear a child. *Journal of Family Law,* 1982, *20,* 263–291.

Bruch, C. S. Property rights of de facto spouses including thoughts on the value of homemakers' services. *Family Law Quarterly,* 1976, *10,* 101–136.

Buhrle v. *State,* 627 P.2d 1374 (Wyo. 1981).

Caban v. *Mohammed,* 441 U.S. 380 (1979).

City of Akron v. *Akron Center of Reproductive Health, Inc.,* 103 S. Ct. 2481 (1983).

Clark, H. H., Jr. *The law of domestic relations.* St. Paul: West Publishing, 1968.

Clark, H. H., Jr. *Cases and problems on domestic relations* (3d ed.). St. Paul: West Publishing, 1980.

Cleary, E. W. (Ed.). *McCormick's handbook of the law of evidence.* St. Paul: West Publishing, 1972.

Clingempeel, W. G., & Repucci, N. D. Joint custody after divorce: Major issues and goals for research. *Psychological Bulletin,* 1982, *92,* 102–127.

Connell, M. J. Property division and alimony awards: A survey of statutory limitations on judicial discretion. *Fordham Law Review,* 1981, *50,* 415–449.

Crouch, R. E. *Interstate custody litigation: A guide to use and court interpretation of the Uniform Child Custody Jurisdiction Act.* Washington, D.C.: Bureau of National Affairs, 1981.

Crutchfield, C. F. Nonmarital relationships and their impact on the institution of marriage and the traditional family structure. *Journal of Family Law,* 1981, *19,* 247–261.

Douthwaite, G. *Unmarried couples and the law.* Indianapolis, Ind.: Allen Smith, 1979.

Fox, S. J. Philosophy and the principles of punishment in the juvenile court. *Family Law Quarterly,* 1974, *8,* 373–384.

Fox, S. J. *Juvenile courts in a nutshell* (2d ed.). St. Paul: West Publishing, 1977.

Freed, D. J., & Foster, H. H., Jr. Divorce in the fifty states: An overview. *Family Law Quarterly,* 1981, *14,* 229–284.

Freed, D. J., & Foster, H. H. Family law in the United States: An overview. *Family Law Quarterly,* 1983, *16,* 289–383.

Gardner, R. A. Joint custody is not for everyone. *Family Advocate,* 1982, *5*(2), 7–9; 45–46.

In re Gault, 387 U.S. 1(1967).

Goldstein, J., Freud, A., & Solnit, A. J. *Beyond the best interests of the child.* New York: Free Press, 1973.

Goldstein, J., Freud, A., & Solnit, A. J. *Before the best interests of the child.* New York: Free Press, 1979.

Graham, K. Dipping a hand in dad's pocket. *Atlanta Constitution,* May 17, 1983, p. 3B.

Grisso, T., & Vierling, L. Minors' consent to treatment: A developmental perspective. *Professional Psychology,* 1978, *9,* 412–417.

Guernsey, T. F. The psychotherapist-patient privilege in child placement: A relevancy analysis. *Villanova Law Review,* 1981, *26,* 955–966.

H. L. v. *Matheson,* 456 U.S. 398 (1981).

Handel, W. W., & Sherwyn, B. A. Surrogate parenting. *Trial,* April 1982, pp. 57–60; 77.

Hennessey, E. F. Explosion in family law litigation: Challenges and opportunities for the bar. *Family Law Quarterly,* 1980, *14,* 187–201.

Hetherington, E. M., Cox, M., & Cox, R. Divorced fathers. *Family Coordinator,* 1976, *25,* 417–428.

Hicks, M. W., Hansen, S. L., & Saur, W. G. Family law and family studies: Professors' views. *Family Coordinator,* 1977, *26,* 481–485.

Ibn-Tamas v. *United States,* 407 A.2d 626 (D.C. Cir. 1979).

Irving, H. H. *Divorce mediation: A rational alternative to the adversary system.* New York: Universe Books, 1981.

Jacobstein, J. M., & Mersky, R. M. *Fundamentals of legal research* (2d ed.). Mineola, N.Y.: Foundation Press, 1981.

Katz, S. N. *Child snatching: The legal response to the abduction of children.* Chicago: American Bar Association Press, 1981. (a)

Katz, S. N. Legal remedies for child snatching. *Family Law Quarterly,* 1981, *15,* 103–147. (b)

Kearns, D. L. Divorce mediation: Models, problems, and proposals, Unpublished manuscript, Georgia State University, 1983.

Kent v. United States, 383 U.S. 54 (1966).

Klaff, R. L. The tender years doctrine: A defense. California Law Review, 1982, 70, 335–372.

Krause, H. D. Family law in a nutshell. St. Paul: West Publishing, 1977.

Lassiter v. Department of Social Services of Durham County, 452 U.S. 18 (1981).

Lavori, N. Living together, married or single: Your legal rights. New York: Harper & Row, 1976.

Loving v. Virginia, 388 U.S. 1 (1967).

McCarty v. McCarty, 453 U.S. 210 (1981).

Maccoby, E. E., Kahn, A. J., & Everett, B. A. The role of psychological research in the formation of policies affecting children. American Psychologist, 1983, 38, 80–84.

McKeiver v. Pennsylvania, 403 U.S. 528 (1971).

Marvin v. Marvin, 18 Cal. 3d 660, 134 Cal. Rptr. 815, 557 P. 2d 106 (1976).

Mazur-Hart, S. F., & Berman, J. J. Changing from fault to no-fault divorce: An interrupted time series analysis. Journal of Applied Social Psychology, 1977, 7, 300–312.

Melton, G. B. Toward "personhood" for adolescents: Autonomy and privacy as values in public policy. American Psychologist, 1983, 38, 99–103.

Mills v. Habluetzel, 102 S.Ct. 1549 (1982).

Mnookin, R. H., & Kornhauser, L. Bargaining in the shadow of the law: The case of divorce. Yale Law Journal, 1979, 88, 950–997.

Moore v. City of Albany, 98 N.Y. 396 (1895).

Mothers losing out on child support, Atlanta Constitution, July 8, 1983, p. 6A.

Mulvey, E. P. Family courts: The issue of reasonable goals. Law and Human Behavior, 1982, 6, 49–64.

National Conference of Commissioners on Uniform State Laws. Uniform Marriage and Divorce Act. Family Law Quarterly, 1971, 5, 205–251.

Orr v. Orr, 440 U.S. 268 (1979).

Parham v. J. R., 442 U.S. 584 (1979).

Pearson, J., & Thoennes, N. The benefits outweigh the costs. Family Advocate, 1982, 4, 26; 28–32.

Pickett v. Brown, 103 S.Ct. 2199 (1983).

Planned Parenthood Association of Kansas City, Mo., Inc. v. Ashcroft, 103 S. Ct. 2517 (1983).

Planned Parenthood of Central Missouri v. Danforth, 428 U.S. 52 (1976).

Podolski, A. L. Abolishing baby buying: Limiting independent adoption placement. Family Law Quarterly, 1975, 9, 547–554.

Quilloin v. Walcott, 434 U.S. 246 (1978).

Reynolds v. United States, 98 U.S. 145 (1879).

Roe v. Wade, 410 U.S. 113 (1973).

Santosky v. Kramer, 102 S.Ct. 1388 (1982).

Schechter, L. F. The violent family and the ambivalent state: Developing a coherent policy for state aid to victims of family violence. *Journal of Family Law,* 1981, *20,* 1–42.

Scherer v. *Scherer,* 249 Ga. 635, 292 S. E. 2d 662 (1982).

Schulman, J. Who's looking after the children? *Family Advocate,* 1982, *5*(2), 2–4.

Sepler, H. J. Measuring the effects of no-fault divorce laws across fifty states: Quantifying a zeitgeist. *Family Law Quarterly,* 1981, *15,* 65–102.

Sharp, S. B. Divorce and the third party: Spousal support, private agreements, and the state. *North Carolina Law Review,* 1981, *59,* 819–866.

Shultz, M. M. Contractual ordering of marriage: A new model for state policy. *California Law Review,* 1982, *70,* 204–334.

Silberman, L. J. Professional responsibility problems of divorce mediation. *Family Law Quarterly,* 1982. *16,* 107–145.

Simon, R. J., & Altstein, H. *Transracial adoption.* New York: John Wiley & Sons, 1977.

Simon, R. J., & Altstein, H. *Transracial adoption: A follow-up.* Lexington, Mass.: D. C. Heath, 1981.

Slovenko, R. *Psychiatry and law.* Boston: Little, Brown, 1973.

Stanley v. *Illinois,* 406 U.S. 645 (1972).

State v. *Thomas,* 66 Ohio St. 2d 518, 423 N.E. 2d 137 (1981).

State Bar of Georgia, Legal Status of Women Committee of the Younger Lawyers Section. *Handbook for battered women.* Atlanta: State Bar of Georgia, 1981.

Steinberg, J. L. Toward an interdisciplinary commitment: A divorce lawyer proposes attorney-therapist marriages or, at the least, an affair. *Journal of Marital and Family Therapy,* 1980, *6,* 259–268.

Straus, M., Gelles, R., & Steinmetz, S. *Behind closed doors: Violence in the American family.* New York: Anchor Press/Doubleday, 1980.

Strickman, L. P. Marriage, divorce and the Constitution. *Family Law Quarterly,* 1982, *15,* 259–348.

Surrogate rejects deformed baby. *Atlanta Journal and Constitution,* January 23, 1983. p. 5A.

Thar, A. E. The admissibility of expert testimony on battered wife syndrome: An evidentiary analysis. *Northwestern University Law Review,* 1982, *77,* 348–373.

Uniform Laws Annotated (Vol. 9): *Matrimonial family and health laws.* St. Paul: West Publishing, 1979. (a)

Uniform Laws Annotated (Vol. 9A): *Matrimonial, family and health laws.* St. Paul: West Publishing, 1979. (b)

U.S. Bureau of the Census. *Statistical abstract of the United States: 1984* (104th ed.). Washington, D.C.: U.S. Government Printing Office, 1983.

Walker, L. *The battered woman.* New York: Harper & Row, 1979.

Wallerstein, J. S., & Kelly, J. B. *Surviving the breakup: How children and parents cope with divorce.* New York: Basic Books, 1980.

Weiss, R. S. Issues in the adjudication of custody when parents separate. In G. Levinger & O. C. Moles (Eds.), *Divorce and separation.* New York: Basic Books, 1979.

Weithorn, L. A., & Campbell, S. B. The competency of children and adolescents to make informed treatment decisions. *Child Development,* 1982, *53,* 1589–1598.

Weitzman, L. J. *The marriage contract: Spouses, lovers, and the law.* New York: Free Press, 1981.

Weitzman, L. J. Changing families, changing laws: Ten major trends that have altered the lifestyles of parents and children. *Family Advocate,* 1982, *5,* 2–7; 40–41.

Weitzman, L. J., & Dixon, R. B. Child custody awards: Legal standards and empirical patterns for child custody, support and visitation after divorce. *U.C.D. Law Review,* 1979, *12,* 473–521.

Weitzman, L. J., & Dixon, R. B. The alimony myth: Does no-fault divorce make a difference? *Family Law Quarterly,* 1980, *14,* 141–185.

Weyrauch, W. O. Metamorphoses of marriage. *Family Law Quarterly,* 1980, *13,* 415–440.

In re Winship, 397 U.S. 358 (1970).

Zablocki v. *Redhail,* 434 U.S. 374 (1978).

Section Eleven

Conclusion and Epilogue

Chapter 46

The Status and Future of Family Psychology and Therapy

LUCIANO L'ABATE

There is more to family psychology and therapy than can be found between these covers. It will take more than this *Handbook* to do justice to the field. This is just a start, and like all beginnings, it has been difficult and it is incomplete. It is, however, a step toward establishing the legitimacy of family psychology as a proper field of psychological study and practice.

Many topics could not, for a variety of reasons, be included, especially the whole issue of divorce and its consequences on the personality development of all family members. Death and dying in the family is another topic that deserves attention. In short, more space and time have been devoted to the inception of the family than to its termination. Topics that flow from many chapters were not covered: adolescent suicide, sibling rivalry, eating and psychosomatic disorders, and so forth. The gamut is too broad to be covered in just one or two volumes.

The purpose of this final chapter is to tie some loose ends and prognosticate and pontificate about some of the directions that family psychology and therapy could follow. This chapter attempts to emphasize a topic that has already been discussed by several of this *Handbook*'s contributors, especially Doane (Chapter 30), Johnson and Notarius (Chapter 12), L'Abate (Chapter 40), Sloan & L'Abate (Chapter 13), and Swensen (Chapter 11)—that is, the primacy of emotional experience within the family.

THE PRIMACY OF EMOTIONAL EXPERIENCE

The publication of recent works concerning emotions (cited in the chapters already listed) is part of correcting an earlier emphasis on cognitive processes at the expense of affective ones. This process of correction will, one hopes, produce a more balanced view of behavior. We do not need all of the evidence summarized in these publications to acknowledge the importance of emotions and emotionality in family psychology. After all, is not the family the product of supposedly "irrational" factors such as falling in love and being in love? The family may rightfully be called the very, perhaps the only, context in which emotions matter. Members stay in a family because they "love" one another. They live together because of illogical and primarily subjective feelings of comfort, caring, and nurturance. Of course, families do stay together for instrumental reasons—finances, convenience, and habit. On the other hand, many of these instrumental services could be secured commercially, often at lower cost. The family, then, is where emotions are experienced, practiced, and—under certain conditions—expressed. The family is the arena, the gymnasium so to speak, for emotional experience. The negotiation of distance that goes on continually among family members provides the exercise that is necessary to the growth and feeding of emotionality, with all the attendant dangers and pleasures. It is in the family that most defeats and victories are shared. It is in the family that most losses are mourned. It is in the family that we behave naturally, without the facade of public self-presentation.

It is no accident that most suicides, murders, and extreme forms of psychopathology occur within the family. By the same token, it is no accident that the greatest pleasures occur within the family. It is from this position, then, that most of the groundwork in family psychology needs to be done. As Lewis and Michalson (1983) reiterated, we do not as yet know a great deal about how we acquire emotional labels, how these labels are a function of intellectual and nonintellectual factors, or how these experiences develop, vary, and progress through the individual, marital, and family life cycles. The major task of family psychology has thus only begun. Emotionality is important not only in its own right, for all the reasons stated; it is also the arena where researchers and practitioners can meet. What we know about emotionality in the family has come from the study of pathological families (Doane, Chapter 30, & Johnson & Notarius, Chapter 12, of this *Handbook;* Vaughn & Leff, 1981); but there is much that we do not know about normative, functional emotionality in optimal, well-functioning families. When we can measure emotionality as we measure intellectual and cognitive functions, a great breakthrough will be made. If one prediction can be made about family psychology, it is that the role of emotions will be given much more prominence than it has been accorded in the past.

Arguments in favor of the primacy of emotions on logical, developmental, and experimental grounds can be found in Clark and Fiske (1982), Epstein (1983), Field and Fogel (1982), Pervin (1983), and particularly in Lewis and Michalson (1983). Psychoanalytic perspectives on affect can be found in the work edited by Cantor and Glucksman (1983), among many others. All of these sources, in one way or another, argue for the primacy of emotions. Although it would be impossible to review all the arguments here, an attempt has been made to summarize them to stress the importance of emotions in family life.

First, emotions control the distance between and among intimates as well as acquaintances (L'Abate, Chapter 40 of this *Handbook*). We choose mates, lovers, friends, and colleagues because we like, love, or simply accept them; we reject, shorten, and devalue relationships with persons whom we do not like. We make friends—and enemies— on the basis of purely emotional factors that are corrected and modulated by cognitive considerations; that is, we may dislike the boss, but to survive, we control and inhibit our real feelings. Feelings, therefore, are the very stuff that families are made of. This argument, a logical one, is buttressed by developmental and empirical findings. It is clear that response matching, among other variables, is determined by positive affect as well as by similarity (Maxwell & Pringle, 1981). Affect is an important consideration in Gottman's (1979) work on marital interaction.

Averill (1982) contended that emotions, which are subjective, are passions that happen to us as reactions to threat, loss, hurt, frustration, or rejection. Using anger as a paradigm for the study of emotions in general, however, Averill (like many other investigators in this area) bypassed completely the role of the family context in the origin and maintenance of emotional experience. Even Lewis and Michalson (1983), who have come closest to a consideration of family contexts, limited themselves to the role of the mother and, at best, "socialization," making no further qualifications. This will be the area in which the researcher and the clinician will be able to profit from each other's experience.

Second, the primacy of emotional experience can be argued on developmental grounds. Simply put, the infant reacts according to hedonic pleasure and pain, learning in time to differentiate more specific emotions (L'Abate 1964; Lewis & Michalson, 1983). Third, the importance of emotional primacy can be maintained from the study of seriously dysfunctional families, such as those of schizophrenics (as indicated in Doane, Chapter 30 of this *Handbook,* and as substantiated by the work of Vaughn and his associates). Families of schizophrenic patients tend to express their emotions either not at all or negatively— through criticisms, put-downs, accusations, and recriminations (Vaughn & Leff, 1981; Vaughn, 1982).

Experimentally, of course, the issue of emotional primacy may not be as clear as it may seem from the preceding arguments (Lewis & Michalson, 1983). However, the controversy about whether emotions precede cognitions or vice versa can be settled by considering individual differences (L'Abate, in press). Some individuals and families bypass, short-circuit, and devalue emotional experiences. Other individuals and families use, enjoy, and value emotional experiences. Others rely on little but emotions.

Lewis and Michalson (1983) have provided a most up-to-date review of the field of emotions. Their theorizing about, and empirical efforts to measure, fear, anger, happiness, social affiliation, and competence represent the benchmark for further research on the genesis and maintenance of emotions in the family. Their outstanding contribution deserves more attention than can be given here. Unfortunately, they, like many other researchers in the field of emotions (Averill, 1982; Epstein, 1983; Pervin, 1983), still cling to the view of emotions in a vacuum, despite frequent disclaimers: "Socialization factors probably play a more complex role in the emotional life of children and adults than has previously been acknowledged and . . . they may be responsible for some aspects of psychopathology not normally considered" (Lewis & Michalson, p. 226).

In most references, labeling emotions "positive" and "negative" derives from the failure, among others, to distinguish between emotional states and experiences. Because the relationship between and among states, experiences, and expressions is by no means linear, emotional expression cannot be predicted from emotional states or experiences. To label emotional states and experiences either negative or positive is an unnecessary value judgment and creates a false dichotomy. How can we label feelings of shame negative and feelings of joy positive? Which emotional experiences or states are positive and which are negative? If these two labels must be used, they might be better applied to the external manifestations or the expressions of such experiences (helpful, hurtful, constructive, or destructive labels would seem more useful when considering emotions in a specific context). As Lewis and Michalson recognized:

> A good way to begin the study of the acquisition of affect labels . . . is by studying the language of children's principal caretakers. By determining the context of the affect labels used around children, investigators may be better able to relate that context both to the children's use of affect terms and to their expressions and experiences of those emotions. (p. 208)

The work of Harter (1982) is an attempt to clarify an area that Lewis and Michalson found seriously lacking in the field of emotions: the learning of emotional labels.

From the preceding considerations, the following definition of emotions is submitted: *Emotions are subjective, passionate reactions to internal and external events.* From this definition, the following characteristics of emotions can be derived:

1.   Emotions are subjective experiences that are phenomenological and idiosyncratic; that is, they vary within individuals and from individual to individual. Each individual has a peculiar way of reacting emotionally. As subjective experiences, emotions should be inferred from behavior or described by self-report.

2.   Emotions are reactive to internal and/or external events that elicit reactions that the individual cannot control. These reactions may occur at levels that are not readily visible—physiological, cerebral, cardiovascular, visceral, or muscular. Yet, the individual does react at some level to threat, loss, stress, trauma, insult, or defeat, as well as to happy events, successes, reunions, victories, or personal or family enhancements.

3.   To the extent that emotions are passionate reactions (Averill, 1982), they are uncontrollable; that is, the individual may not seem to react externally, but because one cannot help but react to pleasurable or painful events, an internal reaction (at whatever physiological level) does occur.

4.   To the extent that emotions are idiosyncratic and different from individual to individual, they are extremely variable.

5.   Although we cannot help reacting subjectively to pleasurable or painful events, the external reaction to such events must be sharply distinguished. We need to monitor our external reactions as demanded by laws, civility, courtesy, and other cultural and ethical restraints. What we experience is one thing. How we choose to manifest a subjective experience is another. Even when subjective experiences are apparently the same, the external reactions of two persons will vary. Given a disapproving glance, one person may walk away; the other may take out a gun and shoot!

LEVELS OF BEHAVIOR IN THE FAMILY

A second area that requires conceptual clarification is the level of analysis. The idea of levels of interpretation has been neglected in the psychological literature, even though it has consistently been stressed because of its importance to family behavior (Scarr, 1983).

As noted earlier (by L'Abate, Chapter 40), behavior occurs at different levels of interpretation. Interpretation can be made at descriptive and at explanatory levels. Descriptive levels deal with clearly visible, reproducible behaviors. These behaviors can be filmed, videotaped, photographed, and recorded. Explanatory levels, on the other hand, are inferred and hypothetical in the sense that they are not as visible as behaviors at descriptive levels. Among the descriptive levels, at least two should be distinguished: presentational and phenotypical. The presentational level is the first impression—that is, the face (or front) that one needs to present to be accepted or to prolong a desired or desirable relationship. The phenotypical level appears after the first impression has worn out its welcome, so to speak.

The presentational level may or may not wear off. Its permanency, or durability, depends on how deeply imbedded it is. In some cultures, individuals are thought to make a "good" impression through manners or clothes or speech. Part of the acquired status comes through self-presentation. More specifically, most families try hard to appear "normal" and take great pains to maintain that fiction, even to the extent of producing a psychotic scapegoat (i.e., "We would be a very normal family if it weren't for so and so"). Maintaining a facade of "normality" is an important facet of presentational behavior.

Presentational behavior is related to what social psychologists call social comparison processes. How much do social comparison processes have to do with personality development within the family (Jellison & Arkin, 1977; Schlenker & Leary, 1982)? L'Abate (1976) postulated that personality differentiation occurs on a continuum of likeness that ranges from symbiosis to sameness, similarity, differentness, oppositeness, and autism (alienation). From this continuum was derived the A–R–C model, which links personality development to family functioning and dysfunctioning.

If, indeed, there is a self-presentational level, there must be other levels beneath it (Hughes, 1984; L'Abate, Chapter 40, and Sloan & L'Abate, Chapter 13 of this *Handbook;* Zigler & Glick, 1984)! As mentioned earlier, many families wish to see themselves as "normal" except for the symptom. Many symptomatic families are indeed convinced that they function quite well except for the symptomatic behavior. The need to appear normal reaches extreme intensity in psychosomatic and psychotic families. Among other research, at least two findings from Gottman's (1979) study of marital interaction support the notion of presentational versus phenotypical levels of description. First, Gottman found that subjects treated strangers more positively than they treated spouses. We tend to be nicer to people we do not know than we are to people we know. The best foot is put forward outside rather than inside the home. By the same token, we tend to be "nastier" to our loved ones than we are to people we do not care about. Second, Gottman found that couples were "more negative" at home (where their interactions were tape-recorded) than they were in the laboratory (where they were observed by outsiders). The second finding substantiates the first, supporting the idea that we present a more positive facade outside than inside the family. In short-lived, superficial relationships, we tend to be more positive, perhaps not ourselves. At home we are more ourselves; we can let go and be more negative than when we are outside the family.

Emotions and levels of behavior

Emotions can be viewed according to levels of interpretation. Some emotions—hurt, shame, guilt, fear, despair—may be considered genotypical; that is, they occur at a very private, recondite level of behavior, a level that is not readily accessible to the person experiencing the feelings or to the external observer. Other emotions (such as anger) occur at a phenotypical level, and some emotions (such as smiling) may occur at a presentational level. Some emotions are faked to reinforce a desired facade. The idea of levels in emotional experience is supported by Berkowitz's (1983) review of the evidence for predispositions to aggression, a position that is consistent with a layered view of emotions.

Aggression and violence

Psychologists have devoted much attention to aggression (Averill, 1982; Berkowitz, 1983; Buss, 1961). Yet, studying aggression in a vacuum has produced a separate literature on violence and abuse in the family (Thaxton, Chapter 28, and Berger, Chapter 29 of this *Handbook*), almost without roots leading to aggression. One can read both categories side by side and find that writers on aggression fail to refer to "real" violence, or what happens within a family. Those who write about family violence fail to cite the work of psychologists who are studying aggression. As a result, the typical psychological study of aggression—in a vacuum—is artificial and futile. Considerable energy is expended to find the causes of aggression, but rarely are the causes related to family modeling (except by Patterson, chap. 44 of this *Handbook*, and in recent work by Wahler & Fox, 1982, and Reid, Patterson & Loeber, 1982). No wonder aggression is seen as a mysterious happening, one without correlates or antecedents! Aggression is the external manifestation of anger, which may or may not result from hurt (Sloan & L'Abate, Chapter 13 of this *Handbook*).

CREATION AND TESTING OF MODELS

Among the many empirical tasks that face researchers in family psychology and therapy are the creation and testing of models. As reviewed throughout this book and elsewhere (L'Abate, in press), models function as *(a)* visual or verbal condensations and representations of more complex and abstract behaviors; *(b)* classifications of seemingly unclassifiable behaviors (diagnostic function); *(c)* testable reductions of seemingly untestable properties; and *(d)* links between theory and practice. In addition, models in family psychology should link individual with family functioning and dysfunctioning.

In addition to the comments of several of this *Handbook's* contributors (Miller & Sobelman, Chapter 1; Kaye, Chapter 2; Warburton & Alexander, Chapter 43) about the role of models in family theory and therapy, Siomopoulos (1983), in reviewing the role of models in anthropology, linguistics, archeology, and semiotics, considered models the outcome of *structuralism,* which is a school of thought concerned with the organization rather than the origin of systems. Siomopoulos attributed to Piaget three conceptions that are necessary for an interdisciplinary epistemology: wholeness, transformation, and self-regulation.

Discussing the role of models in family interaction and psychopathology, Helmersen (1983) concluded that we need models that "can account for the relationship between intrafamily phenomena and their social context" (p. 83). Helmersen's review is crucial as a summary of past work (see Doane, Chapter 30; Sanua, Chapter 27 of this *Handbook*). As a jumping-off point for future work, the review is recommended to both students and researchers.

The creation of such models will lead to testing *(a)* their validity and reliability, *(b)* their comparative influences in how well they encompass and account for the observable variables, *(c)* how they agree with other, established empirical observations (L'Abate & Wagner, Chapter 33 of this *Handbook*), and *(d)* how they can then be extended to therapy. For instance, exercises that families are to practice at home have been derived from such models. The models are tested diagnostically through pencil and paper tests (Chapter 33) and interventionally through structured enrichment (Chapter 39) of this *Handbook*), or with less structure through homework exercises in family therapy (L'Abate, in press).

Among the models that have been developed (see Tables 1 and 2), a model of competence in interpersonal relations is especially noteworthy. The E–R–A–Aw–C model has allowed us to consider emotionality the primary component that governs interpersonal distance among intimates (L'Abate, in press; L'Abate & Frey, 1981; L'Abate, Frey, & Wagner, 1982). The E–R–A–Aw–C model was derived from considering the components that are most important and necessary (albeit insufficient!) to describe, understand, and function in intimate relationships. Emotionality (E) covers the aspects of behavior that we call emotions, feelings, affect, or moods. Rationality (R) covers the aspects of behavior that fall under the rubric of cognitive, intellectual, and logical styles. E deals chiefly with distance (i.e., intimacy among family members);

Table 1

Possible models of personality functioning-dysfunctioning in the family: summary

A. Structural models
    1. Intimate relationships: A–R–C.*
       a. Apathy: atrophy, abuse.
       b. Reactivity: repetitiousness, rebuttals.
       c. Conductivity: creativity, change.
    2. Interpersonal competence.
       a. E–R–A–Aw–C.
          (1) Emotionality: distance/intimacy.
          (2) Rationality: self-concept, problem solving.
          (3) Activity: roles and responsibilities.
          (4) Awareness: reflection, change.
          (5) Context: spatial, temporal.
       b. Functions of the model.
          (1) Classification of theoretical and therapeutic orientations (see Table 3).
          (2) Classification of interpersonal behaviors.
          (3) Process of negotiation.
          (4) Nature of love.
    2. Priorities.†
       a. Intra- versus extrafamilial.
       b. Personal-interpersonal: A–B–C.
          (1) Attachments.‡
          (2) Beliefs and values.
          (3) Commitments.
       c. Resources exchanged.§
          (1) Having.
          (2) Doing.
          (3) Being.
    4. Power sharing and decision making.
       a. Authority-responsibility.
       b. Orchestration-instrumentation.
       c. Negotiation potential = Ills $\times$ Skills $\times$ Wills.
          (1) Ills = style (Model 1).
          (2) Skills = competencies (Model 2).
          (3) Wills = priorities (Model 3).
    5. Control: Who influences whom?
       a. Rules and regulations (implicit-explicit).
       b. Freedom and restraints.
       c. Disciplinary practices.
B. Historical models.
    1. Evolutionary-genetic.
    2. Generational.
    3. Developmental.
C. Cultural models.
    1. Anthropology.
    2. Sociology.
    3. Economics.

---

* L'Abate, L., "Styles in Intimate Relationships: The A–R–C Model," *Personnel and Guidance Journal* 61 (1983), pp. 277–283.
† L'Abate, L., *Understanding and Helping the Individual in the Family* (New York: Grune & Stratton, 1976).
‡ L'Abate, L., Chapter 40 of this *Handbook*.
§ L'Abate, L., Sloan, S., Wagner, V., and Malone, K., "The Differentiation of Resources," *Family Therapy* 7 (1980), pp. 237–246.

Table 2

Theoretical levels of interpretation and understanding and theory testing

	Theory			Theory Testing	
	Levels of analysis				Interventional
Interpretation	Understanding	Models	Diagnostic	Structured	Less structured
Descriptive: Overt-manifest; visible-observable.	Self-presentational: Facade, first impression. Phenotypical: Close, prolonged relationships; actual functioning under stress.	1. Styles (A–R–C). 4. Power sharing and decision making. 5. Control.	Paper and pencil tests	Enrichment programs (general, and specifically derived from models).	Systematic Homework Assignments (SHWAs) derived from models to be used in marital and family therapy.*
Explanatory: Covert, latent, invisible-unobservable.	Phenotypical: Attributional, inferential, hypothetical. Historical-developmental. Generational. Genetic.	2. Interpersonal competencies (E–R–A–Aw–C). 3. Priorities.			

* L'Abate (1985).

R modulates and controls how distance (i.e., intimacy) is expressed outwardly through actions (A), which are verbal and nonverbal behaviors, roles, habits, and interpersonal relationships. Aw stands for awareness, defined as the reflection on, and the consideration of, past behavior and the correction of it. Thus, Aw has a corrective feedback function that is based on our ability to reflect on the consequences and implications of our actions (A). C stands for context, the physical and interpersonal setting that gives the meaning and specificity that allow us to understand behavior. Most of our meaningful and important activities occur within a family context (Table 3).

The E–R–A–Aw–C model allows us to differentiate among the emotional states that belong specifically to E: emotional experiences, which encompass emotional states (E) plus the ability to label them appropriately or at least linguistically (R), and emotional expression, which implies an external manifestation (i.e., A). Equating emotionality and structure is not as far-fetched as it may at first appear. Siomopoulos (1983) viewed affect as structure. However, it should be qualified that this structure is relevant specifically to interpersonal situations, even though the work of Bower (1981) suggests that emotionality is important to learning and perhaps to nonpersonal situations.

The E–R–A–Aw–C model functions in various ways (see Table 3), as:

1. An eclectic classification of various therapeutic movements (Hansen & L'Abate, 1982): According to this scheme, emphasis on E relates to humanism (phenomenology, existentialism, and experientialism); emphasis on R relates to psychodynamic-psychoanalytic schools (rational-emotive, reality, and transactional analysis); emphasis on A relates to behaviorism (radical, social learning, and role theories); emphasis on Aw relates to transcendental meditation, Gestalt, and social

Table 3

The process and components of interpersonal competence

	Language systems		
General	*Information*	*Eclectic (L'Abate)*	*Major theoretical emphases*
Structure	Input	Emotionality	Humanism
Function (process)	Throughput	Rationality	Psychodynamic-cognitive
Outcome	Output	Activity	Behaviorism
Change mechanism	Feedback	Awareness	Gestalt
Context	Context	Context	Family therapies

perspectivism; and emphasis on C relates to family therapy approaches (systemic, strategic, structural).

2.   A diagnostic classification of primary modes of intimate relating that takes us away from the recent debate (Lewis & Michalson, 1983) about the primacy of E over R or the primacy of R over E: As discussed in greater detail elsewhere (Epstein, 1983; L'Abate, in press; Pervin, 1983), some individuals and families (Vaughn & Leff, 1981; Vaughn et al., 1982) completely short-circuit E, thus magnifying either R (obsessively) or A (impulsively). Some individuals and families revel in E and place very little value on R, and A-oriented families put either R or E secondary to their style of living.

3.   A model of negotiation based on the principle that in most family issues, emotions (E) need to be expressed nonjudgmentally and responsibly (in "I" statements) before the family can go on to a more rational (R) discussion of pros and cons in the available courses of action (A): A reasonable amount of time is necessary for the persons in the particular context (C) to evaluate the course of action that has been adopted and to acknowledge their feelings about it.

4.   A definition of love, made up of all five components (L'Abate, 1975): *(a)* seeing the good, which involves R; *(b)* caring, which implies physical presence and nurturance (A); *(c)* intimacy, defined as the sharing of hurt (E); *(d)* awareness (Aw) of consistencies and contradictions in feelings and expressions of love; *(e)* according to the varying spatial and temporal contexts (C) of the family life cycle.

In addition to the A–R–C and the E–R–A–Aw–C models (see Table 1), three other models have been developed (L'Abate, 1985). The model of family priorities has already been mentioned in the *Handbook* (L'Abate & Wagner, Chapter 33). The model of power and negotiation in families *(a)* defines power as authority (who makes the decisions) and responsibility (who carries them out); *(b)* categorizes decisions as orchestrational (big decisions, such as jobs and moves) or instrumental (decisions about daily routines, the mundane); and *(c)* defines negotiation potential as Ills × Skills × Wills (Ills = the functionality of the system [A–R–C]; Skills = the competence of the system [E–R–A–Aw–C]; and Wills = the motivation of the system [priorities]. The content—*what* is negotiated—is defined by a subsidiary model—doing, having, and being—which has been derived from the experimental work of Foá and Foá (1974) (Table 1).

RAPPROCHEMENTS RATHER THAN RUPTURES

Many basic rapprochements need to be considered by family psychologists for the survival and progress of their field: *(a)* between family psychology and the rest of psychology, *(b)* between family psychologists and family sociologists, *(c)* between academician-researchers and clinicians, and *(d)* between therapists and preventers. These rapprochements should be conceptual as well as professional.

Family psychology and psychology

A number, if not all, of the chapters in the *Handbook* have been connected to the general field of psychology, especially developmental, social, and personality psychology. They are, perhaps in that order, the fields of specialization that are most directly relevant to family psychology and therapy.

Family psychologists and family sociologists

Most of us work within a rather parochial circle of similarly inclined colleagues and reference sources, reading within our discipline and within our fields of interest. Very few of us have a chance to read and become acquainted with contributors from other disciplines. Most of us get along perfectly well without interdisciplinary relationships. On the borderlines between disciplines, however, it is important to know what is going on if we are to grow professionally.

Family psychologists cannot afford not to relate to family sociologists. First, the subject matter—the family—overlaps. The overlap exists whether the family is composed of different personalities or subsystems (as the psychologist views it) or is an overall system (as the sociologist—who was there long before the psychologist discovered the family—views it). Second, the overlap in subject matter does not mean an overlap in methods. In fact, it may be said that different viewpoints produce different ways of observing and measuring (Scarr, 1983): that is, psychologists study individuals within the family; sociologists supposedly study the family qua family, as a unit. The differences in viewpoints and methodology make it crucial to compare results. A certain degree of convergence and correspondence should exist between the two approaches. One approach, in a way, validates the other. In this respect, each approach is dependent on the other. Third, any psychological theory of individual and family functioning and dysfunctioning will need to be isomorphic with a sociological theory of the family. The two cannot go their separate ways.

Family psychologists have a great deal to learn, theoretically and methodologically, from family sociologists; the sooner this learning occurs, the better off we—all of us—will be. Family psychologists will need to become acquainted with, and master, various models of family functioning and dysfunctioning that have been developed by family sociologists, such as the circumplex model developed by Olson and his associates (referred to in several chapters) and the model developed by McCubbin and his associates. This knowledge also implies the mastery of more complex statistical analyses, such as multivariate, path, and qualitative (analyses that, as indicated in Chapter 31, have not been well known to psychologists).

The insularity and parochialism of psychologists are inappropriate for family psychologists. To survive and prosper, family psychologists will need to rub elbows with, become friends with, and establish intimate working relations with family sociologists. Psychologically related models, such as the ones reviewed in the *Handbook,* will need to be developed so that they can be compared and contrasted with sociological models of family functioning and dysfunctioning.

"Scientists" and practitioners

The split between academic and clinical psychologists has been the overt or covert source of many struggles as psychology has yielded to the differentiation that is inevitable in a complex system. Such a split will not, one hopes, be repeated in family psychology. Splits along lines of specialization are preferable to a split between academicians and practitioners. Ideally, family psychology will stay united, its researchers, teachers, and practitioners talking and meeting with one another continually.

Clinical family psychologist or family therapist?   Some issues in the training of family psychologists and therapists have been reviewed in Chapter 41. What is relevant here is the distinction between a clinical family psychologist and a family therapist. The title "clinical family psychologist" will be supported as a specific title that is preferable to the more generic title "family therapist." Family therapist may apply to any professional who specializes in family therapy, regardless of disciplinary specialization; hopefully, a clinical family psychologist would have other skills in addition to those of a family therapist.

Family therapy is now so fashionable that thousands of mental health specialists—psychiatrists, clinical psychologists, social workers—have joined the bandwagon. In addition to the traditional professions, a proliferation of other professionals such as pastoral counselors, applied family sociologists, and counselors have joined in. Family therapy, then, is a ubiquitous profession, not specific to a particular discipline. In fact, it can be argued that psychology is the latecomer; that is, very few universities offer an academic or a clinical specialization in family psychology or therapy.

What then is the specific contribution that psychology, as a science and a profession, can make to family therapy? What distinguishes psychologists from other professionals who work in this growing field? Clearly, psychologists cannot claim seniority: The formal structure of our professional association does not even recognize family therapy. The American Psychological Association has only recently (1984) accepted a Division of Family Psychology. Psychologists cannot claim better clinical preparation: Even though most psychologists render professional services to couples and families (VandenBos & Stapp, 1983), most of them received no formal training in family therapy (which raises an ethical question about clinical psychologists practicing without formal training). Psychologists, then, can claim neither seniority nor better professional preparation than other professionals in family therapy. The single area in which we can claim a specific contribution is preparation in research. In this area, psychologists can indeed perform unique services to family therapy.

Therapists and preventers

Most therapists are not interested in prevention (L'Abate, 1981). The preventer seems to be a different kind of individual, one who (for reasons not yet understood) likes to work with more functional relationships. Eventually, we may discover that the value systems of therapists and preventers differ also. Therapists follow a private practice model: the most services for the few who are in need. Preventers follow a public health model: the most services for the greatest number. These two value systems can and should be reconciled theoretically, humanly, and organizationally. How this reconciliation will come about remains to be seen. If such reconciliation is not possible, perhaps therapy and prevention will have to be considered two tracks of the same service delivery system.

As Chapter 39 made clear, prevention (already an important part of intervention) is becoming increasingly important. Unfortunately, many therapists, both individual- and family-oriented, do not see that prevention and preventive activities are as important as crisis intervention; they view therapy as an aspect of prevention. That view, however, is not what is meant here by prevention—a view of service delivery that is completely different from the private practice view. Because of this separation, psychologists may need to train persons who see themselves as preventers rather than therapists (Ganahl, Ferguson, & L'Abate, Chapter 41 of this *Handbook*).

Two aspects of prevention are worthy of note: the presumptuous and presumptive connotations of the term *prevention*. As Warren (1983) concluded in his review of Bond and Joffe (1982), "Although the idea of prevention may strike many as presumptuous, in the long run it remains the only logical and cost-effective course of action for a society that is truly concerned with its own societal problems" (p. 794).

In the sense that it may promise more than it can deliver, prevention may indeed be presumptuous. We cannot know that we have done something preventive until we can explore—many years later—whether the desired outcome has been achieved. The term *prevention* is, of course, presumptive in the sense that we presume, or expect, that whatever we are doing will eventually produce a positive outcome—months, even years, later. Prevention is really a promissory note, not an established outcome. It is indeed grounded in faith rather than in fact. The hope for prevention is apparently greater than the facts of "cure"; that is, it may often be too late to cure, or to fix what is broken. There is nothing wrong with proceeding on faith as long as it does not become a cult!

In their survey of service providers in psychology, VandenBos and Stapp (1983, p. 1336) found that the three major problems were anxiety, depression, and interpersonal, marital, or family problems, followed by problems concerning work, health or psychosomatic illness, substance abuse, mental retardation, and schizophrenia and other psychoses. Can we say that any one of these problems does not relate to the family?

Furthermore, the scope of the task is so immense that individually oriented interventions (e.g., psychotherapy) are a drop in the bucket. Not only will family-oriented approaches be needed but family preventive approaches (Guerney et al., Chapter 39 of this *Handbook*) will be needed sorely.

CONCLUSION

The future of family psychology may not be assured by institutional recognition and status, but it will be assured by the consistency of its findings and the consequence of its theoretical and practical trends. The worst that may happen to this field is that clinicians and therapists may preempt academicians and researchers from the recognition they deserve. To the extent that scholars and practitioners work together, family psychology will be assured a firm place in psychology. To the extent that internecine and petty rivalries are permitted to split family psychology, progress will be slowed—but not derailed.

As Scarr (1983) concluded in her presidential address to Division 7 (developmental psychology):

> There is no need to choose a single lens for psychology when we can enjoy a kaleidoscope of perspectives. In our intellectual population we

should construct the richest account we can of human behavior, which will include variables from several levels of analysis and alternative theoretical accounts. Because we *do* construct science and reality, we might as well give it breadth, depth, and some excitement. (p. 34)

Family psychology adds another lens to psychology. Family therapy adds another approach to the treatment and prevention of psychopathology.

REFERENCES

Averill, J. R. *Anger and aggression: An essay on emotion.* New York: Springer-Verlag, 1982.

Berkowitz, L. Aversely stimulated aggression: Some parallels and differences in research with animals and humans. *American Psychologist,* 1983, *38,* 1135–1144.

Bond, L. A., & Joffe, J. M. (Eds.). *Facilitating infant and early childhood development: Primary prevention of psychopathology series.* Hanover, N.H.: University Press of New England, 1982.

Bower, K. S. Mood and memory. *American Psychologist,* 1981, *36,* 129–148.

Buss, A. H. *The psychology of aggression.* New York: John Wiley & Sons, 1961.

Cantor, M. B., & Glucksman, M. L. (Eds.). *Affect: Psychoanalytic theory and practice.* New York: John Wiley & Sons, 1983.

Clark, M. S., & Fiske, S. T. (Eds.). *Affect and cognition: The seventeenth annual Carnegie symposium on Recognition.* Hillsdale, N.J.: Lawrence Erlbaum Associates, 1982.

Epstein, S. A research paradigm for the study of personality and emotion. In M. M. Page (Ed.), *Personality—current theory and research: 1982 Nebraska Symposium on Motivation.* Lincoln: University of Nebraska Press, 1983. Pp. 91–154.

Field, T., & Fogel, A. (Eds.). *Emotion and early interaction.* Hillsdale, N.J.: Lawrence Erlbaum Associates, 1982.

Foá, U., & Foá, E. *Societal structure of the mind.* Springfield, Ill.: Charles C Thomas, 1974.

Gottman, J. M. *Marital interaction.* New York: Academic Press, 1979.

Hansen, J. C., & L'Abate, L. *Approaches to family therapy.* New York: Macmillan, 1982.

Harter, S. A cognitive-developmental approach to children's understanding of affect and trait labels. In F. C. Serafica (Ed.), *Social-cognitive development in context.* New York: Guilford Press, 1982. Pp. 27–61.

Helmersen, P. *Family interaction and communication in psychopathology: An evaluation in recent perspectives.* New York: Academic Press, 1983.

Hughes, M. C. Recurrent abdominal pain and childhood depression: Clinical observations of 23 children and their families. *American Journal of Orthopsychiatry,* 1984, *54,* 146–155.

Jellison, J., & Arkin, R. Social comparison of abilities: A self-presentational approach to decision making in groups. In J. M. Suls & R. L. Miller (Eds.), *Social comparison pro-*

cesses: Theoretical and empirical perspectives. New York: Halsted Press, 1977. Pp. 235–237.

L'Abate, L. *Principles of clinical psychology.* New York: Grune & Stratton, 1964.

L'Abate, L. A positive approach to marital and familial intervention. In L. R. Wolberg & M. L. Aronson (Eds.), *Group therapy 1975: An overview.* New York: Stratton Intercontinental, 1975. Pp. 63–75.

L'Abate, L. *Understanding and helping the individual in the family.* New York: Grune & Stratton, 1976.

L'Abate, L. Skill training programs for couples and families. In A. S. Gurman & D. P. Kniskern (Eds.), *Handbook of family therapy.* New York: Brunner/Mazel, 1981. Pp. 631–661.

L'Abate, L. Styles in intimate relationships: The A–R–C model. *Personnel and Guidance Journal,* 1983, *61,* 277–283.

L'Abate, L. *Systematic family therapy.* New York: Brunner/Mazel, 1985.

L'Abate, L., & Frey, J., III. The E–R–A model: The role of feelings in family therapy reconsidered: Implications for a classification of theories of family therapy. *Journal of Marital and Family Therapy,* 1981, *7,* 143–150.

L'Abate, L., Frey, J., III, & Wagner, V. Toward a classification of family therapy theories: Further elaborations and implications of the E–R–A–Aw–C model. *Family Therapy,* 1982, *9,* 251–262.

L'Abate, L., Sloan, S., Wagner, V., & Malone, K. The differentiation of resources. *Family Therapy,* 1980, *7,* 237–246.

Lewis, I., & Michalson, L. *Children's emotions and moods: Developmental theory and measurement.* New York: Plenum Press, 1983.

Maxwell, G. M., & Pringle, J. K. Towards the measurement of postural congruence in social interaction. *New Zealand Psychologist,* 1981, *10,* 45–54.

Pervin, L. A. The stasis and flow of behavior: Toward a theory of goals. In M. M. Page (Ed.), *Personality—current theory and research: 1982 Nebraska Symposium on Motivation.* Lincoln: University of Nebraska Press, 1983. Pp. 1–53.

Reid, J. B., Patterson, G. R., & Loeber, R. The abused child: Victim, instigator, or innocent bystander? In D. J. Bernstein (Ed.), *Nebraska Symposium on Motivation: 1981.* Lincoln: University of Nebraska Press, 1982. Pp. 47–68.

Scarr, S. The danger of having pet variables. *APA Newsletter* (Div. 7), Spring 1983, pp. 24–34.

Schlenker, B. R., & Leary, M. R. Social anxiety and self-presentation: A conceptualization and model. *Psychological Bulletin,* 1982, *92,* 641–669.

Siomopoulos, U. *The structure of psychopathological experience.* New York: Brunner/Mazel, 1983.

VandenBos, G. R., & Stapp, J. Service providers in psychology: Results of the 1982 APA human resources survey. *American Psychologist,* 1983, *38,* 1330–1352.

Vaughn, C. E., & Leff, J. P. Patterns of emotional response in relatives of schizophrenic patients. *Schizophrenia Bulletin,* 1981, *7,* 43–44.

Vaughn, C. E., Family factors in schizophrenic relapse: A replication. *Schizophrenia Bulletin,* 1982, *8,* 425–426.

Wahler, R. G., & Fox, J. J. Response structure in deviant child-parent relationships: Implications for family therapy. In D. J. Bernstein (Ed.), *Nebraska Symposium on Motivation: 1981.* Lincoln: University of Nebraska Press, 1982. Pp. 1–46.

Warren, S. F. From intervention to prevention: A revolution in child psychology? *Contemporary Psychology,* 1983, *28,* 792–794.

Zigler, E., & Glick, M. Paranoid schizophrenia: An unorthodox view. *American Journal of Orthopsychiatry,* 1984, *54,* 43–70.

Selected Bibliography

Lyn Thaxton

Akins, F. R., Akins, D. L., & Mace, G. S. *Parent-child separation: Psychosocial effects on development: An abstracted bibliography.* New York: Plenum Press, 1981. Covers articles and books, primarily ones published since 1960, on the consequences of parental separation and deprivation on the developing child and adolescent. Main topics include maternal or paternal absence due to desertion, military duty, imprisonment, paternal institutionalization, and divorce. Author and subject indexes.

Beck, D. R. *Marriage and the family under challenge: An outline of issues, trends, and alternatives* (2d ed.). New York: Family Service Association of America, 1976. Annotated bibliography by Emily Bradshaw (pp. 47–96), focusing on scholarly journal literature.

Child abuse and neglect research: Projects and publications. Springfield, Va.: National Technical Information Service, May 1976–present. Identifies and describes current research projects and publications selected from books, journals, and other "readily accessible" sources. Publications are indexed by author and subject.

Curtis, J., & Green, J. *Premarital, marital and family therapy: An annotated bibliography.* (Counseling & Psychotherapy Monograph Series No. 3.) Jonesboro, Tenn.: Pilgrimage Press, 1980. Compiled from classified annotated bibliographies of books of interest to family specialists, compiled annually, 1970–1979, for the Southeastern Council on Family Relations. Includes many popular and religious titles as well as scholarly works.

Davis, L. G. *The black family in the United States: A selected bibliography of annotated books, articles, and dissertations on black families in America.* Westport, Conn.: Greenwood Press, 1978. Over 300 entries are grouped by type (books, articles, etc.) and subdivided by subject (economic status, education, sex, etc.). Author and selective keyword subject indexes.

Dunmore, C. J. *Black children and their families: A bibliography.* Palo Alto, Calif.: R & E Research Associates, 1976. Lists published materials on the black American child under the subjects of adoption, education, health, family life, ghetto life, mental health, and sex and family planning. Bibliographies and reference works listed separately.

Enriching relationships: A guide to marriage and family enrichment literature. Salisbury, N.C.: Sell, 1980. Divided into sections on premarital, marital, and family enrichment literature. Salisbury, N.C.: Sell, 1980. Divided into sections on premarital, marital, and family enrichment. Lists articles, books, theses, dissertations, and Educational Resources Information Center (ERIC) documents.

Garoogian, A. *Child care issues for parents and society: A guide to information sources.* Detroit: Gale Research, 1977. Annotated listing of books, pamphlets, periodicals, audiovisual materials, organizations, and free and inexpensive materials under such topics as child development, exceptional child, and health. Indexes by author, title, subject, and organization/source of information.

Glick, I. D. *Family therapy and research: An annotated bibliography of articles, books, videotapes, and films published 1950–1979* (2d ed.). New York: Grune & Stratton, 1982. Emphasizes material relevant to psychiatry, psychology, and social work under the headings of family therapy, family therapy outcome, family research, family description, types of families, and surveys of the literature. Author index.

Hill-Scott, K. *The relationship between child care and family functioning: An annotated bibliography* (Public Administration Series: Bibliography No. P 343). Monticello, Ill.: Vance, 1979. This bibliography, covering the period 1972 through 1977, is divided into two sections. The first is a section of major works, with annotations, divided into six groups: family structure and function; maternal employment and its effects; the parent as a child-care consumer; the effects of child care on the mother-child dyad; parent involvement in child care; and child care and public policy issues. The second section is an exhaustive unannotated listing, arranged alphabetically by author.

Inventory of marriage and family literature. Beverly Hills, Calif.: Sage Publications, 1900/1964–present. Previously titled *International bibliography of research in marriage and the family.* Computer-produced bibliography of books and articles, arranged by topics such as organizations and services to families; family relationships and dynamics; and families with special problems. Author and keyword title indexes.

Kalisch, B. J. *Child abuse and neglect: An annotated bibliography.* Philadelphia: J. B. Lippincott, 1978. Comprehensive interdisciplinary listing of books, chapters, articles, documents, reports of special investigative committees, conference proceedings, doctoral dissertations, and pamphlets. Arranged by topics, including prediction, detection and prevention, causative factors, manifestations, treatment, sexual abuse, and legal issues. Author and selective keyword subject indexes.

Lystad, M. *Violence at home: An annotated bibliography.* Rockville, Md.: National Institute of Mental Health, 1974. A selective annotated bibliography, including books, articles, essays, and dissertations, on such subjects as theories of violence and aggression, violence of parent to child, and family violence and socialization.

Marion, R. L., & McCaslin, T. L. *Family support counseling for parents of exceptional children: An annotated and categorical bibliography.* Austin, Tex.: National Educational Laboratory Publishers, 1977. Lists books and articles under a variety of different subjects, including specific handicaps such as mental retardation and learning disabilities, death and dying, sex education, and resources for parents. Many articles cover topics, such as parental attitudes, which are related to, but not specifically about, counseling.

McKenney, M. *Divorce: A selected annotated bibliography.* Metuchen, N. J.: Scarecrow Press, 1975. Classed arrangement, with subject and author indexes. Most entries with brief annotations. Includes such topics as children of divorce and psychological and social aspects of divorce.

Milden, J. W. *The family in past time: A guide to the literature.* New York: Garland, 1977. Annotated bibliography of English-language materials published prior to the end of 1975, including books, articles, unpublished papers, and theses. Classified arrangement with author index. Sections on methodology and theory; family in European history, American history, and non-Western history; and family history projects.

Peck, T. P. *The troubled family: Sources of information.* Jefferson, N.C.: McFarland, 1982. This guide is divided into five parts: (1) a directory of government organizations concerned with families; (2) a directory of private organizations; (3) a directory of other relevant organizations, primarily research-related; (4) a bibliography of printed materials, including journal articles, books, documents, specialized materials, and doctoral dissertations, primarily published between 1976 and summer 1981; and (5) additional information sources. The bibliography is divided into such topics as battered spouses, finances, and runaways and is selectively annotated. Indexes by name, subject, and organization.

Ralston, E. J. *Family structures of drug abusers* (Public Administration Series: Bibliography No. P 557). Monticello, Ill.: Vance, 1980. Intended as a "comprehensive presentation of the relevant literature available on the family structures and dynamics of the drug abuser and their families," this bibliography, with annotations, is arranged alphabetically by author and covers major journal articles.

Schlesinger, B. *The multi-problem family: A review and annotated bibliography.* (3d ed.). Toronto: University of Toronto Press, 1970. Annotated bibliography, arranged by country with author index, preceded by review articles on the concept of the multiproblem family, community treatment programs, and the multiproblem family in Canada.

Schlesinger, B. *The one-parent family: Perspectives and annotated bibliography* (4th ed., rev.). Toronto: University of Toronto Press, 1978. References are grouped under such headings as desertion and separation, divorce, widowhood, the unmarried parent, and remarriage. The introductory essays include methodological considerations for research in the area.

Schulman, J. B., & Prall, R. C. *Normal child development: An annotated bibliography of articles and books published 1950–1969.* New York: Grune & Stratton, 1971. Includes listing of materials that focus on research-determined norms of behavior and attitudes characteristic of children between 3 and 18. Arranged under headings such as adjustment, family relationships, and cognitive. Author index.

Sell, K. D. *Divorce in the United States, Canada, and Great Britain: A guide to information sources.* Detroit: Gale Research, 1978. Annotated bibliography of a wide variety of both published and unpublished material on divorce, including reference material, periodical articles, dissertations, government documents, news media, audiovisual materials, and literature. Indexes by name, title, and subject.

Shack, J. R. *An annotated and indexed bibliography of behavior management with children.* Chicago: Loyola University, 1973. Author listing of books, articles, and dissertations, compiled from *Psychological Abstracts* (through the November 1972 issue). Subject index and cross-index of primary and secondary authors.

University Research Corporation. *Family counseling: An annotated bibliography.* Cambridge, Mass.: Oelgeschlager, Gunn, & Hain, 1981. Coverage is primarily from the 1970s through the present. Sections include models, theories, and concepts of family counseling; applications and the practice of family counseling; research studies; programs, service delivery, training and supervision; and prevention and education. Keyword subject and title indexes.

Wakefield Washington Associates. *Family research: A source book, analysis, and guide to federal funding.* Westport, Conn.: Greenwood Press, 1979. A two-volume listing, with abstracts, of government-sponsored research projects sponsored by such agencies as the Department of Health, Education and Welfare, Department of Housing and Urban Development, and Department of Labor. Indexes by investigators, performing organizations, and subjects.

Williams, T. M. *Infant care: Abstracts of the literature.* Washington, D.C.: Consortium on Early Childbearing and Childrearing, Child Welfare League of America, 1972; Supplement, 1974. Lengthy abstracts of both published and unpublished materials, arranged under the topics infant development; the infant-adult relationship; childrearing patterns; infant education, intervention, and day care; and theoretical and methodological issues. Author index.

Young, M. E. *Family counseling: A bibliography with abstracts: Search period covered, 1964–July 1975.* Springfield, Va.: National Technical Information Service, 1975. Covers federally sponsored research projects. Includes projects related to the involvement of family members in counseling individuals. Also includes reports on counselor training and program effectiveness. Emphasis is on disadvantaged and handicapped families.

Dissertations

American doctoral dissertations. Ann Arbor, Mich.: University Microfilms, 1965/1966–present. A listing of all doctoral dissertations accepted by American and Canadian universities.

Comprehensive dissertation index, 1861–1972. Ann Arbor, Mich.: University Microfilms, 1973. Serves as an author and keyword title index to *American doctoral dissertations* and *Dissertation Abstracts International.* Five-year supplement, 1973–1977; annual supplements, 1978 to date.

Dissertation Abstracts International. Ann Arbor, Mich.: University Microfilms, 1938–present. A compilation of abstracts of dissertations submitted to University Microfilms by a varying number of cooperating universities. Beginning with Volume 27, published in two sections: A (humanities and social sciences); B (science and engineering). Some European dissertations included. Keyword title and author indexes.

Handbooks, encyclopedias, and reviews

Advances in family intervention, assessment and theory. Greenwich, Conn.: JAI Press, 1980–present. Articles in the first volume reflect a mixture of empirical studies on family interaction and assessment and theory-oriented papers.

Annual review of family therapy. New York: Human Sciences Press, 1980–present. Intended to provide an organized overview of the current literature and major issues in family therapy. The first volume includes representative articles published during the past few years and some original contributions not published elsewhere; will limit itself to the literature of a given year in the future. Sections of the first volume are theory, technique, depression, divorce, clinical, and research.

Burr, W. R. (Ed.). *Contemporary theories about the family* (2 vols.). New York: Free Press, 1979. Essays by eminent sociologists detailing research-based theories on the family. Volume 1 covers inductively constructed theories on the family and change, family interaction, and the family and problems. Volume 2 covers general sociological and sociopsychological theories (e.g., symbolic interaction and general systems) deductively applied to families.

Gurman, A. S., & Kniskern, D. P. *Handbook of family therapy.* New York: Brunner/Mazel, 1981. Intended to develop a comprehensive presentation of all major models of family therapy. Sections include the historical perspective; psychoanalytic and object relations, intergenerational and behavioral approaches; enrichment and divorce; and research.

Hoffman, M. L. *Review of child development research.* New York: Russell Sage Foundation, 1964–present. The stated purpose of this series is to disseminate advances in scientific knowledge about children among practitioners in social work, clinical psychology, child psychiatry, and related areas. Another purpose is to help the practitioner increase understanding of the scientific study of child development in order to evaluate his or her own work. Each volume is not intended to be comprehensive but instead to focus on topics for which a significant body of research literature is available.

Howells, J. (Ed.). *Advances in child psychiatry.* New York: International Universities Press, 1979–present. Selection of papers collected at the Institute of Family Psychiatry. Covers not only family therapy but also family psychopathology, family diagnosis, family symptomatology, and vector therapy.

Wolman, B. B. (Ed.). *International encyclopedia of psychiatry, psychology, psychoanalysis, and neurology* (12 vols.). New York: Aesculapius, 1977. Volumes 1–11 contain signed articles that vary in length from one paragraph to 30 pages. Biographies are included. The majority of entries contain suggestions for further reading. Volume 12, a name and subject index, also lists the articles included. Among the articles are ones on family therapy from Adlerian, Jungian, family systems, and psychoanalytic perspectives.

Indexing and abstracting periodicals

Child Development Abstracts and Bibliography. Chicago: University of Chicago Press for Society for Research in Child Development, 1927–present. Abstracts articles from over 100 American and international periodicals and book reviews covering biology, medicine, psychology, and education. Arrangement is by broad subject with subject and author indexes.

Current Contents: Social and Behavioral Sciences. Philadelphia: Institute for Scientific Information, 1971–present. Weekly publication that includes tables of contents of more than 1,300 journals, including many in psychology and psychiatry. Keyword title and author indexes.

Current Index to Journals in Education. New York: Macmillan, 1969–present. Indexes over 700 journals in education and education-related fields, including child development and exceptional children. The main entry section contains abstracts; there are also author and subject indexes. A thesaurus of ERIC descriptors lists and shows the interrelationships among subject headings used in this index and *Resources in Education* (see below).

Exceptional Child Education Resources. Reston, Va.: Council for Exceptional Children, 1969/1970–present. Formerly called *Exceptional Child Education Abstracts.* Includes abstracts from over 200 journals, as well as books, documents, nonprint media, and dissertations. Arranged by document number, with author, title, and subject indexes.

Index to Social Sciences and Humanities Proceedings. Philadelphia: Institute for Scientific Information, 1979–present. Gives an extensive listing of contents of proceedings, as well as indexes by broad category (e.g., family studies, author/editor, sponsor, meeting location, subject, and corporate body with which authors of the conference proceedings are affiliated).

Index to U.S. Government Periodicals. Chicago: Infordata International, 1974–present. A computer-generated index, arranged by authors and subjects interfiled, to over 100 periodicals considered of greatest research value among those published by the federal government. Some periodicals of special interest are *Children Today, Family Economics Review, Schizophrenia Bulletin,* and *Women and Work.*

Psychological Abstracts. Washington, D.C.: American Psychological Association, 1927–present. Abstracts, books, and periodicals under broad subject categories, with author and brief subject indexes in each issue, full author and subject indexes at the end of each six months, and cumulated indexes covering periods of several years. A thesaurus of psychological index terms expedites use.

Resources in Education. Washington, D.C.: U.S. Government Printing Office, 1966–present. Formerly called *Research in Education.* Abstracts of published and unpublished educational research and research-related reports including conference proceedings, government documents, practitioner-related materials, and some books. Emphasis is on unpublished, noncopyrighted materials. The documents résumé section contains abstracts; there are author, subject, and institution indexes.

Sage Family Studies Abstracts. Beverly Hills, Calif.: Sage Publications, 1979–present. Each quarterly issue includes approximately 250 abstracts of books, articles, pamphlets, government documents, speeches, legislative research studies, and "fugitive materials" such as theses and dissertations. Sections include theory and methodology, lifestyles, life cycles, marital and family processes, therapy and counseling, sex roles, and social issues. Author and subject indexes.

Social Sciences Citation Index. Philadelphia: Institute for Scientific Information, 1966/1970–present. An international multidisciplinary index to the literature of the social, behavioral, and related sciences. Indexes every article and every significant editorial item from over 1,000 of the world's most important social sciences journals and covers selectively another 2,200 journals. Includes many important monographs. Also provides access to related articles by indicating references in which a known article by a given author has been cited. In four main sections: citation index, corporate index, source index, and permuterm subject index.

Social Work Research and Abstracts. New York: National Association of Social Workers, 1965–present. Formerly called *Abstracts for Social Workers.* Includes original research papers as well as abstracts of articles. Abstracts include a section on family and child welfare. Author and subject indexes.

Sociological Abstracts. New York: Sociological Abstracts, 1953–present. Contains abstracts of books and articles from over 60 countries; exhaustive coverage. Classified arrangement. Section 1900, the Family and Socialization, is especially useful. Author and subject indexes, including a decennial index covering 1953–1962.

Tests and measurements

Buros, O. K. *The mental measurements yearbook.* Highland Park, N.J.: Gryphon Press, 1938–present. Gives reviews of tests (including excerpts from journal reviews) and bibliography on the construction, use, and validity of specific tests. The Tests and Reviews section is arranged by the type of test (intelligence, multiaptitude, etc.). There is also a section summarizing reviews of books on testing. Indexes include: (1) periodical directory and index, (2) publishers directory and index, (3) index of book titles, (4) index of test titles, (5) index of names, and (6) classified index of tests.

Straus, M. A., & Brown, R. W. *Family measurement techniques: Abstracts of published instruments, 1935–1974* (Rev. ed.). Minneapolis: University of Minnesota Press, 1978. A comprehensive list, arranged by originator, for which are given variables measured, description of test, example of use, length, and citations to studies using tests. Classified sections include husband-wife relationship measures, parent-child and sibling-sibling relationship measures, measures covering both husband-wife and parent-child variables, and sex and premarital relationship measures. Earlier edition, covering 1935–1965, included validity and reliability data but, because the authors believed this information to be often questionable, it was excluded from the later edition.

Appendix A

The Family Psychology Curriculum at Georgia State University

Purpose

The purpose of this specialty is to train Ph.D. students to become leaders in research and training in family psychology and therapy in their theoretical, clinical, and professional applications. The main focus of this specialty is for students to learn to work with couples and families, using a variety of models of evaluation, intervention, and prevention. Research and research methodology are emphasized as the specific contribution that clinical psychologists can make in this field. Research is directed toward testing theoretical and empirical models and methods derived from clinical practice. The student can and should choose from a variety of theoretical and practical viewpoints, as long as this choice is done according to responsible and accepted criteria of scientific and professional practice. Hence, this specialty is theoretically eclectic and practically empirical.

Departmental core and methodology

In addition to two required courses on the biological and cognitive-affective bases of behavior, family psychology students are required to take the following methodology courses or their equivalents:

Advanced Child Development.
Statistics II.
Statistics III.
Research Design.
Single-Case Methodology.
            or
Observational Methodology.

Clinical core

Introduction to Behavior Modification.
Behavior Disorders.

or

Behavioral Disturbances in Children.

Proseminar in Child and Family.

Family psychology core

First year:

Theories of Family Therapy.

Family Evaluation plus one hour of practicum.

Family Enrichment plus one hour of practicum.

Second year:

Personality Development in Marriage.

Human Sexuality.

Marital Interventions plus one hour of practicum.

Third year:

Advanced Family Therapy.

Family Law.

Sociology of the Family.

Supervised Clinical Training.

Enrichment:

Three completed cases, one where role playing has been followed as a client and another two cases as trainer. At least one of these cases should be a family.

Covenant contracting:

Since this is less structured experience than enrichment, three completed cases are expected.

Intimacy workshop:

To train students to work with groups of couples, at least one workshop experience is required.

Practicum in family therapy:

Students should have continuously ongoing cases with quarterly credits from one to three hours.

Internship:

Students are expected to apply to nationally ranking clinical facilities with specific training in family therapy. Please note that no such facility is presently available in the Atlanta area. Consequently, students will need to plan for at least one year of training outside of Atlanta.

Appendix **B**

Michigan State University Training Program in Child and Family Clinical Psychology

Introduction

This program attempts to integrate applied training in child/family clinical psychology (assessment, intervention, consultation, and other professional skills) with the relevant background in general psychology, developmental psychology (theories and facts of normal development, methodology), and clinical theory (development psychopathology, psychodynamic theory, behavior change) and with research training. Thus, we are aiming at the "Boulder model" of the scientist/professional. It represents the joint efforts of the group of interested faculty and the graduate student representative.

We have tried to keep course requirements to a minimum, consonant with general departmental guidelines and current APA requirements for accreditation. We do feel that some breadth of background in general psychology (including personality theory) as well as developmental psychology is important. Ideally, the developmental core courses would cover the lifespan, from infancy through aging, and a range of approaches to social and cognitive development. Specific courses listed in the curriculum should not be taken too literally as requirements; students are encouraged to substitute other relevant background where appropriate and to demonstrate mastery by examination. The intent of the program description is to make clear the expected areas of competence; these competencies may be acquired and demonstrated as the student and his/her guidance committee deem most appropriate.

We have not identified major and minor areas for the doctoral program. Students may elect a major in clinical psychology, including additional course work in the adult and community areas; in that case they will have ample course work for a minor in developmental psychology. Alternatively, students may consider developmental psychology their major area and clinical their minor, in which case they will fulfill the comprehensive and other program requirements of the Developmental Interest Group. Some students may wish to pursue a minor in some other area within the department (e.g., social, physiological, ecological) or outside it (e.g., school psychology, communication, anthropology). Others may elect no minor at all. The choice is up to each student and his/her guidance committee.

The student should refer to the *Graduate Student Handbook* for general departmental guidelines and degree requirements.

However the individual student (in consultation with his/her advisors) may choose to shape the curriculum, research training, and practicum/internship experiences, we believe that the elements of the program we have described, the training resources available in this university and community, the expertise of our faculty, and the highly talented students we are able to recruit will all combine to make up a graduate program in child and family clinical psychology unique in richness and quality.

Outline of program

A. *Course work*

1. Child and Family core curriculum:
    a. Basic Development—three courses.
    b. Assessment—three courses (see description below).
    c. Practicum—year-long sequence.
    d. Intervention and Psychopathology.
        Child Therapy (theories).
        Conjoint Family Therapy (theories).
        Developmental Psychopathology.
2. Research courses:
    Research Methods in Clinical Psychology (optional for students enrolled in Research Apprenticeship Statistics sequence—three courses.
3. General psychology courses—four courses:
    a. History and Systems—Psychology 805.
    b. General distribution requirements (*1* course from each of the following three areas):
        (1) Biological bases of behavior.
        (2) Cognitive/affective bases of behavior.
        (3) Social bases of behavior.
4. Child/Family Seminar (see description below).
5. Electives: Other clinical courses; advanced seminars in Child/Family clinical (e.g., Family Therapy-Special Problems; Advanced Assessment of Children) or developmental.

B. *Comprehensive examinations*

These should be taken by the beginning of the fourth year in the program, after most of the course work has been completed and *before the dissertation is begun.* Ideally, the student should use the comprehensives in part to explore in depth the background literature for his/her dissertation topic. Another goal of the comprehensive is to demonstrate the student's capacity to *integrate* theory and research in special areas of interest with clinical experience and case material. It is often valuable to include a clinical work sample as part of the comprehensive.

Comprehensive examinations are planned with, and administered by, the doctoral guidance committee, who also approve the doctoral program of study.

C. Research requirements

All students in the child/family program will complete a *master's thesis* and *doctoral dissertation* (see *Graduate Student Handbook* for general departmental requirements). All M.A. requirements, including the thesis, should be completed before the beginning of the third year.

M.A. research.   To facilitate early involvement in research and the development of an M.A. proposal, each incoming child/family graduate student will be assigned to a faculty member as a *research apprentice.* The assignment will be made on the basis of the match between the expressed research interests of the student, when he/she applies to the program, and the interests and ongoing research programs of the faculty. Ordinarily, the research mentor will be a child/family faculty member but may be any member of the department whose interests and expertise are most suitable for the student. If the research mentor is not identified with the child/family program, a faculty member in that area will serve on the student's M.A. committee as program adviser. Any student whose initial apprenticeship assignment is incompatible or does not provide the best available match of interests should seek out another research adviser and transfer *not later than the beginning of the second term of graduate study.* The initial orientation program and the Child/Family Seminar (see below) will be planned so as to acquaint the students with the research interests and current activities of the faculty.

The three-person M.A. program committee should be formed by the beginning of the second term in residence. The M.A. thesis proposal should be developed and the M.A. thesis plan approved by a three-person committee by the end of the first year. The associate chairperson of the department will be asked to monitor students' progress in these matters and give feedback to the Child/Family faculty. If these goals are met, the student should generally have no difficulty in meeting the departmental expectation that the M.A. be completed at the end of the second year.

Doctoral research.   The student should select his/her dissertation research adviser during the third year of study. (See *Graduate Student Handbook* for general description of the structure and functions of the dissertation committee.) In consultation with the research supervisor, a dissertation committee is selected so as to give the student the best possible help and advice with the research problem. The dissertation committee is not necessarily the same as the doctoral guidance committee. The dissertation proposal should ideally be approved by the beginning of the fourth year of graduate study and before a student leaves a block internship, if that option is selected. Ordinarily, students should spend at least a full year developing and conducting the doctoral research and preparing the dissertation. Ideally, the dissertation problem should flow from the student's previous research experience. The dissertation committee supervises the doctoral research and conducts the final oral examination on the dissertation (with the addition of a dean's representative). The doctoral guidance committee certifies that all other requirements for the degree are completed, including the internship.

D. Internship

All students must complete an internship: one year for 40 hours a week or its equivalent. Recommended options: A block internship or two or more half-time internships or some combination of these.

If a block internship is chosen, it should represent a balanced range of experiences including a variety of child problems and modes of intervention. It should not be exclusively child-oriented but should offer some experience with adults, either working with them directly on their own problems or working with them as parents, couples, or families.

If local half-time internships are chosen, at least one of these should be in a community or inpatient setting and the two internships should represent a diversity of settings, problems, and approaches.

At this time, there are several on-campus internships particularly appropriate for Child/Family students: Psychological Clinic (one or two positions), Family Life Clinic (two to four positions), and Pediatrics (one position).

Model program

The following represents a typical program; however, the courses need not be taken in this order (for instance, some students may wish to take an intervention course in the first year and defer an assessment course or part of the developmental core). The general psychology courses and electives will depend on the particular interests and emphasis of the student.

First year

	Credits	Term
Assessment I.	2	F
Assessment II (Special Child and Family Section).	3	W
Assessment III (Special Child and Family Section).	3	S
Developmental Psychology: Infancy.	4	F
Developmental Psychology: Childhood.	4	W
Development Psychology: Adolescence and Youth.	3	S

First year (continued)

	Credits	Term
Research Methods in Clinical Psychology.	4	F
Research apprenticeship.	Variable	
Advanced Psychometrics I.	4	W
Advanced Psychometrics II.	4	S
M.A. research.	8–12	Variable
Child and Family Clinical Seminar.		

Second year

	Credits	Term
Child Psychotherapy.	2–4	F
Theories of Conjoint Family Therapy.	2–4	W
Developmental Psychopathology.	4–6	S or F
	2–5	F
Psychological Clinic Practicum.	2–5	W
	2–5	S
Advanced Psychometrics III.	4	F
Research (continued).	8–12	Variable
Child and Family Clinical Seminar.		Variable

Third and fourth years

	Credits	Term
Additional course work (including general psychology courses, advanced seminars in child and family clinical or developmental, adult clinical courses).	Variable	Variable
Comprehensive examinations.		
Internship.		
Dissertation research.	30	Variable

Child and family assessment sequence

First term:

General interviewing course plus infant assessment techniques (Bayley, Denver Developmental, Brazelton) (one credit).

Second term: Didactic content

1. Introduction to Child and Family Assessment (two weeks).
   a. History.
   b. Ethics and values.
   c. Developmental issues.
   d. Classification and diagnosis.
   e. Approaches to understanding assessment data.
2. Assessment of Intelligence (three weeks).
   a. Concepts of intelligence.
   b. Intelligence tests: WISC–R; BINET.
   c. Clinical issues: Giftedness, retardation.
   d. Preschool developmental assessment.
3. Personality Assessment (two weeks).
   a. Projective tests.
   b. Play in assessment.
   c. Clinical issues: Assessment of neurosis; psychosis.
4. Behavioral Assessment (two weeks).
   a. Systematic observation.
   b. Home and school observations.
   c. Behavioral checklists.

Third term: Didactic content

5. Family Assessment (five weeks).
   a. The family as a system.
   b. Family interviews and observations.
   c. Other family assessment techniques.
6. Assessment of Learning and Organic Problems (three weeks).
   a. Organic problems.
   b. Learning problems.
   c. Neuropsychological assessment.
   d. Assessment of learning problems.
   e. Achievement and its relationship to intelligence.
7. Synthesis and Integration (two weeks).
   a. Approaches to synthesis/choices of assessment procedures.
   b. Systematic approaches—SOMPA.
   c. Multidisciplinary approaches.
   d. Special populations—handicaps.
   e. Interpretives.
   f. Reports/communication of results.
   g. Research issues in assessment.

Practicum content (integrated with preceding topics)

Tests and procedures covered:

Unit 2
WISC–R, WPPS
Binet

McCarthy
Merill-Palmer
Gesell (Yale RDs)

Unit 3	Family projectives
TAT (CAT)	Interpersonal systems
KFD–DAP	(Benjamin, Olson, etc.)
Sentence completion	*Unit 6*
Unit 4	Bender
Behavioral checklists	Beery
Observation schedules	Memory for designs
Unit 5	ITPA, PIAT, WRAT
Family interviews	*Unit 7*
Family interaction tasks	SOMPA

All students will be assigned a normal family at the beginning of the year; will study the family, using the various approaches covered in 830 and 832; and will be responsible for an integrated report on the family at the end of the year.

Revised practicum sequence for Child/Family students

General assumptions:

1. The Child/Family student will take 12–20 credits of practicum.

2. Students interested in Child/Family Clinical should enroll for a minimum of two credits each term of the second year. These two credits will represent at least two cases each term seen in the context of the Psychological Clinic; students will be expected to fulfill clinic administrative requirements.

3. The remainder of the practicum requirement would be fulfilled by enrolling during the second year for two or more additional credits per term of any of the options offered by Child/Family faculty (additional practica may be taken in the third year). Some of these options would involve seeing clients in the Psychological Clinic, but others would involve other on- and off-campus settings. Some practicum experiences *should* be in an interdisciplinary setting (see options listed below), and the student is required to function as a member of an interdisciplinary team. Interdisciplinary practicum experiences should generally be available to the more advanced students, after they have gained their initial exposure to clients in the Psychological Clinic.

4. Integrated with more specific skill training, all first- and second-year students in the program should have the experience of following at least one family through the academic year. First-year students, individually or in pairs, might be assigned to normal volunteer families. By the end of the year, they would complete a comprehensive assessment of the family and one or more children in the family across a range of social settings (day care, school, home, etc.). Second-year students would be assigned clinic-referred families for comprehensive assessments, perhaps leading into interventions. They might also follow children with a handicapping condition and their families.

5. The vertical team would be a preferred supervision arrangement for most faculty. This would mean that a faculty supervisor would typically meet regularly with a group of students including one or two from the first-year

class, one or two from the second-year, and one or more third/fourth-year students. (Some third-/and fourth-year students would also be interns in such settings as Psychological Clinic, Family Life Clinic, Pediatrics, etc.; the vertical team meetings would be supplementary to their internship arrangements.) The vertical teams would review the students' work with their normal families (for the first-year students), their clinic-referred families (for the second-year students), and other cases. Some more complex cases, involving several members of a family or several modes of assessment/intervention, might be shared by two or more members of the team. The vertical team provides the opportunity for beginning students to learn by observation and vicariously by participation with the more advanced students; at the same time, the advanced student can get some beginning training in supervision. Some faculty may choose to combine their vertical teams and meet with them jointly. A second-year or advanced student may, in a given term, be a member of more than one vertical team if he or she is enrolled in more than one of the practicum options offered.

Given the preceding assumptions, the practicum requirement could be fulfilled by a combination of the options offered by the various faculty members. Unless otherwise specified, we assume that one case—worked with intensely either in assessment or intervention for the period of one term (or ongoing consultative contact with a program or agency, lasting at least one term)— equals one credit.

A. Assessment options

Individual and family assessment of children: 1–2 students, 1 or more terms.

Evaluation of children in school setting, part of interdisciplinary evaluation team (Ingham Intermediate): 2–3 students, 1 or more terms.

Family assessment: 3–4 students, 1 term, S or F.

Infant biobehavioral and developmental assessment.

Observational methods—including obs, research techniques, in concert with project on adolescent pregnancy.

Intensive diagnostic experience with children aged 0–12 and families: 3 students, 3 terms.

Comprehensive assessment of families: 10–15 students, 3 terms (this presumably includes students from other programs).

Assessment of behavior problems with children: 1–2 students, any term.

B. Intervention options

Group therapy for preschool age children: 5 students for the year or combinations of students for 1 or 2 terms.

Individual, filial, and family therapy of children and parents: 1–2 students, 3 terms (depending on consultation option, whether 1 or 2).

Conjoint family therapy: 6–8 students, 2 or 3 terms, beginning F or W.

Intervention in families whose children have identified handicapping conditions: up to 3 students, 3 terms (in combination with above).

School-based therapy experiences: 3–4 students, 3 terms.

Developing empathic skills with young (3–9 years old) children through play encounters. Techniques of marital conflict resolution, filial therapy, school consultation, parent education: within the 15 students (see above).

Family therapy and therapy with children: up to 2 students, *only* in conjunction with other supervisees.

Treatment of families, couples, individual adolescents: 1–2 students, year-long.

McKinney—assessment/intervention in a pediatric outpatient setting: 1 student, any term, *only* in conjunction with other supervisees (e.g., pediatric residents).

Child/Family Clinical Seminar

All first-year, second-year, and more advanced Child/Family students and interested faculty will meet in a weekly or biweekly brown-bag seminar to discuss professional, ethical, theoretical, and research issues, case presentations, etc. A more detailed plan for this seminar is being developed.

Appendix **C**

Family Internships

Key: S–Separate division of family therapy, distinct from other units.

C–Separate marital and family clinic, not necessarily separate from adult division, etc.

n, n–First number: the importance given to family therapy on a 1–5 scale, 5 being highest importance.

Second number: the number of full and part-time trainers identifying themselves as primarily family or systems oriented.

"—" –No rating or data available re family therapy importance and/or trainers.

*–Non-APA-approved training site.

Albany Medical College/Veterans Administration Medical Center, 45 New Scotland Avenue, Albany, NY 12208, and 113 Holland Avenue, Albany, NY 11206 (Consortium). C, 2, 2

Ball State University, Counseling and Psychological Services Center, Muncie, IN 47306. S, 4, 4, *

Beechbrook, 3737 Lander Road, Cleveland, OH 44124. 5, 11, *

Boulder Mental Health Center, 1333 Iris Avenue, Boulder, CO, 80302. C, 4, 8, *

Community Guidance Center of Mercer County, 65 South Main Street, Building A, Pennington, NJ 08534. 5, 3

D. E. Burrell Community Mental Health Center, Inc., P.O. Box 1611 SSS, Springfield, MO 65805. 5, 3, *

Delaunay Mental Health Center, 5215 N. Lombard Street, Portland, OR 97203–4396. 5, 4, *

Des Moines Child Guidance Center, Inc., 1425 Woodland Avenue, Des Moines, IA 50309. 5, 5

Note: A different, older list is available in Cooper, A., Rampage, C., and Soucy, G., "Family Therapy Training in Clinical Psychology Programs," *Family Process* 20 (1981), pp. 155–166.

Dwight David Eisenhower Army Medical Center, Psychology Service, Department of Psychiatry and Neurology, Fort Gordon, GA 30905. S, 3, 1

Elmcrest Psychiatric Institute, 25 Marlborough Street, Portland, CT 06480. 5, 20

University of Florida, Psychological and Vocational Counseling Center, Gainesville, FL 32601. C, 3, 4, *

Framingham Youth Guidance Center, 88 Lincoln Street, Framingham, MA 01701. 4, 3, *

Harlem Valley Psychiatric Center, Carmel Mental Health Clinic, Route 52, Seavey Plaza, Carmel, NY 10512. S, 5, 8

Hathaway Home for Children, P.O. Box 547, Pacoima, CA 91331. 5, 0

Judge Baker Guidance Center, 295 Longwood Avenue, Boston, MA 02115. S, 4, 1

University of Kansas Medical Center, Wichita, KS. S, 4, 1

Kennedy Memorial Hospital for Children, Psychology Department, 30 Warren Street, Brighton, MA 02135. 5, 2

Kings County Hospital Center, 451 Clarkson Avenue, Brooklyn, NY 11203. C, 3, 3

Louisiana State University Medical Center, Department of Psychiatry and Behavioral Sciences, 1542 Tulane Avenue, New Orleans, LA 70112. C, 3, 8

Madeline Borg Counseling Services, Manhattan West Office, 33 West 60th Street, New York, NY. 5, 2

Manhattan Veterans Administration Medical Center, First Avenue at East 24th Street, New York, NY 10010. S, —, 0

University of Mississippi Medical Center/Veterans Administration Medical Center–Jackson, Department of Psychiatry and Human Behavior, 2500 North State Street, Jackson, MS 39206 (Consortium). C, 4, 4

Mt. Carmel Mercy Hospital, 22621 Mack Avenue, St. Claire Shores, MI 40808. 5, 5, 8, *

Mount Sinai Hospital, 500 Blue Hills Avenue, Hartford, CT 06112. 5, —, *

New Jersey Center for Family Studies, 291 Main Street, Chatham, NJ 07928. S, C, 5, 5, *

University of Medicine and Dentistry of New Jersey, 100 Bergin Street, Newark, NJ 07103. 5, 5, *

New York University–Bellevue Medical Center, Department of Psychiatry, 550 First Avenue, New York, NY 10016. C, 4, 3

University of Oklahoma Health Sciences Center, Department of Psychiatry and Behavioral Sciences Internship Consortium (Children's Memorial Hospital, Oklahoma Memorial Hospital, and Veterans Administration Medical Center), P.O. Box 26901, Oklahoma City, OK 73190 (Consortium). S, C, 4, 4

Southwood Mental Health Center, 950 Third Avenue, Chula Vista, CA 92011. 5, 3, *

Taylor Manor Hospital, Ellicott City, MD 21043. S, 3, 16

University of Texas Health Science Center–San Antonio, 7703 Floyd Curl Drive, San Antonio, TX 78284. 5, 6

Texas Research Institute of Mental Health Sciences, 1300 Moursund Avenue, Houston, TX 77030. C, 4, 6

Topeka State Hospital, 2700 West Sixth Street, Topeka, KS 66606. 5, 2

Veterans Administration Medical Center, Psychology Service, 3350 La Jolla Village Drive, San Diego, CA 92161. C, 3, 3, *

Veterans Administration Medical Center, Augusta, GA 30904. S, 3, 3, *

Veterans Administration Medical Center, Togus, ME 04330. S, C, 5, 1

Veterans Administration Medical Center, 3801 Miranda Avenue, Palo Alto, CA 94304. S, C, 5, 5

Veterans Administration Medical Center, 4150 Clement Street, San Francisco, CA 94121. S, C, 3, 3

Veterans Administration Medical Center, Psychology Service, 1611 Plummer Street, Sepulveda, CA 91343. S, C, 5, 4

Veterans Administration–Edward Hines, Jr., Medical Center, Hines, IL 60141. S, 3, 7

Veterans Administration Medical Center, Psychology Service, 54th Street and 48th Avenue South, Minneapolis, MN 55417. S, 2, 1

Veterans Administration Medical Center, Psychology Service, 1030 Jefferson Avenue, Memphis, TN 38104. C, 4, 9

Veterans Administration Medical Center, 4500 Lancaster Road, Dallas, TX 75216. S, C, 3, 1

Veterans Administration Medical Center, 2002 Holcombe Boulevard, Houston, TX 77211. S, 5, 3

Olin E. Teague Veterans Administration Medical Center, 1901 South First Street, Temple, TX 76501. S. 4, 6

University of Virginia Medical Center, Department of Psychiatry, Charlottesville, VA 22908. C, 3, 2

Walter Reed Army Medical Center, Psychology Service, New Medical Treatment Facility (NMTF). Washington, DC 20012. C, 2, 2

Washington University School of Medicine, Child Guidance Clinic, 369 North Taylor Avenue, St. Louis, MO 63108. 5, 1

University of Wisconsin Center for the Health Sciences, Department of Psychiatry, 600 Highland Avenue, Madison, WI 53706. C, 4, 5

Worcester State Hospital, 305 Belmont Street, Worcester, MA 01604. C, 5, 1

Name Index

Note: Pages 1–660 are in Volume I; pages 661–1457 are in Volume II. Italic numbers indicate reference citations.

I-1

Aldous, J., 157, 164, 165, *174*, 261, *281*, 449, 510, 515, *518*, 519, *520*, 564, *581*, 698, 699, *733*, 755, *773*
Alexander, J. A., 1320, 1321, 1324, 1325, 1327, 1328, 1332, 1335, 1336, 1338, 1341, 1342, 1343
Alexander, J. B., 1228, 1241
Alexander, J. F., 127, *129*, 234, 235, 236, 243, 245, *247*, 366, *375*, 813, 821, 823, 826, 827, 831, *840*, *841*, *842*, 967, 986, 996, *1000*, 1076, 1078, 1079, 1080, 1084, 1086, 1091, 1102, 1346, 1355, 1372, 1375, *1376*
Alexander, J. W., 539, *552*
Al-Issa, I., 849, *868*
Allan, G., 192, *210*
Allen, C. M., 998, 1000
Allen, G., 158, *171*
Allen, W., 663, 664, 666, 671, 689, *695*
Allman, C. R., 1129, *1148*
Allport, F., 6, *35*
Allport, G. W., 102, *129*
Allred, M., 1292, 1303, *1309*
Alpert, J. L., 508, *518*
Als, H., 596, *616*, *621*, *622*
Altman, I., 362, 364, 366, 367, 368, *373*, *374*, *375*, 411, 412, 418, *422*, *427*, 1220, 1245
Altsteen, H., 1397, *1412*
Alvarez, M., 591, *617*
Alverez, M. D., 106, *132*
Amatea, E., 1256, *1273*, 1292, *1309*
American Bar Association, 1394, *1409*
American Psychological Association, 1249, 1255, 1257, 1258, 1261, *1273*
Ames, G. J., 592, *617*
Amish, P., 908, 909, *933*, *936*
Ammons, P., 308, *311*
Amster, L. E., 299, *311*
Anaquost, E., 888, *896*
Ancher, K. N., 1346, 1358, *1376*
Anderson, B. J., 562, *583*, 603, 605, *620*
Anderson, C., 467, *493*
Anderson, C. W., 449, *518*
Anderson, D., 1048, 1071
Anderson, L., 1111, *1125*, 1256, *1273*, 1292, *1309*
Anderson, R., 74, *98*
Anderson, S. A., 117, *138*, 993, 1000, 1001
Anderson, S. H., 1227, 1241
Andolfi, M., 1161, *1175*, 1288, 1291, *1309*
Andrulis, D. P., 857, *868*
Andry, R. G., 231, *247*
Angelo, C., 1161, *1175*
Angst, J., 126, *131*

Angyal, A., 1288, *1309*
Annis, H. M., 233, 234, *247*
Annon, J., 1108, 1124
Anolik, S. A., 232, *247*
Anthony, E. J., 825, *840*, 865, *868*, 1270, 1280
Anthony, J., *247*
Antill, J. K., 117, 118, *129*
Antrobus, J., 1155, 1159, 1173, *1177*
Anzalone, M. K., 588, 607, 610, *617*
Apfel-Savitz, R., 414, *426*
Aponte, H., 744, *773*
Appel, W., 832, *840*
Applebaum, A. S., 447, *462*
Applebaum, M., 1081, 1082, 1103
Aptheker, H., 667, 674, *695*
Araoz, D. C., 791, *807*
Arasteh, J. D., 566, *579*
Arbeit, S. A., 576, *579*
Ardrey, R., 1222, 1241
Arel, B., 1301, *1309*
Arendt, H., 170, *171*
Arias, I., 1061, 1071
Aries, P., 623, *653*
Arieti, S., 852, *868*
Arkin, R., 1422, 1433
Arling, G., 293, *311*, 326, 342, *351*
Arling, G. L., 902, 912, *934*
Armin, R., 474, *494*
Arnie, K. A., 640, *657*
Arnstein, H. S., 572, *579*
Aronovich, J., 1282, *1309*
Aronowitz, S., 161, *171*
Aronson, E., 125, *129*
Arrington, A., 965, 975, 984
Ashby, W. K., 14, *35*
Ashe, M. L., 761, *780*
Asher, H. B., 630, *653*
Asher, S. J., 328, *352*, 1035, 1068
Ashton, G. C., 221, *254*
Atchley, R., 193, *214*
Atchley, R. C., 284, 285, 286, 287, 288, 289, 291, 292, 296, *311*, *319*
Athanasiou, R., 432, *434*, *462*, 466, *492*
Atkinson, J. R., 305, *318*
Atkinson, J. W., *808*
Attneave, C., 18, *37*, 744, *773*, 1271, 1273, 1279
Atwood, G. E., 611, *615*
Auerback, H. H., 1060, 1068
Auerswald, E., 157, *171*
Aug, H. G., 539, *552*
Aug, R. G., 625, 629, *654*
Ault, M. H., 982, 984
Austad, C. C., 649, *654*

Note: Pages 1–660 are in Volume I; pages 661–1457 are in Volume II. Italic numbers indicate reference citations.

Note: Pages 1–660 are in Volume I; pages 661–1457 are in Volume II. Italic numbers indicate reference citations.

Brown, B. B., 368, *374*
Brown, D. J., 786, 787, *809*
Brown, E., 417, *423*
Brown, G., 414, *423*
Brown, G. E., 120, *130*
Brown, G. W., 398, *401*, 539, *551*, 926, *929*, 1143, *1149*
Brown, J. V., 975, 977, 983, 984
Brown, R., 68, *71*
Brown, R. A., 1345, *1377*
Brown, R. W., 1443
Browning, C. J., 232, *248*
Browning, R. M., 982, 984
Bruch, C. S., 1387, *1409*
Brudenell, G., 810, 820, *840*
Brunnquell, D., 901, 905, 916, 918, 922, *930*
Bruzzese, D., 1259
Bryant, B. K., 191, 193, 202, 203, 204, 207, *210*
Bryson, C. H., 1024, 1026, 1029
Bryson, C. L., 850, *870*
Bryson, J. B., 716, 717, 718, 730, 731, *734*
Bryson, R., 716, 717, 718, 730, 731, *734*
Bryson, R. B., 716, 718, 730, 731, *734*
Buck, R., 116, *137*, 381, 385, 386, *401*
Buckley, P., 1299, *1315*
Bucksbaum, S., 854, *871*
Budd, L. G., 117, 118, *137*
Buhler, C., 160, *172*
Buhrle v. *State* 1389, *1409*
Bullock, D., 1300, *1310*
Bullock, R., 414, *423*
Bumagin, V. E., 288, 289, 298, 300, *312*
Bunker, B., 729, *734*
Burbeck, T. W., 392, 393, *401*
Burchinal, L. G., 342, *355*, 625, 654
Burgess, R. L., 107, 111, 112, 113, *133*, 524, *551*, 911, 912, *930*
Burgess, R. S., 918, 919, 925, 926, 930
Burka, J. B., 1187, *1210*
Burke, E., 117, 118, *130*, 234, *253*, 411
Burke, K., *171*, *172*
Burke, R., 411, 419, *423*, 724, 725, 727, 728, *734*
Burke, R. J., 117, 130
Burlingham, D., 184, *210*
Burns, C. W., *841*
Burnside, I. M., 307, *312*
Buros, O. K., 1442
Burr, W. R., ix, xii, 115, *130*, 436, 437, 457, *463*, 1440
Bursk, B. J., 94, *99*, 292, 295, *315*
Burton, R. V., 1350, *1378*

Busch-Rossnagel, N., 160, 163, 164, 540, *554*
Bushing, B. C., 234, *248*
Buss, A., 163, *172*
Buss, A. H., 1423, 1433
Busse, E. W., 120, 121, *130*, 300, 302, 303, 309, *312*
Busse, K., 120, 130
Busse, M., 120, 130
Busse, T. V., 120, 130
Butler, D., 106, *136*
Butler, E., 778
Butler, J. F., 923, *930*
Butler, M., 717, 730, *734*
Butler, M. C., 233, *250*
Butler, R. N., 290, 291, 292, 296, 302, 303, 306, *312*, 315
Butterwieser, E., 1234, 1244
Buttrick, R., 110, *134*
Buzas, H. P., 1146, *1149*
Byassee, J., 764, *774*
Byles, J., 1251, 1267, 1291, *1310*
Byng-Hall, J., 415, *423*, 1227, 1242, 1301, 1305, *1316*
Byrne, D., 116, 125, *130*
Byrne, D. A., 362, *374*
Byrne, D. G., 864, *870*

C

Cabianca, W. A., 561, *582*
Caille, P., 1251, 1266, 1268, 1269, 1271, 1282, 1292, *1310*
Cain, R. L., 562, *583*, 598, 603, 605, *620*
Cairns, R. B., 975, 984, 1074, 1081, 1082, 1086, 1096, 1103, 1375, *1376*
Caldwell, B., 526, *551*, *552*
Caldwell, B. M., 749, 763, *774*
Calhoun, L. C., 623, 643, *654*
Camp, B., 1153, 1169, *1175*
Campbell, D. T., 982, 984, 1037, 1055, 1069, 1088, 1099, 1103, 1227, 1242, 1267
Campbell, E. Q., 219, 220, 236, *248*
Campbell, J. D., 1350, *1378*
Campbell, S., 197, *213*, 543, *551*
Campbell, S. B., 1399, *1413*
Campbell, S. S., 236, *254*
Campos, J. J., 589, *616*
Cannon, K. L., 288, *318*
Cannon, S. R., 234, *248*
Cannon, W., 38, 46, *72*
Canter, F. M., 218, *254*
Cantor, M. B., 1433
Cantwell, D., 1154, 1155, 1156, *1175*, *1177*

Note: Pages 1–660 are in Volume I; pages 661–1457 are in Volume II. Italic numbers indicate reference citations.

Caplan, G., 323, *352*, 815, *841*, 849, *868*
Caplan, P., 1165, *1176*
Caplow, T., 259, *281*
Capra, F., 1250, 1258, 1268
Carew, J. V., 527, *551*
Cargan, L., 330, 331, *353*
Carkhuff, R., 1294, *1310*, *1314*
Carlos, L. M., 863, *877*
Carlson, B. E., 878, 895, *897*
Carlson, N. A., 633, 634, *658*
Carr, J., 755, 767, 768, *774*
Carroll, E. E., 567, *582*
Carruth, F. B., 305, *312*
Carson, R., 995, 1001
Carter, D. L., 901, *935*
Carter, E., 165, 167, *172*, 743, 744, 745, 775, 992, *1003*, 1165, *1175*, 1286, 1290, *1310*
Carter, E. A., 241, *248*
Carter, H., 687, *695*
Carter, R., 1291, *1311*
Carter, R. M., 887, 892, *897*
Cartwright-Smith, J., 395, *402*
Carveth, W. B., 333, 342, *352*, 545, 551
Cassell, J., 323, *352*
Cassell, J. C., 323, 344, *352*, *354*
Cassirer, E., 21, 23, *35*
Castellan, N. J., 1093, 1096, 1103
Catalano, R., 546, *555*
Cate, R. M., 258, *281*
Catlin, N., 832, *841*
Cattell, R., 544, *552*
Cattell, R. B., 117, 118, 120, *129*, *130*, *131*, 992, 1001
Caudill, M., 948, *957*
Caufield, C., 902, 904, 905, 914, 921, *930*
Cautela, J. R., 992, 1001
Cavan, P., 817, *841*
Cavanaugh, J., 1184, *1210*
Cecchin, G., 991, 1004, 1136, 1137, *1150*, 1264, 1269, 1279, 1284, 1287, 1293, 1301, 1302, *1310*, *1315*, 1320, 1343
Cerreto, M., 111, *136*, 995, 1005
Cetingok, M., 863, *871*
Chadwick, B. A., 703, 707, *733*
Chafetz, J. S., 386, *401*
Chafetz, M. E., 234, *248*
Chaleff, A., 911, *934*
Chalmers, M. A., 1234, 1244
Chamberlain, P., 1344, 1347, 1355, 1357, 1358, 1361, 1363, 1365, 1366, 1367, 1368, 1369, *1376*, *1377*, *1378*
Chan, F. A., 467, *493*, 1119, 1120, 1125
Chandler, M., 163, 172
Chandler, M. J., 548, *555*, 635, *658*

Chapman, R., 1109, 1111, 1112, 1124
Chapple, E., 410, 411, *423*
Char, W., 221, *254*
Charles, A., 560, *583*
Charles, E., 1299, *1315*
Chase-Lansdale, L., 598, 600, *619*
Cheal, D. J., 337, *352*
Chein, I., 232, *248*
Cherlin, A., 728, *734*
Cherlin, A. J., 567, *579*
Chesney, A. T., 467, 470, 474, 475, 487, 488, 489, 491, *494*, 1119, 1120, 1125
Chess, S., 256, 542, 543, *556*, 758, 777, 1156, 1157, *1178*
Chester, R., 641, 645, *654*
Chevret, M., 652, *654*
Child, I. L., 848, *875*
Chilman, C. S., 242, *248*, 509, *519*
Chiriboga, D., 157, *175*
Chiriboga, D. A., 289, 290, *312*, *316*, 342, 343, *352*
Chodoff, P., 940, 948, *955*
Chodorow, N., 513, *519*
Chomsky, N., 47, 68, *72*
Chopra, S. L., *807*
Christensen, A., 128, *134*, 964, 965, 971, 972, 973, 974, 975, 978, 980, 984, 996, 1002, 1109, 1126
Christensen, H. T., 454, *462*, 566, *579*
Christenson, C. V., 289, *312*
Christenson, J. A., 510, *579*
Christy, P., 117, 118, *136*
Church, J., 226, *256*
Cicirelli, V. G., 94, *99*, 177, 180, 184, 186, 188, 192, 193, 198, 200, 201, 202, 203, 205, 206, 207, 208, *210*, *211*, 294, *312*, 336, 337, 349, *352*, 826, *841*
Cimbalo, R. C., 367, *374*
Claiborn, C. D., 127, *138*
Clark, A., 471, 495, 515, *519*
Clark, A. L., 472, 483, 488, *493*
Clark, C. G., 884, 894, *899*
Clark, H. H., Jr., 1381, 1384, 1385, 1396, *1409*
Clark, J. C., 830, 832, *841*
Clark, M. S., 112, 113, *130*, *354*, 1419, 1433
Clark, R. A., *808*
Clarke, A. D., 849, *868*
Clarke, A. N., 849, *868*
Clarke-Stewart, K. A., 526, 527, 529, 530, 531, *551*, 599, 602, 613, *616*
Clausen, J., 157, 160, 162, *172*, 848, *868*
Clausen, J. A., 177, *211*, 232, *248*
Clayton, R. R., 86, *99*, 431, *434*, 440, 442, 454, 458, *462*

Note: Pages 1–660 are in Volume I; pages 661–1457 are in Volume II. Italic numbers indicate reference citations.

Cleary, E. W., 1389, *1409*
Cleary, P. D., 562, *581*
Cleghorn, J., 1286, 1291, 1292, 1298, 1299, *1310*
Cleveland, D., 762, 763, *775*
Cleveland, M., 643, *658*
Cleveland, S. E., 1222, 1243
Clifford, W. B., 636, *654*
Cline, V. B., 1325, 1336, 1342
Clinebell, C., 405, *423*
Clinebell, H., 405, *423*
Clingempeel, W. G., 123, *130*, 1402, *1409*
Clore, G. L., 362
Cobb, J. A., 970, 974, 986, 987, 1355, *1378*
Cobb, S., 163, 258, *280*, 343, 350, *352*, 700, *735*
Cobliner, W. G., 627, 629, *654*
Cochran, M., 546, *551*
Cochrane, C., 1259, 1279
Coddington, R. D., 626, *654*
Coffins, P., 813, *841*
Cohen, B. H., 755, *779*
Cohen, C., 852, *868*
Cohen, D., 299, *313*
Cohen, F., 700, 701, 702, 720, *734*
Cohen, J., 821, 822, 823, 827, 828, 830, 834, *841, 842*, 980, 984, 1021, 1022, 1024, 1025, 1026, 1029
Cohen, L. T., 589, *616*
Cohen, M. B., 1135, 1139, *1149*
Cohen, M. I., 904, 910, 916, *930*
Cohen, M. W., 1297, *1310*
Cohen, R. A., 1135, 1139, *1149*
Cohen, R. S., 980, 984
Cohen, S. E., 526, *551*
Cohen, S. L., 856, *869*
Cohen, S. P., 88, *99*
Cohen, S. Z., 286, 297, 312
Cohler, B. J., 84, 86, *99*, 299, 300, *312*, 372, *374*, 864, *870*, 1236, 1237, 1242
Cohn, P. M., 437, 439, 448, 455, *463*
Cohn, R. M., 567, *579*
Coho, A., 342, *352*
Coie, J. D., 576, *579*
Coie, L., 576, *579*
Colapinto, J., 1263
Colarusso, C. A., 786, *807*
Cole, A. L., 472, *493, 494*
Cole, C. M., 467, *493*, 1119, 1120, 1125
Cole, J. O., 1128, *1149*, 1325, 1336, 1342
Cole, R. E., 538, *549*
Cole, S. P., 569, 572, *581*
Coleman, J., 225, 240, 246, *248*, 511, *519*
Coleman, K. H., 887, 893, *897*
Coleman, M., 120, *130*

Coles, R., 822, *841*
Colletta, N. C., 279, *280*, 538, *551*
Colletti, G., 762, *775*
Collins, A. M., 1328, 1342
Collins, J., 288, *319*, 1130, *1149;* 1203, *1210*
Collmer, C., 536, 538, 549, *554*
Collmer, C. W., 900, 903, 904, 924, 925, *934*
Colman, L., 637, 639, *654*
Combrink-Graham, L., 167, 168, *172*
Comly, H., 1156, *1176*
Condran, J. G., 703, 714, *734*
Cone, J. D., 971, 974, 985
Conger, J. J., x, xi, xii, 218, 224, 226, 229, 239, *248, 254*, 449, *521*
Conger, R. D., 911, 918, 919, 925, 926, *930*
Conger, R. E., 996, 1003, 1346, 1355, 1356, *1378*
Connell, M. J., 1391, *1410*
Connolly, P. R., 1223, 1241
Connors, C., 1164, 1165, *1175*
Connors, K., 563, *579*
Conrad, P., 1155, 1158, 1175
Conrad, W., 1156, *1175*
Consensus Development Conference, 562, *571*
Constantine, J., 359, *374*
Constantine, J. A., 1078, 1103, 1269, *1274*
Constantine, L., 359, *374*, 1285, 1287, 1288, 1293, *1310*
Conway, D., 119, *135*
Cook, J. J., 757, *775*
Cook, N., 548, *556*
Cook, T. D., 1081, 1099, 1103
Cookerly, J. R., 1056, 1069
Coombs, R., 259, 277, *280*
Cooper, A., 1250, 1268
Cooper, K. J., 864, *868*
Coopersmith, S., 533, *551*
Cope, D. R., 641, *654*
Copitch, D., 920, *936*
Corea, G., 560, *579*
Corigliano, A., 1161, *1175*
Cormican, E. J., 285, 301, *312*
Cornblatt, B., 865, *869*
Cornelison, A., 13, *36*
Cornelison, A. R., 852, *872*, 1080, 1105
Corrales, R. G., 755, 765, 773, *775*
Corter, C., 190, *210*
Coser, R. L., 731, *734*
Costa, L. A., 1196, *1210*
Cotter, P. R., 292, 294, *313*
Cottrell, L. S., 19, *35*
Coufal, J., 1192, 1193, 1194, *1210, 1212*

Note: Pages 1–660 are in Volume I; pages 661–1457 are in Volume II. Italic numbers indicate reference citations.

Note: Pages 1–660 are in Volume I; pages 661–1457 are in Volume II. Italic numbers indicate reference citations.

Duhl, B., 1271, 1274
Duhl, F., 1271, 1274
Duke, M. P., 1223, 1224–1225, 1241
Dumas, J. E., 1346, 1355, 1375, *1379*
Duncan, P., 232, 237, *249*
Duncan, R. P., 716, *734*
Duncan-Jones, P., 864, *870*
Dunkas, N., 863, *869*
Dunkle, R. E., 303, *313*
Dunlap, K., 1136, *1149*
Dunlop, K. H., 720, *734*
Dunlop, W. R., 750, 754, *775*
Dunmore, C. J., 1436
Dunn, J., 185, 187, 190, 191, 193, 199, 200, 201, 203, 207, 208, *211, 212*
Dunn, J. F., 542, *552*
Dunne, E. E., ix, x, xii
Dupree, L. W., 306, 308, *313*
Durkin, H. P., 1195, 1196, *1211*
Duvall, E., 165, *172*, 324, *353*, 741, *775*
Duvall, E. M., 504, 515, *519*, 559
Dyer, E. D., 569, 574, *580*
Dynes, R. R., 515, *519*
Dysart, R. R., 968, 985

E

Earls, F., 627, *655*
Earp, J., 907, *930*
Earp, J. A., 545, *555*
Ebbin, A. J., 922, *930*
Eberle, P. A., 882, *897*
Ebstein, R., 391, *403*
Eckels, E., 370, *376*
Edelbrock, C. S., 1352, *1376*
Edgerton, R. B., 863, *869*
Edwards, B. L., 715, *739*
Edwards, G. F., 680, *695*
Edwards, J. M., 995, 1002
Edwards, J. N., 111, *131*, 466, 483, 487, *494*
Edwards, R. L., 626, *658*
Egeland, B., 538, *552*, 901, 902, 906, 916, 917, 918, 922, 924, 925, 926, *930*
Eggert, L., 258, *282*
Ehrenreich, B., 169, *172*
Ehrmann, W., 458, *462*
Eichler, L., 342, *353*
Eichler, L. S., 561, 564, 581, 588, 607, 610, 612, *617*
Eidelson, R. J., 117, 118, *131*
Eiduson, B. T., 539, *552*, 812, 815, 816, 817, 818, 820, 821, 822, 823, 824, 825, 827, 828, 829, 830, 831, 832, 835, 836, 837, 839, *841, 843, 844*

Eisdoufer, C., 299, *312*
Eisenberg, J. C., 860, *871*
Eisenberg-Berg, N., 229, *249*
Eisenstadt, S., 163, *173*
Ekstein, R., 1300, *1311*
Elardo, R., *552*
Elder, G., 154, 157, 160, 163, 164, 166, 167, *173*
Elder, G. H., 117, 137, 222, 227, 228, 243, *249*, 546, 552
Elder, G. H., Jr., *249*, 264 n
Elkhaim, M., 1282, *1310*
Elkind, D., 223, 229, 239, *249*
Elliot, F. A., 882, *897*
Ellis, A., 417, 418, *423*, 997, 1002
Ellis, G. J., 178, *193*
Ellis, H., 467, 468, 469, 480, *494*
Elman, M. R., 718, 722, *734*
Elmer, E., 904, 907, 909, 917, 922, 924, *930, 932*
Elms, A., 1285, *1311*
Elster, A. B., 627, *657*
Elwood, R., 1059, 1061, 1065, 1070
Ely, A. L., 1049, 1052, 1055, 1059, 1069, 1203, *1211*
Embree, A., 147, 148, *172*
Emery, R., 1156, *1175*, 1064, 1069, 1071
Emmelkamp, P., 1040, 1041, 1042, 1043, 1062, 1068
Emmons, M. L., 1042, 1068
Emms, E. M., 344, *355*
Ende, R. N., 1232, 1242
Engel, M. L., 1252, 1274, 1283, 1284, *1311*
Engelin, R., 1257, 1274
England, P., 728, *739*
English, D., 169, *172*
Ensminger, M. E., 691, *696*
Entwisle, D. R., 558, 560, 561, 562, 563, 564, 565, 567, 568, 569, 570, 571, 573, 574, 576, *580*
Epperson, A., 334, *354*
Epstein, C., 718, 731, *734*
Epstein, L. J., 302, 303, *313*
Epstein, M., 1282, *1316*
Epstein, N., 229, *254*, 1040, 1042, 1043, 1050, 1052, 1053, 1059, 1064, 1069, 1264, 1268, 1269, 1270, 1274, 1279, 1280
Epstein, N. B., 308, *313*
Epstein, S., 1419, 1420, 1428, 1433
Erbaugh, J., 303 n, *311*
Ericksen, E. P., 703, 708, *735*
Ericksen, J. A., 703, 708, *735*
Erickson, K. R., 262, 263, *280*
Erickson, M., 1292, *1311*, 1320, 1342

Note: Pages 1–660 are in Volume I; pages 661–1457 are in Volume II. Italic numbers indicate reference citations.

Note: Pages 1–660 are in Volume I; pages 661–1457 are in Volume II. Italic numbers indicate reference citations.

Fink, E. L., 123, *131*
Finkelhor, 205, *211*
Firestone, G., 1156, *1175*
Firestone, P., 1156, *1175*, 1153
First, E., 1274
Firth, J., 117, *130*
Fisch, R., 1041, 1072, 1117, 1127, 1137, 1161, *1176*
Fischer, C. S., 266, 267, 270, 271, 275, *281*, 331, 332, 338, 339, *353*
Fischer, E. H., 856, *869*
Fischer, J. L., 390, *403*
Fischer, L. R., 341, 342, *353*, 516, 519
Fischner, W., 305, *317*
Fishbein, M., 347, 348, *353*
Fisher, B. L., 1028, 1029, 1082, *1103*
Fisher, E., 789, *807*
Fisher, L., 866, *869*, 942, 947, 956, 1266, 1269, 1274, 1332, 1342
Fisher, S., 1222, 1225, 1242, 1243
Fishler, K., 751, 763, *776*
Fishman, C., 42, *72*, 168, *175*
Fishman, H. C., 793, *808*, 1076, 1078, 1079, 1105
Fiske, D. W., 1055, 1069, 1363, *1376*
Fiske, M., 79, 94, 95, *99*
Fiske, S. T., 1419, 1433
Fitts, W. H., 998, 1002
Fitzgerald, H. E., 623, 633, *658*
Fitzgerald, N. M., 258, *281*
Flaherty, D., 589, *622*
Fleck, S., 13, *36*, 397, *402*, 852, *869*, *872*, 1080, 1105
Fleece, E. L., 395, *402*
Fleischman, M. J., 1073, *1106*, 1346, 1347, 1356, 1357, 1358, 1359, *1376*, *1378*
Fleiss, J. L., 1092, 1093, 1103
Fleming, B., 1064, 1069
Fleming, J. B., 888, *897*
Fletcher, J., 344, *355*
Flomenhaft, K., 1261, 1277, 1291, *1311*
Flores, E. T., 123, *131*
Flowers, C., 629, *655*
Flowers, J. V., 1225, 1242
Floyd, H. H., Jr., 218, *250*
Flynn, W. R., 904, 923, *931*
Foa, E., 422, *424*, 1428, 1433
Foa, E. B., 127, *131*
Foa, U., 422, *424*, 1428, 1433
Foa, U. G., 127, *131*
Fodor, E. M., 122, *131*
Fogel, A., 1419, 1433
Foley, J. M., 1092, 1104
Follete, W. C., 1061, 1065, 1070
Follingstad, D., 232, *248*

Fomufod, A. K., 916, *931*
Fontana, V. J., 904, 910, *931*
Foote, N. N., 19, *35*
Ford, B. O., 689, *695*
Ford, C. S., 215, *250*
Ford, D., 1290, *1311*
Forehand, R., 974, 984, 1346, 1374, *1378*
Forgatch, M. S., 1344, 1345, 1355, 1361, 1365, 1366, 1367, 1368, 1369, 1370, 1371, 1374, *1376*, *1377*, *1378*
Form, W. H., 142, *211*
Forman, B. D., 230, *250*
Forman, S. G., 230, *250*
Forssman, H., 566, *580*
Forsyth, D., 1292, 1294, *1311*
Forsyth, D. R., 103, *131*
Forsythe, A., 822, 825, 829, 835, *842*
Foster, H. H., Jr., 1390, 1391, 1392, 1393, 1399, 1400, 1403, 1404, *1410*
Foster, M., 167, *173*
Foster, M. A., 716, 717, 719, 720, *735*, *740*, 742, 746, 761, 767, 771, *774*, *776*
Foster, R., 643, *658*
Foster, S. L., 971, 974, 985
Foundation for Child Development, 565, *580*
Fournier, D. G., 967, 984, 989, 1001, 1269
Fowle, C., 754, *776*
Fowlkes, M., 745, 767, *774*
Fox, G. L., 122, *123*, *131*, 449, *519*, 626, 628, *655*, 739
Fox, J. J., 1423, 1434
Fox, K. D., 703, *737*
Fox, R., 1258, 1259, 1274, 1279, 1291, *1315*
Fox, S. J., 1406, 1407, 1408, *1410*
Fraiberg, S., 914, *931*
Framo, J. L., 31, *35*, 102, 103, *131*, *132*, 230, 243, *250*, 414, *423*, 1074, 1109, 1110, 1115, 1117, 1125, 1252, 1263, 1264, *1275*
Frank, E., 467, 478, *494*, 1111, 1114, 1125
Frank, G. H., 850, 851, 852, *869*, 1266, *1275*, 1282, *1311*
Frank, J. D., 1328, 1342, 1374, *1377*
Frankel, A. S., 1225, 1243
Frankel, F., 414, *426*
Frankel, J., 596, *622*
Frankena, S., 1291, 1302, *1312*
Frankl, V., 1136, *1149*
Franklin, G., 1271, 1278, 1291, 1295, *1314*
Franks, D. D., 652, *655*
Franz, W., 563, *579*
Franzini, L. R., 643, *656*
Fraser, F. C., 755, *776*

Note: Pages 1–660 are in Volume I; pages 661–1457 are in Volume II. Italic numbers indicate reference citations.

Frazier, E. F., 665, 666, 667, 671, 672, 674, 675, 676, 677, 678, 679, 680, 682, 694, 695
Frazier, S. H., 1128, *1149*
Fredericksen, N., 927, *931*
Freed, D. J., 1390, 1391, 1392, 1393, 1399, 1400, 1403, 1404, *1410*
Freedman, D., 572, *584*
Freeman, T., 572, *580*
Freeston, B. M., 753, *776*
Freiderich, W. L., 750, 754, *776*
French, J. R. P., 700, *735*
Frenkel-Brunswick, E., 448, *462*
Frenken, J., 1041, 1069
Freud, A., 185, *210,* 219, 238, *250,* 1230, 1243, 1398, 1402, *1410*
Freud, S., 8, 54, *72,* 80, 154, 467, *493,* 524, 847, 850, 851, *869*
Freud, S. A., 533, *552*
Frey, J., 387, *402,* 415, 417, 418, 419, *424, 425*
Frey, J., III, 1424, 1434
Fried, M., 862, *869*
Fried, M. H., 153, *173*
Fried, M. N., 153, *173*
Friedeman, J. S., 289, *313*
Friedenberg, E., 157, 160, *173*
Friederich, W. N., 750, 751, 754, *776,* 916, 917, *937*
Friedlander, S., 75, *99,* 360, 361, *374*
Friedman, A. S., 1134, 1136, *1149*
Friedman, E., 150, *173*
Friedman, E. H., 215, 216, *250*
Friedman, H., 395, 401, *402*
Friedman, J., 414, *424*
Friedman, L. C., 379, *404*
Friedman, S. B., 904, 917, 921, 922, 931, *933*
Friest, W. P., 1187, *1214*
Frieze, I. H., 103, 111, *139,* 449, *519*
Friis, H., 294, *318*
Frodi, A. M., 598, *619,* 905, 916, 920, *929, 931*
Frodi, M., 598, *619*
Fromm, E., 188, *212,* 407, 417, *424*
Frommer, E., 539, *552*
Fromm-Reichmann, F., 17, *35,* 961, 985, 1135, 1139, *1149*
Fruchtman, L. A., 885, *898*
Fulcomer, M. C., 310, *312*
Fulmer, R. H., 244, *250*
Fulton, W., 650, *659*
Furlong, M. J., 510, *519*
Furniss, T., 1266, 1269, 1275

Furstenberg, F. F., 816, *842*
Furstenberg, F. F., Jr., 183, *212,* 568, 580

G

Gabrielson, P., 1363, *1377*
Gadlin, H., 289, *312,* 405, *424*
Gaensbauer, T. J., 917, *931*
Gagnon, J. H., 436, *464*
Gaind, R., 401, *402*
Gaines, R., 902, 904, 907, 910, 916, 923, 924, *931*
Gaines, T., 1291, *1315*
Galbraith, R. C., 126, *132*
Galdston, R., 904, 907, 908, 918, 923, *931*
Galinsky, E., 153, *173*
Gallagher, B. J., 511, *519*
Gallagher, D. E., 303, *313*
Gallagher, J., 156, *172,* 749, 952, 757, 761, 771, *774*
Gallant, D., 864, *870*
Galligan, R. J., 1074, 1104
Gallimore, R., 204, *214*
Gallope, R. A., 1009, 1015, 1016, 1029
Ganahl, G. F., 1198, 1211, 1250, 1270, 1271, 1275
Ganong, L., 120, *130*
Gans, B. M., 286, 297, *312*
Gantman, C., 236, *250*
Garbarino, J., 901, 925, 926, *931*
Gardner, R. A., 1401, 1402, *1410*
Garduque, L., 533, *555*
Garfield, R., 1291, *1311*
Garfield, S., 1295, *1311,* 1340, *1342*
Garland, T. N., 716, 717, 718, 731, *738*
Garlington, W., 1257, 1274
Garmezy, N., 851, 864, 865, 866, *869, 870*
Garner, A., 759, *780*
Garooglan, A., 1437
Garrigan, J., 1269, *1275,* 1291, 1292, 1293, 1298, *1311*
Garrison, H. H., 702, 716, *737*
Garrison, V., 853, *870*
Garvey, C. S., 839, *842*
Gassner, S., 1260, 1275
Gath, A., 754, 755, 762, 763, *776*
Gatz, M., 11, *37*
Gear, G., 782, *807*
Gecds, V., 94, *99*
Geerken, M. R., 572, *581*
Geiser, R. L., 902, *931*
Geiss, S. K., 1048, 1069
Gelfand, D. E., 292, 294, *313*
Gelfand, D. L., 857, *869,* 1082, *1104*
Geller, J. D., 75, *99,* 360, 361, *374*

Note: Pages 1–660 are in Volume I; pages 661–1457 are in Volume II. Italic numbers indicate reference citations.

Note: Pages 1–660 are in Volume I; pages 661–1457 are in Volume II. Italic
numbers indicate reference citations.

Note: Pages 1–660 are in Volume I; pages 661–1457 are in Volume II. Italic numbers indicate reference citations.

Hetherington, E. M., 231, 237, 243, *251*,
   825, *842*, 1262, *1276*, 1402, *1410*
Hetherington, M. E., 625, 626, *656*
Hetznecker, W. H., 755, *779*
Hewett, F., 1153, *1176*
Hickey, I., 301, 304, *313*
Hickman, M. E., 1040, 1049, 1052, 1054,
   1055, 1070
Hicks, M. W., 1380, *1410*
Higa, M., 948, 957
Higuchi, A. A., 908, 914, 920, 927, *930*
Hilberman, R., 877, 879, *897*
Hill, B., 284, *314*
Hill, C., 419, *426*
Hill, C. T., 117, 118, 119, *133*, 279, *281*,
   432, *434*, 437, *462*
Hill, J., 223, 225, 239, 244, *256*
Hill, M. J., 234, *248*
Hill, R., 165, 166, *174*, 259, 260, 261, 262,
   281, 283, 335, 336, 337, *354*, 449, 510,
   515, *518*, *519*, *520*, 557, 564, 565, 569,
   581, 995, 996, 1004
Hill, R. D., 117, 119, *133*
Hill-Scott, K., 1437
Hiltz, S. R., 298 f, 299 n, *314*
Hinchliffe, M., 1129, 1130, 1131, 1132,
   1134, 1143, *1149*
Hinchliffe, M. K., 386, 387, *402*
Hinde, R., 1220, 1243
Hinde, R. A., 179, 181, *212*
Hingtgen, J. N., 850, *870*
Hirari, H., 129, *132*
Hirn, K. F., 288, 289, 298, 300, *312*
Hirsch, S. H., 18, *37*
Hirsch, S. R., 401, *402*, 851, *870*, 940, *956*,
   961, 988
Hirschi, T., 1349, *1377*
Hobbs, D. F., 559, 569, 572, 574, 577, *581*
Hobbs, D. R., Jr., 569, *581*
Hobbs, N., 720, *736*, 1159, 1163, 1176,
   1253, 1276
Hoch, Z., 467, 470, 474, 475, 479, 486, 489,
   494
Hochman, J., 234, *251*
Hock, E., 547, *553*
Hockey, A., 648, *656*
Hodgman, C. H., 234, *251*
Hodgson, J., 1266, 1276
Hoepfner, R., 1332, 1342
Hof, L., 1187, 1196, *1212*
Hofeller, K. H., 879, *897*
Hofferth, L., 626, *657*
Hofferth, S. L., 565, *581*, 724, *737*
Hoffman, L., 32, *36*, 119, 122, *133*, 157,
   167, 168, *174*, 215, 221, 239, 240, 241,

242, 244, *251*, 410, *424*, 994, 995,
   1002, 1268, 1276
Hoffman, L. W., 449, 506, 507, 514, 515,
   520, 546, 547, *553*, 564, 569, 571, *581*
Hoffman, M., 533, *553*
Hoffman, M. L., 228, 229, 251, 449, 506,
   507, *520*, 611, *617*, 1440
Hoffman-Plotkin, D., 902, 918, *932*
Hofstadter, D., 58, 62, *72*
Hogan, 1320, 1342
Hogan, B. K., 1134, *1149*
Hogan, D., 1134, *1149*
Hogan, D. P., 557, *581*
Hogan, R., 75, *99*
Holahan, C. K., 639, *656*, 722, 723, 731,
   735
Holden, R. H., 751, *775*
Holland, D., 241, *251*
Hollenbach, M. G., 855, *870*
Hollenbeck, A. R., 120, *133*
Hollender, M. H., 1118, 1125
Holley, J., 417, *424*
Hollingshead, A. B., 855, 867, *870*
Hollingsworth, J. S., 750, 754, *775*
Hollingsworth, L. S., 782, 785, *808*
Hollister, M., 745, *777*
Holloway, E., 1263, 1264, 1276, 1288,
   1294, *1312*
Holm, G., 643, *658*
Holman, T. B., 115, *133*, 334, *354*
Holmes, T. H., 1035, 1070, 1166, *1176*
Holroyd, J., 751, *777*
Holstein, C. E., 228, *251*
Holt, G., 511, *519*
Holt, K., 750, 755, 762, 767, *777*
Holtzmann, W. H., 220, *254*
Homans, G., 995, 1002
Homans, G. C., 107, 111, *133*, 362, *374*
Homatidis, S., 1165, *1176*
Honeycutt, J. M., 470, 489, *494*
Hong, S., 648, *656*
Hood, J., 703, *736*
Hooper, D., 386, *402*, 1129, 1130, 1131,
   1132, 1134, 1142, *1149*
Hoopes, M. H., 1028, 1029, 1103
Hoover-Dempsey, K. V., 720, *736*
Hopkins, L., 309, *314*
Hopkins, L. P., 309, *314*
Hopkins, P., 309, *314*
Hopkins, R. P., 830, 832, *842*
Hoppe, S. K., 859, *871*
Hops, H., 970, 985, 986, 995, 1003, 1041,
   1043, 1044, 1045, 1047, 1059, 1070,
   1071, 1072
Hops, W., 970, 985

Note: Pages 1–660 are in Volume I; pages 661–1457 are in Volume II. Italic
numbers indicate reference citations.

Horall, B. M., 787, *808*
Horn, D., 1251, 1267, 1291, *1310*
Horn, J. M., 120, *135*
Hornung, C. A., 725, *736*
Horowitz, M. J., 303 n, *314*, 1222, 1225, 1243
Horst, L., 594, *619*
Horst, P., 474, *494*
Horton, P. J., 594, *619*
Hosford, R., 1263, 1264, 1276, 1288, 1294, *1312*
Houghton, P., 645, *656*
House, A. E., 1354, *1379*
House, J. S., 325, 344, *354*
Houseknecht, S. K., 641, 644, *656*, 728, *736*
Hovestadt, A., 1271, *1278*, 1291, 1295, *1314, 1316*
Howard, A., 232, *253*
Howard, J., 97, *99*, 357, 359, *374, 777*
Howard, K. I., 238, *254*
Howells, J. G., 850, 853, *871*
Howells, J. J., 1231, 1243, 1441
Howenstine, R. A., 75, *99*, 360, 361, *374*
Hoyer, W. J., 286, *314*
Hsu, J., 221, *254*
Hubbard, R. W., 305, *315*
Huber, J., 713, 731, *735, 736*
Hubert, J., 570, *581*
Hudgins, W., 233, *252*
Huesmann, L. R., 108, 114, 115, *133, 135*, 362, *374*
Huges, S., 168, *174*
Hughes, M. C., 1422, 1433
Hughes, S. F., 743, 745, *777*
Hughsten, C. A., 307, *315*
Humphrey, M., 647, *656*
Hunt, D. E., 1022, 1023, 1029
Hunt, D. G., 233, *252*
Hunt, J., 526, *556*
Hunt, J. G., 727, *736*
Hunt, L. L., 727, *736*
Hunt, M., 483, 484, 489, *494*
Hunter, R. S., 904, 908, 910, 912, 916, 923, 924, *932*
Hunter, W. W., 309, *315*
Huntington, D. S., 1233, 1243
Hurley, D. J., 688, *696*
Hurley, J. R., 904, *933*
Hurvitz, N., 1258, 1276
Huser, W. R., 723, *736*
Huston, T. L., 107, 111, 112, 113, 116, 128, *133, 134, 135*, 179, *212*, 258, 266, 270, 272, 276, *281, 282*, 1109, 1126
Hutton, S. P., 1020, 1021, 1024, 1029
Huygen, F., 1250, 1276

Hwang, C-P, 598, *619*
Hyde, J. S., 289, *315*
Hyer, W. J., 286, *314*
Hyman, C. A., 918, *932*
Hyman, H. K., 297, 301, *318*

I

Ickes, W. J., 104, *132*
Idol-Maestas, L., 1156, *1176*
Ihinger, M., 179, 181, 182, 183, 191, 203, 206, 207, *212*
Iizuka, R., 652, *656*
Inazu, J. K., 122, 123, *131*
Ingham, M., 589, *616*
Insel, J., 1156, *1175*
Inselberg, R. M., 625, *656*
Irving, H. H., 333, *354, 1410*
Itil, T. M., 863, *871*
Ivey, A., 1292, 1294, *1311*
Iwakani, E., 965, 984

J

Jablonsky, A., 864, *874*
Jacklin, C. M., 513, *521*
Jacklin, C. N., 1233, 1234, 1244
Jackson, D., 961, 984, 1078, 1086, 1103, 1106, 1251, 1260, 1265, 1276, 1318, 1342
Jackson, D. D., 12, 13, 14, 18, 19, 33, *35, 36*, 111, 122, *133, 134*, 473, 474, 476, 488, 494, 793, *809*, 992, 1104, 1117, 1125, 1136, 1148, 1236, 1245
Jackson, E., 1040, 1042, 1043, 1050, 1052, 1053, 1059, 1069
Jackson, J. A., 122, *133*
Jackson, J. S., 684, 687, *696*
Jackson, R., 759, *780*
Jacob, T., 123, *132*, 223, 225, 231, 239, 243, *252, 257*, 589, 594, *617*, 852, *871*, 939, 956, 961, 964, 971, 978, 985, 1276
Jacobsen, R. B., 730, *737*
Jacobson, N. S., 995, 1002, 1045, 1053, 1057, 1059, 1061, 1064, 1065, 1070, 1187, 1212
Jacobson, R., 987, 995
Jacobstein, J. M., 1381, 1382, *1410*
Jacoby, A. P., 569, *581*
Jaffe, D., 360, *374*
Jaffe, D. T., 823, *842*, 1129, 1148
James, W. H., 470, 471, 475, 481, *493*
Jameson, J. D., 860, *871*
Jamison, P. H., 643, *656*
Janoff-Bulman, R., 106, *135*

Note: Pages 1–660 are in Volume I; pages 661–1457 are in Volume II. Italic numbers indicate reference citations.

Note: Pages 1–660 are in Volume I; pages 661–1457 are in Volume II. Italic numbers indicate reference citations.

Kalish, R. A., 187, *212*
Kallman, J. R., 1194, *1216*
Kalmuss, D. S., 882, *897*
Kamarovsky, M., 388, *402*
Kamerman, S. B., 720, *736*, 1187, *1212*
Kamiko, T., 166, *174*
Kandel, D. B., 223, 228, 234, *252*
Kandel, H., 1153, *1175*
Kanouse, D. E., 104, *133*
Kanter, B., 547, *553*
Kanter, D., 50, 51, *72*, 410, *425*
Kanter, J. F., 453, *464*
Kanter, R. M., 360, *374*, 811, 823, *842*
Kantner, J. F., 626, *656*
Kantor, D., 89, 90, *100*, 181, *212*, 608, *617*, 1282, *1312*
Kantor, E., 1225, 1226, 1227, 1243
Kaplan, B. H., 344, *354*
Kaplan, F., 762, *777*
Kaplan, H., 762, 768, *778*
Kaplan, H. S., 289, *315*, 1108, 1109 n, 1119, 1125, 1126
Kaplan, R. M., 643, *656*
Kaplan, S., 610, *621*
Kaplan, S. J., 193, *214*
Karan, D. N., 1028, 1029
Karasu, T., 1299, *1315*
Karoly, P., 1346, 1358, 1359, *1377*
Karpel, M., 408, *425*
Kasahara, Y., 948, *957*
Kasanin, J., 16, 36
Kaschak, E., 449, *521*
Kasl, S. V., 728, *736*
Kaslow, F., 818, *843*, 1269, *1276*, 1291, 1297, *1312*
Kassinove, H., 120, *138*
Kastenbaum, R., 506, *520*, 596, *616*, 751, 757, *779*
Katovsky, M., 531, *551*
Katz, M. H., 722, 726, *736*, *738*
Katz, S. N., 1404, *1410*
Kauffman, C., 611, *617*
Kaufman, A., 1165, *1176*
Kaufman, E., 234, *253*
Kaufman, I., 902, *932*
Kaufman, N., 1164, 1165, *1175*
Kavanagh, K., 1344, 1355, 1361, 1363, 1365, 1366, 1367, 1369, *1376, 1377*
Kawakita, Y., 867, *872*
Kawash, G. F., 118, *138*
Kaye, K., 38, 43, 47, 56, 59, 60, 61, 62, 68, *72*
Kazdin, A., 1153, 1169, *1176*
Keane, T. M., 395, *402*
Kearns, D., 166, *174*, 745, 746, 768, *777*

Kearns, D. L., 1394, *1411*
Kearsky, R., 525, *553*
Keasey, C. B., 533, *554*
Keefe, S. E., 865, *871*
Keegan, J., 164, *174*
Keeley, S. M., 1346, 1367, *1376*
Keenan, V., *780*
Keeney, B., 159, *174*, 742, 747, 753, *777*, 1251, 1266, 1267, 1268, *1269, 1276*
Keeney, B. P., 242, *253*
Kegan, R., 76, 80, 95, *100*
Keith, P. M., 724, *736*
Keith, S. J., 854, *871*
Kellam, S. G., 691, *696*
Keller, J. F., 307, *315*, 832, *841*
Keller, M., 227, *253*
Kelley, H. H., 104, 106, 107, 108, 111, 114, 115, 127, 128, *133, 136, 138*, 276, *281*, 995, 1004, 1093, 1104, 1109, 1116, 1124, 1126
Kellner, H., 1116, 1124
Kelly, G., 1019, 1029
Kelly, G. A., 1230, 1243
Kelly, J., 1166, *1178*
Kelly, J. B., 838, *844*, 1402, *1412*
Kelly, J. R., 334, *354*
Kelly, K., 785, 786, *808*
Kelly, P., 543, *553*
Kelman, H. R., 747, *777*
Kempe, C. H., 904, 911, 916, 922, 924, 925, 932
Kemper, T., 449, *463*, 544, 547, *553*
Kemph, J. P., 902, *936*
Kempster, S., 1299, 1302, *1310*
Kendrick, C., 180, 185, 187, 190, 191, 193, 194, 199, 200, 201, 203, 207, 208, *211*, 212
Keniston, K., 823, 832, *843*, 847, 860, *871*
Kennell, J., 916, *931*, 932
Kenny, D. A., 1096, 1097, 1104
Kensey, A. C., 289, *315*
Kent, J. T., 902, 917, 918, *933*
Kent, R. N., 975, 976, 977, 987
Kerckhoff, A. C., 287, *315*
Kerlinger, F. N., 1098, 1104
Kernberg, P. F., 855, *871*
Kersey, F., 1292, 1303, *1309*
Kessen, W., 586, 587, *617*
Kessler, R. C., 562, *581*, 723, 724, 727, *736*
Key, W. H., 339, *353*
Khatami, M., 1133, 1135, *1150*
Kidd, R. F., 104, *132*
Kiesler, D., 1263, *1276*
Kiesler, D. J., 1085, 1104
Kiesler, G. A., 1060, 1070

Note: Pages 1–660 are in Volume I; pages 661–1457 are in Volume II. Italic numbers indicate reference citations.

Note: Pages 1–660 are in Volume I; pages 661–1457 are in Volume II. Italic numbers indicate reference citations.

Note: Pages 1–660 are in Volume I; pages 661–1457 are in Volume II. Italic numbers indicate reference citations.

Note: Pages 1–660 are in Volume I; pages 661–1457 are in Volume II. Italic numbers indicate reference citations.

Note: Pages 1–660 are in Volume I; pages 661–1457 are in Volume II. Italic numbers indicate reference citations.

Note: Pages 1–660 are in Volume I; pages 661–1457 are in Volume II. Italic numbers indicate reference citations.

Notarius, C., 116, *132*
Notarius, C. I., 378, 386, *402, 403,* 995,
   997, 1002, 1003, 1085, 1104
Notman, M. I., 629, *657*
Nowicki, S., 1223, 1224–1225, 1241
NSPCC School of Social Work, 889, *898*
Nuckolls, K. B., 344, *354*
Nugent, J., 379, *404*
Nunnally, E., 309, *317*
Nunnally, E. W., 1199, 1200, 1201, 1205,
   1214
Nurse, S. M., 904, 911, 922, 923, 924, 925,
   934
Nydegger, C. N., 373, *375*
Nye, F. I., 94, *99,* 111, 112, *136,* 231, 232,
   254, 564, *583,* 723, 724, 725, 728, *737,*
   998, *1003*

O

Obestone, A., 1301, *1314*
O'Conner, P., 725, *739*
O'Connor, W. D., 764, *779*
O'Dell, S., 1361, *1377*
Oden, M. M., 782, *809*
O'Donnel, W. J., 534, *554*
Oerter, R., 169, *175*
Offer, D., 219, 220, 221, 222, 224, 225, 230,
   241, *254*
Offer, J. B., 220, 239, *254*
Ogbu, J. U., 691, 692, *696*
O'Hare, C., 1301, *1314*
Ohi, M., 652, *656*
O'Leary, K. D., 128, *131,* 976, 986, 1036,
   1046, 1048, 1051, 1052, 1053, 1054,
   1055, 1056, 1057, 1059, 1060, 1061,
   1063, 1064, 1069, 1071, 1082, 1105,
   1126
O'Leary, S. E., 600, *620*
Oles, H., 506, *522*
Oliker, S. J., 275, *281*
Olivens, D., 1354, 1372, *1377*
Oliver, J. E., 904, 910, 911, 916, 922, *928,*
   934
Olson, C. L., 1053, 1071
Olson, D., 51, *72,* 405, *426,* 795, *808,* 1261,
   1266, 1269, *1278*
Olson, D. H., 93, *100,* 230, 234, 235, *254,*
   255, 259, *282,* 732, *738,* 969, 986, 989,
   991, 999, 1001, 1003, 1020, 1030,
   1226, 1244, 1320, 1324, 1343
Olson, D. N., 851, *872*
Olson, J. J., 292, *313*
Olson, O. D., 967, 984
Olweus, D., 544, *554*

O'Malia, L., 884, 894, *899*
O'Malley, S. S., 1336, 1343
Oman, M., 848, *869*
O'Neill, M. S., 967
O'Neill, R. E., 762, *779*
Opler, M. K., 854, 856, *872, 874*
Orlinsky, D. E., 359, 360, 369, 370, 371,
   375
Orlofsky, J., 407, *426*
Orne, M. T., 973, 986
Ornstein, R. E., 819, *843*
O'Rourke, J. F., 966, 968, 970, 975, 986
O'Rourke, M., 301, 304, *317*
O'Rourke, V., 1250, *1278*
Orvis, B. R., 106, *136*
Ory, J. G., 907, *930*
Osborne, E., 305, *317*
O'Shea, G., 539, *552*
O'Shea, M., x, xii, 1291, *1313*
Ostrom, C. W., 1100, 1105
Ostrov, E., 238, *254*
O'Tauma, L., 1164, *1177*
Otto, H. A., 1195, *1214*
Overall, J., 1130, *1150*
Owen, M. T., 598, *619*
Owens, D. J., 912, *934*
Ozarin, L. D., 859, *872*

P

Padilla, A. M., 863, *871*
Page, R., 769, 770, 771, *776*
Painter, S. L., 563, *585*
Paisley, W., 717, 730, *734*
Paitich, D., 232, *256*
Pallak, M. S., 908, *929*
Palmore, E. B., 286, 287, 309, *317*
Palumbo, J., 646, *656*
Panzarine, S., 627, *657*
Paolino, T. J., 110, *136*
Paolucci, B., 334, *353*
Papajohn, J., 858, *873*
Papanek, H., 719, *738*
Papenfuh, R., 232, *253*
Papp, P., 992, *1003*
Parelman, A., 421, *426*
Parens, H., 1237, *1244*
Pargament, K. I., 11, *37*
Parham v. J. R., 1399, *1411*
Parikh, B., 228, *255*
Park, R. E., 677, 678, 679, *696*
Parke, R., 165, 173
Parke, R. D., 529, 536, 538, 541, 544, 549,
   554, 600, 601, *620, 621,* 900, 901, 903,
   904, *905,* 921, 924, 925, *930, 934*

Note: Pages 1–660 are in Volume I; pages 661–1457 are in Volume II. Italic numbers indicate reference citations.

793, 805, *808*, 991, *1003*, 1016, *1030*, 1230, *1244*, 1270, *1277*
Phinney, J. S., 389, *403*
Piaget, J., 46, 59, 66, *72*, 80
Picket v. *Brown*, 1396, *1411*
Pierce, J. V., 788, *809*
Pierce, R., 1294, *1314*
Pierce, R. A., 396, *403*
Piercy, F., 1271, *1278*, 1290, 1291, 1295, 1303, *1314*, *1316*
Pilisuk, M., 350, 351, *355*
Pilon, D., 119, 121, *135*
Pine, F., 1226, 1236, 1244
Pinkerton, T. C., 862, *875*
Pinsof, W. M., 128, *137*, 1073, 1081, 1083, 1084, *1106*, 1252, 1261, 1263, 1264, *1278*, 1282, 1283, 1290, 1292, 1297, 1303, *1314*
Piotrkowski, C. S., 547, *555*, 722, 726, 728, *736*, *738*
Pittman, F. S., 894, *898*, 1261, *1277*
Platt, J., 1166, *1178*
Pleck, J., 421, *426*
Pleck, J. H., 573, 574, *583*, 698, 702, 703, 710, 719, 725, *738*, *739*
Plemons, J. K., 508, *521*
Plomin, R., 527, 543, *553*, *555*
Plotkin, R. C., 902, 903, 905, 908, 909, *933*, *936*
Podolski, A. L., 1397, *1411*
Pohlman, E., 641, *657*
Poindexter, E., 236, *250*, 978, *985*
Polanski, N. A., 1234, 1235, *1244*
Pollack, C. B., 904, 908, 911, 923, 924, 925, *935*
Pollack, S., 1263, *1278*
Pollack, W. S., 586, *610*, 611, *621*
Pollane, C., 995, 996, 1001
Pollin, W., 236, *255*, 941, *957*, 978, *987*
Poloma, M. M., 716, 717, 718, 731, *738*
Pomeroy, W. B., 289, *315*
Ponzetti, J. J., 887, 892, *897*
Pope, K. S., *375*
Popper, K., 1288, *1314*
Porges, S., 163, *175*, 1165, *1177*
Porter, B., 1064, *1071*
Porterfield, A. L., 381, 382, 383, *402*
Portner, J., 629, *658*, 991, *1003*
Poston, D. L., Jr., 641, *657*
Potter, H. R., 703, 704, *738*
Pottharst, K., 1256, 1264, 1265, *1278*
Potts, D. A., 915, *932*
Powell, B., 514, *521*, 723, 724, *738*
Powell, D. H., 1224, *1245*
Powell, D. R., 350, *356*, *555*

Powell, G. S., 1183, *1214*
Power, E., 902, 916, *931*
Power, T. G., 596, *621*
Powers, J., 406, *426*
Prall, R. C., *1439*
Prasad, A., 120, 121, *137*
Prasad, M. B., 120, *137*
Prasinos, S., 230, *255*
Prata, G., 991, *1004*, 1136, 1137, *1150*, 1264, 1269, 1279, 1284, 1286, *1315*, 1320, *1343*
Prentice, N. M., 228, 233, 235, *252*
Prescott, J., 467, 491, *494*
Prescott, S., 217, *248*, 878, 881, 889, *898*
Press, S., 1137, *1150*, 1282, *1315*
Presser, H. B., 627, 632, *657*
Preston, A., 531, *551*
Preston, J., 1189, 1190, *1214*
Prestwich, T. L., 720, *739*
Pretzer, J., 1064, *1069*
Price, G., 544, *555*
Price, J. D., 119, 122, *134*
Price, R. A., 117, 118, *134*
Price-Bonham, S., 279, *282*
Prigogine, I., 1282, *1310*
Pringle, J. K., 1419, *1434*
Prinz, R. J., 977, *987*, 1187, *1215*
Prochaska, J., 883, *898*
Proutz, J. H., 889, *898*
Provenzano, F. J., 540, *555*
Prusoff, B. A., 1130, 1134, *1150*
Puckett, J., 409, *426*
Pulliam, G., 1291, *1310*
Pulvino, C. J., 783, *809*

Q

Quarantelli, E. L., 339, *355*
Quarm, D., 702, *734*
Quay, H. C., 237, *255*, 625, *657*, 996, 1003, 1165, *1177*
Querec, L. J., 559, *583*
Quick, A. D., 684, *696*
Quinlan, D., 560, *580*
Quinn, P. E., 652, *657*
Quinn, W. H., 293, 295, 300, *317*

R

Ra, J. B., 119, 122, *137*
Rabkin, J. G., 926, *934*
Rabkin, L., 1264, *1278*
Race, G. S., 117, *138*, 999, *1004*
Rachman, S. J., 1038, 1039, *1071*
Racusin, C., 449, *522*

Note: Pages 1–660 are in Volume I; pages 661–1457 are in Volume II. Italic numbers indicate reference citations.

Note: Pages 1–660 are in Volume I; pages 661–1457 are in Volume II. Italic numbers indicate reference citations.

Note: Pages 1–660 are in Volume I; pages 661–1457 are in Volume II. Italic numbers indicate reference citations.

Note: Pages 1–660 are in Volume I; pages 661–1457 are in Volume II. Italic numbers indicate reference citations.

Note: Pages 1–660 are in Volume I; pages 661–1457 are in Volume II. Italic numbers indicate reference citations.

Note: Pages 1–660 are in Volume I; pages 661–1457 are in Volume II. Italic numbers indicate reference citations.

Note: Pages 1–660 are in Volume I; pages 661–1457 are in Volume II. Italic numbers indicate reference citations.

Note: Pages 1–660 are in Volume I; pages 661–1457 are in Volume II. Italic numbers indicate reference citations.

Walters, J., 230, 232, 243, 253, 256, 372, 376, 449, 506, *522*
Walters, L. H., 180, *214*, 449, 506, *522*
Walters, R., 544, *549*
Walters, R. H., 234, *247*
Walton, M., 1304, *1316*
Waltz, M., 1298, *1316*
Waltzer, H., 651, *659*
Wampler, K. S., 1183, 1199, 1201, 1214, *1216*
Wampold, B. E., 379, 384, *403*
Wandersman, L. P., 548, *522*
Wang, H. S., 289, *317*
Ward, C., 303 n, *311*
Waring, E. M., 391, *404*, 474, 488, 490, 491, *495*
Waring, J. M., 288, 292, 310, *314*
Warkentin, J., 482, *495*
Warnyea, J. A., 562, *579*
Warren, N. J., 386, *403*
Warren, S. F., 1431, 1435
Warshak, R., 544, *555*
Waskow, I., 1268, 1280
Wasli, E., 414, *427*
Wasserman, S., 904, 908, *936*
Wasserman, T., 120, *138*
Waterman, J., 912, *929*
Waters, E., 528, *549*
Watson, J., 559, *584*
Watt, N., 1270, 1280
Watts, B. H., 750, *779*
Watzlawick, P., 14, 33, *36*, 793, 794, 795, *809*, 969, 988, 992, 997, 1004, 1041, 1072, 1078, 1086, 1106, 1109, 1117, 1127
Waxler, C. Z., 977, 978, 988
Waxler, N. E., 103, *138*, 396, 397, *403*, 852, 862, *872*, 875, 941, 944, 953, *956, 957*, 978, 986, 1078, 1105, 1132, *1150*, 1282, 1314
Waxler, P. H., 1220, 1245
Way, A., 306, *318*
Weakland, J. H., 13, 18, *35, 37*, 391, *404*, 961, 984, 1041, 1072, 1078, 1103, 1109, 1117, 1127, 1136, 1137, *1148*, 1161, *1176*, 1236, 1245
Weakland, K., 851, 860, *868*
Weary, G., 104, *132*
Weaver, C. N., 432, *434*
Webber, P. L., 122, *137*
Weber, T., 1287, *1313*
Wechsler, D., 1164, *1178*
Wechsler, H., 232, *256*
Wedderburn, D., 294, *318*
Weed, J. A., 567, *584*

Weeks, G., xi, xii, 1136, 1137, 1138, *1150*, 1172, 1178, 1187, *1213*
Weeks, K., 720, *736*
Weiber, J. D., 823, 824, 825, 844
Weick, K. E., 103, *138*, 967, 988
Weigert, E. B., 1135, 1139, *1149*
Weiman, R. J., 1203, *1216*
Weinberg, R. A., 122, 123, *132, 137*
Weinberg, S. L., 509, *522*
Weiner, B., 104, 105, 106, *133, 139*
Weiner, I. B., 223, 227, 242, 244, 245, *249, 256*
Weiner, M. F., 361, 364, *377*
Weiner, N., 722, 725, *739*
Weingarten, H., 117, 119, *134*
Weingarten, K., 635, 638, 639, *655*, 702, 706, *740*
Weinman, M. L., 630, *659*
Weinraub, M., 596, 601, *619, 622*
Weinrott, M. R., 762, *780*, 1349, 1374, *1378*
Weinstein, K., 296, 297, *317*
Weinstock, C. S., 449, *522*
Weintraub, S., 1156, *1175*, 1269, *1274*
Weir, T., 411, 419, *423*, 724, 725, 727, 728, *734*
Weis, D. L., 474, *495*
Weisberg, C., 388, *402*
Weisberg, D. K., 360, *374*, 823, *842*
Weishaus, S., 287, *320*
Weisner, T. S., 182, 204, *214*, 812, 813, 816, 818, 819, 822, 823, 824, 825, 826, 827, 828, *842, 843, 844*
Weiss, D. J., 981, 988
Weiss, G., 1169, *1175*, 1156, *1177*
Weiss, J. L., 864, *870*
Weiss, L., 413, *425*
Weiss, R. L., 116, *130*, 334, *352, 356*, 379, *404*, 768, 780, 970, 984, 985, 995, 997, 1003, 1005, 1041, 1043, 1044, 1045, 1047, 1059, 1070, 1072, 1078, 1106
Weiss, R. S., 298, *314*, 1399, 1400, *1412*
Weissman, M., 414, *423*
Weissman, M. M., 538, *556*, 1130, 1134, 1136, *1149, 1150, 1151*
Weisz, G., 414, *427*
Weithorn, L. A., 1399, *1413*
Weitz, S., 1219, 1245
Weitzman, J., 894, 895, *899*
Weitzman, L. J., 1380, 1387, 1391, 1400, *1413*
Welch, S., 723, 727, *740*
Weller, L., 222, *256*
Wellish, D. K., 830, 831, *844*
Wells, G. L., 106, *132*

Note: Pages 1–660 are in Volume I; pages 661–1457 are in Volume II. Italic numbers indicate reference citations.

Note: Pages 1–660 are in Volume I; pages 661–1457 are in Volume II. Italic numbers indicate reference citations.

Note: Pages 1–660 are in Volume I; pages 661–1457 are in Volume II. Italic numbers indicate reference citations.

Subject Index

Note: Pages 1–660 are in Volume I; pages 661–1457 are in Volume II. Italic numbers indicate reference citations.

Note: Pages 1–660 are in Volume I; pages 661–1457 are in Volume II. Italic numbers indicate reference citations.

Note: Pages 1–660 are in Volume I; pages 661–1457 are in Volume II. Italic
numbers indicate reference citations.

Note: Pages 1–660 are in Volume I; pages 661–1457 are in Volume II. Italic numbers indicate reference citations.

Note: Pages 1–660 are in Volume I; pages 661–1457 are in Volume II. Italic numbers indicate reference citations.

Note: Pages 1–660 are in Volume I; pages 661–1457 are in Volume II. Italic numbers indicate reference citations.

Note: Pages 1–660 are in Volume I; pages 661–1457 are in Volume II. Italic
numbers indicate reference citations.

This book has been set VideoComp in 10 and 9 point Gael, leaded 2 points. Section numbers are set in 18 point Spectra Extra Bold, section titles in 18 point Spectra. Chapter numbers are 24 point Spectra Extra Bold, and chapter titles are 18 point Spectra. The size of the type page is 27 by 46 picas.